T0393089

THE ROUTLEDGE INTERNATIONAL HANDBOOK OF ONLINE DEVIANCE

Covering a wide range of interactions in the digital society, including invasive social media platforms, new forms of victimisation and cultural resistance, this volume is a comprehensive exploration of the current state of sociological and criminological scholarship focused on online deviance.

Understanding deviance broadly, the handbook acknowledges both conventional normative approach and a constructionist approach to the topic, putting into sharp relief the distinctions between cybercrime and online deviance on the one hand and wider concerns of digital harms related to online interactions on the other. The handbook is divided into five captivating sections, each delving into a unique aspect of online deviance. The first section lays the groundwork with essential theories and methods for exploring this digital phenomenon. In the second section, "Gender, Sex, and Sexuality," you'll find fascinating empirical research on how these aspects are expressed in online spaces considered deviant. The third section, "Violence and Aggression," uncovers the dark side of online communication, examining hate speech, cyberstalking, and other forms of digital violence. The fourth section, "Platforms, Communities, and Culture," takes you into the world of online communities and networks that are often labeled as deviant by society. Lastly, the fifth section, "Contextualizng Online Deviance," highlights research in which a terrestrial location is impactful to the online phenomena studied.

Providing a window into future scholarship over the next several years and acknowledging the ephemeral nature of research on digital technology, *The Routledge International Handbook of Online Deviance* is essential reading for students and scholars of Criminology and Sociology focused on deviant online behaviour. It will also appeal to those working in related areas within Internet/Digital Studies, Media/Communication Studies, Psychology, and Cybersecurity.

Roderick S. Graham is Associate Professor in the Department of Sociology and Criminal Justice at Old Dominion University.

Stephan G. Humer is Professor and Director of the Internet Sociology Department at Fresenius University of Applied Sciences, Berlin. He was the first Chairman of Netzwerk Terrorismusforschung e. V. (Terrorism Research Network) and is now acting as Coordinator of Advanced Research.

Claire Seungeun Lee is Associate Professor in the School of Criminology and Justice Studies at the University of Massachusetts Lowell where she is a member of the Center for Internet Security and Forensics Education and Research (iSAFER), the Center for Terrorism and Security Studies, and the Center for Public Opinion. She is also a core personnel of the University's Center for Asian American Studies.

Veronika Nagy is Assistant Professor at the Willem Pompe Institute for Criminal Law and Criminology, the Netherlands. Nagy's research interests include surveillance, digital inequality, criminalization, and self-censorship.

ROUTLEDGE INTERNATIONAL HANDBOOKS

THE ROUTLEDGE INTERNATIONAL HANDBOOK OF ONLINE DEVIANCE

Edited by
Roderick S. Graham
Stephan G. Humer
Claire Seungeun Lee
Veronika Nagy

Routledge
Taylor & Francis Group

LONDON AND NEW YORK

Designed cover image: gettyimages.com

First published 2025
by Routledge
4 Park Square, Milton Park, Abingdon, Oxon OX14 4RN

and by Routledge
605 Third Avenue, New York, NY 10158

Routledge is an imprint of the Taylor & Francis Group, an informa business

British Library Cataloguing-in-Publication Data
A catalogue record for this book is available from the British Library

Library of Congress Cataloging-in-Publication Data
Names: Graham, Roderick, 1975– editor. | Humer, Stephan G., editor. |
Lee, Claire S., editor. | Nagy, Veronika, editor.
Title: The Routledge international handbook of online deviance /
[edited by] Roderick S. Graham, Stephan G. Humer, Claire S. Lee
and Veronika Nagy.
Description: Abingdon, Oxon ; New York, NY : Routledge, [2025] |
Series: Routledge international handbooks | Includes bibliographical
references and index.
Identifiers: LCCN 2024014935 (print) | LCCN 2024014936 (ebook) |
ISBN 9781032234472 (hardback) | ISBN 9781032234557 (paperback) |
ISBN 9781003277675 (ebook)
Subjects: LCSH: Computer crimes—Handbooks, manuals, etc. | Deviant
behavior—Social aspects. | Internet—Social aspects.
Classification: LCC HV6773 .R69 2025 (print) | LCC HV6773 (ebook) |
DDC 364.16/8—dc23/eng/20240417
LC record available at https://lccn.loc.gov/2024014935
LC ebook record available at https://lccn.loc.gov/2024014936

ISBN: 978-1-032-23447-2 (hbk)
ISBN: 978-1-032-23455-7 (pbk)
ISBN: 978-1-003-27767-5 (ebk)

DOI: 10.4324/9781003277675

The Open Access version of chapter 2 was funded by University of Lausanne.

CONTENTS

Contents

Contents

FIGURES

TABLES

CONTRIBUTORS

Marcelo F. Aebi is a professor of criminology at the University of Lausanne, School of Criminal Sciences, Switzerland. He specializes in comparative criminology and is responsible for the Council of Europe Annual Penal Statistics (SPACE) and co-author of the *European Sourcebook of Crime and Criminal Justice Statistics*.

Jan Christoffer Andersen is a doctoral research fellow at the University of Oslo, Norway. His research explores trends, narratives, and radicalization within the incel community by focusing on everyday stories, stigma, and the subcultural characteristics of online incel culture.

Susanne Ardisson holds a professorship in Communication and Social Media Management at the Fresenius University of Applied Sciences in Hamburg. Ardisson has been working as strategic PR and communications consultant in international companies for more than 17 years. She is Founder and Managing Director of the Berlin-based communication agency Kommunikationsmanufakt.

Susana Avalos is a doctoral candidate in the Department of Sociology and Criminal Justice at Old Dominion University, USA. They research transgender people's spatial experiences in public, private, and online spaces.

Diāna Bērziņa is a researcher in criminology at Maastricht University, The Netherlands. Her research area is art and heritage crime. Currently, her focus is on the exploration of human–object relationships in spaces that mostly are not seen as criminogenic and/or often escape criminology theorization attempts.

Danielle Blunt is a co-founder of and researcher with Hacking//Hustling sex worker collective, USA. She is also a Senior Civic Media Fellow at the Annenberg Innovation Lab at the University of Southern California.

Nicola Bozzi is a lecturer in Digital Innovation Management at Kings College London, United Kingdom. His research area is the reimagination of collective identities through digital media and art. His scholarship develops a conceptual approach to investigate this topic in the context of social media cultures, considering infrastructural affordances—in particular, tagging—as inherently entangled in issues of representation.

Stefano Brilli is a postdoctoral research fellow at the Department of Communication Sciences, Humanities, and International Studies of the University of Urbino Carlo Bo, Italy. His research focuses on digital cultures and performing arts audiences. His main research interests include the study of performative practices in digital culture, performing arts audiences, and sociology of arts.

David Buil-Gil is a senior lecturer in Quantitative Criminology in the Department of Criminology of the University of Manchester, United Kingdom. He is also an academic lead for Digital Technologies and Crime at the Manchester Centre for Digital Trust and Society. His areas of interest cover geographic criminology, small area estimation applications in criminology, measurement error in crime data, new methods for data collection, and cybercrime.

Elisabeth Carter is Associate Professor of Criminology in the Department of Criminology, Politics, and Sociology at Kingston University, United Kingdom. She is a criminologist and forensic linguist who works at the intersection of language and the law. She examines the interactional, ethical, and social drivers manipulated by criminals, revealing the intricate balancing act between power and persuasion, credibility and vulnerability in fraud and financial abuse.

Francisco Javier Castro-Toledo is CEO and Co-founder of Plus Ethics and Co-founder and Head of EU-funded Programmes of PARADIGMA Innovation. His research interests focus on ethics analysis applied to security and cybersecurity, SSH research design, and epistemology.

Wing Hong Chui is Chair Professor of Social Work and Criminology and Head at the Department of Applied Social Sciences, The Hong Kong Polytechnic University. He is also the Co-Director of the Policy Research Centre for Innovation and Technology at the same university. His research interests include youth studies, social work, and criminology and criminal justice.

Thomas Dearden is Associate Professor of Sociology at Virginia Tech, USA. Dearden specializes in research technology and crime and corporate crime. He has conducted research and statistical analysis for organizations across the globe, including the Polynesian Cultural Center in Hawaii, Food for Life Vrindavan in Uttar Pradesh, India, and Pay Tel in North Carolina. Dearden's research focuses on technology, crime, and corporate crime.

Hannah DeLacey is a doctoral candidate at the Van Vollenhoven Institute, University of Leiden, The Netherlands. She performs socio-legal research on the adult webcam industry in the United States. Her work explores how the adult webcam industry is regulated and the working experiences of performers.

Martina Dove is an independent researcher who explores fraud prevention, specializing in fraud vulnerability, individual characteristics that make people vulnerable to fraud, and the scam techniques used by fraudsters.

Awni Etaywe is a linguistics lecturer and forensic linguistics research-theme leader at Charles Darwin University's NT Academic Centre for Cyber Security and Innovation, Australia. His areas of focus are cyber-mediated terrorism and digital deviance. His research establishes evidence of crimes (e.g., threats, incitements) and their moral and social motivations, delves into the language of violent extremism's influence on social networks, and maximizes intelligence yield.

Manolo Farci is Associate Professor of Cultural and Gender Studies at the Department of Communication Sciences, Humanities, and International Studies at the University of Urbino Carlo Bo, Italy. His primary research interests revolve around the study of masculinity, with a specific focus on anti-feminism and the radicalization of misogynistic and pro-male communities in digital media.

Gloria Fernández-Pacheco Alises is a professor in criminology at Loyola University, Andalusia, Spain. She is also the coordinator of the Research Group on Migrations at Loyola University Andalusia. Her research areas include juvenile delinquency, ethnic minorities and victimization, hate crimes, cybervictimization, and risk assessment tools.

Taylor Fisher is a doctoral candidate in the department of criminology at the University of South Florida, United States. Her research focuses on the interaction between cyber environments and social science theories to understand the human factors in cybercrime. Her primary research areas include cybersecurity, cybercrime, digital/network forensics, and applying criminological theory to online environments.

Alice Fox is a lecturer in the department of science, technology, and society at Stanford University, USA. She studies the interrelational dynamics of socio-technical systems and artifacts. She frequently relies upon new and emerging theories and methods within and between post-phenomenology, post-humanism, Constructed Grounded Theory, and Thinking with Theory.

Matthijs Gardenier is Doctor in Sociology. His research is on social movements, political violence, and social media. He completed a PhD on the sociology of crowds and on crowd policing at the University of Montpellier. Since then, he has been working on anti-migrant movements and on conservative participation to security and policing, with a focus on vigilantism. From 2019 to 2021, he conducted a British Academy Newton International Fellowship at the University of Manchester on anti-migrant groups in Dover and in Calais. Matthijs Gardenier has also been teaching at the Universities of Montpellier and of Brasilia (Brazil) since 2012. He has also produced several sociological documentaries.

Ana Belén Gómez-Bellvís is the co-founder and Head of Research and Innovation of PARADIGMA, and lecturer in criminal law at Miguel Hernández University, Spain. Her research interests focus on empirical criminal law, punitive populism, intuitions of justice, democracy, and compliance.

Roderick S. Graham is an associate professor in the department of sociology and criminal justice at Old Dominion University.

Ari Haasio is Principal Lecturer of Business and Culture at Seinäjoki University of Applied Sciences, Finland.

Kevin Haines is Bedford Row Capital's head of social policy in the United Kingdom. He most recently led the criminology department at the University of Trinidad and Tobago as a criminologist and before that, the University of Swansea.

Aaron Hammes is a postdoctoral fellow in the humanities at Case Western Reserve University, USA. He is also the co-founder of Support Ho(s)e collective.

Sten Hansson is an associate professor of communication at the University of Tartu, Estonia. His research explores political blame games, government communication, and disinformation.

J. Tuomas Harviainen is a professor of information studies and interactive media, specializing in information practices, at Tampere University, Finland. He is an information systems, management, and game studies scholar who also dabbles in service research, sexology, and the cognitive study of religion.

James Hawdon is Professor and Director of the Center for Peace Studies and Violence Prevention at Virginia Tech, USA. Hawdon's research investigates the role of communities in promoting, deterring, or reacting to crime, violence, and tragedies.

Marju Himma is an associate professor of journalism studies at the University of Tartu, Estonia. Himma's research embraces contextual factors that lead to publishing misinformation or disinformation in journalism.

Nina Käsehage is an associate professor and currently working as a senior researcher at the Institute for Philosophy and Life Design-Ethics-Religious Studies at the University of Potsdam, Germany. She is affiliated with the European Expert Network on Terrorism (EENeT). Her research interests include religious fundamentalism, jihadism, gender and violence discourses, qualitative research on religion, scientific ethics, and the psychology of religion.

Paul Vinod Khiatani is Research Assistant Professor (Sociology, Anthropology and Philosophy) at the Department of Applied Social Sciences, The Hong Kong Polytechnic University. Among others, his research interests include social movements, youth studies, and Hong Kong studies.

Kristjan Kikerpill is on the faculty of social sciences at the Institute of Social Studies, University of Tartu, Estonia. His research interests include crime-as-communication in mediated environments and critical data studies.

Laura Kobsch completed a Bachelor's degree in Library and Information Management and a Master's degree in Information, Media, and Libraries at the Hamburg University of Applied Sciences (HAW). From October 2019 to December 2023, she worked as a research assistant at Fresenius University of Applied Sciences. Since December 2023, she has worked as Instructional Designer at the Carl Remigius Fresenius Education Group.

Tommi Kotonen is a postdoctoral researcher in the department of social sciences and philosophy at The University of Jyväskylä, Finland. His research interests include crises, political extremism, political violence, political language and rhetoric, far-right movements, and far-right culture.

Heikki Kovalainen is a postdoctoral researcher at Tampere University Institute for Advanced Social Research, Finland. He is also affiliated with the Center of Excellence "Reason and Religious Recognition" based at the University of Helsinki, Finland. His research works at the intersections of the private and the public, exploring ways to make sense of the alleged tension between self-regard and other-regard in contemporary societies, drawing from moral and social philosophy.

Anita Lavorgna is an associate professor in the department of political and social sciences at the University of Bologna. Anita's research pivots around cybercrimes and digital social harms.

Claire Seungeun Lee is an associate professor in the School of Criminology and Justice Studies, where she is a member of the Center for Internet Security and Forensics Education and Research, the Center for Terrorism and Security Studies, and the Center for Public Opinion. She is also a Core Personnel of the Center for Asian American Studies at the University of Massachusetts, Lowell, USA.

Eric Rutger Leukfeldt holds the special chair of Governing Cybercrime at the University of Leiden, established and managed by the Netherlands Institute for the Study of Crime and Law Enforcement (NSCR). He also serves as the director of the Centre of Expertise Cybersecurity at The Hague University of Applied Sciences. Dr. Leukfeldt has spearheaded numerous cybercrime studies for government and private entities, examining the intricacies of cybercriminal operations, nationwide cybercrime victimization, and law enforcement strategies against cybercrime.

Stuart Lucy is a ERSC funded PhD candidate at the University of Southampton, United Kingdom. Stu's research concerns the formative gendered life experiences of involuntary celibate men that identify as 'incel' and how these experiences and their subjective perspectives relate to the decision to identify with the incel community.

Syed Mahfujul Haque Marjan is a doctoral candidate in the department of sociology at the University of North Texas, United States. His research interests include criminology, social inequality, immigration, and Islamist terrorism.

Paula C. Martins is a professor at the Institute of Education at the University of Minho, Portugal.

Sílvia M. Mendes is an associate professor with habilitation at the School of Economics and Management of the University of Minho, Portugal. She is also an integrated member of the Research Center in Political Science at the University of Minho. Her work is at the intersection of Public Administration, Public Policy, and Political Behavior.

Veronika Nagy is an assistant professor at the Willem Pompe Institute for Criminal Law and Criminology, The Netherlands. She is ethnographer, working on surveillance awareness, digital inequality, criminalization, and self-censorship. Her current research is focusing on datafication and social harms of data littering in the migration context.

Shivangi Narayan is an independent researcher of police, policing, data and AI based in Delhi, India, and currently affiliated with a three-year project: "Algorithmic Governance and Cultures of Policing—Comparative perspectives from Norway, India, Brazil, Russia and South Africa" (AGOPOL 21–24). She has a PhD in sociology from Jawaharlal Nehru University, New Delhi. Her book, "Predictive Policing and the Construction of the Criminal" was published by Palgrave Macmillan in August 2023.

Roberta L. O'Malley is an assistant professor of criminology at University of South Florida. Dr. O'Malley's research focuses on the overlap between technology, violence, and deviance. Her primary research interests include violent offending, cyber-violence, cyber-crime, technology-facilitated sexual offending, deviant online communities, and sexual violence.

Petr Oskolkov is a postdoctoral researcher at the Moskowitz School of Communication and in the Department of Middle Eastern Studies and Political Science at Ariel University, Israel. He is also an affiliated research fellow at the Begin-Sadat Center for Strategic Studies, Bar-Ilan University, Israel. His current research focuses on far-right communication on social media. He has published on post-Soviet and European nationalisms, far-right movements, and ethnic politics, in such journals as *Nations and Nationalism, Ethnopolitics,* etc.

Nicolas Trajtenberg is a lecturer in criminology in the department of criminology of the University of Manchester, United Kingdom. His research focuses on cross-cultural criminology, prison violence, attitudes towards punishment, and measurement in criminology.

Katalin Parti is Associate Professor in the department of sociology at Virginia Tech, USA. Parti's research focuses on offenders and victims of cybercrime, sexual violence, and online scams targeting vulnerable populations. She is a member of the Cybercriminology Lab at Virginia Tech, and member of the Social Emotional Research Consortium at Bridgewater State University, MA, USA.

Helidth Ravenholm is an anthropological consultant and owner of Culture Contact, France.

Sybille Reinke de Buitrago is Academic Manager of the Institute for Criminality and Security Research, Germany. She is Non-Resident Fellow at the IFSH, Germany and affiliated with the European Expert Network on Terrorism (EENeT). Her research interests include perception, identity, emotions, discourse and meaning-making in interstate and intergroup relations, political behavior, and political violence.

Oscar Ricci is a postdoctoral researcher in the department of sociology and social research at the University of Milano-Bicocca, Italy.

Robert A. Roks is an associate professor of criminology in the Erasmus School of Law, the Netherlands. His research interests include street culture, street gangs, outlaw motorcycle gangs, and organized crime, with a preference for qualitative research methods and exploring alternative ways of collecting data (social media, digital communication, and (rap) music).

Aleš Bučar Ručman is an associate professor at the University of Maribor, Slovenija. His research interests include the sociology of deviance with a focus on various forms of deviance, the social construction of deviance and crime, (in)formal social control mechanisms, and violence.

Vincenzo Scalia is a senior lecturer in the department of sociology at the University of Florence, Italy. He has worked with the Emilia Romagna local administration on urban security and organized crime policies and has been an observer of Italian Prisons for the Associazione Antigone since 2001.

Kanika Sharma is an assistant professor in criminology at the West Bengal National University of Juridical Sciences in India. Her research interests include addressing gender-related, technological, and marginalized community issues, employing a multidisciplinary approach to tackle complex social and justice challenges.

Piotr Siuda is an associate professor on the Faculty of Social Communication and Media, Kazimierz Wielki University, Poland. His research interests include internet studies, video games, esports, and media literacy.

'Shawn Smith is a criminologist and associate professor in the Department of Criminal Justice at Radford University, USA. He specializes in traditional and experimental crime modeling and public policy development. His current research interests include urban-to-rural comparisons in crime theory, emerging technologies in criminal justice, and digital victimization.

Troy Smith is a national security professional and director at Targeted Evidence-Based Research Solutions Ltd, Trinidad and Tobago. Dr. Smith's research has focused on cybercrime and problematic social media use, including developing a TikTok addiction scale.

Lea Stahel is a postdoctoral researcher and senior assistant at the department of sociology at the University of Zurich, Sweden. She studies the effect of digitization on society from a sociological and communication studies perspective. She publishes on digital hostility, journalism, social norms, and social structure, among other topics.

Lisa Sugiura is a reader in Cybercrime and Gender in the School of Criminology and Criminal Justice at the University of Portsmouth, United Kingdom. Her research focuses on online gender-based violence and concentrates on human interaction with technology and the human dimensions of cybercrime and cybersecurity. Her projects have explored how people use the Internet to obtain pharmaceuticals and illegal drugs, the impact of cyber threats on local communities, harassment and abuse on social media, the role of technology in domestic abuse, and online misogyny.

Ajda Šulc is an assistant lecturer in methodology and sociology on the Faculty of Criminal Justice and Security, University of Maribor. Her main research interests are media and migrations, hateful discourse in online communication, and peer violence.

Maryja Šupa is an associate professor at Vilnius University, Lithuania. Šupa's interests include online crime research, machine learning in law enforcement and social control, and deviance in emerging technologies.

Morena Tartari is Associate Professor of Criminology and Policing in the Department of Social Sciences at Northumbria University. Morena has international research experiences, which intertwine sociology, criminology, communication, and psychology.

Pamela Ugwudike is Professor of Criminology in the Faculty of Social Sciences at the University of Southampton. Pamela's research explores the ethics and governance of AI, with a focus on the technologies deployed by justice systems.

Steve van de Weijer is a senior researcher at the Netherlands Institute for the Study of Crime and Law Enforcement (NSCR). His research interests include perpetrators and victims of cybercrime, the life course and criminal careers of offenders, intergenerational transmission, biosocial criminology, and national foreign prisoners.

Jeroen van den Broek is a doctoral candidate at the Erasmus School of Law, Erasmus University Rotterdam, The Netherlands.

Aaron H. L. Wong is Research Assistant at the Department of Applied Social Sciences, The Hong Kong Polytechnic University. His main research interests are in criminal law and criminal justice.

ACKNOWLEDGMENTS

As we present this editorial volume on Online Deviance, we are deeply indebted to the numerous individuals and institutions whose invaluable contributions have played a pivotal role in shaping this publication. The collaborative effort and support we have received underscore the interdisciplinary nature of this field, highlighting the significance of a collective endeavor in addressing the complexities of interdisciplinary research online.

First and foremost, we extend our sincere gratitude to all universities of our co-editors, whose commitment has been instrumental in bringing this volume to fruition. The indispensable support from our respective research departments has equipped us with the necessary resources and encouragement to navigate the intricacies of this global academic endeavor, addressing sociological and criminological research from a variety of perspectives.

Our heartfelt appreciation extends to the multitude of peers and colleagues who generously shared their insights, advice, and guidance throughout the editorial process. Their diverse perspectives enriched the content of this volume and contributed to the robustness of the scholarly discourse within. The collaborative spirit within the academic community has been pivotal in shaping the depth and breadth of our exploration into online deviance.

We express our deepest gratitude to the authors of the selected chapters. Your meticulous attention to detail and openness to adapting to editorial reviews have been crucial in refining the quality of the content. We acknowledge and value the time, effort, and patience invested by each contributor, as the editorial process unfolded over an extended period. Your commitment to excellence is clearly evident in the polished and insightful chapters that grace these pages.

In addition to the many contributors and collaborators who have shaped this editorial volume on Online Deviance, we extend our heartfelt thanks to the student assistants of Utrecht University, who played a pivotal role in the seamless execution of various administrative tasks. Their dedication and support, notably from Katerina Guseva, have significantly contributed to the success of this project.

Katerina Guseva's outstanding administrative support in managing submissions deserves special recognition. Her efficiency, attention to detail, and proactive approach have not only facilitated the submission process but have also ensured the seamless coordination of the various components that constitute this comprehensive volume. Katerina's commitment to excellence and her remarkable organizational skills have made an indelible mark on the success of this project.

To all the authors who have dedicated their time and expertise to present their contributions at various international conferences, we express our sincere appreciation. Your invaluable contribution has been essential to the promotion of this editorial volume. We deeply appreciate your commitment to managing the logistical aspects of the panels and ensuring the smooth execution of presentations.

Our gratitude further extends to the editorial team at Routledge for their unwavering support and commitment to the success of this project. Their expertise and guidance have proven invaluable, contributing to a seamless editorial process and facilitating the transformation of the contributions into a cohesive and impactful volume.

A special mention goes to the manuscript editor, Medha Malaviya, whose professionalism and effective communication have played a pivotal role in coordinating the various elements of this editorial journey. Medha's dedication to maintaining clarity and coherence throughout the process has been instrumental in bringing together the diverse voices within this volume.

The collaborative effort between the academic and administrative teams of all authors has been crucial in navigating the complexities of compiling and editing an extensive volume on online deviance. The synergy between the academic community and administrative support has undoubtedly enhanced the overall quality and efficiency of this publication.

Recognizing the crucial role played by our partners, who graciously accepted our late evening calls and worked through challenges to organize this international and transnational project, we express our gratitude for your tireless efforts in supporting the editorial process under all circumstances. It is through such collective endeavors that the academic community can continue to produce impactful and meaningful contributions to the understanding of online deviance and its multifaceted implications.

We extend our deepest appreciation to all who have played a role in making this editorial volume on Online Deviance a reality. Your contributions have not only advanced the academic discourse in this field but have also enriched the broader understanding of the challenges and opportunities presented by online deviant behaviors. This collaborative effort stands as a testament to the strength of our scholarly community and its collective commitment to advancing knowledge in this evolving and dynamic field.

PREFACE

The evolution of the digital age has undeniably transformed the landscape of human inter-actions, ushering in an era where online activities have become integral to our daily lives. As scholars immersed in the sociological and criminological realms, we stand witness to the profound impact of internet use on social dynamics. It is within this evolving context that *The Routledge Handbook on Online Deviance* emerges as a compendium of contemporary sociological and criminological scholarship, aiming to delineate the intricate web of online deviance that has become increasingly relevant in our interconnected world.

The overarching goal of this handbook is to address the gap in multidisciplinary scholar-ship related to online harms. The digital realm, with its myriad manifestations, has given rise to diverse forms of deviant behavior, necessitating a comprehensive exploration that transcends the traditional boundaries of sociological and criminological inquiry. Our approach is broad, acknowledging the diverse perspectives that different disciplines con-tribute to the study of online phenomena. Whether referred to as cyber, digital, or online behavior, we recognize the interconnectedness of these actions with offline interactions in the intricate fabric of connected societies.

Within the pages of this editorial volume, we conceive of online deviance in its broad-est sense—an umbrella term encompassing behavior that diverges from normative societal expectations or elicits negative evaluations from others. By embracing this inclusive defi-nition, our aim is to create a nuanced understanding of the multifaceted nature of online deviance and its far-reaching implications.

The thematic structure of this handbook reflects our commitment to comprehensive-ness, featuring chapters that delve into deviant social phenomena arising from internet use across diverse contexts. From theories and concepts to methods and data, from gender, sex, and sexuality to violence and aggression, lies and deception to communities and culture, and finally, regional perspectives—each section represents a facet of the intricate tapestry of online deviance. In doing so, we endeavor to capture the breadth and depth of this phe-nomenon, exploring the various networks, structures, and techniques that underpin deviant actions.

Beyond the conventional considerations of legal, social, political, and economic dimen-sions, we have selected contributions from a wide spectrum of disciplines, approaches, and themes, and in varied formats. This inclusive approach reflects our belief that a comprehensive understanding of online deviance requires insights from diverse fields of study. We recognize that textualities, language, and culture play pivotal roles in shaping online interactions; therefore, we showcase contributions that shed light on these nuanced aspects.

In seeking to compile this handbook, we extend our gratitude to the contributors who have embraced the challenge of unraveling the complexities of online deviance. Their diverse perspectives and expertise contribute to the richness of this volume, reflecting the collaborative spirit that defines our scholarly community.

The Routledge Handbook on Online Deviance is more than a collection of chapters; it is a testament to the evolving nature of deviant behaviors in the digital age. As editors, we are honored to present this volume to scholars, practitioners, students, and enthusiasts alike, hoping it sparks further dialogue, exploration, and understanding of the intricacies that define the realm of online deviance.

INTRODUCTION

Internet use is radically shifting our social relations around the globe. While connected devices such as smartphones and computers were considered pure data transmitters in inter-personal relations, the structural transformative effects of technology were clearly under-estimated (Lucas et al., 2013). Not only have the traditional forms of law enforcement, such as policing and public surveillance, shifted toward a more neoliberal-state corporate control culture, but social deviance has also taken on new forms through advanced internet technologies. In the last few years with the recognition of the large-scale implications of digitalization, several disciplines have opened up to research the different aspects of Inter-net use (Collins et al., 2012). While Science and Technology Studies (STS) (Moats, 2019), Media and Communication Studies, and Computer Science have explosively developed in the last decennia (Derksen et al., 2012), policy-oriented studies such as law and criminology remain relatively reserved in this process (Lee, 2008). Technophobia, mono-disciplinarity, epistemic limitations, and methodological nationalism are regular explanations for the sluggish response of scientists engaged with digital nonconformity (Pasculli, 2020; Rabaka, 2010; Stratton et al., 2017; Wortley et al., 2019); however, as later critics suggest, there is an ever-growing pressure to engage with a tech-savvy, concise, explorative, interdiscipli-nary approach that can explain the consequences of online social behavior (Smith et al., 2017; Pease, 2003; Yar, 2012b). As the editors' introduction shows, this book makes a modest commitment to invite researchers working in the social sciences to a collaboration that develops new directions for a better understanding of online social problems.

The first online deviance-related studies were started by mainstream academics who transmitted their criminological methods to study online victimization by developing a new terrain on Internet use in criminology (Wall, 2003). These studies cover cybercrime offenses, algorithmic decision-making, or Artificial Intelligence (AI) use, classifying abusive platform users, online illegal markets, radicalization, or sexual violence, considering the World Wide Web as an instrumental medium or a social context of criminal offenses (Bar-ton et al., 2013; Karpf, 2012). Some of these scholars focus on the prevention and modus operandi of Internet crimes (Wall, 2007; Loader et al., 2013), but their core concepts remain similar to those of traditional offline studies (Yar, 2012a). Currently, in response to the emerging cyber scholarship (Gillespie, 2015; Jewkes, 2013), a critical counternarrative has

DOI: 10.4324/9781003277675-1

developed, relying on the epistemologies of digital sociology and the heritage of critical surveillance studies (Burden et al., 2003; Steinmetz, 2023). Consequently, criminologists have observed a growing dichotomy between normative and social constructivist researchers (Leman-Langlois, 2013; Steinmetz, 2022) and have alleged an increasing division between internet researchers in different methodological domains (Gordon et al., 2022; McGuire, 2017). To counter the eclecticism of this field, our editorial volume seeks to provide a comprehensive selection of contributions, including diverse epistemic frameworks and topics. This aims to offer a reflection on the limitations of *Online Deviance Research* in the field of criminology. By emphasizing both the strengths and weaknesses of different objectives, we hope to invite readers to develop their own perspectives, contributing to the vivid dialogue of Internet researchers in a creative, inclusive, interdisciplinary manner. As editors of this book, our goal was not to define but to open the frame of such dialogue by structuring our selection under the title of "online deviance."

In order to elucidate this approach, this introduction will elaborate on the comprehensive use of deviance in the social sciences (Joinson, 2005) and rationalize the reasons behind the differentiation of the notions of cyber, digital, and online deviance (Denegri-Knott & Taylor, 2005). By relying on the state of the art of Internet scholarship, this introduction seeks to highlight the conceptual limitations of current studies and justify the need for a more reflective (Wall, 1999), comprehensive (Gradon, 2013), and open Internet scholarship in criminology. Lastly, a short outline of the different sections and a brief reflection on the selected objectives are provided.

Against dichotomies

Offender versus victim, online versus offline, legal versus illegal, quantitative versus qualitative, objective versus subjective realities of deviance. Can we break through these well-established suffocating binaries in our social scientific research? We propose that in order to open the scientific arena of this debate, the first step is to reach a mutual recognition of the limitations of each objective. Therefore, we need to employ broader concepts that allow us to initiate a constructive dialogue on the needs of *new criminology*. The concept of deviance might be considered a safe starting point (Stalans & Finn, 2016). Although crime and deviance are regularly used interchangeably, especially in criminology, this book hopes to accentuate the essential need to extend research objectives beyond the legal construct of crime and highlight the role of a clear conceptual distinction between lawbreaking and social deviance in the future Internet scholarship of criminologists.

Mainstream criminology is traditionally associated with positivist epistemologies, in which normative ideas about crime and harms are generally framed by geopolitically embedded and often outdated legal frameworks (Duff, 2014). These law enforcement-oriented studies rely on jurisdictional dichotomies of victims and perpetrators, and their theoretical reflection mainly focuses on individual decisions (Pratt et al., 2010). Such normative social scientific scholarship in criminology proposes that universal standards or norms define what is right and wrong (Hass et al., 2016). These studies often emphasize the existence of a shared set of values and moral principles within a society, and in the context of the Internet, they might focus on identifying and defining what constitutes criminal behavior online based on established societal norms and concepts (Duff, 2004). For example, hacking, identity theft, and online fraud could be considered deviant because they violate widely accepted norms related to privacy, property, and trust. These assumptions often rest on importing concepts from the offline into the online social domain, often without questioning the relevance of existing legislation. In this framework, online crime is considered a regulated form of deviance, a violation of the written laws set by local authorities that may result in formal punishment. Crimes, in the normative sense of the term, are subject to legal sanctions imposed by law enforcement agencies, including imprisonment, fines, probation, and in some cases, capital punishment. However, due to the dynamic global nature of these activities, online interactions cannot be treated by local law enforcement strategies, as they cross national borders and challenge the protocols of legal infrastructures. While teaching and scholarship tend to distinguish between deviance resulting in a state response (crime) and the myriad forms of responses from individuals and non-state-sponsored organizations, these two forms of responses are also increasingly entangled. Online deviance, therefore, helps investigate social behavior that departs from societal norms and expectations, including its legal implications. It encompasses a broader range of actions that may not necessarily be illegal but are considered socially unacceptable or outside the norm. It also highlights how transgressive deviant actions might become formally criminalized or turn into normative actions.

Normative criminological studies face another similar challenge in the study of online deviance. Normative scholars propose that some universal standards or norms define what is right and wrong, emphasizing the existence of a shared set of values and moral principles within a society (Wincup, 2009). However, these social norms might be radically different in digitally connected networks. In the context of the Internet, normative theories might focus on identifying and defining what constitutes criminal behavior online based on established societal norms among user groups. Yet it is even more complicated to define the harms associated with hacking, identity theft, and online fraud, the social context when it could be considered deviant, and to pinpoint when they violate norms regarding privacy (see chapters on sexting), property (i.e., Non-Fungible Token ((NFT) markets), and trust (e.g., online surveillance). Considering the importance of legislative references to crime, we also seek to provide space to demonstrate the limitations of current legal constructions (Phillips & Chagnon, 2021) and emphasize that the reactive nature of penal policies is sometimes too sluggish to provide a relevant scope for research in the digital era. This is because new forms of deviance are not always comparable to previous offline defenses.

Yet, it is this relativist interpretation of behavior that is regularly contested. Common normative approaches in criminology rely on their interpretation of social deviance on the severity of harm and the public/formal response, while constructivists underscore the role of power relationships in the process of labeling someone as deviant (Triplett & Upton, 2015). According to Goode:

> what is considered deviant is a matter of degree; the key here is the likelihood of attracting censure, and the quantum of censure ranges from mild to extreme, from a negative remark to social isolation, rejection, hostility, condemnation, and denunciation—and, at its most extreme end point, execution by the state or, at one time, a lynch mob.
>
> *(Goode 2015, p. 4)*

However, interactionists would argue that deviance is not solely a matter of intensity regarding its social response in online environments or the severity of deviance in terms of harm (Clifford & White, 2017), but also involves many other situational factors. While social media use is a general reference to informal responses of users who employ a variety of strategies, such as ignoring, muting, unfollowing, and blocking someone as an expression of disapproval (Greer, 2010), other cultural, economic, geopolitical, and social aspects need to be distinguished (Neal, 2014; Sandywell, 2013).

Erich Goode defines deviance as "acts, beliefs, and characteristics that violate major social norms and attract, or are likely to attract, condemnation, stigma, social isolation, censure, and/or punishment by relevant audiences" (Goode, 2015, p. 4). Clearly, exhibiting acts, beliefs, or characteristics that are just different—perhaps in the sense that they diverge from the numerical majority—does not inherently constitute deviance. While deviance involves the violation of norms, it cannot be simplistically equated to merely being "not the norm." Indeed, in many instances, what is rare is what is valued, as illustrated by numerous social media influencers presenting a unique and aspirational body or lifestyle for the followers (Lawrence, 2022). Moreover, what is considered deviance is not ultimately determined by external texts or historical precedents—such as state law, tradition, or religious doctrine. One must link deviance to an audience, individuals who observe the behavior and collectively define it as violating a norm. In the simplest sense, we understand what deviance is through the response of an audience, defined in relation to established societal norms that can vary across cultures, historical periods, and social groups (O'Brien & Yar, 2008). What is considered deviant in one context may be acceptable in another (Ferrel, 2017). This relativity challenges the universality of deviance and questions the objectivity of labeling certain behaviors as inherently deviant (Lageson & Maruna, 2018).

Social responses of online users are often studied on a continuum of severity from ignoring to blocking. However, these responses are intricately intertwined with a normative framework specific to contextual factors where the interpretation of transgression evolves, continuously shifting over time. This is notably evident in discussions surrounding queerness, race, or religion. In our digital age, various subcultures with unique norms flourish within many online communities and social networks. Scholars such as Nancy Baym in *Personal Connections in the Digital Age* (Baym, 2015) and Mary Chayko in *Portable Communities: The Social Dynamics of Online and Mobile Connectedness* (Chayko, 2008) have each made important scholarly contributions by exploring how norms are shaped and enforced in online collectives.

This discussion does not mean that all groups and their definitions of right and wrong are equal. Some groups wield the power to establish their definitions as societal norms, even as less powerful groups resist these definitions. Some scholars conceptualize this dynamic using terms such as heteronormativity or racial normativity, with the former signifying a default position of cisgendered heterosexuality and the latter, particularly in Western countries, referencing whiteness. A particularly severe response from individuals online is what has been called "cancel culture," defined by Norris (2023) as "collective strategies by activists using social pressures to achieve cultural ostracism of targets (someone or something) accused of offensive words or deeds" (p. 148). These strategies often manifest in online spaces, where individuals express their displeasure with posts, comments, and replies.

These responses to deviance—the condemnations, stigmatizing, attempts at social isolation, censuring, and punishments—are understood by sociologists and criminologists as instances of an array of mechanisms in societies to ensure conformity called social control (Chriss, 2018). Similarly, broader structural factors such as poverty, inequality, and systemic discrimination play a fundamental role in the meaning-making of transgressive behavior (Mann & Warren, 2018).

According to Becker (1966), the process of labeling individuals as deviant can contribute to their continued deviant behavior and even to the amplification of transgressive harms (Conyers & Calhoun, 2015). Therefore, interactionists in Internet research emphasize the role of societal reactions in shaping the identity of the labeled individual by emphasizing how violators of norms in turn deal with societal reactions and maintain a certain kind of identity in the face of such reactions. These critics argue that the concept of deviance is closely tied to power dynamics and social control, suggesting that the definition of deviance is often influenced by those in power, such as the dominant culture, political institutions, or economic elites. Labeling theory, a significant perspective in the sociology of deviance, posits that the process of labeling individuals as deviant can contribute to their continued deviant behavior (Sternberg, 2000). As is illustrated by some theoretical chapters included here, this approach highlights the role of societal reactions in shaping the identity of the labeled individual and enables to explore the role of those who weaponize the stigma, regularly discussed in Digilantism studies. Yet critics argue that this perspective overlooks the structural factors that may contribute to primary deviance and places too much emphasis on individual agency (Denegri-Knott, 2004). This raises questions about how we should use the concept of deviance as a tool to complete research or to explore it as an instrument, maintaining the existing power structures rather than objectively identifying harmful or disruptive behavior. In summary, social deviance serves not only as a broad constructivist concept providing a situational research framework for labeling processes but also as a means to understand legislatively framed developments on rights, harms, and penal restrictions associated with online behavior.

The selected chapters explore social deviance from normative as well as social constructivist or realist perspectives. As previously discussed, explanatory or normative approaches, such as cybercrime studies, seek to develop general laws or propositions elucidating the causal factors that predict when victimization occurs or the conditions that facilitate its presence. These propositions can then be applied to various nonconformist behaviors within any given context. This approach is most amenable to a quantitative research design, with its emphasis on constructing hypotheses and deductively testing them through statistical modeling. As will be illustrated in this volume, this is one of the most methodologically progressive approaches in online research.

Meanwhile, constructionist approaches:

> are concerned with how judgments of deviance come about how certain behavior, beliefs, and characteristics come to attract condemnation, and how specific persons come to be censured and stigmatized.
>
> *(Goode, 2015, p. 8)*

Constructionist approaches are focused on exploring how deviance is socially constructed within a given context. The emphasis lies in both understanding the process of defining what qualifies as deviant in a setting and understanding the meaning actors attribute to that process. This approach predominantly adopts a qualitative orientation, with an emphasis on generating thick descriptions through the collection and analysis of the symbolic outputs of online users. Videos and images, posts and replies, emojis and memes, likes and follows are all symbolic outputs that can provide insights into the process of meaning-making. Deviance is approached from a critical constructivist perspective (see DeKeseredy, 2022; Ruggiero, 2021), meaning that the forces in a society that create deviance—or more specifically, the forces that define some acts, beliefs, and characteristics as deviant and others as normative. An emphasis is placed on how powerful groups, often through a society's institutions, impose ideologies, laws, and policies on marginalized groups that in effect *make* the beliefs, traits, and behaviors of marginalized groups deviant. A central question of this approach is, "who makes the rules in the first place?" The answer to this question reveals hidden sources of power or calling into question accepted ideologies and power relations. Scholars adopting this approach draw from a variety of methods, using qualitative social science methods as well as legal analysis and historical-comparative approaches.

The dynamic of power and negotiation outlined here highlights a central assumption at the core of a sociological understanding of deviance: that the perception of what is considered deviant is socially constructed. While it is beyond the scope of this introduction to delve into the processes through which individuals and groups collectively form definitions of what is acceptable or unacceptable (see Andrews, 2012), it is important to note that there is no intrinsic quality embedded in an act, belief, or characteristic that would consistently lead an audience to evaluate it as deviant. Instead, what is considered deviant is a product of our social interactions. We develop common-sense notions of what is right and wrong—and deviant—through repetitive interactions with family, friends, the institutions in which we are embedded, and the media we consume. Online refers to a social environment produced by information and communication technologies. In this environment, people interact with each other and with other computer technologies (bots, artificial intelligence, dynamic HTML, and so on). With this definition in hand, we can simply apply it to Goode's definition of deviance. Therefore, online deviance refers to acts, beliefs, and characteristics *occurring in a social environment produced by information and communication technologies*, which violate major social norms and attract, or are likely to attract, condemnation, stigma, social isolation, censure, and/or punishment from relevant audiences.

As the book title illustrates, besides the use of deviance as a broader domain of criminological research, this editorial volume expands its core framework beyond the boundaries of cyber or digital criminology by consolidating these objectives under the umbrella concept of *online deviance*. In line with the current objectives of Internet studies, we also claim that the online-offline dichotomy in social scientific research should be contested, and the social assemblages of Internet use be explored through new and liquid conceptual designs (Carrington & Larkin, 2016). The existing dichotomies in social scientific research mentioned here, particularly in studying the behavior of Internet users, have been extensively debated and scrutinized. With the increasing number of devices used by the growing internet society, the complexities of online-offline divisions associated with drawing clear boundaries between these two spheres are gradually acknowledged, recognizing the increasingly intertwined nature of online and offline interactions. The notion of a clear boundary between the virtual and physical worlds is challenged by the concept of hybrid realities, where individuals seamlessly move between online and offline environments. This fluidity complicates the task of isolating and studying online behaviors as distinct from offline behaviors. Moreover, this online-offline dichotomy often hinges on the debate between technological determinism and social relativism. Some argue that online platforms shape users' behaviors, while others contend that user practices and societal norms influence the design and development of digital technologies. This tension raises questions about the extent to which online behaviors are a product of the technology itself or the social context in which they are embedded. This concern is also manifested in methodological issues when scholars attempt to categorize and measure online and offline behaviors separately. The reliance on self-reporting, surveys, and other traditional research methods may not fully capture the nuances of online interactions, leading to a potential misrepresentation of user behavior. Online platforms offer individuals opportunities to construct and present identities distinct from their offline personas. This fluidity challenges researchers to navigate the complexities of identity formation and self-presentation in both online and offline contexts. As the following selected case studies will illustrate, understanding the interplay between these realms is crucial for a comprehensive analysis of user behavior. In addition, the concept of *context collapse*, wherein different social spheres converge in online spaces, complicates the distinction between online and offline interactions. Users bring aspects of their offline lives into online platforms and vice versa, eroding the boundaries that traditionally separated these domains. This collapse necessitates a more holistic approach to studying behavior that considers the interconnectedness of these contexts.

Through the selected contributions in this volume, we aim to illustrate the inherent problems in this dichotomy and emphasize key themes and perspectives that have emerged in academic discourse. In summary, we have opted for the term "online deviance" as the broad category of phenomena worthy of consideration for this handbook. The name "online deviance" is an arbitrary one, primarily because "online" is more readily understood and encompasses both the normative aspect of the term "cyber" as well as the techno-social objectives of what we refer to as digital deviance (Carrabine et al., 2020). With the term online deviance, we generally refer to the technical attributes of social interactions that are fundamentally related to Internet connectedness. Due to the broad scope of such phenomena, we have identified online deviance as a comprehensive term for our explanation.

Content outline

This handbook was organized by the editorial team into five sections, covering five core domains of online deviance.

The first section, *Foundations*, is devoted primarily to covering the different epistemic frameworks used in researching online deviance and exploring the different qualitative and quantitative methodologies applied in researching online deviance. While it cannot comprehensively cover all the frameworks used by criminologists, this section provides some reflections on the different schools currently engaged with online deviance. It begins with a theoretical exploration by Troy Smith and Kevin Haines, who discuss the applicability of routine activities theory to understanding online victimization. The authors critically examine the contributions and limitations of this framework and propose future avenues for research within it.

David Buil-Gil, Nicolas Trajtenberg, and Marcelo F. Aebi, noting the questionable accuracy of cybercrime data coming from government arrest and court records, reviews the measures of cybercrime and cyber deviance in the crime surveys administered by national governments to their citizens. The authors identify opportunities for scholars to utilize the data collected by these surveys to advance our understanding of online victimization and offending. Moreover, the authors give methodological recommendations to improve the recording of cybercrime and cyberdeviance in those surveys.

As social science has entered this subject in response to growing concerns about online harm, classical theories continue to dominate this area of research. The majority of studies rely on Rational Choice-based assumptions regarding online behavior, translating explanations of traditional social deviance into online "settings." Routine Activity Theory, originally formulated by Lawrence E. Cohen and Marcus Felson, is still highly popular among cybercrime scholars. It posits that crime occurs when three elements converge: a motivated offender, a suitable target, and the absence of a capable guardian. In the context of online deviance, routine activities are considered in studies on social media, online drug markets, sex trafficking, arms trade, or engaging in forums that create opportunities for various cybercrimes, including cyberbullying, hacking, and identity theft.

Building upon the very same indeterministic idea, Routine Activity Theory seems to provide a general framework for many cybercrime-oriented topics, focusing specifically on the modus operandi of crimes on the web, by emphasizing how the routine activities of individuals create opportunities for online criminal activities such as data fraud or even stealing security intel.

While this approach generally denies the importance of power structures, cultural issues, and contextual differences, it is popular in describing the role of technology in facilitating cybercrime, considering factors like the accessibility of hacking tools, vulnerabilities in online systems, and the increasing connectivity of net users. Several studies in this branch link this knowledge to policy advice, funded by Situational Crime Prevention theories, and propose policing strategies to reduce opportunities for crime. Accordingly, this approach focuses on designing systems and environments that discourage or prevent deviant behaviors, such as implementing secure coding practices, encryption, and user authentication measures. In short, these objectives propose that by addressing vulnerabilities in online systems and platforms, we can reduce the likelihood of cybercrimes like hacking and data breaches.

Scholars studying group behavior online often turn to Bandura's theory as well, explaining online social interrelations as part of a social learning process influenced by the online environment and the behaviors of others. While this theory is relevant for understanding the spread of cybercriminal techniques and the adoption of deviant online behaviors, it does not consider the transformative role of technologies, such as access to connected devices, etc.

Lately, there has also been a growing interest in Strain Theory, initially proposed by Robert K. Merton, who suggests that deviance arises from the strain between societal goals and the means available to achieve them. In the online realm, this approach implies that individuals may turn to deviant behaviors due to the strain caused by limited opportunities or challenges in achieving online success through conventional means. Consequently, criminals might engage in online deviance as a response to perceived strain, such as financial difficulties or a lack of status in the virtual world. Numerous studies have found that online groups, like Telegram chat groups, engage with illegal activities, such as selling banned visual content or personal data of others.

The concept of Neutralization, developed by Gresham Sykes and David Matza, is generally applied in all positivist studies on online deviance that emphasize how internet users rationalize or justify deviant behavior as a response to perceived provocations such as exposing reflections on online harassment, hacking, or spreading malicious content. These studies often focus on specific social groups or networks where subcultural theories are applied. Online groups, like closed chat rooms or game communities, are mainly discussed within the framework of countercultures. This concept is originally associated with the subculture theory of Cohen and Cloward, who suggest that online subcultures, such as hacking communities or online radicalization groups, may foster deviant behavior in the virtual space. Within specific online communities, individuals adopt and reinforce deviant norms and values to establish a sense of belonging.

These explanations are often close to the scope of studies that apply control theories focusing on the strength of social bonds and the effectiveness of social controls. These studies, often targeting young male offenders, analyze the role of offline institutions (e.g., family, school, etc.), and the effectiveness of online policing and regulations in order to explain the impact of online deviance in a specific context. By revealing weak social bonds or inadequate online controls, these studies aim to contribute to various forms of online deviance, from cyberbullying to cyberterrorism.

While most explorative Internet studies focused on such issues, there is a growing interest in extending these classical criminological frameworks to cover social phenomena that cannot be explained by these objectives.

Theories from STS and Media and Communication studies, such as ideas from Latour and Deleuze that have become more prevalent and social constructionist frameworks, have extensively taken ground in online social studies. These approaches differ fundamentally from positivist reviews, arguing that reality is not an objective truth but rather a product of social interactions, language, and shared meanings. Considering the current framework on online deviance, these perspectives suggest that what is considered deviant is not inherent but constructed through social processes, and therefore we first need to examine how online behaviors are labeled as deviant through discourse, media representation, and institutional categorizations and then highlight how these constructions influence societal responses. Stuart Lucy presents a gendered theory of incel digital deviance, shedding light on the dynamics of victimhood and perpetration within the involuntary celibate subculture. The chapter provides insights into the unique aspects of online spaces where gendered theories play a crucial role.

Ethical considerations take the spotlight in Francisco Javier Castro-Toledo and Ana Belén Gómez-Bellvís's chapter, where they examine the ethics of covert surveillance in online deviance research, specifically through the use of honeypots. This exploration sheds light on the challenges and ethical dilemmas associated with studying online deviant behavior.

These objectives are not only directly focused on individual actions online but also on contextual frameworks and narratives such as media outlets, platform economies, online censorship, and online state corporate data governance. These approaches explore the harms of social media, traditional news outlets, and other online platforms and explain how these contribute to the construction of deviance by deconstructing the ways media representations amplify certain behaviors, create moral panics, and influence public perceptions of what is considered deviant.

In these studies, the focus is not on crime but on how the media portrays crimes, such as hacktivism, or online activism, and warns about the impact of these representations on public attitudes and policy responses. By critically reflecting on the role of technological determinism, many constructivist internet scholars reflect on the ways technology influences societal values, norms, and behaviors. These perspectives contribute to research that highlights the harms of technological advancements that contribute to the construction of new forms of deviant behavior. As some chapters selected here will illustrate, by investigating the introduction of new technologies, such as cryptocurrency or anonymization tools, we can elaborate on the landscape of online deviance and how it influences societal perceptions.

There is currently a growing group of academics who rely on critical constructionist theories and emphasize the role of power in shaping discourse and defining deviance. According to these qualitative researchers, in digital environments, power dynamics influence who gets to define what is deviant and how these definitions are disseminated. As examples from critical security studies and surveillance criminology showcase these problems, a new trend reveals how powerful actors, such as Google, Amazon, Facebook, or even federal governments or influential online communities, shape discourses around online behaviors, influencing which actions are labeled as deviant and which are normalized. These studies put more emphasis on the role of the online environment and pinpoint the challenges related to fluidity and ambiguity where we try to apply traditional theories consistently. Critical constructionist theories also account for the intersectionality of online identities, examining how factors such as race, gender, and socioeconomic status influence the construction and perception of online deviance. Also, due to the rapid evolution of online spaces, these studies adopt a more reflective stance on their positionality, recognizing the need for constant adaptation of theories to capture emerging forms of deviance. Lastly, online deviance often transcends national borders, requiring a more global perspective. New online studies recognize the growing concern around the global nature of the Internet and try to figure out how traditional frameworks can be adjusted based on localized cultural contexts.

As will be illustrated in the selected chapters, all theoretical objectives have methodological implications. While positivist research, in particular victim-oriented studies, tends to rely on quantitative research tools, constructivists generally engage with the narratives, symbols, and other representations of data collection methods.

This volume starts the discussion with a general reflection on rational choice-based studies online, showing cases of how they measure victimization and cybercrime, and what the ethical implications of normative online research are when we actively trigger deviant responses, as has been shown by the study on honeypots.

While the categories of victim and perpetrator may seem very clear-cut for many, Stuart Lucy and Martina Dove provide two case studies in which we can explore the challenging angles of such dichotomies. Their chapters provide the bridge to a more complex concern on validity, and as Party et al. and Smith will illustrate, we shall critically consider the use of surveys when we dive into deviance online. Martina Dove focuses on the intriguing phenomenon of "grooming to defraud," uncovering the tactics employed by perpetrators to deceive individuals for financial gain in online environments. Katalin Parti, Thomas Dearden, and James Hawdon contribute by examining the validity of paid panel survey research in studying cybercrime victimization and offending. Their work addresses the intricacies of global online market research, sampling, and data collection. 'Shawn Smith assesses the impact of social capital theory on digital victimization patterns using data from the Oxford Internet Surveys. This chapter provides valuable insights into the role of social relationships in shaping online victimization experiences.

In the last part of the first section, we collected some critical chapters in order to provide a fresh view on ethical issues, and through a few examples of online bullying, online deception, and online activism, we hope to open new doors to discuss the issues of online positionality, research politics, and risks for future academic debates. Aleš Bučar Ručman and Ajda Šulc explore the methodological and ethical considerations inherent in cyberbullying research, offering a comprehensive overview of challenges and best practices in studying this pervasive online phenomenon.

The chapter "Contextual factors of online deception and harmful information: Multidisciplinary perspectives" by Kristjan Kikerpill, Elisabeth Carter, Marju Himma, and Sten Hansson explores the diverse manifestations of online deviance, emphasizing the need to transcend disciplinary compartmentalization for a comprehensive understanding. The examination of context-dependent messages as the primary vehicle for harmful online communication, along with case studies on social engineering attacks and misinformation dissemination, highlights the multidimensional impact of individual, situational, and social-structural factors on online deviance.

Vincenzo Scalia takes a unique approach by analyzing the labeling of online activists, using Julian Assange as a case study. The concept of "cyber outsiders" is introduced, providing a lens through which online activism is examined. The section concludes with Troy Smith, Eric Rutger Leukfeldt, and Steve van de Weijer advocating for a shift from focusing on risk factors to promoting positive online behaviors. Their integrated behavioral change approach aims to foster a safer online environment.

Lastly, from a more culturally critical perspective, there are two chapters included. One of them is Maryja Šupa's chapter, which highlights the need for a more culturally sensitive approach. The other one was written by Veronika Nagy on the concern of accountability in decision-making when we explore the hyper-visible context of digital authorities. Maryja Šupa explores the cultural contexts of online offending, investigating how cultural factors influence and shape various forms of deviant behavior in the digital realm.

The section provides a rich and multifaceted exploration of cybercrime and digital deviance, encompassing theoretical frameworks, methodologies, ethical considerations, and cultural perspectives. Each chapter contributes unique insights, collectively forming a comprehensive overview of the complexities within this dynamic field of study.

The second section, *Gender, Sex, and Sexuality*, presents empirical research on expressions of gender, sex, and sexuality in online spaces that are considered deviant. The selected chapters provide an extensive overview of controversial aspects of online behavior, deviance, and societal perceptions related to gender and sexuality. The authors explore a range of topics, providing nuanced insights into the dynamics of cyberspace and its impact on individuals and communities. In the first chapter, Ana Belén Gómez-Bellvís and Francisco Javier Castro-Toledo investigate the gender gap in online deviance. The authors explore whether cyberspace is democratizing cybercrime, with a particular emphasis on gender dynamics within the realm of digital piracy.

After this study, Roberta L. O'Malley examines the phenomenon of online sextortion, analyzing its characteristics and challenges. The chapter provides insights into the nature of sextortion, shedding light on potential pathways forward to address and mitigate this form of online exploitation.

On the topic of "Online sex work: Deviance and innovation," Aaron Hammes and Danielle Blunt explore the intersection of online platforms and sex work, highlighting the innovative aspects of this evolving industry. The authors discuss how online spaces have influenced the nature of sex work, shaping both deviant and innovative practices.

The chapter "The struggle with stigma in sex work: Webcam models' strategies for stigma management" by Hannah DeLacey examines strategies employed by webcam models to manage and navigate societal stigma in their line of work.

Graham employs sentiment analysis to investigate men's comments on a sex work forum. By analyzing the emotional tone of these interactions, the chapter aims to provide insights

11

into the perspectives and attitudes of forum participants. From a very different perspective on masculine norms, Manolo Farci and Oscar Ricci explore an online controversy within the Italian manosphere, focusing on discussions related to feminism. In one of the last chapters on gender and intersections, Susana Avalos explores the use of online forums by trans people, conducting a qualitative exploration of how online forums are used by trans individuals. Susana gives unique insights into the experiences of trans people in online spaces, particularly focusing on fears of transphobia and the dynamics of support networks. Other than self-identity, safety, and perception of deviance concerning sexual minorities, Helidth Ravenholm's chapter explores the concept of "Other as self" in the context of sexual minorities. Here she examines how identity, safety, and perceptions of deviance intersect within the experiences of sexual minorities navigating online spaces. Nina Käsehage and Sybille Reinke de Buitrago's chapter "Female extremists and the role of gender, sex and sexuality" delves into online deviance by (1) examining theoretical approaches and empirically evaluating the roles of gender, sex, and sexuality among female perpetrators/extremists and (2) analyzing deviance in relation to societal norms. Drawing from qualitative empirical data within the female right-wing and jihadist milieu, the chapter explores the development of perceptions regarding gender, sexuality, emotions, and religion, offering insights into expressions of juvenile protest, quests for belonging, and unique religious interpretations. The chapter concludes with recommendations and prevention lessons aimed at mitigating radicalization and polarization in Western societies.

Collectively, these chapters offer a comprehensive understanding of the intricate relationships between gender, sex, and sexuality in the digital realm, providing valuable insights into the diverse facets of online behavior and its societal implications.

The third section, Violence and Aggression, delves into the intricate and multifaceted realm of online violence and aggression. The chapters in this section scrutinize various aspects of aggressive online behavior among adults, cyber incitement to hatred and violence, the weaponization of followers, caste-based hate speech, ethnic-based cyberbullying victimization, and the examination of provocations, threats, and conflicts within the online drill culture. Acts of violence through communication can leave lasting psychological harm on its victims or potentially justify future political violence against a group. This includes cyberbullying and cyberstalking—especially against women. It also includes various forms of hate speech, including racist, xenophobic, queerphobic, and other forms of speech meant to dehumanize, otherize, or further marginalize oppressed groups. *Deviant communications* in online spaces violate the expected norms of social interaction. This includes forms of trolling, flaming, and deception, such as spreading misinformation or generating disinformation.

In this section, several conceptual interpretations of violence are selected. Gloria Fernández-Pacheco Alises, Paula C. Martins, and Sílvia M. Mendes engage with ethnic-based cyberbullying victimization research in Portugal. Their chapter discusses the implications for criminology, offering a comprehensive understanding of the impact of cyberbullying on diverse communities. In "Moral Disaffiliation in Cyber Incitement to Hatred and Violence," employing a discourse-semantic approach, Awni Etaywe explores moral disaffiliation in cyber incitement to hatred and violence, shedding light on the linguistic and semantic aspects that contribute to the promotion of aggressive behaviors in online spaces. Alice Fox introduces the concept of follower weaponization, offering insights into how the dynamics of followership contribute to the reimagining of violence in the contemporary technological landscape. In "Attacks on Refugee Reception Centres in Finland Between 2015 and

2017—A Case Analysis of Hive Terrorism," Tommi Kotonen and Heikki Kovalainen reflect on anti-refugee arson attacks in Finland between 2015 and 2017, with an emphasis on connections to digital environments, particularly Facebook groups. The analysis follows the idea of "hive terrorism," where structures are comparatively fluid and influenced by content on social media. This idea is challenging for authorities to anticipate, as the authors state in their contribution. Shivangi Narayan introduces some reflections on caste-based hate speech. Her critical contribution investigates the manifestation of hate speech online and its implications, highlighting the nuances of caste-related aggression in the digital sphere. From a cultural criminological perspective, Robert A. Roks and Jeroen van den Broek focused on the online drill culture in Rotterdam, Netherlands in "What happens on the digital street, stays on the digital street?" This chapter explores provocations, threats, and conflicts within this digital subculture, questioning the notion of digital anonymity and its implications for online behaviors. Lea Stahel provides a thorough literature review and proposes an explanatory model that integrates individual, situational, and social status determinants to understand the driving forces behind aggressive online behavior among adults.

Section 4 of the editorial volume, "Platforms, Communities, and Culture," explores a diverse range of topics related to the intersection of online platforms and communities and describes empirical research on online networks that can be defined as deviant by wider societal communities. Social scientists need to conduct a nuanced analysis of the complex and multifaceted interplay between culture and communities in online deviance research. It is crucial for researchers, policymakers, and other stakeholders to understand how culture and communities influence online deviance in order to develop effective prevention and intervention strategies. This analysis will explore various aspects, including the definition of online deviance, cultural factors, community dynamics, and the implications for social scientific research. Diverse legal and regulatory approaches to online activities exist in different cultures. Some countries may have strict laws against certain online behaviors, while others may have more lenient or ambiguous regulations. These legal variations impact the prevalence of online deviance within specific cultural contexts. Moreover, cultural differences in technology adoption play a role in shaping online interactions. For example, cultures with high internet penetration and advanced technological infrastructure may experience different forms of online deviance compared to those with limited access. As will be demonstrated, online deviance frequently manifests within specific digital communities. These communities can be forums, social media platforms, or other online spaces where individuals with shared interests gather. Cultural factors within these communities contribute to the definition and acceptance of deviant behaviors. Subcultures and countercultures within online spaces may embrace behaviors considered deviant in mainstream culture. Understanding the dynamics of these subcultures is crucial for comprehending the motivations and justifications for online deviance within specific community contexts. Cultural and community influences on social identity and group dynamics also play an essential role in shaping online deviant behavior. Therefore, cultural sensitivity is essential in designing research methodologies. Researchers must consider the diverse ways online deviance is perceived and defined across cultures, and their findings should guide the development of policies, educational programs, and technological solutions that respect cultural diversity and community dynamics. Accordingly, the fourth section encompasses studies that delve into various aspects of digital culture, deviant subcultures, and the dynamics of online spaces.

This section's fourth chapter, *Collective Criminal Efficacy in Online Illicit Communities* by Taylor Fisher, investigates the concept of collective criminal efficacy, and the focus is on understanding how individuals within these communities collectively contribute to criminal activities and the dynamics that facilitate such collaboration. The necessity of a holistic view is emphasized, especially for policymakers, to do justice to the phenomenon. A similar approach is used on social networks in the chapter written by Susanne Ardisson and Laura Kobsch, which explores the process of opinion formation among the Baby Boomer generation through social networks. The study investigates how information is disseminated, shared, and shaped within this demographic to influence opinions and perspectives. In their study on "Narratives of Blame and Absolution," Anita Lavorgna, Morena Tartari, and Pamela Ugwudike employ a unique methodology. The chapter critically analyzes framing practices and explores blame and absolution in the context of digital risks associated with harmful sharenting practices. Here, sharenting refers to the overuse or inappropriate use of social media by parents regarding their children. Jan Christoffer Andersen and Lisa Sugiura's contribution, "Interacting with Online Deviant Subcultures: Gendered Experiences of Interviewing Incels," explores the experiences of interacting with online deviant subcultures, with a specific focus on interviewing incels (involuntary celibates). The study sheds light on different aspects of this fieldwork, specifically the tensions in understanding this unique community that both researchers experienced during their work. Reflection of this kind has a decisive effect, particularly in security studies and related research fields. It can make a helpful contribution to appropriate research approaches and strategies. Diāna Bērziņa's chapter, "Legitimization of Grey Activities in Online Space: An Example of Metal Detectorists," examines the legitimation of "grey activities" within online spaces, using metal detectorists as an example. The study analyzes and describes how these communities legitimize their activities within the digital realm. Bērziņa concludes that these highly efficient ways of (re)defining actions might have severe consequences for the development and the application of laws and rules: The inherent standardization and acceptance processes that characterize this milieu can lead to direct threats to accepted social norms. In "Characteristics of the Dark Web's Online Drug Culture," Ari Haasio, Piotr Siuda, and J. Tuomas Harviainen investigate the characteristics of the online drug culture within the dark web. The study offers valuable insights into the dynamics, practices, and trends associated with the illicit drug trade on the dark web. These contributions collectively provide a comprehensive exploration of the intricate relationships between online societies.

The fifth section, *Contextualizing Online Deviance*, offers a comprehensive exploration of responses to online deviance. It examines the multifaceted strategies employed globally to address and combat digital misbehavior. In an era dominated by rapid technological advancements, this section underscores the significance of understanding the dynamic interplay between legal, activist, and socially vigilant responses in mitigating the impact of deviant behaviors on the digital landscape.

To grasp the nuances of responses, the last section begins by providing a contextual framework for online deviance. It elucidates the evolving nature of digital transgressions, encompassing a broad spectrum from cybercrimes to unconventional online activities that challenge societal norms. By delving into the complexities of deviant behaviors, the section lays the groundwork for exploring varied responses, including *Legal Responses, Activist Initiatives, Social Vigilance,* and *Regional Perspectives.* In "Branding the 'Bandito Influencer': Studying Cross-Platform Fame and Deviance in the Cases of Er Brasiliano and 1727wrldStar," Nicola Bozzi and Stefano Brilli investigate the evolution of Italian criminal influencers on social media in an equally lucid and dense manner, portraying two controversial figures who played a part in shaping the online phenomenon of "bandito influencers." The authors provide relevant context to the phenomenon of digital celebrification in a notorious environment. Additionally, they guide the reader to new insights that challenge the idea of an inclusive social narrative as an inevitable result of online fame.

Shifting the focus to social responses, the chapter scrutinizes the gendered dimensions of online deviance. "Female Extremists and the Role of Gender, Sex and Sexuality" by Nina Käsehage and Sybille Reinke de Buitrago explores how gender dynamics intersect with extremism in digital spaces. Furthermore, the examination of anti-migrant groups in Calais and Dover, as discussed Matthijs Gardenier's chapter, "Anti-migrant Groups in Calais and Dover: Protecting Online Resources While Engaging in Digital Vigilantism and Hate Speech," uncovers the complexities of digital vigilantism fueled by socio-political motivations. Its goal is to propose a new approach to understanding digital anti-migrant mobilization. Gardenier states that this is urgently necessary since there is no division between digital and non-digital activities—nowadays, everything is interwoven.

Moving beyond legal avenues, the chapter by Aaron H. L. Wong and his colleagues explores the role of activism in countering online deviance. A critical examination of doxxing, as seen in "Doxxing as a Deviant Behaviour: A Critical Analysis of Hong Kong's Criminal Law Reform Against Doxxing Activities," unravels the complexities surrounding this form of online harassment. In his chapter, Syed Mahfujul Haque Marjan shows how the legal dimension of combating online deviance is scrutinized through a lens that spans various jurisdictions. The chapter delves into the intricacies of legal frameworks, drawing attention to the challenges and opportunities presented by hybrid political systems. His case study, providing insights from Bangladesh, offers in-depth analyses of harmful legal responses. It sheds light on the abuses of legislative measures rapidly evolving to shape and control digital landscapes. Petr Oskolkov's chapter delves into the realm of nationalism, offering insights into how online spaces become breeding grounds for extremist ideologies. "Studying Nationalism in an Online Setting: A Russian Far-Right Community on the Vkontakte Social Media Platform" aims to examine contemporary manifestations of far-right ideological activities and the mobilization of support within online communities. The fundamental assumption is that the expanded possibilities for transmitting extreme viewpoints and active involvement in radical activities in the digital environment, based on a diverse range of digital strategies, probably show only the tip of the iceberg.

Lastly, the final section ends by presenting a collection of regional perspectives, each offering a unique vantage point on responses to online deviance. From the analysis of a Russian far-right community to the examination of attacks on refugee reception centers in Finland, the diverse case studies provide a global panorama of challenges and strategies, emphasizing the need for nuanced approaches tailored to regional contexts.

Bridging gaps and charting the way forward

This introduction wraps up by synthesizing key insights from different approaches to online deviance. It outlines the interconnectedness of several disciplines, advocating for a holistic and adaptive approach to address the ever-evolving landscape of online deviance. As the subsequent chapters delve into specific cases and themes, this introduction serves as a foundational guide, encouraging readers to explore the intricate tapestry of responses shaping the digital realm.

Why is this handbook needed?

Online deviance as a phenomenon is rather ubiquitous. Online deviance as a distinct collection of phenomena is not given proper consideration within the two disciplines that are best suited for its analysis: sociology and criminology. The question is, why? There are at least two reasons.

First, online deviance is often conflated with cybercrime. This conceptual confusion falls under the premise that any analysis of crime is also an analysis of deviance, as the former assumes the latter. As such, the scholarly community has invested considerable energy in understanding forms of cybercrime, and this focus may have taken away from an investment in non-criminal deviant behavior online. Consider an early volume edited by one of the most prominent scholars of cybercrime, David Wall. Wall's scholarship has been enormously influential, and his cybercrime typology of cybertrespass, cyberviolence, cyberpornography, and cyber deception and theft is one that many have adopted in their writing and teaching. Wall's edited volume *Crime and Deviance in Cyberspace* (Wall, 2009) is a collection of groundbreaking chapters that, to my reading, were almost exclusively about crime. Even work exclusively about deviance surrenders to this logic. Similarly, *The Routledge Handbook of Deviant Behavior* (Bryant, 2012) was oriented around the subject of deviance and features a section entitled "Crimes of the Times," which includes chapters on cybercrime and identity theft, but no section, much less a chapter, is devoted exclusively to online deviance.

A second reason may be that whenever the phenomenon of online deviance is named and discussed, it is subsumed under a broader category of deviance. Epitomizing this approach is *The Routledge Handbook on Deviance* (Brown & Sefiha, 2017), which has a section devoted to online deviance alongside other subcategories of deviance such as occupational deviance, cults, and sexuality. Similar to conflating online deviance with cybercrime, considering online deviance as a subcategory of deviance broadly construed is theoretically justifiable. In the abstract, we are talking about deviance, after all. However, scholars have recognized over time that cybercrime as the priority of criminal justice research in the Anglo-Saxon academic focus maintained its hegemonic position and cultural explanations, and critical studies remained in a marginal position of digital scholarship. One can find outlets like the *International Journal of Cybercriminology*, the *International Journal of Cybersecurity Intelligence and Cybercrime*, the *International Journal of Information Security and Cybercrime*, and the *Journal of Digital Forensics, Security, and Law*, among others, devoted to the phenomenon of cybercrime. This has not yet happened for online deviance.

And so we have a curious state of affairs in sociology and criminology in which a rather ubiquitous phenomenon touches the lives of almost anyone who has used the Internet—who has not stumbled upon a webpage or community online that violated your sense of what is normative, interacted with an account that turned out to be a troll, lost their composure and "flamed" someone, had a fraudulent account send them a direct message attempting to scam them, been upset with changes in policies on a platform, or come across racist, sexist, or queerphobic comments on social media platform?

This is not simply a cosmetic concern. To the extent that this lack of visibility and focus diminishes scholarly interest and output, the quantity and quality of academic insight may suffer. This volume, *The Routledge International Handbook of Online Deviance*, addresses this lack of visibility and serves as a critical invitation. To our knowledge, this is the first handbook devoted solely to the phenomenon of online deviance. We hope readers enjoy our collection of chapters.

References

Amman, M., & Meloy, J. R. (2023). Incitement to violence and stochastic terrorism: Legal, academic, and practical parameters for researchers and investigators. *Terrorism and Political Violence.* https://doi.org/10.1080/09546553.2022.2143352

Andrews, T. (2012). What is social constructionism? *Ground Theory Review: An International Journal, 1*(11). Retrieved from https://groundedtheoryreview.com/2012/06/01/what-is-social-constructionism/.

Barton, A., Corteen, K., Scott, D., & Whyte, D. (2013). Introduction: Developing a criminological imagination. In *Expanding the criminological imagination* (pp. 1–14). Willan.

Baym, N. K. (2015). *Personal connections in the digital age* (2nd ed.). Polity Press.

Becker, H. (1966). *Outsiders: Studies in the sociology of deviance.* Free Press.

Brown, S. E., & Sefiha, O. (Eds.). (2017). *Routledge handbook on deviance* (1st ed.). Routledge. Retrieved from https://doi.org/10.4324/9781315648057

Bryant, C. D. (Ed.). (2012). *Routledge handbook of deviant behavior* (0 ed.). Routledge. Retrieved from https://doi.org/10.4324/9780203880548

Burden, K., & Palmer, C. (2003). Internet crime: Cyber crime—A new breed of criminal?. *Computer Law & Security Review, 19*(3), 222–227.

Carrabine, E., Cox, P., Crowhurst, I., Di Ronco, A., Fussey, P., Sergi, A., South, N., Thiel, D., & Turton, J. (2020). *Criminology: A sociological introduction.* Routledge.

Carrington, K., & Larkin, A. (2016). The politics of doing imaginative criminological research. *Liquid Criminology: Doing Imaginative Criminological Research*, 188.

Chayko, M. (2008). *Portable communities: The social dynamics of online and mobile connectedness.* SUNY Press.

Chriss, J. J. (2018). Social control: History of the concept. In M. Deflem (Ed.), *The handbook of social control* (1st ed., pp. 7–22). Wiley. Retrieved from https://doi.org/10.1002/9781119372394.ch1

Clifford, K., & White, R. (2017). *Media and crime: Content, context and consequence.* University Of Tasmania.

Collins, E., Bulger, M. E., & Meyer, E. T. (2012). Discipline matters: Technology use in the humanities. *Arts and Humanities in Higher Education, 11*(1–2), 76–92.

Conyers, A., & Calhoun, T. C. (2015). The interactionist approach to deviance. *The Handbook of Deviance*, 259–276.

DeKeseredy, W. S. (2022). *Contemporary critical criminology* (2nd ed.). Routledge.

Denegri-Knott, J. (2004). Sinking the online "music pirates:" Foucault, power and deviance on the web. *Journal of Computer-Mediated Communication, 9*(4), JCMC949.

Denegri-Knott, J., & Taylor, J. (2005). The labeling game: A conceptual exploration of deviance on the Internet. *Social Science Computer Review, 23*(1), 93–107.

Derksen, M., Vikkelsø, S., & Beaulieu, A. (2012). Social technologies: Cross-disciplinary reflections on technologies in and from the social sciences. *Theory & Psychology, 22*(2), 139–147.

Duff, A. S. (2004). The past, present, and future of information policy: Towards a normative theory of the information society. *Information, Communication & Society, 7*(1), 69–87.

Duff, A. S. (2014). *A normative theory of the information society.* Routledge.

Gillespie, A. A. (2015). *Cybercrime: Key issues and debates.* Routledge.

Goode, E. (2015). *The handbook of deviance.* Wiley-Blackwell.

Gordon, F., McGovern, A., Thompson, C., & Wood, M. A. (2022). Beyond cybercrime: New perspectives on crime, harm and digital technologies. *International Journal for Crime, Justice and Social Democracy, 11*(1), i–viii.

Gradon, K. (2013). Crime science and the internet battlefield: Securing the analog world from digital crime. *IEEE Security & Privacy, 11*(5), 93–95.

Greer, C. (2010). News media criminology. *The SAGE Handbook of Criminological Theory*, 490–513.

Hass, A., Moloney, C., & Chambliss, W. (2016). *Criminology: Connecting theory, research and practice.* Routledge.

Jewkes, Y. (Ed.). (2013). *Crime online.* Routledge.

Joinson, A. N. (2005). Deviance and the internet: New challenges for social science. *Social Science Computer Review, 23*(1), 5–7.

Karpf, D. (2012). Social science research methods in Internet time. *Information, Communication & Society, 15*(5), 639–661.

Lageson, S. E., & Maruna, S. (2018). Digital degradation: Stigma management in the internet age. *Punishment & Society*, 20(1), 113–133.

Lee, R. M., Fielding, N., & Blank, G. (2008). The Internet as a research medium: An editorial introduction to the Sage handbook of online research methods. In N. G. Fielding, R. M. Lee, & G. Blank (Eds.), *The Sage handbook of online research methods* (pp. 3–20). Sage.

Leman-Langlois, S. (Ed.). (2013). *Technocrime: Technology, crime and social control*. Willan.

Loader, B. D., & Thomas, D. (Eds.). (2013). *Cybercrime: Law enforcement, security and surveillance in the information age*. Routledge.

Lucas Jr, H., Agarwal, R., Clemons, E. K., El Sawy, O. A., & Weber, B. (2013). Impactful research on transformational information technology: An opportunity to inform new audiences. *MIS Quarterly*, 371–382.

Mann, M., & Warren, I. (2018). The digital and legal divide: *Silk Road*, transnational online policing and southern criminology. In K. Carrington, R. Hogg, J. Scott, & M. Sozzo (Eds.), *The Palgrave handbook of criminology and the global south* (pp. 245–260). Palgrave Macmillan.

McGuire, M. R. (2017). Technology crime and technology control: Contexts and history. In *The Routledge handbook of technology, crime and justice* (pp. 35–60). Routledge.

Moats, D. (2019). From media technologies to mediated events: A different settlement between media studies and science and technology studies. *Information, Communication & Society*, 22(8), 1165–1180.

Neal, S. (2014). Cybercrime, transgression and virtual environments. In *Crime* (pp. 71–104). Willan.

Norris, P. (2023). Cancel culture: Myth or reality? *Political Studies*, 71(1), 145–174. https://doi.org/10.1177/00323217211037023

O'Brien, M., & Yar, M. (2008). *Criminology: The key concepts*. Routledge.

Pasculli, L. (2020). The global causes of cybercrime and state responsibilities: Towards an integrated interdisciplinary theory. *Journal of Ethics and Legal Technologies (JELT)*, 2(1), 48–74.

Pease, K. (2003). Crime futures and foresight: Challenging criminal behaviour in the information age. In D. Wall (Ed.), *Crime and the Internet* (pp. 30–40). Routledge.

Phillips, N. D., & Chagnon, N. (2021). Lost in the mediascape: Embracing uncertainties and contradictions at the cultural nexus of crime and media. In *Theorizing criminality and policing in the digital media age* (Vol. 20, pp. 151–167). Emerald Publishing Limited.

Pratt, T. C., Holtfreter, K., & Reisig, M. D. (2010). Routine online activity and internet fraud targeting: Extending the generality of routine activity theory. *Journal of Research in Crime and Delinquency*, 47(3), 267–296.

Rabaka, R. (2010). *Against epistemic apartheid: WEB Du Bois and the disciplinary decadence of sociology*. Lexington Books.

Ruggiero, V. (2021). *Critical criminology today: Counter-hegemonic essays* (1st ed.). Routledge. Retrieved from https://doi.org/10.4324/9781003182412

Sandywell, B. (2013). On the globalisation of crime: The Internet and new criminality. In *Handbook of internet crime* (pp. 38–66). Willan.

Smith, G. J., Bennett Moses, L., & Chan, J. (2017). The challenges of doing criminology in the big data era: Towards a digital and data-driven approach. *British Journal of Criminology*, 57(2), 259–274.

Stalans, L. J., & Finn, M. A. (2016). Understanding how the internet facilitates crime and deviance. *Victims & Offenders*, 11(4), 501–508.

Steinmetz, K. F. (2022). Crime in the age of the smart machine: A Zuboffian approach to computers and crime. *International Journal for Crime, Justice and Social Democracy*, 11(1), 225–238.

Steinmetz, K. F. (2023). *Against cybercrime: Toward a realist criminology of computer crime*. Taylor & Francis.

Sternberg, J. (2000). Virtual misbehavior: Breaking rules of conduct in online environments. *Proceedings of the Media Ecology Association*, 1, 53–60.

Stratton, G., Powell, A., & Cameron, R. (2017). Crime and justice in digital society: Towards a 'digital criminology'?. *International Journal for Crime, Justice and Social Democracy*, 6(2), 17–33.

Taylor, J. (2023, September 6). Australia's e-safety regulator warned Twitter about rise in online hate speech during voice debate. *The Guardian*. Retrieved from https://advance-lexis-com.proxy.lib.odu.edu/api/document?collection=news&id=urn:contentItem:693V-HSS1-DY4H-K01D-00000-00&context=1516831

Triplett, R., & Upton, L. (2015). Labeling theory: Past, present, and future. In A. R. Piquero (Ed.), *The handbook of criminological theory* (pp. 271–289). Wiley Blackwell.

Wall, D. (1999). Cybercrimes: New wine, no bottles?. In P. Davies, P. Francis, & V. Jupp (Eds.), *Invisible crimes: Their victims and their regulation* (pp. 105–139). Palgrave Macmillan.

Wall, D. (Ed.). (2003). *Crime and the internet*. Routledge.

Wall, D. (2007). *Cybercrime: The transformation of crime in the information age* (Vol. 4). Polity.

Wall, D. S. (2009). *Crime and deviance in cyberspace*. Ashgate.

Wincup, E. (2009). Researching crime and criminal justice. *Criminology*, 103–125.

Wortley, R., Sidebottom, A., Tilley, N., & Laycock, G. (2019). What is crime science. In R. Wortley, A. Sidebottom, & N. Tilley (Eds.), *Routledge handbook of crime science* (pp. 1–29). Routledge.

Yar, M. (2012a). E-Crime 2.0: The criminological landscape of new social media. *Information & Communications Technology Law*, 21(3), 207–219.

Yar, M. (2012b). Sociological and criminological theories in the information era. In *Cyber-safety: An introduction*. Eleven International Publishing.

PART I

Foundations

1

ROUTINE ACTIVITIES THEORY AS A FRAMEWORK FOR EXPLAINING ONLINE VICTIMIZATION

A discussion of contributions, limitations and future work

Troy Smith and Kevin Haines

Introduction

The study of cybercrime victimization has gained significant attention in recent years due to the increasing use of technology and the internet. Cybercrime victimization refers to the experience of harm or loss resulting from illegal activities that are facilitated using technology or the internet (Marttila et al., 2021). Examples of cybercrime include online identity theft, hacking, phishing, cyberstalking and the distribution of malware. Researchers in the field have primarily employed normative theories and positivist approaches to understanding the causes and consequences of cybercrime victimization (Renaud et al., 2021). Normative theories are frameworks that prescribe how people should behave based on socially constructed values and norms. These theories provide a normative guide for decision-making in moral or ethical dilemmas, but they can also limit the scope of investigation in empirical research (Bachman & Schutt, 2019). Positivist approaches aim to establish objective facts and causal relationships through systematic observation and experimentation. Therefore, it assumes that social phenomena, including crime, can be studied objectively and systematically using quantitative methods (Hagan, 2016). However, this approach may oversimplify complex phenomena and ignore the subjective experiences of victims (Holt & Bossler, 2016). Through the combination of these approaches, researchers seek to use empirical observation and analysis to explain and predict human behavior which is contrary to accepted moral and ethical norms or causes one to become a victim of such behavior (Wall, 2017). The use of these theories and approaches has produced significant insights into the nature of cybercrime victimization.

In this context, the Routines Activities Theory (RAT) has been proposed as a potential approach to understanding the dynamics of cybercrime victimization and has become one of the most employed approaches (Ahmad & Thurasamy, 2022; Smith & Stamatakis, 2020). This approach has allowed some insight into the antecedents of cybercrime victimization,

DOI: 10.4324/9781003277675-3

which has been used in the development of crime reduction strategies. However, limitations and potential misuses of this approach exist (Jaishankar, 2011). The RAT is a theoretical framework that emphasizes the role of normative lifestyle activities in shaping the opportunities for crime and victimization (Cohen & Felson, 1979). The RAT has been used to explain cybercrime victimization by focusing on individuals' online routines and lifestyle choices that increase their attractiveness or suitability in relation to an offender, i.e., a victim-centered approach (Bossler & Holt, 2013). The theory suggests that the convergence of three elements (motivated offenders, suitable targets, and the absence of capable guardians) increases the likelihood of victimization (Cohen & Felson, 1979). As such, the RAT presents a micro-theoretical framework that seeks to explain the relationship between the normative behavior of victims and the rational decision-making process of offenders that leads to a crime event.

· Despite its potential benefits, the RAT has also been subject to criticism for neglecting the role of social structures, power relations in shaping victimization patterns and its applicability in cyberspace due to its reliance on spatiotemporal relationships (Smith & Stamatakis, 2020). Therefore, it is crucial to not only understand the application of the RAT and the insight it has brought but also to critically review its limitations and potential misuse in the study of cybercrime victimization. In this chapter, possible methodological and theoretical issues in the application of the RAT to cybercrime victimization are discussed. Further, recommendations are made for improvement in its application with implications for more in-depth, valid and diverse insight into cybercrime victimization. The overall aim of this chapter is to stimulate a critical review of current cybercrime research approaches using the RAT.

An overview of the routine activities theory

The RAT has a central place in victimology research as it has been able to broadly define the factors leading to susceptibility/vulnerability to crime (Argun & Dağlar, 2016; Louderback & Roy, 2018). The theory was originally focused on explaining the crime increases of the 1960s and 1970s, which were attributed to lifestyle changes (Tilley et al., 2015). The article, titled *Social Change and Crime Rate Trends: A Routine Activity Approach*, was published by Cohen and Felson (1979) and has been cited over 9690 times in the last 40 years according to Google Scholar. Tilley et al. (2015) state that the RAT has demonstrable universal application as it provides a generalizable framework for explaining crime trends and patterns. The RAT as a derivative of the rational choice theory focuses on the pivotal role opportunity plays in crime or disorder (Clarke, 2018). In addition, the RAT implies that crime is normal and/or the existence of a motivated offender is a constant, thus the occurrence of a crime event depends on the opportunities available (Bock et al., 2017; Kringen & Felson, 2014; Miró-Llinares, 2014). This suggests previous criminal intent is unnecessary for a crime event to occur; rather, an individual may simply determine that at a given moment the potential benefits outweigh the risks and that they are sufficiently capable of overcoming barriers to the crime event (Clarke, 1999). Unlike most criminology theories, the RAT avoids speculation about the offenders' motivation.

The RAT approach proposes that crime occurs when a motivated offender is in proximity to a suitable target that has insufficient guardianship because of the individual's 'routine activities' (Cohen & Felson, 2003; DeGarmo, 2011). Routine activities can be defined as generalized temporal and spatial patterns of recurrent and prevalent social activities, which provide for basic population and individual needs, whatever their biological or cultural origins and generalized patterns of social activities in society (Cohen & Felson, 1979; Wikström, 2018). Therefore, RAT extends the understanding of the criminal event to be a result of a person's lifestyle in relation to a convergence of factors (personal and situational) in time and space (Madero-Hernandez, 2019; Pratt & Turanovic, 2015). The RAT then predicts that crime occurs because of routine activities leading individuals into situations favorable for the convergence in time and space of a motivated offender, an attractive target and a lack of capable guardianship.

Therefore, crime is the result of a rational choice based on a mental assessment of social situations; i.e., RAT provides a perspective, predicting how changes in situational conditions influence the probability of a crime event (de Jong et al., 2019; Howell et al., 2019). This suggests that crime is a non-accidental/non-random phenomenon. The combination or convergence of a motivated offender, an attractive target and a lack of capable guardianship provide an opportunity for criminal or deviant activity and the propensity for someone to exploit this opportunity. This in turn increases both the risk of victimization and actual victimization rates (Kringen & Felson, 2014; Miró-Llinares, 2014; Smith & Stamatakis, 2020). Due to its previous success with terrestrial crime, there have been multiple efforts to operationalize RAT in victimology research, which aims to explain cybercrime victimization (Ilievski, 2016; Ngo & Paternoster, 2011; Maimon et al., 2023; Reyns et al., 2011; Smith, 2022).

Tenets of the routine activities theory as it relates to victim selection

To better understand RAT and its generalizability, its possible limitations when being applied to cybercrime, its conceptualization in this study and its applicability to policy development, one must become acquainted with the tenets of a motivated offender, target suitability and capable guardianship explained in greater detail in the following paragraphs.

Target suitability

A suitable target can be animate or inanimate and thus includes persons, objects or places. In the examination of RAT, various constituent properties have been identified that can estimate target suitability. The tenet of target suitability, which is a latent variable and cannot be measured directly, must be measured/inferred using observable variables (Curado et al., 2014; Engel & Schutt, 2014; Garger, 2011; Wachs et al., 2020). The VIVA and CRAVED models present target suitability as a composite made up of several elements from which observable variables can be derived for empirical analysis of the RAT (Leukfeldt & Yar, 2016; Yar, 2005). The applicability of this concept has been cited by researchers and indicate that strategies decreasing target suitability reduce crime opportunities, leading to lower crime rates (Tilley & Sidebottom, 2018; van Ours & Vollaard, 2013).

These models of target suitability that describe its constituent properties are represented by the acronyms VIVA and CRAVED. The acronym VIVA represents the properties of Value, Inertia, Visibility and Access. This model speaks to the qualities of the target which make them attractive to the offender. The qualities are defined as follows:

- Value

This is a subjective property based on the standpoint of a potential offender. As such, targets can vary, as what is considered valuable varies among offenders. In this aspect, cybercrime and conventional crime are similar, as valuations are dependent on the needs/goals of the offender and lead to variability in target suitability.

- Inertia

This traditionally refers to physical factors that may prevent predation or make it difficult (Felson, 1998). In cyberspace, this concept can be considered regarding data volume, which affects portability as it will determine storage requirements, time for data transfer and technology requirements.

- Visibility

This speaks to the need for the potential offender to be aware of the potential target. Valuation and assessment of Inertia can only occur after the offender becomes aware of the target. Therefore, a positive correlation between visibility and suitability of the target must exist (Bennett, 1991). From an online perspective, a target's visibility will be determined by the time spent online; the amount of personal information placed online and the level of public access to the online resources used. However, some crimes only require the potential victim to place an initial set of information which becomes indefinitely available, such as in the case of identity theft.

- Accessibility

This can be defined as the ability of an offender to reach/acquire the target and then escape (Felson, 1998). Consideration of accessibility between targets online and offline converge regarding security devices/resources providing a barrier to access. Passwords and other authentication measures that restrict access to vulnerable targets and their information form the cyber-spatial equivalents of barriers in terrestrial space. Notably, just like in conventional crimes, barriers can be overcome using social engineering or specialized resources e.g., locks vs. lock-picks and passwords vs. password sniffers.

Work on target suitability has been expanded to consider not only motivation but also other factors that must be deliberated when committing a crime, such as concealing and disposing of stolen items (Clarke, 1999; Petrossian & Clarke, 2014). The attributes identified in the CRAVED model are defined as follows:

- Concealable—Targets that are easily identifiable and cannot be concealed after the criminal acts are less desirable to offenders. Further, for crimes that do not involve direct contact, such as financial or cybercrimes, the ability to conceal the occurrence of the offense is most important.
- Removable—This suggests that targets that can be easily moved are more likely to be selected by offenders. Similarly, it can speak to the ease of movement of the item targeted by the offender, whether it is a physical item or data.

- Available—The visibility and accessibility of a potential victim or target item by a motivated offender.
- Valuable—The most valuable goods are more likely to be targeted by offenders. Operationalizing the concept of value in some scenarios can be difficult, as what determines victim/target value will differ from one offender to the next.
- Enjoyable—Offenders will target products that can bring them pleasure over other goods of similar value.
- Disposable—Offenders target victims and engage in behaviors that will make it easier to control and dispose of the victim or evidence during and after the criminal act.

Lack of capable guardianship

Guardianship refers to the capability of preset barriers (physical or symbolic) in the form of persons and/or systems to prevent crime from occurring either directly or indirectly (intentionally or unintentionally) through the disruption of the interaction between a motivated offender and a suitable target (Hollis-Peel et al., 2011; Tseloni et al., 2004). Effective guardianship reduces the opportunity to commit criminal acts and/or makes the act unattractive to a rational actor when they weigh the risk against the possible benefit (Miethe & Meier, 1994).

The concept of guardianship can be categorized in different ways based on how it is applied and how it performs its function (Hsieh & Wang, 2018). First, guardianship can take the form of both formal and informal social controls (Bossler & Berenblum, 2019; Hsieh & Wang, 2018; Yar, 2005). Informal social guardians exercise informal control over other users through warnings, information sharing and parental control (Smith et al., 2006). Formal guardians include network administrators and systems security staff and self-regulation policies and protocols imposed by organizations (Grabosky & Smith, 2001). Second, studies in the field of conventional crime (Fisher et al., 1998) define guardianship in two categories: physical and social guardianship. Physical guardianship refers to automated systems that exercise perpetual vigilance, such as antivirus software, anti-malware and intrusion detection systems—making it difficult for offenders to access targets (Choi, 2008). Social guardianship refers to family, neighbors, friends and social programs or the presence of law enforcement agencies (Fisher et al., 1998).

To improve RAT's ability to explain criminality, the elements with the potential to prevent crime have been further specified. The persons/entities who act as a barrier to a crime, referred to collectively as controllers, have been subdivided according to whether they supervise the offender, target or place. These controllers are referred to as 'handlers', 'guardians' and 'managers' (Hollis-Peel et al., 2011). The term handlers is linked to social guardianship as it refers to persons who exert informal social controls, which can prevent the occurrence of crime by monitoring potential offenders (Sampson et al., 2010). The focus of guardians is the protection of the potential targets/victims for whom they are responsible (Felson, 2006; Sampson et al., 2010). Managers monitor and supervise geographic spaces, i.e., places/locations. The principal concern of managers is the functioning of locations (Felson & Boba, 2010; Sampson et al., 2010).

Overall, the theory defines the necessary elements of a crime as the spatiotemporal convergence of a motivated offender, a suitable target and the absence of suitable guardianship. This means that even with spatiotemporal convergence the potential controllers—handlers, guardians and managers—must be absent or inadequate for a criminal event to occur (Miethe & Meier, 1994; Tewksbury & Mustaine, 2003).

An overview of empirical results of cybercrime victimization studies based on the routine activities theory

This section identifies some of the antecedents and correlates of cybercrime victimization identified by studies in which the RAT was the theoretical framework used.

Demographic factors

Researchers have made some general observations regarding sociodemographic factors and their relation to cybercrime victimization. For instance, there is no statistically significant relationship between age and the risk of hacking victimization (Choi, 2018; Ngo & Paternoster, 2011). The evidence for the effect of sex on the risk of hacking victimization is less decisive, with mixed results among researchers (Bossler & Holt, 2009; Ngo & Paternoster, 2011). However, women experience a greater risk of cyberstalking than their male counterparts, which may be attributable to them being exposed to potential offenders during school and social-related activities outside of cyberspace (Fisher et al., 2002). In the case of online fraud victimization, persons under the age of 20 are less likely to become a victim. Additionally, males and females have varying levels of risk depending on the theme of the online fraud i.e., the scenario presented by the offender (Internet Crime Complaint Center, 2012). In the case of online harassment and cyberbullying, females have a higher probability of becoming a victim (Bossler et al., 2012; Chen et al., 2017; Pelfrey & Weber, 2013; Wolak et al., 2012). The effectiveness of ethnicity as a predictor for cyberbullying victimization has also revealed mixed results (Bossler et al., 2012; Pelfrey & Weber, 2013; Wolak et al., 2012).

Time spent online

Studies have shown that routine activities such as online shopping, which increase an individual's time online, increase the risk of online fraud victimization (Holt & Turner, 2012; Pratt, et al., 2010). Similarly, there is a positive correlation between time spent engaging in online communication (such as chat rooms, social networking sites and e-mails) and the risk of victimization (Choi, 2018; Marcum et al., 2010; van Ouytsel et al., 2018). It is postulated that the increased risk of victimization due to spending more time online, as in the previous two cases, is because of increased exposure to motivated offenders online, since higher levels of content make them more interesting and hence more attractive to offenders (Marcum et al., 2010; van Ouytsel et al., 2018). In some cases, time spent online is possibly more important than the suitability of the target and the absence of suitable guardianship (Bossler & Holt, 2009; Marcum, 2008).

Online activities

The specific activities of online shopping, banking and communication increase the likelihood of cyberbullying (Jansen & Leukfeldt, 2016; van Wilsem, 2013) and online fraud

(Pratt et al., 2010). Interestingly, while time spent online increases the probability of receiving a phishing attack, it does not necessarily lead to becoming a victim (Hutchings & Hayes, 2009). A sample of respondents between the ages of 10 and 17 found that the use of chat rooms, family-related problems and sex-related conversations online increased the risk of victimization (Mitchell et al., 2007; Ybarra et al., 2007). Similarly, the use of social networking, webcams and online shopping sites increases the risk of becoming a victim of cybercrime through the threat vectors of e-mail or online chats (van Wilsem, 2011). While time spent online is a key factor in increasing the risk of cybercrime victimization, it is not the only online routine activity with this effect. Risky online behavior such as frequenting unknown websites and downloading media from the Internet also leads to a greater risk of victimization (Choi, 2008; Reyns, 2013). Additionally, it is not only time spent online that increases risk but also the exposure of personal information online (Marcum, 2008; Marcum et al., 2010). While research has indicated that online communications and disclosure of personal information had a significant effect on the risk of victimization, there are contradicting results that showed they only have a minimal effect (Ngo & Paternoster, 2011).

Deviant behavior

An individual's deviant behavior and lack of self-control have also been considered as observable variables to measure target suitability (Jansen & Leukfeldt, 2016; Mesch & Dodel, 2018; van Ouytsel et al., 2018). Respondents in delinquent behavior surveys that address the use of pirated media, accessing online pornography and cyberbullying, showed a statistically positive relationship between delinquent behavior and the risk of victimization (Bossler & Holt, 2009; Choi, 2008; Hinduja & Patchin, 2009; Holt & Copes, 2010; Wolfe et al., 2007; Ybarra et al., 2007). Further research has shown that the involvement of peers in delinquent behavior significantly increases the risk of victimization, not just personal direct involvement. The involvement of peers in delinquent behavior can expose individuals to secondary exposure to malware (Bossler & Holt, 2009, 2010). However, delinquent behavior/lifestyle does not appear to be an effective predictor for all types of cybercrime. For instance, research shows no statistically significant relationship between delinquent behavior/lifestyle and the risk of credit card fraud (Bossler & Holt, 2010). The increase in the risk of victimization by persons engaging in a delinquent lifestyle may be due to a reluctance to utilize the legal system. Persons involved in delinquent behavior fail to consider the possibility of increased vulnerability due to their activities and the possible need for security software to limit this vulnerability, resulting in an underestimation of the increased risk due to their behavior (Mustaine & Tewksbury, 1998).

Guardianship (social and technical measures)

The latent variable of capable guardianship has been measured using a variety of subcategories including social, digital/technical and personal by researchers in the literature with varying results. The effectiveness of guardianship as a mechanism for decreasing the risk of victimization has been inconsistent (Bossler & Holt, 2009; Choi, 2008; Marcum et al., 2010; Ngo & Paternoster, 2011). Forms of digital guardianship such as antivirus, anti-spyware and firewalls have been found to reduce the risk of becoming a victim of cybercrime (Choi, 2008). Additionally, research has shown that users with security software were more likely to report malware infections (Ngo & Paternoster, 2011). This means that even if the software did not eliminate the risk, it could potentially lessen the damage to the system by making the user aware of the intrusion. This evidence in isolation would suggest that compliance with online safety technology plays an essential role in decreasing the probability of victimization in cyberspace (Marcum et al., 2010). However, most studies found no statistically significant relationship between digital guardianship and risk of victimization, particularly infection by unwanted software (Fleming et al., 2006; Marcum, 2008), cyberbullying (Marcum et al., 2010; Ngo & Paternoster, 2011) and phishing (Hutchings & Hayes, 2009). This may suggest that the nature of the cybercrime determines the potential role or importance of guardianship in the crime event.

Like digital guardianship, tests on the effect of social guardianship on the risk of victimization have delivered mixed results. Cybercrimes such as online harassment, cyberstalking and malware infection were found to be significantly affected by social guardianship (Bossler & Holt, 2009; Bossler et al., 2012; Reyns et al., 2011). One contribution to this decreased risk of victimization, particularly among adolescents, is the active monitoring and mediation of Internet activity by parents, which was found to decrease the occurrence of risky online activities and exposure to inappropriate material online (Lwin et al., 2008). However, this protective effect was found to diminish with the increasing age of the adolescent (Lwin et al., 2008). Nonetheless, one study has provided contradictory evidence that social guardianship in the form of parental controls/regulation, network administrators, systems security staff and online citizens, which introduce informal social controls, did not significantly affect the probability of becoming a victim of cybercrime (Moore et al., 2010).

Assessment of the relationship between personal guardianship and the risk of victimization in the form of computer literacy has also had mixed results (Bossler et al., 2012; Bossler et al., 2012; Grzybowski, 2012; Smith & Stamatakis, 2021; van Wilsem, 2013). Evidence suggests that computer literacy decreases the chance of online harassment and the risk of hacker intrusions (Bossler et al., 2012; van Wilsem, 2013). However, studies also show that computer literacy does not reduce the risk of online harassment (Ngo & Paternoster, 2011; van Wilsem, 2013). One study found that higher levels of computer literacy increased the risk of spyware and adware victimization (Yucedal, 2010). This finding may be a testament to the issues encountered with cross-sectional studies, as it may be that spyware and adware victimization lead to persons gaining/seeking computer literacy, i.e., the causal pathway/relationship is unclear.

Limitations and misuse of the routine activities theory

Overall, studies show an inconsistency regarding the efficacy of the RAT in explaining cybercrimes. Some have shown promising results for the transferability of the RAT to cybercrime (Choi, 2008, 2018; Leukfeldt & Yar, 2016; Marcum et al., 2010) while others have found little or no empirical support for the applicability of the RAT to cybercrime (Bossler & Holt, 2009; Ngo & Paternoster, 2011; Reyns et al., 2011; Rodriguez et al., 2017). As such, researchers have opined that it may be unlikely that the RAT will explain cybercrime victimology in totality. However, due to the generality of the theory, there is the sustained expectancy that with modification it could be applied with success (Choi, 2008; Reyns et al., 2011; Yar, 2005). The following subsection identifies and discusses the methodological and theoretical issues that must be considered and addressed in relation to the use of the RAT in explaining cybercrime.

A discussion of the theoretical issues related to the application of the RAT to cybercrime victimization

Temporal and spatial considerations in cyberspace

The literature is filled with conflicting debates over the correlation between cybercrime and 'terrestrial crime' (Henson, 2020). On one hand, some argue that cybercrime is a new and distinctive form of crime but in principle remains essentially the same as a traditional crime (Grabosky, 2001). This argument suggests that traditional offenders have merely adjusted their tactics to utilize the advantages that cyberspace offers, i.e., the nature of criminality remains the same but has just been adapted to take advantage of a new operating environment (Bossler & Holt, 2014). However, other scholars argue that the uniqueness of the cyber environment creates key differences between cybercrimes and traditional crimes (Yar, 2005). These differences can affect the applicability of general criminological theories previously used to explain terrestrial crimes (Malby, 2013). However, within the boundaries of the ongoing debate, researchers have proposed that RAT could be adapted to account for the spatiotemporal differences between terrestrial space and cyberspace (Ahmad & Thurasamy, 2022; Miró-Llinares, 2011; Yar, 2005). The potential applicability of RAT in its unmodified form is limited by the difficulty of applying the spatial and temporal assumptions required to the virtual environment (Holt & Bossler, 2009; Ilievski, 2016; Yar, 2005).

Scholars such as Yar (2005) argue that spatiotemporal intersection is critical to the implementation of the RAT, and since cyberspace is essentially anti-spatial and anti-temporal, the RAT cannot be used to explain online victimization. In cyberspace victims and offenders can interact without intersection in physical space or ever being on the same website or online platform at the same time. In the early stages of cybercrime research, many researchers simply chose to overlook this important premise of intersection and applied traditional theories without explaining why they would/should work when applied to online crimes (Marcum et al., 2010; Pratt et al., 2010). However, Eck and Clarke (2003) did propose a perspective through which interactions in cyberspace could be mapped to the traditional understanding of victim-offender interaction. They proposed that cybercrime should be considered a system problem with the offender and victim sharing the same system (network, platform and/or online service). As such, the victim and offender can be considered to interact within the shared network. Although this rationalizes the aspect of spatial interaction (partially), the fact remains that the offender performs an event at one time and the victim experiences the event (or its effects) at another time (maybe even months after) (Henson, 2020). This means that the behavior at the time of victimization may not be reflective of the victim's behavior before or after and would not be known to the offender to form part of any assumed rational decision to engage in a crime event. In addition, given the equidistance of points online the victim may be anywhere in the world with cultural and social variables unknown to the offender. These two factors associated with the vastness of cyberspace and temporal differences suggest that it may be unlikely for the offender to be fully aware of the victim or when the individual would interact with the crime event, which undermines the assumption of the RAT that the crime event is a rational decision based only on opportunity.

Assumption of rationality

Some have suggested that the RAT's assumption of rationality arising from its derivation from the Rational Choice Theory ignores the effect of emotional, psychological, social and developmental factors on decision-making (DeLisi & Conis, 2012; Jiang et al., 2018; Katz & Quade, 1989; Stohr & Walsh, 2012; Walsh & Jorgensen, 2017; Wright & Beaver, 2005). This rational choice approach to applying the RAT supposes that actors independently choose their actions based on an assessment of the utility or rewards to be gained versus the potential risk or consequences. Walsh and Jorgensen (2017) point out that the assumption that everyone is rational equates to rationality being constant, and therefore cannot explain the variability of human behavior.

Scholars have also detected that criminal behavior suggests 'bounded' rationality where the decision to offend is based on the offender's perceptions, which are biased by the normalization of their habitual deviant behavior (Aldag, 2013; Stohr & Walsh, 2012). Further, the assumption of rational choice potentially limits the theory's ability to explain 'expressive' crimes such as interpersonal violence (which would include expressive cybercrimes such as cyberstalking, cyberbullying and revenge pornography), with the same power as those based on material or economic gain (Bennett, 1991; Miethe et al., 1987). In these forms of crimes emotion (e.g., lust, anger), psychological deviations (e.g., impulsivity) and social pressures play an important role.

Researchers have also presented the importance of the possible effects of conscience and normative commitments on decision-making, particularly as it relates to 'rational' choice (Clarke & Felson, 2017; Flanigan, 2019). Normative commitment can be a result of personal morality, where one obeys the law because it is aligned with their moral code, and/or legitimacy, where one feels that the authority enforcing the law has the right to dictate behavior (Flanigan, 2019). The deliberations of researchers suggest that rational choice presents a valid picture of factors leading to a criminal event; however, it fails to present a complete picture as it does not adequately account for what makes one become a motivated offender.

The misuse of the RAT can also lead to erroneous conclusions and recommendations. For example, an approach that assumes that individuals always act rationally may lead to the blame and stigmatization of victims of cybercrime, rather than addressing the root causes of cybercrime victimization. Similarly, the positivist approach that underlies the RAT assumes that individuals are solely influenced by external factors, which neglects the role of individual agency and decision-making in shaping online behaviors. This may be particularly important in understanding the complexity and diversity of human behavior relating to the willingness to engage in protective behavior online, which is dependent on normative beliefs, past experiences, emotions (e.g., fear), psychological deviations (e.g., self-control) and appraisals (ability to cope and threat) (van't Hoff-de Goede et al., 2021; Smith & Leukfeldt, 2023). Further, the generalizability that positivists cling to in their comparison to constructivism presents its own issues. Positivists focus on objective variables (deemed to be measurable), such as age, gender and socioeconomic status, and sacrifice the subjective experiences and perceptions of individuals for the desired generalizability (Hagan, 2016). The results of these studies can create the idea that there can be a one-size-fits-all approach, which may not be applicable to all individuals and situations.

Cyberspace as a medium for crime

Another issue is the assumption of the RAT that crime is a random event that occurs due to the convergence of motivated offenders and suitable targets in the absence of capable guardianship. As argued by Holt and Bossler (2015), this assumption may not hold true in the case of cybercrime, because online criminal activity is often premeditated, organized and involves specialized skills and resources. Therefore, the conventional notion of 'opportunity' as a driver of crime may not be relevant in the case of cybercrime.

The application of the RAT usually assumes that offender motivation is a constant and focuses on the opportunity for crime. The issue with this approach is that it still assumes that the offender requires a victim to fit specific profiles and that the completion of the crime event is dependent on a rational decision-making process (Henson, 2020). However, many cyber-attacks target vulnerabilities in systems and data rather than people. Therefore, the crime requires minimal interpersonal interaction (limited dependence on victim participation) and thereby makes routine activities immaterial (Pratt et al., 2014). Hence, cyber-crimes can have completely innocent victims (a victim who did not in any way facilitate their victimization). For example, if an individual's cloud storage provider is hacked, the individual may report being hacked on a survey but would not have in any way contributed to their victimization. This suggests that rather than victimization being explained by human behavior it is either dependent on technological vulnerabilities or a nexus between opportunities provided by technology and the user. As such, the application of the RAT only provides a partial explanation of the crime event, particularly in the case of 'true' cybercrimes, in which the target is technology or data held within a networked system (Smith & Haines, 2023a). In addition, the RAT relies on traditional notions of visible offenders rather than invisible offenders who often rely on automated technical systems to commit crimes. Further, the RAT assumes that the victim has complete control over their guardianship, which is not always the case in the digital world where many security measures are out of the individual's control.

Overall, it neglects the important role technology plays in crime, both as a tool for committing the crime (e.g., malware) or the vulnerability targeted. For example, malware targets a specific vulnerability and not a type of person and may spread via networks or target systems which have weaknesses unknown and out of the control of the individual. Therefore, the application of the technology removes the individual from the equation as they do not need to engage in any specific actions to predispose them to victimization nor does the offender need to select any specific type of target but rather simply build and release their malware into the wild and wait for successful crime events.

The RAT ignores the importance of psychological, social and environmental factors

The RAT has been criticized for its normative approach to assessing crime and victimization. The theory assumes that certain behaviors are normative and that deviations from these behaviors are criminal and as such all cybercrime is the result of deviant motivations. This approach has been criticized for neglecting the social and historical context of crime and victimization. It is argued that the RAT assumes that victimization is a result of individual actions and choices, rather than the result of broader social and economic factors. In the context of cybercrime victimization, this approach can be particularly problematic.

Cybercrime victimization is not solely the result of individual actions and choices but is influenced by the broader technological and economic context in which it occurs. For example, the increasing use of technology and the growing reliance on digital platforms for communication and commerce have created new opportunities for cybercrime as it has naturally led to increased time spent online. Increasing amounts of time are spent online engaging in financial transactions, education and within online social communities, which generally increase accessibility. The degree to which a population will be online and engage in these activities is dependent on factors such as technological infrastructure and affordability of technology (average income of the society vs price of technology). In addition, social and cultural factors which affect normative belief relating to the role of online vs offline social interaction and the need to maintain interconnectedness and approval within a community will affect the use of various forms of technology (Cheng et al., 2021). This in turn affects target suitability factors such as accessibility and disclosure of personal information. Further, the prevalence of cybercrime may be influenced by differences in legal frameworks, law enforcement capabilities or economic conditions across countries or regions. Similarly, social factors such as norms, values and trust can shape individuals' attitudes and behaviors related to cybersecurity. Neglecting these factors can limit the explanatory power of RAT-based cybercrime studies and lead to inaccurate or biased conclusions.

A discussion of the methodological issues related to the operationalization of the RAT in cybercrime victimization studies

Overgeneralization—collective vs individual (or categorical) examination of cybercrime

Inconsistency in empirical evidence has been attributed to the variations in the types of cybercrime examined. Rodriguez et al. (2017) speculated based on the results of their empirical study that the predictors of cyber-victimization may be dependent on the nature of the cybercrime it seeks to predict; for example, cyber-dependent crimes may have a stronger correlation to technological variables such as antivirus software and cyber-enabled protocols, which are computer focused and dependent on social interaction variables (e.g., level of use of social networks).

Further, the effectiveness of RAT may also be affected by the nature or motivation of the crime; i.e., an observed lower efficacy of RAT can be based on the 'expressive' nature of the crime rather than technology. Also, some cybercrimes can have multiple push factors, such as hacking, which can be 'expressive' or driven by material or economic gain (Cross & Shinder, 2008; Murphy, 2019; Woo, 2003). Jiang et al. (2018) opined that in society the spatial distribution of motivated offenders, vulnerable victims or capable guardians is not homogeneous or random. Pratt and Turanovic (2015) promote geography as a factor in the probability of victimization, as individuals who engage in activities that increase the risk of victimization must still converge with a motivated offender in the absence of capable guardianship, which will have a different default probability based on their geographic location. As such, the results of studies will be dependent on the types of crimes grouped together, which crime is dominant in that region and the preferred threat vector of the offenders. This means that the exclusion of offender-related variables in studying victimization confounds the results and that results should not necessarily be generalizable outside the geographical space in which the study was done.

Thus, the RAT will likely not fully adapt to all typologies but will rather have differing levels of successful prediction with specific cybercrimes (Holt & Bossler, 2009; Wall, 2001; Rodriguez et al., 2017). This trend suggests the existence of intrinsic differences between types of cybercrimes. The works of Smith and Haines (2023b) and Akdemir and Lawless (2020) suggest that different typologies of cybercrime have different etiologies. Specifically, Smith and Haines (2023b) demonstrated that the explanatory power of the rate was negatively corre-lated to the dependence of the crime on technology (or conversely, as the importance of inter-personal interaction to commit the crime decreased so did the explanatory power of the RAT).

Operationalization of the RAT

One of the main issues is the difficulty in operationalizing the concepts of RAT when it comes to cybercrime. The RAT homogenizes offenders and victims as rational actors with similar characteristics and motivations. As noted by Holt and Bossler (2015), the concepts of 'suitable targets' and 'motivated offenders' in RAT are hard to apply in the context of cybercrime because the targets and offenders are often anonymous and geographically dis-persed. Furthermore, RAT does not consistently consider the differences in victims' vulner-ability and the extent to which they can protect themselves from cybercrime. This problem is exacerbated by the absence of clear and consistent definitions for these constructs. This makes it challenging to identify specific individuals or entities that can be classified as 'suit-able targets' or 'motivated offenders', which can limit the accuracy and generalizability of RAT-based cybercrime studies (Holt & Bossler, 2016).

Further, many studies' analyses focus on select aspects of the RAT and not the concept in its entirety. This neglects the interconnectedness of the various factors that lead to opportu-nity and the underlying need for all available information to make a 'true' rational (reflec-tive) decision. A potentially major issue is the recurring assumption used that a motivated offender can be taken as a constant when examining victimization. This assumption ignores the diversity of cybercriminals and their varied motives, including financial gain, revenge or activism (Holt & Bossler, 2015; Smith & Haines, 2023b). However, it is the motivations of the offender that determine what makes a target suitable (e.g., expressive vs instrumental crimes) or if the suitability of the target even refers to a human subject (or rather a technical vulnerability). In expressive crimes, the offender seeks to target a specific person or persons with a specific profile because of some underlying emotional or psychological motive. As such, the offender may seek to engage in the action even if the risk would be considered high when assessed logically.

Curry and Tittle (1998) identified that the RAT doesn't clarify categories of 'routine' activities or social conditions that can affect the probability of victimization. Jiang et al. (2018) state that there is a potentially limitless range of 'routine' activities, which may also be affected by an individual's lifestyle. Researchers have also identified similar issues with the specific class of routine activities referred to as risky behaviors (Choi & Lee, 2017; Bossler & Holt, 2013). Scholars have opined that these behaviors can be subjective as they are classed as 'risky' based on the cybercrime examined and sometimes the culture in which it is studied, which makes an unambiguous cyber risk profile improbable (Smith et al., 2022; van't Hoff-de Goede et al., 2021).

Lastly, researchers have cited the problematic nature of using proxy measures to assess the concepts of the RAT (Bolden, 2014; Hollis et al., 2013; Walklate, 2018). At least two sets of researchers have stated that the measure of lifestyles depends on an assumed correlation of structured variables such as age, sex and time spent in a specific activity, which is further plagued by a systematic disregard for power relations (Shillair et al., 2015; Walklate, 2018).

Data collection

The reliance on self-reported surveys and official crime statistics to study cybercrime also poses methodological challenges. According to Akers and Sellers (2013), self-reported surveys may not capture the full extent of cybercrime because many victims may not be aware that they have been victimized, or they may not report the incident to the authorities for fear of embarrassment or retaliation. Similarly, official crime statistics may not accurately reflect the prevalence of cybercrime because many incidents go unreported or undetected.

Most studies dependent on self-report surveys are subject to errors in memory or the participant's desire to give socially desirable answers. Van't Hoff-de Goede et al. (2021) suggest that the degree to which internet users can protect themselves against cybercrime remains unknown largely because how people say or think they behave online is not always the same as how they behave in real situations.

The inconsistency identified in the literature regarding the relationship between guardianship and victimization has also been attributed to the lone use of cross-sectional research designs (Bossler & Holt, 2009; Choi, 2008; Ngo & Paternoster, 2011). For example, the design of cross-sectional studies limits the ability to determine the temporal relationship between security software acquisition and infection/compromise. Past studies have also failed to address the other variables such as the timely installation of software updates, tracking and initiating software notifications and turning off security software to engage in delinquent behavior online, such as media piracy.

Conclusion and recommendations for future work

The study of cybercrime victimization is a complex and ever-evolving field that requires careful consideration of the theoretical approaches and the methodology used to apply them in research. The application of theory is essential as it provides the framework to turn anecdotal evidence about human behavior and interactions into a systematic understanding of societal behavior and norms. It should be the base from which the scientific method is applied and suitable methodologies developed. While current approaches using the RAT have been useful in understanding the nature of cybercrime victimization, the degree to which this is valid and applicable in policy development is questionable due to possible shortfalls in the application of the theory and a failure to redefine aspects of the theory to better align with the new platform of crime (cyberspace). It even begs the question of whether the modernization of the theory is sufficient and if a new theory should be developed for this phenomenon. As noted by Holt and Bossler (2015), it is essential to develop a more comprehensive and nuanced theoretical framework that considers the unique characteristics of cybercrime and the evolving nature of the technology-mediated criminal activity.

A review of the literature clearly shows several opportunities for expanding current knowledge through the modification of past methodologies in several ways. First, there is a need for examination of understudied forms of cybercrime such as malware, hacking and online fraud (Bossler & Holt, 2014; Reyns, 2015) since the focus has primarily been given to person-based forms of cybercrime such as cyberbullying (Marcum et al., 2010; Moore et al., 2010; Navarro & Jasinski, 2012) and online harassment (Bossler & Holt, 2009).

Second, most studies have only partially operationalized the theoretical framework of RAT, i.e., using one or two rather than all three of the concepts of a suitable target, motivated offender and capable guardianship. This has highlighted the ability of the individual latent variables to predict victimization but does not allow insight into how they simultaneously affect the risk of victimization.

Third, there is a need to add credence to observations made by past researchers into RAT by broadening the range of countries surveyed, increasing the sample size and choosing samples that are more likely to be representative of the target country's population. As the reach of the Internet increases and the targets of cybercriminals become broader, it is important to examine online routines from a variety of countries and groups (Reyns, 2015). This is especially necessary since the studies have consistently used non-probability samples and/or random sampling with low response rates from special populations, limiting the ability to make inferences about trends in the general population. Therefore, research within regions such as the Caribbean will add data and trend analysis for a developing geographic region compared to the data collected in the larger continents with differing social, economic, cultural and legal profiles (Smith & Stamatakis, 2021). The small scope of previous research also requires more studies to substantiate the hypothesis that behavior is more significant than sociodemographic variables in its effect on the risk of cyber victimization.

Fourth, future studies should study seek to examine several cybercrimes simultaneously rather than individually and compare them based on their taxonomical grouping as attempted by Akdemir and Lawless (2020) and Smith and Haines (2023b). Further, they should seek to build predictive models of operative risk both at the individual level and for cybercrime in general. There remains a considerable gap in efforts to identify etiological differences between cyber-enabled and cyber-dependent crimes. Given the inconsistencies demonstrated in the literature, this line of inquiry can potentially explain or provide one explanation for the observed differences.

Lastly, cybercrime research has predominantly focused on positivist approaches; however, the use of constructivist approaches can offer an additional dimension that is important to developing a comprehensive understanding of the phenomenon (Renaud et al., 2021). This combination can help in understanding the social, cultural and psychological factors that influence people's attitudes toward cybercrime victimization (locus of control and threat/coping appraisal). Additionally, this combination can provide insights into the situational factors that make individuals more susceptible to cybercrime victimization. Overall, combining these approaches can help scholars understand how social and cultural factors affect routines and decision-making processes that may lead to cybercrime victimization. Such an understanding of social and cultural factors will help policymakers in developing effective interventions to address cybercrime victimization. Understanding the cultural and social norms that influence people's attitudes towards cybercrime victimization can help in developing interventions that address the social stigma associated with being a victim of cybercrime. This can include public awareness campaigns that promote the reporting of cybercrime victimization without shame or embarrassment.

References

Ahmad, R., & Thurasamy, R. (2022). A systematic literature review of routine activity theory's applicability in cybercrimes. *Journal of Cyber Security and Mobility*. https://doi.org/10.13052/jcsm2245-1439.1133

Akdemir, N., & Lawless, C. (2020). Exploring the human factor in cyber-enabled and cyber-dependent crime victimisation: A lifestyle routine activities approach. *Internet Research*. Retrieved from z-wcorg/.

Akers, R. L., & Sellers, C. S. (2013). *Criminological theories: Introduction, evaluation, and application*. Oxford University Press.

Aldag, R. (2013). *Bounded rationality and satisficing (Behavioral decision-making model)*. SAGE Publications, Inc.

Argun, U., & Dağlar, M. (2016). Examination of routine activities theory by the property crime. *International Journal of Human Sciences*, 13(1), 1188.

Bachman, R. D., & Schutt, R. K. (2019). *The practice of research in criminology and criminal justice* (7th ed.). SAGE Publications, Inc.

Bennett, R. (1991). Routine activities: A cross-national assessment of a criminological perspective. *Social Forces*, 70(1), 147–163.

Bock, K., Shannon, S., Movahedi, Y., & Cukier, M. (2017). *Application of routine activity theory to cyber intrusion location and time* [2017 13th European Dependable Computing Conference (EDCC)] (pp. 139–146). Institute of Electrical and Electronics Engineers. https://doi.org/10.1109/EDCC.2017.24

Bolden, C. (2014). Friendly foes: Hybrid gangs or social networking. *Group Processes & Intergroup Relations*, 17(6), 730–749.

Bossler, A., & Holt, T. (2009). Examining the applicability of lifestyle-routine activities theory for cybercrime victimization. *Deviant Behavior*, 30(1), 1–25.

Bossler, A., & Holt, T. (2010). The effect of self-control on victimization in the cyberworld. *Journal of Criminal Justice*, 38(3), 227–236.

Bossler, A., & Holt, T. (2014). An assessment of the current state of cyber crime scholarship. *Deviant Behavior*, 35(1), 20–40.

Bossler, A. M., & Berenblum, T. (2019). Introduction: New directions in cybercrime research. *Journal of Crime and Justice*, 42(5), 495–499. https://doi.org/10.1080/0735648X.2019.1692426

Bossler, A. M., & Holt, T. (2013). Examining the relationship between routine activities and malware infection indicators. *Journal of Contemporary Criminal Justice*, 29(4). https://doi.org/10.1177/1043986213507401

Bossler, A. M., Holt, T. J., & May, D. C. (2012). Predicting online harassment victimization among a juvenile population. *Youth and Society*, 44(4), 500–523.

Chen, L., Ho, S., & Lwin, M. (2017). A meta-analysis of factors predicting cyberbullying perpetration and victimization: From the social cognitive and media effects approach. *New Media, & Society*, 19(8), 1194–1213.

Cheng, C., Lau, Y., Chan, L., & Luk, J. W. (2021). Prevalence of social media addiction across 32 nations: Meta-analysis with subgroup analysis of classification schemes and cultural values. *Addictive Behaviors*, 117, 106845. https://doi.org/10.1016/j.addbeh.2021.106845

Choi, K. (2008). Computer crime victimization and integrated theory: An empirical assessment. *International Journal of Cyber Criminology*, 2(1), 308–333.

Choi, K., & Lee, J. (2017). Theoretical analysis of cyber-interpersonal violence victimization and offending using cyber-routine activities theory. *Computers in Human Behavior*, 73, 394–402.

Choi, S. (2018). *A Lifestyle-Routine Activity Theory (LRAT) approach to cybercrime victimization: Empirical assessment of SNS lifestyle exposure activities* [Seoul National University]. Semantic Scholar. Retrieved from www.semanticscholar.org/paper/A-Lifestyle-Routine-Activity-Theory-(LRAT)-Approach-%EC%B5%9C%EC%A7%80%EC%84%A0/9d3068ee418806c2729e1a05a54f8aeaaf58197d

Clarke, R. (2018). *The theory and practice of situational crime prevention*. Oxford University Press.

Clarke, R. V. G. (1999). *Hot products: Understanding, anticipating and reducing demand for stolen goods*. Home Office, Policing and Reducing Crime Unit, Research, Development and Statistics Directorate.

Clarke, R. V. G., & Felson, M. (2017). *Routine activity and rational choice*. Retrieved from http://search.ebscohost.com/login.aspx?direct=true&scope=site&db=nlebk&db=nlabk&AN=1620798

Cohen, L., & Felson, M. (2003). Routine activity theory. In *Criminological theory: Past to present* (2nd ed.). Roxberry Publishing Company.

Cohen, L. E., & Felson, M. (1979). Social change and crime rate trends: A routine activity approach. *American Sociological Review*, *44*(4), 588–608.

Cross, M., & Shinder, D. (2008). *Scene of the cybercrime* (Vol. 1). Syngress Pub. Retrieved from http://public.eblib.com/choice/publicfullrecord.aspx?p=405213

Curado, M., Teles, J., & Maroco, J. (2014). Analysis of variables that are not directly observable: Influence on decision-making during the research process. *Revista Da Escola de Enfermagem*, *48*(1), 146–152.

Curry, G., & Tittle, C. (1998). Control balance: Toward a general theory of deviance. *Social Forces*, *76*(3).

DeGarmo, M. (2011). Understanding the comparisons of routine activities and contagious distributions of victimization: Forming a mixed model of confluence and transmission. *International Journal of Criminology*, *4*(1), 584–603.

de Jong, E., Bernasco, W., & Lammers, M. (2019). Situational correlates of adolescent substance use: An improved test of the routine activity theory of deviant behavior. *Journal of Quantitative Criminology*, *36*(4), 823–850. https://doi.org/10.1007/s10940-019-09433-w

DeLisi, M., & Conis, P. (2012). *Violent offenders: Theory, research, policy, and practice*. Jones & Bartlett Learning.

Eck, J., & Clarke, R. (2003). Classifying common police problems: A routine activity approach. *Crime Prevention Studies*, *16*, 7–39.

Engel, R. J., & Schutt, R. K. (2014). Conceptualization and measurement. In *Fundamentals of social work research* (pp. 68–70). SAGE Publications. Retrieved from http://public.ebookcentral.proquest.com/choice/publicfullrecord.aspx?p=1995891

Felson, M. (1998). *Crime and everyday life: Insights and implications for society*. Pine Forges Press.

Felson, M. (2006). Those who discourage crime. In J. Eck & D. Weisburd (Eds.), *Crime prevention studies* (Vol. 4, pp. 53–66). Criminal Justice Press.

Felson, M., & Boba, R. (2010). *Crime and everyday life*. Sage.

Fisher, B., Cullen, F., & Turner, M. (2002). Being pursued: Stalking victimization in a national study of college women. *Criminology, & Public Policy*, *1*(2), 257–308.

Fisher, B., Sloan, J., Cullen, F., & Lu, C. (1998). Crime in the ivory tower: The level and sources of student victimization. *Criminology*, *36*(3), 671–710.

Flanigan, E. T. (2019). Do we have reasons to obey the law? *Journal of Ethics & Social Philosophy*, 1–40.

Fleming, M. J., Greentree, S., Cocotti-Muller, D., Elias, K. A., & Morrison, S. (2006). Safety in cyberspace: Adolescents' safety and exposure online. *Youth and Society*, *38*(2), 135–154.

Garger, J. (2011). *Latent constructs in social science research*. John Garger. Retrieved from https://johngarger.com/articles/methodology/latent-constructs-in-social-science-research

Grabosky, P. (2001). Computer crime: A criminological overview. *Forum on Crime and Society*, *1*(1), 35–53.

Grabosky, P., & Smith, R. (2001). Telecommunication fraud in the digital age: The convergence of technologies. In *Crime and the internet* (1st ed., pp. 29–43). Routledge.

Grzybowski, M. (2012). *An examination of cybercrime and cybercrime research: Self-control and routine activity theory*. Arizona State University.

Hagan, M. (2016). *The user experience of the internet as a legal help service: Defining standards for the next generation of user-friendly online legal services* [SSRN Scholarly Paper]. Retrieved from https://papers.ssrn.com/abstract=2942478

Henson, B. (2020). Routine Activities. In T. J. Holt & A. M. Bossler (Eds.), *The Palgrave handbook of international cybercrime and cyberdeviance* (pp. 469–489). Springer International Publishing. Retrieved from https://doi.org/10.1007/978-3-319-78440-3_23

Hinduja, S., & Patchin, J. W. (2009). *Bullying beyond the schoolyard: Preventing and responding to cyberbullying*. Corwin Press.

Hollis, M. E., Felson, M., & Welsh, B. C. (2013). The capable guardian in routine activities theory: A theoretical and conceptual reappraisal. *Crime Prevention and Community Safety*, *15*(1), 65–79.

Hollis-Peel, M., Reynald, D., Bavel, M., Elffers, H., & Welsh, B. (2011). Guardianship for crime prevention: A critical review of the literature. *Crime, Law and Social Change*, *56*(1), 53–70. https://doi.org/10.1007/s10611-011-9309-2

Holt, T., & Bossler, A. (2009). Examining the applicability of lifestyle-routine activities theory for cybercrime victimization. *Deviant Behavior, 30*(1), 1–25. http://dx.doi.org.ezproxy.uky.edu/10.1080/01639620701876577

Holt, T., & Bossler, A. (2015). *Cybercrime in progress* (1st ed.). Routledge. Retrieved from https://doi.org/10.4324/9781315775944

Holt, T., & Copes, H. (2010). Transferring subcultural knowledge on-line: Practices and beliefs of persistent digital pirates. *Deviant Behavior, 31*(7), 625–654.

Holt, T., & Turner, M. (2012). Examining risks and protective factors of on-line identity theft. *Deviant Behavior, 33*(4), 308–323.

Holt, T. J., & Bossler, A. M. (2016). *Cybercrime in progress: Theory and prevention of technology-enabled offenses.* Crime Sciences Series. Routledge.

Howell, C., Burruss, G., Maimon, D., & Sahani, S. (2019). Website defacement and routine activities: Considering the importance of hackers' valuations of potential targets. *Journal of Crime and Justice, 42*(5), 536–550. https://doi.org/10.1080/0735648X.2019.1691859

Hsieh, M., & Wang, S. (2018). Routine activities in a virtual space: A Taiwanese case of an ATM hacking spree. *International Journal of Cyber Criminology, 12*(1), 333–352.

Hutchings, A., & Hayes, H. (2009). Routine activity theory and phishing victimisation: Who gets caught in the 'net'? *Current Issues in Criminal Justice, 20*(3), 433–451.

Ilievski, A. (2016). An explanation of the cybercrime victimisation: Self-control and lifestyle/routine activity theory. *Innovative Issues and Approaches in Social Sciences, 9*(1), 30–47. https://doi.org/10.12959/issn.1855-0541

Internet Crime Complaint Center (IC3). (2012). *2011 Internet crime report.* Retrieved from https://www.ic3.gov/Media/PDF/AnnualReport/2011_IC3Report.pdf

Jaishankar, K. (Ed.). (2011). *Cyber criminology: Exploring internet crimes and criminal behavior* (1st ed.). Routledge. Retrieved from https://doi.org/10.1201/b10718

Jansen, J., & Leukfeldt, R. (2016). Phishing and malware attacks on online banking customers in the Netherlands: A qualitative analysis of factors leading to victimization. *International Journal of Cyber Criminology.* https://doi.org/10.5281/zenodo.58523

Jiang, B., Mak, C., Zhong, H., Larsen, L., & Webster, C. (2018). From broken windows to perceived routine activities: Examining impacts of environmental interventions on perceived safety of Urban Alleys. *Frontiers in Psychology, 9.*

Katz, J., & Quade, V. (1989). The seductions of crime. *Human Rights, 16*(1), 24–51.

Kringen, J. A., & Felson, M. (2014). Routine activities approach. In G. Bruinsma & D. Weisburd (Eds.), *Encyclopedia of criminology and criminal justice* (pp. 4544–4551). Springer. Retrieved from https://doi.org/10.1007/978-1-4614-5690-2_586

Leukfeldt, E., & Yar, M. (2016). Applying routine activity theory to cybercrime: A theoretical and empirical analysis. *Deviant Behavior, 37*(3), 263–280. https://doi.org/10.1080/01639625.2015.1012409

Louderback, E., & Roy, S. (2018). Integrating social disorganization and routine activity theories and testing the effectiveness of neighbourhood crime watch programs: Case study of Miami-Dade County, 2007–15. *British Journal of Criminology, 58*(4), 968–992.

Lwin, M., Stanaland, A., & Miyazaki, A. (2008). Protecting children's privacy online: How parental mediation strategies affect website safeguard effectiveness. *Journal of Retailing, 84*(2), 205–217.

Madero-Hernandez, A. (2019). Lifestyle exposure theory of victimization. In F. P. Bernat & K. Frailing (Eds.), *The encyclopedia of women and crime* (1st ed., pp. 1–3). Wiley. https://doi.org/10.1002/9781118929803.ewac0334

Maimon, D., Howell, C. J., Perkins, R. C., Muniz, C. N., & Berenblum, T. (2023). A routine activities approach to evidence-based risk assessment: Findings from two simulated phishing attacks. *Social Science Computer Review, 41*(1), 286–304. https://doi.org/10.1177/08944393211046339

Malby, S. (2013). *Comprehensive study on cybercrime.* United Nations (p. 165). UNODC. Retrieved from www.sbs.ox.ac.uk/cybersecurity-capacity/content/unodc-comprehensive-study-cybercrime

Marcum, C. (2008). Identifying potential factors of adolescent online victimization in high school seniors. *International Journal of Cyber Criminology, 2*(2), 346–367.

Marcum, C., Ricketts, M., & Higgins, G. (2010). Assessing sex experiences of online victimization: An examination of adolescent online behaviors using routine activity theory. *Criminal Justice Review, 35*(4), 412–437.

Marttila, E., Koivula, A., & Räsänen, P. (2021). Cybercrime victimization and problematic social media use: Findings from a nationally representative panel study. *American Journal of Criminal Justice*, 46(6), 862–881. https://doi.org/10.1007/s12103-021-09665-2

Mesch, G., & Dodel, M. (2018). Low self-control, information disclosure, and the risk of online fraud. *American Behavioral Scientist*, 62(10), 1356–1371.

Miethe, T., & Meier, R. (1994). *Crime and its social context: Toward an integrated theory of offenders, victims, and situations.* State University of New York Press.

Miethe, T. D., Stafford, M. C., & Long, J. S. (1987). Social differentiation in criminal victimization—A test of routine activities/lifestyle theories. *American Sociological Review*, 52(2), 184–194.

Miró-Llinares, F. (2011). The criminal opportunity in cyberspace: Application and development of routine activity theory for the prevention of cybercrime, (13), 7:01–7:55. *Revista Electrónica De Ciencia Penal y Criminología*, 13(7), 1–55. Retrieved from http://criminet.ugr.es/recpc/index.html

Miró-Llinares, F. (2014). Routine activity theory. In *The encyclopedia of theoretical criminology* (pp. 1–7). Blackwell Publishing Ltd. https://doi.org/10.1002/9781118517390/wbetc198

Mitchell, K., Finkelhor, D., & Wolak, J. (2007). Youth internet users at risk for the more serious online sexual solicitations. *American Journal of Preventive Medicine*, 32, 532–537.

Moore, R., Guntupalli, N., & Lee, T. (2010). Parental regulation and online activities: Examining factors that influence a youth's potential to become a victim of online harassment. *International Journal of Cyber Criminology*, 4, 685–698.

Murphy, R. (2019). *Behind the screen: Types of hackers and their motivations.* Cybershark. Retrieved from www.blackstratus.com/behind-the-screen-types-of-hackers-and-their-motivations/

Mustaine, E., & Tewskbury, R. (1998). Predicting risk of larceny theft victimization: A routine activity analysis using refined lifestyle measures. *Criminology*, 36, 829–857.

Navarro, J., & Jasinski, J. (2012). Going cyber: Using routine activities theory to predict cyberbullying experiences. *Sociological Spectrum*, 32(1), 81–94.

Ngo, F., & Paternoster, R. (2011). Cybercrime victimization: An examination of individual and situational level factors. *International Journal of Cyber Criminology*, 5(1), 773–793.

Pelfrey, W. V., & Weber, N. L. (2013). Keyboard gangsters: Analysis of incidence and correlates of cyberbullying in a large urban student population. *Deviant Behavior*, 34(1), 68–84.

Petrossian, G. A., & Clarke, R. V. (2014). Explaining and controlling illegal commercial fishing: An application of the CRAVED theft model. *British Journal of Criminology*, 54, 73–90.

Pratt, T. C., Holtfreter, K., & Reisig, M. D. (2010). Routine online activity and internet fraud targeting: Extending the generality of routine activity theory. *Journal of Research in Crime and Delinquency*, 47(3), 267–296. https://doi.org/10.1177/0022427810365903

Pratt, T., & Turanovic, J. (2015). Lifestyle and routine activity theories revisited: The importance of "risk" to the study of victimization. *Victims and Offenders*, 11(3), 335–354. https://doi.org/10.1080/15564886.2015.1057351

Pratt, T. C., Turanovic, J. J., Fox, K. A., & Wright, K. A. (2014). Self-control and victimization: A meta-analysis. *Criminology*, 52(1), 87–116.

Renaud, K., Zimmermann, V., Schürmann, T., & Böhm, C. (2021). Exploring cybersecurity-related emotions and finding that they are challenging to measure. *Humanities and Social Sciences Communications*, 8(1), 75. https://doi.org/10.1057/s41599-021-00746-5

Reyns, B. (2013). Online routines and identity theft victimization: Further expanding routine activity theory beyond direct-contact offenses. *Journal of Research in Crime and Delinquency*, 50(2), 216–238.

Reyns, B. (2015). A routine activity perspective on online victimisation. *Journal of Financial Crime*, 22(4), 396–411. https://doi.org/10.1108/JFC-06-2014-0030

Reyns, B., Henson, B., & Fisher, B. (2011). Being pursued online: Applying cyberlifestyle—Routine activities theory to cyberstalking victimization. *Criminal Justice and Behavior*, 38(11), 1149–1169. https://doi.org/10.1177/0093854811421448

Rodriguez, J., Oduber, J., & Mora, E. (2017). Routine Activities and Cybervictimization in Venezuela. *Latin American Journal of Safety Studies*, 20, 63–79.

Sampson, R., Eck, J. E., & Dunham, J. (2010). Super controllers and crime prevention: A routine activity explanation of crime prevention success and failure. *Security Journal*, 23(1), 37–51.

Shillair, R., Cotten, S., Tsai, H., Alhabash, S., LaRose, R., & Rifon, N. (2015). Online safety begins with you and me: Convincing internet users to protect themselves. *Computers in Human Behavior*, 48, 199–207.

Smith, C. B., McLaughlin, M. L., & Osborne, K. K. (2006). Conduct control on usenet. *Journal of Computer-Mediated Communication, 2*(4).

Smith, T. (2022). Assessing the effects of COVID-19 on online routine activities and cybercrime: A snapshot of the effect of sheltering in place. *Caribbean Journal of Multidisciplinary Studies, 1*(1), 36–60. Retrieved from https://cjms.utt.edu.tt/ojs/index.php/cjms/article/view/15

Smith, T., & Haines, K. (2023a). A doubled-edged sword called cyberspace: Introducing the concept of cybercrime. In P. K. Roy & A. K. Tripathy (Eds.), *Cybercrime in social media: Theory and solutions.* Taylor & Francis Group.

Smith, T., & Haines, K. (2023b). Examining the etiology of cybercrime: Comparing the utility of the routine activities theory using a model-comparison approach. *Caribbean Journal of Multidisciplinary Studies, 1*(2).

Smith, T., Leukfeldt, E. R., & van de Weijer, S. (2022). *Risky online behaviors scale validation and identification of behavioral sub-groups: An assessment using classical test theory and the Rasch model* [Conference Presentation]. Annual Human Factor in Cybercrime Conference, Clearwater, Florida.

Smith, T., & Leukfeldt, R. (2023). Moving from risk factors to positive online behaviors: An integrated behavioral change approach. In R. Graham, S. Humer, C. Lee, & V. Nagy (Eds.), *Routledge international handbook of online deviance* (p. 2023). Routledge.

Smith, T., & Stamatakis, N. (2020). Defining cybercrime in terms of routine activity and spatial distribution: Issues and concerns. *International of Cyber Criminology, 14*(2), 433–459. https://dx.doi.org/10.5281/zenodo.4769989

Smith, T., & Stamatakis, N. (2021). Cyber-victimization trends in Trinidad & Tobago: The results of an empirical research. *The International Journal of Cybersecurity Intelligence and Cybercrime, 4*(1), 46–63. https://doi.org/10.52306/04010421JINE3509

Stohr, M., & Walsh, A. (2012). *Corrections: The essentials.* SAGE Publications.

Tewksbury, R., & Mustaine, E. E. (2003). College students' lifestyles and self-protective behaviors: Further considerations of the guardianship concept in routine activity theory. *Criminal Justice and Behavior, 30*, 302–327.

Tilley, N., Farrell, G., & Clarke, R. V. (2015). Target suitability and the crime drop. In *The criminal act: The role and influence of routine activity theory.* Palgrave Macmillan. https://doi.org/10.1007/978-1-137-52502-4

Tilley, N., & Sidebottom, A. (2018). Situational crime prevention. In G. Bruinsma & D. Weisburd (Eds.), *Encyclopedia of criminology and criminal justice* (pp. 4864–4874). Springer. Retrieved from https://doi.org/10.1007/978-1-4614-5690-2_549

Tseloni, A., Wittebrood, K., Farrell, G., & Pease, K. (2004). Burglary victimization in England and Wales, the United States and the Netherlands. *British Journal of Criminology, 44*(1), 66–91.

van Ours, J., & Vollaard, B. (2013). *The engine immobilizer a non-starter for car thieves.* CESifo. Retrieved from www.cesifo-group.de/ifoHome/publications/working-papers/CESifoWP/CESifoWPdetails?wp_id=19073347

van Ouytsel, J., Ponnet, K., & Walrave, M. (2018). Cyber dating abuse victimization among secondary school students from a lifestyle-routine activities theory perspective. *Journal of Interpersonal Violence, 33*(17), 2767–2776. https://doi.org/10.1177/0886260516629390

van Wilsem, J. (2011). Worlds tied together? Online and non-domestic routine activities and their impact on digital and traditional threat victimization. *European Journal of Criminology, 8*(2), 115–127.

van Wilsem, J. (2013). "Bought it, but never got it" assessing risk factors for online consumer fraud victimization. *European Sociological Review, 29*(2), 168–178.

van't Hoff-de Goede, M. S., Leukfeldt, E. R., van der Kleij, R., & van de Weijer, S. G. A. (2021). The online behaviour and victimization study: The development of an experimental research instrument for measuring and explaining online behaviour and cybercrime victimization. In M. Weulen Kranenbarg & R. Leukfeldt (Eds.), *Cybercrime in context: Vol. I* (pp. 21–41). Springer International Publishing. Retrieved from https://doi.org/10.1007/978-3-030-60527-8_3

Wachs, S., Michelsen, A., Wright, M. F., Gámez-Guadix, M., Almendros, C., Kwon, Y., Na, E.-Y., Sittichai, R., Singh, R., Biswal, R., Görzig, A., & Yanagida, T. (2020). A routine activity approach to understand cybergrooming victimization among adolescents from six countries. *Cyberpsychology, Behavior, and Social Networking, 23*(4), 218–224. https://doi.org/10.1089/cyber.2019.0426

Walklate, S. (2018). *Handbook of victims and victimology* (2nd ed.). Routledge.

Wall, D. (Ed.). (2001). *Cybercrimes and the internet* (1st ed.). Routledge.

Wall, D. (Ed.). (2017). *Crime and deviance in cyberspace* (1st ed.). Routledge. Retrieved from www.myilibrary.com?id=1019851

Walsh, A., & Jorgensen, C. (2017). Crime as choice: Rationality. In *Emotion, and criminal behavior* (p. 93). Sage Publications.

Wikström, R. (2018). *The evolution of technology*. Retrieved from www.oxfordbibliographies.com/view/document/obo-9780195396607/obo-9780195396607-0010.xml

Wolak, J., Finkelhor, D., & Mitchell, K. J. (2012). How often are teens arrested for sexting? Data from a national sample of police cases. *Pediatrics, 129*(1), 4–12.

Wolfe, S. E., Higgins, G. E., & Marcum, C. D. (2007). Deterrence and digital piracy: A preliminary examination of the role of viruses. *Social Science Computer Review, 26*(3), 317–333.

Woo, H.-J. (2003). *The hacker mentality: Exploring the relationship between psychological variables and hacking activities* [Dissertation, The University of Georgia].

Wright, J., & Beaver, K. (2005). Do parents matter in creating self-control in their children? A genetically informed test of Gottfredson and Hirschi's theory of low self-control. *Criminology, 43*(4).

Yar, M. (2005). The novelty of "cybercrime": An assessment in light of routine activity Theory. *European Journal of Criminology, 2*(4), 414. https://doi.org/10.1177/147737080556056

Ybarra, M., Mitchell, K., Finkelhor, D., & Wolak, J. (2007). Internet prevention messages: Targeting the right online behaviors. *Archives of Pediatrics & Adolescent Medicine, 161*(2), 138–145.

Yucedal, B. (2010). *Victimization in cyberspace: An application of routine activity and lifestyle exposure theories*. Kent State University. Retrieved from http://rave.ohiolink.edu/etdc/view?acc_num=kent1279290984

2

MEASURING CYBERCRIME AND CYBERDEVIANCE IN SURVEYS

David Buil-Gil, Nicolas Trajtenberg and Marcelo F. Aebi

Introduction

Crime researchers have been preoccupied with the accuracy of crime measures at least since the early 19th century. As soon as the first national court statistics were published in France, Alphonse de Candolle (1830 [1987], 1832 [1987]) pointed out that they were likely affected by a variety of factors external to crime events, including whether incidents are identified by someone, if the person responsible is identified and if the court has enough evidence to convict the offender. Since then, many have studied the extent to which crime estimates recorded from different data sources accurately reflect the volume and nature of crime in society (Biderman & Reiss, 1967; Coleman & Moynihan, 1996; Skogan, 1977). Currently, the development of digital technologies is leading researchers and practitioners worldwide to recognize that measuring cybercrime and cyberdeviance is even more challenging than measuring more traditional forms of criminal and deviant behavior (Aebi et al., 2022; Caneppele & Aebi, 2019; Decker, 2020; Furnell et al., 2015). For instance, using data from the Crime Survey for England and Wales 2019–2020, the UK Office for National Statistics (2021) estimated that while 49% of violence, 45% of robbery, 37% of theft and 33% of damage incidents are reported to the police, public authorities are only informed of 13% of cyber-enabled frauds and 4% of computer misuse incidents (including computer viruses and unauthorized access to personal information). This chapter addresses the measurement of cybercrime with a focus on estimates obtained from surveys. It describes, categorizes and compares the measures of cybercrime and cyberdeviance included in the main national crime surveys, and discusses the opportunities and limitations of these measures to generate accurate estimates to study the prevalence, incidence, distribution and nature of cybercriminal and cyberdeviant behavior.

The chapter builds upon the comprehensive conceptualization of cybercrime presented by McGuire and Dowling (2013), which is used as a primary criterion for cybercrime counting in the UK and other countries. According to them, cybercrime can be defined as a set of offences that are dependent on or enabled by computers, computer networks or other forms of information and communication technologies. Policy documents distinguish cyber-dependent crimes (i.e., offenses that can only be committed through digital systems,

DOI: 10.4324/9781003277675-4

which mainly include malware, hacking and denial of service attacks) from cyber-enabled crimes (i.e., traditional crimes which have increased in scale or reach due to the use of digital technologies, including cyber-enabled fraud as well as other cyber-enabled predatory offences and crimes against individuals). This definition is nonetheless restricted to those behaviors categorized as 'criminal' by the criminal law, thus excluding other forms of online deviant behavior with harmful consequences (Graham & Smith, 2020). Although the distinction between 'cybercrime' and 'cyberdeviance' is not always clear-cut (Cioban et al., 2021), most national surveys have tended to focus on criminal behaviors. Less attention has been given to cyberdeviant behavior such as cyber-enabled bullying, online harassment, online hate speech or online gambling (Castaño-Pulgarín et al., 2021; Chun et al., 2020; Lee, 2018). In addition, researchers are warning about the challenges posed by hybrid crimes, which are crimes that take place both online and offline; for example, when an adolescent is bullied at school and on social media (Aebi, 2022).

Both cyber-enabled and cyber-dependent crime figures have seen rapid increases at least since the early 2000s (EUROPOL, 2021) and spiked in the aftermath of the COVID-19 pandemic (Buil-Gil et al., 2021a). Estimates from the International Telecommunication Union (2021), the United Nations' specialized agency for information and communication technologies, show that 4.9 billion people (63% of the world's population) had access to the internet in 2021, compared to 1 billion in 2005. This increase seems mainly related to the exponential growth of smartphones, which multiplied the number of potential offenders and victims of cybercrime. With the increase in cybercrime and cyberdeviance, it becomes urgent to adequately understand its volume, characteristics and distribution to study its causes and consequences, and in turn design and evaluate prevention strategies. There is a growing need for reliable data on cybercrime offending and victimization. While police-recorded cybercrime data is regularly criticized for failing to capture the vast majority of cybercrime incidents (Caneppele & Aebi, 2019; Correia, 2022; Decker, 2020), crime surveys probe representative population samples about their experiences with crime and deviance and are often used to obtain estimates of cybercrime prevalence and incidence (Furnell et al., 2015; Reep-van der Bergh & Junger, 2018) and to study the precursors of victimization (Holt & Bossler, 2008; Leukfeldt & Yar, 2016) and offending (McGuire & Dowling, 2013; Weulen Kranenbarg, 2022). Survey data offer apparent advantages over more traditional sources of cybercrime and cyberdeviance data, but surveys are not free from limitations, and temporal and cross-national comparisons are not always possible.

Data sources to measure cybercrime and cyberdeviance

A variety of data sources have traditionally been used to measure crime. Crime researchers, police forces and policy makers use data recorded from criminal justice statistics, calls for police services, ambulance dispatches and victimization and self-report surveys to study the nature and volume of crime (Aebi et al., 2002; Bottoms et al., 1987; Huey & Buil-Gil, 2024). While all these data sources offer important information about crime, none of them allow for error-free crime measurements. Different data sources are affected by different kinds of measurement error and fail to capture many crimes that happen in society. To mention some examples, police records do not document incidents that are not reported to the police or those that the police deem not serious enough; health emergency services' statistics only measure incidents that result in physical injuries; victim surveys fail to capture so-called 'victimless' crimes (e.g., drug offenses, tax fraud) and vital offenses; and

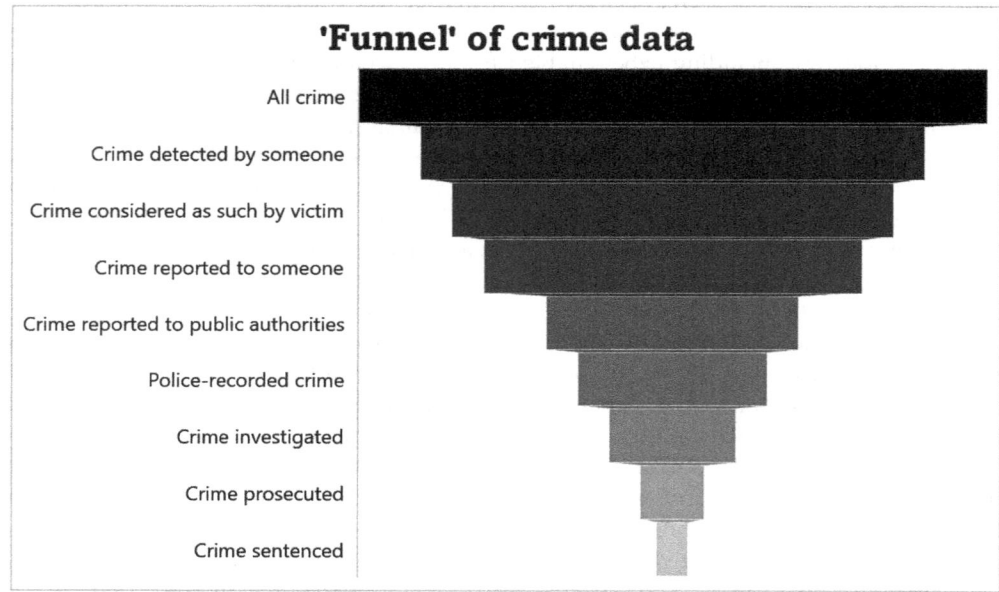

Figure 2.1 'Funnel' of crime data

self-report studies are often limited to delinquent and deviant behavior in adolescents. As a consequence, estimates of crime obtained from different sources often show remarkably different trends (Lynch & Addington, 2006) and spatial distributions (Buil-Gil et al., 2022).

Crime data users often prioritize data sources that are closer to the crime event in terms of legal procedure, as crime records shrink through the stages of the criminal justice system process. This is often referred to as the 'Sellin's dictum'—"the value of a crime rate for index purposes decreases as the distance from the crime itself in terms of procedure increases" (Sellin, 1931, p. 346). The dwindling of crime records through the legal procedure stages is commonly visualized as the 'funnel' (Figure 2.1) or the 'sieve' of crime statistics (Chopin & Aebi, 2020). In this regard, crime surveys, which probe representative population samples about their direct experiences with crime, are typically assumed to allow for more valid estimates of 'all crime' than official sources of crime data.

Similarly, a variety of sources of data have been used in research and practice to measure and study cybercrime. Public administrations increasingly publish aggregated statistics of known online crimes. Some of the most widely known examples of open-access cybercrime data repositories and reports are the annual report of the FBI's Internet Crime Complaint Center IC3 in the US,[1] the interactive data dashboard of Action Fraud in the UK,[2] the annual Internet Organized Crime Threat Assessment of EUROPOL's European Cybercrime Centre EC3[3] and the Australian Cyber Security Centre Annual Cyber Threat Report.[4] The European Sourcebook of Crime and Criminal Justice Statistics publishes cross-national records of cyber-enabled fraud, and for some countries cyber-dependent crime, recorded each year in official statistics and national surveys in European countries (Aebi et al., 2021). The non-governmental organization Private Rights Clearinghouse provides detailed descriptions of data breaches sentenced in US courts.[5]

Alongside official cybercrime records, private organizations, mainly technology and cybersecurity software companies, are increasingly developing their own estimates of cybercrime based on data sources often unavailable to public administrations (Furnell et al., 2015). McAfee, one of the largest security software companies, publishes data aggregates about ongoing and emerging ransomware threats identified by the company in an interactive data dashboard called MVISION Insights.[6] F-Secure, a cybersecurity company with headquarters in Finland, set up a network of honeypots to identify malware trends and publishes aggregated data in its annual Attack Landscape report.[7] F-Secure also publishes data recorded from surveys with IT decision makers in the private sector. A network of honeypots is also used by Broadcom, an American software company, to record data and publish descriptive statistics about cyber-dependent threats.[8] Broadcom also utilizes email processing technology to identify and share data about spam, phishing and email malware trends. All these sources of data published by private initiatives provide highly important information about ongoing and emerging cyber-dependent and in some cases cyber-enabled crimes, and can serve to identify changes in trends. Nonetheless, private organizations seldomly publish microdata about specific incidents, and there is often a lack of transparency about methodologies used to estimate and forecast crime threats, which makes this data of very limited use for the more advanced statistical techniques needed to understand the nature of cybercrime. This opacity regarding data sharing practices in the private sector is most probably due to the interest of businesses in protecting highly competitive market shares against organizational competitors, and perhaps due to data privacy implications (Young et al., 2019). Academic organizations are also developing similar initiatives and sharing the data through user agreements and online requests. As an example, the Cambridge Cybercrime Centre records data about underground and extremist online forums, defaced websites, investment scams, denial of service attacks, phishing, spam and malware.[9] The Korea University's Hacking and Countermeasure Research Lab records data about malware, hacking and attacks against Internet of Things devices.[10]

There is also a growth of digital platforms that record crowdsourced data about cybercrime and cyberdeviance. A variety of platforms exist that allow individuals to report details of individual incidents, thus allowing others to protect themselves against similar threats. 'Ransomwhere' is an open code website that allows victims of ransomware to share details about the incident, including free text descriptions of each crime and the Bitcoin address where the ransom was requested or paid.[11] Bitcoin Abuse offers similar functionalities.[12] These data sources are open-source, easily accessible and sometimes record information over long periods of time (Gundur et al., 2021). The main issue with crowdsourced datasets of incidents is that these are recorded from non-probability samples, and the mode of production of these data may contribute to severe self-selection biases and overrepresentation of so-called 'super-contributors' (Solymosi & Bowers, 2018). Unsolicited online data recorded from encrypted 'darknets' is also used to analyze drug markets (Enghoff & Aldridge, 2019; Paquet-Clouston et al., 2018), and social media data to analyze cyber-enabled hate crime (Burnap & Williams, 2016), but may be of limited use to analyze most other types of cybercrime.

While many different sources of cybercrime data are becoming available and used in research and practice to understand online crime and deviance, many argue that surveys are today the most fit-for-purpose tool to study the volume, distribution and characteristics of cybercrime and cyberdeviance.

Crime surveys

Since the 1930s, social surveys have been used to measure a variety of aspects of people's social and political lives, including voting intentions, opinion polls, market preferences, trust in government agencies and social attitudes. A door-to-door inquiry about burglaries conducted in Aarhus, Denmark, in 1730, is often considered a predecessor of contemporary victimization surveys (Wolf & Hauge, 1975; cited in Sparks, 1981). In 1945, the Gallup Poll included measures of personal crime victimization in the last 12 months, including theft, burglary, robbery, assault, trespassing and fraud, in a social survey conducted in Finland (Aebi & Linde, 2014). Nonetheless, the first survey specifically designed to measure crime and victimization was sponsored by the US President's Commission on Law Enforcement and Administration of Justice in 1965 (Ennis, 1967). The 'Attitudes and Experience Questionnaire: Victimization Study' asked a sample of US respondents about their experiences with crime, namely with burglary, car theft, robbery, larceny, malicious mischief or arson, counterfeiting, rape, other sex crimes, assault, threat, auto offenses, intrafamilial violence, consumer fraud, building violations, bribing, homicide and kidnapping. It also included follow-up measures about details of the victims and offender, crime reporting to the police, consequences of crime and perceptions about the police.

Since then, victimization surveys have become a common instrument at the national (Aebi & Linde, 2014), local (Maguire, 1997) and international levels (van Dijk et al., 2007). Some of the main national victimization surveys are the US National Crime Victimization Survey (NCVS), the Crime Survey for England and Wales (CSEW; formerly known as British Crime Survey), the Mexico National Survey on Victimization and Perception of Public Safety (ENVIPE), the Netherlands Safety Monitor and the Chilean National Urban Survey on Citizen Security (ENUSC). The International Crime Victims Survey (ICVS) recorded data across many countries worldwide in 1989, 1992, 1996, 2000 and 2004/2005.[13] Victimization surveys have been key for the advancement of explanations of victimization (Hindelang et al., 1978; Pratt et al., 2010; Tilley & Tseloni, 2016) and revictimization risk (Farrell & Pease, 1993; Osborn & Tseloni, 1998), fear of crime (Brunton-Smith & Sturgis, 2011), crime reporting (Kemp et al., 2023; Tarling & Morris, 2010) and the geographic distribution of crime in communities (Cernat et al., 2022; Osborn et al., 1992; Sampson & Groves, 1989). Most victimization surveys only began including measures of cybercrime in the late 2010s (Reep-van der Bergh & Junger, 2018).

Aside from victimization surveys, self-reported delinquency studies have also been instrumental for the study of crime and deviance. These are surveys in which respondents are asked about instances in which they have been actively involved in crime or deviant behavior (Hindelang et al., 1981; Junger-Tas & Marshall, 1999). Self-report offending studies have been key for measuring juvenile delinquency and developing and testing some of the main theories of criminal and deviant behavior. Wallerstein and Wyle (1947) surveyed nearly 1,700 adults in New York and found that most respondents had committed at least one offense in the last year, but these were mostly trivial incidents. Short and Nye (1958) found little relationship between socio-economic status and self-reported delinquency. Gold (1970) found that most self-reported youth delinquent behavior was committed with other peers. Hirschi (1969) used cross-sectional self-report offending surveys to study the link between juvenile crime and social control. Longitudinal self-report surveys have also gained traction in criminological research. A key example is the US National Youth Survey, which started in 1976 following 1,725 adolescents aged 11 to 17 and became the National

Youth Survey Family Study in 2000 (Elliott et al., 1985). Lauritsen (1993) analyzed this survey and found that juvenile delinquency is strongly concentrated in a very small proportion of the households sampled. Another noteworthy example of cross-national self-report delinquency survey is the International Self-Report Delinquency Study, which has been conducted four times since the beginning of the 1990s (Junger-Tas, 2010). Self-report offending surveys have also been utilized to study active involvement in cybercrime (e.g., Allen et al., 2005; Weulen Kranenbarg et al., 2019), as will be described in more detail. On the contrary, research has shown that their main limitation is that their validity is doubtful with adult populations unless they are somehow "captive", as is the case with inmates or drug addicts enrolled in heroin prescription programs (Aebi, 2006).

The next two sections describe, categorize and compare the measures of cybercrime and cyberdeviance included in some of the main national victimization and self-report offending surveys, and discuss the opportunities and limitations of these measures to generate accurate estimates to study the nature of cybercrime and cyberdeviance.

Measuring cybercrime victimization using surveys

Individual and household crime surveys

To better understand the measurement of cybercrime in victimization surveys, we have selected a sample of population surveys and extracted information from them using a standardized form. More specifically, after consulting with colleagues and experts in victimization survey data, we have selected a set of surveys that meet the following criteria:

(a) national victimization surveys, thus excluding surveys with a local and regional focus and general social surveys;
(b) surveys that record random samples representative of the national population, thus excluding non-probability samples;
(c) surveys that recorded data annually or biannually, thus excluding surveys undertaken only at one point in time;
(d) surveys that provide meta-data and questionnaire documentation in either English, Spanish, Dutch or French (languages spoken by authors or collaborators); and
(e) where possible, at least one national crime survey on each continent.

The sample, presented in Table 2.1, does not seek to be exhaustive nor representative of national victimization surveys worldwide. It includes the NCVS and the CSEW, which are by far the most quoted surveys in the scientific literature, as well as the national crime surveys in the Netherlands, Mexico, Chile, South Africa and New Zealand. Our review does not include the Korean Crime Victims Survey—the only Asian survey that meets the criteria presented earlier[14]—because we did not obtain access to its methodological documentation in English, Spanish, Dutch or French. We also note that some of the countries included in our sample undertake other surveys that may include indicators of cybercrime and cyberdeviance (e.g., CSEW questionnaire for persons aged under 16, the Chilean Survey of Local Authorities, New Zealand Crime and Safety Survey), but the focus of our analysis is the main crime survey in each country.

For each survey, we record information about whether and how they record information about victimization related to different types of cybercrime. We summarize this information in Table 2.2. All surveys measure both the prevalence and incidence of

Table 2.1 National crime surveys of individuals or households included in analysis

Name	Name in original language	Acronym	Country	Frequency	Round analyzed	Sample
Crime Survey for England and Wales		CSEW	England and Wales	Annual	2019–20	33,734 households (aged 16 or more)
Safety Monitor	'Veiligheidsmonitor'	VM	Netherlands	Every 2 years	2019	135,000 adults (aged 15 or more)
National Crime Victimization Survey (Identity Theft Supplement)		NCVS-ITS	USA	Every 2 years	2018	102,400 respondents (aged 16 or more)
National Survey of Victimization and Perception of Public Safety	'Encuesta Nacional de Victimización y Percepción de Seguridad Pública'	ENVIPE	Mexico	Annual	2021	102,297 households (aged 18 or more)
National Urban Survey on Citizen Security	'Encuesta Nacional Urbana de Seguridad Ciudadana'	ENUSC	Chile	Annual	2021	22,180 households (aged 15 or more)
Victims of Crime Survey		VOCS	South Africa	Annual	2017	33,000 households (aged 16 or more)
New Zealand Crime and Victims Survey		NZCVS	New Zealand	Annual	2021	6,244 residents (aged 15 or more)

Table 2.2 Measures of cybercrime victimization included in sampled national crime surveys of individuals or households*

	Cyber-dependent crime			Cyber-enabled financial crime				Cyber-enabled personal crime/deviance	
	Malware	*Hacking*	*Spam/phishing*	*Online shopping fraud*	*Online banking fraud*	*ID fraud*	*Advance fee fraud*	*Hate crime*	*Online harassment*
CSEW	"computer or other internet-enabled device been infected or interfered with, for example by a virus"	"stolen personal information or details held on computer or in online accounts (e.g. email, social media)"		"anyone tricked or deceived you out of money or goods, in person, by telephone or on-line"	"personal information or account details used to obtain money, or buy goods or services without your permission or knowledge"	As a result of crime . . . "personal information or details accessed or used without permission"	Was crime related to . . . "chance to make investment with guaranteed high return"	For crimes registered . . . "incident motivated by offender's attitude towards . . . (race, religion, sex, disability, etc.)"	"anyone put personal, obscene or threatening information about you on internet on more than one occasion and which caused you fear, alarm or distress"

(Continued)

Table 2.2 (Continued)

	Cyber-dependent crime		Cyber-enabled financial crime					Cyber-enabled personal crime/ deviance	
	Malware	Hacking	Spam/phishing	Online shopping fraud	Online banking fraud	ID fraud	Advance fee fraud	Hate crime	Online harassment
VM		"hacked into or logged into computer, email account, website, or profile site (e.g., Facebook, Twitter)"		"been cheated when buying or selling goods or services, e.g., purchased goods were not delivered"		"identity fraud. This involves using someone's personal data for financial gain without permission (e.g., withdrawing money, taking loans)"			"bullying, stalking, blackmail or threats" If yes, was it: "embarrassing or hurtful website or profile about you", "messages under your name on Internet forum or social media", "extorted, blackmailed"
NCVS-ITS		If personal information misused by	If personal information misused by		"someone, without your permission,	"misuse of account such as telephone, cable, gas			

(Continued)

Table 2.2 (Continued)

Cyber-dependent crime		Cyber-enabled financial crime					Cyber-enabled personal crime/deviance		
Malware	*Hacking*	*Spam/phishing*	*Online shopping fraud*	*Online banking fraud*	*ID fraud*	*Advance fee fraud*	*Hate crime*	*Online harassment*	
	someone else . . . was it accessed "Someone hacked into my computer"	someone . . . "I responded to scam email/phone call"		used or attempted to use your existing checking or savings account, including any debit or ATM cards"	or electric accounts, online payment account, insurance, entertainment account"; "other fraudulent purpose, such as filing fraudulent tax return, getting medical care, applying for a job or benefits"				

(Continued)

Table 2.2 (Continued)

	Cyber-dependent crime		Cyber-enabled financial crime					Cyber-enabled personal crime/deviance	
	Malware	Hacking	Spam/phishing	Online shopping fraud	Online banking fraud	ID fraud	Advance fee fraud	Hate crime	Online harassment
ENVIPE				"paid money for product or service that you never received (consumer fraud)"		"someone used your checkbook, credit card or bank account without your consent to make payments or obtain money from account (bank fraud) or gave you counterfeit cash"			
ENUSC	"remotely destroying your hard drive or content in computer"			"fraud while buying online"	"forged your identify to access your bank account or credit card"	"forged your identity in email accounts or social media"		For crimes registered . . . "believe it was motivated by your personal character-istics or believes? Nationality, sex . . ."	"threats through internet or email"; "harassment trough inappropriate or obscene messages, communications, unrequested images, or sexual requests"
VOCS				"Consumer fraud" within last 5 years and last 12 months					

(Continued)

54

Table 2.2 (Continued)

	Cyber-dependent crime		Cyber-enabled financial crime					Cyber-enabled personal crime/deviance	
	Malware	*Hacking*	*Spam/phishing*	*Online shopping fraud*	*Online banking fraud*	*ID fraud*	*Advance fee fraud*	*Hate crime*	*Online harassment*
NZCVS	"computer or Internet-enabled device been infected or interfered with, for example by a virus or someone accessing without permissions"			"tricked or deceived you, in order to obtain money, goods or a service"	"used or attempted to use bank card, credit card, cheque card or other document without your permission, to obtain money, or buy goods or services"				

*The wording of some questions has been shortened

victimization and include survey weights to allow estimates of crime for the target population. All these surveys also included measures of crime reporting, hence enabling analyzing the proportion of incidents that are known to public authorities each year (van de Weijer et al., 2019).

As can be seen in Table 2.2, the way in which cybercrime is measured varies extensively from survey to survey. With regard to cyber-dependent crime, while three surveys included measures that may in some cases refer to malware victimization, the CSEW is the only to include a question specifically designed to measure this type of crime. The NZCVS, for example, probes respondents about instances where computer devices are infected or interfered with by a virus or someone else, hence referring to either cases of malware or hacking. Similarly, the ENUSC probes about the remote destruction of hard drive or content in computer, which may also refer to both malware and hacking victimization. With the exception of ENVIPE and VOCS, all other surveys include indicators that can be used to measure at least one type of cyber-dependent crime. The only survey to include an indicator of phishing victimization is the NCVS-ITS. Yet this question is only asked to those who had previously answered that their information had been misused by someone else. Some surveys also include follow-up questions for each crime reported, such as the methods used by offenders to access the data, devices affected and changes in behavior and prevention measures taken after the incident, in the CSEW.

The measurement of cyber-enabled crime also varies across crime surveys. We recorded measures of cyber-enabled financial crime (i.e., those that target a financial gain) and cyber-enabled personal crime (i.e., those that seek to harm someone). With the exception of the NCVS-ITS, all other surveys included at least one measure that may in some cases refer to online shopping fraud. However, the only survey that measures specifically *online* shopping fraud is the ENUSC. The CSEW question, for example, includes both incidents committed via telephone and online. The VM, ENVIPE and NZCVS include all forms of shopping fraud in the same question, and the VOCS measure refers to all kinds of consumer fraud, which may also refer to online banking fraud and ID fraud. It is true, however, that most of these questionnaires include follow-up measures for each crime reported, which allows distinguishing cyber-enabled frauds from those committed offline and via telephone. The VOCS, for instance, asks respondents if the consumer fraud refers to "banking fraud (e.g., internet)", "identity fraud", "illegal duplication of bankcard/ATM fraud", amongst other options. Likewise, the ENVIPE asks whether frauds took place online.

All surveys include at least one measure of either online banking fraud or ID fraud, but item wording varies extensively across surveys, and in some cases, it is not clear if the measure refers to the illegal access and use of personal information to access finances through online banking (i.e., online banking fraud) or for other purposes. The VM, for example, probes about the use of personal data for financial gain, "withdrawing money, taking loans, etc.", and the ENVIPE asks about the use of data to "make payments or obtain money from your account (bank fraud) or gave you counterfeit cash". Even though some government agencies such as the UK Action Fraud recommend these to be treated as separate crime types, this distinction is not clearly defined in any of the surveys explored. The CSEW is the only survey to include a measure of advance fee fraud, which can be cyber-enabled in some cases, but this measure is included as a follow-up question for victims only.

With regard to cyber-enabled personal crime, only two surveys, the CSEW and the ENUSC, included a follow-up question to victims of crime to disentangle whether each crime was motivated by racial, religious, gender or other types of hatred. This measure is also included in the main questionnaire of the NCVS, but not in the Identity Theft Supplement. However, these indicators do not allow distinguishing cyber-enabled hate crime from traditional forms of hate crime. Analysts would need to first subset those crimes that took place on the internet, and then explore how many of those were motivated by hate towards certain population groups. The CSEW, VM and ENUSC also included measures of cyber-enabled harassment, though as can be seen in Table 2.2 the design and wording of these questions is remarkably different, hence making cross-national comparisons difficult. In Mexico, each year the National Survey on the Availability and Use of Information Technologies at Home (MOCIBA) also includes measures of cyber-harassment,[15] but these are not included in the ENVIPE. The ENVIPE includes measures of threats and extortion in general terms.

Most of these surveys also include a number of other key indicators. The VM measures how information was intercepted in the first place (e.g., email, internet, ATM), and the CSEW includes items to capture satisfaction with the police response. Questions about the harms of each crime are included in most surveys. The CSEW and ENUSC also include measures of perceptions about cybercrime trends and worry about cybercrime. The VOCS includes a set of questions about concerns about hate crime, fraud and identity document theft.

Business crime surveys

A first *International Commercial Crime Survey* was conducted in eight European countries in 1994 using a standardized questionnaire pilot-tested in four other countries, used later in several others and then adapted to focus on corruption, fraud and extortion before being used for a second wave of the survey—renamed the *International Crime Business Survey*—in nine Central-East European cities in 2000 (Alvazzi del Frate, 2004). This international effort was discontinued, but its results, combined with those obtained in countries that conduct national crime business surveys, highlight the need for such studies, which must be conducted using questionnaires that include cybercrimes at a time when a substantial part of economic transactions take place online (Dupont, 2019; Junger et al., 2020). Some estimate that the financial losses suffered by businesses due to cybercrime may greatly exceed that suffered by individuals. For instance, in 2017, the UK Annual Fraud Indicator estimated that frauds were responsible for £140 billion losses for the private sector, £40 billion losses for the public sector and £6.8 billion losses for individuals (Crowe, 2017). Taking into account the magnitude of these losses and knowing the limitations of official crime statistics (Kemp et al., 2023), several national governments have launched recurring business cybercrime surveys. In this chapter, we analyze three that have been conducted at least two times and have been used in research and policy making (Buil-Gil et al., 2021b; Rantala, 2008): the UK Cybersecurity Breaches Survey, the US National Computer Security Survey and the Canadian Survey of Cyber Security and Cybercrime. We exclude surveys undertaken by cybersecurity businesses and consultancy companies and surveys undertaken only at one point in time (e.g., in 2021, a Eurobarometer included measures of corporate cybercrime victimization across 27 European Union countries[16]). Details about the three surveys included for analysis are presented in Table 2.3.

Table 2.3 National crime surveys of businesses included in analysis

Name	Acronym	Country	Frequency	Round analyzed	Sample
Cyber Security Breaches Survey	CSBS	UK	Annual	2021	1,419 businesses, 487 charities and 378 education institutions
National Computer Security Survey	NCSS	USA	2001 and 2005	2005	7,818 businesses
Canadian Survey of Cyber Security and Cybercrime	CSCSC	Canada	Every 2 years	2021	12,158 businesses

While these three surveys are not representative of how business cybercrime victimization is measured elsewhere, a comparison of their questionnaires may reveal inconsistencies in the way business cybercrime victimization is measured in these three countries, and potentially also elsewhere. Australia, for example, includes measures of business cybercrime victimization in its Small Business Survey, and in Mexico the National Survey of Victimization of Businesses (ENVE) also asks victimized companies whether each incident took place offline or online (e.g., in the case of fraud and extortion). In order to keep our search manageable, we did not include in our analysis other business victimization surveys in UK, USA and Canada that may also include measures of cybercrime, such as the UK Cyber Security Longitudinal Survey.[17]

Table 2.4 presents the item wording used in these three surveys to measure five types of cyber-dependent crime (i.e., malware, hacking, Denial of Service (DoS), website defacement and spam/phishing), two types of cyber-enabled crime (i.e., fraud and identity theft) as well as unauthorized access to data by someone inside or outside the organization. The crime types included in business surveys are quite different from those included in household surveys, mirroring the variations and nuances in the types of crimes suffered by organizations and individuals. For instance, questions about website defacements and unauthorized access to data are not included in household surveys, and those on fraud are more generic in business surveys than in household surveys.

In terms of the design of these surveys, while the CSBS and NCSS directly pose a question for each type of crime, the CSCSC has a generic filter question about whether the company suffered any kind of cybercrime attack that had an impact on the business and, if that is the case, it poses follow-up questions for each type of cybercrime. Specifically, the CSCSC asks all businesses in the sample whether they suffered concrete cybersecurity incidents that aimed to disrupt the business or web presence, steal personal information, steal money or demand a ransom, steal or manipulate intellectual property, access unauthorized areas, monitor business activity or any other motive. Only those businesses that answer affirmatively are then asked about the "method" to execute the attack—which more closely matches the crime definitions of the CSBS and NCSS. Thus, while the CSBS and NCSS ask about crime types, the CSCSC asks first about the motive of the incident and then about the

Table 2.4 Measures of cybercrime victimization included in national crime surveys of organizations*

| | Cyber-dependent crime | | | | | Cyber-enabled financial crime Other | | | |
	Malware	Hacking	DoS	Website defacement	Spam/ phishing	Fraud	Identity theft	Unauthorized access (internal)	Unauthorized access (external)
CSBS	"Computers becoming infected with ransomware"; "with other malware (e.g viruses or spyware)"	"Hacking or attempted hacking of online bank accounts"	"Denial of service attacks, i.e. attacks that try to slow or take down website, applications or services"	"Takeovers or attempts to take over website, social media accounts or email accounts"	"Phishing attacks, i.e. staff receiving fraudulent emails or arriving at fraudulent websites"		"People impersonating organisation in emails or online"	"Unauthorised accessing of files or networks by staff, even if accidental"	"Unauthorised accessing of files or networks by people outside organisation"
NCSS	"intercept computer viruses before they could infect computer systems"; "detect viruses which infected computer systems"	"company detect any other computer security Incidents"; If yes . . . "hacking"	"detect any incidents of denial of service (noticeable interruption of Internet connection or e-mail service)"		"company detect any other computer security Incidents" If yes . . . "phishing"	"someone inside or outside this company used a computer to commit fraud against this company"		"someone inside or outside company used a computer to obtain intellectual property from this company"; "someone inside or outside company used a computer to obtain personal or financial information from this company"	

(Continued)

Table 2.4 (Continued)

| | Cyber-dependent crime | | | | | Cyber-enabled financial crime | | Other | |
	Malware	Hacking	DoS	Website defacement	Spam/ phishing	Fraud	Identity theft	Unauthorized access (internal)	Unauthorized access (external)
CSCSC	For crimes registered ... "what the method ...": "ransomware"; "other malicious software"	For crimes registered ... "what the method ...": "exploiting software, hardware or network vulnerabilities"; "hacking or password cracking"	For crimes registered ... "what the method ...": Denial of service or Distributed denial of service"	For crimes registered ... "what the method ...": "disruption or defacing of web presence"		For crimes registered ... "what the method ...": "scams or fraud"	For crimes registered ... "what the method ...": "identify theft"	For crimes registered ... "what the method ...": "abuse of access privileges by a current or former internal party"	

*The wording of some questions has been shortened

method. The combination of these two measures can then be used to estimate crime prevalence (Bilodeau et al., 2019). Looking more closely at the item wording, we also observe that while the CSCSC measures incidents that did have an impact on the business, the CSBS and NCSS also consider attempted attacks that were detected but did not have significant impacts.

In practice, there are relevant differences in the types of crimes included in the surveys as well as in most of their definitions. Regarding malware, the CSBS and CSCSC differentiate ransomware from other types of malware whilst the NCSS refers to computer viruses. The NCSS asks about hacking in general, the CSBS about hacking of bank accounts, and the CSBS about the exploitation of computer or network vulnerabilities and "hacking or password cracking". Measures of DoS exist in the three surveys, but the definitions provided in the CSBS and NCSS vary as the former describes attacks on websites, applications or services, while the latter refers to attacks targeting internet connection or e-mail services. The CSBS and the CSCSC measure website defacement, which is excluded from the NCSS, while the latter and the CSBS include phishing, which is excluded from the CSCSC. Identity theft is included as such in the CSCSC, whilst the CSBS refers to someone impersonating the organization online, and the NCSS excludes that cyber-offense. Another key difference between the household and business surveys studied here is that the former differentiate between different types of fraud, but the NCSS and the CSCSC refer to fraud in general terms.

Finally, all three surveys include measures of unauthorized access to files and data, but there are two important differences in the way it is measured. First, regarding the target of the intrusion, the CSBS refers to files or networks, the NCSS to either intellectual property or personal or financial information and the CSCSC to abuse of access privileges more generally. Second, regarding the person responsible for the unauthorized access, the CSBS differentiates internal from external threats (Williams et al., 2019), the NCSS includes both types of actors in the same question, and the CSCSC only refers to insiders. Both the NCSS and the CSCSC also include a follow-up question about whether the suspect is an insider or outsider.

Aside from the offenses included in Table 2.4, the CSBS also measures unauthorized listening of videos or messages, and the NCSS measures electronic vandalization or sabotage of computer systems as well as the use of the latter to commit embezzlement. All three surveys also include questions about the cybersecurity measures applied by the organization, cybersecurity priorities, investment in cybersecurity, online presence, crime reporting and consequences of each incident.

Measuring cybercrime offending and deviance through self-report delinquency studies

Self-report delinquency studies are the main alternative to measure the frequency, distribution and nature of cybercrime (e.g., Allen et al., 2005; Weulen Kranenbarg et al., 2019). As explained in the Introduction, research on the validity of self-reported delinquency studies has shown that they are mainly valid with adolescents. Here we include information about how some of the main extant self-report crime surveys measure cybercrime offending and deviance. We have purposively selected three of the main self-report crime surveys that are openly available, have been conducted at least twice and include clear questionnaire

Table 2.5 Self-report offending surveys included in analysis

Name	Acronym	Country	Frequency	Round analyzed	Sample
Offending, Crime and Justice Survey	OCJS	UK	Annual, 2003 to 2006	2006	5,354 respondents aged 10 to 29
Youth Delinquency Survey	YDS	Netherlands	Quinquennial	2015	1,471 respondents aged 12 to 23
International Self-Report Delinquency Study	ISRD4	Cross-national	1991/91, 2006/08, 2012/19, 2021/22	2021/22	Varies by country (respondents aged 13 to 17)

documentation. As in the previous sections, Table 2.5 summarizes the main characteristics of the surveys, while Table 2.6 presents the measures of cybercrime and cyberdeviance included in them.

Again, while these three surveys are not representative of how self-reported cybercrime offending is measured elsewhere, a comparison of their questionnaires discloses inconsistencies in the way active involvement in juvenile cybercrime and cyberdeviance is measured in three of the main self-report studies. Beyond these three surveys, the measurement of cybercrime offending is scarce and mostly confined to small and non-representative samples or case studies. There are, however, emerging initiatives to record data on self-reported cybercrime offending, such as Virginia Tech's Longitudinal Survey of Cybercriminology (Dearden & Parti, 2021).

One of the first nationally representative surveys to include measures of cybercrime offending and deviance was the OCJS, which was conducted between 2003 and 2006 in the UK (Allen et al., 2005). The survey included measures of cyber-dependent crimes such as malware, hacking and digital piracy, as well as cyber-enabled behaviors such as online harassment and online credit card fraud. This survey also asked respondents whether they had accessed deviant forums or websites (i.e., "visited a website that showed you how to commit a crime, or might have helped you commit a crime" and "visited a website that might be thought of as racist, either because you supported their views or because you were thinking of becoming a member") and whether they had bought stolen goods on the internet.

The YDS also includes measures of cybercrime offending (van der Laan et al., 2021). Its first two waves focused on a more limited set of online crime items such as digital piracy (i.e., downloading online material illegally), online threats/harassment and sending computer viruses; but the third wave extended the range of cyber-enabled offenses to hacking, DoS and online shopping fraud (Rokven et al., 2018). The YDS is also the only survey to include measures of identity theft ("impersonated somebody else on the internet") and distribution of online child sexual exploitation material ("distributed sexual material of minors through your smartphone or over the internet"), which has not been included in Table 2.6 due to space restrictions.

Table 2.6 Measures of cybercrime offending included in self-report crime surveys*

	Cyber-dependent crime			Cyber-enabled financial crime			Cyber-enabled deviance	Cyber-enabled personal crime/deviance
	Malware	Hacking	DoS	Digital piracy	Online banking fraud	Online shopping fraud	Hate speech	Online harassment
OCJS	"used internet to send viruses on purpose to other computers"	"used internet to hack intro other computers? by hacking we mean using a computer to illegally get access to another computer's files"		"used internet to download software, music or films that you knew to be pirated or unauthorized"	"bought anything over the internet using payment card or card details that did not belong to you, without the card owner's permission"			"sent email message to someone in order to harass, scare or threaten them"; "sent voice or text message on your phone ..."
YDS	"intentionally sent out viruses through e-mail or over the internet"	"logged on to somebody else's computer, email or social media account without informed consent"; "changed someone's account password (computer or social media) to prohibit them from accessing"; "logged on onto somebody else's computer, email or social media account without informed consent, and manipulated or deleted information"	"tried to disrupt a website or email account by sending out large amounts of data"			"sold something through internet, but not sending out goods after receiving payment"; "bought something through internet, but not paying for goods after receiving items"		"threatened someone through text messages, e-mails or in chat boxes"; "threatened someone through social media, such as WhatsApp, Facebook, Twitter, etc."

(*Continued*)

Table 2.6 (Continued)

	Cyber-dependent crime				Cyber-enabled financial crime		Cyber-enabled personal crime/deviance	
	Malware	Hacking	DoS	Digital piracy	Online banking fraud	Online shopping fraud	Hate speech	Online harassment
ISRD4		"hacked or broken into a private account or computer to acquire data, get control of an account, or destroy data"				"used internet, e-mail or social media to dupe or deceive others (like phishing, selling worthless or illegal things, etc.) to make money"	"sent hurtful messages or comments on social media about someone's race, ethnicity or nationality, religion, gender identity, etc."	

*The wording of some questions has been shortened

Finally, the ISRD is probably the only *cross-national* self-report offending survey to include measures of online offending, which were introduced in its third wave (Haen-Marshall et al., 2022). Table 2.6 presents the main cybercriminal and cyberdeviant behaviors measured in its fourth wave, which included a larger variety of cybercrime types as well as improved wording for the offenses previously included. These include hacking and cyber-enabled behaviors such as online hate speech, online shopping fraud and sharing intimate images of others online (the latter not included in the table).

Table 2.6 shows that measurement varies extensively across surveys. Although all of them include measures of both cyber-enabled and cyber-dependent crime and deviance, the specific types of behaviors vary significantly. For example, when it comes to cyber-enabled crime and deviance, online hate speech and intimate posting are only measured in the ISRD. Distribution of child pornography and identity theft were only measured in the YDS. In addition, digital piracy and access to deviant websites were only included in the OCJS, while online harassment is only absent in the ISRD. Other cyber-enabled offenses like online shopping fraud are included in at least two of the surveys, but not only is there variation in how the items are formulated but also in the number of questions included (e.g., while the YDS probes about committing online shopping fraud both as seller and buyer, the ISRD includes a general question about deceiving others for money). With regard to cyber-dependent offenses, hacking is measured in all the surveys. However, while the OCJS and ISRD use more general questions about hacking into others' devices without their consent, the YDS provides a more exhaustive measurement of this behavior. Concretely, it includes multiple items that interrogate not only about illegally accessing email accounts or websites but also distinguishing between logging into computers to block access and to manipulate or destroy information.

The three surveys measure the prevalence of cybercriminal and cyberdeviant behavior (i.e., percentage of respondents involved in each type of behavior) but differ in the type of period prevalence measured. The YDS refers to lifetime prevalence (crime and deviant behaviors committed at any point in time) and the OCJS measures the last 12 months' prevalence, while the ISRD-4 measures both. In addition, the ISRD-4 also measures the incidence or frequency of offending (i.e., the number of times the offence was committed by the respondent). Furthermore, in the case of hacking, the ISRD-4 also includes additional follow-up questions about the motivation, *modus operandi*, detection by authorities or victim and rate of success (Haen-Marshall et al., 2022). All these measures can be particularly useful for the development of typologies of cyber offenders (Weulen Kranenbarg, 2022).

Ways forward and conclusions

Cybercrime has been on the rise since the 1990s (Caneppele & Aebi, 2019), and so is the need for researchers and public administrations to better estimate its prevalence, incidence, distribution and nature. The limitations of police statistics as measures of crime are widely known and seem even more severe—in terms of the volume of unrecorded offenses— in the case of cybercrimes (Decker, 2020; van de Weijer et al., 2019). The problem of under-recording may be even more acute for crimes suffered by organizations (Kemp et al., 2023). From that perspective, victimization surveys with national representative samples are seen as the main alternative to obtain more valid and reliable estimates of cybercrime and cyberdeviance (Aebi et al., 2022; Reep-van der Bergh & Junger, 2018). Self-reported delinquency studies can provide information on juvenile cybercrime and cyberdeviance from the point of view of the offenders and, if accompanied by a victimization module, on the incidents suffered by the younger generations. Surveys also provide information on many other variables that are absent from police or court recorded crimes, related to the personal characteristics of individuals, their everyday activities, cybersecurity practices and so on, which allow identifying key risk factors and testing different theories of online crime and deviance (Holt & Bossler, 2008; Leukfeldt & Yar, 2016). In addition, surveys conducted regularly can also be key to assessing temporal changes in overall criminal behavior (Caneppele & Aebi, 2019).

While we have seen a rapid increase in the number of crime surveys that include measures of cybercrime since the early 2010s, our scoping review has identified a series of practices that could be refined to better measure online victimization and offending, and to enable cross-national and temporal comparisons. Overall, it seems reasonable to state that cybercrime and cyberdeviance is measured less adequately than more traditional crime types. This might be in part due to the ever-changing nature of cyberspace. For instance, music downloading seemed a major threat to intellectual property rights in the 1990s and early 2000s, until streaming services radically changed the way we interact with music. Similarly, online social media platforms follow each other constantly, in such a way that once survey items have been tested and seem valid for one of them, there is a new social media platform that dominates the market, hence making the previous questions irrelevant. Consequently, survey administrators must be constantly on guard to capture the set of crimes that probably represent the major criminal and deviant behaviors taking place in hybrid societies (Aebi, 2022). Our review of victimization surveys and self-reported delinquency studies is based on a purposively selected sample and therefore is not representative of how cybercrime and cyberdeviance is measured across the world, but it allows us to identify a series of inconsistencies across and within surveys that are likely to apply to other surveys at the national and local levels.[18]

One of the main implications of this review is that cross-national comparisons of cybercrime victimization are nowadays extremely challenging, if not impossible. Different surveys have different designs, consider different cybercrime types and conceptualize and operationalize cybercrime and cyberdeviance in different ways. Cross-national comparisons of online offending and deviance, at least of hacking, distribution of intimate images of others, online shopping fraud and hate speech committed by persons aged 13 to 17, are enabled by the ISRD (Haen-Marshall et al., 2022; Junger-Tas, 2010). In many cases, measures of cybercrime do not allow temporal comparisons, because these have only been included recently or have been changed in recent years. The fear of changing questions and thus losing historical series is one of the main reasons why some ongoing victimization surveys still do not include questions on cybercrime, often combined with the fear of increasing respondent fatigue and ultimately non-response or attrition bias (Guzy & Leitgöb, 2015; Hart et al., 2005). While we understand these concerns, cybercrime is undoubtedly an issue important enough both in terms of its prevalence and incidence, as well as because of its harms (Agrafiotis et al., 2018), to warrant its own measurement in crime surveys.

Our review suggests that the different sets of cybercrimes included in various surveys are not necessarily related to the main cybersecurity issues faced in each country. At best, these could be explained by policy priorities which are not described in the documentation of surveys. The review also allows us to suggest that household victimization surveys should, at the very least, include direct measures of malware, hacking, spam/phishing, online shopping fraud, online banking fraud (if possible, distinguishing between online banking and credit card fraud), ID fraud, advance fee fraud, online hate crime and online harassment. Business surveys should also include measures of DoS, website defacements and internal threats, while self-reported delinquency studies should not forget digital piracy. Importantly, where possible these measures should be designed to match official definitions of crime, to enable estimates of the 'dark figure of crime', but always considering that their main role is probably to allow for cross-national and temporal comparisons. Additionally, surveys should include items to measure other forms of online deviant behaviors that are not necessarily categorized as 'criminal' (e.g., hate speech, harassment, bullying, etc.), which are already considered in a few of the sampled studies. Considerations such as whether questions refer to completed or attempted incidents, whether they refer to "at any point in time" or the last 12 months, whether they measure prevalence or incidence, and the wording of items more generally, should where possible also consider the measurement of cybercriminal and cyberdeviant behavior in other countries. In this regard, the creation of international networks of researchers and survey administrators may be essential in the future (e.g., Aebi et al., 2022). Finally, measures of cybercrime and cyberdeviance could be further refined by applying more sophisticated item validation measures and considering measurement invariance and item response theory (Murray et al., 2021; Osgood et al., 2002).

All things considered, both in terms of research and policy and practice, it is essential for national governments to come together and launch a new ICVS with a set of measures of cyber-dependent and cyber-enabled crime. The design of the ICVS with indicators of cybercrime and cyberdeviance would be key for a more accurate assessment of the extent and nature of cybercrime at a global scale, as well as potentially unearthing important cross-national patterns in victimization, and serve as a unique opportunity to capture these key measures in countries without instituted national crime surveys, especially in the Global South. While crime surveys are not free from limitations and are known to be affected by issues such as memory failures, social-desirability bias, underestimation or exaggeration of situations, telescoping and measurement non-invariance (Schneider, 1981; Skogan, 1975), they are still the best data source available to complement official statistics and better understand cybercrime and cyberdeviance. Ideally, future research should not only focus on describing differences in item wording and survey design across surveys, but also apply advanced psychometric assessment of cybercrime measures to ensure they enable reliable and valid estimates of cybercrime and cyberdeviance, both for national and international studies.

Notes

1 Annual reports of the Internet Crime Complaint Center IC3. www.ic3.gov/Home/AnnualReports
2 Interactive data dashboard of Action Fraud. www.actionfraud.police.uk/data
3 Internet Organized Crime Threat Assessment of EUROPOL. www.europol.europa.eu/publications-events/main-reports/iocta-report
4 Australian Cyber Security Centre Annual Cyber Threat Report. www.cyber.gov.au/acsc/view-all-content/reports-and-statistics

5 Private Rights Clearinghouse's data breaches dataset. https://privacyrights.org/data-breaches
6 McAfee's MVISION Insights dashboard. www.mcafee.com/enterprise/en-us/lp/insights-preview.html
7 Reports published by F-Secure. www.f-secure.com/en/press/media-library/reports
8 Reports published by Broadcom. www.broadcom.com/support/security-center/publications/archive
9 Access to data recorded by the Cambridge Cybercrime Centre can be requested through. www.cambridgecybercrime.uk/
10 Access to data recorded by the Korea University's Hacking and Countermeasure Research Lab can be requested through. https://ocslab.hksecurity.net/Datasets
11 Ransomwhere data. https://ransomwhe.re/
12 Bitcoin Abuse database. www.bitcoinabuse.com/api-docs
13 International Crime Victims Survey. https://wp.unil.ch/icvs/
14 To our knowledge, the Korean Crime Survey is the only recurring victimization survey in Asia, while non-recurring national crime surveys were undertaken in Thailand between 2006 and 2012, in Philippines in 2012 and in Kazakhstan in 2018.
15 Mexico's National Survey on the Availability and Use of Information Technologies at Home. www.inegi.org.mx/programas/mociba/2020/
16 2021 Eurobarometer on cybervictimization of organisations. https://eucrim.eu/news/survey-on-the-experience-of-smes-with-cybercrime/
17 Cyber Security Longitudinal Survey. www.gov.uk/government/publications/cyber-security-longitudinal-survey
18 The Islington Crime Survey, in the UK, and the Barcelona Victimization Survey, in Spain, are two examples of local crime surveys that also include measures of cybercrime.

References

Aebi M. F. (2006). *Comment Mesurer la Délinquance?* Armand Colin.

Aebi, M. F. (2022). Lessons learned from a council of Europe's conference on measuring cybercrime. In M. F. Aebi, S. Caneppele, & L. Molnar (Eds.), *Measuring cybercrime in Europe: The role of crime statistics and victimisation surveys* (pp. 7–18). Eleven.

Aebi, M. F., Caneppele, S., Harrendorf, S., Hashimoto, Y. Z., Jehle, J., Khan, T. S., Kühn, O., Lewis, O., Molnar, L., Smit, P., Þórisdóttir, R., & National Correspondents. (2021). European sourcebook of crime and criminal justice statistics 2021 (6th ed.). *Series UNILCRIM*, 1. UNILCRIM.

Aebi, M. F., Caneppele, S., & Molnar, L. (Eds.). (2022). *Measuring cybercrime in Europe: The role of crime statistics and victimisation surveys*. Eleven.

Aebi, M. F., Killias, M., & Tavares, C. (2002). Comparing crime rates: The international crime (victim) survey, the European sourcebook of crime and criminal justice statistics, and interpol statistics. *International Journal of Comparative Criminology*, 2(1), 22–37.

Aebi, M. F., and Linde, A. (2014). National victimization surveys. In G. Bruinsma & D. Weisburd (Eds.), *Encyclopedia of criminology and criminal justice* (pp. 3228–3242). Springer.

Agrafiotis, I., Nurse, J. R., Goldsmith, M., Creese, S., & Upton, D. (2018). A taxonomy of cyber-harms: Defining the impacts of cyber-attacks and understanding how they propagate. *Journal of Cybersecurity*, 4(1), tyy006.

Allen, J., Forrest, S., Levi, M., Roy, H., & Sutton, M. (2005). *Fraud and technology crimes: Findings from the 2002/3 British crime survey and 2003 offending, crime and justice survey* [Online Report 34/05]. Home Office.

Alvazzi del Frate, A. (2004). The international crime business survey: Findings from nine central—Eastern European Cities. *European Journal on Criminal Policy and Research*, 10(2), 137–161.

Biderman, A. D., & Reiss, A. J. (1967). On exploring the "dark figure" of crime. *The ANNALS of the American Academy of Political and Social Science*, 374(1), 1–15.

Bilodeau, H., Lari, M., & Uhrbach, M. (2019). *Cyber security and cybercrime challenges of Canadian businesses, 2017* [Report 85–002-X]. Statistics Canada.

Bottoms, A. E., Mawby, R. I., & Walker, M. A. (1987). A localised crime survey in contrasting areas of a city. *The British Journal of Criminology, 27*(2), 125–154.

Brunton-Smith, I., & Sturgis, P. (2011). Do neighborhoods generate fear of crime? An empirical test using the British crime survey. *Criminology, 49*(2), 331–369.

Buil-Gil, D., Brunton-Smith, I., Pina-Sánchez, J., & Cernat, A. (2022). Comparing measurements of violent crime in local communities: A case study in Islington, London. *Police Practice and Research, 23*(4), 489–506.

Buil-Gil, D., Lord, N., & Barrett, E. (2021b). The dynamics of business, cybersecurity and cyber-victimization: Foregrounding the internal guardian in prevention. *Victims & Offenders, 16*(3), 286–315.

Buil-Gil, D., Zeng, Y., & Kemp, S. (2021a). Offline crime bounces back to Pre-COVID levels, cyber stays high: Interrupted time-series analysis in Northern Ireland. *Crime Science, 10*(26).

Burnap, P., & Williams, M. L. (2016). Us and them: Identifying cyber hate on twitter across multiple protected characteristics. *EPJ Data Science, 5*(11).

Candolle, A. de (1830/1987). Considérations sur la statistique des délits. *Déviance et Société, 11*(4), 352–355.

Candolle, A. de (1832/1987). De la statistique criminelle. *Déviance et Société, 11*(4), 356–363.

Caneppele, S., & Aebi, M. F. (2019). Crime drop or police recording flop? On the relationship between the decrease of offline crime and the increase of online and hybrid crimes. *Policing: A Journal of Policy and Practice, 13*(1), 66–79.

Castaño-Pulgarín, S. A., Suárez-Betancur, N., Vega, L. M. T., & López, H. M. H. (2021). Internet, social media and online hate speech. systematic review. *Aggression and Violent Behavior, 58*, 101608.

Cernat, A., Buil-Gil, D., Brunton-Smith, I., Pina-Sánchez, J., & Murrià-Sangenís, M. (2022). Estimating crime in place: Moving beyond residence location. *Crime & Delinquency, 68*(11), 2061–2091.

Chopin J., & Aebi M. F. (2020). The level of attrition in domestic violence: A valid indicator of the efficiency of a criminal justice system? *European Journal of Criminology, 17*(3), 269–287.

Chun, J., Lee, J., Kim, J., & Lee, S. (2020). An international systematic review of cyberbullying measurements. *Computers in Human Behavior, 113*, 106485.

Cioban, S., Lazăr, A. R., Bacter, C., & Hatos, A. (2021). Adolescent deviance and cyber-deviance. A systematic literature review. *Frontiers in Psychology, 12*, 748006.

Coleman, C., & Moynihan, J. (1996). *Understanding crime data: Haunted by the dark figure.* Open University Press.

Correia, S. G. (2022). Making the most of cybercrime and fraud crime report data: A case study of UK action Fraud. *International Journal of Population Data Science, 7*(1), 09.

Crowe. (2017). *Annual frau indicator 2017. Identifying the cost of fraud to the UK economy.* Crowe UK.

Dearden, T. E., & Parti, K. (2021). Cybercrime, differential association, and self-control: Knowledge transmission through online social learning. *American Journal of Criminal Justice, 46*, 935–955.

Decker, E. (2020). Full count?: Crime rate swings, cybercrime misses and why we don't really know the score. *Journal of National Security Law and Policy, 10*, 583–604.

Dupont, B. (2019). The cyber-resilience of financial institutions: Significance and applicability. *Journal of Cybersecurity, 5*(1).

Elliott, D. S., Huizinga, D., & Ageton, S. S. (1985). *Explaining delinquency and drug use.* SAGE.

Enghoff, O., & Aldridge, J. (2019). The value of unsolicited online data in drug policy research. *International Journal of Drug Policy, 73*, 210–218.

Ennis, P. H. (1967). *Criminal victimization in the United States. A report of a national survey.* US Government Printing Office.

EUROPOL. (2021). *Internet Organised Crime Threat Assessment (IOCTA) 2021.* Publications Office of the European Union.

Farrell, G., & Pease, K. (1993). *Once bitten, twice bitten: Repeat victimisation and its implications for crime prevention* [Crime Prevention Unit Series Paper No. 46]. Home Office Police Department.

Furnell, S., Emm, D., & Papadaki, M. (2015). The challenge of measuring cyber-dependent crimes. *Computer Fraud & Security, 10*, 5–12.

Gold, M. (1970). *Delinquent behavior in an American city*. Brooks.

Graham, R. S., & Smith, S. K. (2020). *Cybercrime and digital deviance*. Routledge.

Gundur, R. V., Berry, M., & Taodang, D. (2021). Using digital open source and crowdsourced data in studies of deviance and crime. In A. Lavorgna & T. J. Holt (Eds.), *Researching cybercrimes* (pp. 145–167). Palgrave Macmillan.

Guzy, N., & Leitgöb, H. (2015). Assessing mode effects in online and telephone victimization surveys. *International Review of Victimology, 21*(1), 101–131.

Haen-Marshall, I., Birkbeck, C. H., Enzmann, D., Kivivouri, J., Markina, A., & Steketee, M. (2022). *International Self-Report Delinquency (ISRD4) study protocol: Background, Methodology, And Mandatory Items For the 2021/2022 survey* [ISRD Technical Report 4]. Northeastern University.

Hart, T. C., Rennison, C. M., & Gibson, C. (2005). Revisiting respondent "fatigue bias" in the national crime victimization survey. *Journal of Quantitative Criminology, 21*(3), 345–363.

Hindelang, M. J., Gottfredson, M. R., & Garofalo, J. (1978). *Victims of personal crime: An empirical foundation for a theory of personal victimization*. Ballinger Publishing.

Hindelang, M. J., Hirschi, T., & Weis, J. G. (1981). *Measuring delinquency*. SAGE.

Hirschi, T. (1969). *Causes of delinquency*. University of California Press.

Holt, T. J., & Bossler, A. M. (2008). Examining the applicability of lifestyle-routine activities theory for cybercrime victimization. *Deviant Behavior, 30*(1), 1–25.

Huey, L., & Buil-Gil, D. (Eds.). (2024). *The crime data handbook*. Bristol University Press.

International Telecommunication Union. (2021). *Measuring digital development: Facts and figures 2021*. ITU Publications.

Junger, M., Wang, V., & Schlömer, M. (2020). Fraud against businesses both online and offline: Crime scripts, business characteristics, efforts, and benefits. *Crime Science, 9*(13).

Junger-Tas, J. (2010). The significance of the International Self-report Delinquency Study (ISRD). *European Journal on Criminal Policy and Research, 16*, 71–87.

Junger-Tas, J., & Marshall, I. H. (1999). The self-report methodology in crime research. *Crime and Justice, 25*, 291–367.

Kemp, S., Buil-Gil, D., Miró-Llinares, F., & Lord, N. (2023). When do businesses report cybercrime? Findings from a UK study. *Criminology & Criminal Justice, 23*(3), 468–489.

Lauritsen, J. L. (1993). Sibling resemblance in juvenile delinquency: Findings from the national youth survey. *Criminology, 31*(3), 387–409.

Lee, B. H. (2018). Explaining cyber deviance among school-aged youth. *Child Indicators Research, 11*(2), 563–584.

Leukfeldt, E. R., & Yar, M. (2016). Applying routine activity theory to cybercrime: A theoretical and empirical analysis. *Deviant Behavior, 37*(3), 263–280.

Lynch, J. P., & Addington, L. A. (Eds.). (2006). *Understanding crime statistics: Revisiting the divergence of the NCVS and UCR*. Cambridge University Press.

Maguire, M. (1997). Crime statistics, patterns, and trends: Changing perceptions and their implications. In M. Maguire, R. Morgan, & R. Reiner (Eds.), *The Oxford handbook of criminology* (2nd ed., pp. 135–188). Oxford University Press.

McGuire, M., & Dowling, S. (2013). *Cyber crime: A review of the evidence* [Research Report 75]. Home Office.

Murray, A. L., Eisner, M., Ribeaud, D., Kaiser, D., McKenzie, K., & Murray, G. (2021). Validation of a brief self-report measure of adolescent bullying perpetration and victimization. *Assessment, 28*(1), 128–140.

Office for National Statistics. (2021). *Table D10: Percentage of CSEW incidents reported to the police or action fraud, year ending December 1981 to year ending March 2020 CSEW*. Retrieved from www.ons.gov.uk/peoplepopulationandcommunity/crimeandjustice/datasets/crimeinenglandandwalesannualtrendanddemographictables/current (Last accessed 02 April 2022).

Osborn, D. R., Trickett, A., & Elder, R. (1992). Area characteristics and regional variates as determinants of area property crime levels. *Journal of Quantitative Criminology, 8*, 265–285.

Osborn, D. R., & Tseloni, A. (1998). The distribution of household property crimes. *Journal of Quantitative Criminology, 14*, 307–330.

Osgood, D. W., McMorris, B. J., & Potenza, M. T. (2002). Analyzing multiple-item measures of crime and deviance I: Item response theory scaling. *Journal of Quantitative Criminology, 18*, 267–296.

Paquet-Clouston, M., Décary-Hétu, D., & Morselli, C. (2018). Assessing market competition and vendors' size and scope on AlphaBay. *International Journal of Drug Policy, 54*, 87–98.

Pratt, T. C., Holtfreter, K., & Reisig, M. D. (2010). Routine online activity and internet fraud targeting: Extending the generality of routine activity theory. *Journal of Research in Crime and Delinquency, 47*(3), 267–296.

Rantala, R. (2008). *Cybercrime against businesses, 2005. Special report, bureau of justice statistics.* US Department of Justice.

Reep-van der Bergh, C. M. M., & Junger, M. (2018). Victims of cybercrime in Europe: A review of victim surveys. *Crime Science, 7*, 5.

Rokven, J. J., Weijters, G., Beerthuizen, M. G., & van der Laan, A. M. (2018). Juvenile delinquency in the virtual world: Similarities and differences between cyber-enabled, cyber-dependent and offline delinquents in the Netherlands. *International Journal of Cyber Criminology, 12*(1), 27–46.

Sampson, R. J., & Groves, B. W. (1989). Community structure and crime: Testing social disorganization theory. *American Journal of Sociology, 94*(4), 774–802.

Schneider A. L. (1981). Methodological problems in victim surveys and their implications for research in victimology. *The Journal of Criminal Law and Criminology, 72*(2), 818–838.

Sellin, T. (1931). The basis of a crime index. *Journal of Criminal Law and Criminology, 22*(3), 335–356.

Short, J. F., & Nye, F. I. (1958). Extent of unrecorded juvenile delinquency: Tentative conclusions. *The Journal of Criminal Law, Criminology, and Police Science, 49*(4), 296–302.

Skogan W. G. (1975). Measurement problems in official and survey crime rates. *Journal of Criminal Justice, 3*(1), 17–31.

Skogan, W. G. (1977). Dimensions of the dark figure of unreported crime. *Crime & Delinquency, 23*(1), 41–50.

Solymosi, R., & Bowers, K. (2018). The role of innovative data collection methods in advancing criminological understanding. In G. J. N. Bruinsma & S. D. Johnson (Eds.), *The Oxford handbook of environmental criminology* (pp. 210–237). Oxford University Press.

Sparks, R. F. (1981). Surveys of victimization-an optimistic assessment. *Crime and Justice, 3*, 1–66.

Tarling, R., & Morris, K. (2010). Reporting crime to the police. *The British Journal of Criminology, 50*(3), 474–490.

Tilley, N., & Tseloni, A. (2016). Choosing and using statistical sources in criminology: What can the crime survey for England and Wales tell us? *Legal Information Management, 16*(2), 78–90.

van de Weijer, S. G. A., Leukfeldt, R., & Bernasco, W. (2019). Determinants of reporting cybercrime: A comparison between identity theft, consumer fraud, and hacking. *European Journal of Criminology, 16*(4), 486–508.

van der Laan, A. M., Rokven, J., Weijters, G., & Beerthuizen, M. (2021). The drop in juvenile delinquency in the Netherlands: Changes in exposure to risk and protection. *Justice Quarterly, 38*(3), 433–453.

van Dijk, J. J. M., van Kesteren, J., & Smit, P. (2007). *Criminal victimisation in international perspective. key findings from the 2004–2005 ICVS and EU ICS.* WODC.

Wallerstein, J. S., & Wyle, C. J. (1947). Our law-abiding law-breakers. *Probation, 25*, 107–112.

Weulen Kranenbarg, M. (2022). When do they offend together? Comparing co-offending between different types of cyber-offenses and traditional offenses. *Computers in Human Behavior, 130*, 107186.

Weulen Kranenbarg, M., Holt, T. J., & van Gelder, J. (2019). Offending and victimization in the digital age: Comparing correlates of cybercrime and traditional offending-only, victimization-only and the victimization-offending overlap. *Deviant Behavior, 40*(1), 40–55.

Williams, M. L., Levi, M., Burnap, P., & Gundur, R. V. (2019). Under the corporate radar: Examining insider business cybercrime victimization through an application of routine activities theory. *Deviant Behavior*, 40(9), 1119–1131.

Young, M., Rodriguez, L., Keller, E., Sun, F., Sa, B., Whittington, J., & Howe, B. (2019). Beyond open vs. Closed: Balancing individual privacy and public accountability in data sharing. In *Proceedings of the conference on fairness, accountability, and transparency* (pp. 191–200). Association for Computing Machinery.

3

THE VICTIM-PERPETRATOR?

A gendered theory of incel digital deviance

Stuart Lucy

Introduction

Twenty-first century user-generated online socialization has fundamentally altered the identity of individuals, as disembodied digital and embodied physical experiences coexist along a continuum of subjective experience. The digital and physical self intersect symbiotically, as each affects the other (Powell et al., 2018). Alongside the innovations and progressive achievements produced by this contemporary digital interconnectivity, there also exists the capacity to perform disembodied deviant behaviour as anonymous, and largely unaccountable, actors. As individual subjective immersion into digital deviance deepens, so does the propensity for the development of sophisticated, amorphous, and perverse networks that surpass traditional geographical boundaries. These may serve to intensify extreme, radical, or combative sociopolitical positions that seek to identify, demonize, and attack targeted Others (Graham & Smith, 2020). The aim of this chapter is to discuss one such example of reactionary, digitally embodied deviant actors: involuntary celibates, or 'incels', utilizing a combination of criminological frameworks applied through a poststructural gendered lens to conceptualize this relatively novel and growing online community. This theoretical exploration was undertaken during an ongoing PhD investigating the (in)formative gendered mechanisms operant in the process of adherence to incel ideology, and participation in the community's online spaces. The purpose of this analysis is to offer a gendered criminological framework that considers the complex and contradictory position of incel online deviance through a victim-offender overlap.

'Incel' is predominantly a digital identity—individuals converging within a variety of online social media consisting of heterosexual men and adolescents self-defined by an inability to achieve heterosexual sociosexual intimacy and connection (O'Malley et al., 2022). Incels ascribe to a biologically determined, antifeminist, misogynistic, and self-deprecating gendered ideology (Lindsay, 2022), viewing the world through a social sexual hierarchy in which genetically determined physical features dictate one's opportunity to have sex and attract a long-term partner, achievements perceived as central to a successful and happy life (Sugiura, 2021). Incels place themselves at the bottom of this rigidly constructed hierarchy based on a subjectively supposed failure to meet prescribed ideals of attractiveness (Burton,

DOI: 10.4324/9781003277675-5

2022). The incel identity is suggested to manifest mainly through digital forum-based activity, in which various instances of deviance arise, including but not limited to cyberbullying/stalking, harassment of women, the malicious release of personal information (doxing), sharing of extreme and illegal pornography, and participation in symbolically violent misogynistic memetic and subcultural discourse (Ging, 2019a). There have also been an increasing number of instances of physical violence enacted upon the general public, in some cases specifically targeting women. Following these acts of violence linked to the community and its associated ideology, the identity has received an increasing level of academic interest (Tastenhoye et al., 2022). The incel community is frequently investigated through a sociological lens of gendered power, born from critical studies of men and masculinities, analyzing performances of maleness relative to broader structures of patriarchy and hierarchies of competing masculinities. Investigation has predominantly involved qualitative analysis of data derived from dedicated incel forums and websites (Ging & Murphy, 2021). While useful in understanding the mechanics of these spaces, the potentially performative nature of the forums and analysis of static posts prevents deeper analysis of individual experiences and subjectivities of the embodied men behind the keyboards and screens. Further, the complexity of digital (and offline) deviance performed by individuals, oftentimes with claimed experience of significant mental health conditions and various incidents of discrimination (Costello et al., 2022; Moskalenko et al., 2022; Speckhard & Ellenberg, 2022), suggests that a delicate approach is warranted in understanding the complexity of these individuals. A poststructural theory of discourse offers a framework with which to interrogate the multiple and potentially contradictory identities of incels and serves as a foundation with which to apply extant criminological theories to the incel individual through a gendered lens. Emerging literature detailing the victim-offender overlap (Berg & Mulford, 2020; Reingle Gonzalez, 2014) provides a theoretical framework within which this lens may be applied to understand the deviancy of cyber communities such as incels. In line with strain theories, gendered subjects bound to pervasive traditional male ideology (Pleck, 1995) and socially dictated mandates to achieve masculine status (Agnew, 2001), may experience direct and indirect psychological dysfunction (and potential physical injury through adolescent peer assault) resulting from an inability to assume the required masculine performances. This gendered strain can produce an over-conformity to traditional male ideology, resulting in instances of misogyny, antifeminism, and violence as well as isolation, self-harm, and suicide (American Psychological Association, Boys and Men Guidelines Group, 2018)—behaviors documented by a variety of incel-related research (e.g. Daly & Laskovtsov, 2021; Maxwell et al., 2020; Sparks et al., 2022; Sugiura, 2021). Incels' negative psychic and physical experiences as a direct and indirect result of strain derived from a pervasive gendered ideology, an ideology which directly informs acts of perpetrated deviance, demonstrates a victim-offender overlap in which certain individuals are affected by and effect gendered deviance in parallel.

The chapter begins first with an outline of the incel identity, community, and ideology before moving on to an examination of the various fields of academic investigation that have taken place following instances of incel-associated real world violence. After discussing the critical study of men and masculinities' contributions to mapping the many masculine performances found in incel digital media, the limitations of the predominant form of qualitative methodology applied to incel forum data is critiqued, demonstrating its inability to draw out the subjectivities and experiences of the individuals who make up the online community. The poststructural theory of discourse is then offered as an alternative to the structural gendered investigation of incels, to provide a foundation that incorporates gender into a position that recognizes multiple, complex, and at times, contradictory subjective identities that define the individual. Existing criminological victim-offender and strain theories (Agnew, 1992; Pleck, 1995; Reingle Gonzalez, 2014) are then applied to the incel experience, building on a poststructural foundation to conceptualize the duality of a gendered victim experience that directs and informs the over-conformity of individuals to traditional male ideology and masculine discourse producing deviant gendered action. The chapter concludes with the suggestion that gendered criminological models and supporting methodologies that approach the individual as a subjective, fluid, and complex identity may provide an opportunity to understand this specific instance of digital deviance from a position that affords insight into the motivations and mechanisms behind the assumption of an incel identity.

The incel phenomenon

The original inception of the incel identity, created towards the end of the twentieth century, is accredited to a Canadian bisexual woman who wishes only to be known as Alana. Keen to connect with peers, both male and female, in an inclusive digital forum to reciprocally support anyone experiencing negative emotional and cognitive experiences resulting from a life absent of romantic and sexual connection (Kassam, 2018), 'incel' was a constructive and progressive designation intended to recognize sociosexual challenges within a supportive space (Byerly, 2020). The mutation of the incel identity gradually occurred over the following two decades as a subset of young heterosexual men and male adolescents within the original community began to break away, banned from associated inclusive digital spaces for espousing a militant, misogynistic, and rejectionist identity visible in contemporary incel digital forums today (Ging, 2019b; Nagle, 2016). The evolution of this community was facilitated by the imageboard environs of online sites such as 4Chan, unregulated arenas in which hypermasculine, misogynous rhetoric merged with indistinguishable acts of supposed irreverent and ironic humor known colloquially as trolling and 'shitposting' (Nagle, 2017). Similar to many internet users, incels are active in numerous user-generated social media arenas and consequently, incel rhetoric spread to more mainstream sites such as Reddit (Cottee, 2021). Following Reddit's update of terms of service in an attempt to eradicate hate-fueled and -filled content, the banning of incel specific subforums such as 'r/incels' and 'r/braincels' led to the community's convergence within purpose-built homosocial forum-based websites, buttressed by an increasing number of YouTube channels, Facebook groups and incels active on Twitter (Sugiura, 2021).

Appropriated from the 1999 film *The Matrix*, incel ideology originates from a binary metaphoric construct of consumption of a blue or red pill, conveying ignorance or realization respectively of the gendered 'truth' of Western society. Consuming their 'redpill' and discovering said truth is to acknowledge and thus internalize belief in a biologically determined, sociosexual ordering in which genetically defined determinants such as height, muscularity, shoulder width, and hairline dictate male heterosexual success (Conley, 2020; Ging, 2019a; Nagle, 2017; O'Malley et al., 2022). Connected to this is the belief that women, through feminism and liberal political influence, have molded Western liberal democracy into a gynocentric order which benefits women and subjugates men, and thus men must react in a multitude of ways to achieve their desired ends of societal and interpersonal mastery and, ultimately, sex (Van Valkenburgh, 2021). Incels accept this ideology as foundational, extending it to the '*black*pill', a nihilistic evolution that accepts defeat in light of this dark 'truth', as men genetically predisposed to fail in meeting the required standards of women. Internalizing a self-denigrating identity as inferior 'subhumans', many incels adopt a fatalistic defeatism supposing a physicality too unattractive to ever achieve heterosexual intimacy (Cottee, 2021). Placing themselves at the bottom of the biologically determined sexual hierarchy perceived as the core tenet of social ordering, incels ubiquitously denounce the people above them. Subsequent ideological rhetoric creates mythical exemplars of hypersexualized men and women, named Chad and Stacy respectively, castigated for their dominant success in the sociosexual milieu. This resentment extends to lower ranked 'beta' women for their supposed self-subjugation to Chads and to hierarchically corresponding beta men for self-subjugation to manipulative and hypergamous, financially exploitative women whose biologically driven desire is inexorably transfixed upon highly prized alpha-male Chads (Menzie, 2020; Thorburn et al., 2022). This radical, gendered, and hypersexualized view of the world utilizes cherry-picked and distorted evolutionary psychology to support their claims of sexual biological determinism, used as a justification for the profound and explicit denigration of all women, manifest in the symbolic violence of hyper-misogynous rhetoric found in digital incel spaces. Incels simultaneously direct deviance internally through glorified and encouraged self-loathing, which taken to its extreme can precondition suicidal tendencies (Daly & Laskovtsov, 2021), as well as externally through sharing of illegal and extreme pornography, doxing, cyberstalking/bullying, harassment, and the explicit misogynistic denigration of women (Ging, 2019a).

Academic investigation

The incel community has attracted significant academic interest following increasing instances of associated physical violence. In 2014, a 22-yr-old male perpetrated the Isla Vista, California mass shooting—killing six and injuring 14—leaving behind a detailed and lengthy part-autobiography/part-manifesto which asserted, without directly referring to, incel ideology (Vito et al., 2017). In 2018, a self-identifying incel committed a van attack in Toronto in which 10 people lost their lives, with an additional 16 injured, prior to which the perpetrator posted via Facebook a message specifically referring to an 'incel rebellious uprising' (O'Donnell & Shor, 2022; Zimmerman et al., 2018). Given this explicit reference in a mass killing, the potential threat of incels catalyzed numerous academic lenses of investigation including terrorism studies, cultural studies, and critical feminist and masculinity frameworks. The nature of these varying themes of investigation examined the philosophical positionality of incel ideology and action, the loci of incel socialization and content of media produced by perpetrators of violence that had adopted the identity (Andersen, 2022; Tastenhoye et al., 2022). The predominant method of inquiry within incel-associated research has involved some form of thematic content analysis of a select portion of textual data obtained from either defunct or active incel digital forums (Ging & Murphy, 2021).

Initial security and terrorism analyses framed incel ideology as politically minded quasi-extremism differing from traditional conceptual frameworks, as incel in-group self-loathing distinctively departed from Islamic or traditional far-right radical dualist ideologies (Baele et al., 2019). Subsequent inquiry named incel ideology and incels as violent extremism (Jaki et al., 2019), as a single-issue terrorist group (O'Donnell & Shor, 2022), an atypical terrorism lacking coercive properties of comparative terrorist groups (Cottee, 2021), and as indicative of gendered, normalized spectral misogynistic violence culminating in sporadic stochastic terroristic acts (Lindsay, 2022). While recent investigation continues to advocate for the securitization of incels (Roose & Cook, 2022; Tomkinson et al., 2020), contrasting positions highlight the complexity and difficulty in applying traditional models of security and terrorism to incels, given their idiosyncrasies and heterogeneity and that a 'terrorist or not' dichotomy fails to effect mitigation of risk from their attacks (Brzuszkiewicz, 2020; Leidig, 2021; Nardone, 2022). Recognition that heterogeneity exists within the online community, with levels of extremist language varying across digital incel space (Baele et al., 2023; Perliger et al., 2023), suggests that individual-level analyses may serve to offer insight as to why some incels commit physical violence, while others remain in digital space with a spectrum of non-violent deviant engagement.

The critical study of men and masculinities also investigated incels via their online content, often utilizing qualitative thematic analysis of forum data theorized through the construct of multiple masculinities. Briefly, R. W. Connell's (1995) theory of multiple masculinities outlines a structure of competing masculinities, with the promotion of a particular configuration of performative male action above others: hegemonic masculinity, culturally exalted, and exemplifying the 'right' way to be a man—think James Bond or David Beckham. As a culturally sensitive presentation of masculinity, forever reformulating and adapting to sociocultural shifts, it ensures the continuation of patriarchy and the dominance of some men over women by socially, culturally, and politically legitimizing the subordinate position of women and other men (Messerschmidt, 2018). Hegemonic masculinity can only exist in relation to other masculinities and femininity. For there to be an exemplar of all that it is to be the right type of man, all rejected qualities, such as effeminateness, must be placed into a relative position of subordinated masculinity. Complicit masculinities also exist, performances in which one may not necessarily adopt the hegemonic form but fail to challenge it, benefiting through a patriarchal 'dividend' that legitimizes the sustained domination of men over women. (Connell, 1995; Connell & Messerschmidt, 2005). The fourth type of masculinity, marginalized masculinity, refers to men who lack attributes to be able to conform to hegemonic masculinity such as their race, (homo)sexuality, or (working) class status. As an approach connecting gender and power, this theory describes how sociopolitical ideals perpetrate the continual domination of men over women through cultural scripts that strategically promote and denounce particular performances of men in different arenas. Numerous applications within the investigation of online instances of incel masculine deviance have produced varying conclusions with regards to the different masculinities present in these spaces. Various scholarly analyses examining incel forum content via thematic analysis have identified the presence of hegemonic (Maxwell et al., 2020; Preston et al., 2021; Scheuerman, 2021; Vito et al., 2017), subordinate (Halpin, 2022; Lindsay, 2021), and marginalized (Vallerga & Zurbriggen, 2022) presentations of masculinity. Using an abductive thematic analysis of 9,062 comments posted to the incel forum incels.co, Preston et al. (2021) noted that incels' policing of other men's behaviour through structuring of rigid male hierarchies and equating masculine worth to heterosexual success were both indicative of the subjectivities of hegemonic masculinity. Analysis of the manifesto left by the perpetrator of the Isla Vista mass shooting by Vito et al. (2017) suggested that although he challenged hegemonic masculine norms, his construction of masculinity via physical embodiment and sexual prowess simultaneously reproduced hegemonic masculinity. In a literature review of the study of the incel phenomenon, Scheuerman (2021) found research suggesting that incels both reject and conform to hegemonic masculinity through constructions of sexual prowess and dominance regarded as masculine, despite their inability to achieve these due to a self-perceived insufficiency. Lindsay (2021) analyzed 250 threads over a three-month period from the forums incels.co and r/braincels, using thematic analysis to identify key themes, narratives, and ideas. According to this analysis, incels construct a monstrous, feminine Other to justify their violence against women. This was seen as reclamation of their masculinity; a liberation from their position of subordinated men, unable to live up to the hegemonic norms culturally endorsed within a patriarchal society valuing male sexual prowess and dominance. Vallerga and Zurbriggen (2022) analyzed just one day of posts on r/incels, suggesting incels were both unable to live up to hegemonic norms, but considered doing so to be dangerous, rejecting aspects of such a dominant identity and instead positing themselves as a marginalized masculinity that, as a relational construction, still reinforced hegemonic masculine dominance. Using reflexive thematic analysis, Thorburn et al. (2022) assessed the top 10 posts, from 45 parent threads, across a 14-day period from the forum incels.is, applying Connell's (1995) multiple masculinities model to guide coding of the data. Analysis led the authors to identify incels' digital performances of maleness within this forum as subordinate to the hegemonic norms of more socially and successful Chad alpha males. Hierarchically competitive masculine performances presented within the forum created an inverted version of hierarchical masculine structure in which the most subordinated presentations of maleness, that is, the furthest from the hegemonic norm, were exalted. Conversely, the least subordinate, possessing traits and features most associated with traditional forms of desirable masculinity (e.g. tall, muscular, good-looking etc.), were derided as 'fake incel' identities. Ging (2019a) extends this identification of multiple, sometimes contradictory, digital masculine performance, suggesting the presence of an incel 'hybrid' masculinity. A concept derived from work by Demetriou (2001), hybridity highlights the capacity for hegemonic presentations of masculinity to subsume elements of subordinate or marginalized masculinity, reconfiguring into a revised hegemonic form that appears to demonstrate features of marginalized or subordinate masculinity while remaining hegemonic. For Ging, incel masculinity, encapsulated within a conceptualization of geek identity, remains hegemonic, evidenced through the digital deviancy performed by these individuals via online harassment, doxing, cyberstalking/bullying of women, and the explicit and pernicious misogyny espoused in these spaces. Incels retain and express traditional aspects of hegemonic maleness whilst they appropriate, internalize, and reproduce presentations of subordinate forms of masculinity, maintaining a hegemonic configuration through action that exerts continual dominion over women viewed as the inferior gender. Individual testaments of incels' subordination or marginalization as a victim in the hands of feminism, and the sociosexual ordering of contemporary society, serves as a ruse: a dummy performance masking heteronormative patriarchal misogyny bound within incel digital action. This hybridity was supported by Glace et al. (2021) in their analysis of the top 400 posts of the now-defunct r/incels forum hosted on Reddit. They noted a hybrid masculinity that discursively distanced from hegemonic masculinity via claims of subordinate male status and victimization, establishing a critical consciousness by strategically borrowing language from marginalized groups as they iterated performances of symbolically violent and virulent antifeminism and misogyny. These direct applications and amplifications of Connell's (1995) masculinities model demonstrates within incel digital space a variety of positions of masculinity; a continuum of gendered practices performed as men and male adolescents navigating a dialogical and dialectical relationship with masculinity. Lacking the necessary perceived requisites to acquire or achieve positions of power, to be celebrated and exalted as the correct way to 'be' a man, incels nevertheless interact with tenets of hegemonic masculinity through gendered deviance specifically targeted at women, giving meaning to their male identity. Unable to fulfil the required demands, the amorphous digital incel community presents a variety of masculine positions bound to, but incapable of, a desired masculine performance—and by extension, its identity-confirming status.

The thematic analysis of forum data employed across a variety of investigations mentioned thus far has resulted in numerous useful ways of looking at incels. It has, however, also led to analyses that arguably homogenize the community as the subjective individual experiences of the community are read, via forum analysis, as collective. Further, the utilization of blocks of posts captures only a snapshot of one spatiotemporal digital moment or limited period in a forum(s), a performative space not necessarily indicative of the true character of its participants, resulting in the generalization of a broad and diverse group of individuals as a synchronous, homogenous, mass. As theories of security, terrorism, gender, and masculinity are applied to, or derived from, data deemed to be representative of the incel phenomenon, the sum of individuals therein become bound to categorical assessments of violent extremism (or not) and structural gendered models of power. The identities and individual experiences behind the data points remain absent from view, leading to the theorization of incels en masse, then compared to established understandings of existing group-derived extremism/terrorism, offering minimal nascent constructs beyond existing conceptual boundaries. While the lens of gender provides a means with which to ascribe an identity to the individuals, much associated analysis does so from a structural position that lacks the facility for deeper interrogation of an on-/offline complexion; of who the individual incel is and how their formative experiences have led to a susceptibility to, and perpetration of, the so frequently documented digital deviance and virulent misogyny. Studies that applied additional or alternative methodologies to the thematic analysis of select forum data suggest a complex gendered interaction between experience and performance. A survey of 272 self-identifying incels by Speckhard and Ellenberg (2022) revealed an elevated incidence of several complex mental health conditions compared to non-incel populations, including depression, anxiety, bipolar, autistic spectrum, and post-traumatic stress disorders. Participants also discussed the presence of perceived physical deficits linked to traditional masculine traits such as height, muscularity, or jawline. Further, engagement with incel forums was felt by participants to consequentially exacerbate many experienced mental health issues. The authors conclude that whilst much of the literature linking the sense of emasculation within the incel community has been linked to constructions of masculinity, as discussed here, these feelings could alternatively and equally be analyzed as psychological challenges. Noting Pleck's (1995) gender role strain paradigm (GRsP), Speckhard and Ellenberg suggest that mental health issues could arise from the internalized effects of a perceived failure to meet the masculine ideal. Using the same dataset, Moskalenko et al. (2022) expand this analysis by demonstrating that the majority of incels rejected radical or violent incel ideology, further suggesting that adherence to radical ideology is potentially associated with experience of autism spectrum disorder and/or bullying. In studies that directly interviewed incels, both Sugiura (2021) and Daly and Reed (2021) documented participants' struggle with masculine identity and expectations. The latter study noted that this challenge was deemed to lead to perceptions of marginalization and that incels experienced negative emotionality because of inceldom. In a recent investigation that analyzed the connection between misogyny and unwanted celibacy in the wider population, Grunau et al. (2022) suggest that misogyny and hostile attitudes toward women by heterosexual men was significantly and positively correlated with unwanted celibacy. That is, it was the experience of sexlessness that could be driving misogyny as a byproduct of high male sexual desire, suggesting that previous gendered experiences may drive future gendered behaviour.

Beyond qualitative digital thematic methodologies, incels become a complex heterogeneous ensemble of subjective men driven by their experiences. When the individuals behind coalesced digital performances are engaged, we discover a significant prevalence of self-reported and professionally diagnosed mental health disorders and negative gendered life course experiences; traumatic adverse childhood incidents, vulnerable isolation, and masculine identities indentured to psychologically dysfunctional prescriptions of being a man. The gendered lens of incel identity construction suggests that the deviance found within the community may well be a reactionary consequence of an assumed perception of failure to meet the traditional masculine ideology operant in gender role strain (Pleck, 1995). The strain to meet gendered expectations may drive incels towards digital spaces that offer solace and a sense of community, but in doing so, incubate animosity and afford opportunity to enact digital deviance. The personal experiences and perspectives captured in investigations that attempt to interrogate the individual, away from potentially performative forums with requisites that may exaggerate, coerce, or misrepresent individual sentiment, suggest perceived and actual negative experiences formative of a subjective gendered identity instrumental in subsequent deviant action(s). An enhanced explanation of the deviance of the incel identity perhaps requires the incorporation of structural gendered interpretations into a theoretical criminological model that provides space to recognize simultaneous subjective, onto-formative negative encounters, experienced from a subordinate position relative to normative expectation and understanding of masculinity, and perpetuation of digital (and physical) deviance informed by that experience. This suggests a potential to approach deviant groups of males such as incels from a position using existing criminological constructs that recognizes the interconnecting complexity of victim and perpetrator identities, whilst retaining the gendered lens of the critical study of masculinity. The concurrent duality of identities present in such a theoretical direction commands the application of a poststructural toolkit (Whitehead, 2002), building upon evidence of gendered deviant action concurrently present alongside subjective perceptions and experiences of subordinate and 'failed' masculinity that has been so far provided by the investigation of incels.

Poststructural discursive identity

Poststructural theory allows interrogation of the individual at the subject level, offering a toolbox of ideas useful for deconstructive interpretation of structural formations and interactions individuals are bound within (Gutterman, 2001). Regarding the incel identity, community, and resulting deviance, rather than seeking explanation through an angle of structural gendered power between the sexes, this form of consideration permits recognition and examination of multiple, potentially contradictory, identities, discourses, and performances that comprise the incel subject.

Intersectionality reminds us that the individual is constituted of numerous subjectivities, including race, class, sexuality, and gender. With that in mind, the male subject, while indeed embroiled within a gendered relational power dynamic, also holds numerous other conflating and seemingly contradictory positions and identities based on a variety of additional impactive discourses. Discourse, understood in the Foucauldian sense, serves as both a linguistic structure and, crucially, a signifying identity *practice*, marking and enabling the individual, producing the subject through construction of a multifaceted being (Foucault, 1969). This operationalization of discourse allows us to understand how social norms and the values placed upon them are constructed, producing contingent, unstable identities based upon individual perception and interpretations that become internalized, and subsequently performed, by the subject. We may, as individuals, be some things sometimes, other things at different times, or many things at the same time. Discourses possess authoritative validating potential within a relational societal milieu (Howarth & Stavrakakis, 2000), which enables the subject to pursue an identity project in order to construct their 'self'— formulating dominant 'truths' about race, sexuality, and power that result from gradations of dominance placed upon the identities within these domains (Whitehead, 2006). Concerning gender, Brittan (1991) offers a useful perspective to understand how particular gendered discourses become operational and effective within the social milieu, resulting in male domination that underscores traditional structural theories of patriarchy and hegemony. 'Masculinism' refers to pervasive reproductive discourse(s) that provides justification for the naturalization, through gender essentialism, of male domination, configurations of hegemonic action outlined in Connell's (1995) theory of multiple masculinities. Differences between men and women are taken as fundamental within masculinism discourse—men as socially and sexually dominant, women subordinate and receptive—with heterosexual normativity a fundamental enabler of particular male action. The discourse of masculinity shapes the attributes that the individual must embody to 'be' a man. Whilst far-reaching, such exigencies may or may not be achievable and thus cannot possibly be adopted and successfully performed by everyone. This means during construction and subsequent articulation of the male self, power over women and other men becomes a fluid, contestable, perpetually negotiated dynamic among males undergoing constantly reformative subjective identity work. Rather than hierarchical, power becomes circular or networked, existing dialectically with varied resistance to it (Foucault, 2020). Power is not always held by all men all the time, nor is it permanent once possessed. Power is unstable as new and competing discourses vie for dominance. The male individual, then, far from the ubiquitous proprietor of power and oppression, instead is embroiled with numerous discourses that may conflict and contradict, existing in relative and concurrent positions of dominance and resistance; power and powerlessness; oppressor and oppressed.

Such a poststructural theorization of masculinity and power licenses understanding of the male individual as spatiotemporally contingent; as potentially powerless and powerful depending on particular discourses of identity, experiences, performances, and specific subjective realities relative to the particular social milieu they inhabit. This then provides the capacity to interpret and explain the contradiction of 'powerful powerlessness' of the individual(s) within a structure, cognizant of the multiple discourses that inform their subjective identity and any subsequent powerful/less performances or experiences that may occur. This theoretical foundation of multiple formative realizations coexisting in an individual offers a lens with which to comprehend the simultaneous complexity of the incel position. While they are perpetrators of gendered digital deviancy through symbolic violence in acts of misogyny, cyberstalking, doxing, and online harassment of women, incels also experience the pain (Kross et al., 2011) of adverse life events such as psychological and/or physically violent peer assault, social rejection or isolation, and associated psychological dysfunction (Costello et al., 2022; Moskalenko et al., 2022; Speckhard & Ellenberg, 2022) resulting from failure to meet socially prescribed standards of expected masculinity. This concurrent opposing state offers a nuanced gendered comprehension of incel deviance at the individual, subjective level, recognizing the formative discourse(s) that simultaneously produces experiences of both psychological dysfunction and social ostracization while catalyzing acts of misogyny, harassment, cyberbullying, and other digital forms of deviant behaviour.

Towards the individual INCEL

The utilization of gender-based lenses applied to the incel community has informed the research community of the presence of numerous conflicting and contradictory masculine performances in the digital forums in which the analyses occurred. This research, however, groups large numbers of individuals together, collating posts and threads to produce a homogenous, potentially superficial appraisal, that may overlook numerous aspects operant in the formation and performances of an individual's incel identity. Reductive analyses of static moments or periods in digital forums risks a myopia focused upon biological essentialism, misogyny, female objectification, dominance, and sexual aggressiveness, resulting in the construction of a narrative of the 'perpetrator incel'. Studies that extend beyond this methodology and structural view of gender to the individual identify socially constructed self-loathing and hopelessness that is inextricably bound to a perception of masculine failure, adverse childhood experiences, depression, anxiety, and other significant mental health conditions (Daly & Reed, 2021; Justin et al., 2022; Sparks et al., 2022; Speckhard & Ellenberg, 2022). Structural gender theory focuses upon meso-level analysis of masculinities in relation to hegemony and patriarchy, and whilst it is certainly a useful lens to understand the gendered existence of groups in incel digital space, this type of critical ontology inhibits a framework premised upon individual psychological issues permitting a gendered victim-perpetrator dialectic. If we instead view incels as individuals formed by multiple influences, including those that dictate expectations of heterosexual masculinity, it becomes possible to (cautiously) give space to a form of 'victimhood' that catalyzes and instructs their perpetration of digital deviance. Failure to achieve the socially prescribed correct physical and social standards, inscribed into the individual's understanding of an acceptable male identity, leads to a broad array of psychological dysfunction readily documented through interaction with incels. Coupled with social rejection, isolation, and loneliness, this gendered perception of persecution contributes towards, but does not justify, the fueling of the community's deviance. The very same discourses they fall victim to underpin the perpetration they subsequently commit. Formative gendered identity discourses, such as Brittan's (1991) masculinism, provide an unseen benefit to these individuals as men in a male-dominated society, but conversely produces negative experiences. These individuals are physically and verbally assaulted for their failures as men and experience the failure in fundamental heteronormative masculine formative discourse: the inability to be sexually active. This prevalent and influential gendered ideology bound in formative discourse is intrinsic to a subjective existence within a gendered social environment. For those unable to attain the demands of this discourse; men lacking the desired and required physicality, social competency, or heterosexual success to 'be a real man', repeated and sustained exposure to identity determinative ideology can become harmful to the conceptualization of self, and regarding subsequent deviance, also lead to the harm of others. So damaging is this traditional male ideology that the American Psychological Association (APA) released an unprecedented 36-page report concerning psychological practice with boys and men, detailing the pervasive effects of discourse associated with traditional masculine ideology upon psychological development, behaviour, and mental and physical health. The report linked adherence to traditional masculine ideology to misogyny, anti-femininity, sexual harassment, and violence, alongside self-deprecating behaviors including isolation, self-harm, and suicide (American Psychological Association, Boys and Men Guidelines Group, 2018; Whitehead, 2021).

To understand an incel's identity as a complex interrelated duality, a 'victim' to the same insidious masculine discourse(s) that are simultaneously perpetrated through their online deviant action, requires a model permitting a nuanced interpretation of this deviant performative masculine identity. Using poststructural tools to conceptualize identity builds upon the historical foundations of gender and power, permitting examination of the actions of incels cognizant of the determinative discourse they encounter, internalize, and signify through digitally disembodied acts. Incels then become actualized as reproductive perpetrators of the narratives, discourse, and behaviors they as 'failed' men fall victim to during their subjective formative identity projects. To interrogate incel deviance in such a delicate and nuanced light, inquiry demands the capacity to recognize and consider that their experience as a failure, according to traditional masculine ideology discourse, can be catalytic and contributory to the perpetration of deviant and violent gendered action. To produce this framework of the 'victim-perpetrator incel' we turn to criminological literature regarding the victim-offender overlap, utilizing general strain theory (Agnew, 1992, 2001) and the gender role strain paradigm (Pleck, 1995) to outline the nature of incels' gendered 'victimhood' and its connection to their instigation of digital deviance.

The victim-offender incel paradigm

The development of criminological research regarding victims and offenders has generally progressed as two parallel bodies of inquiry. This binary limited recognition that often these individuals are not distinct types of identity, rather each position frequently overlapped; victims often go on to offend, while offenders demonstrate susceptibility to victimization (Berg & Mulford, 2020; Jennings et al., 2010; Reingle Gonzalez, 2014). Here, it is the directional relationship concerning the propensity for victims to become offenders with which we are concerned. Evaluating previous victimization as a predictor for latter offending, academic investigation of human trafficking (Baxter, 2020), violent crime (Jennings et al., 2012), and property crime (Hay & Evans, 2006) consistently identified the presence of previous experiences of victimization in those that commit offences in the same category of crime. While this theoretical framework of overlap has predominantly been used to understand victim-offender associations with matching crimes, often in overlapping geographical locales and class structures, here the framework serves to recognize the connection between the gendered identity and nature of deviance experienced and committed. The victim incel and the perpetrator incel are products of an ideology, an ideology that asserts men are superior and dominant, entitled to treat and access women as they see fit, an ideology that further states that only certain presentations of masculinity are valid indicators of being a man. The experience(s) of gendered subjugation that incels may have been exposed to in their formative years, and the psychological dysfunction that arose as a result—and the misogyny, cyberstalking, cyberbullying, and harassment of women that they perpetrate—are all intrinsically connected to the same traditional male ideology discourse. Further, incels also *internally* perpetrate, through suicide, self-harm, self-loathing, and denigration they exert upon themselves and each other (Daly & Laskovtsov, 2021).

Similar to individuals who were originally victims of violent crime, proceeding then to become violent offenders themselves (Jennings et al., 2012), incels inflict harm on others after they themselves have experienced strain and harm, a product of the internalized gendered discourse producing both identities.

To theorize the identified victim-offender overlap (VOO), various criminological theories have been offered as an explanation for the propensity of victims of crime to become perpetrators. Agnew's (1992, 2001) general strain theory is one such framework offering capacity with which to interpret conceptually the duality of the offending victim incel. General strain theory suggests specific strenuous life experiences predispose individuals to commit crimes. Strain is defined as "resulting from any relationship or event in which the individual is not treated as he or she would like or experiences undesired outcomes" (Hay & Evans, 2006, p. 262). This may include failure to achieve valued goals and the removal of desired, or the presence of undesired, outcomes or circumstances (Agnew, 1992). Following critique of the difficulty in falsifying the theory due to the generality and plurality of the constitutional nature of a strain, Agnew's (2001) revision specified four criteria to refine the strain concept. For a strain to be operant, the individual experiencing it must consider it unjust, perceive it as significantly impactive based upon the individual's life perspective, be associated with low conventional social controls, such as weak proximity to parental or teacher supervision, and incentivize a form of criminal coping. Experiencing strain results in negative emotionality, specifically anger, motivating the individual to perform retributive corrective action(s). This anger is mediated by individual factors such as a low level of self-control and poor social support systems. To refine the generality of the numerous possible strains upon an individual, the revision lists 10 which meet the four definitional criteria that are most likely to motivate offending: parental rejection; excessive/strict supervision or discipline; child abuse; negative school experiences; working in secondary labor market roles; homelessness; adolescent peer abuse; experience of discrimination; failure to achieve core goals; and criminal victimization. If we consider the research of incels discussed earlier, detailing negative formative life experiences (e.g. Costello et al., 2022; Moskalenko et al., 2022; Speckhard & Ellenberg, 2022), it is likely many of these strains will have been present in an individual's developmental life-course. A significant portion of the incel community self-report levels of education conducive to work attainment in the secondary labor market, with a large majority reporting sustained adolescent peer abuse and experiences of discrimination (Moskalenko et al., 2022). Many incels reported physical abuse as part of the sustained peer abuse received, which would fall into the category of violent criminal victimization. Further, it could be argued that the continual sociosexual rejection and isolation incels widely report due to the ascetic discrimination of 'lookism', whether real or imagined, creates a subjectively perceived strain that could well be as psychologically degrading as other forms of discrimination. As a minimum, we can assert that social rejection produces a psychic experience neurologically aligned to physical pain (Kross et al., 2011). Finally, when referring to the failure to achieve core goals, Agnew (2001) explicitly examples one such goal as gaining "masculine status" (p. 343), with offending depicted as a way to (re)acquire confirmation of male status. This is a core goal that research has demonstrated incels to hold, and a failure they subjectively experience, thus it becomes possible to apply to incels, through a gendered lens, Agnew's principle of anger-inducing strain as a precursor to offending.

The gendered strain of a failure to affirm masculine status relates directly to the statement made by the American Psychological Association, Boys and Men Guidelines Group

(2018) regarding the damaging effects of masculine ideology on men and boys. Attempts to conform to traditional masculine ideology discourse leads to an array of negative physical, mental, and psychological health outcomes placing significant strain on the individual as they undertake their male identity project. The "standard model" (Levant & Powell, 2017, p. 15) of research in the psychology of men and masculinities, informing the APA's report on boys and men, is the gender role strain paradigm (GrSP). Developed by Joseph Pleck (1995), the paradigm acknowledges that the male gender role, and consequential masculine identity, is socially constructed, here conceptualized as done so through discourse. Four core tenets of the subject-formative traditional male ideology discourse have been identified: absence of femininity, respect through material achievements, stoic absence of weakness, and acceptance of violence through risk and adventure seeking (David & Brannon, 1976). The restrictive, reductive, and dysfunctional nature of traditional male ideology can produce either a discrepancy strain resulting from failure to perform to the standard of the stipulated tenets, or a dysfunction strain when successfully reproducing the specific gendered behaviors and actions (Pleck, 1995). Based on incels' perceptions of their failure to achieve valid maleness mediated through their lack of sexual intercourse and romantic success, a principle of heterosexual masculinity readily acknowledged in the masculinity literature (e.g. Connell, 1995; Kimmel, 2008, 2017; Pascoe. 2007), it is reasonable to believe the incel community represents a collective of individuals suffering from discrepancy strain. A core tenet of the GrSP states that violation, whether actual or imagined, leads to the tendency of individuals to over-conform to traditional male ideology (Levant & Powell, 2017; Pleck, 1995). We may understand the incel blackpill as an example of this over-conformity, simultaneously acting as a mechanism with which subsequent deviant perpetration is enabled and justified within the community. Incels vehemently cling to biological determinism and a rigid sociosexual hierarchy that grants masculinity-affirming dominant status over women via a proclaimed intellectual superiority in knowing this 'truth'. This ideological positioning simultaneously rejects women and femininity from their spaces, enshrines material achievements through reverence of looks, money and status (Sugiura, 2021), and encourages and permits violence through deviant online action. Incels as individual male subjects fall victim to the consequences of discourse that produces both the psychological strain instructing their status and actions as gendered perpetrators. Prevalent traditional male ideology discourse prohibits their valid existence as men, due to the discrepancy between an actual and imposed male identity, fueling an over-conformity that results in gendered acts of harassment, doxing, cyberbullying/stalking, and extreme and explicit misogyny. In addition to this significant and impactive discrepancy strain, previously discussed gendered strains outlined by Agnew (2001) would likely add to the psychological dysfunction experienced by these individuals, with many arising because of the effects of masculine discourse. Homosocial peer abuse in adolescence often results from failure to conform to traditional male ideology (Fleming et al., 2014; Levant & Powell, 2017), suggesting that this violent criminal victimization that many incels experience in the form of physical peer abuse (Speckhard & Ellenberg, 2022) may also derive from the dominant male discourse incels are unable or unwilling to adopt and perform. Repeated social and sexual rejection should perhaps also be considered forms of strain if we consider the subjective 'injustice' likely perceived by the individual given the assumed normative life course of initiating successful heterosexual courtship in adolescence and young adulthood (Donnelly et al., 2001).

For the discourse-violating male subject, transgression from traditional masculine ideology results in a victim status; that is, individuals experience a variety of documented psychological dysfunction and physical repercussions. This produces an over-conformity to aspects of the very discourse responsible for their negative experience. As incels perpetrate online, gendered, deviant actions, they also continue to self-victimize through over-conformity to the traditional male ideology discourse that undergirds this behaviour. Whilst many incels claim an intellectual superiority in forum performances, having consumed the blackpill, this truth is in reality over-conformity to traditional male ideology; a reactive response to the gendered strain of failing to meet the goal of masculine status, and the psychological and physical adverse experiences they have endured as a result. These individuals internalize biologically deterministic sociosexual beliefs that fuel simultaneous perceptions of themselves and women as inferior, judging themselves against the pervasive expectations of dominant male discourse in their self-assessment as physically substandard men, producing a perpetual cycle of self-reinforcing, self-victimization, and justification for, and perpetration of, digital deviance.

Conclusion

Incels are a relatively new phenomenon, a contemporary digital identity emerging from a collective male reaction to the evolving socioeconomic shifts and feminist progressive political action in hitherto male-dominated spheres (Messner, 1998; Van Valkenburgh, 2021). Whilst in its infancy, the online and offline deviance of the community has catalyzed numerous fields of study that have assessed the threat of incels to wider society as well as investigated the internal mechanics of the group. The critical study of men and masculinities has offered a useful foundational gendered insight into the numerous, often contradictory performances of masculinity in the online spaces in which they coalesce. However, the predominant qualitative methodology employing various versions of thematic analysis upon spatiotemporally static data, acquired from a limited number of incel digital forums, prevents deeper exploration of the subjective individuals behind an anonymous, amorphous, digital collective. Together, this gendered meso-level analysis of incel masculinities in relation to power structures and patriarchy lacks capacity to determine if and how the deviance of incels arises from individual, psychological experience(s) collectively espoused in these performative forums. An alternative poststructural interpretation of discourse, as formative and signifying upon an individual's fluid and relational gendered identity project, permits numerous contradictory positions and subjective realities to be experienced and performed at once. Building on structural foundations of gendered analysis while adopting this poststructural standpoint to interrogate the digital deviance of incels allows interrogation of identity projects through masculine discourse(s), reflective in subjective understandings and expectations of what it means to be a 'real' man. Taking an individual-level, critically empathetic approach to the incel male subject enables the complexity and contradictory presentations of their viewpoints, perspectives, and performances to be interrogated in such a way that we can consider separately and in relation the harmful gendered experiences and deviant outputs bound to these individual's identities.

Emerging literature concerning the criminological framework of the victim-offender overlap lends itself well to the juxtaposition of a reductive and pervasive gendered discourse that, in certain men, may result in psychic and physical pain whilst also underpinning consequential deviant activity. Rather than instances of street-level crime to which the VOO is more commonly associated, here masculine ideology becomes an operant mechanism that inflicts harm upon individuals who go on to perpetrate gendered deviance towards others (and themselves). General strain theory highlights specific instances in which this pervasive gendered discourse may be a direct and indirect cause of instances of strain, such as failure to meet the core goal of masculine status or violent criminal victimization via homosocial peer assault. Further, the gender role strain paradigm suggests failure to meet the requirements of traditional male ideology may not only lead to a pernicious discrepancy strain, but that this strain produces an over-conformity to an ideology that the American Psychological Association suggests leads to misogyny, anti-femininity, sexual harassment, violence, isolation, self-harm, and suicide—behaviors documented by a variety of incel-related research. The numerous gendered strains that these individuals experience produce an over-conformity to the very problematic object of masculine discourse from which much of their pain arises. The blackpill ideology inherent to incels' collective identity likely reflects a reactive response to the strain and pain experienced as subjectively failed men bound to internalized traditional male ideology and dominant masculine discourse. This then serves as a justification mechanism for the perpetration of digital deviance to others via online misogyny, doxing, and cyberbullying/stalking, as well as the self-reinforcing self-victimization they place on themselves as biologically inferior men.

To understand the interrelation between the incel victim experience via direct and indirect consequences of traditional male ideology and the gendered deviance that may result from internalized over conformity to this masculine discourse facilitated via the blackpill, future investigation must redirect towards comprehensive engagement with the incel subject. Offline or on-/offline combination methodologies must seek to interrogate the individual as a subjective identity project in relation to the dominant and operant discourses that affect their lives. Exploring any gendered strain(s) incurred from the consequences of failure to achieve masculine status prescribed by traditional male ideology, and how this relates to perceptions of self and actions perpetrated, will lead to a nuanced understanding that extends beyond digital community performances. Traditional male ideology and dominant gendered discourse now digitally networked via pills, forums, and social media provide an incubator for digital deviance as well as offline violence. To attempt to minimize expansion of the incel community and the associated deviance, academic, security, and medical spheres must integrate understandings of incels as more than an object of misogynistic malevolence or disciples of violent extremist ideology. So that we may reduce instances of both on- and offline deviance, criminological frameworks must recognize incels as a complex, contradictory, and perhaps inevitable, result of a technologically facilitated gendered identity production mechanism. Interwoven into widespread and formative masculine discourse, the identities of strained male subjects can be psychologically shaped through traditional male ideology, reactive over-conformity, and facilitative online communities, resulting in the perpetration of deviance imbued by the very ideology and discourse to which they have fallen victim.

References

Agnew, R. (1992). Foundation for a general strain theory of crime and delinquency. *Criminology*, *30*(1), 47–88. https://doi.org/10.1111/j.1745-9125.1992.tb01093.x

Agnew, R. (2001). Building on the foundation of general strain theory: Specifying the types of strain most likely to lead to crime and delinquency. *Journal of Research in Crime and Delinquency*, *38*(4), 319–361. https://doi.org/10.1177/0022427801038004001

American Psychological Association, Boys and Men Guidelines Group. (2018). *APA guidelines for psychological practice with boys and men*. American Psychological Association. Retrieved from www.apa.org/about/policy/psychological-practice-boys-men-guidelines.pdf

Andersen, J. C. (2022). The symbolic boundary work of Incels: Subcultural negotiation of meaning and identity online. *Deviant Behavior*, 1–21. https://doi.org/10.1080/01639625.2022.2142864

Baele, S. J., Brace, L., & Coan, T. G. (2019). From "Incel" to "Saint": Analyzing the violent world-view behind the 2018 Toronto attack. *Terrorism and Political Violence*, 33(8), 1667–1691. https://doi.org/10.1080/09546553.2019.1638256

Baele, S. J., Brace, L., & Ging, D. (2023). A diachronic cross-platforms analysis of violent extremist language in the Incel online ecosystem. *Terrorism and Political Violence*, 1–24. https://doi.org/10.1080/09546553.2022.2161373

Baxter, A. L. A. (2020). When the line between victimization and criminalization blurs: The victim-offender overlap observed in female offenders in cases of trafficking in persons for sexual exploitation in Australia. *Journal of Human Trafficking*, 6(3), 327–338. https://doi.org/10.1080/23322705.2019.1578579

Berg, M. T., & Mulford, C. F. (2020). Reappraising and redirecting research on the victim—Offender overlap. *Trauma, Violence, & Abuse*, 21(1), 16–30. https://doi.org/10.1177/1524838017735925

Brittan, A. (1991). *Masculinity and power*. Wiley-Blackwell.

Brzuszkiewicz, S. (2020). 'Incel Radical Milieu and external locus of control. *The International Centre for Counter-Terrorism—The Hague (ICCT) Evolutions in Counter-Terrorism*, 2, 1–20.

Burton, A. G. (2022). Blackpill science: Involuntary celibacy, rational technique, and economic existence under neoliberalism. *Canadian Journal of Communication*, e20220725. https://doi.org/10.3138/cjc.2022-07-25

Byerly, C. M. (2020). Incels online reframing sexual violence. *The Communication Review*, 23(4), 290–308. https://doi.org/10.1080/10714421.2020.1829305

Conley, J. (2020). *Efficacy, nihilism, and toxic masculinity online: Digital misogyny in the incel subculture* [Masters dissertation, The Ohio State University].

Connell, R. W. (1995). *Masculinities*. Polity.

Connell, R. W., & Messerschmidt, J. W. (2005). Hegemonic masculinity: Rethinking the concept. *Gender and Society*, 19(6), 829–859.

Costello, W., Rolon, V., Thomas, A. G., & Schmitt, D. (2022). Levels of well-being among men who are Incel (Involuntarily celibate). *Evolutionary Psychological Science*, 8(4), 375–390. https://doi.org/10.1007/s40806-022-00336-x

Cottee, S. (2021). Incel (E)motives: Resentment, shame and revenge. *Studies in Conflict & Terrorism*, 44(2), 93–114. https://doi.org/10.1080/1057610X.2020.1822589

Daly, S. E., & Laskovtsov, A. (2021). 'Goodbye, my friendcels': An analysis of incel suicide posts. *Journal of Qualitative Criminal Justice & Criminology*. https://doi.org/10.21428/88de04a1.b7b8b295

Daly, S. E., & Reed, S. (2021). "I think most of society hates us": A qualitative thematic analysis of interviews with incels. *Sex Roles*, 86. https://doi.org/10.1007/s11199-021-01250-5

David, D., & Brannon, R. (1976). *The forty-nine percent majority: The male sex role*. addison-Wesley.

Demetriou, D. Z. (2001). Connell's concept of hegemonic masculinity: A critique. *Theory and Society*, 30(3), 337–361. https://doi.org/10.1023/A:1017596718715

Donnelly, D., Burgess, E., Anderson, S., Davis, R., & Dillard, J. (2001). Involuntary celibacy: A life course analysis. *The Journal of Sex Research*, 38(2), 159–169. https://doi.org/10.1080/00224490109552083

Fleming, P. J., Lee, J. G. L., & Dworkin, S. L. (2014). "Real men don't": Constructions of masculinity and inadvertent harm in public health interventions. *American Journal of Public Health*, 104, 1029–1035. https://doi.org/10.2105/AJPH.2013.301820

Foucault, M. (1969). *Archaeology of knowledge and the discourse on language*. Panthenon Books.

Foucault, M. (2020). *The history of sexuality: 1*. Penguin Books.

Ging, D. (2019a). Alphas, betas, and incels: Theorizing the masculinities of the manosphere. *Men and Masculinities*, 22(4), 638–657. https://doi.org/10.1177/1097184X17706401

Ging, D. (2019b). Bros v. Hos: Postfeminism, anti-feminism and the toxic turn in digital gender politics. In D. Ging & E. Siapera (Eds.), *Gender hate online understanding the new anti-feminism* (pp. 45–67). Palgrave Macmillan. Retrieved from https://doi.org/10.1007/978-3-319-96226-9_3

Ging, D., & Murphy, S. (2021). Tracking the pilling pipeline: Limitations, challenges and a call for new methodological frameworks in incel and manosphere research. *AoIR Selected Papers of Internet Research*. https://doi.org/10.5210/spir.v2021i0.12174

Glace, A. M., Dover, T. L., & Zatkin, J. G. (2021). Taking the black pill: An empirical analysis of the "Incel". *Psychology of Men & Masculinities, 22,* 288–297. https://doi.org/10.1037/men0000328

Graham, R., & Smith, S. (2020). *Cybercrime and digital deviance.* Routledge.

Grunau, K., Bieselt, H. E., Gul, P., & Kupfer, T. (2022). *Unwanted celibacy is associated with misogynistic attitudes even after controlling for personality.* PsyArXiv. Retrieved from https://doi.org/10.31234/osf.io/qv4a9

Gutterman, D. (2001). Postmodernism and the interrogation of masculinity. In S. Whitehead & F. Barrett (Eds.), *The masculinities reader* (pp. 55–72). Blackwell Publishers.

Halpin, M. (2022). Weaponized subordination: How incels discredit themselves to degrade women. *Gender & Society, 36*(6), 813–837. https://doi.org/10.1177/08912432221128545

Hay, C., & Evans, M. M. (2006). Violent victimization and involvement in delinquency: Examining predictions from general strain theory. *Journal of Criminal Justice, 34*(3), 261–274. https://doi.org/10.1016/j.jcrimjus.2006.03.005

Howarth, D., & Stavrakakis, Y. (2000). Introducing discourse theory and political analysis. In D. Howarth, A. Norval, & Y. Stavrakakis (Eds.), *Discourse theory and political analysis* (pp. 1–23). Manchester University Press.

Jaki, S., De Smedt, T., Gwozdz, M., Panchal, R., Rossa, A., & Pauw, G. (2019). Online hatred of women in the Incels.me Forum: Linguistic analysis and automatic detection. *Journal of Language Aggression and Conflict, 7.* https://doi.org/10.1075/jlac.00026.jak

Jennings, W., Higgins, G., Tewksbury, R., Gover, A., & Piquero, A. (2010). A longitudinal assessment of the victim-offender overlap. *Journal of Interpersonal Violence, 25,* 2147–2174. https://doi.org/10.1177/0886260509354888

Jennings, W., Piquero, A., & Reingle Gonzalez, J. (2012). On the overlap between victimization and offending: A review of the literature. *Aggression and Violent Behavior—AGGRESS VIOLENT BEHAVIOR, 17.* https://doi.org/10.1016/j.avb.2011.09.003

Justin, K., Shepler, D., & Kinel, J. (2022). She's just not that into me: Sexual self-concept among heterosexual men who identify as involuntary celibates. *Journal of Social, Behavioural & Health Sciences, 16*(1), 117–133.

Kassam, A. (2018). Woman behind 'incel' says angry men hijacked her word 'as a weapon of war'. *The Guardian.* Retrieved from www.theguardian.com/world/2018/apr/25/woman-who-invented-incel-movement-interview-toronto-attack

Kimmel, M. (2008). *Guyland the perilous world where boys become men.* Harper Perennial.

Kimmel, M. (2017). *Angry white men: American masculinity at the end of an era.* Hachette.

Kross, E., Berman, M. G., Mischel, W., Smith, E. E., & Wager, T. D. (2011). Social rejection shares somatosensory representations with physical pain. *Proceedings of the National Academy of Sciences of the United States of America, 108*(15), 6270–6275. https://doi.org/10.1073/pnas.1102693108

Leidig, E. (2021). *Why terrorism studies miss the mark when it comes to incels.* ICCT. Retrieved from www.icct.nl/publication/why-terrorism-studies-miss-mark-when-it-comes-incels

Levant, R. F., & Powell, W. (2017). The gender role strain paradigm. In R. F. Levant & Y. J. Wong (Eds.), *Psychology of Men and Masculinities.* American Psychological Association. Retrieved from https://doi.org/10.1037/0000023-000

Lindsay, A. (2021). Incel violence as a reclamation of masculinity and defence of patriarchy on three distinct levels. *New Zealand Sociology, 36*(1), 25–49. https://doi.org/10.3316/informit.850259762614973

Lindsay, A. (2022). Swallowing the black pill: Involuntary celibates' (Incels) anti-feminism within digital society. *International Journal for Crime Justice and Social Democracy, 11*(1), 210–224. https://doi.org/10.5204/ijcjsd.2138

Maxwell, D., Robinson, S. R., Williams, J. R., & Keaton, C. (2020). "A short story of a lonely guy": A qualitative thematic analysis of involuntary celibacy using reddit. *Sexuality & Culture, 24*(6), 1852–1874. https://doi.org/10.1007/s12119-020-09724-6

Menzie, L. (2020). Stacys, Beckys, and Chads: The construction of femininity and hegemonic masculinity within incel rhetoric. *Psychology & Sexuality.* https://doi.org/10.1080/19419899.2020.1806915

Messerschmidt, J. W. (2018). *Hegemonic masculinity formulation, reformulation, and amplification.* Rowman & Littlefield.

Messner, M. A. (1998). The limits of "the male sex role": An analysis of the men's liberation and men's rights movement discourse. *Gender & Society*, *12*(3), 255–276. https://doi.org/10.1177/0891243298012003002

Moskalenko, S., González, J., Kates, N., & Morton, J. (2022). Incel ideology, radicalization and mental health: A survey study. *The Journal of Intelligence Conflict and Warfare*, *4*, 1–29. https://doi.org/10.21810/jicw.v4i3.3817

Nagle, A. (2016). *The new man of 4chan | Angela nagle*. The Baffler. Retrieved from https://thebaffler.com/salvos/new-man-4chan-nagle

Nagle, A. (2017). *Kill all normies: Online culture wars from 4chan and tumblr to trump and the alt-right*. Zero Books.

Nardone, A. (2022). Misogynist incel violence as a post-organizational threat: Addressing a new challenge for the current counter-terrorism strategies. *ITSS Verona Magazine*, *1*(2).

O'Donnell, C., & Shor, E. (2022). "This is a political movement, friend": Why "incels" support violence. *The British Journal of Sociology*, *n/a*(n/a). https://doi.org/10.1111/1468-4446.12923

O'Malley, R. L., Holt, K., & Holt, T. J. (2022). An exploration of the involuntary celibate (Incel) subculture online. *Journal of Interpersonal Violence*, *37*, NP4981—NP5008. https://doi.org/10.1177/0886260520959625

Pascoe, C. J. (2007). *Dude, you're a fag: Masculinity and sexuality in high school*. University of California Press.

Perliger, A., Stevens, C., & Leidig, E. (2023). *Mapping the ideological landscape of extreme misogyny*. International Center for Counterterrorism. Retrieved from www.icct.nl/publication/mapping-ideological-landscape-extreme-misogyny

Pleck, J. (1995). the gender role strain paradigm: An update. In R. F. Levant & W. S. Pollack (Eds.), *A new psychology of men* (pp. 11–32). Basic Books.

Powell, A., Stratton, G., & Cameron, R. (2018). *Digital criminology: Crime and justice in digital society*. Routledge.

Preston, K., Halpin, M., & Maguire, F. (2021). The black pill: New technology and the male supremacy of involuntarily celibate men. *Men and Masculinities*, *24*(5), 823–841. https://doi.org/10.1177/1097184X211017954

Reingle Gonzalez, J. (2014). Victim-offender overlap. In J. Mitchel Miller (Ed.), *Encyclopedia of Theoretical Criminology* (1st ed., p. 3). https://doi.org/10.1002/9781118517390.wbetc139

Roose, J. M., & Cook, J. (2022). Supreme men, subjected women: Gender inequality and violence in jihadist, far right and male supremacist ideologies. *Studies in Conflict & Terrorism*, 1–29. https://doi.org/10.1080/1057610X.2022.2104681

Scheuerman, J. (2021). The anatomy of inceldom: An analysis of incels through the lens of gender. *Themis: Research Journal of Justice Studies and Forensic Science*, *9*(1). https://doi.org/10.31979/THEMIS.2021.0903

Sparks, B., Zidenberg, A., & Olver, M. (2022). *Involuntary celibacy: A review of incel ideology and experiences with dating, rejection, and associated mental health and emotional sequelae*. Retrieved from https://doi.org/10.13140/RG.2.2.25352.70408

Speckhard, A., & Ellenberg, M. (2022). Self-reported psychiatric disorder and perceived psychological symptom rates among involuntary celibates (incels) and their perceptions of mental health treatment. *Behavioral Sciences of Terrorism and Political Aggression*, 1–18. https://doi.org/10.1080/19434472.2022.2029933

Sugiura, L. (2021). *The Incel rebellion*. Emerald Publishing Limited.

Tastenhoye, C. A., Ross, N. E., Dupré, J., Bodnar, T. V., & Friedman, S. H. (2022). Involuntary celibates and forensic psychiatry. *The Journal of the American Academy of Psychiatry and the Law*. https://doi.org/10.29158/JAAPL.210136-21

Thorburn, J., Powell, A., & Chambers, P. (2022). A world alone: Masculinities, humiliation and aggrieved entitlement on an incel forum. *The British Journal of Criminology*, *XX*, 1–17. https://doi.org/10.1093/bjc/azac020

Tomkinson, S., Harper, T., & Attwell, K. (2020). Confronting Incel: Exploring possible policy responses to misogynistic violent extremism. *Australian Journal of Political Science*, *55*(2), 152–169. https://doi.org/10.1080/10361146.2020.1747393

Vallerga, M., & Zurbriggen, E. (2022). Hegemonic masculinities in the 'manosphere': A thematic analysis of beliefs about men and women on The Red Pill and Incel. *Analyses of Social Issues and Public Policy*. https://doi.org/10.1111/asap.12308

Van Valkenburgh, S. P. (2021). Digesting the red pill: Masculinity and neoliberalism in the mano-sphere. *Men and Masculinities, 24*(1), 84–103. https://doi.org/10.1177/1097184X18816118

Vito, C., Admire, A., & Hughes, E. (2017). Masculinity, aggrieved entitlement, and violence: Considering the Isla vista mass shooting. *NORMA, 13*(2), 86–102. https://doi.org/10.1080/1890213 8.2017.1390658

Whitehead, S. (2002). *Men and masculinities: Key themes and new directions.* Polity.

Whitehead, S. (2006). *Men & masculinities* (1st ed.). Routledge.

Whitehead, S. (2021). *Toxic masculinity: Curing the virus: Making men smarter, healthier, safer.* Andrews UK Ltd.

Zimmerman, S., Ryan, L., & Duriesmith, D. (2018). *Who are Incels? Recognizing the violent extremist ideology of 'Incels'.* Women in International Society. Retrieved from https://wiisglobal.wpengine.com/wp-content/uploads/2018/09/Policybrief-Violent-Extremists-Incels.pdf

4
ETHICS OF COVERT SURVEILLANCE IN ONLINE DEVIANCE RESEARCH USING HONEYPOTS

Francisco Javier Castro-Toledo and Ana Belén Gómez-Bellvís

Introduction

Over the last decade, interest in the use of honeypots as an online research tool has grown among social and behavioural researchers to explore in a different way criminological issues such as unauthorised access (Maimon et al., 2013; Testa et al., 2017; Wilson et al., 2015), pornography consumption (Pritchar et al., 2021) or child exploitation in online sites (Açar, 2017; Vendius, 2015), among other deviant behaviours (Perkins & Howell, 2021). Use of digital decoys of different sorts are a powerful resource within the field of cybersecurity to develop more effective prevention strategies based on the undercover and real-time collection of data on cyberattackers' routines on vulnerable targets (Vetterl, 2020).

While these technical characteristics of honeypots are certainly their methodological strength, they also represent their ethical weakness. Therefore, this chapter starts from the acknowledgement that this normative dimension has not been sufficiently analysed for the field of online deviance analysis, despite the very important ethical challenges and risks that arise from the use of these online tools for covert surveillance. Hence, the next sections aim to meet the following objectives: 1) identify the particularities of honeypots as an online social and behavioural methodology of great interest, 2) address two of the main ethical risks associated with the use of honeypots in online deviance research (namely, the use of deception and the breach of users' expectations of privacy) and 3) outline a framework for the ethical use of honeypots in online deviance research. Specifically, we will advocate that a concrete use of honeypots is ethically responsible when it meets at least the following three requirements: (1) it addresses an issue of public interest, (2) it is methodologically necessary and (3) it uses full simulated targets.

Use of honeypots in online deviance research

Following the recent work of Prichard et al. (2022), 'honeypots' can be broadly defined as "computers or Internet sites that mimic likely targets of online attacks or other deviant contacts, and are used as 'bait' to detect, analyse and/or counteract such unwanted activity" (p. 5). Stated differently, honeypots act as an easy target for cyber attackers, but in reality

DOI: 10.4324/9781003277675-6

they are a decoy in which the attacker is trapped into performing some illicit operations that, by generating specific signatures, can then be tracked and analysed for the purpose of enhancing the real system (Gupta & Gupta, 2018). This is therefore a defensive technique capable of reinforcing those traditional lines of firewall and defence intrusion detection systems that could not, by themselves, provide an analytical and preventive solution to the recent increase in this type of cyber-attacks (Gupta et al., 2016; Zhang & Gupta, 2016). Nonetheless, its technical approach is not new. According to the historical overview of its use elaborated by Vetterl (2020), such tools were first implemented by Stoll (1989, cited in Vetterl, 2020), who described it as a non-production-value fake system environment that was used solely to monitor incoming connections and track attackers. However it was Spitzner (2003) who a decade later popularised the term 'honeypot' as a "security resource whose value lies in being probed, attacked or compromised" (p. 40).

Vetterl et al. (2019) explains that the classifications of honeypot types have been various throughout their evolution, respond to different purposes and encompass a very wide range of deviant behaviours within the cybercrime domain (Perkins & Howell, 2021). One of the issues most addressed through the experimental use of honeypots is the possible deterrent effects of online warning messages. These include, firstly, the use of targeted messages to impact active online behaviours, including system roaming and file manipulation, and whether these effects are consistent between intruders with administrative and non-administrative access (Maimon et al., 2013; Testa et al., 2017; Wilson et al., 2015). Similarly, Moneva et al. (2022) used warning messages where appropriate, to reduce distributed denial of service (DDoS) attacks. Applied to other online deviant behaviours, Prichard et al. (2022) have used honeypots to evaluate the potential positive deterrent effects of some types of automated messages on Internet users trying to access "barely legal" pornography. On this latter kind of use, Bleakley (2019) critically describes how, notably due to the reliance on certain lax restrictions, some US police departments have used controlled covert infiltration techniques, some through the use of honeypots, on online forums dedicated to child exploitation with some success. Açar (2017; and broadly on proactive undercover policing and online child sex crimes, see Vendius, 2015), posits some methods based on the analysis of metadata and content data from Voice-over-IP (VoIP) communications by the private sector and the use of fully automated chatbots for undercover webcam child prostitution operations. Lastly, it is worth mentioning those studies on vulnerabilities in the victim's computer, where the victim is sent a link to a compromised web server that has a browser exploit kit that identifies a dozen vulnerabilities in the computer and forces the victim to load malicious software (Bueno, 2011).

Honeypots involve advanced social and law enforcement research techniques and mechanisms to identify new trends and patterns in cyberattackers in real time and in a straightforward manner (Pritchard et al., 2021). But that has not prevented some important criticisms suggesting that honeypots cannot collect any information about the attacker's demographics, motivations, motives or technical skill (Bossler, 2017), among other methodological limitations. These technical limitations compromise researchers' ability to make inferences, increase the risk of making incorrect assumptions about cyberattackers and condition their use as a complement to other social research designs (Holt, 2017). What is worth highlighting here, however, is how little ethical attention honeypots have received from researchers who have made use of them, beyond a few very brief general considerations. This is despite the enormous sensitivity and challenges that we will see in the next sections of the chapter.

Two main ethical issues in honeypots' use

To date, the most systematic effort to address the emerging ethical issues with the use of honeypots is David Dittrich's work, "The Ethics of Social Honeypots" (2015), (also see Rowe & Rushi, 2016; Pattison, 2020; Vetterl et al., 2019), which examined some of the specific legal and ethical limits of these covert social and behavioural research tools. In this section, and for reasons of limited extension, only two of the most relevant ethical risks will be considered: namely, deception and the breach of privacy expectations of the individuals under observation.

Use of deception

Broadly speaking, to deceive is to make people accept as true what is false or to give a false impression (Nicks et al., 1997). Now, if there is a way to define the use of honeypots, it seems to be that honeypots are a tool based on the deception of participants who do not even know that they are participating in a study. To avoid this risk, the main codes of ethics for social and behavioural research articulate the principle of respect for persons or autonomy: that is,

> participation as a research subject is voluntary and derives from informed consent; treat people as autonomous agents and respect their right to determine their own self-interest; respect people who are not the subject of the research and yet are affected; people with diminished autonomy, who are unable to decide for themselves, have the right to be protected.
>
> *(Kenneally & Dittrich, 2012, p. 5)*

Put differently, human participants are guaranteed the right to full disclosure of the purposes of the research as promptly as is appropriate for the research process, as well as the right to the opportunity to have their concerns about the purpose and use of the research fully addressed (Braswell et al., 2017).

Against this background, one of the most controversial issues in the use of honeypots are all those practices of observing people's behaviour in their natural context whilst assessing the limited extent to which researchers have obtained informed consent from their participants (Castro-Toledo, 2020; Podschuweit, 2021; Roulet et al., 2017): namely (1) participants give consent on the basis of false information, or (2) participants do not give consent and thus receive no information at all (Sieber, 1982). The Menlo Report (Kenneally & Dittrich, 2012) explicitly recommends:

> Appropriate Respect for Persons in such deception research can typically be achieved by debriefing the subjects after the research is completed. Debriefing is typically required when deception is used in order to mitigate harm resulting from loss of trust in researchers by those subjects who were deceived.
>
> *(p. 8)*

Nevertheless, Dittrich (2015) qualifies this position with respect to honeypots, which are tools intended to be deployed in online environments with massive user traffic. This would therefore technically impede collecting informed consent from the affected users or being able to inform them in an adequate manner.

Such an approach has been adopted by researchers when they foresee the risk that those who are aware that they are being observed may decide to act differently compared to their usual environment, notably when it comes to criminal or simply anti-social behaviour, and thus invalidate the results of the study (Hagan, 1997, Maxfield, 2015; Maxfield & Babbie, 2014). In the field of the criminal justice system, several studies have shown how the importance of discretion in the criminal justice process and the hidden nature of many daily decisions seem to support the increased use of these covert and non-consensual observation techniques in an effort to unravel how police, prosecutors and prison staff perform their duties (Açar, 2017; Miller & Gordon, 2014; Vendius, 2015). Alongside these pragmatic reasons, others have been added, such as the degree of intervention of the researchers in the context of observation. In this regard, Braswell et al. (2017) are right to introduce the ethically sensitive qualification that if a studied behaviour could have occurred without researcher intervention, then the absence of consent seems less problematic than those research designs in which researchers introduce ad hoc elements to produce some kind of response in the observed persons. By introducing elements of provocation of the cyberattack (i.e. the decoy), the use of honeypots would therefore fall into this second group, which significantly increases their sensitivity.

Breaches in users' privacy expectations

Among the main consequences of the use of deception as a social and behavioural research strategy, like honeypots by default, we can highlight the important breaches in the privacy expectations of users under covert observation. Indeed, this ethical risk is very challenging as the European research context is highly safeguarded by the limits and possibilities in the correct application of the General Data Protection Regulation (Castro-Toledo & Miró Llinares, 2021). Its greatest relevance lies in the strong consolidation of its normative framework, as the right to data protection is enshrined in the *EU Charter of Fundamental Rights* (see Chapter II) and in the *Treaty on the Functioning of the European Union* (Art. 16), which assert the right to privacy of individuals by giving them control over how information about them is collected and used. For the sake of this chapter, however, as far as research activities are concerned, data protection imposes an obligation on researchers to provide research subjects with detailed information about what will occur with the personal data being collected (European Comission, 2018b). In the case of honeypots, the absence of informed consent is completely incompatible with the proper exercise of these obligations of the researchers.

On the other hand, research on deviant online behaviour requires large amounts of data of different nature, and the current model is one of massive and automatic data collection (Hughes et al., 2021). As Zook et al. (2017) point out, however, we should not forget that all the data from Internet research data on social or behavioural phenomena relate to human individuals. In other words, the data collected, processed and used by the researcher are from real people who deserve to be protected from possible harm (in respect of the harm minimisation principle). In response to this, it is often pointed out that an important issue in internet research ethics is the distinction between public and private online sites (Buchanan & Ess, 2016; Rosenberg, 2010; Zimmer, 2010; Bromseth, 2002). Arguably, the use of honeypots for data collection in public cyberspaces is less problematic than private online environments (e.g. closed forums, social networks with restricted access profiles, etc.). However, this differentiation is often problematic because it is mediated by individual and cultural definitions and expectations (Buchanan, 2010; McKee & Porter, 2009). Moreover, people's privacy is not only related to genuinely private online environments, but may include public environments of online interaction and encounters with other users. On this, the European Court of Human Rights (ECtHR) has noted that there are areas of interaction between people, even in a public context, which may fall within the realm of private life ECtHR (2019, 2020). In the light of this, Kuyumdzhieva (2018) suggests that, when determining whether data is open for use or should be considered private, the online environment in which it is published and the reasonable expectations of privacy that the user may have should be taken into account. This reasonable expectation of privacy, according to the European Fundamental Rights Agency (FRA, 2019), refers to the extent to which individuals can expect to have privacy in public spaces (online or offline) without being subject to surveillance.

Lastly, there is another ethical consideration closely related to data collection and users' privacy expectations, namely that covert research, which also applies to honeypots, often unintentionally yields findings outside the scope of the original research questions. This forces researchers to resolve, in certain circumstances, the dilemma between preserving confidentiality or disclosing information to the relevant authorities. Consistent with the European Standards of Integrity in Social Science and Humanities Research (European Commission, 2018a), they state that criminal activities witnessed or discovered in the course of research should be reported to the responsible and appropriate authorities, even if this means compromising previous commitments to participants to maintain confidentiality and anonymity. Hence, researchers should consider from the design of the honeypot the potential sensitivity of the data collected and whether users could be harmed (physical, social, psychological, economical, etc.) if their data is publicly communicated. Informing participants about the limits of confidentiality that can be offered (i.e., the consent information sheet should cover the policy on incidental findings) usually mitigates this risk of incidental findings and their potential negative impacts. Unfortunately, these kinds of measures are not applicable in the context of honeypots.

A proposed ethics framework for the use of honeypots in online deviance research

The literature on the specific uses of honeypots for the analysis and prevention of certain online deviant behaviours that we identified in the first section of this chapter justifies their use from a purely pragmatic perspective, whereas the ethical perspective has not been treated with such detail and care. Regarding this issue, in the previous two sections we have been able to analyse how, from an ethical perspective, the use of honeypots poses very important challenges (among them, deception and privacy breaches) that cannot be satisfactorily addressed due to the inherent technical nature of the tool. This is why in this last section we want to propose three ethical requirements for the responsible deployment of this type of covert online surveillance tools, which can help to complement other specific previous ethical models (Dittrich, 2015). We can state that the use of honeypot methodologies is ethically responsible when it meets at least the following three requirements: (1) it addresses an issue of public interest, (2) it is methodologically necessary and (3) it uses full simulated targets. In the following, we will look at what each of the three requirements consists of and, using the model of ethical guidance based on the identification of key questions used elsewhere (Castro-Toledo & Miró Llinares, 2021), we will outline both some guiding questions for researchers to assess the ethical suitability of the use of honeypots in their specific research, and some challenges that will warrant further attention in the future.

Addressing an issue of public interest

The first of the ethical requirements to be met is that the use of honeypots, due to their sensitivity, will be more justifiable in those cases of research aligned with supranational or national governmental strategies and interests of analysis, prevention and mitigation of online criminal phenomena or other types of related behaviours. For instance, the European Commission (EU) or Europol (through the European Cybercrime Center, EC3) have produced numerous publications and calls for public R&D funding that outline and justify their cybersecurity priorities on the basis of the identification of specific threats and vulnerabilities of European citizens (just to mention a few: the EU Cybersecurity Strategy, the European Union Strategy for a Security Union or Cluster 3 of the Horizon Europe R&D programme). The same applies at the national level. In consequence, the right application of this requirement should lead us to reject any honeypot research proposal motivated exclusively by private interests or private organisations failing to directly address matters of public interest.

In order to meet this requirement, there are several questions that researchers may ask themselves. Three are outlined here:

1. Are the purposes of the research project in which honeypots will be used aligned with the strategic cybersecurity prevention priorities of the government agencies in the location where the research will be conducted?
2. Is the research project funded by a supranational, international, national or local public agency?
3. If not (1), does it involve any other deviant online behaviour that has recently increased significantly in prevalence and is causing significant social alarm?

In turn, there are several challenges to this first requirement worthy of note in the following: (a) it could be the case that government agencies' cybersecurity agendas may be compromised by a lack of material legitimacy (e.g. lack of citizen support, undemocratic or tyrannical governments, lobbyist interference); (b) or that procedures for identifying public cybersecurity interests are not sufficiently accurate (overestimating or underestimating their seriousness), leading to significant blind spots in the mapping of threats and vulnerabilities.

Methodological necessity of honeypots

A second ethical requirement for the responsible use of honeypots in social and behavioural research is the existence of a methodological necessity for their use. In the field of criminological research ethics (Alexander & Ferzan, 2019; Banks, 2018; Arrigo, 2014; Miller & Gordon, 2014; Pollock, 2014; Roberson & Mire, 2009;Braswell et al., 2017; Kleinig, 2008) necessity, as a principle, is strongly established. In general terms, to apply it correctly, it is necessary to check whether there is a need to use honeypots. There are three elements to consider: (a) the circumstances surrounding the cybersecurity problem, (b) the need to use the honeypots, and (c) whether there are less intrusive alternative means of addressing the topic of research. The development of these measures requires an analysis of proportionality. In this sense, proportionality is first and foremost a question of appropriateness between the objectives to be achieved and the means employed to achieve them. The principle of proportionality is closely linked to the notion of balance, which requires that the use of this tool should not be the only cybersecurity and online deviance behavior prevention response.

In assessing the fulfilment of this second requirement, researchers can be guided by four questions:

1. Have less intrusive and less harmful methodological alternatives been adequately evaluated before using the intended honeypots?
2. Is the purpose/s of the intended use of honeypots clearly defined?
3. Is the use of honeypots to be limited to a specific time?
4. Is there provision for limiting the use of honeypots to specific cyberplaces?

As with the first requirement, the methodological necessity of honeypots poses a significant challenge that we might call "the responsible researcher's dilemma". Very broadly describing this, it could be the case that the researcher is confronted with the choice between (a) using honeypots and collecting higher-quality empirical evidence (especially with respect to the external validity of the data) or (b) using less intrusive (i.e., less ethically sensitive) methodologies, but collecting lower-quality data.

Full target simulation

Lastly, we believe it is important to introduce a third ethical requirement for the responsible use of honeypots. More specifically, it is necessary for the decoys used by researchers to be entirely simulated targets of a real potential victim. This seems obvious insofar as the technical tendency of all the studies we have referenced in the first part of this chapter use simulated decoys. But here we want to emphasise the idea that the rationale for this requirement should not be sought in the pragmatics of target simulation (e.g., absence of actual damage or loss), but rather in the false representation to the potential attacker that a cyber-attack is taking place when in fact it is not. That is essentially the traditional continental idea of reverse error in the field of criminal law, which is connected with the total absence of liability on the part of the perpetrator of the false attack (Esmein, 2000; Spencer & Pedain, 2005). To put it another way, although the use of honeypots is intended to trigger certain antisocial behaviour in some users in order to gather specific information, researchers have the obligation to ensure that the user who tries to perpetrate a crime does not do so because there is no real victim. In this sense, the only question to be asked about this requirement is: has a decoy been used that fully simulates the vulnerabilities of a real target?

For its part, we already introduced in the previous section some keys to understanding the challenge associated with this third requirement. With Braswell et al. (2017), the ethical sensitivity of research is related to the degree of intervention and interference of researchers in the behaviour of the people under observation. The case of honeypots is highly problematic because, even without engaging the liability of the attackers with criminal consequences, honeypots do induce deviant behaviour online, even without any real objective. In short, the researcher who makes use of honeypots must therefore face the paradox of wanting to prevent deviant behaviour by provoking it beforehand.

General remarks

This chapter has pointed out that the use of covert research methodologies, including the use of honeypots, offers a number of advantages over other kinds of analytical strategies (especially those based on self-reporting), as it allows for a direct and more naturalised observation of both users' online behaviour in general and deviant behaviour in particular (Vetterl, 2019). This avoids issues such as behavioural simulation or social desirability, among other threats to the ecological validity of the research design and data quality (Maxfield, 2015; Maxfield & Babbie, 2014; Hagan, 1997). However, this advantage is possible because the people under observation do not even know that their online routines are being monitored in real time for later evaluation. Certainly, this feature of honeypots constitutes both their strength in technical terms and their most acute weakness in the sense of ethical and moral responsibility of the researchers. On this point, the specialised cybersecurity literature discussed in the first section of the chapter generally lacks significant gaps in terms of critical and rigorous ethical reflection on when a particular use of honeypots is responsible in the context of an investigation of deviant online behaviour.

Looking at this background, in this chapter we have evaluated some of the most serious risks with the most serious implications from a research ethics perspective due to their potential violation of some of the ethical principles guiding research in information and communication technologies (Kenneally & Dittrich, 2012). The first of these is the use of deception in honeypot research, in which researchers deliberately lie or mislead participants in the online research environment so that the true purpose of the study remains unknown to them. This ethical risk mainly violates the principle of respect for the autonomy of individuals, which could be ensured by collecting informed consent. Unfortunately, cyber-deception techniques (Rowe & Rrushi, 2016), such as the use of honeypots, hinder the possibility of adequately informing participants and obtaining their informed consent a posteriori. If possible, measures must be put in place to minimise or mitigate any social, emotional or psychological harm resulting from the disclosure of the real purposes of the study (Podschuweit, 2021; Roulet et al., 2017). In turn, the second of the ethical risks analysed is the significant breach of users' privacy expectations under covert online surveillance. On this issue, we have shown the profound incompatibilities between the current European regulatory model of personal data protection (see GDPR) and the use of these online research tools. In turn, we have also pointed out that user privacy expectations must be taken into consideration by researchers in an ethical model that goes beyond the distinction between public/private online sites (Buchanan & Ess, 2016, Rosenberg, 2010; Zimmer, 2010; Bromseth, 2002) and that pays special attention to the production of incidental research findings (such as real criminal activity) that could lead to the reporting to authorities and could result in legal action against users (European Commission, 2018a). In a practical sense, while technically complex in honeypot use cases, researchers should consult the relevant terms and conditions of the online platforms they will use to collect their data and, if there is an expectation of privacy, should seek permission from users (or, alternatively, the website administrator) to use the data and obtain their informed consent, albeit after the event (European Comission, 2018b).

To conclude, all the challenges outlined so far have led us to raise the requirements of moral possibility for the use of these tools. In this case, we agree with the idea of their usefulness in terms of scientific rationality; however, the ethical challenges they face are numerous and far-reaching. That is why this chapter ends with a proposal for a 'minima moralia' that defines the ethical requirements for a responsible use of honeypots in the context of online deviant behaviour of interest to us. More specifically, it has been justified that an ethical use of these tools must meet three requirements: it must address a matter of public interest, it must be methodologically necessary and finally, it must use fully simulated objectives. Meeting these three requirements would therefore help researchers to better justify the responsible use of these tools in the context of social and behavioural research.

References

Açar, K. V. (2017). Webcam child prostitution: An exploration of current and futuristic methods of detection. *International Journal of Cyber Criminology*, *11*(1), 98–109.

Alexander, L., & Ferzan, K. K. (Eds.). (2019). *The Palgrave handbook of applied ethics and the criminal law*. Palgrave Macmillan.

Arrigo, B. A. (Ed.). (2014). *Encyclopedia of criminal justice ethics*. SAGE Publications.

Banks, C. (2018). *Criminal justice ethics: Theory and practice*. Sage Publications.

Bleakley, P. (2019). Watching the watchers: Taskforce Argos and the evidentiary issues involved with infiltrating Dark Web child exploitation networks. *The Police Journal*, *92*(3), 221–236.

Bossler, A. M. (2017). Need for debate on the implications of honeypot data for restrictive deterrence policies in cyberspace. *Criminology & Public Policy*, *16*, 679.

Braswell, M. C., McCarthy, B. R., & McCarthy, B. J. (2017). *Justice, crime, and ethics*. Taylor & Francis

Bromseth, J. C. (2002). Public places—Public activities. Methodological approaches and ethical dilemmas in research on computer-mediated communication contexts. *SKIKT'Researchers—Researching IT in Context*, 33–61.

Buchanan, E. (2010). Internet research ethics: Past, present, future. In C. Ess & M. Consalvo (Eds.), *The Blackwell handbook of internet studies*. Oxford University Press.

Buchanan, E., & Ess, C. (2016). Ethics in Digital Research. In M. Nolden., G. Rebane, & M. Schreiter (Eds.), *The Handbook of social practices and digital everyday worlds* (pp. 375–383). Springer.

Bueno, P. (2011). *Updates on zeroaccess and BlackHole front*. Retrieved from http://isc.sans.edu/diary.html?storyid=12079

Castro-Toledo, F. J. (2020). Exploring some old and new ethical issues in criminological research and its implications for evidence-based policy. *Spanish Journal of Legislative Studies*, *2*, 1–11.

Castro-Toledo, F. J., & Miró-Llinares, F. (2021). Researching cybercrime in the European Union: Asking the right ethics questions. In *Researching cybercrimes* (pp. 327–345). Palgrave Macmillan.

Dittrich, D. (2015). The ethics of social honeypots. *Research Ethics*, *11*(4), 192–210.

ECtHR. (2019). *López Ribalda and Others v. Spain*. Retrieved from https://hudoc.echr.coe.int/fre#{%22itemid%22:[%22002-12630%22]}

ECtHR. (2020). *Guide on article 8 of the European convention on human rights right to respect for private and family life, home and correspondence*. Council of Europe, Strasbourg.

Esmein, A. (2000). *A history of continental criminal procedure: With special reference to France*. The Lawbook Exchange, Ltd.

European Commission. (2018a). *Ethics in social science and humanities*. Retrieved from https://ec.europa.eu/info/sites/info/files/6._h2020_ethics-soc-science-humanities_en.pdf

European Commission. (2018b). *Ethics and data protection*. Retrieved from https://ec.europa.eu/info/sites/info/files/5._h2020_ethics_and_data_protection_0.pdf.

FRA. (2019a). *Facial recognition technology: Fundamental rights considerations in the context of law enforcement*. Retrieved from https://fra.europa.eu/en/publication/2019/facial-recognition-technology-fundamental-rights-considerations-context-law

Gupta B. B., Agarwal, D. P., & Yamaguchi S. (2016). *Handbook of research on modern cryptographic solutions for computer and cyber security*. IGI Global. Retrieved from https://doi.org/10.4018/978-1-5225-0105-3

Gupta, B. B., & Gupta, A. (2018). Assessment of honeypots: Issues, challenges and future directions. *International Journal of Cloud Applications and Computing (IJCAC)*, *8*(1), 21–54.

Hagan, F. E., & Hagan, F. E. (1997). *Research methods in criminal justice and criminology* (pp. 347–48). Allyn and Bacon.

Holt, T. J. (2017). On the value of honeypots to produce policy recommendations. *Criminology & Public Policy, 16,* 737.

Hughes, J., Chua, Y. T., & Hutchings, A. (2021). Too much data? Opportunities and challenges of large datasets and cybercrime. *Researching Cybercrimes,* 191–212.

Kenneally, E., & Dittrich, D. (2012). *The Menlo Report: Ethical principles guiding information and communication technology research.* U.S. Department of Homeland Security.

Kleinig, J. (2008). *Ethics and criminal justice: An introduction.* Cambridge University Press.

Kuyumdzhieva, A. (2018). Ethics challenges in the digital era: Focus on medical research. In Z. Koporc (Ed.), *Ethics and integrity in health and life sciences research* (pp. 45–62). Emerald Publishing Limited.

Maimon, D., Kamerdze, A., Cukier, M., & Sobesto, B. (2013). Daily trends and origin of computer-focused crimes against a large university computer network: An application of the routine-activities and lifestyle perspective. *The British Journal of Criminology, 53*(2), 319–343. https://doi.org/10.1093/bjc/azs067

Maxfield, M. G. (2015). *Basics of research methods for criminal justice and criminology.* Cengage Learning.

Maxfield, M. G., & Babbie, E. R. (2014). *Research methods for criminal justice and criminology.* Cengage Learning.

McKee, H. A., & Porter, J. (2009). *The ethics of internet research: A rhetorical, case-based process.* Peter Lang Publishing.

Miller, S., & Gordon, I. A. (2014). *Investigative ethics: Ethics for police detectives and criminal investigators.* John Wiley & Sons.

Moneva, A., Leukfeldt, E. R., & Klijnsoon, W. (2022). Alerting consciences to reduce cybercrime: A quasi-experimental design using warning banners. *Journal of Experimental Criminology,* 1–28.

Nicks, S. D., Korn, J. H., & Mainieri, T. (1997). The rise and fall of deception in social psychology and personality research, 1921 to 1994. *Ethics & Behavior, 7*(1), 69–77.

Pattison, J. (2020). From defence to offence: The ethics of private cybersecurity. *European Journal of International Security, 5*(2), 233–254.

Perkins, R. C., & Howell, C. J. (2021). Honeypots for cybercrime research. In *Researching cybercrimes* (pp. 233–261). Palgrave Macmillan.

Podschuweit, N. (2021). How ethical challenges of covert observations can be met in practice. *Research Ethics, 17*(3), 309–327.

Pollock, J. M. (2014). Ethical dilemmas and decisions in criminal justice. Nelson Education.

Prichard, J., Wortley, R., Watters, P. A., Spiranovic, C., Hunn, C., & Krone, T. (2022). Effects of automated messages on internet users attempting to access "barely legal" pornography. *Sexual Abuse, 34*(1), 106–124.

Roberson, C., & Mire, S. (2009). *Ethics for criminal justice professionals.* CRC Press.

Rosenberg, A. (2010). Virtual world research ethics and the private/public distinction. *International Journal of Internet Research Ethics, 3*(1), 23–37.

Roulet, T. J., Gill, M. J., Stenger, S., & Gill, D. J. (2017). Reconsidering the value of covert research: The role of ambiguous consent in participant observation. *Organizational Research Methods, 20*(3), 487–517.

Rowe, N. C., & Rrushi, J. (2016). *Introduction to cyberdeception* (pp. 721–725). Springer International Publishing.

Sieber, J. E. (1982). Deception in social research I: Kinds of deception and the wrongs they may involve. *IRB: Ethics & Human Research, 4*(9), 1–5.

Spencer, J. R., & Pedain, A. (2005). *Approaches to strict and constructive liability in continental criminal law. In Appraising strict liability.* Oxford University Press.

Spitzner, L. (2003). *Honeypots: Tracking hackers.* Addison-Wesley.

Testa, A., Maimon, D., Sobesto, B., & Cukier, M. (2017). Illegal roaming and file manipulation on target computers: Assessing the effect of sanction threats on system trespassers' online behaviors. *Criminology and Public Policy, 16*(3), 689–726. https://doi.org/10.1111/1745-9133.12312

Vendius, T. T. (2015). Proactive undercover policing and sexual crimes against children on the internet. *European Review of Organised Crime, 2*(2), 6–24.

Vetterl, A. (2020). *Honeypots in the age of universal attacks and the internet of things* [Doctoral dissertation, University of Cambridge].

Vetterl, A., Clayton, R., & Walden, I. (2019). Counting outdated honeypots: Legal and useful. In *2019 IEEE Security and Privacy Workshops (SPW)* (pp. 224–229). IEEE.

Wilson, T., David, M., Bertrand, S., & Michel, C. (2015). The effect of a surveillance banner in an attacked computer system additional evidence for the relevance of restrictive deterrence in cyberspace. *Journal of Research in Crime and Delinquency, 52*, 829–855

Zhang Z., & Gupta B. B. (2016). *Social media security and trustworthiness: Overview and new direction in future generation computer systems.* Elsevier.

Zimmer, M. (2010). "But the data is already public": On the ethics of research in Facebook. *Ethics and Information Technology, 12*(4), 313–325.

Zook, M., Barocas, S., Boyd, D., Crawford, K., Keller, E., Gangadharan, S. P., Goodman, A., Hollander, R., Koenig, B. A., Metcalf, J., Narayanan, A., Nelson, A., & Pasquale, F. (2017). Ten simple rules for responsible big data research. *PLoS Computational Biology, 13*(3), e1005399.

5

GROOMING TO DEFRAUD

Martina Dove

Introduction

Once upon a time, scams were expensive to execute. Scammers had to either send a letter or a fax, make a phone call (before phone calls were free) or go door to door, hoping to engage a potential victim in a conversation, which may or may not result in compliance. For example, Nigerian scams were first executed by post and then later on, via phone or fax (Glickman, 2005). All of this carried a considerable cost to a scammer, either in time or funds. This changed with the invention of the internet, which created unique opportunities for online deviance: online aggression and bullying, false impersonations (e.g., catfishing), child pornography, software piracy, hacking into unauthorized areas to steal data or hijack an organizations' resources (e.g., ransomware attacks), phishing and other scams. (Attrill, 2015; Attrill-Smith & Wesson, 2020; Deora & Chudasama, 2021; Holt & Bossler, 2014; Palmieri et al., 2021; Peterson & Densley, 2017; Reshmi, 2021). The list is quite extensive.

Executing scams online is not only easy and efficient but is also relatively risk- and cost-free. A scammer can cast a wide net by sending multiple phishing emails in hopes of identifying the most vulnerable victims (Smith, 2010). Some scams are even thought to operate solely to identify people who may be more willing to engage with scams, and whose details are then sold on to other scammers, so they can be exploited over and over (Herley, 2012). As a result, most scams now operate in digital environments, online or via text messages. This affords a degree of anonymity to a scammer and makes execution more streamlined, as scammers can easily pretend to be someone else online. In real life or face-to-face, this is harder. Online fraud is also more difficult to prosecute (Button, 2012; Button et al., 2015). For example, a scammer may be located in a different country than the victim, making it harder to pinpoint jurisdiction in order to prosecute the crime. It also makes it harder to investigate, as different international agencies need to collaborate to make this happen (Cross, 2019). This could be why fraud has been steadily increasing and evolving in recent times (Gee & Button, 2019).

Another reason why digital environments are popular with scammers is the intimacy and emotional involvements they foster. Online relationships evolve more quickly due to frequency of communication and disclosure as intimate details are typically shared early

DOI: 10.4324/9781003277675-7

on. With high self-disclosure, intimacy level also increases, and this is especially true when communication takes place online or via text (Jiang et al., 2011). Additionally, in digital environments, scammers control the narrative, appearing as an ideal partner, something that would be harder in real life where contextual factors are also available. This creates an advantage for scammers, as strong emotional connection and trust with the victim is established quickly, which ensures that compliance is guaranteed at a later date (Buchanan & Whitty, 2014; Whitty, 2013).

The amount of effort a scammer invests in designing and executing a scam can have a great impact on the return. Even a little bit of research or information gathering before targeting the intended victim adds credibility to a request, such as in the cases where scammers gather information about company employees and the CEO before targeting company staff with requests to pay invoices (Button et al., 2017). Similarly, romance scams can go on for many months.

Now, new scam techniques have started to emerge, centering around building trust and laying the groundwork before the scam is executed, and some are extremely sophisticated, insidious, and based on intricate lies. One such example of this are 'pig butchering scams', so called because scammers invest time in feeding their victims lies, sometimes for months, in order to build trust before leaving victims with big losses (FBI, 2022; Podkul, 2022). Typically, victims are sent a text or a social media message, pretending to be a wrong number or a distant acquaintance, and engaged in deceptive conversation, with scammers concocting elaborate stories in order to encourage potential victims to invest money in fake crypto investments or similar ventures (Dove, 2022b).

Even scams that are perpetrated face-to-face are getting more inventive. Recent documentaries on high-profile scammers outlined just how deep deception can go. Some scammers go the extra mile to persuade, using 'status symbols' such as expensive cars, planes or other desirable and expensive items, in order to convince the victim that the narrative that they are trying to construct is real. Some even involve other people to lie on their behalf to enhance credibility (Morris, 2022; Pressler, 2022; Shane, 2021).

The reason these scams are successful is grooming. The scammer will take a long time grooming the victim, spinning an engaging narrative and constructing a specific persona. Sometimes this 'persona' mimics the victim's circumstances to appear more similar and likeable (Dove, 2020), and sometimes the persona is focused on wealth and generosity in order to evoke assumptions, stereotypes and social norms, which help aid compliance: for example, in the case of the Tinder Swindler and Anna Delvey, with personae created focused on the projection of a wealthy lifestyle (Morris, 2022; Shane, 2021). Many romance scams also have a grooming component, such as employing elaborate deception and persona construction (Carter, 2021; Koon & Yoong, 2013; Whitty, 2013; Whitty & Buchanan, 2012a), as do some investment scams (Dove, 2018, 2022a). Additionally, some sextortion scams also use elaborate lies and persona construction to induce fear and aid compliance.

Construction of the specific narrative (e.g., a wealthy persona) ensures more lucrative returns in the end. The closer they get to the victim emotionally, earning the victim's trust slowly, the more likely it is that the victim will ignore any warning signs and go along with the scam. In fact, scams that use deceptive and insidious grooming techniques are so lucrative that criminals are starting to engage in human trafficking in order to establish 'scam centers', where human trafficking victims are forced to enter in lengthy deceptive communications with victims (McCready, 2022).

This chapter outlines the types of online scams which rely heavily on lies and grooming, as a specific compliance technique. Additionally, it breaks down levels of deception, deceptive techniques, narratives and lies to show how they persuade. While most of the cases mentioned occurred in digital environments, some cases span both digital and real-life environments.

Levels of deception in fraud

Some level of deception is needed for any fraud to be successful, but sophistication and purpose are not always the same. Some frauds, like phishing emails, rely on relatively simple deceptive tactics, such as mimicking the legitimate companies' logos and using well-known persuasion techniques, such as evoking strong emotions (e.g., fear, greed, excitement) and using scarcity or urgency to encourage compliance. A scammer may lie that the victim's account was compromised and needs immediate attention. This creates urgency and panic. Or they may purport that the victim has won a prize of some sort, such as a lottery, a voucher or a tax rebate. Some try to persuade by constructing simple narratives, where a scammer may pretend to be a corrupt bank official needing a partner in getting money out of the country, or a wealthy widow who is trying to give the money away (Dove, 2020).

Other phishing emails pretend to be relatively mundane emails, such as delivery carriers trying to pinpoint the correct details to deliver the package. While these types of communications are based on lies and specific narratives (e.g., lottery win, free flights, account being compromised, etc.), the deception and narratives they contain are relatively simple. They work by evoking visceral states, such as greed, fear, excitement, in order to encourage quick and impulsive responses (Dove, 2020; Langenderfer & Shimp, 2001; Loewenstein, 1996). Evoked visceral states then influence quick information processing, which bypasses careful consideration and focuses on peripheral cues (Cacioppo et al., 1986; Langenderfer & Shimp, 2001; Petty et al., 1986). With such frauds, visual cues are very successful, such as company logos, which can be quickly associated with legitimate companies to enhance the credibility of the communication (Blythe et al., 2011).

However, many scammers know that more can be gained if they invest the time to earn the trust of the potential victim. To earn that trust, fraudsters must create and maintain successful narratives over a longer period, which are constructed through carefully chosen lies with the purpose of building a deep interpersonal connection. For example, it is not uncommon for fraudsters to use lies to appear similar to the victim, to mimic their circumstances (e.g., going through divorce, being a single parent), interests or background (Dove, 2018, 2020; Lea et al., 2009; Whitty, 2013). There is a specific reason for this. As human beings, we rely on our social connections. We help others and others help us. Once we trust someone, we are more likely to help them. In fact, research suggests that people struggle to believe that those who are known to them could be deceptive (Bond & DePaulo, 2006). Perhaps because once trust is extended, anything that is not congruous with that trust may have an impact on self-esteem (e.g., I didn't assess this person correctly). Therefore, once there is a period of conversation in which personal information is exchanged and the fraudster creates a narrative that creates a backdrop to eventual exploitation, it is more likely that the victim will go along with a plan and ignore warning signs.

Many types of frauds rely on long-term deception or grooming, in which a scammer tells specific lies and often provides proof. The lies contribute to the construction of a carefully chosen narrative, which makes the scam more believable. There can be several layers of deception during this process of grooming, some explicit and some implicit. More explicit ways of deceptions are direct lies, giving the victim false information to create a desired 'persona' and creating a specific narrative (Carter, 2021; Dove, 2018, 2022a; Whitty & Buchanan, 2012b). This often involves other people, such as individuals who are brought in to support the narrative by reiterating lies told to the victim (Dove, 2018; Morris, 2022; Whitty & Buchanan, 2012b).

In addition to direct lies, a more subtle or implicit deception is employed as a backdrop to the narrative, which happens when a fraudster embodies a lifestyle that supports the narrative they are trying to uphold, which obviously adds credibility to their lies. They may rent expensive properties, have expensive vehicles or other items, such as designer clothes, and go on expensive holidays. They may even take the victim with them in the early stages to establish trust and aid compliance in the future. They may speak of 'staff', such as assistants or security guards, which supports this lifestyle construction, or involve third parties to corroborate the narrative by playing a specific part (Konnikova, 2016; Monroe, 2018; Morris, 2022; Shane, 2021).

In many frauds that use grooming, once the victim is groomed to accept and trust the constructed persona, fraudsters may orchestrate a critical incident. This incident is often a catalyst for financial exploitation. Fraudsters may pretend they are in distress and need help, have been in an accident, state that someone is after them or that they are temporarily without funds (Carter, 2021; Minn, 2017; Morris, 2022; Whitty, 2015). Or in financial frauds, they may pretend the victim's account is at risk (Dove, 2022a). Often, the victim offers to help without being asked. The critical incident and the lengthy grooming create a perfect situation for exploitation. A critical incident subtly influences the potential victim to act, and the trust earned through the grooming stage ensures that any warning signs are easily dismissed. Not all frauds that rely on grooming will have this deceptive component, but many do, especially romance frauds.

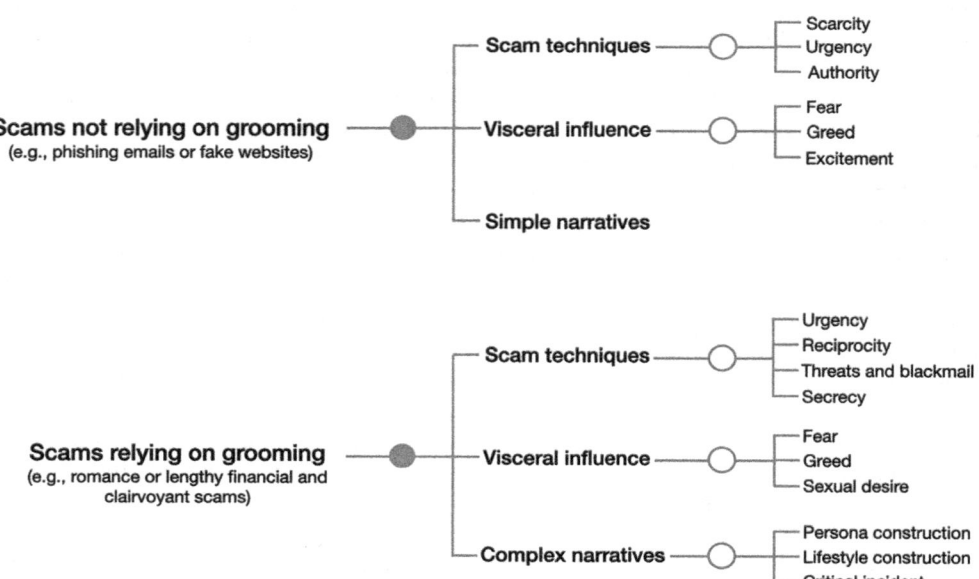

Figure 5.1 Differences between scams utilizing grooming as a technique and those that do not

Persona construction through different types of frauds

Scam 'personas' often vary according to a particular fraud (e.g., romance vs. financial) but can also vary greatly depending on the potential victim. In some cases, such as the 'pig butchering' scams, the scammer often adapts the narrative and the persona (e.g., a friend, a romance partner or an advisor) by starting more neutrally, and mapping out the scam according the victim's responses (Dove, 2022b).

One victim of financial fraud was groomed by two skillful fraudsters, pretending to be fraud investigators looking into cases of insider fraud. They told the victim that her bank account was at risk from the corrupt bank employees and asked the victim to help with the investigation. They called the victim often and over a period of about a month, with updates on the case. By doing so, they constructed a strong persona that a victim could trust and have complete faith in. They also appealed to secrecy by telling the victim that anyone at the bank could potentially be involved in insider fraud, pulling the victim further into the circle of trust (Dove, 2022a).

Romance scams are no different. Often, fraudsters tell multitudes of lies in order to create specific personas they think will appeal to the intended victim. For example, Koon and Yoong (2013) examined email correspondence between a victim and a perpetrator of a romance scam, in which a fraudster created a favorable persona over several emails. Through carefully orchestrated lies, the fraudster alluded to being someone who is new to online dating and somewhat naïve about finding a partner online. This serves to disarm the victim, making it seems as if they have control of the relationship as the love interest is inexperienced and therefore non-threatening. The authors also note that repeated references to religious beliefs and impressive educational backgrounds allude to someone who has good morals and is a good and credible person. Furthermore, the scammer also spent time describing their family as a 'well-to-do family' that is nurturing and well-educated. These lies are not merely used to describe the scammer's character but also create a richer narrative, a reality that a victim can picture themselves being a part of.

In Carter's (2021) analysis of romance fraud correspondence, a different, specific persona emerged: a successful boxing promoter. The scammer took the time of talking about emotional aspects that come from disappointments that go with establishing a career in the boxing world. Financial decisions and struggles that go along with this were frequently mentioned to the victim. The grooming stage lasted 6 months and during this time, the victim was being lied to in small increments, leading to distorted reality. This grooming stage is a segue to what comes next: a request for funds.

These stories are not isolated; in fact, the narrative and persona construction is a typical tactic in romance frauds (Cross, 2022; Fight Cybercrime, n.d.; Whitty, 2013; Whitty & Buchanan, 2012b). Other successful romantic scams rely on a strong, wholesome persona, but this can vary according to gender and sexual orientation. For example, fraudsters construct personas that target specific qualities women and men look for in a partner or which trigger certain stereotypes (Whitty, 2015).

Women frequently encounter romance fraudsters that pretend to be army generals, businessmen, investors etc. They are either divorced, widowed or raising a child alone, which may be a tactic to evoke more sympathy. They pretend to be in a successful career and often talk about their business deals with a victim (Minn, 2017; Whitty, 2015; Whitty & Buchanan, 2012b). Female personas with which fraudsters target men are almost the complete opposite. They are often young women, sometimes single mothers raising a child.

They are in low-paying jobs (e.g., nurse, teacher or a student), struggling to survive and in need of help (Whitty, 2015).

Whitty (2015) also found that there is a distinct persona which is used to target homosexual men. This persona is frequently a fairly young man, but professions tend to vary a great deal. Sometimes a persona is poor and living in countries where poverty is prevalent. At other times, the persona is a man in a semi-professional job or with a successful career. Although slightly different than grooming in romance and financial frauds, clairvoyant scams also rely on lies and deception to distort reality. To enhance credibility and status, some clairvoyants purport to have celebrities as clients and pretend to care deeply for the victim, fostering longer-term friendships that often keep victims engaged for periods of time (Button et al., 2009; Carter, 2015; CBS News, 2013; Lea et al., 2009).

There are other frauds that employ lies and construct specific personas and narratives to elicit quick compliance. In frauds where a fraudster is not willing to or cannot invest a considerable amount of time to sufficiently groom the victim through careful persona construction, they often rely on fear and threats. These threats can be explicit or implicit. For example, in some sextortion frauds perpetrated via email, fraudsters prepare the victim to accept their fate by listing explanations for why going to the police would be pointless. The persona of a successful and clandestine hacker is created by mentioning usernames on the dark web or similar exploits. Fraudster may also say that they cannot be traced or that they are in another country; therefore, the crime will be difficult to prosecute if a victim decides to report it to the police (Dove, 2019).

These lies appear somewhat convincing and act as a way of inducing helplessness. Helpless victims will be more likely to accept their fate and pay the ransom (Abramson et al., 1978; Dove, 2019, 2020, 2021; Seligman, 1972). Even more sinister are other types of sextortion scams, where victims are persuaded to share intimate photos with a perpetrator, which are often sold or misused. In a recent documentary, many victims recounted how they were groomed over time, by someone they thought was a love interest, to eventually provide intimate photos. When they tried to resist, victims were told their friends are doing it too and if they wanted to report it, the police would not help them (Howard & Grazer, 2022).

Wolf in sheep's clothing—lifestyle construction

Many fraudsters invest money in constructing a lifestyle and context which adds credibility to the scam and aids compliance, as a victim may use this non-verbal information to judge whether the fraudster is trustworthy. Lifestyle construction is not as explicit as persona construction, in which a fraudster lies to the victim over time; it is more subtle and deceptive, relying on cues that people pick up unconsciously. Just as certain professions, such as army or police officers and doctors are seen as more trustworthy (Cialdini, 2014; Lea et al., 2009; Whitty & Buchanan, 2012a), someone who embodies an expensive lifestyle may be viewed as wealthy and financially stable, and not in need of funds. This may disarm a potential victim and encourage dismissal of warning signs.

In Konnikova's (2016) book, which explains how fraudsters operate, this is called the 'put-up' stage, in which a fraudster adopts a certain lifestyle. This lifestyle bolsters the persona they are creating and adds credibility to the lies they tell to build a specific narrative. For example, in a recent documentary about a successful fraudster, 'The Tinder Swindler', victims spoke of a charming and successful businessman who would frequently take them to expensive venues and hotels, where they would witness him spending big sums of money. Or they would be taken on a trip in a private plane. He also had a bodyguard who would often accompany him, adding credibility to lies being told to victims (Hassan, 2022; Morris, 2022).

This stage acts as a context and trust-building exercise. Many people would not immediately believe everything they are told by a stranger, especially someone they met online. There are many fraud warnings around which specifically concentrate on warning victims about fraudsters that ask for money. Therefore, many potential victims may have their guard up at first and only start to trust the narrative being communicated consistently and over time. The process of building trust is accelerated by witnessing elements that support the lies being told, such as a wealthy lifestyle. Typically, if we are told something and we can also observe this to be true at the same time, we can quickly verify what was said (Gilbert, 1991). Therefore, a lifestyle construction is crucial for a successful deception and eventual fraud compliance. If a victim believes that a fraudster is wealthy, their guard is likely to be down when they are asked for money and they will be less risk-averse. For example, a potential victim may rationalize the request for funds from someone who appears to have money as a 'temporary lack of funds' and not a 'permanent lack of funds', making them more comfortable with lending or giving money.

Critical incident

Not all frauds use critical incidents as a catalyst to financial abuse, but some do and these incidents can be very convincing and persuasive, so it is worth mentioning them. Once a victim has been groomed over time, during which a persona was constructed and trust has been established, fraudsters often construct 'an incident' in which something urgent comes up, usually a pressing financial problem or crisis, which needs immediate attention (Carter, 2021; Dove, 2022a; Morris, 2022; Whitty, 2015). This is done to encourage compliance. Fraudsters may say they were in an accident or were hurt in some way. They may have other people corroborate the story (e.g., sending pictures, having someone pretend to be a doctor and calling the victim, etc.). This corroboration serves to immediately mitigate any suspicions that may arise. The incident itself is an important part of the fraud because it puts the victim under a visceral influence (i.e., heightened state of stress or fear), compromising judgments and rational thinking. In this state, people are more likely to act impulsively and ignore risks (Langenderfer & Shimp, 2001; Loewenstein, 1996; Slovic & Peters, 2006).

The request for funds can be explicit, such as an outright request to loan funds to help with the crisis, or implicit, where a victim offers to help because they believe this seems reasonable at that moment (Cialdini & Goldstein, 2004). It may seem inconceivable, but by that time, most victims that have been groomed over a long time, have strong emotional bonds and trust the narrative that the fraudster has concocted. The request is usually large at this point and may feel uncomfortable, but many victims feel they are doing this for the good of the relationship (Morris, 2022; Whitty, 2013; Whitty & Buchanan, 2012b). If the victim starts doubting or refuses to cooperate, the fraudster may threaten to end the relationship, evoking further fear (Whitty, 2013; Whitty & Buchanan, 2012b).

In the case of financial fraud, this critical incident may vary. One victim, who was groomed to believe she was helping fraud investigators investigate insider fraud at her local bank, was told that a corrupt senior bank official is trying to organize a transfer of funds from the victim's account. Scammers she was speaking to also told her that although they know this is about to happen, they cannot stop the transfer without her help. And in order to protect her savings, she has to act quickly and transfer her savings into another account, which they had access to. This incident on its own sounds unbelievable, but after months of grooming through careful and strategic injection of lies and persona construction, and with added fear evoked by the incident, it can seem believable (Dove, 2022a). The victim's defenses are already down since the trust was built over the course of weeks, and fear ensures that careful thinking is compromised. When presented with a solution by 'trusted persons', the solution can lower anxiety and stress that the critical incident caused, leading the victim to accept it.

Another financial fraud victim was told, after investing a sum of money into bogus shares and having lengthy and frequent conversations with a fake 'investment broker', that a merger was about to happen (critical incident). The fraudster suggested they should invest more money because the merger will increase victim's return on investment, and it would be a shame to miss out. This evoked greed, which is also a form of visceral influence, and the victim ended up borrowing more money and investing more (Dove, 2018).

Other financial frauds also have the same web of lies that slowly ensure the victim does not object to or disagree with what is being orchestrated, but many have different narratives or incidents. Some victims are also groomed to lie to bank employees, if they ask any questions, when money transfers or withdrawals are being arranged by the victim (Dove, 2022a; Tims, 2021).

In sextortion frauds which are disseminated via email, 'the incident' is presented at the beginning. The fraudster usually asserts that the victim was caught in some shameful act, such as cheating on their partner or visiting porn sites. The fraudster may also tell the victim that they were recorded in the act, and the recording or evidence will be sent to their work colleagues, friends and family (Dove, 2019, 2021). Even though these emails cast a wide net, they are incredibly harmful and effective, because the victim has no way of knowing whether the fraudster is telling the truth, especially if a fraudster was successful in constructing a convincing persona (e.g., a skillful hacker who operates undetected on the dark web). This will likely evoke fear and stress, making the victim feel they have no other recourse but to pay the ransom.

In clairvoyant scams, an incident may be part of the 'reading'. Victims are told that bad luck was placed on them and are asked for money to lift the curse or bad luck (Button et al., 2009; CBS News, 2013; Lea et al., 2009). This can be particularly harmful for people who are recently bereaved and are already going through grief and stress due to bereavement, who seem to be the most vulnerable to this type of fraud (Lonsdale et al., 2016). Many victims also enter an emotionally dependent relationship with a 'clairvoyant' who may keep the bad luck narrative alive for a while. This ensures that victims are in a perpetual state of fear and allowing the fraudster to keep defrauding them over and over (Dove, 2018).

Conclusion

In summary, this chapter illustrated that when it comes to fraud, the lies that fraudsters tell are not merely lies; they have a higher purpose. Their purpose is to construct a persona that is believable and likeable, create a narrative around it and at the right time, present an additional challenge which is difficult to solve without the victim's help, encouraging compliance.

Furthermore, this chapter demonstrated that persona construction in such frauds is a crucial part of deception, especially when constructed by employing cues that point to a certain lifestyle or status. It subliminally influences trust and prepares the victim for eventual victimization. As such, fraud relying on grooming is not merely an act of dishonesty, just a couple of lies that are made up on a whim. It is a pervasive threat which utilizes manipulative and deceptive practices, completely distorting the victim's reality.

The battle against fraud is never-ending with criminals always one step ahead, adapting and evolving their techniques to stay ahead of prevention. However, the key to prevention is knowledge. Understanding the mechanics of the grooming process and raising awareness of these harmful and deceptive practices brings us one step closer to stripping fraudsters of their power and reducing the number of potential victims.

References

Abramson, L. Y., Seligman, M. E., & Teasdale, J. D. (1978). Learned helplessness in humans: Critique and reformulation. *Journal of Abnormal Psychology*, 87(1), 49–74. https://doi.org/10.1037/0021-843X.87.1.49

Attrill, A. (2015). *The manipulation of online self-presentation: Create, edit, re-edit and present.* Springer.

Attrill-Smith, A., & Wesson, C. (2020). The psychology of cybercrime. In T. J. Holt & A. M. Bossler (Eds.), *The Palgrave handbook of international cybercrime and cyberdeviance* (pp. 653–678). Springer International Publishing. Retrieved from https://doi.org/10.1007/978-3-319-78440-3_25

Blythe, M., Petrie, H., & Clark, J. A. (2011). F for fake: Four studies on how we fall for phish. *Proceedings of the SIGCHI Conference on Human Factors in Computing Systems*, 3469–3478. https://doi.org/10.1145/1978942.1979459

Bond, C. F., & DePaulo, B. M. (2006). Accuracy of deception judgments. *Personality and Social Psychology Review*, 10(3), 214–234. https://doi.org/10.1207/s15327957pspr1003_2

Buchanan, T., & Whitty, M. T. (2014). The online dating romance scam: Causes and consequences of victimhood. *Psychology, Crime & Law*, 20(3), 261–283.

Button, M. (2012). Cross-border fraud and the case for an "Interfraud." *Policing: An International Journal of Police Strategies & Management*, 35(2), 285–303. https://doi.org/10.1108/13639511211230057

Button, M., Blackbourn, D., & Tunley, M. (2015). 'The not so thin blue line after all?' Investigative resources dedicated to fighting fraud/economic crime in the United Kingdom. *Policing: A Journal of Policy and Practice*, 9(2), 129–142. https://doi.org/10.1093/police/pau037

Button, M., Lewis, C., & Tapley, J. (2009). *Fraud typologies and victims of fraud* (p. 40). National Fraud Authority. Retrieved from https://researchportal.port.ac.uk/portal/files/1926122/NFA_report3_16.12.09.pdf

Button, M., Shepherd, D. W. J., & Blackbourn, D. (2017). *Annual fraud indicator 2017: Identifying the cost of fraud to the UK economy*. Centre for Counter Fraud Studies. Retrieved from https://researchportal.port.ac.uk/portal/files/18878333/Annual_Fraud_Indicator_report_1_2017.pdf

Cacioppo, J. T., Petty, R. E., Kao, C. F., & Rodriguez, R. (1986). Central and peripheral routes to persuasion: An individual difference perspective. *Journal of Personality and Social Psychology*, 51(5), 1032–1043.

Carter, E. (2015). The anatomy of written scam communications: An empirical analysis. *Crime, Media, Culture*, 11(2), 89–103. https://doi.org/10.1177/1741659015572310

Carter, E. (2021). Distort, extort, deceive and exploit: Exploring the inner workings of a romance fraud. *The British Journal of Criminology*, 61(2), 283–302. https://doi.org/10.1093/bjc/azaa072

CBS News. (2013, November 14). Sylvia Mitchell update: "Sorry" NYC psychic gets 5 to 15 years in prison for conning clients. *CBS News*. Retrieved from www.cbsnews.com/news/sylvia-mitchell-update-sorry-nyc-psychic-gets-5-to-15-years-in-prison-for-conning-clients/

Cialdini, R. B. (2014). *Influence: Science and practice.* Pearson Education Limited.

Cialdini, R. B., & Goldstein, N. J. (2004). Social influence: Compliance and conformity. *Annual Review of Psychology, 55*(1), 591–621. https://doi.org/10.1146/annurev.psych.55.090902.142015

Cross, C. (2019). 'Oh we can't actually do anything about that': The problematic nature of jurisdiction for online fraud victims. *Criminology & Criminal Justice*, 1748895819835910. https://doi.org/10.1177/1748895819835910

Cross, C. (2022). Meeting the challenges of fraud in a digital world. In M. Gill (Ed.), *The handbook of security* (pp. 217–238). Springer International Publishing. Retrieved from https://doi.org/10.1007/978-3-030-91735-7_11

Deora, R., & Chudasama, D. (2021). Brief study of cybercrime on the internet. *Journal of Communication Engineering & Systems, 11*, 1–6. https://doi.org/10.37591/JoCES

Dove, M. (2018). *Predicting individual differences in vulnerability to fraud* [Ph.D., University of Portsmouth]. Retrieved from https://researchportal.port.ac.uk/portal/en/theses/predicting-individual-differences-in-vulnerability-to-fraud(cad05d23–5626–478c-975c-764cf41ce683).html

Dove, M. (2019). *Persuasive elements in (s)extortion correspondence demanding cryptocurrency* [SSRN Scholarly Paper ID 3616205]. Social Science Research Network. Retrieved from https://papers.ssrn.com/abstract=3616205

Dove, M. (2020). *The psychology of fraud, persuasion and scam techniques understanding what makes us vulnerable* (1st ed.). Routledge.

Dove, M. (2021, September 21). *Sextortion scams—How they persuade and what to watch for.* The State of Security. Retrieved from www.tripwire.com/state-of-security/security-data-protection/sextortion-scams-how-they-persuade-and-what-to-watch-for/

Dove, M. (2022a, June 16). *Grooming lies and their function in financial frauds.* The State of Security. Retrieved from www.tripwire.com/state-of-security/security-data-protection/grooming-lies-function-financial-frauds/

Dove, M. (2022b, August 15). *5 tips for spotting and avoiding Pig butchering scams.* The State of Security. Retrieved from www.tripwire.com/state-of-security/security-data-protection/cyber-security/tips-for-spotting-and-avoiding-pig-butchering-scams/

FBI. (2022, April 5). *FBI Oregon tech Tuesday: Building a digital defense against a new cryptocurrency scam: Pig butchering* [Press Release]. Federal Bureau of Investigation. Retrieved from www.fbi.gov/contact-us/field-offices/portland/news/press-releases/fbi-oregon-tech-tuesday-building-a-digital-defense-against-a-new-cryptocurrency-scam-pig-butchering

Fight Cybercrime. (n.d.). Romance scams. *Fightcybercrime.Org.* Retrieved August 27, 2022, from https://fightcybercrime.org/scams/imposter/romance-scams/

Gee, J., & Button, M. (2019). *The financial cost of fraud 2019* (p. 28). Crowe and Centre for Counter Fraud Studies. Retrieved from www.crowe.ie/wp-content/uploads/2019/08/The-Financial-Cost-of-Fraud-2019.pdf

Gilbert, D. T. (1991). How mental systems believe. *American Psychologist, 46*(2), 107–119. https://doi.org/10.1037/0003-066X.46.2.107

Glickman, H. (2005). The Nigerian "419" advance fee scams: Prank or peril? *Canadian Journal of African Studies/Revue Canadienne Des Études Africaines, 39*(3), 460–489. https://doi.org/10.1080/00083968.2005.10751326

Hassan, J. (2022, February 7). 'Tinder Swindler' con artist, subject of new Netflix documentary, banned from dating app. *Washington Post.* Retrieved from www.washingtonpost.com/arts-entertainment/2022/02/06/tinder-bans-tinder-swindler-netflix-hayut-leviev/

Herley, C. (2012). Why do Nigerian scammers say they are from Nigeria? *Microsoft Research, in Weiss*, 14.

Holt, T. J., & Bossler, A. M. (2014). An assessment of the current state of cybercrime scholarship. *Deviant Behavior, 35*(1), 20–40. https://doi.org/10.1080/01639625.2013.822209

Howard, R., & Grazer, B. (2022). *Web of make believe: Death, lies and the internet.* Netflix. Retrieved from www.netflix.com/title/81122462

Jiang, L. C., Bazarova, N. N., & Hancock, J. T. (2011). The disclosure—Intimacy link in computer-mediated communication: An attributional extension of the hyperpersonal model. *Human Communication Research, 37*(1), 58–77. https://doi.org/10.1111/j.1468-2958.2010.01393.x

Konnikova, M. (2016). *The confidence game: Why we fall for it . . . every time* (1st ed.). Viking.

Koon, H. T., & Yoong, D. (2013). Preying on lonely hearts: A systematic deconstruction of an Internet romance scammer's online lover persona. *Journal of Modern Languages, 23*(1), Article 1.

Langenderfer, J., & Shimp, T. A. (2001). Consumer vulnerability to scams, swindles, and fraud: A new theory of visceral influences on persuasion. *Psychology & Marketing, 18*(7), 763–783. https://doi.org/10.1002/mar.1029

Lea, S. E. G., Fischer, P., & Evans, K. M. (2009). *The psychology of scams: Provoking and committing errors of judgement.* Office of Fair Trading. Retrieved from https://ore.exeter.ac.uk/repository/handle/10871/20958

Loewenstein, G. (1996). Out of control: Visceral influences on behavior. *Organizational Behavior and Human Decision Processes, 65*(3), 272–292. https://doi.org/10.1006/obhd.1996.0028

Lonsdale, J., Schweppenstedde, D., Strang, L., Stepanek, M., & Stewart, K. (2016). *National trading standards—Scams team review:* RAND Corporation. Retrieved from www.rand.org/pubs/research_reports/RR1510.html

McCready, A. (2022, July 13). From industrial-scale scam centers, trafficking victims are being forced to steal billions. *Vice.* Retrieved from www.vice.com/en/article/n7zb5d/pig-butchering-scam-cambodia-trafficking

Minn, H. (2017, February 1). How a university professor was scammed of £140,000 by man she met on dating site. *Mirror.* Retrieved from www.mirror.co.uk/tv/tv-news/phillip-schofield-shocked-university-professor-9735938

Monroe, R. (2018, March 6). The perfect man who wasn't. *The Atlantic.* Retrieved from www.theatlantic.com/magazine/archive/2018/04/our-time-com-con-man/554057/

Morris, F. (2022). *The tinder swindler.* Netflix. Retrieved from www.netflix.com/title/81254340

Palmieri, M., Shortland, N., & McGarry, P. (2021). Personality and online deviance: The role of reinforcement sensitivity theory in cybercrime. *Computers in Human Behavior, 120,* 106745. https://doi.org/10.1016/j.chb.2021.106745

Peterson, J., & Densley, J. (2017). Cyber violence: What do we know and where do we go from here? *Aggression and Violent Behavior, 34,* 193–200. https://doi.org/10.1016/j.avb.2017.01.012

Petty, R. E., Cacioppo, J. T., Kao, C. F., & Rodriguez, R. (1986). Central and peripheral routes to persuasion: An individual difference perspective. *Journal of Personality and Social Psychology, 51*(5), 1032–1043.

Podkul, C. (2022). What's a pig butchering scam? Here's how to avoid falling victim to one. *ProPublica.* Retrieved from www.propublica.org/article/whats-a-pig-butchering-scam-heres-how-to-avoid-falling-victim-to-one

Pressler, J. (2022, February 8). *How an aspiring 'it' girl tricked New York's party people—And its banks.* The Cut. Retrieved from www.thecut.com/article/how-anna-delvey-tricked-new-york.html

Reshmi, T. R. (2021). Information security breaches due to ransomware attacks—A systematic literature review. *International Journal of Information Management Data Insights, 1*(2), 100013. https://doi.org/10.1016/j.jjimei.2021.100013

Seligman, M. E. (1972). Learned helplessness. *Annual Review of Medicine, 23*(1), 407–412.

Shane, M. (Director). (2021, April 22). Anna Delvey takes Manhattan. In *Generation hustle.* IMDB.

Slovic, P., & Peters, E. (2006). Risk Perception and Affect. *Current Directions in Psychological Science, 15*(6), 322–325. https://doi.org/10.1111/j.1467-8721.2006.00461.x

Smith, R. G. (2010). Identity theft and fraud. In *Handbook of internet crime* (pp. 273–301). Routledge.

Tims, A. (2021, April 17). Haunted by shame: Victims of bank transfer scams tell of lasting trauma. *The Guardian.* Retrieved from www.theguardian.com/money/2021/apr/17/bank-transfer-scams-fraud-victims

Whitty, M. T. (2013). The scammers persuasive techniques model: Development of a stage model to explain the online dating romance scam. *The British Journal of Criminology, 53*(4), 665–684. https://doi.org/10.1093/bjc/azt009

Whitty, M. T. (2015). Anatomy of the online dating romance scam. *Security Journal, 28*(4), 443–455. https://doi.org/10.1057/sj.2012.57

Whitty, M. T., & Buchanan, T. (2012a). The online romance scam: A serious cybercrime. *Cyberpsychology, Behavior, and Social Networking, 15*(3), 181–183. https://doi.org/10.1089/cyber.2011.0352

Whitty, M. T., & Buchanan, T. (2012b). *The psychology of the online dating romance scam.* University of Leicester. Retrieved from https://fido.nrk.no/d6f57fd73b9898b42c8c322c961c8255f370677f-bac5272b71d86047a5359b66/Whitty_romance_scam_report.pdf

6

PERSPECTIVES OF PAID PANEL SURVEY RESEARCH IN CYBERCRIME VICTIMIZATION AND OFFENDING

Validity of global online market research sampling and data collection

Katalin Parti, Thomas Dearden and James Hawdon

Introduction

Surveys are standard tools used to gather representative data on myriad topics, including the study of online deviance and cybercrime. However, the increased use of the internet has led to the increased use of non-probability samples by researchers. Topics such as teen cybervictimization (Wright et al., 2021), problematic social media use and cybervictimization (Marttila et al., 2021), differential association and self-control and cybercrime (Dearden & Parti, 2021), cyber hatred (Reichelmann & Costello, 2021), cybercrime and institutional anomie theory (Dearden et al., 2021), and cybercrime and COVID (Hawdon et al., 2020; Kemp et al., 2021) have been studied using the non-probability data collected from online panels and tools such as Mechanical Turk.

Criminologists have long expressed concerns about measuring crime (Quetelet, [1839], 1969). Since crime rates fluctuate, insufficient policies exist, and official statistics are limited, the use of victim surveys is common and provides a needed alternative to official data (Decker, 1977; Lynch, 2014). Typically, victim surveys are used to inform criminological theories and to shape crime policies, particularly in Anglo-Saxon countries. These data are valuable as a counter to official data because they allow citizens direct participation in the documenting of the "crime problem." Moreover, since the official agencies providing protective services have a direct interest in how the "crime problem" is presented, using self-reported assessments of victimization protects against this bias by allowing the collection of data concerning crime and public safety to be separated from those agencies charged with providing protective services. However, despite their importance and development over time, victim surveys still present limitations that make measuring crime difficult. Nevertheless, these surveys can provide valuable data for analyzing victims' behaviors and needs, but their value is a direct function of the accuracy with which they measure the concepts they aim to measure.

DOI: 10.4324/9781003277675-8

This chapter aims to evaluate online surveys as sources for estimating rates of online offending. We do this by comparing data collected by two leading industry panel research companies, juxtaposing the results with FiveThirtyEight, an American company focusing on opinion poll analysis. We use polls from the 2020 US presidential election as a baseline of analysis.

Literature review—characteristics of non-probability sampling

Although most studies are performed using samples, census-based estimates are preferred whenever possible (Suresh et al., 2011; Rothman et al., 2013), independent of whether samples represent any target population. It would be nice to know how many people actually engage in cybercrimes and what the actual rate of victimization is; however, there are several theoretical and practical reasons that prevent researchers from carrying out census-based surveys. Barriers to census-based data include ethical issues (it may be unethical for researchers to include a greater number of individuals than is required to answer the research question), budgetary limitations and the costs of census surveys, logistical challenges with the required staff and equipment, the amount of time required of respondents to complete a census-based survey may be excessive, and unknown target population size (the actual pool of actors engaging in cybercrime is difficult to estimate). These reasons explain why samples are far more likely to be used than census-based studies.

When it comes to sampling practices, there are two major sampling types: probabilistic and non-probabilistic. In probabilistic samples, every individual in the population has an equal likelihood of being selected into the sample. In non-probabilistic samples, the likelihood of selecting every individual from the target population to the sample is unknown or zero, which results in coverage error. Therefore, the results are usually not generalizable to the target population. Cybercrime researchers often use convenience samples such as classes of students (Back et al., 2018; Meldrum et al., 2019; Ngo & Paternoster, 2011; Bossler, 2021; Holt & Bossler, 2008), purposive sampling such as asking the opinion of experts in a particular field (Priya, 2021; Montoh et al., 2021; Correia, 2022; Ncubukezi et al., 2020), snowball sampling where current research participants help recruit future participants (Holt, 2007; Holt et al., 2017; Kinkade et al., 2013; Li & Chen, 2014; Steinmetz, 2015), or quota sampling (Reichelmann et al., 2021; Costello et al., 2021; Dearden et al., 2021; Parti et al., 2022). In quota sampling, the population is first classified by age, gender, race/ethnicity, etc., then sampling units are selected to complete each quota (for an overview, see Martinez-Mesa et al., 2016).

Panel vendors use non-probabilistic quota samples. These vendors are organizations that sample and recruit potential respondents who have agreed to complete surveys for various forms of compensation. Once contracted by a researcher, the vendor then identifies a specified target audience of potential participants and invites them to complete a survey. Questions typically include survey items tapping participants' opinions, preferences, and behaviors. These vendors allow researchers to accrue survey responses while protecting respondents' anonymity as the vendors manage the sampling, selecting, and inviting panelists while verifying identities and compensating participating panelists for completing the survey. Once the data is collected, the vendor delivers the survey data to the researchers. Researchers can get data expeditiously from respondents who previously signed up for survey participation. Offering data in a relatively short time at reasonable prices while managing the complexities of sampling and data collection, the use of panel vendors is quite attractive in social research. Compared to college samples, online panels provide access to participants with a wide range of demographics given how widespread digital devices are connected to the internet (e.g., smartphones, tablets, laptops, etc.). Even difficult-to-reach populations, such as marginalized communities and specific age groups, can be available via panel vendors for researchers, albeit not without challenges (Ibarra et al., 2018). Of course, one of the greatest attractions of online panel data is the relatively low expense of collecting it. Participants who sign up to be included in the online panels can be paid between $2 and $10 for completing a survey (Craig et al., 2013) or receive other rewards such as donations to charities in their name, "status points" from the vendor, or other inexpensive gifts.

Nevertheless, there are also drawbacks of online surveys. First, panel vendors cannot guarantee sample representativeness. Panel samples tend to over-represent higher educated, white, non-Hispanic, and younger populations, whose income exceeds the national median. For example, Craig et al. (2013) found that panel vendor samples underrepresent low socioeconomic respondents. Higher-income populations have access to better (faster and more reliable) internet connections at home, which probably explains their higher participation rate. This non-coverage bias affects quota sampling practices since only those with internet access can opt-in to online survey participation. Approximately 89.8% of the US population had access to the internet in 2022 (InternetWorldStats, 2022); however, younger, more educated, and high-income people were the most likely to have internet access. According to the Pew Research Center (2021), 96% to 99% of adults under 65 maintain daily access to broadband internet, whereas only 75% of people 65 and above do. While the once-pronounced gender and racial/ethnicity gaps in internet access are no longer significant (e.g., 94% of men and 93% of women; 93% of white, 91% of black, and 95% of Hispanics have access to the internet), only 57% of households with less than $30,000 income have broadband internet compared to 92% of households with $75,000 or higher income (Pew Research Center, 2021). Education also patterns one's chances of connecting to the World Wide Web: while 98% of college graduates are connected, only 71% of those without a high school diploma are (Perrin & Atske, 2021). Furthermore, online surveys show biases toward English-speaking, literate, non-visually impaired, and persons with low time costs (Eysenbach & Wyatt, 2002; Liu et al., 2010; Craig et al., 2013). When these demographic and socioeconomic characteristics cumulate in intersectional disadvantages, underprivileged communities and societal groups will be left out of panel vendor samples (Perrin & Atske, 2021). These biases may affect generalizability.

Characteristics of Dynata and Qualtrics (prolific or middleman services)

In research examining data quality and representativity juxtaposing selected platforms (e.g., Amazon Mechanical Turk or MTurk, CloudResearch, Prolific), online platforms such as MTurk, where research participants use the platform as their primary source of income but spend just a few hours per week on surveys, did not provide quality data. These studies concluded that MTurk and other online platforms offer convenience samples at a reasonable price, but the quality of survey responses is low (Porter et al., 2019; Thompson & Pickett, 2020; Wang et al., 2015; Yeager et al., 2011). In addition, MTurk users can be highly active to the point that they are considered professional survey takers, which could further hamper data quality (Chandler et al., 2014; Keith et al., 2017).

Survey platforms such as MTurk, CloudResearch, Prolific, and SurveyMonkey are *self-service platforms* that provide researchers with complete control over the sampling and administering of their study. These platforms apply river sampling, routing, or banners to attract survey participants. Panel vendors such as Qualtrics and Dynata are *middleman services* (Eyal et al., 2021) that handle sampling and administration of the study on behalf of the researchers. Prolific panel vendors can also run the study independently through common industry software platforms (such as Qualtrics and QuestionPro), and they invite panel members who have previously agreed to take online surveys based on set population characteristics (e.g., age, sex, education, etc.). Among other advantages, middleman services score higher in honesty, attention checks, and internal reliability (Cronbach's alpha between different sites; Eyal et al., 2021). Moreover, many participants (41–42%) of self-service platforms said they use the site as their primary source of income, but only 7% of Qualtrics users did so (Eyal et al., 2021). Studies suggest an inverse relationship between hours spent on the site and data quality, with self-service platform users showing relative high frequency in usage (eight hours a week or more) and providing lower quality data than middleman services with less than two hours a week (Eyal et al., 2021). Overall, Qualtrics and Dynata provide higher data quality than self-service platforms, yet many of their participants fail attention-check questions and cheat when given the opportunity. Furthermore, these panels are more expensive than self-service panels such as MTurk (Eyal et al., 2021). Still, Qualtrics and Dynata have the highest data quality among these types of online survey providers (Eyal et al., 2021).

Studies have also tested whether probability-based selection occurs with panel vendors. Kimball (2019) found that prolific panel vendors such as Qualtrics and Dynata provide much more reliable data than self-service panels. Kimball (2019) tested sample composition in eight US states as well as on a nationwide sample. A demographic survey was fielded by prolific panels and MTurk. Demographic composition showed significant differences in some states compared to the US census data. Although basic demographics such as gender, race/ethnicity, and party affiliation only showed significant differences from census data in one or two in nine studies, educational attainment was significantly different from census data in half of the eight states. The age distribution showed the highest variability and diversion: MTurk was skewed towards a younger demographic because it was low in older age cohorts, whereas the prolific panels had a more normal distribution by age (Kimball, 2019). The study shows that panel vendors provide a demographic composition closer to the US census than self-service platforms.

In the current analysis, we compare two samples from prolific panel vendors, Dynata (formerly SSI Research Now) and Qualtrics, with data from the US Census and FiveThirtyEight, a company that reports on results from opinion polls while adjusting for the quality of the survey. Dynata and Qualtrics are commercial, prolific panelists operating globally with locations in the Americas, Europe, and Asia-Pacific, and are recognized as the leaders in the market research industry. After the panel companies are contacted by researchers/clients, they recruit participants and implement the survey compiled and designed by the clients.

Prolific commercial panel vendors use sampling quotas to obtain panel diversity. Prolific panelists may deliver samples from their own panel or leverage various technologies and platforms to aggregate/blend participants from a combination of sample sources (ESOMAR, 2021). These sources include opt-in databases of individuals who agreed to complete research projects and undertake other non-market research activities (such as watching ads, downloading an app, completing marketing offers, also known as loyalty programs, or getting rewards on "Get Paid To" sites). The "opt-in for market research" process requires respondents to submit an initial registration form requesting participation in market research studies. Potential participants build their profiles from a standardized list of questions. Panel vendors then select from the profiles that best fit the case specifications. There is a double opt-in requirement, meaning that those who do not reconfirm will not be contacted to participate in a survey.

To ensure data validation, Qualtrics replaces respondents who finish in less than half the median survey completion length (ESOMAR, 2012). Then, within seven days of completion of sample quotas, the company sends the database to the client to check data quality and if any additional data replacement is needed to address any sampling biases and improve quality. The company and the client can also work together as the data are being collected to monitor any potential issues. For example, if the sample appears to be over-representing females, the vendor can increase its efforts to recruit males.

Characteristics of FiveThirtyEight

FiveThirtyEight is an American company that focuses on opinion poll analysis. Taking its name from the number of electors in the United States Electoral College (538), it was founded as a polling aggregation website in 2008. During the presidential primaries and general election of 2008, the site compiled polling data through a unique methodology called sabermetrics to "balance out the polls with comparative demographic data" (Romano, 2008a; Romano, 2008b). Each poll is weighted based on the pollster's historical track record, sample size, and recentness of the poll (Silver, 2008). Since the 2008 election, the site has published articles on various topics in current politics and political news, typically creating or analyzing statistical information. These included monthly updates on numerous topics, including the prospects for turnover in the Senate; federal economic policies; Congressional support for legislation; public support for health care reform; global warming legislation; LGBT rights; elections around the world; marijuana legalization; and numerous other topics. The site and its founder are best known for election forecasts, including the 2012 presidential election in which FiveThirtyEight correctly predicted the vote winner of all 50 states and the District of Columbia.

Research questions

We aim to answer the research questions:

RQ1) Do panel sample data accurately reflect the nation in terms of demographic characters when compared to US Census data?
RQ2) How reliably did each panel and FiveThirtyEight predict the results of the 2020 US presidential election?

By answering these research questions, we seek to highlight the generalizability of panel surveys and the reliability of panel vendors for cybercrime researchers.

Sample and methods

We requested samples from two prominent panel vendors, Dynata and Qualtrics, two weeks before the 2020 US presidential elections. We requested that the sample quotas meet the following requirements: 1,300 adult respondents representing the American population

Table 6.1 Sample sizes for total and remaining sample after dropping respondents

	# Participants starting the survey	# Participants not accepting IRB consent	Dropped # speeders (under 180s)	Remaining sample
Dynata	1,717	120	197	1,400
Qualtrics	1,490	114	105	1,271
Total	3,207	234	302	2,671

by age, sex, race, and ethnicity. In addition to questions about typical demographics such as age, sex, race, ethnicity, and education, the survey included items about participants' online presence, online activities, the use of computers in terms of both frequency and activities, familiarity with computers, cybercrime victimization, and cybercrime offending. We also asked about the respondents' voting preferences in the upcoming presidential elections. In the following analysis, we concentrate on common demographic information and the preferences in the presidential election.

The data from Dynata was collected between Oct 19, 2020, and Oct 27, 2020. Overall, 1,717 participants started the survey. One-hundred-twenty individuals who started the survey were dropped because they did not consent to participate as required by standard Institutional Review Board (IRB) ethical considerations. In addition, 197 participants were dropped from the sample because they completed the survey in less than 180 seconds and were considered "speeders." Dropping these respondents resulted in a final sample of 1,400.

Qualtrics data was collected between Oct 19, 2020, and Oct 26, 2020, and included 1,490 participants. Like the Dynata data, some participants were initially dropped from the data, including 114 who did not consent to the research per IRB requirements. In addition, 105 respondents were dropped because they completed the survey faster than 180 seconds (see Table 6.1). The final Qualtrics sample had 1,271 respondents.

Results: evaluating the quality of the data

To judge the accuracy of the two samples, we begin by comparing the general demographic information of our samples with US Census data. To do so, we use Pearson's chi-square tests, and the results can be found in Table 6.2. Based on these results, both Dynata and Qualtrics do reasonably well returning a sample that reflects the nation's demographic profile. First, both samples are well within expected margins of error in terms of sex and most racial/ethnic categories. The Qualtrics sample significantly under-represented the Hispanic or Latino population and slightly over-represented the Black or African American population. Both samples significantly over-represented people of American Indian and Alaska Native origins.

Next, we compare age categories to the US census. Because our samples were limited to those 18 or older, the census figures reported here are derived from the US census instead of those reported by the census. The following numbers are the people in the respective age category as a percentage of the total US population 18 and over, rather than the people in the category as a percentage of the total US population. Given this adjustment, age categories were reasonably well represented in both samples, at least for those between the ages of 35 and 74. Both samples over-sampled those ages 20 to 34 while under-sampling those 75 years old or over. Dynata performed slightly better reflecting those 75 and over,

Table 6.2 Sample and US census comparisons on key demographic variables

	Dynata	Qualtrics	US Census (Percent of Population over 18)
Median age	41 (n/a)	42 (n/a)	38.2 (+/–0.1)
Persons 20 to 34, percent	30.3**	28.5*	26.5
Persons 35 to 54 years, percent	35.0	32.7	33.1
Persons 55 to 74 years, percent	26.2	29.8	28.4
Persons 75 years and older, percent	5.1**	3.3***	8.3
Female persons, percent	51.3	51.6	50.5
White alone, percent	73.7	75.0	75.8
Black or African American, percent	14.3	15.5*	13.6
Asian alone, percent	5.8	5.6	6.1
American Indian, Alaska Native	3.3***	2.5***	1.3
Hawaiian and Pacific Islander, percent	1.1***	0.3	0.3
Hispanic or Latino, percent	18.5	13.1***	18.9
High school or equivalent degree, percent	19.5***	28.5	26.7
Some college, no degree, percent	22.7	24.8***	20.3
Bachelor's degree, percent	29.2***	29.8***	20.2
Graduate or professional degree, percent	25.5***	14.8*	12.7
Employed, percent	59.3*	53.9***	59.6 (+/–0.1)
Median household income (in 2020 dollars)	$50–75 000 (n/a)	$50–75 000 (n/a)	$64,995 (+/–$128)

***p<.000; **p<.010; *p<.050; n/a: no p values

while Qualtrics provided a slightly better sample for those between 20 and 34. This under-sampling of the older population and over-sampling of the younger population is unsurprising given the relationship between age and internet use. These biases, slight as they may be, should be taken into consideration when trying to predict social phenomena related to age.

In terms of education, both samples return somewhat biased samples, but in different ways. The Dynata sample significantly under-represented those with a high school or equivalent degree, and substantially over-represented those with a bachelor's degree and those with a graduate or professional degree. The only educational grouping the Dynata sample accurately reflected the nation's population was for those with some college. Qualtrics did not perform much better in terms of education, as it only accurately reflected the nation for those with a high school degree or equivalent, although it only slightly over-represented those with a graduate or professional degree. It significantly over-represented those with some college and those with a bachelor's degree. It is interesting to note that the samples did not differ in terms of the percentage of respondents with a bachelor's degree. This educational category is clearly over-represented in both samples.

The Dynata sample more accurately represented the employment status of the nation. It did not significantly differ from the nation in terms of employment (59.3% for the sample, 59.6% for the nation). The Qualtrics sample, however, under-represented the employed, as only 53.9% of that sample reported being employed. This under-representation may reflect that in previous studies 7% of Qualtrics users said completing surveys was their primary source of income (Eyal et al., 2021); however, we lack the data to verify this possible explanation.

Finally, in terms of income, it appears that both samples did reasonably well. It is difficult to accurately test the representativeness of income since our survey collected data in income ranges instead of actual dollar amounts. Collecting income in ranges is a common practice in survey research as people frequently will skip the income question unless ranges are provided. Nevertheless, the fact that the nation's median household income is approximately the mid-point of the median-range of the samples is encouraging.

Overall, the two samples appear to reasonably reflect the nation's demographics, although there are important shortcomings in terms of education and employment. Given the likely correlation between these factors and important topical concerns—voter preference and cybercrime in our case—this is worrisome and casts concerns about the true representativeness of the samples. It is however possible to perfectly balance any desired demographic variable through both vendors. This aim can be achieved by not interviewing individuals whose demographic profile matches those of the established quotas that have been filled. Of course, this approach changes the nature of the survey design as demographic questions would need to be at the beginning of the survey. It also can significantly affect the price of the survey. Weights to correct for over- or under-sampling certain groups can also be constructed to correct for sampling biases. Yet, the data here suggest that setting basic quotas on sex and race/ethnicity can result in a sample that reasonably reflects the general population.

Next, we consider the accuracy of the polling services by comparing a question asking who respondents planned to vote for in the 2020 presidential election to the election's final results. Respondents were asked the question, "If the 2020 election were held today, would you vote for: a) Donald Trump, b) Joe Biden, c) some other candidate, or d) will not vote/not sure." We only analyze here those who specified a candidate. We do this since most polls reported are of likely voters, and because the data were collected between October 19, 2020, and October 26, 2020, within weeks of the actual election. We also compare data from FiveThirtyEight's collected polls. We use the reported predictions from the end of our data collection period, October 26, 2020 (FiveThirtyEight, 2020). As reported by FiveThirtyEight's "Who's ahead in the national polls," 52.3% of likely voters were predicted to vote for Joseph Biden, 42.8% for Donald Trump, and 3.1% for other candidates. Because FiveThirtyEight does not report undecided and not all polls report other candidates, we adjusted the reported percentages to reflect 100% of the total votes. Doing this resulted in predictions of Biden receiving 53.3%, Trump 43.5%, and other candidates 3.2% of the vote. The predictions from the two samples and FiveThirtyEight are reported in Table 6.3, along with the results of the actual election as reported by the Federal Election Commission (FEC, 2020).

Table 6.3 Comparison of Dynata, Qualtrics, FiveThirtyEight, and actual election results

Source	Joe Biden	Difference from Biden Actual	Donald Trump	Difference from Trump Actual	Other candidate	Difference from Other Actual
Actual Results	51.3%		46.9%		1.8%	
Dynata	50.4%	−0.9	46.5%	−0.4	3.1%	+1.3
Qualtrics	53.8%	+2.5	42.1%	−4.8	4.1%	+2.3
FiveThirtyEight	53.3%	+2.0	43.5%	−3.4	3.2%	+1.4

The numbers in Table 6.3 indicate that all three predictions were reasonably accurate, and all three sources accurately predicted the eventual winner. Yet it is clear from the data that the Dynata sample outperformed both the Qualtrics sample and FiveThirtyEight's polls-only data. Dynata was within 1.0% of the actual results for both President Biden and former President Trump, and it only over-predicted votes for other candidates by 1.3%. It was the only source of data that did not over-estimate the share of the vote that would eventually go to President Biden, and it nearly perfectly predicted the vote for former President Trump. Both Qualtrics and FiveThirtyEight underestimated the vote that would go to then-president Trump.

Results: estimating cybercrime

Now that we are confident that our samples are reasonably reflective of the general population, we can ask what percentage of Americans are victimized by or engage in cybercrime. To measure cybervictimization, respondents were asked if they had been a victim of seven different types of cybercrime in the 12 months preceding the survey. In this chapter, we operate with a reactivist or relativist definition of deviance (Meier, 2007) when defining cybercrime. That said, to investigate the prevalence and patterns of cybervictimization and offending, we included behaviors that are clearly normatively "deviant" or illegal such as "hacking," identity theft, or publishing someone's intimate images without permission, but we also considered behaviors that are likely to elicit negative social reactions that can be considered "mildly deviant." An example of such an act would be excluding someone from an online community. Therefore, all the included "offending" types will likely provoke normative response if someone is victimized. As such, our definition of cybercrime is a compound of normative and reactivist definitions of deviant activities. Hence, to measure cyber-offending, respondents were asked if they engaged in any of 10 behaviors in the 12 months preceding the survey. Table 6.4 reports the number and percentages of respondents who were victimized or engaged in cybercrime for each survey.

Looking at Table 6.4, it becomes obvious that the two samples produce different estimates of involvement with cybercrime. Respondents in the Dynata sample consistently report less victimization and less cyber-offending than do the respondents in the Qualtrics sample. In fact, rates of victimization and offending in the Qualtrics sample are approximately twice those in the Dynata sample, on average. The differences between the two samples are more pronounced for offending than for victimization. For offending, respondents in the Qualtrics sample are approximately 2.2 times more likely to report committing the offense than are those in the Dynata sample, and at times the estimate is 2.4 times higher in the Qualtrics sample than in the Dynata sample. This is the case for three offenses: hacking into an unauthorized area of the Internet, distributing malicious software, and posting nude photos without the person's permission. The two samples' estimates of victimization are relatively closer, with Qualtrics respondents being approximately 1.6 times more likely than Dynata respondents to report being a victim of cybercrime, on average.

Finally, to provide global estimates of the extent to which Americans are victimized by cybercrimes, we code respondents as either experiencing any of these cybercrime victimizations or not. We also code respondents as either engaging in any of the cybercrimes or not. Calculating estimates from each sample using these global measures of victimization and offending generates the estimates presented in Table 6.5. However, realizing that our samples over-represent young people and under-represent older people and knowing that age

Table 6.4 Sample-based cybervictimization and cyber-offending data

	Dynata		Qualtrics	
	Count	Percent	Count	Percent
Cybervictimization				
Lost money due to an email, website, or other computer scam	162	13.0%	324	23.4%
Had your identity used by someone else to start a bank account, credit card, or loan	125	10.0%	230	16.6%
Had unknown transactions in your bank/investment account, credit card, or other online payment system	208	16.6%	332	24.0%
Received notification from a company or organization that your private information, such as name, social security, credit card or password, has been stolen or posted publicly	192	15.1%	317	22.9%
Experienced hurtful comments, pictures, or videos about you posted online	168	13.5%	301	21.6%
Experienced unwanted sexual comments or advances online	182	14.6%	276	19.8%
Had a computer virus or malware that affected how your computer operated	154	12.3%	300	21.7%
Cyber-offending				
Posted hurtful information about someone on the internet	118	9.4%	306	22.0%
Threatened or insulted others through email or instant messaging	97	7.8%	214	15.4%
Excluded someone from an online community	132	10.5%	299	21.5%
Hacked into an unauthorized area of the internet	74	5.9%	192	13.9%
Distributed malicious software	80	6.4%	214	15.4%
Illegally downloaded copyrighted files or programs	117	9.3%	247	17.8%
Illegally uploaded copyrighted files or programs	80	6.4%	193	13.9%
Used someone else's personal information on the internet without their permission	91	7.2%	213	15.4%
Bought prescriptions (without a prescription) or other drugs on online pharmacies or websites	97	7.7%	219	15.8%
Posted nude photos of someone else without his/her permission	81	6.5%	221	15.9%

Table 6.5 Estimates of global cybervictimization and cyber-offending from two samples using unweighted and weighted data

	Victimization		Offending	
	Unweighted Data	Data Weighted on Age	Unweighted Data	Data Weighted on Age
Dynata	37.2%	35.8%	18.4%	17.1%
Qualtrics	46.5%	45.4%	31.6%	30.8%

is related to cyber-offending and cybervictimization, we also re-estimate these figures after weighting the data so that it accurately reflects the US population in terms of age. These estimates are also presented in Table 6.5.

The estimates in Table 6.5 reflect the same pattern as those in Table 6.4 in that the respondents in the Qualtrics sample were more likely to report being a victim of or engaging in cybercrime than the respondents in the Dynata sample. However, the discrepancy between the two samples is smaller using this global measure than when individual crimes were reported. The Qualtrics estimate of victimization was only 1.3 times higher than the Dynata estimate, and the estimate of offending was only approximately 1.7 times higher in the Qualtrics sample as compared to the Dynata. Unsurprisingly, the data that is weighted by age provide lower estimates of cybercrime involvement than the unweighted data. This is expected since both samples under-represented youth and over-represented the older population. The correlation between age and cybervictimization and cyber-offending in both samples is negative, so using the unweighted data would over-estimate cybercrime involvement because it includes a disproportionate number of younger respondents who are disproportionately more likely to be both victims and offenders.

Discussion

In this chapter, we considered the validity of panel data used for cybercrime offending and victimization analysis. Analyzing data from two of the leading prolific panel vendors, Dynata and Qualtrics, we compared essential demographic characteristics of the samples to current US Census data. In addition, we utilized a control question about the likelihood of voting for the presidential candidates in the 2020 election, considering FiveThirtyEight, an American company rating polls by quality. Furthermore, we consider potential differences and future implications of utilizing panel vendors' non-probability samples for measuring cybercrime.

Samples collected by the two prolific panel vendors, Dynata and Qualtrics, did not show significant differences: the 1,400 US adult population samples were completed within a week, and the demographic variables showed little difference from actual US Census data, partly confirming previous studies. The differences observed in the panels' age, racial/ethnicity, education, and employment components indicated a slightly higher rate of 65–74 years of age individuals but a lower representation of 75+ individuals in the panels compared to then-current US Census data. This result is similar to previous research scrutinizing quota sampling (Eyal et al., 2021). Next, both panels performed well representing sex. In contrast to Kimball (2019), our samples did not under-represent racial and ethnic minorities. Comparing our sample to the US census, both samples accurately reflected the White and Asian populations, and Dynata also accurately reflected the Hispanic and Black or African American populations. Hispanic or Latinx individuals were under-represented in the Qualtrics sample. Both panel samples over-represented highly educated individuals, similar to previous research findings (Craig, 2013; Szolnoki & Hoffmann, 2013). The most striking difference was the rate of overrepresentation of people with college and professional degrees in the panels. Apparently, individuals with higher socioeconomic status (Craig, 2013; Szolnoki & Hoffmann, 2013)—a composition of better education and older age in our sample—are indeed more likely to participate in panel surveys. Employment status was also slightly under-represented in the Qualtrics sample, as it showed a 5.7% difference over-representing unemployed participants. Regarding income differences, the median household income of panel participants was very similar to the US Census median.

There are several issues to consider when trying to answer why specific demographics are over-represented or under-represented in profile panels. First, interest in participating in surveys might differ by the survey topic, and this selection bias can dramatically influence survey results (see Shropshire et al., 2009). For example, women are more concerned about social and health care-related issues than are men (Bidmon & Terlutter, 2015; Rainie & Fox, 2000). Second, broadband internet access, an inherent necessity of taking part in online surveys, is not equally available for everyone. In the United States and elsewhere, internet access is positively associated with being male, being younger, having higher income and more education, being White or Asian, and not being Hispanic (Horrigan, 2010; Bethlehem & Biffignandi, 2012). However, measuring internet penetration has become more challenging since people can get reliable internet over their phones (Horrigan, 2010), and many survey platforms such as Qualtrics now design their surveys to be visually appealing and well-functioning on mobile phones. Still, out of all of these differentiating characteristics, our samples seriously over-represented only higher educated individuals. Panel vendors typically field a survey until the requested quotas are filled, and we cannot tell why participants took the survey at an earlier or later stage. As such, we cannot tell whether early and later survey-takers differ in their motives for participating in the survey. Future research should consider asking participants directly about why they completed a particular survey, including cybercrime-related social surveys. Fourth, when turning to panel vendors, researchers should also consider that recruitment rates for panel survey participation are 33% or less (nonresponse bias; Callegaro & DiSogra, 2009), which undoubtedly creates bias in the samples and decreases their representativeness.

The study's second goal was to determine how reliably each panel predicted the result of the US presidential election. Our samples were also compared to the predictions reported by FiveThirtyEight. All three sources accurately predicted Joseph Biden as the winner, but Dynata provided the most accurate results. Qualtrics and FiveThirtyEight both under-estimated the share of the vote that President Trump would eventually receive, possibly indicating a bias in these data sources. It is possible that both sources under-sampled the groups most likely to vote for then-president Trump. This potential problem notwithstanding, our results indicate that panel vendor surveys can predict the outcomes of an upcoming presidential election with similar levels of accuracy as more traditional methods of polling potential voters. While no polling will achieve 100% accuracy, all of these sources accurately reflected the final results within expected margins of error.

Regarding data quality and representativeness, we can conclude that the panel samples' demographic composition is slightly different from that of the US Census; however, the samples overall provided reasonable reflections of the nation's demographic profile. Nevertheless, survey participants' drives and motivations are unknown, and these could include money (or the small rewards offered by panel vendors), general interest in participating in social surveys, or specific interest in participating in a survey about cybercrime victimization and offending. Since the channels of circulating the polls gathered by FiveThirtyEight and our panel vendors were slightly different (with FiveThirtyEight polls being circulated not exclusively online but also over dial-up services), we can expect more accuracy in FiveThirtyEight polls. However, panel surveys still offer a great deal of advantages to researchers, including quota sampling for a reasonable price, which produces more reliable results compared to other non-probability sampling techniques such as convenience sampling on college campuses or snowball sampling.

Although our samples from these non-probabilistic panel vendors reasonably reflected US demographics and presidential election results, there are issues to consider when selecting panel vendors. Although prolific panels utilize a sample that's larger and more aligned with the US census than other non-probabilistic samples, realistically, every participant has the potential to provide poor-quality data if they are incorrectly screened. Panel vendors admittedly (Fawson & Lorch, 2021) try to build in quality checks to the process, such as fraud or cheating prevention, by employing machine learning or AI, reasonable rewards, accuracy screeners, and mobile-friendly surveys. According to ESOMAR (2015) recommendations for enhancing data quality, agencies must validate each research participant's claimed identity, and providers must ensure that research participants complete the same survey only once. However, researchers could also take actions to enhance data quality as well. For example, applying a good online questionnaire design can provide clarity and motivation to complete the survey once it is started. The longer the survey, the more likely research participants will disengage and potentially drop out before finishing the survey. This process is known as "survey fatigue" (Shropshire et al., 2009). Repeated matrix or grid-style questions can result in straight-lining and other patterned responses. Furthermore, a phenomenon known as primacy, where questions with a large number of answer categories can result in research participants choosing responses from the top of the list more often than the bottom, can also be problematic. Conversely, the use of images can increase respondent interest and data quality (Witte et al., 2004). In addition to the application of good survey design, building speed checks and attention check questions into the survey can identify a large number of problematic participants and enhance response validity (for standardized reporting checklists, see Cheung et al., 2017; DeSimone et al., 2015; Keith et al., 2017).

Cybercrime researchers face additional challenges compared to social researchers with other interests. Studies of cybercrime found that participants with the highest income level were largely unavailable, and the recruitment of older people took longer than for the rest of the sample (Miller et al., 2020). Moreover, gathering data about people's engagement in crimes and deviant activities presents further challenges. According to Hutchings and Holt (2018), researchers tend to conceptualize cybercrime and deviant cyber activities, such as hacking, cyberbullying, and cyberstalking differently. This can complicate the collection of data on these topics and make comparisons across samples difficult or impossible. In addition, there are ethical issues associated with researching cybercrime, as recruiting offenders and convincing them to participate in research can be challenging (Hutchings & Holt, 2018). Considering that participant honesty is compromised in asking about illegal and ambiguous activities, we recommend using triangulation (multimode design) to ensure data reliability. We believe that a mix of cross-sectional surveys or longitudinal panel measurements, supported by qualitative research techniques such as interviews and focus groups, would provide a good balance for studying cybercrime and its impact on society.

In conceptualizing "cybercrime," we followed a broader approach of deviance that included normative illegal as well as relative or reactionist deviant activities. Other research may utilize a more constructivist definition of deviance and ask why certain offenses are defined as crimes while others that are equally or even more harmful are not, whose interests are served by defining some but not other behaviors as crimes, whether the act is harmful, and what reactions they provoke. Yet, we maintain that even constructivist studies of crime and deviance require accurate data. For example, studies concerning the creation and sustaining of moral panics (e.g., Hawdon, 2001; Bonn, 2010) need good estimates of the "problem" to establish if a constructed moral panic was a disproportionate response to the potential harm posed by the targeted behaviour and group. Therefore, the focus on respondents' perceptions of what they considered to be "crimes," "deviant," and "harmful" is important.

Another limitation to the current research is that we only included US samples in the analysis. First, the commercial survey platforms can only be utilized in countries where these platforms are available (i.e., in countries with developed economies). In contrast, countries with lower GDPs and non-capitalist cultures are typically not represented; hence, part of the global population is excluded from the possibility of professional panel-based data collection. This is clearly an issue of coverage bias related to the use of these vendors. Yet, it should be noted that collecting data using other methods would also be difficult in many of the nations that are not covered by online panels. Moreover, a significant number of US users are registered in the commercial platforms under scrutiny, which increases reliability and cost effectiveness of panel research. Furthermore, the presence and availability of fairly accurate census polls in the US provided opportunity for comparison. In addition, the fact that our data was collected at the same time of the presidential election allowed us to directly compare our prediction of that event with the actual results provided an excellent test of the data's accuracy and utility. Still, professional panels have limitations. In addition to the coverage bias mentioned earlier, there is a likely selection bias due to marginalized populations not being able to reach online platforms and consequently being under-represented. Coverage biases may also be introduced by educational level, race and ethnicity, income, and other factors. While these biases can be estimated and steps to correct them can be taken, they are nevertheless issues that must always be considered when using survey research data.

Finally, it is important to note that our two samples provide very different estimates of cybercrime involvement. Despite both being reflecting the demographic characteristics of the country reasonably well and providing relatively accurate predictions of the 2020 presidential election, respondents from the Qualtrics sample were significantly more likely to report being victims of cybercrime and engaging in cyber-offenses than the Dynata respondents. This difference is likely a function of who participated in the survey. As noted, topical interest is an important determinant of survey participation (Shropshire et al., 2009), and we suspect that interest in cybercrime may have varied between the two samples. Given that the surveys used to collect the data were identical, other survey design factors could not have influenced these estimates. Unfortunately, we are unable to definitively know why the estimates varied so much, but the fact that they did should give researchers pause when trying to use surveys to estimate rates of cybercrime involvement. This problem dramatically highlights the need for the collection of high-quality data on cybercrime using techniques such as those used to collect the National Crime Victimization Survey (NCVS). While collecting these data are extremely expensive, our estimates of the extent to which Americans experience cybercrime victimization or participate in cybercrime will be questionable and open to the errors that plague all survey research.

Conclusion

The issues to consider when applying panel samples are responsiveness, loss of attention, attrition due to survey length and ambiguities, and failure to maintain sociodemographic diversity. However, some studies do not require representativeness to ensure internal validity. For example, experimental designs that test theory-driven hypotheses within a defined population sampled by a panel vendor can legitimately test the hypotheses. Before deciding on prolific panel vendors, we recommend that researchers proactively ask questions about panels and carefully consider the strengths and drawbacks of online survey features, including quota sampling.

References

Back, S., Soor, S., & LaPrade, J. (2018). Juvenile hackers: An empirical test of self-control theory and social bonding theory. *International Journal of Cybersecurity Intelligence & Cybercrime*, 1(1), 40–55. Retrieved from www.doi.org/10.52306/01010518VMDC9371

Bethlehem, J., & Biffignandi, S. (2012). *Handbook of web surveys*. Wiley & Sons.

Bidmon, S., & Terlutter, R. (2015). Gender differences in searching for health information on the internet and the virtual patient-physician relationship in Germany: Exploratory results on how men and women differ and why. *Journal of Medical Internet Research*, 17(6), e156. https://doi.org/10.2196/jmir.4127.

Bonn, S. A. (2010). *Mass deception. Moral Panic and the US war on Iraq*. Rutgers University of Press.

Bossler, A. M. (2021). Perceived formal and informal sanctions in deterring cybercrime in a college sample. *Journal of Contemporary Criminal Justice*, 37(3), 452–470. https://doi.org/10.1177/10439862211001630

Callegaro, M., & DiSogra, C. (2009). Computing response metrics for online panels. *Public Opinion Quarterly*, 72(5), 1008–1032. https://doi.org/10.1093/poq/nfn065

Chandler, J., Mueller, P., & Paolacci, G. (2014). Nonnaïveté among Amazon Mechanical Turk workers: Consequences and solutions for behavioral researchers. *Behavior Research Methods*, 46(1), 112–130. https://doi.org/10.3758/s13428-013-0365-7

Cheung, J. H., Burns, D. K., Sinclair, R. R., & Sliter, M. (2017). Amazon Mechanical Turk in organizational psychology: An evaluation and practical recommendations. *Journal of Business and Psychology*, 32(4), 347–361. https://doi.org/10.1007/s10869-016-9458-5

Craig, B. M., Hays, R. D., Pickard, A. S., Cella, D., Revicki, D. A., & Reeve, B. B. (2013). Comparison of US panel vendors to online surveys. *Journal of Medical Internet Research*, 15(11), e260. Retrieved from www.jmir.org/2013/11/e260/

Correia, S. G. (2022). Making the most of cybercrime and fraud crime report data: A case study of UK Action Fraud. *International Journal of Population Data Science*, 7(1), 9–17. https://doi.org/10.23889/ijpds.v7i1.1721

Costello, M., Restifo, S. J., & Hawdon, J. (2021). Viewing anti-immigrant hate online: An application of routine activity and social structure-social learning theory. *Computers in Human Behavior*, 124. https://doi.org/10.1016/j.chb.2021.106927

Dearden, T. E., & Parti, K. (2021). Cybercrime, differential association, and self-control: Knowledge transmission through online social learning. *American Journal of Criminal Justice*, 46, 935–955. https://doi.org/10.1007/s12103-021-09655-4

Dearden, T. E., Parti, K., & Hawdon, J. (2021). Institutional anomie theory and cybercrime—Cybercrime and the American dream, now available online. *Journal of Contemporary Criminal Justice*, 37(3), 311–332. https://doi.org/10.1177/10439862211001590

Decker, S. H. (1977). Official crime rates and victim surveys: An empirical comparison. *Journal of Criminal Justice*, 5, 47–54.

DeSimone, J. A., Harms, P. D., & DeSimone, A. J. (2015). Best practice recommendations for data screening. *Journal of Organizational Behavior*, 36(2), 171–181. https://doi.org/10.1002/job.1962

ESOMAR. (2012). *28 questions to help buyers of online samples*. ESOMAR World Research. Retrieved July 24, 2022, from https://swiss-insights.ch/wp-content/uploads/2020/05/ESOMAR-28-Questions-to-Help-Buyers-of-Online-Samples-September-2012.pdf

ESOMAR. (2015). ESOMAR/GRBN guideline for online sample quality. *Global Research Business Network*. Retrieved July 24, 2022, from https://grbn.org/wp-content/uploads/2016/12/Online_Sample_Quality_Guideline.pdf

ESOMAR. (2021). Questions to help buyers of online samples. *ESOMAR Global Research*. Retrieved July 24, 2022, from https://esomar.org/uploads/attachments/ckqqecpst00gw9dtrl32 xetli-questions-to-help-buyers-of-online-samples-2021.pdf

Eyal, P., Rothschild, D., Gordon, A., Evrden, Z., & Damer, E. (2021). Data quality for platforms and panels for online behavioral research. *Behavioral Research Methods*, 54, 1643–1662. https://doi.org/10.3758/s13428-021-01694-3

Eysenbach, G., & Wyatt, J. (2002). Using the Internet for surveys and health research. *Journal of Medical Internet Research*, 4(2), e13. https://doi.org/10.2196/jmir.4.2.e13

Fawson, B., & Lorch, J. (2021, March 29). The new dynamics of online sample quality. *Greenbook*. Retrieved July 24, 2022, from www.greenbook.org/mr/market-research-trends/the-new-dynamics-of-online-sample-quality/

FEC. (2020). Official 2020 presidential general election results. *Federal Election Commission*. Retrieved August 26, 2022, from www.fec.gov/resources/cms-content/documents/2020presgeresults.pdf

FiveThirtyEight. (2020). Who's ahead in the national polls? *FiveThirtyEight*. Retrieved August 26, 2022, from https://projects.fivethirtyeight.com/polls/president-general/2020/national/

Hawdon, J. (2001). The role of presidential rhetoric in the creation of a moral panic: Reagan, Bush, and the war on drugs. *Deviant Behavior*, 22(5), 419–445.

Hawdon, J., Parti, K., & Dearden, T. E. (2020). Cybercrime in America amid COVID-19: The initial results from a natural experiment. *American Journal of Criminal Justice*, 45, 546–562. https://doi.org/10.1007/s12103-020-09534-4

Holt, T. J. (2007). Subcultural evolution? Examining the influence of on- and off-line experiences on deviant subcultures. *Deviant Behavior*, 28(2), 171–198. https://doi.org/10.1080/01639620601131065

Holt, T. J., & Bossler, A. M. (2008). Examining the applicability of lifestyle-routine activities theory for cybercrime victimization. *Deviant Behavior*, 30(1), 1–25. https://doi.org/10.1080/01639620701876577

Holt, T. J., Freilich, J. D., & Chermak, S. M. (2017). Exploring the subculture of ideologically motivated cyber-attackers. *Journal of Contemporary Criminal Justice*, 33(3), 212–233. https://doi.org/10.1177/1043986217699100

Horrigan, J. B. (2010). Broadband adoption and use in America. Results from an FCC survey. *Federal Communications Commission*. Retrieved July 24, 2022, from https://transition.fcc.gov/Diversity-FAC/032410/consumer-survey-horrigan.pdf

Hutchings, A., & Holt, T. J. (2018). Interviewing cybercrime offenders. *Journal of Qualitative Criminal Justice & Criminology* [Preprint]. https://doi.org/10.21428/88de04a1.1fdab531

Ibarra, J. L., Agas, J. M., Lee, M., Pan, J. L., & Buttenheim, A. M. (2018). Comparison of online survey recruitment platforms for hard-to-reach pregnant smoking populations: Feasibility study. *Journal of Medical Internet Research Protocols*, 7.

Internet World Stats. (2022). Internet users and 2020 population in North America. *Internet World Stats*. Retrieved July 24, 2022, from www.internetworldstats.com/stats14.htm#north

Keith, M. G., Tay, L., & Harms, P. D. (2017). Systems perspective of Amazon Mechanical Turk for organizational research: Review and recommendations. *Frontiers in Psychology*, 8, 1359. https://doi.org/10.3389/fpsyg.2017.01359

Kemp, S., Buil-Gil, D., Moneva, A., Miro-Llinares, F., & Diaz-Castano, D. (2021). Empty streets, busy internet: A time-series analysis of cybercrime and fraud trends during COVID-19. *Journal of Contemporary Criminal Justice*, 37(4), 480–501. https://doi.org/10.1177/10439862211027986

Kimball, S. H. (2019). Survey data collection; Online panel efficacy. A comparative study of Amazon MTurk and research now SSI/Survey monkey/Opinion access. *Journal of Business Diversity*, 19(2). https://doi.org/10.33420/jbd.v19i2.2054

Kinkade, P., Bachmann, M., & Bachmann, B. (2013). Hacker Woodstock: Observations of an off-line cyber culture at the Chaos Communication Camp 2011. In T. J. Holt (Ed.), *Crime on-line: Correlates, causes, and context* (2nd ed., pp. 27–53). Carolina Academic Press.

Li, W., & Chen, H. (2014). Identifying top sellers in underground economy using deep learning-based sentiment analysis, *2014 IEEE Joint Intelligence and Security Informatics Conference* (pp. 64–67). https://doi.org/10.1109/JISIC.2014.19

Liu, H., Cella, D., Gershon, R., Shen, J., Morales, L. S., Riley, W., & Hays, R. D. (2010). Representativeness of the patient-reported outcomes measurement information system Internet panel. *Journal of Clinical Epidemiology*, 63(11), 1169–1178. https://doi.org/10.1016/j.jclinepi.2009.11.021

Lynch, J. (2014). The evolving role of self-report surveys of criminal victimization in a system of statistics on crime and the administration of justice. *Statistical Journal of the IAOS*, 30(3), 165–169.

Martinez-Mesa, J., Gonzalez-Chica, D. A., Duquia, R. P., & Bastos, J. L. (2016). Sampling: How to select participants in my research study? *Anais Brasileiros de Dermatologia*, 91(3), 326–330. http://dx.doi.org/10.1590/abd1806-4841.20165254

Marttila, E., Koivula, A., & Räsänen, P. (2021). Cybercrime victimization and problematic social media use: Findings from a nationally representative panel study. *American Journal of Criminal Justice*, 46, 862–881. https://doi.org/10.1007/s12103-021-09665-2

Meier, R. F. (2007). Deviance, normative definitions of. In R. F. Meier & C. M. Cain (Eds.), *The Blackwell encyclopedia of sociology* (pp. 1116–1117). Wiley. Retrieved from https://doi.org/10.1002/9781405165518

Meldrum, R. C., Boman, J. H., & Back, S. (2019). Low self-control, social learning, and texting while driving. *American Journal of Criminal Justice*, 44, 191–210. https://doi.org/10.1007/s12103-018-9448-4

Miller, C. A., Guidry, J. P. D., Dahman, B., & Thomson, M. D. (2020). A tale of two diverse Qualtrics samples: Information for online survey researchers. *Cancer Epidemiology Biomarkers Preview*, 29(4), 731–735. https://doi.org/10.1158/1055-9965.

Montoh, A., Mirahyanti, G. A., & Rantung, T. (2021). Cyber security analysis on small medium enterprise's online shop. *International Journal of Information Technology and Education*, 1(1). https://ijite.jredu.id/index.php/ijite/article/view/14

Ncubukezi, T., Mwansa, N., & Rocaries, F. (2020). A review of the current cyber hygiene in small and medium-sized businesses. *15th International Conference for Internet Technology and Secured Transactions (ICITST)* (pp. 1–6). https://doi.org/10.23919/ICITST51030.2020.9351339

Ngo, F. T., & Paternoster, R. (2011). Cybercrime victimization: An examination of individual and situational level factors. *International Journal of Cyber Criminology*, 5(1), 773–793.

Parti, K., Dearden, T., & Hawdon, J. (2022). Understanding the overlap of online offending and victimization: Using cluster analysis to examine group differences. *Victims & Offenders*, 17(5), 712–734. https://doi.org/10.1080/15564886.2022.2036655

Perrin, A., & Atske, S. (2021, April 2). 7% of Americans don't use the internet. Who are they? *Pew Research Center*. Retrieved July 25, 2022, from www.pewresearch.org/fact-tank/2021/04/02/7-of-americans-dont-use-the-internet-who-are-they/

Pew Research Center. (2021, April 7). *Internet/Broadband Fact Sheet*. Retrieved July 24, 2022, from www.pewresearch.org/internet/fact-sheet/internet-broadband/

Porter, C. O., Outlaw, R., Gale, J. P., & Cho, T. S. (2019). The use of online panel data in management research: A review and recommendations. *Journal of Management*, 45(1), 319–344. https://doi.org/10.1177/0149206318811569

Priya, P. (2021). Effectiveness of planned teaching programme on knowledge regarding cybercrime among higher secondary students in selected school of Indore district in the year 2015–16. *GFNPSS Global Nursing Journal of India*, 4(2). Retrieved August 26, 2022, from https://ssrn.com/abstract=3930173

Quetelet, L. A. J. (1839/1969). *A treatise on man and the development of his faculties*. Scholars Facsimiles and Reprints.

Rainie, L., & Fox, S. (2000, November 26). The online health care revolution. *Pew Research Center*. Retrieved August 26, 2022, from www.pewresearch.org/internet/2000/11/26/the-online-health-care-revolution/

Reichelmann, A. V., & Costello, M. (2021). When patriot becomes hate-triot: The relationship between American identity and the production of cyberhate. *American Journal of Criminal Justice*, 46, 956–979. https://doi.org/10.1007/s12103-021-09659-0

Reichelmann, A. V., Hawdon, J., Costello, M., Ryan, J., Blaya, C., Llorent, V., Oksanen, A., Räsänen, P., & Zych, I. (2021). Hate knows no boundaries: Online hate in six nations. *Deviant Behavior*, 42(9), 1100–1111. https://doi.org/10.1080/01639625.2020.1722337

Romano, A. (2008a). Where we were on June 16, 2004–and what it means for November 4, 2008. *Newsweek*. Retrieved July 24, 2022, from https://web.archive.org/web/20080620173241/http://www.blog.newsweek.com:80/blogs/stumper/archive/2008/06/16/the-electoral-map-is-obama-outperforming-kerry-or-is-mccain-outperforming-bush/comments.aspx

Romano, A. (2008b). Making his pitches: Nate Silver, an all-star in the world of baseball stats, may be the political arena's next big draw. *Newsweek*. Retrieved July 25, 2022, from https://web.archive.org/web/20080619111251/http:/www.newsweek.com/id/140469

Rothman, K. J., Gallacher, J. E., & Hatch, E. E. (2013). Why representativeness should be avoided. *International Journal of Epidemiology*, 42(4), 1012–1014. https://doi.org/10.1093/ije/dys223

Shropshire, K., Hawdon, J., & Witte, J. C. (2009). Web-survey design: Balancing measurement, response, and topical interest. *Sociological Methods and Research*, 37(3), 344–370. https://doi.org/10.1177/0049124108327130

Silver, N. (2008, March 1). *Frequently asked questions, last revised 8/7/08*. FiveThirtyEight. Retrieved July 24, 2022, from https://fivethirtyeight.com/features/frequently-asked-questions-last-revised/

Steinmetz, K. F. (2015). Craft(y)ness: An ethnographic study of hacking. *The British Journal of Criminology*, 55(1), 125–145. https://doi.org/10.1093/bjc/azu061

Suresh, K., Thomas, S. V., & Suresh, G. (2011). Design, data analysis and sampling techniques for clinical research. *Annals of Indian Academy of Neurology*, 14(4), 287–290. https://doi.org/10.4103/0972-2327.91951

Szolnoki, G., & Hoffmann, D. (2013). Online, face-to-face and telephone surveys—Comparing different sampling methods in wine consumer research. *Wine Economics and Policy*, 2(2), 57–66. https://doi.org/10.1016/j.wep.2013.10.001.

Thompson, A. J., & Pickett, J. T. (2020). Are relational inferences from crowdsourced and opt-in samples generalizable? Comparing criminal justice attitudes in the GSS and five online samples. *Journal of Quantitative Criminology*, 36(4), 907–932. https://doi.org/10.1007/s10940-019-09436-7

Wang, W., Rothschild, D., Goel, S., & Gelman, A. (2015). Forecasting elections with non-representative polls. *International Journal of Forecasting*, 31(3), 980–991. https://doi.org/10.1016/j.ijforecast.2014.06.001

Witte, J. C., Pargas, R., Mobley, C., & Hawdon, J. (2004). The effects of images in web surveys: A research note. *Social Science Computer Review*, 22(3), 363–369. https://doi.org/10.1177/0894439304264531

Wright, M. F., Wachs, S., Yanagida, T., Sevcikova, A., Dedkova, L., Bayraktar, F., Aoyama, I., Kamble, S. V., Machackova, H., Li, Z., Soudi, S., Lei, L., & Shu, C. (2021). Associations between severity and attributions: Differences for public and private face-to-face and cyber victimization. *American Journal of Criminal Justice*, 46, 843–861 (2021). https://doi.org/10.1007/s12103-021-09660-7

Yeager, D. S., Krosnick, J. A., Chang, L., Javitz, H. S., Levendusky, M. S., Simpser, A., & Wang, R. (2011). Comparing the accuracy of RDD telephone surveys and internet surveys conducted with probability and non-probability samples. *Public Opinion Quarterly*, 75(4), 709–747. https://doi.org/10.1093/poq/nfr020

7

ASSESSING THE WEIGHT OF SOCIAL CAPITAL THEORY IN DIGITAL VICTIMIZATION PATTERNS VIA THE OXFORD INTERNET SURVEYS

'Shawn Smith

Introduction

Long gone are the days when online experiences were a largely solitary affair. The Internet today is every bit a social experience; the fact that access is relegated to web-enabled devices and networks does not make it any less so. With early and rapid adoption of socialization routines facilitated by communication innovations of the Web 2.0 era (e.g., instant message boards, chat rooms, social media) came the drive to reassess preexisting constructivist ideas of social interaction and the meaning extracted from such notions. The work advancing new pathways of theory development in this area is ongoing, but current literature already reveals both significant gains and limitations inspiring scholars to expand analysis and comprehension of digital socialization models and their various effects on online user experiences. To that end, this chapter focuses on what can be learned from expanding the current discourse surrounding victimization experiences in digital settings.

Firstly, we must acknowledge that inquiries concerning negative experiences in digital settings, and specifically that which results from cybercrime offending, have typically centered on the perpetrator. What strategies does the romance scammer employ in the swindling of selected targets? What factors precede acts of cyberbullying? How do online crime syndicates succeed in evading law enforcement? Such ponderings dominate the critical cybercrime landscape.

Yet, what of the cybervictim? What conceptual premises might serve to advance the study and comprehension of victimization patterns within cybercrime scholarship? Are there precepts of existing ecological theories worth exploring toward clearer understanding of digital victimization encounters? The research highlighted in this chapter represents part of a growing effort to address such questions, and more broadly expands the direction of cybercrime scholarship to include the experiences and perspectives of the "microlevel" user.

Scholarship centering on digital victimization, or *cybervictimization*—the process of victimizing others through the use of information and/or communication technologies (Roberts, 2009)—is warranted and sorely needed, given the weight of current literature

DOI: 10.4324/9781003277675-9

suggesting that those who fall prey to deviant behaviors online suffer just as much as any other victim, and perhaps more so. As noted in Cross and colleagues' (2016) study of the experiences of online fraud victims:

> Consistent with prior research . . . the overwhelming majority of participants in this study reported profound emotional and psychological impacts following their victimization. Participants described the fraud as 'devastating', 'soul-destroying', or as an event that 'changed [their] attitude to life'. One admitted having 'a bit of a nervous breakdown' following the fraud, and another claimed the impacts were such that 'it was the first thing I thought about when I woke up and the last thing I thought of before I went to sleep'. Participants described a number of (often interconnected) emotional responses following the fraud. The most common were shame or embarrassment, distress, sadness and anger. Others described stress, worry, shock and loneliness.
>
> *(Cross et al., 2016, p. 4)*

Further worth noting is the substantial financial impact of such victimization. From 2017 to 2021, the U.S. Federal Bureau of Investigations averaged 552,000 complaints of Internet offenses and over 3.74 billion dollars in total losses for each year (FBI Internet Crime Complaint Center, 2021). Comparatively, UK reports of credit card theft, purchase of misrepresented products, and solicitation of bank account information (phishing) rose by at least 5% respectively from 2003–2013 (Dutton et al., 2013), and at an estimated loss of 190 million pounds in 2013 (UK Finance, 2018). These trends remained mostly stable or had risen considerably as of 2022 (Jones, 2022).

Additionally, when compared to victims of offline criminal activity, digital victims often face a tougher challenge in recovering from their victimization. Avoiding reminders of the trauma experienced can be exponentially more difficult for the digital victim (Clevenger & Navarro, 2021; Clevenger et al., 2018), given that remnants of the crime committed against them (i.e., lost personal information, explicit photographs, disparaging comments on message boards) can remain on the Internet and/or connected devices indefinitely. Revenge porn pics can be shared infinitely and remain on countless servers. Identity theft and online fraud victims lose more than just tangible assets; they experience heightened fear/anxiety and lost confidence in a range of other social interactions that many never fully recover from (Abdulai, 2020; Virtanen, 2017; Whitty & Buchanan, 2016). They may also be subjected more often to victim blaming, as some scholars suggest we often assign excessive blame to the cybervictim because we desire to distinguish ourselves from said victim as a coping mechanism (Joyce, 2021). We need to see the cybervictim as somehow complicit in their own targeting, for if we cannot then we risk seeing ourselves in the victim and drawing the conclusion that we are similarly susceptible to such offenses (Joyce, 2021).

These observations notwithstanding, and consistent with the broader history of criminological research in the U.S. and abroad, studies of cybercrime tend to center around some aspect of either the offender or the offending behavior itself. Victim experiences and victimization overall receive comparatively less attention. Consider that cybercrime scholarship published from 2000–2022 reveals that the terms "victim(s)" and "victimization" as foci represent approximately only 7% of total studies published[1] in journals dedicated to the discipline. More light should be shed on such topics given the upward trending of cybervictimization during this same time span (Petrosyan, 2023). Toward advancing cybercrime and digital victimization scholarship, theories surrounding the phenomena must grow as well.

At present, apart from advancements in cyber-routine activities theory (cyber-RAT), theoretical developments focusing on the victims of digital offenses and discovery of factors influencing their experiences are lacking. The research featured in this chapter posited that *social capital theory* particularly warrants closer attention. Does social capital, as represented by trust, organizational participation, and social bonds (the nature and extent of one's formal and informal bonds to friends, family, and other familiars within a social setting) negatively correlate with digital victimization? Or can it also result in increased likelihood of certain victimization occurrences? Such are the types of questions addressed in the following pages.

Digital victimization and routine activities (Ellison et al., 2007; Valenzuela et al., 2009)

Where victimization has been highlighted in cybercrime scholarship, studies centered around routine activities theory (RAT) tend to dominate. This is not without some justification, as the merits of the theory in explaining a variety of online and ICT-based offending have been well-documented (Dodel & Mesch, 2017; Graham & Triplett, 2017; Holt & Bossler, 2009; Kirwan et al., 2018). Often categorized as "cyber-RAT", the research of Kyung-shick Choi and colleagues (2008, 2010, 2017) is especially noteworthy here.

This body of work posits that the more frequent and predictable one's interactions with information and communication technologies (ICTs) are, especially when such interactions are considered "risky" and conducted against a backdrop of insufficient safeguards and motivated offenders, the more likely they will find themselves targeted and experience some form of victimization facilitated through digital means. Examples of ineffective guardianship might include out-of-date or missing virus protections, unsophisticated user credentials, and/or the lax security measures commonplace with WiFi hotspots in public places. Offender motivation can come in numerous ways as well, including but not limited to jilted ex-lovers, radicalized youths, and greedy scammers in search of easy targets. Again, considerable work in this ilk already exists, and this author notes the observations of online financial fraud (Hutchings & Hayes, 2009; Williams, 2016), romance scams (Saad et al., 2018), identity theft (Hutchings & Hayes, 2009; Reyns, 2013; Williams, 2016), and grooming (Wachs et al., 2020) that demonstrate the RAT perspective have been used extensively to argue that the behavior of digital victims tends to be patterned and easy to exploit for prospective offenders.

The offender in this model benefits from the lack of willingness of victims to come forward, and victims tend to be reluctant in reporting their experiences for a variety of reasons. Common among them are a tendency for victims and law enforcement alike to trivialize the full impact of the offending act upon the victim, as well as victims' own self-shaming for falling prey to the offense committed against them (Cross et al., 2016; Halder & Jaishankar, 2011). Underreporting also leads to inaccuracies in the documentation of such crimes, and thus lowering the likelihood of proper safeguards being identified and implemented since the full scope of offending activity becomes much harder to ascertain.

Within both RAT and cyber-RAT literature, gender has warranted particular concern for cybercrime scholars (Henson et al., 2011; Popovic-Citic et al., 2011) in light of varying observations on the propensity of men and women to fall prey to certain online attacks. For instance, despite indications of nearly identical amounts of Internet usage (Pew Research Center, 2017; Popovic-Citic et al., 2011), males have been found more susceptible to cyberbullying (Festl & Quandt, 2016; Popovic-Citic et al., 2011; Zhou et al., 2013), violent threats (Nasi et al., 2015), and online identity theft (Reyns, 2013), while female users have been found prone to mobile-phone bullying (Holt, Fitzgerald, et al., 2016), sexual harassment/solicitation online (Holt, Bossler, et al., 2016; Khurana et al., 2015; Nasi et al., 2015; Saha & Srivastava, 2014), romance scams (Saha & Srivastava, 2014), and other online offenses centered around intimacy and/or deep emotional interactions (Marganski & Fauth, 2013; Saha & Srivastava, 2014).

The likelihood of sexual solicitation (i.e., sexting requests), online harassment, and (in contrast to some studies of roughly the same timeframe), general cyberbullying tends to be higher for females active online versus male cohorts (Holt et al., 2016). Communicating with strangers and posting pictures increases likelihood of sexual victimization online for male users (Holt et al., 2016), while for female audiences the deviant activity of their peers (i.e., viewing sexually explicit material) tended to increase their risk for such victimization (Holt et al., 2016). Communication with strangers, along with prolonged online social activity has also been shown to increase frequency of cyberbullying experienced by female Internet users, while such communication only demonstrated higher victimization for males online when exposed to antisocial media content (Festl & Quandt, 2016). In fact, among both males and females, increased interactivity with strangers and prolonged socializing via outlets like social networks, chatrooms, and message boards have been shown to correlate strongly with a variety of online victimizations (Henson et al., 2011).

Concerning age as a correlate, there is strong evidence that many forms of digital victimization skew toward younger audiences (Bernat & Godlove, 2012; Campbell & Moore, 2011; Fazio & Sgarbi, 2016; Nasi et al., 2015). However, here again conflicting findings are observed. Some scholars have found older audiences become more susceptible to online information theft and fraud when offenders target higher incomes and/or financial activity volume, and in combination with either greater online shopping activity or inexperience with the threats associated with such activities (Jorna, 2016; Reyns, 2013; Williams, 2016). Such exceptions notwithstanding, the prevailing literature generally supports the position that young people are more prone to most online victimization threats.

One major reason for the youth skew in digital victimization concerns the behavioral patterns of younger Internet users. According to the Pew Research Center (2017), Internet users aged 18–29 tend to manage multiple online profiles, access the Internet through multiple devices, and are more willing to accept strangers into their social networks. Each of these behaviors has been associated with higher reports of several negative experiences, including online harassment, cyberstalking, and unwanted online contact both sexual and nonsexual in nature (Henson et al., 2011; Reyns et al., 2016).

Additionally, it is becoming ever more clear that demographic traits like age and gender are by no means solely attributable to the perils one experiences online, and merely being online does not increase one's risk of digital victimization (Reyns et al., 2016). Rather, what you do or are likely to do in such settings underscores much of what is currently observed as digital victimization. As such, an increasingly popular perspective is that certain online activities one regularly engages in tend to attract a specific type of offender at a particular point in time.

Williams (2016), for instance, highlighted the heightened risk of victimization stemming from online commercial activity (i.e., buying and selling goods online), online forum activity, and Internet usage in public settings—all resulting in greater influence over victimization risk than demographic characteristics like age. Among targets chosen by age, the tendency for cybercriminals to prey on younger victims is underscored by the conjunction between both high engagement with digital technologies, and either profound unawareness or (if aware) lack of concern for the dangers of prolonged exposure to the Internet through multiple devices that makes many younger Internet users such suitable targets (Fazio & Sgarbi, 2016).

Compelling as it is, cyber-RAT draws criticisms similar to traditional routine activities theory for its presumption that offenders always assess targets and opportunities from a rational choice position (Kitteringham & Fennelly, 2020), as well as its reliance upon a "spatial" understanding of offending and victimization—a contradiction to the inherently non-spatial nature of the Internet (Leukfeldt & Yar, 2016; Vakhitova et al., 2019; Yar, 2005). Results from cybercrime studies implementing RAT have also proven inconsistent (Williams, 2016), as difficulty in applying certain elements of the theory abounds (Leukfeldt & Yar, 2016). Thus, toward a fuller understanding of digital victimization paradigms, there is justification for consideration of alternative conceptual frameworks. One such framework, *social capital theory*, draws specific attention in this chapter given its preexisting ties to conventional victimization models offline. Does social capital hold relevance in models of digital victimization experiences? If so, how do these models compare with traditional models of social capital and victimization, and what expansion of scholarship concerning digital victimization patterns results from such models?

Conceptualizing digital social capital

While definitions can vary greatly, the core premise of social capital maintains that social bonds carry a variety of attributes that can be leveraged by individuals within a collective toward the benefit of a singular member or the entire collective. Common among these traits are generalized trust, reciprocity, volunteerism, and civic engagement, and social capital is observed when one or more of these traits are applied towards a shared cause or goal deemed important to the collective. The nature of social capital varies by whether it resides amongst members united within a mostly homogenous collective (*bonding social capital*), individuals gathered in more heterogenous groupings (*bridging social capital*), or those residing at different hierarchical levels (*linking social capital*). Individuals and groups alike use social capital as a means of achieving goals (Putnam, 1995, 2000), and the commodity is grounded in relationships and behavioral norms defined by the aforementioned traits (Coleman, 1988, 1990; Halpern, 2005; Neal, 2011; Portes, 1998; Putnam, 2000; Woolcock, 2010). It is an asset in and of itself, as well as an augmentation for other resources.

The latter 20th century experienced a resurgence of interest in social capital theory, and its progression as a focal point of scholarly discourse is documented several times over, due in no small measure to a trio of seminal theorists: James Coleman, Robert Putnam, and Pierre Bourdieu. For Coleman, social capital existed in three basic forms: 1.) the combination of established obligations, expectations, and trustworthiness, 2.) information channels allowing the production of social ties conducive in producing or enhancing information and goal attainment, and 3.) established norms and sanctions of behavior supported by neighborhood residents (Coleman, 1990; Portes, 1998). Putnam defined the concept as the connections between and across groups of social actors that facilitate survival and/or advancement within social settings, along with the norms of generalized trust, reciprocity, and collective action that arise from such connections (Putnam, 2000). Bourdieu's interpretation held that social capital was "the aggregate of the actual or potential resources which are linked to possession of a durable network of more or less institutionalized relationships of mutual acquaintance or recognition" (Bourdieu, 1985, p. 248). He understood social capital as both the connections between social actors that provide mutually beneficial resources, and the quality of these resources. Bourdieu also believed that the resources "which accrue from membership in a group are the basis of the solidarity which makes them possible" (Bourdieu, 1985, p. 249).

Echoing across each of their distinct interpretations is the notion that social capital is linked to social structure and the capacity to incite specific actions from individuals within said structure (Coleman, 1990; Portes, 1998). Simply put, where individuals find reason and means to organize themselves, collective action among said individuals can and often will occur; it is here that social capital lives. Co-opting their work, and with an emphasis on Coleman's and Bourdieu's contributions, the author proffers that virtually any online community can be described in this way. The Internet is home to countless formal organizations and informal groups galvanized by shared goals. These Internet-enabled communities foster social capital by way of shared interests and the forging of collective identities (Kaakinen et al., 2018; Walther & Jang, 2012), which in turn can be engaged for a common good.

Digital social capital was fully observed when, in the investigation and capture of Luka Magnotta for the murder and dismemberment of Concordia University student Jun Lin, online communities of amateur Internet sleuths shed light on Luka's escalating violence patterns (Global News Staff, 2012; Lewis, 2019; Minsky, 2014). In response to a self-produced and posted video of the grisly torture and murder of several kittens by Magnotta himself (in disguise) prior to Lin's murder, users across numerous social media and message platforms were compelled to act in identifying and bringing Magnotta to justice. Emboldened by an unofficial but widely recognized online behavioral standard that "you don't f*ck with cats", these groups—notably, the Facebook group, *Find the Kitten Vacuumer . . . For great justice*—rapidly formed to engage in an international-scale campaign of open-source intelligence gathering and digital forensic investigation (Lewis, 2019). In fact, most accounts of the case acknowledge the role of such informal Internet groups in tipping off law enforcement as to Magnotta's existence and activity even before he was officially investigated for Lin's murder.

Though devoid of any personal connection to or knowledge of Lin, these user groups were nonetheless bonded by an overarching desire to serve a common good by tracking down his killer and putting an end to the violence already witnessed in the previous kitten tortures. In the cohesion and resourcefulness demonstrated by these groups in coordinating months of evidence gathering to track down and expose Magnotta, we saw the capacity of virtual communities to act upon what can only be described as a dynamic blend of bonding and bridging social capital. Further, in true functionalist fashion, these groups also represented a particular consensus on certain established rules of order governing healthy online experiences, and the propensity of online communities to resolve deviations from the behavioral standards deemed acceptable in the spaces they frequent by identifying and seeking the removal of a divergent linked to material or behavior perceived as offensive and/ or detrimental to said order.

Indeed, across the vast and ever-changing expanse that is the Internet, the presence of such collective behaviors bound by shared ideals is a constant. From online social movements like #MeToo to criminal collusion on the dark web, the Internet is home to countless examples of group activity threaded together by shared ideals and objectives. As such, the premise of social capital as theorized by scholars like Coleman and Bourdieu is plausible as a digital construct. Sociologist Chris Julien (2015) surmised as much:

> Social capital exhibits itself in new ways online. It does not remain unchanged in its adaptation to internet culture and communication. Because of the current ubiquitous accessibility of the internet, online interactions themselves contain and extend social capital. As social capital is the aggregate of resources that are connected to member-ship in a specific group, this resource can proliferate on the internet and through the ties and memberships that individuals have there.
>
> *(Julien, 2015) (Bourdieu, 1985)*

Social media platforms like Instagram and Facebook, as well as more nuanced platforms like Discord and Nextdoor.com, allow social bonds to form virtually, and even extend friendship networks in ways otherwise impractical due to the limitations of physical boundaries. Activity in such networks has also been associated with offline manifestations of social capital, and there is some suggestion of overlap between social capital in both online and terrestrial settings (Ellison et al., 2007; Kaakinen et al., 2018; Valenzuela et al., 2009).

Empirical support of digital social capital can be found in Valenzuela and colleagues' (2009) discovery of positive correlations between social network site frequency (notably Facebook) and social trust, civic engagement, and political participation, respectively. Among young voters, online and offline voting participation and activism co-occurs with various measures of social media activity (Bode, 2008; Park, 2015; Zhang & Lin, 2014). Usage of social networking sites like Facebook have also been linked with higher levels of bonding, bridging, and linking social capital (Ellison et al., 2007), and more broadly online and offline social capital have been observed as complimentary where pro-social behavior—voluntary acts intended to benefit other individuals or groups—are a focus (Bosancianu et al., 2013). However, as per the extant victimization literature, social capital does not always produce positive outcomes.

Linking digital victimization and social capital

As with ecological studies of residential neighborhoods, where many have remarked the outcomes of social capital can be both beneficial and detrimental, the author asserts that social capital is just as likely to foster positive and negative experiences online. Some types of victimization may actually flourish under conditions where social capital is high (Medina, 2015). For instance, in Bouchard and colleagues' analysis of school-based victimization (2012), they observed how social capital could impact violent victimization even while failing to influence other forms (i.e., theft victimization). They further suggested that certain social capital-based models could produce even stronger effects on violent victimization than those derived from routine activities premises (Bouchard et al., 2012).

Regarding specific components of social capital, trust features prominently in online romance and fraud scams as a key instrument in the emotional manipulation associated with forging false intimacy (Kopp et al., 2015; Rege, 2009; Whitty, 2013, 2015). Friendship networks have been implicated in studies of "carders"—data thieves who primarily prey on bank and credit cardholders (Soudjin & Zegers, 2012); such offenders are known to collude within like-minded hacker networks found throughout social media spaces

(Al-khateeb et al., 2016). Online social capital has further been implicated in fostering exclusionary spaces, and supporting harmful acts like flaming, trolling, and similar forms of cyberviolence (Burnap et al., 2014; Julien, 2015; Kaakinen et al., 2018).

These insights notwithstanding, gaps in the digital victimization literature have become apparent. For starters, studies modeling the experiences of individual users are less common than macrolevel studies such as what is found in cybersecurity research (where the focus tends to be on the targeting and impact of digital offending on large-scale organizations and government institutions). Some of the bias stems from longstanding preference in research funding towards cybersecurity interests, while some of the scarcity can be attributed to reporting issues among victims themselves (e.g., unawareness of being victimized, uncertainty about reporting procedures, reluctance to report). With respect to exploration of alternative theories like social capital, the prevailing literature is also lacking here for reasons yet to be addressed. However, existing data sources like the 2013 Oxford Internet Surveys provide opportunities to address these gaps and invite positivist speculation on the connection between social capital and victimization experiences online.

OxIS 2013 offered a robust array of measures and sample audiences to address the central questions posed in this chapter. The survey series has been a reputable authority of insight on a variety of intellectual "cyber-concerns", including regulation and governance of the Internet and concerns related to privacy, risk, and trust since 2003. The 2013 iteration was compiled from dual-stage stratified sampling of roughly half of all urban and rural geographic output areas, and represented roughly 2,600 urban and rural residents across the UK (Dutton et al., 2013). Additionally, along with being demographically comparable to the UK national audience in terms of age, gender, and income, this iteration of OxIS carried a particularly robust array of measures[2] consistent with recent empirical work in cybercrime victimization—most notably Reyns and colleagues' study of online stalking (Reyns et al., 2016), Henson's probe of fear of interpersonal violence online (Henson et al., 2013), and Holfeld and Sukhawathanakul's exploration of cybervictimization among adolescents (Holfeld & Sukhawathanakul, 2017).

For estimating social capital, several indicators of trust and socialization in the survey—both prominent measures in social capital models—provided important preliminary groundwork that social capital might be present among these users. Participant responses to these items suggested digital means were preferred for maintaining connections with friends and family (versus older methods such as writing letters). They expressed general confidence in building social connections online; just under 58% reported being at least fairly confident in making new online friends. Responses also indicated moderate generalized trust towards people they communicate with online, Internet service providers, and society overall. Given the ubiquity of phones in present society, and especially smartphones, it was not surprising that using a phone was reported as a preferred method of staying in touch with loved ones both near and far (41% opted to phone weekly with distant friends and relatives; 50% reported opting for this method weekly with loved ones in close physical proximity).

Such mass incorporation of digital technology into the socialization routines of microlevel users comes with considerable victimization risks, and analysis from the OxIS data supported this assertion as well. Computer virus attacks and phishing infractions targeting bank information were the most common negative experiences reported (29% and 18.4% respectively). Binary logistic regression modeling between demographic traits and reported victimization revealed top UK earners (annual income starting at £40K) were especially likely to experience computer virus infractions (ExpB = 1.668; p < .01), while age groups ranging from Millennials to the youngest Gen-Xers (roughly 30–42 years in age) were almost 38% more likely to experience banking-related phishing attacks versus any other cohort (ExpB = 1.376; p < .05). The youngest audience, 14–17-year-olds, were 63% less likely to experience such attacks (ExpB = .366; p < .05)—likely attributable to their lack of significant banking profiles and activity at that age.

18–29-year-olds were more likely to experience harassment through email (ExpB = 1.588; p < .01) and online purchase fraud (ExpB = 1.713; p < .01). The latter fraud, along with credit card information theft, was also more prevalent among £20K—£30K annual income earners: ExpB = 1.512 (p < .05) and ExpB = 1.967 (p < .01), respectively. In contrast, the poorest income group (annual income of £12.5K or lower) were 40% less likely to experience such purchase fraud (ExpB = .604; p < .05) and 84% less likely to have credit card information stolen (ExpB = .155; p < .01). As with the associations observed between age and phishing attacks, the graduated increase in fraud victimization experienced by higher income groups may simply be the result of increased likelihood in meeting the preconditions for such victimization (i.e., greater disposable income and asset attainment).

As noted previously, social media is an area where digital social capital can flourish, and it is plausible activity in such spaces could be leveraged as resources for preempting the victimization events captured in the OxIS 2013 and/or providing a means of coping with such events afterwards. Through various social media connections, communities of concerned users might find and cultivate solidarity with one another, as well as discover additional inspiration to address wrongful acts such as was demonstrated in the aforementioned "kitten killer" campaign that ultimately exposed Luka Magnotta and his role in Jun Lin's murder. Child victimization and protection organizations like the National Center for Missing and Exploited Children regularly engage with social media via posting and content management to publicize their services and alert audiences of threats to children online. Victims of cybercrime regularly seek out support through online groups like the Cybercrime Support Network and Victim Support Scotland to cope with their experiences, build solidarity, and warn others.

However, evidence from further analysis of the OxIS data revealed much contradiction to the premise of social media as a positive force; the data revealed profound *increases* in odds for experiencing each victimization type when social media activity was accounted for. Specifically, the amount of social media one accesses exponentially raised the risk of experiencing each one of the five victimization events measured. The risk was most pronounced for receiving computer viruses (Exp$B$ = 1.223; p < .01), experiencing online fraud (Exp$B$ = 1.233; p < .01), and having credit card details stolen (Exp$B$ = 1.241; p < .01). The odds of experiencing these events grew even stronger when accounting for frequency of social media usage. Across all five models, higher frequencies of social media usage resulted in an even greater likelihood of experiencing each cybervictimization event.

These findings are consistent with several studies citing the connection between social media activity and digital victimization. Despite its notable positive impacts on agenda-setting, political participation, and social activism (especially among younger audiences), a popular concern with social media usage is the potential for exposure to cyberbullying, risky behaviors, and online addiction (Valenzuela et al., 2009). Indeed, there is empirical support for the notion that elevated social media profiles and activity levels result in higher victimization (Kim et al., 2022; Sampasa-Kanyinga & Hamilton, 2015). Cyberbullying, stalking, hate speech, and other forms of harassment appear prominently in studies of social media networks (Cimke & Cerit, 2021; Kim et al., 2022; Wachs et al., 2020), as does increased experience with online fraud (Leukfeldt & Yar, 2016; Wilsem, 2013).

Clearly, great caution is needed in theorizing digital victimization patterns based upon social capital where social media activity is a proxy. At minimum, it would seem premature to assume the interactions facilitated through social media result in any measure of social capital that consistently results in reduced victimization occurrences. Furthermore, social media exposure and frequency have not always produced strong patterns of digital victimization (Ngo & Paternoster, 2011; Vakhitova et al., 2019). Some even contend victimization patterns associated with social media activity are not so much outcomes governed by digital social capital, but rather are manifestations of the *guardianship* component underlying cyber-RAT (Vakhitova et al., 2019).

Alongside concerns stemming from social media activity, additional scrutiny of digital victimization models featuring social capital might be warranted due to how relatively new conceptualization of socialization is as a construct of online behavior. Compared with thousands of years of development in human civilization characterized by social interaction devoid of Internet access, socialization online is still very much a concept-in-progress. As such, theoretical applications of concepts like social capital are still vetted more clearly offline. Accordingly, it would be prudent to also consider traditional interpretations of social capital with respect to digital victimization modeling.

Case in point: formal and informal organizational participation—well established among social capital proxies—was adequately captured among OxIS 2013 measures. Bearing in mind these measures did not specify whether participation entailed maintaining an online presence or required interaction with ICTs as a facet of participation, we nonetheless found the odds ratios between these measures and digital victimization strikingly consistent with those revealed with social media activity. Involvement in trade unions, for instance, suggested increased likelihood of receiving computer viruses ($\text{Exp}B = 1.554$; $p < .05$) and suffering phishing attacks related to credit card details ($\text{Exp}B = 1.988$; $p < .01$). The latter experience with phishing also holds true for involvement in political/campaigning organizations ($\text{Exp}B = 1.928$; $p < .05$) and charity/social aid organizations ($\text{Exp}B = 2.058$; $p < .01$). Participation in charities and/or social aid groups also suggested an increased likelihood of experiencing online harassment by 88% ($\text{Exp}B = 1.888$; $p < .01$).

Concerning participation in sports and/or social clubs, these activities demonstrated statistical significance in all but one victimization model (phishing attacks). Respondents were 68% more likely to experience online harassment ($\text{Exp}B = 1.679$; $p < .01$), 42% more likely to suffer a computer virus ($\text{Exp}B = 1.421$; $p < .01$), 71% more likely to experience online purchase fraud ($\text{Exp}B = 1.710$; $p < .01$), and 89% more likely to have credit card details stolen ($\text{Exp}B = 1.891$; $p < .01$) when involved in a sports or social club. Whether such participation directly causes any of the victimizations reported or is merely the result of some underlying causal factor is unknown. However, here again we find some weight for the possible role of guardians previously highlighted in the extant RAT-themed literature on victimization.

Socialization via sports teams and social clubs carries potential for access to resources for warding off threats or gaining comfort after experiencing a victimization event (Evans et al., 2016; Vakhitova et al., 2019; Vakhitova et al., 2021). The rationale from a social capital lens is that the camaraderie and empathy embedded within informal social bonds are fostered more easily amongst individuals connected under a common set of goals, such as you would find among members of a team or club. Teammates, coaches, fellow club members and supporters of the organizations are then thought to become more capable of and willing to serve as resources of aid should one within their collective find themselves on the receiving end of a negative encounter (e.g., cybercrime targeting). Whether this actually happens or not with respect to digital victimization has yet to be determined, as direct assessments are scarce across the social capital literature. However, RAT studies where sports team and/or social club activity are offered as proxies of guardianship tend to confirm that such associations are indeed viable sources of capable guardians and result in lower risk of digital victimization (Vakhitova et al., 2019; Vakhitova et al., 2021)—a contradiction to the higher likelihood ratios observed in this chapter.

Perhaps the link between social capital and victimization in digital settings is best understood as a three-pronged paradigm where additional factors must "activate" the relationship, and ultimately dictate if social capital or any of its component parts will influence exposure to a digital victimization event. As per Evans and colleagues' research of bullying and cyberbullying in team sports (Evans et al., 2016), where they learned both forms of victimization are more prevalent among participants with weaker connections to their fellow teammates, one such intervening factor may be the *quality* of peer connections upheld within these collectives. They suggest that simply being on a sports team does not result in access to the protective social capital that results from bonds with willing guardians. Rather, one must also have cultivated their social ties within the team dynamic in such a way that social capital—in this case, a firmer sense of social cohesion and obligation to protect—is formed. Having forged these stronger ties, participants should be better positioned to capitalize upon any protective advantages available through their involvement in the collective, while those with weaker ties would likely receive either no such benefits or with diminished effect.

Similarly, it may well be the case that the trust and solidarity one can cultivate through social media connections would only serve to aid in lowering victimization risk online if those bonds are forged with users willing and capable of fulfilling a guardianship role. This would represent an activation of social capital consistent with prevailing theory. Otherwise, these same bonds could be just as easily exploited by prospective offenders adept at infiltrating such communities and pinpointing targets while remaining undetected. In fact, in the absence of tethers to such guardians, heightened online socialization (be it through social media or some other outlet) might be more likely to increase a user's exposure to prospective offenders—many of whom we already know often enjoy a certain amount of social capital via collusion in the effort to acquire such victims.

Conclusion

The research and discourse in this chapter sought to contribute to literature on digital victimization by ascertaining the relevance of factors drawn from social capital theory. To that end, analysis of the OxIS 2013 data did successfully convey important suggestions about the relevance of certain factors for a variety of victimization models. For starters, this work revealed social capital is not always conducive to lower victimization, and this is as much true with targets acquired in digital settings as those in physical spaces. While models incorporating trust were surprisingly unsupported in this research, various forms of socialization and organizational participation yielded quite a bit of evidence of correlation with digital victimization. Such interactions have been known to facilitate several types of victimization, along with reducing many others—patterns consistent with traditional social capital. In this respect, one could say Julien's (2015) premise that social capital exists similarly in the digital world is not only accurate, but so too are its effects on certain phenomena mimicked.

Worth noting is that, though clearly an integral part of social capital as a 21st—century concept, socialization via social media destinations was not particularly high for these survey participants. Most averaged just under two social media destinations regularly managed, and minimal engagement within those outlets. While consistent with observations in recent years that the popularity of social media activity appears to be levelling off (Dutton et al., 2013), it is also true that mainstay destinations like Facebook, Instagram, and LinkedIn have found themselves competing for users more each year with niche sites like Gab.com and Nextdoor.com. Thus, social capital as represented by socialization via social media may no longer be adequately measured by the mainstays alone. The limited activity here may also result from growing wariness among UK audiences towards social media platforms in light of their popularity as spaces for targeting potential victims in numerous cybercrime offenses.

These insights notwithstanding, there were also important limitations in the data and analysis worth noting. For starters, as Fukuyama (2001) precisely noted, social capital is greatly hampered by the absence of agreement on how to measure it. This is no less a concern when considering the digital rendition of the concept. More than likely, it is best defined as the sum of its parts, and thus some omnibus measurement effort is warranted. To the extent that we can reasonably define and properly identify versions of features like trust, socialization, and social bonding online as digital social capital, we can begin to advance the framework of digital victimization theory as many scholars have done with routine activities theory online. Therein lies the first of several challenges ahead in implementing social capital as a scheme for digital victimization modeling—consensus on what should be incorporated into the formula.

In this respect, the constraints of the OxIS for measuring social capital were significant. While it was easily the best option among studies of digital experiences that also contained proxies of social capital, the OxIS 2013 was not a dedicated exploration of the concept. Thus, an argument could be made for devising a similar study with measures more explicitly aimed towards a direct and comprehensive operationalization of social capital—one that distinguishes between variations of bonding, bridging, and linking social capital. (Fukuyama, 2001)

Another consideration would be to address social capital's premise as a commodity intricately tied to both group membership and participation (Bourdieu, 1985; Julien, 2015; Putnam, 1995, 2000). A more concise delineation between one's group networks in digital settings and the reciprocal exchanges that occur for said individual in those networks would serve to further clarify how victimization is impacted. In such an effort, a more direct implementation of social capital—for instance, the Internet Social Scales conceived by Park et al. (2015)—may be useful.

Noting that the OxIS was a study of individual UK residents, a strong case could be made for measuring core concepts like social capital, victimization, and Internet behavior in general as phenomena experienced at an aggregate level. Incorporating units of analyses such as local authority designations or wards might allow for determining stronger models and clearer relationships, as employed in recent work like Rubin's (2016) treatise on reconceptualizing linking social capital in disaster situations, or Bishop's (2017) exploration of social capital's significance in insolvency solutions across England and Wales.

Ultimately, studies designed to specifically measure social capital are sorely lacking. Even with the utility of mass surveys like OxIS, we can only approach an approximation of true social capital. Indirect measures can only carry the advancement of this concept in digital victimization studies so far. Efforts should continue towards explicit measurement of social capital in its various forms.

Digital victimization also stands to gain valuable exposure and clarity through scholarly efforts to expand models of its influential factors and outcomes. As of this publication, such work has been narrow in theoretical rigor, especially with regards to theories outside of the routine activities framework. Considering the ever-growing presence of cybercrime offending and victimization trends in the modern era, along with the advent of virtual communities within the lexicon of ecological scholarship centered around human interactions (Su Wong, 2009), the material presented in this chapter adds to necessary discourse on digital victimization and influences from social capital and its numerous components.

Notes

1 Based upon a literature search of peer-reviewed publications, conducted May 23, 2023, and compiled from the following databases: Academic Search Complete, Computers & Applied Sciences Complete, Criminal Justice Abstracts with Full Text, and SocINDEX with Full Text. Search terms included were the following: cybercrime, computer crime, hacking, cyber security, and cybersecurity.
2 Victimization measures in the OxIS 2013 consisted of self-reports of negative online experiences via dichotomous responses (1 = "Yes"; 0 = "No") to the following items: *received obscene or abusive e-mails, received a virus onto your computer, bought something which was misrepresented on a website, had your credit card details stolen via use on the Internet*, and *been contacted by someone online asking you to provide bank details*.

References

Abdulai, M. (2020). Examining the effect of victimization experience on fear of cybercrime: University students' experience of credit/debit card fraud. *International Journal of Cyber Criminology, 14*(1), 17.
Al-khateeb, S., Conlan, K. J., Agarwal, N., Baggili, I., & Breitinger, F. (2016). Exploring Deviant Hacker Networks (DHN) on social media platforms. *Journal of Digital Forensics, Security, and Law, 11*(2), 14.
Bernat, F., & Godlove, N. (2012). Understanding 21st century cybercrime for the "common" victim, *89*(2). Retrieved from www.crimeandjustice.org.uk/publications/cjm/article/understanding-21st-century-cybercrime-%E2%80%98common%E2%80%99-victim
Bishop, P. (2017). Spatial variations in personal insolvency choices: The role of stigma and social capital. *Urban Studies, 54*(16), 16.
Bode, L. (2008, February 25). *Don't judge a Facebook by its cover: Social networking sites, social capital and political participation* [Annual Meeting of the Midwest Political Science Association, Chicago, IL].
Bosancianu, C. M., Powell, S., & Bratovic, E. (2013). Social capital pro-social behavior online and offline. *International Journal of Internet Science, 8*(1), 20.
Bouchard, M., Wang, W., & Beauregard, E. (2012). Social capital, opportunity, and school-based victimization. *Violence and Victims, 27*(5), 15.
Bourdieu, P. (Ed.). (1985). *The forms of capital*. Greenwood.
Burnap, P., Williams, M. L., Sloan, L., Rana, O., Housley, W., Edwards, A., Knight, V., Proctor, R., & Voss, A. (2014). Tweeting the terror: Modelling the social media reaction to the Woolwich terrorist attack. *Social Network Analysis and Mining, 4*(1), 14.
Campbell, J., & Moore, R. (2011). Self-perceptions of stalking victimization and impacts on victim reporting. *Police Practice and Research, 12*(6), 13.

Choi, K.-S. (2008). Computer crime victimization and integrated theory: An empirical assessment. *International Journal of Cyber Criminology, 2*(1), 27.

Choi, K.-S. (2010). *Risk factors in computer-crime victimization.* LFB Scholarly Publishing LLC.

Choi, K.-S., & Lee, J. R. (2017). Theoretical analysis of cyber-interpersonal violence victimization and offending using cyber-routine activities theory. *Computers in Human Behavior, 73,* 8.

Cimke, S., & Cerit, E. (2021). Social media addiction, cyberbullying and cyber victimization of university students. *Archives of Psychiatric Nursing, 35,* 4.

Clevenger, S., & Navarro, J. (2021). The "third-victimization": The cybervictimization of sexual assault survivors and their families. *Journal of Contemporary Criminal Justice, 37*(3), 22.

Clevenger, S., Navarro, J. N., Marcum, C. D., & Higgins, G. E. (2018). *Understanding victimology: An active-learning approach.* Routledge.

Coleman, J. (1988). Social capital in the creation of human capital. *American Journal of Sociology, 94*(Suppl), 15.

Coleman, J. (1990). *Foundations of social theory.* Harvard University Press.

Cross, C., Richards, K., & Smith, R. G. (2016). *The reporting experiences and support needs of victims of online fraud* [Trends and Issues in Crime and Criminal Justice, Issue]. Retrieved from https://aic.gov.au/publications/tandi/tandi518

Dodel, M., & Mesch, G. (2017). Cyber-victimization preventive behavior: A health belief model approach. *Computers in Human Behavior, 68,* 8.

Dutton, W. H., Blank, G., & Groselj, D. (2013). *Culture of the internet: The internet in Britain* [Oxford Internet Survey 2013, Issue]. University of Oxford.

Ellison, N. B., Steinfeld, C., & Lampe, C. (2007). The benefits of facebook "friends": Social capital and college students' use online social network sites. *Journal of Computer-Mediated Communication, 12*(4), 26.

Evans, B., Adler, A., MacDonald, D., & Cote, J. (2016). Bullying victimization and perpetration among adolescent sport teammates. *Pediatric Exercise Science, 28*(2), 7.

Fazio, L. D., & Sgarbi, C. (2016). Unwanted online attentions among an Italian students sample. *European Journal on Criminal Policy and Research, 22*(2), 15.

FBI Internet Crime Complaint Center. (2021). *Internet crime report 2021.* Retrieved from https://www.ic3.gov/Media/PDF/AnnualReport/2021_IC3Report.pdf

Festl, R., & Quandt, T. (2016). The role of online communication in long-term cyberbullying involvement among girls and boys. *Journal of Youth Adolescence, 45*(9), 14.

Fukuyama, F. (2001). Social capital, civil society, and development. *Third World Quarterly, 22*(1), 13.

Global News Staff. (2012, May 31). Timeline of events: The Luka Magnotta case. *Global News.* https://globalnews.ca/news/251318/timeline-of-events-the-luka-rocco-magnotta-case/

Graham, R., & Triplett, R. (2017). Capable guardians in the digital environment: The role of digital literacy in reducing phishing victimization. *Deviant Behavior, 38*(12), 11.

Halder, D., & Jaishankar, K. (2011). Cyber gender harassment and secondary victimization: A comparative analysis of the United States, the UK, and India. *Victims and Offenders, 4*(4), 13.

Halpern, D. (2005). *Social capital.* Polity Press.

Henson, B., Reyns, B. W., & Fisher, B. S. (2011). Security in the 21st Century: Examining the link between online social network activity, privacy, and interpersonal victimization. *Criminal Justice Review, 36*(3), 16.

Henson, B., Reyns, B. W., & Fisher, B. S. (2013). Fear of crime online? Examining the effect of risk, previous victimization, and exposure on fear of online interpersonal victimization. *Journal of Contemporary Criminal Justice, 29*(4), 23.

Holfeld, B., & Sukhawathanakul, P. (2017). Associations between internet attachment, cyber victimization, and internalizing symptoms among adolescents. *Cyberpsychology, Behavior, and Social Networking, 20*(2), 7.

Holt, T. J., & Bossler, A. M. (2009). Examining the applicability of lifestyle-routine activities theory for cybercrime victimization. *Deviant Behavior, 30,* 24.

Holt, T. J., Bossler, A. M., Malinski, R., & May, D. C. (2016). Identifying predictors of unwanted online sexual conversations among youth using a low self-control and routine activity framework. *Journal of Contemporary Criminal Justice, 32*(2), 20.

Holt, T. J., Fitzgerald, S., Bossler, A., Chee, G., & Ng, E. (2016). Assessing the risk factors of cyber and mobile phone bullying victimization in a nationally representative sample of singapore youth. *International Journal of Offender Therapy and Comparative Criminology, 60*(5), 17.

Hutchings, A., & Hayes, H. (2009). Routine activity theory and phishing victimization: Who gets caught in the 'net? *Current Issues in Criminal Justice, 20*(3), 20.

Jones, P. (2022, September 26). Nature of crime: Fraud and computer misuse year ending March 2022. *Office for National Statistics*. Retrieved from https://www.ons.gov.uk/peoplepopulationandcommunity/crimeandjustice/articles/natureoffraudandcomputermisuseinenglandandwales/yearendingmarch2022

Jorna, P. (2016). The relationship between age and consumer fraud victimisation. *Trends & Issues in Crime and Criminal Justice*, 17. Retrieved from https://aic.gov.au/publications/tandi/tandi519

Joyce, M. (2021). Cybercrimeology. In *From frankenstein to Hulk: Understanding cybervictimology*. Retrieved from www.cybercrimeology.com/episodes/from-frankenstein-to-hulk-understanding-cybervictimology

Julien, C. (2015). Bourdieu, social capital, and online interaction. *Sociology, 49*(2), 18.

Kaakinen, M., Keipi, T., Oksanen, A., & Rasanen, P. (2018). How does social capital associate with being a victim of online hate? Survey evidence From the United States, the United Kingdom, Germany, and Finland. *Policy and Internet, 10*(3), 21.

Khurana, A., Bleakley, A., Jordan, A. B., & Romer, D. (2015). The protective effects of parental monitoring and internet restriction on adolescents' risk of online harassment. *Journal of Youth Adolescence, 44*(5), 8.

Kim, S., Garthe, R., Hsieh, W.-J., & Hong, J. S. (2022). Problematic social media use and conflict, social stress, and cyber-victimization among early adolescents. *Child and Adolescent Social Work Journal*.

Kirwan, G. H., Fullwood, C., & Rooney, B. (2018). Risk factors for social networking site scam victimization among malaysian students. *Cyberpsychology, Behavior, and Social Networking, 21*(2), 5.

Kitteringham, G., & Fennelly, L. J. (2020). Environmental crime control. In L. J. Fennelly (Ed.), *Handbook of loss prevention and crime prevention* (pp. 207–222). Elsevier.

Kopp, C., Layton, R., Sillitoe, J., & Gondal, I. (2015). The role of love stories in romanc scams: A qualitative analysis of fradulent profiles. *International Journal of Cyber Criminology, 9*(2), 13.

Leukfeldt, E. R., & Yar, M. (2016). Applying routine activity theory to cybercrime: A theoretical and empirical analysis. *Deviant Behavior, 37*(3), 17.

Lewis, M. (2019). *Don't F**K with cats: Hunting an internet killer*. Netflix.

Marganski, A., & Fauth, K. (2013). Socially interactive technology and contemporary dating: A cross-cultural exploration of deviant behaviors among young adults in the modern, evolving technological world. *International Criminal Justice Review, 23*(4), 20.

Medina, J. C. (2015). Neighborhood firearm victimization. *Violence and Victims, 30*(1), 16.

Minsky, A. (2014). Luka Magnotta guilty of first-degree murder, sentenced to life in prison. *Global News*. Retrieved from https://globalnews.ca/news/1735929/jury-reaches-verdict-in-luka-magnotta-trial/

Nasi, M., Oksanen, A., Keipi, T., & Rasanen, P. (2015). Cybercrime victimization among young people: A multi-nation study. *Journal of Scandinavian Studies in Criminology and Crime Prevention, 16*(2), 8.

Neal, D. L. (2011). *Social capital and urban crime*. LFB Scholarly Publishing.

Ngo, F., & Paternoster, R. (2011). Cybercrime victimization: An examination of individual and situational level factors. *International Journal of Cyber Criminology, 5*(1), 20.

Park, C. S. (2015). Pathways to expressive and collective participation: Usage patterns, political efficacy, and political participation in social networking sites. *Journal of Broadcasting & Electronic Media, 59*(4), 18.

Park, S., Kim, E.-M., & Na, E.-Y. (2015). Online activities, digital media literacy and networked individualism of Korean youth. *Youth & Society, 47*(6), 20.

Petrosyan, A. (2023). Annual number of incoming complaints about internet crime on the IC3 website from 2000 to 2022. *Statistica.com*. Retrieved from www.statista.com/statistics/267546/number-of-complaints-about-us-internet-crime/

Pew Research Center. (2017). *Internet and broadband fact sheet*. Retrieved from www.pewinternet.org/fact-sheet/internet-broadband/

Popovic-Citic, B., Djuric, S., & Cvetkovic, V. (2011). The prevalence of cyberbullying among adolescents: A case study of middle schools in Serbia. *School Psychology International*, *32*(4), 12.

Portes, A. (1998). Social capital: Its origins and applications in modern sociology. *Annual Review Sociology*, *24*, 23.

Putnam, R. D. (1995). Bowling alone: America's declining social capital. *Journal of Democracy*, *6*(1), 13.

Putnam, R. D. (2000). *Bowling alone: The collapse and revival of American community*. Simon & Shuster.

Rege, A. (2009). What's love got to do with it? Exploring online dating scams and identity fraud. *International Journal of Cyber Criminology*, *3*(2), 18.

Reyns, B. W. (2013). Online routines and identity theft victimization: Further expanding routine activity theory beyond direct-contact offenses. *Journal of Research in Crime and Delinquency*, *50*(2), 23.

Reyns, B. W., Henson, B., & Fisher, B. (2016). Guardians of the cyber galaxy: An empirical and theoretical analysis of the guardianship concept from routine activity theory as it applies to online forms of victimization. *Journal of Contemporary Criminal Justice*, *32*(2), 20.

Roberts, L. D. (2009). Cyber-victimization. In R. Luppicini & R. Adell (Eds.), *Handbook of research on technoethics* (pp. 575–592). IGI Global. Retrieved from https://doi.org/10.4018/978-1-60566-022-6.ch037

Rubin, O. (2016). The political dimension of "linking social capital": Current analytical practices and the case for recalibration. *Theory and Society*, *45*(5), 20.

Saad, M. E., Abdullah, S. N. H. S., & Murah, M. Z. (2018). Cyber romance scam victimization analysis using routine activity theory versus apriori algorithm. *International Journal of Advanced Computer Science and Applications*, *9*(12), 6.

Saha, T., & Srivastava, A. (2014). Indian women at risk in the cyber space: A conceptual model of reasons of victimization. *International Journal of Cyber Criminology*, *8*(1), 12.

Sampasa-Kanyinga, H., & Hamilton, H. A. (2015). Social networking sites and mental health problems in adolescents: The mediating role of cyberbullying victimization. *European Psychiatry*, *30*(8), 6.

Soudjin, M., & Zegers, B. (2012). Cybercrime and virtual offender convergence settings. *Trends in Organized Crime*, *15*(2/3), 19.

Su Wong, F. (2009). *Virtual communities: Bowling alone, online together*. Peter Lang Publishing, Inc.

UK Finance. (2018). *Fraud the facts 2018: The definitive overview of payment industry fraud*. Retrieved from https://www.ukfinance.org.uk/system/files/2021-11/Fraud-the-facts-August-2018.pdf

Vakhitova, Z. I., Alston-Knox, C. L., Reynald, D. M., & Townsley, M. K. (2019). Lifestyles and routine activities: Do they enable different types of cyber abuse? *Computers in Human Behavior*, *101*, 12.

Vakhitova, Z. I., Go, A., & Alston-Knox, C. L. (2021). Guardians against cyber abuse: Who are they and why do they intervene? *American Journal of Criminal Justice*.

Valenzuela, S., Park, N., & Kee, K. F. (2009). Is there social capital in a social network site?: Facebook use and college students' life satisfaction, trust, and participation. *Journal of Computer-Mediated Communication*, *14*(4), 27.

Virtanen, S. M. (2017). Fear of cybercrime in Europe: Examining the effects of victimization and vulnerabilities. *Psychiatry, Psychology, and Law*, *24*(3), 15.

Wachs, S., Michelsen, A., Wright, M. F., Gámez-Guadix, M., Almendros, C., Kwon, Y., Na, E.-Y., Sittichai, R., Singh, R., Biswal, R., Görzig, A., & Yanagida, T. (2020). A routine activity approach to understand cybergrooming victimization among adolescents from six countries. *Cyberpsychology, Behavior, and Social Networking*, *23*(4), 6.

Walther, J. B., & Jang, J.-W. (2012). Communication processes in participatory websites. *Journal of Computer-Mediated Communication*, *18*(1), 14.

Whitty, M. T. (2013). The scammers persuasive techniques model: Development of a stage model to explain the online dating romance scam. *British Journal of Criminology*, *53*, 19.

Whitty, M. T. (2015). Anatomy of the online dating romance scam. *Security Journal*, *28*, 12.

Whitty, M. T., & Buchanan, T. (2016). The online dating romance scam: The psychological impact on victims—Both financial and non-financial. *Criminology & Criminal Justice*, *16*(2), 18.

Williams, M. (2016). Guardians upon high: An application of routine activities theory to online identity theft in europe at the country and individual level. *British Journal of Criminology*, *56*, 29.

Wilsem, J. V. (2013). 'Bought it, but never got it' assessing risk factors for online consumer fraud victimization. *European Sociological Review, 29*(2), 10.

Woolcock, M. (2010). The rise and routinization of social capital, 1988–2008. *Annual Review of Political Science, 13*, 21.

Yar, M. (2005). The novelty of 'cybercrime': An assessment in light of routine activity theory. *European Journal of Criminology, 2*(4), 20.

Zhang, X., & Lin, W.-Y. (2014). Political Participation in an Unlikely place: How individuals engage in politics through social networking sites in China. *International Journal of Communication, 8*.

Zhou, Z., Tang, H., Tian, Y., Wei, H., Zhang, F., & Morrison, C. (2013). Cyberbullying and its risk factors Chinese high school students. *School Psychology International, 34*(6), 17.

8

METHODOLOGICAL AND ETHICAL CONSIDERATIONS IN CYBERBULLYING RESEARCH

Aleš Bučar Ručman and Ajda Šulc

Introduction

Most authors understand cyberbullying simply as bullying via information-communication technology (Gladden et al., 2014; Kowalski et al., 2008; Olweus, 2017). This is also how cyberbullying is contextualized in the general English-speaking environment, which is clear from the definition in Oxford English Dictionary. Cyberbullying is defined as "the use of information technology to bully a person by sending or posting text or images of an intimidating or threatening nature" (Oxford University Press, n.d.). From this aspect, cyberbullying is seen as one of several forms of general bullying, i.e., negative intentional actions of one or several perpetrators, repeated several times or carried out for a long time against a victim who feels discomfort (Olweus, 1993). This basic definition set by a pioneer in bullying research, Dan Olweus, later added an important specific of power or strength imbalance between the perpetrator and the victim, causing the latter to have a hard time defending her- or himself. Based on this, we can distinguish bullying from general violence or aggression among equally powerful individuals (Griffin & Gross, 2004; Olweus & Limber, 2018; Smith et al., 2012). On the other hand, we cannot set the criteria so straightforwardly for cyberbullying since the actions performed in the cyber environment are significantly changing some fundamental aspects of communication and personal relations. Consequently, what seems to be a simple definition at first glance turns out to be one of reasons for several methodological issues in cyberbullying research, causing inconsistencies among worldwide studies in the conceptualization and operationalization of the construct.

As far as cyberbullying as a phenomenon is concerned, debates about it started around 30 years ago, when the term was (supposedly) first mentioned in New York Times article in 1995 and discussed and defined in 2003 when Bill Belsey created the first website on the topic (i.e., www.cyberbullying.ca/). The first scientific research started in North America at the beginning of the century (Smith, 2018)—the Cyberbullying Research Center has been surveying American middle and high school students since 2002 (Patchin, 2022). Research in European countries followed soon after and surpassed US activities after 2012, with an increasing number of EU programs funding cyberbullying research (Smith, 2019). The growing number of studies in the last decade might help detect the prevalence and nature

DOI: 10.4324/9781003277675-10

of cyberbullying among children and adolescents, but only if the results are valid. Nevertheless, the methodological quality of research in this field is still severely under-discussed, which opens some essential concerns about the validity, reliability and comparability of different studies. Authors reviewing previous empirical literature note a significant predominance of quantitative, cross-sectional studies reporting prevalence rates and negative consequences from self-reported surveys and witness behaviour from experiments as the second most widely used method (Chan et al., 2021; Smith, 2019). However, vast divergences in results (Patchin & Hinduja, 2012; Smith, 2019) indicate the need for consistent methodology based on methodological studies on cyberbullying research that we currently lack. There are some studies either researching or at least considering the quality of the research, but those are scarce. For example, some of the earliest authors addressing this were Tokunaga (2010), who discussed the importance of definition and operationalization of the construct; Topcu and Erdur-Baker (2010), and Cetin et al. (2011) were studying the quality of measuring instruments with additional qualitative methods, and statistical validity analyses, such as Del Rey et al. (2015) did on an international sample. A significant contribution was also made by studies researching either the terminology (e.g., Nocentini et al., 2010) or definitions used by children and adolescents for this type of behaviour (e. g. Betts & Spenser, 2017; Naruskov et al., 2012; Nocentini et al., 2010; Vandebosch & Van Cleemput, 2008). Some latter studies also address cyberbullying research methodology, mainly conceptualizations and research methods used (Bauman et al., 2012; Olweus & Limber, 2018; Vandebosch & Green, 2019a).

The starting point of this chapter is characterized by an acceptance of the positivistic notion that social phenomena can be researched and measured, though this requires diligent and systematic work at all stages of research. Effective research planning, precise conceptualization, careful operationalization and rigorous analysis contribute to the validity, reliability and generalizability of research. However, accepting only one theoretical approach often overlooks other conclusions and findings. Therefore, in our approach, we also include other theoretical perspectives and question the methods used in cyberbullying research through the lenses of interactionism and critical theory. Our investigation is guided by the following research questions: What are the fundamental characteristics of research methods and approaches used in the study of cyberbullying? How do researchers employ different methods? Are specific methods predominantly used, or they use a combination and complementary use of various methods (i.e. mixed method approach)? What insights can we gain about the methodological approach from existing methods, and how can we overcome the potential pitfalls and limitations? Since cyberbullying includes sensitive topics (victimization and harm) and a vulnerable population (school children and youth), we also consider the basic ethical recommendations for cyberbullying research.

The research methods employed to address the aforementioned questions involve a precise examination of existing cyberbullying studies, with a specific focus on their research methods. We shed light on these cyberbullying studies by critically evaluating their research methods and approaches, taking into account insights from methodological references. We incorporated the research method inference (Barakso et al., 2014), which leads to amalgamation of the existing knowledge about cyberbullying research methods and general knowledge about social science research methods. Our approach follows a causal inference perspective, exploring potential (negative) consequences associated with specific cyberbullying research methods and proposing potential modifications to overcome such challenges.

In the following sections we discuss research dilemmas connected to terminology and conceptualization, qualitative and quantitative research methods, reflect on the need for mixed methods approach and finally present ethical considerations within cyberbullying research.

Conceptualization and terminology

Terminology

In the English language, the term *cyberbullying* has been widely used and agreed upon by most researchers and the general public. Nevertheless, there are still some inconsistencies in the use of the term. Rare authors tend to use several expressions to describe a general concept of cyber violence, with cyberbullying being one of them—besides aggression, violence, harassment and similar (e.g., Baić et al., 2017; Popovac & Leoschut, 2012; Turan et al., 2011). Popovac and Leoschut (2012, p. 1) —argue that all those terms, with the added adjective "on-line" or "cyber", "refer to violence and aggression perpetrated through ICTs". Similarly, some authors also use stalking, mobbing, abusing and teasing when discussing what could be described as cyberbullying (Nocentini et al., 2010; Smith et al., 2012). They do not seem to distinguish between violence and bullying on-line; even though for traditional bullying (i.e. bullying in the physical world), authors tend to agree that it represents a specific *form* of violence and is, therefore, a much narrower concept. If we understand cyberbullying as a type of bullying, there should be a clear distinction from general violence via ICT. The first stage of this distinction is, in fact, the use of correct and distinguishing terms and appropriate definition of the concept.

What seems to be a more challenging task is a translation of *(cyber-)bullying* to other languages that do not have a specific single term that would describe such actions and can sometimes only describe them with a definition (Završnik, 2013). In most languages, there have been attempts to translate it with expressions that can vary even among authors from the same country but also seem to indicate different types of violence across languages. A term used in one language can emphasize a different aspect of the concept compared to the term used in another language, which is primarily due to cultural differences and perceptions of violence or aggression (Smith et al., 2012). Since there is no identical expression in most languages, they usually use either too wide (referring to violence or aggression in general) or too specific terminology that narrows the meaning to only a part of the behaviour. One of the possible solutions some authors use is importing the English term *(cyber-) bullying* into national languages.[1] Still, others warn this might lead to insufficient consideration of cultural context specific to a particular society (Canty et al., 2014).

Using the appropriate term in non-English languages is an important starting point in addressing and researching the problem but should not be decided on without consideration. For example, discussions in focus groups or interviews with representatives of the target population before the start of the data collection turn out to be significantly helpful in addressing this issue.

Defining the concept

Additional inconsistencies identified among researchers worldwide refer to the concept's definition and operationalization. Regarding the definition, most authors agree that

151

cyberbullying is a form of bullying and should therefore be considered as such, with all its inclusion criteria. These include intentional and repetitive aggressive acts, carried out by an individual or a group. In this process, a victim has a hard time defending him/herself, and victimization is committed by ICT (Smith et al., 2008). However, this relatively simple and exact definition faces some inconsistency in further operationalization, because some of the characteristics get different meanings when transferred into cyberspace (Dooley et al., 2009). First, the intent to harm might be more abstract than in the physical world, where the perpetrator gets direct feedback about the victim's emotional response to his actions. With indirect communication via ICT, there is a chance of misinterpretation of actions by the victim or bystander. The latter might understand a particular communication as hostile, or even cyberbullying, even though the "victim" does not perceive it as such. This might be the case when slightly aggressive wording is regularly used between friends who do not feel victimized by it (Bauman, 2012). A meaningful proposal for adaptation to these specifics is to form the criteria as an act that is intended to harm or can be recognized as an act that *could* hurt someone and which actually *caused* a negative effect on the victim (The Council of Europe, 2018). Second, the repetition in cyberspace does not necessarily demand several repetitions of acts by perpetrators but is more or less reflected as repetitive or long-lasting victimization based on sharing, liking or otherwise spreading harmful content in cyberspace. The feeling of powerlessness and shame of the victim and his or her social and emotional damage is repetitive (Dooley et al., 2009; Gaffney et al., 2019). It is, therefore, too narrow to understand it as simply as *repeating* acts. Third, the power imbalance does not solely depend on physical strength or social power, as in traditional bullying. It is mainly the consequence of better ICT skills, the anonymity of the perpetrator, and the potential of uncontrollable spread of derogatory content to a vast number of users, giving the victim a hard time stopping it or acting against it (Bauman, 2012; Smith et al., 2012; The Council of Europe, 2018). For the victim, this might reflect a feeling of intense insecurity from not knowing who has seen the content or even believing it has been seen by many peers and having no power to stop the spread.

Literature review reveals that most researchers do define cyberbullying as described here. However, they still do not consider some of its criteria or specifics when measuring it. Within operationalization, authors should primarily consider the victim's feelings, especially when measuring with self-report instruments. Asking about the act itself, or acts witnessed by a third party unfamiliar with the communication dynamics, might lead to mistakenly measuring playful teasing between friends, a single act of violence that did not cause a significant adverse effect for a victim or another much broader concept of cyber aggression as cyberbullying. Several systematic reviews of cyberbullying instruments used in existing studies (Berne et al., 2013; Frisén et al., 2013; Vivolo-Kantor et al., 2014) found that most instruments did not offer adequate definitions. They were missing at least one of the crucial criteria of cyberbullying, and authors rarely reported the reliability or validity of their data. Even more, Chun et al. (2020) found that only 23% of studies used at least one additional method directed towards the development of valid scales used in surveys, while others either modified pre-existing scales or simply generated them without additional steps to ensure the quality. Olweus and Limber (2018) argued that because of such operationalization divergences, many of the previous study results on cyberbullying are, in fact, incomparable or even contradictory. The measured occurrence of cyberbullying involvement among children and adolescents ranges from only 1% to 50% (Olweus, 2017) or even 72% (Juvonen & Gross, 2008). This might mainly be due to the non-consistent time frame of measured involvement—from "in last week" to "anytime" or a different understanding of the repetitiveness and impact on the victim, but also because of significantly different samples (Olweus, 2017; Ybarra, 2012).

However, not all authors agree on the definition of cyberbullying that derives from the conventional bullying concept. For example, Law et al. (2012a) argue that because of the aforementioned specifics of cyberbullying criteria, cyberbullying can be hardly distinguished from general cyber aggression. Further, almost every aggression in cyberspace might meet these criteria. All aggressive acts of a person who is anonymous or has good ICT skills show a power imbalance. Similarly, any content that spreads or can potentially spread through the internet is consequently repetitive from the potential victimization point of view. In another study, Law et al. (2012b) try to justify this perspective with the findings that perpetrators in cyberspace are significantly different from those in traditional bullying. In the cyber environment, weaker and introverted students also carry out aggression. Additionally, there are considerably more people involved as both victims and perpetrators in the on-line world, and they tend to understand some of the elements of cyber aggression differently than the supposedly identical elements of traditional bullying.

Divergences in definitions and understandings of the concept are causing even more inconsistencies among studies questioning the validity of some of the previous findings. The dilemma about cyberbullying being part of bullying or not can be solved by the conclusions of Menesini et al. (2013). They found that when children assess whether a particular behaviour is considered cyberbullying, the most important criterion is the imbalance of power—which is similar to traditional bullying. Those findings might indicate that children themselves understand cyberbullying as a subset of bullying, and therefore inclusion of bullying criteria within the conceptualization of cyberbullying research is in accordance with children's perception of the concept.

Specifics of cyberbullying research

Discussions on peer cyberbullying are not new, but from the methodological point of view, this field is still underdeveloped. Non-existent agreement on the usage of terms (especially in non-English speaking countries) and conceptualization is just a part of what makes researching this concept complex. Never-ending changes in technology, communication and interpersonal relations trends in the cyber world require constant follow-up. It is important to note that young people tend to develop their relationships in the cyber world differently than in the physical world and that these represent an essential part of their everyday life (Spears & Zeederberg, 2012). Children are sometimes reluctant to honestly report involvement in deviant acts on-line because they are worried about possible restrictions on their ICT use from their parents (Mishna & Van Wert, 2012). To overcome this, participants must be assured that their involvement in the research is anonymous, that their honest answers are encouraged and that no penalties or sanctions are associated with their participation in the survey. This can be done with the explanation that their answers are important for better understanding and responding to cyberbullying (McCarry, 2012), and especially within qualitative methods, enabling them to speak about "what they heard or know" instead of asking them directly about their own experiences (Mishna & Van Wert, 2012).

In addition to these specifics, researching cyberbullying among peers targets a specific population of children and adolescents. Researchers must be aware that young people might understand and form their relations differently than adults, especially on-line. When planning the research and analysing the results, we must proceed from their understanding of the processes, acts and the concept itself. The researchers must be well informed and up to date with ICT to be taken seriously and to understand the meaning of some specifics (Mishna & Van Wert, 2012).

Quantitative research methods

Until now, cyberbullying has been predominately researched with quantitative methods. Smith and Berkkun (2017) report that 93% of the studies collected exclusively quantitative data, while only 7% used qualitative or mixed methods. While questionnaires and experiments offer an essential insight into the incidence of cyberbullying and causal relationships, their limitations need to be taken into account.

By far the most common quantitative research method used is the *survey*. Children and adolescents are asked about their victimization, perpetration or witnessing cyberbullying events, along with their characteristics, risk factors, consequences, attitudes towards particular behaviour and similar issues. It allows a researcher to identify the prevalence of behaviour and types of cyberbullying, its location and correlations with respondents' characteristics (Espinoza & Juvonen, 2012; Vandebosch & Green, 2019b). If sampled appropriately, findings can be generalized to the population, re-calculated and statistically assessed for possible errors (Creswell, 2013). In addition, survey data enables the calculation of validity and reliability measures, such as Factor analysis and Cronbach alpha coefficient (Card, 2012), which can be an important contribution to the research quality verification.

However, survey results might be prone to some crucial measurement errors. Since surveys are usually self-administered, some respondents might interpret specific questions differently than they are meant or find them too complicated. Additionally, because they typically ask direct questions about victimization or perpetration for studying prevalence, we should expect limited willingness to answer honestly, especially from children and adolescents. As we discussed, the frequency estimate of children's involvement significantly depends on how the concept is operationalized. For example, Ybarra et al. (2012) found that when young people are asked about their experiences with acts that might be categorized as cyberbullying, they report higher prevalence rates as compared to the direct question about victimization. With follow-up questions asked to check for misclassification, authors found that questions based on a list of acts probably measure another concept, which is broader than cyberbullying. It is therefore crucial either to ask directly about victimization or to ask additional questions to confirm that the person did feel like a victim and that other criteria were also met. On the other hand, a direct question about whether a person has cyberbullied someone else might feel too intrusive and deflect the respondent from confessing his perpetration. Concerning this dilemma, ensuring respondents' anonymity and gaining their trust is crucial. As surveys for children and adolescents are usually conducted in schools, it might be essential to eliminate the possible influence of other students' or teachers' presence to ensure the respondents do not worry about negative consequences for their honesty and therefore give mainly socially desirable answers. Another critical issue, especially with younger participants, is the length of the survey. Galesic and Bosnjak (2009) found that the longer the survey, the fewer respondents complete the questionnaire and that questions at the end are answered faster and more superficially.

Generally, it is vital to ensure that the questionnaire will produce valid and reliable data. Using valid scales that enable additional calculation of validity and reliability measures is one way to improve quality. Still, the adequacy and comprehensibility of the survey content cannot be guaranteed without additional qualitative methods. Before conducting a survey, a researcher should follow at least some of the recommended guidelines for developing the used scales, which include expert reviews, pilot studies, focus group interviews and similar (Chun et al., 2020). Especially in a field such as cyberbullying, which lacks adequate methodological discussions and solutions, research solely with the survey can hardly ensure valid data.

The second quantitative research method that has been less often used for researching cyberbullying is an *experiment*. Unlike a survey, experiments allow testing for causal relationships between chosen variables by manipulating specific interferences in a controlled environment that creates a better foundation for validity. Therefore, it is possible to measure the exact impact of certain events; for example, of different types or circumstances of cyberbullying, on how involved children emotionally experience it (Espinoza & Juvonen, 2012) or how bystanders react to it (Schacter et al., 2016). Although this is an important and possibly valid contribution to exploring relationships, one can only test specifically elaborated hypotheses with exactly specified interferences to be researched. To create such a controlled environment, the researcher must be familiar with existing characteristics that she/he can alter and the dynamics in peer relationships that might be important in cyberbullying events. This requires a certain degree of familiarity with the phenomenon, either from a comprehensive literature review or from preceding in-depth qualitative research.

Qualitative research methods

Although quantitative research in cyberbullying is more often used than qualitative (Smith, 2019), this does not mean that qualitative methods are not appropriate for such research. On the contrary, as Hennink et al. (2020) suggest qualitative research can be used for various aims, and we can connect many of them directly to cyberbullying research. For example, we can get insight into behaviour, beliefs, opinions and emotions from the study participants' perspective—something closely related to Weber's sociological approach entitled *Verstehen*. Qualitative methods step into the background of social phenomena and gather material for writing stories through participants' eyes, and through this enlighten specific phenomena with details. As Hammarberg et al. (2016) say, "these data are usually not amenable to counting or measuring" or, in other words, cannot be gathered by quantitative methods. Further, qualitative research helps to detect the meaning people give to their experiences (e.g., consequences of being a victim, perpetrator or witness of cyberbullying). Qualitative research also helps to understand social interactions, norms, and values (e.g., why cyberbullying happens, how and when young people perceive a specific situation as cyberbullying and how other people react when they are informed about cyberbullying). Finally, according to Hennink et al. (2020), qualitative research is used to examine new and also sensitive topics. Cyberbullying fulfils both criteria. One of the basic characteristics of cyberspace is its constant change and implementation of new technologies. New devices, programs and applications are constantly developed, and new forms of cyberbullying are following this path. Further, research showing the negative consequences and impacts of cyberbullying on victims and perpetrators (Kowalski et al., 2014) clearly illustrates this topic's sensitivity. As summarized by Dennehy et al. (2020), cyberbullying is a serious public health problem and a known risk to young people's health and well-being.

Qualitative research uses various methods to gather data. Most commonly, authors use various types of (individual) interviews. It depends on the focus of their research and who is included in the sample. To gather victims' voices, they include youngsters who were already exposed to cyberbullying (Ranney et al., 2020; Wang et al., 2019). For a broader understanding of the phenomena and its conceptualization they interview youngsters in general (i.e., potential victims, perpetrators and bystanders) (Rafferty & Vander Ven, 2014). Sometimes they include other people familiar with the topic, e.g., public school administrators (Young et al., 2017). Aside from individual interviews, researchers use focus groups (Navarro & Serna, 2016; Vandebosch & Van Cleemput, 2008). Interviews are mainly conducted face-to-face, though in some cases, researchers use on-line support and even survey forms with open-ended questions (Rafferty & Vander Ven, 2014). Another approach includes the use of written vignettes about cyberbullying, combined with writing down responses (Evans et al., 2016) and the use of vignettes (Berne et al., 2014) or video materials or films (Dobson, 2019) to encourage the discussion in focus groups. Green et al. (2022) conclude that in recent decades qualitative research in cyberbullying has matured and moved to a more holistic approach with co-participatory methodologies. A higher amount of qualitative research also opened the possibility of conducting in-depth literature reviews (Thornberg, 2011) and qualitative meta-studies, which offer a synthesis of various research on cyberbullying (Dennehy et al., 2020; Green et al., 2022).

Qualitative research provides many possibilities for the collection of data, though not all of them are appropriate for cyberbullying research.[2] Aside from the well-known rule that there is no research without intense pre-planning and pre-training of researchers, researchers have to constantly bear in mind that studying traumatic events and processes—such as cyberbullying—can be very challenging for participants and researchers as well (Fahie, 2014). Throughout the study, researchers must consider the position of (possible) victims and prevent secondary victimization. There are various options for collecting data more efficiently and without additionally exposing the victims (e.g. individual interviews are in these cases preferable over the focus groups). Researchers have to plan their study and organize the approach in a way that prevents the confrontation of possible victims and offenders. However, focus groups can offer a better understanding of some issues than individual interviews (e.g., a general conceptualization and classification of specific acts of cyberbullying among young people). In these situations, the composition of groups has to be carefully planned. Greater anonymity among groups of strangers compared to acquaintances can lead to more detailed discussions (Hennink et al., 2020). Collection of qualitative data can also be organized with information technology—from assembling and studying the existing stories and narratives, photos, records of on-line exchanges, and other digital traces of cyberbullying to the use of technology for conducting interviews (Green et al., 2019).[3] Cyberbullying researchers can also apply another helpful method for collection of qualitative data, which was used decades ago by Cohen (1972) in his research on moral panic, i.e. students writing anonymous essays on various perspectives on cyberbullying—updated to the current situation, this can be done through the use of on-line forms.

Mixed methods research

As we discussed earlier, every method has its benefits and limitations. Quantitative data gives us essential insight into the prevalence of certain behaviours or attitudes and causal relationships among specific elements, which can be generalized to a population if collected from a representative sample. Meanwhile, qualitative methods allow exploring the motives, meanings and interpretations of those involved (Espinoza & Juvonen, 2012). Qualitative methods are also recommended for researching topics that are either under-researched in general or when previous research does not yet allow a comprehensive understanding of the concept and the key elements that define it (Creswell, 2013). However, as Green et al. (2022) conclude, qualitative studies are typically not considered generalizable or replicable. They claim that qualitative methods are frequently triangulated (or, more precisely, mixed or combined)[4] with other research approaches, strengthening the findings and making them applicable to other situations. Smith (2019: 9) clearly sees "the need for more longitudinal studies, and also more qualitative and mixed methods approaches" in cyberbullying research. Combining different research methods can significantly increase the depth and integrity and, above all, the quality of collected data.

The need for integration of methods in the first place originates in inconsistent operational definitions, as well as a non-existent adequate translation for *cyberbullying* in some languages. Consequentially, there is a high chance of unintentionally measuring different concepts among studies or even among respondents in the same study. To prevent that, it is important to first harmonize the understanding of studied concepts among participants, as well as among researchers, and clarify some conceptual and operational dilemmas to ensure consistency (Mishna & Van Wert, 2012). This requires a process-oriented research method or pilot study to be conducted before the actual data collection. Proceeding from the ever-changing trends in ICT use among young people, this approach also reduces the possibility that any of the possibly undiscovered forms of cyberbullying, which previous knowledge and thus survey questionnaires did not detect yet, would not be investigated (Smith, 2019). In fact, this applies to a broader field of children's interpersonal relations, especially in cyberspace, that might be subjected to their specific way of experiencing certain behaviours, as well as to the research conducted on children in general. It is advised to perform interviews or focus groups with the target population beforehand to assure that the measuring instrument, planned for the actual research, is clearly formulated, uses vocabulary appropriate and comprehensible for a specific age and is relevant in terms of content (Balakrishnan, 2017; Purdy & Mc Guckin, 2015).

An additional argument for using a mixed-methods approach relates to meaningfulness in addressing different responders in the sense of data source combination. Depending on who we want to include, we need to implement various data collection methods adapted to their roles in researched events or relationships. When researching with children, measurement instruments or even methods should be adapted to their age, developmental, cognitive, communication and social capacities (Heary & Hennessy, 2002). On the other hand, if we also want to include the aspects of parents, teachers or other actors, one will want to use different methods and focus on different content than with children (Vandebosch & Van Cleemput, 2008). Grown-ups who work with children can also significantly contribute to the research plan in the first steps of the research, especially if they are aware of the dynamics of children's relations.

Since cyberbullying is a specific topic, highly dependent on children's subjective understanding of events and relations, respondents from the target population can also contribute significantly to interpretation of previously collected quantitative or qualitative data. They can explain certain contexts that are better known to them than to adult researchers (Shaw et al., 2011). Since the implementation of such sequential explanatory research design is fairly simple, it is relatively often used by researchers studying cyberbullying with mixed methods.

Ethical considerations

Research in social sciences needs special ethical considerations. This complex and demanding task requires attention at each research step and goes beyond the space we can dedicate to it in this section. Therefore, we address the topic with brief guidelines for ethical considerations when conducting cyberbullying research. It can be used as a starting point for further elaboration on this matter. We focus on specifics of cyberbullying research ethics and do not address general issues that should be known and respected in all research (i.e., issues of plagiarism, authorship, conflict of interest, distribution of results, etc.).

Social scientists are often directly connected with the people they are researching, and their actions could negatively affect individuals. Many classical studies conducted in the past are considered unethical nowadays, and researchers would be prevented from running them. Research in cyberbullying, which by definition involves sensitive, possibly even traumatic events and, at the same time, young people, calls for additional caution and consideration. Research has to be evaluated through the perspective of beneficence and protection from the risk of significant, long-lasting harm and unreasonable burdens (Israel & Hay, 2006). Therefore, at each level, preventive measures must be taken. For example, in the initial phase of the literature review, researchers need to carefully examine all possible negative effects of their research and prepare clear answers to various "what if" situations. At the beginning of the research the detailed description of research has to be evaluated and must receive ethical clearance by ethics review committees consisting of experts from various disciplines of social sciences and with no conflict of interest. Some scholars argue in favour of a more flexible approach; for example, Godfrey-Faussett (2022) defends a "dialogic and situational approach to ethics regulation", which allows researchers to delay and re-negotiate some decisions. Although this seems appealing, less rigid and adjustable, we believe cyberbullying research should generally stay within the boundaries of a pre-planned, predicted and approved research agenda.

Anonymity has been considered as general guidance to research ethics, though there are some exceptions when such clearing of names, and with them identities, leads to the disempowerment of specific groups (Gordon, 2019; Moore, 2012). Further, Godfrey-Faussett (2022) described cases when participants wanted their voices to be heard. Despite various arguments in favour of alternative approaches to a decision to anonymize collected data, cyberbullying research should be guided by a commitment to anonymity. Exposing victims' or perpetrators' identities could cause secondary victimization or lead to retaliation. Breach of anonymity represents a repetition of the same form of harm, i.e. public exposure of a specific situation or (mis)information. For all those cases where victims want to be heard, the research and later publications enable them to present their cases indirectly through their contribution to research. However, they should use other communicational channels if they wish to connect them with their personal details and reveal their identities. Participants should also be informed in advance (informed consent) about the measures taken to guarantee their anonymity and how and where the data (e.g., recordings, gathered materials) will be archived, and who will have access to them. All described steps create trust between participant and researcher.

Researchers must be prepared in advance for situations when specific actions should be according to the law and/or their judgement reported to authorities or situations where authorities would later investigate activities and they would demand researchers' cooperation and access to the un-anonymized data. Research practice shows that some researchers are willing to breach the vow of confidentiality (e.g., to prevent further harm), though there are others who are willing to defend the confidentiality even in courts and despite being threatened with prison time or even jailed for obstruction of justice or contempt of court (see Brajuha & Hallowell, 1986; Palys & Lowman, 2000; Scarce, 1995). Research teams have to decide which ethical approach and corresponding decisions regarding cooperation with authorities will be followed in their research. It is nearly impossible to give general guidance on this matter. Differences in legislation among states and variations in authorities' reactions and demands, specifics of different research topics level of support of research institutions are among the elements that can influence such decisions. However, all research teams must get familiar with legislation and policy demands regarding their research and expected actions from them (e.g., if they are obliged to report a discovered case of cyberbullying) and follow one general ethical norm: Honest communication with participants and a commitment to fulfilling promised guarantees are essential. The decision on which type of confidentiality (absolute or limited confidentiality) is granted to participants must be taken in advance and communicated with participants before gaining their consent to participate in a study. In practice, this means that in case of limited confidentiality, all participants of cyberbullying research are informed about possible exceptions to confidentiality and made aware of potential consequences in case of self-incrimination or exposed victimization which victims did not want to report. To avoid such issues, especially the latter ones, which can be seen as secondary victimization through research, alternative measures can be used (e.g., descriptions of events in the third person).

Research ethics presupposes informed consent, which includes the following elements: participants receive information about the study; they can comprehend this information and afterward express voluntary agreement to participate in research. Researchers are obliged to disclose key information about the study and present it to participants in advance. This includes the data on the research organization and the team conducting the research, the process of anonymization, approach to confidentiality, possible risks of self-incrimination, archiving of data and voluntary participation, which includes the right to end participation at any moment of research, etc. Cyberbullying research (usually) includes a specific population—children and adolescents. The age group of included students varies depending on the study's theoretical framework, though practically all studies include minors. Ruiz-Canela et al. (2013) argue that the general approach in the current research environment is to see adolescents as children and therefore demand parental consent for their participation in research. An overview of legal requirements and guidance of codes of ethics for the participation of minors in research in European Union member states reveals different approaches among countries. In some cases, parental or legal guardian permission is needed for all participants under the age of 18 years, and in other cases, under 15 or 14 years (European Union Agency for Fundamental Rights, 2014). Research teams must be familiar with these ethical requirements and adjust their approach. However, even when legal requirements are fulfilled, additional consideration should be given to specifically sensitive matters such as cyberbullying.[5]

Despite different arguments in favour of giving minors a voice and including them in a shared deliberative process among them, parents and researchers (Kuther & Posada, 2004), the distinction between adolescents and children has to be made. Inclusion of children in research without parental consent can be problematic (and ethical codes generally prohibit it); a situation with adolescents is more complex, and there is no uniform solution. Insisting on parental consent for adolescents until the legal age of 18 years neglects the abilities of youth to make important decisions and can lead to paradoxical situations when mature minors are in most countries already considered responsible for crimes, can under special conditions drive a car, travel alone, in some countries even vote in municipal and national elections, but cannot decide to participate in a professional low-risk research study. Not to mention instances involving stigmatized issues, such as research on adolescent minors and sexually transmitted diseases, as well as studies focused on gender and sexual minorities (Fisher et al., 2016; Macapagal et al., 2017), runaway, street or homeless minors, with no contact or fragile relationships with parents (Stablein & Jacobs, 2011). Conditioning inclusion of all minors to research with parental consent either excludes them from research or might exacerbate their relationship with parents or even harm them.[6] Inclusion of parental consent for cyberbullying studies (especially self-report research) with mature minors as participants could lead to similar situations as described by Macapagal et al. (2017), who found out that most respondents from sexual and gender minority groups would not have participated in the studies about sex and sexuality if a guardian's permission was required. It can be assumed that potential perpetrators of cyberbullying and hidden victims would hesitate to join a study if they had to inform and ask their parents for permission. After the decision about the need for parental consent is taken, researchers have to check the situation in their country, the school's policy and other requests to decide on the most appropriate and acceptable form of parental consent (e.g., the decision for active or passive consent) (Hollmann & McNamara, 1999; Jason et al., 2001; Spence et al., 2015).

Some studies used specific low-cost incentives (e.g. gifts such as pens, coffee mugs), although we believe this is unnecessary and participation in a study should be voluntary and without material reward. Motivation should be guided by self-interest to do something good through participation in research. Cyberbullying researchers should pay special attention to the prevention of secondary victimization through research. This also includes careful consideration of when to use individual or focus groups and recruiting participants for qualitative focus group discussions. The general aim is to prevent the confrontation between (possible) bully and victim and avoid public exposure of victims or perpetrators. Interviews must be conducted in private and discreet locations known to respondents. Another possibility is to conduct interviews on-line, maybe even using audio calls only. Another detail that needs consideration through the ethical perspective is intrusiveness of research. Disruptions of schedule should be minimized and research timing adjusted to the availability of students (see Humphrey & Symes, 2010). An important part of the preparation for cyberbullying research is the detection of possible distress caused by cyberbullying and (indirectly) provoked by research questions. Researchers must have the information to refer participants to professional help.

Conclusion

With the development of ICT and especially with the internet's intrusion and occupation of practically all aspects of our lives, negative and harmful processes followed this path and adjusted to this situation. Aside from all the positive opportunities given by ICT, these new technologies quickly became (ab)used also for bullying. The first cyberbullying research reaches back approximately two decades. In all these years, it has become clear which the most used methods for cyberbullying research and the most significant challenges, problems and opportunities are. Numerous studies in recent years have given us insight into the prevalence and nature of cyberbullying among children and adolescents.

However, the results differ significantly and show an extremely heterogeneous, if not even inconsistent, picture. Further, some cyberbullying research aspects are only vaguely addressed and reflected.

What can we conclude about the fundamental characteristics of research methods and approaches used in the study of cyberbullying? Firstly, there is terminological confusion and difficulties in translating the term to other languages besides English. In the past this problem was known among bullying researchers, though nowadays, the additional word in the label (cyber) the situation is even worse. Literal translation, even if it is technically accurate and professionally correct, can be highly confusing, particularly for younger participants. Secondly, there is no overall definition of cyberbullying, and there is a lack of precise operationalization. Some authors put under the label of cyberbullying various acts which in fact do not fulfil cyberbullying criteria and include more severe episodes of internet violence. Further, some authors use various inappropriate labels to describe and refer to cyberbullying (e.g., cyber aggression, cyber violence, on-line violence). In many cases, the definitions of cyberbullying are not appropriate and are missing key elements of cyberbullying. Theoretical approaches are so versatile and even include contradictory perspectives. Some researchers understand cyberbullying as a form of general bullying, whereas others claim it is a specific and separate phenomenon. With inconsistency and contradictions in definitions, operationalization cannot measure similar indicators, and end results lead to incomparable data. Thirdly, cyberbullying research is marked by the dominance of the quantitative research approach, which presents only part of the whole process and overlooks needed details. Recent years show some increase in the use of qualitative approach (mainly individual interviews and focus groups), which could pave the way for further inclusion of various qualitative research methods and ideally mixed method approach to study this issue. Fourthly, there is a lack of studies and discussions on the ethical aspects of cyberbullying research. Cyberbullying research teams must rely on general guidance for social science research ethics or on elaborations connected to other similar research topics (e.g., research ethics on bullying, peer violence and delinquency). Cyberbullying research ethic principles have to provide guidance on basic aspects of such studies (e.g., when to apply for ethical approval, which participants can be included, what type of consent can be used, is parental/guardian consent needed) to more specific ones (what level of anonymity and confidentiality can be guaranteed to participants, how to prevent secondary victimization, how to react in case of participant's unease and discomfort triggered by research).

For reliable and valid results in cyberbullying research, all of these specifics should be considered and carefully evaluated. The whole process should be thought through—from using the correct terminology to defining and conceptualizing the construct, choosing and combining qualitative and quantitative methods and research instruments and considering ethical considerations. This can contribute to the better quality of the collected data, give insight into researched phenomenon and establish a professional relationship with participants without negative consequences for them.

Notes

1 In research conducted in 2022 in Slovenia with children and adolescents, all the boys and older students claimed they use the English term *cyberbullying* when referring to it in conversational language among themselves. They explained there is no perfect translation and can therefore perfectly describe the concept only with the original English term. Younger girls, on the other hand, were not familiar with it (see Šulc, 2023).

2 For example, despite the success of application of drawing and later discussions about the pictures that children had drawn in bullying research (Bosacki et al., 2006; Andreou & Bonoti, 2010), this method would not be recommended for cyberbullying research. Cyberbullying involves students who are usually older than victims of classical bullying and are therefore already capable of expressing emotions, feelings, ideas, values.

3 Authors of this chapter conducted the collection of data on bullying and cyberbullying of people with disabilities and it proved extremely useful that victims had a possibility to engage in individual online interview with audio call only. In the initial moment of the interview researchers used cameras to create the contact, though some participants decided not to show their faces at all, which guaranteed them a higher level of anonymity.

4 Triangulation as a research approach has been criticized in recent years. As Fetters and Molina-Azorin (2017) elaborate, triangulation has many meanings, so many that it is already impossible to understand exact idea behind the label unless clearly defined by authors. Further, their criticism shows that triangulation in its essence "suggests that the multiple sources of data *will* confirm each point/ location/truth." (ibid.: 8, emphasis in original). We believe that instead of using methods that are expected to come to a junction, we should use research approach that addresses the same phenomena through different methods (qualitative *and* quantitative) and gives us the data to present a story through different though complementary perspectives. This can be labeled as an integrated or mixed-method approach.

5 Ruiz-Canela et al. (2013) developed a practical decision tree guide regarding parental permission in research with adolescents, which can be used as guidance in various research on adult minors.

6 The American Psychological Association took an official position on this matter in a resolution (APA, 2018) which supports inclusion of mature minors in research without parental permission, when it could potentially harm the mature minor and when alternative and appropriate research protections are in place.

References

American Psychological Association [APA]. (2018). *APA resolution on support for the expansion of mature minors' ability to participate in research*. Retrieved from www.apa.org/about/policy/resolution-minors-research.pdf

Andreou, E., & Bonoti, F. (2010). Children's bullying experiences expressed through drawings and self-reports. *School Psychology International, 31*(2), 164–177. https://doi.org/10.1177/0143034309352421

Baić, V., Ivanović, Z., & Simeunovic-Patic, B. (2017). Distribution and characteristics of cyber violence among elementary school students—Survey results in Serbia. *Journal of Psychological and Educational Research, 25*(1), 93–114.

Balakrishnan, V. (2017). Unraveling the underlying motives SCulPT-ing cyberbullying behaviours among Malaysian young adults. *Computers in Human Behaviour, 75*, 194–205. https://doi.org/10.1016/j.chb.2017.04.062

Barakso, M., Sabet, D. M., & Schaffner, B. F. (2014). *Understanding political science research methods: The challenge of inference*. Routledge.

Bauman, S. (2012). Why it matters. In S. Bauman, D. Cross, & J. Walker (Eds.), *Principles of cyberbullying research: Definitions, measures, and methodology* (pp. 23–25). Routledge.

Bauman, S., Cross, D., & Walker, J. (2012). *Principles of cyberbullying research: Definitions, measures, and methodology*. Routledge.

Berne, S., Frisén, A., & Kling, J. (2014). Appearance-related cyberbullying: A qualitative investigation of characteristics, content, reasons, and effects. *Body Image, 11*(4), 527–533. https://doi.org/10.1016/j.bodyim.2014.08.006

Berne, S., Frisén, A., Schultze-Krumbholz, A., Scheithauer, H., Naruskov, K., Luik, P., Katzer, C., Erentaite, R., & Zukauskiene, R. (2013). Cyberbullying assessment instruments: A systematic review. *Aggression and Violent Behavior, 18*, 320–334. https://doi.org/10.1016/j.avb.2012.11.022

Betts, L. R., & Spenser, K. A. (2017). "People think it's a harmless joke": Young people's understanding of the impact of technology, digital vulnerability and cyberbullying in the United Kingdom. *Journal of Children and Media, 11*(1), 20–35. https://doi.org/10.1080/17482798.2016.1233893

Bosacki, S. L., Marini, Z. A., & Dane, A. V. (2006). Voices from the classroom: Pictorial and narrative representations of children's bullying experiences. *Journal of Moral Education, 35*, 231–245. https://doi.org/10.1080/03057240600681769

Brajuha, M., & Hallowell, L. (1986). Legal intrusion and the politics of fieldwork. *Urban Life, 14*(4), 454–478. https://doi.org/10.1177/0098303986014004005

Canty, J., Stubbet, M., Steers, D., & Collings, S. (2014). The trouble with bullying—Deconstructing the conventional definition of bullying for a child-centred investigation into children's use of social media. *Children & Society, 30*(1), 48–58. https://doi.org/10.1111/chso.12103

Card, N. A. (2012). Psychometric considerations for cyberbullying research. In S. Bauman, D. Cross, & J. Walker (Eds.), *Principles of cyberbullying research: Definitions, measures, and methodology* (pp. 188–201). Routledge.

Cetin, B., Yaman, E., & Peker, A. (2011). Cyber victim and bullying scale: A study of validity and reliability. *Computers & Education, 57*, 2261–2271. https://doi.org/10.1016/j.compedu.2011.06.014

Chan, T. K. H., Cheung, C. M. K., & Lee, Z. W. Y. (2021). Cyberbullying on social networking sites: A literature review and future research directions. *Information & Management, 58*(2). https://doi.org/10.1016/j.im.2020.103411

Chun, J., Lee, J., Kim, J., & Lee, S. (2020). An international systematic review of cyberbullying measurements. *Computers in Human Behavior, 113*. https://doi.org/10.1016/j.chb.2020.106485

Cohen, S. (1972). *Folk devils and moral panics.* MacGibbon and Kee.

Council of Europe. (2018). *Mapping study on cyberviolence.* Council of Europe. Retrieved from www.coe.int/en/web/cybercrime/-/t-cy-mapping-study-on-cyberviolence-recommendations

Creswell, J. W. (2013). *Research design: Qualitative, quantitative, and mixed methods approaches* (4th ed.). Sage Publications.

Del Rey, R., Casas, J. A., Ortega-Ruiz, R., Schultze-Krumbholz, A., Scheithauer, H., Smith, P., Thompson, F., Barkoukis, V., Tsorbatzoudis, H., Brighi, A., Guarini, A., Pyzalski, J., & Plichta, P. (2015). Structural validation and cross-cultural robustness of the European cyberbullying intervention project questionnaire. *Computers in Human Behavior, 50*, 141–147.

Dennehy, R., Meaney, S., Walsh, K. A., Sinnott, C., Cronin, M., & Arensman, E. (2020). Young people's conceptualizations of the nature of cyberbullying: A systematic review and synthesis of qualitative research. *Aggression and Violent Behavior, 51*. https://doi.org/10.1016/j.avb.2020.101379

Dobson, A. S. (2019). 'The things you didn't do': Gender, slut-shaming, and the need to address sexual harassment in narrative resources responding to sexting and cyberbullying. In H. Vandebosch & L. Green (Eds.), *Narratives in Research and Interventions on Cyberbullying among Young People* (pp. 147–160). Springer. Retrieved from https://doi.org/10.1007/978-3-030-04960-7_10

Dooley, J., Pyzalski, J., & Cross, D. (2009). Cyberbullying versus face-to-face bullying: A theoretical and conceptual review. *Zeitschrift fur Psychologie, 217*(4), 182–188. https://doi.org/10.1027/0044–3409.217.4.182

Espinoza, G., & Juvonen, J. (2012). Methods used in cyberbullying research. In S. Bauman, D. Cross, & J. Walker (Eds.), *Principles of cyberbullying research: Definitions, measures, and methodology* (pp. 112–124). Routledge.

European Union Agency for Fundamental Rights [FRA]. (2014). *Child participation in research.* Retrieved from https://fra.europa.eu/en/publication/2019/child-participation-research#publication-tab-0

Evans, Y., Selkie, E., Midamba, N., Ton, A., & Moreno, M. (2016). Proposed solutions for addressing cyberbullying: A qualitative study of adolescents. *Journal of Adolescent Health, 58*(2). https://doi.org/10.1016/j.jadohealth.2015.10.158

Fahie, D. (2014). Doing sensitive research sensitively: Ethical and methodological issues in researching workplace bullying. *International Journal of Qualitative Methods, 13*, 19–36. https://doi.org/10.1177/160940691401300108

Fetters, M. D., & Molina-Azorin, J. F. (2017). The journal of mixed methods research starts a new decade: Principles for bringing in the new and divesting of the old language of the field. *Journal of Mixed Methods Research, 11*(1), 3–10. https://doi.org/10.1177/1558689816682092

Fisher, C. B., Arbeit, M. R., Dumont, M. S., Macapagal, K., & Mustanski, B. (2016). Self-consent for HIV prevention research involving sexual and gender minority youth: Reducing barriers through evidence-based ethics. *Journal of Empirical Research on Human Research Ethics, 11*(1), 3–14.

Frisén, A., Berne, S., Schultze-Krumbholz, A., Scheithauer, H., Naruskov, K., Luik, P., Katzer, C., Erentaite, R., & Zukauskiene, R. (2013). Measurement issues: A systematic review of cyberbullying instruments. In P. K. Smith & G. Steffgen (Eds.), *Cyberbullying through the new media: Findings from an international network* (pp. 37–62). Psychology Press.

Gaffney, H., Farrington, D. P., Espelage, D. L., & Ttofi, M. M. (2019). Are cyberbullying intervention and prevention programs effective? A systematic and meta-analytical review. *Aggression and Violent Behavior, 45*, 134–153. https://doi.org/10.1016/j.avb.2018.07.002

Galesic, M., & Bosnjak, M. (2009). Effects of questionnaire length on participation and indicators of response quality in a web survey. *Public Opinion Quaterly, 73*(2), 349–360. https://doi.org/10.1093/poq/nfp031

Gladden, R. M., Vivolo-Kantor, A. M., Hamburger, M. E., & Lumpkin, C. D. (2014). *Bullying surveillance among youths: Uniform definitions for public health and recommended data elements.* National Center for Injury Prevention and Control, Centers for Disease Control and Prevention in U. S. Department of Education. Retrieved from https://files.eric.ed.gov/fulltext/ED575477.pdf

Godfrey-Faussett, T. (2022). Participatory research and the ethics of anonymisation. *Education Sciences, 12*(4), 260. https://doi.org/10.3390/educsci12040260

Gordon, R. (2019). 'Why would I want to be anonymous?' Questioning ethical principles of anonymity in cross-cultural feminist research. *Gender & Development, 27*(3), 541–554. DOI: 10.1080/13552074.2019.1664044

Green, D. M., Taddeo, C. M., Price, D. A., Pasenidou, F., & Spears, B. A. (2022). A qualitative meta-study of youth voice and co-participatory research practices: Informing cyber/bullying research methodologies. *International Journal of Bullying Prevention, 4*, 190–208. https://doi.org/10.1007/s42380-022-00118-w

Green, L., Van Royen, K., & Vermeulen, A. (2019). Narrative research methods, particularly focused upon digital technology use in everyday life. In H. Vandebosch & L. Green (Eds.), *Narratives in research and interventions on cyberbullying among young people* (pp. 47–60). Springer. Retrieved from https://doi.org/10.1007/978-3-030-04960-7_4

Griffin, R. S., & Gross, A. M. (2004). Childhood bullying: Current empirical findings and future directions for research. *Aggression and Violent Behavior, 9*, 379–400. https://doi.org/10.1016/S1359-1789(03)00033-8

Hammarberg, K., Kirkman, M., & de Lacey, S. (2016). Qualitative research methods: When to use them and how to judge them. *Human Reproduction, 31*(3), 498–501.

Heary, C. M., & Hennessy, E. (2002). The use of focus group interviews in pediatric health care research. *Journal of Pediatric Psychology, 27*(1), 47–57.

Hennink, M., Hutter, I., & Bailey, A. (2020). *Qualitative research methods (2E).* Sage.

Hollmann, C. M., & McNamara, J. R. (1999). Considerations in the use of active and passive parental consent procedures. *The Journal of Psychology, 133*(2), 141–156. https://doi.org/10.1080/00223989909599729

Humphrey, N., & Symes, W. (2010). Responses to bullying and use of social support among pupils with autism spectrum disorders (ASDs) in mainstream schools: A qualitative study. *Journal of Research in Special Educational Needs, 10*(2), 82–90.

Israel, M., & Hay, I. (2006). *Research ethics for social scientists: Between ethical conduct and regulatory compliance.* Sage.

Jason, L. A., Pokorny, S., & Katz, R. (2001). Passive versus active consent: A case study in school settings. *Journal of Community Psychology, 29*(1), 53–68. https://doi.org/10.1002/1520-6629(200101)29:1<53::AID-JCOP4>3.0.CO;2-6

Juvonen, J., & Gross, E. F. (2008). Extending the school grounds? Bullying experiences in cyberspace. *Journal of School Health, 78*(9), 496–505. DOI: 10.1111/j.1746–1561.2008.00335.x

Kowalski, R. M., Giumetti, G. W., Schroeder, A. N., & Lattanner, M. R. (2014). Bullying in the digital age: A critical review and meta-analysis of cyberbullying research among youth. *Psychological Bulletin, 140*(4), 1073–1137. https://doi.org/10.1037/a0035618

Kowalski, R. M., Limber, S. P., & Agatston, P. W. (2008). *Cyber bullying: Bullying in the digital age.* Blackwell Publishing.

Kuther, T., & Posada, M. (2004). Children and adolescents' capacity to provide informed consent for participation in research. *Advances in Psychology Research, 32*, 163–173.

Law, D. M., Shapka, J. D., Domene, J. F., & Gagné, M. H. (2012a). Are cyberbullies really bullies? An investigation of reactive and proactive on-line aggression. *Computers in Human Behavior*, 28(2), 664–672. https://doi.org/10.1016/j.chb.2011.11.013

Law, D. M., Shapka, J. D., Hymel, S., Olson, B. F., & Waterhouse, T. (2012b). The changing face of bullying: An empirical comparison between traditional and internet bullying and victimization. *Computers in Human Behavior*, 28(1), 226–232. https://doi.org/10.1016/j.chb.2011.09.004

Macapagal, K., Coventry, R., Arbeit, M. R., Fisher, C. B., & Mustanski, B. (2017). "I won't out myself just to do a survey": Sexual and gender minority adolescents' perspectives on the risks and benefits of sex research. *Archives of sexual behavior*, 46(5), 1393–1409. https://doi.org/10.1007/s10508-016-0784-5

McCarry, M. (2012). Who benefits? A critical reflection of children and young people's participation in sensitive research. *International Journal of Social Research Methodology*, 15(1), 55–68. https://doi.org/10.1080/13645579.2011.568196

Menesini, E., Nocentini, A., Palladino, B. E., Scheithauer, H., Schultze-Krumbholz, A., Frisén, A., Berne, S., Luik, P., Naruskov, K., Ortega-Ruiz, R., Calmaestra, J., & Blaya, C. (2013). Definitions of cyberbullying. In P. K. Smith & G. Steffgen (Eds.), *Cyberbullying through the new media: Findings from an international network* (pp. 23–36). Psychology Press.

Mishna, F., & Van Wert, M. (2012). Qualitative Studies. In S. Bauman, D. Cross, & J. Walker (Eds.), *Principles of cyberbullying research: Definitions, measures, and methodology* (pp. 238–258). Routledge.

Moore, N. (2012). The politics and ethics of naming: Questioning anonymisation in (archival) research. *International Journal of Social Research Methodology*, 15(4), 331–340. https://doi.org/10.1080/13645579.2012.688330

Naruskov, K., Luik, P., Nocentini, A., & Menesini, E. (2012). Estonian students' perception and definition of cyberbullying. *A Journal of the Humanities & Social Sciences*, 16(4), 323–343. https://doi.org/10.3176/tr.2012.4.02

Navarro, R., & Serna, C. (2016). Spanish youth perceptions about cyberbullying: Qualitative research into understanding cyberbullying and the role that parents play in its solution. In R. Navarro, S. Yubero, & E. Larrañaga (Eds.), *Cyberbullying across the globe: Gender, family, and mental health* (pp. 193–218). Springer Science + Business Media. Retrieved from https://doi.org/10.1007/978-3-319-25552-1_10

Nocentini, A., Calmaestra, J., Schultze-Krumbholz, A., Scheithauer, H., Ortega, R., & Menesini, E. (2010). Cyberbullying: Labels, behaviours and definition in three European countries. *Journal of Psychologists and Counsellors in Schools*, 20(2), 129–142. https://doi.org/10.1375/ajgc.20.2.129

Olweus, D. (1993). *Bullying at school: What we know and what we can do*. Blackwell Publishers Ltd.

Olweus, D. (2017). Cyberbullying: A critical overview. In B. J. Bushman (Ed.), *Aggression and violence: A social psychological perspective* (pp. 225–240). Routledge.

Olweus, D., & Limber, S. P. (2018). Some problems with cyberbullying research. *Current Opinion in Psychology*, 19, 139–143. https://doi.org/10.1016/j.copsyc.2017.04.012

Oxford University Press. (n.d.). *Cyberbullying*. Oxford English Dictionary.

Palys, T., & Lowman, J. (2000). Ethical and legal strategies for protecting condential research information. *Canadian Journal of Law and Society*, 15, 39–80. https://doi.org/10.1017/S0829320100006190

Patchin, J. W. (2022, June 22). *Summary of our cyberbullying research (2007–2021)*. Cyberbullying Research Center. Retrieved from https://cyberbullying.org/summary-of-our-cyberbullying-research

Patchin, J. W., & Hinduja, S. (2012). *Cyberbullying prevention and response: Expert perspectives*. Routledge.

Popovac, M., & Leoschut, L. (2012). Cyber bullying in South Africa: Impact and responses. *CJCP Issue Paper*, 13.

Purdy, N., & Mc Guckin, C. (2015). Cyberbullying, schools and the law: A comparative study in Northern Ireland and the republic of Ireland. *Educational Research*, 57(4), 420–436. https://doi.org/10.1080/00131881.2015.1091203

Rafferty, R., & Vander Ven, T. (2014). "I hate everything about you": A qualitative examination of cyberbullying and on-line aggression in a college sample. *Deviant Behavior*, 35(5), 364–377. https://doi.org/10.1080/01639625.2013.849171

Ranney, M. L., Pittman, S. K., Riese, A., Koehler, C., Ybarra, M. L., Cunningham, R. M., Spirito, A., & Rosen, R. K. (2020). What counts?: A qualitative study of adolescents' lived experience with online victimization and cyberbullying. *Academic Pediatrics, 20*(4), 485–492. https://doi.org/10.1016/j.acap.2019.11.001

Ruiz-Canela, M., Lopez-del Burgo, C., Carlos, S., Calatrava, M., Beltramo, C., Osorio, A., & de Irala, J. (2013). Observational research with adolescents: A framework for the management of the parental permission. *BMC Medical Ethics, 14*, 2. https://doi.org/10.1186/1472-6939-14-2

Scarce, R. (1995). Scholarly ethics and courtroom antics: Where researchers stand in the eyes of the law. *The American Sociologist, 26*(1), 87–112. https://doi.org/10.1007/BF02692012

Schacter, H. L., Greenberg, S., & Juvonen, J. (2016). Who's to blame?: The effects of victim disclosure on bystander reactions to cyberbullying. *Computers in Human Behavior, 57*, 115–121. https://doi.org/10.1016/j.chb.2015.11.018

Shaw, C., Brady, L. M., & Davey, C. (2011). *Guidelines for research with children and young people.* NCB Research Centre.

Smith, P. K. (2018). *Snapshot: How research on cyberbullying has developed.* ACAMH. Retrieved from https://static.acamh.org/app/uploads/2018/02/Infomatics_Bridge_Feb18-3snapshot.pdf

Smith, P. K. (2019). Research on cyberbullying: Strengths and limitations. In H. Vandebosch & L. Green (Eds.), *Narratives in research and interventions on cyberbullying among young people* (pp. 9–27). Springer.

Smith, P. K., Barrio, C., & Tokunaga, R. (2012). Definitions of bullying and cyberbullying: How useful are the terms? In S. Bauman, J. Walker, & D. Cross (Eds.), *Principles of cyberbullying research: Definition, methods, and measures* (pp. 64–86). Routledge.

Smith, P. K., & Berkkun, F. (2017). How research on cyberbullying has developed. In C. Mc Guckin & L. Corcoran (Eds.), *Bullying and cyberbullying: Prevalence, psychological impacts and intervention strategies* (pp. 11–27). Nova Science.

Smith, P. K., Mahdavi, J., Carvalho, M., Fisher, S., Russell, S., & Tippett, N. (2008). Cyberbullying: Its nature and impact in secondary school pupils. *Journal of Child Psychology & Psychiatry, 49*, 376–385. https://doi.org/10.1111/j.1469-7610.2007.01846.x

Spears, B., & Zeederberg, M. (2012). Emerging methodological strategies to address cyberbullying: Online social marketing and young people as co-researchers. In S. Bauman, D. Cross, & J. Walker (Eds.), *Principles of cyberbullying research: Definitions, measures, and methodology* (pp. 166–179). Routledge.

Spence, S., White, M., Adamson, A. J., & Matthews, J. N. (2015). Does the use of passive or active consent affect consent or completion rates, or dietary data quality? Repeat cross-sectional survey among school children aged 11–12 years. *BMJ Open, 5*(1), e006457. https://doi.org/10.1136/bmjopen-2014-006457

Stablein, T., & Jacobs, S. (2011). Waiving parental consent when researching at-risk youth. *Sociological Studies of Children and Youth, 14*, 205–226. https://doi.org/10.1108/S1537-4661(2011)0000014014

Šulc, A. (2023). *Methodological approaches to the analysis of cyberbullying* [Doctoral dissertation, University of Ljubljana].

Thornberg, R. (2011). 'She's Weird!' - The social construction of bullying in school: A review of qualitative research. *Children & Society, 25*(4), 258–267. https://doi.org/10.1111/j.1099-0860.2011.00374.

Tokunaga, R. S. (2010). Following you home from school: A critical review and synthesis of research on cyberbullying victimization. *Computers in Human Behavior, 26*(3), 277–287. https://doi.org/10.1016/j.chb.2009.11.014

Topcu, C., & Erdur-Baker, O. (2010). The Revised Cyber Bullying Inventory (RCBI): Validity and reliability studies. *Procedia Social and Behavioral Sciences, 5*, 660–664. https://doi.org/10.1016/j.sbspro.2010.07.161

Turan, N., Polat, O., Karapirli, M., Usyal, C., & Gokce Turan, S. (2011). The new violence type of the era: Cyber bullying among university students: Violence among university students. *Neurology, Psychiatry and Brain Research, 17*(1), 21–26. https://doi.org/10.1016/j.npbr.2011.02.005

Vandebosch, H., & Green, L. (2019a). *Narratives in research and interventions on cyberbullying among young people.* Springer.

Vandebosch, H., & Green, L. (2019b). Introduction. In H. Vandebosch & L. Green (Eds.), *Narratives in research and interventions on cyberbullying among young people* (pp. 1–6). Springer.

Vandebosch, H., & Van Cleemput, K. (2008). Defining cyberbullying: A qualitative research into the perceptions of youngsters. *Cyberpsychology & behavior: The impact of the Internet, Multimedia and Virtual Reality on Behavior and Society, 11*(4), 499–503. DOI: 10.1089/cpb.2007.0042

Vivolo-Kantor, A. M., Martell, B. N., Holland, K. M., & Westby, R. (2014). A systematic review and content analysis of bullying and cyber-bullying measurement strategies. *Aggression and Violent Behavior, 19*, 423–434. https://doi.org/10.1016/j.avb.2014.06.008

Wang, C. W., Musumari, P. M., Techasrivichien, T., Suguimoto, S. P., Chan, C. C., Ono-Kihara, M., Kihara, M., & Nakayama, T. (2019). "I felt angry, but I couldn't do anything about it": a qualitative study of cyberbullying among Taiwanese high school students. *BMC Public Health, 19*. https://doi.org/10.1186/s12889-019-7005-9

Ybarra, M. (2012). Measurement: Why it matters. In S. Bauman, D. Cross, & J. Walker (Eds.), *Principles of cyberbullying research: Definitions, measures, and methodology* (pp. 183–187). Routledge.

Ybarra, M. L., Boyd, D., Korchmaros, J. D., & Oppenheim, J. (2012). Defining and measuring cyberbullying within the larger context of bullying victimization. *Journal of Adolescent Health, 51*(1), 53–58. https://doi.org/10.1016/j.jadohealth.2011.12.031

Young, R., Tully, M., & Ramirez, M. (2017). School administrator perceptions of cyberbullying facilitators and barriers to preventive action: A qualitative study. *Health Education & Behavior: The Official Publication of the Society for Public Health Education, 44*(3), 476–484. https://doi.org/10.1177/1090198116673814

Završnik, A. (2013). Kibernetsko nadlegovanje: Pojem, metode in pojavnost po svetu in v Sloveniji. In M. Ambrož, K. Filipčič, & A. Završnik (Eds.), *Zbornik za Alenko Šelih: kazensko pravo, kriminologija, človekove pravice* (pp. 427–448). Pravna fakulteta.

9

CONTEXTUAL FACTORS OF ONLINE DECEPTION AND HARMFUL INFORMATION

Multidisciplinary perspectives

Kristjan Kikerpill, Elisabeth Carter, Marju Himma
and Sten Hansson

Introduction

Context has both a constitutive and interpretive dimension (Rigotti & Rocci, 2006), which means that it allows us to interpret incoming messages (regardless of their origin) as well as to create messages that fit certain frames of interpretation in an effort and attempt to elicit particular responses. Thus, while lies and deception in online contexts (see Hancock, 2009) are often discussed using varying terminology (Kalbfleisch & Docan-Morgan, 2019; Hansson et al., 2021), the inroads to terminological overlap as well as the importance of context in the delivery and receipt of information are less explored. To address the theoretical-terminological overlap and differences between discussions of 'lies and deception' and 'information disorder', this chapter first provides the relevant theoretical background for both, including a comparative table listing often-used terms on either side of the aisle. Secondly, the chapter introduces three levels of contextual factors that impact both the crafting and receipt of messages: the individual, situational, and social-structural context factors. These contextual factors are then illustrated with the help of four case studies focussing on online fraud, deceptive content in journalism, and communication-related vulnerabilities in crisis situations.

Theoretical background: lies, deception, information disorder, and context

Enquiries into lies and deception must cover three important categories: (1) the ontology of lies and deception ("what they are"), (2) their creation ("how are lies and deception crafted and presented"), and (3) detection ("how to avoid being misled by lies and deception"). As with all forms of communication, all three categories are inextricably connected to the contexts in which the (potentially) deceptive messages function (Carter, 2014; Kalbfleisch & Docan-Morgan, 2019).

The first of the aforementioned categories is a contested topic that has generated extensive discussions (Kalbfleisch & Docan-Morgan, 2019) throughout human history and,

DOI: 10.4324/9781003277675-11

more recently, in various fields of research (McGlone & Knapp, 2019, pp. 9–10). Moreover, the titled category of "lies and deception" itself is subject to further distinctions, i.e., which types of lies and deception exist, and what, if anything, distinguishes lies from deception. On the latter issue, there seems to be at least some agreement that deception is a broader category than lying, i.e., lies are a type of deception (see Levine, 2014; Kalbfleisch & Docan-Morgan, 2019, pp. 31–32). Another aspect considered when distinguishing lies from deception is intentionality. While some authors suggest that "deception may or may not be a deliberate act, whereas a lie is always deliberate" (Frank & Svetieva, 2013, p. 123), others characterise both lies and deception as deliberate communicative acts (Levine, 2014). As a shorthand, it may therefore be useful (1) to consider lies as one form of deception and (2) to think of both lies and the broader category of deception as deliberate communicative acts, which (3) also leaves room for the unintentional creation of misconceptions, e.g., false impressions. The latter is important due to the way in which encoding, and decoding occur in communication (Hall, 1973), i.e., the meaning of a message may vary depending on how it is interpreted by the recipient. Although different combinations of meaning-making and the veracity of information play a role in what constitutes "harmful content" online (see e.g., Woods & Perrin, 2019, p. 39), i.e., content which is not necessarily deemed illegal but may bring about adverse effects for the user, lies and deception comprise an important portion of such content.

Following Hancock (2009), the creation of lies and deception online can be broken down into two broad categories: identity-based and message-based (digital) deceptions. Identity-based digital deceptions flow from the "false manipulation or display of a person or organisation's identity" (Hancock, 2009, p. 290), while for message-based deceptions, the crux of the manipulation occurs within the content of messages exchanged between senders and receivers. For the deceptions to be effective, an open channel needs to exist between the sender and receiver regardless of the particular media used for dissemination or display (Kikerpill, 2021). Understandably, identity- and message-based deceptions are not mutually exclusive (Hancock, 2009). Conversely, these two broad categories are often combined to enhance the efficacy of the deception both offline and online (e.g., Carter, 2015; Kikerpill, 2021). For instance, the use of deepfakes, i.e., fake audio and video content created with the assistance of machine learning techniques (e.g., Kikerpill, 2020), currently operates as the technological pinnacle of combining identity- and message-based deceptions. The use of audio and video deepfakes is a concern in political deception and disinformation as well as blackmail and fraud (Kikerpill, 2020; Cross, 2022). However, these will likely be surpassed in deceptive efficacy by generative artificial intelligence solutions that allow even more believable text- and image-based deceptions to be created (see Fadilpašić, 2023). When significant control over identity and message manipulations is further enforced by exploiting relevant contextual factors, it allows for the creation of authentifakes, i.e., intentionally deceptive representations of someone or something that has an unnatural accordance with the expectations, wishes, and desires of target audiences in particular social contexts (Kikerpill, 2023b). These particular contexts of exploitation can range from personal, e.g., romantic relationships (Carter, 2021), to global (Hansson et al., 2021). Given the myriad identity, message, and context combinations available for actors engaged in deception online, a considerable strain is placed on the detection of such activities and content.

The importance of detecting lies comes from their sheer volume in everyday life. Previous research has suggested that people tell about one to two lies a day (DePaulo et al.,

1996). However, the distribution of lying has been shown to be heavily skewed (Serota et al., 2010), i.e., a small number of prolific liars account for a majority of the lies told, and this finding has been replicated across a number of more recent studies (see Serota et al., 2021). In online environments, a significant amount of false information is also spread by non-human actors, e.g., social bots (Shao et al., 2018). Since humans have great difficulties differentiating between the activities of social bots and genuine human users (see Himelein-Wachowiak et al., 2021), they often end up making things worse with respect to the quantities of false information being shared online and the speed with which it occurs (Vosoughi et al., 2018). While technical tools exist to mitigate the dissemination of misleading information online (e.g., Choraś et al., 2021), humans themselves, by default, assume the truthfulness of incoming communication: if nothing triggers suspicion or scepticism that leads a person to actively decide not to believe something, the truth-default state remains intact (Levine, 2019).

For decades, deception detection research operated from what have come to be called "cue theories" (see Levine & McCornack, 2014), i.e., the detection of lies or deception supposedly relied on observable behavioural cues of the speaker or communicator. However, results from the application of such theoretical approaches obtained deception detection rates at only slightly-better-than-chance levels (Blair et al., 2010). In contrast, "non-cue theories" such as the truth-default theory (Levine & McCornack, 2014, p. 434; Levine, 2019) place detection-related emphasis on the content of information that is being communicated and the context within which the information was produced. Outside-the-lab detection of lies and deception relies on comparing what is communicated with some type of evidence, or on confessions (Park et al., 2002). Although people look for both behavioural cues and non-behavioural information when detecting lies in everyday life, non-behavioural information has been found to be more useful to this particular end (Sánchez et al., 2021). In fact, situational familiarity and the provision of contextual information raises deception detection rates considerably, e.g., from the slightly-better-than-chance rates to 75% accuracy (Blair et al., 2010; Levine, 2019, pp. 263–268). Hence, understanding the context within which false information is or may be created and disseminated is crucial for improved deception detection.

In addition to approaches that could be categorised as traditional in terms of terminology used, media scholars and policy makers are increasingly concerned about 'information disorder'—the unprecedentedly broad and fast diffusion of various forms of false and harmful information in modern societies due to complex socio-political, cultural, and technological changes (Wardle & Derakhshan, 2017; Freelon & Wells, 2020; Jungherr & Schroeder, 2021; Kapantai et al., 2021; Hansson et al., 2021).

Disinformation refers to intentionally fabricated, manipulated, imposter, and misleading content. Advertising and propaganda can be both intentionally and unintentionally misleading. Misinformation can be presented in a false context to create false connections, but it can be intentional or unintentional, e.g., inaccurate misinterpretation (Rubin, 2019). Malinformation is intended to be malicious, to harm the subject and the receiver (Zhou & Zafarani, 2020). Where misinformation and disinformation result in deception, malinformation is generally considered to be different in that regard, i.e., malinformation covers categories such as hate speech, leaks, and harassment (Wardle & Derakhshan, 2017; Caramancion et al., 2022). Hence, disinformation can be distinguished from misinformation on the basis of intent to mislead, and from malinformation as including the element of deception. Fake news—a term often encountered in current academic parlance, but increasingly falling out of favour due to issues with its precise definition (see Habgood-Coote, 2019)—could be used as a genre describing the deliberate creation of pseudo-journalistic disinformation; fake news may also refer to a label that describes the political instrumentalisation of the term to delegitimise news media (Egelhofer & Lecheler, 2019; Mourão & Robertson, 2019). While fake news constitutes intentionally deceptive content, it is just one of the phenomena of information disorders—a concept embracing mis-, mal- and disinformation in its various forms (Tandoc Jr et al., 2018; Wardle & Derakhshan, 2017).

To clarify certain positions of terminology, we present a side-by-side comparison of often-used concepts in the well-established camp of 'lies and deception', and the emerging discussions on 'information disorder' (see Table 9.1).

Contextual factors

Sociologists who study vulnerability distinguish between three kinds of dynamic and interacting factors that can make people more prone to suffering adverse effects due to various hazards: (1) individual, such as impairments or limited skills, (2) situational, such as complications or obstacles arising from a particular event, and (3) social-structural factors, such as inadequate government policies and various historically, culturally, and politically constructed forms of inequality in society (Hansson et al., 2020). The extent to which people could become susceptible to online deception and harmful information can also be seen as being shaped by these three types of factors. We will discuss these in turn.

Contextual factors are a key tool for fraudsters aiming to convince their target to believe the actions they are taking (which ultimately will lead to their financial detriment) are reasonable and desirable. 'Genre mapping' (Carter, 2015) is where the fraudster draws on familiar words and phrases from legitimate sources such as sales or marketing communications, for example "hurry while this offer lasts", in order to provoke urgent action without causing alarm; harnessing their communicative styles to provoke feelings of familiarity and the reassurance this brings in order to manipulate an individual's fundamental inclination to trust (Fischer et al., 2013). This is supported by Oliver and colleagues (2015), who found persuasive deception techniques stemmed from drawing on overarching interactional cues to legitimacy, such as using glossy leaflets or official-looking documents usually found in genuine marketing and sales literature. Together with the general understanding that lies are easier to produce and harder to detect when the deceiver incorporates elements of the truth in their talk (Carter, 2013), drawing on contextual factors to disguise fraudulent interactions as legitimate can be considered a powerful tool of deception that is difficult for the target of that deception to identify (Carter, 2024).

Individual factors

Much is written about individual factors relating to victimhood of deceptions and deceptive practices; however, these tend to focus on the individual deficiencies of the victim rather than on the characteristics and techniques of the criminal intent of inflicting financial or psychological harm (Carter, 2021). In relation to fraud, Carter (2023) identifies this focus on victims and examining their cognitive or social deficiencies, or lack of awareness in the framework of their vulnerability to fraud victimhood as a contributing factor in the shame experienced by victims (Cross, 2015). The shame experienced in victimhood and through societal expectations of effective self-protection from fraud presents a significant barrier to

Table 9.1 A comparative view of terminology: lies and deception, and information disorder

Lies and deception		Comparative view	Information disorder	
Deception	A superordinate category of intentionally misleading the recipient that involves lies as well as other intentional forms of creating misconceptions, e.g., camouflage or mimicking	In 'information disorder' discussions, disinformation covers a broad array of different types of intentionally false content described as harmful. In 'lies and deception' discussions, the sub- and superordinate relationship between lies and deception have led some to consider 'lies' as primarily concerning verbal statements, while acknowledging that deception can be achieved in numerous other ways. As an older and better established category of discussion, 'lies and deception' have produced various subcategories of 'lie' such as bald-faced lies or, more recently, false implicature. By excluding the creation of unintentional misconceptions, the terms in this bracket concern intentionally misleading messages of various forms, which cause harm to recipients	Disinformation	The intentional spreading of knowingly false content such as imposter content (deceit concerns the source of information), and manipulated or fabricated content (deceit concerns the truthfulness of the content itself, and includes images, video, and sound content), and the use of false contexts (taking statements out of context and/ or presenting them in contexts dissimilar from statement's original context in an effort to mislead recipients)
Lies	A concept within the broader category of intentional deception, which is often related to *statements*, i.e., by commission (intentionally contributing false statements) or omission (intentionally leaving out parts of statements)			
Malicious lies	Intentionally misleading statements or omissions used to gain some benefit with a concurrent assumption that others are knowingly harmed by such lies			
Bald-faced lies	Lies that are known to be lies both by the sender and the recipient but are nonetheless told to avoid accountability or admitting guilt			
False implicature	Using an otherwise truthful statement in specific contexts to lead recipients to make false implications			

(Continued)

Table 9.1 (Continued)

Lies and deception	Comparative view	Information disorder	
	Categories of information only included in discussions of 'information disorder' because the aim of this type of information or content is to cause harm without the need to involve deception	**Malinformation**	Disseminating truthful information for the distinct purpose of causing harm, e.g., hate speech or specifically timed information leaks
Unintentional creation of misconceptions	Situations in which the sender has no intention to lie or deceive, but a misconception is created for the recipient nonetheless. Can be described by the phrase "it is not what it looks/sounds like"	**Misinformation**	Unintentionally spreading untrue information, often by accident, that results from outdated information or mistranslation
	Misconception can be created, and misinformation spread, without an intention to deceive recipients. Misconceptions emphasise the varied interpretations recipients can attach to information being processed, while misinformation often originates from outdated information or poor information sharing practices, e.g., a lack of fact-checking		
'Noble' lies	Intentionally misleading statements or omissions used to avoid causing harm in particular situations		
	A contested category in 'lies and deception', which must be separated from disinformation because the stated aim of noble lies is to avoid causing harm to others		

reporting this crime (Button et al., 2013); rates currently sit around 15% (Crime Survey for England and Wales, 2019). Carter's (2021, 2023) work has started to redefine the trajectory of academic endeavour (and the associated impacts on criminal justice practice) to "step away from traditional perceptions of victims as different, vulnerable individuals" (Carter, 2023, p. 16). One would not, for example, ascribe individual actions or traits as a contributory or causal factor of domestic violence or rape. Indeed, the psychological harm visited upon victims of fraud has been described as akin to rape (Whitty & Buchanan, 2016). This reframing of fraud as a type of grooming akin to coercive control and domestic violence and abuse highlights that anyone can be 'vulnerable' to fraud—there is not a special combination of individual factors that will lead to or directly cause victimhood; the manipulation of a seemingly limitless combination of individual situations, contexts, and social-structural factors by serious organized criminals is what does.

Fraud is, of course, a distinct area of criminality that sits apart from other types of acquisitive criminality and deceptions in terms of modus operandi and unique dual financial and psychological harm (Whitty & Buchanan, 2016). In the context of digital communication, however, especially in relation to behavioural conditions, in combination with limited knowledge of information disorders, individual factors gain significance. Hansson et al. (2020, p. 6) state that individual factors arise from personal, physical, mental, emotional, or behavioural conditions that could make it difficult or impossible for people to send, receive, understand, or react to information about hazards. For example, the unperceptiveness of one's personal bias may hinder recognizing hazards in the case of harmful strategic narratives (Ventsel et al., 2023). The results show that, especially in times of high uncertainty and post-factual information ecology, if citizens believe that global threats do not affect them personally, they may be less likely to comply with regulations communicated by the authorities (Van der Meer et al., 2022). The increasing number of fact-checking initiatives has led to studying their impact on correcting false information, indicating that partisans trust or distrust a fact-checking message based on whether the message benefits or harms their supporting party. Since trust and belief in the content is strongly related to political and social identity, fact-checking and labelling dis- and misinformation do not seem to have a beneficial effect on an individual's credibility perceptions (Scharrer et al., 2022; Sun, 2022). Hence, accepting or objecting to fact-checking initiatives is one example where the individual, situational, and social-structural levels intersect, but the key is in the individual's knowledge and bias.

Situational factors

Situational factors are diverse and complex. In disaster contexts, situational aspects may affect access to communication channels or create misinterpretations due to exposure to false information (Hansson et al., 2020). However, in non-crisis situations, the diversity of potential forms of situational factors increases further still. Here, we highlight two dimensionally different aspects.

US conspiracy theorist and radio host Alex Jones was ordered to pay $49.3m in damages after intentionally claiming that the Sandy Hook school shooting in 2012 was a hoax orchestrated by the government to strip Americans of gun rights and that the parents of the dead children were "crisis actors". While the trial was about defamation, the intention behind spreading false information was deliberate and driven by financial benefit (BBC, 2022). In this case, the situational factors set a favourable scene for spreading disinformation, i.e. the context of a tragedy is used as a vehicle for peddling outrageous claims to soothe a particular audience already primed for such illogical explanations to emerge.

Another example can be brought from a common situation of malfunctioning card payments, online banking, or digital authentication services. In highly digitalized countries like Estonia, malfunctioning of digital services can easily be interpreted as a result of hostile cyberattacks. As everyday life depends on several digital services, this sort of disturbance forms a favourable basis for mal- and disinformation. As a result, the credibility of institutions is undermined, and in worst cases, people make drastic cash withdrawals, jeopardizing banks' available cash reserves, i.e., initiate a 'bank run'.

The factor connecting both cases is trust. In Alex Jones' case, the aim was to undermine the trust in government. In case of dis- and misinformation on malfunctioning of digital services, the objective is to use people's distrust towards digital services with the intention of pushing them towards harmful actions on the personal and societal level. In Jones' case, the spreading of particular disinformation relied on the salience of the tragic event as such, which also emphasizes the aspect of social timing as a method of ensuring salience for disseminating harmful information or potential scams (see Kikerpill, 2023a).

Social-structural factors

The dissemination of falsehoods online is incentivized by economic factors—especially the digital advertising industry, which makes significant profits from the viral spread of hoax news (Braun & Eklund, 2019)—as well as the socio-political developments in the Western countries, such as the growing distrust in news media and the deepening of political contentiousness (Freelon & Wells, 2020). Individuals' susceptibility to online false information is significantly shaped by several macro-level factors: the overall level of polarization and populist communication, the level of media trust and shared news consumption, and the strength of public service media organizations (Humprecht et al., 2020).

In modern democracies, governments are proposing various policy responses to the threats posed by intentional production and dissemination of false information (Tenove, 2020; Miller & Vaccari, 2020; Torpan et al., 2021). These include legislative measures to regulate media organizations to limit people's exposure to falsehoods, development of media literacy education programmes and public information campaigns aimed at making citizens more resilient to deception, and attempts at fact-checking and refuting incorrect information.

However, governments themselves may be the sources and disseminators of false, misleading, and potentially harmful content online. Politicians may try to sway their voters by producing polarizing content that is not based on facts. Government officeholders may use misleading or manipulative rhetoric in their social media postings in an attempt to present their policies in a positive light, avoid blame for their misdeeds, and hold on to power (Hansson & Page, 2022, 2023; Hansson, 2024). Importantly, manipulative rhetoric entails not only spreading outright lies: manipulators may omit relevant information or, the other way round, provide too much (possibly irrelevant) information to mystify the listeners/readers (Hansson, 2015). Untruthful communication by policymakers is detrimental to democracy in at least four ways: it reduces freedom and equality in society, weakens accountability, undermines citizens' trust in democratic institutions, and jeopardizes the ability to compromise (Hansson & Kröger, 2021).

The spreading of falsehoods and harmful narratives is also part of international politics. Major challenges to Western democracies arise from the uses of disinformation in international influence activities, such as those propagated by the Russian Federation as a part of its 'information warfare' against its neighbours and NATO allies (Lanoszka, 2016; Miskimmon & O'Loughlin, 2017). Russian state-funded media channels, such as RT and Sputnik, construct and spread narratives of fear and blame regarding international security issues to intimidate and confuse Western audiences and sow distrust among NATO members (Ventsel et al., 2021; Hansson et al., 2023). These channels design their content in a way that encourages Western audiences to share their disinformation online (Wagnsson, 2022). Their messages may be further amplified by trolls and bots and recycled in other genres, such as memes (Manor, 2019). The pro-Kremlin disinformation may harm the situational awareness of citizens who are exposed to it in the context of military aggression that is accompanied by hostile foreign influence, such as Russia's war against Ukraine (Golovchenko et al., 2018, Erlich & Garner, 2021). The strategic spreading of disinformation narratives as a form of online deviance may be difficult to pin down, and policymakers need to consider a mix of strategies to respond to them (Hellman & Wagnsson, 2017).

Case studies

The following four case studies are presented to exemplify some specific ways in which individual, situational, and social-structural contextual factors influence the creation, dissemination, and receipt of various types of information. The case studies aim to show the instrumental use of context within message delivery in order to achieve ends such as fraud victimization, deception via journalistic content, and the multifaceted dissemination of harmful information during crises.

Consumer fraud and situational factors

Fraud is defined as the causing of proprietary damage to another person by knowingly causing a misconception of existing facts for the purpose of proprietary benefit (Riigi Teataja, 2022). As the definition suggests, fraud is rooted in and dependent upon communication, i.e., it is "essentially a crime of interaction" (Harrington, 2012, p. 396). With respect to these interactions, message contexts have both a constitutive and interpretive dimension (Rigotti & Rocci, 2006). Thus, alongside the impact that the surrounding social environment has or can have on the interpretation of received messages, the content of such messages can be made more believable by exploiting external contextual references and by timing the dissemination of fraud messages on the basis of certain salient social events (Kikerpill & Siibak, 2021; Steinmetz et al., 2021; Taodang & Gundur, 2022).

The prevalence of online fraud in particular coincided with a shift towards the digitalization of interactions that were previously premised on face-to-face communication, e.g., in retailing. The geography of retailing experienced a paradigm change in the early 2000s with the emergence of e-commerce (see Rodrigue, 2016), which transformed retail exchanges, offerings, settings, as well as how different actors engage in the activity of purchasing goods (Hagberg et al., 2016). Since all activities in retailing, with the exception of the receipt of physical goods, can be managed via mediated environments, we are increasingly participating in activities in the form of action-as-communication (Kikerpill, 2021), i.e., looking for deals, picking a vendor, making the purchase, and choosing delivery times are all achieved through data entry and technology-mediated communication, not by walking from shop to shop and looking at prices.

Within this broader communicative context, the practice of observing (online) "commercial holidays" such as Amazon Prime Day (Stewart, 2022) brings with it the need to be aware of and detect crime-as-communication, i.e., criminal actors interjecting themselves into legitimate mediated interactions that people perform in the course of everyday life. The near-immediate access to recipients offered by modern communications technologies means that people are largely alone in the initial process of determining the veracity of incoming messages (Kikerpill, 2021). In the Amazon Prime Day example, the detection of criminal communication therefore relies heavily on contextual factors such as the geographical availability of specific offers or delivery options, cultural acceptance of and participation in these types of sales events, and the temporal aspects of the event itself (Kikerpill, 2023a). More specifically, while Amazon Prime Day began as a 24-hour sales event that included 9 countries, it now spans 20 countries and lasts for two days (Johnston, 2022). Hence, the geographical reach of services and options offered has increased over time, which inadvertently extends the number of people for whom the Amazon Prime Day event can function as a legitimizing context when assessing the veracity of incoming offers and messages, including in the form of native advertising in which the advertisement's format is fashioned to reflect primary content (Wu et al., 2016).

Even though the geographical reach of the event has increased, taking part in Prime Day offerings also runs on a cultural and individual component, e.g., "people everywhere, but Americans in particular, love sales; they love deals" (see Stewart 2022, para. 5). In other words, people's willingness to look for commercial deals on set dates depends in part on their developing cultural surroundings (Sklair, 2015). Taken together, the social-structural factors of accessibility and the culture of consumerism drive e-commerce participation, which subsequently creates opportunities for cybercriminal exploitation. Since crime goes where people go (Posick, 2018), any changes in the dates of "commercial holidays" come to be reflected in the criminal activity it attracts. In 2020, Amazon Prime Day was moved to October instead of its usual summertime occurrence (Whitney, 2021), the news of which prompted rapid preparations by scammers looking to victimize consumers (Bolster, 2021). Hence, red letter days in so-called "criminal calendars" (Kikerpill, 2023a) can be expected to shift together with the events that function as the situational context for relevant cybercrimes. Indeed, emerging criminological research has shown that salient social events can be effectively used as contextual cues when vying for the attention of potential victims (see Steinmetz et al., 2021, p. 5).

Overall, the observance of social-structural (access and culture of consumerism) and situational factors (timing) in the crafting of scam messages, which reference sales events such as Amazon Prime Day, add credibility to criminal content that spreads alongside legitimate information and offers.

Romance fraud and individual factors

Deception is a requirement for fraudulent interactions, as the purpose and intent of fraudsters is to persuade the recipient (target victim) to act in a way that is financially and psychologically harmful to themselves, while maintaining a façade of performing an entirely different, often beneficial, action or task: in the case of romance fraud, the mutual seeking of an individual connection that will lead to a romantic relationship. Drawing on the personal in all types of fraud is a useful tool as it enables the fraudster's interactions to appear individualized in terms of content and detail, which increases the appearance of credibility.

In romance fraud, it's also normalized through the wider contextual expectations of providing personal information in efforts to build rapport and getting to know the other person; a practice that invites reciprocal and continued interaction in order for both parties to engage in a functional conversation within the context of a developing romantic relationship.

Similarities and assimilations

Individualizing communications can involve the fraudster focusing on themes and topics that align with the victim's own personal preferences, opinions, and experiences, assimilating these as their own or revealing similarities with their own lives. It can also present as the fraudster drawing on their fictitious vulnerabilities or details about their personal lives. The following extract is between Debbie (the fraudster) and Peter (the victim), where Debbie has convinced Peter to transfer money to her amidst their developing romantic relationship.

> Debbie: "Haven't been with anyone since I lost my hubby. It's been my only marriage so far and the only serious relationship I've been able to build. Sorry to hear about your divorce. It's never easy, is it?"

This façade of similarity also extends to their expectations of the recipient; shown here, after Peter transfers money to Debbie, she uses this to her advantage in terms of developing her own character traits. First, she claims that she will repay him in kind, reinforcing her credibility in her role as a grateful girlfriend receiving a gift:

Debbie (Fraudster): "I do need to spoil you . . . I strongly believe in the principle of reciprocation x x. X"
Peter: "You do not give to receive—you in my life will be enough to spoil me XxX trust me XxX. Money on its way £100 transferred Babes XxX"

She then uses the victim's phrase to claim 'alignment' with his philosophical perspective, which also frees her from future negotiating narratives around (not) repaying the money.

Debbie: "Yes you're so right . . . you give to create joy. not just because you wish to get something back . . . it's amazing to see how much we align babes xxx thanks much my love xxxx"

Distancing

Disguising deception is essential to the fraudster as the victim is required to engage with the fraudulent content for their exploitation to occur. Fraudsters conceal their true intentions by distancing themselves from the responsibility of the message they are delivering, by distancing themselves from being a fraudster, or disguising their requests of the victim as beneficial to them or mutually beneficial.

This is a way in which deceptions can be delivered in a manner which is less likely to be discovered. General interactional distancing is not verifiable in the way that unequivocal direct claims or statements are, and therefore do not allow judgement on their truth or falsehood, or draw suspicion in the way that direct falsehoods might in these contexts (Carter, 2014). By the fraudster framing themselves as the messenger rather than the source of the information, questions or suspicions relating to that issue are intuitively directed towards the 'other' from whom the message appears to originate (Carter, 2015). The recipient therefore may continue engaging with the fraudster where they may have otherwise stopped, if the fraudster's legitimacy were in question. This distancing behaviour is examined in the following extract.

Harnessing higher deities distances the fraudster from the source; positioning the fraudster (Harry in the following extract) as messenger rather than protagonist, elevates the source of the information as unavailable to scrutiny, and legitimizes the fraudster with qualities of faith that would be appreciated and understood by recipients with similar religious inclinations. It also personalizes the communication by focussing on the victim as the particular individual chosen for the fraudster.

Harry: "How can I ever Thank God for the grace to send me someone like you to share everything with, to rely on, to have confidence. Even now without ever having met, you show so much trust in me my dearest one that overwhelms me".

The fraudster scripts the victim (Helen) as sent from God, with all the attendant virtues and expectations (generosity, faith when in doubt, and so on) this entails. Distancing is also performed through bringing potential 'red flags' into plain sight (Carter, 2024). He reframes trusting someone 'even' without having met as a positive personal attribute of the victim, as a particular demonstration of trust that has had a profound positive effect on him. The fraudster's display of vulnerability and linking the victim's behaviours with his emotions is a type of 'visceral response', which individualizes the communication that draws victims into the situation and makes it difficult for them to leave, rewards personally risky behaviours with praise, and normalizes ignoring potential concerns, much like in coercive relationships and domestic abuse (Carter, 2021).

Harry: "You cannot imagine how much I prayed and asked God for sending me the partner he meant for me during the last months. When I finally decided to surrender, not to force anything, not taking any actions, you came into my life my dear, totally unexpected."

Framing his actions as benign, inert, and their connection as a result of the actions of God rather than his active seeking of a partner reinforces the implicit suggestion that he is non-threatening, non-predatory. There is also the inevitability of the relationship, with undertones of possessiveness framed in an overarching lack of accountability for his feelings and actions, and the victim as designed for him.

Deceptive content in journalism

Different forms of information disorder may seep into journalistic content for myriad reasons. This case study focusses on the biased production of deceptive scientific evidence (Weatherall et al., 2020) and native advertising (Amazeen & Wojdynski, 2020), i.e., two different lines of potential deception that share a persuasive intent, and the effects and impacts of which are greater when published in news media.

In 2016, a local NGO—the Institute of Social Studies—was established in Estonia. The NGO mainly produced public opinion surveys focussing on controversial political issues.

Results from the aforementioned surveys were distributed as press releases that resembled news articles. Estonian online news portals published these texts without fail on each occasion. While the reports and press releases resembled scientific research, analyses of the methods used revealed a strong bias in terms of research design and process. Only 22% of the survey questions adhered to standards expected from a sociological survey (Laube, 2018), indicating deliberate bias and skewed results (ERR, 2017; Ott, 2019). The disseminated results often matched respective agendas of national-conservative politicians, and the NGO disclosed having received funding from entrepreneurs known to be supporters and sponsors of a national-conservative political party.

While the aforementioned constitutes a model example of deceptive political initiative, it is neither exceptional nor new. The so-called 'tobacco strategy' making use of similar tactics of producing faux scientific research appears in accordance with a particular agenda (Oreskes & Conway, 2010). Weatherall and colleagues (2020) describe the causal link between biased production, i.e., the scientific-looking deceptive information, and the impact it has on public opinion and individual beliefs. The effect is notable, because scientists are viewed as essential predictors of perceived trustworthiness (Reif et al., 2020). Thus, reliance on the social authority of researchers and their work allows the production of faux science that, in turn, finds its way into journalistic content.

Lies and deception that evade the journalistic fact-checking filter find fruitful soil on all three levels of vulnerability. On the individual level, journalists and audiences lack the skills necessary for verifying information. In particular, journalists are not well-versed in methods of sociological study and lack mathematical skills necessary for evaluating or analysing raw or pre-processed data (Kõuts-Klemm, 2019). While core fact-checking-related journalistic skills ought to eliminate most avenues to inadvertently disseminating false information, implementing such skills often relies on trust and previous communicative patterns, which creates blind trust in the journalistic source and leaves important gaps in the fact-checking filter (Himma-Kadakas & Ojamets, 2022). The ability to use technologies, media, and contexts for the purpose of gathering resources and information, and exchanging different meanings, embodies the concept of transliteracy (Sukovic, 2017), which forms the basis for how individual audience members cope with potentially false or deceptive information. To recognize the potential deception, e.g., fabrications or manipulations presented as research, and to verify or debunk the information, a person must possess knowledge and skills in scientific literacy as well as in numeric, news, media, information, and digital literacies. Unsurprisingly, audiences tend to struggle with detecting false content, which may be magnified by salient social circumstances such as crises (Almenar et al., 2021). Moreover, the self-perceived knowledge of different literacies may not actualize as fact-checking practices (Jones-Jang et al., 2021).

Situational factors promoting the publication of deceptive information originate in the operational routines of news media organizations. Given the time pressures entailed by online work routines, and the tensions involved in producing content in competitive media houses, deceptive information enters the publishing cycle of online news portals more easily in comparison with legacy media (Himma-Kadakas, 2017; Himma-Kadakas & Ojamets, 2022). Knowledge of journalistic work routines and related pitfalls increases the probability of successful deception.

Social-structural factors that influence deceptive content that finds its way into journalistic content are easy to explain rationally, but difficult to detect in practice. While the political and business agendas behind biased content production have long-term implications on public opinion, native advertising may create a significant immediate effect which, over time, undermines the credibility of journalism as such. One potential pathway for deception's entry into news media comes in the form of native advertising as sponsored and persuasive content. This type of content could undermine journalistic credibility because native advertising is often indistinguishable from editorial content and can, with respect to relevant audiences, function like fact-based news. Although native advertising must be disclosed as an advertisement (Federal Trade Commission, 2015; Riigi Teataja, 2019), audiences are often deceived by poor disclosure labelling (Ferrer-Conill et al., 2021) or because they lack the ability to recognize and critically assess the content in question (Amazeen & Wojdynski, 2019). Wu and colleagues (2016) showed that priming individuals with a definition of native advertising increases their ability to recognize the content as advertising, including its persuasive intent, and makes people take a more critical approach towards such content. Thus, providing this type of information proves useful in media literacy training as it increases people's resilience against deceptive content. Even so, it does not address the issue of commercial pressure placed on newsrooms to accept native advertising. Since sponsored content is often managed separately from editorial content, persuasive content not subject to fact-checking gets published alongside journalistic articles and contributes to the diminishing credibility of journalism (Schauster et al., 2016).

Improving transliteracy for the purposes of increasing resilience towards deceptive information does obtain some results, but little attention has thus far been paid to the processes that facilitate the dissemination of deceptive content in journalistic channels. The problem highlighted here centres on journalism's inability to detect deceptive intentions and fabricated information that is brought on by the intertwined effects from all three levels of vulnerability. Hence, deceptive information becomes legitimized, is published as news or as indistinguishable from it, and potentially creates a greater impact than it would in the case of smaller-scale dissemination (e.g., in alternative or social media groups).

COVID-19 information disorder

Major disasters and crises create contexts in which people are exposed to increasing streams of emotionalized, unverified, and often-contradictory messages from multiple channels. Hansson et al. (2021) charted various messages and information behaviour that put people's lives, health, or property in harm's way at the outset of the pandemic in six European countries. They found six types of harmful information. First, there were messages that discouraged appropriate protective actions against catching/spreading the virus, such as observing lockdown measures and wearing a face covering. Second, there were stories and advertisements promoting the use of false (or harmful) remedies against the virus, for example claiming that the novel coronavirus could be treated by consuming sodium bicarbonate or by smoking. Third, some stories misrepresented the transmission mechanisms of the virus, for instance falsely claiming that the virus is spread by bacteria and can be kept away by high temperature. Fourth, there were messages that downplayed the risks related to the pandemic, for example falsely claiming that the coronavirus outbreak would end in a matter of weeks or that the virus did not even exist. Fifth, scammers exploited individuals' anxieties and ignorance during the outset of the pandemic by tricking them into buying fake protection against the virus and by using the pandemic as a pretence to invade their privacy. For instance, scammers tried to sell fake coronavirus tests and enter people's homes to 'install coronavirus filters' but actually stole their valuables. Sixth, some individuals and groups, such as refugees, were victimized as the alleged spreaders of the virus by harassment/hate speech.

Hansson et al. (2021) observed that in multiple cases, harmful information was originally published in local news media, non-mainstream news websites, or some social media profiles, but later disseminated more widely, including internationally, via social media. The authors concluded that exposure to these types of information may pose a threat to people's lives or wellbeing irrespective of whether the creator/sender intended to cause harm or simply saw it as a benevolent piece of advice or a joke. Importantly, people's vulnerability to harmful information is heavily shaped by social and structural factors related to politics, power, and social inequality. During a crisis, authorities may fail to provide accurate risk information and behavioural guidance quickly enough, and in a manner tailored to the needs of various groups in society, providing fertile ground for rumourmongering and the diffusion of harmful speculation. Moreover, the risk of falling victim to scams or hate speech is higher in societies with no effective policy measures in place to combat (cyber) crime and xenophobia.

Conclusion

This chapter has highlighted the theoretical-terminological overlap, and differences, between broader discussions focussing on 'lies and deception' and 'information disorder'. While the 'lies and deception' camp has more fully developed what 'information disorder' refers to as disinformation, the 'information disorder' camp has successfully added the concept of mal-information, i.e., the use of truths to cause harm. As online communication depends on the exchange of context-dependent messages, the chapter also reviewed and analysed three levels of contextual factors impacting information dissemination: the individual, situational, and social-structural contextual factors. Furthermore, four case studies were presented to highlight the various forms and real-life situations in which informational exchanges serve malicious ends. More specifically, the chapter focussed on online fraud in romantic and consumer contexts, highlighting the ways in which manipulation occurs on both on the level of individual talk as well as driven by salient social (commercial) events. Furthermore, the chapter showed how deceptive content seeps into journalistic practice, and crisis situations bring out the individual and situational communication-related vulnerabilities of communities. In future studies, researchers could use the theoretical-terminological work in this chapter for further narrowing the divide between the camps of 'lies and deception' and 'information disorder' to better understand the different malicious uses of information and the context within which it is delivered.

References

Almenar, E., Aran-Ramspott, S., Suau, J., & Masip, P. (2021). Gender differences in tackling fake news: Different degrees of concern, but same problems. *Media & Communication*, 9(1), 229–238. https://doi.org/10.17645/mac.v9i1.3523

Amazeen, M. A., & Wojdynski, B. W. (2019). Reducing native advertising deception: Revisiting the antecedents and consequences of persuasion knowledge in digital news contexts. *Mass Communication & Society*, 22(2), 222–247. https://doi.org/10.1080/15205436.2018.1530792

Amazeen, M. A., & Wojdynski, B. W. (2020). The effects of disclosure format on native advertising recognition and audience perceptions of legacy and online news publishers. *Journalism*, 21(12), 1965–1984. https://doi.org/10.1177/1464884918754829

BBC. (2022, August 6). Alex Jones must pay $49.3m for Sandy Hook hoax claim. *BBC News*. Retrieved from www.bbc.com/news/world-us-canada-62444302

Blair, J. P., Levine, T. R., & Shaw, A. S. (2010). Content in context improves deception detection accuracy. *Human Communication Research*, *36*(3), 423–442. https://doi.org/10.1111/j.1468-2958.2010.01382.x

Bolster Blog. (2021, June 16). *Amazon scams up 7X leading up to prime day*. Retrieved from https://bolster.ai/blog/amazon-scams-up-7x-leading-up-to-prime-day/

Braun, J. A., & Eklund, J. L. (2019). Fake news, real money: Ad tech platforms, profit-driven hoaxes, and the business of journalism. *Digital Journalism*, *7*(1), 1–21. https://doi.org/10.1080/21670811.2018.1556314

Button, M., Tapley, J., & Lewis, C. (2013). 'The 'fraud justice network' and the infra-structure of support for individual fraud victims in England and Wales'. *Criminology & Criminal Justice*, *13*(1), 37–61. https://doi.org/10.1177/1748895812448085

Caramancion, K. M., Li, Y., Dubois, E., & Jung, E. S. (2022). The missing case of disinformation from the cybersecurity risk continuum: A comparative assessment of disinformation with other cyber threats. *Data*, *7*(4), art 49. https://doi.org/10.3390/data7040049

Carter, E. (2013). *Analysing police interviews: Laughter, confessions and the tape*. Bloomsbury.

Carter, E. (2014). Deception in different contexts. In T. R. Levine (Ed.), *Encyclopedia of deception* (pp. 265–268). Sage.

Carter, E. (2015). The anatomy of written scam communications: An empirical analysis. *Crime, Media, Culture: An International Journal*, *11*(2), 89–103. https://doi.org/10.1177/1741659015572310

Carter, E. (2021). Distort, extort, deceive and exploit: Exploring the inner workings of a romance fraud. *British Journal of Criminology*, *61*(2), 283–302. https://doi.org/10.1093/bjc/azaa072

Carter, E. (2023). Confirm not command: Examining fraudsters' use of language to compel victim compliance in their own exploitation. *British Journal of Criminology*. https://doi.org/10.1093/bjc/azac098

Carter, E. (2024). *The language of romance crimes: Interactions of love, money and threat*. Cambridge University Press. https://doi.org/10.1017/9781009273008

Choraś, M., Demestichas, K., Giełczyk, A., Herrero, Á., Ksieniewicz, P., Remoundou, K., Urda, D., & Woźniak, M. (2021). Advanced Machine Learning techniques for fake news (online disinformation) detection: A systematic mapping study. *Applied Soft Computing*, *101*, 107050. https://doi.org/10.1016/j.asoc.2020.107050

Crime Survey for England and Wales. (2019). *Crime in England and Wales: Year ending March 2019 — Office for National Statistics*. Office for National Statistics. ons.gov.uk

Cross, C. (2015). No laughing matter: Blaming the victim of fraud. *International Review of Victimology*, *21*(2), 187–204. https://doi.org/10.1177/0269758015571471

Cross, C. (2022). Using artificial intelligence (AI) and deepfakes to deceive victims: The need to rethink current romance fraud prevention messaging. *Crime Prevention & Community Safety*, *24*, 30–41. https://doi.org/10.1057/s41300-021-00134-w

DePaulo, B. M., Kashy, D. A., Kirkendol, S. E., Wyer, M. M., & Epstein, J. A. (1996). Lying in everyday life. *Journal of Personality & Social Psychology*, *70*(5), 979–995. https://doi.org/10.1037/0022-3514.70.5.979

Egelhofer, J. L., & Lecheler, S. (2019). Fake news as a two-dimensional phenomenon: A framework and research agenda. *Annals of the International Communication Association*, *43*(2), 97–116. https://doi.org/10.1080/23808985.2019.1602782

Erlich, A., & Garner, C. (2021). Is pro-Kremlin disinformation effective? Evidence from Ukraine. *The International Journal of Press/Politics*. https://doi.org/10.1177/19401612211045221

ERR. (2017, March 30). *Sotsioloogide ühisavaldus ajendatult MTÜ Ühiskonnauuringute Instituudist*. ERR. Retrieved from www.err.ee/587088/sotsioloogide-uhisavaldus-ajendatult-mtu-uhiskonnauuringute-instituudist

Fadilpašić, S. (2023, April 26). How hackers use generative AI in their attacks and what we can do about it. *Make Use Of*. Retrieved from www.makeuseof.com/how-hackers-use-generative-ai-in-their-attacks/

Federal Trade Commission. (2015, December 22). *Native advertising: A guide for businesses*. Federal Trade Commission. Retrieved from www.ftc.gov/business-guidance/resources/native-advertising-guide-businesses

Ferrer-Conill, R., Knudsen, E., Lauerer, C., & Barnoy, A. (2021). The visual boundaries of journalism: Native advertising and the convergence of editorial and commercial content. *Digital Journalism*, *9*(7), 929–951. https://doi.org/10.1080/21670811.2020.1836980

Fischer, P., Lea, S. E., & Evans, K. M. (2013). Why do individuals respond to fraudulent scam communications and lose money? The psychological determinants of scam compliance. *Journal of Applied Social Psychology*, *43*(10), 2060–2072. https://doi.org/10.1111/jasp.12158

Frank, M. G., & Svetieva, E. (2013). Deception. In D. Matsumoto, M. G. Frank, & H. S. Hwang (Eds.), *Nonverbal communication: Science & applications* (pp. 121–144). Sage.

Freelon, D., & Wells, C. (2020). Disinformation as political communication. *Political Communication*, *37*(2), 145–156. https://doi.org/10.1080/10584609.2020.1723755

Golovchenko, Y., Hartmann, M., & Adler-Nissen, R. (2018). State, media and civil society in the information warfare over Ukraine: Citizen curators of digital disinformation. *International Affairs*, *94*(5), 975–994. https://doi.org/10.1093/ia/iiy148

Habgood-Coote, J. (2019). Stop talking about fake news! *Inquiry: An Interdisciplinary Journal of Philosophy*, *62*(9–10), 1033–1065. https://doi.org/10.1080/0020174X.2018.1508363

Hagberg, J., Sundstrom, M., & Egels-Zandén, N. (2016). The digitalization of retailing: An exploratory framework. *International Journal of Retail & Distribution Management*, *44*(7), 694–712. https://doi.org/10.1108/IJRDM-09-2015-0140

Hall, S. (1973). *Encoding and decoding in television discourse* [Discussion Paper]. University of Birmingham. Retrieved from https://core.ac.uk/download/pdf/81670115.pdf

Hancock, J. T. (2009). Digital deception: Why, when and how people lie online. In A. N. Joinson, K. Y. A. McKenna, T. Postmes, & U.-D. Reips (Eds.), *The Oxford handbook of internet psychology* (pp. 289–302). Oxford University Press.

Hansson, S. (2015). Calculated overcommunication: Strategic uses of prolixity, irrelevance, and repetition in administrative language. *Journal of Pragmatics*, *84*, 172–188. https://doi.org/10.1016/j.pragma.2015.05.014

Hansson, S. (2024). Coercive impoliteness and blame avoidance in government communication. *Discourse, Context & Media*, *58*, 100770. https://doi.org/10.1016/j.dcm.2024.100770

Hansson, S., & Kröger, S. (2021). How a lack of truthfulness can undermine democratic representation: The case of post-referendum Brexit discourses. *The British Journal of Politics and International Relations*, *23*(4), 609–626. https://doi.org/10.1177/1369148120974009

Hansson, S., Madisson, M. L., & Ventsel, A. (2023). Discourses of blame in strategic narratives: The case of Russia's 5G stories. *European Security*, *32*(1), 62–84. https://doi.org/10.1080/09662839.2022.2057188

Hansson, S., Orru, K., Siibak, A., Bäck, A., Krüger, M., Gabel, F., & Morsut, C. (2020). Communication-related vulnerability to disasters: A heuristic framework. *International Journal of Disaster Risk Reduction*, *51*, 101931. https://doi.org/10.1016/j.ijdrr.2020.101931

Hansson, S., Orru, K., Torpan, S., Bäck, A., Kazemekaityte, A., Meyer, S. F., Ludvigsen, J., Savadori, L., Galvagni, A., & Pigrée, A. (2021). COVID-19 information disorder: Six types of harmful information during the pandemic in Europe. *Journal of Risk Research*, *24*(3–4), 380–393. https://doi.org/10.1080/13669877.2020.1871058

Hansson, S., & Page, R. (2022). Corpus-assisted analysis of legitimation strategies in government social media communication. *Discourse & Communication*, *16*(5), 551–571. https://doi.org/10.1177/17504813221099202

Hansson, S., & Page, R. (2023). Legitimation in government social media communication: The case of the Brexit department. *Critical Discourse Studies*, *20*(4), 361–378. https://doi.org/10.1080/17405904.2022.2058971

Harrington, B. (2012). The sociology of financial fraud. In K. K. Cetina & A. Preda (Eds.), *The Oxford handbook of the sociology of finance* (pp. 393–410). Oxford University Press.

Hellman, M., & Wagnsson, C. (2017). How can European states respond to Russian information warfare? An analytical framework. *European Security*, *26*(2), 153–170. https://doi.org/10.1080/09662839.2017.1294162

Himelein-Wachowiak, M., Giorgi, S., Devoto, A., Rahman, M., Ungar, L., Schwartz, H. A., Epstein, D. H., Leggio, L., & Curtis, B. (2021). Bots and misinformation spread on social media: Implications for COVID-19. *Journal of Medical Internet Research*, *23*(5), e26933. https://doi.org/10.2196/26933

Himma-Kadakas, M. (2017). Alternative facts and fake news entering journalistic content production cycle. *Cosmopolitan Civil Societies: An Interdisciplinary Journal, 9*(2), 25–40. https://doi.org/10.5130/ccs.v9i2.5469

Himma-Kadakas, M., & Ojamets, I. (2022). Debunking false information: Investigating journalists' fact-checking skills. *Digital Journalism,* 1–22. https://doi.org/10.1080/21670811.2022.2043173

Humprecht, E., Esser, F., & Van Aelst, P. (2020). Resilience to online disinformation: A framework for cross-national comparative research. *The International Journal of Press/Politics, 25*(3), 493–516. https://doi.org/10.1177/1940161219900126

Johnston, B. (2022, January 4). *Prime Day 2022: Everything you need to know.* Retrieved from www.expertreviews.co.uk/amazon-prime-day

Jones-Jang, S. M., Mortensen, T., & Liu, J. (2021). Does media literacy help identification of fake news? Information literacy helps, but other literacies don't. *American Behavioral Scientist, 65*(2), 371–388. https://doi.org/10.1177/0002764219869406

Jungherr, A., & Schroeder, R. (2021). Disinformation and the structural transformations of the public arena: Addressing the actual challenges to democracy. *Social Media & Society, 7*(1), 2056305121988928.

Kalbfleisch, P. J., & Docan-Morgan, T. (2019). Defining truthfulness, deception, and related concepts. Historical perspectives on the study of lying and deception. In T. Docan-Morgan (Ed.), *The Palgrave handbook of deceptive communication* (pp. 29–40). Palgrave Macmillan.

Kapantai, E., Christopoulou, A., Berberidis, C., & Peristeras, V. (2021). A systematic literature review on disinformation: Toward a unified taxonomical framework. *New Media & Society, 23*(5), 1301–1326. https://doi.org/10.1177/1461444820959296

Kikerpill, K. (2020). Choose your stars and studs: The rise of deepfake designer porn. *Porn Studies, 7*(4), 352–356. https://doi.org/10.1080/23268743.2020.1765851

Kikerpill, K. (2021). *Crime-as-communication: Detecting diagnostically useful information from the content and context of social engineering attacks.* University of Tartu Press.

Kikerpill, K. (2023a). Chapter 4: Scanning for scams: Local, supra-national and global events as salient contexts for online fraud. In D. Radovanović (Ed.), *Digital literacy and inclusion.* Springer Nature. Retrieved from https://doi.org/10.1007/978-3-031-30808-6.

Kikerpill, K. (2023b). (M)asking for a return: Social hypocrisy and social engineering. In L. Magalhães & C. O. Martins (Eds.), *Masks and human connections: Disruptive meanings and cultural challenges* (pp. 47–59). Palgrave Macmillan. Retrieved from https://doi.org/10.1007/978-3-031-16673-0_4

Kikerpill, K., & Siibak, A. (2021). Mazephishing: The COVID-19 pandemic as credible social context for social engineering attacks. *Trames Journal of the Humanities & Social Sciences, 25*(4), 371–393. https://doi.org/10.3176/tr.2021.4.01

Kõuts-Klemm, R. (2019). Data literacy among journalists: A skills-assessment based approach. *Central European Journal of Communication, 12*(3), 299–315. https://doi.org/10.19195/1899-5101.12.3(24).2

Lanoszka, A. (2016). Russian hybrid warfare and extended deterrence in eastern Europe. *International Affairs, 92*(1), 175–195. https://doi.org/10.1111/1468-2346.12509

Laube, K. (2018). *MTÜ Ühiskonnauuringute Instituudi küsitlusuuringute sõnastus ja nende uuringutulemuste kajastus Eesti uudisajakirjanduse veebiväljaannetes* [Bachelor's thesis, 84. University of Tartu].

Levine, T. R. (2014). Truth-Default Theory (TDT): A theory of human deception detection. *Journal of Language & Social Psychology, 33*(4), 378–392. https://doi.org/10.1177/0261927X14535916

Levine, T. R. (2019). *Duped: Truth-default theory and the social science of lying and deception.* University of Alabama Press.

Levine, T. R., & McCornack, S. A. (2014). Theorizing about deception. *Journal of Language & Social Psychology, 33*(4), 431–440. https://doi.org/10.1177/0261927X14536397

Manor, I. (2019). *The digitalization of public diplomacy.* Springer.

McGlone, M. S., & Knapp, M. L. (2019). Historical perspectives on the study of lying and deception. In T. Docan-Morgan (Ed.), *The Palgrave handbook of deceptive communication* (pp. 3–28). Palgrave Macmillan.

Miller, M. L., & Vaccari, C. (2020). Digital threats to democracy: Comparative lessons and possible remedies. *The International Journal of Press/Politics, 25*(3), 333–356. https://doi.org/10.1177/1940161220922323

Miskimmon, A., & O'Loughlin, B. (2017). Russia's narratives of global order: Great power legacies in a polycentric world. *Politics & Governance, 5*(3), 111–120. https://doi.org/10.17645/pag.v5i3.1017

Mourão, R. R., & Robertson, C. T. (2019). Fake news as discursive integration: An analysis of sites that publish false, misleading, hyperpartisan and sensational information. *Journalism Studies, 20*(14), 2077–2095. https://doi.org/10.1080/1461670X.2019.1566871

Oliver, S., Burls, T., Fenge, L. A., & Brown, K. (2015). "Winning and losing": Vulnerability to mass marketing fraud. *Journal of Adult Protection, 17*(6), 360–370. https://doi.org/10.1108/JAP-02-2015-0002

Oreskes, N., & Conway, E. M. (2010). Defeating the merchants of doubt. *Nature, 465*(7299), 686–687. https://doi.org/10.1038/465686a

Ott, M. (2019, January 25). *Teaduspesu*. Sirp. Retrieved from https://sirp.ee/s1-artiklid/c21-teadus/teaduspesu/

Park, H. S., Levine, T. R., McCornack, S. A., Morrison, K., & Ferrera, M. (2002). How people really detect lies. *Communication Monographs, 69*(2), 144–157. https://doi.org/10.1080/714041710

Posick, C. (2018). *The development of criminological thought: Context, theory and policy*. Routledge.

Reif, A., Kneisel, T., Schäfer, M., & Taddicken, M. (2020). Why are scientific experts perceived as trustworthy? Emotional assessment within TV and YouTube videos. *Media & Communication, 8*(1), 191–205. https://doi.org/10.17645/mac.v8i1.2536

Rigotti, E., & Rocci, A. (2006). Towards a definition of communication context. Foundations of an interdisciplinary approach to communication. *Studies in Communication Sciences, 6*(2), 155–180.

Riigi Teataja. (2019). *Consumer protection act [of the republic of Estonia]*. Retrieved from www.riigiteataja.ee/en/eli/520032019016/consolide

Riigi Teataja. (2022). *Penal code [of the republic of Estonia]*. Retrieved from www.riigiteataja.ee/en/eli/510052022003/consolide

Rodrigue, J.-P. (2016). The distribution network of Amazon and the footprint of freight digitalization. *Journal of Transport Geography, 88*, 102825. https://doi.org/10.1016/j.jtrangeo.2020.102825

Rubin, V. L. (2019). Disinformation and misinformation triangle: A conceptual model for "fake news" epidemic, causal factors and interventions. *Journal of Documentation, 75*(5), 1013–1034. https://doi.org/10.1108/JD-12-2018-0209

Sánchez, N., Masip, J., & Herrero, C. (2021). How people [try to] detect lies in everyday life. *Trames Journal of the Humanities & Social Sciences, 25*(4), 395–419. https://doi.org/10.3176/tr.2021.4.02

Scharrer, L., Pape, V., & Stadtler, M. (2022). Watch out: Fake! How warning labels affect laypeople's evaluation of simplified scientific misinformation. *Discourse Processes*, 1–16. https://doi.org/10.1080/0163853X.2022.2096364

Schauster, E. E., Ferrucci, P., & Neill, M. S. (2016). Native advertising is the new journalism: How deception affects social responsibility. *American Behavioral Scientist, 60*(12), 1408–1424. https://doi.org/10.1177/0002764216660135

Serota, K. B., Levine, T. R., & Boster, F. J. (2010). The prevalence of lying in America: Three studies of self-reported lies. *Human Communication Research, 36*(1), 2–25. https://doi.org/10.1111/j.1468-2958.2009.01366.x

Serota, K. B., Levine, T. R., & Docan-Morgan, T. (2021). Unpacking variation in lie prevalence: Prolific liars, bad lie days, or both? *Communication Monographs*. https://doi.org/10.1080/03637751.2021.1985153

Shao, C., Ciampaglia, G. L., Varol, O., Yang, K.-C., Flammini, A., & Menczer, F. (2018). The spread of low-credibility content by social bots. *Nature Communications, 9*, 4787. https://doi.org/10.1038/s41467-018-06930-7

Sklair, L. (2015). Culture-ideology of consumerism. In D. T. Cook & J. M. Ryan (Eds.), *The Wiley Blackwell encyclopedia of consumption and consumer studies*. John Wiley & Sons Ltd. Retrieved from https://doi.org/10.1002/9781118989463.wbeccs089

Steinmetz, K., Pimentel, A., & Goe, W. R. (2021). Performing social engineering: A qualitative study of information security deceptions. *Computers in Human Behavior, 124*, 106930. https://doi.org/10.1016/j.chb.2021.106930

Stewart, E. (2022, July 14). *We all just fell for Amazon's made-up holiday yet again*. Vox. Retrieved from www.vox.com/the-goods/2022/7/14/23203964/amazon-prime-day-2022-deals-capitalism-discounts

Sukovic, S. (2017). *Transliteracy in complex information environments*. Elsevier/Chandos Publishing.

Sun, Y. (2022). Verification upon exposure to COVID-19 misinformation: Predictors, outcomes, and the mediating role of verification. *Science Communication, 44*(3), 261–291. https://doi.org/10.1177/10755470221088927

Tandoc Jr, E. C., Lim, Z. W., & Ling, R. (2018). Defining "fake news". *Digital Journalism, 6*(2), 137–153. https://doi.org/10.1080/21670811.2017.1360143

Taodang, D., & Gundur, R. V. (2022). How frauds in times of crisis target people. *Victims & Offenders.* https://doi.org/10.1080/15564886.2022.2043968

Tenove, C. (2020). Protecting democracy from disinformation: Normative threats and policy responses. *The International Journal of Press/Politics, 25*(3), 517–537. https://doi.org/10.1177/1940161220918740

Torpan, S., Hansson, S., Rhinard, M., Kazemekaityte, A., Jukarainen, P., Meyer, S. F., Schieffelers, A., Lovasz, G., & Orru, K. (2021). Handling false information in emergency management: A cross-national comparative study of European practices. *International Journal of Disaster Risk Reduction, 57*, 102151. https://doi.org/10.1016/j.ijdrr.2021.102151

Van der Meer, T. G. L. A., Brosius, A., & Hameleers, M. (2022). The role of media use and misinformation perceptions in optimistic bias and third-person perceptions in times of high media dependency: Evidence from four countries in the first stage of the COVID-19 Pandemic. *Mass Communication & Society.* https://doi.org/10.1080/15205436.2022.2039202

Ventsel, A., Hansson, S., Madisson, M. L., & Sazonov, V. (2021). Discourse of fear in strategic narratives: The case of Russia's Zapad war games. *Media, War & Conflict, 14*(1), 21–39. https://doi.org/10.1177/1750635219856552

Ventsel, A., Hansson, S., Rickberg, M., & Madisson, M.-L. (2023). Building resilience against hostile information influence activities: How a new media literacy learning platform was developed for the Estonian defense forces. *Armed Forces & Society.* https://doi.org/10.1177/0095327X231163265

Vosoughi, S., Roy, D., & Aral, S. (2018). The spread of true and false news online. *Science, 359*(6380), 1146–1151. https://doi.org/10.1126/science.aap9559

Wagnsson, C. (2022). The paperboys of Russian messaging: RT/Sputnik audiences as vehicles for malign information influence. *Information, Communication & Society.* https://doi.org/10.1080/1369118X.2022.2041700

Wardle, C., & Derakhshan, H. (2017). *Information disorder: Toward an interdisciplinary framework for research and policy making.* Council of Europe. Retrieved from https://firstdraftnews.org/wp-content/uploads/2017/11/PREMS-162317-GBR-2018-Report-de%CC%81sinformation-1.pdf

Weatherall, J. O., O'Connor, C., & Bruner, J. P. (2020). How to beat science and influence people: Policymakers and propaganda in epistemic networks. *The British Journal for the Philosophy of Science, 71*(4), 1157–1186. https://doi.org/10.1093/bjps/axy062

Whitney, L. (2021, June 17). Amazon prime day scams resurface for 2021. *TechRepublic.* Retrieved from www.techrepublic.com/article/amazon-prime-day-scams-resurface-for-2021/

Whitty, M. T., & Buchanan, T. (2016). The online dating romance scam: The psychological impact on victims—Both financial and non-financial. *Criminology & Criminal Justice, 16*, 176–94. https://doi.org/10.1177/1748895815603773

Woods, L., & Perrin, W. (2019, April). *Online harm reduction—A statutory duty of care and regulator.* Carnegie UK Trust. Retrieved from https://d1ssu070pg2v9i.cloudfront.net/pex/carnegie_uk_trust/2019/04/08091652/Online-harm-reduction-a-statutory-duty-of-care-and-regulator.pdf

Wu, M., Huang, Y., Li, R., Bortree, D. S., Yang, F., Xiao, A., & Wang, R. (2016). A tale of two sources in native advertising: Examining the effects of source credibility and priming on content, organizations, and media evaluations. *American Behavioral Scientist, 60*(12), 1492–1509. https://doi.org/10.1177/0002764216660139

Zhou, X., & Zafarani, R. (2020). A survey of fake news: Fundamental theories, detection methods, and opportunities. *ACM Computing Surveys, 53*(5), 1–40. https://doi.org/10.1145/3395046

10

CYBER OUTSIDERS

Julian Assange and the labelling of online activists

Vincenzo Scalia

Introduction

The Australian media activist and journalist Julian Assange, one of the founders of the Wikileaks site, is a controversial figure of contemporary history (Maurizi, 2021). Assange was arrested on the 11th of April 2019 inside the Ecuadorian embassy he had been living in as a refugee since June 2012, after the president of the Latin American country deprived him of his refugee status. He was eventually detained in London's Belmarsh prison by the British government, as the United States government is seeking his extradition (Crouch, 2019). Washington claims (Global Freedom of Expression, 2023) that Assange is liable of a high treason accusation for putting USA security at risk. Such a charge would result in a 175-year jail sentence. On the other hand, among Western civil society, many have protested the arrest and extradition request (Melzer, 2023), contending that the prosecution of Julian Assange contradicts the most outstanding standpoints of Western democracies, such as freedom of speech and freedom of the press.

This chapter will use the case of Julian Assange as the starting point for a reflection about the web as a new space (Hayward, 2012) wherein the borders between legal and illegal, legitimate and illegitimate, licit and illicit behaviours are drawn. One can argue that the internet can be seen as a social framework wherein different groups and individuals, endowed with different interests, values and aims, engage in power-related conflicts. The outcome of such clashes is the division of society between the *insiders*, who set up the rules, and the *outsiders*, who are criminalized as they do not fit into the pattern of rules that has been set up (Becker, 1963). The web is a double-edged sword; on the one hand it can be seen as a tool allowing the free flow of interactions between its users, on the other hand it is a tool of social control by the most powerful social groups; that is, the corporations and the State, whose use of the web aims at shaping and controlling the choices of global consumers. This conflict results in the production and enactment by the outsiders of those practices that aim at challenging and overturning the dominating pattern of rules. One can define such practices as *counter-surveillance*, or the possibilities of controlling the controllers provided by the web. Julian Assange, like other web activists, has thus wielded a counter-power, as he has used the web both to get hold of secret information and to make

DOI: 10.4324/9781003277675-12

the public aware of the way governments works by circulating the material he found. The practice that Assange and his Wikileaks partners have enacted makes them outsiders, as it triggers the reaction of the states that suffered the hacking of their security sites. The problem is that those who react against Assange are the same social groups that set the security rules and, at the same time, committed those global crimes that whistleblowers have revealed (Ruggiero, 2016). Assange violated the rules of secrecy, but at the same time, he put into practice the freedom of speech (ACLU, 2023b). Moreover, if transparency is supposed to be one of the standpoints of democracy, its violation could help those who want to advocate the abolition of state secrets in the pursuit of their aim. In order for the public to assess the quality of its leaders, information about indiscriminate killings of civilians or about surveillance through the use of IT become crucial resources. This being the case, one could argue that Assange was *labeled* as a deviant and a criminal because of his opposition to the current political and economic *status quo* that set and enforced the rules of the web.

This chapter will use Assange as a starting point to discuss the definition of online deviance. The first part will analyse the ambiguities of the web under the penal aspect. It will be possible to see from the outset how the web follows some patterns of control produced and enforced by powerful groups (IT majors, entrepreneurs and the state) for sake of controlling web surfers and orienting their market choices. In the second part, an in-depth discussion on the Assange case will bring to the fore the issue of social control in connection with relational surveillance and its potential of resistance to power. The latter concept draws on the ideas of Michel Foucault (1980), who argues that in order to resist the dominating narrative of power, it is necessary both to elaborate on and to enact an alternative set of strategies that make room for an alternative pattern of values and interests.

The process of labelling will be analysed through a three-stage scheme I propose to adapt: *slandering*, referring to the attacks on the reputation of Julian Assange; *isolation*, which consists of political pressure on Assange's potential supporters; and finally, that of *repression*, concerning what follows the arrest. In all three stages it will be possible to see a combination of the State's repressive force with ideological elements, such as that of national security, or instrumentally using such issues as sexual violence, which eventually proved flawed. The definition of Assange's practice as *counter-surveillance* and his consequent labelling as deviant and a criminal by the social groups who hold power will be discussed in the third part. A conclusion will be dedicated to a reflection of the penal implications on the web: virtual space is like the social space, with deviance being a definition forged by those who hold the internet under their control. The real solution is that of pushing further for democratization and transparency.

The ambiguities of the net

The bursting affirmation of the IT-based network as the fulcrum of social relations has led some scholars to speak of the "third space": like the natural environment and society, we find ourselves in a context characterized by its own rules, by independent dynamics, by peculiar conflicts, by completely new representations and identities. In terms of crime, new opportunities would also be produced within the third space, ranging from online scams to child pornography, passing through the so-called "cyber-terrorism". In other words, the network, in addition to increasing and modifying relational possibilities, also has the effect of producing new moral panic, with new moral entrepreneurs ready to stir up the bugbear of new threats to be exorcised by implementing measures. The securitization of the network is also felt on the political level. Since the third space is structured from the outset as a public space which accessible to everyone without relevant censorship, two types of political struggles are produced within it: the first concerns the use of the network to create and disseminate alternative political practices. Not surprisingly, many of the recent social movements, such as Occupy and the Arab Spring, have been born and spread online. The second concerns resistance and insubordination towards a power that also manifests itself in cybernetic forms, as in the case of whistleblowers who operate through the use of encrypted platforms or through the use of the deep web. The hackers, or Julian Assange and Edward Snowden, might be included within this typology of web surfers. Therefore, a deeper perspective on network security is created, where control strategies and moral panic intertwine directly with the prevention and repression of the emergence of alternative discourses and practices. To better understand the relation between alternative uses of the web and the repressive practices enacted by the stakeholders (majors, governments, platform owners), it is necessary to create a more in-depth analysis, in order to also consider crime-related issues.

How real is the cybercrime threat? Is the definition of *cybercriminals* a way of labelling whistleblowers? How is it distinguished from other types of crime? How is the dialectic between freedom and security articulated? Some authors (Gottschalk, 2010) respond by depicting the identity of the cybercriminal. They refer to an individual with specific skills, jealous of his criminal identity, using the network for his illicit purposes and a member of criminal networks. The existence of such a criminal threat would require the need to control and limit the use of the network. The creation of a cyber-police that uses the most sophisticated technology would serve this purpose well.

James Treadwell (2012), Goldsmith and Brewer (2015) are concerned with criticizing this approach by highlighting its limits. The first underlines how the network constitutes a real bazaar: it is possible to find the most varied actors operating in different fields. The Internet, Treadwell tells us, is characterized precisely by its fluidity: not only it is possible to adopt multiple identities, but one can choose to operate simultaneously within legal and illegal domains, thanks to the guarantee of anonymity. This also applies to illegal activities. On the internet, as in the social space, mostly minor crimes are committed, and the perpetrators, as shown by a study of some workers in the East End of London, are not habitual criminals, nor do they possess sophisticated skills (Treadwell, 2012, cit.). They carry out small-scale fraud when they are in economic difficulties, and intermittently as well as individually. The latter move along the same path as Treadwell, speaking of the existence of a real "digital drift". The network users pursue a multiplicity of behaviours, implemented in an unstructured way and often according to instrumental purposes. Consequently, the bonds that are created on the network denote a certain transience, which makes it difficult to talk about the existence of criminal networks.

These analytical approaches, although important, leave out two aspects of cybercrime that are crucial as they mirror the debate on crime that crosses the non-virtual public sphere: how much security must be guaranteed to users of the network? Who has to guarantee it? To what extent does security clash with civil liberties or justify the choice to classify some practices? The state, through its preventive and repressive apparatuses, comes back into play, staging the issues of social control and the relationship between freedom and security. These aspects denote direct political implications: in the second space the security discourse has catalysed the repression of dissent, and in the third, the cyber-criminal threat can become a blunt weapon to wield towards ever-wider types of non-compliant behaviour.

As Giorgio Agamben (2017) points out, drawing on the work of Carl Schmitt (1982), states thrive on the establishment of a pattern based on the friend-enemy dialectic; that is, translated into the criminological language proposed by Howard Becker (1963, cit.), the distinction between insiders and outsiders. Assange, Manning and Snowden are the *enemies* to be dealt with accordingly. The construction of what one could define as *cyber-enemies*, though, must be understood within the contradictions that arise inside the web.

State regulation of the network presents a qualitatively relevant problem, which Daniel Geer (2016) connects with the so-called "digital physics". Unlike the material space, the third space is characterized by its fluidity, volatility and unpredictability; these characteristics intersect with the protection of civil liberties and the free market. Consequently, individuals and economic actors are unwilling to provide vital information about their existence and their interests to the actors' social control, which would make it problematic to implement all kinds of security measures on the net.

In reality, according to Lee Tien (2016), the reading of the network as a free and uncontrolled flow of relations and information turns out on second glance to be limited, insofar as the network works according to the principle of regulation. As a house orients and determines our movements according to its conformation, so the network orients our digital paths, creating the conditions for an ex-ante control based on the pre-determination of cybernetic navigation. Unlike the physical-social environment, where sanctions are imposed ex-post, the computer limits and directs our drift into the digital space right from the start. We follow from the beginning the directories of the web, and we are immediately told not to use abusive or offensive language, images or footage.

It is within this pre-regulated framework that space is created for a new form of surveillance: horizontal, imperceptible, pervasive; in other words, as David Lyon (2007, 2009, 2016) defines it, it is relational. Surveillance refers to all those activities aimed both at preventing and repressing any formal or informal breach of the rules that keep the social fabric together. The activity of watching the way members of a society behave allows those actors vested with formal and legitimized power to intervene in order to suppress the risk of anomic drifts (Durkheim, 2000). Surveillance is strongly related to power relations as the dominating social groups, or the insiders, make and enforce the rules against the marginal social groups, or the outsiders (Becker, 1963). Surveillance can thus be defined as an activity aimed at reproducing the existing force relations and the uneven power distribution within the social spectrum.

There are two different kinds of surveillance (Wood & Monahan, 2019): the first is formal; that is, all those activities of control that are carried out by the state through its apparatuses by relying on legal entitlements (Weber, 1971): police, magistrates and the army wield formal social control to deploy a surveillance one can define as vertical due to its being wielded from the top, i.e., state power, to the bottom, i.e., society. Vertical surveillance requires a high degree of obedience, both to the rules and their enforcers. Whereas it is possible for the members of society to change those who make the rules to eventually indirectly change the rules, it is not possible to dodge formal rules, the violation of which entails sanctions from fining to imprisonment. Other authors (Cohen, 1985), depict a wider spectrum of formal surveillance by using the concept of social control (Cohen, 1985). This concept also encompasses those agencies whose aims are ostensibly those of support and care, as in the case of a welfare state. Here we also find relations of subjugation and domination, as individuals are required to adhere to the dominating system of values and aims.

Another form of surveillance is the informal one; that is, surveillance wielded by the group of peers, neighbours, family, religious groups and work colleagues, or the social capital in which individuals are embedded (Coleman, 1988). This is a horizontal kind of surveillance which usually requires individuals' cognitive adherence to the rules underpinning inter-individual interaction, although in this case it is also possible to formally abide by the rules while enacting a secret deviance. Michel Foucault (1980) defines both horizontal and vertical surveillance as disciplinary powers, as they both draw on social relations to produce a web of domination that is deployed across society. The aim of disciplinary power is producing docile bodies that comply with the discipline required by industrial society. On the trail of Foucault's reflections, Gilles Deleuze (1999) defines contemporary society as a society of control, mostly relying on a web of mutual surveillance to make sure that individuals comply with rules and expectations that are moulded and conveyed through the media. In Deleuze's view, society has assimilated control to the point of letting technology catalyse surveillance and report what happens to the agencies in charge of social control.

The social networks we frequent, the people we chat with, the sites we visit, can be monitored by digital control systems that make use of a wider-ranging security question to monitor both actors and communications considered "a risk". This is the case with the "Carnivore" project (Deflem & Ventura, 2005), a surveillance program prepared by the FBI and approved by the US Congress in the aftermath of September 11th. Law enforcement agencies can monitor, with the approval of the district attorney and for limited periods of time, those individuals and those portions of the network suspected of terrorism. The surveillance authorization can be renewed if the investigation reveals something that leads to believing that the suspicions are well-founded, which thus requires further investigation supplements. The Carnivore project has been severely contested by organizations active in the defense of civil rights (Deflem & Ventura, 2005, cit., p. 59), not only because it violates privacy and freedom of expression, but also because it is aimed above all at American citizens of Arab origin or of Muslim religion, leading to the a priori criminalization of entire sections of the population.

Alongside the Carnivore project, as Edward Snowden revealed in 2013, there are other network control programs developed and implemented by the National Security Agency, which are characterized by being much more sophisticated and articulated (Lyon, 2016, cit., p. 72). The internal security agency is in fact characterized as the main actor of relational surveillance, whose control programs do not only concern alleged Muslim terrorists but affect the entire population. The network surveillance work therefore aims to monitor every form of communication, relationship and practice that goes against the regulation architecture, and it monitors the activities of alternative groups and networks. In this context, figures like Snowden and Assange are dangerous, as they not only reveal the details of the current interweaving of power but also demonstrate the possibility of overturning the security flow through using the network in the opposite direction to the conventional one, which wants to create a docile, controllable and tameable user. Relational surveillance brings about the possibility of counter-surveillance in the use of tools of control provided by the web to produce and enact practices of resistance against power. This kind of practice consists of the detection, as well as of the revelation, of the crimes committed by *the powerful*, such as white-collar crimes and state crimes (Green & Ward, 2006) and of the social harm they cause (Whyte et al., 2015). As a consequence, the practices enacted by Julian Assange and WikiLeaks can be defined as counter-surveillance. They are an opposition not only to the existing power relations but also to the practices of control implemented both by political actors, such as the state, and by economic actors like contractors, private companies, and the IT majors through the manipulation of Big Data (Lyon, 2019). Assange, with the help of Edward Snowden and Chelsea Manning, enacted a counter-manipulation as he accessed the Big Data provided by the governments and made them public.

In other words, there is no difference between the social space and the cyberspace: in both cases, the definition of what is legal and what is not is the outcome of a conflict with the state embodying the interests of the insiders and enforcing the law against the outsiders (Poulantzas, 1977). The state, at the same time, holds back from prosecuting more serious crimes, as well as itself committing some peculiar crimes related to prevention, to repression or to war crimes.

As in the material space, the moral panic around some small-scale crimes provides the right to implementation of repressive measures that pass through the criminalization of specific sectors of society. In the network the alarm for cybercrimes, amplified by the fear of terrorism, becomes the Trojan horse for repressive action and for the implementation of new forms of social control, as well as for the repression of new forms of dissent. On the other hand, it is the very fluidity of the web that allows the production and dissemination of dissenting knowledge and practices, both through individual actions, such as those of Snowden, and through the creation of more structured experiences, such as Wikileaks. This flow of social relations in the web is deemed dangerous by the rule makers, whose legitimacy could be put at risk by the revelation of misdeeds that contradict the official impartiality and neutrality of the state conveyed by all the official narrations.

The making of a villain: slandering, isolation and repression. Assange as *homo sacer*

The criminalization of Julian Assange, as well as of those media activists who revealed state secrets via the web, marks an unprecedented event in contemporary history: in 1971, the *New York Times* got hold of and eventually published the Pentagon Papers about the Vietnam War, revealing the US Army's raids against North Vietnam and exposing the White House to further stigmatization that increased the anti-war movement (Sheehan, 1971). Three years later, the *Washington Post* made the public aware of Richard Nixon's administrative misdeed in the Watergate case (Bernstein & Woodward, 1972). These cases, like the Abu Ghraib abuses scandal of 2004 (Greenberg & Dreitel, 2005), were made public and widely discussed without provoking any reaction by the United States government under the assumption that both freedom of the press and freedom of speech, two standpoints of Western democracy, provided the rights to publicize unknown state practices. The case of Julian Assange has seen a different approach, based on the criminalization and prosecution of the Australian media activist. It is this crucial to analyse this difference from a criminological point of view, as it poses the question: "Why is Julian Assange criminalized, unlike his colleagues of the past?" In following Howard Becker's labelling theory, this case fits into the concept of *social reaction* (Becker, 1960, pp. 803–810). Becker argues that crime is not an objective phenomenon. An act is deemed criminal when it is defined as such by those who make the rules (*insiders*). Secondly, the definition of crime would be ineffective without a social reaction to behaviour that is defined as criminal. For example, if the use of marijuana is illegal, a police officer seeing a group of people smoking dope in the park can choose either to sanction them or to just warn them that such a practice is not legal and force them out of the park. In following this pattern, one can follow an articulation of the criminalization process in three stages: firstly, there is no such thing as a set of social phenomena one can define as *crimes*; as a consequence of this, the definition of either an event or a behavior as criminal is the consequence of the reaction, either by society or by institutional agencies; thirdly, criminals are drawn from the ranks of those groups outside of mainstream society; that is, the *outsiders*. In the case of Julian Assange, all these conditions are fulfilled.

Assange's activism was immediately portrayed as a crime by the American government after the release by Wikileaks, on the 5th of April 2010 (Maurizi, 2021, p. 35), of the video showing the killing of civilians in Iraq, dating back to three years before. The video had been provided by a US soldier in Iraq, Bradley Manning, who was later to be sentenced and to become Chelsea Manning after her decision to change sex. Its worldwide circulation through the web left public opinion puzzled, as it damaged the reputation of the USA government. The Obama administration overreacted to that, claiming that by circulating the video, Wikileaks had put the security of the USA at risk. Assange was charged with high treason under the Espionage Act the federal government had enacted in 1935. Assange consequently ceased to be a media activist and a journalist to become a criminal.

Such an overreaction is the consequence of the massive defamation the American government had been facing since the early 2000s, when the second Gulf War left Western public opinion perplexed because of the flaky evidence that Iraq's dictator, Saddam Hussein, had weapons of mass destruction. Moreover, the news of the serious violations of human rights in the prisons at Guantanamo and Abu Ghraib (www.aclu.org) had made things worse for the American government. Wikileaks had also circulated documents that proved the brutalities.

The two more important reasons for the criminalization of Julian Assange, though, might be related to the means Wikileaks used and to the nature of the organization itself. To the first point, Wikileaks had used the web both to get the material from Chelsea Manning and to circulate it. Unlike the *New York Times* and the *Washington Post*, who had relied upon "deep throats" providing them with restricted information, Assange and Wikileaks had made extensive use of the web in a subjective way: their use of the Tor software to dodge the online control and get hold of material due to their connection with hackers, as well as the use of the web to spread the information faster, contradicted the architectural regulation of the web. Assange has taken seriously the potential of the web as a free space, thus trespassing the paths for its use set up both by the software producers and by its institutional users: the market and the state. As a consequence, Assange is an *outsider*, as he follows a different set of rules and his idea of the use of the web is different than the prevailing one. His project, and that of Wikileaks, is not that of controlling the web surfers and orienting their market choice. Assange uses the web with the purpose of informing worldwide public opinion by making use of the potentiality of cybernetics, including the involvement of hackers, communication through encrypted software such as Tor and the circulation of classified material (Melzer, 2023, cit.). The purpose of Wikipedia is radically different from that of the USA government, but the latter are in the position of setting and enforcing the rules.

The labelling process, though, cannot happen without those *rituals of degradation* (Garfinkel, 1956) that deprive a person of their own identity and reputation to be stigmatized by the others (Goffman, 1963). This is what we call the first stage of Assange's labelling, which is *slandering*. The strategy of degradation consists of a false accusation of a serious crime that causes the rise of moral panic and triggers moral repulsion against a person. Such an accusation will prove successful to persuade the reluctant part of the public that the stigmatized person is a villain rather than a person entitled to their rights. For Julian Assange, slandering meant the accusation of sexual violence. That accusation, dating back to late 2010 when Assange was in Sweden, was later to be dropped by the Swedish magistrates (*www.theguardian.com/media/2017/may/19/swedish-prosecutors-drop-julian-assange-investigation*). After Assange's arrest in London in 2019, the British prosecutor took the same decision.

Although the charges were eventually dropped (in 2017), the shadow of such a serious accusation hung for 9 years over the spokesman of Wikileaks, paving the way for the second stage of his labelling: *isolation*. This stage recalls the *secondary deviance* Lemert (1951) refers to and Becker has drawn upon. Whereas *primary deviance* relates to the deviant act, the secondary stage relates to the reaction society and enforcement agencies enact once an individual (or a group) has been labeled as deviant. The stigmatization of deviants means their marginalization from mainstream society. Their behaviour will be stigmatized to draw a line between them and the society of insiders. Assange was indeed denied the possibility to move freely across the world: the US government issued an extradition warrant for high treason, along with the Swedish government's international warrant for the accusations of sexual violence. Two of the most important Western states made Julian Assange a wanted criminal, with the Swedish warrant striking a blow against his reputation as an activist. Sweden has had a long tradition of human rights-oriented policies and has been known for decades as one of the most attentive states to women's rights. A warrant issued by Sweden for sex-related crimes, for a media-activist claiming to campaign for human rights, is more effective at marring the reputation than an American warrant (Maurizi, 2021, cit., p. 87). Whereas the latter is questionable as the border between high treason and freedom of press blurs, the Swedish warrant, as well as reducing Assange's movements across the Western world, casts doubt about his credibility as an activist, thus weakening both his campaigns and arguments he was the victim of an unjustified prosecution. The only chance he had was to seek refuge inside the Ecuadorian embassy in London, after applying for political asylum in the Latin American country on the 19th of June 2012. As Rafael Correa, president of Ecuador from 2007 to 2017, was sympathetic to Wikileaks' cause, Assange could live in the Ecuadorian embassy, although it was difficult for him to leave the premises because of the risk of being arrested (*www.washingtontimes.com/news/2012/aug/16/uk-we-wont-allow-julian-assange-to-leave-britain/*). As Western countries aligned themselves to the Swedish and American desiderata, Assange was spied on (Maurizi, cit., p. 130–164), with bugs and cameras being illegally installed inside the embassy. After Correa left the presidency, it was possible for British intelligence to infiltrate some agents under cover inside the embassy until Assange's asylum was revoked in 2019, thus making it possible to arrest him on the 12th of April. The isolation and arrest of Julian Assange makes the argument about labelling even stronger. While Assange was banned from travelling and forced to seek refuge in an embassy, living for seven years like a prisoner, the state crimes (Kauzlarich, 2001) committed by the British government, in the violation of Assange's privacy and the violation of Ecuador's embassy sovereignty until 2017, are not considered as the insiders, in this case the British government, makes the rules by and for itself (Ruggiero, 2016) and works out self-acquittal strategies based either on outright or on interpretive denial (Cohen, 2006). Such an uneven power relation produces an insider/outsider dichotomy, which turned out to be disadvantageous for Assange, who then faced the stage of *repression*.

Julian Assange has been jailed since the 19th of April 2022. The charges of sexual violence were dropped, but he is awaiting the final verdict about his extradition to the USA.

While the legal battle outside is raging as the extradition warrant was signed on the 16th of June by the British Home Minister Priti Patel (www.theguardian.com/media/2022/jun/17/julian-assange-extradition-to-us-approved-by-priti-patel), his solicitors have appealed the decision, both to the British Supreme Court and to the European Court of Human Rights, claiming that Assange is detained under inhumane conditions (*www.ecchr.eu/en/publication/the-detention-of-julian-assange-is-inhumane/*). The Belmarsh prison, where Assange is being held, is a Category A prison, hosting people convicted or accused of having committed serious crimes, such as sex offenders, terrorists and murderers. The British prison Ombudsman (*www.justiceinspectorates.gov.uk/hmiprisons/inspections/?location=belmarsh*) has several times in his yearly reports addressed the poor living conditions in the prison, indicating the repeated and disproportionate use of force by the prison staff. Julian Assange suffered from the harsh conditions of detention in Belmarsh, and a stroke hit him in December 2021. Moreover, his pathologies are against a prolonged state of detention under harsh conditions. Apart from the inhumane life conditions inside prison, Assange has yet to be tried for the alleged accusation by the US government. Moreover, he does not have a criminal record for crimes like terrorism or homicide. While he is awaiting extradition, the reason why he is being kept under such conditions needs to be reflected upon.

Assange is being accused of putting the USA's security at risk for circulating classified materials about the war. While public opinion worldwide could appreciate that it is hard to detect a relation between the documents circulated through Wikileaks and the security of the USA, Assange's responsibility does need to be ascertained in a trial that grants him the possibility of defending himself under habeas corpus and the Bill of Rights. Assange has indeed served a long pre-trial detention of three years and a half as this chapter is being drafted. Moreover, the state of detention is impacting his health. It appears the stage of repression articulates in two stages: that of the pre-trial detention Assange is currently experiencing, and the stage after he will be sentenced to jail by the US courts if extradited.

The US reaction looks more like a reprisal than a reaction against a violation of state secrets. There are indeed more complex dynamics behind it. Firstly, the issue of uneven power relations between insiders and outsiders is at stake. The US government calls a violation of security what a consistent portion of worldwide public opinion calls freedom of the press and of speech. There is no objective or a shared definition of freedom and crime. The borders between are legitimate. Thanks to the help of those *moral entrepreneurs* Becker refers to as agencies mobilizing public opinion about an issue (1963, cit.), the labelling process proves successful. Assange is labelled a villain by the US government. This label is accepted by the British government, which detains him under inhumane conditions and has agreed to his extradition (Melzer, 2023, cit., p. 143).

Secondly, labelling implies that the attention of public opinion is deflected from the heinous crimes that were committed during the Gulf War. It's likely, as the Chilcot report of 2017 demonstrated definitively that Tony Blair and his government deceived British public opinion to declare war on Iraq (*www.gov.uk/government/publications/the-report-of-the-iraq-inquiry*), that the British government is pursuing the same aim. A scapegoat, an enemy or a case to be put in front of public opinion will give governments the possibility of hiding evidence and crafting new justifications for what they did.

Thirdly, this paves the way for the self-acquittal of states. Their control of the bureaucratic machines, their legislation, their network of relations (Ruggiero, 2016, cit.) allow them to call an International Governmental Crime (Kauzlarich, 2001), or crimes committed outside a state jurisdiction by violating international laws, an act committed for sake of national security. The exercise of fundamental rights will thus become a crime for the state's parameters, whereas the social harm (Whyte et al., 2015) caused by a war, the indiscriminate killing of civilians, the environmental disasters and other violations of human rights will be denied or hidden.

Fourthly, there is an outright conflict in the definition of acts and behaviors, as well as the enforcement of rules. This is because what is at stake is the control of a new space, the web, to be structured as a public space. Whereas the states and the majors pursue their aim of architectural regulation to force the surfers into pre-order paths, interests, aims and values, Assange and Wikileaks advocate an open, plural, complex and public access and use of the web, attempting to make the web the new arena of civil liberties. Their activities are by this token a danger for those who are in control of the web, particularly the states. This is because Assange and Wikileaks propose a different approach of resistance, one that does not imply the use of political violence (Ruggiero, 2006).

The relational quality of IT-based surveillance provides new potentialities to fight and counterbalance the control and subjugation attempts that surveillance capitalism conveys. Both on a micro and on a macro level, it is possible to enact and develop a plurality of strategies for counter-surveillance, or those practices that both individuals and groups implement to protect their liberties by controlling the controller. On a micro level, counter-surveillance is a widespread practice that all of us are involved in daily. To check a Facebook page or a university site in order to gather information about someone we know is an act of counter-surveillance, as it enables us to know many things we need about a person: residence, where they are at a certain time, lifestyle, political ideas, sexual orientations and so on. All this information is provided spontaneously by the users, who often neglect the issue of privacy and security. In any case, they make it possible for anyone with a basic knowledge of IT to easily acquire a significant amount of information about as many people as possible. On a macro level, it is necessary to possess more sophisticated skills, such as the use of more advanced search engines (like Tor) or the know-how to hack and crack the websites of governmental agencies and corporations. Another requirement is that of a network, both among hackers and crackers and those who work within the surveillance network and can leak classified news. The case of Julian Assange and Wikileaks matches all these requirements; firstly, because of the use of Tor, which allows for developing an underground connection between the sources and the members of Wikileaks. Secondly, Assange and his group possess those skills that enable them to hack the IT systems containing the information to be made public. Finally, the cases of Chelsea Manning and Edward Snowden demonstrate the importance of a network of infiltrators inside the surveillance apparatus; Manning was a soldier and Edward Snowden worked for Booz Allen Hamilton, one of the sub-contractors spying on the public on behalf of the American government. It was thanks to this articulated organization that Wikileaks was able to obtain the news about state crimes and circulate the information among the public. In other words, Assange and his partners exploited the potentialities of relational surveillance at its best. As watchful and disrespectful of civil liberties as surveillance can be, its contradictions allow those being surveyed the possibility of resisting and counteracting such surveillance, both by creating an alternative network to that of the dominating political and economic power, and by using the information acquired through this network to reveal the abuses committed by the dominating rulers against the public, thus enforcing a real democracy. Finally, as a consequence of this, the current rule-makers have been floundering, as they are facing an unprecedented challenge with new means and new contents. Such a vacillating power tries to restore its foundation based on the *homo sacer* (Agamben, 2017), or the right to rule over life and death that power is founded upon. The border between outsiders and insiders, good citizens and villains, makes up a structural aspect of every society. When the border blurs it is necessary to reaffirm it in a radical way, by creating an enemy and punishing him (in this case) for the alleged danger he is accused of having created. In the case of Julian Assange, the friend/enemy, insider/outsider appears to have worked successfully. Consequently, the possibility and the practice of an open, free, plural web have been turned into crimes to be prosecuted with the harshest measures possible, such as confinement in a maximum-security prison and the threat of 175 years of jail for Assange, whereas Edward Snowden lives in Russia. Punishment and repression appear to be the answers that states provide to those who put fundamental liberties into practice. Julian Assange has not killed, injured or harmed anybody. He is accused of robbing or stealing information but, more than this, of publicizing it. One could argue we are facing a new kind of crime that has much to do with the virtual nature of the web. Fraud, identity thefts, forgeries and industrial espionage are being committed on the web. Assange did not commit any of these crimes. He obtained classified materials, but he did not do so for sake of making a profit or to advantage one market competitor against another. His criminalization and imprisonment appear to have slowed the activities of whistleblowers, as there is no notice of either new state crimes or of crimes of the powerful being leaked to public opinion. As illegal as his way of acquiring information might appear, it has much to do with the tricks of the trade, as journalists very often get hold of information (and use it) in ways that do not follow standard procedure. The trade-off between acquisition of material and publication has been positive up to now, as the interest of the public has been accomplished. In the case of Assange, the question is not *how to punish*, but *why punish?* The answer is because the Australian media-activist has committed a deviant act where the US government, in order to criminalize it, retrieved a law dating back to 1937. Moreover, Assange has followed the principles outlined by the freedom of information. More than this, he is not the first journalist or press-activist to do so. This important part of the labelling theory, that of enforcing a different kind of punishment, must be discussed under a different light. Following Becker's arguments on the use of marijuana (1953), which focuses on the connection between the drug and the social group that makes use of it, in his words African American jazz musicians, it is possible to argue that *decriminalization*, rather than *diversion*, should be the path to be followed in the case of Julian Assange and other media activists. Freedom of speech and freedom of the press are two standpoints of the social space. It is time to extend them to the virtual space.

Conclusions

The story of Julian Assange seems to give a negative answer to our initial question, as it looks like any attempt to make classified news public ends up being criminalized.

Some authors (Delagasnerie, 2020) have argued that the activism of Wikileaks proves that the only possibility of resisting power nowadays lies in the deployment of a strategy based on underground resistance. As surveillance is very invasive, activists must carry out their sabotaging of power by keeping and developing secret identities and activities. We believe this is not the case for Wikileaks for two reasons: firstly, because Assange and all his partners have always made public what they were doing and why. In the second case, their activity consists precisely of revealing to the public what the power conceals, thus reaffirming the value of public discourse against the arcana imperii, or the idea that a state's security relies on the performance of secret activities by those vested with power. Norberto Bobbio (1987, cit., p. 63) argued that the security of power relies on the insecurity of citizens. Assange and Wikileaks have endorsed Bobbio's theorization by overthrowing it: the more insecure power is, the more citizens feel secure: Tony Blair's lies about the Gulf War, Guantanamo, Abu Ghraib, the bombing of Iraq and Afghanistan, as well as the news about financial and environmental crimes leaked by Wikileaks, reveal the real aspects of power, and at the same time show its weak spots, by empowering the public with the resource of information. Moreover, Wikileaks and Assange suggest making a fluid, democratic and open use of the web, unlike some other attempts, such as the Rousseau platform adopted by the Italian populist 5 Star Movement (Stockman & Scalia, 2020) to use the web to produce a plebiscitarian form of politics. The issue of privacy and freedom of speech, both in an active way (use of the web by the internet surfers) and in a passive way (protection of privacy from manipulation and surveillance) has been recently at stake once again, as Twitter/X was taken over by Elon Musk (Gallagher, 2022).

The American government considers Assange, Manning and Snowden as criminals because they revealed state secrets in violation of the web. While we appreciate that Julian Assange and his partners might not have respected the law completely, they did not behave any differently from those governments that had been spying on private individuals and sold information to private operators without obtaining consent. Finally, the real crimes, as many human rights organizations and civil society groups have pointed out, are those committed in Guantanamo, in Abu Ghraib and in the rendition protests (ACLU, 2023a). Such crimes need someone to push the boundaries of legality to reinforce civil liberties and democracy. Julian Assange and Wikileaks are the ones who have done this.

References

Agamben, G. (2017). *Homo sacer*. Quodlibet.

Becker, H. (1953). Becoming a Marijuana user. *The American Journal of Sociology, 69*, 235–242.

Becker, H. (1960). Normative reaction to normlessness. *American Sociological Review, 25*, 803–810.

Becker, H. (1963). *Outsiders*. Free Press.

Bobbio, N. (1987). *The future of democracy. A defence of the rules of the game* (R. Griffin, Trans.). University of Minnesota Press. (Original work published 1984). Retrieved from https://archive.org/details/futureofdemocrac00bobb.

Cohen, S. (1985). *Visions of social control*. Transaction.

Cohen, S. (2006). *Stati di negazione*. Carocci.

Coleman, J. (1988). Social capital in the creation of human capital. *American Journal of Sociology, 94* (Supplement: Organizations and Institutions: Sociological and Economic Approaches to the Analysis of Social Structure, 95—S120). Retrieved from www.jstor.org/stable/2780243.

Deflem, M., & Ventura, H. (2005). Governmentality and the war on terror: FBI project carnivore and the diffusion of disciplinary power. *Critical Criminology, 13*, 55–70.

Delagasnerie, G. (2020). *L'Arte della Rivolta*. Stampa Alternativa.

Deleuze, G. (1999). *Principio Metamorfosi. Verso un'antropologia dell'artificiale*. Mimesis.

Durkheim, E. (2000). *La Divisione del Lavoro Sociale*. Edizioni di Comunità.

Foucault, M. (1980). *Power/knowledge*. Harvester Wheatsheaf.

Garfinkel, H. (1956). Condition of successful degradation ceremonies. *American Journal of Sociology, 61*(5), 420–424.

Geer, D. (2016). *Cybercrime. Digital cops in a networked environment*. New York University Press.

Goffman, E. (1963). *Stigma: Notes on the management of spoiled identity*. Prentice Hall.

Goldsmith, A., & Brewer, R. (2015). Digital drift and the criminal interaction order. *Theoretical Criminology, 19*(1), 112–130.

Gottschalk, P. (2010). *Policing cybercrime*. Boon Boon.

Green, P., & Ward, T. (2006). *State crimes*. Pluto Press.

Greenberg, K., & Dreitel, J. (Eds). (2005). *The torture papers. The road to Abu Ghraib*. Cambridge University Press.

Hayward, K. J. (2012). Five spaces of cultural criminology. *British Journal of Criminology, 53*(3), 441–462.

Kauzlarich, D. (2001). Towards a victimology of state crime. *Critical Criminology, 10*, 173–194.

Lemert, E. (1951). *Social pathology. A systematic approach to the theory of sociopathic behavior*. McGraw-Hill.

Lyon, D. (2007). *Massima Sicurezza*. Raffaello Cortina.

Lyon, D. (2009). *Oltre il Panopticon*. Raffaello Cortina.

Lyon, D. (2016). *Surveillance after Snowden*. Wiley.

Lyon, D. (2019). *The culture of surveillance*. Polity.

Maurizi, S. (2021). *Il Potere Segreto*. Chiarelettere.

Melzer, N. (2023). *The trial of Julian Assange*. London.

Poulantzas, N. (1977). *Il potere nella società contemporanea*. Editori Riuniti.

Ruggiero, V. (2006). *La Violenza Politica*. Laterza.

Ruggiero, V. (2016). *Perché i Potenti Delinquono*. Feltrinelli.

Schmitt, C. (1982). *Le categorie del politico*. Il Mulino.

Stockman, C., & Scalia, V. (2020). Democracy and the five stars movement. *European Politics and Society, 21*(5), 603–617.

Tien, L. (2016). Architectural regulation and the evolution of social norms. In D. Geer (Ed.), *Cybercrime: Digital cops in a networked environment* (pp. 37–58). New York University Press.

Treadwell, J. (2012). From the car boot to booting it up? eBay, online counterfeit crime and the transformation of the criminal marketplace. *Criminology and Criminal Justice, 2*, 175–191.

Weber, M. (1971). *Il Lavoro Intellettuale come Professione*. Einaudi.

Whyte, S. (Ed.). (2015). *Why is Britain corrupt?* Pluto Press.

Wood, M., & Monahan, T. (2019). Platform surveillance. *Surveillance and Society, 17*(1–2), 1–6.

Websites

American Civil Liberties Union. (2023a). *Guantanamo bay detention camp*. Retrieved from www.aclu.org/issues/national-security/detention/guantanamo-bay-detention-camp

American Civil Liberties Union. (2023b). *Letter urging DOJ to Drop the charges against Julian Assange*. Retrieved from www.aclu.org/documents/letter-urging-doj-drop-charges-against-julian-assange (accessed 12 August 2023).

Bernstein, C., & Woodward, B. (1972, August 1). *Bug supsect got campaign funds*. Retrieved from www.washingtonpost.com/wp-srv/national/longterm/watergate/articles/080172-1.htm

Crouch, D. (2019, April 11). *Julian Assange faces US extradition after arrest at Ecuadorian embassy*. Retrieved from www.theguardian.com/uk-news/2019/apr/11/julian-assange-arrested-at-ecuadorian-embassy-wikileaks.

Gallagher, R. (2022, December 2). *Twitter firings gutted its compliance teams. Now it risks investigations and big fines*. Retrieved from www.latimes.com/business/story/2022-12-02/twitter-shrunk-compliance-teams-risks-investigations-fines

Global Freedom of Expression. (2023). *USA vs. Assange*. Retrieved from https://globalfreedomofexpression.columbia.edu/cases/the-government-of-us-of-america-v-assange/ (accessed 12 August 2023).

Sheehan, N. (1971, June 13). *Vietnam archives. Pentagon study traces 3 decdes of growing U.S. Involvement*. Retrieved from www.nytimes.com/1971/06/13/archives/vietnam-archive-pentagon-study-traces-3-decades-of-growing-u-s.html

11
MOVING FROM RISK FACTORS TO POSITIVE ONLINE BEHAVIORS
An integrated behavioral change approach

Troy Smith, Eric Rutger Leukfeldt and Steve van de Weijer

Introduction

From the positivist perspective, as is applicable in this chapter, online deviance can be collectively defined as voluntary inappropriate behavior that may be criminal or violate societal norms (provoke disapproval, anger or indignation), which use or target networked systems (Ford et al., 2018; Thio et al., 2013). This form of deviance is examinable in a process framework of antecedents, behaviors and outcomes (Cioban et al., 2021; Ford et al., 2018). This approach assumes that deviance is absolutely real and distinguishable from conventional behavior where offenders and so to their victims may be modeled as observable objects with actions determined by social factors (Thio et al., 2013).

The term cybercrime encapsulates online deviant behaviors which are contrary to existing legal frameworks; i.e., formalization and association of penalties to behaviors considered contrary to societal norms/beliefs (McGuire & Dowling, 2013). Cybercrime as a form of online deviance has been increasing and is projected to continue to increase as the reach of networked systems continues to grow and integrate with critical infrastructure and almost every aspect of the daily lives of users inclusive of entertainment, communication, banking, shopping, medical services and school (Bossler & Berenblum, 2019; Coffey et al., 2018; Sarre et al., 2018). Online deviance and cybercrime can have significant effects on victims psychologically, emotionally, financially and even physically (Anderson et al., 2012; Karaymeh et al., 2019; Leukfeldt et al., 2019; Reyns et al., 2018).

Until recently, the fight against cybercrime was dominated by technical solutions to prevent victimization (Leukfeldt, 2017). However, technical models alone are not sufficient to tackle the cybercrime problem. Victimization can generally be traced back to human behavior, even if the initial threat vector is based on the exploitation of technical vulnerabilities (Jansen, 2018; van't Hoff-de Goede et al., 2021). It has been stated and demonstrated that to fully understand cybercrime or cybersecurity and develop holistic proactive protection strategies, the so-called human factor (i.e., behavioral and psychosocial factors) must be understood along with the technical aspects (Hadlington, 2017; Hassandoust & Techatassanasoontorn, 2020; Maalem Lahcen et al., 2020).

DOI: 10.4324/9781003277675-13

To date, research into the human factor of cybercrime has predominantly taken a positivist approach focused on target hardening using the scientific method, data and empirical evidence to predict behavioral patterns and activities that increase the risk of victimization (Cioban et al., 2021; Ford et al., 2018; Leukfeldt & Yar, 2016). Overall, these studies have found that risk-increasing behaviors are numerous and can be inconsistent between cybercrimes (Akdemir & Lawless, 2020; Holt et al., 2020; Leukfeldt & Yar, 2016; Smith & Stamatakis, 2021). Further, it has been demonstrated that risky behaviors are very broad as they can include routine activities such as emailing or using social media. This means that like the argument presented by constructivists on deviant behavior, risky behavior may not have any intrinsic characteristics unless it is thought to have these characteristics and as such is subjective (Becker, 1963).

There is a growing perspective that an investigation of protective behavior (safe online behavior/cyber-hygiene/cyber-safety) and the determinants of this behavior are more apt for parsimonious and effective crime reduction strategies (Cain et al., 2018; Leukfeldt, 2014; van't Hoff-de Goede et al., 2021). Therefore, it is important to understand factors that affect human behaviors which are conducive to increased cybersecurity (rather than the behaviors themselves) and consequently a reduction of risk as this may provide a finite set of actions as compared to avoidance of 'risky' behaviors (Jansen & Leukfeldt, 2016). The choice to engage in protective behaviors or the avoidance of risk-increasing behavior is itself the product of various social and psychological factors, although the factors influencing these behaviors may not be consistent in size, direction or 'relevance' across behaviors. As such, it is equally important to identify categories of protective behaviors and determinants of these behaviors.

Contrary to the majority of previous studies, this chapter diverges from a variable-centric approach, which primarily focuses on target hardening methods and the identification of behaviors that increase risk. Instead, it proposes a person-centric perspective that emphasizes understanding the factors inspiring and facilitating users to adopt protective behaviors. Grounded in the positivist paradigm, the approach asserts that a victim's protective behavior is a tangible reality, distinguishable from other behavioral patterns, and measurable. It proposes that these behaviors and their relationships can be systematically modeled. However, it also acknowledges that an individual's engagement in a particular behavior is influenced by an interplay of psychological and social factors. This approach does not adopt a purely deterministic stance. While it recognizes that actions can be influenced by forces beyond an individual's control, it posits that the outcome of non-reflective reasoning is a product of free will. This free will operates within the confines of an individual's interpretation and evaluation of social factors, coupled with psychological precursors. Therefore, the chapter posits that the decision to partake in protective online behavior is the outcome of an assessment of factors associated with the utility and feasibility of such behavior. This assessment, however, is bound by psychosocial constraints (Howell, 2021; Maalem Lahcen et al., 2020; van't Hoff-de Goede et al., 2021). The research methodology implemented in the generation of this chapter entailed an exhaustive review of existing literature, aiming to identify the key determinants of safe online behavior and vulnerability to victimization. This comprehensive analysis included both empirical studies and theoretical works, providing a multifaceted understanding of the subject. The chapter also underlines the limitations of self-report surveys, highlighting the need for more robust measures to accurately capture actual behavior in the digital domain. This chapter, therefore, sets the stage for a nuanced exploration of protective online behaviors, inviting readers to engage with a fresh perspective on mitigating online deviance.

The problem with risky behavior as a predictor in the study of cybercrime

Due to the increasing social, psychological and economic effects of cybercrime, research and supporting literature have increased over the last 20 years (Bossler & Berenblum, 2019; Weulen Kranenbarg et al., 2019; Reyns et al., 2018). Extensive empirical research has been conducted, which has established a relationship between unsafe or risky online behaviors and victimization (Jansen, 2018; Jansen & Leukfeldt, 2016; Smith et al., 2022). Activities such as sharing passwords, clicking links in emails from unknown senders, sharing personal information on SMS and communicating with strangers online have been identified as some of the risky behaviors that can lead to victimization (Akdemir & Lawless, 2020; Choi & Lee, 2017; Jansen & Leukfeldt, 2016; Smith & Stamatakis, 2021). Further, an individual's deviant behavior, such as downloading pirated content or visiting pornographic websites and lack of self-control (psychological deviation) have also been generally identified as being related to an increased risk of victimization as they increase target suitability (Bossler & Holt, 2010; Jansen & Leukfeldt, 2016; Mesch & Dodel, 2018; van Ouytsel et al., 2018). Overall, these results suggest that to some degree individuals are selected based on their suitability (characteristics and/or behaviors) as victims.

While the importance of risky or unsafe behavior in understanding victimization is irrefutable, there are two key issues with its application in the development of cybersecurity strategies. First, the range of behaviors that may be classified as 'risky' are extensive and include what may be deemed necessary activities today. For instance, engaging in online-banking and shopping has been demonstrated to be related to an increased risk of victimization (e.g., Pratt et al., 2010; van Wilsem, 2013). Similarly, activities that have become commonplace in society, particularly among adolescents and young adults, have also been identified as risk increasing. For example, the use of SMS, other online communication mediums such as email and even time spent browsing the Internet have been identified as risky behaviors in past studies (Leukfeldt & Yar, 2016; Smith & Stamatakis, 2020, 2021). Although these behaviors in themselves may not be intrinsically risk-increasing, they can be associated with maladaptive responses to social media and Internet use that eventually lead to addiction-like behaviors and other risk behaviors, such as disclosure of personal information online, that increase risk of victimization (Hadlington, 2017; Ngo et al., 2020; Smith & Short, 2022). Second, there has been notable inconsistency in the significance of different 'risk' behaviors among cybercrimes and between studies. This has been attributed to the asymmetric nature of the Internet, which allows a single attacker to target large groups at even the international level with little effort (Chu et al., 2010; Gordon & Qingxiong, 2003). The broad brush used by cybercriminals in offenses, such as hacking and phishing, suggests that victimization is ubiquitous, and while some victims are selected due to their suitability and lack of capable guardianship measures, others simply fall into traps laid for whoever may stumble into them (Choi & Lee, 2017; Bossler & Holt, 2013). Also, some researchers such as Akdemir and Lawless (2020) and Smith (2021) have empirically demonstrated that victimization patterns differ between cyber-enabled and cyber-dependent crimes. As such, it is likely impossible to develop a totally unambiguous risk profile for the range of criminal events classified as cybercrimes.

Contrary to theories of victim facilitation that suggest that characteristics or activities of the victim precipitate the crime, there may be innocent cybercrime victims (i.e., they become victims not because of any specific pattern of behavior). This is contrary to the generally accepted assumption that the interaction between a victim and an offender is balanced and requires contribution from both parties (Scott, 2016). In this, case Mendelsohn's (1976) typology of crime victims describes an 'innocent victim' as someone who did not contribute to the victimization and is in the wrong place at the wrong time (Sanchez, 2022). For example, if a provider's cloud storage network is hacked due to an exploitable weakness in their systems the resulting victims who are the users of the service would not have necessarily engaged in any risky activity but would be victims to the loss in confidentiality, integrity and/or accessibility of their data. This is in comparison to the 'victim with minor guilt' often referenced in cybercrime research who does not actively participate in their victimization but contributes to some minor degree by engaging in activities associated with a higher risk of victimization (Sanchez, 2022). Several researchers have highlighted cybercriminals as being opportunistic and casting a wide net, making everyone a potential victim (Leukfeldt, 2014; van't Hoff-de Goede et al., 2021; Smith & Stamatakis, 2021). Therefore, cyberspace may be considered intrinsically criminogenic with the capacity for direct and indirect victimization, which makes the development of a generalizable profile of high-risk characteristics or routine activities improbable (Leukfeldt & Yar, 2016; Reyns, 2015; van de Weijer & Leukfeldt, 2017; van't Hoff-de Goede et al., 2021).

Taken together, previous studies suggest that individuals become more attractive and more likely to become victims based on their suitability as defined by their risky behavior online and their lack of capable guardianship. However, the insufficient consistency among cybercrimes and the range of behaviors that can be considered risky are broad and overlap with common daily routines (van't Hoff-de Goede et al., 2021). Therefore, an important condition with practical implementation possibilities for reducing online victimization is safe online behavior or cyber-hygiene (Cain et al., 2018; Maalem Lahcen et al., 2020; van Bavel et al., 2019; van't Hoff-de Goede, 2021). These measures of self-protection restrict the likelihood of a crime event by reducing target suitability and/or increasing guardianship i.e., target hardening. This approach to crime prevention is important as it empowers the user with their own self-protection, which can work in tandem with measures implemented at the administrative, corporate or national levels (Maimon et al., 2022).

Protective online behavior (cyber-hygiene/cyber-safety measures)

Cyber hygiene is the amalgamation of various existing target hardening practices, which can mitigate the risk of online victimization (Cain et al., 2018; Maennel et al., 2018; Vishwanath et al., 2020). While there are numerous definitions in academic and non-academic literature, Maennel et al. (2018) presented a conceptual framework and formal definition based on a comprehensive literature review. Maennel et al. (2018, p. 6) defined cyber hygiene as "a set of practices aiming to protect [individuals] from negative impact to [their] assets from cybersecurity related risks." This definition highlights the main tenet of cyber hygiene, which is the human factor in the reduction of cyber-related risk. Users of networked technology must actively engage in routine protective behaviors which are known to reduce the risk of online victimization. These behaviors are based on the user's risk assessments and take different forms based on their specific computing environment.

Research within the last decade has identified categories or behavioral clusters of cyber-security best practices based on comprehensive reviews of the extant literature (Cain et al., 2018; Fausett et al., 2020; van't Hoff-de Goede et al., 2021). The identified categories are the use of security software, updating software, password/credential creation and management, browser and network practices, social media usage, data and personal information control, backing-up important files, being alert online, handling emails and device management (Cain et al., 2018; Fausett et al., 2020; van't Hoff-de Goede et al., 2021). The choice of categories highlights the underlying nature of cyber hygiene as a union of standard practices regarding technology and human behavior (Maennel et al., 2018).

Cybersecurity best practice categories can be translated into specific cyber hygiene practices. For example, the category of 'use of security software' is reflected by the installation and regular updating of anti-virus software to protect and secure Internet-enabled devices and information stored on these devices. In relation to password/credential creation and management, users are also advised to use long and complex passwords (including random symbols, letters and numbers), which should be changed regularly and be different for each platform (Cain et al., 2018; Hoonakker et al., 2009). Complex passwords make guessing or the use of brute force attacks extremely difficult, while different passwords limit the damage if one platform is compromised (Ashford, 2009; Dawson & Stinebaugh, 2010). It is also good cyber hygiene to avoid the use of public Wi-Fi networks or use virtual proxy networks (vpn) as cybercriminals can potentially intercept communication and gain access to sensitive data (Cain et al., 2018; Karaymeh et al., 2019). The adoption of cyber hygiene practices appropriate for a given operating environment does not eliminate the risk but is correlated with reduced risk of online victimization experiences (Cain et al., 2018).

Contrary to expectations, research has shown that users—even those deemed knowl-edgeable about cybercrime and cybersecurity—are often limited in their use of proper cyber hygiene. Several studies found that many individuals do not have anti-virus soft-ware installed and at least two in every five that do neglect to update it (Cain et al., 2018; Hadlington, 2017; van Schaik et al., 2018). Studies also show that more than half of the users reuse passwords across platforms and may share their passwords with others (Alo-hali et al., 2018; Cain et al., 2018; Grawemeyer & Johnson, 2011). One study found that approximately 33 percent of users share their passwords (Furnell, 2005). These same pat-terns of poor cyber-hygiene are also recorded for disclosure of personal information on SNS and connecting to public Wi-Fi (Arachchilage & Love, 2014; Christofides et al., 2012; Debatin et al., 2009; Maimon et al., 2022).

It remains unclear why some individuals fail to adopt self-protective behaviors, particu-larly in situations where information on risk is publicly (readily) available. Thus, there is considerable academic and practical utility in the development of a theoretical model capa-ble of explaining the decision-making process involved in the adoption of self-protective behavior. Such an explanatory model can be used in the development of strategies for behavioral modification that leads to greater levels of cyber hygiene.

Explaining human behavior online: an integrated reasoned-action and motivation approach

The use of a positivist approach to the study of cybercrime remains important because it allows researchers to objectively measure and quantify factors that lead to the desired outcome (protective behavior), which is more digestible to those responsible for policy and intervention efforts. In addition, the development of the interventions is enhanced by the scientific method and empirical evidence's ability to facilitate an understanding of the causal relationship of the dependent variable (outcome) with individual and contextual factors. While a constructivist approach elucidates the subjective experience and perception of individuals, which may be important in the context of remote groups or exploring underlying mechanisms, it does not provide the high level of generalizability and predictive power given by the positivist approach, which is required for high-level policy development.

The integration of the positivist approach with reason-based assessment allows for a more comprehensive understanding of the various factors that influence individuals' online behavior. The Rational Actor Model (RAM) contextualizes the observable rational relationships of social factors and social norms with behavioral outcomes. However, although minimized by positivists, the RAM allows researchers to consider that while social factors outside the control of individuals can lead to action, their effect can be obstructed by psychological deviations and emotions. For example, research has shown that fear can motivate individuals to engage in protective behavior, while low self-control can lead to impulsive and risky online behavior. Therefore, it is important to understand the interplay between rational decision-making, social factors, psychological deviations and emotions in shaping an individual's behavior. The integrated approach presented here also highlights that the decision to engage in a specific behavior is not the end of the process. Returning to the positivist approach in the context of reasoned-action, the transition from intent to act to action is affected by external forces which can be outside the control of the individual. For example, one may intend to engage in protective behavior but lack the opportunity and capacity to engage in the desired activity.

The following sub-sections provide an overview of Protection Motivation Theory (PMT) (Floyd et al., 2000; Howell, 2021; Norman et al., 2005), the Capability Opportunity Motivation-Behavior Framework (COM-B) (Michie et al., 2011) and the Reasoned-Action Approach (RAA) (Fishbein & Ajzen, 2010) inclusive of operational definitions of constructs and their reflective indicators. These models have been used extensively to explain behaviors with the intent to develop behavior change interventions (Jansen & Leukfeldt, 2016). These frameworks suggest that a person's choice to engage in protective habits is determined by several constructs of motivation, knowledge, opportunity and capability to engage in safe online behavior (Coventry et al., 2014; Michie et al., 2011). Although the three models are all evaluated as motivational models, they represent different dimensions in the prediction of human social behavior. The theories are reviewed in the given order to first establish the rational link between the reason-based decision-making process, then the link between intent and actual behavior, then introduces COM-B, which provides an understanding of the importance of environment/social factors on motivation that leads to the discussion on the antecedents of PMT (coping and threat appraisal).

Reason-based framework

The assumptions of classical realism are captured in an analytical theory known as RAM. While there are accepted limitations to human rationality in the process of decision-making, it remains applicable to victimology due to its explanatory power. However, the limitations of RAM must be considered in its application as there are several. First, human decision-making can be prone to deviation from what would be a rational procedure due to psychological factors such as low self-control, loss aversion and tendencies to oversimplify complex realities and to disproportionally focus on satisficing information (Stein, 2012, p. 139). Second, neuroscience studies suggest that emotions precede reason as rational thought is first processed in relation to paradigms such as fear and as such influence the cognitive brain (McDermott, 2004, p. 693). Lastly, RAM assumes to some degree individual thought and does not account for the social factors which affect choices, which include the desire to align with existing norms.

Protection Motivation Theory

Central to these models is the Protection Motivation Theory (PMT), first proposed by Rogers in 1975 in the realm of health psychology. The PMT provides a robust theoretical foundation for understanding self-protective behavior in the face of perceived threats. In recent years, PMT has gained traction in the information security domain, with several scholars examining its ability to explain online behavior (e.g., Boerman et al., 2017; Hanus & Wu, 2016; Jansen & Leukfeldt, 2016; van Bavel et al., 2019; van't Hoff-de Goede et al., 2021). PMT is a social cognitive model that predicts an increased intent to engage in protective behavior given the anticipation of a negative outcome (Milne et al., 2000; Weinstein, 1993). In the context of cybersecurity, a person's willingness to behave more cautiously and engage in behaviors to protect themselves online is influenced by the level of motivation to do so due to a desire to avoid security threats and the associated consequences. This approach is one part of the reason-based approach to the analysis of behavior, as it focuses on the threat vs coping dynamic that contributes to behavioral intention, which according to the Theory of Planned Behavior (Fishbein & Ajzen, 2010) is strongly predictive of actual behavior.

In general, PMT proposes that end-users are motivated to engage in self-protective behavior based on threat and coping appraisal, which implies a rational choice based on an assessment of possible threats and the ability to cope with negative outcomes. Threat appraisal refers to the process of identifying the level of belief that the threat is a serious concern (i.e., threat severity) and their susceptibility to the threat (i.e., threat vulnerability) (Milne et al., 2000); i.e., is there a sufficient risk to worry about? The summative effect of threat severity and threat vulnerability is a persuasive fear response motivating the user to have the intent to engage in protective behavior (Boss et al., 2015; Hassandoust & Techatassanasoontorn, 2020). Coping appraisal is defined as the process of considering the user's response efficacy (i.e., the probability that the intended action will be sufficient), self-efficacy (i.e., the user's belief in their capacity to engage in the required coping response) and the costs of accomplishing the adaptive response believed to be necessary in relation to the threat appraisal (Floyd et al., 2000). The fear of victimization and the coping appraisal results in an end-user's intent to engage in protective behavior to prevent harm, given that the cost of response does not outweigh the available resources and perceived benefit (Floyd et al., 2000; Westcott et al., 2017).

The application of PMT in the study of online behavior has had mixed results with some empirical evidence being contradictory to theoretical expectations. Studies have found a significant relationship between coping appraisal and protective online behavior as the PMT predicts (e.g., Crossler & Belanger, 2014; Jansen & van Schaik, 2017; van Bavel et al., 2019). Threat appraisal has been found to have an overall significant effect, though it was less than that of coping appraisal (van Bavel et al., 2019). However, studies examining the dimensions of threat appraisal have had mixed results with studies finding that perceived vulnerability was not related to safe online behavior (Jansen, 2018; Crossler & Belanger, 2014) while a significant relationship existed between perceived severity and online behavior (Jansen, 2018; Jansen & van Schaik, 2017). However, these results did not consider the importance of risk attitudes, which were found to be a significant predictor of online behavior (van Bavel et al., 2019). Risk attitudes are themselves dependent on antecedents of victimization such as past experiences, locus of control and threat awareness. This points out a potential flow in previous approaches, which can lead to the spurious interpretation of the relationship between the tenets of PMT and online behavior. The facets of motivation given by PMT should be examined in the context of factors such as the antecedent of victimization.

Reasoned-Action Approach

To provide context and establish the relationship between the reason-based approach as constrained by factors outside the control of the individual, the RAA is presented. It specifically contextualizes the appraisals of beliefs and perceptions highlighted in PMT and COM-B that motivate the user to have the intent to engage in protective behavior; the RAA suggests that intent predicts the actual change in behavior (Jansen & Leukfeldt, 2016). The RAA is concerned with the determinants of intended behavior resulting from a rational decision-making process (Fishbein & Ajzen, 1975). Where the intent to engage in protective behavior is moderated by action control, i.e., opportunity and capacity to engage in the desired activity (Fishbein & Ajzen, 2010). Further, an individual's behavioral intention is guided by their attitude towards the behavior and their subjective norm (Hooper & Blunt, 2020). The latter captures the individual's desire to comply with how a significantly influential or entrusted other suggested they should behave, i.e., perception of social pressures (Ajzen & Fishbein, 1980). Overall, the theory suggests that the behavioral intention resulting from the influence of attitudes toward behavior and subjective norms is a good predictor of actual behavior (Maalem Lahcen et al., 2020).

The RAA is considered a unified approach and can be extended to a myriad of behaviors (and relatable to other motivation-based behavioral theories) including online behaviors (Jansen & Leukfeldt, 2016). In part, this flexibility is because it is considered a general model and does not specify the operative belief for a given behavior, allowing the researcher to specify the salient belief of the individuals under investigation (Davis et al., 1989). However, the RAA requires that intent and actual behavior not be highly correlated, such as when the temporal gap between their expression is minimal. Assessment when the gap between intent and actual behavior are minimal effectively corroborates the attitudinal basis for current behavior rather than assessing the model's ability to predict behavioral change (Yousafzai et al., 2010). Studies applying RAA to online behavior are limited with the authors finding only one study by Jansen and van Schaik (2016) testing this relationship. The researchers found that their model based on RAA explained high levels of variance for positive/protective behavior ($R^2 = 0.66$) online as well as for perception of risk ($R^2 = 0.62$).

The RAA overlaps with PMT and COM-B in the aspect of its theoretical approach, remaining broad enough to allow the addition of other factors related to behavioral change. The RAA, like PMT and COM-B, relates motivation to intent as a factor of the user's attitude (belief or perception) toward performing the target behavior (Fishbein & Ajzen, 1975). However, PMT specifies the appraisal process and COM-B the antecedents of these processes leading towards the user's attitude toward behavior. Similarly, there is an overlap in the concepts of perceived behavioral control and active control (environment) in the RAA with the construct of opportunity (social and material) in COM-B. In both cases, the constructs are defined by the injunctive norms (perception of what is acceptable or required), descriptive norms (whether others are engaging in the same activity and to what degree) and the resources (finance, time and tools) necessary to engage in the protected activity. However, the RAA specifies the moderating effect of opportunity and capability on the relationship between intent and behavior.

Another aspect of the RAA is the power of control, which is defined by the user's capacity and autonomy to engage in protection behavior. Power of control determines the user's actual control or ability to engage in the intended behavior. One additional dimension of this power of control not captured by PMT and COM-B introduced in this study is self-control. Researchers have argued that self-control is related to online behavior as persons with low self-control are impulsive and are less prone to risk avoidance (Bossler & Holt, 2010; Ngo & Paternoster, 2011). In addition, self-control has a direct effect on motivation (Bossler & Holt, 2010; van't Hoff-de Goede et al., 2021; van Wilsem, 2013). However, it is proposed that self-control moderates the relationship between intent and online behavior, as low self-control leads to a tendency toward immediate or near-term pleasure regardless of the known risk to longer-term interests (Gottfredson, 2017).

Framing social and environmental factors as antecedents of reasoned-action

This chapter presents a critical theoretical discussion geared toward understanding the behavioral outcome of protective behavior resulting from a reason-based assessment of motivational factors and their antecedents, given the capability and opportunity for an individual to do so. It may be argued that 'protective behavior' is not absolute but rather subjectively defined. However, whether the act is specifically defined as protective or otherwise it remains that the individual did 'something', and the focus herein is the motivation to engage in desired action rather than the action itself. This section presents the theory and empirical evidence that this 'something' is the result of sociological (environment) and psychological (deviations, learning), which contribute to the reason-based decision-making process. However, rather than assume that these factors, which are considered beyond the control of the individual, directly lead to behaviors it is proposed that they contribute to an overall reasoned process that guides how the individual exercises free will. This is from both the perspective of moving from intent to action and in the factors which are considered in the rational decision-making process.

COM-B *theory of change*

The Capability Opportunity Motivation-Behavior (COM-B) model for behavior change cites capability (C), opportunity (O) and motivation (M) as three key factors capable of changing behavior (B). Capability is defined as the individual physical and psychological capacity to engage in the intended behavior, i.e., perceived behavioral control. Opportunity describes all the factors which are external to the individual that prompt, enable or make the behavior feasible, which again are beyond the control of the individual. Motivation is defined as the result of the cognitive processes that encourage or direct behavior. Therefore, to perform a particular behavior or engage in the required behavioral change, one must feel they are both psychologically and physically able to do so (Capability), have the social and physical opportunity for the behavior (Opportunity) and want or need to carry out the behavior more than other competing behaviors (Motivation) (Michie et al., 2011, 2014). Or more simply, an individual who is motivated and has the intent to engage in a particular behavior must also have the capacity and conducive environmental conditions. Thus, it introduces the nexus between the deterministic nature of the positivist approach and reason-based assessment.

Previous studies have suggested that a user's knowledge regarding computer literacy and online safety practice (i.e., Countermeasure Awareness) is indicative of their capability to engage in such activity (Alohali et al., 2018; Arachchilage & Love, 2014; Downs et al., 2007). Assessment of the relationship between knowledge of online safety practice and the risk of victimization in the form of computer literacy and knowledge of cybersecurity has also had mixed results (Alohali et al., 2018; Arachchilage & Love, 2014; Grzybowski, 2012; Bossler & Holt, 2013; Marcum, 2008; Ngo & Paternoster, 2011; Shillair et al., 2015; Ovelgönne et al., 2017; van Wilsem, 2013; Yar, 2005). Evidence suggests that computer literacy decreases vulnerability to online harassment, phishing and the risk of hacker intrusions, as they are more adept at identifying potential threats/attacks (Arachchilage & Love, 2014; Reyns et al., 2012; van Wilsem, 2013). However, other studies suggested that computer literacy does not reduce the risk of online harassment (Ngo & Paternoster, 2011; van Wilsem, 2013). One study found that higher levels of computer literacy increased the risk of spyware and adware victimization (Yucedal, 2010). Similarly, a few researchers found that persons who considered themselves highly knowledgeable about information technology (IT) exhibit lower levels of protective behavior (Cain et al., 2018; Ovelgönne et al., 2017). However, this was contrary to the findings of Alohali et al. (2018), which suggested that IT experts were less likely to engage in risky online behaviors.

The COM-B framework also suggests that knowledge and motivation in isolation may be insufficient to lead to safe online behavior. Rather, the user's desired change must be facilitated by the social and material environment, which provides the opportunity to act (Michie et al., 2011). The social environment refers to subjective norms as a function of the user's belief that specific individuals or groups will support persons engaging in a behavior or the action is considered normal or common within the community, i.e., normative beliefs (Lewis et al., 2008; Yzer, 2017). Further, attitudes toward engaging in behavioral change is connected to the user's belief of whether the locus of control lies with them, i.e., do they believe they are responsible for their self-protection (Maalem Lahcen et al., 2020)? Studies examining the effect of the social environment in relation to online behaviors have been extremely limited (Maalem Lahcen et al., 2020). The material environment refers to the availability of finances, time and tools to support safe practices. Finances are necessary to acquire some necessary security resources, and time is needed for implementation. The actual acquisition of tools strengthens self-confidence in displaying the 'new' behavior (Herath & Rao, 2009). This suggests that the overall ease or difficulty of performing the intended behavior acts as a behavioral control. However, the literature shows a dearth of studies examining the relationship between the material environment and online behavior at the individual level.

Antecedents of threat and coping appraisal

While the foundations of the Protection Motivation Theory (PMT) are rooted in threat and coping appraisal processes, several antecedents to these processes have been recognized. These antecedents could be integrated into an augmented version of the PMT, thereby offering a more comprehensive theoretical framework for understanding the motivations underlying behavioral change (Westcott et al., 2017). In behavior analysis, antecedent events are simply phenomena that occur (or exist) immediately prior to a particular behavior of interest. These antecedents represent the positivist factors that are considered outside the control of the individual (and outside the sphere of free will) such that if left alone the individual would have a repeatable outcome (Thio et al., 2013).

Even though the literature on PMT recognizes the importance of the sources of information that users use to weigh the importance of threats and their abilities to address such threats (Milne et al., 2000), the antecedents of threat and coping appraisals are frequently neglected in the literature (Hanus & Wu, 2016; Hassandoust & Techatassanasoontorn, 2020). The antecedents such as threat awareness and past experiences provide the basis that influences the formation of cognitive processes in the PMT (Hanus & Wu, 2016; Milne et al., 2000). Three key factors have been presented as determinants of online behavior, namely past victimization experiences, locus of control and threat awareness (Hanus & Wu, 2016; Hassandoust & Techatassanasoontorn, 2020; van't Hoff-de Goede et al., 2021). These factors are thought to contribute to the cognitive process involved in threat and coping appraisal that will direct motivation.

Past victimization experiences. Research has shown that the incorporation of prior victimization experience into the conventional PMT model increases the model's explanatory power (Tsai et al., 2016; van't Hoff-de Goede et al., 2021). Past experiences are important predictors of future behavior as they shape belief and perception (Folkes, 1988; Pachur et al., 2012; Vance et al., 2012). It should be noted that these experiences can be internal or external, i.e., occurrences experienced by the individual directly or those experienced through individual social interactions. Biases associated with past experiences can facilitate accurate thinking, as in victimization it provides a base for identifying experiences that the individual wishes to avoid. A user's desire for risk avoidance tends to be higher even at the subconscious level if they have experienced the negative consequence associated with the risk. Where the desire for risk avoidance may be subjectively higher based on the individual's perception of the level of discomfort, disruption or negative emotions caused by the event (Christofides et al., 2012; Debatin et al., 2009; Vance et al., 2012).

However, the converse may also be true as dependence on past experiences can also have a limiting effect on cognition. This availability heuristic leads to future outcomes being perceived based on historical information, which causes 'errors' that limit an individual's ability to think divergently and generate new ideas from a subconscious level (Folkes, 1988; Pachur et al., 2012). For example, if someone has not been engaged in protective online behavior but has not been a victim of cybercrime (to their knowledge), they may assume based on past experiences that protective behavior is unnecessary. This mode of thinking could be fortified if, in their social environment, others who have been engaging in some degree of protective behavior have succumbed to cybercrimes. Further, there is heterogeneity among studies, with some suggesting that a negative experience may not always lead to a change in behavior (Cain et al., 2018).

Locus of Control. The term 'locus of control' or ownership appraisal refers to the sense of responsibility that individuals assume towards their own safety and/or the weight given to different sources of information (Hamilton et al., 2016; Kassianos et al., 2016; Rotter, 1966). The locus of decision-making can be attributed to the individual (i.e., internal locus of control or inward expert) or official sources/entrusted others (i.e., external locus of control) (Hamilton et al., 2016; Wallston et al., 1978). Where an individual places their locus of control determines how they perceive or interpret information about threats from external sources and the level of responsibility they take for self-protection (Debatin et al., 2009; Jansen, 2018; Oakley et al., 2020; Workman et al., 2008). Studies by Jansen (2018) and Workman et al. (2008) identified a positive significant relationship between locus of control and online self-protection. First, the way an individual perceives information on a possible risk is determined by the weight they place on the source of information (Hamilton et al., 2016). If a person believes the source is reliable and deemed to have the knowledge and resources to provide such information, they are more likely to weigh this information strongly in their threat appraisal. Second, an individual with a strong external locus of control is expected to attribute responsibility to 'entrusted others' such as the state. Therefore, even if they perceive high vulnerability and severity being associated with the threat, they will not necessarily be motivated to act as they will defer the responsibility (van't Hoff-de Goede et al., 2021).

Threat Awareness. Another factor traditionally presented is fear-appeal, which is defined as persuasive measures developed to cause fear by explaining the harmful consequences that will occur if protective behavior is not adopted (Floyd et al., 2000). However, in this study, the term threat awareness is presented in place of fear-appeal in line with the study by Hanus and Wu (2016). Threat awareness can be defined as an individual's knowledge of particular security threats to which they may be susceptible, and their commitment to learning about threat and technology-based problems is referred to as their level of threat awareness (Dinev & Hu, 2007; Hanus & Wu, 2016; Siponen, 2000; Thomson & von Solms, 1998). The prevailing consensus in the literature suggests that instilling fear in the target audience is not a long-term solution. Instead, more sustainable strategies should encompass identification and elucidation of threats to end-users, coupled with the promotion of positive outcome expectancy associated with protective behavior (Hanus & Wu, 2016; Tunner et al., 1989; Westcott et al., 2017). In addition, this threat awareness approach informs the end-users how this self-protective posture might be achieved (Westcott et al., 2017).

Individuals with greater threat awareness are better able to identify security risks in the context of their interactions with networked technology and are more conscious about protective behaviors which may reduce those risks (Herold, 2010; Peltier, 2000). As such they tend to interact with technology in a secure manner (Dinev & Hu, 2007; Hanus & Wu, 2016). Threat awareness impacts PMT's threat appraisal as it results in more accurate anticipation of the vulnerability and risks associated with threats (Hanus & Wu, 2016). Further, it provides a more accurate understanding and a solid base for weighting the likelihood of being impacted by threats and the severity of their negative impact (Hanus & Wu, 2016). Additionally, individuals will have more of the necessary information to determine their ability to handle the impact of the threat which forms part of their assessment of relative severity.

It has also been suggested that threat awareness counteracts the perception of 'benefits' or maladaptive rewards associated with avoiding protective behavior (Boss et al., 2015; Hanus & Wu, 2016). For example, individuals may request firewalls, implemented by their internet service provider, to be removed to enable the functioning of BitTorrent clients for the reward of downloading pirated content. In this case, they may not be aware of or choose to ignore the threat of increased vulnerability to viruses and other cyberattacks due to lower threat awareness. Threat awareness is also related to the cognitive process involved in assessing one's ability to cope with the identified threats. Knowledge about information technology, associated threats and protective mechanisms increases an individual's belief in their capacity to engage in the desired protective behavior (self-efficacy) and more accurately assess the cost-benefit ratio associated with such action (Boss et al., 2015; Dinev & Hu, 2007; Ifinedo, 2012). Individuals with high self-efficacy have a greater tendency to engage in protective behaviors due to a greater belief in their capabilities to exercise control over potential threats (Ifinedo, 2012). However, if the demand for resources necessary to engage in the protective action is deemed too high, individuals tend to be reluctant to adopt those behaviors (Ifinedo, 2012; Milne et al., 2000). This consideration itself is not done in isolation and is also linked to their perception of their personal threat, i.e., is the likelihood of them becoming a victim sufficiently proportional to the required effort or resources?

From intent to actual behavior: an integrated model of reasoned-action, social and psychological factors

The study proposes that intent to engage in protective behavior results from a combination of reasoned-action (threat and coping appraisal) which are dependent on social factors (prior victimization and threat awareness), psychological (locus of control) and emotional factors (fear of victimization). Further, the resulting intent does not necessarily result in action and is further dependent on the ability to engage in the action. The ability to engage in the action is determined by psychological deviations such as self-control, opportunity (to engage in the action) and capability to do so. Therefore, an integrated model of behavior is introduced which utilizes the previously presented theories to provide different aspects of the same reality and assumes that the determining factors are measurable (normative). Such a model can give 'true' insights into the broader reality by integrating insights from the different theories to explain the role of structures, events and agents.

The integrated approach presented here uses RAA as an overall framework to explain the structural relationship of PMT and COM-B while integrating the antecedents of coping and threat appraisal (past victimization experiences, locus of control and threat awareness). Further, it allows PMT and COM-B as determinants of behavioral intent to engage in safe online behavior to be linked to actual online behavior, a relationship which according to the RAA is moderated by action control. Action control is defined by the user's opportunity and capability to engage in safe online behavior as well as their capacity for self-control. Therefore, the approach allows the researcher to go beyond the nomological models of PMT and COM-B and includes other factors known to affect human social behavior.

The RAA states that attitudes toward the behavior, perceived norms, and perceived behavioral control determine people's intentions, while people's intentions predict their behaviors (Fishbein & Ajzen, 2010). These dimensions of intention as defined by the RAA can be equated to the summative effect of the constructs of the PMT, beliefs affected by past victimizations, locus of control and threat awareness. This approach assumes a strong correlation between behavioral intention to adopt behavioral recommendations and the adoption of actual behavior. While this approach has garnered strong support and the correlation is supported with empirical evidence, it possibly overstates the relationship between

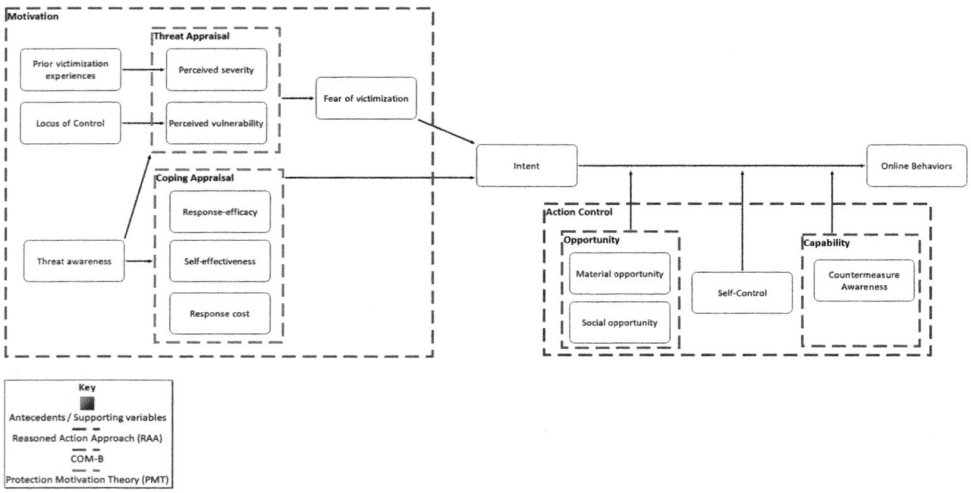

Figure 11.1 Structural model of integrated PMT/COM-B/RAA variables

intention to act and action, particularly where maintaining the action is important (Howell, 2021; Tsai et al., 2016; van Bavel et al., 2019). Research has shown that users may fail to act on a threat simply because they neither have the time nor the skill to respond (Bulgurcu et al., 2010; Reid & Van Niekerk, 2016). There is a notable gap between intention and actual behavior, with research showing that the likelihood of intention leading to actual behavior is close to 50% (Sheeran, 2002; Sheeran & Webb, 2016; Sniehotta et al., 2005).

Importantly, the RAA provides the reality that the conversion of intent to actual online behavior is moderated by Action Control, which can be defined by the capability and opportunity to engage in safe online behavior as well as self-control (Maalem Lahcen et al., 2020). This accounts for the fact that intent does not necessarily translate to actual behavior and is indeed constrained by other factors (Sniehotta et al., 2005). Given that cyber-hygiene requires continued adherence to maintain a cyber-secure posture (sustained response), the factors affecting the relationship between intent and actual behavior must be considered (Crossler et al., 2013).

The integrated model based on the theoretical assessment outlined here is presented in Figure 11.1.

Discussion

This chapter argues for a substantial shift in our understanding and application of protective behavior models, specifically within the context of online deviance. Historically, much of the research in this field has focused on identifying factors that lead to an individual's intent to engage in desired or protective behavior. However, our study underscores the critical need to move beyond this somewhat narrow scope. We posit that an effective model must encompass not just the intent but also the actual execution and maintenance of desired behaviors.

This argument arises from an observable disparity between behavioral intent and actual behavior. This gap, although substantial, is often overlooked in the literature, resulting in a simplified view of online behaviors. A limited number of studies have utilized actual behavior as the dependent variable, thereby providing a more accurate depiction of the relationship between motivation and behavior (van Bavel et al., 2019; van't Hoff-de Goede et al., 2021; Woon et al., 2005; Workman et al., 2008). By focusing on actual behavior, these studies lend weight to our assertion that the study of protective behavior needs to embrace a broader, more nuanced approach.

From an intervention standpoint, it is essential to acknowledge that the nature of interventions hinges on the root causes of the behavior or non-behavior. Our review of the literature suggests that these causes can vary significantly among different groups (Kirlappos et al., 2015). This variance implies that a one-size-fits-all approach to intervention design may not be effective. Instead, interventions need to be tailored to the specific needs and circumstances of the target group.

In light of these findings, this chapter promotes an integrated approach to the study of protective behavior. This approach advocates for interventions that enhance reasoned behavior assessment and consider a broad range of factors, including the reasoning process, social and psychological factors, intent, norms and environmental influences. It encourages further exploration of the impact of these internal and external factors on actions and behaviors related to victimization.

The proposed modeling process is ideally suited for structural equation modeling. This statistical technique can quantify relationships among various factors and inform the design of interventions aimed at inducing behavioral change. By using this method, researchers can gain valuable insights into the complex interplay of factors that influence protective behavior.

However, this chapter also highlights a significant limitation of the current research methods in the study of online deviance, particularly regarding protective behavior. It cautions researchers and policymakers to consider that an individual's planned, desired or portrayed behavior may not always align with their actual behavior. Self-report surveys, a common tool in this field, may not accurately capture this discrepancy. Hence, there is a need for more robust measures to capture actual behavior in the digital realm accurately.

Finally, this chapter introduces a paradigm shift in the study of online deviance: instead of focusing on identifying risk factors that facilitate victimization, it argues for the need to determine positive behaviors that may reduce risk. This perspective, emphasizing the promotion of positive behaviors over the elimination of negative ones, has not been extensively explored in the existing literature but holds significant potential for future research. Thus, this chapter offers a fresh perspective on the study of online deviance and protective behavior. Advocating for a broader, more nuanced approach to this field of study opens up new avenues for research and intervention design. It is our hope that this new perspective will lead to more effective strategies to mitigate online deviance and reduce victimization risk.

Conclusion

This research contributes to the burgeoning field of online deviance studies by pivoting the focus from the traditional perspective of risk factors to fostering positive online behaviors. By proposing an integrated behavioral change approach, it underscores the critical distinction between intent and actual behavior. The study further emphasizes the importance of decision support systems in aiding behavior execution and maintenance, which can significantly reduce the risk of victimization from cybercrime.

The societal relevance of this research is significant. In an era characterized by digital interactions forming an integral part of daily life, understanding the factors influencing safe online behavior and susceptibility to victimization is crucial. The approach proposed in this chapter promotes interventions that enhance reasoned behavior assessment, taking into account a broad spectrum of factors—from reasoning processes to normative influences to environmental factors. This comprehensive perspective on online behavior provides a robust foundation for developing effective policy measures and designing interventions to mitigate online deviance.

From an academic standpoint, this research broadens the existing literature on online deviance by introducing a novel perspective that emphasizes positive behaviors reducing victimization risk. This viewpoint aligns with the emerging shift in epistemology from normative to more interpretive and constructivist approaches in the study of online deviance. Nevertheless, it also highlights the continued relevance and utility of established normative models, suggesting a balanced and integrated approach for future research.

In conclusion, the integrated behavioral change approach advanced in this research offers a promising pathway for future studies and practical interventions in the domain of online deviance. By shifting the focus toward fostering positive behaviors, it introduces a fresh perspective that holds substantial potential for effectively combating cybercrime. The societal and academic implications of this approach underscore the profound relevance of this work in our increasingly digital world, where the threat of cybercrime continues to grow and evolve.

References

Ajzen, I., & Fishbein, M. (1980). *Understanding attitudes and predicting social behavior.* Prentice-Hall.

Akdemir, N., & Lawless, C. J. (2020). Exploring the human factor in cyber-enabled and cyber-dependent crime victimization: A lifestyle routine activities approach. *Internet Research, 30*(6), 1665–1687. https://doi.org/10.1108/INTR-10-2019-0400

Alohali, M., Clarke, N., Li, F., & Furnell, S. (2018). Identifying and predicting the factors affecting end-users risk-taking behavior. *ICS Information & Computer Security, 26*(3), 306–326. Retrieved from z-wcorg/.

Anderson, R., Barton, C., Böhme, R., Clayton, R., van Eeten, M. J. G., Levi, M., Moore, T., & Savage, S. (2013). Measuring the cost of cybercrime. In R. Böhme (Ed.), *The economics of information security and privacy* (pp. 265–300). Springer. https://doi.org/10.1007/978-3-642-39498-0_12

Arachchilage, N., & Love, S. (2014). Security awareness of computer users: A phishing threat avoidance perspective. *Computers in Human Behavior, 38*, 304–312.

Ashford, W. (2009, September 7). Millions of web users at risk from weak passwords [Blog]. *Computer Weekly.* Retrieved from www.computerweekly.com/Articles/2009/09/07/237569/ Millions-of-web-users-at-risk-from-weak-passwords.htm?printerfriendly=true07

Becker, H. S. (1963). *Outsiders: Studies in the sociology of deviance.* Free Press Glencoe.

Boerman, S. C., Kruikemeier, S., & Zuiderveen Borgesius, F. J. (2017). Online behavioral advertising: A literature review and research agenda. *Journal of Advertising, 46*(3), 363–376. https://doi.org/1 0.1080/00913367.2017.1339368

Boss, S. R., Galletta, D. F., Lowry, P. B., Moody, G. D., & Polak, P. (2015). What do systems users have to fear? Using fear appeals to engender threats and fear that motivate protective security behaviors. *MIS Quarterly, 39*(4), 837–864. https://doi.org/10.25300/MISQ/2015/39.4.5

Bossler, A., & Berenblum, T. (2019). Introduction: New direction in cybercrime research. *Journal of Crime and Justice.* https://doi.org/10.1080/0735648X.2019.1692426

Bossler, A., & Holt, T. (2010). The effect of self-control on victimization in the cyberworld. *Journal of Criminal Justice, 38*(3), 227–236.

Bossler, A., & Holt, T. (2013). Examining the relationship between routine activities and malware infection indicators. *Journal of Contemporary Criminal Justice, 29*(4). https://doi.org/10.1177/1043986213507401

Bulgurcu, B., Cavusoglu, H., & Benbasat, I. (2010). Information security policy compliance: An empirical study of rationality-based beliefs and information security awareness. *MIS Quarterly, 34*(3), 523. https://doi.org/10.2307/25750690

Cain, A. A., Edwards, M. E., & Still, J. D. (2018). An exploratory study of cyber hygiene behaviors and knowledge. *Journal of Information Security and Applications, 42*, 36–45. https://doi.org/10.1016/j.jisa.2018.08.002

Choi, K. S., & Lee, J. R. (2017). Theoretical analysis of cyber-interpersonal violence victimization and offending using cyber-routine activities theory. *Computers in Human Behavior, 73*, 394–402. https://doi.org/10.1016/j.chb.2017.03.061

Christofides, E., Muise, A., & Desmarais, S. (2012). Risky disclosures on Facebook: The effect of having a bad experience on online behavior. *Journal of Adolescent Research, 27*(6), 714–731. https://doi.org/10.1177/0743558411432635

Chu, B., Holt, T., & Ahn, G. (2010). *Examining the creation, distribution, and function of malware on-line.* Bibliogov.

Cioban, S., Lazăr, A. R., Bacter, C., & Hatos, A. (2021). Adolescent deviance and cyber-deviance. A systematic literature review. *Frontiers in Psychology, 12*, 748006. https://doi.org/10.3389/fpsyg.2021.748006

Coffey, J., Haveard, M., & Golding, G. (2018). A case study in the implementation of a human- centric higher education cybersecurity program. *Journal of Cybersecurity Education, Research and Practice, 2018*(1).

Coventry, L., Briggs, P., Blythe, J., & Tran, M. (2014). *Using behavioral insights to improve the public's use of cyber security best practices* (10.13140/RG.2.1.2387.3761). Retrieved from www.gov.uk/government/uploads/system/uploads/attachment_data/file/309652/14-835-cyber-security-behavioural-insights.pdf

Crossler, R. E., & Belanger, F. (2014). An extended perspective on individual security behaviors: Protection motivation theory and a unified security practices (USP) instrument. *Data Base for Advances in Information Systems, 45*, 51–71.

Crossler, R. E., Johnston, A. C., Lowry, P. B., Hu, Q., Warkentin, M., & Baskerville, R. (2013). Future directions for behavioral information security research. *Computers & Security, 32*, 90–101. https://doi.org/10.1016/j.cose.2012.09.010

Davis, F. D. (1989). Perceived usefulness, perceived ease of use, and user acceptance of information technology. *MIS Quarterly, 13*(3), 319. https://doi.org/10.2307/249008

Dawson, L., & Stinebaugh, J. (2010). *Methodology for prioritizing cyber-vulnerable critical infrastructure equipment and mitigation strategies* (No. SAND2010–1845, 1028958; pp. SAND2010–1845, 1028958). https://doi.org/10.2172/1028958

Debatin, B., Lovejoy, J. P., Horn, A.-K., & Hughes, B. N. (2009). Facebook and online privacy: Attitudes, behaviors, and unintended consequences. *Journal of Computer-Mediated Communication, 15*(1), 83–108. https://doi.org/10.1111/j.1083-6101.2009.01494.x

Dinev, T., & Hu, Q. (2007). The centrality of awareness in the formation of user behavioral intention toward protective information technologies. *Journal of the Association for Information Systems, 8*(7), 386–408. https://doi.org/10.17705/1jais.00133

Downs, J. S., Holbrook, M., & Cranor, L. F. (2007). Behavioral response to phishing risk. *Proceedings of the Anti-Phishing Working Groups 2nd Annual ECrime Researchers Summit on—ECrime '07* (pp. 37–44). https://doi.org/10.1145/1299015.1299019

Fausett, C., Christovich, M., & Keebler, J. (2020). Best practices for cyber hygiene: A systematic literature review. *The 2021 Student Research Symposium.* Retrieved from https://commons.erau.edu/db-srs/2020/poster-session-grad/6

Fishbein, M., & Ajzen, I. (1975). Belief, attitude, intention and behavior. In *Del 1: An introduction to theory and research.* Addison-Wesley.

Fishbein, M., & Ajzen, I. (2010). *Predicting and changing behavior* (0th ed.). Psychology Press. Retrieved from https://doi.org/10.4324/9780203838020

Floyd, D. L., Prentice-Dunn, S., & Rogers, R. W. (2000). A meta-analysis of research on protection motivation theory. *Journal of Applied Social Psychology*, 30(2), 407–429. https://doi.org/10.1111/j.1559-1816.2000.tb02323.x

Folkes, V. (1988). The availability heuristic and perceived risk. *Journal of Consumer Research*, 15(1), 13–23.

Ford, D. P., Garmsiri, M., Hancock, A. J., & Hickman, R. D. (in press). A review and extension of cyber-deviance literature: Why it likely persists. In R. N. Landers (Ed.), *Technology in motivation and performance*. Cambridge University Press.

Furnell, S. (2005). The Problem of Computer Insecurity. In S. Furnell (Ed.), *Computer insecurity: Risking the system* (pp. 1–15). Springer. Retrieved from https://doi.org/10.1007/1-84628-270-5_1

Gordon, S., & Qingxiong, M. (2003). *Convergence of virus writers and hackers: Fact or fantasy?* Symantec.

Gottfredson, M. (2017). Self-Control Theory and Crime. In M. Gottfredson (Ed.), *Oxford research encyclopedia of criminology and criminal justice*. Oxford University Press. Retrieved from https://doi.org/10.1093/acrefore/9780190264079.013.252

Grawemeyer, B., & Johnson, H. (2011). Using and managing multiple passwords: A week to a view. *Interacting with Computers*, 23(3), 256–267. https://doi.org/10.1016/j.intcom.2011.03.007

Grzybowski, M. (2012). *An examination of cybercrime and cybercrime research: Self-control and routine activity theory*. Arizona State University.

Hadlington, L. (2017). Human factors in cybersecurity; examining the link between Internet addiction, impulsivity, attitudes towards cybersecurity, and risky cybersecurity behaviours. *Heliyon*. https://doi.org/10.1016/j.heliyon.2017.e00346

Hamilton, K., Shih, S.-I., & Mohammed, S. (2016). The Development and Validation of the Rational and Intuitive Decision Styles Scale. *Journal of Personality Assessment*, 98(5), 523–535. https://doi.org/10.1080/00223891.2015.1132426

Hanus, B., & Wu, Y. (2016). Impact of Users' Security Awareness on Desktop Security Behavior: A Protection Motivation Theory Perspective. *Information Systems Management*, 33(1), 2–16. https://doi.org/10.1080/10580530.2015.1117842

Hassandoust, F., & Techatassanasoontorn, A. A. (2020). Understanding users' information security awareness and intentions. In *Cyber influence and cognitive threats* (pp. 129–143). Elsevier. Retrieved from https://doi.org/10.1016/B978-0-12-819204-7.00007-5

Herath, T., & Rao, H. R. (2009). Protection motivation and deterrence: A framework for security policy compliance in organisations. *European Journal of Information Systems*, 18(2), 106–125. https://doi.org/10.1057/ejis.2009.6

Herold, R. (2010). *Managing an information security and privacy awareness and training program*. CRC Press.

Holt, T. J., van Wilsem, J., van de Weijer, S., & Leukfeldt, R. (2020). Testing an integrated self-control and routine activities framework to examine malware infection victimization. *Social Science Computer Review*, 38(2), 187–206. https://doi.org/10.1177/0894439318805067

Hoonakker, P., Bornoe, N., & Carayon, P. (2009). Password authentication from a human factors perspective: Results of a survey among end-users. *Proceedings of the Human Factors and Ergonomics Society Annual Meeting*, 53(6), 459–463. https://doi.org/10.1177/154193120905300605

Hooper, V., & Blunt, C. (2020). Factors influencing the information security behaviour of IT employees. *Behaviour & Information Technology*, 39(8), 862–874. https://doi.org/10.1080/0144929X.2019.1623322

Howell, C. (2021). *Self-protection in cyberspace: Assessing the processual relationship between thoughtfully reflective decision making, protection motivation theory, cyber hygiene, and victimization* [Dissertation, University of South Florida]. https://scholarcommons.usf.edu/etd/8794

Ifinedo, P. (2012). Understanding information systems security policy compliance: An integration of the theory of planned behavior and the protection motivation theory. *Computers & Security*, 31(1), 83–95. https://doi.org/10.1016/j.cose.2011.10.007

Jansen, J. (2018). *Do you bend or break?: Preventing online banking fraud victimization through online resilience*. Retrieved from z-wcorg/.

Jansen, J., & Leukfeldt, R. (2016). Phishing and malware attacks on online banking customers in the Netherlands: A qualitative analysis of factors leading to victimization. *International Journal of Cyber Criminology*. https://doi.org/10.5281/zenodo.58523

Jansen, J., & van Schaik, P. (2017). Comparing three models to explain precautionary online behavioural intentions. *Information & Computer Security*, 25(2), 165–180. https://doi.org/10.1108/ICS-03-2017-0018

Karaymeh, A., Ababneh, M., Qasaimeh, M., & Al-Fayoumi, M. (2019). Enhancing data protection provided by VPN Connections over Open WiFi networks. *2019 2nd International Conference on New Trends in Computing Sciences (ICTCS)*, 1–6. https://doi.org/10.1109/ICTCS.2019.8923104

Kassianos, A. P., Raats, M. M., & Gage, H. (2016). An exploratory study on the information needs of prostate cancer patients and their partners. *Health Psychology Research*, 4(1). https://doi.org/10.4081/hpr.2016.4786

Kirlappos, I., Parkin, S., & Sasse, M. A. (2015). "Shadow security" as a tool for the learning organization. *ACM SIGCAS Computers and Society*, 45(1), 29–37. https://doi.org/10.1145/2738210.2738216

Leukfeldt, E. R. (2014). Phishing for suitable targets in the Netherlands: Routine activity theory and phishing victimization. *Cyberpsychology, Behavior, and Social Networking*. https://doi.org/10.1089/cyber.2014.0008

Leukfeldt, E. R. (2017). *Research agenda the human factor in cybercrime and cybersecurity*. Eleven International Publishers.

Leukfeldt, E. R., & Yar, M. (2016). Applying routine activity theory to cybercrime: A theoretical and empirical analysis. *Deviant Behavior*, 37(3), 263–280. https://doi.org/10.1080/01639625.2015.1012409

Leukfeldt, R., Notté, R., & Malsch, M. (2019). *Cybercrime has serious consequences for its victims*. Retrieved from www.nscr.nl/en/gevolgen-cybercrime-zeer-ingrijpend-voor-slachtoffers/

Lewis, K., Kaufman, J., & Christakis, N. (2008). The taste for privacy: An analysis of college student privacy settings in an online social network. *Journal of Computer-Mediated Communication*, 14(1), 79–100. https://doi.org/10.1111/j.1083-6101.2008.01432.x

Maalem Lahcen, R. A., Caulkins, B., Mohapatra, R., & Kumar, M. (2020). Review and insight on the behavioral aspects of cybersecurity. *Cybersecurity*, 3(1), 10. https://doi.org/10.1186/s42400-020-00050-w

Maennel, K., Mäses, S., & Maennel, O. (2018). Cyber hygiene: The big picture. In N. Gruschka (Ed.), *Secure IT systems* (Vol. 11252, pp. 291–305). Springer International Publishing. Retrieved from https://doi.org/10.1007/978-3-030-03638-6_18

Maimon, D., Howell, C. J., Jacques, S., & Perkins, R. C. (2022). Situational awareness and public Wi-Fi users' self-protective behaviors. *Security Journal*, 35(1), 154–174. https://doi.org/10.1057/s41284-020-00270-2

Marcum, C. (2008). Identifying potential factors of adolescent online victimization in high school seniors. *International Journal of Cyber Criminology*, 2(2), 346–367.

McDermott, R. (2004). The feeling of rationality: The meaning of neuroscientific advances for political science. *Perspectives on Politics*, 2(04), 691–706. https://doi.org/10.1017/S1537592704040459

McGuire, M., & Dowling, S. (2013). *Cyber crime: A review of the evidence: Summary of key findings and implications*. Home Office. ISBN: 9781782462453 1782462457

Mendelsohn, B. (1976). Victimology and contemporary society's trends. *Victimology*, 1(1), 8–28.

Mesch, G., & Dodel, M. (2018). Low self-control, information disclosure, and the risk of online fraud. *American Behavioral Scientist*, 62(10), 1356–1371.

Michie, S., Atkins, L., & West, R. (2014). *The behaviour change wheel: A guide to designing interventions*. Silverback Publishing.

Michie, S., van Stralen, M. M., & West, R. (2011). The behaviour change wheel: A new method for characterising and designing behaviour change interventions. *Implementation Science*, 6(1), 42. https://doi.org/10.1186/1748-5908-6-42

Milne, S., Sheeran, P., & Orbell, S. (2000). Prediction and intervention in health-related behavior: A meta-analytic review of protection motivation theory. *Journal of Applied Social Psychology*, 30(1), 106–143. https://doi.org/10.1111/j.1559-1816.2000.tb02308.x

Ngo, F. T., & Paternoster, R. (2011). Cybercrime victimization: An examination of individual and situational level factors. *International Journal of Cyber Criminology*, 5(1), 773–793.

Ngo, F. T., Piquero, A. R., LaPrade, J., & Duong, B. (2020). Victimization in cyberspace: Is it how long we spend online, what we do online, or what we post online? *Criminal Justice Review*, 45(4), 430–451. https://doi.org/10.1177/0734016820934175

Norman, P., Boer, H., & Seydel, E. (2005). Protection motivation theory. Predicting health behaviour. In *Predicting Health Behaviour* (pp. 81–127). Open University Press.

Oakley, M., Mohun Himmelweit, S., Leinster, P., & Casado, M. (2020). Protection motivation theory: A proposed theoretical extension and moving beyond rationality—The Case of Flooding. *Water, 12*(7), 1848. https://doi.org/10.3390/w12071848

Ovelgönne, M., Dumitraş, T., Prakash, B. A., Subrahmanian, V. S., & Wang, B. (2017). Understanding the relationship between human behavior and susceptibility to cyber attacks: A data-driven approach. *ACM Transactions on Intelligent Systems and Technology, 8*(4), 1–25. https://doi.org/10.1145/2890509

Pachur, T., Hertwig, R., & Steinmann, F. (2012). How do people judge risks: Availability heuristic, affect heuristic, or both? *Journal of Experimental Psychology: Applied, 18*(3), 314–330. https://doi.org/10.1037/a0028279

Peltier. (2000). Security awareness program. In *Information security management.* Auerbach Publications.

Pratt, T., Holtfreter, K., & Reisig, M. (2010). Routine online activity and internet fraud targeting: Extending the generality of routine activity theory. *Journal of Research in Crime and Delinquency, 47*(3), 267–296. https://doi.org/10.1177/0022427810365903

Reid, R., & Van Niekerk, J. (2016). Decoding audience interpretations of awareness campaign messages. *Information & Computer Security, 24*(2), 177–193. https://doi.org/10.1108/ICS-01-2016-0003

Reyns, B. (2015). A routine activity perspective on online victimisation. *Journal of Financial Crime, 22*(4), 396–411. https://doi.org/10.1108/JFC-06-2014-0030

Reyns, B., Fisher, B., Bossler, A., & Holt, T. (2018). *Opportunity and self-control: Do they predict multiple forms of online victimization?* https://doi.org/10.1007/s12103-018-9447-5

Reyns, B. W., Henson, B., & Fisher, B. S. (2012). Stalking in the twilight zone: Extent of cyberstalking victimization and offending among college students. *Deviant Behavior, 33*(1), 1–25. https://doi.org/10.1080/01639625.2010.538364

Rotter, J. B. (1966). Generalized expectancies for internal versus external control of reinforcement. *Psychological Monographs: General and Applied, 80*(1), 1–28. https://doi.org/10.1037/h0092976

Sanchez, S. (2022). Victims and victim typologies. In *Introduction to the American criminal justice system* (pp. 42–43). Southern Oregon University. Retrieved from https://openoregon.pressbooks.pub/ccj230/chapter/1-14-victims-in-the-cj-system/#return-footnote-2351-3

Sarre, R., Lau, L., & Chang, L. (2018). Responding to cybercrime: Current trends. *Police Practice and Research, 19*(6), 515–518.

Scott, H. (2016). *Victimology: Canadians in context* (2nd ed.). Oxford University Press.

Sheeran, P. (2002). Intention—Behavior relations: A conceptual and empirical review. *European Review of Social Psychology, 12*(1), 1–36. https://doi.org/10.1080/14792772143000003

Sheeran, P., & Webb, T. L. (2016). The intention-behavior gap: The intention-behavior gap. *Social and Personality Psychology Compass, 10*(9), 503–518. https://doi.org/10.1111/spc3.12265

Shillair, R., Cotten, S. R., Tsai, H.-Y. S., Alhabash, S., LaRose, R., & Rifon, N. J. (2015). Online safety begins with you and me: Convincing internet users to protect themselves. *Computers in Human Behavior, 48*, 199–207.

Siponen, M. T. (2000). A conceptual foundation for organizational information security awareness. *Information Management & Computer Security, 8*(1), 31–41. https://doi.org/10.1108/09685220010371394

Smith, T. (2021). *All cybercrimes were not created equal: Assessing cybercrime using a routine activities theory model- comparison approach* [Viva Voce]. Oral defence hosted by Office of Research, Impact and Postgraduate Studies, University of Trinidad and Tobago, Tamana Campus. Retrieved from https://utt.edu.tt/index.php?articles=1&article_key=8354&wk=1

Smith, T., & Short, A. (2022). Needs affordance as a key factor in likelihood of problematic social media use: Validation, Latent Profile Analysis and comparison of TikTok and Facebook problematic use measures. *Addictive Behaviors*, 107259. https://doi.org/10.1016/j.addbeh.2022.107259

Smith, T., & Stamatakis, N. (2020). Defining cybercrime in terms of routine activity and spatial distribution: Issues and concerns. *International of Cyber Criminology, 14*(2), 433–459. https://dx.doi.org/10.5281/zenodo.4769989

Smith, T., & Stamatakis, N. (2021). Cyber-victimization trends in Trinidad & Tobago: The results of an empirical research. *The International Journal of Cybersecurity Intelligence and Cybercrime, 4*(1), 46–63. https://doi.org/10.52306/04010421JINE3509

Sniehotta, F. F., Scholz, U., & Schwarzer, R. (2005). Bridging the intention—Behaviour gap: Planning, self-efficacy, and action control in the adoption and maintenance of physical exercise. *Psychology & Health*, 20(2), 143–160. https://doi.org/10.1080/08870440512331317670

Stein, E. (2012). *Analítica existencial e psicanálise: Freud, Binswanger, Lacan, Boss—Conferências* (1st ed.). Ijuí: Editora Unijuí.

Thio, A., Taylor, J., & Schwartz, M. D. (2013). *Deviant behavior* (A. Thio, Ed., 11th ed.). Pearson.

Thomson, M. E., & von Solms, R. (1998). Information security awareness: Educating your users effectively. *Information Management & Computer Security*, 6(4), 167–173. https://doi.org/10.1108/09685229810227649

Tsai, H.-Y. S., Jiang, M., Alhabash, S., LaRose, R., Rifon, N. J., & Cotten, S. R. (2016). Understanding online safety behaviors: A protection motivation theory perspective. *Computers and Security*, 59, 138–150.

Tunner, J. F., Day, E., & Crask, M. R. (1989). Protection motivation theory. *Journal of Business Research*, 19(4), 267–276. https://doi.org/10.1016/0148-2963(89)90008-8

van Bavel, R., Rodríguez-Priego, N., Vila, J., & Briggs, P. (2019). Using protection motivation theory in the design of nudges to improve online security behavior. *International Journal of Human-Computer Studies*, 123, 29–39. https://doi.org/10.1016/j.ijhcs.2018.11.003

van de Weijer, S. G. A., & Leukfeldt, E. R. (2017). Big Five Personality Traits of Cybercrime Victims. *Cyberpsychology, Behavior, and Social Networking*, 20(7), 407–412. https://doi.org/10.1089/cyber.2017.0028

van Ouytsel, J., Ponnet, K., & Walrave, M. (2018). Cyber dating abuse victimization among secondary school students from a lifestyle-routine activities theory perspective. *Journal of Interpersonal Violence*, 33(17), 2767–2776. https://doi.org/10.1177/0886260516629390

van Schaik, P., Jansen, J., Onibokun, J., Camp, J., & Kusev, P. (2018). Security and privacy in online social networking: Risk perceptions and precautionary behaviour. *Computers in Human Behavior*, 78, 283–297. https://doi.org/10.1016/j.chb.2017.10.007

van Wilsem, J. (2013). "Bought it, but never got it" assessing risk factors for online consumer fraud victimization. *European Sociological Review*, 29(2), 168–178.

van't Hoff-de Goede, M. S., Leukfeldt, E. R., van der Kleij, R., & van de Weijer, S. G. A. (2021). The online behaviour and victimization study: The development of an experimental research instrument for measuring and explaining online behaviour and cybercrime victimization. In M. Weulen Kranenbarg & R. Leukfeldt (Eds.), *Cybercrime in context*: Vol. I (pp. 21–41). Springer International Publishing. https://doi.org/10.1007/978-3-030-60527-8_3

Vance, A., Siponen, M., & Pahnila, S. (2012). Motivating IS security compliance: Insights from Habit and Protection Motivation Theory. *Information & Management*, 49(3–4), 190–198. https://doi.org/10.1016/j.im.2012.04.002

Vishwanath, A., Neo, L. S., Goh, P., Lee, S., Khader, M., Ong, G., & Chin, J. (2020). Cyber hygiene: The concept, its measure, and its initial tests. *Decision Support Systems*, 128, 113160. https://doi.org/10.1016/j.dss.2019.113160

Wallston, K. A., Strudler Wallston, B., & DeVellis, R. (1978). Development of the Multidimensional Health Locus of Control (MHLC) Scales. *Health Education Monographs*, 6(1), 160–170. https://doi.org/10.1177/109019817800600107

Weinstein, N. D. (1993). Testing four competing theories of health-protective behavior. *Health Psychology*, 12(4), 324–333. https://doi.org/10.1037/0278-6133.12.4.324

Westcott, R., Ronan, K., Bambrick, H., & Taylor, M. (2017). Expanding protection motivation theory: Investigating an application to animal owners and emergency responders in bushfire emergencies. *BMC Psychology*, 5(1), 13. https://doi.org/10.1186/s40359-017-0182-3

Weulen Kranenbarg, M., Ruiter, S., & Van Gelder, J.-L. (2021). Do cyber-birds flock together? Comparing deviance among social network members of cyber-dependent offenders and traditional offenders. *European Journal of Criminology*, 18(3), 386–406. https://doi.org/10.1177/1477370819849677

Woon, I., Tan, G., & Low, R. (2005). A protection motivation theory approach to home wireless security, 31. ICIS. Retrieved from https://aisel.aisnet.org/icis2005/31

Workman, M., Bommer, W. H., & Straub, D. (2008). Security lapses and the omission of information security measures: A threat control model and empirical test. *Computers in Human Behavior*, 24(6), 2799–2816. https://doi.org/10.1016/j.chb.2008.04.005

Yar, M. (2005). The novelty of "cybercrime": An assessment in light of routine activity theory. *European Journal of Criminology*, 2(4), 414. https://doi.org/10.1177/147737080556056

Yousafzai, S. Y., Foxall, G. R., & Pallister, J. G. (2010). Explaining internet banking behavior: Theory of reasoned action, theory of planned behavior, or technology acceptance model?: INTERNET BANKING BEHAVIOR. *Journal of Applied Social Psychology*, *40*(5), 1172–1202. https://doi.org/10.1111/j.1559-1816.2010.00615.x

Yucedal, B. (2010). *Victimization in cyberspace: An application of routine activity and lifestyle exposure theories*. Kent State University. Retrieved from http://rave.ohiolink.edu/etdc/view?acc_num=kent1279290984

Yzer, M. (2017). Reasoned action as an approach to understanding and predicting health message outcomes. In M. Yzer (Ed.), *Oxford research encyclopedia of communication*. Oxford University Press. Retrieved from https://doi.org/10.1093/acrefore/9780190228613.013.255

12

THE CULTURAL MILIEUS OF ONLINE OFFENDING

Maryja Šupa

Introduction

"It's the nineties, and anything can be hacked."
— *TVTropes.org on Hollywood hacking*[1]

Many studies of technically complex online offences, such as unauthorised access to computer systems, manipulation of data and information systems, creation of malware, or denial of service, focus on offenders—interpreting them as criminals, members of deviant communities, or both. The issue is complicated by the fact that sometimes technically skilled *online offending* is conflated with *hacking*, a contested term (see Jordan, 2017; Raymond, 2003), and at other times with offences that occur online but do not require detailed knowledge of computer systems, e.g., digitally distributed spam, scam, copyright infringement, doxxing, or social engineering.

Study results show that the question "Who are online offenders?" is deceptive in its simplicity. As in the parable of the blind men and the elephant, various approaches to answering this question present a rather fragmented and contradictory picture. Rational-choice approaches in criminology rely on demographic variables and individual motivation to construct a universal portrait of the online offender, while constructivist ethnographers observe hacker subcultures that are most often only nominally related to illicit activity. In public discourse, the mass media provides mythologised portraits of offenders—from teenage geniuses operating in bedrooms to patriotic hackers fighting a perpetual cyberwar. One of the reasons for this fragmentation is that there is a vast diversity of cultural milieus within which online offences are carried out, as well as the cultural viewpoints from within which they are researched (see Cross, 2018 for a reflection from the researcher's point of view). Online offenders are complex global actors rooted in local cultures which remain largely invisible and under-researched. Therefore, this chapter suggests re-framing online offenders in terms of the wider cultural milieus in which they operate.

The structure of this chapter is as follows. It begins with a more detailed critical exposure of currently existing characterisations of online offenders. They are divided into two

DOI: 10.4324/9781003277675-14

parts: the outsider view and the insider view. The outsider view is based on research about the characterisation of online offenders based on data from the criminal justice system and mainstream myths based on media portraits of hackers. The insider view presents research based on ethnographic data and content analysis from communities allegedly involved or associated with online offending. The critical exposure provides a summary of currently existing research and indicates knowledge gaps that lead to the current fragmentation of knowledge in this area. It is followed by a theoretical synthesis of key premises from cultural criminology, concepts from other fields of critical technology studies, and examples of empirical evidence found in existing studies. They are used to propose four directions for developing a culturally aware analysis of online offending, which are presented next.

First, uneven distribution of power is connected to the concept of post-colonial computing from human-computer interface design to ask how online offending may be explained using the notions of centre and periphery and global North and global South. Second, a focus on online offending as a transnational process indicates that it is made up of multiple intercultural interactions within globally operating offender networks, and between offenders and their targets from different locations. Third, local cultures are significant for understanding offenders' motives, value systems, and future prospects. These may vastly differ based on geographical location and participation in local, face-to-face social networks. Finally, a rethinking of how online offending relates to mainstream and popular culture challenges the view that contemporary online offending is a subcultural phenomenon. It has rather succumbed to a blurring of the boundaries between popular culture and deviant subcultures. Ideas presented in the chapter may serve as ideas for further academic inquiry in the critical paradigm within digital criminology. It is also an invitation to revise the positivist approach and enrich current methodologies with the quantifiable aspects of cultural contexts.

The outsider view of online offenders

The *outsider* view of online offenders is defined as a view that is based on measures of their characteristics without direct contact or close interaction with offenders as research subjects. Academic research relies on two major sources of data representing the outsider view of online offending: criminal justice institutions and mass media. Criminal justice institutions, such as law enforcement agencies and courts, provide statistics, court case materials, and operational data about countering online offences. The mass media produce news stories and portraits of offenders in popular culture, such as film, literature, or music. All of these sources suggest divergent conclusions about offenders' characteristics, motivations, and modus operandi in both criminal justice and the collective imagination.

The criminal justice system catalogues online offenders in units of social and demographic statistics, such as age, gender, types of offences, modus operandi, and outcomes of their cases in court, such as punishment (among others, Cai et al., 2018; Grivna & Drápal, 2019; Hutchings & Collier, 2019; Kikerpill, 2019; Hartel et al., 2022). The demographic framing is apparent in the types of data that are typically collected during the criminal justice process and made available in court case material from different countries. The results paint a diverging (sometimes comically so) picture of offenders. On one end of the spectrum are local opportunists undertaking technologically unsophisticated offences (Grivna & Drápal, 2019; Hutchings & Collier, 2019), followed by more sophisticated offending at the national level (Kikerpill, 2019). The opposite side of the spectrum comprises complex international networks of offenders uniting technologically advanced and non-technical individuals (Nguyen, 2021; Leukfeldt et al., 2017). The range indicates that the prosecution of online offenders and their pathways through the criminal justice systems are highly selective. They depend on the resources of local law enforcement agencies, as well as their political priorities. Furthermore, selectivity in criminal justice affects not only *who* is punished for online offending but also the amount and type of punishment, ranging from negligible to substantial (Hartel et al., 2022; Grivna & Drápal, 2019; Dawei, 2021; Sun et al., 2015).

Pop-cultural portraits of hackers reveal them as heroic or, less often, villainous figures (Gordon, 2010), rife with tropes and stereotypes. Wall (2008) has outlined four distinct stages of hackers' portrayal in film: the older eccentric, the teenage genius, the romanticised rebel, and finally, the state agent. A common thread in all of these media portraits has been the appeal to futurism and production of unrealistic ideas about what online offending is (and is not). Coined by Wall (2008, p. 865), the increasingly mainstream "new haxploitation narrative" reverses the previously seen roles of the offender and the state or the hero and the anti-hero in crime story narratives. Adding to these problematic portrayals is the *Hollywood hacking*[2] trope in fictional depictions of hacking: online offending actions are displayed in a simplified, unrealistic, or outright fictional manner.

In contrast, news media reports focus strongly on the negative connotations of online offending as dangerous and criminal (Pei et al., 2022). It is in rare cases that specific personalities like Edward Snowden or collectives like Anonymous are presented as heroes (Kubitschko, 2015, p. 389). It has also been suggested that in many cases media reports may address the potential of "hacking incidents that never happened" rather than real offences (Vegh, 2005). Thus, news media accounts are not a source of a more realistic counterbalance to the hacker myths from popular culture. Coincidentally, contradictions between offences reported by the media and those actually prosecuted have already been noted by Wall (2008, p. 862) who emphasised this contradiction as a form of "social science fiction".

Since 9/11, a new media framing of online offences has emerged: images of the terrorist hacker (Vegh, 2005) and the patriotic hacker (Karatgozianni, 2010; Dilworth & Stempel, 2010, p. 40). After a long period of presenting online offending as a global and placeless endeavour, at the beginning of the 21st century the media brought at least some online offenders back into a geopolitical context, where state relations and local identities regained their significance. Within this framing, online offenders are *othered* either as highly unique, hero-villain individuals or allegedly highly skilled and superior representatives of rival states. For example, in the United States, *The New York Times* frequently connected online offending to Russian, Chinese, Iranian, and North Korean actors (Pei et al., 2022, p. 9). Karatgozianni (2010) also found evidence of the problematic mythologisation of Russian hackers as allegedly highly skilled. These developments in the news media echo the increasing role of the state as an agent of online offending in recent film narratives (Wall, 2008, p. 865). Thus, the mainstream imagination morphs online offenders (or those capable of online offending) into genius individuals roaming a global and borderless network and into a localised and geopolitically partial framing. State borders define online affiliations, and actors are increasingly faceless and state-sponsored rather than individually motivated.

Problematically, criminal justice data and mass media accounts present online offenders from specific institutional perspectives. They are driven and biased by criminal justice selectivity and media agenda-setting. As sources of data, they provide valuable insights about law enforcement and the media, but fall short of telling a coherent story about perpetrators of online offences.

The insider view of online offenders

In contrast to the outsider view, the insider view is present in studies constructing a bottom-up approach to understanding online offenders. However, they also have limitations. Ethnographies of hacker culture (Steinmetz, 2015; Steinmetz, 2016) focus on groups that are deviant but not necessary illicit (often guilty by association), strongly integrated into the information and knowledge economy and based around the ideals of open source, information freedom, and decentralised power. The results of these studies present hacking as tinkering, innovation, and a creative and skilful approach to technology. If there is offending involved, it is the result of ambiguous or inappropriate legislation, or legal grey areas rather than criminal intent. Although examples of successful online research with hard-to-reach offender groups do exist (see e.g., Ferguson, 2017) there is a lack of in-depth ethnographies of actual online offenders and groups to which they belong.

In a divergent approach, research focusing on online hacking forums is usually based on large amounts of publicly available scraped post data, such as the Cambridge Cybercrime Centre's CrimeBB database (Pastrana, 2018). These studies (among many others, Holt, 2013; Kigerl, 2018; Bhalerao et al., 2019; Pete et al., 2020) classify topics discussed in online communities to reveal the social hierarchies within criminal or potentially criminal networks, and crime scripts—activities before, during, and after carrying out an offence (e.g., Hutchings & Holt, 2015). However, some of their key findings indicate that the division between offenders and non-offenders is blurry. Online hacking forums draw together diverse communities without clear prerequisites of technical skills or offending experience. At times, members may take chances of offending due to opportunistic availability, boredom (Collier et al., 2021), or other context-dependent reasons. At other times they may participate in discussions and activities altogether unrelated to offending. Their participation in online environments often embodies the drift between offending and conventional behaviour. The results of studies about online hacking forums seldom reveal the motivations and cultural contexts in which the (potential) offenders are situated. The forums are under-researched as a *cultural* phenomenon, although they are cultural artefacts.

From the insider perspective, cultural contexts of actual online offending remain largely under-researched. Ethnographies directly engaging online offender groups barely exist, while content analysis of online forums rarely addresses their cultural background.

The cultural approach to online offending

As outlined previously, currently existing insider and outsider views of online offenders are fragmented: they are contradictory and do not offer a coherent and nuanced narrative about actors involved in online offending. The dominant theoretical paradigm is positivist. It includes rational choice, routine activity theory, and more recently, crime script analysis (for an overview of rational choice and its derivatives as the dominant direction in the criminology of online offences, see Maimon & Lourderback, 2019). Within this paradigm, online offending is understood as an individual action based on a rational analysis of potential rewards and punishments. While it aims to explain individual motivation and is used to offer preventive measures, this approach overlooks factors external to the individual. In contrast, a socio-cultural approach to online offending has not yet been utilised to its full potential. Rather than focusing on individuals, it considers the bigger picture: the cultural, social, economic, and political contexts of online offending. This approach offers a distinction between the local and the global factors underlying online offending. It also questions the relationship of mediatisation and popular culture with online offending.

As a theoretical background, cultural criminology, the contemporary offshoot of critical criminology, offers key theoretical propositions that may be adapted in digital criminology.

First, cultural criminologists interpret crime and punishment as one of the key sources of symbolic capital and power (Ferrell et al., 2008, p. 206). They are used in the official criminal justice system and well beyond it; for example, in the privatisation of security or development of vigilantism. In regard to digital criminology, this proposition implies that control over the internet, construction of what constitutes online offences, and responsibility for punishment are all a part of the struggle for symbolic power to master information technology and use it for the purposes of privileged interest groups. The privatisation of online security is extended using algorithmic governance by the private corporations providing online services. Grassroots online spaces, such as online hacking forums, are not only community spaces, but also participants in the wider process of establishing or disrupting norms around the use of existing and newly developing technologies. Exploration of power imbalances contributes towards a digital criminology that continues the reflection and critique of the dominant principles of social control.

Second, cultural criminology focuses on the expressions and transformations of norms and deviance in late modernity. The process is defined by uncertainty, multiple identities and values, mediatisation, and capitalistic production and consumption (Ferrell et al., 2008, pp. 5–17). Multiple identities are forged in globally and locally enacted social relations and must adapt to rapid change (Ferrell et al., 2008, p. 56) within which norms are negotiated. Observation of online offending as it unfolds offers insights into the other side of this coin: at which point, how and why norms are transgressed and what social meanings are attributed to online deviant activity. Images of offenders and offending in the mass media, on social networking, in online games, augmented reality, and other interactive environments contribute to co-created meanings. This co-creation is expressed interactively through memes, online folklore, algorithmic art, and other artefacts, merging the deviant back into popular culture. The merging of pop-culture and deviant activities (Presdee, 2010) are therefore directly relevant to digital criminology.

Third, an important methodological principle of cultural criminological research is expressed as criminological *Verstehen*, in reference to Max Weber's sociological approach. It refers to the in-depth understanding of social interactions, meaning-making, and negotiations about norms. This approach allows understanding contradictions between the values, lifestyle, and decisions of different social actors (Ferrell, 1997, p. 21). Traditionally this approach has emphasised the use of methods such as ethnography and media content analysis. However, to transfer the principle of *Verstehen* to digital criminology implies a reconsideration of research objects and methods that best fit them. It requires methodological innovations that allow capturing and rigorously analysing ongoing online interactions and co-created meanings. Although much content is published online and publicly accessible, there are also interactions that do not persist, requiring approaches such as instant ethnography or ethnographic content analysis (Ferrell et al., 2008, pp. 179–191), which refers to observation of rapidly changing social interactions. Another promising approach is media archaeology, the exploration of archival data and mining for volatile and vulnerable data sources. Suitable empirical research in the digital realm is thus crucial for delivering results that fulfil the first two propositions.

There have already been attempts to extend these theoretical propositions to digital criminology. Majid Yar (2018) has called for a *cultural criminology of the internet*, pointing out that online communication enables "the production and reproduction of transgressive, subaltern or deviant subcultures" (p. 123). Online hacking forums may be one such

227

space, where community interactions produce and reproduce deviance related to technology. Some studies (Holt et al., 2014; Siu et al., 2021) suggest that a large part of the content in online hacking forums does not directly express or discuss illicit activity. Instead, the forums offer spaces enabling broader discussion themes, including technical but not illicit (e.g. programming languages, software, hardware) themes and non-technical themes including discussions of music, film, politics, and pornography. The latter demonstrates direct links between forum members and cultural aspects from their everyday life.

Another relevant cultural viewpoint is Keith Hayward's (2012) identification of the internet as one of the five spaces that may be addressed in cultural criminology. Hayward viewed the internet as a space of (tele)presence, convergence, and virtuality (p. 456). He has discussed the convergence of online and offline actions which are increasingly interdependent. The divide between physical and "cyber", or online and offline has since become blurred and erased in many highly populated, highly connected, predominantly urban spaces. The more users find themselves permanently online, the more convergence there is between their online and offline personas. There is also less difference between subjective cultural experiences offline and online. In addition to constant connectivity, the digitalisation of popular culture has contributed to the blurring of subcultural and pop-cultural boundaries. As a result, many spaces that have previously been called the digital underground or internet culture have embraced mainstream discourse.

Despite these two theoretical additions, there is still a gap in coherent and empirically grounded research of the cultural aspects of online offending. Filling this gap with theoretically sound research and extensive empirical results would show how interweaving cultural contexts define the similarities and differences in online offending as a social practice. Within broader cultural contexts media myths co-exist with the characteristics and motivations of individual offenders, while criminal justice priorities are shaped by political and financial powers. The confluence of global and local, mainstream and subcultural worldviews and consumption patterns creates unique settings for offences.

Based on the key propositions from cultural criminology, subsequent sections explore four directions for a culturally informed digital criminology. They are based on a synthesis of the propositions with critical terms from other disciplines and empirical findings from studies of online offences and offenders which have addressed at least some of their cultural aspects. Power struggles and the uneven distribution of power are presented through a global dimension with ideas from postcolonial computing. The problem of late modern identities is expressed in the tension inherent in online offending as set activities carried out globally but coupled with the specific local cultures and social relations of the offenders. Identities are further expressed in the blurring of boundaries between the mainstream and subcultural belonging of online offenders. Criminological *Verstehen* points to the importance of understanding meanings and co-creation of norms as a hands-on research experience enabling the exploration of cultural themes in digital criminology.

Symbolic capital and power: insights from postcolonial computing

Several researchers have criticised dominant computer hardware and software design practices and the tensions and divides between technology adoption in the Global North and Global South. They offer an alternative approach, *postcolonial computing* (Irani et al., 2010) or *decolonial computing* (Ali, 2016). This perspective points out that technologies are developed in and exported from specific locations because of global power configurations.

The global spread of technologies is seen as a re-occurring colonial practice which may or may not be co-opted to local requirements and peculiarities. Computing as colonisation has been criticised from a variety of points of view and places, including Kenya (Wyche et al., 2015), Bangladesh (Sultana & Ahmed, 2019), and South Africa (Kwet, 2019), among others.

Online offending is often framed by the Global North as an offence against consumers and their ability to successfully continue consuming (an attitude apparent in e.g. Krebs, 2014) rather than a strictly technological threat. The "costs" of online offending are frequently expressed in monetary terms, indicating consumption as the key criterion defining online victimhood. However, the postcolonial point of view refocuses on the cultural impact of online offending. It may be re-framed as a silent retaliation of the Global South against the Global North's *digital empire*, a term discussed by Ulrich Beck in the context of risks to digital freedom (see Beck, 2015). For instance, the trope of online *piracy* may be interpreted as a product of the colonisation of local digital spaces by corporate empires.

There is thus a contradiction between interpretations: online offending as barrier to consumption, and online offending as piracy against the digital empires. It reflects a seminal concept from postcolonial theory: the divide of the centre and the periphery. Victims from the Global North represent the centre and the interests of its powers, while offenders from the Global South represent the periphery. The technical and social skills of the offenders rarely allow them to move from periphery to centre, despite the growth of the global IT industry and online crime prevention tactics such as "influence policing" campaigns in the UK during which targeted online ads with warnings had been served to algorithmically detected online offenders (Collier et al., 2021, pp. 117–120). From the point of view of the colonising corporate centres, online offending is an economic problem requiring technical solutions provided by law enforcement agencies and private security companies. The perspective of the periphery re-frames it as a primarily social and political problem, requiring social and political solutions based on an in-depth understanding of the contexts from which the offences originate. Only then in turn would it be reasonable to expect changes to technology design as suggested by Irani et al. (2010).

Postcolonial computing also pays attention to how specific legal regimes are spread and enforced globally in parallel with technological advancement, e.g., intellectual property rights and patent legislation in IT and the right-to-repair in increasingly connected everyday devices. Recent critique of the global regimes of datafication and breaches of privacy and access to information is based around exploitative extraction of value from data (Zuboff, 2019). Legislative resistance to it may be seen in, for example, the Max Schrems cases against Google and Facebook (Mann, 2018), or the operation of Sci-hub in India (Mohan & Gupta, 2021).

Transnational and global aspects of online offending

Online offences are highly transnational because of how they are organised. The offenders and victims may be in locations far away from each other, and the technical infrastructure is spread around the world. This is especially true when offences are undertaken by organised crime groups operating for profit. For instance, in Vietnam, unsuspecting participants were recruited to operate fraudulent VoIP calls for the financial gain of scam network managers (Nguyen, 2021). Based on the languages they spoke, they were assigned to call victims in different regions. Online and offline social ties, casual local connections, and shared language(s) (Leukfeldt et al., 2017) are crucial enablers of offender recruitment. When international organised crime networks absorb online offences, they become too multiple and complex to be qualified as occurring strictly online. What makes these offences stand out in comparison to offline crime is rather the ways of administering, communicating, and managing a technologically diffuse and remotely orchestrated crime network, as well as the impact on information and data.

Little is known about political views and geopolitical affiliations of online offenders. However, there is a variety of contexts in which country names are mentioned in online hacking forums, implying complex mental maps of stereotypes, technological divides, and political sensitivities about the global potential of offenders' operations. Smirnova and Holt (2017) have shown that some states, especially English-speaking Canada, UK, and the US dominate as sources of data illicitly sold in some online marketplaces. However, the data is sold and bought by agents from a wide variety of countries (Smirnova & Holt, 2017). Evidence of the uneven distribution of offences shows that it is not a uniform global phenomenon, dependent just on the technological possibility of connecting with any person or system in the world. Rather, it reflects global digital divides, uneven distribution of access to specific online services (such as social networking, data storage, or online banking), uneven consumption patterns, uneven demand, and uneven profitability of online offences.

Some online offenders are sponsored by states or act in support of state interests without formal endorsement, allegedly in exchange for remuneration, lenient persecution, or permission to stay online. Such cases range from highly targeted, like the development of Stuxnet software (Collins & McCombie, 2012), to grassroots-associated hacktivism, such as operations on behalf of or in support of Ukraine in its war against Russia (Baezner, 2018; Soesanto, 2022). In such cases offending (attacks on infrastructures, defaced websites, data leaks, unauthorised access to systems) is repackaged as "cyberwarfare". The activities become performative, and their actors participate in war as a global cultural spectacle. Many acts of "cyberwarfare" do not correspond to an armed conflict but are congruent with the previously discussed media narratives of "patriotic hacking". In a Baudrillardian reversal of meanings, the global potential of online offending implodes to hyperlocal and perhaps somewhat dated images of statehood. Performativity and re-framing of offences as war carry these activities outside the perceived scope of the criminal justice system and contribute to the mediatisation of contemporary conflicts.

The rooting of online offending in local cultures

The globalisation of online offending is complemented by local cultures within which the offenders operate. There is an expanding body of research on local forms of online offending from across the world (among many others, Broadhurst & Chang, 2013; Olayemi, 2014; Leukfeldt et al., 2017; Lazarus & Okolorie, 2019; Kshetri, 2015; Kshetri, 2019; Nguyen & Luong, 2020; Kranenbarg, 2020; Lusthaus & Varese, 2021). This literature reveals feedback loops between transnational online offences and the local practices they are inevitably intertwined with—the motivations, value systems, and opportunities of the offenders and the structures of social and legal institutions in which they are embedded. For example, the Yahoo boys in Nigeria are a subculture specialising in online scams, with at least some influence of local spiritual or magic practices used to facilitate online offending (Lazarus & Okolorie, 2019). In the Macedonian town of Veles, teenagers and young adults who are sometimes credited with the invention of "fake news" have been motivated by a combination of poverty and critical outlook on the rule of law (Hughes & Waismel-Manor, 2020).

Global advances in technological design are directly related to cultural change and social change (Irani et al., 2010, p. 1314). They are influenced by specific cultural milieus and in turn exert influence on cultural milieus in other settings. New forms of crime emerge when new technologies become available en masse, but they also depend on co-occurring cultural and social changes. Offenders adapt to how users build trust online, what types of digital data they decide to store on remote platforms, how they understand information security, privacy, and norms of online behaviour—all depending on their cultural background. Aesthetics as well as technical frameworks determine the design trends of convincing-looking phishing websites and defacement notices or alternative characters used for evading spam filters.

On the receiving end, the victims or survivors of online offences are also culturally embedded. Scammers all over the world exploit specific cultural tropes such as romantic love or rags-to-riches (the desire for quick enrichment is something the victims may have in common with the perpetrators). Fake news manufacturers rely on monetisation driven by advertising, an essential product of information capitalism. They are enabled by the culturally defined fears and anxieties of their target audiences in the United States and other countries. Financial crime relies on the difference in levels of protection in products created in different corporate cultures, e.g., the differences in money transfer security in the United States and the European Union.

"Intercultural encounters between designers and users" in the field of technological production (Irani et al., 2010, p. 1319) have a corresponding relationship in the intercultural encounters between offenders and their targets. Most targets of online offending do not become victims, e.g., they have systems that are resilient to generic attacks, they do not engage with spam or scam schemes, and they are resilient to phishing or social engineering. They are thus neither victims nor survivors, and additional exchange of meanings, partially dependent on technology and partially defined by culture, needs to take place for such a target to become a victim. The negotiation and crossing of cultural boundaries, such as language, hardware and software use cases, or corporate cultures, takes place in every potential online offence.

The pop-cultural and subcultural sensitivities of online offenders

In addition to being embedded in local cultural milieus, online offenders also participate in the consumption and distribution of global popular culture, which may serve as a backdrop for practising and discussing technical skills. For instance, some online hacking forums that are strongly focused on illicit online activities contain multiple spaces dedicated to non-technical discussions (Šupa et al., work in progress). Often such forums offer separate spaces for discussing different cultural topics, such as the more prevalent music, world news, film and TV, games, graphic art, and, less often, psychoactive substances, sports, food, and sexuality. They span a broad variety of genres and styles, including highly popular mainstream ones. Such discussions serve as social glue, a means of building trust and long-term acquaintanceship among community members (Yip et al., 2013).

Mainstream popular culture is thus one of the subjects bringing together members of online hacking forums despite divergent technical backgrounds and local cultures. In order to participate in these discussions, it is necessary that the users know what they are discussing. The acceptance and knowledge of mainstream culture, especially music and film, indicates that potential online offenders more readily consume popular culture rather than resist it. It counters the view of online offenders as mainly niche subcultural actors acting against and in tension with *the mainstream*. In some communities there are further examples, such as distribution of celebrity porn (objectified twice, first as sexualised depictions of women and second as illicitly shared digital files within the mission of *freeing information*). Such examples form *the invisible mainstream* (Šupa et al., work in progress): cultural consumption patterns that are mainstream but remain inapparent in live everyday interactions. In the case of communities focusing on sharing digital content, often in conflict with the current system of copyright, the demand for popular culture is the key driving force that enables and attracts offenders. Cultural consumption is thus not a matter of subcultural resistance or demonstration of uniqueness for such communities, but rather a matter of a common core of meanings and communal coherence.

Previous decades of online (counter)cultures have been associated with literary and artistic genres such as cyberpunk, but also cypherpunk (Jarvis, 2021), cyberdadaism (Nason & Troy Innocent, 1991) and other artistic interpretations of information technology. Such interpretations are almost entirely absent from contemporary debates in online communities that focus on technology and possibly offending. Even anime, which is strongly promoted in some of the communities, is represented by predominantly mainstream series. In locations where online offending corresponds to a locally prominent subculture with its own physical spaces and cultural markers there are also clear indicators of their links to pop-cultural consumption and even production, e.g., when Nigerian Yahoo boys become founders of hip-hop labels (Lazarus, 2018). Therefore, there is evidence of ties between online offenders' everyday life and consumption of global popular culture. It points to a problematic blurring of boundaries between popular culture and allegedly deviant subcultures. The exaggerated othering of online offenders as different from the rest of society is another result of mythologised media images.

Conclusions

In summary, current theoretical and empirical literature shows useful contours of the cultural milieus of online offending, but lacks a systematic and interconnected approach to the topic. There are four conclusions offered in this chapter.

First, the current academic narrative about online offenders is fragmented and contradictory, reflecting the fragmentation inherent in institutional accounts of online offending: criminal justice statistics and mass media myths. Ethnographies of hacker culture are usually not related to offending behaviour, and content analysis rarely addresses online communities as a cultural phenomenon. Theoretically, much of this research is based on rational choice approaches which interpret offending as an individual choice based on perceived costs and benefits, and may contribute practically to the development of prevention.

Second, a culturally aware approach offers an opportunity to account for the overlooked context and address online offending as locally rooted action which has global impact. This chapter builds upon several key propositions from cultural criminology to set the theoretical background and discuss it in light of critical concepts and promising results from existing studies. The result is an invitation to explore four potential directions for a more culturally aware digital criminology.

Third, a critical analysis of power relations may be carried out as an examination of colonising effects of the development and global spread of technology, as well as legal and punitive practices related to the use of technology. Online offending may be seen as the result of global power relations between digital centres and peripheries, and responsive to changes in these domains. It is important to examine both the globality and locality of online offending to understand the underlying tensions. Encounters between offenders and their targets, some of whom become victims, are often intercultural. They rely on a range of cultural assumptions from both sides in addition to the technologies used for offending. Online offenders may also have political and geographical affiliations which motivate their participation in offences that are repackaged as the spectacle of "cyberwar". Finally, the blurring of pop-cultural and subcultural boundaries is apparent in the engagement of online offenders or potential offenders with popular culture. As consumers, they may be culturally closer to their targets and victims than to mythologised images of offender subcultures.

Finally, addressing the cultural backgrounds of online offending from the perspectives of both offenders and their targets carries out the principle of criminological *Verstehen*. The key takeaway for digital criminology is the significance of cultural background to the understanding and interpreting online offending as social practices that occur within broader societal systems and have an impact on them.

Notes

1 https://tvtropes.org/pmwiki/pmwiki.php/Main/HollywoodHacking
2 https://tvtropes.org/pmwiki/pmwiki.php/Main/HollywoodHacking

References

Ali, S. M. (2016). A brief introduction to decolonial computing. *XRDS: Crossroads, The ACM Magazine for Students, 22*(4), 16–21.

Baezner, M. (2018). *Cyber and information warfare in the Ukrainian conflict.* Center for Security Studies (CSS), ETH Zürich.

Beck, U. (2015). The digital freedom risk: Too fragile an acknowledgment. *Quaderns de la Mediterrània, 22.*

Bhalerao, R., Aliapoulios, M., Shumailov, I., Afroz, S., & McCoy, D. (2019). Mapping the underground: Supervised discovery of cybercrime supply chains. In *2019 APWG symposium on electronic crime research (eCrime)* (pp. 1–16). IEEE.

Broadhurst, R., & Chang, L. Y. C. (2013). Cybercrime in Asia: Trends and challenges. In J. Liu, S. Jou, & B. Hebenton (Eds.), *Handbook of Asian criminology* (pp. 49–64). Springer.

Cai, T., Du, L., Xin, Y., & Chang, L. Y. (2018). Characteristics of cybercrimes: Evidence from Chinese judgment documents. *Police Practice and Research, 19*(6), 582–595.

Collier, B., Thomas, D. R., Clayton, R., Hutchings, A., & Chua, Y. T. (2021). Influence, infrastructure, and recentering cybercrime policing: Evaluating emerging approaches to online law enforcement through a market for cybercrime services. *Policing and Society, 32*(1), 103–124.

Collins, S., & McCombie, S. (2012). Stuxnet: The emergence of a new cyber weapon and its implications. *Journal of Policing, Intelligence and Counter Terrorism, 7*(1), 80–91.

Cross, C. (2018). Marginalized voices: The absence of Nigerian scholars in global examinations of online fraud. In K. Carrington, R. Hogg, J. Scott, & M. Sozzo (Eds.), *The Palgrave handbook of criminology and the global south* (pp. 261–280). Palgrave Macmillan.

Dawei, S. (2021). Sentencing disparity in China: A descriptive research on auxiliary cybercrime stipulated by amendment IX of criminal law. *Iustum Aequum Salutare, 17*(2), 209–240.

Dilworth, S. W., & Stempel, P. A. (2010). The art of cyberwar. *Reporter, 37*(3), 36–42.

Ferguson, R. H. (2017). Offline 'stranger' and online lurker: Methods for an ethnography of illicit transactions on the darknet. *Qualitative Research*, *17*(6), 683–698.

Ferrell, J. (1997). Criminological Verstehen: Inside the immediacy of crime. *Justice Quarterly*, *14*(1), 3–23.

Ferrell, J., Hayward, K., & Young, J. (2008). *Cultural criminology: An invitation*. Sage.

Gordon, D. (2010). Forty years of movie hacking: Considering the potential implications of the popular media representation of computer hackers from 1968 to 2008. *International Journal of Internet Technology and Secured Transactions*, *2*(1/2), 59–87.

Gřivna, T., & Drápal, J. (2019). Attacks on the confidentiality, integrity and availability of data and computer systems in the criminal case law of the Czech Republic. *Digital Investigation*, *28*, 1–13.

Hartel, P., Wegberg, R., & van Staalduinen, M. (2022). Investigating sentence severity with judicial open data. *European Journal on Criminal Policy and Research*, 1–21.

Hayward, K. J. (2012). Five spaces of cultural criminology. *British Journal of Criminology*, *52*(3), 441–462.

Holt, T. J. (2013). Exploring the social organisation and structure of stolen data markets. *Global Crime*, *14*(2/3), 155–174.

Holt, T. J., Smirnova, O., Strumsky, D., & Kilger, M. (2014). Case study: Advancing research on hackers through social network data. In C. D. Marcum & G. E. Higgins (Ed.), *Social networking as a criminal enterprise* (pp. 145–163). Routledge.

Hughes, H. C., & Waismel-Manor, I. (2020). The Macedonian fake news industry and the 2016 US Election. *Political Science and Politics*, *54*(1), 19–23.

Hutchings, A., & Collier, B. (2019). Inside out: Characterising cybercrimes committed inside and outside the workplace. In *Proceedings of the 4th IEEE European symposium on security and privacy workshop on attackers and cyber—Crime operations* (pp. 481–490). IEEE.

Hutchings, A., & Holt, T. J. (2015). A crime script analysis of the online stolen data market. *British Journal of Criminology*, *55*(3), 596–614.

Irani, L., Vertesi, J., Dourish, P., Philip, K., & Grinter, R. E. (2010). Postcolonial computing: A lens on design and development. In *Proceedings of HCI 2010: HCI for all* (pp. 1311–1320). IEEE.

Jarvis, C. (2021). Cypherpunk ideology: Objectives, profiles, and influences (1992–1998). *Internet Histories*, *6*(3), 315–342.

Jordan, T. (2017). A genealogy of hacking. *Convergence: The International Journal of Research into New Media Technologies*, *23*(5), 528–544.

Karatgozianni, A. (2010). Blame it on the Russians: Tracking the portrayal of Russian hackers during cyber conflict incidents. *Digital Icons: Studies in Russian, Eurasian and Central European New Media*, *4*, 127–150.

Kigerl, A. (2018). Profiling cybercriminals: Topic model clustering of carding forum member comment histories. *Social Science Computer Review*, *36*(5), 591–609.

Kikerpill, K. (2019). Work, prey, love: A critical analysis of Estonian cybercrime case law 2014–2019. *Proceedings Estonian Academy of Security Sciences*, *18*, 109–137.

Kranenbarg, M. W. (2020). Global voices in hacking (multinational views). In T. J. Holt & A. M. Bossler (Eds.), *The Palgrave handbook of international cybercrime and cyberdeviance* (pp. 771–792). Springer International Publishing.

Krebs, B. (2014). *Spam nation: The inside story of organized cybercrime—From global epidemic to your front door*. Sourcebooks.

Kshetri, N. (2015). Cybercrime and cybersecurity issues in the BRICS economies. *Journal of Global Information Technology Management*, *18*(4), 245–249.

Kshetri, N. (2019). Cybercrime and cybersecurity in Africa. *Journal of Global Information Technology Management*, *22*(2), 77–81.

Kubitschko, S. (2015). Hackers' media practices. *Convergence: The international journal of research into new media technologies*, *21*(3), 388–402.

Kwet, M. (2019). Digital colonialism: US empire and the new imperialism in the Global South. *Race and Class*, *60*(4), 3–26.

Lazarus, S. (2018). Birds of a feather flock together: The Nigerian cyber fraudsters (Yahoo boys) and hip hop artists. *Criminology, Criminal Justice, Law & Society*, *9*(2), 63–80.

Lazarus, S., Okolorie, G. U. (2019). The bifurcation of the Nigerian cybercriminals: Narratives of the Economic and Financial Crimes Commission (EFCC) agents. *Telematics and Informatics*, *40*, 14–26.

Leukfeldt, E. R., Kleemans, E. R., & Stol, W. P. (2017). A typology of cybercriminal networks: From low—Tech all—Rounders to high—Tech specialists. *Crime, Law and Social Change*, *67*(1), 21–37.

Lusthaus, J., & Varese, F. (2021). Offline and local: The hidden face of cybercrime. *Policing: A Journal of Policy and Practice, 15*(1), 4–14.

Maimon, D., & Louderback, E. R. (2019). Cyber—Dependent crimes: An interdisciplinary review. *Annual Review of Criminology, 2*(1), 191–216.

Mann, M. (2018). The Max Schrems litigation: A personal account. In E. Fahey (Ed.), *Studies in European economic law and regulation* (pp. 75–89). Springer International Publishing.

Mohan, M. P. R., & Gupta, A. (2021). *Right to research and copyright law: From photocopying to shadow libraries*. Indian Institute of Management.

Nason, D., & Innocent, T. (1991). Cyber dada manifesto. *Leonardo, 24*(4), 486.

Nguyen, T. V. (2021). The modus operandi of transnational computer fraud: A crime script analysis in Vietnam. *Trends in Organized Crime, 25*(2), 226–247.

Nguyen, T. V., & Luong, H. T. (2020). The structure of cybercrime networks: Transnational computer fraud in Vietnam. *Journal of Crime and Justice*, 1–22.

Olayemi, O. J. (2014). A socio-technological analysis of cybercrime and cyber security in Nigeria. *International Journal of Sociology and Anthropology, 6*(3), 116–125.

Pastrana, S., Thomas, D. R., Hutchings, A., & Clayton, R. (2018). CrimeBB: Enabling cybercrime research on underground forums at scale. In *Proceedings of the 2018 world wide web conference on world wide web—18*. ACM Press.

Pei, J., Li, D., & Cheng, L. (2022). Media portrayal of hackers in "China Daily" and "The New York Times": A corpus-based critical discourse analysis. *Discourse and Communication, 16*(5), 598–618.

Pete, I., Hughes, J., Chua, Y. T., & Bada, M. (2020). A social network analysis and comparison of six dark web forums. In *2020 IEEE European symposium on security and privacy workshops (EuroS&PW)* (pp. 84–493). IEEE.

Presdee, M. (2010). *Cultural criminology and the carnival of crime*. Routledge.

Raymond, E. S. (Ed.). (2003). Hacker. *The Jargon File, version 4.4.7*. Retrieved from www.catb.org/jargon/html/H/hacker.html

Siu, G. A., Collier, B., & Hutchings, A. (2021). Follow the money: The relationship between currency exchange and illicit behaviour in an underground forum. In *2021 IEEE European symposium on security and privacy workshops* (pp. 191–201). IEEE.

Smirnova, O., & Holt, T. J. (2017). Examining the geographic distribution of victim nations in stolen data markets. *American Behavioral Scientist, 61*(11), 1403–1426.

Soesanto, S. (2022). *The IT army of Ukraine: Structure, tasking, and Eco-System*. Center for Security Studies (CSS), ETH Zürich.

Steinmetz, K. F. (2015). Craft(y)ness: An ethnographic study of hacking. *British Journal of Criminology, 55*(1), 125–145.

Steinmetz, K. F. (2016). *Hacked: A radical approach to hacker culture and crime*. New York University Press.

Sultana, S., & Ahmed, S. I. (2019). Witchcraft and HCI: Morality, modernity, and postcolonial computing in rural Bangladesh. In *Proceedings of the 2019 CHI conference on human factors in computing systems*. ACM.

Sun, J. R., Shih, M. L., & Hwang, M. S. (2015). Cases study and analysis of the court judgement of cybercrimes in Taiwan. *International Journal of Law, Crime and Justice, 43*(4), 412–423.

Vegh, S. (2005). The media's portrayal of hacking, hackers, and hacktivism before and after September 11. *First Monday, 10*(2).

Wall, D. S. (2008). Cybercrime and the culture of fear. *Information, Communication and Society, 11*(6), 861–884.

Wyche, S., Dillahunt, T. R., Simiyu, N., & Alaka, S. (2015). "If God gives me the chance I will design my own phone": Exploring mobile phone repair and postcolonial approaches to design in rural Kenya. In *Proceedings of the 2015 ACM international joint conference on pervasive and ubiquitous computing—UbiComp 15* (pp. 63–473). ACM Press.

Yar, M. (2018). Toward a cultural criminology of the internet. In K. Steinmetz & M. R. Nobles (Eds.), *Technocrime and criminological theory* (pp. 116–132). Routledge.

Yip, M., Webber, C., & Shadbolt, N. (2013). Trust among cybercriminals? Carding forums, uncertainty and implications for policing. *Policing and Society, 23*(4), 516–539.

Zuboff, S. (2019). *The age of surveillance capitalism: The fight for a human future at the new frontier of power*. Profile Books.

PART II

Gender, sex, and sexuality

13

GENDER GAP AND ONLINE DEVIANCE BEHAVIOR: IS CYBERSPACE DEMOCRATIZING CYBERCRIME?

The case of digital piracy

Ana Belén Gómez-Bellvís and Francisco Javier Castro-Toledo

The gender gap and (online) deviance

One of the few agreements in criminological research is the gender gap in crime in the sense that men engage more in crime than women in physical space (Steffensmeier & Allan, 1996; Heimer, 2000; Daigle et al., 2007; Moffit et al., 2001; Serrano Maíllo, 2009; Realpe Quintero & Serrano Maíllo, 2016; Barberet, 2014; Cerezo-Domínguez & Díez-Ripollés, 2015). This gap becomes wider and more evident with respect to more violent crimes[1] (Lauritsen et al., 2009; Heimer et al., 2009), regardless of the debate as to whether arrest and incarceration statistics or self-reported crime surveys can give a better or worse accounting of this gap (Heimer & De Coster, 1999), as well as that which is beginning to take place regarding the narrowing of the gender gap in relation to more violent crimes, possibly due to the crime drop.[2]

However, cyberspace, where we carry out an important part of our daily lives, represents a different area of criminal opportunity in which several types of crimes take place that: i) either already existed and take advantage of cyberspace as a new means, or ii) new crimes have been created that can only be committed through ICTs and the Internet (Wall, 2010). In this sense, it is worth asking whether this gender gap has also been transferred to cyberspace, considering that cyberspace has certain characteristics that clearly differentiate it from physical space, such as anonymity, distance from the victim, the low perception of being detected and punished, etc. (Morris et al., 2009). This question is especially relevant if we take into consideration that an element that is essential to most crimes in which men are statistically more involved is missing in cyberspace: a certain amount of physical violence.

Accordingly, at least two new questions arise in relation to the gender gap and cybercrime that have not been studied as much in the literature. The first is whether the gender gap clearly observed in physical space also exists in cyberspace. If so, the second question is whether the same criminological explanations are valid, as well as whether other factors related to the very realm of cyberspace may play a role.

DOI: 10.4324/9781003277675-16

As is the case with physical space, research has tended to show that cybercrime offenders have characteristics in common and one of these would be gender, in the sense that the majority are male (Hutchings & Chua, 2016). For example, some studies have found a gender gap in the case of cyberharassment (Barlett & Coyne, 2014); also, in relation to software piracy (Hinduja, 2007, Higgins, 2006), digital piracy (Donner, 2016; Udris, 2016), or especially in the case of hacking behavior (Bachman, 2010; Turgeman-Goldschmidt, 2005; Schnell & Dodge, 2002; Udris, 2016; Holt, 2020). So, it is easily assumed that cybercrime could be also a male phenomenon. However, it is necessary to bear in mind that cybercrime, like crime, is a macro-category that serves to encompass a multitude of deviance behavior of a very different nature, and that it is not so much a question of whether cybercrime is a male thing, but in which type of cybercrime such a gap exists and try to explain why it is for every specific deviance behavior (Lazarus et al., 2021). As Hutchings and Chua (2016) explain, this gap depends on the concrete online deviance behavior. Thus, the authors show that women commit cybercrimes, but tend to commit those that do not require special technical skills and engage in activities that are considered "less serious". As for the explanation the authors give for these results, they indicate that they are related to the lack of women's participation in crime in general, together with the gender gap that exists in what they call the computer sciences.

The case of digital piracy

One of the most analyzed cybercrimes in criminological literature is digital piracy. This term covers different conducts that have in common the infringement of the copyright of a certain work such as movies, series, shows, music, TV, sports, software, etc. (e.g., by downloading, streaming, stream-ripping, uploading, hyperlinking, etc., without the right holder consent). The fact that these behaviors are committed by a significant part of the population and across Western societies makes it a particularly interesting one to analyze from a criminological perspective (Brown & Holt, 2018). At the same time, it is one of the most suitable cybercrimes to analyze if cyberspace could have narrowed the gender gap for several reasons: i) because it can be carried out from any location; ii) it does not require great technical skills; iii) it is a behavior that does not require violence; iv) the victim is much more diluted than, for example, a specific victim of theft in physical space (Morris et al., 2009; Wingrove et al., 2011). In other words, digital piracy is a cybercrime that arguably lacks the main characteristics that would differentiate it from crimes committed more frequently by men.

There are some studies that show that men engage more in digital piracy than women (e.g., Holt et al., 2012; Moon et al., 2010; Moon et al., 2013; Higgins, 2006). Nevertheless, other studies have been warning that the gender gap in digital piracy has been narrowing for the last two decades (Odell et al., 2000). For instance, Al-Rafee & Cronan (2006) found that, although men were more accepting of digital piracy, the difference between men and women was not statistically significant. Similar results were obtained by Robertson et al. (2011). In the latter study, the authors hypothesized that based on what the literature had collected so far on the narrowing of the gender gap in digital piracy, there would be no gender differences between men and women in terms of prevalence, a hypothesis that their results confirmed. Thus, several studies have shown that gender has no effect on the behaviors assessed (Holt & Morris, 2009: Higgins et al., 2008; Morris et al., 2009; Wolfe & Higgins, 2009).

Notwithstanding the foregoing, recent studies still indicate that there are gender differences in digital piracy prevalence, especially when attention is paid to the object or type of work being pirated. Udris (2016) analyzed data from the second *International Self-Report Delinquency Study* (ISRD-2) on hacking behavior and illegal downloading. Among his results, he found that the differences in prevalence between genders are not as high as for hacking behavior, an essentially male behavior (8.29% vs. 2.58%); but there is still a difference, albeit smaller, between men and women in the online deviance behavior of illegal downloading (54.6% vs. 42.4%). Likewise, with respect to software piracy, studies indicate that this behavior is also carried out more by men than by women (Hinduja, 2003, 2007). Along these lines, while Cox and Collins (2014) found that women and older men were less likely to engage in digital piracy behavior, they also found that women were less likely to pirate movies than music. Similarly, Smallridge and Roberts (2013) found that gender was a predictor of intellectual property infringing behavior in the sense that men are more likely to engage in digital piracy behaviors, but not for all kinds of pirated content. Specifically, gender was only significant for movie, game, and software piracy.

In a recent study we conducted, we analyzed in a representative sample of the Spanish population the behavior of illegally downloading the following types of works from the Internet: music, audiovisual content (e.g., movies, series, documentaries, etc.); books or articles to read; video games; soccer games or other sports, and software. (Gómez-Bellvís & Miró Llinares, 2021). The results showed an issue that could provide an answer to the question of why such mixed results occur in the literature on the gender gap in digital piracy. The answer may be that both those who observe that the gap has narrowed and those who obtain that the gap is maintained are right, because according to our results the gap is maintained but only with respect to piracy of certain content. According to this study, there was no statistically significant difference between men and women in the illegal downloading of music, books, or video games. But it also showed that there was a statistical difference in the case of illegal downloading of audiovisual content, soccer or other sports games, and software (Gómez-Bellvís & Miró Llinares, 2021).

Some explanations from criminology

General overview

Why women engage in crime less frequently than men is therefore an obvious and necessary line of research, and we could say that it is also a star topic in criminology. Thus, Feminist Criminology[3] has played a central role in this line of research, especially since the work of Adler (1975) and Simon (1975).

Although there are several criticisms from Feminist Criminology (Barberet, 2014) in relation to research on "crime and gender" (Barberet & Larraui, 2019; Serrano Tárraga, 2021; Serrano Maíllo, 2009), there is one that we are interested in highlighting here: The discussion on whether traditional criminological theories explaining crime are sufficient to explain women's crime, since it is precisely the low prevalence of women in the commission of crimes that has resulted in theories based on male crime (Daigle et al., 2007; Marganski, 2020).

Indeed, since research on the relationship between crime and gender began, it has also questioned whether traditional criminological theories were neutral in their explanation and therefore generalizable, or whether instead new theories had to be derived that focused on explaining only female crime in attention to its particularities (Sánchez, 2004; De Coster et al., 2013; Kruttschnitt, 2013; Serrano Maíllo, 2009; Barberet, 2014).

Following the literature review carried out by Kruttschnitt (2013), who follows up the previous review by Steffensmeier and Allan (1996) in the *Annual Review of Sociology*, there have been three ways of approaching the question. The first is those studies that have worked with the central concepts of the theories and found that the causal mechanisms are the same in men and women, despite the differences in prevalence (Bell, 2009). The second is to analyze whether each specific theory is sufficiently adequate to also explain female crime, highlighting in the literature the testing of the General Strain Theory and the self-control theory of Gottfredson and Hirschi (1990).[4] Regarding the former, it explains that men and women are subject to different stresses, namely that men are exposed to stresses and stressful emotional responses that lead to delinquency (Broidy & Agnew, 1997). As for the second, it explains that the gender difference in crime is explained by the different education and social-ization of men and women (Bartolomé et al., 2009). In a nutshell, the theory of self-control understands that the crime commission will depend largely on the level of self-control of the individual and how impulsive he/she is. But this self-control is gestated from family educa-tion and socialization processes. In this sense, this theory explains that to the extent that parents tend to control their daughters more than their sons, women will develop higher lev-els of self-control than men (Gottfredson & Hirschi, 1990). However, testing the hypotheses put forward by these theories in terms of gender, as Kruttschnitt (2013) explains, has led to mixed findings.[5] Finally, the third research approach has sought to examine whether the same structural covariates can explain the rates of female offending (e.g., poverty, unequal income, female-headed households, unemployment, marriage-divorce, etc.). According to the studies analyzed by Kruttschnitt (2013) these variables have "largely" the same effects on female and male crime rates. As a result, state-of-the-art analysis of the issue leads the author to indicate that, when faced with the question of whether we need to derive sepa-rate theories to explain gender-specific crime, there is scientific evidence available showing that most of the core elements of the theoretical correlates of crime (poor parenting, low self-control, delinquent peers, etc.) are gender-invariant.[6]

While it is therefore not unreasonable to claim that men commit more crimes than women and that the core elements of crime theories can explain crime in general, can the same be said for cybercrime?

What about digital piracy as an online deviance behavior: are the same explanations valid?

In the field of cybercrime, there has also been a tendency to test traditional criminological theories that would also consider the gender issue as would have been indicated for the theory of self-control (Higgins & Nicholson, 2020). This theory that puts the focus on poor self-control as a cause of crime would indicate for the case of digital piracy that those who engage in these behaviors do so because they do not have the ability to control themselves from downloading and accessing content for free, which has also been found to be a predic-tive factor in the literature (Higgins & Nicholson, 2020). Studies such as those by Higgins et al. (Higgins et al., 2012 for music piracy; Higgins et al., 2006 for movie piracy; Higgins, 2006 for software piracy) have shown a positive relationship between infringing behavior and low self-control. As to whether this theory can explain the gender gap, the few studies show mixed results. For example, in the case of Higgins' (2006) study analyzing software piracy behavior, it was found on the one hand that men committed these behaviors more than women and on the other hand that self-control was lower in men than in women. These results would support what was established in terms of gender by the theory of Gottfredson and Hirschi (1990). In contrast, Donner's (2016) more recent study finds that, although men commit more digital piracy behaviors than women, the self-control variable is gender-invariant, leading him to conclude that according to his data, self-control would not be sufficient to explain the gender gap by itself.

Another criminological theory that has been used to explain copyright infringement in cyberspace is that of social learning (Akers, 1998), and that applied to digital piracy understands that this behavior is related to the subject's association with those who pirate (Jennings & Bossler, 2019), and with whom he/she shares the same values about digital piracy. In fact, the literature has found that this association with peers is a strong predictor of digital piracy (Burrus et al., 2019; Lee et al., 2018; Nodeland & Morris, 2020; Sanhi & Gupta, 2019; Hinduja & Ingram, 2009; Burrus et al., 2019). Likewise, support for intellectual property violations also gains importance (Burrus et al., 2019; Morris & Higgins, 2010). Nodeland and Morris (2018) tried to analyze the variables of social learning theory and self-control regarding several behaviors in cyberspace. Among them: trying to discover someone's password on a social network, on an educational website, online banking, or email account; using a social network to retaliate against someone to make them feel bad; accessing files without authorization; adding, deleting, or changing or printing someone else's file from their computer without their knowledge; or downloading software, videos, or music. According to the authors, "the results suggest that association with peers either online or offline who support participation in cybercrime significantly influences participation in this behavior" (p. 11). In relation to the gender gap, this theory would indicate that women commit less crime because the socialization processes are different in men than in women. Thus, for example, Higgins (2006) found that social learning theory had the capacity to reduce the gender gap in software piracy, insofar as men are more exposed to peers who also pirate. However, Morris et al. (2009) found that the impact of the various theories of crime measured in their study (including social learning) was equivalent in men and women.

Since we are dealing with deviant behaviors that take place online and in the cyberspace environment, in which it is vital to have at least some basic skills, it is necessary to ask whether variables that have to do with cyberspace itself would account for the gender gap in cybercrime. Thus, as Hutchings and Chua (2016) pointed out in their study, the gender gap found in online deviant behaviors may be due to the gender gap with respect to computer skills.

The difference in prevalence has also been explained by other postulates such as formal or technical knowledge or online socialization. The literature has shown that the field of computer science has been mainly dominated by men. In the meta-analysis carried out by Whitley (1997) it was found that men and boys showed greater gender stereotypes in relation to computers and computing, as well as in relation to self-efficacy to carry out these activities. These stereotypes also extend to other issues related to cyberspace. For example, Cheryan et al. (2009) showed that video games were perceived as a man's game, and this perception may affect women's interest in joining such environments. Another factor that may influence cybercrime is the socialization that takes place in cyberspace, which in turn may be conditioned by the amount of time individuals spend on the Internet (Higgins & Marcum, 2011; Richie & Freiburger, 2014). As Donner (2016, p. 6) puts it:

> for cybercriminals, the Internet can facilitate diversion in a number of ways. For example, the more time individuals spend on the Internet, the more opportunity they have to immerse themselves in the online world, socialise with peers (through social networks, games, chats, etc.) and increase their computer skills.

In fact, since the 1990s some studies also indicate a gender gap in Internet use. Morahan-Martin (1998) found that men made much more use of the Internet than women and attributed this gender gap to the fact that men are more experienced and have more favorable attitudes toward computers than women, and that certain male stereotypes may also have carried over into cyberspace. While more recent studies have shown that the gender gap in Internet or computer use has narrowed considerably with men and women having similar access, they still seem to find that men go online more frequently and spend more time on the Internet than women (Wasserman & Richmond-Abbott, 2005; Imhof et al., 2007).

There are also gender differences in terms of what the Internet is used for. For example, Odell et al. (2000) found that more girls than boys used the Internet for email and university-related tasks, but more men than women used the Internet for visiting pornographic websites, shopping, checking the news, playing games, and listening to or downloading music. The type of studies the subjects were studying at university also seemed to play a role. Those with backgrounds in business management and administration, mathematics, and pure sciences spent more time on the Internet, followed by those studying education, communication, humanities, and social sciences. In a similar direction, Li and Kirkup (2007) found that men use more email or chat rooms, play more video games, and have more confidence in their own skills than women.

Focusing on digital piracy, in the study by Gómez-Bellvís and Miró Llinares (2021), different theoretical frameworks were analyzed with the aim of observing whether the variables of each were distributed differently between men and women, taking into account that they had found a gender gap in terms of digital piracy of audiovisual content, soccer matches or other sports, and software, and having found that this gap was nonexistent in the case of illegal downloading of music, books, and video games. In this study, they analyzed variables from the deterrence approach (perceived certainty and perceived severity); variables from the social influence approach (descriptive and prescriptive norm); moral judgment on downloading behavior; self-efficacy variables; daily Internet use; and subscription to paid platforms (e.g., HBO).

Regarding the theoretical frameworks tested, they found that the variables were similarly distributed in men and women. Similarly, neither time spent on the Internet nor subscriptions to paid platforms were different in men and women. The only variable that was statistically different between genders was perceived self-efficacy. That is: women perceive themselves as less capable or having fewer technical skills to carry out digital piracy behaviors than men.

In this sense, the authors find that the gender gap persists in digital piracy, but with respect to content related to a specific leisure activity (audiovisual content and soccer matches) and with regard to behaviors for which the predominant explanatory factors are moral judgment and perceived self-efficacy. Regarding the audiovisual content, the authors hypothesize that it may be due to the fact that women have less time to spend on this type of leisure. Although it is a hypothesis that deserves much more attention to analyze this cybercrime by focusing on the gender perspective, the fact is that data from official institutions find that women spend two hours more per day than men attending to home and family matters, and this means that they have on average one hour and thirty-seven minutes less per day than men of free time (Gómez-Bellvís & Miró Llinares, 2021). As for the illegal downloading of soccer matches, the authors attribute the gender difference to the gender stereotypes that still reach the infringement of property rules in the field of sports. And as far as illegal software downloading is concerned, according to this study women would download less software than men because they understand it to be worse in a moral sense than men do, and also because they perceive that they have fewer technical skills than men do (Gómez-Bellvís & Miró Llinares, 2021).

Likewise, one result stands out from this study: the non-existence of the gap in the illegal downloading of video games, an area that the literature has pointed out as masculine. However, this would be in line with the idea that has been pointed out in some reports on the progressive incorporation of women in this field. Thus, in a report on the video game sector in Spain in 2019 showing the profile of gamers, Out of fifteen million players, 42% are women (AEVI, 2019).

Conclusion

We said at the beginning that cyberspace is an area of criminal perpetration different from the physical space, with characteristics that differentiate it substantially and give rise to the question of whether the so-called gender gap is transferred into this place. From a descriptive and prevalence point of view, studies indicate that the gap is transferred to a certain extent. While there are behaviors that remain essentially male-dominated such as hacking, it is also true that women commit other types of deviant behaviors online (Hutchings & Chua, 2016). In any case, the fact that in cyberspace certain elements that are related to crime especially committed by men in physical space disappear raises the question of whether cyberspace democratizes the commission of crime.

In this sense, and although it will depend on each specific cybercrime, in the case of digital piracy it is observed that, while the gender gap has narrowed for many behaviors, the gap still occurs with respect to others. As for the reasons for this gap, according to the latest studies, it is difficult to find them solely based on traditional criminological approaches. Nor does the explanation relating to the profile of the Internet user seem plausible. While it is true that in the late 1990s and early 2000s, studies reported that women accessed the Internet less than men, or that men spent more time online, women now tend to access the Internet more or less equally with men and spend approximately the same amount of time on the Internet. According to this, it would be interesting to carry out a deeper analysis of the issue from feminist criminology, with the aim of analyzing the reasons for this gap and going beyond the core elements of traditional theories which, as we have seen, the literature suggests are gender invariant.

Notes

1 Thus, criminological literature has shown that while men tend to be involved in behavior such as vandalism, gangs, weapons offenses, or offenses directly involving physical aggression, women are more involved in anti-social behavior such as fraud, prostitution, or verbal aggression (Steffensmeier & Allan, 1996; Piquero et al., 2005; Piquero, 2000, among others).

2 Something that some authors have already hypothesized and tried to show is due not so much to women committing more violent crimes, but rather to the crime drop that is occurring in crimes committed by men (Beatton et al., 2018).

3 Although, as Barberet and Larraui (2019, p. 275) explain, there are various currents of Feminist Criminology, it is not a concept that refers to a single movement, trend, and postulates. However, all feminist currents would share six main principles: "(1) demonstrate that women 'exist', whether as transgressors, victims and criminal justice practitioners; (2) emphasize that gender is not just a variable but a system, as patriarchy—the subordination of women to men—is a form of discrimination; (3) affirming that masculinity is a subject of feminist study, since in terms of the aetiology of crime, traditional 'toxic' masculinity—that which emphasizes aggressiveness, risk-taking, dominance, physical strength and ambition and cultural values—can be criminogenic; (4) practice reflexivity, what we know or accept as knowledge is often the result of power, privilege and domination, and is never completely objective; (5) be guided by the aims of action research, so that our feminist research methods focus on the possibility and necessity of change, serves women (to promote gender equality) rather than being done merely about women; and (6) be concerned that research should not compromise women's safety, security and dignity". In a narrower sense, Lazarus et al. (2021) understand feminist epistemology to be based on at least two assumptions: the first is the unequal power relationship between men and women; and the second is the difference in men's and women's perceptions and experiences of the world.

4 It is also interesting to note that more recent literature attempts to test other theories such as rational choice or situational action theory. In this sense, Neissl et al. (2019), through the analysis of 735 interviews from Russia and Ukraine, found that the variables of this theory (risk and reward) operate in a very similar way between men and women. On the other hand, Weerman et al. (2015) investigated the extent to which Situational Action Theory could explain gender differences in offending, based on the Study of Peers, Activities, and Neigborhoods (SPAN), taking into account variables such as morality, self-control, unsupervised peer activity, and peer deviance, as well as family and school relationships and parental surveillance. According to their results, the authors confirmed that there were differences in delinquency levels between boys and girls, namely that boys were three times more delinquent than girls, and that there were also differences in the independent variables that could explain the gap. Thus, girls were more supervised by their parents, and had on average higher levels of self-control and morality, as well as fewer rule-breaking peers. In addition, from their regression analyses they found that the core elements of the Situational Action Theory served to explain both female and male delinquency.

5 Specifically, he refers to studies that would show that the confirmation of the hypotheses is partial and depends on other variables. Thus, with respect to the General Strain Theory, he states: "when the stress-delinquency relationship is measured with the presence of adverse life events only, the relationship holds for general delinquency regardless of the respondent's gender. However, when emotional responses to negative life events are modelled as mediating variables, both emotional and behavioural responses to stress vary significantly by gender" (p. 296). He also refers to the mixed results of self-control theory. He explains that "although results vary somewhat depending on measures of self-control and antisocial behaviour, there is evidence of gender invariance in the effects of low self-control on delinquency. However, the way in which self-control interacts with opportunities to offend may differ by gender" (p. 296).

6 A similar conclusion was reached by Smith and Paternoster (1987) when they suggested that at that time the criticism about the need to derive specific theories was somewhat premature insofar as empirical knowledge on the issue was still scarce, but that, in any case, the fact that the theories would be based on male offending did not mean that they could not explain female offending. In this sense, Moffit et al. (2001) already indicated in their study that, on the one hand, gender differences in crime are more a matter of degree than of quality and, on the other hand, that in reality the risk factors for criminality are valid for both genders.

References

Adler, F. (1975). *Sisters in crime*. Waveland Press.

AEVI. (2019). *La industria del videojuego en España. Anuario 2019*. Retrieved from www.aevi.org.es/web/wp-content/uploads/2020/04/AEVI-ANUARIO-2019.pdf (Last accessed 11 May 2023).

Akers, R. (1998). *Social learning and social structure: A general theory of crime and deviance.* Northeastern University Press.

Al-Rafee, S., & Cronan, T. P. (2006). Digital Piracy: Factors that influence attitude toward behavior. *Journal of Business Ethics, 63*, 237–259.

Bachman, M. (2010). The risk propensity and rationality of computer hackers. *International Journal of Cyber Criminology, 4*, 643–656.

Barberet, R. (2014). *Women, crime and criminal justice. A global enquiry.* Routledge.

Barberet, R., & Larrarui, E. (2019). Métodos de investigación feministas. En R. Barberet, R. Bartolomé, & E. Fernández-Molina (Coords.), *Metodología de investigación en Criminología.* Tirant lo Blanch.

Barlett, C., & Coyne, S. M. (2014). A meta-analysis of sex differences in cyber-bullying behavior: The moderating role of age. *Aggressive Behavior, 40*, 474–488.

Bartolomé, R., Montañés, M., Rechea, C., & Montañés, J. (2009). Los Factores de Protección frente a la Conducta Antisocial: ¿Explican las diferencias en violencia entre chicas y chicos?. *Revista Española de Investigación Criminológica, 7.*

Beatton, T., Kidd, M. P., & Machin, S. (2018). Gender crime convergence over twenty years: Evidence from Australia. *European Economic Review, 109*, 275–288.

Bell, K. E. (2009). Gender and gangs. A quantitative comparison. *Crime & Delinquency, 55*(3), 363–387.

Broidy, L., & Agnew, R. (1997). Gender and crime: A general strain theory perspective. *Journal of Research in Crime and Delinquency, 34*(3), 275–306.

Brown, S. C., & Holt, T. J. (Eds.). (2018). *Digital piracy: A global, multidisciplinary account.* Routledge.

Burrus, G. W., Holt, T. J., & Bossler, A. (2019). Revisiting the suppression relationship between social learning and self-control on software piracy. *Social Science Computer Review, 37*, 178–195.

Cerezo-Domínguez, A. I., & Díez-Ripollés, J. L. (2015). La perspectiva de género en el tratamiento y prevención de la delincuencia femenina. En F. Miró Llinares, J. R. Agustina Sanllehí, J. E. Medina Sarmiento, & L. Summers (Eds.), *Crimen, oportunidad y vida diaria. Libro homenaje al Profesor Dr. Marcus Felson.* Dykinson.

Cheryan, S., Plaut, V. C., Davies, P. G., & Steele, C. M. (2009). Ambient belongin: How stereotypical cues impact gender participation in computer science. *Journal of Personality and Social Psychology, 97*, 1045–1060.

Cox, J., & Collins, A. (2014). Sailing in the same ship? Differences in factors motivating piracy of music and movie content. *Journal of Behavioral and Experimental Economics, 50*, 70–76.

Daigle, L. E., Cullen, F. T., & Wright, J. P. (2007). Gender differences in the predictors of juvenile delinquency. assessing the generality-specificity debate. *Youth Violence and Juvenile Justice, 5*(3), 254–286.

De Coster, S., Heimer, K., & Cumley, S. R. (2013). Gender and theories of delinquency. En F. T. Cullen & P. Wilcox (Eds.), *The Oxford handbook of criminological theory* (pp. 313–330). Oxford University Press.

Donner, C. M. (2016). The gender gap and cybercrime: An examination of college students' online offending. *Victims & Offenders, 11*(4), 556–577.

Gómez-Bellvís, A. B., & Miró Llinares, F. (2021). Por qué incumplen ellas las normas penales en Internet? Aproximación al "género del cibercrimen" desde el análisis de las infracciones de piratería intelectual. *Revista General de Derecho Penal, 36*, 1–47.

Gottfredson, M. R., & Hirschi, T. (1990). *A general theory of crime.* Stanford University Press.

Heimer, K. (2000). Changes in the gender gap in crime and women's economic marginalization. En *Criminal justice 2000. The nature of crime: Continuity and change* (pp. 427–483). United States Department of Justice, Office of Justice Programs.

Heimer, K., & De Coster, S. (1999). The gendering of violent delinquency. *Criminology, 37*, 277–317.

Heimer, K., Lauritsen, J. L., & Lynch, J. P. (2009). The national crime victimization survey and the gender gap in offending: Redux. *Criminology, 47*(2).

Higgins, G. E. (2006). Gender differences in software piracy: The mediating roles of self-control theory and social learning theory. *Journal of Economic Crime Management, 4*(1), 1–30.

Higgins, G. E., Fell, B. D., & Wilson, A. L. (2006). Digital piracy: Assessing the contributions of an integrated self-control theory and social learning theory. *Criminal Justice Studies: A Critical Journal of Crime, Law, and Society, 19*, 3–22.

Higgins, G. E., & Marcum, C. D. (2011). *Digital piracy: An integrated theoretical approach*. Carolina Academic Press.

Higgins, G. E., Marcum, C. D., Freiburger, T., & Ricketts, M. (2012). Examining the role of peer influence and self-control on downloading behavior. *Deviant Behavior: An Interdisciplinary Journal, 33*, 412–423.

Higgins, G. E., & Nicholson, J. (2020). The general theory of crime. In *The Palgrave handbook of international cybercrime and cyberdeviance* (pp. 567–581). Palgrave Macmillan.

Higgins, G. E., Wolfe, S. E., & Marcum, C. D. (2008). Digital piracy: An examination of three measurements of self-control. *Deviant Behavior, 29*(5), 440–460.

Hinduja, S. (2003). Trends and patterns among online software pirates. *Ethics and Information Technology, 45*, 49–61.

Hinduja, S. (2007). Neutralization theory and online software piracy: An empirical analysis. *Ethics and Information Technology, 9*(3), 187–204.

Hinduja, S., & Ingram, J. R. (2009). Social learning theory and music piracy: The differential role of online and offline peer influences. *Criminal Justice Studies, 22*(4), 405–420.

Holt, T. J. (2020). Computer hacking and the hacker subculture. In T. J. Holt & A. M. Bossler (Eds.), *The Palgrave handbook of international cybercrime and cyberdeviance* (pp. 725–742). Springer International Publishing. Retrieved from https://doi.org/10.1007/978-3-319-78440-3_36

Holt, T. J., Bossler, A. M., & May, D. C. (2012). Low self-control, deviant peer associations, and juvenile cyberdeviance. *American Journal of Criminal Justice, 37*(3), 1–18.

Holt, T. J., & Morris, R. G. (2009). An exploration of the relationship between MP3 player ownership and digital piracy. *Criminal Justice Studies, 22*(4), 381–392.

Hutchings, A., & Chua, Y. T. (2016). Gendering cybercrime. En T. Holt (Ed.), *Cybercrime through an Interdisciplinary Lens*. Routledge.

Imhof, M., Vollmeyer, R., & Beierlein, C. (2007). Computer use and the gender gap: The issue of acces, use, motivation, and performance. *Computers in Human Behavior, 23*(6), 2823–2837.

Jennings, K., & Bossler, A. M. (2019). Digital piracy. En T. Holt & A. M. Bossler (Eds.), *The Palgrave handbook of international cybercrime and cyberdeviance*. Cyberdeviance. Retrieved from https://doi.org/10.1007/978-3-319-90307-1_44–1

Kruttschnitt, C. (2013). Gender and crime. *Annual Review of Sociology, 29*, 291–308.

Lauritsen, J. L., Heimer, K., & Lynch, J. P. (2009). Trends in the gender gap in violent offending: New evidence from the national crime victimization survey. *Criminology, 47*(2), 361–399.

Lazarus, S., Button, M., & Kapend, R. (2021). Exploring the value of feminist theory in understanding digital crimes: Gender and cybercrime types. *The Howard Journal of Crime and Justice, 2022*. https://doi.org/10.1111/hojo.12485

Lee, B., Paek, S. Y., & Fenoff, R. (2018). Factors associated with digital piracy among early adolescents. *Children and Youth Services Review, 86*, 287–295.

Li, N., & Kirkup, G. (2007). Gender and cultural differences in Internet use: A study of China and the UK. *Computers & Education, 48*(2), 301–317.

Marganski, A. (2020). Feminist theories in criminology and the application to cybercrmies. In T. J. Holt & A. M. Bossler (Eds.), *The Palgrave handbook of international cybercrime and cyberdeviance* (pp. 623–651). Palgrave Macmillan.

Moffit, T., Caspi, A., Rutter, M., & Silva, P. A. (2001). *Sex differences in antisocial behavior. Conduct disorder, delinquency, and violence in the Dunedin longitudinal study*. Cambridge University Press.

Moon, B., McCluskey, J. D., & McCluskey, C. P. (2010). A general theory of crime and computer crime: An empirical test. *Journal of Criminal Justice, 38*(4), 767–772. https://doi.org/10.1016/j.jcrimjus.2010.05.003

Moon, B., McCluskey, J. D., McCluskey, C. P., & Lee, S. (2013). Gender, general theory of crime and computer crime: An empirical test. *International Journal of Offender Therapy and Comparative Criminology, 57*(4), 460–478. https://doi.org/10.1177/0306624X11433784

Morahan-Martin, J. (1998). The gender gap in internet use: Why men use the internet more than women—A literature review. *CyberPsychology & Behavior, 1*(1), 3–10.

Morris, R. G., & Higgins, G. E. (2010). Criminological theory in the digital age: The case of social learning theory and digital piracy. *Journal of Criminal Justice, 38*(4), 470–480.

Morris, R. G., Johnson, M. C., & Higgins, G. E. (2009). The role of gender in predicting the willingness to engage in digital piracy among college students. *Criminal Justice Studies, 22*(4), 393–404.

Neissl, K., Botchkovar, E. V., Antonaccio, O., & Hughes, L. A. (2019). Rational choice and the gender gap in crime: Establishing the generality of rational choice theory in Russia and Ukraine. *Justice Quarterly*, 36(6), 1096–1121.

Nodeland, B., & Morris, R. (2018). A test of social learning theory and self-control on cyber offending. *Deviant Behavior*, 41–56. https://doi.org/10.1080/01639625.2018.1519135

Nodeland, B., & Morris, R. (2020). A test of social learning theory and self-control on cyber offending. *Deviant Behavior*, 41(1), 41–56.

Odell, P. M., Korgen, K. O., Schumacher, P., & Delucchi, M. (2000). Internet use among female and male college students. *CyberPsychology & Behavior*, 3(5), 855–862.

Piquero, A. (2000). Frequency, specialization, and violence in offending careers. *Journal of Research in Crime & Delinquency*, 37(4), 392–418.

Piquero, N. L., Gover, A. R., MacDonald, J. M., & Piquero, A. R. (2005). The influence of delinquent peers on delinquency: Does gender matter? *Youth & Society*, 36(3), 251–275. https://doi.org/10.1177/0044118X04265652

Realpe Quintero, M. F., & Serrano Maíllo, A. (2016). La brecha de género en la criminalidad. Un test de la teoría del poder-control mediante modelos de ecuaciones estructurales con datos del Estudio de Delincuencia Juvenil de Cali. *Revista Electrónica de Ciencia Penal y Criminología, RECPC, 18–21*, 1–19.

Richie, M., & Freiburger, T. L. (2014). Creating identity on social network sites. En C. D. Marcum & G. E. Higgins (Eds.), *Social networking as a criminal enterprise* (pp. 9–26). CRC Press.

Robertson, K., McNeill, L, Green, J., & Roberts, C. (2011). Illegal downloading, ethical concern, and illegal behavior. *Journal of Business Ethics*, 108, 215–227.

Sánchez, M. N. (2004). La mujer en la teoría criminológica. *La Ventana*, 20), 240–266.

Sanhi, S. P., & Gupta, I. (2019). *Piracy in the digital era. Psychosocial, criminological and cultural factors*. Springer.

Schnell, B. H., & Dodge, J. L. (2002). *The Hacking of America: Who's Doin It, Why and How*, Quorum Books.

Serrano Maíllo, A. (2009). *Introducción a la Criminología* (6ª ed.). Dykinson.

Serrano Tárraga, M. D. (2021). *Delincuencia femenina. Un estudio sobre tendencia, control y prevención diferenciales desde la perspectiva de género*. Tirant lo blanch

Simon, R. (1975). *Women and crime*. Lexington Books.

Smallridge, J. L., & Roberts, J. R. (2013). Crime specific neutralizations: An empirical examination of four types of digital piracy. *International Journal of Cyber Criminology*, 7(2), 125–140.

Smith, D. A., & Paternoster, R. (1987). The gender gap in theories of deviance: Issues and evidence. *Journal of Research inc Rime and Delinquency*, 24(2), 140–172.

Steffensmeier, D., & Allan, E. (1996). Gender and crime: Toward a gendered theory of female offending. *The Annual Review of Sociology*, 22, 459–487.

Turgeman-Goldschmidt, O. (2005). Hackers Accounts: Hacking as a social entertainment. *Social Science Computer Review*, 23, 8–23.

Udris, R. (2016). Cyber deviance among adolescents and the role of family, school, and neighborhood: A cross-national study. *International Journal of Cyber Criminology*, 10(2), 127–146.

Wall, D. A. (2010). The internet as a conduit for criminal activity. In A. Pattavina (Ed.), *Information technology and the criminal justice system* (pp. 77–98). Sage.

Wasserman, I. M., & Richmond-Abbott, M. (2005). Gender and the internet: Causes of variation in access, level, and scope of use. *Social Science Quarterly*, 86(1), 252–270.

Weerman, F. M., Bernasco, W., Bruinsma, G. J. N., & Pauwels, L. J. R. (2015). Gender differences in delinquency and situational action theory: A partial test. *Justice Quarterly*. http://dx.doi.org/10.1080/07418825.2015.1064987

Whitley, B. E. (1997). Gender differences in computer-related attitudes and behavior: A meta-analysis. *Computer in Human Behavior*, 13(1), 1–22.

Wingrove, T., Korpas, A. L., & Weisz, V. (2011). Why were millions of people not obeying the law? Motivational influences of non-compliance with the law in case of music piracy. *Psychology, Crime & Law*, 17(3), 261–276.

Wolfe, S. E., & Higgins, G. E. (2009). Explaining deviant peers associations: An examination of low self-control, ethical predispositions, definitions, and digital piracy. *Western Criminology Review*, 10(1), 43–55.

14

SEXTORTION ONLINE

Characteristics, challenges, and pathways forward

Roberta L. O'Malley

Introduction

In 2012, Canadian teenager Amanda Todd posted a video to YouTube describing the extreme harassment she experienced from Aydian Coban, a 44-year-old male from the Netherlands, who had blackmailed Todd for years by threatening to publicly disseminate intimate images of her unless she performed additional sexual acts online (Yousif, 2022). Tragically, several weeks after posting her video, Todd, then 15 years old, took her own life due to the incessant torment she experienced at the hands of Coban and her peers when he leaked her private images online. Coban went on to target several other minor girls and adult women around the world in similar blackmail campaigns. He was eventually sentenced to 11 years in prison by a Dutch court in 2017 and was convicted of extortion, possession of child pornography, child luring, and criminal harassment against Todd by the Supreme Court in New Westminster, British Columbia in 2022 (Uguen-Csenge, 2022).

In another example, James Krey, a Florida police officer, threatened to distribute sexual images and videos of his ex-girlfriend to his friends and her co-workers unless she agreed to continue their relationship. When she refused, Krey used the images to coerce her into quitting her job and moving from her home. Eventually, Krey distributed these videos and images to the victim's co-workers, leading to his arrest and imprisonment (Olmeda, 2018). In a final example, a 17-year-old boy took his own life when a cybercriminal lured him into an online webchat and threatened to release sexual images of him unless he paid 5,000 dollars USD (Campbell & Kravarik, 2022).

These three cases are instances of an alarming form of online abuse known colloquially as sextortion, which occurs when an offender threatens to disseminate a victim's intimate images, videos, or information unless the victim complies with the offender's demands (O'Malley & Holt, 2022). As evidenced by the examples, sextortion demands are varied and may include demands for money (FBI, 2021; O'Malley, 2023), sexual contact, the production of more sexual images (Acar, 2016; Kopecký, 2017; O'Malley & Holt, 2022; O'Malley et al., 2023; Wittes et al., 2016b), or to remain in an unwanted relationship (Draucker & Martsolf, 2010; Wolak & Finkelhor, 2016). In addition, the relationship between victim and perpetrator, as well as the offender's motivation for blackmailing the

DOI: 10.4324/9781003277675-17

victim, vary substantially. Thus, sextortion crimes are linked by a common offender ruse—using the threat of publishing sexual images and information to blackmail victims—but occur within the context of different interpersonal crimes, such as intimate partner violence, cyber fraud, and child sexual exploitation (Liggett, 2019; O'Malley & Holt, 2022).

Due to sextortion's overlapping contexts, homing in on one contextual definition of sextortion is difficult and nuanced. For instance, the Federal Bureau of Investigation (FBI) has published several public service announcements warning parents, citizens, and local law enforcement agencies of rising numbers of sextortion incidents, using the "sextortion" moniker to describe both sextortion used by adult strangers online to target minor children for the purpose of sexual exploitation (Department of Justice, 2016; FBI, 2022) as well as financially motivated sextortion that primarily targets adult men and minor boys and is perpetrated by overseas cyber criminals (FBI, 2021, 2022). This chapter will explore the unique aspects of sextortion, describe its connection to other forms of image-based sexual abuse, explore offender characteristics, identify victim impacts, and discuss the legal and investigative challenges associated with sextortion.

Overview of image-based sexual abuse and sextortion

The integration of technology into sexual and gender-based violence has received increasing attention from law enforcement, politicians, and scholars. These types of offenses are known as technology-facilitated sexual violence (TFSV), and they refer to the range of behaviors in which digital technologies are used to support virtual and off-line sexual harms (Henry & Powell, 2016b; Powell & Henry, 2017). Research focused on TFSV has emphasized the importance of focusing on a continuum of abusive behavior that resembles traditional crime with new technological tools (Eaton et al., 2017; Henry & Powell, 2016b, 2016a; McGlynn, Rackley, & Houghton, 2017; Powell & Henry, 2016). In Henry and Powell's (2016b) conception, TFSV contains several key dimensions: 1) harassing or violent acts that involve unwanted sexual attention, 2) gender- and sexuality-based harassment, 3) cyberstalking, 4) image-based abuse, and 5) use of technology to facilitate offline coercive sexual experiences.

Within TSFV, image-based sexual abuse (IBSA) captures the specific behaviors in which sexually explicit videos and images are non-consensually produced, manufactured, distributed, or misused in a way to punish, humiliate, or coerce another person's behavior (McGlynn et al., 2017; McGlynn & Rackley, 2018; Walker & Sleath, 2017). Behaviors that fall into this continuum include revenge pornography, non-consensual pornography, pressure to create sexually explicit material, surreptitiously recording or taking sexual images of another person (colloquially referred to as "up skirting" or "down blousing"), and manufacturing fake pornographic images or "deep fakes" (Flynn et al., 2022; Henry & Powell, 2016b; McGlynn et al., 2017; Powell & Henry, 2017).

Sextortion is a form of IBSA in which the threat to distribute images, videos, and intimate information is used to coerce the behavior of others. Sextortion may overlap with other forms of IBSA, TFSV, and offline gender-based violence. For example, some victims of sextortion may experience co-occurring forms of sexual harassment, cyberstalking, intimate partner violence, and nonconsensual pornography as well as sextortion (Henry et al., 2020; Henry et al., 2021; McGlynn & Rackley, 2018; Walker et al., 2021). In other ways, sextortion is distinct from other forms of IBSA. Compared to revenge pornography and other forms of nonconsensual pornography, images or videos may never be distributed during a sextortion. Instead, the power and control that an offender holds over the victim by threatening to distribute intimate material is central to sextortion, and this uncertainty as to whether or not the image will be disseminated creates fear and compliance in the victim (O'Malley & Holt, 2022; O'Malley, 2023). In addition, sextortion overlaps with several crime types, including other forms of TFSV, child exploitation (Acar, 2016; Department of Justice, 2016; Kopecký, 2017; O'Malley et al., 2023; Wittes et al., 2016b), intimate partner violence (Henry et al., 2020; Woodlock, 2017), and cyber fraud (Cross et al., 2022; FBI, 2021; Ward, 2021b). Since sextortion is associated with multiple offenses, it is important to understand the nexus between sextortion and other forms of cyberviolence. This holistic view can inform both research and policy concerning sexual violence, gender-based violence, and technology.

Current research estimates the prevalence of sextortion between 4% (Lenhart et al., 2016) and 17.38% (Snaychuk & O'Neil, 2020). In a meta-analysis conducted by Patel and Roesch (2022), the pooled prevalence rate of receiving threats or blackmail associated with intimate images or videos was 7.22%. For adolescents, other studies have found a prevalence rate between 2.6% (Gámez-Guadix et al., 2022) and 5% (Patchin & Hinduja, 2018), and a survey of 1,631 cyber sextortion victims found that the majority (46%) were under the age of 18 years old at the time of their victimization (Wolak & Finkelhor, 2016). A recent national survey of American children found that 3.5% of minors reported being victimized by sextortion and 11% reported being a victim of some form of IBSA (Finkelhor et al., 2022).

Limited surveys exist to measure the prevalence of sextortion offending. One survey conducted on over 4,000 Australian adults found that 4.6% had threatened to distribute intimate images (Powell et al., 2018). Similarly, Patchin and Hinduja (2018) found that about 3% of teenagers in their United States sample have perpetrated sextortion, and a large survey of Spanish adolescents found that 0.7% of their sample had perpetrated sextortion (Gámez-Guadix et al., 2022).

Sextortion offenders

Sextortion is unique in its implementation. A qualitative analysis of 152 sextortion cases conducted by O'Malley and Holt (2022) found that different types of offenders use sextortion to fulfill diverse goals and motivations. Using a sample of news media articles and court cases, the authors outlined four categories of offenders that differed substantially in their target selection, demands, and potential motivations for using sextortion to coerce victim behavior. These categories of offenders included intimately violent cyber sextortion offenders, minor-focused cyber sextortion offenders, cybercrime sextortion offenders, and transnational criminal cyber sextortion offenders (O'Malley & Holt, 2022).

Other research also reports high incidences of the use of sextortion by former intimate partners (Eaton et al., 2017; Patchin & Hinduja, 2018; Wolak & Finkelhor, 2016; Woodlock, 2017), as well as sextortion campaigns in which stranger adults specifically target minor children (De La Hoz, 2021; Kopecký, 2017; Nilsson et al., 2019; O'Malley et al., 2023; Powell et al., 2018; Wittes et al., 2016b). In addition, sextortion perpetrated by transnational criminal organizations and other international actors motivated by financial gain has expanded in the last four years (FBI, 2021; National Crime Agency, 2018; Ward, 2021a, 2021b), and will be referred to as financial sextortion in this chapter (O'Malley, 2023).

Sextortion perpetrated by romantic partners and known acquaintances

Most IBSA victim-survivors report knowing their offender, usually because they were in a former romantic, sexual, or dating relationship with their abuser (Citron & Franks, 2014; Dardis & Richards, 2022; Henry et al., 2018, 2020; Ruvalcaba & Eaton, 2020). Former dating relationships between victims and offenders are a common dynamic for most sextortion offenses perpetrated against both adults and minors (Dardis & Richards, 2022; Eaton et al., 2022; Finkelhor et al., 2022; Henry et al., 2018; Wolak & Finkelhor, 2016). Within dating relationships, sexual images and videos may be generated consensually, recorded without the victim's knowledge, or pressured from victims (Dardis & Richards, 2022). Indeed, it is not uncommon for men and women to send sexually explicit images, videos, or messages—colloquially referred to as "sexts"—within new or established relationships (Mori et al., 2020). However, for some, these images are weaponized by offenders in order to coerce compliance. In addition, perpetrators may target victims online through romance scams, where victims are lured into relationships, manipulated into believing the relationship is real, and coerced into sending money as a sextortion demand later on (Cross et al., 2022).

According to a large national survey of Australian adults, 11.1% of their sample reported perpetrating IBSA against others and 4.9% specifically admitted to sextortion, with men being significantly more likely than women to self-report engaging in IBSA and sextortion (Powell et al., 2018). In addition, self-reported perpetrators also noted that they were more likely to target known individuals, such as former romantic partners, friends, or family members (Powell et al., 2018). In a large survey of American adults, Ruvalcaba and Eaton (2020) found that 65.38% of self-reported IBSA perpetrators targeted former or current romantic partners. These results showcase that most forms of IBSA and sextortion are perpetrated by others known to the victim.

Intimately violent forms of sextortion and IBSA are also common among minor victims. Wolak and colleagues' (2018) survey of minor sextortion victims found that approximately 60% of victims knew their offender, usually because they were a current or former romantic partner. Similarly, Finklehor et al.'s (2022) survey of American children found that 31.4% of sextortion incidents were perpetrated by individuals under the age of 18 years old, and that 31.6% of sextortion offenders were former or current intimate partners to victims (Finkelhor et al., 2022). Thus, in many cases, sextortion against minors is perpetrated by other minors known to the victim.

Due to the close dating relationships between victims and offenders, sextortion, as well as other forms of IBSA, can be considered an extension of intimate partner violence. In several cases, sextortion is deployed as a form of punishment when the victim leaves the relationship or the perpetrator feels like they are losing control over the victim (O'Malley & Holt, 2022). As seen in the introductory example of James Krey, offenders may use sextortion to force victims to comply with a variety of demands aimed at controlling their behavior, such as pressuring them to communicate with the offender, stay in the relationship, move, or resign from their jobs (O'Malley & Holt, 2022). In some instances, former romantic partners may use sextortion to coerce the victim into producing more sexual images or engaging in unwanted sexual contact (Dardis & Richards, 2022).

According to Eaton and colleagues' (2020) content analysis of media articles, nonconsensual pornography can be considered a form of intimate partner violence, as it has been perpetrated using all eight of the abuse metatactics described within the Power and Control Wheel. In addition, Eaton and colleagues' (2022) representative survey of 2,006 Americans during the COVID-19 pandemic found that pre-pandemic reports of sexual intimate partner violence significantly predicted sextortion victimization during the pandemic. Similarly, Dardis and Richards' (2022) survey of 493 undergraduate students found that victims who experienced nonconsensual distribution of sexual images by a former romantic partner reported significantly more co-occurring forms of interpersonal violence from their perpetrator than those who were victimized by non-romantic partners. Thus, it appears that IBSA and sextortion perpetrated by former romantic partners occur within an overall pattern of intimate partner violence in which images are utilized by perpetrators to control, threaten, and humiliate victim-survivors (Dardis & Richards, 2022; Eaton et al., 2020; Woodlock, 2017).

Adult strangers who target and sexually exploit minor children

Most concerning, although less common than sextortion perpetrated by known romantic partners or acquaintances (Finkelhor et al., 2022; Patchin & Hinduja, 2018), minor children may be targeted by adult strangers online (Wittes et al., 2016b; Wolak & Finkelhor, 2016). As a result, sextortion has been labeled "the most significantly growing threat to children" within the 2016 National Strategy for Child Exploitation Prevention and Interdiction (Department of Justice, 2016, p. 75).

The use of sextortion by adult strangers against minor children has more in common with other online sexual solicitation and child sexual abuse material offenses than with most forms of IBSA. Online sexual solicitation is defined as the use of the Internet and/or other digital technologies to communicate with children for sexual purposes (Seto et al., 2012). According to a large national survey, approximately 22.5% of youth experience unwanted sexual solicitation online, and 5.4% experienced online sexual exploitation and grooming from adults (Finkelhor et al., 2022). Female adolescents, in particular, are at increased risk of online sexual abuse and unwanted sexual solicitations (Finkelhor et al., 2009; Whittle et al., 2013). Although the rate of unwanted sexual solicitations online has decreased significantly over the last decade (Madigan et al., 2018; Mitchell et al., 2013), the sexual exploitation of children continues to be a pervasive global issue and a major concern for law enforcement.

Minors are generally targeted by adult strangers online, who often impersonate children in order to communicate with their victims (Acar, 2016; O'Malley & Holt, 2022; O'Malley et al., 2023; Wittes et al., 2016b). Offenders will often use grooming tactics to increase trust and manipulate their victims into disclosing private information, engaging in explicit conversations, and sending sexually explicit images (Kopecký et al., 2015; O'Malley et al., 2023). Once a victim provides an offender with a sexually explicit image, the offender will use that image to sextort the victim. In most cases, the sextortion demands are sexual. Most common, offenders will demand their victims create and send more sexual images (O'Malley et al., 2023; Wittes et al., 2016b; Wolak & Finkelhor, 2016).

Within the sextortion offense, demands often escalate, meaning that adult offenders will coerce children into producing increasingly explicit images that may place them in physical harm (O'Malley & Holt, 2022; O'Malley et al., 2023). This is highly concerning because self-generated images, such as those provided, coerced, and exchanged during sextortion campaigns, are the fastest-increasing form of new child sexual abuse material available online and on the Dark Web (Smith, 2012, 2014). These types of sextortion threats are not uncommon in the overall literature concerning online child grooming. For instance, several studies outlining the linguistic properties and persuasion tactics used by groomers highlight the use of threats, pressure, and nagging to coerce children into sending images (Craven et al., 2006; Joleby et al., 2021; Kloess et al., 2019; McAlinden, 2006; O'Connell, 2003; Winters et al., 2020).

Minor victims targeted by adults online may also experience demands that lead to physical sexual abuse. For instance, some offenders may use sextortion to physically force minor children to meet for sexual activity (O'Malley & Holt, 2022; O'Malley et al., 2023). In addition, some offenders have demanded their victims abuse other minor children around them, such as friends or siblings, and send documentation of the abuse to the offender (O'Malley & Holt, 2022). As a result, offenders, despite being geographically distant from victims, can inflict wide-ranging damage to children that represents a form of "remote sexual assault" (Wittes et al., 2016b, p. 2). Due to the overlap between sextortion, child sexual abuse material, and online sexual exploitation of children, it is likely that some offenders are motivated to use sextortion to generate large collections of child abuse material due to a sexual interest in children (O'Malley & Holt, 2022). However, this is not the case for all offenders who have sextorted children online (O'Malley & Holt, 2022). For instance, some offenders report not being attracted to children and instead using sextortion in order to exert power and control over others. In these cases, offenders may target minors because they believe them to be impressionable and easy to control (O'Malley & Holt, 2022).

Cybercrime sextortion offenders

Similar to other forms of IBSA, cybercrime sextortion offenders tend to specifically target young adult females (Eaton et al., 2017; O'Malley & Holt, 2022; Ruvalcaba & Eaton, 2020). In these instances, offenders may use theft, scams, trickery, or technological skills to uncover sexually explicit images of their victims (O'Malley & Holt, 2022). For example, offenders may use hacking or social engineering schemes to gain access to social media accounts, webcams, emails, or cloud storage to find sexual images or videos. In some cases, these campaigns resemble ransomware attacks in which victims are locked out of their accounts and told that they will only be able to regain control if they comply with the offender's demands. Similar to minor-focused sextortion, these demands generally involve the creation of additional sexually explicit images or videos (O'Malley et al., 2022).

Limited research exists that focuses on sextortion perpetrated by strangers online in which images are accessed through technological skills such as theft and hacking. However, this form of sextortion closely resembles other large-profile instances of nonconsensual pornography, such as when several female celebrities were victimized by cloud server hacks and had their intimate images subsequently "leaked" or published across the Internet (Citron, 2014; Citron & Franks, 2014; Freeth, 2021). These campaigns often launch a large-scale spread of images that accompany pervasive harassment campaigns by cyber-mobs, which force victims to disengage online, fear for their safety, and even lose valuable friendships and employment opportunities (Citron, 2014; Citron & Franks, 2014).

Further, victims may be threatened with the release of manufactured of doctored images, such as "deepfakes," where technology can superimpose innocuous images onto pornographic ones (Chesney & Citron, 2019; Flynn et al., 2022). The simplification and wide accessibility of these AI-powered tools indicate that any user, even those with minimal technological skill, can manufacture pornographic images and use them to threaten and exploit victims (Flynn et al., 2022). Large-scale harassment campaigns that include the distribution of images or the creation of deepfakes not only harm individual victims, but harm the minoritized social groups in which they belong (Citron, 2014). Most victims of these types of cyberattacks are women and racial and sexual minorities (Citron, 2014; Citron & Franks, 2014). As a result, other members of these minority social groups are sent the message that they do not belong in online spaces and that their ability to engage freely is unequitable (Citron, 2014).

Financial sextortion offenders

Financial sextortion is one of the most rapidly increasing forms of sextortion (FBI, 2021; Ward, 2021b). While women are most often victimized by other forms of sextortion (Citron, 2014; O'Malley & Holt, 2022; Wittes et al., 2016b; Wolak & Finkelhor, 2016), financial sextortion is unique in that it primarily targets adult men between the ages of 20–39 years-old (FBI, 2021). The Internet Criminal Complaint Center (IC3), operated by the Federal Bureau of Investigation in the United States, received over 16,000 sextortion complaints in 2021, with associated losses of nearly $8 billion dollars USD (FBI, 2021). In addition, hotline reports of financial sextortion, also referred to as webcam blackmail, to the United Kingdom's Revenge Porn Hotline increased by 40% from 2020 to 2021 (Ward, 2021b). Distinct from other forms of sextortion, the main demand is financial payment of a ransom to prevent the distribution of images.

Within financially motivated sextortion, offenders will use false personas online to lure victims into engaging in sexually explicit conversations or video chats. Once a victim complies, offenders will use the image or recording of the webcam encounter to threaten the victim (O'Malley, 2023; O'Malley & Holt, 2022). Oftentimes, offenders will gather information about the victim using their social media accounts, taking screenshots of the victim's friends, followers, family members, and place of work in order to increase the severity of their threats. It is generally suspected that most perpetrators of financially motivated sextortion are part of international cybercrime organizations (O'Malley, 2023; O'Malley & Holt, 2022; Ward, 2021b). Thus, financially motivated forms of sextortion overlap with the context of other cyber scams.

Sextortion victimization

Victimization studies of IBSA and sextortion hint at an interesting intersection between gender, age, and sexuality. For example, some studies on sextortion argue that women are more often victimized by IBSA and sextortion than men (Eaton et al., 2017; Henry & Powell, 2015; O'Malley & Holt, 2022; Wolak & Finkelhor, 2016). However, other studies find either similar reports of victimization among men and women (Gámez-Guadix et al., 2022; Lenhart et al., 2016) or slightly higher numbers of men reporting IBSA and sextortion (Powell & Henry, 2019). One reason why the rates of male victimization may be higher in more recent surveys could be the rapid increase in financial sextortion, which specifically targets men and minor boys. In addition, other surveys have found that LGB adults and youth are more likely than heterosexual adults and youth to be victimized by IBSA and sextortion (Citron & Franks, 2014; Henry, Flynn, & Powell, 2019; Lenhart et al., 2016; Patchin & Hinduja, 2018).

Due to the high incidence of female victimization and the significant overlap between IBSA and intimate partner violence, most research on TFSV and IBSA takes a gender and feminist perspective. These perspectives do not discount the high number of male victims of IBSA and sextortion; however, they do argue that the experience of TFSV and IBSA may be different for men and women, and this difference 1) reflects the social context of gender inequality, generally, and 2) mirrors the ways in which women navigate several sources of gender- and sexual-based coercion on- and offline (Citron, 2014; Henry & Powell, 2016b, 2018; Powell & Henry, 2017).

Sextortion is unique in that it impacts victims differently based on age and gender. Many of these gender differences emerge with respect to offender demands and outcomes. For instance, women are more likely than men to have their images nonconsensually shared or distributed (Patel & Roesch, 2022; Powell & Henry, 2016). In addition, when women and girls are targeted, demands are often sexual or include various forms of behavioral coercion, such as demanding the victim remain in an unwanted relationship or maintain communication with the offender. However, when heterosexual men are targeted, the demands are usually financial (O'Malley, 2023; O'Malley & Holt, 2022). Thus, while sextortion seems to impact men and women at similar rates (Powell & Henry, 2019), the qualitative experience of IBSA and sextortion may be distinct by gender and should be further explored in qualitative and quantitative research. Furthermore, in O'Malley and colleagues' (2023) analysis of 130 adult offenders who specifically targeted minor children, approximately 73.08% specifically targeted minor girls, mirroring extant data on online sexual solicitation offenders, who are more likely to target minor girls (Whittle et al., 2013).

Psychological impacts of sextortion and IBSA

The impacts of IBSA, particularly when images and videos are non-consensually distributed, are profound and represent a constellation of psychosocial challenges for victim-survivors. One large survey of American adults found that those who had their intimate images non-consensually distributed reported significantly worse mental health outcomes compared to non-victims (Eaton et al., 2017). Champion and colleagues' (2022) mixed-methods study of 337 technology-facilitated sexual violence victims found that those who experienced IBSA reported significant mental health issues related to depression and anxiety. Mandau's (2020) research on 157 adolescent female victims of IBSA found that the majority reported several negative emotions in response to the abuse, such as fear, worry, sadness, self-harm, and suicidal thoughts. This is especially troubling since themes of fear, hopelessness, helplessness, embarrassment, and self-harm are prevalent within at least three high-profile cases of suicide among young sextortion victims (Nilsson et al., 2019). Indeed, additional research on TFSV found that victims were at increased risk of suicide (Champion et al., 2021). Interviews with adult female victims of IBSA found that those who had their images distributed experienced similar negative reactions such as suicidal ideation, depression, and anxiety (Bates, 2017). Similarly, McGlynn and colleagues' (2021) interviews with 75 adult victims of IBSA found that victim-survivors reported the experience as devastating, highly disruptive to their social lives, having a continuous impact on their lives, and causing feelings of social isolation. Additional studies on nonconsensual image distribution finds that victims report fear of going out in public, fear of applying to jobs, fear of beginning new relationships, and fear of seeking help for their victimization (Campbell et al., 2022).

Qualitative analyses of financial sextortion victim-survivors' online narratives indicate strong initial reactions of fear, self-blame, and anxiety (O'Malley, 2023). In addition, victims of financial sextortion are also likely to experience emotions such as shame and embarrassment as well as endorse suicidal thoughts (O'Malley, 2023). For some victim-survivors, feelings of anxiety are long-lasting (O'Malley, 2023). These results reflect other qualitative interviews with victim-survivors, which illuminate several emotional reactions to being threatened, such as embarrassment, anger, and humiliation (Walsh & Tener, 2022). In addition, some victim-survivors of sextortion describe the emotional instability related to their inability to control the sextortion and not knowing if or when their images will be disseminated (Walsh & Tener, 2022).

IBSA victimization also includes several social consequences. For example, sextortion survivors, usually women and girls, report losing relationships with friends, relatives, or intimate partners due to the sextortion (Walsh & Tener, 2022; Wolak & Finkelhor, 2016). Others report socially withdrawing from friends and experiencing harm to their reputations (Campbell et al., 2022; Walsh & Tener, 2022). IBSA victimization may also result in victims having to change schools or jobs (Wolak & Finkelhor, 2016) or experiencing a decrease in educational or occupational functioning (Champion et al., 2022; Wolak & Finkelhor, 2016) as well as loss of employment (Citron, 2014; 2015). In addition, victims of technology-facilitated sexual violence were significantly more likely to experience cyberbullying, which subsequently increased their suicide risk (Champion et al., 2021).

Victim-survivors of financial sextortion are also likely to limit their online engagement after their sextortion, which has long-term implications for them to feel connected in digital spaces (O'Malley, 2023). When victim-survivors are forced to hide their identity or fully disengage online due to fear and harassment, they are unable to access the economic and social benefits of a connected world (Citron, 2011). In addition, victims of sextortion often report feeling fear that their abuser will return and resume their threats (O'Malley, 2023; Walsh & Tener, 2022). As a result, IBSA victimization, including sextortion, can cause substantial disruptions in the lives of victim-survivors, and these harms are not trivial.

Minor children who are sexually extorted by stranger adults online may also report compounding psychopathology around the abuse. Oftentimes the sextortion of minors includes the creation of self-generated abusive material. In addition, adult abusers will escalate their demands to include more egregious forms of exploitation (O'Malley et al., 2023). These coerced, self-generated images may eventually siphon into the overall child sexual abuse material that circulates online (Liggett et al., 2020; Smith, 2012). Victims of child sexual abuse material report feeling fearful that they will be recognized by others, which causes them to experience social anxiety (Canadian Centre for Child Protection, 2017; Gewirtz-Meydan et al., 2018, 2019). Compounding this social anxiety is the fear associated with knowing their abuse images are publicly available online, and that they are unable to control who sees or uses these images. Thus, knowing that others may be viewing their images is a constant source of re-traumatization. For victims who have their images distributed online the offense never ends but is instead recurring every time a new perpetrator views their CSAM (Canadian Centre for Child Protection, 2017; Leonard, 2010).

Legal and investigative challenges in sextortion

New policies and legislation have been created to combat certain forms of IBSA such as revenge porn. For instance, 48 U.S. states and the District of Columbia have laws against nonconsensual pornography (Cyber Civil Rights Initiative, 2023). In addition, several countries, such as Australia, England and Wales, Scotland, Northern Ireland, France, Malta, Germany, Italy, Canada, Japan, Philippines, Singapore, and Israel have enacted laws criminalizing IBSA (The Center for Internet & Society, 2018; South China Morning Post, 2019; Tidman, 2019). However, most legislation focuses on image distribution, leaving cyber sextortion victims with limited avenues to seek justice (Citron & Franks, 2014; McGlynn et al., 2017; Najdowski, 2017; Walker & Sleath, 2017; Wittes, et al., 2016a). To account for this, at least eight U.S. states have enacted sextortion-specific legislation (Cyber Civil Rights Initiative, 2023), along with England and Wales and Western Australia (The Center for Internet & Society, 2018). In the creation of new IBSA laws, experts caution lawmakers against focusing too narrowly on language specific to "revenge pornography", such as including language around offender intent to humiliate, cause emotional distress, or harm victims, which may not account for the nuanced ways in which IBSA is perpetrated and thus make prosecution more difficult (Citron, 2014; Citron & Franks, 2014; Najdowski, 2017; McGlynn & Rackley, 2018).

Investigation and prosecutorial gaps in sextortion

Some scholars have argued that a sentencing gap exists between sextortion cases against minors versus adults (Wittes et al., 2016b, 2016a). For instance, most minor-focused sextortion offenders are charged with crimes related to child pornography as well as extortion (Marcum et al., 2021; Wittes et al., 2016b). In the U.S., child pornography carries harsh punishments, usually between 15 to 30 years imprisonment. As such, offenders who target children are likely to receive much harsher sentences than those who target adults. In those latter cases, prosecutors often rely on creative charging schemes that draw on several different interpersonal and cybercrimes, such as computer intrusion, cyberstalking, and harassment (Marcum et al., 2021; Wittes et al., 2016b). In the absence of sextortion laws, these creative charging schemes mean that perpetrators who sextort adults are given much lighter sentences or plead to adjacent crimes such as computer intrusion (Wittes et al., 2016b, 2016a).

For example, Cameron Scot Bivins-Breeden was arrested for sextorting a minor girl and pled guilty to production of child pornography and enticement of a minor. As a result, he was sentenced to 288 months in prison (United States v. Cameron Scot Bivins-Breeden, 2014). On the other hand, Adam Paul Savader hacked the accounts of several women, stole their sexual images, and threatened them with distribution if they did not produce more sexually explicit images. Savader plead guilty to cyberstalking and internet extortion, earning him a sentence of 30 months (United States v. Adam Paul Savader, 2014). Thus, when minor children are sextorted by adults, child pornography and sexual exploitation charges are a straightforward and effective legal avenue to ensure arrest and punishment. However, adult victims of sextortion must rely on adjacent crimes, such as cyberstalking and harassment, which may not apply for all sextortion instances, leaving many victims with limited options when it comes to bringing their abuser to justice (Citron, 2014; Citron & Franks, 2014). One solution, promoted by Wittes and colleagues (2016a, 2016b), is to advocate for federal sextortion legislation that protects adult victims of sextortion and accounts for the various ways in which sextortion is utilized by different kinds of offenders.

An additional legal challenge comes from dealing with minor offenders of IBSA. According to victimization surveys, minor youth victims of IBSA and sextortion are most often targeted by other minors (Finkelhor et al., 2022; Wolak & Finkelhor, 2016; Wolak et al., 2018). Although these offenses include the production and distribution of sexual images of children, most scholars and legal analysts argue that charging minors with child pornography offenses is overly harsh, extreme, and inappropriate (Coburn et al., 2015; Shariff & DeMartini, 2015). Indeed, research finds that law enforcement officers are also reluctant to arrest minor children who misuse images of other minor children unless certain aggravating factors are present, such as reckless distribution and intents to harm (Wolak et al., 2012). Dodge and Spencer's (2018) interviews of Canadian police officers also found that when IBSA incidents are reported, officers use their discretion to avoid charging minor children with child pornography offenses, and instead engage in alternative, extra-judicial strategies to address IBSA, such as informal conversations, scare tactics, and education.

Challenges for law enforcement

Technology has globalized cyber sextortion, facilitating greater access to victims and increased anonymity for offenders. This has created substantial investigative challenges for law enforcement, such as the need for multi-agency cooperation, specialized cybercrime units, and advanced technological resources (Brenner, 2012; Department of Justice, 2016). For instance, Henry and colleagues' (2018) interviews with 52 Australian stakeholders found that most report jurisdictional challenges, issues in procuring evidence, and lack of police resources as barriers in investigating and prosecuting IBSA. While these issues are common for all forms of cybercrime (Brenner, 2012), sextortion in particular may struggle from an investigative gap. For instance, one media outlet reported that while financial sextortion is quickly increasing in the United Kingdom, only about 1% resulted in a charge or summons (Jack, 2022). It is likely that this low arrest rate is due to the fact that most perpetrators of financial sextortion operate overseas, where identification and apprehension of criminals becomes more challenging. In addition, law enforcement is generally more motivated and better supported in their global efforts to investigate and identify adult perpetrators who exploit minor children online, but not those offenses that specifically target adult men and women (Henry et al., 2018), despite the fact that young adult men and women are primary targets for IBSA and sextortion (FBI, 2021; Lenhart et al., 2016; Powell & Henry, 2019).

Despite investigative and prosecutorial challenges associated with sextortion, international cooperation has been successful in taking down large international cybercrime organizations (Interpol, 2014), and there seems to be strong investment in cross-jurisdictional investigations for sextortion perpetrated against minors (Powell & Henry, 2018). One way to facilitate better relationships between victims and law enforcement is to invest in more training for officers about IBSA and sextortion. For instance, law enforcement officers may not receive training in IBSA, such as revenge pornography, and may not feel confident in responding to these types of crimes (Bond & Tyrrell, 2020). Specifically, Bond and Tyrrell's (2020) survey of British police officers and staff found that nearly half of the officers did not feel confident collecting digital evidence associated with IBSA and that most never received specialized training in IBSA. Thus, one place to strengthen law enforcement responses is to increase training in both online interpersonal crimes and digital evidence collection.

Moving towards prevention

Sextortion is a form of IBSA that occurs in multiple and overlapping contexts. Although all sextortion crimes are connected by the act of threatening to publicly distribute sexual images, videos, or information in order to coerce and control others, different profiles of offenders use sextortion to accomplish their own distinct goals, which in turn impacts their victim selection. As such, it is difficult to define sextortion using generalized language as if it were one specific type of crime without also mentioning the nuanced ways in which it is perpetrated.

This concept is exemplified in the diverse scholarship surrounding IBSA and sextortion. On one hand, several notable research and policy papers focus on the use of sextortion by stranger adults online to target minor children (e.g. Acar, 2016; Kopecký, 2017; O'Malley et al., 2023; Wittes et al., 2016a). However, this context is only one of many ways in which victim-survivors experience sextortion. Victimization studies of both minor children and adults showcase that most are targeted by known acquaintances or former romantic partners, highlighting the strong overlap between sextortion and intimate partner violence (e.g. Eaton et al., 2022; Finkelhor et al., 2022; Wolak & Finkelhor, 2016). Alternatively, neither form of sextortion specifically captures cases that are financially motivated, which predominately impact men and are usually perpetrated by overseas cyber criminals (FBI, 2021; O'Malley, 2023; Ward, 2021a, 2021b).

As a result, research and stakeholders must both clarify the type of sextortion under investigation as well as create educational and prevention campaigns that acknowledge the various ways in which one may be victimized by sextortion. For example, preventative education that targets children should cover awareness of all forms of IBSA, such as nonconsensual distribution of images, sextortion, nonconsensual sexting, and nonconsensual recording of others. In addition, education campaigns targeted towards children should focus on the use of sextortion and IBSA by peers and acquaintances as well as its overlap with dating violence. Other educational material used to prevent the online sexual solicitation of minors by adult strangers online are also useful and would include curriculum aimed at familiarizing children with Internet safety procedures (such as not accepting friend requests from strangers online and how to recognize suspicious profiles) and recognizing grooming behaviors (O'Malley et al., 2023).

Successful intervention and prevention of sextortion and IBSA require multi-pronged initiatives that target law enforcement, law making, education, technology, and online platforms. For instance, increased training on sextortion and IBSA is critical in ensuring that victim-survivors report their victimization and receive appropriate assistance and responses. So far, very few victims—minors or adults—report their sextortion to law enforcement (Patchin & Hinduja, 2018; Powell & Henry, 2019; Wolak et al., 2017). One specific improvement in this area would be to provide law enforcement officers with specialized training in IBSA and sextortion that 1) capitalized on their required training in intimate partner violence and 2) increases their knowledge of their local IBSA and extortion laws (Bond & Tyrrell, 2020; Henry et al., 2018; Powell & Henry, 2018). In addition, increased cybercrime training for line officers would facilitate their investigative capacity by increasing their confidence in investigating technology-facilitated crimes and gathering digital evidence (Holt et al., 2019).

Technological cooperation is also critical for both 1) identifying and removing nonconsensual pornography and child abuse images and 2) serving as a mechanism for reporting. For instance, AI-enabled interventions such as PhotoDNA can crawl the Internet to identify and remove child sexual abuse images. In addition, the National Center for Missing and Exploited Children launched "Take it Down," a free service that will allow minor children to prevent the spread of their intimate images using image hashing, which will flag and remove images from participating websites (NCMEC, 2023). A similar service exists for those over the age of 18 years old who wish to reduce the spread of their intimate images (StopNCII, 2023). Expanding the number of participating websites and social media companies using software like PhotoDNA, Take it Down, and Stop NCII would give victims of IBSA and sextortion pathways for reducing the dissemination of their intimate images. Furthermore, advocating for better reporting structures within dating applications and other social media applications would allow victim-survivors to report fraudulent, harassing accounts that are threatening them. Having a specific reporting category for IBSA would ensure that these cases are escalated within the reporting and safety structures present on social media applications (O'Malley, 2023). Finally, social media and dating applications can also participate in education and public service campaigns by warning users about risky online behavior, how to identify and report suspicious profiles, and how to report harassment.

Legal approaches to preventing and intervening in sextortion crimes are also necessary. While most U.S. states and several countries have criminalized the nonconsensual distribution of intimate images, not all states have sextortion-specific laws. This may leave some victims unable to obtain justice in instances where they are threatened with the dissemination of images, but those images are never distributed. Although several adjacent laws, such as those prohibiting extortion, harassment, cyberstalking, child pornography, invasion of privacy, and revenge pornography cover several elements of sextortion, having dedicated local and federal laws combating sextortion would provide clear guidelines for law enforcement officers. Therefore, lawmakers and policymakers should be encouraged to reevaluate and update existing laws to account for the ever-changing technological landscape of interpersonal crimes and consider adding legislation that specifically criminalizes sextortion. Indeed, eight U.S. states, such as Alabama, Georgia, and New York, have created new sexual extortion laws (Cyber Civil Rights Initiative, 2023) while other states, such as California, include the threat to disseminate explicit images within their existing extortion laws (California Penal Code Section 518–527).

Conclusion

The Internet and digital technologies have rapidly reshaped interpersonal crimes. In particular, the malicious misuse of intimate images has garnered academic, legal, and public interest. Although the concept of sexual extortion is not new, the integration of technology is critical to our understanding of how sexual extortion has changed during the information age. Specifically, images can be distributed with ease, and their spread is virtually impossible to control. As a result, the reputational harm and potential for further harassment means that victim-survivors of IBSA are constantly re-victimized every time their image is shared or viewed. In addition, Internet technologies afford substantial anonymity to offenders, meaning that identifying and arresting offenders is a herculean effort for law enforcement. It is likely that offenders capitalize on both the anonymity of the Internet and public fear of nonconsensual pornography by using sextortion to threaten, terrorize, and coerce compliance from victims. Thus, this new iteration of sexual extortion is closely tied to the realities of our digitally connected world. As such, it is critical that laws are updated to reflect the realities of this form of abuse and that law enforcement invests in appropriate training and resources to assist officers in investigating sextortion offenses. Finally, intervention and prevention must reach victims in the spaces they congregate by offering information and digital reporting structures to minimize the spread of images and flag fraudulent profiles. Combating IBSA and sextortion in the digital world requires investment and collaboration between technology, social media applications, and law enforcement agencies. Breaking the silos that separate these three entities will ensure a safer and more equitable future for online activity.

References

Acar, K. V. (2016). Sexual extortion of children in cyberspace. *International Journal of Cyber Criminology, 10*(2), 973–5089. https://doi.org/10.5281/zenodo.163398/

Bates, S. (2017). Revenge porn and mental health: A qualitative analysis of the mental health effects of revenge porn on female survivors. *Feminist Criminology, 12*(1), 22–42. https://doi.org/10.1177/1557085116654565

Bond, E., & Tyrrell, K. (2020). Understanding revenge pornography: A national survey of police officers and staff in England and Wales. *Journal of Interpersonal Violence*, 1–16. https://doi.org/10.1177/0886260518760011

Brenner, S. W. (2012). *Cybercrime and the law: Challenges, issues, and outcomes.* Northeastern University Press.

California Penal Code Section 518–527. Retrieved from https://leginfo.legislature.ca.gov/faces/codes_displayText.xhtml?lawCode=PEN&division=&title=13.&part=1.&chapter=7.&article=

Campbell, J. K., & Kravarik, J. (2022 May 23). A 17-year-old boy died by suicide hours after being scammed. The FBI says it's part of a troubling increase in 'sextortion' cases. *CNN*. Retrieved from www.cnn.com/2022/05/20/us/ryan-last-suicide-sextortion-california/index.html

Campbell, J. K., Poage, S. M. C., Godley, S., & Rothman, E. F. (2022). Social anxiety as a consequence of non-consensually disseminated sexually explicit media victimization. *Journal of Interpersonal Violence, 37*(9–10), NP7268–NP7288. https://doi.org/10.1177/0886260520967150

Canadian Centre for Child Protection. (2017). *Survivors' survey executive summary 2017.* https://www.jamesmarshlaw.com/wp-content/uploads/2018/09/C3P_SurvivorsSurveyExecutiveSummary2017_en.pdf

Champion, A. R., Oswald, F., Khera, D., & Pedersen, C. L. (2022). Examining the gendered impacts of technology-facilitated sexual violence: A mixed methods approach. *Archives of Sexual Behavior, 51*(3), 1607–1624. https://doi.org/10.1007/s10508-021-02226-y

Champion, A. R., Oswald, F., & Pedersen, C. L. (2021). Technology-facilitated sexual violence and suicide risk: A serial mediation model investigating bullying, depression, perceived burdensomeness, and thwarted belongingness. *Canadian Journal of Human Sexuality, 30*(1), 125–141. https://doi.org/10.3138/CJHS.2020-0044

Chesney, B., & Citron, D. (2019). Deep fakes: A looming challenge for privacy, democracy, and national security. *California Law Review, 107*, 1753–820.

Citron, D. K. (2011). Civil rights in out information age. In S. Levmore & M. C. Nussbaum (Eds.), *The offensive internet: Speech, privacy, and reputation* (pp. 31–49). Harvard University Press.

Citron, D. K. (2014). *Hate crimes in cyberspace.* Harvard University Press.

Citron, D. K. (2015). Protecting sexual privacy in the information age. In J. Scott & J. Horwitz (Eds.), *Privacy in the modern age: The search for solutions* (pp. 47–54). The New Press.

Citron, D. K., & Franks, M. A. (2014). Criminalizing revenge porn. *Wake Forest Law Review, 49*, 345–391.

Coburn P., Connolly D., & Roesch R. (2015). Cyberbullying: Is federal criminal legislation the solution? *Canadian Journal of Criminology and Criminal Justice, 57*(4), 566–579.

Craven, S., Brown, S., & Gilchrist, E. (2006). Sexual grooming of children: Review of literature and theoretical considerations. *Journal of Sexual Aggression, 12*(3), 287–299. https://doi.org/10.1080/13552600601069414

Cross, C., Holt, K., & O'Malley, R. L. (2022). "If u don't pay they will share the pics": Exploring sextortion in the context of romance fraud. *Victims and Offenders.* https://doi.org/10.1080/15564886.2022.2075064

Cyber Civil Rights Initiative. (2023). *48 States + DC + two territories now have laws against nonconsensual pornography.* Retrieved from https://cybercivilrights.org/nonconsensual-pornography-laws/

Dardis, C. M., & Richards, E. C. (2022). Nonconsensual distribution of sexually explicit images within a context of coercive control: Frequency, characteristics, and associations with other forms of victimization. *Violence Against Women.* https://doi.org/10.1177/10778012221077126

De La Hoz, G. T. (2021). New trends in online crime using social networking sites and Apps against children and adolescents: Police-based longitudinal research. *International Journal of Cyber Criminology*, 15(1), 31–49. https://doi.org/10.5281/zenodo.4766531

Department of Justice. (2016). *The national strategy for child exploitation prevention and interdiction*. Retrieved from www.justice.gov/psc/file/842411/download

Dodge, A., & Spencer, D. C. (2018). Online Sexual violence, child pornography or something else entirely? Police responses to non-consensual intimate image sharing among youth. *Social and Legal Studies*, 27(5), 636–657. https://doi.org/10.1177/0964663917724866

Draucker, C. B., & Martsolf, D. S. (2010). The role of electronic communication technology in adolescent dating violence. *Journal of Child and Adolescent Psychiatric Nursing*, 23(3), 133–142. https://doi.org/10.1111/j.1744-6171.2010.00235.x

Eaton, A. A., Jacobs, H., & Ruvalcaba, Y. (2017). *2017 Nationwide online study of nonconsensual porn victimization and perpetration: A summary report*. Retrieved from www.cybercivilrights.org/wp-content/uploads/2017/06/CCRI-2017-Research-Report.pdf

Eaton, A. A., Noori, S., Bonomi, A., Stephens, D. P., & Gillum, T. L. (2020). Nonconsensual porn as a form of intimate partner violence: Using the power and control wheel to understand nonconsensual porn perpetration in intimate relationships. *Trauma, Violence, & Abuse*, 1–15. https://doi.org/10.1177/1524838020906533

Eaton, A. A., Ramjee, D., & Saunders, J. F. (2022). The Relationship between sextortion during COVID-19 and pre-pandemic intimate partner violence: A large study of victimization among diverse U.S. men and women. *Victims & Offenders*, 1–18. https://doi.org/10.1080/15564886.2021.2022057

FBI. (2021). *FBI warns about an increase in sextortion complaints*. Retrieved from www.ic3.gov/Media/Y2021/PSA210902

FBI. (2022, December 20). *Sextortion crimes on the increase: Talk to your kids now*. Retrieved from www.justice.gov/usao-wdpa/pr/sextortion-crimes-increase-talk-your-kids-now

Finkelhor, D., Ormrod, R., Turner, H., & Holt, M. (2009). Pathways to poly-victimization. *Child Maltreatment*, 14, 316–329. http://dx.doi.org/10.1177/1077559509347012

Finkelhor, D., Turner, H., & Colburn, D. (2022). Prevalence of online sexual offenses against children in the US. *JAMA Network Open*, 5(10), E2234471. https://doi.org/10.1001/jamanetworkopen.2022.34471

Flynn, A., Powell, A., Scott, A. J., & Cama, E. (2022). Deepfakes and digitally altered imagery abuse: A cross-country exploration of an emerging form of image-based sexual abuse. *The British Journal of Criminology*, 62(6), 1341–1358. https://doi.org/10.1093/bjc/azab111

Freeth, B. (2021, November 24). Jennifer Lawrence says 'trauma' of having her nude photos leaked will last 'forever'. *Cosmopolitan*. Retrieved from www.cosmopolitan.com/uk/body/a38328843/jennifer-lawrence-trauma-nude-photo-leak/

Gámez-Guadix, M., Mateos-Pérez, E., Wachs, S., Wright, M., Martínez, J., & Íncera, D. (2022). Assessing image-based sexual abuse: Measurement, prevalence, and temporal stability of sextortion and nonconsensual sexting ("revenge porn") among adolescents. *Journal of Adolescence*. https://doi.org/10.1002/JAD.12064

Gewirtz-Meydan, A., Lahav, Y., Walsh, W., & Finkelhor, D. (2019). Psychopathology among adult survivors of child pornography. *Child Abuse and Neglect*, 98, 104189. https://doi.org/10.1016/j.chiabu.2019.104189

Gewirtz-Meydan, A., Walsh, W., Wolak, J., & Finkelhor, D. (2018). The complex experience of child pornography survivors. *Child Abuse & Neglect*, 80, 238–248. https://doi.org/10.1016/j.chiabu.2018.03.031

Henry, N., Flynn, A., & Powell, A. (2018). Policing image-based sexual abuse: Stakeholder perspectives. *Police Practice and Research*, 19(6), 565–581. https://doi.org/10.1080/15614263.2018.1507892

Henry, N., Flynn, A., & Powell, A. (2019). Image-based sexual abuse: Victims and perpetrators. *Australian Institute of Criminology Trends & Issues in Crime and Criminal Justice*, 572.

Henry, N., Flynn, A., & Powell, A. (2020). Technology-facilitated domestic and sexual violence: A review. *Violence Against Women*, 26(15–16), 1828–1854. https://doi.org/10.1177/1077801219875821

Henry, N., McGlynn, C., Flynn, A., Johnson, K., Powell, A., & Scott, A. J. (2021). *Image-based sexual abuse: A study on the causes and consequences of nonconsensual nude or sexual imagery.* Routledge.

Henry, N., & Powell, A. (2015). Embodied harms: Gender, shame, and technology-facilitated sexual violence. *Violence Against Women, 21*(6), 758–779. https://doi.org/10.1177/1077801215576581

Henry, N., & Powell, A. (2016a). Sexual violence in the digital age: The scope and limits of criminal law. *Social & Legal Studies, 25*(4), 397–418. https://doi.org/10.1177/0964663915624273

Henry, N., & Powell, A. (2016b). Technology-facilitated sexual violence. *Trauma, Violence, & Abuse,* 1–14. https://doi.org/10.1177/1524838016650189

Holt, T. J., Lee, J. R., Liggett, R., Holt, K. M., & Bossler, A. (2019). Examining perceptions of online harassment among constables in England and Wales. *International Journal of Cybersecurity Intelligence &, 2*(1), 24–39. https://doi.org/10.52306/02010319LFQZ1592

Interpol. (2014, May 2). Coordinated operation strikes back at 'sextortion' networks. *Interpol Press Release.* Retrieved from https://www.interpol.int/en/News-and-Events/News/2014/INTERPOL-coordinated-operation-strikes-back-at-sextortion-networks

Jack, P. (2022, August 19). Record number of blackmail crimes reported to police. *Evening Standard.* Retrieved from https://uk.news.yahoo.com/record-number-blackmail-crimes-reported-150316575.html?guccounter=1&guce_referrer=aHR0cHM6Ly93d3cuZ29vZ2xlLmNvbS88&guce_referrer_sig=AQAAAHGltwY7tNhHvD52gTVN4IHWRs2ALPE5ovRnvbCZYEcpthMLYVcdtNxJ8In2xSoigmg98DO20g8tCmehvvsno5ire7PvrcD6h3dTgBh8qZnGKIhcXPmGyaYemCs_NdUHZLwEBQQNV_qv7I70mDpqColryqA5c0n5Bm99zOEB7AHA

Joleby, M., Lunde, C., Landström, S., & Jonsson, L. S. (2021). Offender strategies for engaging children in online sexual activity. *Child Abuse and Neglect, 120*, 145–2134. https://doi.org/10.1016/J.CHIABU.2021.105214

Kloess, J. A., Hamilton-Giachritsis, C. E., & Beech, A. R. (2019). Offense processes of online sexual grooming and abuse of children via internet communication platforms. *Sexual Abuse: Journal of Research and Treatment, 31*(1), 73–96. https://doi.org/10.1177/1079063217720927

Kopecký, K. (2017). Online blackmail of Czech children focused on so-called "sextortion" (analysis of culprit and victim behaviors). *Telematics and Informatics, 34*, 11–19. https://doi.org/10.1016/j.tele.2016.04.004

Kopecký, K., Hejsek, L., Kusa, J., Polak, M., & Maresova, H. (2015). Specifics of children communication and online aggressors within the online assaults on children (analysis of selected utterances). *2nd International Multidisciplinary Scientific Conference on Social Sciences and Arts, 1*, 195–202. https://doi.org/10.5593/SGEMSOCIAL2015/B11/S1.026

Lenhart, A., Ybarra, M., & Prince-Feeny, M. (2016). *Nonconsensual image sharing: One in 25 Americans has been a victim of revenge porn.* Retrieved from www.independent.co.uk/news/people/icloud-celebrity-nude-leak-jennifer-lawrence-kate-upton-man-pleads-guilty-a7334031.html

Leonard, M. M. (2010). "I did what I was directed to do but he didn't touch me": The impact of being a victim of internet offending. *Journal of Sexual Aggression, 16*(2), 249–256. https://doi.org/10.1080/13552601003690526

Liggett, R. (2019). Exploring online sextortion offenses: Ruses, demands, and motivations. *Sexual Assault Report, 22*(4), 58–62.

Liggett, R., Lee, J. R., Roddy, A., & Wallin, M. (2020). The dark web as a platform for crime: An exploration of illicit drug, firearm, CSAM, and cybercrime markets. In T. J. Holt & A. M. Bossler (Eds.), *The Palgrave handbook of international cybercrime and cyberdeviance.* Palgrave.

Madigan, S., Villani, V., Azzopardi, C., Laut, D., Smith, T., Temple, J. R., Browne, D., & Dimitropoulos, G. (2018). The prevalence of unwanted online sexual exposure and solicitation among youth: A meta-analysis. *Journal of Adolescent Health, 63*(2), 133–141. https://doi.org/10.1016/j.jadohealth.2018.03.012

Mandau, M. B. H. (2020). "Snaps", "screenshots", and self-blame: A qualitative study of image-based sexual abuse victimization among adolescent Danish girls. *Journal of Children and Media, 15*, 431–447. https://doi.org/10.1080/17482798.2020.1848892

Marcum, C. D., Higgins, G. E., Tsai, T. M., & Sedlacek, J. (2021). Exploration of prosecutor experiences with non-consensual pornography. *Deviant Behavior, 42*(5), 646–658. https://doi.org/10.1080/01639625.2020.1821410

McAlinden, A. M. (2006). 'Setting "em up": Personal, familial and institutional grooming in the sexual abuse of children. *Social and Legal Studies*, 15(3), 339–362. https://doi.org/10.1177/0964663906066613

McGlynn, C., Johnson, K., Rackley, E., Henry, N., Gavey, N., Flynn, A., & Powell, A. (2021). 'It's torture for the soul': The harms of image-based sexual abuse. *Social and Legal Studies*, 30(4), 541–562. https://doi.org/10.1177/0964663920947791

McGlynn, C., & Rackley, E. (2018). Image-based sexual abuse. *Oxford Journal of Legal Studies*, 37(3), 534–556.

McGlynn, C., Rackley, E., & Houghton, R. (2017). Beyond "revenge porn": The continuum of image-based sexual abuse. *Feminist Legal Studies*, 25, 25–46. https://doi.org/10.1007/s10691-017-9343-2

Mitchell, K. J., Jones, L. M., Finkelhor, D., & Wolak, J. (2013). Understanding the decline in unwanted online sexual solicitations for U.S. Youth 2000–2010: Findings from three youth internet safety surveys. *Child Abuse and Neglect*, 37(12), 1225–1236. https://doi.org/10.1016/j.chiabu.2013.07.002

Mori, C., Cooke, J. E., Temple, J. R., Ly, A., Lu, Y., Anderson, N., Rash, C., & Madigan, S. (2020). The prevalence of sexting behaviors among emerging adults: A meta-analysis. *Archives of Sexual Behavior*, 49(4), 1103–1119. https://doi.org/10.1007/S10508-020-01656-4

Najdowski, C. J. (2017). Legal responses to nonconsensual pornography: Current policy in the United States and future directions for research. *Psychology, Public Policy, and Law*, 23, 154–165. https://doi.org/10.1037/law0000123

National Center for Missing and Exploited Children. (2023). *Take it down*. Retrieved from https://takeitdown.ncmec.org/

National Crime Agency. (2018, May 24). Record numbers of UK men fall victim to sextortion gangs. *National Crime Agency Press Release*. Retrieved from https://www.nationalcrimeagency.gov.uk/news/1360-record-numbers-of-uk-men-fall-victim-to-sextortion-gangs

Nilsson, M. G., Tzani-Pepelasis, C., Ioannou, M., & Lester, D. (2019). Understanding the link between sextortion and suicide. *International Journal of Cyber Criminology*, 13(1), 55–69. https://doi.org/10.5281/zenodo.3402357

Olmeda, R. (2018, January 17). Cop guilty of threatening to release nude photos of ex-girlfriend. *South Florida Sun Sentinel*. Retrieved from www.sun-sentinel.com/2018/01/17/cop-guilty-of-threatening-to-release-nude-photos-of-ex-girlfriend/

O'Connell, R. (2003). *A typology of cybersexploitation and online grooming practices*. Cyberspace Research Unit, University of Central Lancashire. http://www.jisc.ac.uk/uploaded_documents/lis_PaperJPrice.pdf

O'Malley, R. L. (2023). Short-term and long-term impacts of financial sextortion on victim mental well-being. *Journal of Interpersonal Violence*, Online First. https://doi.org/10.1177/08862605231156416

O'Malley, R. L., & Holt, K. M. (2022). Cyber sextortion: An exploratory analysis of different perpetrators engaging in a similar crime. *Journal of Interpersonal Violence*, 37, 258–283. https://doi.org/10.1177/0886260520909186

O'Malley, R. L, Holt, K., Holt, T. J., & Rodriguez, J. (2023). Minor sextortion by adult strangers online: A crime script analysis of media and court documents. *Criminology & Public Policy*, 22, 779–802.

Patchin, J. W., & Hinduja, S. (2018). Sextortion among adolescents: Results from a national survey of U.S. Youth. *Sexual Abuse*, 1–25. https://doi.org/10.1177/1079063218800469

Patel, U., & Roesch, R. (2022). The prevalence of technology-facilitated sexual violence: A meta-analysis and systematic review. In *Trauma, Violence, and Abuse* (Vol. 23, Issue 2, pp. 428–443). SAGE Publications Ltd. Retrieved from https://doi.org/10.1177/1524838020958057

Powell, A., & Henry, N. (2016). Technology-facilitated sexual violence victimization. *Journal of Interpersonal Violence*, 1–29. https://doi.org/10.1177/0886260516672055

Powell, A., & Henry, N. (2017). *Sexual violence in the digital age*. Palgrave.

Powell, A., & Henry, N. (2018). Policing technology-facilitated sexual violence against adult victims: Police and service sector perspectives. *Policing and Society*, 28(3), 291–307. https://doi.org/10.1080/10439463.2016.1154964

Powell, A., & Henry, N. (2019). Technology-facilitated sexual violence victimization: Results from an online survey of Australian adults. *Journal of Interpersonal Violence*, 34(17), 3637–3665. https://doi.org/10.1177/0886260516672055

Powell, A., Henry, N., Flynn, A., & Scott, A. J. (2018). Image-based sexual abuse: The extent, nature, and predictors of perpetration in a community sample of Australian adults. *Computers in Human Behavior*. https://doi.org/10.1016/j.chb.2018.11.009

Ruvalcaba, Y., & Eaton, A. A. (2020). Nonconsensual pornography among U.S. Adults: A sexual scripts framework on victimization, perpetration, and health correlates for women and men. *Psychology of Violence*, 10(1), 68–78. https://doi.org/10.1037/vio0000233

Seto, M. C., Wood, J. M., Babchishin, K. M., & Flynn, S. (2012). Online solicitation offenders are different from child pornography offenders and lower risk contact sexual offenders. *Law and Human Behavior*, 36, 320–330. https://doi.org/10.1037/h0093925

Shariff, S., & DeMartini, A. (2015). Defining the legal lines: Egirls and intimate images. In J. Bailey & V. Steeves (Eds.), *eGirls, eCitizens* (pp. 282–307). University of Ottawa Press.

Smith, S. (2012). *Study of self-generated sexually explicit images and videos featuring young people online*. Retrieved from www.iwf.org.uk/sites/default/files/inline-files/IWF_study_self_generated_content_online_011112.pdf

Smith, S. (2014). *Briefing paper-preliminary analysis of new commercial CSAM website accepting payment by bitcoin*. Retrieved from www.iwf.org.uk/sites/default/files/inline-files/Preliminary_analysis_into_commercial_CSAM_distributor_accepting_bitcoin_sanitised_not_restricted_01014.pdf

Snaychuk, L. A., & O'Neill, M. L. (2020). Technology-facilitated sexual violence: Prevalence, risk, and resiliency in undergraduate students. *Journal of Aggression, Maltreatment and Trauma*, 29(8), 984–999. https://doi.org/10.1080/10926771.2019.1710636

South China Morning Post. (2019, May 7). *Singapore outlaws revenge porn and cyber-flashing in clampdown on digital sexual offences*. Retrieved from www.scmp.com/news/asia/southeast-asia/article/3009232/singapore-outlaws-revenge-porn-and-cyber-flashing

StopNCII. (2023). *What do you do if someone is threatening to share your intimate images?* Retrieved from https://stopncii.org/

The Centre for Internet & Society. (2018). *Revenge porn laws across the world*. Retrieved from https://cis-india.org/internet-governance/blog/revenge-porn-laws-across-the-world

Tidman, Z. (2019, April 4). Italy criminalises revenge porn with prison sentences of up to six years. *The Independent*. Retrieved from www.independent.co.uk/news/world/europe/revenge-porn-italy-five-star-league-red-code-bill-a8853591.html

Uguen-Csenge, E. (2022 August 6). Dutch man Aydian Coban convicted of sexually extorting B.C. Teen Amanda Todd. *CBC*. Retrieved from www.cbc.ca/news/canada/british-columbia/aydin-coban-amanda-todd-trial-verdict-1.6541210

United States of America v. Adam Paul Savader case no: 13CR20522–1 (E.D. Michigan, 2014).

United States of America v. Cameron Scot Bivins-Breeden case no: 3:19-cr-00025 (E.D. Virginia, 2014).

Walker, K., & Sleath, E. (2017). A systematic review of the current knowledge regarding revenge pornography and non-consensual sharing of sexually explicit media. *Aggression and Violent Behavior*, 36, 9–24. https://doi.org/10.1016/j.avb.2017.06.010

Walker, K., Sleath, E., Hatcher, R. M., Hine, B., & Crookes, R. L. (2021). Nonconsensual Sharing of Private Sexually Explicit Media Among University Students. *Journal of Interpersonal Violence*, 36(17–18), NP9078–NP9108. https://doi.org/10.1177/0886260519853414

Walsh, W. A., & Tener, D. (2022). "If you don't send me five other pictures I am going to post the photo online": A qualitative analysis of experiences of survivors of sextortion. *Journal of Child Sexual Abuse*, 1–19. https://doi.org/10.1080/10538712.2022.2067093

Ward, Z. (2021a). Intimate image abuse, an evolving landscape. *Revenge Porn Helpline*. Retrieved from https://revengepornhelpline.org.uk/assets/documents/intimate-image-abuse-an-evolving-landscape.pdf?_=1639471939

Ward, Z. (2021b). RPH report 2021: The rise of sextortion. *Revenge Porn Helpline*. Retrieved from https://revengepornhelpline.org.uk/assets/documents/art2.pdf?_=1653315991

Whittle, H., Hamilton-Giachritsis, C., Beech, A., & Collings, G. (2013). A review of young people's vulnerabilities to online grooming. *Aggression and Violent Behavior*, 18(1), 135–146. https://doi.org/10.1016/j.avb.2012.11.008

Winters, G. M., Jeglic, E. L., & Kaylor, L. E. (2020). Validation of the sexual grooming model of child sexual abusers. *Journal of Child Sexual Abuse*, 29(7), 855–875. https://doi.org/10.1080/10538712.2020.1801935

Wittes, B. B., Poplin, C., Jurecic, Q., & Spera, C. (2016a). *Closing the sextortion sentencing gap: A legislative proposal*. Retrieved from www.brookings.edu/wp-content/uploads/2016/05/sextortion2.pdf

Wittes, B. B., Poplin, C., Jurecic, Q., & Spera, C. (2016b). *Sextortion: Cybersecurity, teenagers, and remote sexual assault*. Retrieved from https://www.brookings.edu/articles/sextortion-cybersecurity-teenagers-and-remote-sexual-assault/

Wolak, J., & Finkelhor, D. (2016). *Sextortion: Findings from a survey of 1,631 victims*. Retrieved from www.missingkids.com/content/dam/ncmec/en_us/documents/2016crimesagainstchildrenresearchcentersextortionresearch.PDF

Wolak, J., Finkelhor, D., & Mitchell, K. J. (2012). How often are teens arrested for sexting? data from a national sample of police cases. *Pediatrics, 129*, 4–12. https://doi.org/10.1542/peds.2011-2242

Wolak, J., Finkelhor, D., Walsh, W., & Treitman, L. (2018). Sextortion of minors: Characteristics and dynamics. *Journal of Adolescent Health, 62*, 72–79. https://doi.org/10.1016/j.jadohealth.2017.08.014

Woodlock, D. (2017). The abuse of technology in domestic violence and stalking. *Violence Against Women, 23*(5), 584–602. https://doi.org/10.1177/1077801216646277

Yousif, N. (2022, October 15). Amanda Todd: Dutchman sentenced for fatal cyber-stalking. *BBC*. Retrieved from www.bbc.com/news/world-us-canada-63218797

15

ONLINE SEX WORK

Deviance and innovation

Aaron Hammes and Danielle Blunt

Introduction: online sex work deviance, sanction, and innovation

Deviant behavior is inherently innovative in the ways it reacts to and resists social norms, and, under carceral capitalism, policing follows deviant innovation and resource accumulation. Out of necessity and ingenuity, sex workers have been and continue to be early adopters and innovators of technology, breaching new physical and digital spaces and rendering them more desirable and accessible. When policed out of physical spaces due to presumptions of deviant behavior, sex workers innovate new technologies, building much of the backbone of the internet. Further criminalization and policing have created categories of social deviance that compel the movement and innovation of sex workers in order to survive. There exists a significant literature gap concerning online sex work in social deviance thinking, as criminalized/highly gendered labor of this variety is undertheorized in general. Despite many categories of online sex work in the US (such as porn and camming) being ostensibly legal, this chapter theorizes ways in which private actors and corporations are deputized into a carceral system within the expanding web of gendered criminalization, which seeks to outlaw and police deviance in the various technologies that this same deviance helped build. Sex workers occupy various socially deviant subject positions, both offline and on, but it is the latter venue which is under scrutiny in this political moment.

The most recent and widespread version of this deputization in the United States took place under the passage of the Stop Enabling Sex Traffickers Act (SESTA) and the Fight Online Sex Trafficking Act (FOSTA), which were proposed as measures to hold websites liable for the content published on them, purportedly as a means to shut down "sex trafficking" advertising. What is notable about these bills from a social deviance perspective is that they took advantage of moral/sex panic without any one specific moral crusader or entrepreneur. The moral entrepreneurs who motivated passage of the bills included entities as diverse as crusading journalists, celebrities with no particular personal interest other than further building their brands, and organizations which claim to be centered on anti-trafficking but in effect are sex work abolitionists. Furthermore, this legislation passed with almost unanimous bipartisan support despite national campaigns from both sex worker rights organizations and internet freedom coalitions. The signing into law of

DOI: 10.4324/9781003277675-18

FOSTA-SESTA is illustrative of a specific brand of symbolic politics which conflates sex trafficking with sex work, ignoring that all labor under capitalism is vulnerable to exploitation and exists on a spectrum of choice, circumstance, and coercion. Those in the sex trades who experience violence do so predominantly as the direct result of criminalization, stigma, and policing and surveillance. As is the case with much symbolic politics, the impacts of FOSTA-SESTA and adjacent statutory and criminal legislation has been to further gentrify the internet, chill speech, and make working conditions both on- and offline less safe for both sex working individuals and those most vulnerable to labor exploitation and trafficking in and adjacent to the sex trades.

In this chapter, when we describe policing, we try to be explicit regarding distinctions between policing at the state level, the platform level (the deputization of private actors and corporations), and the deputization of individuals (who may be weaponizing content moderation systems to maliciously deplatform sex workers). The vagueness of FOSTA-SESTA and increased platform liability has led to mass platform response, which mirrors what happens in physical spaces and is an extension of state control, deputizing private actors to do the work of the state in places where the law can't touch. Denying access to the technologies that keep sex workers safe pushes them further toward the margins and further codifies new categories of deviance as criminal.

For various (deviant) communities and subjects, the internet has been both refuge (advertising and vetting for sex workers, and community knowledge sharing and solidarity for queer and trans folks) and nightmare (increased policing and surveillance, doxing and outing of deviant actors, deplatforming and de-monetization), but the criminalization of online deviance is selective and highly reflective of broader phobias and state fetishes around "defending" marriage, hetero/homonormativity, and women's bodily and economic autonomy. As this population and venue is so undertheorized, this study will take advantage of "classic" sociological theory, including Stanley's Cohen's "moral panics" and Howard Becker's "outsiders" concepts, as well as the work of more contemporary technology theorists. As sex workers have adapted to the broadening web of online criminalization, we in turn look at sex worker artist collectives' responses and tools of resistance to imagine liberatory futures. This chapter considers social deviance theories and thinking around sex worker access and movement to, as well as erasure from, online spaces and the ways in which marginalized, deviant, and criminalized communities are resisting. As discourse around sex work decriminalization is becoming more mainstream, online platforms continue to punish sex workers in whorephobic attempts to mitigate their risk. This chapter proposes that new theories of deviance are needed to consider more capaciously the simultaneous and often competing needs for visibility and anonymity within online sex work.

Brief history of sex work in the United States and movement online

Sex workers have historically made new physical and digital spaces habitable and desirable through their presence and offerings. In the face of sanction, sex work has responded by facilitating both movement (predominantly of women, and particularly migrant women and women of color) and the adoption and development of communication technologies, including: taking advantage of trains as a technology and industry, which helped facilitate the institution of brothels in the American West during the gold rush; urbanization and the creation of city brothels, which were some of the first spaces to install phone lines; and pornographers innovating photography, home video, cable TV, and the internet. As journalist Patchen Barss (2010) writes in *The Erotic Engine*, "Pornographers were the technological pioneers who figured out how to make money from a new medium before the mainstream saw any profit potential" (p. 53).

Nonetheless, focusing on concepts such as online deviance or digital gentrification risks erasing pre-existing, institutionalized forms of discrimination, such as racial and gendered capitalism, rather than framing online and digital spaces as extensions of extant spaces to act out these processes. None of the deviant behaviors and identities around sex work are novel; the adoption and spread of newer technologies has simply translated deviance and the policing thereof into new online spaces. As long as capitalism has existed, deviant communities have been targeted and marginalized through violent processes of erasure, denial of access to resources, and incarceration. The maintenance of capitalism is dependent on the unpaid and underpaid labor of marginalized communities. In the 16th and 17th centuries, sex workers and other deviant women were persecuted in the witch hunts as part of "capitalist disciplining of women". In the US, women were not able to open bank accounts until the 1970s and were unable to open a line of credit without their husband's approval until the 1980s. This restriction of the flow of capital to deviant women (and those gendered as women) and other marginalized communities continues to this day with the policing of sex work on- and offline. Deviance has always been policed because deviant innovation strays away from capitalist forms of wealth and power accumulation. However, with the advent of new technologies, the policing of public space adopts new technologies, too, and has moved online.

In *Times Square Red, Times Square Blue*, a landmark ethnography of changing Midtown Manhattan, Samuel Delaney discusses how the process of gentrification is reliant on the violent dismantling of visible sex work, such as peepshows and street-based sex workers, hiding them from public view. In the study, Delaney charts an example of technological innovation: the peep show becomes the pornographic theater. This allowed for the relatively safer dissemination of erotic materials and public, nonreproductive/recreational sex until the state "caught up" and disavowed it. In 1985, under the guise of "public safety," sex work was heavily policed and pushed out of Times Square in New York City, forcing sex workers into more dangerous working conditions. Delaney focuses on the socio-cultural dynamics of this shift, but his study also sheds light on how policing and "quality of life" discourse recode deviance around the use of both "public" space (such as parks and train stations) and "private" space (pornographic movie theaters).

As they continued to be policed out of physical spaces, many sex workers who had access to internet resources began to move online and innovate online spaces. Sex workers were some of the first users of proto-internet bulletin board systems (BBSs), paving the way for a more accessible and widely available web. Livia Foldes writes in "Sex Workers Built the Internet":

From the web's earliest days, sex workers' labor enticed potential users to overcome the hurdles of expensive hardware and clunky interfaces. The promise of real-time erotic interaction drove consumer demand for faster modems, clearer webcams, and greater bandwidth. And, for better or worse, the adult industry's technical and social innovations—including cookies, web analytics, affiliate marketing, and seamless online payments—demonstrated the commercial potential of a risky new technology.

As the internet became more accessible and widely available, sex workers used the web to create bad-date lists, online advertising and classified ads, photo and video streaming, and secure online paygates. These innovations led to a decrease in the need for third-party management, such as pimps and madams, meaning more of the money sex workers earned stayed in their hands. This is all to say: sex workers are at once the innovators who use the medium to make their work safer and more advanced in service delivery, and simultaneously the "bad actors" of internet commerce and spaces, emblematic of lawless permissiveness and moral panic.

Since sex workers have worked and advertised online, police have used sex worker advertisements to set up stings. Private companies such as Thorn have used sex worker advertisements to develop facial recognition technologies and databases of sex workers. And moral panics have led to the shuttering of countless sex worker advertisement websites. In 2010, Craigslist took down their "Erotic Services" section after warnings from the Justice Department. In 2014, the government shut down the sex worker advertising platform MyRedbook, followed by a string of other advertising platforms, including RentBoy in 2017 and Backpage in 2018, the week before FOSTA-SESTA was signed into law.

Despite legislators arguing that FOSTA-SESTA was necessary in order to take down websites like Backpage, the site was seized by the FBI before the bill was signed into law. Platform response to FOSTA-SESTA was immediate and devastating. Having already preemptively shuttered one avenue for sex work advertising, Craigslist took down their Personal Section and put up the following notice: "Any tool or service can be misused. We can't take such risk without jeopardizing all our other services, so we have regretfully taken Craigslist personals offline. Hopefully we can bring them back some day." Countless other websites followed, with the free and the niche sites closing first, meaning that those already unable to afford an ad on pricier "mainstream" sites were the most impacted. Hacking// Hustling's report "Erased: The Impact of FOSTA-SESTA and the Removal of Backpage" found that after April of 2018, many workers faced increased economic instability (72.5% of online respondents), many workers couldn't afford to place an ad for their services (46% of online respondents), sex workers were having a harder time connecting with community, and the law chilled sex worker speech. One sex worker respondent to the study noted, "Everything I know about being safe in sex work is because I was able to speak to other sex workers online." Sex workers also reported financial discrimination (33% of online respondents reported losing access to a payment app) and barriers to banking (78% of street-based workers reported being unbanked).

Similar to "broken windows" policing, the use of condoms as evidence, and "walking while trans" bans (couched in anti-loitering laws), platform policing and content moderation systems employ overly broad algorithmic captures that use behaviors as a proxy for the subject position "prostitute." Due to the categorization of many forms of sex work as "high-risk" deviance, the identity of sex worker is algorithmically constructed to further police sex work at the level of the platform, similar to the racist and transphobic policing tactics used to police sex work and deviance on the streets. None of these practices are new, of course, instead falling into a lineage of predictive policing and profiling which stretches back at least to the beginning of the 20th century. In each of the associated algorithmic practices, if policing fails to "find" crime amongst presumed deviant populations, it will construct it. Predictive policing and platform algorithmic profiling of sex workers further constructs deviance by over-capturing and using behaviors as proxies for sex work, regardless of their legality or relationship to actual sex work. The more capacious the definitions of illicit and illegal activity, the more discretion afforded to civic and private actors, and finally, the broader the application of (online) deviance.

Sex workers who work online navigate the paradoxical needs for anonymity, in order to be safe, and visibility, in order to make money. Online sex work and the increasing reliance on social media requires a certain level of visibility that necessitates deviant communities move out of underground spaces into those more visible/public that may exacerbate exposure to violent harm (doxxing, outing, etc.). With this increased visibility comes increased policing and criminalization, and sex workers are forced to navigate and try to adapt to an online ecosystem of disappearing platforms, account deletions, and de-monetization—all of which result in increased violence, isolation, chilled speech, houselessness, and labor exploitation. This deviance dynamic echoes both Robert Merton's concept of blocked structural opportunities and at least one branch of critiques thereof. Whereas sex workers are certainly forced to innovate in constructing and discovering online practices and spaces to keep themselves safer, the appropriation, sanction, and criminal legal dismantling of said practices and platforms calls into question the goals themselves: who decides how the internet is to be used, what renders particular usages of an internet platform or marketing outlet deviant, and how and to what extent ought it to be regulated? In many cases, access to the very technologies that sex workers innovated are denied to sex workers and used to exacerbate harm, invisibilize marginalized communities, and spread sensationalized media on sex trafficking in the absence of sex worker and survivor voices.

Becker and diffuse moral entrepreneurship

Any contemporary consideration of social deviance must take into account interactionist theories; that is, those that consider both the rule-makers (and enforcers) and rule-breakers. One of the pioneers of this family of theories, Howard Becker (2018), refers to deviance as a "double-barreled term" (p. 2) in that both society and his titular "outsiders" label each other as deviant. As we consider the presumed rule-breakers, sex working people who advertise and/or labor on the internet, we must first decide how they come to be labeled as deviant. The simplest answer is that sex work is generally deemed deviant in the United States: many, though far from all, forms of labor within the sex trades are criminalized, subject to sanction, or otherwise stigmatized. Despite the diversity of more and less formal sanctions, sex work criminalization has coalesced around a few sites which are instructive in considering the deviance of the online sex trades.

The first site is women's bodily and economic autonomy. The formal criminalization of sex work in the United States is generally traced to the Mann Act (also known as the White-Slave Traffic Act) of 1910, legislation premised on halting trafficking, but in effect limiting unmarried women's ability to cross state lines for any reason. Unmarried, or even simply unaccompanied, women were folded into the category of potential prostitute, and a moral panic around white slavery offered an opportunity to prescribe limits on their independence. The second site is im/migrant sex work, which was actually sanctioned earlier than the Mann Act, via the Page Act of 1875, which prohibited the "importation" of women into the United States for the purposes of prostitution. A century and a half later, illegal migrancy remains a headline political issue, from the Obama administration's deportation of over 400,000 migrants in 2012 to Trump's border wall. The third site is around race and class. In the late 19th and early 20th centuries, sex work was one of the few forms of employ in which Black women could earn as much as or more than their white counterparts. Today, "Quality of Life" ordinances around loitering and the use of public space more broadly disproportionately target women of color, trans women, and cash-poor women in general. In the case of online sex work, access to better protected sites and anonymized advertising requires certain levels of technical expertise and payment for ads. Criminalization breaks down the "democratization" of the internet for some of the most precariously positioned sex working people.

One could debate the extent to which criminalization of behavior or in this case of employ, stems from labels of deviance, or the reverse. But the aforementioned sites (women's autonomy, migrancy, and race and class) are ripe for moral panic and othering, and thus labels of deviance are somewhat self-reinforcing. Is sex work particularly statistically deviant? This depends on how one defines sexual labor. Since at least as far back as Emma Goldman's 1910 "The Traffic in Women," feminist thinkers have considered the extent to which marriage contracts constitute a form of sexual labor. The idea of exchanging sexual services for money, goods, shelter, protection, or other services is both ancient and widespread. Is sex work pathologically deviant? It is the often the presumption of either psychological or emotional trauma or pathology, and/or the argument that sex workers are "vectors of disease" that justifies sanction. Yet there is little effort from the state and its criminal legal system or medical industries to ameliorate these issues, and equally little data to suggest higher STI infection rates among sex workers, other than perhaps those placed in the most precarious situations due to lack of access to contraception or the ability to screen or refuse clients. Are sex workers deviant because they reduce social stability or organization (the "functional view")? This, too, is a complicated consideration. On one hand, criminalization and sanction reduce individual stability and the ability for criminalized laborers to organize themselves. Most of the unsafe working conditions sex workers face and, as a result, the most "deviant" situations in which they find themselves, can be traced to criminalization, from justified fear of police to the lack of recourse when facing violent clients or managers. This naturally extends to internet-based sanctions and restrictions, which have served to drive many of the most precariously situated sex working people off the internet and into less-safe working conditions, or simply out of work altogether. But on the other hand, sex work at least symbolically does serve to destabilize certain forms of social organization and presumed stability on which the state depends: reproductive sex (that is, vaginal intercourse between partners biologically capable of carrying a pregnancy to term), the marriage pact (which the state fetishizes to the point of now even endeavoring to allow certain categories of homosexual union), and, as referenced earlier, non-cis male economic and bodily autonomy (as these are forms of employ wildly overrepresenting queer, of color, migrant, trans, disabled, and cash-poor women, femmes, and nonbinary people making money independent of phobic state and commercial systems). Finally, are sex workers, particularly those who use the internet for their work, deviant due to failure to obey group rules? The "rules" of the internet continue to be made, and some of the most drastic, whether the decisions of private entities or state mandate, have been in response to the ingenuity and enterprise of sex working people. From Craigslist's aforementioned shuttering of its "Adult Services" section in 2010, to the 2015 raid of RentBoy.com, to the 2018 shutdown of Backpage.com and the passage of FOSTA-SESTA a week later, to more recent legislation such as the EARN IT act governing online liability, there is a clear pattern of state intervention into the labor practices of online sex workers, generally under the auspices of anti-trafficking lobbying and politicking.

Becker's interactionist theories remain instructive when considering the categories of services that fall under the umbrella of online sex work. He defines deviance as "not a quality that lies in behavior itself, but in the interaction between the person who commits an act and those who respond to it" (p. 14). The interaction as regards the internet, however, is often obscure, which in part allows rule-makers and rule-enforcers to equivocate sex work and trafficking. Melissa Gira Grant (2014) has referred to sex work as a "talking crime" (p. 37) as neither the sex nor the exchange of currency or anything else is itself illegal. But solicitation takes on a more abstract form via the internet, where obscenity and anti-prostitution laws have less-clear jurisdictions and platforms overcomply to reduce their own liability. Thus, in one sense, online sex workers are more definitively labeled deviant than their offline counterparts (though the ability or relegation to remain "completely" offline is often the result either of a certain privilege or massive disadvantage). Deplatforming, doxxing, and outing—labeling, for lack of a better term—can be far more permanent, indelible, and yet outwardly invisible in cyberspace.

Becker also notes that deviance "is always the result of enterprise" (p. 162), both on the part of the rule-maker and the rule-breaker. Online sex work is a useful test case for his concepts of deviant careers and moral entrepreneurs, as well as the enterprise which motivates each of them. Becker writes of a series of "career contingencies" that contribute to the shape of a deviant career. That is, deviant behavior that moves from primary to secondary status and becomes part of a lasting label. These include the objective facts of social structure and changes in the perceptions, motivations, and desires of the individual deviant actor (p. 24). Becker further suggests that "the treatment of deviants denies them the ordinary means of carrying on the routines of everyday life open to most people" (p. 35). In the case of online sex workers, many have experience in the "offline" trades, and the risks of in-person work and/or advertising has made the internet a safer, more reliable tool to mediate their labor. "Ordinary means" would here include basic labor protections assumed by most workers: safety guidelines, recourse to authorities for labor practice violations, ability to organize, etc. Their deviant careers are more often than not the result of these means failing in other, perhaps more socially acceptable modes of employ. If the deviant (and/or criminal) label follows them onto the internet, then the "objective facts" of the deviant career likely propels them to alternative paths of less resistance—working with exploitative managers, less-safe and unvetted clients, and outdoors or in less-safe and desirable locales.

Gira Grant also writes about the gentrification of the internet and its impact on the market for sex workers, but this begs the question: is the internet public space? The stakes of this question for sex workers and online deviance are multifaceted. Jean Camp and Y.T. Chien (2000) offer one instructive distinction in considering whether and to what extent the internet is public and how that might govern the state's reaction to internet pornography. Under a "media rubric" (p. 9), the government would be responsible for keeping pornography off the internet, much as some argue it should censor sex work advertising and solicitation more broadly. But under a "spatial concept" (ibid), the government has only a basic responsibility to ensure public safety, and the internet becomes a market of content "that is competitive and non-exclusionary" (ibid). The former view renders all content in some way "public," in that it is accessible via a medium anyone can log on to, while the latter contends more directly with the way in which the internet, and internet sex work particularly, challenges public/private and global/local distinctions, among others. We will offer a few models for how the internet as a public space has been theorized later in this chapter, but suffice it to say the construction of online deviance is highly predicated upon the extent to which given behaviors and ideas are considered public.

In public space or not, the question regarding sex work remains: short of the presumption of the possibility (and proven fallacy) of complete eradication of sex work, i.e. "ending demand" for sexual services and the income they provide, when and where is sex work not deviant? Even those services which are technically legal elicit specific varieties of deplatforming and shadowbanning, as we'll see later in this chapter, and thus online sex working people (and, importantly, those presumed to be) occupy a deviant subject position which transcends or supersedes their actual labor. Whether they do so in the commons of the internet has more to do with how their work might face sanction and prohibition than whether it is in any way deviant.

On the rule-maker side, Becker suggests that enforcement "requires explanation" (p. 122). This explanation tends to emanate first from a moral entrepreneur, appealing to both rule-creators and rule-enforcers, who endeavors to make the rule public for enforcement. So much of the discourse around online sex work (and for that matter, trafficking) is expository and sensationalistic. Yet the moral entrepreneurs are diffuse, from anti-prostitution and anti-porn feminists to evangelicals and politicians from both major electoral parties. Moral entrepreneurs comprise both rule-creators (politicians at the most formal levels, District Attorneys, police, lobbyists, journalists, and various NGOs in less codified ways) and rule-enforcers (again, police and other vestiges of the criminal legal system, but also the website operators who often preemptively ban and deplatform the workers who helped build their brands). Finally, it is worth reinforcing the varying degrees of personal interest of the enforcers. There have been various cases of extremely dubious interest from saviorism (such as Nicolas Kristof's campaigns through his position as NY Times staff writer, or Rashida Jones's fetishization of "amateur" pornography) to careerist (NGOs generate millions of dollars and jobs, as well as political influence, from their lobbying around sex work criminalization).

The designation of outsider and the deviance of online sex workers is ultimately the result of what Becker refers to as "collective action" (p. 182). Any gentrification of the internet regarding sex workers only follows from the gentrification of "public spaces" in cities and towns. Once again, the (criminal) deviance of online sex workers questions the extent to which the internet is public, and what it means if it is not. In sex work more generally, the infraction of norms begins as wholly moral: recreative sex is a threat to the normative institutions of marriage, nuclear/biological family, and Abrahamic religion. From there, however, are the more nuanced expressions of deviance, from broader economic self-sufficiency to highly specialized forms of erotic labor and fetish provision. In the wake of the recent (and ongoing) COVID-19 pandemic, more and more people have considered online sex work in response to Becker's query: "Instead of asking why deviants want to do things that are disapproved of, we might better ask why conventional people do not follow through on the deviant impulses they have" (pp. 26–27). Gira Grant similarly wonders why media, government, and individuals often obsess over why people go into sex work, without asking why others do not. That is, if two subjects face similar concerns with employment, financial or housing security, or other related concerns, why does one subject engage in sex work and the other not? The rise of sex worker use of online platforms such as TikTok, Instagram, and OnlyFans has further challenged how to define the deviance of online sex work, making it subject to both harder and softer sanctions while being engaged in by a growing and diversifying population.

In the end, Becker reformulated and refocused his ideas around labeling theory in response to what he saw as various misuses thereof. In considering the prospects for defining deviance moving forward, he saw theoretical, rather than technical trouble:

> We can construct workable definitions either of particular actions people might commit or of particular categories of deviance as the world (especially, but not only, the authorities) defines them. But we cannot make the two coincide completely, because they do not do so empirically.
>
> *(p. 185)*

Cohen and irregular moral panic

The difficulties in demarcating consistent features of the coding of online sex worker deviance are various: the different modalities of use of the internet (advertising via more or less specialized websites and platforms, livestreaming performances, sales of prerecorded videos or images, to name a few), the spectrum of legality and sanction (from corporatized pornography distribution to individual accounts on various platforms to "tube" sites, which exist in a liminal state of a mixture of stolen footage, sex worker monetized content, and freely distributed "amateur" videos), and the friction between the massive consumption of online sex work (certainly hardly statistically deviant) and the continued persecution of the workers (from the aforementioned laws and more informal sanctioning to doxxing and public outing). The rise of "tube" sites destroyed pre-existing porn site payment models. The rise of OnlyFans and other paywalled fan sites marked a shift in more people returning to paying for their porn. The continued demonetization of adult websites via Visa/Mastercard pushes sex work into a further deviant and marginalized space with less access to resources. While Becker and interactionist theories help us consider in what ways online sex work satisfies conceptions of social deviance, the media (both social and more or less formal journalistic varieties) uniquely dictate these forms of deviance. As noted earlier, online sex work challenges conceptions of the internet as a public space; the way that public perceptions are conditioned is central to its being considered deviant (or not). Physical spaces can be more easily classified, according to various heuristics, as either public or private. The internet, as Camp and Chien note, is an entity in which "the public space, the private sector space, and the personal spaces merge seamlessly" (p. 3).

Stanley Cohen's (2011) foundational study of media exaggeration and threat-conditioning, *Folk Devils and Moral Panics*, has been subject to over- and (arguable) misuse to at least the extent of Becker's work in the ensuing decades. Here, we consider the relative peculiarity of the shuttering of websites and legislation around online sex work through the lens of moral panic (though sex panic may be a more apt designation here). Cohen describes a "media inventory" (p. 49) that builds toward moral panic and subsequent reaction by rule-makers and enforcers. This sequential model begins with the exaggeration and distortion of the issue, followed by prediction of its results, and finally symbolization into a comprehensible paradigm and public vernacular. In the case of online sex work, the exaggeration is of the link between sex work advertising and online services and sex trafficking (or what is sometimes coded in media as "sex slavery," a symptom of the lurid symbolization required to pass legislation). Mainstream media often fails to discriminate between sex work and instances of labor exploitation within the sex trades, and collapses both into a rhetoric of sex trafficking. Any actual instance of force, fraud, or coercion is either painted in the most extreme terms or exploded into unverifiable (and often willfully falsified) statistics in the service of promoting specific political agendas. The sex worker, wherever they may fall on the spectrum of choice, circumstance, or coercion, is also written out of this account, either reframed as a traitor to feminism, self-deluded, or oblivious to their own exploitation. Thus, sex work is distorted as trafficking and vice versa, leading to the prediction that this social problem will (continue to) astronomically increase if not choked at the source: internet advertising. But it is the symbolization that is of most interest in the current chapter: what does the online sex worker symbolize in the "public" or political imagination?

Cohen expands on Edwin Lemert's "societal control culture" in thinking through what we might today call a carceral orientation toward deviance. These mechanisms are constituted of "laws, procedures, programs and organizations which in the name of a collectivity help, rehabilitate, punish or otherwise manipulate deviants" (Cohen, 2011, p. 77). They can include both official institutions and "typical modes and models of understanding and explaining the deviance" (ibid). When it comes to sex working people (and, for that matter, self-identifying trafficking survivors), "help" generally means the rescue industry, either abolitionist[1] NGOs, religiously-affiliated organizations, or governmental programs which rarely focus on direct service provision or aftercare (i.e. housing, employment, childcare). "Rehabilitate" is a mixed concept regarding sex work: there are state-mandated "john schools" for clients in certain municipalities, and parallel programs for the workers themselves (such as NYC's Human Trafficking Intervention Courts). But for the online sex worker who has little or no in-person contact with clients, the only "rehabilitation" would be changing one's identity or else embracing a more or less public label. Thus, the deviance of online sex work predominantly faces either punishment (from various corners) or manipulation (changing the way the internet can be used).

There is no single moral entrepreneur when it comes to online sex work, and the construction of deviance can seem self-contradictory, depending on which parties are promoting it and for what ends. Cohen notes the concept of "sensitization" in reaction to deviance, which "involves not only redefinition but also the assignment of blame and the direction of control measures towards a specific agent thought to be responsible" (p. 81). FOSTA-SESTA have had no demonstrable impact on curbing sex trafficking, yet have caused a massive amount of harm for sex workers who advertise online. The construction of deviance allows for sex workers to be framed as collateral damage or "unintended consequences" of such bills, even as sex workers' rights groups vociferously denounced what the effects would be. As such, online sex workers are subject to both commercial and ideological exploitation. In the former case, sex workers are often the early adopters who help build various platforms and sites (such as Tumblr), which were only too happy to distance themselves as federal enforcement heated up. Cohen defines the latter as instances in which the "deviant used for societally defined ends without any regard to the consequences of this on the deviant" themselves (p. 157).

But none of this necessarily explains why the online sex worker makes such a particularly apt receptacle for sanction and symbolization. Cohen gestures toward symbolic politics in his work, but focuses primarily on (presumed) youth violence and resulting unrest. Online sex workers labor at the nexus of the narrative/fantasy capacities of the internet and the moral panic of faceless sex traffickers prepared to steal and sell young women. Cohen notes, "The manipulation of appropriate symbols—the process which sustains moral campaigns, panics and crusades—is made much easier when the object of attack is both highly visible and structurally weak" (pp. 225–226). The deviance of online sex work is reinforced by its visibility. The workers are presumed to be reducible to their work, or else robbed of all agency under the mantle of "trafficking victim." The structural weakness is the ultimate independence of almost all online sex work—the few sites and platforms which better protect users' information or retain lawyers are often the most expensive. There is no actual labor solidarity available, making online sex workers perfect candidates for Cohen's "folk devils" as media, politicians, and other entities seek to deploy them as such.

In *Sex, Trafficking and Scandal: The Transformation of Journalism*, Gretchen Soderlund writes about how scandalous representations of sex work and "white slavery" sold more papers and reformists constructed a moral panic that led to moral crusaders policing sex work. A similar moral crusade was used to pass FOSTA-SESTA under language that aimed to stop sex-trafficking, but where it deviates is in how sex workers publicly responded and how many mainstream journalists covered FOSTA-SESTA from a sex worker-centered perspective. The media response to FOSTA-SESTA marks a shift in how sex work was covered by mainstream media, including media coverage from sources like Teen Vogue, receiving unprecedented pushback and media coverage, largely due to sex worker organizing. It is not necessarily that "better" media coverage tempers the moral panic; however, it is more that sex-worker-centered media makes visible the stories behind deviant communities and highlights sex worker struggles.

Models for considering the internet as public space

The misconception that there are discrete categories of, and impenetrable borders between, online and offline sex work persists in a variety of venues. All sex work that happens online (such as camming, OnlyFans, porn) is produced in a physical space and much of offline sex work (such as escorting, sugar babying) is advertised and found through online marketing and advertisements. The policing of sex work follows a similar path, where the use of digital evidence and surveillance is used in the prosecution of offline sex work, and the lived physical impacts of not having equitable access to social media, financial technologies, or the tools to operate a business online (such as increased vulnerability, houselessness, etc.). The pandemic further collapsed the boundary between online and offline sex work and home/work by bringing online sex work in closer proximity to home as many sex workers were forced to share space with family/roommates while continuing to make an income and continuing to labor.

As this chapter has repeatedly noted, the potential, ascribed, or actual deviance of online sex work rests heavily on the extent and ways in which the internet is considered "public," and whether it is a medium, a space, a combination thereof, or something else entirely. As far back as 1996, Anne Branscomb theorized the internet as an "information agora," a kind of multipurpose commons which operates under a rather tenuous, shifting set of dictates and proscriptions regarding its use. The agora is, of course, a space, and Camp and Chien build out some key considerations to consider in the regulation of digital spaces. Though they favor the spatial metaphor, they note the oddness of the internet's being both ubiquitous and personal (p. 1), as well as exhibiting characteristics of simultaneity (i.e., being in two places at once), permeability (e.g., work/home boundary), and exclusivity (in this instance, such as intranets) (ibid). Most compelling for this chapter is the ways in which each is reflected in the regulation of sex work. The simultaneity of online video and cam content, as well as various forms of electronic correspondence with sex working people, is rather obvious. But more insidious is the way in which anti-prostitution metaphors around "selling one's body" are wholly ignorant of the simultaneity of these forms of emotional and physical labor: sex workers simultaneously retain possession of their bodies while using them in myriad ways in exchange for currency, goods, or services (as in many other industries). The work/home boundary is particularly permeable for on-call and cam workers, whose deviance is perhaps attenuated by having the ability to work from the relative safety and privacy of their own spaces. That said, one's online persona or avatar bleeding into the personal "space" of one's government identity is a particular risk for online deviants who face both increased risk of doxxing and are coerced by platforms to share personally identifying information. Exclusivity is a double-edged sword for criminalized online deviants attempting to monetize their deviant behavior—it is arguably a particular class marker when an online worker can subsist strictly on client referrals and/or intranet-type, firewalled, and paywalled sites. So if the internet is a public space, it is a bifurcated one, allowing participation in the commons from the physical privacy of one's home.

At another register, perhaps the internet is a set of interlocking territories, some overlapping, some with harder borders. What is deviant in one territory is not in another, and jurisdictions are often unclear or simply asserted until annexed or challenged. Rebecca MacKinnon (2012) refers to the "sovereigns of cyberspace," online platforms that Zeynep Tufekci (2016) recognizes as harbingers of "the growth of privately owned spaces that functioned as public commons" (p. 66). As the agora is privatized, the task of how to account for and deal with the deviants becomes more pressing. In the case of sex workers, this has meant platform over-response in content moderation through the construction of "high-risk" communities to minimize platform liability. Platforms do not differentiate between sex work and femininity and both are policed and often conflated with trafficking, resulting in the restriction of access to online banking, deplatforming, shadowbanning, and various other sanctions.

Tufekci offers another metaphor which perhaps better reflects these practices in reaction to various deviant practices: the internet as "algorithmic walled garden" (p. 68). The walls are erected by some of the aforementioned sovereigns, resulting in most users sticking to the trusted curations of Facebook and Google. Of course, there is a massive market for sex workers to present their wares and services in these gardens, and the friction of deviance tends to occur when their ingenuity is suddenly outed or deemed unsafe. As noted earlier in this chapter, sex workers make new spaces desirable, but as these platforms become mainstream with larger potential for commercial success, sex workers and other deviant communities' content is suppressed or removed to keep undesirables out of these walled gardens. Content moderation practices that determine content to be too "high-risk" or "low-quality" further enforce the process of what feminist media studies scholar Jessa Lingel (2023) calls the "gentrification of the internet."

Relatedly, there is the metaphor of the "architecture" of the internet and the code on which it is built. Where does this metaphor leave the deviants? Especially when deviance and sex work are being algorithmically coded and placed in "high-risk" categories. Clearly not in wholly separate structures, and not really underground, either, as sex workers have always been part of the commons. Generally speaking, the internet-as-public suggests a question regarding causation: do we consider the internet public due to the way it is used and governed (form following function), or do we govern and use it a certain way due to presumptions of its being public (function following form)?

Paradox of visibility: dangers and opportunities offered by online space

The internet presents both unique opportunities and dangers for sex working people. For many sex workers who have access, the internet is a harm reduction tool that places more distance between client and sex worker, and more time to make decisions. Many sex workers use the internet to vet clients, share bad-date lists and harm reduction working tips with other sex workers, and build community and organize. Despite all the ways that sex workers use the internet to mitigate harm, the visibility of online sex work opens sex workers up to a host of new potential harms such as increased state and platform surveillance, online harassment, doxxing, outing, and the necessity of revealing personally identifiable information, all of which further codify the sex worker as a deviant body under platform and state surveillance.

In earlier online sex work and advertising, less verification was needed to make money, meaning that sex workers had to disclose less personally identifying information. It was easier to work without placing ads with photos, having social media, or maintaining an online brand. This afforded a more ephemeral nature to sex work, where sex workers who were working online had more anonymity, and the ability to move in and out of sex work without the identity of a sex worker following them around. Since FOSTA-SESTA, the websites where sex workers make money or advertise for in-person work require increasingly demanding identity verification, including 3D biometric scans of faces. How this information is used is an opaque practice, but when sex workers report being stopped at borders and having their ads pulled up by border agents, it is likely that there are undisclosed private/state relationships and cross-sharing of this information.

With online sex work, many workers are navigating complicated relationships with visibility: where visibility is needed to make money and that visibility also increases your exposure to various other harms. The publicity of online sex work, and the increase of online sex work during the pandemic, creates a heightened category of online deviance where one's deviant status is no longer private, ephemeral, or underground.

Finally, and arguably most importantly, sex workers themselves are both combatting and wielding their status as online deviants. Through innovative uses of technology, shifting media narratives, and artistic and academic interventions, sex worker collectives are pushing back against whorephobic legislation, the loss of online spaces, and the exclusion of sex work from art and academia.

The sex worker collective Hacking//Hustling emerged from the silence of the tech sector and academia in response to FOSTA-SESTA and the removal of Backpage, responding to how this silence contributes to violent legislation and platform policing. Hacking//Hustling "is a collective of sex workers, survivors, and accomplices working at the intersection of tech and social justice to interrupt violence facilitated by technology." Hacking//Hustling demanded that sex worker voices were present and centered in conversations on future tech legislation, such as The Earn It Act. The first event sponsored by Hacking//Hustling was a presentation by Danielle Blunt and Melissa Gira Grant (2018), 'Dystopia Now: Erasing the Internet by Erasing Sex Workers at Data and Society,' an organization that routinely leaves sex work out of their analysis of gig work, care work, and online labor. This event was followed by Hacking//Hustling: A Platform for Sex Workers in a Post-SESTA World, a two-day workshop at Eyebeam with a panel discussion on sex work and technology followed by peer-led harm reduction programming and a community art exhibition. Hacking//Hustling also started collecting data on the impact of FOSTA-SESTA and the removal of

Backpage, which became some of the only data on the impact for the three years follow-ing FOSTA-SESTA being signed into law. Over the last five years, Hacking//Hustling has intervened in the Academy through sex-worker led publications, conferences at institutions like Cornell and Harvard, and building cross-movement responses to increasing gendered criminalization among queer and trans communities, people seeking abortion care, and substance users seeking survival and bodily autonomy.

Decoding Stigma is another working group that seeks to build "a cross-institutional coa-lition of laborers, futurists, advocates, artists, designers, technologists, researchers, teach-ers, and students who want to compel conversations about sex and sex work at the tech school." Both Hacking//Hustling and Decoding Stigma wield deviance through occupying space as out sex workers and accomplices within the Academy, strategizing ways to be out as a way to resist stigma and build solidarity with other workers.

Veil Machine is a sex worker artist collective exploring "Intimacy through lies. Authen-ticity through commodification. The digital as the real." Their work plays with the ephem-erality of online sex work as highlighted in their 2020 performance "E-viction." "E-viction" was a 12-hour "virtual whorehouse/whore gallery" where you could explore and engage with sex worker artists before the platform self-destructed at midnight. The collective describes the performance as "a direct response to our urgent need for a digital public sphere and the challenges of sex worker survival in COVID-19." Viewers are invited in as voyeurs, participants, and deviants and seduced by intimately curated sex worker perfor-mances, art, and political education before the finale when the platform itself self-destructs. These viewers are left alone against a blank, glowing screen in their physical spaces without access to the performances or the community that had been built throughout the event. In their press release the collective writes, "E-Viction is a self-destructing platform where sex workers and artists create intimate encounters and exchanges to imagine a world beyond SESTA/FOSTA . . . before dramatizing the otherwise invisible censorship of sex workers by self-destructing." Veil Machine continues to host sex worker art salons, artist talks, and performance intensives.

Artist and sex worker Lena Chen and a team of sex workers and allies created the interactive game *OnlyBans* as an intervention to teach people about digital surveillance and how marginalized bodies and sex workers are policed online. In the game, players assume the role of a sex worker amidst a cacophony of "content moderation algorithms, shadow-banning, "real name" policies, facial recognition software, and other threats based on actual experiences of sex workers" and try to make an income. The participant is invited into the role of the deviant, the game highlighting the experiences and images that sex workers shared with the game developers.

Despite rampant erasure, sex workers are demanding and taking up space with their interventions in art and within the academy. Both E-viction and OnlyBans create artistic interventions that put the viewer or player into the role of the deviant to somaticize the feelings of platform punishment, stigma, isolation, and erasure, making visible for civilians the harm of deplatforming and financial discrimination.

Whether lecturing in leather, having a submissive hold note cards when presenting at an award ceremony, or using conference stages and hashtags to hustle, Danielle Blunt, sex worker and one of the co-authors of this chapter, wields their status as an online deviant when interfacing with the academy. After being invited to the Lesbians Who Tech confer-ence to speak on the impact of FOSTA, presenters Danielle Blunt and Daly Barnett were asked to change the title of their talk from 'Health Equity in the age of SESTA' to 'From

Spreading Hate on 8chan to the Safety of Sex Workers, How & Where do We Draw the Line'. Instead, the two gave an incendiary talk calling the organizers of the conference out for partnering with tech companies:

> Since my ad space has been systematically eliminated by officials who do not care about queer communities' safety or survival, let me use this platform and leave you with this. As a queer dominatrix, I also offer a reduced rate for queers who need, and it doesn't involve partnering with organizations like Palantir, that uphold systems that we should all be actively trying to dismantle. Please visit my website if you'd like to book a session.

Having a whore co-write this chapter on sex work and online deviance and share personal experiences further wields the deviant status by resisting tokenization and the status of solely a subject to be studied rather than a co-creator of knowledge and expertise.

Conclusion

Social deviance theories have historically emerged out of interest in deviant groups and subcultures (street gangs, radical political formations, cognitively and affectively differently abled people, queer and trans people, etc.) or specific deviant behaviors or ideologies (school shooters, pedophiles, extreme body modifiers, flat earthers, etc.). In the case of sex work and sex workers, various moral entrepreneurs, phobic public institutions, and sociocultural forces construct and reinforce presumed deviant and sanctionable behavior. The cyclical progress of sex worker as community member, fallen woman, feminist icon or enemy, and/or subject of fetish or violence (or both at once) is reproduced in the internet age. Also reproduced is sex working subjects' innovation toward survival strategies and political resistance at both the individual and community levels. Sex workers are hardly a miner's canary for internet policy; their deviant activity in regards to the internet is always reducible to a safer, less precarious working existence, and one that intersects with their non-sex working life to the extent they desire. What makes the coding of online deviance regarding sex work a ripe area for theorizing, then, are a few factors.

First, the amount of legal red tape around both the criminalized and ostensibly legal forms of online sex work is matched perhaps only by the attention anti-trans or anti-reproductive choice legislation has garnered over the past few years. In the case of federal legislation such as FOSTA/SESTA and EARN-IT, the laws and statutes largely serve to further conflate sex work and labor trafficking, narrowing the former to coerced and/or uncompensated labor, and the latter to the tiny sliver represented by sexual labor under force, fraud, or coercion erasing the complexities of experiences of those who trade sex. As we have seen in the past few years, tech often gets regulated through stoking moral panics about child safety (in the case of sex work, but also anti-trans and anti-reproductive choice movements alike). In more local and municipal cases, the sex worker becomes a lightning rod for social ills and "bad work." Of course, the internet is only federal insofar as the government claims jurisdiction over certain activities taking place on the web, and local insofar as workers use it to attract and vet clients locally. In either case, the ubiquitous availability of online sexual services far outstrips the government's ability to snuff them out—just as anti-trans, anti-queer, or anti-choice legislation simply serves to make the world less safe for deviant subjects and their communities, broadly construed, so do anti-sex work bills in all their forms. Stigmatization contributes to the criminalization of one's livelihood.

Second, sex working subject positions—and particularly those most precarious and reactive to deviant designations—overlap with a variety of other deviant subject positions. The overrepresentation of queer and trans, disabled, cash-poor, migrant, and of color subjects in sex work reflects the full breadth of the "deviance" of the sex worker. The internet has the potential to be both a site of refuge and a tool of surveillance, designations with which the aforementioned subjects are often quite familiar. From FBI wiretaps of civil rights leaders back to the Underground Railroad, contemporary technology can be wielded to oppress and liberate in equal measure. Sex workers, having faced some form of codified, federal censure in the US for a century, have always used technology (trains and cars, telegrams and phones, prophylactics and contraceptives, experience-enhancing substances and bondage equipment) as elemental to their work and their survival. When it comes to the internet, the uses are as varied as the sale of goods (pornographic video or image, apparel, or toys), advertising for services both offline and online, and performance both widely broadcast and one-on-one. Who deploys the internet for these practices, how they differ from their "non-deviant" counterparts, and the extent to which any of them is deemed deviant, criminal, or otherwise worthy of remark and labeling, is a vast and under-considered field of inquiry for deviance studies. It also bears out the last category of interest.

Finally, the difficulty of classifying "sex worker" as a single or even immediately related set of subject positions, despite a spectrum of common interests, renders the category a useful testing ground for deviance theories. Interactionist theories of deviance, as noted earlier, focus on encounters between deviant actors and various respondents, be they rule-makers, moral crusaders, or simply norm-following (which is often to say, norm-policing) publics. If we consider the continuum of legality alone, the difficulty of definition reveals itself. To begin with, the "porn loophole" is the most obvious avenue for non-criminalized online sex work: it is legal to record sexual acts for pay under a variety of state and municipal jurisdictions. While these workers may be socially deviant, they are certainly not criminally so, at least currently. Cam work and online, live erotic performance tests some of these limits, as how money is being transacted may be subject to a different set of statutes, including overreaching obscenity laws and banking regulations which serve to restrict free speech online by limiting what content can be sold or discussed, even in otherwise technically legal contexts. As with many forms of online sex work, the level of protection from legal sanction is proportionate to the worker's financial means to access better-protected sites. In these instances, social deviance is limited to how "social" the work actually is (i.e., who knows about it and what can they do about it?). Finally, the category of advertising online is perhaps the most spectral: workers on certain platforms (including private, operator-owned sites) are nearly immune to fear of legal consequence while others are relegated to using coded language and rightly fear entrapment, banning, and outing/doxxing. Obviously, these lines are no more firmly drawn than any other when it comes to sex work deviance, but class position and various "whorearchies" are often more than suggestive of levels of deviance. This stratification across subject position(s) and identities is part-and-parcel to harm reduction and decriminalization efforts and social deviance studies alike. Should the online sex worker's deviance ever be evacuated from the criminal category and solely within the range of the social, phobic publics would be forced to confront their phobias and what underpins them in far more complicated ways. This is perhaps the highest aim of social deviance studies.

References

Barss, P. (2010). *The erotic engine: How pornography has powered mass communication, from gutenberg to Google.* Anchor Canada.

Becker, H. (2018). *Outsiders: Studies in the sociology of deviance.* Free Press.

Berg, H. (2021). *Porn work: Sex, labor, and late capitalism.* The University of North Carolina Press.

Blunt, D., & Ariel, W. (2020). Erased: The impact of FOSTA-SESTA. Hacking//hustling. *Hacking//Hustling 2020.* Retrieved from https://hackinghustling.org/wp-content/uploads/2020/02/Erased_Updated.pdf

Blunt, D., & Ariel, W. *Erased: The impact of FOSTA-SESTA & the removal of backpage.* Retrieved from https://hackinghustling.org/erased-the-impact-of-fosta-sesta-2020/ (accessed 23 May 2021).

Blunt, D., & Barnett, D. (2019). *From spreading hate on 8chan to the safety of sex workers, how & where do we draw the line.* Lesbians Who Tech & Allies, New York, NY.

Blunt, D., Emily, C., Shanelle, M., & Ariel, W. (2020). *Posting into the void. Hacking//hustling.* Retrieved from https://hackinghustling.org/wp-content/uploads/2020/09/Posting-Into-the-Void.pdf

Branscomb, A. W. (1996). Cyberspaces: Familiar territory or lawless frontiers. *Journal of Computer-Mediated Communication, 2*(2), 1–38.

Camp, J., & Chien, Y. T. (2000). The internet as public space: Concepts, issues, and implications in public policy. *ACM Sigcas Computers and Society, 30*(3), 13–19.

Cohen, S. (2011). *Folk devils and moral panics: The creation of the mods and rockers.* Routledge.

Delaney, S. (2019). *Times square red, times square blue.* New York University Press.

Emma, G. (2002). The traffic in women. *Hastings Women's Law Journal, 13*(9).

Foldes, L. *Sex workers built the internet.* Retrieved from https://parsons.edu/dt-2022/sex-workers-built-the-internet/ (accessed 21 May 2023).

Gira Grant, M. (2014). *Playing the whore: The work of sex work.* Verso.

Gira Grant, M., & Danielle, B. (2018). *Dystopia now: Erasing the internet by erasing sex workers* [Data and Society's Future Perfect Conference organized by Ingrid Burrington].

Hacking//Hustling. (2018, September 20). A platform for sex workers in a post-sesta world. *Eyebeam Assembly.* Retrieved from www.youtube.com/watch?v=8capdFOA1FE&t=1s.

Hacking//Hustling. (2021). *Train, tits, and text: Sex work, technology, and movement.* Retrieved from https://hackinghustling.org/trains-texts-and-tits-sex-work-technology-and-movement/

Lingel, J. (2023). *The gentrification of the internet: How to reclaim our digital freedom.* University of California Press.

MacKinnon, R. (2012). *Consent of the networked: The worldwide struggle for internet freedom.* Basic Books.

Soderlund, G. (2013). *Sex trafficking, scandal, and the transformation of journalism, 1885–1917.* University of Chicago.

Stardust, Z., Gabriella, G., & Chibundo, E. (2020, December 16). What can tech learn from sex workers: Sexual ethics, tech design & decoding stigma. *Berkman Klein Center for Internet and Society/Medium.* https://medium.com/berkman-klein-center/what-can-tech-learn-from-sex-workers-8e0100f0b4b9.

Tiidenberg, K., & Van Der Nagel, E. (2020). *Sex and social media.* Emerald Group Publishing.

Tufekci, Z. (2016). As the pirates become CEOs: The closing of the open internet. *Daedalus, 145*(1), 65–78.

16

THE STRUGGLE WITH STIGMA IN SEX WORK

Webcam models' strategies for stigma management

Hannah DeLacey

Introduction

Sex work is portrayed in the media as inherently linked to exploitation, enslavement, and criminal activities, and the media helps to shape the stigma around sex work (Benoit et al., 2020; Desyllas, 2013; Weitzer, 2018). Sex workers are commonly stereotyped as dirty, criminal, a threat to the public, or vectors of disease (Abel, 2011), and the 'whore stigma' is widely ingrained in society (Pheterson, 1993). Previous research on sex work and stigma has primarily focused on in-person forms of sex work such as stripping, escorting, and full-service sex work. In this chapter, I explore a relatively new form of sex work: webcamming.

Webcamming started in the 1990s and has since evolved into a global industry (Jones, 2020; Senft, 2008). Webcam models earn money via tips or pay-per-minute shows, and the viewer(s) may have a lot of control over the performances (Jones, 2020; Sanders et al., 2020). Part of the appeal of webcamming is that it is live, interactive, 'amateur', and personalized. Models draw in fans eager to interact with them and their unique personalities (Nayar, 2017).

Some research has shown that there are differences between the experiences of webcam models and other types of sex workers. Jones (2021) described how respondents felt webcamming was more socially acceptable than in-person sex work such as stripping or escorting because it took place online in a virtual space. In their comparative work on students who do sex work in the UK and Australia, Simpson and Smith (2021) found that there were major differences in the experiences of escorts and webcam models and how the Internet shaped their experiences of stigma. Escorts could use the Internet to increase their privacy and avoid stigma. At the same time, for webcam models, it made them more visible and therefore increased their exposure and experiences of stigma.

This chapter aims to understand whether and how webcam models experience stigma, and how they manage it using stigma management techniques. The chapter also aims to uncover whether the online realm creates or mitigates opportunities for stigma compared to other forms of sex work. More broadly, this work will shed light on the ongoing challenges experienced by webcam models and how they work despite their limited control over their working conditions and the constant legal and political threats to their work.

DOI: 10.4324/9781003277675-19

This chapter starts with an overview of stigma and sex work. Then it will describe respondents' experiences of stigma and their stigma management techniques.

Stigma and sex work

Goffman (1986) described stigma as "an attribute that is deeply discrediting". People who are stigmatized can feel like they are less accepted or valued in society, and Goffman described this as having a "spoiled identity" (Goffman, 1986). Link and Phelan (2001) took Goffman's definition a step further by including "power" and "discrimination" as key factors that shape how people are stigmatized. Stigma is relational and complex, and how people experience it is shaped by time, place, context, and power relationships (Link & Phelan, 2001).

In the United States and most places around the world, sex work is highly stigmatized, which has potentially harmful consequences for sex workers (Sallmann, 2010; Weitzer, 2018). Sex work has an occupational stigma, which means that the stigma is attached to the work itself (Blithe & Wolfe, 2017; Goffman, 1986), but workers often internalize the negative discourses about themselves because of their work (Corrigan & Watson, 2002).

A great portion of previous research on sex work and stigma has looked at stigma's impact on health, safety, and violence (e.g., Benoit et al., 2020; Jiao & Bungay, 2019; Krüsi et al., 2016; Pinsky & Levey, 2015). Prostitution is illegal in almost all of the United States. Its criminalization is rooted in sex work stigma (Nencel et al., 2021) and reflects the broader socio-cultural beliefs that all sex work is exploitation and synonymous with human trafficking (Weitzer, 2018). Because of this stigma, sex workers are seen as both degenerates and victims in need of saving (Koken, 2012). Laws and policies which further increase their stigmatization and vulnerability are made without their input (DeLacey, 2022; Musto et al., 2021). Even if people want to transition out of the sex industry, it can be difficult to access the mainstream labor market due to the stigma of (formerly) being in the sex industry (Berg, 2016; Ham & Gerard, 2014; Koken, 2012), and women may face even more challenges than men (Berg, 2016). Moreover, it can be difficult to find work that offers the same flexible schedule and high income, especially in the mainstream market.

The fear of stigma or being stigmatized can shape the behavior of sex workers and their willingness to be open about their work. Some sex workers may not disclose their job because of anticipated stigma (Ham & Gerard, 2014; Pitcher, 2015; Quinn & Chaudoir, 2009). Consequently, this can result in social isolation due to keeping their work secret from those around them and the resulting lack of social support (Begum et al., 2013; Koken, 2012; Toubiana & Ruebottom, 2022). Selectively coming out can lead to strained relationships for sex workers, leading some to go back into 'the closet'. Moreover, those around them are at risk of vicarious stigma (Morrison & Whitehead, 2007). Some sex workers cope with stigma by selectively disclosing their employment information to a few close friends or family members (Ham & Gerard, 2014) or by sharing it only with people who are also sex workers (Koken, 2012).

In Benoit et al. (2020), the authors described how Canadian sex workers reframed or rejected stigma by highlighting the positive benefits of their work. Reframing helps reduce stigma by focusing on the important aspects of the work, such as helping people, being valuable to society, and having many personal benefits such as a flexible work schedule and high income (Morrison & Whitehead, 2005). In Benoit et al. (2020), sex workers also reflected on how their work positively impacted their self-esteem, sexual identity, self-confidence, and feelings of empowerment. They described how sex workers saw their work as a viable profession because it gave them power and control over their lives and a sense of independence. Other research found that many sex workers reported that they enjoy their work, find it emotionally fulfilling, and are proud of their services (e.g., Adams, 2020; Jones, 2020; Koken et al., 2004).

Different forms of sex work may be more or less stigmatized, and some describe this hierarchical organization as the 'whorearchy' (Herrmann, 2022; Knox, 2014; McNeill, Maggie, 2012). "The whorearchy is arranged according to intimacy of contact with clients and police. The closer to both you are, the closer you are to the bottom (Knox, 2014)." Webcam models sit near the top of the whorearchy: webcamming is seen as less dirty than other forms of sex work because it takes place online and it is legal (Rodriguez, 2022; Scortino, 2016; Weitzer, 2009). Sex workers involved in multiple aspects of the industry may strategically present only one part of their work because of their higher social standing—such as identifying as a porn star instead of an escort, even if they do both (Berg, 2016). Sex workers may differentiate themselves from other sex workers in the same line of work to manage stigma (Herrmann, 2022; Parreira, 2021; Sanders, 2005).

Methods

I collected the data for this article as part of my larger doctoral research project on the adult webcam industry in North America. This chapter is based on interviews with 22 webcam models in the United States, and one in Canada. Participants were recruited through social media platforms (n = 20), referral sampling (n = 2), and in person (n = 1). When I refer to participants, I include their pseudonym, age at the time of the interview, and their reported approximate length of time working in the industry (e.g. Anna, 28, 1 year).

I identified potential participants on social media by looking at social media profiles and the type of content that they posted. In doing so, I surmised that they would likely be webcam models. Then I sent a message to them explaining that I was looking for webcam models who lived in the United States or Canada to interview as part of my doctoral research. Most messages were not read (likely due to message filtering on social media) or not responded to. If people asked questions, I answered them thoroughly; I tried to be as transparent as possible about who I am and my research. I shared my full real name, links to my university profile, and social media accounts (which used my real name as the screen name).

In my initial message, I stated that I was searching for webcam models. I allowed people to self-report that they were webcam models, and I did not ask them to verify by sending a link to their profile. I did this to protect their privacy and identity. Many of the people I spoke with were very concerned about being identified and wanted to participate in the study anonymously.

How people defined being a webcam model differed. Some worked exclusively on platforms designed for webcam models (e.g., Chaturbate, MyFreeCams, and LiveJasmin). In contrast, others performed live-shows one-on-one with clients via non-adult video chat platforms (e.g., Skype, Snapchat). Moreover, most of the people I spoke with were also (formerly) involved in other forms of sex work, such as selling content, phone sex, stripping, and full-service sex work. None of the models I spoke with worked at a webcam studio.[1]

Interviews all took place over video chat platforms. The interviews lasted between 45 minutes and 4.5 hours, with the majority of interviews lasting between 2 and 2.5 hours. A few respondents opted not to turn their cameras on during the interview. I kept my camera on in all but one instance when the respondent specifically requested to speak "on the phone[2]". I thought it was important for respondents to see me so that they could verify my identity and see my facial reactions and body language.[3] Respondents were informed at the beginning of the interview how their data would be used, and that they could discontinue the interview at any time. During the interviews, I also verbalized that it would be okay for the participants to end the interview if they wanted to, even if I had not covered all the topics I wanted to ask them about. However, we continued the interview if they indicated they still had time to speak.

Interviews were semi-structured, and I had broad categories of topics I wanted to speak with respondents about, such as general working experiences, interactions with viewers, the use of social media, online communities, and privacy concerns. However, I also adapted the questions during the interviews based on the respondents' areas of expertise or to reflect their experiences. Some respondents brought up stigma on their own, or I asked direct questions about stigma based on the context of the conversation. In some interviews, I did not ask directly about stigma, but it became visible while analyzing the interviews. Overall, the interviews felt more like conversations. The respondents were very open, and many of them spoke at length without much intervention from me.

It is important to note that almost all of the interviews took place during the height of the COVID-19 pandemic (2020–2021).[4] Some respondents were in lockdown during the interview, and almost everyone had limited social contact and/or limited time spent outside the home. Due to health concerns, I was in a very strict lockdown during the interviews, and sometimes respondents were the only people I had spoken with that day. I believe that this shared experience helped create rapport with many of the respondents.

Respondent demographics

	N
Age	
18–20	1
21–25	8
26–30	9
31–35	1
36–40	2
Older than 41	2
Gender	
Male	3
Female	19[5]
Non-binary	1
Length of time in the industry	
Less than one year	7
1–2 years	9
3–5 years	2
6–10 years	0
10+ years	5
Education (highest level attended)	
Not specified	1
High school	2
Trade school	2
Bachelor's	14
Master's/equivalent	2
PhD	2

The amount of time that respondents worked as webcam models varied. Some did it occasionally for a few hours at a time; others worked full-time or up to 16 hours a day. Some respondents reported their working hours specifically in terms of hours spent live-streaming on a webcam platform. In contrast, others included all the additional time spent advertising, communicating with clients, building social networks, creating content, and other work-related activities. The income of participants was difficult to determine due to factors such as fluctuations in income, being new to the industry and unable to calculate an average, and lumping together income from all sources of adult work. Some participants also did not disclose their income. Most participants (n=13) earned more than $3000 per month, and of those, five earned more than $10,000 per month; one reported over $25,000 per month, and another reported earnings in the "mid six figures annually".

Coding

I thematically coded interview transcripts using ATLAS.ti. I applied codes that described how stigma was experienced by webcam models, how they managed stigma, and factors that shaped how they experienced or managed stigma. Following this, I broke each of these codes into more specific groups to illustrate central themes of how participants managed stigma.

Experiences of stigma

Performers experienced stigma on a personal level. They were also aware of the more wide-spread social stigma attached to sex work, and the negative portrayals of sex work in the media which shape the common discourse about sex work (Weitzer, 2018). They also said that they heard stories of things that had happened to other performers and read news stories about people who had lost their jobs because their OnlyFans account was discovered.

Many participants talked about how they thought through their decision to become a performer in light of the stigma attached to them. When Veronica (30, 11 years)[6] started, she knew that this was a major decision, and if she were going to do it, she would have to go *all in* because her image would be online indefinitely. Other respondents also discussed webcamming and the potential implications with their partners before starting, partly because stigma can be attached to those who affiliate with a stigmatized person (Morrison & Whitehead, 2007; Pryor & Reeder, 2011). Before starting to webcam, Quinn (24, 1 year) talked with her boyfriend about the long-term implications of webcamming, and each of them 'came out' to their friends and family.

Anna also carefully weighed the decision to become a webcam model and felt secure with her choice because her husband supported her.

Anna: So it was after I made that decision that I was comfortable with it and being married helped because I was like, "I'm not scared. As long as my husband doesn't care, I don't care what people say".

(Anna, 28, 1 year)

Katherine (30, a few months) was very aware of the sex work stigma, which shaped her life in her community. She lived in a conservative area, and she had to be extremely secretive about working as a sex worker, or it could jeopardize her other businesses, and her relationships with friends and family.

290

Katherine: I wouldn't be able to run my business here. Essentially, it would just deteriorate. People just make terrible assumptions around sex work and they're like, "Oh, they're on drugs! They're doing this because they're desperate for money!"

(Katherine, 30, a few months)

Social media sites were cited as a major challenge for respondents. Social media is widely used by webcam models to advertise and communicate with clients (Jones, 2020; Stuart, 2022). However, performers were constantly under pressure because of the ever-changing rules on the websites and efforts to remove sex workers from many platforms. Twitter and Reddit were mentioned as more sex worker-friendly sites, but other platforms such as Instagram were known to be very strict about their use by sex workers, and performers were regularly banned or shadow banned[7] from various social media sites. Emma (26, 2 years) described how platform policies were weaponized against her. It became known among people in her hometown that she was working as a webcam model. She said that some of the women she knew were jealous and felt like she was trying to lure their boyfriends, so they reported her posts on Instagram, even though the posts complied with community guidelines. Instagram then flagged Emma's account, and she said this led to her account being constantly under scrutiny from the platform.

The sex work stigma also created problems for models to access banking and payment processors. Many payment processors, such as PayPal or Cash App, explicitly forbid their services from being used for adult services (Beebe, 2022). Webcam models in this study reported that they still used these payment processors but with the knowledge that their accounts could be frozen and they could lose their money (Blunt et al., 2020). Veronica (30, 11 years) talked at length about the challenges faced by adult performers and having access to payment processors.

Veronica: I think that the systemic stigma is a different one than the stigma we face as performers, and I know many performers who have had their bank accounts shut down with no reasoning, with no notice. . . . There's various banks that are particular about that, that always do it. . . . Some days it feels like there's fewer safe spaces for us, and other days it feels like we're making moves forward and it's going to be okay. In the middle of all that, you just kind of juggle and hope for the best. Try to think of what could happen and prevent it before it happens.

(Veronica, 30, 11 years)

Veronica acknowledged that many businesses face similar problems with the banking system and that companies need to "adapt or die". However, she also described the broader systemic issues and how they are influenced by religious organizations that have an outsized influence on laws and policies that impact the adult industry. The refusal of banks and payment processors to work with the adult industry is linked to a stigma against sex work, pressure from outside organizations who conflate all sex work with trafficking or exploitation, and the belief that the adult industry is 'high-risk' (Bernstein, 2018; Cole, 2018a; Stokes, 2021). The adult industry continues monetizing its products by using businesses that act as a middleman to guarantee payments (e.g., CCBill; Epoch) in exchange for a high fee, which cuts into the profits of adult performers (Graver, 2022). Adult platforms are also at constant risk of being demonetized (Cole, 2021, 2022). More broadly, stigma shapes how the adult industry can operate, such as limiting businesses' access to mainstream services, and it shapes the laws which govern the adult industry and the policies on platforms (Beebe, 2022; Stegeman, 2021; Voss, 2012).

Respondents said that they felt that there were ongoing cultural shifts and that digital sex work was becoming more widely known and accepted in culture (see also: van der Nagel, 2021). This shift was linked to online communities of sex workers and other sexually open individuals speaking publicly, and celebrities' mainstreaming of the sex industry and blurring the lines between adult performers and mainstream content. Veronica (30, 11 years) has been in the adult industry for over a decade. She said that she has felt a noticeable shift in stigma due to the rise of OnlyFans.[8]

Veronica: So with the whole rise and trendiness of OnlyFans, we've seen a lot of mainstream Instagram influencers pop in the space, dip their toe in the water. And then we've seen also in the last, you know, maybe three to five years, a lot of sex workers get mainstream brand deals for things on Instagram like Fashion Nova collaborations and stuff. . . . So we're in an exciting time where I think the more that line gets blurred, the more stigma kind of falls off a little bit piece by piece. So I think it's changing, but those things always come at a slow pace.

(Veronica, 30, 11 years)

Blaire (34, 1.5 years) recounted a story of overhearing people at the bar talking about a friend who did OnlyFans.

Blaire: I was out with a friend, like a few weeks ago, and I was just kind of like listening in, eavesdropping like a nosy bitch, let's be honest, and started hearing like, "Oh, she has an OnlyFans." "Yeah? How much money is she making off of that?" "Oh, when did she start it?" Like? Wait a minute, how do you know that she has an OnlyFans? How do you know how much money she's making? How do you know her subscriber count? Like, how do you know this? . . . It's normal. And in just such a weird way, it's part of zeitgeist.

(Blaire, 34, 1.5 years)

Based on their conversation, it was clear to her that it was something normal and socially acceptable in their friend group. However, these changes were not visible to all performers. Whitney (26, 2 years) came from a conservative background, and she spoke extensively about the stigma about sex work and pornography in her social group and where she lived.

Whitney: I think most people . . . don't understand it and are disgusted by it. Same with, you know, anything in the porn industry. And everyone consumes porn, basically everyone. It's very hypocritical. . . . I think that the general vibe in the US is definitely sex-negative. Maybe . . . in modern, like, cities like Austin or Seattle or whatever. Like, there's some communities of sex positivity, but most people just like don't have a lot of sex and judge people who do have a lot of sex and [they] hate porn and hate sex work and think everyone's being sex trafficked, but yet at the same time everyone is, like, addicted to porn.

(Whitney, 26, 2 years)

Despite her currently pessimistic view, Whitney (26, 2 years) had hopes that the culture, laws, and stigma would eventually change with new generations.

Whitney: It's just like all the lawmakers are old, prudish men and women who are terrified of, like, sex and terrified of their own bodies and also religious. So like, yeah, once they die, maybe it'll get better, like, that's all, that's the only hope I have is, like, these old lawmakers dying.

(Whitney, 26, 2 years)

Broadly, the experiences of webcam models that I spoke with show how they experience stigma at a personal and societal level, as well as systemically through the various institutions with which they are forced to interact to do their work.

Stigma management techniques

Information control

Respondents strategically controlled the information they shared with others to mitigate the effect of the occupational stigma associated with webcamming. Unlike other research on sex work, all the respondents in my research were open to at least one person in their life about their work. However, respondents had different levels of openness with people around them and different motivations or triggers for 'coming out'.

Passing and concealment

Sex work is an invisible stigma, meaning that it is a stigma that is not based on visible characteristics, and it is possible to be concealed (Benoit et al., 2020; Koken et al., 2004). The stigmatized person can often decide whether to disclose their stigmatized status. Passing is when a person does not reveal their stigmatized identity, and they *pass* for a member of an unstigmatized group. Deciding whether to share their stigmatized identity can be crucial for information control (Goffman, 1986; Koken, 2012).

Most of the respondents were only open to people in their close groups of friends or family members. Respondents used a variety of cover stories to explain what they did for work. For example, Natalie (24, 3.5 years) told people she was a creative director and model, and Blaire (36, 1.5 years) told people she did content creation and marketing.

Parents and in-laws were the people respondents most commonly concealed their work from. Blake (20, 6 months) was very open with most people in his life about webcamming, except for his parents. He decided not to tell them to protect them and because he did not think they would understand.

Blake: I don't want my parents knowing because they grew up in rural [North America, HD], and they don't quite understand that kind of thing, like even if I did explain it to them in like a proper way, then they don't quite understand it because they're a little bit old school.

(Blake, 20, 6 months)

Unfortunately, due to trying to protect his parents, he could not cam as much as he would have liked to. He could only do it when they were out of town or when he was staying with his friends. These restrictions potentially impacted his ability to be a successful webcam model due to his inability to be online regularly.

Becky (22, 2 months) didn't want to come out to her parents because they would be concerned about her. She knew they loved her unconditionally but would not accept her work and would pressure her to quit.

Becky: [My parents would say, HD] "We will accept you if you find your self-worth and stop doing this." So, it wouldn't be, like, "We, we don't accept [you] anymore." But it's almost like they would treat it as, like, "You're walking down the broken path." . . . Like, "You don't need to be doing this. Like, you have support, like, are we not doing enough for you? Why are you choosing to do something so negative?"

(Becky, 22, 2 months)

Some respondents benefitted from their parents not being tech-savvy. Blaire (34, 1.5 years) told her father that she was a content creator, and since she knew that he would not have the wherewithal to look for her work online, she felt safe.

Doxing, or having one's personal information released online (Cole, 2018b; Jones, 2020; Swords et al., 2021), is a real concern for webcam models as well as other sex workers. Doxing can give people with ill intentions the tools to stalk, blackmail, harass, or physically harm sex workers. It can also result in the sex worker being outed. Given these risks, many respondents went to great lengths to conceal their identity. For example, Samantha (26, 1 year) did not show her face on camera, and she covered any marks that could be identifiable. She knew that if her work was discovered, it would have a very negative impact on her future career in a niche male-dominated STEM field.

One of the 'least out' participants was Vicky (49, 1 year). She was aware that it was inevitable that she would be exposed, and she was prepared for it to happen. However, she was not worried about her friends finding out.

Vicky: I also think that if any of my friends found out and they were, like—I'm going to be 50 years old [in a few months, HD], and I think they'd just be, like, "Really? You go girl!"

(Vicky, 49, 1 year)

She went on to say that because of her age, appearance, and stage of life, she did not feel the same pressures as she expected someone younger would. She took pride in the fact that she was successful as a webcam model.

Vicky: I could just be like "I had cancer and I'm going to go in bed and die", you know? But I didn't. Instead, I'm online and people are paying me!

(Vicky, 49, 1 year)

By concealing their work as webcam models, these respondents could avoid the occupational stigma of webcamming in much of their lives. Respondents were motivated to conceal their work to protect themselves from the stigma and to protect people they cared about from discomfort and vicarious stigma. However, concealing their work came with downsides, such as limiting when they could work, the kind of content they could make, and how much they could advertise. It also led to personal discomfort and exacerbated feelings of shame.

Coming out

Respondents had various reasons for coming out to their friends and family members, and they had different levels of openness with the people in their lives. Coming out can be valuable for sex workers because they no longer have to be secretive about a portion of their life, thus increasing their social support (Lee, 2015). However, it can also negatively affect their relationships (Morrison & Whitehead, 2007).

For some respondents, coming out came with a lot of forethought and consideration of how the information would impact those they cared about. Sophie (23, 3 years) had a brother on the autism spectrum. She talked to him about her work so that he did not find out from someone else, so she could make sure that he knew she was happy and safe.

However, not all respondents had the luxury of planning how to come out to their friends or family. Becky (22, 2 months) didn't intend to come out to her sister about her work. However, one night when she was filming content, her sister urgently needed a ride to the ER. Becky didn't have time to change out her outfit and makeup, so she was forced to explain the situation to her sister on the drive to the hospital.

Becky: But she [my sister, HD] thought it was hilarious. She thought it was so funny because she and I are very open about things like that and so she was just like "Oh my . . ." I think she posted that on her Snapchat story. She was, like, "This is hilarious! . . . What a great sister, like, pausing her OnlyFans shoot to take me to the emergency room!"

(Becky, 22, 2 months)

When Jenna (25, 1 year) started working as a webcam model, she tried to hide it from her family, with whom she did not have a great relationship. However, Jenna felt that keeping it a secret was too much of a burden because she always had to lie.

Jenna: So I told them [my mom and sister, HD]; it was really not pretty. It left me a mess and feeling just awful about myself and took me a long time to get out of that.

(Jenna, 25, 1 year)

However, after some time, Jenna was happy that she was out. She no longer had to expend energy lying about her life, and she could be honest with her family. Jenna intended to be open with her friends and any future romantic partners moving forward as well. It was more important to her to live freely than to try to hide from sex work's occupational stigma. Melanie (26, 2.5 years) shared a similar viewpoint and said she would be open with all potential romantic partners. Melanie felt that it was better to be honest and that it would help weed out people with whom she was not compatible.

From the beginning, Veronica knew that she would have to be open about being a webcam model because everything would always be online, and she knew that there was a strong stigma attached to sex work. She was thankful that she had support from her friends and family from the start.

Veronica: But I just felt like I had the [whore, HD] stigma attached regardless because I'm an attractive woman in society, so I might as well capitalize on it. Seems silly not to. And then I had a really good support system. My boyfriend at the time, I asked him how he felt about me going into webcam, he supported it. And then my mom at the time, she actually picked out my first stage name. She was all for it. She had me, she had my back.

(Veronica, 30, 11 years)

However, Veronica was soon forced to come out completely because a viewer online was threatening her. Her experience demonstrates that some people may be compelled to come out before they want to.

Veronica: There was this guy on cam that was just trolling me so hard. And he actually came into my Twitter DMs and threatened to, you know, dox me and publish my real name and my real location if I didn't give him like all my content now and forever for free. And I was, like, "Mmm . . . it's going to be a hard no. I'm just going to dox myself." And I put my real name out there and I've been [using my real name, HD] ever since.
Hannah: In order to avoid being blackmailed, you just put it out there?
Veronica: I don't play with terrorists.

(Veronica, 30, 11 years)

By associating herself with her real name and being as open as possible, Veronica could take power away from the person threatening her, and anyone else who might try to do this in the future.

Other respondents also said they were open about their work because it gave them a layer of protection against harm from people who wanted to blackmail or dox them. Emma (26, 2 years) said that she felt protected from being blackmailed because most of the people in her life already knew what she was doing and were supportive. Paige (29, 10 years) shared similar sentiments and was completely out to her parents and most other people in her life.

Paige: But my main safety concern is that, like, someone's going to find out who I am and then try to blackmail me by telling my parents. But if my parents already know, I'll be, like, "You're wasting my dad's time. You're not going to get money. My dad already knows what the fuck is going on!"

(Paige, 29, 10 years)

The decision to come out to friends or family was often shaped by the expectation of how they would react. For Paige (29, 10 years), it was an easy decision because her parents both worked in different facets of the sex industry. However, some respondents did not expect that they would receive support from their parents or friends because they had more conservative backgrounds and beliefs, held disparaging ideas about sex work, or did not understand what webcamming was.

Only a handful of respondents were open with people outside their social circles or openly identified as a webcam model. By being honest with people in their immediate social circle, respondents could gain social support, feel less shame, expend less energy lying, and protect themselves from being blackmailed by viewers. However, being open to wider society did not always come with added benefits. There were also many risks associated with it, such as the impact it could have on future careers or being ostracized. It could increase harassment and the associated dangers. Those who were open tended to be very successful career models, and it would have been difficult for them to conceal their work.

Reframing and resistance

Respondents used the stigma management technique of reframing—or putting their work into positive terms—to counteract the stigma associated with them or their work (Benoit et al., 2020; Weitzer, 2018). Many of the performers reported that they earned a good living, especially compared to what they would have earned in other forms of employment. Katherine (30, a few months) said that before doing sex work, she worked multiple jobs and was still barely able to earn enough to support herself. Natalie (24, 3.5 years) shared a similar story. She had worked over 60 hours a week as a bartender but struggled to earn enough.

Natalie: I set up an OnlyFans and I ended up making like I think $10,000 in a day . . . That was like months of work for me that I made in the day. So I was, like, "Yeah, ok, I'm quitting—I'm doing this."

(Natalie, 24, 3.5 years)

The potential income[9] that could be earned while webcamming shaped people's beliefs about the work and their desire to continue working as a webcam model. Whitney (26, 2 years) felt that webcamming was extremely stigmatized and personally had a lot of disparaging beliefs about adult content. However, earning $150 an hour helped her justify her work and reject the uncomfortable feelings. The earning potential also influenced others' perceptions of webcamming. When some of the participants told their friends about how much they earned as webcam models, some of their friends also started doing it.

Favorable working conditions were another reason webcam models cited as a valuable part of their work. Unlike other forms of work, webcam models worked for themselves, and they did not face the same pressures put on them by bosses or hostile working environments.[10] Before webcamming full-time, Vicky (49, 1 year) worked in a high-pressure corporate environment. She described the work environment as abusive. In contrast, the people she spoke with on webcam were pleasant—or she could block them. This gave her a sense of autonomy and power over her working environment and whom she interacted with.

Several respondents said that they liked webcamming because it allowed them to accommodate their physical and mental health challenges.[11][12] The labor market is not designed for people with different physical or mental health needs, which often limits the opportunities for people or makes maintaining employment challenging (Beatty, 2012). There are very few opportunities outside of sex work that come with a similarly high-earning potential and flexible schedule while working a limited number of hours per week (Jones, 2021).

Jenna (25, 1 year) struggled to work at a corporate job and manage her mental health. Webcamming allowed her to work when she wanted and improved her quality of life.

Jenna: I work probably 10–15 hours a week and make about 600, 700 dollars. . . . Yeah, it's awesome. It's like the only time I've been able to, able to put myself first in anything where I can be, like, "Hey, I feel bad today, I don't have to have a panic attack about telling my boss that I am having suicidal thoughts!" [laughing]. Like I can just give myself a day off. And it's really, really, really empowering. I can't imagine—kind of keep thinking about how maybe I'm a little bored you know because I do have that science mind, but I just can't give up the freedom. I love it!

(Jenna, 25, 1 year)

Megan (23, 1 year) reflected on sex work more broadly and how it benefits people from various backgrounds.

Megan: I think a lot of people in the sex work community are in sex work because they need that sort of independence because of like mental health problems and, like, it's very just difficult to have a regular job, and then that gets even more complicated when it's, like, like, women, but even more so POC [people of color, HD] and even more so, like, queer POC; like, there's a lot of abuse that goes on and, like, probably a lot of workplaces and it's just, like, in a lot of ways, sex work is safer.

(Megan, 23, 1 year)

Respondents also described the positive benefits that webcamming had for them on a personal level. Veronica (30, 11 years) spoke at length about webcamming's positive impact on herself and her self-esteem. She went through a difficult phase at the end of high school and dealt with many body image issues. She said that being on webcam for hours a day and receiving a constant stream of positive comments from people helped her change how she viewed herself. Other respondents shared similar stories of how webcamming positively impacted their self-image and improved their mental health. Anna (28, 1 year) went so far as to call her fans her "cheerleaders" and said they gave her a lot of emotional support.

Sexual pleasure was a motivator for a number of respondents to work as webcam performers, and it was cited as one of the benefits of webcamming (Jones, 2020). Sexual pleasure came not only from orgasms[13] but also from the pleasure of being watched, desired, and exploring sexual fantasies. Quinn (24, 1 year) used her adult work to explore and discover new aspects of her sexuality. She enjoyed fulfilling the clients' requests and filming content with new partners with divergent desires. Vicky (49, 1 year) said that she had a long history of having erotic conversations and video chats with people, and she started webcamming when she learned that she could also earn money from it.

Vicky: I was doing it recreationally for a long time, you know, and then, you know, 'cause I was spending so much time on it, like, recently . . . that's when I was, like, "You know, I can charge for this!"

(Vicky, 49, 1 year)

She equated going to work with going to the bar for a fun night.

Vicky: So, like, while other people would be, like, "Oh, it's Friday, let's go to the pub and have a drink." And I don't drink, you know . . . so instead I'm, like, "Well, nobody's here", so instead of me wanting to go out, I want to go onto my camera. So I'm getting dressed up and I feel like I'm going to Cheers, that bar, like, where everybody knows your name.

(Vicky, 49, 1 year)

Vicky enjoyed the process of getting dressed up for her 'night out' and carrying on multiple simultaneous conversations with her viewers. She found pleasure in performing erotically for the viewers and making them feel good about themselves and their sexual desires. She paid specific attention to men to whom she was attracted. To Vicky, webcamming was her job, part of her social life, and a way to express and indulge her sexual desires.

Many respondents highlighted their work's value for viewers, and they felt that webcamming was an important service. For example, Emma (26, 2 years) said that her shows allowed people to explore their fantasies in a safe space, which she believed had positive benefits for their mental health.

Emma: One of the most liberating parts of this job is allowing people to explore parts of their sexuality that they can't normally explore in their normal day-to-day lives. And that's why I really don't like, like, people who look down on others who pay for porn, or . . . pay for cam models. . . . They're given a safe space and an understanding individual to really play out fantasies that they've probably had their entire lives and they've never had an outlet for it. And they finally found somebody that they want to explore that outlet with and I think it's like a really vital part of, like, mental health and being able to, like, like, expressing those feelings and those thoughts.

(Emma, 26, 2 years)

Veronica (30, 11 years) also considered webcam models' work to be therapeutic. She said that webcam models became especially important during the COVID-19 pandemic when people were isolated and working from home or out of work. Many people turned to webcam models during the lockdowns for emotional support (Zane, 2020).

Respondents also highlighted the professionalization of webcamming and the skills required to be successful (Koken et al., 2004; Nayar, 2017; Rodriguez, 2022). Webcamming may be seen as 'easy money' to people outside the industry (van der Nagel, 2021). However, many models put a lot of time and effort into developing a personal brand, advertising, maintaining contact with clients, developing their skills, and planning performances. There is a lot of behind-the-scenes work that takes place to present a so-called "amateur" performance (Nayar, 2017).

Megan: I think I wish people knew that it is, takes a lot of work, and it's not like something you can do without a brain. And it's not just sexuality or, like, flashing; it's really calculated and takes a lot of organization.

(Megan, 23, 1 year)

Respondents spoke about how much time they spent planning new shows and setting up their camming room. Layla (26, 1 month) was part of an online discussion group for cam models, and they frequently shared fun cam show ideas. Jim (71, 30+ years) dedicated much of his time to learning about the adult industry, maintaining connections with people in the industry, developing and marketing content, and attending industry events. Respondents demonstrated that webcamming, to them, was a serious job that required a lot of skill and dedication. These experiences challenge the pervasive belief that sex work is unskilled or a profession that someone would not willingly choose to do.

There are online communities of webcam models and other adult performers who share information about camming amongst themselves and to a wider audience. These communities support one another with their businesses and on a more personal level (Jones, 2020; Sanders et al., 2018; Simpson & Smith, 2021). Some models spent time developing (free) educational material and mentoring (new) models or advising on help forums. The educational material and advice covered many topics, such as structuring shows, interacting with clients, marketing and branding, content creation, and taxes. Others used their online presence to communicate with people outside the adult industry. By being open and vocal about their work in public spaces such as social media, sex workers could counteract the misinformation about their work.

Respondents were aware of the stigma associated with webcamming and sex work more broadly but focused on the positive aspects of the work[14] (Koken et al., 2004). Performers said that webcamming was accessible and accommodating to their physical and mental health challenges, which was not something they found in other forms of employment. Some of the other beneficial factors respondents highlighted were their ability to earn a high income, a flexible working schedule, it boosted their self-esteem, and they felt like they were helping others (Jones, 2020). Models also challenged the stigma associated with camming through professionalizing their work, highlighting the skills required to be successful, and integrating into and supporting the larger community of adult content creators (Jones, 2020; Sanders et al., 2018; Simpson & Smith, 2021).

Limitations

A major limitation of this research is that I could only speak with people willing to talk with me. Most people I contacted did not reply to my messages (over 250 people were contacted). Many people I contacted were skeptical about my intentions and asked me to verify my identity. Understandably, people would be skeptical or cautious about answering a message with a request for an interview from a stranger online. Moreover, sex workers may be unwilling to participate in research due to negative past experiences, distrust of academic research (Stuart, 2022), or concerns about speaking to a researcher from an unfamiliar European university. I tried to combat some of these issues before reaching out to participants by making myself very visible and easy to find on social media.

As this research was exploratory in nature and examined the occupational stigma of webcamming, there were several areas that could not be explored in depth and warrant further research. This chapter only included webcam models from the United States and Canada, which are very specific social and cultural contexts. This research was primarily based on interviews with white or white-presenting cis-gendered women. Other research on sex work and stigma indicates that there may be differences in the working experiences of people from different racial or ethnic backgrounds and of varying gender identities (e.g., Jones, 2021; Koken et al., 2004; Morrison & Whitehead, 2007). Moreover, additional areas of investigation include, for example, the representation of webcamming in the media, other people who work in the adult industry (e.g., studio operators, webcam platform employees), geographical location and local culture, and social connections within the adult industry.

Finally, stigma was not originally the focus of my research, but it was a common topic throughout many of the interviews. These conversations triggered interesting thoughts about the experiences of online sex workers compared to the body of literature on in-person sex workers, and I decided to explore it further for this chapter. Since this was exploratory research, it is not representative of the community of sex workers or online sex workers as a whole. However, it provides an interesting starting point from which to explore this population and these themes further.

Conclusion

In this chapter, I explored webcam models' experiences of stigma and the stigma management techniques they employ. Webcam models I spoke with experienced stigma in various ways, including within their personal relationships, wider society, systemically, and at a legal and policy level. These experiences shaped how they expected to be treated and, in turn, how open they were about their work. To mitigate the impacts of stigma, webcam models used stigma management techniques such as information control and reframing.

All of the respondents in this research were open to at least one person in their life, and many were out to all of their friends and family. By coming out and being honest, webcam models could gain social and emotional support and shed the burden of being *in the closet*. However, few respondents were completely open about being sex workers in their day-to-day lives. There is still a strong stigma associated with sex work, and being a sex worker or a former sex worker can (unfortunately) have consequences for future employment opportunities, relationships, and other aspects of life. Because of the risk of being outed or doxed, webcam models employed various strategies to protect their real identities.

Respondents in this research also managed stigma by reframing their work to challenge or counteract the extent to which they experienced stigma. Some of these methods included focusing on the benefits of webcamming, such as a flexible work schedule, high income, and accessibility for people with different physical and mental health challenges. Respondents also highlighted the positive impact that webcamming had on their emotional well-being and self-image, and the value of the services they provided for the clients (e.g., Adams, 2020; Begum et al., 2013; Benoit et al., 2020; Koken et al., 2004). Reframing and rejection of stereotypes were common stigma management techniques used by sex workers in other studies (Benoit et al., 2020; Koken et al., 2004). In Benoit et al. (2020), sex workers of all types rejected the stigma because sex work provided them with a comfortable life, and they "rejected the notion that sex work was fundamentally different from other jobs". Sex workers also reframed their work as a helping profession that was good for people and provided an important service to society.

Does the online environment mitigate experiences of stigma, or does it create new opportunities for it? I would argue that it does both. Working in an online environment alleviates some of the 'whore stigma' (Pheterson, 1993) attached to webcam models, as they perform a legal form of sex work and do not interact with clients in person. The stigma attached to full-service sex workers is in part linked to a risk of disease and that it is considered immoral, exploitative, or synonymous with human trafficking (Budhwani et al., 2021; Oldenburg et al., 2014; Weitzer, 2007). Many of these risks and the stigma are alleviated by working independently in an online environment.

Webcam models I spoke with were largely accepted by the people in their lives to whom they disclosed their work. They felt that society was becoming more accepting of digital forms of sex work in general. Notably, two respondents I spoke with also did in-person full-service sex work. Both said they were a lot more cautious about disclosing this aspect of their work, highlighting that they felt the stigma attached to in-person work was greater than online sex work.

A notable difference between online and in-person sex workers was their experiences of harassment for being sex workers. Webcam models can block people harassing them in their chat rooms or on social media.[15] However, in-person sex workers do not have the same luxury, and they can face great danger to their physical and mental health due to this harassment and potential violence (Wong et al., 2011).

I would argue that the online domain creates new opportunities for stigmatization. Some forms of sex work can be performed without an online presence or a limited one (e.g., massage parlor, stripping, full-service sex work). Webcamming takes place completely online and includes live-streaming video for hours at a time. Webcam models may also do other forms of digital content creation and use social media. By conducting their work in a digital space, they are at a heightened risk for digital surveillance (Blunt et al., 2020; Fukushima, 2020; Sanders et al., 2018). Online work means that a performer's image is on the Internet, which can lead to greater problems for them in the future, long after they have discontinued their careers, due to stigmas against sex work(ers) and sexuality more broadly. This can be further exacerbated by platforms that record and resell content or users who reupload and distribute content (Cole, 2017; Stuart, 2022). This burden is felt even more by performers with intersecting marginalized identities (Blunt et al., 2020; Blunt & Stardust, 2021; Jones, 2020).

Like other sex workers, stigma shapes the laws and policies which govern the work of webcam models. In the case of brothel workers in Nevada (Blithe & Wolfe, 2017), laws control the movement of sex workers, the space they can operate in, and their behavior while working, while simultaneously prioritizing the interests of business owners and the community. A similar dynamic is observed for sex workers who operate in online spaces. Policies and terms of service (TOS) on platforms are shaped by laws which are often created based on stereotypes and stigma. These laws and policies prioritize the interests of people from certain groups without consideration of the working conditions of sex workers, or they actively work to de-platform and erase sex workers in online spaces (Blunt et al., 2020; Blunt & Stardust, 2021; van der Nagel, 2021).

Unfortunately, there is still a widespread pervasive stigma which can have a negative impact on performers. Though the strength and resilience of sex workers is something to be admired, it is important to move beyond putting the burden on them to 'counteract' or 'manage' stigma and to start to dismantle the wider social structures which create this burden of stigma in the first place (Simpson & Smith, 2021). Moving forward, I hope that laws and society begin to reflect the valuable contributions that these workers make and the importance of the services that they provide.

Notes

1 Webcam models can either work from home using their own equipment or they can work from a place called a webcam studio. Webcam studios typically offer a place to work and the tools needed to livestream (e.g., camera, Internet). They may also offer training, support, and other amenities

such as a gym, hairstylist, and makeup artist. Webcam studios are uncommon in North American and more common in places such as Eastern Europe and South America (Matache, 2018; Franco, 2022).

2   We spoke using a video chat platform that he requested and neither of us turned on our cameras. I met this respondent in person, so he already knew who I was and was comfortable with me.

3   My cat, Mila, was present for many of the interviews. She was frequently a topic of discussion, as were the pets of the respondents. She helped develop rapport with respondents, and comforted a respondent who began to cry. Her commentary can frequently be heard in the recordings of the interviews. Photos of Mila are available @ScreamingMila.

4   1 interview took place in 2019.

5   One participant identified as female but was questioning her gender identity.

6   (Pseudonym, age, reported approximate length of time in the industry).

7   Shadow ban is a term used to describe when a user's account no longer shows up in the search results but they are still able to use or access their account. Others can only find their account if they have a direct link (Cole, 2018b).

8   OnlyFans.com is a subscription-based platform where users pay a monthly fee to access the content created by different content creators, including photos, videos, livestreams, and they can also send direct messages to creators. The platform allows all forms of content but it is primarily used for adult content (van der Nagel, 2021).

9   There are great differences in the amount earned by webcam models, and there are not reliable publicly available statistics on the income of webcam models. In this research, over half of the respondents (n = 13) earned over $3000 per month, and five respondents reported earning over $10,000 per month. A survey completed by ReadySetCam.com found that in 2022, the average webcam model earned $1,043 per week while working 18 hours, and the top earning cam models in the United States earned up to $6,000 per week (Ramer, 2022).

10 Jones (2020, pg. 84) described how webcamming is far from a "feminist, queer, or economic utopia" and that there are problematic aspects of the working environment. However, when compared to other forms of work, there are many aspects of webcamming that make it preferrable (Berg, 2016).

11 Over half of the respondents in this study reported physical or mental health challenges, and a number of them explicitly stated that these were motivating factors for working as a webcam model.

12 Hacking and Hustling found that 50% of online sex workers had a physical or mental health problem which prevented them from participating in the mainstream workforce (as cited in: Blunt et al., 2020).

13 Many of the respondents I spoke with said that they did not have orgasms while working. Their reasons varied from finding it distracting or tiring, to feeling like it impacted their personal sexual life, or just not wanting to. Despite the lack of orgasm, many participants still found their work to be sexually or emotionally pleasurable. Moreover, I feel that it is important to note that orgasms are not essential for pleasurable sex or sexual experiences. I would encourage the reader to explore pleasure-oriented sex rather than goal-oriented sex, and to develop a broader definition of what 'sex' is (e.g., Constantinides et al., 2019; Nagoski, 2015).

14 It must be noted that there are downsides to webcamming, such as stigma, low or inconsistent earnings, harassment from viewers, and the fact it can be physically and mentally exhausting. The respondents that I spoke with were generally very positive about their work and spoke at length about how much they enjoyed it. However, I was only able to speak with performers who were willing to speak with me, and this could mean that those who do not enjoy webcamming as much did not participate in this study. Moreover, respondents could have shaped the information that they shared because they were talking to a researcher, and for myriad other reasons (e.g., Nayar, 2017).

15 It is important to note that blocking users who are harassing or otherwise bothering performers is not always effective. Platforms may have a time-limited ban period, users may create new accounts, or they may contact performers through other means such as social media. Respondents I spoke with did not report harassment or stalking, but it is commonly discussed in other sources as a major risk of being a webcam performer (e.g., Fustich, 2017; Jones, 2020; Sanders et al., 2018).

References

Abel, G. (2011). Different stage, different performance: The protective strategy of role play on emotional health in sex work. *Social Science and Medicine, 72*, 1177–1184. https://doi.org/10.1016/j.socscimed.2011.01.021

Adams, S. (2020). Sex work saved my life. *TSQ: Transgender Studies Quarterly, 7*(2), 272–273. https://doi.org/10.1215/23289252-8143463

Beatty, J. E. (2012). Career barriers experienced by people with chronic illness: A U.S. Study. *Employee Responsibilities and Rights Journal, 24*(2), 91–110. https://doi.org/10.1007/s10672-011-9177-z

Beebe, B. (2022). "Shut up and take my money!": Revenue chokepoints, platform governance, and sex workers' financial exclusion. *International Journal of Gender, Sexuality and Law, 2*(1), 140–170. https://doi.org/10.19164/ijgsl.v2i1.1258

Begum, S., Hocking, J. S., Groves, J., Fairley, C. K., & Keogh, L. A. (2013). Sex workers talk about sex work: Six contradictory characteristics of legalised sex work in Melbourne, Australia. *Culture, Health & Sexuality, 15*(1), 85–100. https://doi.org/10.1080/13691058.2012.743187

Benoit, C., Maurice, R., Abel, G., Smith, M., Jansson, M., Healey, P., & Magnuson, D. (2020). 'I dodged the stigma bullet': Canadian sex workers' situated responses to occupational stigma. *Culture, Health & Sexuality, 22*(1), 81–95. https://doi.org/10.1080/13691058.2019.1576226

Berg, H. (2016). 'A scene is just a marketing tool': Alternative income streams in porn's gig economy. *Porn Studies, 3*(2), 160–174. https://doi.org/10.1080/23268743.2016.1184478

Bernstein, E. (2018). *Brokered Subjects: Sex, Trafficking, and the Politics of Freedom*. University of Chicago Press. Retrieved from https://doi.org/10.7208/chicago/9780226573809.001.0001

Blithe, S. J., & Wolfe, A. W. (2017). Work—Life management in legal prostitution: Stigma and lockdown in Nevada's brothels. *Human Relations, 70*(6), 725–750. https://doi.org/10.1177/0018726716674262

Blunt, D., Coombes, E., Mullin, S., & Wolf, A. (2020). *Posting into the void* (p. 87). Hacking and Hustling. Retrieved from https://hackinghustling.org/wp-content/uploads/2020/09/Posting-Into-the-Void.pdf

Blunt, D., & Stardust, Z. (2021). Automating whorephobia: Sex, technology and the violence of deplatforming: An interview with Hacking//Hustling. *Porn Studies, 8*(4), 350–366. https://doi.org/10.1080/23268743.2021.1947883

Budhwani, H., Hearld, K. R., Butame, S. A., Naar, S., Tapia, L., & Paulino-Ramírez, R. (2021). Transgender women in Dominican Republic: HIV, stigma, substances, and sex work. *AIDS Patient Care and STDs, 35*(12), 488–494. https://doi.org/10.1089/apc.2021.0127

Cole, S. (2017, August 24). A redditor archived nearly 2 million gigabytes of porn to test Amazon's 'unlimited' cloud storage. *Vice.* Retrieved from www.vice.com/en/article/a33j5a/a-reddit-or-archived-nearly-2-million-gigabytes-of-porn-to-test-amazons-unlimited-cloud-storage

Cole, S. (2018a, June 28). Patreon is suspending adult content creators because of its payment partners. *Vice.* Retrieved from www.vice.com/en_us/article/vbqwwj/patreon-suspension-of-adult-content-creators

Cole, S. (2018b, November 16). A New Zealand woman was charged for doxing a sex worker online. *Vice.* Retrieved from www.vice.com/en/article/mbygqp/new-zealand-woman-charged-for-doxing-a-sex-worker-online

Cole, S. (2021, December 2). Another porn site says banks forced it to stop paying sex workers. *Vice.* Retrieved from www.vice.com/en/article/jgmm9g/avn-stars-porn-site-monetized-content-banks

Cole, S. (2022, February 10). Sex workers detail the financial damages of Mastercard's discrimination. *Vice.* Retrieved from www.vice.com/en/article/88gvpk/sex-worker-mastercard-discrimination-survey

Constantinides, D. M., Sennott, S. L., & Chandler, D. (2019). *Sex therapy with erotically marginalized clients: Nine principles of clinical support*. Routledge, Taylor & Francis Group.

Corrigan, P. W., & Watson, A. C. (2002). Understanding the impact of stigma on people with mental illness. *World Psychiatry: Official Journal of the World Psychiatric Association (WPA), 1*(1), 16–20.

DeLacey, H. (2022). A critical analysis of the enactment of the allow states and victims to fight online sex trafficking act of 2018. *International Journal of Gender, Sexuality and Law, 2*(1), 100–139. https://doi.org/10.19164/ijgsl.v2i1.1257

Desyllas, M. C. (2013). Representations of sex workers' needs and aspirations: A case for arts-based research. *Sexualities, 16*(7), 772–787. https://doi.org/10.1177/1363460713497214

Franco, L. (2022, May 18). Colombia's "camgirls" slowly start to break taboos. *El País*. Retrieved from https://english.elpais.com/society/2022-05-18/profession-webcammer.html#

Fukushima, A. (2020). In: The role of technology in human trafficking and anti-trafficking. *Global Alliance against Trafficking in Women*. Retrieved November 11, 2022, from www.youtube.com/watch?v=uvAbn1WwB0M&feature=youtu.be

Fustich, K. (2017, November 15). *The internet is leaving cam girls vulnerable*. Retrieved August 28, 2020, from www.dailydot.com/irl/cam-girls-vulnerable/

Goffman, E. (1986). *Stigma: Notes on the management of spoiled identity* (1st Touchstone ed). Simon & Schuster.

Graver, R. (2022, April 25). Why banks and payment processors shun perfectly legal businesses. *Coindesk*. Retrieved August 28, 2020, from www.coindesk.com/layer2/paymentsweek/2022/04/25/why-banks-and-payment-processors-shun-perfectly-legal-businesses/

Ham, J., & Gerard, A. (2014). Strategic in/visibility: Does agency make sex workers invisible? *Criminology & Criminal Justice*, 14(3), 298–313. https://doi.org/10.1177/1748895813500154

Herrmann, T. (2022). Colleagues, councils, and club owners: The materialisation of the whorearchy inside British strip clubs. In T. Sanders, K. McGarry, & P. Ryan (Eds.), *Sex work, labour and relations* (pp. 73–96). Springer International Publishing. Retrieved from https://doi.org/10.1007/978-3-031-04605-6_4

Jiao, S., & Bungay, V. (2019). Intersections of stigma, mental health, and sex work: How Canadian men engaged in sex work navigate and resist stigma to protect their mental health. *The Journal of Sex Research*, 56(4–5), 641–649. https://doi.org/10.1080/00224499.2018.1459446

Jones, A. (2020). *Camming: Money, power, and pleasure in the sex work industry*. New York University Press. Retrieved from https://doi.org/10.18574/nyu/9781479842964.001.0001

Jones, A. (2021). Cumming to a screen near you: Transmasculine and non-binary people in the camming industry. *Porn Studies*, 8(2), 239–254. https://doi.org/10.1080/23268743.2020.1757498

Knox, B. (2014, July 2). Tearing down the whorearchy from the inside. *Jezebel*. Retrieved August 30, 2020, from https://jezebel.com/tearing-down-the-whorearchy-from-the-inside-1596459558

Koken, J. A. (2012). Independent female escort's strategies for coping with sex work related stigma. *Sexuality & Culture*, 16(3), 209–229. https://doi.org/10.1007/s12119-011-9120-3

Koken, J. A., Bimbi, D. S., Parsons, J. T., & Halkitis, P. N. (2004). The experience of stigma in the lives of male internet escorts. *Journal of Psychology & Human Sexuality*, 16(1), 13–32. https://doi.org/10.1300/J056v16n01_02

Krüsi, A., Kerr, T., Taylor, C., Rhodes, T., & Shannon, K. (2016). 'They won't change it back in their heads that we're trash': The intersection of sex work-related stigma and evolving policing strategies. *Sociology of Health & Illness*, 38(7), 1137–1150. https://doi.org/10.1111/1467-9566.12436

Lee, J. (Ed.). (2015). *Coming out like a porn star: Essays on pornography, protection, and privacy*. ThreeL Media.

Link, B. G., & Phelan, J. C. (2001). Conceptualizing stigma. *Annual Review of Sociology*, 27(1), 363–385. https://doi.org/10.1146/annurev.soc.27.1.363

Matache, S. (2018, June 15). Inside the studios for Romania's booming sex cam industry. *Vice*. Retrieved from https://www.vice.com/en/article/3k4ymn/inside-the-studios-for-romanias-booming-sex-cam-industry

McNeill, Maggie. (2012, May 10). Whorearchy. *The Honest Courtesan*. Retrieved June 20, 2022, from https://maggiemcneill.com/2012/05/10/whorearchy/

Morrison, T. G., & Whitehead, B. W. (2005). Strategies of stigma resistance among Canadian gay-identified sex workers. *Journal of Psychology & Human Sexuality*, 17(1–2), 169–179. https://doi.org/10.1300/J056v17n01_10

Morrison, T. G., & Whitehead, B. W. (2007). "Nobody's ever going to make a fag *Pretty Woman*: Stigma awareness and the putative effects of stigma among a sample of canadian male sex workers. *Journal of Homosexuality*, 53(1–2), 201–217. https://doi.org/10.1300/J082v53n01_09

Musto, J., Fehrenbacher, A. E., Hoefinger, H., Mai, N., Macioti, P. G., Bennachie, C., Giametta, C., & D'Adamo, K. (2021). Anti-trafficking in the time of FOSTA/SESTA: Networked moral gentrification and sexual humanitarian creep. *Social Sciences*, 10(2), 58. https://doi.org/10.3390/socsci10020058

Nagoski, E. (2015). *Come as you are: The surprising new science that will transform your sex life*. Simon & Schuster Paperbacks.

Nayar, K. I. (2017). Working it: The professionalization of amateurism in digital adult entertainment. *Feminist Media Studies*, *17*(3), 473–488. https://doi.org/10.1080/14680777.2017.1303622

Nencel, L., Bjønness, J., & Skilbrei, M.-L. (2021). Reconfiguring stigma in sex work studies and beyond. In J. Bjønness, L. Nencel, & M.-L. Skilbrei (Eds.), *Reconfiguring stigma in studies of sex for sale* (1st ed., pp. 1–16). Routledge. Retrieved from https://doi.org/10.4324/9780429464805-1

Oldenburg, C. E., Biello, K. B., Colby, D., Closson, E. F., Mai, T., Nguyen, T., Nguyen, N. A., & Mimiaga, M. J. (2014). Stigma related to sex work among men who engage in transactional sex with men in Ho Chi Minh City, Vietnam. *International Journal of Public Health*, *59*(5), 833–840. https://doi.org/10.1007/s00038-014-0562-x

Parreira, C. (2021). The lady and the Tramp. Management of stigma in the Nevada Brothel. In J. Bjønness, L. Nencel, & M.-L. Skilbrei (Eds.), *Reconfiguring Stigma in Studies of Sex for Sale* (1st ed., pp. 169–184). Routledge. Retrieved from https://doi.org/10.4324/9780429464805-1

Pheterson, G. (1993). The whore stigma: Female dishonor and male unworthiness. *Social Text*, *37*, 39. https://doi.org/10.2307/466259

Pinsky, D., & Levey, T. G. (2015). 'A world turned upside down': Emotional labour and the professional dominatrix. *Sexualities*, *18*(4), 438–458. https://doi.org/10.1177/1363460714550904

Pitcher, J. (2015). Sex work and modes of self-employment in the informal economy: Diverse business practices and constraints to effective working. *Social Policy and Society*, *14*(1), 113–123. https://doi.org/10.1017/S1474746414000426

Pryor, J. B., & Reeder, G. D. (2011). HIV-related stigma. In *HIV/AIDS in the Post-HAART Era: Manifestations, treatment and epidemiology* (pp. 790–806). PMPH-USA.

Quinn, D. M., & Chaudoir, S. R. (2009). Living with a concealable stigmatized identity: The impact of anticipated stigma, centrality, salience, and cultural stigma on psychological distress and health. *Journal of Personality and Social Psychology*, *97*(4), 634–651. https://doi.org/10.1037/a0015815

Ramer, J. (2022, May 2). How much do cam girls make? (2022 Cam girl salary report). *Ready Set Cam*. Retrieved August 28, 2020, from https://readysetcam.com/blogs/camming-101/how-much-do-cam-girls-make

Rodriguez, T. (2022). *Taboo to trendy: How is onlyfans breaking boundaries and creating narratives*. Southeastern Louisiana University. Retrieved from www.proquest.com/docview/2658639313?pq-origsite=gscholar&fromopenview=true. Retrieved: 30/09/2020.

Sallmann, J. (2010). Living with stigma: Women's experiences of prostitution and substance use. *Affilia*, *25*(2), 146–159. https://doi.org/10.1177/0886109910364362

Sanders, T. (2005). "It's just acting": Sex workers' strategies for capitalizing on sexuality. *Gender, Work and Organization*, *12*(4), 319–342. https://doi.org/10.1111/j.1468-0432.2005.00276.x

Sanders, T., Brents, B. G., & Wakefield, C. (2020). *Paying for sex in a digital age: US and UK perspectives* (1st ed.). Routledge. Retrieved from https://doi.org/10.4324/9780429454370

Sanders, T., Scoular, J., Campbell, R., Pitcher, J., & Cunningham, S. (2018). *Internet sex work*. Springer International Publishing. Retrieved from https://doi.org/10.1007/978-3-319-65630-4

Scortino, K. (2016, May 23). Sex worker and activist, Tilly Lawless, explains the whorearchy. *Slutever*. Retrieved from https://slutever.com/sex-worker-tilly-lawless-interview/. Retrieved: 20/03/2022.

Senft, T. M. (2008). *Camgirls: Celebrity and community in the age of social networks*. Lang.

Simpson, J., & Smith, C. (2021). Students, sex work and negotiations of stigma in the UK and Australia. *Sexualities*, *24*(3), 474–490. https://doi.org/10.1177/1363460720922733

Stegeman, H. M. (2021). Regulating and representing camming: Strict limits on acceptable content on webcam sex platforms. *New Media & Society*, 146144482110591. https://doi.org/10.1177/14614448211059117

Stokes, R. (2021, September 21). How banks are controlling your wanks. *Vice*. Retrieved March 3, 2022, from www.vice.com/en/article/v7eaw4/banks-influence-on-sex-life.

Stuart, R. (2022). Webcam performers resisting social harms: "You're on the web masturbating . . . it's just about minimising the footprint." *International Journal of Gender, Sexuality and Law*, *2*(1), 171–198. https://doi.org/10.19164/ijgsl.v2i1.1259

Swords, J., Laing, M., & Cook, I. R. (2021). Platforms, sex work and their interconnectedness. *Sexualities*, 13634607211023013. https://doi.org/10.1177/13634607211023013

Toubiana, M., & Ruebottom, T. (2022). Stigma hierarchies: The internal dynamics of stigmatization in the sex work occupation. *Administrative Science Quarterly*, *67*(2), 515–552. https://doi.org/10.1177/00018392221075344

van der Nagel, E. (2021). Competing platform imaginaries of NSFW content creation on OnlyFans. *Porn Studies*, *8*(4), 394–410. https://doi.org/10.1080/23268743.2021.1974927

Voss, G. (2012). 'Treating it as a normal business': Researching the pornography industry. *Sexualities*, *15*(3–4), 391–410. https://doi.org/10.1177/1363460712439650

Weitzer, R. (2007). The social construction of sex trafficking: Ideology and institutionalization of a moral crusade. *Politics & Society*, *35*(3), 447–475. https://doi.org/10.1177/0032329207304319

Weitzer, R. (2009). Sociology of sex work. *Annual Review of Sociology*, *35*(1), 213–234. https://doi.org/10.1146/annurev-soc-070308-120025

Weitzer, R. (2018). Resistance to sex work stigma. *Sexualities*, *21*(5–6), 717–729. https://doi.org/10.1177/1363460716684509

Wong, W. C. W., Holroyd, E., & Bingham, A. (2011). Stigma and sex work from the perspective of female sex workers in Hong Kong: Stigma and female sex workers in Hong Kong. *Sociology of Health & Illness*, *33*(1), 50–65. https://doi.org/10.1111/j.1467-9566.2010.01276.x

Zane, Z. (2020). What it's like to be a cam girl when everyone's self-isolating. *Men's Health*. Retrieved March 06, 2022, from www.menshealth.com/sex-women/a31741068/cam-girls-social-distancing-coronavirus-covid-19/

17

A SENTIMENT ANALYSIS OF MEN'S COMMENTS ON A SEX WORK FORUM

Roderick S. Graham

Introduction

In the United States, there is an ongoing debate about legalizing sex work. On one hand, many groups in society see sex work as an inherently exploitative, negative element in society and want the practice to remain prohibited. Sex work is routinely policed by local law enforcement as a quality-of-life issue (Cohen, 2019). Additionally, links have been made by organizations and scholars between the presence of sex work and sex trafficking (Gould, 2014; Matthews, 2015; Morselli & Savoie-Gargiso, 2014). As such, both formal law enforcement and non-profit agencies have invested heavily in the policing of sex work. On the other hand, sex workers' rights organizations are advocating for the legalization of sex work. One argument is that legalization or decriminalization protects women from abuse by allowing sex workers to report violence from clients and others looking to take advantage of a marginalized group (Baratosy & Wendt, 2017; Shaver et al., 2011). Another is that legalization will enable populations of women to pursue meaningful careers in sex work. This argument is gaining currency as more middle-class white women are entering sex work (Bernstein, 2007).

As sex work advocacy grows, legislators and voters will need to evaluate the potential impacts of its legalization. One possible negative impact is men's views of women. Paralleling a pornography consumption argument, some groups in society believe the availability and visibility of sex work will lead to more men objectifying women and committing acts of sexual violence (Peter & Valkenburg, 2009; Willis et al., 2022).

This research addresses this argument. One way of doing this is to explore spaces where sex work is currently legal and use those insights to help us understand what *may* happen under a similar regulatory regime in the United States. The current research is grounded in this reasoning. The United Kingdom has a regulatory regime in which sex work is legal (however, many ancillary activities that make the sale of sex possible, such as advertising services or owning a brothel, are prohibited.) Given the cultural similarities between the US and the UK, studying the sentiments of men in London may provide a window into how men perceive sex work in the United States. A sex worker review forum entitled (to be discussed in more detail in the following) called *International Sex Guide* provides that opportunity.

DOI: 10.4324/9781003277675-20

Theoretical overview

Hegemonic masculinity

How can we make sense theoretically of sentiments expressed by men on an online sex work forum?

One approach is Connell's hegemonic masculinity (Campos et al., 2020; Connell, 2012; Connell, 2005; Connell & Messerschmidt, 2005; Demetriou, 2001; Wedgwood, 2009; Yang, 2020). Hegemonic masculinity refers to the set of gendered behaviors that embody "the currently most honored way of being a man, it require[s] all other men to position themselves in relation to it, and it ideologically legitimate[s] the global subordination of women to men." (Connell & Messerschmidt, 2005, p. 832).

What differentiates hegemonic masculinity is not the number of people who perform these behaviors but its idealized status—it is the most valued and exalted form of masculinity. In other words, hegemonic masculinity is not normal, but it is normative. Connell argues that there is a hierarchy of masculinities, with hegemonic masculinity placed at the apex. Other expressions of masculinities are less valued. The practices of effeminate men, gay men, and working-class men, are "subordinated masculinities", and the practices of racial minorities are "marginalized masculinities". Nevertheless, masculinities from hegemonic to marginalized are understood to be in contradistinction and superior to femininities. While most men do not embody the ideals of hegemonic masculinity, they accrue a "patriarchal dividend" as a result of female subordination (Yang, 2020).

Connell and her frequent collaborator Messerschmidt have described a fluid, multilevel process that can only be understood within a historical context. Types of hegemonic masculinity are rooted in a historical and social context—what is hegemonic today may not have been so yesterday; what is hegemonic in a particular corporation in Peru is different than on a soccer pitch in Manchester. This complexity can be understood as variations on a singular theme of "heterosexual 'play boy', stoic, competitive, dominant, aggressive, risk-taker, independent, physically strong and invincible, capable of overpowering women and other men" (Campos et al., 2020, p. 1844). Moreover, there is an interplay between masculinities at the local, regional, and global levels—again, along variations of a theme. A male actor can be the embodiment of hegemonic masculinity at a regional level, such as a popular male Nollywood (Nigerian Hollywood) actor. This actor then becomes a reference point for men locally throughout the region.

It is this multilevel fluidity that provides an entry point into the current study. The sentiments expressed in an online forum are not random data points or idiosyncrasies. The sentiments expressed on a discussion forum are a combination of global and regional masculinities and the unique, context-dependent masculine expressions that arise through repeated interactions in a space devoted to the pursuit of sex workers in London. The forum, then, should have variations on a theme of hegemonic masculinity as it is embedded in global and regional contexts, yet have unique expressions of masculinity befitting its environment and subject matter.

Sex work research and male clients

Women providing sexual services for men has traditionally been the locus of academic inquiry into sex work. In recent decades, there has been increased interest in understanding the male clients (Birch et al., 2017; Brooks-Gordon, 2010; Jones & Hannem, 2018;

Joseph & Black, 2012; Kong, 2016; Milrod & Monto, 2017). Exploring this research will provide key context moving forward. Specifically, the insights from this particular study can be compared with the themes from previous research on male clients. This section is focused on two main themes from this literature—the complexity of masculine expression and the desire for intimacy.

The first theme is the acknowledgment of the complexity of masculinity present in sex work encounters. Scholars have found that the motivations for procuring a prostitute are varied and multilayered. There may be a stereotype that men who seek prostitutes are seeking an experience in which they get to display their "manliness" and treat women as sexual objects. These tendencies would suggest hegemonic masculine traits—traits that increase the inequalities between men and women. However, the motivations for seeking a prostitute are varied. For example, Kong (2016) argued that men seeing sex workers in Hong Kong "can be understood as an escape and resistance to the normative and hegemonic model of companionate sexuality" (p. 105). Kong theorized the procuring of sex work, as a type of "edge work", voluntary high-risk and thrilling activities. As hegemonic masculinity is historically situated, Kong argues that the procuring of sex workers is a resistance to the dominant companionate love model idealized in Hong Kong society.

Joseph and Black (2012), using survey data of male clients of prostitutes, identify and explore two types of masculine attitudes. One type of masculinity they identify is a "consumer" masculinity. Men who typify this category are looking for a sexual release with a prostitute and are not interested in a relationship. A second type are men who exhibit "fragile" masculinities. These men feel awkward and unattractive around women and have a history of rejection. Joseph and Black argue that fragile masculinities are potentially dangerous. Men with these attitudes are using prostitution to enact domination over women. Moreover, these men are more likely to accept rape myths and have committed sexual assault. Joseph and Black's research reveals a complexity in the relationship between male clients and sex workers—supporting the arguments of some feminists who believe prostitution is inherently sexist as it reduces women to sexual objects, and sex workers who believe prostitution is a commercial act that benefits provider and client.

A second theme is the prevalence of emotional intimacy in client-prostitute relations. This is somewhat related to the first theme, in that a variation of masculinity is the seeking of emotional support, and not merely the display of sexual dominance. Scholars are finding that the seeking of intimacy is becoming a major aspect of the sex work experience. Men are looking for more than a simple physical activity; they're looking for a multifaceted experience that includes socializing and sharing. Sanders (2008) used interviews with clients to argue that sex worker clients use traditional scripts of romance and courtship in the process of becoming a "regular" to one sex worker. Meanwhile, Milrod and Monto (2017) used a questionnaire of older male clients (60–84) to examine patterns of buying sex work within this demographic. They found that many older clients sought out an all-time favorite provider, and that contrary to prior studies, they saw an increase in the frequency of purchasing sexual activities with age.

Similarly, Jones and Hannem (2018), using interviews with clients of escorts, developed a four-category typology of regulars, hybrids, searchers, and industry insiders. The key insight from these authors is the integration of an intimacy component, where some clients resist seeking sexual variety and instead focus on developing emotional bonds. For example, a "regular" seeks out the same client and develops courting rituals similar to a regular relationship, whereas a "a searcher" is someone needing intimacy who has yet to find the right escort.

In an analysis of interviews done with male clients of prostitutes, Birch et al. (2017) identified three themes. One theme, which the authors link to hegemonic masculinity, is of a man needing the services of a prostitute because they are not getting their sexual needs met elsewhere. When this attitude is employed by first-time customers, the purchase is linked to "building confidence" for future sexual activities. Two other themes emerged, both of which the authors linked to subordinate masculinities. A second theme was seeking the intimacy of a romantic relationship. Men were attending to their emotional needs by procuring a prostitute and treating the prostitute as they would an intimate partner. A third theme is buying this intimacy. These men needed emotional support but understood the intimacy they were getting was a commodity.

Bernstein (2007), in her work on middle-class women sex workers, notes that the dynamics of their profession create situations where intimacy is integral to the process. Unlike streetwalkers whose labor is for a specific act that may take 15 minutes, the sex workers she interviewed worked by the hour. This hour is meant to be an "experience" for the client, filled with either manufactured or real intimacy.

The research on male clients juxtaposed with the theoretical formulations of hegemonic masculinity presents a few conclusions relevant for the current research. Granting that hegemonic masculinity is normative but not normal, one would expect a diversity of masculinities. For this same reason, a desire for intimacy does not fit with the idealized versions of manhood but are nonetheless present.

Research questions

Will we see these themes replicated on the International Sex Guide website? On one hand, the anonymity of a website may allow men to avoid some of the normative influences of hegemonic masculinity and express masculinity in more varied ways. On the other hand, a space designed for the procurement of sexual services and reviews of those services may foster a level of objectification that reproduces at the least hegemonic practices of sexual domination, and at worst toxic practices supporting sexual violence. The two questions asked in this study are:

1. *What sentiments are expressed by men in an online sex work forum?* Are users speaking positively or negatively about their experiences with sex workers? What are the common emotions expressed?
2. *Have these sentiments changed over time?* A snapshot of sentiments in a narrow time frame may not provide an accurate picture of the general sentiment on the forum. Positive or negative sentiments could change over time.

Data

The space under consideration is the "International Sex Guide". The International Sex Guide is a website for individuals looking for reviews about sex workers and suggestions for where and how to find them. Additionally, users report their experiences in specific places with specific sex workers. The site is organized by geographic area, with separate forums dedicated to a region, country, or large city. The London thread is the focus of the research. The London thread of the "International Sex Guide" has been in operation since 2002 and is still active at the time of this writing. This extended time frame provides a unique opportunity to explore changes over time.

What is sentiment analysis and why use it?

Sentiment analysis is a form of natural language processing, the branch of artificial intelligence focused on using computers to understand human language. Sentiment analysis is also called opinion mining. The method is still relatively new, but examples are available in several disciplines (Burnap & Williams, 2015; Compagner et al., 2021; Udanor & Anyanwu, 2019). Because it is relatively new, a brief discussion is in order. For a more in-depth analysis, see Liu (2012).

A sentiment analysis extracts and quantifies the emotional polarity from a text. The unit of analysis can be a set of words, sentences, blocks of text such as tweets or posts online, or documents. As an automated process that attempts to quantify emotion, sentiment analysis is most applicable to extensive text collections such as thousands of tweets or customer reviews. It is also well suited for providing answers that need to be quantitative, such as comparing the degree of like or dislike or the change in sentiment over time.

The process of sentiment analysis is relatively straightforward. The text to be analyzed is called a corpus. The algorithms that take a corpus as input and produce a numerical value as output can be called an extraction method. There are several extraction methods. However, the basic process is similar for all. A corpus is compared to a dictionary of words, called a lexicon. The lexicon is composed of words that are associated with emotional states (e.g., "dejected", "prosperous", "stimulating") that have been given a numerical value of positive or negative. Dejected is a negative word and will be given a value less than zero, while prosperous and stimulating would be given a value greater than 1. Some lexicons also score words by specific emotions such as anger, disgust, joy, and trust. These scores are then used to generate an overall measure of sentiment for the unit of analysis—the sentence, the tweet, the entire document. In the simplest sense, words are counted, and if the number of negative words outnumbers the number of positive words, then the sentence or document is seen as some degree of positive.

Sentiment analysis is well suited to providing insight into sex work. There are at least two reasons for this. First, as the amount of data increases, so does the value of using a computer-automated process. How much time does a qualitative researcher have to invest in reading and evaluating the comments on a discussion forum of upwards of 15,000 posts and 90,000 lines of text? Or the 85,000 tweets that may be associated with a given hashtag during a month? One way around this is to select a sample from the universe of posts. However, given a standard of 10% for a representative sample, the sample may still not be small enough for intensive qualitative analysis. Sentiment analysis allows a researcher to make some sense of large collections of data, after which more in-depth analysis can be done.

Second, sex work is *work*, in which ultimately a service is provided (Lucas, 2005; Robertson et al., 2014; West & Austrin, 2005). Sociological studies have traditionally focused more on the actors who are a part of the buying and selling of this product. Some scholars may even object to framing sex work as a service, as they may see this as dehumanizing (Gutiérrez, 2014). However, the individuals in the scene—the clients and the customers—understand sex work primarily as a type of business transaction. If we understand sex work as a service, then sentiment analysis becomes more appropriate as we want to know the opinions about this service. These opinions can be used by groups working closely with this population—scholar-activists, policymakers, law enforcement, and interest groups.

Data

Data was collected from a website entitled *International Sex Guide*. The *International Sex Guide* hosts forums that allow users to ask and answer questions about the sex work scene of most major metropolitan areas of the world. For example, one can click on the forum link for "India" and will be presented with a series of India-related threads, including "Calcutta", "Bangalore", and "A Photo Guide [of Indian Escorts]".

The thread of focus was the London thread in the United Kingdom Forum, hereafter called *London International*. Major conversational themes include asking where one can find sex workers, how to avoid scams, and the prices of services. A significant number of conversations also took the form of field reports, where a client discusses their experiences. These experiences often detailed the process of searching for sex workers, negotiating payment, and the graphic details of the sex act.

Web crawling software was used to collect posts from *London International* and place them into a data frame for analysis. A sample of the most important elements of the data frame is presented in Table 17.1. For this study, the focus is on the data in the "Post Reply" column. Replies instead of original posts are used because there is always a unique entry in each row. The text in the "Post Reply" column ranges from short phrases to entries several paragraphs long. In total, there are 6971 post replies from 5/16/2002 until 8/2/2020. The units of analyses are the post replies.

Methods

Data will be analyzed using sentiment analysis. Sentiment analysis is a form of natural language processing, the branch of artificial intelligence focused on using computers to understand human language. Sentiment analysis is also called opinion mining. The method is still relatively new, but examples are available in several disciplines (Burnap & Williams, 2015; Compagner et al., 2021; Udanor & Anyanwu, 2019), often where scholars want to understand customer's views and attitudes about a service. For an in-depth analysis, see (Liu, 2012).

Sentiment analysis is well suited to providing insight into sex work. There are at least two reasons for this. First, sentiment analysis allows a researcher to make some sense of

Table 17.1 Sample elements scraped from London International

Post Number	Title of Post	Date	Username for Post Reply	Post Reply	Username for Original Post Message	Original Post Message
1	Title	08-10-19, 14:09	User3	Reply 4	User Y	Original 2
2	Title	08-09-19, 11:45	User2	Reply 3	User Y	Original 2
3	Title	08-05-19, 06:01	User2	Reply 2	User X	Original 1
4	Title	08-05-19, 03:45	User1	Reply 1	User X	Original 1

large collections of data, after which more in-depth analysis can be done. Second, sex work is ultimately transactional—a service is being provided (Lucas, 2005; Robertson et al., 2014; West & Austrin, 2005). Some scholars may object to framing sex work as a service, as they may see this as dehumanizing (Gutiérrez, 2014). However, if we understand sex work as a service, then sentiment analysis becomes more appropriate as we want to know the opinions about this service.

This study used the R statistical program and the Syuzhet sentiment analysis package (Jockers, 2020). The Syuzhet package provides the researcher with four different extraction methods—Syuzhet, Afinn, Bing, and NRC. Each method uses a different lexicon and algorithm for computing sentiments. The 6971 post replies from *London International* will be analyzed using all four of these methods. Using a variety of methods is a way to cross-validate findings and draw more reliable conclusions.

Another approach taken to validity, paralleling face validity, is to compare the sentiment scores from *London International* to two well-known documents—the American Declaration of Independence and the "I Have a Dream" speech by Martin Luther King, Jr. in 1963. These two documents will be analyzed at the sentence level, with the Declaration of Independence having an N = 34 and the "I Have a Dream Speech" having an N = 84. This is a novel approach, but the lack of emotion in the Declaration of Independence and the well-known crescendo of emotion evidenced in the "I Have a Dream" speech allow us to judge the validity of the four extraction methods. The sentiment scores computed should mirror our expectations of these two documents.

Results

Descriptive statistics

Table 17.2 shows the most frequent terms from users on *London International*. This frequency distribution describes a corpus of text that focused on finding sex workers. Top words include "good", "time", "great", "hour", and "massage." On the one hand, this is expected, as it is the express purpose of *London International*. On the other hand, one can imagine many negative scenarios that would have been reflected in the conversations in the forum. If men were frequently posting negative comments about sex workers, top words may have included insults about women's intelligence, personality, or references disparaging their bodies. If men were frequently talking negatively about the process of procuring sex work, top words may have included words connoting fraud or a low quality of service. Negative conversations and the words used in them are undoubtedly a part of *London International*, and a qualitative study could tease these out. But at a macro level, these words are too infrequent to appear in a frequency distribution.

What sentiments are expressed by men in an online sex work forum?

The median and mean sentiment scores for the *London International* corpus, using all extraction methods, are positive. Context can be gained by comparing sentiment scores across different corpora. As scored by the four extraction methods, the Declaration of Independence is a neutral document, with little emotion. Median sentence scores hover around 0. Two methods produce scores precisely at 0 (Syuzhet and Bing), while the Afinn method

Table 17.2 Most frequent words* from London International**

	Word	Frequency		Word	Frequency		Word	Frequency
1	one	3131	21	even	1082	41	anyone	862
2	good	2950	22	many	1082	42	way	856
3	time	2677	23	Soho	1068	43	try	851
4	like	2617	24	got	1064	44	say	840
5	get	2375	25	experience	1062	45	another	839
6	don't	1574	26	first	1056	46	agency	836
7	know	1504	27	looking	1043	47	look	824
8	great	1417	28	around	1012	48	went	817
9	hour	1399	29	thanks	990	49	lot	771
10	back	1376	30	best	948	50	day	743
11	massage	1363	31	bit	946			
12	really	1326	32	I've	946			
13	find	1325	33	street	944			
14	much	1224	34	service	941			
15	see	1202	35	two	913			
16	nice	1159	36	guys	909			
17	well	1157	37	now	908			
18	place	1129	38	said	906			
19	sex	1123	39	minutes	895			
20	think	1109	40	going	870			

* Some words were removed from this list because they were very frequent and/or did not add to the overall understanding ("http", "https", "can", "just", "want", "will", "also", "London", "girl", "girls").

**Total count for all words in the corpus = 25185

produces a score of –1, and NRC produces a score of 1. Similarly, mean scores are a little above 0 (Syuzhet and NRC) or below 0 (Bing and Afinn). Comparing the Declaration of Independence with *London International* places into sharp relief the polarity differences, with the former being neutral and the latter being positive.

Comparing scores from the "I Have a Dream" speech provides more context. The overall sentiment in King's speech is measured consistently as positive. Looking at just mean scores, all four measures are consistently above 0. Similarly, three of the four median scores are above 0, with only the Bing method producing a neutral score. We can say that the emotional sentiment of the "I Have a Dream" speech is overall positive, but not as positive as *London International*.

The measures for "I Have a Dream" and the Declaration of Independence help demonstrate to some extent how positive the comments are on *London International* by comparing the same corpus across the same extraction method. For example, for the Syuzhet extraction method, the mean sentence sentiment score in the Declaration of Independence is 0.21. The score is more than twice as high for the "I Have a Dream Speech" at 0.52. Meanwhile, the difference between the "I Have a Dream Speech" and *London International* is fivefold. This magnitude of difference is paralleled across mean and medians for all four extraction methods.

Table 17.3 Sentiment analysis comparisons using different extraction methods*

Extraction Method	Declaration of Independence		"I Have A Dream"		London International	
	Median	Mean	Median	Mean	Median	Mean
Syuzhet	0	0.21	0.5	0.52	1.65	2.55
Bing	0	–0.18	0	0.33	1	2.14
Afinn	–1	–0.35	1	1.14	3	5.07
NRC	1	0.79	1	0.58	2	2.92

*Unit of analysis was the sentence for Declaration of Independence (N = 34) and the I Have a Dream Speech (N = 84). The unit of analysis for London International was the post (N = 6971).

Table 17.4 Emotions extracted using the NRC method

Emotions	Declaration of Independence	I Have a Dream	London International
Anger	18 (.10)	42 (.13)	5828 (.07)
Disgust	12 (.07)	23 (.07)	4044 (.05)
Fear	32 (.17)	45 (.14)	6755 (.08)
Sadness	24 (.13)	58 (.18)	6500 (.08)
Anticipation	27 (.15)	58 (.18)	17147 (.20)
Joy	15 (.08)	72 (.22)	15594 (.19)
Surprise	9 (.05)	18 (.06)	8357 (.10)
Trust	47 (.26)	9 (.03)	20053 (.24)
Sum	184 (100)	325 (100)	84278 (100)

Emotions

The NRC extraction method also allows the researcher to classify words in each corpus into eight basic human emotions—anger, disgust, fear, sadness, anticipation, joy, surprise, and trust. This process provides insight into the underlying emotional structure of the positive and negative polarities discussed earlier. Not all words, such as conjunctions or names, can be classified into an emotion. However, 184 words were labeled in the Declaration of Independence, 325 for "I Have a Dream", and 84278 for London International.

Emotion extraction results are in Table 17.4. The first column of the table lists emotions, with the first four emotions underpinning negative sentiment and the remaining four words underpinning positive sentiment. For the Declaration of Independence, the three most common emotions are trust (.26), fear (.17), and sadness (.15). For the "I Have a Dream" speech, the three most common emotions are joy (.22), anticipation (.22), and sadness (.18). There is a mix of emotions connected to both positive and negative sentiments in both these documents.

The greater levels of overall positive sentiment in London International are reflected in its emotion distribution. The three most common emotions are trust (.24), anticipation (.20), and joy (.19). These are all associated with positive emotions. More telling is the relative lack of words associated with negative emotions—anger (.07), disgust (.05), fear (.08), and sadness (.08). This difference is shown more clearly in Figure 17.1. Compared to the two control documents, the words associated with negative emotions take up far less of the total number of labeled words in London International.

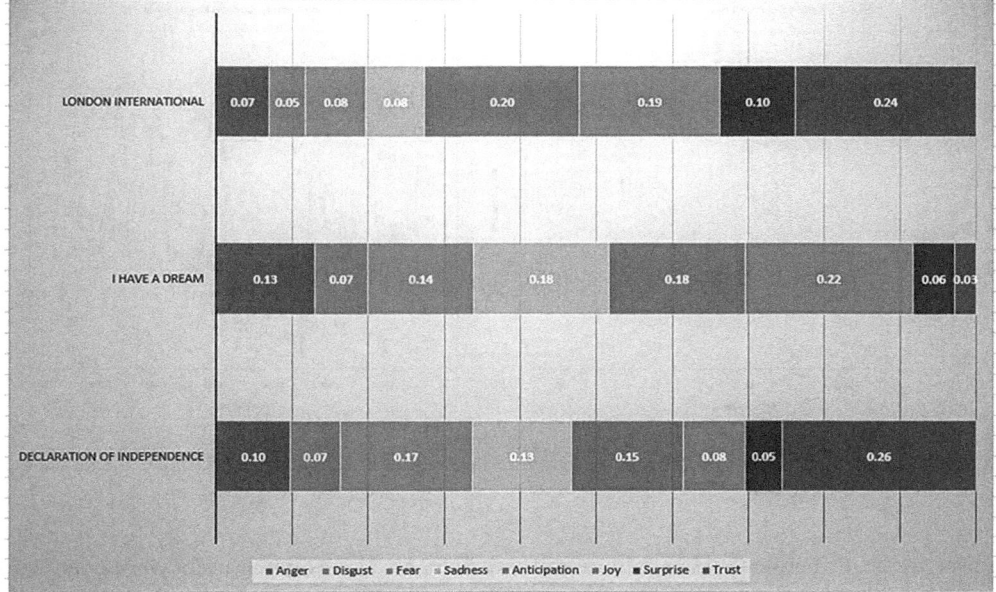

Figure 17.1   Visual representation of emotions extracted using the NRC method

Have sentiments changed over time?

At the time of web scraping, *London International* listed posts beginning in mid-2002 and was still active when data collection concluded in 2020. This length of time spans about two decades and allows an opportunity to explore changes in sentiment over time. These analyses suggest that while the four extraction methods produce slightly different results, they point to the same conclusions. Therefore, in this portion of the analysis, only the sentiment data from the Syuzhet extraction method will be used. Additionally, only the "I Have a Dream" speech will be used to provide context.

A rolling mean will be displayed visually on a line graph to observe changes over time more clearly. A rolling mean is calculated by first getting the mean of an initial subset, or window, of data. For example, the first 20 observations in a set of data could be the initial window. New values are calculated and plotted by shifting the window forward, removing the last number in the subset and including the next number in the series. A rolling mean is one of many "smoothing" methods that removes the volatility observed in time series data. Figure 17.2 shows the rolling means of Syuzhet sentiment scores for the "I Have a Dream Speech" (subset window = 3) and for *London International* (subset window = 200). For the former, time is measured in the progression of sentences. For the latter, it is measured in the progression of postings.

The rolling mean for the "I Have a Dream" speech has fluctuations in sentiment, with several positive peaks. The speech ends on a high, quantifying the well-known rhetorical flourish of Dr. King's speech. Turning to *London International*, fluctuations in sentiment are also exhibited. There are some periods—postings at the 2500 mark—where users were not as positive as other times—postings around the 5500 mark. Notably, the rolling mean

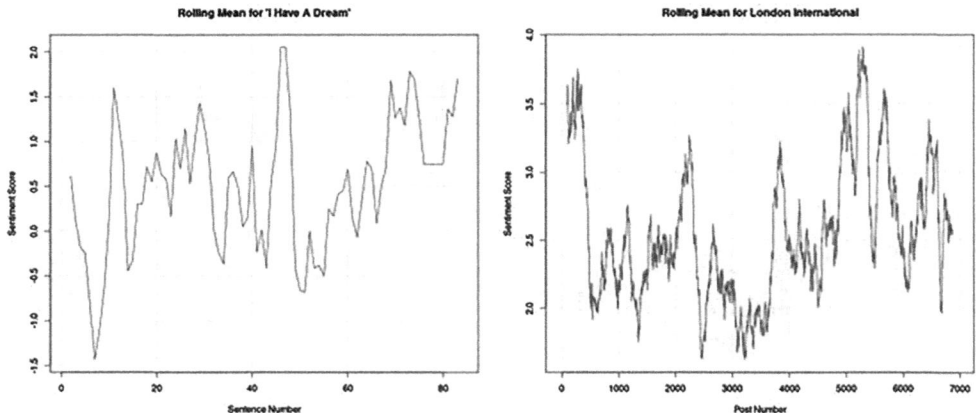

Figure 17.2 Rolling means for "I Have a Dream" and London International: Using Syuzhet extraction method

values are never below 0. Thus, although there were occasions when users were commenting negatively about some aspect of sex work, the overall sentiments throughout the two decades can be described as consistently positive.

Discussion

Some qualifications about the scope of this study are in order before concluding. First, the sentiments are best understood as being about the transactional nature of sex work, with an emphasis on the process of procuring services and evaluating those services. This is a working assumption given the site's primary focus and a preliminary reading of comments by the researcher. This point needs to be made because many of the issues surrounding sex work have to do with how the industry may have adverse effects on women in the wider society who are not sex workers. Namely, a higher prevalence of sex work activity and greater visibility of sex workers may lead to societal shifts towards a greater objectification of women. The present study cannot speak to this issue, as perceptions about the process of sex work and sex workers diverge from perceptions about the larger category of women.

Second, as a case study, any generalizations must be taken with caution. Different discussion forums will have different dynamics. Moreover, this discussion forum is specifically about men seeking sex workers in London, with a large portion of men coming from out of town. Men traveling to a different destination for sex work services is not uncommon. Indeed, given the dynamics of sex work, this may be somewhat normative. However, it must be stated that the discussions on this forum would be different than discussions on sex work forums with different aims.

Having made these two qualifications, the purpose of this research note was to report the early results from an exploration of an online sex work forum. The first question this study sought to answer was: what sentiments are expressed by men in an online sex work forum? Evidence from four sentiment extraction methods and an emotion extraction algorithm suggest that positive sentiments are expressed on this forum. The users in this forum express emotions such as anticipation, joy, and trust much more than emotions such as anger, disgust, and sadness.

The second question asked whether these sentiments changed over time. Calculating rolling mean values from the initial post in 2002 to the last post collected in 2020 shows that while there have been fluctuations, those fluctuations are best characterized as more or less positive. Despite the cultural and social changes over the past two decades, the conversations around procuring sex from sex workers have remained ones characterized by positive sentiment.

The next step in this research is to explore more closely what it is about sex work that produces the trends discussed here. This following study will be qualitative and will add to the literature on hegemonic masculinity (Connell, 2012; Connell & Messerschmidt, 2005; Demetriou, 2001). Specifically, conversations on the forum where men speak about their experiences with sex workers will be identified and analyzed for indicators of masculinity. Are men looking to assert sexual dominance over a woman? Do they reduce sex workers to purely sexual objects? These are indicators of hegemonic masculinity. On the other hand, they may also find value not in raw sexual activity but in sharing intimacy and affection. Conversations of this type would challenge dominant notions of masculinity.

References

Baratosy, R., & Wendt, S. (2017). "Outdated laws, outspoken whores": Exploring sex work in a criminalised setting. *Women's Studies International Forum, 62*, 34–42. https://doi.org/10.1016/j.wsif.2017.03.002

Bernstein, E. (2007). Sex work for the middle classes. *Sexualities, 10*(4), 473–488. https://doi.org/10.1177/1363460707080984

Birch, P., Baldry, E., & Hartley, V. H. (2017). Procuring sexual services: Evidencing masculinity diversity and difference through sex work research. *Sexuality & Culture, 21*(4), 1106–1119. https://doi.org/10.1007/s12119-017-9439-5

Brooks-Gordon, B. (2010). Bellwether citizens: The regulation of male clients of sex workers. *Journal of Law and Society, 37*(1), 145–170. https://doi.org/10.1111/j.1467-6478.2010.00499.x

Burnap, P., & Williams, M. L. (2015). Cyber hate speech on twitter: An application of machine classification and statistical modeling for policy and decision making: Machine classification of cyber hate speech. *Policy & Internet, 7*(2), 223–242. https://doi.org/10.1002/poi3.85

Campos, L., Bernardes, S., & Godinho, C. (2020). Food as a way to convey masculinities: How conformity to hegemonic masculinity norms influences men's and women's food consumption. *Journal of Health Psychology, 25*(12), 1842–1856. https://doi.org/10.1177/1359105318772643

Cohen, B. (2019). Police enforcement of street prostitution as a quality-of-life offense: New York City, United States, and Frankfurt am Main, Germany. *Deviant Behavior, 40*(5), 526–543. https://doi.org/10.1080/01639625.2018.1431096

Compagner, C., Lester, C., & Dorsch, M. (2021). Sentiment analysis of online reviews for selective serotonin reuptake inhibitors and serotonin—Norepinephrine reuptake inhibitors. *Pharmacy, 9*(1), 27. https://doi.org/10.3390/pharmacy9010027

Connell, R. W. (2005). *Masculinities* (2nd ed.). University of California Press.

Connell, R. W. (2012). Masculinity research and global change. *Masculinities and Social Change, 1*(1), 4–18. https://doi.org/10.4471/MCS.2012.01

Connell, R. W., & Messerschmidt, J. W. (2005). Hegemonic masculinity: Rethinking the concept. *Gender & Society, 19*(6), 829–859. https://doi.org/10.1177/0891243205278639

Demetriou, D. Z. (2001). Connell's concept of hegemonic masculinity: A critique. *Theory and Society, 30*(3), 337–361.

Gould, C. (2014). Sex trafficking and prostitution in South Africa. *The ANNALS of the American Academy of Political and Social Science, 653*(1), 183–201. https://doi.org/10.1177/0002716214521557

Gutiérrez, E. J. D. (2014). Prostitution and gender-based violence. *Procedia—Social and Behavioral Sciences, 161*, 96–101. https://doi.org/10.1016/j.sbspro.2014.12.016

Jockers, M. (2020). *Syuzhet package* (1.06). Retrieved from https://github.com/mjockers/syuzhet

Jones, Z., & Hannem, S. (2018). Escort clients' sexual scripts and constructions of intimacy in commodified sexual relationships: Escort clients' sexual scripts. *Symbolic Interaction, 41*(4), 488–512. https://doi.org/10.1002/symb.379

Joseph, L. J., & Black, P. (2012). Who's the man? Fragile masculinities, consumer masculinities, and the profiles of sex work clients. *Men and Masculinities, 15*(5), 486–506. https://doi.org/10.1177/1097184X12458591

Kong, T. S. K. (2016). Buying sex as edgework: Hong Kong male clients in commercial sex. *British Journal of Criminology, 56*(1), 105–122. https://doi.org/10.1093/bjc/azv040

Liu, B. (2012). *Sentiment analysis and opinion mining.* Morgan & Claypool.

Lucas, A. M. (2005). The work of sex work: Elite prostitutes' vocational orientations and experiences. *Deviant Behavior, 26*(6), 513–546. https://doi.org/10.1080/01639620500218252

Matthews, R. (2015). Female prostitution and victimization: A realist analysis. *International Review of Victimology, 21*(1), 85–100. https://doi.org/10.1177/0269758014547994

Milrod, C., & Monto, M. (2017). Older male clients of female sex workers in the United States. *Archives of Sexual Behavior, 46*(6), 1867–1876. https://doi.org/10.1007/s10508-016-0733-3

Morselli, C., & Savoie-Gargiso, I. (2014). Coercion, control, and cooperation in a prostitution ring. *The ANNALS of the American Academy of Political and Social Science, 653*(1), 247–265. https://doi.org/10.1177/0002716214521995

Peter, J., & Valkenburg, P. M. (2009). Adolescents' exposure to sexually explicit internet material and notions of women as sex objects: Assessing causality and underlying processes. *Journal of Communication, 59*(3), 407–433. https://doi.org/10.1111/j.1460-2466.2009.01422.x

Robertson, A. M., Syvertsen, J. L., Amaro, H., Martinez, G., Rangel, M. G., Patterson, T. L., & Strathdee, S. A. (2014). Can't buy my love: A typology of female sex workers' commercial relationships in the Mexico—U.S. Border region. *The Journal of Sex Research, 51*(6), 711–720. https://doi.org/10.1080/00224499.2012.757283

Sanders, T. (2008). Male sexual scripts: Intimacy, sexuality and pleasure in the purchase of commercial sex. *Sociology, 42*(3), 400–417. https://doi.org/10.1177/0038038508088833

Shaver, F. M., Lewis, J., & Maticka-Tyndale, E. (2011). Rising to the challenge: Addressing the concerns of people working in the sex industry: Rising to the challenge. *Canadian Review of Sociology/Revue Canadienne de Sociologie, 48*(1), 47–65. https://doi.org/10.1111/j.1755-618X.2011.01249.x

Udanor, C., & Anyanwu, C. C. (2019). Combating the challenges of social media hate speech in a polarized society: A Twitter ego lexalytics approach. *Data Technologies and Applications, 53*(4), 501–527. https://doi.org/10.1108/DTA-01-2019-0007

Wedgwood, N. (2009). Connell's theory of masculinity—Its origins and influences on the study of gender. *Journal of Gender Studies, 18*(4), 329–339.

West, J., & Austrin, T. (2005). Markets and politics: Public and private relations in the case of prostitution. *The Sociological Review, 53*(2_Suppl), 136–148. https://doi.org/10.1111/j.1467-954X.2005.00577.x

Willis, M., Bridges, A. J., & Sun, C. (2022). Pornography use, gender, and sexual objectification: A multinational study. *Sexuality & Culture, 26*(4), 1298–1313. https://doi.org/10.1007/s12119-022-09943-z

Yang, Y. (2020). What's hegemonic about hegemonic masculinity? Legitimation and beyond. *Sociological Theory, 38*(4), 318–333. https://doi.org/10.1177/0735275120960792

"I DO NOT BELIEVE THAT TALKING ABOUT THIS KIND OF STUFF IS A WAY TO DIMINISH FEMINIST BATTLES." AN ONLINE CONTROVERSY IN THE ITALIAN MANOSPHERE

Manolo Farci and Oscar Ricci

Introduction

In the past 10 years there have been intense debates in masculinity studies about transformations in men's behavior and their impact on gender relations. A significant part of these debates is dedicated to trying to understand how white heterosexual masculinities are produced and buttressed in Internet settings, as demonstrated by the increasing amount of knowledge about the heterogeneous nature of the so-called manosphere (Schmitz & Kazyak, 2016; Marwick & Caplan, 2018). "Manosphere" comprises a loose confederacy of online subculture groups that post hateful speech through blogs, subreddits, tweets, websites, forums, and other online spaces:

> a strange vanguard of teenage gamers, pseudonymous swastika-posting anime lovers, ironic South Park conservatives, anti-feminist pranksters, nerdish harassers and meme-making trolls whose dark humor and love of transgression for its own sake made it hard to know what political views were genuinely held and what were merely, as they used to say, for the lulz.
>
> *(Nagle, 2017, p. 2)*

These groups utilize disparate and seemingly opposing strategies in how they frame their opinions: some communities blame society for systematically working on "the pussification of men" (Blais & Dupuis-Déri, 2012) and encourage the return of an hegemonic masculinity (Connell, 1995), the only one that can stand against the "women's evil narcissistic nature"; others offer images and narratives of white male as victim (Savran, 1998) that suffers general oppression from a political and criminal justice perspective and strives for social legitimacy by using the tactful and non-discriminatory vocabulary typically associated with feminism, such as "equality", "fairness", and "justice" (Schmitz & Kazyak,

DOI: 10.4324/9781003277675-21

2016). In this sense, the omnipresent reference to terms like misandry allows ideologically diverse communities to appropriate the language of leftist identity politics and share a victimized stance which then helps them to sustain their own ideologies and beliefs.

Although it cannot be subsumed within a single entity, many scholars describe the manosphere as an online network of deviant subculture groups concentrated in hating women (Ging, 2017; Liang, Lin, 2017; Lilly, 2016). In these spaces men can receive support from other men with similar feelings and experience to learn how, and to be applauded for deviating from social norms. According to Lawson (2019), the behaviors of some of the major groups can be associated with the classic deviant strategies theorized by Robert Merton, characterized by rebellion, retreat, and innovation. It is thus that, for instance, the PUA's adapt through innovation (accept the goal, but reject the means), the MGTOW choose to retreat (reject the goal and the means) by choosing not to date or live with women, while the Incels rejects goals and means, and creates new ones through extreme or violent anti-feminist acts. Sugiura (2021) also connects the manosphere with the concept of deviance. In her book she explores the possibility that in becoming a member of groups belonging to the manosphere there are issues related to neurodivergence: many Incels are thought to be on the autistic spectrum, demonstrating characteristics such as problems in socially interacting with others and having unusual and prolonged emotional reactions. It could well be the case that those with autism spectrum disorder (ASD) are more vulnerable to the lure of the ideas espoused within the Incel community; however similar to the stereotyping of all hackers as autistic (Bolgan et al., 2016; Seigfried-Spellar et al., 2015), making such connections as an explanation for deviance or criminality leads to stigmatization and alienation (Sugiura, 2021, p. 21). We must be careful, however, that the deviant label applied to manosphere groups does not result in completely portraying this phenomenon. First, while it is often discussed as a coherent object with a cohesive set of beliefs, the manosphere is not a monolith (Sharkey, 2021). Although there is no doubt that the worldview as expressed in online men's communities constitute a very specific shared perspective that has all the features of an extremist mindset (Baele et al., 2019), the broad assumptions about misogyny and violence do not fully encapsulate differences of opinion within the manosphere. Obviously, there are members of the manosphere who fundamentally distrust and dislike women and engage in deviant acts of misogyny, who believe that rape is a made-up crime, that feminism is an ideology of hate, akin to Nazism, or that false rape accusations against men have reached epidemic proportions. However, a good part of those who engage in men's online communities express considerable ambivalence toward predominant standards of masculinity and reject traditional gender ideology, which assumes men to be naturally rough, tough, and sexually aggressive, and women to be passive, caring, and good. In some way, they seem to support many of the same things that feminists want, including acceptance of alternative masculinities, and apparently reject all the poisonous practices associated with the term *toxic masculinity*. Like feminists, they argue that a rigid notion of socially acceptable male/female behavior has negative consequences for men, limiting their self-expression (Seidler, 1989) and creating unrealistic expectations of physical strength and financial success (Kaufman, 1994). Focusing more on the costs of being male, these pro-male groups attract those mostly younger men who feel disempowered by the shift in gender roles in recent decades (Gotell & Dutton, 2016). As Messner states, while overt hatred of women continues to mark many men's communities on the Internet, we are witnesses of the emergence of a kinder, gentler form of men's rights discourse that is likely to resonate best with educated middle-class white men who do not want to appear to be backwards misogynists (Messner, 2016).

The aim of this chapter is to understand whether the apparently progressive sensibility that marks this new form of men's rights discourse offers nothing but a new gateway to the misogynistic ideology of the Incel and MGTOW. In order to engage with this topic, we have chosen to analyze the rise of online pro-male communities in the Italian context. Nowadays, most of the research on this phenomenon focuses on the US context, and in rare cases on other Anglophone realities (such as Australia and Canada). Conversely, in Italy there are few studies exploring the manosphere, except for Vingelli (2017) and Farci and Righetti (2019), who reconstruct, respectively, the network of Italian online groups of men's rights activists and their antifeminist rhetoric, Cannito and Mercuri (2021), who analyze the politics of fatherhood on an Italian Facebook group, Dordoni and Magaraggia (2021), who look at interactions, representations, and discourses circulating within an Incel and Red Pill Italian community, Scarcelli (2021), who demonstrates that everyday conversations among teenagers in private WhatsApp groups often echo the languages, contents, and practices of the manosphere, and Farci and Ricci (2021) who focus on the pro-masculinity discourses of some online influencers. This shortage is generally attributed to the scant institutionalization of gender studies in universities and the lack of discussion in both the academic and public arenas regarding the rapidly changing world of masculinities among Italian men (Piccone, 2000). While there are still few academic works on the manosphere, the last decade has witnessed the emergence of a growing number of antifeminist and men's rights groups on the Italian web. One of the most famous examples of the increasing occurrence of men's issues on the Net is the case of Marco Crepaldi. Marco Crepaldi is a social psychologist who runs channels on YouTube and Twitch, where he talks about male issues, such as body shaming, violence against men, social isolation, and feminism. In June 2020, he made some controversial statements on the social difficulties experienced by straight white males, which caused a large, polarized debate on Italian social media. Marco Crepaldi was chosen for several reasons. First, even though he often perpetuates the same antifeminism rhetoric carried on by more conservative MRA movements, his anti-sexist discourses seem to differ both from the *heteropaternalism* of fathers' rights groups and from the anti-woman rhetoric and explicit misogyny of communities like Incels (*Involuntary Celibate*) or Red Pillers. Second, although it is not possible to prove that he is representative of the entire manosphere population, his work indicates the emergence of a new strand of moderate discourse of men's issues that put together people who are convincedly anti-feminist with others who seem to be really worried about men's issues. The first part of the chapter analyzes his channel's main content, reviewing forty videos he made on the topic of men's issues from July 2019 until the break on 4 June 2020. The second part explores how the controversy that erupted in late May and early June was interpreted by young adults who, although not belonging to specific pro male groups suchs as Incel or Red Pillers nor having a specific vocation for political activism, are nonetheless interested in debating some of the men's issues discussed by Marco Crepaldi.

A therapist for men?

During the first week of June 2020, the Crepaldi case broke out. Marco Crepaldi is a social psychologist who in 2013 decided to start a blog and then a YouTube channel to raise awareness of the issue of Hikikomori, a Japanese term that defines individuals who choose to shut themselves up at home by refusing all contact with the outside world (Crepaldi, 2019). Between the end of 2019 and the beginning of 2020, Crepaldi inaugurated

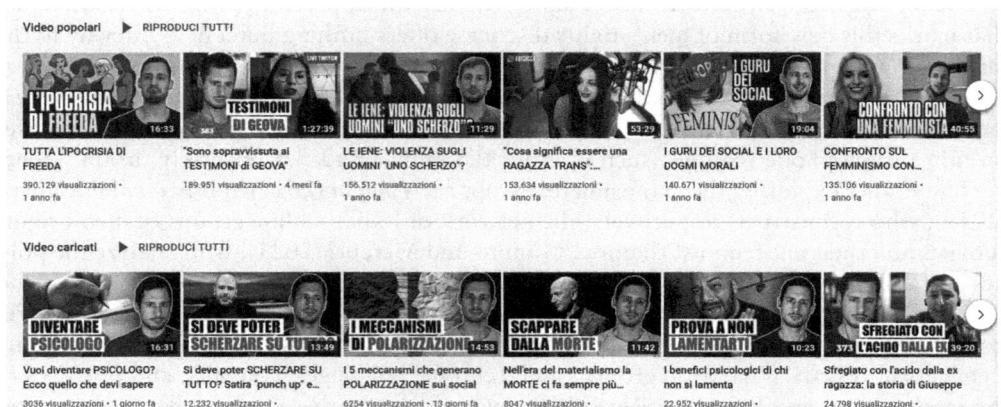

Figure 18.1   Marco Crepaldi's YouTube

Source: Among the videos we can note: "All the hypocrisy of Freeda", "Does is violence against men a joke", "What it means to be a trans girl", "Confrontation on feminism"

an additional space on YouTube where he addresses more specifically issues related to the male universe, such as sexuality and the Incel subculture, violence or discrimination against men, body shaming, or bigorexia.

Between the end of May and the beginning of June 2020, following a series of Stories posted on Instagram in which he had spoken of "hostility towards the male, in particular the white heterosexual male" and used the term "Nazi-feminism", the YouTuber faced a shitstorm on Twitter, which led him to decide to suspend, at least temporarily, his dissemination activities on the Internet on issues related to male discrimination.

Although Crepaldi's interest in masculinity is more recent than his studies on the Hikikomori, the analytical bases applied to the two phenomena both refer to psychological studies on the sex role, which were particularly widespread in the 1960s and 1970s thanks to feminist-inspired male liberation movements (Pleck, 1981). According to the YouTuber, in fact, in any cultural context women and men function as beings socialized to their gender role, which would represent a social construct "created by society" and "determined by social expectations". In this sense, any difference between masculinity and femininity would be defined by a set of conditioning and role expectations. In the case of men, particularly Incel and Hikikomori, these social constraints include the pressure to conform to the group, to be brilliant with peers or to get good grades, to build an important career, as well as pressures of a sexual nature. Right from his theoretical premises, Crepaldi tries to distance himself from any form of biological reductionism that characterizes the manosphere's thinking. Nevertheless, his mode of thinking inevitably falls into a return essentialism in which the masculine (but also the feminine), although understood as a product of culture, ends up corresponding to two natural categories (Petersen, 1998). To imagine that a person's sexual experience is automatically shaped by socialization mechanisms is to assume the existence of a universal concept of masculine and feminine, which would be added to nature almost automatically in order to give us a gender. The social pressures on men would thus be reduced to a set of attributes unchanged in time and space, a kind of gender script to which all males would inevitably be led to adhere.

Using the concept of gender role as an interpretative resource, Crepaldi's reasoning thus comes to naturalize a precise scenario of polarization and sexual complementarity between men and women. In such a scenario, women would have an advantage "in being able to manage sex with much less anxiety, in having much less suffering in selecting partners"; moreover, they would be "much more selective, and therefore the physical aspects become much more impactful in the selection of men, than in the selection of women". This view of sexuality would be confirmed in realities such as Tinder, where girls appear to be more available and sexually promiscuous, but it is always other males—who in Incel jargon are called *chads*—who benefit from this horizon of unexpected sexual possibilities (Kimmel, 2008). Although the YouTuber never indulges in homohysterical or explicitly sexist attitudes (Anderson, 2011), it is clear that the cultural model of heterosexuality he refers to is very similar to that prevalent in the Pick Up Artist (PUA) and Incel communities (O'Neill, 2018; Van Valkenburgh, 2018). Crepaldi keeps well clear of the often-caricatured jargon that connotes these two phenomena of the manosphere. Yet, he too comes to imagine sex as a male physical necessity conditioned by evolutionary imperatives (Hollway, 1984), an insatiable urgency driven by instincts (Ferrero Camoletto & Bertone, 2010)—instincts that if not properly suppressed would risk erupting into phenomena of open misogyny. Male sexuality thus becomes a paradoxical impulse that must be kept under control, even though it is in some respects uncontrollable. It is the dilemma of the respectability script that has historically marked men's relationship with sex (Bertone & Ferrero Camoletto, 2009). Although there is a natural exuberance of male desire, the ideal man is the bourgeois male who knows how to curb his passions and follow the path of moderation and reasonableness; in this way, he differs from the predatory sexuality of other males, such as those belonging to the working classes, those with less cultural capital, or who are otherwise marginalized. Crepaldi does the same with his calm, nice-guy talk: he does not deconstruct the roots of the male stereotypes that fuel the Incels' shouted claims, but merely dissociates himself from their behavior, offering his audience a comforting way to feel morally different, without ever really questioning himself. This is the same mechanism we find when the YouTuber connects sexuality to the phenomenon of male homosociality. Like so many users who frequent the manosphere sharing the belief that relationships with the opposite sex are the best way to gain mastery (Pascoe, 2007) and measure one's personal fulfillment (O'Neill, 2018), Crepaldi argues that emotional relationships are a way to "maintain a social status that allows men to be appreciated". In this view, women would be objectified as scarce resources to be contended for in order to increase their self-confidence and the consideration of their peer group. This would explain the feeling of irretrievable dependence on the feminine that many male movements supporting the Red Pill philosophy complain about openly and often violently, and that the YouTuber's reflection seems to implicitly imply. A dependence that ends up being justified by referring to the presumed sexual advantage that women have over so-called beta males, and that would make them cruelly more selective in terms of partners (Marchi, 2018), but which would derive from the instrumental logic with which many men look at their intimate life and ties with the opposite sex.

In this sort of dystopian imagining that is very reminiscent of Michel Houellebecq's novels, in which sex is everywhere but males are condemned to a state of enforced sexual pauperization, if one does not want to abandon oneself to frustration and resentment (Bratich & Banet-Weiser, 2019), according to Crepaldi one will have no choice but to work on oneself to improve, to be able to acquire those characteristics that successful people have in the sexual sphere: to accept, in short, the rules of the game, however ruthless they may appear.

The YouTuber borrows here one of the interpretative repertoires that the Pick Up Artists share with the Red Pillers: the idea that the whole of existence can be explained as a social universe of generalized competition, where every relationship is subject to the monetizable mechanisms of supply and demand and each individual is driven to see in himself a human capital to be valued, like a company selling a service on a market (Dardot & Laval, 2009).

It then becomes crucial for Crepaldi to understand how men can decide to free themselves from the constrictive cage of their gender roles, if around them the alleged mechanisms of female sexual selectivity would seem to precisely reward those virtues, such as fight, strength, vigor, and virility, which would confirm the most normative stereotypes of masculinity. It is here that in order to overcome the contradiction between the possession of its own explanatory theory—the concept of gender role—and the everyday common sense that would seem to deny this same theory, Crepaldi's thought makes a further dialectical twist, and relies on totally different discursive resources, which refer to the tradition of men's studies (even if the YouTuber seems unaware of it). When, for example, he pays attention to the way in which the pressures of gender roles drive men to suppress the whole range of emotions, needs and possibilities seen as inconsistent with the power of masculinity, he is simply reiterating positions widely expressed by the male liberation movements of the 1970s, which strongly denounced the social costs of masculinity (Kaufman, 1994; Seidler, 1989). There is, however, a substantial reversal with respect to the emancipatory objectives of the profeminist movements: while for them traditional roles had to be rejected because they guaranteed male power over women, on the contrary, for Crepaldi, they must be abandoned because they give women greater control over men, forcing them to adhere to gender roles that are psychologically lethal for them (Clatterbaugh, 1996). It is as if the male subject is trapped in a vicious circle: although he is distancing himself from the image of the hard, pure male he had in the past, this de-virilization does not correspond to what women instinctively look for in him. Traditional masculinity can be said to be thus denied, only to be recovered as a victimizing posture through which men attempt to cope with the reality of their own powerlessness in the face of women's power of sexual choice (Messner, 1997).

Even after the controversy he faced in late May and early June 2020, Crepaldi continues to present himself as a moderate social psychologist. The fact that he does not consider himself an activist for men's rights or distance himself from many assumptions circulating in the manosphere, as we have said, makes him particularly exemplary of a discourse on masculinity that escapes the radicalism that characterizes other men's movements and structures itself instead as a kind of everyday ideology with dilemmatic and contradictory characters. And it is precisely in the light of this dilemmatic nature that it becomes even more interesting to analyze the debate that has been widely raised after the controversy in which it has been involved.

Research design

To investigate how young adults have interpreted the meanings of the controversy against Marco Crepaldi, we decided to conduct twenty focus groups. We conducted focus groups for several purposes. Our first goal was to create interactive data. Focus groups are conversations in which everyone in the group concentrates on one particular subject. As such, participants mostly talk to each other rather than the researcher and tend to speak in a way that is more ordinary, so focus groups are an ideal way to access some sort of "natural language" (Wilkinson, 1998). Second, focus groups lead to better disclosure. Research on focus groups has shown that people are more likely to self-reveal and share personal experiences in a group than in an individual context (Morgan & Krueger, 1993), especially because they can feel empowered and supported in a group surrounded by their own (Farquhar & Das, 1999). Focus groups are also particularly useful for investigating issues that are perceived as sensitive (Renzetti & Lee, 1993; Rubin, 2004). Furthermore, we wanted to use a method that was characterized by non-hierarchical relationships between researchers and researchers (Kitzinger, 1994). Because focus groups are designed to provide opportunities for an interactive exchange of views, they are less subject to researcher influence (Morgan & Krueger, 1998; Johansson & Klinth, 2008). We also expected research participants to be able to affirm their programs in a group of their peers and to negotiate meanings through discussion (Kitzinger & Farquhar, 1999; Kitzinger, 1994). The focus group allows participants to spontaneously express, reject, and change opinions through group norms in a particular context (Halkier, 2010; Liong & Chan, 2020). We have limited the size of our focus groups to six participants each to encourage discussion (Wilkinson, 1998). This ensured that participants were comfortable discussing topics that might be considered sensitive in a traditional focus group made up of people who do not know each other in advance (Barbour, 2007; Ravn, 2018). They were first contacted by university mail, followed by snowballing, a technique that is popular in qualitative studies (Bowling, 1997) and is considered acceptable for initial investigations. It involves asking the first members of a target group to suggest other people they know who are in the target group.

The participants were chosen on a volunteer basis; the prerequisite for acceptance was that they knew who Marco Crepaldi was and they were interested. A semi-structured questionnaire was used with only three questions. The groups were asked to discuss what they knew about Marco Crepaldi, how they knew him, and what they thought about the whole case.

The focus group meeting was held in the Webex platform; all participants were assured of confidentiality, and they consented to videotaping the conversation. After the initial questions, the group was left to take the conversation in any direction, with occasional requests from the researchers. Most focus groups lasted approximately 90 minutes; names and other identifying characteristics were anonymized. We organized 20 focus groups, with a total of 108 people present. 55 were female and 53 were male, the mean age was 23 years, with a range from 20 to 25.

All speech was transcribed and subjected to a "thematic decomposition" (Stenner, 1993) to divide the transcript into coherent "themes", thus obtaining a series of frames through which to frame the multiple representations of the discursive production built around the story of the YouTuber at the center of our focus. In other words, an attempt was made to identify the different ways in which the focus group participants provided narrative paths, possible interpretations, and points of view.

The themes

Even though over the course of the focus groups several issues emerged, we focused on four that seemed particularly relevant: the problem of defining what feminism Crepaldi is talking about; the existence of a supposed female sexual advantage in relationships; the fact that thanks to the controversy about Crepaldi many people became aware of the issue of male problems and the general question of how to define Crepaldi thought; and Crepaldi himself.

What kind of feminism are we talking about?

One of the themes that appears in every focus group concerns the problematic definition of feminism that emerges from the arguments of Marco Crepaldi. This is not very surprising, considering that one of the triggering reasons that caused the shitstorm was the term "Nazi-feminist", used by Marco Crepaldi in one of his Instagram stories. But when Crepaldi uses the term "feminism", what exactly is he talking about? Many comments tend to point out that Crepaldi's speech lacks a clear understanding of what exactly the feminist movement is:

Giorgia (22 years old):   I mean, I really do not understand what kind of feminism he is talking about. He clearly hasn't read so much about gender studies or feminist stuff.

Lucrezia (21 years old):   I think he makes some confusion about at least two types of feminism: one that is an academic one, and one that is a mediatic one.

This final comment, with its clear distinction between media feminism and non-media feminism, is reflected in many other remarks, and is often expanded by adding a distinction between media feminism *tout court* and "digital" feminism, generally considered the worst way in which feminism can come about. In fact, the internet is considered by many to be the main cause of the decay of issues that elsewhere find a qualitatively better discursive space:

Laura (20 y.o.):   I agree with Lucrezia, and I must add that I think that rather than a "mediatic one" we should be talking about a "digital one", considering that basically this kind of feminism is basically spread on digital media.

Diego (21 y.o.)   It is really too easy for him to accuse this kind of feminism; this is not feminism, this is mediatic garbage.

We see in these observations how Crepaldi is accused of having chosen as a target a feminism born and raised exclusively on the Internet. The place that is most frequently mentioned as an example of the wrong target chosen by Crepaldi is undoubtedly *Freeda*, a social publisher that since 2017 has tried to become the "reference point for women between 18 and 34 years old". Freeda is always quoted as a negative example of feminism, as we can see in the following comments:

Luca (23 y.o.):   In my opinion, feminism that comes from digital media is the worst one, take Freeda for example.[1]

Marzia (25 y.o.):   Come on, guys, Freeda is owned by the Berlusconi family; no wonder it is spreading the worst bullshit.

Marco (21 y.o.):   Freeda. That's not feminism for sure.

The fact that Freeda seems to represent so well the supposed decadence of the feminist discourse, however, leads several focus group participants to question why this site, so criticized and yet so successful, could somehow have gained so much space in the field of feminism:

Chiara (24 y.o.):   I agree that Marco Crepaldi is quite wrong in attacking so much this kind of feminism, but we have to ask ourselves why Freeda is so popular nowadays.

Lucia (21 y.o.):   In my opinion, the problem is that the "Freeda feminism" is basically the only one that matters; most of my friends know something about feminism just looking on those pages.

Lorenzo (22 y.o.):   But are you sure that there is another feminism that is so much better than this one? In my opinion, this is the mainstream feminism, and it is not so different from the academic one.

The idea that Crepaldi has, for many focus group participants, mistaken in identifying what the "right" feminism is constitutes the main reason for the disapproval of his words, and the justification for the issues that followed. One of the issues at stake, in fact, is to decide whether the controversy that has resulted from his words has been deserved or not.

Gregorio (24 y.o.):   I mean, I don't think the whole idea of the shitstorm is very well thought. First of all, it gives him so much more visibility, and secondly the violence of it can persuade some people that he is somehow right.

Livia (20 y.o.):   Well, actually, I think that the shitstorm is wrong on any level we can consider. This shitstorm makes us look not very different from the people we are criticizing.

In the criticism of the shitstorm, we therefore see at least two main modalities. The first one considers the shitstorm as being instrumentally wrong on a political level; the second one condemns the shitstorm as wrong, as an incorrect tool to be used regardless, for principle and morals reasons.

Is there a female sexual advantage?

There is another theme where we see the emergence, as in the case of the discussion on feminism, of a mostly negative judgment on various digital platforms: the supposed female sexual advantage. We have seen in the treatment of Crepaldi's thought how the alleged female sexual advantage is one of his strong points. This same topic has emerged several times from focus groups, and has almost always been related to the development of different digital platforms:

Marco (21 y.o.)   Well, come on people, we cannot pretend there isn't a female sexual advantage; consider for instance the simp phenomenon.

The word "Simp" is one of the many neologisms belonging to the digital culture. According to the dictionary.com definition, this word describes "men who are seen as too attentive and submissive to women, especially out of a failed hope of winning some entitled sexual attention or activity from them".[2]

The problem of the supposed female advantage would derive from an excessive focus on some digital dynamics, considered decidedly detached, or in any case emphasized compared to offline relational dynamics. As a matter of fact, we had several comments (especially by men) focusing on the power of online dating platforms, considered a tool that allow women to exploit men's desire:

Pietro (22 y.o.):   Well, I give you an idea: use Tinder with a fake female identity, you will see what kind of different results you will get.

Giulio (21 y.o.): If you are a man on Tinder, you are lucky if you get one like in a while; if you are a woman you will get likes every five minutes.

This opinion is, however, strongly challenged by many focus group participants (both men and women), who think that focusing just on online practice is a wrong way of thinking, because it places too little weight on offline relationships:

Lucia (24 y.o.): If you think that using Tinder is a correct way of looking at human relationships, you have a problem.

Marco (22 y.o.): We must draw a line when we are talking about online dynamics: very often we overestimate the importance of them.

So, we see here essentially the same criticism raised from the previous theme regarding what kind of feminism Crepaldi was targeting: in that case the problem was focusing on a mostly media-based feminism, and more precisely on a feminism propagated on and by digital media; in this case the supposed female advantages are deduced from a dating app. This discourse develops further by analyzing the pervasiveness of another platform: OnlyFans. OnlyFans is a digital platform that allows the sharing of generic content by different content creators, but which gradually, and especially during the pandemic, has become the most widespread platform for sharing amateur erotic content. When the discussion moved to OnlyFans, we noticed two things: 1) the comments became much more intense; 2) there was no criticism of the diverse importance of online and offline relationships:

Marco (20 y.o.): If you are a man and you fail at your job, you don't have any other option; if you are a woman, you can always open an OnlyFans. No matter how beautiful or ugly you are, you will always find a man who is willing to pay you.

Giulia (23 y.o.): I think OnlyFans is really something new, something we have not witnessed before. I have to say that I don't believe that the possibility of selling our body online has to be considered a privilege, but at the same time I understand people that see in OnlyFans a great female power.

Lucia (25 y.o.) We have to admit it: the possibility of opening an OnlyFans is a female privilege; hiding it is not doing any good to the woman cause.

I didn't know about all this before the shitstorm

This theme is composed by focus group participants who claim that through this controversy they have managed to encounter issues they knew nothing about. Through the media exposure following the statements of Marco Crepaldi, several people have heard for the first time about gender issues related to the male role, or even about gender issues *tout court*:

Manlio (19 y.o.): I had never heard the name of Marco Crepaldi before the shitstorm took place. Actually, it was quite interesting, I had never even heard of these topics.

Lucia (21 y.o.):   Thanks to Marco Crepaldi, I came into contact with a topic I knew nothing about. Of course, I don't agree with many things, but I think it was very interesting to discover information on the male world that helped me to demythologize it a bit.

Therefore, we see how a large number of the participants of the focus group, especially the males, have become aware of gender issues thanks to Marco Crepaldi and the shitstorm that hit him. Not only that: in some cases, this controversy was an opportunity to face for the first time personal problems that are difficult to externalize:

Luigi (25 y.o.):   Look, it is easier to talk about this kind of stuff now that I'm older, but when I was younger, let's say during my teenage years, I suffered many of the problems Crepaldi is talking about. I was a very shy teenager, and shy is not a peculiarity you want to have to prove you are a real man. I had several opportunities to have sexual intercourse with women, but I was afraid, and you don't want to be afraid of having sexual intercourse if you are a real man. There is a lot of pressure that can hit men too, and this doesn't mean that being a woman is easier. But I think that acknowledging that males can have problems too is a thing that can help men and women.

Milena (24 y.o.)   I totally agree with Luigi. Generally speaking, I think Crepaldi is wrong when he attacks feminism, almost suggesting that feminism is the cause of male problems, but it is very true that I know plenty of men who suffer from typically male-oriented problems, and I do not believe that talking about this kind of stuff is a way to diminish feminist battles.

Is he the Italian Jordan Peterson? Is he an Incel?

The last theme we are going to analyze is the one composed of comments focused on the definition of who Crepaldi really us and what his thoughts really represent. Basically, the focus group participants raised two interesting comparisons: one with the Canadian psychologist Jordan Peterson and another one with the Incel movement. The comparison with Jordan Peterson is particularly intriguing because it allows us to underline affinity and divergence with the figure who in recent years has probably had the most media coverage in the field of the manosphere:

Valeria (19 y.o.):   He reminds me a little bit of Jordan Peterson, but at the same time I can see that there are several differences even though I cannot tell you really which one.

Lucia (23 y.o.):   Even though they have some topics in common I also see some very important differences, one for all: Peterson is clearly a right-wing man, with Crepaldi I wouldn't be so sure.

Giacomo (22 y.o.):   Yes, it is more difficult to collocate Crepaldi on the political spectrum, but I would say he is definitely closer to the left rather than the right.

The opinion that Crepaldi is closer to the political left than to the political right finds almost all the participants in the focus groups in agreement, causing some observation about the appropriateness of the shitstorm:

Lucia (23 y.o.): No wonder that nowadays most people find feminism too intransigent. They shitstormed Marco Crepaldi, who is not exactly Hitler, with the most violent terms.

Giacomo (22 y.o.): I mean if you attack a person in such a violent manner, and this person is not clearly an enemy, a fascist, or an incel, I tend to think that you can be way less tolerant than him.

Also in regard to the supposed placement of Marco Crepaldi in the Incel sphere, nearly all the participants in the focus groups agree with Giacomo: Crepaldi is not an Incel; at most, some of his fans can be:

Marzia (26 y.o.): He is surely not an incel, although some of his followers are very close to that type of guy.

Olga (20 y.o.): At first, I thought he looked a lot like them, but having seen some of his YouTube content I would say that he is far more moderate than them.

Milo (22 y.o.): He is definitely not an Incel, and actually I think that most of the people who attack him defining him an Incel are a lot more similar to the Incel than Marco Crepaldi himself. They are using the same incel tactics to get rid of a person who is not thinking exactly how they deem he should think.

Marina (23 y.o.): Look, he's not Jordan Peterson; he is not an incel. It's a pity that they trashed him so violently, not just because I feel sorry for him, but because it would have been a wonderful opportunity to discuss male issues. Look for instance at what just happened in our focus group! It has been really interesting listening to some males talking about their problems. I think occasions like this one could really help males and females to get along more easily.

Lorenzo (24 y.o.): I think that one of the problems when we address men's issues is just this constant referring to incels. Incels do exist, it's true, but they are a very small fraction of men, and they are also a very small fraction of the men who are discussing men's issues online in recent years. Labeling every man who talks about male issues online as an incel I don't think does any good for men, women, or feminism at large.

The juxtaposition with Jordan Peterson or with Incel thought patterns therefore helps us to better frame Marco Crepaldi's political position. In particular, the idea that emerges from the people interviewed in the focus groups is that most of those who took part in the shitstorm considered Marco Crepaldi much more intolerant than he really is. In this sense, the whole story leaves many of the interviewees disappointed, convinced that it would have been possible to make a better use of this event to deepen the issues connected to male problems in an original way.

Discussion and conclusions

While contemporary pro male movements are often thought to be a coherent object with a cohesive set of beliefs, our research suggests that when people discuss male issues there is a heterogeneity of opinions that cannot be completely encapsulated in the rhetoric of the manosphere. Even though a great part of Marco Crepaldi's content recall themes and concepts usually shared in these misogynistic communities—albeit mitigated by an apparently progressive sensibility—what people get from his discourses is often steeped in ambivalence. In that sense, we have identified two subject positions emerging from our data. The concept of subject positions holds that people make sense of who they are by locating themselves within culturally circulating discourses and narratives (Fairclough, 1992). The first subject-position that our participants tend to assume in order to make sense of Marco Crepaldi's discourse is a *defensive* one. As our research confirms, this position seems to emerge as a reaction to the wide circulation of feminism in popular and commercial media, such as digital spaces like blogs, Instagram, and Twitter, as well as broadcast media. Popular feminism is part of the larger attention economy, where its sheer accessibility—through shared images, likes, clicks, followers, retweets, and so on—is a key component of its popularity. In such a context, it is inevitable that the feminist issues that receive the most attention are precisely those that end up reaffirming a neoliberal version of entrepreneurial femininity, that retrieves historically feminist concepts, such as empowerment and choice, in order to *depoliticize* them, without challenging deep structures of inequities (McRobbie, 2008). In this sense, critique of the business of platforms such as *Freeda* that emerged in our focus groups might seem similar to that which many activists have been ascribing for years to postfeminism. Despite the substantive knowledge gap about what feminism is/was among younger people, participants in our focus groups are aware of the distinction between media feminism *tout court* and the so-called "digital" feminism more than Crepaldi himself. Nevertheless, even if they are capable of distinguishing between different kind of feminism, many participants consider the popularity of digital feminism as proof of the internet's progressive *feminization* (Duffy, 2017). Even though the history of the Internet is deeply embedded in masculine codes and values (see van Zoonen, 2002), many participants share the idea that girls on the Internet have more power than men, considering the success of *influencers* on Instagram, the greater female opportunities in *dating* apps such as Tinder, or the recent rise of social media platforms such as OnlyFans. The alleged feminization of the Internet tends to favor in many younger users an unrealistic perception of women's real status: though the evidence suggests that men are in the driver's seat when it comes to sex, they think that women have all the power in the romantic sphere, especially the privilege to compare and choose (Kimmel, 2008). Such a posture is particularly appealing to those mostly younger men who feel disempowered by the shift in gender roles of the recent decades and is confirmed by the results of our research. Indeed, in order to contrast this false belief, many men seem to respond with a sort of *possessive reinvestment* in their own masculinity; that is, the claim of an idea of masculinity made of moral cynicism, self-mastery, and impenetrability to any conditioning of the feminine. Even though many participants do not explicitly mention the idea of "taking the Red Pill", their discourses are imbued with the themes of individualism, rationalism, and self-discipline that circulate in the manosphere. This is demonstrated by the derogatory term "Simp". The concept of the "Simp", in fact, indicates all those males who have lost control of themselves, who carry out feminist social demands not because they are really interested, but because they are unable to stand up to the manipulative power of female sexuality (White, 2019). This confirms how, for a certain generation of young men, a substantive knowledge gap about what feminism is, combined with continued exposure to postfeminism ideas on digital platforms has arguably created the perfect conditions for anti-feminist ideas to thrive (Ging, 2019).

The second subject-position can be labeled as *adaptive*. Mimicking the discursive practices of popular feminism, such as attention to the mechanisms of gendered socialization processes, the emphasis on the social costs of sexual roles, the exploitation of the therapeutic language of empowerment and self-awareness pushes men to seek a new mutual recognition based on the sharing of their own specific condition of discrimination. As the earlier analysis makes clear, Crepaldi represents one example of this trend. In order to distance himself from the overt anti-feminist and misogyny of groups such as Incel or Red Pillers, as well as from the conservative *heteropaternalism* that has traditionally characterized the more historical anti-feminism of father's rights groups, he seems to mimic what Banet-Weiser (2018) calls the *sentimental earnestness* of popular feminism. Sentimental earnestness is a specific mode of address exploited in many recent feminist campaigns that present girls and women as being "in crisis"—a crisis due to insecurity or a lack of self-confidence, among other things. Crepaldi mirrors the same logic but in a way that distorts and transforms the target of empowerment so that it is men who are discriminated against and in need of recuperation and reparation. It goes without saying that this kind of *affective engagement* is highly controversial because it leads to a falsely symmetrical call for women's and men's liberation from oppressive sex roles and discredits any feminist analysis of structural and political inequalities between sexes as unnecessary and unreasonable. As we saw earlier, by focusing their attention on how men are disadvantaged by gender role stereotypes, many pro-male groups may provide fuel for male backlash against feminism under the guise of male suffering (Schmitz & Kazyak, 2016). That said, his style seems to be appreciated by many participants who took part in our focus group. According to them, offering a narrative that excludes the idea of male privilege could help vulnerable men to better cope with their social anxieties and feelings of powerlessness (Jefferson, 2002). In that sense, Crepaldi might represents a way to come to terms with the reality of male discomfort and prevent it from feeding into more violent deviant subcultures of the manosphere. As our results show, Crepaldi's YouTube channel attracts members who have witnessed or experienced some kind of discomfort resulting from the pressures exerted on them by hegemonic masculinity—the pressure to not appear weak or effeminate, pressure to be strong or to be a leader. Unbeknownst to them, they have likely spent more time pondering gender theory than have most other men.

Following Marco Crepaldi, they try to adapt their ideas about gender equality (the ideas that feminists have been battling for decades), without necessarily having to identify themselves as feminists or to delve into feminist thought. Of course, this behavior also has its ugly side, because it can provide fuel for male backlash against feminism under the guise of male suffering. Nevertheless, when our participants talk about male problems, a good part of their arguments revolves around the rejection of patriarchal notions of gender essentialism, which assume men to be naturally rough, tough, and sexually aggressive. A lot of people who adopt this narrative genuinely care about gender equality. So, to our participants, it is incorrect to label every man who talks about male issues online as an Incel. At the same time, it is wrong to consider Crepaldi the Italian version of Jordan Peterson. This is confirmed by the arguments our participants express regarding the shitstorm against him. For many, addressing the YouTuber with phrases like "cry white man" risks confirming the popular gender stereotypes that men don't cry. In that sense, their discourses seem to echo Segal's terms (1990) that it is playing masculinity's own game to suggest that men do not experience fear, trauma, and bodily shattering, much like a woman.

In conclusion, the data we have collected show us how the case of Marco Crepaldi introduces an element of novelty in the theorization of the *deviant* nature of the manosphere in that, while on one hand his activity risks reactivating certain consolidated mechanisms of hegemonic or toxic masculinity (Connell & Messerschmidt, 2005), on the other hand it seems to open up spaces for negotiation with respect to certain feminist demands.

Of course, rarely can the topics discussed by Crepaldi and our participants be considered explicitly pro-feminist. On the contrary, Crepaldi himself is responsible for downplaying the existence of men's institutionalized power. That said, it is inaccurate to ignore that a good part of his argument is addressed to criticizing patriarchal gender ideology, an ideology that feminists have been battling for decades. In this context, the assimilation of elements of feminist culture into heterosexual masculinities may be considered different from a repackaging of forms of domination (Ingram & Waller, 2014) or a masquerade behind which pro-male groups try to attract educated middle-class white men who do not want to appear to be backwards misogynists (Messner, 2016). On the contrary, it is important to consider that there are contradictory ideas circulating in the *pro-male* groups, and members can use different, and often conflicting, discourses to make sense of their investment in these groups. Although the manosphere is now considered an identity category in popular debates, it is possible to distinguish activists who are convincedly anti-feminist from those who are really worried about men's issues (Allan, 2016). Focusing on such heterogeneity could be a crucial first step in bridging the divide between the pro-male groups and feminism, which are still seen as opposing sides in the fight for gender equality.

Notes

1 www.freedamedia.com/?fbclid=IwAR0OjtZTtHHp9YyLFa4P9tNK85A8sKqDgkROuL5Ox-uCeTZF9LTnU2NGAsc
2 www.dictionary.com/e/slang/simp/

References

Allan, J. A. (2016). Phallic affect, or why men's rights activists have feelings. *Men and Masculinities*, *19*(1), 22–41. https://doi.org/10.1177/1097184X15574338

Anderson, E. (2011). *Inclusive masculinity: The changing nature of masculinities*. Routledge.

Baele, S. J., Brace, L., & Coan, T. G. (2021). From "Incel" to "Saint": Analyzing the violent worldview behind the 2018 Toronto attack. *Terrorism and Political Violence*, *33*(8), 1667–1691. https://doi.org/10.1080/09546553.2019.1638256

Banet-Weiser, S. (2018). *Empowered: Popular feminism and popular misogyny*. Duke University Press Books.

Barbour, R. (2007). *Doing focus groups*. Sage.

Bertone, C., & Ferrero Camoletto, R. (2009). Beyond the sex machine? Sexual practices and masculinity in adult men's heterosexual accounts. *Journal of Gender Studies*, *18*(4), 369–386. https://doi.org/10.1080/09589230903260035

Blais, M., & Dupuis-Déri, F. (2012). Masculinism and the antifeminist countermovement. *Social Movement Studies*, *11*(1), 21–39. https://doi.org/10.1080/14742837.2012.640532

Bolgan, S., Mosca, D., McLean, C., & Rusconi, E. (2016). Systemizers are better code-breakers: Self-reported systemizing predicts code-breaking performance in expert hackers and naïve participants. *Frontiers in Human Neuroscience*, *10*, 229. https://doi.org/10.3389/fnhum.2016.00229

Bowling, A. (1997). *Research methods in health*. Open University Press.

Bratich, J., & Banet-Weiser, S. (2019). From pick-up artists to Incels: Con(Fidence) games, networked misogyny, and the failure of neoliberalism. *International Journal of Communication, 13,* 5003–5027.

Cannito, M., & Mercuri, E. (2021). Fatherhood and gender relations in the manosphere: Exploring an Italian non-resident fathers' online forum. *European Journal of Cultural Studies, 25*(4), 110–129. https://doi.org/10.1177/13675494211036967

Clatterbaugh, K. (1996). *Contemporary perspectives on masculinity: Men, women, and politics in modern society.* Westview Press.

Connell, R. W. (1995). *Masculinities.* Polity Press.

Connell, R. W., & Messerschmidt, J. W. (2005). Hegemonic masculinity: Rethinking the concept. *Gender & Society, 19*(6), 829–859. https://doi.org/10.1177/0891243205278639

Crepaldi, M. (2019). *Hikikomori. I giovani che non escono di casa.* Alpes.

Dardot, P., & Laval, C. (2009). *La nouvelle raison du monde: Essai sur la société néolibérale.* Editions La Découverte.

Dordoni, A., & Magaraggia, S. (2021). Modelli di mascolinità nei gruppi online Incel e Red Pill: Narrazione vittimistica di sé, deumanizzazione e violenza contro le donne. *AG About Gender—Rivista internazionale di studi di genere, 10*(19), 35–67. https://dx.doi.org/10.15167/2279-5057/AG2021.10.19.1268

Duffy, B. E. (2017). *(Not) Getting paid to do what you love: Gender, social media, and aspirational work.* Yale University Press.

Fairclough, N. (1992). *Discourse and social change.* Polity.

Farci, M., & Ricci, O. (2021). Io onestamente oggi non vorrei rinascere maschio. Il caso marco Crepaldi. *AG About Gender—Rivista internazionale di studi di genere, 10*(19), 167–198. https://doi.org/10.15167/2279-5057/AG2021.10.19.1269

Farci, M., & Righetti, N. (2019). Italian men's rights activism and online backlash against feminism. *Rassegna Italiana Di Sociologia, 4*(2019), 765–781. https://doi.org/10.1423/96115.

Farquhar, C., & Das, R. (1999). Are focus groups suitable for "sensitive" topics? In R. Barbour & J. Kitzinger (Eds.), *Developing focus group research: Politics, theory and practice* (pp. 47–64). Sage.

Ferrero Camoletto, R., & Bertone, C. (2010). Coming to be a man: Pleasure in the construction of Italian men's (Hetero)sexuality. *Italian Studies, 65*(2), 235–250. https://doi.org/10.1179/0161462 10X12593180182775

Ging, D. (2017). Alphas, betas, and incels: Theorizing the masculinities of the manosphere. *Men and Masculinities, 22*(4), 638–657. https://doi.org/10.1177/1097184X17706401

Ging, D. (2019). Bros v. Hos: Postfeminism, anti-feminism and the Toxic Turn in digital gender politics. In D. Ging & E. Siapera (Eds.), *Gender hate online: Understanding the new anti-feminist* (pp. 45–67). Palgrave Macmillan.

Gotell, L., & Dutton E. (2016). Sexual violence in the "manosphere": Antifeminist men's rights discourses on rape. *International Journal for Crime, Justice and Social Democracy, 5*(2), 65–80. https://doi.org/10.5204/ijcjsd.v5i2.310.

Halkier, B. (2010). Focus groups as social enactments: Integrating interaction and content in the analysis of focus group data. *Qualitative Research, 10,* 71–89. https://doi.org/10.1177/1468794109348683

Hollway, W. (1984). Gender difference and the production of subjectivity. In J. Henriques, W. Hollway, C. Urwin, C. Venn, & V. Walkerdine (Eds.), *Changing the subject psychology, social regulation and subjectivity* (pp. 227–263). Methuen.

Ingram, N., & Waller, R. (2014). Degrees of masculinity: Working and middle-class undergraduate students' constructions of masculine identities. In S. Roberts (Ed.), *Debating modern masculinities: Change, continuity, crisis?* (pp. 35–51). Palgrave Macmillan

Jefferson, T. (2002). Subordinating hegemonic masculinity. *Theoretical Criminology.*, *6*(1), 63–73. https://doi.org/10.1177/1362480602006001

Johansson, T., & Klinth, R. (2008). Caring fathers: The ideology of gender equality and masculine positions. *Men and Masculinities, 11*(1), 42–62. https://doi.org/10.1177/1097184X06291899.

Kaufman, M. (1994). Men, feminism, and men's contradictory experiences of power. In H. Brod & M. Kaufman (Eds.), *Theorizing masculinities* (pp. 142–163). Sage.

Kimmel, M. S. (2008). *Guyland: The perilous world where boys become men.* Harper.

Kitzinger, J. (1994). The methodology of focus groups: The importance of interaction between research participants. *Sociology of Health and Illness, 16*(1), 103–121. https://doi.org/10.1111/1467-9566. ep11347023

Kitzinger, J., & Farquhar, C. (1999). The analytical potential of "sensitive moments" in focus group discussions. In R. Barbour & J. Kitzinger (Eds.), *Developing focus group research: Politics, theory and practice* (pp. 156–173). Sage.

Lawson, S. L. (2019). *Theorizing deviance: Sociology of crime and deviance in the manosphere* [Master thesis, University of Toronto]. Retrieved from www.academia.edu/41606360/SOC212_Theorizing_Deviance_Sociology_of_Crime_and_Deviance_in_the_Manosphere (accessed 27 June 2023).

Liang Lin, J. (2017). Antifeminism online MGTOW (Men Going Their Own Way). In U. Frömming, S. Köhn, & S. Fox (Eds.), *Digital environments: Ethnographic perspectives across global online and offline spaces* (pp. 77–81). Bielefeld.

Lilly, M. (2016). *The world is not a safe place for men': The representational politics of the manosphere* [Master thesis, University of Ottawa]. Retrieved from https://ruor.uottawa.ca/handle/10393/35055 (accessed 27 June 2023).

Liong, M., & Chan, L. S. (2020). Walking a tightrope on (Hetero)Sexuality: Performatively vigilant masculine subjectivity in response to sexualized culture. *Men and Masculinities, 23*(2), 225–41. https://doi.org/10.1177/1097184X17753267

Marchi, F. (2018). *Contromano. Critica dell"ideologia politicamente corretta*. Zambon Editore.

Marwick, A. E., & Caplan, R. (2018). Drinking male tears: Language, the manosphere, and networked harassment. *Feminist Media Studies, 18*(4), 543–59. https://doi.org/10.1080/14680777.2018.1450568

McRobbie, A. (2008). *The aftermath of feminism: Gender, culture and social change*. Sage.

Messner, M. A. (1997). *Politics of masculinities: Men in movements*. Sage.

Messner, M. A. (2016). Forks in the Road of men's gender politics: Men's rights vs feminist allies. *International Journal for Crime, Justice and Social Democracy, 5*(2), 6–20. https://doi.org/10.5204/ijcjsd.v5i2.301

Morgan, D. L., & Krueger, R. A. (1993). When to use focus groups and why. In D. L. Morgan (Ed.), *Successful focus groups: Advancing the state of the art* (pp. 1–19). Sage.

Morgan, D. L., & Krueger, R. A. (1998). *The focus group kit*. Sage.

Nagle, A. (2017). *Kill all normies: Online culture wars from 4Chan And Tumblr to Trump and the alt-right*. Zero Books.

O'Neill, R. (2018). *Seduction: Men, Masculinity and mediated intimacy*. Polity Press.

Pascoe, C. J. (2007). *Dude, You're a Fag: Masculinity and sexuality in High School*. University of California Press.

Petersen, A. (1998). *Unmasking the Masculine: 'Men' and 'Identity' in a Sceptical Age*. Sage.

Piccone, S. (2000). Gli Studi Sulla Mascolinità. Scoperte e Problemi Di Un Campo Di Ricerca. *Rassegna Italiana Di Sociologia, 1*(2000), 81–108. https://doi.org/10.1423/2531.

Pleck, J. H. (1981). *Myth of masculinity*. MIT Press.

Ravn, S. (2018). "I would never start a fight but . . .": Young masculinities, perceptions of violence, and symbolic boundary work in focus groups. *Men and Masculinities, 21*(2), 291–309. https://doi.org/10.1177/1097184X17696194

Renzetti, C. M., & Lee, R. M. (1993). *Researching sensitive topics*. Sage.

Rubin, R. (2004). Men talking about Viagra: An exploratory study with focus groups. *Men and Masculinities, 7*(1), 22–30. https://doi.org/10.1177/1097184X03257439

Savran, D. (1998). *Taking it like a man: White masculinity, masochism, and contemporary American culture*. Princeton University Press.

Scarcelli, C. M. (2021). Manosphere periferiche. Ragazzi, omosocialità e pratiche digitali. *AG About Gender—Rivista internazionale di studi di Genere, 10*(19), 1–34. https://doi.org/10.15167/2279-5057/AG2021.10.19.1278

Schmitz, R. M., & Kazyak E. (2016). Masculinities in cyberspace: An analysis of portrayals of manhood in men's rights activist websites. *Social Sciences, 5*(2), 18–28. https://doi.org/10.3390/socsci5020018

Segal, L. (1990). *Slow motion: Changing masculinities, changing men*. Virago.

Seidler, V. J. (1989). *Rediscovering MASCULINITY: Reason, language and sexuality*. Routledge.

Seigfried-Spellar, K. C., O'Quinn, C. L., & Treadway, K. N. (2015). Assessing the relationship between autistic traits and cyberdeviancy in a sample of college students. *Behaviour & Information Technology, 34*(5), 533–542. https://doi.org/10.1080/0144929X.2014.978377

Sharkey, G. (2021.) Failure to thrive: Incels, boys and feminism. *Continuum, 36,* 37–51. https://doi.org/10.1080/10304312.2021.1958160

Stenner, P. (1993). Discoursing jealousy. In E. Burman & I. Parker (Eds.), *Discourse analytic research: Repertoires and readings of texts in action* (pp. 114–132). Taylor & Francis/Routledge.

Sugiura, L. (2021). *The incel rebellion: The rise of the manosphere and the virtual war against women.* Emerald Publishing Limited.

Van Valkenburgh, S. P. (2018). Digesting the red pill: Masculinity and neoliberalism in the manosphere. *Men and Masculinities, 24*(1), 1–20. https://doi.org/10.1177/1097184X18816118.

Van Zoonen, L. (2002). Gendering the internet claims, controversies and cultures. *European Journal of Communication, 17,* 5–23. https://doi.org/10.1177/0267323102017001605

Vingelli, G. (2017). Patriarchy strikes back: A case study on men's rights movements in Italy. In J. Ros Velasco (Ed.), *Feminism: Past, Present and Future Perspectives* (pp. 175–197). Nova Publishing.

White, M. (2019). *Producing masculinity: The internet, gender, and sexuality.* Routledge.

Wilkinson, S. (1998). Focus groups in health research: Exploring the meanings of health and illness. *Journal of Health Psychology, 3,* 329–349. https://doi.org/10.1177/135910539800300304

19

"IS MY FEAR OF TRANSPHOBIA JUST A LITTLE OUT OF CONTROL?"

A qualitative exploration of the use of online forums by trans people

Susana Avalos

Introduction

"We shouldn't have to feel trapped," says Ash[1] (trans woman), who is sharing her personal experiences with being out full time[2] to support a member who feels that the "world will always hate her" for being trans. Several other trans men and trans women join in on the conversation offering similar advice while sharing their personal experiences navigating everyday life as a trans person. Historically, transgender[3] people, also referred to as trans, have been viewed as "abnormal," "illegitimate," and "inferior" due to widely held hetero-cis-normative beliefs[4] (Worthen, 2016). These beliefs put trans people at elevated risk of transphobic harm (acts of violence, discrimination, or prejudice committed against trans people) and other negative outcomes. For instance, trans people experience harassment, abuse, discrimination, victimization, and criminalization at higher rates than cisgender[5] people (James et al., 2016; Walker et al., 2018). These adverse experiences place trans people at an economic disadvantage and put them at a higher risk of negative health outcomes such as depression, anxiety, low self-esteem, self-harming behaviors, and suicidality than cisgender people (Cipolletta et al., 2017; Ross & Scholl, 2016; Walker et al., 2018).

Online spaces are found to be valuable spaces where information that is otherwise unavailable or hard to access can be easily obtained, especially for marginalized people (Mehra et al., 2004). However, relative to other marginalized communities, much remains unknown about the use of online spaces by trans people. Extant research, while limited, shows that trans people use social media platforms to find information related to their identity (Cipolletta et al., 2017; Liamputtong et al., 2020), resources (Ross & Scholl, 2016), safety from sexual violence (Noack-Lundberg et al., 2020) and peer support (Hawkins & Haimson, 2018). Missing from the literature is how trans people use online spaces for support regarding perceived or attempted transphobic harm and the potential benefits using these spaces has on their safety and well-being. Given that roughly 1.6 million people ages 13+ identify as trans in the U.S. (Herman et al., 2022), exploring online spaces' potential uses and benefits is important for this special population.

DOI: 10.4324/9781003277675-22

This chapter explores how trans people support and empower one another, how online spaces may reduce the emotional and psychological distress associated with high rates of abuse, discrimination, and harassment, and the role of online trans communities in preventing or reducing existing or future victimization. To better understand how trans people navigate their daily adverse experiences and the role of the internet in facilitating a livable life, it is crucial to understand the potential benefits of using online spaces in reducing feelings of social isolation, exclusion, self-doubt, and fear. Doing so could help inform service providers on potential coping mechanisms trans people could use to prevent negative transphobic experiences and overcome the associated psychological and emotional distress.

Literature review

Trans people's social experiences

Relative to the cisgender population, trans people are vulnerable to multiple types of gender-based violence, discrimination, and poly-victimization. For instance, trans people are vulnerable to sexual assault and physical assault, intimate partner violence, non-partner sexual assault, anti-trans family violence, etc., over their life course (Messinger et al., 2021). The risk of victimization is elevated when trans people are women, are less visually conforming, and/or are "out" about being trans (Messinger et al., 2021). While all trans people may experience one or more forms of discrimination and abuse, trans people of color experience "deeper and broader patterns of discrimination" compared to white trans people (James et al., 2016, p. 4). Specifically, research shows that trans women of color experience higher levels of violence, poverty, incarceration, substance use, mental health conditions (depression, anxiety, suicidality, etc.), and victimization compared to white trans women due to the country's history with racism (Jackson et al., 2022).

Additionally, trans people are denied equal treatment or services in places of public accommodation because people disagree with their gender identity. For example, trans people report being discriminated against or harassed by staff or employees in areas of public transportation, gyms, retail stores, restaurants, government assistance programs, nursing homes, courts, legal services from attorneys, drug or alcohol programs, domestic violence shelters, etc. (James et al., 2016). These experiences with violence and discrimination make trans people fear that they will be mistreated or attacked should they seek public accommodations. Indeed, they may avoid these places altogether to limit potentially uncomfortable or violent confrontations. Together, these experiences contribute to trans people's social exclusion and isolation.

Trans people's experiences with the criminal legal system

The violence and discrimination committed against trans people is not limited to the actions of the general population. Research shows criminal legal actors can also be hostile toward trans people (James et al., 2016). When interacting with criminal legal actors, trans people, especially trans people of color, are discriminated against by police, court officials, and correctional staff (Buist & Stone, 2014). Police are found to harass and assault (physically and sexually) trans people during police stops (Grant et al., 2011; James et al., 2016).

Specifically, trans women of color are subject to frequent police stops and searches as they are presumed to be sex workers (Carpenter & Marshall, 2017). These police stops are believed to be based on historically stigmatizing beliefs of trans people as sexually deviant and perverse (Buist & Lenning, 2022). Indeed, Black (33%) and multiracial (30%) trans women report that officers assumed they were sex workers when stopped or pulled over (James et al., 2016). This type of police profiling happens often enough that the term "walking while trans" was coined (Carpenter & Marshall, 2017). As a result, trans people, largely due to transphobia, cissexism, and racism, are disproportionately visible in the criminal legal system (Avalos, 2022). Research shows that one in five trans women are incarcerated in their lifetime (Ezie & Saenz, 2020).

Historically, carceral spaces are gendered and sex-segregated, meaning people are placed based on their gender assigned at birth (Mogul et al., 2011). Research shows that 60% of all trans people who have been incarcerated have been incorrectly placed (Lambda Legal, 2014). Consequently, once in carceral spaces, trans people are subject to high harassment and violent victimization rates by correctional staff and other incarcerated people, especially when they are trans women. For example, trans people are five times more likely to be sexually assaulted by correctional staff and nine times more likely to be sexually assaulted by other incarcerated people than their cisgender counterparts (James et al., 2016). Relative to their white trans counterparts, Black trans women are subject to higher sexual and physical assault rates (James et al., 2016). Due to unclear and conflicting policies, trans people are also more likely to be placed in solitary confinement, which is known for causing severe psychological and emotional distress to incarcerated people (Malkin & DeJong, 2019; Rosenberg & Oswin, 2015; Sexton et al., 2010).

Finally, in court settings, trans people are vulnerable to mistreatment, discrimination, and abuse by court officials, judges, attorneys, and juries are often uninformed or misinformed about trans identities, whether they are victims, offenders, or in need of court services (Braunstein, 2017; James et al., 2016). For example, when dealing with custody matters, trans parents believe they are less likely to get custody of their children because people disagree with their trans identity (Grant et al., 2011). Based on their negative experiences with criminal legal actors and within the criminal legal system, trans people do not feel comfortable or safe interacting with criminal legal actors. Mistreatment by all members of society, lack of access to resources, income, and discrimination in employment, healthcare, legal settings, and housing are reasons some trans people may seek community-based support from readily available resources such as online spaces.

Uses and benefits of online spaces

For many Americans, internet access is integral to daily life. The internet is used to access news, education (e.g., to do homework, online classes), remote jobs, resources, and to connect with family, friends, acquaintances, etc. It is estimated that 92% of U.S. households own a computer, 85% own a smartphone, 63% own a tablet, and 85% have access to broadband internet (Martin, 2021). As internet use has increased over the decades, scholars have explored its value, potential, and consequences (Barry, 2018). Research has found problematic internet consumption behaviors, such as media addiction, are associated with poor mental health outcomes (El Asam et al., 2019; LaRose et al., 2003; Marchant et al., 2017). Further, the internet can be used to disseminate misinformation intentionally

(Waszak et al., 2018). Conversely, online spaces are valuable locations where people seek out information that cannot be obtained through traditional means, specifically for minoritized and marginalized populations (Mehra et al., 2004).

Data on trans people's internet use is limited, as most government agencies do not collect information regarding gender identity. However, one study shows that among trans participants, three-quarters used the internet to gather information about their identities, resources, and community (Hill, 2005). For trans people, the internet can be a safe space to engage in meaningful conversations and relationships (Ross & Scholl, 2016). The internet provides access to resources that are otherwise difficult to obtain, facilitates the spread of information (and counters misinformation), and helps trans people educate themselves and others about their identities.

Trans youth are specifically found to be drawn to using online spaces as they are vulnerable to discrimination (bullying, school policies such as sports and bathroom bans), violence, and trauma that socially isolate them and make them vulnerable to self-harming behaviors (Grossman & D'Augelli, 2006, 2007; Hellen, 2009; Meadow, 2018). Online spaces are described as safe spaces to engage in conversations regarding their identity, health, and safety (Austin et al., 2020; GLSEN et al., 2013) and improve trans youth's well-being (Austin et al., 2020). Similarly, trans adults have positive outcomes when using trans-inclusive spaces. Trans-inclusive online spaces are easily accessible and convenient and reduce trans people's feelings of isolation and exclusion (Hawkins & Haimson, 2018). As such, trans adults find these spaces to be therapeutic and positively impact their identity and well-being (Hawkins & Haimson, 2018; Ross & Scholl, 2016).

In sum, online spaces allow trans people (adults and youths) to connect with others going through similar experiences and contribute to trans people's sense of self-discovery (Ross & Scholl, 2016). These spaces are found to be important for identity formation, peer support, and for locating resources. While the literature explores issues related to health, transition, and safety from sexual violence, little research explores narratives of resilience among trans people, specifically how they navigate everyday transphobic harassment, discrimination, and violence using trans-inclusive online spaces and the benefit of using these spaces.

Current study

Although prior research demonstrates trans people, namely trans youth, benefit from online spaces, minimal research has explored trans people's help-seeking behaviors regarding attempted or perceived transphobic harm. Online communities provide opportunities to discuss interests and fears and disclose behaviors on- and offline. While the results may not be generalizable to other contexts or trans experiences, the information obtained may be invaluable from a research standpoint. Their posts can be used to inform other trans people of potential coping mechanisms to limit exposure to adverse experiences.

These data are derived from a larger project that explored trans people's resilience strategies. This study utilized a sample of 19 discussion threads and 202 comments posted by members across two online forums. These forums are trans-inclusive spaces as they are considered safe and supportive spaces where trans and other gender minorities could engage in conversations with minimal risk of being cyberbullied or harassed. A qualitative analysis was performed based on an online forum analysis of users' posts that sought advice or support related to their safety and transphobic harm.

Methods

This study is situated within unobtrusive research, a method that assesses actual behavior rather than reported behavior and is repeatable, accessible, inexpensive, and safe for researchers and other people as observations are made discreetly in a non-disruptive way (Lee, 2019; Kellehear, 2020). As the internet has become a preferred method of communication, online data collection methods have increased in visibility (Im & Chee, 2006). Among those methods, online forum analyses are the most frequently used qualitative internet research and are described as the most appropriate method for conducting a qualitative analysis (Im & Chee, 2012). Online forum analyses allow the researcher(s) flexibility to collect data over long periods of time, reduce safety concerns, and do not require subject participation (Im & Chee, 2006). While no participants were actively recruited for this study, IRB approval was obtained by the author from their institution to conduct an online forum analysis.

Forum selection

Forums were located by searching "transgender forums" on Google. The Google search yielded a variety of trans-specific online forums, many of which were support forums for trans adults, youths, or family members (partners, parents, grandparents, siblings, children, etc.). While most forums were open to the public, some required membership to be viewed. For all forums observed, membership was required to post. During the application process, individuals are asked a combination of open-ended and closed-ended questions to ensure people who are prejudiced against trans people do not join these sites. Due to privacy concerns, some forums explicitly state that they do not allow research to be conducted on their site, or there is a statement requiring researchers to ask for permission beforehand. For this study, two forums[6] that allowed researchers (without the need for permission) and were open to the public domain were analyzed. Qualitative data were derived from observations of these two trans-specific online forums. Participants self-selected into the forums and participated in asynchronous discussions relevant to their identity, needs, and concerns. From there, discussion board threads were selected based on their relevance to the research aims.

Analytic strategy

Across the forums, trans people could seek support for various topics, ranging from health, relationships, coming out, transitioning, family support, etc. On these forums, people select the discussion board threads they identify with the most based on their gender identity or needs. For instance, if someone is interested in getting support for their non-binary, genderqueer, or trans identity, there are specific discussion board threads they may choose. The focus of this study was on trans people; therefore, only the discussion board threads relevant to trans people were analyzed. To narrow down threads specific to violence, discussion board threads under the categories of "discrimination" and "hate" were chosen. From there, keywords such as "hate," "afraid," "transphobia," "help," and "safety" were selected, and the threads analyzed. A pseudonym was assigned to ensure anonymity and privacy if a quote was taken.

Using grounded theory (GT) as an analytical strategy (Chun Tie et al., 2019), the threads were thematically analyzed and open-coded on Microsoft software (Word). The GT method is structured while allowing the researcher(s) flexibility to analyze data while building emerging theories (Ruppel & Mey, 2015). The GT method is particularly useful for interpreting qualitative data but is also applicable to quantitative data (Chun Tie et al., 2019). To date, there are no extant theories explaining how trans people use online spaces to navigate the adverse experiences they face in public or private spaces, nor are there any theories explaining the role of online trans communities in developing coping mechanisms necessary to overcome such adverse experiences. Given the GT method's flexibility, it was possible to explore how online trans communities develops agency and how involvement in these spaces increases trans people's feelings of safety and well-being.

Sample characteristics

The subject population is trans people, the group most suited to weigh in on trans people's perceptions of and responses to transphobic harm. This group includes, but is not limited to, trans women and trans men, non-binary, intersex, two-spirit, or gender non-conforming people. While some trans people identify as a man or woman, others do not and may instead identify as other gender identities. On these forums, trans youth can post and engage in conversations under specific categories labeled for trans youth. However, on the analyzed threads, most of the forum members who posted were determined to be trans adults based on self-reported information. On these forums, most members voluntarily share their gender identity markers below their pictures (male or female, trans man or woman, non-binary, genderqueer, etc.), pronouns (she/her, he/him, they/them, etc.), and terms associated with their sexuality (lesbian, gay, bisexual, straight, etc.). Some members also voluntarily share additional information on their discussion board posts, such as age and location (or region).

Across 19 threads, 202 comments were analyzed. Most members posting questions on discussion boards self-identified as trans women ($N = 13$), trans men ($N = 4$), non-binary ($N = 4$), a transsexual woman[7] ($N = 1$), and an androgynous[8] individual ($N = 1$). Since gender identity markers were shared in every thread analyzed, it was possible to collect this information. The gender identity markers were similar for the members who commented on the posts, $N = 138$ for trans women, $N=17$ for trans men, $N = 1$ for transsexual woman, $N = 6$ for non-binary people, and $N = 1$ for androgynous. Additional demographic information was unavailable unless the members voluntarily shared that information when asking or responding to discussion posts.

Findings

An analysis of these forums demonstrates that these online spaces can have a prosocial influence on trans people. Discussions among forum members foster the development of problem-focused (a strategy that aids with the development of potential solutions to manage stress effectively), appraisal-focused (a strategy that challenges assumptions by modifying the way one thinks), and emotion-focused coping strategies (a strategy that alleviates distress associated with a certain situation) when responding to transphobic violence (Baker & Berenbaum, 2007; Senanayake et al., 2018). Together, these coping strategies enable trans people to develop potential solutions for effectively managing the emotional and psychological distress associated with their adverse experiences.

Moving through physical spaces

Grounded theory analysis reveals three themes for moving through physical spaces: learning self-defense, hypervigilance, and utilizing selective listening and inattention. Two sub-themes were identified for selective listening and inattention: walking confidently and practicing mindfulness. In this context, physical spaces were described as public or private outdoor or shared spaces, such as malls, bars, restaurants, bedrooms, and homes. An analysis of the forums demonstrated that the members' fears were centered around leaving the comfort of their safe space (a location where trans people do not have to worry about having negative interactions with people). Members had many concerns regarding transphobic harm when leaving their safe spaces, as discussed here.

Learning self-defense

For forum members, the looming threat of being victimized determines whether they leave the comfort of their safe space. Savanna (trans woman) fears being victimized now that she is beginning her transition (male to female) and seeks advice on whether she should purchase a weapon or take self-defense classes to defend herself. Specifically, she posts that she fears being the victim of trans bashing (i.e., being physically, sexually, emotionally, or verbally victimized because someone disagrees with her gender identity). While some members supported using a weapon, most advocated for non-lethal methods of protecting themselves, such as learning hand-to-hand combat (karate, jujitsu) and or using mace, tasers, whistles, or not engaging at all. In this context, learning self-defense is a problem-focused coping mechanism for managing the stress associated with their fears of being victimized.

One member discussed how dangerous it is for a trans person to defend themselves, especially with a weapon, because "there is no such thing as defending yourself when you're trans." This belief is consistent with research that shows a trans person is likely to be blamed for their own victimization or not believed by police officials, especially if they are a Black trans person (Buist & Stone, 2014; Carpenter & Marshall, 2017; Donovan & Barnes, 2018; Guadalupe-Diaz & Jasinski, 2017). Whether members on these forums were aware of how police officials have mishandled cases involving trans people remains unknown. Still, most members advocated using non-lethal methods of self-defense because it is less dangerous than using a gun or a knife (i.e., they can be potentially arrested and or the perpetrator may take it away) and costs less.

While these were the common suggestions, some members brought up how inaccessible self-defense courses could be as some places are not accepting of trans people. In response, Stella (trans woman) suggests not engaging at all. Rather, she suggests they stand their ground (use intimidating stances) and speak up for themselves, an effective preventative measure used by cisgender women when seeking to resist being sexually victimized (Hollander, 2009). Another member (Mary, a trans woman) asks Savanna if her fears are real or if they are a projection of what she sees in the media. She asks:

> Is it really a problem where you live? Or is it a fear conjured up by reading what happens to some trans people in bad places? At some point you need to ask yourself, is my fear of transphobia out of control?

Mary attempts to challenge Savanna's thoughts regarding trans bashing and whether there is a need to purchase a weapon or take self-defense classes. In recent years, there has been an attempt to shift away from identity-based anti-violence narratives (narratives that include discussions of statistics of violence committed against trans people) because these narratives unintentionally give off the impression that trans lives are unlivable (trans people believe they are too vulnerable and fear victimization, so they avoid leaving their safe spaces; Westbrook, 2020). It is unknown if these new efforts by trans activists and advocates influence Mary's point of view, but it is important to note nonetheless. Future research should explore these types of exchanges between trans people to understand the impact moving beyond discourses of violence has on trans people's feelings of safety and overall well-being.

Hypervigilance

For some trans people who have a heightened fear of being victimized, they may choose to invest their money in protection rather than their transition. This was the case for Savanna (mentioned earlier). In her post, she expressed sadness for delaying her transition because she needed to purchase a weapon or take self-defense classes to feel safe. Extant research shows that trans people experience high rates of depression, anxiety, and overall distress based on a number of factors (e.g., social exclusion, isolation, internalized transphobia, etc.), including the transition process (Budge et al., 2013). Research indicates that the further an individual is in their transition process, the better their well-being is (Budge et al., 2012). In choosing to delay her transition to purchase a weapon or take self-defense courses for her safety, Savanna prolonged any distress she may be experiencing related to her gender identity.

In response to her concerns about where to allocate her funds, some members provided coping strategies with no monetary cost, specifically that of being hyper-vigilant of her surroundings. To members, being hyper-vigilant consisted of being alert in new, unlit, or dark places, not wearing headphones, and not taking shortcuts in unfamiliar neighborhoods. Anis (trans woman) suggested she not go out alone into unfamiliar neighborhoods or bars and, if she did go out, go to a heavily populated public place, like a mall, to reduce the possibility of "ending up as a statistic." In offering this advice, Anis and other members offer a problem-focused coping strategy for managing the stress associated with their fears of victimization.

Selective listening and inattention

As mentioned earlier, trans people are at increased risk of being victimized relative to cisgender people. With the heightened risk and the fear of trans bashing, members sought advice on responding to a person believed to be a threat. Most members advocated for the use of selective listening and inattention because, according to the members, transphobes (people prejudiced against trans people) will make hateful comments just to get them (trans people) to engage in a confrontation. Members consistently suggested to keep on walking and ignore the comments. Jesse (trans woman), responding to Jude's (transsexual woman) fear of leaving her safe zone, points out that because of transphobia (negative feelings, attitudes, or actions toward trans people) and toxic masculinity (unhealthy traditional gender roles where men are expected to be masculine, assertive, dominant, etc.), there will always be some "lout who needs to prove his superiority." Hence, the best thing they can do to protect themselves from harm is to keep walking. Regarding walking, members were explicit in their advice that they *walk confidently* (i.e., with direction and purpose) by mimicking cisgender women when in potentially harmful situations. One member suggested going to a mall and watching how cisgender women walk and talk so that they (trans women) "blend in" as much as possible.

Practicing mindfulness. Since ignoring comments was a consistent recommendation, members also suggested taking the time to process their emotions. Members suggest being aware of the negative feelings and practicing remaining calm. To do so, the advice was to practice mindfulness (an emotion-focused and appraisal-focused coping strategy). Practicing mindfulness was described as taking deep breaths, centering yourself, and concentrating on making yourself feel better by using positive thoughts when someone gets aggressive or confrontational rather than engaging with them. In this context, utilizing selective listening and inattention, walking confidently, and practicing mindfulness are preventative measures that can reduce the risk of victimization.

Overcoming perceived or attempted harm: how members build resilience

Two themes were identified when exploring how trans people respond to negative interactions or experiences and how they build resilience: encouragement and seeking therapy. For the encouragement theme, three sub-themes were identified: sharing personal experiences, humor, and pride. An analysis of the forums demonstrates that most of the fears shared are that of being potentially victimized, harassed, or discriminated against because of people's negative responses to their trans identity. Specifically, trans women were the most concerned about having negative interactions or experiences with transphobic people. The fears trans women experience are consistent with the literature that shows trans women are at higher risk of being violently victimized, harassed, or discriminated against (Blondeel et al., 2018; Flores et al., 2021; Messinger & Guadalupe-Diaz, 2020; Silva et al., 2022).

Among the members, there is a deep desire to live a life without the worry of being a victim of trans bashing. Through sharing personal experiences, the members uplift and inspire one another to be resilient. For the purpose of this chapter, resilience is conceptualized along similar lines as Momen and DeKeseredy (2020) as the ability to change or adapt to adverse circumstances, the capacity to overcome and recover from adverse experiences, and the ability to take a proactive approach when faced with adverse experiences. Their narratives are shared next.

Encouragement

Sharing personal experiences. When engaging in conversations involving attempted harm or perceived harm (the belief they will become a victim of a hate crime), some members made it a point to uplift the struggling members. For instance, Lynn (trans woman) posts about feeling hopeless because no matter what she does, she feels that the world will always hate her. Lynn is tired of the negativity toward her because people disagree with her gender identity, but she does not want to give up hope. Hence, she asks members to provide encouraging advice to overcome negative thoughts and self-talk. In response, members share personal experiences with coming out or transitioning part-time or full-time and how they handled similar fears. One member, Ash (trans woman), equates her experience before transitioning as feeling like being in a "straitjacket so tight you can't breathe" and the anger associated with such an experience as feeling like "you're choking to death." She explains that there comes a breaking point when sitting in "dark silence" is no longer an option if there is a desire to be truly and authentically happy, describing her experience after transitioning feeling like "you can finally breathe for the first time in your life."

In sharing how liberating her experience has been, Ash reassures Lynn and others reading the post that she is making the right decision despite the distress she is currently experiencing. Other members joined in, sharing their personal experiences fraught with difficulties, but the outcome was almost always positive post-transition. By sharing their personal experiences, the members encourage one another to be strong and resilient and reassure one another that they are making the best decision for themselves to move forward with the identity that has always been and feels right.

Humor. On the threads analyzed, discussions were centered around traumatic experiences, societal rejection, or fears of victimization. While some members shared personal experiences, others used humor to explain why certain people dislike trans people and what these perpetrators act or look like. One member calls transphobic people "crusty" and simple-minded. Another member explains that transphobic heterosexual, cisgender men attack trans people out of frustration that they cannot treat trans women like cisgender women, stating that because trans women are not "fertile and ready to bear their ugly ass children," men get angry about being unable to subjugate them. In making these comments, these members attempt to lighten the mood and shift the conversation to transphobic people as the problem, not their trans identity. Research shows that humor, when used positively, can be considered a cognitive protective factor linked to positive health outcomes such as improved self-esteem (Kfrerer et al., 2022). In this context, humor appears to be an appraisal-focused coping strategy that serves to challenge and change anti-trans attitudes held by trans people (internalized transphobia) and other people's transphobic views.

Pride. Across threads, members encouraged each other to take pride in their gender. For example, Jude (a Black transsexual woman) posts that it is difficult for her to leave her safe zone (her bedroom and neighborhood) because

> everyone seems to want to attack me, whether it is my pops [her dad] or someone else. Someone always has to say something to try to enable my anger. I know I have power over my emotions, but imma still stand up for myself by simply continuing to be who I am anyhow, no matter what the circumstances are in that or any given moment.

Despite being in a potentially dangerous situation that she is unable to leave, Jude gives herself and, in the process, others the encouragement to keep going. Members point out how valid her feelings and identity are and how strong and powerful she is for making the decision to transition. This type of encouragement to take pride in their gender is evident in threads where transitioning comes up, specifically for those early in their transition journey whose fear is paralyzing. Through sharing personal experiences, these trans folks demonstrate to each other that navigating life as a trans person can be difficult, but it does not have to be incapacitating. By sharing words of encouragement and affirmation, the online community fosters resilience and facilitates the process of taking pride in their gender.

Seeking therapy

Given the nature of the threads being analyzed, seeking therapy was consistently advised by members. This advice was generally under threads where members were interested in transitioning or were early in their transition journeys, whether it was to address internalized transphobia, transphobic views by others, fear of victimization, coping with a negative and traumatic experience, or simply wanting to understand their identity better. Members who were out full time were more likely to advocate for the use of therapy, sharing how their experiences in therapy increased their well-being. For example, Sam (trans woman) shared how her experience in therapy helped her address the internalized transphobia she struggled with during the early stages of her transition journey and put into perspective that not all people view trans people the same way. For members, seeking therapy is necessary to let go of incapacitating fears and build resiliency.

Discussion and conclusions

This chapter explored how trans people use online spaces. The findings demonstrate that online spaces can have a prosocial influence on trans people. Specifically, these forums act as sites of resistance that can help prevent victimization and foster resilience through various coping mechanisms. Within the context of this study, resistance is operationally defined similarly to Robinson and Schmitz (2021) as locations where trans people disrupt, challenge, and change stigmatizing narratives. Through sharing positive experiences and preventative measures (problem-focused, emotion-focused, and appraisal-focused coping mechanisms) members could use to protect themselves, the trans people in these forums cultivate hope for a livable life: that is, a fulfilling life where fear does not incapacitate them.

Across the forums and threads, members supported one another in meaningful ways while simultaneously challenging hetero-cis-normative biases, misogyny, and transphobia. By shifting preconceived ideas of their trans identities as the problem to transphobic people being the problem, the members facilitate the process of accepting and reclaiming their power (taking back control of their lives). In many ways, these members deconstruct stereotypical notions of hetero-cis-normativity while simultaneously building resilience.

Further, given that trans people are economically disadvantaged relative to the general population, the cost-free self-protective measures (hypervigilance, walking with confidence, and utilizing selective inattention and listening) are particularly significant as trans people are provided an opportunity to move forward with their transition, rather than spend their money on weapons. As mentioned, delaying the transition process can have detrimental effects on trans people (mental health problems); therefore, more than saving money and minimizing the risk of victimization, these self-protective measures are critical for improving trans people's overall well-being and, for some, saving their lives.

Consistent with the literature, online forums can create a safe space for actionable choices at the individual level (active resistance against victimization) and demonstrate the importance of the role of the online community in building resilience. In this context, trans people can envision a life of limited exposure to adverse experiences and take a proactive approach to minimize their risk. Since suicide rates and suicidal tendencies are high among trans people relative to the general population (Virupaksha et al., 2016), this change in mindset could positively impact their well-being, thus implying that engagement in these spaces could save trans lives.

Exploring how trans people navigate anti-trans stigma provides critical insight into the role of the online community in developing preventative and protective measures. The results of this analysis can directly benefit service providers, specifically therapists, who work with trans individuals on various issues related to trauma, fear of victimization, identity, etc. Due to the accessibility of these public forums, they may be an essential tool for identifying coping mechanisms that can be effective in alleviating the distress of living in a society where one's gender identity or expression is viewed as wrong or illegitimate. For therapists who provide treatment, these forums could serve as a key resource to help reach the larger population of trans people who face substantial social stigma.

As the internet continues to be necessary for everyday life, future research should explore other potential benefits using these spaces has for other trans and gender minorities. Specifically, future research should explore the nuances between members of trans communities as these findings are not generalizable to all trans experiences. For example, it was found that trans men experienced fewer public safety concerns and were more interested in the public perceptions of their identities and media representation. Future research should also explore the role of the online community in facilitating the process of seeking help regarding topics such as intimate partner violence and suicidal ideation and the role these online spaces may have on desistance from engaging in criminal or deviant behavior.

Notes

1 To ensure anonymity and privacy, all people observed were assigned pseudonyms.
2 The members discussed being out part time (presenting in public as one's authentic gender depending on the situation) or full time (presenting in public as one's authentic gender at all times) when sharing their experiences with transphobia.
3 Individuals whose gender identity and presentation are incongruent with their biological sex (GLAAD, 2021).
4 The belief that being cisgender and heterosexual is normal whereas being non-cisgender and non-heterosexual is abnormal.
5 Individuals whose gender identity and presentation are congruent with their biological sex (GLAAD, 2021).
6 The names of the forums are excluded to facilitate anonymity of the people observed.
7 The term transgender is a common identifier for transgender community members, but some people continue to self-identify with the term transsexual. The term transsexual is outdated; as such, the term should not be used by cisgender people or institutions (GLAAD, 2021).
8 An individual whose gender presentation cannot be distinguished as feminine or masculine (GLAAD, 2021).

References

Austin, A., Craig, S. L., Navega, N., & McInroy, L. B. (2020). It's my safe space: The lifesaving role of the internet in the lives of transgender and gender diverse youth. *International Journal of Transgender Health*, 21(1), 33–44. https://doi.org/10.1080/15532739.2019.1700202

Avalos, S. (2022). The trans experience with the criminal legal system. *Crime and Delinquency*, 1–11. https://doi.org/10.1177/00111287221134914

Baker, J. P., & Berenbaum, H. (2007). Emotional approach and problem-focused coping: A comparison of potentially adaptive strategies. *Cognition and Emotion*, 21(1), 95–118. https://doi.org/10.1080/02699930600562276

Barry, J. J. (2018). *Information communication technology and poverty alleviation: Promoting good governance in the developing world*. Routledge.

Blondeel, K., De Vasconcelos, S., García-Moreno, C., Stephenson, R., Temmerman, M., & Toskin, I. (2018). Violence motivated by perception of sexual orientation and gender identity: A systematic review. *Bulletin of the World Health Organization*, 96(1), 29–41. http://doi.org/10.2471/BLT.17.197251

Braunstein, M. D. (2017). The five stages of LGBTQ discrimination and its effects on mass incarceration. *Miami Race and Social Justice Law Review*, 217–246.

Budge, S. L., Adelson, J. L., & Howard, K. A. (2013). Anxiety and depression in transgender individuals: The roles of transition status, loss, social support, and coping. *Journal of Consulting and Clinical Psychology, 81*(3), 545–557. https://doi.org/10.1037/a0031774

Budge, S. L., Katz-Wise, S. L., Tebbe, E. N., Howard, K. A. S., Schneider, C. L., & Rodriguez, A. (2012). Transgender emotional and coping processes: Facilitative and avoidant coping throughout gender transitioning. *The Counseling Psychologist, 41*(4), 601–647. https://doi.org/10.1177/0011000011432753

Buist, C. L., & Lenning, E. (2022). *Queer criminology.* Routledge.

Buist, C. L., & Stone, C. (2014). Transgender victims and offenders: Failures of the United States criminal justice system and the necessity of queer criminology. *Critical Criminology, 22*(1), 35–47. http://doi.org/10.1007/s10612-013-9224-1

Carpenter, L. F., & Marshall, R. B. (2017). Walking while trans: Profiling of transgender women by law enforcement, and the problem of proof. *William & Mary Journal of Women and the Law, 24*(1), 5–38.

Chun Tie, Y., Birks, M., & Francis, K. (2019). Grounded theory research: A design framework for novice researchers. *SAGE Open Medicine, 7*, 1–8. https://doi.org/10.1177/2050312118822927

Cipolletta, S., Votadoro, R., & Faccio, E. (2017). Online support for transgender people: An analysis of forums and social networks. *Health & Social Care in the Community, 25*(5), 1542–1551. https://doi.org/10.1111/hsc.12448

Donovan, C., & Barnes, R. (2018). Being 'ideal' or falling short? The legitimacy of lesbian, gay, bisexual and/or transgender victims of domestic violence and hate crime. In M. Duggan (Ed.), *Revisiting the 'ideal victim': Developments in critical victimology* (pp. 83–102). Bristol University Press.

El Asam, A., Samara, M., & Terry, P. (2019). Problematic internet use and mental health among British children and adolescents. *Addictive Behaviors, 90*, 428–436. https://doi.org/10.1016/j.addbeh.2018.09.007

Ezie, C., & Saenz, R. (2020). *Abuse and neglect of transgender people in prisons and jails: A lawyer's perspective.* Lambda Legal. Retrieved March 17, 2022, from www.lambdalegal.org/blog/20201125_transgender-people-prisons-jails

Flores, A. R., Meyer, I. H., Langton, L., & Herman, J. L. (2021). Gender identity disparities in criminal victimization: National crime victimization survey, 2017–2018. *American Journal of Public Health, 111*, 726–729. https://doi.org/10.2105/AJPH.2020.306099

GLAAD. (2021). *Glossary of terms: Transgender.* Retrieved March 15, 2022, from www.glaad.org/reference/trans-terms

GLSEN, CiPHR, & CCRC. (2013). *Out online: The experiences of lesbian, gay, bisexual and transgender youth on the internet.* GLSEN. Retrieved March 15, 2022, from *Out Online: The Experiences of LGBT Youth on the Internet | GLSEN*

Grant, J. M., Mottet, L. A., Tanis, J., Harrison, J., Herman, J. L., & Keisling, M. (2011). *Injustice at every turn: A report of the national transgender discrimination survey.* National Center for Transgender Equality and National Gay and Lesbian Task Force. Retrieved March 15, 2022, from https://transequality.org/sites/default/files/docs/resources/NTDS_Exec_Summary.pdf

Grossman, A. H., & D'Augelli, A. R. (2006). Transgender youth: Invisible and vulnerable. *Journal of Homosexuality, 51*(1), 111–128. https://doi.org/10.1300/J082v51n01_06

Grossman, A. H., & D'Augelli, A. R. (2007). Transgender youth and life-threatening behaviours: Suicide and life-threatening behaviors. *Journal of Homosexuality, 37*(5), 527–537. https://doi.org/10.1521/suli.2007.37.5.527

Guadalupe-Diaz, X. L., & Jasinski, J. (2017). "I wasn't a priority, I wasn't a victim": Challenges in help-seeking for transgender survivors of intimate partner violence. *Violence against Women, 23*(6), 772–792. https://doi.org/10.1177/1077801216650288

Hawkins, B. W., & Haimson, O. (2018). Building an online community of care: Tumblr use by transgender individuals. In *Proceedings of the 4th conference on gender & it* (pp. 75–77). AMC Digital Library. https://doi.org/10.1145/3196839.3196853

Hellen, M. (2009). Transgender children in schools. *Liminalis: Journal for Sex/Gender, Emancipation and Resistance, 9*, 81–99. https://research.gold.ac.uk/id/eprint/3531

Herman, J. L., Flores, A. R., & O'Neil, K. K. (2022). *How many adults and youth identify as transgender in the United States?* Williams Institute, UCLA School of Law. Retrieved March 20, 2022, from https://williamsinstitute.law.ucla.edu/wp-content/uploads/Trans-Pop-Update-Jun-2022.pdf

Hill, D. B. (2005). Coming to terms: Using technology to know identity. *Sexuality & Culture, 9*, 24–52. https://doi.org/10.1007/s12119-005-1013-x

Hollander, J. A. (2009). The roots of resistance to women's self-defense. *Violence Against Women, 15*(5), 574–594.

Im, E. O., & Chee, W. (2006). An online forum as a qualitative research method: Practical issues. *Nursing Research, 55*(4), 267–273. http://doi.org/10.1097/00006199-200607000-00007

Im, E. O., & Chee, W. (2012). Practical guidelines for qualitative research using online forums. *Computers, Informatics, Nursing, 30*(11), 604–611. http://doi.org/10.1097/NXN.0b013e318266cade

Jackson, A., Hernandez, C., Scheer, S., Sicro, S., Trujillo, D., Arayasirikul, S., McFarland, S., & Wilson, E. C. (2022). Prevalence and correlates of violence experienced by trans women. *Journal of Women's Health, 31*(5), 648–655. http://doi.org/10.1089/jwh.2021.0559

James, S. E., Herman, J. L., Rankin, S., Keisling, M., Mottet, L., & Anafi, M. (2016). *The Report of the 2015 U.S. Transgender Survey.* National Center for Transgender Equality. Retrieved March 15, 2022, from https://transequality.org/sites/default/files/docs/usts/USTS-Executive-Summary-Dec17.pdf

Kellehear, A. (2020). *The unobtrusive researcher: A guide to methods.* Routledge.

Kfrerer, M. L., Rudman, D. L., Aitken Schermer, J., Wedlake, M., Murphy, M., & Marshall, C. A. (2022). Humor in rehabilitation professions: A scoping review. *Disability and Rehabilitation,* 1–16. https://doi.org/10.1080/09638288.2022.2048909

Lambda Legal. (2014). *Protected and served? The executive summary of Lambda Legal's national survey that explores discrimination by police, courts, prisons, and school security against lesbian, gay, bisexual, transgender (LGBT) people and people living with HIV in the United States.* Retrieved on March 17, 2022, from www.lambdalegal.org/sites/default/files/publications/downloads/ps_executive-summary.pdf

LaRose, R., Lin, C. A., & Eastin, M. S. (2003). Unregulated Internet usage: Addiction, habit, or deficient self-regulation? *Media Psychology, 5*(3), 225–253. https://doi.org/10.1207/S1532785XMEP0503_01

Lee, R. M. (2019). Unobtrusive methods. In P. Liamputtong (Ed.), *Handbook of research methods in health social sciences* (pp. 491–507). Springer Nature.

Liamputtong, P., Noack-Lundberg, K., Dune, T., Marjadi, B., Schmied, V., Ussher, J., Perz, J., Hawkey, A., Sekar, J., & Brook, E. (2020). Embodying transgender: An analysis of trans women in online forums. *International Journal of Environmental Research and Public Health, 17*(18), 1–15. https://doi.org/10.3390/ijerph17186571

Malkin, M. L., & DeJong, C. (2019). Protections for transgender inmates under PREA: A comparison of state correctional policies in the United States. *Sexuality Research and Social Policy, 16*(4), 393–407. https://doi.org/10.1007/s13178-018-0354-9

Marchant, A., Hawton, K., Stewart, A., Montgomery, P., Singaravelu, V., Lloyd, K., Purdy, N., Daine, K., & John, A. (2017). A systematic review of the relationship between internet use, self-harm and suicidal behaviour in young people: The good, the bad and the unknown. *Public Library of Science One, 12*(8), 1–26. https://doi.org/10.1371/journal.pone.0181722

Martin, M. (2021). *Computer and internet use in the United States: 2018.* United States Census Bureau. Retrieved March 10, 2022, from www.census.gov/content/dam/Census/library/publications/2021/acs/acs-49.pdf

Meadow, T. (2018). *Trans kids: Being gendered in the 21st century.* University of California Press.

Mehra, B., Merkel, C., & Bishop, A. P. (2004). The internet for empowerment of minority and marginalized users. *New Media & Society, 6*(6), 781–802. https://doi.org/10.1177/1461444804047513

Messinger, A. M., & Guadalupe-Diaz, X. L. (Eds.). (2020). *Transgender intimate partner violence: A comprehensive introduction.* New York University Press.

Messinger, A. M., Guadalupe-Diaz, X. L., & Kurdyla, V. (2021). Transgender polyvictimization in the U.S. Transgender survey. *Journal of Interpersonal Violence,* 1–27. https://doi.org/10.1177/08862605211039250

Mogul, J. L., Ritchie, A. J., & Whitlock, K. (2011). *Queer (In)justice: The criminalization of LGBT people in the United States.* Beacon.

Momen, R. E., & DeKeseredy, W. S. (2020). Why don't you just leave? Transgender resilience and barriers to escaping abuse. In *Transgender intimate partner violence: A comprehensive introduction* (pp. 91–109). New York University Press.

Noack-Lundberg, K., Liamputtong, P., Marjadi, B., Ussher, J., Perz, J., Schmied, V., Perz, J., Schmied, V., Dune, T., & Brook, E. (2020). Sexual violence and safety: The narratives of transwomen in online forums. *Culture, Health & Sexuality, 22*(6), 646–659. https://doi.org/10.1080/13691058. 2019.1627420

Robinson, B. A., & Schmitz, R. M. (2021). Beyond resilience: Resistance in the lives of LGBTQ youth. *Sociology compass, 15*(12), 1–15. https://doi.org/10.1111/soc4.12947

Rosenberg, R., & Oswin, N. (2015). Trans embodiment in carceral space: Hypermasculinity and the US prison industrial complex. *Gender, Place & Culture, 22*(9), 1269–1286. https://doi.org/10.10 80/0966369X.2014.969685

Ross, K. A., & Scholl, J. C. (2016). Socially supported transition: How transgender individuals use the internet to navigate medical transition. *Iowa Journal of Communication, 48*(1–2), 35–38.

Ruppel, P. S., & Mey, G. (2015). Grounded theory methodology—Narrativity revisited. *Integrative Psychological and Behavioral Science, 49*(2), 174–186. https://doi.org/10.1007/s12124-015-9301-y

Senanayake, S., Harrison, K., Lewis, M., McNarry, M., & Hudson, J. (2018). Patients' experiences of coping with idiopathic pulmonary fibrosis and their recommendations for its clinical management. *Public Library of Science One, 13*(5), 1–14. https://doi.org/10.1371/journal.pone.0197660

Sexton, L., Jenness, V., & Sumner, J. M. (2010). Where the margins meet: A demographic assessment of transgender inmates in men's prisons. *Justice Quarterly, 27*(6), 835–866. https://doi. org/10.1080/07418820903419010

Silva, I. C. B. D., Araújo, E. C. D., Santana, A. D. D. S., Moura, J. W. D. S., Ramalho, M. N. D. A., & Abreu, P. D. D. (2022). Gender violence perpetrated against trans women. *Revista Brasileira de Enfermagem, 75*(2), 1–8. https://doi.org/10.1590/0034-7167-2021-0173

Virupaksha, H. G., Muralidhar, D., & Ramakrishna, J. (2016). Suicide and suicidal behavior among transgender persons. *Indian Journal of Psychological Medicine, 38*(6), 505–509.

Walker, A., Sexton, L., Valcore, J. L., Sumner, J., & Wodda, A. (2018). Transitioning to social justice: Transgender and nonbinary individuals. In C. Roberson (Ed.), *Routledge handbook of social, economic and criminal justice* (pp. 220–233).

Waszak, P. M., Kasprzycka-Waszak, W., & Kubanek, A. (2018). The spread of medical fake news in social media—The pilot quantitative study. *Health Policy and Technology, 7*(2), 115–118. https:// doi.org/10.1016/j.hlpt.2018.03.002

Westbrook, L. (2020). *Unlivable lives: Violence and identity in transgender activism.* University of California Press.

Worthen, M. G. (2016). Hetero-cis—Normativity and the gendering of transphobia. *International Journal of Transgenderism, 17*(1), 31–57. https://doi.org/10.1080/15552739.2016.1149538

20

OTHER AS SELF-IDENTITY, SAFETY AND PERCEPTION OF DEVIANCE CONCERNING SEXUAL MINORITIES

Helidth Ravenholm

Introduction

As we as a global society begin to unravel deviant behaviour online, it is crucial that we first debate thoroughly what deviance even is. Words are a powerful tool of communication, and they have an additional power that we see at work all too frequently—they divide the world, according to the speaker and listener, into acceptable people and Other. Depending on where and when in the world, Other may live relatively peacefully, may even achieve some form of integration; at other times and in other places, Other is presented as an abominable enemy, a representation of all that is inhuman and has no rights, no freedoms and no hope to achieve either while living under this label. Other, in short, is free game for all—and we see this in endless violations of human rights that span anything from the relatively "harmless" acts of mild bullying and harassment to horrific crimes that include torture, forced disappearance and murder.

In today's world, understanding the importance of terminology is especially critical, because globalised meaning leads to globalised decisions. How we define and legislate behaviour, including online and offline hate speech and acting on it, two examples of what we often mean when we discuss deviant behaviour, falls foul of this definition—as does any debate on the extant and emerging technologies that are or may be used to police (and suppress) deviants and deviant behaviour, as well as what we set in legal terms, as all these are bound to how we perceive Otherness and who and how gets represented under the term.

As a rule, minorities comprise the bulk of otherness

While the word "minority" spans numerous—often intersecting—racial, ethnic, religious and mixed identities, I will be focusing on sexual minorities which are, often invisibly, because we over-focus on sexual orientation only, members of those other groups too—e.g. LGBT Muslims (e.g. Sydney Queer Muslims, n.d.; Muslim Youth Leadership Council, 2018; Muslims for Progressive Values, 2019; Imaan, n.d.), Buddhists (e.g. Rainbodhi, 2021; Gay Buddhist Fellowship, 2022) and Christians (e.g. European Forum of Lesbian, Gay, Bisexual and Transgender Christian Groups, 2022; Wakefield, 2022), ethnic minority members and

DOI: 10.4324/9781003277675-23

people with mixed backgrounds. I will look at the LGBT group specifically; while the rainbow umbrella covers many more people and identities, the plights of all differ somewhat. For instance—the demi and aro groups (so aromantic, asexual, demiromantic, demisexual and many monikers in between, such as greysexual, etc.) face problems that, insofar as they are heterosexual and cisgendered, fall rather under criminalisation and decriminalisation/ lack of criminalisation of sexual violence outside and inside marriage and forced marriage than specifically sexual orientation-related violence. While these are obviously serious matters, I feel they require a whole separate discussion, and would dilute the discussion of treatment of minorities with specific *sexual orientation*, who may also be intersecting with these groups as it is. Additionally, I will consider non-traditional, newly emerging modern genders under the broader trans umbrella for specific cases, and otherwise under lesbian, bisexual and gay topics; as the violence experienced and deviance ascribed to them both tend to fall under perceptions of deviance and violence associated with homosexuality, and are approached binarily; remaining narrower in the debate makes more sense than further diversifying it. The self and representation of especially butch women, effeminate men and trans people have traditionally received a wide array of negative emotions and an equally wide array of subsequent negative reactions, and continue to do so now at an arguably higher rate than when one's identity is at least visually correlated with societal, cultural and religious expectations (e.g. Mohan, 2019). People born outside of sexual expectations (e.g. intersex people) and heterosexual cisgendered men and women who fall outside the usual visual expectations of male and female looks, while undoubtedly affected, are affected because of extant prejudices that touch those aforementioned groups, which depend on sex and gender perceptions within the society and culture. Therefore, I will not discuss them specifically, though it is worthwhile to note that hostilely ascribed homosexuality can and does influence everyone, regardless of sex, gender and other markers of self where it is considered a deviant feature. As Betsy Phillips puts so eloquently in the *Nashville Scene*, the debate around and subsequent bathroom bans, when considering numbers of actual trans people in the state, the hostility and bans are likeliest to affect those men and women who fall somewhat outside the expected (visual, self-representative) spectrum of masculinity and femininity, as the debate spurs on hate-fuelled witch hunts reliant on visual cues (Phillips, 2021). While the bans undoubtedly do influence the trans community horrifically because they are singled out as a ready and acceptable target for their perceived deviant behaviour, their numbers (and hopefully survival skills) are such that the moral panic can and must also affect those who are not, in fact, trans as well, and quite likely more often (Hansford, 2022a).

What is a deviant—and who decides that?

There is no one defining characteristic of those perceived as deviants that could be relied upon to establish a firm global rule on what a deviant is. The somewhat vague label of Otherness is the umbrella term for many considered to be deviants when discussing it academically; otherwise, criminality may represent deviance where acts or behaviour are, for relevant or biased reasons, perceived as Otherable, i.e. in conflict with the dominant culture's perspective on what is or is not criminal. It is worthwhile to note that what is criminal often falls into the brackets of what is not normative, and does not necessarily denote an actual active participation in any factual crime—it is merely an act of representing an unwanted form of diversity or diversity in general.

355

Other may not always be determined by others, but also by ourselves, as a conscious adoption of what we believe or know the dominant culture considers to be Other, including where this is criminalised or may have unwanted social consequences (e.g. counterculture, political lesbianism, ideological positions, political religious positions); it may be to express a desire to affirm unbelonging to the dominant culture vs actually unbelonging because we are in a position where we are Othered by others. But for either of these forms of unbelonging to be experienced or adopted, we need framework to form the social "shape" of what Other—and therefore deviance—look like in the first place. Notably, the more rigid the social context, the more our self—as Other or otherwise—depends not on identity-related traits (e.g. group adherence or belonging, likes and dislikes), but on **what we are *not***; under those circumstances, Othering—and criminalisation of diversity (i.e., deviance)—is as definite as our self is, and as unavoidable.

Things as simple as hair or eye colour, disabilities, skin appearance (albinism) and speech can represent Other; a monobrow, for instance, is considered a sure sign of witchcraft in some parts of Slovenia according to one source (Radešček, 1988, 1984). During fieldwork, I have come across stories of people (not exclusively rural or under-educated) who knew someone who "got sick after being looked at" by a person with a monobrow. Witches' teats, or moles of any kind that might resemble any form of devil's mark, were long thought to be a definite sign of that globally recognised kind of Otherness (e.g. for European space—Kramer, 1487). Needless to say, who is a deviant is, even when we Other ourselves deliberately, delineated by a dominant group, both by creating the templates for that which we are (supposed to be) and that which we are not.

The present book discussions—and the wider, necessary discussions of deviance in the world right now—tend to focus on the real and prevalent problem: the rise of online and online-related crime, ranging from cyber and cyber-enabled crime (Interpol, n.d. a) to stalking that turns into a real-world crime to online abuse and bullying. Also not absent are discussions of technological advancements, such as facial recognition technology or FRT (Louradour & Madzou, 2021), medical technology innovations (e.g. McQuillan, 2022), distance learning technology (Human Rights Watch, 2022c), surveillance technology, drones (Ciancaglini, et al., 2020) and phenomena like DeepFakes (Schwartz, 2018; Ciancaglini, et al., 2020) and Deep Voice (Cole, 2018; Damiani, 2019) and the role they might play in our social behaviours. Hate groups and the rise of authoritarianism and authoritarian-related violence are in focus. It is easy to argue, reasonably, that all those acts and phenomena come under the term "deviance", if this term indicates a commonly/globally held regard for human rights that they intend to willingly, actively and violently disregard.

There are two problems with this way of thinking. Firstly, what we consider to be a widely held regard for human rights, while a notion that definitely should be able to connect us all, is relatively new (United Nations, 1948); they are also not held as widely and as universally as we might like and may indeed be applied very poorly (Ring, 2022; United Nations, 2022; United Nations Human Rights, 2022a, 2022b; Human Rights Watch, 2015). Additionally, rigid movements (e.g. extreme religious groups or ideologues), groups and cultures adhering to a rigid perception of self within one's society and notably a rise in authoritarianism on both sides of political spectrum (Healey, 2018) and neo-fascism/neo-Nazism specifically in the past decade or so have the power to shape and reshape the generally socially liberal approach that regard for human rights not only espouses, but also needs to survive.

The second point is no less salient—deviance carries, within the word itself, centuries of bias in meaning and action, legal and otherwise, associated with that meaning. It is impossible to miss the fact that, especially with regard to sexual minorities, original human rights treaties often ignored or omitted enshrining safety for sexual minorities in particular into law, and as such into social consciousness, be it because one's intersection with simply being human was expected to act as a bulwark against violation, regardless of humanity; in practice, being socially withheld from sexual minorities through biased and violent treatment before and after the signing, or felt that those particular rights did not, in fact, warrant being put into law, the intersecting humanity of the people in question regardless, despite possible intersections with other noticeably persecuted groups (e.g. religion, ethnic minority, etc.). While this supposition may seem harsh, it is not baseless—consider the abundance of laws that existed unchanged or were indeed put into effect in the countries that were signatories of these treaties, that specifically targeted and persecuted sexual minorities (Human Dignity Trust, 2022d), or portrayed them as ill for being different than was expected and required (Drescher, 2015). Since that first signing in 1948, subsequent treaties have only recently begun to look at sexual orientation as a protected identity (HRC Staff, 2017; Kirichenko, 2019), and yet, both within the signatories' territories and elsewhere, sexual minorities still often face persecution one way or another (Human Dignity Trust, 2022c; Human Rights Watch, 2022a; Ghoshal et al., 2022); additionally, inclusion of sexual orientation has served as a direct cause of distaste and outright rebellion among the countries where sexual minorities are most widely persecuted when involved in any way in discussion on human rights globally or locally (Ring, 2022; Human Dignity Trust, 2022c; Human Rights Watch, 2022a).

This often leads to a certain amount of looking the other way by many, because being a member of sexual minority within the dominant society comes with implicit bias that is strong and hard to shift; looking the other way while claiming to "understand" cultures that do not wish to protect these minorities, as well as nodding to claims that homosexuality in those cultures "does not exist" or that it is a "Western import", is actually a clear example of this bias, and would be totally unacceptable in cases of religious, racial or ethnic minorities or the rights of women and children nowadays. This is done in the face of nascent or extant groups of native LGBT members fighting desperately not only for their rights, but often for survival, in what may be a "minority genocide" (e.g. Cooper, 2014; Younes, 2022; Human Rights Watch, 2019; Steinmetz, 2019; BBC Staff, 2017; Le Monde avec AFP, 2017; also cf. Younes, 2021b on intersectional issues that make fighting for minority status secondary) that is poorly researched and poorly documented because too few people care, and who, when fleeing their origin countries for the relative safety of the West, often face poor reception, disbelief, claims of not being LGBT or not truly fleeing danger, invasive questions, denial of asylum, general abuse and poverty and deportation (e.g. Brewer, 2020).

With this in mind, and with observing how belonging to LGBT group features around the world in perceptions of deviant behaviour, it is imperative that we ask ourselves when discussing the topic of this chapter—what is deviant behaviour? Who sets the terms? What biases have been included in creating the normative definition[1] which serves as the opposite to what is deviant/Other? And are we aware that those terms, if not clearly determined so that they exclude identities that are only criminal by definition of a dominant group and do not in fact engage as a group in actual criminal behaviour, promote criminalisation and mark as deviant people whose only claim to these labels is that they are perceived as Other by a dominant group? Furthermore, where is our responsibility, ethically at least, if we do not question the label of deviance rather than accept, often blindly and with little information on consequences for minorities, this definition at face value?

Positive deviance and other deviant behaviour—how is the difference made?

To start with, let's look at the phenomenon of deviance. If we consider deviance as an aberrance from the expected, a deviation from commonly used social behaviours, then deviance is neither good nor bad but neutral; it is the context in which it is found—e.g. a brutal crime or an unexpected but harmless trait such as modifying a known recipe—that gives it definition. This is logical but fails where rigid expectations are concerned; to those defining deviance rigidly, harmless may have equal weight to criminal, and the effective, logical difference between the two may not exist. That said, this does not make one deviance as bad as the other—it is merely the perception that equalises them, and not the context in which they are found, perhaps making a case for positive, negative and even neutral deviance discussion.

With this definition in context, it is easy to apply it to what we know of the lives and selves of sexual minorities around the world.

In most societies, we are almost by default raised in the context of the dominant society. As the Making Gay History podcast and other sources (Making Gay History Team, 2022; CBC True Crime, 2022A; Cole, 2000) show us again and again, this may mean that members of sexual minorities grow up with little to no context about their identity, or solely with contexts that may be rigid in perception of a third gender at best[2] or simply criminalises same-sex identity and behaviours. Between no information, barely present information, label of sickness and criminalisation (all of which in some way portray same-sex behaviours as deviant and seek to regulate or police it), growing up without other information means that sexual minority members grow up not only in physically and psychologically unsafe conditions, but also with the feeling of loneliness, confusion and wrongness applied to oneself over not fitting the expectations. This does not in any way lessen their "gayness", just like exposure to LGBT-inclusive topics does not "make one gay"; the false positive appears merely because once people who thought that something was wrong with them initially finally have a word for who they are, identification and self-identification (positive or negative, given the high probability of internalised homophobia) within their social context, and the context of a group of others like themselves, the curtain of seeming and globalised heterosexuality falls decisively from the life they have tried to lead thus far, leaving them and those observing them with the realisation that they are in fact a member of a sexual minority.

Where this behaviour is criminalised in any sense, even just by social perception and lack of acceptance, it may seem that they "chose deviant behaviour" or were "changed" by exposure. Lack of scientific knowledge of why sexual minorities exist can in a sense aid the thinking that there is no "natural reason" for diversity in not only human, but other animal sexual diversity (Kamath et al., 2019); that said, not only is such behaviour already biased by imposing a heterosexist view on what we know of extant diversity; scientific pinpointing of any one or multiple factors has the potential to give rise to numerous near-future high-tech versions of conversion therapy: be it by screening for LGBT in foetuses and elimination of those who seem to be, could be or actually are sexually diverse, or later attempts at "fixing" the diversity. If this sounds far-fetched, there exist even now articles discussing the possibilities (Earp et al., 2014); additionally, many people and organisations take it upon themselves to in some way influence what they think may be LGBT behaviour, even in children (e.g. Kelleher, 2021).

To recognise who we are and be able to live as we are is therefore a form of positive deviance—we may deviate from the expected, but it neither has factual negative consequences for our society nor for ourselves outside of possible social repercussions based on bias; families, too, where existing, are finding ways to adapt when a parent, for instance, comes out as gay or lesbian or trans (e.g. Rowello, 2020). It is worth noting also that LGBT people who try to live as straight—therefore often striving to create those families they might later leave—do so in an effort to avoid being a deviant, or because they are so poorly informed about who they are; should they not have to go through this, neither would their families. Sexually risky behaviours are also connected to a poor understanding of one's identity, internalised homophobia and sexual practices in contexts where being a sexual minority is in some way unsafe—legally or socially (e.g. Stevens et al., 2013; AIDS Accountability International, n.d.).

Contrarily, other behaviours that we label as deviant are technically and factually often criminal. While societies often fail to make a real difference and will occasionally lump accusations together because of the perception that one deviant behaviour must mean a whole palette of deviant behaviour, or because a deviant-labelled group lives in conditions that force it into what is otherwise criminalised behaviour,[3] there is a striking difference between criminal behaviours based on factual deeds and actions and those anchored in social unacceptance.

In contrast with those whose criminalisation is based on Othering, the actors otherwise considered deviant generally have a factual impact on their environment that is not only the result of their existence or differing (sex, gender) behaviour, but is deliberately sought with an intent to harm a third party and/or benefit from that harm. Criminal activities bear multiple consequences—from loss of material goods by the victim(s) to group on group interpersonal violence (e.g. ideological, religious, ethnic, racial tensions), to physical and emotional harm (e.g. beatings, rapes, kidnappings), destruction of property or environment, risk to endangered species for profit, singling out of what represents Other through hate speech, rumour mongering with intent to reputational, emotional, economic or physical harm (e.g. Hansford, 2022b), use of technology to persecute, harass and otherwise inconvenience Other, and so on. While it would be wrong to forget that in many cases there may be reasons for someone to start on a path of crime, those reasons cannot be considered an excuse or logical when dealing with the potential or the results of a crime; they can, and should be, considered when we seek to act preventatively (e.g. address poverty that may push people into wildlife poaching and smuggling (Duffy & St John, 2013; Price, 2020)). Furthermore, we cannot, and should not, allow ourselves to discuss "deviance" in a way that does not, as I have previously stressed, separate these *factual crimes* from *criminalisation of Other*, as this simplification actively feeds into extant, and often implicit, biases inherited through social and cultural instructions we all receive throughout our lives via interactions with others, which inform us not only of what is "acceptable", but also what is not, and what steps are acceptable to deal with that which we do not find acceptable: to wit, persecution of Other becoming, in the long term, sanctionable and acceptable.

Living as a deviant—challenges and safe spaces

For all those considered deviants, and for minorities in general (and it is worth noting that the concepts often intersect), life means unique challenges not experienced by the dominant groups, and frequently, those challenges create a life that is reliant on safe spaces, both for physical, economic and other very easy-to-understand aspects of safety, as well as for the mental safety of being able to be, at least for some time, as we are truly to a full extent. In HR and DEI, the process of passing for something or someone else in one context[4] and switching to being authentically self is referred to as code switching, and one may switch more than one code for more than one situation even without belonging to a minority; as our identities include sub-identities, or parts of one general identity, such as our work behaviour/representation, partner behaviour/representation, pupil behaviour/representation etc., and these too can sometimes clash or intersect, it's safe to say that everyone code switches to a certain extent. Notably, multicultural and multilingual people are more likely to switch than others; but for those whose identities do not mark **them** in their broader society as deviant, code switching is not as intense because "slipping up" carries far fewer consequences. A person may incidentally tell co-workers that they like a singer on one single occasion, and unless there are suppositions applied to that singer and the person that attach to societal perceptions on deviant behaviour (e.g. a man liking Celine Dion or other singers associated with romance and femininity may be perceived as gay, even if they are not), their lives and how they are perceived are not likely to change (e.g. Laguerre et al., 2010, p. 4). Likewise, services that others take for granted, such as the right to expect medical care, being able to shop for goods or expect services that attach to an event (or simply services that may be refused to them when and if their "deviant" identity is revealed), getting education, a job or promotion (e.g. Malta et al., 2019; Itaborahy & Zhu, 2013) as well as simply being able to live with those we love without fear or sanctions, can be withdrawn the moment one's full identity is in the picture. This does not by any means only happen to sexual minorities; but sexual minorities are the most commonly Othered group for various historic reasons (Human Dignity Trust, 2022d; Drescher, 2015) and when their identity is one of minority within minority status or an intersectional minority,[5] the chances for safe spaces become much reduced.

If that is hard to understand, consider that minority members generally tend to greatly rely on each other. The more excluded and Othered someone is, the more they are likely to be ghettoised, as well as tend to self-ghettoise, both as an act of setting physical and imaginary boundaries and to be able to live in as peaceful a way as possible, especially where violence isn't out of question (e.g. Steinmetz, 2019; Laguerre et al., 2010). Throughout history, we see this ghettoisation—which may start from deliberate ghettoisation at one point and slowly develop into self-ghettoisation at another (e.g., Irish settlers and the formation of early gangs in the US (Howell & Moore, 2010)—forming often large, but tightly knit communities that trade, live, die and express their own identities clearly and unabashedly within these owned spaces. I could fill a book with examples, but I will only give a few here—the Jews, both in Europe and in the US, have generally tended to move or be compelled to move together (e.g. ibid); post-Civil War America delineated spaces between the white and non-white people clearly (Borunda, 2020; Miller, 2016), with the laws often deliberately disabling people of even mixed heritage from settling in "white" neighbourhoods; Italian and Hispanic groups, German and Slavic immigrants, religious and ethnic minorities in the West and elsewhere in the world have all given us examples of such habitation, whether on purpose or because they were forced to.

Notably, when the groups live under such conditions, the sense of group identity is almost exaggerated (I will call this self-Othering). Whether we take this to be an act of defiance that seeks to keep one's identity from being predated upon by dominant groups, an act of safekeeping where physical and emotional safety may be paramount or even an incidental power grab by the most rigid members of the group who abuse its plight to try and enforce a type of unity that suits their ideas of this group (e.g. Feld, 2015), the groups are not unlikely to delineate belonging to their own little world vs the larger dominant group by focusing on not only what they are, but what they are not. And under those circumstances, the group often has little tolerance for anyone who does not represent it in a way it feels it should be represented; a good example of this are Black lesbians during the early stages of women's liberation, left behind by the movement that wanted to represent Black women as non-deviant representatives of accepted, normative womanhood (Woolner, 2017). Similarly, nativist, nationalist and other fundamentalist movements tend to deplore those who do not fit a narrative set for the holy past[6] and the future and present that is supposed to be built from it (e.g., white Christian nationalist movements and the perception of a white Christian nationalist past, e.g., Blake, 2022). As sex, gender and sexual orientation and self-representation under those terms tend to be set quite rigidly, they are of course the likeliest to be the target of an otherwise seemingly unified group, or at least a group that seeks to be unified, for whatever reason.

Under any of these circumstances, sexual minority members fare poorly; one may be a member of the same ethnicity, the same religion, the same race and the same background, may share the same wider space and observe the habits of its inhabitants and worship devotedly, but, insofar as they are found out, may not only lose what support network they have due to other parts of their identity, but also be denied access and (self)attribution of those other elements of self, simply because they are Othered by their "failure" to be heterosexual and/or cisgendered. To this end, it is worth noting that Christian, Jewish, Buddhist, Sikh and Muslim LGBT groups are creating support networks of their own, which include outreach and education that not only serves as a soothing reminder to those cast out that their identities are and should be valid in their whole, but also to act as advocates for their members within their original communities (e.g. Sydney Queer Muslims, n.d.; Rainbodhi, 2021; European Forum of Lesbian, Gay, Bisexual and Transgender Christian Groups, 2022; Mohan, 2019). It is, however, often impossible for them to do so in their original countries—many advocate from abroad, where they are theoretically (e.g. Holman, 2019; Advocate.com Editors, 2019; Munhazim, 2020) more likely to be protected than in countries where even the slightest suspicion of belonging to or supporting sexual minorities can mean sanctions, loss of all normal human rights, associated safety, and imprisonment and death (Human Rights Watch, 2022a; Human Dignity Trust, 2022c; Human Rights Watch, 2021a; Younes, 2021a).

Safe spaces are, therefore, paramount to people grappling with such conditions. I would argue that they are not obsolete, even where being LGBT is no longer dangerous, or at least is not supposed to be as dangerous as before; under those circumstances, finding a partner, making friends and general pros of being in a space shared by those who belong to one's community can simply be uplifting and relaxing. That said, extending hospitality to non-minority members can, while perhaps somewhat reducing that effect, also act as a valuable connection-building space, which can effectively reduce stereotyping and Othering in the non-minority community.

For early LGBT communities and communities living in unaccepting places, physical safe spaces can literally be a lifeline (CBC True Crime, 2022a; CBC True Crime, 2022b; Making Gay History Team, 2022; Tang, 2016; United Nations Human Rights, 2022c). Online spaces in particular also have the benefits of anonymity, which is important where there is an active fear of (legal and governmental) persecution (e.g., Nelson, 2021), and do not require one to leave their home, where they may also be safe (especially if they are an adult living alone) or feel safer than if they had to go outside. Particularly where long-term couplehood is not likely to be possible (e.g. AFP, 2017; Notaro, 2017) and where seeking partners for sexual activity is all that one may hope for (cruising), a person may never know whether they are meeting a safe partner or not, and help (be it by a friend or by law enforcement) may not be likely or even possible; this, in turn, means that such meetings carry a certain amount of danger anyhow, even before we begin to consider active entrapment attempts or surveillance by any governmental or affiliated group or person (CBC True Crime, 2022a; CBC True Crime, 2022b; Munhazim, 2020; Making Gay History Team, 2022; Younes, 2021a).

Policing and sanctioning deviance

When deviance is established as Other, the society will seek to be rid of it for multiple purposes:

1. Establishment of firm control

Through setting examples of what happens to detractors, rigid societies will hold fear or anxiety over the members (e.g. BBC Staff, 2017; Cooper, 2014; Human Dignity Trust, 2022c; Human Rights Watch, 2021b; Mohan, 2019; Itaborahy & Zhu, 2013; Steinmetz, 2019; Tang, 2016; Martin, 2014, etc.). This is particularly visible in authoritarian settings, but is by no means absent from other things; like social shunning of someone, passing them over for promotion, declining them work or living space, shaming and ridicule are milder forms of the same rigid behaviour we see even in our own (predominantly liberal and democratic) proverbial back yard. Those deemed deviants, too, are less likely to have fair hearings (e.g. Smithsonian National Museum of African American History & Culture, 2022) and more likely to have the state or someone representing or thinking they have the right to represent the state—or any other dominant group—closely monitoring their familial life, potentially even removing their children or their right to custody or visitation for the reason of deviance, which is considered incompatible with those children's upbringing, or any work that involves or could involve those that the group deems vulnerable—i.e. the people who are not as yet taught the rigid principles to a satisfactory extent, or who may be thought to be capable of "slipping up" (e.g. Healey, 2018). Under those circumstances, it is actually possible to talk about indoctrination—a system of beliefs applied as the sole truth in defiance to all actual facts or free will that could, with different information, challenge the dominant belief.

2. Self-delusion

Without loud or visible detractors, it is possible for a group to communally pretend that a problem does not exist. This is particularly visible in the treatment of trans women of colour—their identities intersect with other categories where it would be easier not to have a problem (e.g. problematic criminalisation and poverty of immigrants or certain racial or ethnic groups), and not having a problem not only means there is no need to look for a solution, but that we as a society can also lull ourselves into thinking that our group works and needs no introspection of any kind. Where a group is anxious to present—to its members as well as outsiders—a seemingly perfect face of unity and harmony, "detractors" in any form—including victims of bias who also showcase this bias exists and its consequences in one—ruin this picture.

3. Lack of information

Many people lack information on diversity even today and even in the West. This is the environment in which superstition, urban legends, conspiracism and misinformation reign supreme and can establish a very effective rule of fear very quickly. Within this is hidden another reason—fear of change, which is linked to the fear of having to re-examine where one's self fits after this change, particularly when that self is created under and used to rigid or rigid-leaning environments. Where the self is linked as much (or even more) to what we are not than what we are, seeing this change looming can be disorienting and disheartening, and it is easy to understand why someone may choose to oppose it—to them, the change really is tantamount to losing an entire self.

Once the need is established, there are four main ways society polices for deviant behaviour.

1. Actual policing of deviant behaviour through groups devoted to that purpose.

Whether they are informal committees or police as we know it, there will be people involved in hunting down the Other. Needless to say, they may also abuse this power, knowing that no one is likely to contradict them because, when Otherness is a crime, it is often hard to pinpoint it at the first glance, and therefore judgement of those who are there to enforce the rules is more likely to be heard than the testimonies of the victim, who is likely to be dismissed on the grounds of trying to evade capture and punishment (e.g. Steinmetz, 2019).

2. Self-policing of behaviour that could be considered deviant—be it to preserve one's safety or that of loved ones, or because of internalised shame (e.g. internalised homophobia).
3. Pattern seeking and confirmation bias in tandem—when we overly focus on something, other things may begin to look just enough like it that they may become relevant. We seek what *seems* to fit, and then assure ourselves that it must because we saw it (confirmation bias).
4. Creation of confirming narratives—be it by looking at a single case, by communally repeating a commonly held "truth", by ascribing events that are fully unconnected (e.g. blaming a group, including the LGBT, for a disease, natural disaster or imagined/perceived "decay" of society (e.g. Baumgart & Farooqi, 2020) or a combination of all or some of these, Other is firmly established as causing some kind of harm that may be more or less visible to the society (e.g. a pandemic or natural disaster are far more visible than the elusive decay of morality or society); furthermore, this harm will be perceived as real even when it is highly questionable (e.g. decay of society), utterly unattributable

(e.g. blaming homosexuality for earthquakes (Laguerre et al., 2010), and will create a seemingly unquestionable position of enmity as the only logical position to have in the normative society.

In all these cases, Other will try to survive while being hunted, online and in the physical world; the amount of aggression and effort depends on both groups in question (the dominant and the Othered). Success and consequences of failure can also differ widely. But one thing they have in common is the perceived need to go after what would, to an outside observer, appear as a waste of time and resources in light of actually criminal actions by others. Needless to say, criminality is generally ascribed in bouts (e.g. CBC True Crime, 2022a; CBC True Crime, 2022b; Tayebi, 2022—this last article is a good example of ascribing further deviance and criminality to a 'deviant' albeit not non-LGBT member). More importantly, actual criminality, even when it is ascribed as a must-have of deviance simply because deviance is deviant (Brower et al., 2015; Strand et al., 2021), is perceived as a lesser offence than going after identity-related issues of the dominant group can be.

One thing to consider when discussing survival of Other in the case of sexual minorities is the notion of taint by association. While not solely applicable to sexual minority response, these are effectively honour killings with a dual role: policing and sanctioning of Other in existence and firm, clear establishing of self as not Other in one's own eyes and the eyes of the observing society. Only recently has the "gay panic defence" started to be outlawed as a form of legal defence (Movement Advancement Project, 2022), and while the laws delineate a step forward in combating discrimination, including that with a deadly end, the practical application can still vary (Human Dignity Trust, 2022c; Human Rights Watch, 2022a). Similarly, killings and corrective rapes of LGBT people around the globe both reflect not only the bias itself but also how imperfectly protection may be applied even where there exist legal protections and recourses; in all those cases, the legal framework cannot and does not get applied because the broader societal behaviours still accept Othering as a valid point of view that must not only be respected but enforced (e.g. Fihlani, 2011; Yurcaba, 2021).

Online spaces and technology—as safety

Especially where involvement in physical world can pose realistic threats, members of same-sex groups often seek and find refuge online, where they can not only search for information regarding their identity but also develop a community of sorts, even if it remains anonymous or semi-anonymous, including by creating personas they may not otherwise be able to create and that do not or should not lead to them in any way, which can be far more difficult in the physical world. Online space can also offer a form of sexual fulfilment—in Pakistan, for instance, homosexuality is criminalised by law and a taboo topic socially, but it leads as a country in accessing gay and trans pornography (Nelson, 2013).

For those seeking partnership, it offers the potential of expressing who they are in a different way than in the physical world. Where in the physical world, designated meeting places and physical representation of self[7] have always been the key to establishing connection with other members of sexual minorities, these can be, for lack of a better word, "outed" very quickly, placing those connected to them in considerable peril. While peril always invariably exists where legal assistance, first responder help, bystander help and even the help of friends and family may not be available for fear of hate crimes or expulsion (e.g., Toksabay, 2012; Yurcaba, 2021), the online world can be both safer and less safe, because it offers a person a non-physical refuge in which to be themselves amongst others like them, seemingly without threat or repercussions, and should serve as a screening test for potential aggressors as well; needless to say, this does not always work as expected, as showcased by predation on especially gay men around the globe at different times, both by people posing as gay men and as incidentally gay criminals. In terms of the latter, it is often hard to determine whether the perpetrator was in fact gay or not—not only are LGBT-related crimes often investigated poorly if at all, but they are also approached with a good dose of bias and lack of knowledge (CBC True Crime, 2022a; CBC True Crime, 2022b; Making Gay History Team, 2022). They do, however, often serve as a form of confirmation bias of innate criminality of the deviants for the broader society.

New technologies can also take into account both openly out members of the LGBT community and those who are not out or cannot be; travel apps, for instance, are being developed specifically with LGBT travellers in mind and delineating safe spaces and gay-friendly zones. Needless to say, as we will see in the next sections, this and other technology, including online space itself, can be turned against this community; either by completely disabling online life (e.g. by banning searches and keeping track of phrases connected to the LGBT community developed to get around the bans, cyberspying (Braga et al., 2018; Bishop et al., 2021); infiltrating the safe spaces in order to commit hate speech or bullying (e.g. Nelson, 2021; Hansford, 2022b; Summers & Liapi, 2022); licit and illicit policing of the online safe spaces; hacking; and of course legal framework criminalising any form of action or association with deviant identity as established by the dominant group (e.g. Younes, 2021a; D'Arcy, 2018).

That is not to say that, despite these measures, the community ceases to exist. If history teaches us anything it is that when people are pushed too far, some push back. Even as far back as previous centuries, some members of the LGBT community found a way to resist the label of deviants,[8] with various results, some of which were undoubtedly tragic while others were (relatively) triumphant; arguably, both have contributed to the development of the LGBT rights global movement and such rights as exist now and might exist in the future. It is possible to categorise these into four broad groups:

- Defiant-accepted group is comprised of people who, through flaunting the deviant label, manage to both defy the extant prejudices and laws and become accepted, be it on a small or large scale (within a familiar circle vs e.g. their state)
- Defiant-unaccepted group is comprised of people who may have flaunted the deviant label and tried to live as their authentic selves, but with bad to disastrous results
- Semi-accepted for passing or emulating is the group that finds a way to fit a societal expectation while somewhat circumventing the deviant label; traditionally, third genders, femme lesbians and effeminate gay men have been found in this group (Cole, 2000).
- Ritualised homosexual behaviours create a time, space and context for acceptable homosexual behaviour that is otherwise labelled deviant (e.g. Allen, 1984; Naga Siu, 2015).

Online spaces and technology—as danger

Before Stonewall, and in many parts of the world still, the LGBT community was (or is) confined to designated places, acts of representation that are understandable to members of the same group and covert private meetings. During the pre-Stonewall times in the

West, many of the clubs and bars that served predominantly the gay members of the LGBT society were mafia-owned due to the criminalisation of homosexuality, which effectively excluded the possibility for the LGBT patrons to be served or safely meet up in less shady places and exposed them to perhaps questionable surroundings and definitely less-than-safe meeting practices (CBC True Crime, 2022a; CBC True Crime, 2022b). Additionally, raids, hate crimes perpetrated by homophobes and bad interpersonal situations going worse, attempts at shutting down or physically destroying these clubs, bars and cafes, predation (both personal and official) by governments and government officials, medical, mental and health-related dangers of covert sexual life, sexual predators and criminals, family and friend violence upon exposure and predation by specific hate groups were and remain a threat that many LGBT members nowadays seek to minimise through use of online spaces and technology. That is not, however, without very similar risks.

If Stonewall became known as a gay bar, similar knowledge can easily spread about an online chatroom, hashtag, search phrase or literally any other form of involvement in online life (Summers & Liapi, 2022; Younes, 2021a). Especially where the governments themselves, affiliated groups or vigilantes take upon themselves to police and sanction deviant behaviour, and homosexuality is considered deviant, there exists a strong incentive to use as much technology as possible to hunt down said deviants, and technology can make these hunts not only easy; it can make it easy to plant false locally incriminating "evidence" on political dissidents, opponents or others (ibid.; Hansford, 2022b; Glaser & York, 2014).

This is also down to the meaning of the word "deviant" and the power it has in criminalisation of both people who are considered Other and people one merely wishes to incriminate to get them into bad public books, or to find a reason for arbitrary arrest or violence, and it features as fodder for gathering votes (e.g. Mijatović, 2021; Reid, 2015; Kamarck, 2019). In China, there have been attempts not only to police local society (Special Procedures of the Human Rights Council, 2022; Human Rights Watch, 2022d; Freedom House, 2022), but also to force the West to agree to the dominant worldview by criminalising "deviance" of Western "dissidents" (National Endowment for Democracy, 2022),[9] which would disable searches for those things the Chinese find objectionable—notably, all searches related to LGBT themes (e.g. Mullin, 2022; Yang, 2022; Freedom House, 2022) as well as information about women's rights and rape-related questions and help forums were included (e.g. Special Procedures of the Human Rights Council, 2022; Human Rights Watch, 2022d; Yang, 2022; Xu & Albert, 2017; Freedom House, 2022) and are included locally. It is worth noting that LGBT-related themes are invariably thrown together with pornography; whatever any one person feels about or believes about pornography and whatever its licit or illicit state in the local or global legal code, it is alarming to consider that sexual orientation is and remains highly sexualised with this sexualisation also being considered deviant, thus both fetishising and forbidding it in the same breath (Mountford, 2009; Cossman, 2014; Shepard, 2020). Where there is little to no exposure to LGBT people and communities, this sexed-up, criminalised perception literally forms all the information a member of that society may have about the community, making it easy for the group to remain criminalised and the dominant views enforced. The common misconception— or rather slander—equating LGBT members with paedophiles, as well as claims about a "pure" society in which moral decay, foreign debauchery and religious and ideological improprieties are creating havoc through having immoral sexual relations form the rest of the opinions. The role of all of this in general is to espouse not only a feeling of self based on that which one is not, but also a perceived fear of this corruption that is then easily seen as necessary to police, sanction and, in the worst cases, erase from existence in word and person.

In this environment of hate, a member of a "deviant" group may not be as safe as they think; it is easy enough to trace a person through their online presence, or to plant technology—be it in the devices we all use or at specific spaces—that serves surveilling purposes. Consider the travel apps—how easy would it be, for instance, for those apps to be found on a traveller's phone or computer, and from there proceed to criminalise them? How easy would it be to plant other incriminating evidence on them (Glaser & York, 2014; Younes, 2021a) to make criminalisation stick and extradition difficult or impossible? How easy would it be to infiltrate the dating or travelling apps (ibid; Flanagan, 2016; Senzee, 2014) in order to police the perceived deviance?

Some of this is daily life for many in the LGBT community. For them and their future safety and rights as humans, understanding how and why the description of the term "deviant" is formed is crucial, as is understanding how equalising the factual crime with criminalisation of Other not only plays out locally, but what global implications it holds for us all—in innovation, in production of technology abroad where the products may become (licitly or illicitly) a tool for spying and suppression, which can quickly and sneakily become a form of minority policing even when it masquerades as an attempt to control factual crime.

What does the future hold? Discussing developing and innovation in queer context

In terms of technology and online space in connection to definition and policing of deviance, it is important to look at extant problems and consider, from this experience, what we can expect in the future.

Drones—the use of drones as surveillance and attack devices is not a matter of the future—in many ways, their use now is a harbinger of things to come. While ubiquitous drones are not normally armed nowadays, it is not impossible to either arm a drone (Ciancaglini et al., 2020; Dilanian, 2021; Orozobekova & Finaud, 2020) or come into possession of one via some form of illicit trade; equally important to consider is their becoming a legally obtainable personal defence weapon, as well as their role in licit control of any environment through constant observation and possibly sanctioning. In Singapore during the pandemic, a larger robotic counterpart was being used experimentally to police deviant behaviour (Cohen & Geddie, 2020). Needless to say, this behaviour depends on definitions of deviance, and minority groups are likely to be targeted somewhere at some point (Mozur, 2019).

FRT—a thorny subject nowadays, FRT or facial recognition technology has many pros and many cons. While it can be useful in reconstruction of events, including crimes, in finding escaped criminals or even children, mentally disabled and elderly who are lost or may not know how to return without help, it is also notorious for misuse, over-enthusiastic expectation of accuracy and inbuilt bias (Najibi, 2020).[10] A recent white paper (Louradour & Madzou, 2021) seeks to discuss ethical use of FRT in terms that, while well-meant, can only be considered naïve at best and underinformed at worst, as it not only fails to acknowledge properly that human rights are not universally respected but also fails to consider that perceptions of deviance that have nothing to do with factual crime are and will likely remain a part of local laws for the foreseeable future, thus raising serious questions about there being a possibility of speaking of global ethical guidelines there at all, as well as the question of production and selling—should the countries that are concerned with ethics and human rights trade in this and other technology with those who are not? Where is our ethical obligation when we are potentially enabling human rights abuses? For LGBT members, FRT can pose a risk of tracking and exposure where sexual minorities are persecuted.

Cyber and cyber-enabled crime—hacking, spying through electronic home devices and phones and inbuilt control devices in computers are some of the cyber and cyber-enabled crimes (Interpol, n.d. A) that can target anyone, including political dissidents and minority members, notably the LGBT members. The aim is to use the cyberspace to harm the victim in some way—through extortion, gathering information on them for various purposes from black market value of personal information to licit policing of deviance to bullying, robbing and otherwise inconveniencing. Not only can minorities be deliberate targets—where they fear exposure, they are also more likely to be vulnerable to illicit or semi-licit (e.g. governmental official with an extortion scheme on the side) crimes, because they often have no one to turn to (Brewster, 2022).

Online space (controlling with or without human factor, policing the internet; doxing)—controlling the online space can happen in two ways—through controlling with or without the human factor (e.g. using AI or actual agents (Wang, 2020) for an official body (e.g. governmental censorship of searches, sites, phrases and behaviours), but also illicitly by vigilantes, hate groups or even disgruntled people we know (notably ex-partners) (Tatum, 2022; Ebel, 2021). Doxing, or finding and dumping personal information on the internet publicly, is a tried and tested method used nowadays, and it is only going to become easier as we spend more time online and use more online-operable tech (e.g. Heater, 2016; Whittaker, 2019; Coldewey, 2016; Greenberg, 2015; Velasco, 2020).[11] This information, of course, may or may not be correct—doxing can use a mishmash of correct and planted information to achieve a result. Where an identity is illegal, this opens up a host of doxing possibilities both ways. The more information is known to be obtainable through easy hacking, the more likely it is that even the planted pieces are likely to be believed, thus creating a convenient way of Othering of political opponents, much like it is already being done (Barr et al., 2021; Freedom House, 2022; Cluley, 2018).

Cameras—There are two ways cameras get used in the matter of deviance—legally, through discriminatory policies using any extant camera as a Big Brother private eye into even private spaces and general lives of the citizens, and illegally, in order to obtain images and footage, be it for extortion, sexual gratification or selling on the black market. Both can affect minorities disproportionally, in part because legal recourse is a risk of being exposed. Policing for the purpose of sanctioning is of course the predominant likely reason for cameras to be used against them (Mozur, 2019; Najibi, 2020).

Medical technology—As stated earlier, there already exist various musings about the future of high-tech medical interventions where sexual minorities are concerned. I would like to add that this technology may or may not be accurate; for developers and users, the ***perception of accuracy*** in the effort to police and sanction or prevent will be enough. Legally, to my current knowledge, no body of text exists that would frame this practice as unethical and forbidden,[12] and it is highly likely that it will be used in some way in the near future as companies seek to develop "acceptable" ways to police and sanction homosexuality, even but not exclusively in the West.

Human chipping (control and tracing)—using implants to ensure tracing or even attempt control is a grisly possibility of the near future. Attempting to create a clear picture of where someone goes, what they are experiencing and doing and attempting to control their actions already exist in some form now; given the preoccupation with homosexuality as something to remove at present and in the past, it is likely that someone at some point will at least attempt to do what sci-fi horror tales have already explored. This also does not seem to have any extant legal system poised to rise against it, but it should (Ibid).

In hate crimes, it is worthwhile to consider: Distance crimes—I consider a distance crime any crime that does not require the physical presence of the perpetrator; technology enables a host of those already, and it will likely continue to do so at a greater pace in the near future. Malicious use of hacking for exposure or harm; drone use for murders, vigilante action and spying; abuse of online-accessible home devices (e.g. fridges, stoves, washing machines (Coldewey, 2016; Greenberg, 2015; Whittaker, 2019), and sexual assault through hacking high-tech toys are problems that are likely to affect us all in the future, but will disproportionally target those communities who, again, will be unwilling to admit to a life that may be portrayed as criminal for their sexuality. I deem it worth elaborating on the abuse through sex toys—as lack of protection (Ilevičius, 2021; Williams, 2020; Winder, 2020) has been established and the availability of high-tech sex toys grows, including in spaces where sex toys themselves may be illegal, the likelihood of hackers abusing the access points, including for the purpose of sexual abuse, grows as well. While this is unlikely to count as rape legally,[13] it would certainly feel like rape to the victim should they suddenly find the toy doing something they or their partner did not program it to do, with or without an open admission by the perpetrator. Comparing the cases of planted cameras and internet sex crimes leaves us with the clear knowledge that the emotional effects would be clear and definite for the victims, even more so if they must remain silent because of criminalisation of their sexual identity, which makes access to legal recourse or mental health help difficult, risky or even impossible.

DeepFakes and DeepVoice—Be it for official or unofficial purposes, DeepFakes and all their technological compatriots offer a valuable tool for incrimination of Other, as well as for feeding narratives. We have already seen some use—and its consequences—in recent times (e.g. Kamarck, 2019; Toews, 2020); in the near future, they are likely to become even more convincing, and our willingness to accept the narratives presented even less based in fact may grow. Including DeepFakes in the debate on deviation is crucial, because deviation, in particular sexual minorities, remains fodder for a number of far-right and other conspiracies, helping give rise to hate crimes based on commonly held "fact" narratives of those groups' members. As visual and vocal fakes can serve as indisputable "proof" of that "fact", it is necessary to remain aware of the role it plays, especially in rising numbers of hate crimes (Woolf, 2022; Langguth et al., 2021).

Future in space and in redevelopment of countries—No debate on deviant behaviour is truly complete without asking ourselves what happens if, as we seek to redevelop our countries, often in an authoritarian image, and even consider colonising space, laws that we have established, which in themselves are not necessarily perfect, may be completely abolished, including if we fail to understand why wording and understanding implicit bias hidden in it matters. To retain human rights, we must understand why some do not have them, and what we are doing, or not doing, to that effect.

Conclusion

Rights are easier to lose than to gain. In our effort to build a better world, we should remember that words matter, and that re-examining them is crucial for our present and our future. In this book, and this chapter, this re-examination will hopefully help us create a dialogue that can contribute to that better world—for all.

Since the research and the writing of this chapter, much has changed. Rights of minorities, including and especially sexual minorities, are never a static matter; they flux between acceptance, tolerance and hate as they are affected by the majoritarian world—the difference is that Othering a minority often presents the parties doing the Othering with easy targets, targets that can be smeared with wild rumours, fears and the acceptance of whom is generally considered to be unimaginable, including in those societies where all or some acceptance has already taken root. We can see this done with other than sexual minorities in cases of tribal belonging in Africa (cf. Crary, 1986; Najimdeen, 2022), in cases of horrific ethnic and religious hate-based violence in Myanmar (cf. Human Rights Watch, 2022b; Hölzl, 2020) and in China (cf. Facing History & Ourselves, 2022; Freedom House, 2022; Amnesty, 2022). But through all this, we should remember that sexual minorities are not in a vacuum of mere existence as a sexual minority—they, we, are people with diverse backgrounds, often intersecting our sexual minority status with other "undesirable" identities, such as race, colour, ethnicity, mixed background and so on. The fight for sexual minority rights has been long and bitter, and it is not without success—currently, the number of countries where being LGBT is criminalised has fallen to 66 (Human Dignity Trust, 2022c[14]); while the number of those where the death penalty still exists for being gay has not changed, and the informal/illicit/not state-sanctioned violence often remains the same for a long time, this is hopeful, especially given the ease with which modern—technology-aided—surveillance is used in rigid contexts. That said, the current times have also seen a rise in hate, often using the online world to cross-pollinate and share hate ideologies; I have argued elsewhere (Ravenholm, 2022) that the modern hate group is a new form of organised crime at an intersection of organised crime, hate group and terrorism, and I believe my suppositions make sense in light of how hate is currently spreading and how it interacts with markers typical for terrorism and organised crime. It is through this hate, this highly organised and politically present hate, that we have seen LGBT (and other minority) rights dwindle in countries where they have peaked with what were full or nearly full rights—the USA (e.g., Madrigal-Borloz & OHCHR, 2022), the UK (e.g., Middleton, 2022), in parts of Europe (e.g., Thoreson, 2022; Council of Europe—Commissioner for Human Rights, 2021), or where the fight seemed at least hopeful if not successful (parts of Africa, e.g., Kenya (Informant, 2023;[15] Kisika, 2023; Kelleher, 2023; Kupemba, 2022)). With that in mind, it is vital that we pay close attention not only to what is considered deviant, and what the basis for such consideration is, but also to who decides who a deviant is or should be, what they "look like"—visual cues are often a basis for rejection and even endangerment, which hurts everyone (e.g., McKee, 2023)—as policing communities doesn't always involve factual crimes, but perception and Othering, which make their way into public and private lives, into societal and cultural perceptions and into law. This means not only exploring bias, conscious or unconscious, but also question, relentlessly, whether it is creeping into how we behave towards others, and what the consequences of that behaviour will be. Lawyers, politicians and legislators are people, and as such consciously and unconsciously, deliberately or accidentally, part of prejudices that our societies teach—but their power, and the power of all who decide to impact those societies, leaves a definite mark on those who are Othered, and that's never been easier than now, with quick, often poorly regulated, advances in technology that come at a time when we are realising that minorities, especially sexual, have mostly been left out of firm international rules about life, safety, equality and human dignity, and that it is somewhat difficult to bring those on board. This difficulty isn't merely about a disagreement with other cultures—it is also a mirror image of the prejudices still alive and well in the West, and the unwillingness of many to consider minority members as worthy of full and encompassing human rights.

Notes

1 Normativity is created by the intersection of social behaviours given the stamp of longevity (even when this longevity is questionable), and the application of a holy past (i.e. a religious and/or ideological narrative—e.g. White Christian American ethnostate enshrined in the reinterpreted Constitution (Blake, 2022), only specific interpretations of religious texts, etc.) which, through repeated and generational applications form what we consider normative for our cultural group. In a sense, society (the group and personal self) depends on repetitive, unquestioned and undisturbed interpretation of the normative+narrative to form a rigid culture. Once normativity is established, it can form a large portion of how we look at things, because it becomes unsafe, unthinkable or both to look at them in any other way. This is very visible in academic discourse through time, which established as fact many now recognised biases (e.g. racial theories), pre-determined archaeological finds expectations (e.g. sex of the body where the burial is found with "male-normative" grave goods) and in legal cases (e.g. assumed criminalisation of specific groups, e.g. by race, immigration status, sexuality, unexpected mourning or shock behaviour, etc.) (Cf. Geertz, 1973).

2 E.g. unwillingness to be pressed to live as a third gender where third gender is available (despite being a part of the dominant cultural landscape, the third gender often still faces marginalisation—(cf. Baumgart & Farooqi, 2020 for how hijra is treated), lesbian, bisexual and gay people who do not want to be forced into sex transition, e.g. Hamedani, 2014).

3 E.g. trans and LGBT members forced into prostitution by being discriminated against, including when looking for work; stealing to survive; other minorities, such as racial or religious, being overlooked in housing and development, education, access to healthcare, etc., are all known factors in the criminalisation pipeline.

4 I am using the term loosely, to indicate mimicry of an accepted dominant society—a good example is Purl (Lester, 2018); in LGBT culture, the term "passing" signifies a person who can pass for a cisgendered or, more often, heterosexual person, much like people of mixed cultural, ethnic and racial backgrounds can "pass" for a different race, ethnicity or nationality through visual cues expected of that group (Cole, 2022).

5 In client work, I define intersectional minorities and minorities within minorities thus: Minorities within minorities—are minorities within an already minority group, e.g., members of an ethnic group that has at least one or more characteristic not held by their own group, the dominant group or both. This may mean that they pursue (religiously, ethnically, racially) mixed relationships, thus becoming pariahs in their own space; they may hold slightly different tribal allegiances, or have different religious affiliations and beliefs (from belonging to specific belief groups to having a different than expected religion), are racially and ethnically mixed, have lived abroad, have a sexual orientation that differs from desired/expected, etc. Even if they hold a characteristic of the dominant society, their other characteristics may still make them undesirable. Unlike the otherwise very similar intersectional minorities, these people tend to have poor to no access to support networks otherwise typical for intersectional minority, because they represent Other to members of those groups regardless of their similarities or associations with them. Intersectional minority—is a minority that has more than one non-majority held characteristic; this may be race and religion, race and ethnicity, ethnicity and religion, ethnicity and tradition, and more. Unlike the minorities within minorities, intersectional minorities, while facing often dogged persecution by the majority or even a specific group (e.g., a religious, ethnic or tribal group involved in domestic and/or international acts of terror that is or isn't addressed by the state and/or global society), they usually have a good support group within their own sphere. While this does not make their overall situation easier, it definitely means that they have some support to rely on in times of need or personal crises.

6 A past that explains a society's culture, traditions and establishes it in its space from a mythical or semi-mythical beginning onwards; often defines Otherness. In rigid societies especially it is not to be doubted or questioned, and it serves as a foil to potential change. I developed this term from observations on Durkheim and Geertz, and Douglas' discussions of purity and danger, in context of fieldwork together with my wife, C. Reid.

7 Cole, 2000, 2022—a note—the discussion was very useful in establishing that little has been researched about diversity of representation among the LGBT community (in particular British non-Caucasian and non-Black men); it is important to remember that this unfamiliarity with representation is used by the Home Office when dealing with "fake" asylum applications, as well as has been used elsewhere (cf. Brewer, 2020; Making Gay History Team, 2022).

8 It would take a full manuscript to fully research and debate all cases of recognised or suspected members of the LGBT community in the past and their stories; therefore I can only suggest to the reader to look up LGBT history and explore from there. A good place to start is the Making Queer History website.

9 It is worth noting that many countries that practice state-sanctioned homophobia have done the same, with various results; possibly the clearest is the impact on private companies looking to obtain/keep revenue in homophobic countries rather than non-homophobic countries as socio-political entities.

10 During the course of this research, I have also come across discussions of FRT specifically aimed at "recognising" LGBT people—by their faces, through use of tech (cf. Lewis, 2018).

11 I first wrote an article on possible crimes utilising smart tech over half a decade ago; while I intended to put it either on my business page or on LinkedIn, I hesitated and finally decided against it. While it is, and was then, logical to assume bad agents may indeed reach the same conclusions as myself, the risk of providing "inspiration" for a crime felt too great. To this day, that article remains unpublished, but much of what I had then considered a possibility—notably unlocking doors—has since come to pass.

12 While much of the West now has laws banning conversion therapy in its many forms, it is not unlikely that an argument for high-tech intervention might be made (cf. Earp et al., 2014).

13 The definition of what counts as rape can be complicated and flexible due to binary, heteronormative, gendered stereotypes and normativity that shape these laws.

14 According to a Forbes article accessed in June 2023 (Wareham, 2023), the number is quoted as 64. Because the figure isn't static and updates aren't as regular as the changes, it is hard to say for sure which number is correct; no site reflects oncoming positive or negative changes or even very recent changes, such as Uganda (Reuters & Obulutsa, 2023).

15 Informant R. is a refugee in Kenya; for his safety, his name is omitted.

References

Advocate.com Editors. (2019, February 14). Ten exiled LGBTQ activists speak. *Advocate.com*. Retrieved August 20, 2022, from www.advocate.com/commentary/2019/2/13/ten-exiled-lgbtq-activists-speak

AFP. (2017, November 21). Secrets and wives: Gay Chinese hide behind "sham marriage." *France 24*. Retrieved June 20, 2022, from www.france24.com/en/20171121-secrets-wives-gay-chinese-hide-behind-sham-marriage

AIDS Accountability International. (n.d.). The marginalisation of LGBT. *Accountability International (Formerly AIDS Accountability International)*. Retrieved August 28, 2022, from www.aidsaccountability.org/del/the-sexual-diversity-initiative/lgbt-project-framework-report/the-marginalisation-of-lgbt/

Allen, M. R. (1984). Ritualized homosexuality, male power and political organization in North Vanuatu: A comparative analysis. In G. H. Herdt (Ed.), *Ritualized homosexuality in Melanesia* (pp. 83–127). University of California Press.

Amnesty. (2022, June 27). China: Uyghur student facing trial highlights government push to jail Muslims. *Amnesty.org*. Retrieved July 25, 2022, from www.amnesty.org/en/latest/news/2022/06/china-uyghur-student-facing-trial-highlights-government-push-to-jail-muslims/

Barr, H., Yoon, L., & Nguyen, E. (2021, June 16). "My life is not your porn" digital sex crimes in South Korea. *Human Rights Watch*. Retrieved July 25, 2022, from www.hrw.org/report/2021/06/16/my-life-not-your-porn/digital-sex-crimes-south-korea

Baumgart, P., & Farooqi, S. (2020, July 17). India's hijras find themselves further marginalized amid the pandemic. *New Atlanticist*. Retrieved June 19, 2022, from www.atlanticcouncil.org/blogs/new-atlanticist/indias-hijras-find-themselves-further-marginalized-amid-the-pandemic/

BBC Staff. (2017, May 16). Chechnya accused of 'gay genocide' in ICC complaint. *BBC*. Retrieved August 27, 2022, from www.bbc.com/news/world-europe-39937107

Bishop, A., Filastò, A., Xynou, M., Dalek, J., Dumlao, N., Kenyon, M., Poetranto, I., Senft, A., & Wesley, C. (2021). *No access: LGBTIQ website censorship in six countries*. OutRight Action International.

Blake, J. (2022, July 24). An 'imposter Christianity' is threatening American democracy. *CNN*. Retrieved July 25, 2022, from https://edition.cnn.com/2022/07/24/us/white-christian-nationalism-blake-cec/index.html

Borunda, A. (2020, September 2). Racist housing policies have created some oppressively hot neighborhoods. *National Geographic*. Retrieved September 27, 2021, from www.nationalgeographic.com/science/article/racist-housing-policies-created-some-oppressively-hot-neighborhoods

Braga, M., Ayed, N., Seglins, D., Sher, J., & Gagnon, M. (2018, April 25). To censor the internet, 10 countries use Canadian filtering technology, researchers say. *CBC News*. Retrieved August 30, 2022, from www.cbc.ca/news/science/citizen-lab-netsweeper-internet-filtering-tech-censorship-1.4631243

Brewer, K. (2020, February 26). 'How do I convince the home office I'm a Lesbian?'. *BBC News*. Retrieved June 22, 2022, from www.bbc.com/news/stories-51636642

Brewster, T. (2022, August 25). An Instagram sextortionist tricked 30 boys into sharing intimate photos, FBI says. One took his own life. *Forbes*. Retrieved August 29, 2022, from www.forbes.com/sites/thomasbrewster/2022/08/25/instagram-sextortionist-fbi-investigation/?sh=332b86096fc3

Brower, T., Lesh, E., & Shay, G. (2015). Jury selection and anti-LGBT bias. Best practices in LGBT-related voir dire and jury matters. Lambda Legal—GHLA.

CBC True Crime. (2022a). The Village podcast. CBC Media Centre. Retrieved from www.cbc.ca/mediacentre/program/the-village

CBC True Crime. (2022b). The village: The Montreal murders. *CBC True Crime*. Retrieved from https://podcasts.apple.com/ca/podcast/the-village-the-montreal-murders/id1528612213

Ciancaglini, V., Gibson, C., Sancho, D., McCarthy, O., Eira, M., Amann, P., & Klayn, A. (2020). *Malicious uses and abuses of artificial intelligence*. Trend Micro Research.

Cluley, G. (2018, April 10). China forces spyware onto Muslim's Android phones, complete with security holes. *BitDefender*. Retrieved August 31, 2022, from www.bitdefender.com/blog/hotforsecurity/china-forces-spyware-onto-muslims-android-phones-complete-with-security-holes

Cohen, T., & Geddie, J. (2020, August 6). Don't stand so close: Singapore trials automated drones to check. *Reuters*. Retrieved August 31, 2022, from www.reuters.com/article/us-health-coronavirus-israel-drones-idUSKCN2521K3

Coldewey, D. (2016, August 9). 'Smart' locks yield to simple hacker tricks. *Tech Crunch*. Retrieved August 31, 2022, from https://techcrunch.com/2016/08/08/smart-locks-yield-to-simple-hacker-tricks/

Cole, S. (2000). *'Don we now our gay apparel' Gay men's dress in the twentieth century*. Berg.

Cole, S. (2018, March 7). 'Deep Voice' software can clone anyone's voice with just 3.7 seconds of audio. *Vice*. Retrieved August 25, 2022, from www.vice.com/en/article/3k7mgn/baidu-deep-voice-software-can-clone-anyones-voice-with-just-37-seconds-of-audio

Cole, S. (2022, July). (H. Ravenholm, Interviewer).

Cooper, T. (2014, December 15). License to harm—Violence and harassment against LGBT people and activists in Russia. *Human Rights Watch*. Retrieved August 7, 2022, from www.hrw.org/report/2014/12/15/license-harm/violence-and-harassment-against-lgbt-people-and-activists-russia

Cossman, B. (2014). Censor, resist, repeat: A history of censorship of gay and lesbian sexual representation in Canada. *Duke Journal of Gender Law & Policy*, 21, 45–66. Retrieved August 30, 2022, from https://scholarship.law.duke.edu/cgi/viewcontent.cgi?article=1246&context=djglp

Council of Europe—Commissioner for Human Rights. (2021, February 9). Report: Human rights of LGBTI people in Europe: Current threats to equal rights, challenges faced by defenders, and the way forward. *Council of Europe—Commissioner For Human Rights*. Retrieved August 9, 2022, from https://rm.coe.int/human-rights-of-lgbti-people-in-europe-current-threats-to-equal-rights/1680a4be0e

Crary, D. (1986, March 23). African continent tormented by tribal conflicts: Problem Has Triggered wars, toppled governments and wrecked courtships. *Los Angeles Times*. Retrieved June 4, 2023, from www.latimes.com/archives/la-xpm-1986-03-23-mn-5583-story.html

Damiani, J. (2019, September 3). A voice Deepfake was used to scam a CEO out of $243,000. *Forbes*. Retrieved August 27, 2022, from www.forbes.com/sites/jessedamiani/2019/09/03/a-voice-deepfake-was-used-to-scam-a-ceo-out-of-243000/?sh=4b8ec10c2241

D'Arcy, P. (2018, September 21). The smart strategy that one LGBTQ forum uses to keep out trolls and bullies. *Ideas.Ted.Com*. Retrieved August 30, 2022, from https://ideas.ted.com/the-smart-strategy-that-one-lgbtq-forum-uses-to-keep-out-trolls-and-bullies/

Dilanian, K. (2021, December 6). Kamikaze drones: A new weapon brings power and peril to the U.S. military. *NBC News*. Retrieved August 20, 2022, from www.nbcnews.com/news/military/kamikaze-drones-new-weapon-brings-power-peril-u-s-military-n1285415

Drescher, J. (2015). Out of DSM: Depathologizing homosexuality. *Behavioral Sciences*, 5(4), 565–575. https://doi.org/10.3390/bs5040565

Duffy, R., & St John, F. A. V. (2013). *Poverty, poaching and trafficking: What are the links?* https://doi.org/10.12774/eod_hd059.jun2013.duffy

Earp, B. D., Sandberg, A., & Savulescu, J. (2014, January). Brave new love: The threat of high-tech "conversion" therapy and the bio-oppression of sexual minorities. *AJOB Neuroscience*, 5(1), 4–12. https://doi.org/10.1080/21507740.2013.863242

Ebel, F. (2021, April 22). Tunisian police are using drones and Facebook to doxx LGBTQ protesters. *Coda Story*. Retrieved August 15, 2022, from www.codastory.com/authoritarian-tech/anti-lgbt-crackdown-in-tunisia/

European Forum of Lesbian, Gay, Bisexual and Transgender Christian Groups. (2022). *European forum of lesbian, gay, bisexual and transgender Christian groups*. Retrieved from www.lgbtchristians.eu/

Facing History & Ourselves. (2022, February 4). The targeting of Uighur Muslims in China—Why is the Chinese government surveilling and detaining members of a minority group? *Facing History & Ourselves (Educator Resources)*. Retrieved August 10, 2022, from www.facinghistory.org/educator-resources/current-events/targeting-uighur-muslims-china

Feld, A. (2015, September 17). 'Self-ghettoization' in the State of Israel. *The Jerusalem Post*. Retrieved August 29, 2022, from www.jpost.com/opinion/self-ghettoization-in-the-state-of-israel-416438

Fihlani, P. (2011, June 30). South Africa's lesbians fear 'corrective rape'. *BBC News*. Retrieved March 21, 2022, from www.bbc.com/news/world-africa-13908662

Flanagan, J. (2016, August 27). The Egyptian police are using Grindr to entrap gay men. *Gay Star News*. Retrieved August 21, 2022, from www.gaystarnews.com/article/egyptian-police-using-grindr-catch-gay-men/

Freedom House. (2022). Freedom In the World 2022 — China. *Freedom House*. Retrieved August 21, 2022, from https://freedomhouse.org/country/china/freedom-world/2022

Gay Buddhist Fellowship. (2022). *Gay Buddhist fellowship*. Retrieved August 2022, from https://gaybuddhist.org/

Geertz, C. (1973). *The interpretation of cultures*. Fontana Press.

Ghoshal, N., Thoreson, R., Sulathireh, T., & Knight, K. (2022, August 10). "I don't want to change myself" anti-LGBT conversion practices, discrimination, and violence in Malaysia. *Human Rights Watch*. Retrieved August 30, 2022, from www.hrw.org/report/2022/08/10/i-dont-want-change-myself/anti-lgbt-conversion-practices-discrimination-and

Glaser, A., & York, J. C. (2014, April 23). LGBTQ Communities in the Arab World face unique digital threats. *Electronic Frontier Foundation*. Retrieved August 30, 2022, from www.eff.org/deeplinks/2014/04/lgbtq-communities-arab-world-face-unique-digital-threats

Greenberg, A. (2015, July 21). Hackers remotely kill a jeep on the highway—With me in it. *Wired*. Retrieved August 20, 2022, from www.wired.com/2015/07/hackers-remotely-kill-jeep-highway/

Hamedani, A. (2014, November 5). The gay people pushed to change their gender. *BBC News (Persian)*. Retrieved August 28, 2022, from www.bbc.com/news/magazine-29832690

Hansford, A. (2022a, August 19). Parents complain cis athlete might be trans because she 'doesn't look feminine enough'. *PinkNews*. Retrieved August 24, 2022, from www.pinknews.co.uk/2022/08/19/trans-athletes-school-sport-utah/

Hansford, A. (2022b, August 26). Swatting: How the terrifying abuse tactic is being used to threaten, intimidate and even kill. *PinkNews*. Retrieved August 24, 2022, from www.pinknews.co.uk/2022/08/26/what-is-swatting-prank-abuse/

Healey, D. (2018). *Russian homophobia from stalin to sochi*. Bloomsbury Academic.

Heater, B. (2016, May 10). Cujo is a firewall for the connected smart home network. *Tech Crunch*. Retrieved August 31, 2022, from https://techcrunch.com/2016/05/10/cujo-is-a-firewall-for-the-connected-smart-home-network/

Holman, R. (2019, March 20). Jean Wyllys, a gay congressman flees Bolsonaro's 'dangerous' Brazil. *France 24*. Retrieved August 30, 2022, from www.france24.com/en/20190320-brazil-jean-wyllys-openly-gay-congressman-rights-activist-exile

Howell, J. C., & Moore, J. P. (2010, May). History of street gangs in the United States. *National Gang Center Bulletin*. Retrieved from www.nationalgangcenter.gov/content/documents/history-of-street-gangs.pdf

HRC Staff. (2017, September 18). Ten ways the United Nations has protected LGBTQ Human Rights. *Human Rights Campaign*. Retrieved August 27, 2022, from www.hrc.org/news/ten-ways-the-united-nations-has-protected-lgbtq-human-rights

Human Dignity Trust. (2022c). Map of countries that criminalise LGBT People. *Human Dignity Trust*. Retrieved August 27, 2022, from www.humandignitytrust.org/lgbt-the-law/map-of-criminalisation/

Human Dignity Trust. (2022d). A history of LGBT criminalisation. *Human Dignity Trust*. Retrieved August 27, 2022, from www.humandignitytrust.org/lgbt-the-law/a-history-of-criminalisation/

Human Rights Watch. (2015, April 20). Government against rights groups. *Ecoi.net*. Retrieved August 9, 2022, from www.ecoi.net/en/document/1154960.html

Human Rights Watch. (2019, May 8). Russia: New anti-gay crackdown in Chechnya. *Human Rights Watch*. Retrieved August 27, 2022, from www.hrw.org/news/2019/05/08/russia-new-anti-gay-crackdown-chechnya

Human Rights Watch. (2021a, April 23). Human Rights watch country profiles: Sexual orientation and gender identity. *Human Rights Watch*. Retrieved August 30, 2022, from www.hrw.org/video-photos/interactive/2021/04/23/country-profiles-sexual-orientation-and-gender-identity

Human Rights Watch. (2021b, September 20). Ghana: LGBT activists face hardships after detention—Extreme anti-LGBT bill stokes hostility. *HRW*. Retrieved August 7, 2022, from www.hrw.org/news/2021/09/20/ghana-lgbt-activists-face-hardships-after-detention

Human Rights Watch. (2022a, August 5). #Outlawed: "The love that dare not speak its name". *Human Right Watch—LGBT Rights*. Retrieved from https://features.hrw.org/features/features/lgbt_laws/index.html

Human Rights Watch. (2022b). Rohingya. *Human Rights Watch*. Retrieved from www.hrw.org/tag/rohingya

Human Rights Watch. (2022c, May 25). "How dare they peep into my private life?" Children's rights violations by governments that endorsed online learning during the COVID-19 pandemic. *Human Rights Watch*. Retrieved August 26, 2022, from www.hrw.org/report/2022/05/25/how-dare-they-peep-my-private-life/childrens-rights-violations-governments

Human Rights Watch. (2022d). China—Events of 2021 (World Report 2022). *Human Rights Watch*. Retrieved August 31, 2022, from www.hrw.org/world-report/2022/country-chapters/china-and-tibet

Hölzl, V. (2020, September 17). Myanmar said the Rohingya lied. New soldier confessions are moment of vindication. *Vice*. Retrieved February 1, 2021, from www.vice.com/en/article/z3edvj/myanmar-rohingya-soldier-confessions

Ilevičius, P. (2021, February 2). Sex toys let cybercriminals hack more than just your secrets. *NordVPN*. Retrieved August 30, 2022, from https://nordvpn.com/blog/sex-toy-hack/

Imaan. (n.d.). *Imaan*. Retrieved from https://imaanlondon.wordpress.com/

Informant R. (2023, April). (H. Ravenholm, Interviewer)[1]

Interpol. (n.d. a). Cybercrime and Cyber-enabled crime. *Interpol*. Retrieved May 30, 2022, from www.interpol.int/var/interpol/storage/images/7/3/7/1/141737-1-eng-GB/CYBER12.jpg

Itaborahy, L. P., & Zhu, J. (2013). *State-sponsored homophobia. A world survey of laws: Criminalisation, protection and recognition of same-sex love* (8th ed.). ILGA—International Lesbian Gay Bisexual Trans and Intersex Association.

Kamarck, E. (2019, July 11). A short history of campaign dirty tricks before Twitter and Facebook (Cybersecurity and Election Interference series). *Brookings.edu*. Retrieved August 31, 2022, from www.brookings.edu/blog/fixgov/2019/07/11/a-short-history-of-campaign-dirty-tricks-before-twitter-and-facebook/

Kamath, A., Monk, J., Giglio, E., Lambert, M., & McDonough, C. (2019, November 20). Why Is same-sex sexual behavior so common in Animals? *Scientific American*. Retrieved August 28, 2022, from https://blogs.scientificamerican.com/observations/why-is-same-sex-sexual-behavior-so-common-in-animals/

Kelleher, P. (2021, February 9). Father forced sex workers to abuse seven-year-old son 'because he didn't want him to be gay'. *Pink News*. Retrieved from www.pinknews.co.uk/2021/02/09/malta-sexual-abuse-sex-worker-audrey-demicoli/

Kelleher, P. (2023, February 24). Kenya's Supreme Court rules in favour of LGBTQ+ rights group in "triumph of justice." *PinkNews*. Retrieved June 4, 2023, from www.thepinknews.com/2023/02/24/kenya-supreme-court-lgbtq-rights/

Kirichenko, K. (2019, October 22). Treaty Bodies | UN treaty bodies advance LGBTI rights. *International Service for Human Rights*. Retrieved August 27, 2022, from https://ishr.ch/latest-updates/treaty-bodies-un-treaty-bodies-advance-lgbti-rights/

Kisika, S. (2023, April 26). Kenyan anti-homosexuality bill would expel LGBTQ refugees. *Washington Blade: LGBTQ News, Politics, LGBTQ Rights, Gay News*. Retrieved June 4, 2023, from www.washingtonblade.com/2023/04/26/kenyan-anti-homosexuality-bill-would-expel-lgbtq-refugees/

Kramer, H. (1487). *Malleus maleficarum*. Britannica Online Encyclopedia and Project Gutenberg Consortia Center. Retrieved from https://cdn.britannica.com/primary_source/gutenberg/PGCC_classics/malleus.htm

Kupemba, D. N. (2022, July 21). Death sentences for three gay men in Nigeria 'opens the door' for more 'draconian judgements'. *PinkNews*. Retrieved from www.pinknews.co.uk/2022/07/21/nigeria-gay-death-sentences/

Laguerre, S., Johnson, C., Fox, S., Dupont, R., & Ferreyra, M. (2010). *The impact of the earthquake, and relief and recovery programs on Haitian LGBT people*. International Gay and Lesbian Human Rights Commission (IGLHRC) & SEROvie.

Langguth, J., Pogorelov, K., Brenner, S., Filkuková, P., & Schroeder, D. J. (2021). Don't trust your eyes: Image manipulation in the age of deepfakes. *Frontiers in Communication*, 6. https://doi.org/10.3389/fcomm.2021.632317

Le Monde avec AFP. (2017, May 17). La Tchétchénie accusée de génocide envers les homosexuels. *Le Monde*. Retrieved August 27, 2022, from www.lemonde.fr/international/article/2017/05/16/des-associations-lgbt-accusent-la-tchetchenie-de-genocide-devant-la-cpi_5128402_3210.html

Lester, K. (Director). (2018). *SparkShorts-S1.E1 'Purl'* [Film] Pixar.

Lewis, P. (2018, July 7). 'I was shocked it was so easy': Meet the professor who says facial recognition can tell if you're gay. *The Guardian*. Retrieved August 29, 2022, from www.theguardian.com/technology/2018/jul/07/artificial-intelligence-can-tell-your-sexuality-politics-surveillance-paul-lewis

Louradour, S., & Madzou, L. (2021). *A policy framework for responsible limits on facial recognition. use case: Law enforcement investigations*. World Economic Forum.

Madrigal-Borloz, V., & OHCHR. (2022, August 30). *United States: UN expert warns LGBT rights being eroded, urges stronger safeguards* [Press release]. Retrieved June 4, 2023, from www.ohchr.org/en/press-releases/2022/08/united-states-un-expert-warns-lgbt-rights-being-eroded-urges-stronger

Making Gay History Team. (2022). *Making gay history*. Retrieved from https://makinggayhistory.com/

Malta, M. A., Cardoso, R. R., Montenegro, L. C. M., De Jesus, J. G., Seixas, M., Benevides, B., Silva, M. M., LeGrand, S., & Whetten, K. (2019). Sexual and gender minorities rights in Latin America and the Caribbean: A multi-country evaluation. *BMC International Health and Human Rights*, 19(1). https://doi.org/10.1186/s12914-019-0217-3

Martin, V. (2014, January 14). UN human rights chief denounces 'draconian' anti-homosexuality law in Nigeria. *UN News*. Retrieved July 19, 2022, from https://news.un.org/en/story/2014/01/459642-un-human-rights-chief-denounces-draconian-anti-homosexuality-law-nigeria

McKee, J. (2023, May 23). Woman with dementia, 86, beat up by thug and put in wheelie bin because he thought she was trans. *PinkNews*. Retrieved June 4, 2023, from www.thepinknews.com/2023/05/23/woman-86-beaten-wheelie-bin-trans/

McQuillan, L. (2022, July 05). Americans are being urged to delete period tracking apps. Should Canadians do the same? *CBC News*. Retrieved from www.cbc.ca/news/health/period-tracker-apps-data-privacy-1.6510029

Middleton, L. (2022, May 12). UK drops in LGBTQ+ rights ranking over trans conversion therapy. *Reuters*. Retrieved June 4, 2023, from www.reuters.com/article/britain-lgbt-rights-idUSL5N2X366R

Mijatović, D. (2021, August 16). Pride vs. indignity: Political manipulation of homophobia and transphobia in Europe. *Council of Europe—Commissioner for Human Rights*. Retrieved August 26, 2022, from www.coe.int/en/web/commissioner/-/pride-vs-indignity-political-manipulation-of-homophobia-and-transphobia-in-europe

Miller, G. (2016, October 17). Newly released maps show how housing discrimination happened. *National Geography*. Retrieved from www.nationalgeographic.com/history/article/housing-discrimination-redlining-maps

Mohan, M. (2019, June 24). The red zone: A place where butch lesbians live in fear. *BBC News*. Retrieved August 26, 2022, from www.bbc.com/news/stories-48719453

Mountford, T. (2009). The legal status and position of Lesbian, Gay, Bisexual and Transgender people in the people's republic of China. *OutRight International*. Retrieved August 31, 2022, from https://outrightinternational.org/sites/default/files/395-1.pdf

Movement Advancement Project. (2022, August 23). Equality maps: Panic defense bans. *Movement Advancement Project*. Retrieved August 30, 2022, from www.lgbtmap.org/equality-maps/panic_defense_bans

Mozur, P. (2019, April 14). One month, 500,000 Face scans: How China is using A.I. to profile a minority. *The New York Times*. Retrieved August 31, 2022, from www.nytimes.com/2019/04/14/technology/china-surveillance-artificial-intelligence-racial-profiling.html

Mullin, K. (2022, July 21). A Chinese social media platform is making it hard to use a popular LGBTQ hashtag. *Quartz*. Retrieved August 31, 2022, from https://qz.com/1597485/weibo-censorship-of-lgbtq-hashatag-les-creates-outcry/

Munhazim, A. Q. (2020, July 10). Suicide of Egyptian activist Sarah Hegazi exposes the 'freedom and violence' of LGBTQ Muslims in exile. *The Conservation*. Retrieved August 30, 2022, from https://the-conversation.com/suicide-of-egyptian-activist-sarah-hegazi-exposes-the-freedom-and-violence-of-lgbtq-muslims-in-exile-141268

Muslim Youth Leadership Council. (2018). I'm Muslim and I might not be Straight: A resource for LGBTQ+ Muslim youth. *Advocates for Youth*. Retrieved June 24, 2022, from www.advocatesforyouth.org/wp-content/uploads/2018/11/Im-Muslim-I-Might-Not-Be-Straight.pdf

Muslims for Progressive Values. (2019). LGBTQI resources. *Muslims for Progressive Values*. Retrieved June 2022, from www.mpvusa.org/lgbtqi-resources

Naga Siu, D. (2015, November 11). Homosexual hazing rituals in a heteromasculine context. *Washington Square News*. Retrieved from https://nyunews.com/2015/11/11/homosexual-hazing-rituals-in-a-heteromasculine-context/

Najibi, A. (2020, October 24). Racial discrimination in face recognition technology. *Harvard University—The Graduate School of Arts and Science*. Retrieved August 31, 2022, from https://sitn.hms.harvard.edu/flash/2020/racial-discrimination-in-face-recognition-technology/

Najimdeen, H. (2022, May 20). African politics, tribal violence, and socio-economic rivalry in Africa. *Politics Today*. Retrieved June 4, 2023, from https://politicstoday.org/african-politics-tribal-violence-and-socio-economic-rivalry-in-africa/

National Endowment for Democracy. (2022, February 22). Censorship, surveillance, and human rights: 10 ways these trends intersect with the 2022 Beijing Winter Olympics. *National Endowment for Democracy*. Retrieved August 21, 2022, from www.ned.org/censorship-surveillance-and-human-rights-1 0-ways-these-trends-intersect-with-the-2022-beijing-winter-olympics/

Nelson, C. (2021, February 26). Queer Nigerians hoped the clubhouse App would be a safe haven. It's become another breeding ground for bigotry. *Time Magazine*. Retrieved August 8, 2022, from https://time.com/5942353/clubhouse-queer-nigerians-community-bigotry/

Nelson, S. C. (2013, June 14). Homosexuality is not tolerated In Pakistan, but the Country leads Google searches for gay porn. *Huffington Post UK*. Retrieved August 30, 2022, from www.huffingtonpost.co.uk/2013/06/14/homosexuality-not-tolerated-pakistan-google-searches-gay-porn_n_3440586.html

Notaro, P. C. (2017, October 17). Marriage of convenience: When a Lesbian marries a gay. *Il Grande Colibri*. Retrieved August 27, 2022, from www.ilgrandecolibri.com/en/marriage-convenience-when-lesbian-marries-gay/

Orozobekova, C., & Finaud, M. (2020). Regulating and limiting the proliferation of armed drones: Norms and challenges. *Geneva: Geneva Centre for Security Policy*. Retrieved August 20, 2022, from https://dam. gcsp.ch/files/doc/regulating-and-limiting-the-proliferation-of-armed-drones-norms-and-challenges

Phillips, B. (2021, May 24). Let's talk about just how dumb Tennessee's antitransgender laws are. *Nashville Scene*. Retrieved July 19, 2022, from www.nashvillescene.com/news/pithinthewind/ lets-talk-about-just-how-dumb-tennessees-antitransgender-laws-are/article_345ca0fa-1ee3–55c1–81ba-2e028b2d1bd5.html

Price, F. (2020, October 23). The link between poverty and poaching. *The Borgen Project*. Retrieved August 25, 2022, from https://borgenproject.org/the-link-between-poverty-and-poaching/

Radešček, R. (1984–1988). *Slovenske ljudske vraže*. Kmečki glas.

Rainbodhi. (2021). *Rainbodhi*. Retrieved August 2022, from https://rainbodhi.org/

Ravenholm, H. (2022, October 14). Redefining organised crime. In Panel "understanding organized crime: Definitions and governance" [Speaker]. *24-hour Conference on Global Organized Crime*. Retrieved from https://oc24.heysummit.com/talks/understanding-organized-crime-definitions-and-governance/

Reid, G. (2015, June 29). Homophobia as a political strategy. *Human Rights Watch*. Retrieved August 31, 2022, from www.hrw.org/news/2015/06/29/homophobia-political-strategy

Reuters, & Obulutsa, G. (2023, May 30). Uganda enacts harsh anti-LGBTQ law including death penalty. *Reuters*. Retrieved June 4, 2023, from www.reuters.com/world/africa/ugandas-museveni-approves-anti-gay-law-parliament-speaker-says-2023-05–29/

Ring, T. (2022, July 8). U.N. Steps up efforts against Anti-LGBTQ+ violence and discrimination. *The Advocate*. Retrieved August 26, 2022, from www.advocate.com/world/2022/7/08/ un-steps-efforts-against-anti-lgbtq-violence-and-discrimination

Rowello, L. (2020, October 9). How LGBTQ parents can handle coming out to their children. *The Washington Post*. Retrieved August 28, 2022, from www.washingtonpost.com/lifestyle/2020/10/09/ parents-come-out/

Schwartz, O. (2018, November 12). You thought fake news was bad? Deep fakes are where truth goes to die. *The Guardian*. Retrieved June 18, 2021, from www.theguardian.com/technology/2018/ nov/12/deep-fakes-fake-news-truth

Senzee, T. (2014, September 18). Egyptian police ensnare gay men using Grindr. *The Advocate*. Retrieved August 21, 2022, from www.advocate.com/world/2014/09/18/egyptian-police-ensnare-gay-men-using-grindr

Shepard, J. M. (2020). The first amendment and the roots of LGBT rights law: Censorship in the early homophile era, 1958–1962. *William & Mary Journal of Race, Gender, and Social Justice, 26*(3), 599–670. Retrieved August 31, 2022, from https://scholarship.law.wm.edu/wmjowl/vol26/iss3/5

Smithsonian National Museum of African American History & Culture. (2022). The Scottsboro boys. *Smithsonian National Museum of African American History & Culture*. Retrieved from https:// nmaahc.si.edu/explore/stories/scottsboro-boys

Special Procedures of the Human Rights Council. (2022, June 10). China must address grave human rights concerns and enable credible international investigation: UN experts. *United Nations Human Rights*. Retrieved August 31, 2022, from www.ohchr.org/en/press-releases/2022/06/ china-must-address-grave-human-rights-concerns-and-enable-credible

Steinmetz, K. (2019, July 26). A victim of the anti-gay purge in Chechnya speaks out: 'The truth exists'. *Time*. Retrieved August 27, 2022, from https://time.com/5633588/anti-gay-purge-chechnya-victim/

Stevens, R., Bernadini, S., & Jemmott, J. B. (2013). Social environment and sexual risk-taking among gay and transgender African American Youth. *Cult Health Sex., 15*(10), 1148–1161. https://doi. org/10.1080/13691058.2013

Strand, C., Svensson, J., Blomeyer, R., & Sanz, M. (2021). *Disinformation campaigns about LGBTI+ people in the EU and foreign influence*. European Parliament.

Summers, C., & Liapi, A. (2022). The online world; A sanctuary or troll-filled nightmare for the LGBTQ+ community. *myGWork.com*. Retrieved August 30, 2022, from www.mygwork.com/en/ my-g-news/the-online-world-a-sanctuary-or-troll-filled-nightmare-for-the-lgbtq-community

Sydney Queer Muslims. (n.d.). *Sydney queer Muslims*. Retrieved June 2022, from https://sydneyqueer-muslims.org.au/

Tang, A. (2016, December 5). In fear after attacks, gay Bangladeshis retreat into closet and flee abroad. *Reuters*. Retrieved August 30, 2022, from www.reuters.com/article/us-bangladesh-lgbt-idUSKBN13U06K

Tatum, M. (2022, June 8). Meet the LGBTQ activists fighting to be themselves online in Malaysia. *MIT Technology Review*. Retrieved August 31, 2022, from www.technologyreview.com/2022/06/08/1053212/lgbtq-activists-online-in-malaysia/

Tayebi, A. (2022, August 30). Iranian Hijab protester Rashno released on bail after being held for over two months. *RFERL.org*. Retrieved August 30, 2022, from www.rferl.org/a/iranian-hijab-protester-rashno-released-bail/32010848.html

Thoreson, R. (2022, February 15). LGBT rights under renewed pressure in Hungary. *Human Rights Watch*. Retrieved June 4, 2023, from www.hrw.org/news/2022/02/15/lgbt-rights-under-renewed-pressure-hungary

Toews, R. (2020, May 25). Deepfakes are going to wreak havoc on society. We are not prepared. *Forbes*. Retrieved June 18, 2021, from www.forbes.com/sites/robtoews/2020/05/25/deepfakes-are-going-to-wreak-havoc-on-society-we-are-not-prepared/?sh=6362e6b17494

Toksabay, E. (2012, January 20). Gay "honor killing" movie shakes Turkey up. *Reuters*. Retrieved August 30, 2022, from www.reuters.com/article/us-turkey-movie-gays-idUSTRE80J0O920120120

United Nations. (1948). United declaration of human rights. *United Nations*. Retrieved 2022, from www.un.org/en/about-us/universal-declaration-of-human-rights

United Nations. (2022, June 7). Press Release—Human rights council adopts four resolutions—Extends mandate of the independent expert on protection from violence and discrimination related to sexual orientation and gender identity. *United Nations*. Retrieved August 26, 2022, from www.ohchr.org/en/press-releases/2022/07/human-rights-council-adopts-four-resolutions-extends-mandate-independent

United Nations Human Rights. (2022a). Fact sheet No.23, Harmful traditional practices affecting the health of women and children. *United Nations Human Rights*. Retrieved August 10, 2022, from www.ohchr.org/sites/default/files/Documents/Publications/FactSheet23en.pdf

United Nations Human Rights. (2022b). OHCHR and women's human rights and gender equality. *United Nations Human Rights*. Retrieved from www.ohchr.org/en/women

United Nations Human Rights. (2022c, May 16). Forcibly displaced LGBT persons face major challenges in search of safe haven. *United Nations OHCHR*. Retrieved August 26, 2022, from www.ohchr.org/en/statements/2022/05/forcibly-displaced-lgbt-persons-face-major-challenges-search-safe-haven

Velasco, J. (2020, June 19). Should you worry about hacked smart home appliances? *Digital Trends*. Retrieved from www.digitaltrends.com/home/hacked-smart-appliances-legitimate-concerns-feature/

Wakefield, L. (2022, January 31). Majority of LGBT+ Christians don't feel safe to be themselves in church, damning report finds. *PinkNews*. Retrieved August 26, 2022, from www.pinknews.co.uk/2022/01/31/lgbt-church-christian-research-ozanne-foundation/

Wang, Y. (2020, September 1). In China, the 'great Firewall' is changing a generation. *Human Rights Watch*. Retrieved August 31, 2022, from www.hrw.org/news/2020/09/01/china-great-firewall-changing-generation

Wareham, J. (2023, April 7). New maps show where it's illegal to Be LGBTQ in 2023. *Forbes*. Retrieved June 4, 2023, from www.forbes.com/sites/jamiewareham/2023/04/07/new-maps-show-where-its-illegal-to-be-lgbtq-in-2023/?sh=8debe327eaad

Whittaker, Z. (2019, July 2). Security flaws in a popular smart home hub let hackers unlock front doors. *Tech Crunch*. Retrieved August 31, 2022, from https://techcrunch.com/2019/07/02/smart-home-hub-flaws-unlock-doors/

Williams, S. (2020, December 31). Hackers in your bedroom: Hackers targeting smart sex toys. *Security Brief New Zealand*. Retrieved August 31, 2022, from https://securitybrief.co.nz/story/hackers-in-your-bedroom-hackers-targeting-smart-sex-toys

Winder, D. (2020, October 6). Sex toy chastity hack could mean a very Awkward emergency room visit. *Forbes*. Retrieved August 31, 2022, from www.forbes.com/sites/daveywinder/2020/10/06/how-this-sex-toy-lockdown-hack-could-mean-an-awkward-emergency-room-visit/?sh=43bc01f4379c

Woolf, M. (2022, June 19). Online hate law should address 'deepfakes' and disinformation: Advisory panel. *Global News*. Retrieved August 31, 2022, from https://globalnews.ca/news/8931856/online-hate-law-should-address-deepfakes-and-disinformation/

Woolner, C. (2017, October 24). "Have we a new sex problem here?" Black queer women in the early great migration. *Process History*. Retrieved August 10, 2022, from www.processhistory.org/woolner-black-queer-women/

Xu, B., & Albert, E. (2017, February 17). Media censorship in China. *Council on Foreign Relations*. Retrieved August 31, 2022, from www.cfr.org/backgrounder/media-censorship-china

Yang, Z. (2022, August 11). China has censored a top health information platform. *MIT Technology Review*. Retrieved August 31, 2022, from www.technologyreview.com/2022/08/11/1057592/china-censored-health-information-platform/

Younes, R. (2021a, August 5). 'Clean the streets of faggots': Governments in the Middle East & North Africa target LGBT people via social media. *The Conversationalist*. Retrieved August 30, 2022, from https://conversationalist.org/2021/08/05/clean-the-streets-of-faggots-governments-in-the-middle-east-north-africa-target-lgbt-people-via-social-media/

Younes, R. (2021b, July 28). The trouble with the 'LGBT Community'. *Human Rights Watch*. Retrieved August 30, 2022, from www.hrw.org/news/2021/07/28/trouble-lgbt-community

Younes, R. (2022, March 22). "Everyone wants me dead"—Killings, abductions, torture, and sexual violence against LGBT people by armed groups in Iraq. *Human Rights Watch*. Retrieved August 7, 2022, from www.hrw.org/report/2022/03/23/everyone-wants-me-dead/killings-abductions-torture-and-sexual-violence-against

Yurcaba, J. (2021, May 11). Gay Iranian man dead in alleged 'honor killing,' rights group says. *NBC News*. Retrieved August 30, 2022, from www.nbcnews.com/feature/nbc-out/gay-iranian-man-dead-alleged-honor-killing-rights-group-says-n1266995

21
FEMALE EXTREMISTS AND THE ROLE OF GENDER, SEX AND SEXUALITY

Nina Käsehage and Sybille Reinke de Buitrago

Introduction

The chapter discusses *Female Extremists and the Role of Gender, Sex and Sexuality*. Considering that the participation of women in extremist movements was long underestimated (cf. Bond et al., 2019; Sjoberg & Gentry, 2011), and the discussion about gender (roles), the multiple forms and meaning of sex and sexuality are barely reflecting contemporary developments related to diversity and the equality of minorities (keywords: LGBQ+ and woke), this chapter offers added theoretical and empirical value. It conducts and presents a classification regarding the aforementioned topic and its entanglement with deviance, the role of emotions, symbols and visuals and religion or 'substitute religion', as socially 'accepted' or rejected by the majority society.

With the help of selected examples resulting from empirical research on the female right-wing and jihadist milieu (cf. Reinke de Buitrago, 2020a, 2020b, 2022[1]), as well as qualitative religious research (interviews) regarding 60 female jihadists in eight European countries (cf. Käsehage, 2024), the present contribution examines communalities and differences between the female extremists. As emotions, symbols and visuals play an important role in terms of female (online-)radicalization, these mechanisms are briefly laid out at the beginning. The discussion related to the bonding between gender, sex, sexuality and religion illustrates the Western (patriarchal) norms and values that frame the environments in which the persons considered in this study grew up and decided on a deviant way of living, self-perception and loving. The chapter applies the concept of religion as a substitute religion to right-wing extremism. The chapter finds that as some female extremists turn, or even return, to values related to gender, sex and sexuality and religion that are in the West considered outdated and too conservative, most Western societies refuse and reject such moves so strongly because they appear *deviant* to the values of 'modernity'.

The selected examples from women as members of right-wing and jihadist groups are the results of two different surveys with slightly different sources and methodological approaches. Both based on being qualitative research and from the same time period, a comparison is nevertheless valuable. The chapter identifies patterns and concentrates on the comparison of various motives of female members. It presents the 'art of living/loving

DOI: 10.4324/9781003277675-24

and believing' as observed from various locations and forms of occurrence in order to distinguish on- and offline behaviour. The discussion follows the themes of (online) deviance, the role of emotions, symbols and visuals, gender (roles), sex and sexuality and religion.

In closing, the chapter offers policy recommendations as useful bases to facilitate a social rethinking of gender, sex and sexuality as 'a whole-of-society' approach.

How female extremists become active participants

(Online) Deviance

This section lays out the understanding of deviance and deviance in the online space. While according to Wallner and Weiss (2019, p. 42) *delinquency* is defined as behaviour that deviates from the norm, e.g. fare dodging, and is sanctioned by criminal law because it consequently constitutes a criminal offense, *deviant* behaviour is defined as any other behaviour that deviates from the norm (Ibid.). *Deviant offenses* are divided into property, property damage, violence and drug-related offenses (cf. ib., pp. 57–58). The present contribution concentrates on the discussion of *(online) deviant violent offenses* or actions committed by violent female members of right-wing and jihadist groups.

Attempts to label something or someone as deviant points to efforts to exert control over that something or someone. To exert control, a differentiation between what is considered deviant and what is not is necessary, which implies and/or produces an Other (see for ex. Resende & Reinke de Buitrago, 2019).

With respect to Battin et al. (1998), the increase in delinquency in adolescence corresponds to the increasing impact of the peer group. Therefore, it could be assumed that negative role models and group pressure contribute to a temporary increase in the tendency to commit delinquent acts (Wallner & Weiss, 2019, p. 55). Although most sporadically delinquent offenses are based on *adolescence limited antisociality*, persistent socially conspicuous teenagers have an increased risk of *life-course persistent antisociality* (Moffitt, 1993). In the nexus of this contribution, the participation in violent extremist groups and the use of violence might thus also be seen as possible expressions of juvenile protest, quests for belonging or the rebellion towards parental religious traditions and intended (religiously motivated) roles for their daughters (cf. Lynch & Argomaniz, 2019).

Structural functionalists such as Durkheim describe deviance as a necessary aspect of social organization. It functions as an affirmation related to cultural norms and values, defines moral boundaries (good vs. evil), leads to social conformity by forcing people to initiate counter reactions against the deviant behaviour and therefore can enable social change (cf. Durkheim, 2002).

Following Durkheim's model, deviant actions lead to crimes that violate the public perception of collective consciousness that most people follow. As a reaction regarding this social deviance, the majority joins forces and exercises social regulations such as the implementations of certain legislation in order to be able to punish the *deviant social actions*. Creating a set of cultural norms and values that are (again) followed by the majority leads in turn to *deviant behaviour* by some individuals who rebel against this social conformity and want to implement their own (social) rules and reality.

By transferring the structural functionalist understanding of deviance onto female extremists, the female interest in violence and their participation in violent groups and in violent actions represents *deviant behaviour* and *deviant actions* from the prevailing social

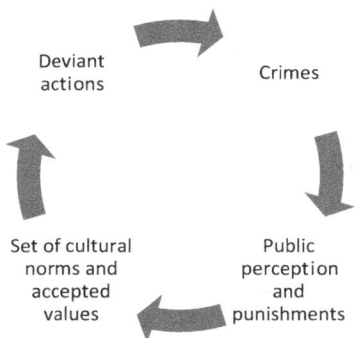

Figure 21.1   Durkheim's model of deviance

Western norms that women—in contrast to men—reject violence as a proven means of action (cf. Winterbotham & Pearson, 2016; King, 2017; Lahoud, 2017). Furthermore, the online space represents fewer emotional and physical hurdles to deviance, including calls for physical self-defence and for violence as means.

The refusal of both the ideological, political or religious 'mainstream' and the way of living of their own parents[2] illustrates the deviance of the female extremists and documents that their (contemporary) 'art of living/loving and believing' is associated with delinquent peers and the adoption of delinquent values in the middle adolescence phase (Wallner et al., 2019, p. 3). *Delinquency* and *deviance* themselves have amplifier functions and lead to a consolidation of corresponding action patterns (Ibid; cf. Wittenberg & Wallner, 2016). Thus, females would inspire themselves as easily as men to follow and engage in deviant actions.

Thus, in accordance with Durkheim (2002), the attempt of the majority of society to 'force' this group to follow the 'normal' Western values and norms may lead to and/or facilitate the *deviant behaviour* and actions of the female extremists. It furthermore has already facilitated a *social change* in three ways:

1) a different public perception of female jihadists and right-wing actors,
2) a re-thinking of radicalization processes of women and
3) an extension of the common C/PVE (countering and prevention of violent extremism) approaches in terms of gender-sensitivity (cf. OSCE, 2019; ICAN, 2021).

When considering *deviance* in the context of *online* space, additional aspects become central. The online space offers new and seemingly easier ways to be deviant. The online world and social media are mostly easily accessible, low-cost and low-barrier, with little social control. Anonymity furthermore lowers inhibitions in expressions, interactions and forms of content. Scholars argue that real-time global communication and content according to user preferences can effectively raise attention to certain messages (Baaken & Schlegel, 2017, pp. 187–188). The set-up of algorithms, for example in YouTube, enables users to easily get in contact with extreme or otherwise problematic content. Some also see a blurring of reality and illusion in the online world, and as especially contested issues are strongly represented in social media, they are easily framed for various ends (Baudrilliard,

2002; Bronfen, 2006). Widely differing understandings of issues can result, along with great potential for distortion and misuse for (political) agendas.

Anyone can use social media to share content and engage online. Extremists engage in and with social media to spread ideas recruit, and mobilize. Scholars even see a "virtual extremist onslaught" (Crosston, 2018, pp. 38–39) and a new dimension of propaganda: once a debate has been initiated, it is easy to foster a high level of interest and excitement (Neumann, 2013, p. 434). Extremists apply various means and strategies, including ideological framings, to further their goals (Al-Rawi & Groshek, 2018). Right-wing groups tend to apply nationalism and nationalist appeals, whereas Islamist groups tend to apply a religious framing. Scholars, however, evaluate actual theological knowledge as highly varying (Schröter, 2018, p. 124), as well as a strong use of deceit in online interaction by Islamist groups (Rudner, 2017; Winter, 2015) in order to subvert Muslims in Western democracies. Neumann (2016, pp. 84–85) adds that ideologies are generally applied to offer simplified explanations of complex issues and to mobilize, including for violence.

The role of emotions in online deviance

Online deviance is a phenomenon that displays and engages emotions. Such emotional framings and appeals are applied in being deviant and to foster deviance in attempts to generate support for the Self (the content creator). Emotional appeals regarding Self and Other, regarding issues and claimed-as-needed-action are purposefully applied to convince, divide, antagonize and/or mobilize and recruit. Emotional representations of Self and Other often include appeals to actively differentiate from mainstream society and behave deviant from societal norms. Such representations often address the needs of belonging by aiming to draw people away from the Other and towards the Self.

Scholars see humans relying on emotions to make sense of their surroundings and to interact with others (Bially Mattern, 2014, pp. 590–591; Mercer, 2014), which is why emotions are significant also in political behavior (Bleiker & Hutchison, 2008). Extremists address emotional and identity needs in their discourse (Barrelle, 2014; Neumann, 2016, p. 64). The manner of Self-Other representation and how they confirm or reject certain identity aspects and their emotional links can therefore shape radicalization processes (Mercer, 2014, pp. 522, 530), a dynamic that can be extended to more general deviant behavior. Self-Other representations can include exaggerated difference and dichotomies, where Self and Other are strategically emotionalized to produce hierarchies of a superior Self and an inferior, threatening Other (Reinke de Buitrago, 2018; Resende & Reinke de Buitrago, 2019), which then is utilized to justify deviance towards the majority society and its norms. Scholars have shown that the use of negative emotions is particularly effective in fostering radicalization (Canetti, 2017; van Stekelenburg, 2017), and by extension (online) deviant behavior. Thus, the way of emotional framing of deviance from the Other's societal norms can accord such deviance attention, a positive notion and attraction, or not. The online space accords anonymity and reduces barriers, which may even foster emotional framings. Via speaking to emotional needs, such as belonging, extremists attempt to draw the audience towards the Self and to motivate deviance towards the majority society as the represented Other, and their norms. As stated, a label of deviant is also an effort to exert control over this Other.

The impact of online narratives of jihadist and right-wing extremists on vulnerable groups

Research underlying this chapter has illustrated that both right-wing extremist and jihadist discourse online employ a strong use of emotions to spread ideology, appeal and convince, pull the audience to one's side and recruit and mobilize (Reinke de Buitrago, 2020a, 2020b, 2022). Online content by these groups, whether text or images, often displays dramatic emotional appeals as well as identity aspects. Emotional framings are meant to evoke emotions, and to stoke the audience with the goal of building dichotomies between the Self (the extremist/s) and the Other (often the majority society, the government, media, or in the case of jihadists whoever they label a non/disbeliever or not a 'true' believer).

Both the right-wing (extremist) and jihadist milieus work with images of victim versus perpetrator for Self and Other, linked to calls to mobilize and rid oneself of the victim status.

Jihadists represent Muslims as victims in Western societies and of non-Muslims, pointing to discrimination or Western military interventions. Being a 'true' Muslim is claimed to be impossible when living under Western norms, and that Western norms and societies thus victimize the 'true' Muslim. The West is generally represented as inferior to Islam and Islamic life, culminating in calls on Muslims to distance and differentiate themselves from the Western life and their norms. Dis/nonbelievers and all non-'true' believers are said to carry blame for not seeing the 'truth' and are thus to be fought by all believers (for example Come to jihad, n.d.; Jihad Explained, n.d.; Why jihad, n.d.). Emotions such as hatred are to be spread when discourse portrays Muslims in the West as surrounded by enemies of Islam; but the portrayal of these enemies as not knowing the 'truth' turns them into the actual victims, and the 'true' Muslim into the superior (Sie verachten dich, 2015). The portrayal of 'true' Muslims as infallible seems attractive, particularly for adolescents (Interview 7, 2018). The negative portrayal of the West and Islam's idealization (Interview 3, 2018; Interview 5, 2018) can foster online deviance vis-à-vis extremism and calls to violence.

Right-wing extremists portray themselves and their home as victims of foreigners, refugees and migrants, and in the last years especially Muslims, but furthermore as victims of their country's migration policies and their government. They claim the 'native' population in the West are at the mercy of the state and liberal, mainstream media (liberal and mainstream are meant negatively). Portrayals and claims of long refugee treks, chaos at borders and of authorities appearing overwhelmed aim at stoking anxiety, hatred and resentment. Linked to this are urgent calls to stem the 'tide' of strangers, to mobilize against governments and their 'open' migration policies and to self-defend—to no longer be at the mercy of states allowing these threats and of the state-colluding media (for example Deutschland meine Heimat, n.d.; Farle, 2018; Weidel, 2018). These strong emotional (negative) framings and the appeals for action call for supporting and engaging in anti-liberal, deviant (and even delinquent) behavior against the norms of the majority society.

Stylizing the Self as victim also comes in the form of utilizing poll results regarding a population's views vis-à-vis foreigners. The claim is that when a government 'allows' 'masses' of foreigners to enter and then subsidizes their living, despite the population's great majority not seeing foreigners as part of their country, or Islam as part of a Western society, the state is prioritizing foreigners over the own population, to the point of the 'native' population being extinguished (for example Patriot, Wo Bist Du, n.d.; Höcke, 2015–2019; Presseportal, 2021). Right-wing actors portray the state as victimizing its own citizens, applying emotions to create division between the 'native' Self and the foreign Other, as well as antagonism towards the state and the colluding media. The goal is to foster deviance serving right-wing objectives. Notions of superiority are meant to appeal to the 'native' We at the cost of societal polarization.

Another typical portrayal is that of women as victims of anarchic, violent (Muslim) men. Such claims are also expressed online with a growing tendency by women in right-wing milieus. Claims express the distortion of events and facts to serve the right-wing agenda (for example German women rise up, n.d.; Identitäre Bewegung: Eine Botschaft, n.d.; Freya über die identitäre Bewegung, n.d.; AfD, 2019). Arguably, women can address other women more effectively by building on experiences of being female and possibly bonding, which may make the content appear more legitimate.

The use of moral shock tactics

Emotions can also be stoked with strong Self-Other contrasts as a method of dramatization. The use of markedly different sounds and colours in videos and online content can create shock or irritation and motivate a reaction—up to (online) deviance.

On the jihadist side, the strong sound, music and colour contrasting frames the claimed opposition to the West and may, together with the calls to live as 'true' Muslims (Sie verachten dich, 2015), facilitate the intended Self-Other differentiation and thereby possibly also deviance from the Western society's norms. The Self's depiction is framed by calm music and lighter colours; the Other's depiction by aggressive, irritating music and sounds as well as darker colours; abrupt changes produce contrast and shock that evoke emotions. Many jihadist videos also imitate the style of Hollywood (with fast cuts and slowing pictures), or ego-shooter games, thus clearly aimed at young people (Interview 5, 2018). Images often show Muslims suffering and war, framed by calls to defend Islam and Muslims (Interview 2, 2018). Emotions thus are significant in both portrayals of and framed calls for deviance.

Right-wing groups aim to evoke emotions via framings of looming catastrophe for Western and European societies. Discourse dramatizes and exaggerates refugee and migration flows and claims a disastrous impact on 'native' populations, effectively extinguishing Western/European (and Christian) populations (for example Deutschland meine Heimat, n.d.; Höcke, 2015–2019; Presseportal, 2021). Respective videos utilize strong colour and music contrasts to evoke positive emotions for the Self and negative emotions towards the Other, working with pride but also anxiety and hatred. Discourse paints a threatened future for Western societies, lest 'the people' rise up and defend themselves against both the foreign threat and their government allowing this threat.

Such representations both build on emotions and evoke emotions by way of facilitating the viewer experiencing a stronger feeling and greater urgency regarding the presented issue. Emotional framings can aid the motivation of online deviance.

The extremists' misuse of psychological vulnerabilities

Girls and young women who joined jihadist groups display symptoms such as an affinity to rage towards others due to post-traumatic stress disorder (PTSD) resulting from former violence experiences, for example in their families, which (partly) explains their interest in violent groups (Käsehage, 2022, p. 12). In that sense, the violence-prone (jihadist) group can function as a container for suppressed emotions of the female jihadists (Meloy & Yakeley, 2014, pp. 347–365).

Extremists furthermore use neuromarketing to target their consumers. This could be observed in terms of the establishing of the new 'brand' Daesh and its online strategy: "Marketers first and foremost need to fundamentally understand both the implicit and explicit emotional associations targeted consumers make with their product's current design, packaging, and brand messaging" (Bolls, 2010). Such 'marketing' relies also on symbols and visuals.

Symbols and visuals in online deviance

Symbols are signs that express or represent meaning, such as an idea or a physical object, in a simplified, condensed manner. Widely known examples are the heart for love, or a red cross on a white background for medical services. For Womack (2005), symbols are a mechanism in and of communication; humans communicate via symbols, also creating new symbols with new meanings. Social media has also added more complexity to means and dynamics of propaganda and persuasion as a communication form (Jowett & O'Donnell, 2012). There are then many more ways to strategically spread ideas, convince and mobilize, including via many new possibilities for creating and presenting symbols and visuals. Scholars have illustrated that exposure to extremist images and videos online can result in emotional desensitizing, which is one of the ways in which the emotional framings shape online radicalization (Neumann, 2013, p. 435).

In the context of online deviance, symbols are something actively created and linked to new meanings in order to express particular views and make particular demands. Examples are Disney figures as Western symbols, representing certain cultural and/or political ideas, being distorted by jihadists, or right-wing extremists using flags, runes and other symbols or characters that have come to signify right-wing ideology. Symbols thus have an emotional dimension and can be applied to evoke emotions.

Visuals are symbols that express meaning, including emotional meaning. Scholars have argued the importance of visuals in processes of sense and meaning making, and in affecting emotions (Bleiker, 2009; Hansen, 2015). Humans use visuals and symbols to express themselves and their views of issues in a shortcut manner, both visuals and symbols expressing meaning in a simplified and condensed way, often with emotional framing. Scholars point out that visuals inform about specific representations of Self and Other and their power relations, including elements of friendship and bonding and of rivalry and hostility (Dodds, 2010; MacDonald et al., 2010, p. 2). In the justification of violence, visuals play a strong role. Scholars evaluate the use of images to legitimize violence as an effective strategy (Schlag & Geis, 2017, p. 193).

The psychology of symbology in the jihadist and right-wing milieus

Regarding ways to influence others via visual means and social media: "[t]he master truth of understanding the interaction between the brain and visual media: *believing is seeing*" (Perlmutter, 2016, p. 10). This explains why extremist organizations such as Daesh have very successful marketing and can convince others to risk their own lives for its 'ideals': "Whereas on a 1–10 scale using visuals and social media to convince someone to change his brand of toothpaste might be considered a 2, convincing him to die for you is an 11" (Ibid: 9).

Though the message of Daesh is visually interlinked with the lives of real individuals, it mobilizes more recruits who can identify with other people's experiences (Ib.).

Jihadists address their audience with visuals of fight, comradery or friendship, community and a safe home in a strong community; right-wing extremists utilize visuals of a threatened home, and of masculinity and traditional notions of womanhood. Style and form come in a great variety (see also Ayad, 2021).

Other types are memes adapted from symbols or existing visuals. Jihadists have used popular Disney figures as Western symbols and re-dressed them in Islamic clothing and appearance—thus appropriated for jihadist aims. These memes are even used by women to remind each other of correct behaviour in Western societies, presenting a deviance from Western norms. This illustrates a more active role for women in the jihadist milieu: a form of enlarged action space. An expert (Interview 6, 2018) calls such use of Western symbols a strategic move due to the expectation to profit from the figures' attractiveness.

Right-wing extremists often integrate images of flags into online content, but also rune characters, '88', swastika variations, a fist with 'White Power' slogans or other symbols and characters associated with right-wing ideology, such as *Thor Steinar* (see for example (Federal Office for the Protection of the Constitution, 2018). Symbols have also evolved to evade legal prosecution, illustrating acts of (online) deviance (especially in countries with tougher legal restrictions on the use of National Socialist symbols).

Gender (roles)[3] and online deviance

The category 'gender' has multiple meanings with a deep impact on both our understanding and expectations regarding different sexual categories and their role in society: for sexuality, in the areas of legalization, in religion(s) and regarding violence. While gender refers to an individual's social identity that is co-shaped by cultural meanings and experiences, sex refers to biological characteristics. According to the definition of the World Health Organization (WHO):

> Gender refers to the characteristics of women, men, girls and boys that are socially constructed. This includes norms, behaviours and roles associated with being a woman, man, girl or a boy, as well as relationships with each other. As a social construct, gender varies from society and can change over time. . . . Gender interacts with but is different from sex, which refers to the different biological and physiological characteristics of females, males and intersex persons, such as chromosomes, hormones and reproductive organs. Gender and sex are related to but different from gender identity. Gender identity refers to a person's physiology or designated sex at birth.
> *(WHO)*

Gender can be seen as fluid concept—always in motion and interacting with various challenges, e.g. in terms of social, cultural, ideological, historical or religious changes (Hopflinger et al., 2012). A major aim of gender studies deals with the roots of gender-related principles resulting in and from patriarchal societies and asymmetric power between genders in earlier times (King & Beattie, 2004).

The impact of religion on gender especially reflects such an entanglement as the result of religiously related impact on people's identity as well as self-perception, which is discussed in the 'Religion' section in this chapter.

Gendered female extremism

Since expectations regarding the 'appropriate' way for women and men to think, dress, feel and behave do shape societies' (stereotypical) understanding of gender roles (King & Beattie, 2004), female extremists' positions seem to challenge the common gender understanding (Duderija, 2010; 2011). Regarding memberships and functions in violent extremist groups, women are usually described as victims of male dominance and power and wives or mothers (Pearson & Winterbotham, 2017; Lahoud, 2017), whereas their roles have actually changed to include perpetrator and fighter (Peresin & Cervone, 2015; Blee, 2002).

Meanwhile, Pearson and Winterbotham (2017, p. 16) point out an important insight regarding Daesh "fostering online relationships with young women":

> 'grooming' narratives might actually apply to women more than men. The finding contextualises community beliefs about the role of the internet in radicalisation. While it was emphasised by the milieu, there appeared to be gender differences in male and female radicalisation, due to both cultural norms and differences in male and female internet use.
>
> *(Ibid)*

Women are still mostly seen as victims and/or followers of men in extremist milieus, less as perpetrators. However, as this chapter argues, women have taken on a more active role (see Bakker & de Leede, 2015; cf. Chatterjee, 2016). The examples of female influencers in the alt-right scene illustrate this change; women are often active participants, including online, where they engage in the spreading of ideology, content creation and ideology mainstreaming for recruitment (Kisyovaa et al., 2022).

The participation of some females in radical Islamic movements is also explained by the unwillingness of 'mainstream' society to accept another way of living; for instance, when a woman decides to wear the veil or refuses the concept of 'Western feminism' (Käsehage, 2018, p. 235). The free decision of some women to live under patriarchal rules is often seen as 'forced' by men, because it deviates from prevailing social values (Käsehage, 2018, p. 236).

One female German Salafist questions the 'mainstream order to be emancipated' through one's appearance as form of counter suppression of these women who are agreeing on patriarchy as divinely willed: "Die Emanzen sagen zu mir: 'Du bist nicht frei!' Dabei hab' ich mich doch für dieses Leben entschieden"[4] (Interview *Umm Rabia*, 2013, p. 7).

Legal gender-bias related to female perpetrators

Beside the social and religious expectations regarding females and gender, Western gender norms related to women also shape the *legal* view on female perpetrators and reflect binary gender expectations (cf. Buckley-Zistel & Zolkos, 2012). With regard to trials related to female Daesh members, Kather et al. (2021) point out that:

> initial investigations and phases of the trials predominantly focused on the religious motives and intent of IS perpetrators, IS gender ideology was left unattended. Upon examination of the language in the indictments against female IS perpetrators, it initially had been around religious ideology justifying their criminal conduct and

involvement. . . . both the religious and gender ideology of IS that has influenced and has a relationship to the criminal conduct of perpetrators. Respectively, this relationship vis-a-vis the involvement of all perpetrators (female and male) in said conduct needs to be adequately investigated, legally categorised and prosecuted.

(Ibid)

This legal imbalance between male and female perpetrator is based on stereotypes regarding long-existing gender roles. Lesser punishments for female Nazis or perpetrators of Rwandan genocide were observed during both the Nuremberg trials and the International Criminal Tribunal for Rwanda respectively, where women played the *carte blanche* of being victims of male dominance (Ibid), thus somehow being less accountable, which was accepted then.

The changing roles of female extremists

Some argue that women play an essential role in jihadist organizations by working to maintain operational capabilities and ideological motivation, including the education of children, which should be understood as political act (von Knop, 2007). Thus, without women, jihadism would falter in the long term.

There is also a religious dimension of gender,[5] as gender is deeply embedded in Islamic traditions, such as regarding morality and politics. A reformist way of thinking about gender equality is presented by reformist Ziba Mir-Hosseini, who argues that the dynamic of Islamic sources allows its harmonization with human rights, diversity and democracy (cf. Mir-Hosseini, 1998, 1999, 2006, 2009). She reflects gender inequality as part of a male Muslim approach in classical fiqh (law) instead of a reflection of a divine will (see Mir-Hosseini, 2003).

In addition, the example of European women (of various backgrounds) going to Syria, Iraq or other places to support the IS (in various roles) evidence both online and offline deviance and a changing role for women. While in many ways women remain below men in status and role, they can engage in more action while deviating from Western norms. Research has shown (Bennhold, 2015) that recruitment efforts exploit girls' and young women's frustrations and dreams, and that after joining jihadist organizations, these young women are active in the organizations' institution-building, including recruitment (Chatterjee, 2016). Studies (Bakker & de Leede, 2015) show women increasingly committing acts of physical violence, including in some cases suicide bombing. Women can thus play a highly active and visible role. While such acts go far beyond deviance, the foundation of such behaviour is deviance from the majority society's norms.

In addition, women have increased their role vis-à-vis other women. As stated earlier—regarding the example of the strategic use of memes (Interview 6, 2018)—women in jihadist groups are themselves more active by way of reminding each other of the 'correct' way of life, including in online discussions and clearly in deviant ways.

On the right-wing side, women are also taking on a more active role (see for example Bakker & de Leede, 2015; Ebner, 2021; Reinke de Buitrago, 2020b, 2022). Women in right-wing extremist groups are active online, as well as in their own YouTube videos, addressing women directly in order to spread ideology, fraternize, mobilize and recruit (for example German women rise up, n.d.; Identitäre Bewegung: eine Botschaft, 2016; Freya über die Identitäre Bewegung, n.d.). They also play an essential role in the groups' support and maintenance, including the bringing up of children.

Females have become active as online influencers in less of a martial style but more modern and mainstream—appearing more harmless. The Identitarian Movement is a good example of a greater role for women. The *120db* campaign exemplifies the specific addressing of females to other females. Other research (Ayaadi, 2021) shows that right-wing extremist content is framed with harmless and attractive content and images and uses platforms such as Instagram for recruitment, to transport their messages.

Arguably, when women address women, they can address female needs and views with more authenticity. When women portray themselves as victims of violence conducted by foreigners/migrants (a key theme in right-wing discourse) and urge the need to self-defend, they can connect to more general fears of women and likely evoke other women more effectively. Therein lies the strategy of enabling identification with the portrayed women and generating support for the group. When women call on other women to mobilize or engage in actions, it arguably presents higher mobilization potential than when men address women.

While women in both milieus clearly remain below men, in status and roles, they have gained more space to act and take influence themselves—also to be a perpetrator.

Sex and sexuality in online deviance

The WHO defines sex as "the different biological and physiological characteristics of females, males and intersex persons, such as chromosomes, hormones and reproductive organs," while the term 'sex' "defines biological traits that society associates with being male or female", and the term 'sexuality' rather describes the "sexual attraction, practices and identity which may or may not align with sex and gender" (Zevallos, 2014).

Analysing this relationship between gender and sex, the expectations regarding different sexes and their roles in society can be understood as influenced by social constructions and values in the same way as gender. This detaches the public expectations regarding female extremists. The link between sexuality and gender rights in terms of (traditional) Muslims is based on the family law and its aim to regulate (fe-)male abilities to express their sexuality freely and to determine binary roles that are defined as biologically determined and 'divinely' justified (cf. Mir-Hosseini, 2003, 2006, 2009). The same understanding regarding the 'perfect' roles for women can also be found in traditional non-religious but social milieus. Both expectations regarding female behaviour in terms of sexuality are also a part of right-wing and radical Islamic milieus (Pearson & Winterbotham, 2017, p. 18) who share the same patriarchal ideas.

With respect to the online radicalization, it can be observed that because "[v]iolent Salafi doctrine does not allow for a public role for women, or for contact between the sexes [a]s a result, radicalisation may take place more frequently online for women rather than men" (Pearson & Winterbotham, 2017, p. 21). The potential role for women has in any case increased with the online space, where women can address other women and remind each other of the 'appropriate' behaviour or coordinate action (done to travel to Syria and Iraq to support the IS, in Bakker & de Leede, 2015).

On the right-wing side, as discussed earlier, women are also taking on a role in recruitment and mobilization, particularly in New Right groups such as the Identitarian Movement. The online space has also given women a greater role: to frame the ideology more to the needs of women, focus on women and their role, mobilize women for activities such as recruiting other women or posting 'evidence' of violence against women by foreigners in attempts to mobilize. These women instrumentalize a deviant view or form of gender for the political goals of the groups in which they take part.

As a result of the rejection of certain duties related to females, sexual violence can be used as a weapon to force women following (male) 'ideals' related to sex and sexuality to reduce their individual freedom and to present their hegemony (cf. Puechguirbal, 2010; Shepherd, 2008). According to Käsehage's European survey related to female jihadists (2022) that expands the research foci in the field of female radicals, all of the women rejected an equal partnership and defined the term 'partnership' depending on their husbands' needs and ideals as the following selected examples underline:

"die Wünsche meines Ehemanns zu erfüllen."[6] (Interview *Umm Naima*, 2014, p. 6)
" die perfekte Frau für ihn zu sein."[7] (Interview *Umm Hisam*, 2013, p. 4)

In the right-wing milieu, women tend to have the role of mother and childrearer still, even if their roles online and offline have also increased. Regarding womens' roles, the right-wing milieu is also divided into more conservative groups with traditional notions, and more modern groups (New Right) that aim at the society's mainstream with more contemporary notions of womanhood (Anastasiadou, 2020).

Sexuality was associated by most of the women with men's pleasure and not described from their own perspective or in view of their own emotions and needs. 18-year-old *Umm Malika* defined sexuality as:

c'est un terrain de jeu pour les hommes. Ils peuvent essayer çe qu'ils veulent et nous [les femmes] devons faire semblant d'aimer ça. Oui, parfois c'est du Plaisir, mais quelques hommes ne se soucient pas de savoir si tu es d'humeur ou situ souffres. Ils veulent que nous soyons leur 'rêve devenu réalité, peu importe comment nous nous, tant qu'ils peuvent parler à leurs amis des 'les plus récent choses' qu'ils sont faites avec nous. . . . Nous ne sommes pas censés parler d'eux, mais bien sûr, ils donnez-nous des notes pour nos performances quand leurs amis sont à proximité.[8]

(Interview Umm Malika*, 2012, p. 7)*

Overall it can be said that the asymmetric demands of obligations regarding sexes and the male claim to control the female body, reflect their aim to gain power over women in order to control their social environment that is defined by their spouses, children, families and their peer groups (here: the extremist Islamist and right-wing milieus) (cf. Kfir, 2015). When Daesh and all extremists apply sexism and misogyny as the defining features of gender relations, the signal appeals to those who yearn for less complicated times when women were neither educated nor employed, neither seen nor heard" (Rasool, 2016, p. 42; cf. Duderija, 2011).

Religion—as socially 'accepted' or rejected by the majority society—in online deviance

From the perspective of a religious sociologist, religion is the result of social interactions, and functions itself as a socio-cultural system through ex- and inclusion of major/minor ideas and groups (Duderija, 2017, p. 259; cf. Hopflinger et al., 2012, p. 621). In the modern age with the increasing urbanization, economic development such as industrialization, the building of democracies and the development of science and technologies, Western societies became more and more secular, and religion and religiosity are seen by some as being in decline (cf. Albrecht & Heaten, 1984).

At the same time, others see democracies as a new market for non-traditional religions such as Christianity, and as a space for atheism and new spiritual beliefs (cf. Iannaccone, 1991). Contrary to the prediction of secularized Western societies, the return of religion was broadly visible in those people who could or would not keep up with the ongoing economic and physical competition and were in search for individual sanctuary and community (cf. Berger, 1999). Some of these believers search for the 'pure' religious truth and often find it in the alleged 'true' religious interpretation of fundamentalist religious groups such as evangelicals or radical Islamic communities (cf. Käsehage, 2021, p. 16). Truth claims are abundant in jihadist discourse, whether it is the 'true' religion, the 'true' path or the knowing of the 'truth' (Reinke de Buitrago, 2020b, 2022). Truth claims are used to convince and to generate support for the speaker and his/her group; they can be attractive via a claimed exclusiveness.

As argued, women in jihadist groups can in fact be seen as actors in their own right, such as taking an active role when it comes to reminding each other of the 'correct' way of life, clothing and behaviour (Interview 6, 2018), and finding their own ways to do so. They thereby contribute to the maintenance of norms and codes for behaviour and thus to deviance from the majority society. Ideas about sex and sexuality are part and parcel of this, which they in turn teach their children as the next generation.

Religion had and still has a deep impact on the construction of gender roles on a symbolic and practical level within the (super-)natural world (cf. Duderija et al., 2020). It shapes different roles for male and female believers and—by doing so—often limits their individual rights as human beings, particularly regarding their sexuality and their professional and familial possibilities and opportunities (Manning, 2012, pp. 336–439).

As the founder of the religion, the Islamic prophet Muhammad was seen as a feminist and the one who was divinely chosen to bring gender equality through the holy scripture (Qur'an) by 'mainstream' Muslims, fundamentalist religious actors try to recover this 'pureness' of the original content (Duderija, 2017, p. 259). The examples of female jihadists in the present chapter illustrate that these females wanted to follow the 'true' Islam represented to them by the jihadist groups they followed. They thus tried to imitate the appearance of a 'true' female believer and decided to wear the abbaya and a face veil. Both the fundamentalist and—in terms of jihadist movements—violence-prone religious interpretation and the covering of their faces and bodies were broadly rejected by the majority Western societies and marked as 'deviant' behaviour (cf. Käsehage, 2024). Whereas this majority position in terms of the rejection of violence is clearly understood, it is questionable from the view of Western societies' citizens to freely choose what to wear. 19-year-old *Umm Fatima* puts this 'dress code' debate like this:

Me dicen: 'No te cubras la cara, eres hermosa.' y yo respondo: 'Pero solo quiero ser hermosa para mi marido.' Pero nadie quiere entenderlo. Está prohibidio llevarlo que se quiera. Bienvenidos en Europa! Bienvenidos en España![9]
(Interview Umm Fatima, *2015, p. 5)*

While religion is less relevant and less associated with right-wing extremism than jihadism, the function of religion also plays a role in the right-wing milieu. Thus, right-wing extremism can be understood as a substitute for religion for some of their adherents (cf. Yendell & Sammet, 2021; cf. Thomik, 2009). Their way to dress and speak demonstrates their (alleged) 'religious' confessions. Wearing clothing with symbols, such as runes, are such expressions; females in right-wing groups follow either a more traditional clothing style or a modern one that does not by itself allow a distinction, depending on the group's orientation.

Given these facts, religion and gender are mutually dependent and need to be analysed together. Religious sources and traditions indeed often function as a landmark or template for (contemporary) gender role constructions.

Conclusions and implications

This chapter has contextualized the findings regarding female online deviance from the disciplinary perspectives of both political science and religious studies. Further added value comes from the consideration of the role of emotions, symbols and visuals, gender, sex and sexuality and religion or substitute religion. The return to 'old-fashioned' religious, social, economic, gender-, sex- and sexuality-related values by some female extremists discussed here is rejected so strongly by the majority in Western societies because they appear *deviant* to the values of 'modernity' that have been established within decades for and by other women. In this sense, the *social deviant actions* and *behaviour* of female extremists frighten the majority and causes them to punish the concerned 'violator' of the established order (cf. Durkheim, 2002). While the online space has given women in both jihadist and right-wing milieus more action space, and while the New Right also follows more modern roles for women, by and large women in both milieus deviate from the majority society's norms and norms for women.

At the same time, the jihadist actors themselves are creating a distinction between themselves, as religiously obedient believers, and the Other (the 'disbelievers', the majority of society) which is in itself discriminatory towards their environment but demands respect and hegemony for them and their peer group only (cf. Reinke de Buitrago, 2020a, 2022; Duderija, 2010). Similar claims of exclusiveness are found in right-wing extremist scenes; this similarity can be explained by the Self/Other differentiation and distinction as inherently dichotomous and the claimed Self's superiority.

Seeing the motives of females to join extremist organizations and their on-/offline recruitment, it is clear that the active role of females is still underestimated. Although various approaches in the field of C/VPE, social work, law enforcement and science have begun to enlarge the view related to gender awareness (cf. Winterbotham & Pearson, 2016), including female radicalization and the distinction between (fe-)male motivations to join violent movements, further needs regarding the prevention of female involvement in extremist groups are identified:

The gap between required gender-equality in science and practice projects and in terms of how leadership positions in radicalization are visible and may have caused a 'limited' view on gender aspects within the research landscape so far. The present contribution tried to illustrate this issue, calling for a change of perspective related to the meaning of gender in extremism.

The questioning of prevailing social, gender-, sex- and sexuality values related to extremist milieus but also regarding Western societies has shaped our understanding of gender roles, sex and sexuality and still informs the assessment of female perpetrators within society and legislation. In that sense, women who prefer patriarchal patterns in their relationships or marriages are alienated by the larger society, a step that can lead to further concentration on the extremist peer group.

In this nexus, the questions arise whether Western societies can tolerate all individual positions related to e.g. the equality of women in the private sphere or whether they tend to over-regulate and force individuals to obey 'mainstream' norms and values—and thereby possibly push some to rebel against the mainstream 'pressure' through radicalization. The border between is blurry, as it is not easy to decide or predict whether some decisions (for instance regarding the wearing of a face-veil by young women) results from a beginning radicalization or their individual religious understanding. This aspect may thus be a test for the 'case-to-case' empathy of democracies and be difficult in general. Likewise, some may take certain government measures as an 'excuse' for deviant actions; assessing the actual motivation with certainty remains difficult.

If commonalities of violent female extremists prevail across milieus, corresponding prevention and awareness approaches should be implemented in terms of C/PVE programmes. C/PVE programs need not only consider the power of symbols and visuals, but also the role of emotions. Prevention measures should lay open extremists' use of emotions and build positive emotions for constructive change. More interdisciplinary working groups are needed; interdisciplinary work should be a more earnest endeavour and even an obligation to generate innovative approaches to understand and prevent female radicalization. Research groups should thus reflect diversity in itself.

Notes

1 Some of this research expands from the project VIDEOSTAR—Video-based Strategies against Radicalization, funded by the Internal Security Fond of the EU.
2 Exceptions are those actors who imitate their parent's bonding to extremist ideologies.
3 Although the term 'gender' does not automatically identify or belong to women, it is used in this sense in public, the media and (sometimes) in science too. The present contribution takes this approach into account.
4 "The feminists tell me: 'You are not free!' But I have chosen this way of life myself." [Author's own translation].
5 Here understood in its binary sense.
6 "Fulfilling the wishes of my husband" [Author's own translation].
7 "To be the perfect wife for him" [Author's own translation].
8 "it's a playground for men. They can try and do whatever they like and we [the women] have to pretend that we like it. . . . Yes, sometimes it is fun, but some men don't care, if [you] are in the mood for it or if it hurts you. They want us to be their 'dream-come-true', no matter if we feel it as long as they can talk with their friends about the 'newest things' they have done with us. . . . We should not exchange about they are, but of course they give us notes for our 'performance' when their colleagues are around" [Author's own translation].
9 "They tell me: 'Don't cover your face, you are beautiful.' and I respond: 'But I want to be beautiful only for my husband.' But nobody wants to hear that. It is forbidden to wear what you want. Welcome to Europe! Welcome to Spain!" [Author's own translation].

References

Albrecht, S. L., & Heaten, T. B. (1984). Secularization, higher education and religiosity. *Review of Religious Research*, 26(1), 43–58.
Al-Rawi, A., & Groshek, J. (2018). Jihadist propaganda on social media: An examination of ISIS related content on Twitter. *International Journal of Cyber Warfare and Terrorism*, 8(4), 1–15.

Anastasiadou, M. (2020, December 7). *Women on the right: Anti-feminists, mothers, fighters*. Heinrich-Böll-Stiftung & Gunda Werner Institute. Retrieved from www.gwi-boell.de/en/2020/12/07/women-right-anti-feminists-mothers-fighters (accessed 4 July 2022).

Ayaadi, K. (2021, August 25). Rechtsextreme Inhalte schön verpackt. *Belltower News*. Retrieved from www.belltower.news/rechte-influencerinnen-rechtsextreme-inhalte-schoen-verpackt-120301/ (accessed 4 July 2022).

Ayad, M. (2021). *Islamogram: Salafism and alt-right online subcultures*. ISD. Retrieved from www.isdglobal.org/wp-content/uploads/2021/11/Islamogram.pdf (accessed 30 June 2022).

Baaken, T., & Schlegel, L. (2017/18). Fishermen or swarm dynamics? Should we understand Jihadist online-radicalization as a top-down or bottom-up process? *Journal for Deradicalization*, 13, 178–212.

Bakker, E., & de Leede, S. (2015). *European female jihadists in Syria: Exploring an under-researched topic*. ICCT Background Note (April), ICCT, The Hague.

Barrelle, K. (2014) 'Pro-integration: Disengagement from and life after extremism'. *Behavioural Sciences of Terrorism and Political Aggression*, 7(2), 129–142. https://doi.org/10.1080/19434472.2014.988165

Battin, S. R., Hill, K. G., Abbott, R. D., Catalano, R. F., & Hawkins, J. D. (1998). The contribution of gang membership to delinquency beyond delinquent friends. *Criminology*, 36(1), 93–115.

Baudrilliard, J. (2002). *Screened out*. Verso.

Becker, H. S. (1963). *Outsiders: Studies in the sociology of deviance*. The Free Press of Glencoe.

Bennhold, K. (2015, August 17). Jihad and girl power: How ISIS lured 3 London girls. *The New York Times*. Retrieved from www.nytimes.com/2015/08/18/world/europe/jihad-and-girl-power-how-isis-lured-3-london-teenagers.html (accessed 4 July 2022).

Berger, P. L. (Ed.). (1999). *The desecularization of the world: Resurgent religion and world politics*. William B. Eerdmans Publishing Company.

Blee, K. M. (2002). *Inside organised racism: Women in the hate movement*. University of California Press.

Bleiker, R. (2009). *Aesthetics and world politics*. Macmillan.

Bleiker, R., & Hutchison, E. (2008). Fear no more: Emotions and world politics. *Review of International Studies*, 34, 115–135.

Bially Mattern, J. (2014). On being convinced: An emotional epistemology of international relations. *International Theory*, 6(3), 589–594. https://doi.org/10.1017/S1752971914000323

Bolls, P. (2010, March 3). Paul Bolls on the psychophysiological assessment of emotions in advertising. *Emotiveanalytics*. Retrieved from www.emotiveanalytics.com/emoblog/?p=43 (accessed 19 May 2012).

Bond, K., Cronin-Furman, K., Loken, M., Lake, M., Parkinson, S., & Zelenz, A. (2019, March 4). The West needs to take the politics of women in ISIS seriously. *Foreign Policy*. Retrieved from https://foreignpolicy.com/2019/03/04/the-west-needs-to-take-the-politics-of-women-inisis-seriously/ (accessed 7 March 2019).

Bronfen, E. (2006). Reality check. Image affects and cultural memory. *Differences*, 17(1), 20–46.

Buckley-Zistel, S., & Zolkos, M. (2012). Introduction: Gender in transitional justice. In *Gender in transitional justice* (pp. 1–33). Palgrave Macmillan. http://dx.doi.org/10.2139/ssrn.2267777

Canetti, D. (2017). Emotional distress, conflict ideology, and radicalization. *PS: Political Science & Politics*, 50(4), 940–943. https://doi.org/10.1017/S1049096517001032

Chatterjee, D. (2016). Gendering ISIS and mapping the role of women. *Contemporary Review of the Middle East*, 3(2), 201–218.

Crosston, M. (2018). Jihadi Johns: Virtual democracy and countering violent extremism propaganda. *Cyber, Intelligence, and Security*, 2(3), 37–55.

Dodds, K. (2010). Popular geopolitics and cartoons: Representing power relations, repetition and resistance. *Critical African Studies*, 2(4), 1–19.

Duderija, A. (2010). Constructing the religious self and the other: Neo-traditional Salafi manhaj. *Islam and Christian—Muslim Relations*, 21(1), 75–93.

Duderija, A. (2011). *Constructing a religiously ideal "believer" and "woman" in Islam: Neo-traditional Salafi and progressive Muslim methods of interpretation*. Palgrave.

Duderija, A. (2017). Tensions between the study of gender and religion: The case of patriarchal and non-patriarchal interpretations of the Islamic tradition hawwa. *Journal of Women in the Middle East and the Islamic World*, 15(3), 257–278.

Duderija, A., Isac Alak, A., & Hissong, K. (2020). *Islam and gender: Major issues and debates*. Routledge.

Durkheim, E. (1895–2002). *Die Regeln der soziologischen Methode*. Frankfurt am Main.

Ebner, J. (2021). *Going dark: The secret lives of extremists*. Bloomsbury.

Federal Office for the Protection of the Constitution. (2018). *Right-wing extremism: Signs, symbols and banned organisations*. Retrieved from www.verfassungsschutz.de/SharedDocs/publikationen/EN/right-wing-extremism/2018-10-right-wing-extremism-symbols-and-organisations.pdf?__blob=publicationFile&v=10 (accessed 30 June 2022).

Hansen, L. (2015). How images make world politics: International icons and the case of Abu Ghraib. *Review of International Studies*, 41(2), 263–288.

Hopflinger, A.-K., Lavanchy, A., & Dahinden, J. (2012). Introduction: Linking gender and religion. *Women's Studies: An Interdisciplinary Journal*, 41(6), 615–638.

Iannaccone, L. R. (1991). The consequences of religious market structure: Adam Smith and the economics of religion. *Rationality and Society*, 3(2), 156–177.

ICAN (International Civil Society Action Network). (Ed.). (2021). *Gender and identity in extremisms. Case studies on the role of gender and identity in shaping positive alternatives to extremisms*. ICAN.

Jowett, G. S., & O'Donnell, V. (2012). *Propaganda & persuasion*. Sage.

Kather, A. L., Sanghvi, N., & Sallach, C. (2021, October 29). How gender stereotypes distort IS trials in Germany. *Justiceinfo.net*. Retrieved from https://www.justiceinfo.net/en/83848-how-gender-stereotypes-distort-is-trials-germany.html (accessed 3 April 2024).

Käsehage, N. (2018). *Die gegenwärtige salafistische Szene in Deutschland. Prediger und Anhänger* (2. Aufl.). LIT.

Käsehage, N. (2021). Introduction. In N. Käsehage (Ed.), *Religious fundamentalism in the age of pandemic* (pp. 7–24). transcript.

Käsehage, N. (2022). Jihadistische Sozialisationsprozesse junger Mädchen aus gewaltaffinen Milieus. In Arbeits- und Forschungsstelle Demokratieförderung und Extremismusprävention (AFS) am Deutschen Jugendinstitut (DJI) (Ed.), *Jugend und islamistischer Extremismus. Pädagogik im Spannungsfeld von Radikalisierung und Distanzierung* (pp. 147–164). Barbara Buderich.

Käsehage, N. (2024). *Frauen im dschihad. Salafismus als transnationale bewegunng*. zu Klampen. [In Progress].

Kfir, I. (2015). Social identity group and human (in)security: The case of Islamic State in Iraq and the Levant (ISIL). *Studies in Conflict and Terrorism*, 38(4), 233–252.

King, A. (2017). Gender and close combat roles. In R. Woodward & C. Duncanson (Eds.), *The Palgrave international handbook of gender and the military* (pp. 305–317). Palgrave Macmillan.

King, U., & Beattie, T. (2004). *Gender, religion and diversity: Cross-cultural perspectives*. Continuum.

Kisyovaa, M.-E., Veilleux-Lepageb, Y., & Newby, V. (2022). Conversations with other (alt-right) women: How do alt-right female influencers narrate a far-right identity?. *Journal for Deradicalization*, 31, 35–71.

Lahoud, N. (2017). Can women be soldiers of the Islamic State? *Survival: Global Politics and Strategy*, 59(1), 61–78.

Lynch, O., & Argomaniz, J. (Eds.) (2017). *Victims and perpetrators of terrorism. Exploring identities, roles and narratives*. Routledge. https://doi.org/10.4324/9781315182490

MacDonald, F., Dodds, K., & Hughes, R. (Eds.). (2010). *Observant states: Geopolitics and visual culture*. I.B. Tauris.

Manning, C. (2012). Gender. In M. Juergensmeyer & W. Clark Roof (Eds.), *Encyclopedia of global religion* (2 vols., pp. 435–438). Sage.

Mead, G. H. (1934). *Mind, self, and society*. University of Chicago Press.

Meloy, J. R., & Yakeley, J. (2014). The violent true believer as a "lone wolf'- Psychoanalytic perspectives on terrorism. *Behavioral Sciences and the Law*, 32(3), 347–365.

Mercer, J. (2014). Feeling like a state: Social emotion and identity. *International Theory*, 6(3), 515–535. https://doi.org/10.1017/S1752971914000244

Mir-Hosseini, Z. (1998). Rethinking gender: Discussions with ulama in the Islamic Republic. *Critique: A Journal for Critical Studies of the Middle East*, 13(3), 45–59.

Mir-Hosseini, Z. (1999). *Islam and gender: The religious debate in contemporary Iran*. Princeton University Press.

Mir-Hosseini, Z. (2003). The construction of gender in Islamic legal thought: Strategies for reform. *Hawwa: Journal of Women in the Middle East and the Islamic World, 1*(1), 1–28.

Mir-Hosseini, Z. (2006). Muslim women's quest for equality: Between Islamic law and feminism. *Critical Inquiry, 32*(2), 629–645.

Mir-Hosseini, Z. (2009). Towards gender equality: Laws and the Shari'a. In Z. Anwar (Ed.), *Wanted: Equality and justice in the muslim family* (pp. 23–63). Musawah. Retrieved from www.musawah. org/wanted-equality-and-justice-muslim-family (accessed 12 June 2022).

Moffitt, T. E. (1993). Adolescence-limited and life-course-persistent antisocial behavior: A developmental taxonomy. *Psychological Review, 100*(4), 674–701.

Neumann, P. (2013). Options and strategies for countering online radicalization in the United States. *Studies in Conflict & Terrorism, 36*(6), 431–459. https://doi.org/10.1080/10576 10X.2013.784568

Neumann, P. (2016). *Der Terror ist unter uns. Dschihadismus und Radikalisierung in Europa.* Ullstein Buchverlage.

OSCE (Organization for Security and Co-operation in Europe). (Ed.). (2019). *Understanding the role of gender in preventing and countering violent extremism and radicalization that lead to terrorism. Good practices for law enforcement* (pp. 1–142). OSCE.

Pearson, E., & Winterbotham, E. (2017). Women, gender and Daesh radicalisation: A milieu approach. *RUSI Journal, 162*(3), 60–72, 1–25.

Peresin, A., & Cervone, A. (2015). The Western *muhajirat* of ISIS. *Studies in Conflict & Terrorism, 38*(7), 495–509.

Perlmutter, D. D. (2016). "Look, look; see the glorious fighters!": The visual persuasion of ISIS and the fanboys of terror. In The Carter Center (Ed.), *Countering daesh propaganda: Action-oriented research for practical policy outcome* (pp. 9–14). The Carter Center.

Phelan, A. (2020). Special issue introduction for terrorism, gender and women: Toward an integrated research agenda. *Studies in Conflict & Terrorism.* https://doi.org/10.1080/10576 10X.2020.1759252

Puechguirbal, N. (2010). Discourses on gender, patriarchy and resolution 1325: A textual analysis of UN documents. *International Peacekeeping, 17*(2), 172–187.

Rasool, E. (2016). Preventing the synapse: Transmission of Daesh religious signals in search of receivers. In The Carter Center (Ed.), *Countering Daesh propaganda: Action-oriented research for practical policy outcome* (pp. 38–42). The Carter Center.

Reinke de Buitrago, S. (2018). Grasping the role of emotions in IR via qualitative content analysis and visual analysis. In M. Clément & E. Sangar (Eds.). *Researching emotions in International Relations: Methodological perspectives on the emotional turn* (pp. 303–324). Palgrave Macmillan.

Reinke de Buitrago, S. (2020a). Mnemonic insecurity: The German struggle with new trends of radicalization. *Interdisciplinary Political Studies, 6*(1), 21–49.

Reinke de Buitrago, S. (2020b). Radikalisierung, online-Diskurse und Emotionen. In S. Koschut (Ed.), *Emotionen in den Internationalen Beziehungen* (pp. 213–230). Nomos.

Reinke de Buitrago, S. (2022). Radikalisierungsnarrative online in der politischen Bedeutungsschaffung: Islamistische und rechtsextremistische/-populistische Narrative in YouTube. In S. Reinke de Buitrago (Ed.), *Radikalisierungsnarrative online: Perspektiven und Lehren aus Wissenschaft und Prävention.* VS Springer.

Resende, E., & Reinke de Buitrago, S. (2019). The politics of otherness. Illustrating the identity/alterity nexus and othering in IR. In J. Edkins (Ed.), *Routledge handbook of critical international relations* (pp. 179–193). Routledge.

Rudner, M. (2017). Electronic jihad: The internet as Al Qaeda's catalyst for global terror. *Studies in Conflict and Terrorism, 40*(17), 10–23. https://doi.org/10.1080/1057610X.2016.1157403

Schlag, G., & Geis, A. (2017). Visualizing violence: Aesthetics and ethics in international politics. *Global Discourse, 7*(2–3), 193–200. https://doi.org/10.1080/23269995.2017.1359995

Schröter, S. (2018). Religiöse Rechtfertigungen des Dschihadismus. In J. Schellhöh, J. Reichertz, V. M. Heins, & A. Flender (Eds.), *Großerzählungen des Extremen. Neue Rechte, Populismus, Islamismus, War on Terror* (pp. 121–136). transcript Verlag.

Shepherd, Laura J. (2008). *Gender, violence and security: Discourse as practice.* Zed Books.

Sjoberg, L., & Gentry, C. E. (Eds.) (2011). *Women, gender, and terrorism.* University of Georgia Press.

Thomik, J. (2009). *Nationalsozialismus als Ersatzreligion: die Zeitschriften "Weltliteratur" und "Die Weltliteratur"/1944 als Träger nationalsozialistischer Ideologie: gleichzeitig ein Beitrag zur Affaire Schneider/Schwerte*. Einhard. https://lccn.loc.gov/2010451395 (accessed 12 June 2022).

van Stekelenburg, J. (2017). Radicalization and violent emotions. *PS: Political Science & Politics*, *50*(4), 936–939. https://doi.org/10.1017/S1049096517001020.

Von Knop, K. (2007). The female jihad: Al Qaeda's women. *Studies in Conflict & Terrorism*, *30*(5), 397–414. https://doi.org/10.1080/10576100701258585

Wallner, S., & Weiss, M. (2019). Prävalenz und Verlauf von Devianz und Delinquenz. In S. Wallner, M. Weiss, J. Reinecke, & M. Stemmler (Eds.), *Devianz und Delinquenz in Kindheit und Jugend Neue Ansätze der kriminologischen Forschung* (pp. 39–61). Springer VS.

Winter, C. (2015). The virtual 'caliphate': Understanding Islamic State's propaganda strategy. *Quilliam*. Foundation. Retrieved from www.quilliamfoundation.org/wp/wp-content/uploads/publications/free/the-virtual-caliphate-understanding-islamic-states-propaganda-strategy.pdf (accessed 14 June 2022).

Winterbotham, E., & Pearson, E. (2016). Different cities, shared stories: A five-country study challenging assumptions around Muslim women and CVE interventions. *RUSI Journal*, *161*(5), 54–65.

Wittenberg, J., & Wallner, S. (2016). Devianz und Delinquenz. In J. Reinecke, M. Stemmler, & J. Wittenberg (Eds.), *Devianz und Delinquenz im Kindes- und Jugendalter: Ungleichheitsdimensionen und Risikofaktoren* (pp. 27–52). Springer VS.

Womack, M. (2005). *Symbols and meaning: A concise introduction*. Alta Mira Press.

World Health Organization. (WHO). *Gender and health*. Retrieved from https://who.int/health-topics/gender#tab1=tab_1 (accessed 12 June 2022).

Yendell, A., & Sammet, K. A. (2021). Religion und Rechtsextremismus. *Zeitschrift für Religion, Gesellschaft und Politik*, *5*, 411–414.

Zevallos, Z. (2014, November 28). Sociology of gender. *The Other Sociologist*. Retrieved from https://theothersociologist.com/sociology-of-gender/ (accessed 12 June 2022).

Primary sources

AfD. (2019, July 10). *Alice Weidel: Frauen und Mädchen sind Leidtragende verfehlter Migrationspolitik der Regierung*. Retrieved from www.afd.de/alice-weidel-frauen-und-maedchen-sind-die-leidtragenden-verfehlter-migrationspolitik-der-regierung/ (accessed 30 June 2022).

Come to jihad. (n.d.). [Video]. *YouTube*. Retrieved from www.youtube.com/watch?v=ll-s3gKfz-s (accessed 7 March 2019).

Deutschland meine Heimat. (n.d.). [Video]. *YouTube*. Retrieved from www.youtube.com/watch?v=81KLQxRtuFM (accessed 3 April 2019).

Farle, R. (2018, January 26). AfD-Politiker platzt der Kragen wegen Familiennachzug und Weltfremdheit der Linken [Video]. *YouTube*. Retrieved from www.youtube.com/watch?v=4P-_WsxltOE (accessed 30 April 2020).

Freya über die Identitäre Bewegung. (n.d.). #120db, Meinungsfreiheit und Rollenbilder #speakup. [Video]. *YouTube*. Retrieved from www.youtube.com/watch?v=QBRlsYucJoE (accessed 20 June 2019).

German women rise up! (n.d.). #120. [Video]. *YouTube*. Retrieved from www.youtube.com/watch?v=RJxU8iiyOS0 (accessed 12 March 2018).

Höcke, B. (2015–2019). *11 Zitate von Björn Höcke, die für den AfD-Chef Jörg Meuthen „nich drüber"sind*. Retrieved from www.watson.de/deutschland/best%20of%20watson/988199781-afd-joerg-meuthen-verteidigt-bjoern-hoecke-gegen-kritik-an-der-grenze-aber-nicht-drueber (Accessed 30 April 2020).

Identitäre Bewegung: Eine Botschaft an die Frauen. (2016). [Video]. *YouTube*. Retrieved from www.youtube.com/watch?v=sTMoGod5d6o (accessed 12 March 2018).

Jihad Explained in One Video—Abu Usamah animated. (n.d.). [Video]. *YouTube*. Retrieved from www.youtube.com/watch?v=AvBUhc7IjP0 (accessed 7 March 2019).

Patriot, Wo Bist Du?—Martin Sellner über App Patriot Peer. (n.d.). [Video]. *YouTube*. Retrieved from www.youtube.com/watch?v=9_UCPniV6so (accessed 3 April 2019).

Presseportal. (2021). *Tino Chrupalla/Alice Weidel: Ideologische Migrationspolitik der Ampel zerreißt Deutschland und Europa*. Retrieved from www.presseportal.de/pm/130241/5083924 (accessed 29 June 2022).

Sie verachten dich ¦ Laufe zurück zu Allah ¦ BotschaftDesIslam. (2015). [Video]. *YouTube*. Retrieved from www.youtube.com/watch?v=CN3BZKdVXtg (accessed 7 March 2018).

Weidel, A. (2018, May 16). *Alice Weidel (AfD) über Kopftuchmädchen*, Co-chair of AfD Bundestag parliamentary group, Speech in Bundestag [Video]. *YouTube*. Retrieved from www.youtube.com/watch?v=Mtu3MMUph4A (accessed 30 August 2018).

Why jihad? (n.d.). [Video]. *YouTube*. Retrieved from www.youtube.com/watch?v=raB-5Cl_oFE (accessed 2 June 2018).

Unpublished interviews that have been conducted by the author Nina Käsehage

2012. Interview *Umm Malika* (21 years), pp. 1–12. France.
2013. Interview *Umm Hisam* (18 years), pp. 1–12. Germany.
2013. Interview *Umm Rabia* (15 years), pp. 1–15. Germany.
2014. Interview *Umm Naima* (20 years), pp. 1–14. Germany.
2015. Interview *Umm Fatima* (19 years), pp. 1–16. Spain.

Unpublished interviews that have been conducted by the author Sybille Reinke de Buitrago

2018. Interview 2. Researcher. March, Germany.
2018. Interview 3. Security official. March, Germany.
2018. Interview 5. Prevention expert. March, Germany.
2018. Interview 6. Security official. March, Germany
2018. Interview 7. Researcher. April 27, Germany.

PART III

Violence and aggression

22

SELF-REPORTED ETHNIC-BASED CYBERBULLYING VICTIMIZATION IN PORTUGAL

Prevalence and implications for criminology

*Gloria Fernández-Pacheco Alises, Paula C. Martins
and Sílvia M. Mendes*

Introduction: ethnic-based cyberbullying

Similar to traditional bullying victimization, cyberbullying may be more likely for victims with ethnic backgrounds (Rodríguez-Hidalgo et al., 2018). There has been abundant research that has studied gender-bias based cyberbullying, focusing on the gender or sexual orientation of victims (Abreu & Kenny, 2018; Price-Feeney et al., 2018). There are, however, few studies that focus on ethnicity. It is striking to see how as time progresses, we obtain more sophisticated means of communication that facilitate interpersonal contact and how this causes violent behaviours among peers to have increasingly high prevalence rates in all corners of an increasingly multicultural world. The internet has become an indispensable medium for communication between people and for the development of social skills—an issue of special relevance for the process of the integration of adolescents with an ethnic background. There are voices that simultaneously describe the internet as a space full of threats and as a space conducive to improving the cognitive abilities and creativity of minors (Livingstone et al., 2011). In truth, cyberspace is currently one of the first areas for relationships between minors, and therefore the probability of victimization for the most vulnerable children and adolescents can increase due to communication difficulties or relative social stereotypes for migrants from the global South. The internet has replaced the traditional areas with the risk of committing criminal acts, thus becoming a prevalent space in the study of peer crime (Miró, 2013).

Cyberbullying refers to the forms of aggression between minors through the internet or mobile devices, "an aggressive and intentional action, developed by a group or an individual using electronic forms of contact, repeated several times over time against a victim who cannot easily defend himself or herself" (Smith et al., 2008, p. 376).

The criminological literature supports that the risk of being a victim of violent behaviour is not distributed homogeneously among the entire population. In this sense, Routine Activity Theory (RAT) explains that instead there are people, groups of people or situations that generate a greater probability of being a victim (Cohen & Felson, 1979). Specifically,

DOI: 10.4324/9781003277675-26

concerning bullying, certain static factors such as age, race or sex are pointed out; other dynamics related to life habits, situational factors or social relationships, explain the special vulnerability to victimization of certain groups (Tamarit et al., 2011). For cybervictimization, unlike school bullying, a high level of anonymity is characteristic and implies immediacy and speed in the expansion of cyber aggression (Del Rey et al., 2015). In turn, anonymity seems to promote a considerable overlap between the roles of a cyberbully and a cyber victim in the youth population, with the dynamics of these roles even sometimes reversed (Ybarra & Mitchell, 2004). Observing this, Baldry et al. (2015) indicate that the processes to become a cyberbully or a cyber victim do not seem to be separate and even share many risk factors. Cyberbullying is also closely related to bullying in the school environment (Baldry et al., 2015; Del Rey et al., 2016).

Ethnic-based cyberbullying consists of "cyberbullying based on a victim's actual or perceived characteristics such as race, ethnicity or national origin" (Henry, 2013). Bias-based cyberbullying due to ethnicity is also called ethnic-based cyberbullying. Therefore, ethnic-based cyberbullying is a form of psychological, verbal or social harassment, depending on the behaviour of the aggressor, which is based on racial or ethnic characteristics and occurs by means of new technologies (Atalan et al., 2021).

Are children and youth from ethnic minorities or ethnic backgrounds more vulnerable to cybervictimization? What are the features of children from an ethnic background who are bullied online?

In general, the victimization of children and adolescents is a phenomenon that is recognized as universal and common to different social and economic groups, regardless of their status (UNICEF, 2014). Although it has many characteristics in common with adult victimization, youth victimization has its own specificity (Martins et al., 2019). In fact, child victimization rates are higher than those of adults (Finkelhor, 2011), but this cannot be explained only by the relative size of the child population. On the other hand, children are subject to a greater diversity of types of violence to the extent that, in addition to being victims of the same types of victimization as adults, they are victimized by specific forms of violence (for example, sexual abuse, child pornography, bullying) in different contexts. They are exposed to violence at home, at school, in their community or in cyberspace, perpetrated by relatives and strangers, whether peers or adults. Cybervictimization rates vary in the literature, with prevalence rates ranging from 2.2% to more than 44% (Patchin & Hinduja, 2012).

In addition, violence in childhood could have a negative impact on the functioning of children, with potentially dramatic consequences (Herrenkohl et al., 2010) that will influence their future trajectories.

On the other hand, the victimization of children and young people is, as stated by the coordinators of the collaborative self-report project *International Self-Report Delinquency Study* (Enzmann, 2010), an indirect way of measuring crime as it reveals a group of special vulnerabilities in relation to crime.

Studies on cyber-victimization in Southern Europe: predictors of cyber-victimization

The first international studies on bullying emerged in Norway in the research of Olweus in the 1980s and 1990s (León del Barco et al., 2013). Subsequently, in terms of Mediterranean countries, studies have been carried out in Italy, Spain and Portugal. In Spain, there are three relevant studies at the national level that have been carried out by public agencies: the Ombudsman research between 1999 and 2006, the Cisneros X Study "Violence and School Harassment" in 2006 and the Reina Sofía Center's "Violence between classmates at school", prepared by Serrano and Iborra in 2005 (Oñate et al., 2007). In Portugal, different studies on child victims of violence in the school environment indicate that bullying between peers is a phenomenon that occurs in all the countries that have been studied and that has clearly negative effects on the victims, such as decreasing their self-esteem. This hinders the integration of minors into the school environment and negatively affects school learning.

Analyses on the victimization of minors and young people in cyberspace could result from an increase in the opportunities for crime and motivations, along with a decrease in the guardians who would prevent the production of a crime (De Haro, 2021). These arguments arise from the perspective of the RAT, which considers cyberspace and new technologies to enhance the strength of criminals as it allows them, with very few resources, to generate a great impact (Yar, 2005). The same offender can attack a victim multiple times or simultaneously attack several victims with extreme ease since there is the possibility of attacking from different computer systems or locations, such as through the use of bots or multiple accounts on social networks (Miró, 2011).

Some studies have focused specifically on the risk factors for victimization, on demographic characteristics, such as the age, gender, nationality of the victims, personality characteristics and patterns of social relationships (Miró, 2013). Other vulnerability factors identified by the literature include years of schooling, previously being a victim of bullying, family environment, ethnicity, certain psychological traits and a lack of friends (Smith et al., 2008).

Regarding the age of the victims of cyberbullying, the conclusions of existing studies are disparate; some studies indicate that victims are more exposed during adolescence (Patchin & Hinduja, 2006), decreasing their exposure risk in later phases, while other authors (Slonje & Smith, 2008) indicate that the percentage of victims is lower among students aged between 15 and 18 years and more pronounced among younger adolescents (aged 12 to 15 years). This increase also seems to be verified by an increase in the age of the population victimized by the phenomenon of sexting.

Gender, on the other hand, is a factor for which contradictory conclusions have been drawn. According to some authors (González, 2013), girls have a greater tendency to be involved in cyberbullying situations as both aggressors and victims due to their innate tendency to engage in emotional rather than physical behaviours. However, while this trend has been verified at younger ages, as boys grow up, they tend to monopolize more aggression than girls. In general, scientific studies seem to demonstrate a trend where girls are more involved in situations of aggression in cyberspace at an early age; however, as the age increases, behaviours become more gender-equalized. In relation to sexting, gender is also a highly studied variable, but with contradictory results. Most studies do not find significant differences between girls and boys who are either victims or perpetrators of this type of behaviour. In this regard, Agustina and Gómez-Durán (2016) point out a distribution of roles based on the purposes of the distribution of digital material, with males typically being the recipients and senders of material disseminated on social networks and females usually being the transmitters and receivers of material within a couple relationship.

Regarding the role of family environment, the research still requires clarification; however, this is likely also an important factor, as an inverse relationship has been revealed between family climate, parental supervision and harassment practices (Broll, 2020). Children from single-parent families seem to be more exposed to victimization, as are those with inconsistent parenting practices, i.e., either very authoritarian or too permissive. That is, while authoritarian parenting practices seem to be associated with aggressive behaviours in cyberspace, indulgent or permissive parenting practices are more associated with cybervictimization. This could be explained by the fact that young people with affective problems are usually more exposed to victimization by cyberbullying (Miró, 2013). In minors with these psychological characteristics, it is also more frequent to find behaviours of dependence on social networks and risk-seeking through the internet, specifically in the use of blogs or chats.

Accordingly, it is not surprising that minors who have been victims of face-to-face harassment have a greater tendency to be victims of cyberbullying (Del Rey et al., 2015). In this regard, students with higher levels of exposure and proximity to social activities within educational centres, such as sports clubs, cultural activities or group events, and students who engage in truancy seem to be more involved in fights or drug trafficking in addition to reporting higher levels of victimization by bullying (APAV, 2020). In contrast, certain factors such as the emotional support of teachers or other students, compliance with the rules of the educational centre or security measures, such as security guards or video surveillance cameras, are elements that lead to lower levels of victimization by harassment in school.

It has been suggested in the literature that victims of harassment could be especially prone to participate in cyberbullying (for example, Smith & Slonje, 2010). Therefore, being a victim of bullying is also a likely predictor of cyber aggression (Yang & Salmivalli, 2013).

Regarding the official victimization statistics in Portugal, there is no national database that gathers data on the victimization of children and young people. The official data come from two main sources: the Portuguese Association for Victim Support (APAV) and the National Commission for the Promotion of the Rights and Protection of Children and Young People (CNPDPCJ). Moreover, there is a partial overlap of data whose scope is unknown since the inclusion criteria of these entities are not mutually exclusive. These agencies also notably differ in terms of the types of victimization they consider (criminal victimization for the APAV and criminal and noncriminal victimization for the CNPDPCJ). According to data from the APAV on the characterization of the criminal victimization of children during the 2013–2018 period, on average, approximately 57.6% of the people served by victim care services were female minors, while 8.52% of the crimes were committed in the school environment, 56.7% at home and 11.83% at the home of the perpetrator. Of the crimes committed against children, 44.7% involved a complaint filed with the authorities. Specifically, crimes committed against minors in the school context had an upwards trend between 2013 (64 reported cases) and 2015 (105 cases), while between 2016 and 2018, they remained constant (an average of 89 cases per year reported to the APAV refer to crimes committed against minors in the school context).

A diagnostic study was conducted in 2012 (Pessoa et al., 2016) on cyberbullying with the objective of contributing to the design of the profiles of aggressors and occasional and frequent victims of cyberbullying among young adolescents. However, its results do not show significant differences based on sociodemographic characteristics, such as age or gender, although they do propose prevention strategies in the educational field.

Concerning this line of research, Portugal has been part of a research project called the *International Self-Reported Delinquency Study (ISRD3)* since 1992. The project periodically evaluates and monitors the international variability of patterns of self-reported criminal behaviour and risk factors and protective factors related to it, in addition to testing different criminological theories applicable in the field of juvenile delinquency. The ISRD3 team (Mendes & Carvalho, 2010) in Portugal has participated in three rounds of the study, conducted between 1992–1993, 2005–2007 and 2015–16 along with 13, 30 and 35 other countries, respectively. Thus, via the third version of the ISRD3 self-reported crime survey in Portugal, in this study, the profiles of minors and young people victimized through cyberspace are analysed.

This study's objective is, therefore, identifying the prevalence figures and victimization profiles of Portuguese youth in urban areas based on the results of the ISRD3. More specifically, the purpose of the study is to determine the prevalence of ethnic-based cyberbullying with respect to other types of victimization among Portuguese youth. The sociodemographic profiles of the victims are taken into account based on gender, age and city size, as well as family characteristics and other demographic and socioeconomic correlations.

As a study hypothesis, it is proposed that the increase in social relationships through the internet has favoured a disproportionate increase in ethnic-based cyberbullying in Portugal in relation to the other types of victimization among minors and young people. Gender, age, ethnic profile and having been a victim or aggressor of various types of victimization thus influence a higher prevalence of cybervictimization in Portugal.

Research design

Data, sample selection and data collection

We use individual-level of the International Self-Reported Delinquency Study-3 (ISRD3) data that have been translated, retro-translated, validated and administered by the authors of this study. The ISRD3 is a standardized self-report questionnaire on victimization and juvenile delinquency. The questionnaire includes items on sociodemographic information, family, school, victimization, leisure and peers, neighbourhood, attitudes and values (prosocial values, self-control and neighbourhood), crime, substance use, force of transmission of norms, procedural justice and gang membership. Online and paper-and-pencil versions of the questionnaire were administered.

A random sample of classes from the 7th to 12th grades was extracted, stratified by type of school (public or private) and grade level at the city level. The focal schools were contacted, and permission was requested to administer the survey to the selected classes in the sample. Once the approval of a school was obtained, the consent of the parents (*opt-in*) was then required for students under 18 years old. Each child took an informed consent form home, and only if they did not expressly give their consent to complete the questionnaire were participants excluded. The students also gave their consent to participate in the study when they were up to 18 years old.

The administration of the survey was carried out during a class session supervised by at least one research assistant. Oral consent was obtained from the students after they were provided written and oral information on the objectives of the study. Anonymity and confidentiality were guaranteed. The research assistants answered any questions of the participants to ensure that the objectives, consent to and questionnaire of the study were well understood.

After receiving prior approval from the Portuguese Data Protection Agency, the Ministry of Education and the Ethics Committee of the University of Minho (Braga), the questionnaire was administered, whenever possible, online. Paper-based administration was used only when a computer was not available to administer the survey or when there were problems with connections to the web platform. Data collection was carried out between October 2015 and June 2016.

Finally, 4,124 students from the 7th to 12th grades participated, corresponding to courses for students between 12 and 21 years of age. They were recruited from 80 educational centres in three cities of different sizes in Portugal: Braga, Oporto and Lisbon. Of these, 75 questionnaires were excluded because the information was incomplete or invalid. Therefore, the final sample comprised 4,048 students.

Variables and study design

Past victimization during the last year as a dependent variable

Our dependent variable is victimization as a function of its different types: extortion or blackmail with aggression, robbery with violence, robbery without violence, hate crime and domestic violence, whether indirect (minors witness violence towards third parties, usually their mother) or direct (towards minors). Cyberbullying is defined as the prevalence throughout one's life or most recent year of "a minor having been seriously mocked in a hurtful way through email or instant messaging, on social networks, on a website, or through text messages sent to his or her mobile phone".

First, the diversity of victimization throughout life was analysed according to the different types of victimization, and then the prevalence during the most recent year was analysed in all cases. Diversity refers to the number of different types of victimization experienced. In other words, it is exposure to different types of victimization (0 = no victimization, 1 = one type of victimization, 2 = two types of victimization, etc.). The severity of the categorization of victimization refers to cases of "mild" and "serious" victimization; "mild" generally corresponds to nonviolent crimes, such as robbery, hate crimes or cybervictimization, which are usually more frequent, while "serious" corresponds to crimes that involve violence and are usually more infrequent (Enzmann et al., 2010), e.g., extortion, robberies with violence or domestic violence, both direct and indirect.

Sociodemographic variables of the study

The independent variables used are demographic and socioeconomic in nature. The demographic variables include the participants' gender, age (categorized by the researchers into two age groups, 12 to 15 years and 16 to 21 years for the analysis), country of birth and parents. On the other hand, the sociodemographic indicators include the participants' type of family (single-parent or not), status as an immigrant or child of immigrants, ethnic minority status, parents' employment status and socioeconomic family level. The sociodemographic variables were *dichotomized* (categorized into two variables) for better between-groups comparative analysis.

Prevalence of victimization and characteristics of cyberbullying among Portuguese minors

The descriptive results show that half of the respondents reported having been a victim of at least one crime throughout their lives. In addition, the majority of victims reported having been exposed to one or two types of victimization. That is, among those who claimed to

Table 22.1 Prevalence by type of victimization throughout life and during the last year

Variables	N	Mean	Dev. typical	Minimum	Maximum
Type of victimization					
Prevalence throughout life					
Total prevalence	4048	0.506	0.500	0	1
Diversity	4010	0.908	1.171	0	7
Extortion	4040	0.081	0.273	0	1
Aggression	4032	0.041	0.198	0	1
Robbery	4038	0.292	0.455	0	1
Hate crime	4032	0.041	0.198	0	1
Direct domestic violence	4028	0.056	0.229	0	1
Indirect domestic violence	4026	0.282	0.450	0	1
Cyberbullying	4034	0.115	0.319	0	1
Prevalence during the previous year					
Extortion	4033	0.070	0.404	0	7
Aggression	4032	0.022	0.237	0	10
Robbery	4018	0.245	0.747	0	12
Hate crime	4023	0.052	0.560	0	20
Cyberbullying	4009	0.271	3.094	0	100
Direct domestic violence	4011	0.200	4.127	0	222
Indirect domestic violence	3942	0.801	8.194	0	365

have been victims of crime, 90% had suffered more than one type of victimization. Regarding the specific types of victimization, robbery (29.2%) and exposure to violence in the family (28.0%) were the most reported types of victimization, followed by cybervictimization, as 11% of the surveyed population claimed to have suffered this type of harassment at some time. Direct family abuse (5.6%), hate crimes and blackmail with aggression (4.1%) were the least reported (Table 22.1). Moreover, among the most frequent types of victimization in the last 12 months were violence in the family environment (80%) and cyberbullying, which was reported by 27% of the minors and young people surveyed, outnumbering the cases of theft (0.24%) and parent-child violence or direct violence (20%).

Characteristics of victims of cyberbullying in Portuguese minors and youth

Bivariate correlation analyses between the demographic variables and victimization variables show that age, gender and size of the city are associated with the prevalence of victimization, indicating an increase in the prevalence of victimization, especially among older male youth and those who live in larger cities.

Concerning the variables of criminal opportunity, living in a larger city seems to be associated with a higher risk of face-to-face victimization than living in a smaller city. Notably, the greatest magnitude regarding the most serious victimizations occurs in Lisbon, which could be explained by its status as the largest city in Portugal, in regard to the prevalence of victimization throughout life. While the highest prevalence of victimization occurred during the previous year among respondents residing in the city of Porto, which is considered medium-size within the country when compared to Braga, a small city. This is explained, based on the theories of criminal opportunity, by the fact that in larger cities, there are greater criminal opportunities since adolescents are able to be far from their sources of supervision and informal social control, as established by the routine activities theory (Cohen & Felson, 1979). Based on this theoretical perspective, crime occurs when motivated offenders come into contact with propitious objectives in the absence of a guardian or protector capable of preventing harm.

On the other hand, the female gender is associated with a lower incidence of victimization in general. While boys are more likely to be victims of serious crimes (especially blackmail with aggression), girls are more likely to be victims of cyber harassment. In the case of cyberbullying, female adolescents report being more victimized. Girls tend to have a profile as victims of harassment behaviours, and boys tend to have a profile as aggressors (León del Barco et al., 2013). The female gender has also been one of the variables identified in the literature as more vulnerable to victimization or at least to feeling more insecure in the face of the probabilities of victimization (Medina, 2003). Female adolescents prefer chats and instant messages when they are aggressors; boys prefer to threaten online and generate hatred on websites (Agustina & Gómez-Durán, 2016). According to the authors, women are usually the emitters and receivers of material within a couple relationship.

Age is significant, with a greater risk of victimization in general. This means that the adolescents in the oldest age group in the sample (16–21 years) showed a greater risk of suffering in-person victimization behaviours throughout their lives than the group of children under 16 years of age. This could be explained by an increase in the risk situations the former face in an evolutionary stage marked by the beginning of social relationships and discoveries (see Table 22.2). Regarding cyberbullying, the results also show a significant

Table 22.2 Lifetime prevalence of victimization by gender and age

Type of victimization	Total N = 4048[a]	Gender		Age group	
		Male *n = 1889*	*Female* *n = 2159*	*12–15* *n = 2196*	*16–21* *n = 1852*
General victimization					
No	2019 (49.9)	936 (49.6)	1083 (50.2)	1216 (55.4)	803 (43.4)[b]
Yes	2023 (50.0)	950 (50.3)	1073 (49.7)	975 (44.4)	1048 (56.6)
Diversity					
None	2019 (49.9)	936 (49.6)	1083 (50.2)	1216 (55.5)	803 (43.4)[b]
1–2 types	1602 (39.6)	747 (39.6)	855 (39.7)	840 (38.3)	762 (41.2)
3 or more than 3 types	421 (10.4)	203 (10.8)	218 (10.1)	135 (6.2)	286 (15.5)
Mild victimization					
No	2118 (52.3)	1006 (53.3)	1112 (51.6)	1263 (57.7)	855 (46.2)[b]
Yes	1922 (47.5)	880 (46.7)	1042 (48.4)	926 (42.3)	996 (53.8)
Serious victimization					
No	3346 (82.7)	1481 (78.5)	1865 (86.5)[b]	1945 (88.8)	1401 (75.7)[b]
Yes	695 (17.2)	405 (21.5)	290 (13.5)	246 (11.2)	449 (24.3)
Cyberbullying					
No	3571 (88.2)	1729 (91.8)	1842 (85.7)[b]	1991 (91.1)	1580 (85.5)[b]
Yes	463 (11.4)	155 (8.2)	308 (14.3)	195 (8.9)	268 (14.5)

[a] Percentage less than 100 for each variable as a result of missing data (<6%).

[b] Level of significance: p <.001.

[c] Level of significance: p <.01.

and increasing trend in bullying behaviours in the older age group. This point thus confirms the results of other studies that point to the increase in age as a predictor of the increase in the probability of victimization through the internet.

Regarding general victimization, sociofamily characteristics seem to be determinant for a greater predisposition to victimization among children who belong to a single-parent family or a family with parents born abroad—to an even greater extent when the mother is of foreign origin. In the case of repeated victimization or having been a victim of crime once or twice, in relation to sociofamily characteristics, only the immigrant origin of the father has an influence.

Severe victimization, specifically extortion, is the form of violence that is best predicted according to our demographic and socioeconomic variables. More specifically, 14% of the violence suffered by young people is explained by a specific set of characteristics. That is, age (older children), gender (male), nationality (immigrant origin), family structure (a single caregiver) and size of the city in which they live (medium or large) put children at higher risk for victimization. Being male and 16 to 21 years old with low income and a single father in a large or medium-sized city explains 20% of the participants' experiences of victimization.

Regarding *cyberbullying*, the results show a lower prevalence in minors and young people with families of at least two members. Therefore, belonging to a single-parent family seems to be a risk factor for cyberbullying, as is the case with general victimization. This variable is also important in terms of the previous year's prevalence in the case of cyberbullying. On the other hand, for this type of virtual behaviour, the immigrant origin of family members does not seem to significantly effect an increase in harassment behaviours through the internet or social networks, as Table 22.3 shows. While other demographic factors differentially influence cybercrime (gender, age, single-parent family), according to the correlations between our variables, ethnic origin does not seem to be a differential factor in the probability of being victimized.

To determine the characteristics that predict the risk of being a victim of cyberbullying in the focal population, logistic regression analysis was performed with the identified variables in the correlations with victimization behaviours. Via this analysis, the variables that are relevant to predicting victimization behaviours are introduced to see what effect each of the variables has on the explanation of this victimization by cyberbullying at some time or during the past year, with the intention of predicting what may happen in the future. That is, the aim is to identify the sociodemographic factors that generate greater vulnerability to victimization by cyberbullying based on the results we have obtained from a representative sample of the Portuguese adolescent population.

Table 22.4 shows the logistic regression coefficients for the model specification presented here regarding both lifetime and past-year victimization. Based on the results of the regression models, sociodemographic variables such as gender, age or family attachment contribute to a higher probability of lifetime cybervictimization. The odds ratio for gender is –0.659 (significant), which suggests that being male (the reference category) is associated with lower odds of cybervictimization compared to being female. The odds ratio for age is 0.477 (significant). This implies that older individuals are associated with higher odds of cybervictimization compared to younger individuals. The odds ratio for "family attachment" is 0.572 (significant), which indicates that lower levels of family attachment are associated with an increased likelihood of cybervictimization. The odds ratio for "ethnic minority" is –0.837 (significant) in the last year, which means that being an ethnic minority

Table 22.3 Lifetime prevalence of victimization by sociofamily characteristics

	Family support		Number of family caregivers		Foreign minor		Immigrant mother		Immigrant father	
	Low n = 508	High n = 3537	<2 n = 867	≥2 n = 3152	No n = 3850	Yes n = 198	No n = 3499	Yes n = 534	No n = 3538	Yes n = 486
General victimization										
No	173 (34.1)	1843 (52.2)[a]	392 (45.3)	1615 (51.3)[b]	1947 (50.6)	72 (36.5)[a]	1776 (50.8)	238 (44.7)[b]	1789 (50.6)	218 (45.0)[c]
Yes	335 (65.9)	1688 (47.8)	474 (54.7)	1532 (48.7)	1898 (49.4)	125 (63.5)	1719 (49.2)	294 (55.3)	1745 (49.4)	266 (55.0)
Diversity										
No	173 (34.1)	1843 (52.2)[a]	392 (45.3)	1615 (51.3)[a]	1947 (50.6)	72 (36.5)[a]	1776 (50.8)	238 (44.7)[a]	1789 (50.6)	218 (45.0)[b]
1–2 types	217 (42.7)	1385 (39.2)	353 (40.8)	1237 (39.3)	1519 (39.5)	83 (42.1)	1381 (39.5)	214 (40.2)	1399 (39.6)	197 (40.7)
≥ 3 types of victimization	118 (23.2)	303 (8.6)	121 (14.0)	295 (9.4)	379 (9.9)	42 (21.3)	338 (9.7)	80 (15.0)	346 (9.8)	69 (14.3)
Victim. mild										
No	188 (37.0)	1927 (54.6)[a]	414 (47.8)	1691 (53.8)[b]	2040 (53.1)	78 (39.6)[a]	1856 (53.1)	257 (48.4)[c]	1876 (53.1)	230 (47.5)[c]
Yes	320 (63.0)	1602 (45.4)	452 (52.2)	1454 (46.2)	1803 (46.9)	119 (60.4)	1638 (46.9)	274 (51.6)	1656 (46.9)	254 (52.5)
Victim. serious										
No	342 (67.3)	3001 (85.0)[a]	682 (78.8)	2644 (84.0)[a]	3207 (83.4)	139 (70.6)[a]	2926 (83.7)	408 (76.7)[a]	2947 (83.4)	381 (78.7)[c]
Yes	166 (32.7)	529 (15.0)	184 (21.2)	502 (16.0)	637 (16.6)	58 (29.4)	568 (16.3)	124 (23.3)	586 (16.6)	103 (21.3)
Cyberbullying										
No	401 (78.9)	3167 (89.9)[a]	742 (85.8)	2806 (89.4)[b]	3403 (88.7)	168 (85.3)	3095 (88.7)	463 (87.2)	3130 (88.7)	420 (87.0)
Yes	107 (21.1)	356 (10.1)	123 (14.2)	334 (10.6)	434 (11.3)	29 (14.7)	393 (11.3)	68 (12.8)	397 (11.3)	63 (13.0)

[a] Percentage less than 100 for each variable as a result of missing data (<6%).
[b] Level of significance: $p < .001$.
[c] Level of significance: $p < .01$.

Table 22.4 Determinants of cybervictimization

VARIABLES	Cyberbullying	
	Ever	Past Year
	Sig. (Exp. B)	Sig. (Exp. B)
Gender	−0.659***(0.108)	0.111 (0.377)
Age	0.477*** (0.105)	0.277 (0.408)
City of Lisbon	0.306** (0.127)	0.687 (0.506)
City of Porto	0.264** (0.123)	0.641 (0.455)
Family attachment	0.572*** (0.164)	−0.109 (0.439)
Social support	0.233* (0.140)	0.719 (0.481)
Single-parent family	0.228* (0.120)	0.707*(0.399)
Immigrant	0.0898 (0.273)	−0.879 (0.673)
Foreign mother	0.0576 (0.178)	0.0555 (0.382)
Foreign parent	0.0345 (0.189)	0.197 (0.436)
Ethnic minority	−0.173 (0.177)	−0.837***(0.305)
Unemployed mother	0.170 (0.139)	−0.0231 (0.444)
Unemployed father	0.0721 (0.175)	0.433 (0.439)
Constant	−2.418***(0.111)	−2.228***(0.463)
Observations	3,906	3,882
Log Likelihood	−2982	−2982
Pseudo R2	0.0459	0.0562

*** p <0.01, ** p <0.05, * p <0.1

is significantly associated with a decrease in odds of experiencing victimization. This is not the case with the variable being an immigrant. The odds ratios for "immigrant" is −0.879 in the last year (nonsignificant), which suggests that being an immigrant is not significantly associated with cybervictimization.

According to the results, the profile of a cyberbullying victim in Portugal is being a female aged between 16 and 21 years from a large- or medium-sized city (Lisbon and Oporto) with a lack of family attachment or inconsistent family style, e.g., a single-parent family, with either a father or mother of migrant origin or an ethnic minority status. It is, however, necessary to specify that the condition of ethnic minorities was relevant only in the case of the prevalence of victimization by cyberbullying during the previous year in an inverse relationship. This means that if we have the presence of young people from ethnic minorities, the probability of cybervictimization is reduced. In general, as the rest of the socioeconomic variables do not appear statistically relevant in the model, they cannot be considered predictive for this type of victimization.

However, the effect of this prediction is not very high. More specifically, 11% of the profiles of people who have been victims of cyberbullying at some point in their lives and approximately 5% in the last year are explained by a specific set of characteristics: age (older children), gender (female), belonging to an ethnic minority and size of the city of residence (medium or large). This necessitates studying in depth the specific characteristics of ethnic-based cybervictimization in Portugal.

Regarding the relationship of ethnic origin to the severity of victimization, extortion is the form of violence where immigrant origin is one of the factors that best predicts the risk of victimization. More specifically, age (older children), sex (male) and nationality (immigrant) determine a greater risk of victimization.

Conclusions

In this study, we have aimed to answer the following question: Are the prevalence rates and characteristics of victimization concerning ethnic-based cyberbullying among minors different from those of other forms of victimization in Portugal?

Accordingly, the ISRD3 self-reported crime survey in Portugal, one of the most frequent types of victimization is cybervictimization, with 11% of the surveyed population claiming to have suffered this type of harassment. This percentage rises to 27% concerning victimization by cyberbullying that has occurred during the last 12 months. The prevalence data confirm the disparity noted in relation to the official statistics of victimization in Portugal (León del Barco et al., 2013). According to these official data, the average percentage of aggressors is 9.1% and of victims 18.1%; this aligns with the variability pointed out by other international studies that have indicated prevalence rates for cyberbullying that range between 2.2% and more than 44% (Patchin & Hinduja, 2012). Regarding official victimization data, there is no national database that gathers data on the victimization of children and young people, entailing an incomplete view that does not allow comparison with other studies using different methodologies. Precisely these methodological gaps were the germ in the 1980s and 1990s of alternative methodologies, such as the self-report survey used in this study, with the intention of completing the information of official agencies that only offered data from reported crimes. Self-report surveys thus offer a much more complete and dynamic image of youth victimization, since the perpetrators or victims themselves are asked about the behaviours they have performed. Moreover, they make it possible to obtain risk profiles among the studied population. We propose, therefore, that the public administrations in charge of conducting victimization surveys explore the methodology of self-report studies to complete the information that they have to be able to more effectively address the criminal phenomena that they use as a means of commissioning the transience of ICT.

Concerning the risk profiles of victimization, belonging to an ethnic minority is a protective factor of experiencing cybervictimization in the last year in Portugal. Knack et al. (2014) refer to a victimization based on ethnicity, which ethnic minorities and immigrant youth often experience as a form of victimization by peers, especially in regard to bullying. Migrant origin seems to primarily be a predictor of the severity of victimization but not of cyberbullying.

In cyberbullying, the best risk factor predictors of victimization are oriented towards the female gender, an age between 16 and 21 years, living in a large or medium-sized city (Lisbon and Oporto) and a lack of family attachment or styles, with inconsistent relatives, e.g., single-parent families. Theories on criminal opportunity have been responsible for explaining why larger cities produce greater criminal opportunities. Furthermore, as has been said in other criminological studies (González, 2013), an intrinsic contextual feature of cyberbullying is that it can be carried out at any time without being limited to the school environment. No prior interaction within an educational circle or peer group is necessary; thus, it is not necessary to know the identity or specific ethnic profile of a victim. This entails an increase in opportunity as an explanatory factor of cybervictimization, i.e., the presence of a motivated criminal, a favourable victim in cyberspace and a lack of guardians (Cohen &

Felson, 1979). While the meeting point in the physical world is the educational centre, in the online world, the meeting points are diffuse but no less concrete: social networks and mobile applications. Therefore, cyberbullying behaviours should also be considered social criminal behaviours (Miró, 2013). Cyberbullying aims to obtain a result or influence with respect to social status, the support of a peer group, or the expression of feelings of anger or revenge in the context of social relationships between peers.

Belonging to an ethnic minority is relevant as a risk factor in the case of the prediction of victimization by cyberbullying during the previous year. Having a foreign father or mother does not seem to have implications for the prevalence of lifetime cybervictimization. However, this is relevant in terms of severe victimization and victimization by hate crime. This finding has important implications for both research on and intervention with multicultural groups.

Regarding research, more research is necessary to test whether ethnicity is a potential mediator of the severity and frequency of various forms of cybervictimization. In this way, the most prone profiles and relationships with respect to hate crime victimization could be identified (Henry, 2013). In current multicultural societies, one's ethnic profile must be determined so that it does not represent a factor of vulnerability in terms of harassment behaviours, both in person and online.

Regarding intervention, as cyberbullying has negative consequences for victims in adolescence, including depression or suicidal ideation (Perren et al., 2010), it is necessary to promote specific interventions that involve more information among families regarding cybervictimization and its effects on minors. Although traditional peer harassment protocols, implemented primarily in the educational field, can serve as guidance on the steps to follow when we encounter cyberbullying behaviours, specific coping strategies can be applied in the family and social support environment to improve the well-being of the victims and cushion negative impacts. The victims themselves can try to face the problem emotionally, and their peers, friends or ethnic group can offer them emotional and instrumental support.

Bibliography

Abreu, R. L., & Kenny, M. C. (2018). Cyberbullying and LGBTQ youth: A systematic literature review and recommendations for prevention and intervention. *Journal of Child & Adolescent Trauma, i*(1), 81–97. https://doi.org/10.1007/s40653-017-0175-7

Agustina J. R., y Gómez-Durán, E. L. (2016). Factores de riesgo asociados al sexting como umbral de diversas formas de victimización. Estudio de factores correlacionados con el sexting en una muestra universitaria. *IDP Revista d'Internet, Dret i Política, 22*, 21–47.

Almeida, P. (2010). A vitimação em Portugal: Apresentação de Dados de um Estudo Nacional. In En MAI (Ed.), *Jornadas de Segurança Interna*. Libro de actas. Ministério da Administração Interna.

Associação Portuguesa de Apoio à Vítima (APAV). (2018, March 1). Estatísticas APAV. *Relatório Anual 2016*. Retrieved from https://apav.pt/apav_v3/images/pdf/Estatisticas_APAV_Relatorio_Anual_2016.pdf

Associação Portuguesa de Apoio à Vítima (APAV). (2019). *Estatisticas APAV: Crianças e Jovens Vítimas de Crime e de Violência 2013-2018*. Retrieved May 8, 2020, from https://apav.pt/apav_v3/index.php/pt/estatisticas-apav

Atalan Ergin, D., Akgül, G., & Güney Karaman, N. (2021). Ethnic-based cyberbullying: The role of adolescents' and their peers' attitudes towards immigrants. *Turkish Journal of Education, 10*(2),139–156. https://doi.org/10.19128/turje.879347

Baldry, A. C., Farrington, D. P., & Sorrentino, A. (2015). "Am I at risk of cyberbullying?" A narrative review and conceptual framework for research on risk of cyberbullying and cybervictimization:

The risk and needs assessment approach. *Aggression and Violent Behavior, 23,* 36–51. https://doi.org/10.1016/j.avb.2015.05.014

Broll, R., y Reynolds, D. (2020). Parental responsibility, blameworthiness, and bullying: Parenting style and adolescents' experiences with traditional bullying and cyberbullying. *Criminal Justice Policy Review, 2020,* 1–22.

Buelga, S., Cava, M. J., y Musitu, G. (2010). Cyberbullying: Victimización entre adolescentes a través del teléfono móvil y de Internet. *Psicothema, 22*(4), 784–789.

Cohen, L. E., y Felson, M. (1979). Social change and crime rate trends: A routine activity approach. *American Sociological Review, 44*(4), 588–608. https://doi.org/10.2307/2094589

Comisión Nacional de Promoción de los Derechos y Protección de los Niños y los Jóvenes (CNPD-PCJ). Retrieved from www.cnpdpcj.gov.pt/inicio

De Haro Olmo, F. J. (2021). Acoso y ciberacoso como fenómeno delictivo. Protocolos de actuación en España. *Scientia Omnibus Portus, 1*(2), 1–14. https://iescelia.org/ojs/index.php/scientia/article/view/6

Del Rey, R., Casas, J. A., Ortega-Ruiz, R., Schultze-Krumbholz, A., Scheithauer, H., Smith, P., Thomson, F., Tsorbatzoudis, H., Brigh, A., Guarin, A., Pyzalski, J., & Plichta, P. (2015). Structural validation and cross-cultural robustness of the European cyberbullying intervention project questionnaire. *Computers in Human Behavior, 50,* 141–147. https://doi.org/10.1016/j.chb.2015.03.065

Del Rey, R., Lazuras, L., Casas, J. A., Barkoukis, V., Ortega-Ruiz, R., & Tsorbatzoudis, H. (2016). Does empathy predict (cyber) bullying perpetration, and how do age, gender and nationality affect this relationship? *Learning and Individual Differences, 45,* 275–281. https://doi.org/10.1016/j.lindif.2015.11.021

Enzmann, M., Marshall, I., Killias, M., Junger-Tas, J., Steketee, M., & Gruszczynska, B. (2010). Self-reported youth delinquency in Europe and beyond: First results of the second international self-report delinquency study in the context of police and victimization data. *European Journal of Criminology, 7*(2), 159–183.

Finkelhor, D. (2011). Prevalence of child victimization, abuse, crime, and violence exposure. En J. W. White, M. P. Koss, & A. E. Kazdin (Eds.), *Violence against women and children: Mapping the terrain* (Vol. 1, pp. 9–29). American Psychological Association.

Garofalo, J. (1987). Reassessing the lifestyle model of criminal victimization. In M. R. Gottfredson y T. Hirschi (Eds.), *Positive criminology* (pp. 23–42). Sage.

González, A., y Campoy, P. (2018). Ciberacoso y cyberbullying; diferenciación en función de los precipitadores situacionales. *Revista Española de Investigación Criminológica, 16,* 1–31, Article 4.

González García, A. (2013). *El ciberbullying o acoso juvenil a través de internet: un análisis empírico a través del modelo del Triple Riesgo Delictivo* [Tesis doctoral, Repositorio Universitat de Barcelona]. Retrieved March 3, 2020, from www.tdx.cat/handle/10803/384709

Hamby, S. L., & Finkelhor, D. (2000). The victimization of children: Recommendations for assessment and instrument development. *Journal of the American Academy of Child and Adolescent Psychiatry, 39*(7), 829–840. https://doi.org/10.1097/00004583-200007000-00011

Henry, J. (2013). Bias-based cyberbullying: The next hate crime frontier?. *Criminal Law Bulletin, 49*(3), 481–503. https://papers.ssrn.com/sol3/papers.cfm?abstract_id=2331371

Herrenkohl, T., Hong, S., Klika, J., Herrenkohl, R., & Russo, M. (2010). Developmental impacts of child abuse and neglect related to adult mental health, substance use, and physical health. *Journal of Family Violence, 28*(2), 191–199.

Knack, N., Vaillancourt, T., Krygsman, A., Arnocky, S., Vitoroulis, I., Hepditch, J., & Blain-Arcaro, C. (2014). Peer victimization: Understanding the developmental correlates of at-risk children and youth. In J. A. Burack & L. A. Schmidt (Eds.), *Cultural and contextual perspectives on developmental risk and well-being: interdisciplinary approaches to knowledge and development* (pp. 107–126). Cambridge University Press. Retrieved from https://doi.org/10.1017/CBO9780511920165

León del Barco, B., Mira, A. R., Verdasca, J. L. C., Felipe Castaño, E., y Gómez Carroza, T. (2013). Cyberbullying en centros de enseñanza básica y secundaria del Alentejo. *Educação, Temas e Problemas, 12,* e13, 239–251.

Livingstone, S., Haddon, L., Görzig, A., & Ólafsson, K. (2011). *Risks and safety on the internet: The perspective of European children: Full findings and policy implications from the EU Kids Online* survey of 9–16 year olds and their parents in 25 countries (pp. 1–171). EU Kids Online, Deliverable D4. EU Kids Online Network.

Martins, P. C., Mendes, S. M., Fernández- Pacheco, G., y Tendais, I. (2019). Juvenile victimization in Portugal through the lens of ISRD-3: Lifetime prevalence, predictors, and implications. *European Journal on Criminal Policy and Research*, *25*, 317–343.

Medina, J. J. (2003). Inseguridad, miedo al delito y policía en España. *Revista Electrónica de Ciencia Penal y Criminología*, *05–03*, 1–21.

Mendes, S., y Carvalho, S. (2010). Portugal. En J. Junger-Tas, I. Marshall, D. Enzmann, M. Killias, M. Steketee, & B. Gruszczynska (Eds.), *Juvenile delinquency in Europe and beyond. Results of the second international self—Report delinquency study* (pp. 205–212). Springer.

Miró, F. (2011). La oportunidad criminal en el ciberespacio. Aplicación y desarrollo de la teoría de las actvidades cotidianas para la prevención del cibercrimen. *Revista Electrónica de Ciencia Penal y Criminología*, *13*(7), 55.

Miró, F. (2013). La victimización por cibercriminalidad social. Un estudio a partir de la teoría de las actividades cotidianas en el ciberespacio. *Revista Española de investigación criminológica (REIC)*, *11*, 1–35, Article 5.

Mrug, S., y Windle, M. (2013). Prospective effects of violence exposure across multiple contexts on early adolescents' internalizing and externalizing problems. *Journal of Child Psychology and Psychiatry*, *51*(8), 953–961.

Oñate, A., y Piñuel, F. (2007). *Informe Cisneros X: Acoso y violencia escolar en España*. Retrieved January 15, 2020, from www.bienestaryproteccioninfantil.es/fuentes1.asp?sec=27&subs=281&cod=2356&page=

Patchin, J. W., e Hinduja, S. (2006). Bullies move beyond the schoolyard a preliminary look at cyberbullying. *Youth Violence and Juvenile Justice*, *4*(2), 148–169.

Patchin, J. W., & Hinduja, S. (Eds.). (2012). *Cyberbullying prevention and response: Expert perspectives*. Routledge.

Perren, S., Dooley, J., Shaw, T., & Cross, D. (2010). Bullying in school and cyberspace: Associations with depressive symptoms in Swiss and Australian adolescents. *Child and Adolescent Psychiatry and Mental Health*, *4*, 28. http://dx.doi.org/10.1186/1753-2000-4-28.

Pessoa, T., Matos, A., Amado, J., Freire, I., y Caetano, A. P. (2016). *Cyberbyllying entre adolescentes y jóvenes portugueses"*. *Comunicación y Pedagogía*, 2016. Retrieved March 4, 2020, from www.centrocp.com/comunicacion-pedagogia-297-298-inclusion-tic/

Price-Feeney, M., Jones, L. M., Ybarra, M. L., & Mitchell, K. J. (2018). The relationship between bias-based peer victimization and depressive symptomatology across sexual and gender identity. *Psychology of Violence*, *8*(6), 680–691. https://doi.org/10.1037/vio0000219

Rodríguez-Hidalgo, A. J., Solera, E., & Calmaestra, J. (2018). Psychological predictors of cyberbullying according to ethnic-cultural origin in adolescents: A national study in Spain. *Journal of Cross-cultural Psychology*, *49*(10), 1506–1522. https://doi.org/10.1177/0022022118795283

Shan-A-Khuda, M., y Schreuders, Z. C. (2019). Understanding cybercrime victimization: Modelling the local area variations in routinely collected cybercrime police data using latent class analysis. *International Journal of Cyber Criminology*, *13*(2), 493–510.

Slonje R., y Smith, P. K. (2008). Cyberbullying: Another main type of bullying?. *Scandinavian Journal of Psychology*, *49*(2), 147–154.

Smith, P. K., Mahdavi, J., Carvalho, M., Fisher, S., Russell, S., y Tippett, N. (2008). Cyberbullying: Its nature and impact in secondary school pupils. *Journal of Child Psychology and Psychiatry*, *49*(4).

Smith, P. K., & Slonje, R. (2010). Cyberbullying: The nature and extent of a new kind of bullying in and out of school. In S. Jimerson, S. Swearer, & D. Espelage (Eds.), *Handbook of bullying in schools* (pp. 249–262). Routledge.

Tamarit Sumalla, J., Luque Reina, E., Guardiola Lago, M. J., y Salinero Echeverría, S. (2011). La victimización de migrantes. Una encuesta a colombianos en Cataluña. *Revista Electrónica de Ciencia Penal y Criminología*, *13–11*, 1–22.

UNICEF. (2014). *Ending violence against children: Six strategies for action*. Retrieved September 11, 2017, from www.unicef.org/publications/files/Ending_Violence_Against_Children_Six_strategies_for_action_EN_2_Sept_2014.pdf

Walters G. D. (2020). Unraveling the bidirectional relationship between bullying victimization and perpetration: A test of mechanisms from opportunity and general strain theories. *Youth violence and Juvenile Justice*, 395–411. https://doi.org/10.1177/1541204020922874

Yang, A., & Salmivalli, C. (2013). Different forms of bullying and victimization: Bully-victims versus bullies and victims. *European Journal of Developmental Psychology*, 723–738. https://doi.org/10.1080/17405629.2013.793596

Yar, M. (2005). The novelty of 'cybercrime': An assessment in light of routine activity theory. *European Journal of Criminology*, 2(4), 407–427. https://doi.org/10.1177/147737080556056

Ybarra, M. L., & Mitchell, K. J. (2004). Youth engaging in online harassment: Associations with caregiver—Child relationships, Internet use, and personal characteristics. *Journal of Adolescence*, 27, 319–336. https://doi.org/10.1016/j.adolescence.2004.03.007

23

MORAL DISAFFILIATION IN CYBER INCITEMENT TO HATRED AND VIOLENCE

A discourse semantic approach

Awni Etaywe

Introduction

Incitement to hatred and terrorist acts is a key aspect of illegal online content (Rediker, 2015) that, unlike one-to-one incitement acts, addresses a wide range of audiences and requires terrorists exploit social bonds (i.e. values) to legitimise violence and achieve their agendas (Malešević, 2019; Etaywe, 2021, 2023a). However, little is known about how terrorists utilise language to mobilise (i.e. activate) these bonds and to discursively construct a moral system in the service of positioning the inciters and incitees and regulating their moral conduct against Others. Contributing to the growing international commitment to counterterrorism, this study proposes the concept of 'disaffiliation' as a communication strategy used in incitement towards outgroups. The chapter empirically examines and showcases how terrorists use language to enact bonding and provide a moral ground for 'disaffiliation'—the process of forging value-disalignment with outgroups—while they incite hatred and violence. It contributes to the limited forensic linguistic research into the moral motivations of terrorist cyber incitement and digital deviance, examining how social 'disaffiliation' is enacted and its moral foundation activated in digital incitement texts in service of enacting moral coercion into violence. This study applies a discourse semantic approach to incitement as a social semiotic practice of 'digital deviance' (Graham & Smith, 2020), drawing on the Affiliation model as grounded in Systemic Functional Linguistics (hereafter, SFL) (explained in 'The discourse semantic approach and procedures of analysis' Section). The chapter demonstrates how the approach adopted can help us obtain empirical insights into the meta-values established in discourse to create relational and treatment/actional social networks and valuable insights into the semiotic resources whereby terrorists turn a conflict into an axiological and ideological issue, and violence into an act of care and vigilance against outgroups' immoral actions. The chapter takes a set of online texts made by the following terrorists as a case study: former al-Qaeda leader Osama bin Laden (hereafter, OBL); former ISIS leader Abu Baker al-Baghdadi (hereafter, al-Baghdadi); and the far-rightist Brenton Tarrant (hereafter, Tarrant).

Criminal investigative analysis (formerly known as criminal profiling) of an offender's actual language has been found to be useful in assessing and revealing the offender's identities and motives for committing a crime (Smith & Shuy, 2002). Such analysis can also help security and

DOI: 10.4324/9781003277675-27

law enforcement agencies to better understand how terrorists communicate and how to communicatively challenge the online terrorists' content as part of the counter terrorism efforts (Braddock, 2019; Taylor & Bean, 2019; Etaywe, 2022b, 2023a). This chapter contributes to threat assessors' fuller understanding of the discursive nature of terrorists' inciting content, enabling new insights into the morality negotiated in digital discourse. This study contributes to cyber-forensic linguistic research – that is, the use of linguistic techniques to maximise intelligence yield and to investigate and aid in establishing evidence of social cybercrimes and their motivations, in which language data forms part of the evidence (Etaywe, 2023a, p. 909) – and to discourse analysis tools used for forensic purposes (for more, see Olsson, 2021; Shuy, 2021). The aim is to showcase how to help investigators to decode extremists' "encoded attitude"—the aggressive attitudes being construed as a result of context activation of attitudinal meaning and meaning activation of attitudinal expressions (Etaywe & Zappavigna, 2021, p. 317)—and to illuminate the patterning and functioning of attitudinal meanings and moral meta-values in discourse. Additionally, the analytical strategy adds a linguistic method to the criminal investigative analysis of offenders' motives for cybercrimes, and to extremists' moral values analysis (MVA) – identifying the predispositions and assumptions upon which an extremist relies to position people within relational and actional (i.e. bonds- and obligations-based) online and offline networks.

The focus of this study is on the role of evaluative, attitudinal meanings in construing an extremist moral system/order in discourse. In so doing, the chapter builds on Thompson and Hunston's (2000, pp. 6–7) argument that "[e]very act of evaluation expresses a communal value-system, and every act of evaluation goes towards building up that value-system. This value-system in turn is a component of the ideology which lies behind every text". This study also adopts the theoretical orientation that: firstly, acts of social (dis)alignment are manifest in the acts of stancetaking (Du Bois, 2007); and secondly, moral and ideological struggles within the context of terrorism are manifest in the attitudinal meanings and social values that are contested in terrorist texts and that can provide clues to the predispositions and assumptions that inform violent actions and identity relationships (Etaywe & Zappavigna, 2021).

Literature review: terrorism, digital presence and morality

The design of the Internet and social media platforms such as Facebook and YouTube is sometimes criticised for bringing affordances that allow for driving hateful and extreme views and leading users towards more extreme content (Munn, 2020). Such affordances are exploited by extremists, be they lone wolves or organisations. Terrorists from jihadism and far-right extremism have increased their online presence for a range of purposes, including orchestrating and livestreaming terrorist attacks, recruitment, fundraising from the group's global diaspora, radicalisation and incitement to hatred and violence (Mandaville, 2007; Conway, 2012; Önnerfors, 2019). This move by terrorists to develop a strategic new media presence began with al-Qaeda and its affiliates' work towards outreaching potential followers (Reid & Chen, 2007). This has allowed terrorists to move from traditional media outlets to the new media alternative, where any Internet user can easily find, for example, a digital archive of bin Laden and al-Zawahiri's messages (see e.g. Dauber, 2009).

Other jihadist and far-right extremist groups have also established their digital presence. For example, ISIS has established its new media arms, such as al-Hayat Media Center, to enable sharing of recruitment videos and communicating via ISIS magazines (e.g. *Dabiq*, *Rumiya*, and *Inspire*) (Wignell et al., 2017). This extremist content can motivate sympathisers worldwide to do what they can, with whatever they have, wherever they are, whenever possible (Atran, 2015, p. 2). In addition, far-right extremists use large online forums such as 4chan which has incubated the initial growth of the alt-right (or alternative right)—an internet-based extreme-right movement that is based in the USA but exists in different parts of the world. Unlike, for example, Twitter/X followers of extremists who are definable, 4chan provides its users with—in Anderson's (2016, p. 44) terms—"unified fields of exchange and communication" and the condition of anonymity which allows for open discussion of violence and extreme ideas without exposing the users' offline identity (Elley, 2021).

Many recent studies of the role of terrorists' use of social media in the radicalisation and recruitment processes illuminate how extremists tap into topics such as group membership, culture, ideals, and the need for self/group improvement, to intimidate opponents and encourage hatred and violence against members of outgroups (e.g. Chen et al., 2008; Youngblood, 2020; Elley, 2021). Recent studies focusing on the patterns of language used in digital extremist discourse show that the strategic use of certain meanings can provide clues to suspect extremist and aggressive identity (e.g. Etaywe & Zappavigna, 2021). This chapter adds to existing literature on the language of terrorist incitement online (e.g. Jaconelli, 2017; Tsesis, 2017) by focusing on the morality of incitement and the link between group membership, values, and patterns of evaluation.

The causes of terrorism include political, ethnonationalist and/or religious elements. Research in the field of law also emphasises that causes of terrorist acts include "intensely moral elements" that require the use of suitable analytical tools "to develop a better understanding of those elements" and to support the prosecution of illegal practices (e.g. Seto, 2002, p. 1263). This chapter will contribute to that requirement. Existing literature on the psychology of terrorism shows that an ideology or a moral system of terrorists serves to provide a set of inviolable beliefs that justify and guide behavioral mandates, and encourage followers to buttress their own identity by means such as attacking others (Borum, 2004). Bandura's (2016) work, which is based on a social cognitive theory of morality (see pp. 24–39), argues that while societies adopt standards of right and wrong, reflecting their values, and implement these standards through legal and societal orders, these moral orders are insufficient to curb an extremist's deviance and violence. Terrorists tend to, for example, provide various moral and social justifications to sanitise their acts, to enhance the construction of their worldviews and agendas, and to enable a selective disengagement from legal and societal orders depending on whom the terrorists favour or include in their social category and whom they disfavour or exclude (Bandura, 2016). Existing literature as such makes dealing with the concept of membership categorisation (e.g. Sacks, 1992) crucial to the linguistic examination of the morality of incitement acts.

This chapter adopts a functional linguistic analytic method. This method provides a linguistic account that characterises an inciter's encoded attitude and endorsed moral reasonings. It can give us "a perspective of meaning-making that is grounded in social practice and in the many varied and complex contexts in which we find ourselves", such as the terrorism contexts (May et al., 2021, p. 1). The discourse semantics-based investigation in this chapter is also informed by recent linguistic literature on the moral foundations of evaluation and acts of impoliteness (e.g. Spencer-Oatey & Kádár, 2016; Kádár, 2017; Kádár et al., 2019), specifically in terrorism context (e.g. Etaywe & Zappavigna, 2021, 2023; Etaywe, 2022a, 2022b, 2023a, 2023b).

Methodology

Data

Nine written incitement texts of terrorist public statements produced by OBL, al-Baghdadi, and Tarrant were analysed in this study, giving a representation of cyber incitement texts by members of the two most lethal transnational terrorist ideologies, the jihadist and the

Table 23.1 Overview of the dataset

Author (group)	Text code	Title/topic
Osama bin Laden (al-Qaeda)	OBL 1	A message to Iraqis in particular, and Muslims in General
	OBL 2	A message to the Muslim Ummah
	OBL 3	A message to the People of Iraq in Particular, and Muslims in General
	OBL 4	A statement on Prince Abdullah bin Abdulaziz's Initiative for Peace with Israel
	OBL 5	A message to the Pakistani people
	OBL 6	A message to the Afghan people
Abubakeral-Baghdadi (ISIS)	al-Baghdadi 1	This is what Allah and His messenger promised us
	al-Baghdadi 2	Give glad tidings to the patient
Brenton Tarrant (Far Right)	Tarrant	The Great Replacement - namely the following sections: Addresses to various groups; Introduction; General Thoughts and Potential Strategies; In Conclusion

far-rightist (Global Terrorism Index, 2020). Table 23.1 shows an overview of the texts made available online—thus not privately owned data—to address a range of audiences in a range of a variety of geographical, sociocultural, political, and ideological contexts.

For example, OBL, former al-Qaeda leader, dedicated himself to a global struggle against the USA and their allies worldwide and mainly in the Middle East. The OBL texts were communicated over 2001–2006, that is, in the period following the 9/11 attacks, and addressed Muslim communities in, for example, Iraq, Saudi Arabia, Afghanistan, Bangladesh and Palestine (see e.g. FBIS Report, 2006, for official translations of OBL's texts). The al-Baghdadi texts were produced during 2016–2018 and made available in English by ISIS's al-Hayat Media Centre and in ISIS English-language magazine *Rumiya*. The manifesto of far-right white supremacist Brenton Tarrant, 'The Great Replacement', is used in this chapter (Tarrant, 2019). The manifesto was published before Tarrant's attack on two mosques in Christchurch, New Zealand, in 2019. The manifesto communicates messages, including incitement of Christians and European men and women against groups of people such as immigrants and democrats.

The discourse semantic approach and procedures of analysis

The discourse semantic approach (see e.g. van Dijk, 1995) to online terrorist inciting texts used in this study is informed by SFL, a linguistic model that views language as a reflection of the society within which it occurs (Halliday, 1973, 1978) and that "consider[s] the social structure [which is of moral essence] as one aspect of the social system" (Halliday & Hasan, 1985, p. 4). This social semiotic perspective allows for capturing the semantic syntagmatic structures of discourse (e.g. lexical structures that signal the themes of morality) and the paradigmatic structures of discourse (e.g. pattern of attitudinal meaning). The chapter argues that these structures are underpinned by the ideologies of text authors which inform: firstly, "the attitudes and other social representations shared by members of groups [and secondly,] the interpretation basis and contextual embeddedness of discourse and its structures" (van Dijk, 1995, p. 243).

The adopted approach allows us to focus on the functions of language which provide the motivations for language form and structure (Halliday, 1978). Within SFL, meaning is construed as a function of human experience and is encoded in language around three types of functions or meanings, termed (meta)functions: ideational meaning, interpersonal meaning and textual meaning. Of relevance to this study are (Martin, 2010, p. 12):

- Interpersonal meaning: which is for enacting social relations and expressing attitudes and building "tenor", that is, it relates to social positioning, and interpersonal relations, affinity, power and solidarity; and
- Ideational meaning: which is for construing our experience and knowledge of the world and building "field", i.e. it focuses on the social process, activity and our participation in life and social processes.

Since the interpersonal meaning cannot be divorced from the ideational meaning (e.g. in the act of evaluation, we always evaluate something or someone) (Halliday & Matthiessen, 2014), we can account for this association by the term coupling, specifically 'evaluative coupling' (Knight, 2010b). This functional approach to text, where language is "doing some job in some context" (Halliday & Hasan, 1985, p. 10), enables working out what a text is doing in terms of moralisation and legitimation of violence, encoding interpersonal meanings and enacting interpersonal relations (e.g. exclusion). This approach to text as a "process" also enables seeing the "continuous process of [particular] semantic choice[s]" (Halliday & Hasan, 1985, p. 10), in incitement texts, as empirical evidence of: (i) how morality and social structure function as a regulator of language behaviour; and (ii) how patterns of linguistic structures reflect morality as not only "an intrapsychic matter [but also] deeply embedded in human relationships, with rights, obligations, emotional involvements, and societal networks of normative codes" (Bandura, 2016, p. 26).

The texts were examined to provide evidence of the extremists' "appraisal signature" (Martin & White, 2005, p. 203)—i.e. the extremists' evaluative style that is realised in the evaluative-coupling disposition (Etaywe & Zappavigna, 2021). The focus of the analysis is on the themes of morality that regulate or underpin disaffiliation, as well as on the act of disaffiliation – that is, how language is used to forge value disalignments and to influence networks of interpersonal relationships, provoke hostility, and encourage violence towards outgroups or their members. Therefore, the inciting texts were first annotated for their evaluative couplings (ideation + evaluative meaning) that realise the patterns of enacted (alternatively, tabled) bonds, and then, the moral foundations of these couplings were described, as explained next. This analysis focus satisfies two conditions set by Spencer-Oatey and Kádár (2016) for an exploration of morality and evaluations in discourse; that is, considering, firstly, which group norms are being activated or drawn on, and secondly, which foundations are used for judgements and moral evaluations.

Disaffiliation analysis: evaluative couplings realising key bonds in discourse

The approach adopted in this analysis builds on the concept of 'affiliation' as grounded in SFL (see e.g. Knight, 2010b), as a social semiotic process of negotiating communal identity and a theorisation of how language users mobilise and couple attitudinal and ideational resources to form social bonds with others. However, unlike affiliation where the focus is on creating bonds and forging alignment with, for example, a group of friends, the concept of disaffiliation here focuses on de-bonding and disalignment with the outgroup—yet based on the ingroup moral system. Similar to the affiliation analysis, the disaffiliation analysis is grounded in the Appraisal framework for analysing linguistic evaluation and ideological positioning of audiences (Martin & White, 2005). The Appraisal framework, specifically the ATTITUDE system, was used to analyse and systematically account for evaluative meanings. The ATTITUDE system encompasses three simultaneously operating sub-systems (see e.g. Etaywe & Zappavigna, 2021):

- Attitude types, which include:
  - AFFECT: resources and features for expressing emotional reactions and states (e.g. hate)
  - JUDGEMENT: resources and features for construing assessments of behaviour with respect to values of social esteem (e.g. one's incapacity) and social sanction (e.g. one's veracity and propriety of their acts) in terms of social rules and regulations
  - APPRECIATION: resources for assessing the value of things, entities, events, processes and products in terms of aesthetic dimensions
- Explicitness (inscribed or invoked); and
- Polarity (positive attitude or negative attitude).

For the purpose of this study, attitude types and polarity are analysed. The main analytical unit used in the disaffiliation analysis to investigate how values are negotiated in texts are couplings of ideational and attitudinal meaning, through which audiences discursively co-identify and exclude victims. An example of an attitude-ideation coupling in the dataset is a negative attitude (shown underlined) targeted at Prince Abdullah of Saudi Arabia (the incited against, shown in bold) for collaboration with the USA on invading Iraq and using the Saudi lands for the invasion, in the following excerpt taken from OBL 2:

Before that, **he** [Prince Abdullah of Saudi Arabia] <u>betrayed</u> the two holy mosques when **he** <u>allowed the Americans to enter the country of the two holy mosques</u> under the false allegations of the need for their assistance [he/—JUDGEMENT].

This ideation-attitude coupling can be said to table (i.e. make available) a bond which we might gloss as 'Prince Abdullah is bad: traitor'. This bond serves as a moral basis for inciting the civil disobedience and the killing of Prince Abdullah, then King Abdullah of Saudi Arabia.

The dataset was annotated for ideation-attitude couplings as follows: AFFECT is dotted-underlined, JUDGEMENT underlined, APPRECIATION double-underlined, and polarity is coded as '+' for positive polarity and '−' for negative polarity. Couplings were annotated following Martin, Zappavigna et al. (2013) square brackets notation style: [ideation: <<>>/ attitude: <<>>] as shown in the prior excerpt. This notation style allows for in-text annotation and suggests that ideational target and attitude are fused together to construe the values that are made available in discourse as: (i) bases for perceptions, legitimisation of violence and exploring "what is at stake when one stance is chosen over another" (Martin & White,

2005, p. 92); and as (ii) an entry point to and linguistic evidence of the social values negotiated, the social action of disaffiliation, and the positioning of outgroups as a threat. This chapter argues that, through these couplings, an inciter attempts to not only align with the incitees but also *to disalign* the ingroup's members with outgroups.

The account of collocative values in each terrorist's texts are grouped into patterns of collocating general 'our' versus 'their' ideational targets (e.g. Christianity, immigrants) with a general positive or negative value. The patterns of collocates assist in realising the overall prosodic structure resulting from this unfolding of collocative values, and providing insights into the unfolding categories of 'our' versus 'their' ideational targets and related attitudes in discourse; thus the field of a text, what or whom a text is taking a stance about, and who is, on one hand, good, victim and incited for violence, and who is, on the other hand, bad, victimiser and incited-against. In Zappavigna et al.'s (2008, p. 171) terms, focus on the characteristic use of couplings in a terrorist context allows for identifying and describing patterns of the collocative values in the paradigmatic options across metafunctions, since patterns of the same type of coupling "are likely to reoccur across a text or a set of texts under analysis", and the syntagmatic options, "since items that are coupled are likely to occur very near each other logogenetically [i.e. as unfolding in a text]".

Moral foundations analysis

The moral grounds that each terrorist tends to endorse are explored to better understand the alleged moral justifications for hostility and incited violence. The moral meta-values underpinning the couplings help us to understand how an activation of a moral foundation can invite an activation of a set of social roles or obligations and a reasoning for violence. Six moral meta-values were considered in order to sensitise us as to the moral assumptions and considerations underpinning evaluative couplings and to the relationship between morality and the disaffiliative function of incitement texts. Each meta-value was taken as a moral basis (i.e. framework) that an inciter tends to construct in their texts. The meta-values are (Haidt & Kesebir, 2010; Ståhl et al., 2016):

1. ingroup/loyalty;
2. authority/respect;
3. purity/degradation;
4. harm/care;
5. fairness/reciprocity;
6. liberty/oppression.

For example, to illustrate how values associated with ingroup/(dis)loyalty may influence the creation of evaluative couplings, consider the excerpt from OBL 2. In this excerpt, OBL negatively evaluates Prince Abdullah for an act of betrayal and loyalty to the Americans at the expense of Muslims and their (Iraqi) lands. The JUDGEMENT-based couplings realise the 'bad/treacherous Prince Abdullah' bond, and they are deployed—in Ståhl et al.'s (2016) terms—in response to signs of disloyalty and to serve the purpose of preserving a strong coalition against outgroups. Put differently, in Haugh's (2015) terms, the ingroup/loyalty meta-value underpins the interpretive and evaluative process and has a bearing on how the inciter expects the ingroup members and rulers to act.

Results and discussion

The analysis revealed the values negotiated in the act of disaffiliation and in the service of incitement, in terms of positive ATTITUDE-based couplings—as linguistic resources—used for aligning with positively charged ingroup ideational targets versus negative ATTITUDE-based couplings used for disaligning with negatively charged outgroup ideational targets. This section first reports on these findings and the key bonds realised in each terrorist's texts, beginning with an overview of key ideational targets and bonds, and then explores the moral meta-values activated in these texts.

Patterns of collocative values and key bonds

OBL, al-Baghdadi and Tarrant tend to set up an 'us versus them' dichotomy, underpinned by repeated couplings associating the outgroup's ideational targets with negative ATTITUDE while the ingroup's ideational targets are coupled with positive ATTITUDE (see Table 23.2 for a detailed account of the linguistic resources used for (dis)alignment; those used for disalignment with outgroups are in bold). For example, in OBL's texts, positive linguistic values are used in the ingroup-centred cluster to align with collocated Muslims, their Tawhid (i.e. monotheist) creed and jihad. In the outgroup-centred cluster, negative values are used to disalign with collocated America, pro-US regimes, non-Muslims and alternative approaches to jihad (e.g. democracy). In al-Baghdadi's texts positive values collocate the Sunnis Muslims, Islam, ISIS, jihad, mujahidin and martyrhood to align with them, as a cluster activated in opposition to the outgroup-centered cluster where negative values collocate with 'outsiders' with whom to disalign. These outsiders include, inter alia, Muslim Shiite and Sunni Muslims non-adherent to ISIS ideology, and America. In Tarrant's manifesto, positive values collocate, for example, with being White, hierarchy and violence with which to align. Negative values, in contrast, collocate with the following to disalign with: immigrants; state, leftists, NGOs and economic elites facilitating immigration; and anti-White terms and ideas such as multiculturalism and democracy.

Focusing on the key bonds activated in discourse, the three terrorists tend to table throughout their texts a set of key bonds at stake, meaning that their beliefs, worldviews and collocative values were relatively stable in their texts. To elaborate, OBL's tabling of the *tawhid* bonds has activated the first bond cluster: the 'good Muslims/monotheists' bond cluster in all his texts (e.g. '*to the best **Ummah** ever raised to humanity . . . to our Muslim Ummah*'). This activation serves to enact solidarity and inclusiveness via forging Islam as a shared identity with the incitees. OBL also tends to construct Muslims as being victimised and humiliated innocents, thus positively constructed unlike their victimisers. This construction has given rise to the second primary bond cluster, the 'victimised Muslims' bond cluster (Example 1). The 'good Muslims' and 'victimised Muslims' bond clusters are activated in opposition to the 'non-believer victimiser' bond cluster which serves in all OBL's texts to disaffiliate with the incited-against threat and the religiously different outgroups, such as the USA and their allies in the war against Iraq, as in Example 2. This bond-based 'we/they' opposition builds a text structure that is—in Maton's (2014, p. 20) terms—"condensed with axiological meanings and charged positively and negatively". OBL's texts enact *jihad* bonds whereby the 'good jihad' cluster is activated as a fourth primary cluster in all OBL's texts. This cluster legitimises and beautifies the invitation of the incitees to pursue jihad as the right path to follow, a duty, an act of heroism and the means to triumph over the non-believer victimisers (Example 3).

Table 23.2 A summary of the linguistic resources used for (dis)alignment

Extremist	Linguistic Resources	Function/Act	Ideations
OBL	Positive ATTITUDE-based couplings	Aligning with (positively charged)	Muslims Tawhid Jihad
	Negative ATTITUDE-based couplings	Disaligning with (negatively charged)	America and pro-US regimes (e.g. Israel, Saudi regime) non-Muslims alternative approaches to jihad (e.g. democracy, parliamentary elections)
Al-Baghdadi	Positive ATTITUDE-based couplings	Aligning with (positively charged)	Ahl as-Sunnah (i.e. the Sunni Muslims); Islam ISIS Jihad; mujahidin; martyrhood
	Negative ATTITUDE-based couplings	Disaligning with (negatively charged)	America; Europe; pro-US regimes and states (e.g. Saudi monarchy, King of Jordan, UAE rulers); Turkey; the Russians non-Muslims; polytheists; apostates; the *Rafida/the Magian* (i.e. Iran and the pro-Iranian militias); the *Nusayri* (i.e. al-Asad regime of Syria and his supporting factions)
Tarrant	Positive ATTITUDE-based couplings	Aligning with (positively charged)	Whiteness; Europeanness Fertility; (better) birthrate; popularism; violence and radicalized solutions
	Negative ATTITUDE-based couplings	Disaligning with (negatively charged)	Immigrants; Marxist; communists; Muslims; state; corporates; leftists; NGOs; economic elites Immigration; replacement; multiculturalism; democracy; Europeanization; capitalist markets; globalist culture; urbanization; industrialization; drug dealing; nihilism; consumerism; individualism

(1) *Since about 80 years ago . . . **our sons** are being killed* [our sons/+ JUDGEMENT], ***its** [our ummah's] **blood** is being shed* [ummah/+ JUDGEMENT], ***its** sanctities are being attacked . . .* [ummah's sanctities/+ JUDGEMENT].

(2) ***They** [Bush and his supporters] came out to fight Islam under the falsifying name of 'fighting terrorism'* [They/—JUDGEMENT].

(3) ***Jihad** is a needed duty . . .* [jihad/+ JUDGEMENT].

Al-Baghdadi's texts, like OBL's, also tend to activate the 'good Muslims/Islam' bond cluster via forging the Sunni identity and Islam as the 'glory-bringer' bond (Example 4). The 'victimised Sunnis' bond cluster is also activated, as in Example 5 where al-Baghdadi constructs the Sunnis in Iraq as undergoing humiliation and disgrace brought about by *the Rafida* (i.e. the rejectionist), the Shiite and pro-Iran militias. While these two key bond clusters enable al-Baghdadi to enact solidarity and inclusiveness, tabling these bonds establishes a basis for activating the 'non-believer victimiser/expansionist' cluster associated with the threatening outgroups. This cluster serves to justify why to reject and exclude outgroups: they victimise the Sunnis and expand at the expense of their regions in Syria, Iraq and elsewhere (Example 5). Like OBL, the construction of 'Us' versus 'Them' within the framework of victimisation is exploited by al-Baghdadi to mobilise the victims and adherents to ISIS ideology into jihad—the fourth bond cluster. Enacting jihad bonds serves to promote jihad as being the vengeful act and the pathway to victory and defending honour and religion (Example 6).

(4) *It was only* **through Islam** *. . . that Allah gave glory to you* [Islam/invoked + APPRECIATION].

(5) **They** *[the Rafida] raid your lands under the pretext of waging war against the Islamic State* [they/-JUDGEMENT], *then they do not depart until they have either killed your men* [they/-JUDGEMENT] *and taken your women and children prisoner* [they/-JUDGEMENT] *or until they have driven them out* [they/-JUDGEMENT].

(6) *O people of Ninawa . . .* Beware *of* **becoming weak in waging jihad** *against your enemy and* **repelling** *them [the Rafidi]* [(being weak to wage jihad)/—AFFECT invoking—JUDGEMENT], *for indeed,* **this** will undo the bonds of Islam and extinguish the light of truth [this (not waging jihad)/—JUDGEMENT].

Tarrant's messages also activate a set of bond clusters, which all imply opposing clusters. These bonds include the 'White West is best yet threatened' by replacement; and the 'good hierarchy and inequality' bond cluster. Enacting these bonds, Tarrant enacts solidarity and inclusiveness and constructs who 'We' are via forging Whiteness and Europeanness as shared master identity. The 'West is best' bonds establish a basis for the 'West' and 'the Rest' as a binary opposition in terms of power relations and civilization via alluding to the historical discourse about the West and Rest (see e.g. Turner & Kühn, 2019; van der Dussen, 2016)—see Example 7. Enacting the 'good hierarchy and inequality' bonds, Tarrant maintains his argument against values and ideas (e.g. diversity, democracy, egalitarianism) as disadvantageous ideas and concepts of White superiority as wrong (Example 8). Like OBL and al-Baghdadi's framing of violent acts, Tarrant's enacting of the 'radicalization/fight is right' bonds (Example 9) serves to propose and negotiate radical actions against those involved in the alleged 'conspiracy' of immigrants' influx targeting Whites. In an act of extreme social cohesion (namely an act of 'identity fusion') (Buhrmester et al., 2018), Tarrant urges violent actions to allegedly defend the White, win the cultural competition against the constructed threats and create a new, stronger society. Tarrant tables the 'fight is right' bonds to promote violence, civil war, killing those facilitating the mass immigration and risk-taking as a must, whereas he considers inaction, gradual change or non-revolutionary change as a defeat. These actions are prescribed so that Whites avoid becoming a minority and thus losing power; which gives rise to two key bond clusters: 'becoming minority is bad'; and 'immigrants, state and corporate entities are anti-White', where immigrants are constructed as *'unarmed invaders'* [(immigrants)/—JUDGEMENT] and the state, leftists and democrat politicians are involved in the act of *'racial replacement'*.

(7) *Unity, purpose, trust, traditions, nationalism and racial nationalism is what provides strength* [unity, purpose, trust . . ./+ JUDGEMENT invoking + APPRECIATION]. *Everything else is just a catchphrase* [Everything else (e.g. diversity, equality)/—APPRECIATION].

(8) **Diversity** *by its very definition belies equality* [diversity/—APPRECIATION].

(9) *Therefore, we must* **destabilize and discomfort** *society wherever possible* [to stabilize . . ./+ JUDGEMENT].

This subsection has offered insights into the key social bonds made present for negotiation in the dataset. The 'We'-oriented versus 'They'-oriented evaluative couplings tend to serve to construct an inter-group conflict as being an axiological and valuation issue, and activate clusters of key bonds. That is, these key bonds serve to function to construct social groups in discourse as oppositional, with the ingroup positioned as (culturally, racially or religiously) superior yet threatened or victimised, the outgroups (and their ideas and abstractions) positioned as a threat or victimiser, and violence and hostile acts as warranted and serving collective values and goals. Put differently, the inter-group relationships are framed in terms of who is responsible for the goings-on, and the incited actions are framed as suggested solutions—as in Tarrant's inciting killing Erdogan, in any visit to Europe, to get rid of a leader of the biggest 'enemy' ethnic and religious group: *'kill Erdogan'*. In addition, ingroup members' failure to act is thus constructed to serve to stimulate fear of the consequences of inaction and laying the "socio-psychological premise" for fear and consequently for hatred and violence (Cap, 2017, p. 1), as in Tarrant's inciting European men's violence and to accept the consequences of carrying out radical actions: *'Accept death: as it is as certain as the setting of the sun at evenfall. Only when you embrace death and the only thing you will have left to fear is inaction'*.

In order to better understand the foundations of enacted bonds, the next subsection reports and discusses the pattern of moral foundations of enacted bonds as endorsed by the three extremists in the dataset. The section also argues for the role of these foundations in justifying and morally coercing the incitees into violence; creating relational and action affiliations; and activating ingroup obligations within a common enterprise that cancels and morally disengages from the incited-against outgroups.

Moral foundations of bonding and debonding

The analysis has provided an account of six meta-values that are repeatedly endorsed by the three terrorists. These meta-values, summarised and explained in Table 23.3, belong to two main taxonomies (for a similar pragmatic categorisation of meta-values, see e.g. Etaywe, 2022a):

- 'Relational links' meta-values: which include ingroup/(dis)loyalty, authority/(dis)respect, and purity/degradation.
- Intergroup or 'interpersonal treatment' meta-values: which include liberty/oppression, harm/care, and fairness/cheating.

Table 23.3 Summary of the meta-values in the dataset

Taxonomies	Themes of moral meta values underpinning evaluation and (de)bonding	Explanation
Relational links taxonomy	Ingroup/(dis)loyalty	This meta-value underpins evaluations and bonds related to obligations of group membership, virtues and practices of self-sacrifice, loyalty, and vigilance against betrayal and shifting coalitions. Evaluation here attests to the presence of expectations about the need to maintain a strong coalition against outgroups.
	Authority/(dis)respect	This meta-value underpins bonds related to social order and obligations of hierarchical social relationships and interactions. Evaluation here attests to the presence of expectations about virtues such as obedience, leadership, followership, respect for traditions, respect of legitimate authority and subversion against an authority considered illegitimate.
	Purity/degradation	This meta-value underpins bonds related to concerns about striving to live in sanctity and distant from physical and spiritual contagion. Evaluation here attests to the presence of expectations about virtues of chastity, control of desires and avoidance of the degradation of entities.
Interpersonal treatment taxonomy	Harm/care	This meta-value underpins bonds about the vulnerability of the ingroup members and the feeling of disliking their pain. Evaluation here is triggered by experiencing signs of suffering and attests to the presence of expectations about the need to care for and defend the ingroup.
	Liberty/oppression	This meta-value underpins bonds concerned with reactions and resentment felt towards those dominating 'Us' or restricting 'Our' right to freedom. Evaluation is deployed in response to hatred and actions of dominators or to signs of restricting 'Our' freedom.
	Fairness/cheating	This meta-value underpins bonds concerned with equality, and with in-kind reciprocal treatment including virtues of altruism, compassion and being considerate of the ill-treatment directed at members of the ingroup. Evaluation here attests to the presence of expectations about the need to maintain fair treatment and prevent exploitation.

Table 23.4 Summary of the frequency of use of meta-values in the dataset

Taxonomy	Moral foundations/ meta-values	Frequency			Total
		OBL	Al-Baghdadi	Tarrant	
Relational links	ingroup/(dis)loyalty	**55**	**55**	**67**	**177**
	authority/(dis)respect	23	20	14	57
	purity/degradation	1	6	15	22
Interpersonal	harm/care	8	34	40	82
treatment	liberty/oppression	25	32	2	59
	fairness/cheating	3	1	14	18

These six meta-values offer insights into how the activation of particular moral foundations draws on the ingroup members' assumptions and predispositions—or alternatively their basic moral perspective (Parvaresh, 2019)—which in turn provide semiotic clues to how certain experiences are responded to and how social roles, expectations, rights and duties are activated. These meta-values reveal that the evaluative couplings in the dataset are not "unregulated outburst[s] of aggression" (Kádár, 2017, p. 31). Instead, they follow an identifiable pattern that function to present each inciter and their incitees as deontic participants motivated by and operating within certain moral frameworks.

Despite similarity in the moral foundations activated in the incitement texts, the frequency of use of each meta-value varies (see Table 23.4). The increased frequency of use of the ingroup/(dis)loyalty meta-value (as emphasised in bold) presents this meta-value as the dominant foundation across the three terrorists' texts and as the key pedestal for polarisation and incitement to violence, as an act of respect for traditions and an act of care and vigilance against outgroup coalitions. The loyalty to ingroup meta-value is thus found to be a locus for the remaining foundations that are contingent on defining who 'We' are (not). In the following, each meta-value is exemplified at a time. Attention in the subsequent subsections is drawn to the evaluative couplings underpinned by each meta-value at a time.

Ingroup/(dis)loyalty

Ingroup/(dis)loyalty underpins bonds related to obligations of group membership, including virtues of self-sacrifice and vigilance against betrayal and shifting coalitions. The evaluative couplings here attest to the presence of expectations about the need to maintain a strong coalition against outgroups. To clarify how values associated with (dis)loyalty may influence the creation of evaluative couplings, consider Examples 10–12 and the JUDGEMENT-based couplings there, with a focus on structure in bold (the JUDGEMENT lexis or expressions are underlined). In Example 10, taken from OBL 2 inciting violence against regimes in Muslim majority countries, OBL negatively evaluates the governments of these countries as being *traitor, collaborator* and thus part of the US coalition that targets Muslims. In Example 11, taken from al-Baghdadi 1 inciting the Sunnis against their rulers, al-Baghdadi describes the rulers as practicing the lowest *forms of treachery*. In Example 12—where Tarrant incites European men and women not to pay taxes to the state that gives the Whites' money to people who *despise* Whites—Tarrant describes the act of non-payment as *a sign of racial loyalty* while taxation is evaluated as a *theft* and the European nations are thus being ruled by non-loyal men and women.

(10) *It is no secret that any government formed by the United States is a **traitor and col-laborator government** like all governments in the region.*

(11) *O Ahl as-Sunna, your **rulers** in the region have practiced the lowest and most despic-able form of **treachery** history has known, for **they sold** your issue and surrendered your affair and your land to your enemy.*

(12) ***Until** our nations are run by **men and women loyal** to our cause[,] taxation should be considered theft, and **refusal to pay taxes a sign of racial loyalty**.*

As such, evaluative couplings seem to be deployed in response to signs of disloyalty and to serve the purpose of preserving a strong union. In other words, what appears to have triggered the considerations of morality in these situations is each terrorist's expectation that people of the ingroup should be vigilant of and move against disloyalty. The negative evaluative couplings concerning outgroups can best be described as *"reactions* to an allegedly immoral/inappropriate action" (Kádár, 2017, p. 33), the realisation of which is grounded in the inciters' and incitees' basic moral perspective. Dis/loyalty can thus under-pin the interpretive and evaluative process (Haugh, 2015), and it has a bearing on how each terrorist reacts and expects the ingroup members to react to social actions. In addition, the activation of the (dis)loyalty foundation invites activation of a set of expectations such as devotion to the cause of the ingroup. However, accusing Others of the unfulfilment of these expectations leads to aggressive, negative evaluation. Drawing on this moral foundation serves to brand OBL and al-Baghdadi as loyal warriors dedicated to Muslims' coalition against Others; and so is Tarrant to his Christian and racial group.

Authority/(dis)respect

Authority/(dis)respect underlies bonds related to social order and obligations of hierarchical social relationships and interactions (see also Haidt, 2012). Evaluative couplings here attest to the presence of expectations about virtues related to leadership and followership, such as respect for traditions and legitimate authority and subversion against illegitimate leadership or authority. Put differently, social values associated with authority/(dis)respect influence how evaluative couplings are formed. Consider Examples 13–16 and the JUDGEMENT-based couplings there. In Example 13, taken from OBL 5 inciting the Pakistani people to support the Afghanis in their jihad against the Americans, OBL perceives *Mullah Mohammad Omar* positively as a leader aligned with Allah's voice, while OBL and the mujahidin are seen as respectful subordinates and followers of that leader. In Example 14, taken from OBL 4 inciting disobeying and toppling Muslim countries' rulers and rejecting Prince Abdullah bin Abdulaziz's initiative for peace with Israel, Prince Abdullah is viewed negatively as someone who disrespects traditions by supporting non-Muslims against the Palestinians through *tricking* and *'false promising'* the Palestinians and *'aborting'* their uprising/jihad. In Exam-ple 15, taken from al-Baghdadi 2 inciting the Sunnis in Syria against the commanders of *Sahwa* (awakening) factions, al-Baghdadi negatively views those commanders and officers as being dishonest, deceivers of their followers, supporting *the Nusayri taghut* (i.e. the Syr-ian regime) and fighting with him against ISIS and the Sunnis. In Example 16, in inciting a swift takeover of European cities and decision-making institutions by pro-popularism and white supremacy, Tarrant negatively views the politicians controlling these cities as being anti-White and thus feels they ought to be changed.

(13) *I convey glad tidings to you brothers, announcing that **we are steadfast** in the path of jihad . . . **under the leadership of our Mujahid emir** [i.e. leader], who **is proud of his religion**, the Commander of the faithful, Mullah Mohammad Omar.*

(14) *By announcing the initiative, **he** [Prince Abdullah of Saudi Arabia] is **following the footsteps of his father** who **aborted** 1936 CE/1354 H Intifada with a **false promise** to the Palestinians from him and the English government, thus **tricking** the Palestinians, **stopping their Intifada**, and **continuing the occupation** until . . . Palestine was handed over to the Jews.*

(15) *Therefore, O soldiers of the Sahwa factions in Syria, is it not time for you to realise what is taking place around you, and what situation **your commanders and the officers of your faction** are leading you to? **They deceived** you and **seduced** you with supporting ahl al-Sunna in Syria after **claiming** to have split away from and opposed the Nusayri taghut. But today, **they** reconcile with him and stand with him side by side in fighting the Khilafa State . . .*

(16) *[I]t's the cities where the **anti-white politicians** and the NGOs make their homes.*

As such, evaluative couplings are deployed in response to signs of 'illegitimate' leadership and to serve to preserve the integrity of (the 'ought to be') established hierarchies. What appears to have triggered the considerations of morality in these instances is the terrorists' expectation that authorities and leaders should work for their own particular social groups; otherwise, authority subversion should be accepted and expected. These considerations operate—in Haidt's (2012, p. 168) terms—by "look[ing] in two directions—up towards superiors [e.g. Allah, Islamic traditions, pro-White traditions] and down towards subordinates". That is, couplings appear to be in response to the perception of leaders' conduct as being a violation of the ingroup traditions and interests, which occasion the negative evaluations of disaligned leaders and reinforce the call for subordinates to align with the inciters' proposals. The evaluative couplings are thus reactions to allegedly immoral actions, which are contrary to participants' moral perspectives. The underpinning authority/(dis)respect serves to support not only OBL's and al-Baghdadi's discourse as being an echo of the concerns of Muslim countries in relation to subversion against illegitimate rulers (see e.g. Miller, 2015), but also Tarrant's discourse as echoing the White supremacists' concerns.

Purity/degradation

Purity/degradation underlies evaluative couplings related to concerns about striving to live in sanctity and distance from contagion. The evaluative couplings here attest to the presence of expectations about the conceptualisation of self (or an ingroup), body or something as an entity that should attain purity, or as a temple that should not be desecrated (for similar arguments, see e.g. Graham et al., 2011; Lai et al., 2014; Parvaresh, 2019).

Consider the JUDGEMENT-based and APPRECIATION-based couplings in Examples 17–19, where JUDGEMENT-lexis or expressions are underlined and APPRECIATION expressions are double-underlined. In Example 17, taken from OBL 4 inciting against the Saudi regime that permitted the Americans' entrance into the land of the two holy mosques, OBL draws on Muslims' perspective about protecting this land from polytheists' desecration, grounded in his understanding of a Quranic verse—from the *At-Tawbah* (i.e. The Repentance) chapter: "O believers! Indeed, the polytheists are 'spiritually' impure, so they should not approach the Sacred Mosque after this year". The same meaning is drawn on in al-Baghdadi 1, where he deploys his understanding of the prophetic saying: *Remember the final will of your prophet SAW that "there cannot exist two religions in the peninsula of the Arabs".* In addition, al-Baghdadi activates the 'purity' value to incite patience and steadfastness in jihad, through presenting the suffering of some defeats as being *'like a doctor'*, and Godly acts to purify the Muslims' souls from arrogance and transgression, which are negatively appreciated attributes, as in Example 18. Couplings in Example 19 also attest to Tarrant's expectations about the chastity of European women and how *'non-White scum'* (i.e. immigrants) are polluting it. The same moral theme underpins Tarrant's evaluations elsewhere (see Example 20) to encourage the incitees to *'isolate'* and *'radicalize'* against the dominating culture of celebrities, pop icons, politicians and priests known for acts of *suicide* and *drug addiction*, ignorance of environmental health, or for being *pedophiles*. Purity/degradation considerations, as such, serve the alleged right to enjoy and protect sanctities and assign blame to those committing acts of desecration and pollution.

(17) *Before* that, *he [Prince Abdullah of Saudi Arabia] betrayed the two holy mosques when **he allowed the Americans to enter the country of the two holy mosques**.*

(18) *[I]f Allah **were to always give victory** to the believers over their enemies **everywhere and always** grant them consolation and domination over their enemies, **their souls would have transgressed and become arrogant**.*

(19) *But what few know is that Rotherham [a UK town associated with a scandal of organised child sexual abuse by immigrants] is just one of an ongoing trend of **rape** and **molestation** perpetrated by **these non-white scum**.*

(20) ***Suicide*** *rates climbing year by year . . . **Drug use** at all levels of society, in all age groups . . . *Pedophile* **politicians**, *pedophile* **priests** and *pedophile* **pop stars**, demonstrating to all the *true depravity* of our age.*

What seems to have triggered the considerations of morality in these situations is the terrorists' expectation that the ingroup entities must be protected. The negative evaluative couplings thus come in reaction to allegedly immoral actions by social actors disaligned with the ingroup. The findings support previous studies that have found notions of purity linked to Western, rightist societies and to Eastern and Muslim societies and their practices of derogation, stigmatisation and discrimination (e.g. Haidt et al., 2009; Smith et al., 2014; Parvaresh & Tayebi, 2018; Parvaresh, 2019). So far, evaluative couplings have been found to be underpinned by relational moral bases. The remaining meta-values, discussed next, focus on providing, regaining and protecting the ingroup's rights as founded in interpersonal treatment meta-values.

Liberty/oppression

The liberty/oppression meta-value underlies bonds concerned with reactions and resentment that an inciter feels towards those dominating 'Our' group or restricting 'Our' right to *freedom*. Evaluative couplings are thus deployed—in Ståhl et al. (2016) terms—in response to hatred and actions of dominators or to signs of restricting 'Our' freedom, and to serve to encourage actions to preserve freedom and to come together in solidarity to topple or overcome the oppressors. Consider the JUDGEMENT-based couplings in Examples 21–23. In Example 21, OBL deploys negative evaluations to serve to motivate ingroup members to come into solidarity, rise and accept death as a solution to be rid of the *tyranny*, *oppression* and *humiliation*, and regain *dignity* and freedom. Al-Baghdadi in Example 22 creates awareness among his incitees about those plotting and *waging war* against the Sunnis' freedom in inciting 'justified' hostility and aggression. Tarrant in Example 23 also manages awareness about the negative role of immigrants and the Marxists, viewing them as *invaders* from whom European cities should be freed.

(21) *O Ummah, Rise up and stand against . . . **tyranny, oppression, aggression, humiliation and contempt**, for . . . our property is not more valuable than our **dignity**, and death is not more difficult for us than to **live in humiliation and contempt**.*

(22) *[H]ere is **the** disbelieving **world** today having mobilized, called out, formed coalitions and parties, and gathered all its strength, partners, allies, and awliya **to wage war against Islam and its people** and **to plot against the believers and their religion**.*

(23) *It's the cities where the struggle lies, it's the cities where the **invaders** have massed, it's the cities where **the** [M]arxists have poisoned the institutions.*

Evaluative couplings attest to the presence of expectations about the right to enjoy and protect freedom. The realisation of outgroups' actions as being immoral appears to be grounded in the ingroup's moral perspective of the right to protect self from restrictions on 'Our' freedom and 'Our' upper hand. Consideration of the liberty/oppression foundation is thus used to serve to promote violence as rational in reaction to the hatred and negative actions of those accused of domination.

Fairness/cheating

Fairness/cheating underpins bonds concerned with *equality*, and with in-kind reciprocal treatment including virtues of altruism, compassion and being considerate of the ill treatment directed at members of the ingroup. Evaluative couplings here attest that what appears to have triggered the considerations of morality is the presence of expectations about the need to maintain fair treatment and prevent exploitation. By reference to these considerations, a terrorist's evaluations come in response to a situation of alleged immoral actions of cheating in saying and doing and alleged inequality. Consider Examples 24–26. In Example 24, in relation to the US war on Iraq, OBL couples the US soldiers and government with negative JUDGEMENT: acts of lying concerning fighting terrorism. Hence, the evaluative couplings respond to signs of cheating and unfairness. The US soldiers are coupled with the unfair cause of fighting, making gains via illegitimate access (e.g. selling arms) and supporting evil (e.g. '*the criminal gang at the White House*', '*usury takers*', and '*capitalists*') to access 'Our' resources (i.e. stealing 'Our' oil). Considerations of the immorality of these US actions also promote OBL as the adversary of unfair capitalism and illegitimate control over Muslims' resources—a negative view of globalisation driven by greed is also identified in Tarrant's texts to urge preservation of the resources and thrift of the White. In Example 25, al-Baghdadi also promotes ISIS as a Sunni group committed to jihad in rejection of the unfair treatment and injustices against the Sunni people. Unlike OBL and al-Baghdadi who incite violence against inequality and unfairness, Tarrant in Example 26 defends inequality and views fairness in treatment as being inappropriate in a diverse society, laying the groundwork for unfair treatment towards people from different ethnicities and cultures. Tarrant's negative APPRECIATION-based couplings, appear to have been triggered by expectations about diversity as a factor of social dis-cohesion and about the need to maintain the superiority of the White over: '*race*[s] *of low intellect, low agency, muddled, muddied masses*'.

(24) *Those [US] soldiers are completely <u>convinced of the injustice and lying</u> of their government. They also <u>lack a fair cause to defend</u>. They only <u>fight for capitalists, usury takers, and the merchants of arms and oil</u>, including the <u>criminal gang</u> at the White House.*

(25) *The Islamic State is not confined to Hajin [a small city in Syria], for the sons of the Sunnah are warriors who <u>do not sleep in the face of injustice</u>.*

(26) *The more diverse a group becomes, <u>the less equal it becomes</u>. Diversity is <u>anathema</u> to equality.*

The couplings nevertheless serve to demand and promote radical acts (i) against equality and in-kind treatment, as in Tarrant's texts or (ii) against unfairness, as in OBL's call to Muslims to '*work hard against this [US led] unjust campaign*'. For the jihadist terrorists, considerations of fairness/cheating constitute—in Rai and Fiske's (2011, p. 57) terms—a motive and a moral premise for the incitees to act and demand "balanced, in-kind reciprocity, equal treatment, equal say, and equal opportunity".

Harm/care

The harm/care foundation underpins bonds about the pain of the ingroup members and the feeling of disliking that pain, and *vulnerability*. Evaluative couplings tend to be triggered by experiencing signs of suffering, and attest to the presence of expectations about the need to care for and defend the ingroup. To clarify how values associated with harm/care may influence how evaluative couplings are formed, consider the JUDGEMENT-based couplings in Examples 27–29 (focus on structures in bold). In Example 27, in inciting suicide attacks such as those of the 9/11 attack on America and justifying them, OBL frames al-Qaeda acts within the 'care' for '*vulnerable sons, brothers and sisters*' frame and in response to decades of *debasement* exercised by the Americans against Muslim majority countries. Similarly, al-Baghdadi in Example 28 draws on this moral foundation to reflect care for those jihadists in captivity in America and elsewhere. Tarrant's couplings in Example 29 appear to be influenced by his feelings of care for alleged future vulnerability and destruction of White societies caused by immigrants (especially those coming from *China, Turkey* and *India*), if not acting against them now and before their '*reaching their own zeniths of power*'.

(27) *Since about 80 years ago, our Ummah has been tasting this humiliation and debasement . . . Yet, **<u>nobody cares</u>** . . . When **these** [9/11 attackers] **<u>defended</u>** their **vulnerable sons, brothers and sisters** in Palestine and in many Islamic countries, the world at large screamed out.*

(28) *To **our brothers** . . . tested with **captivity**: By Allah . . . **<u>we have not forgotten you nor shall we ever forget you</u>**.*

(29) *Also, relying on this time period [2028–2038, until most of the European boomers begin to pass] for our victory holds a second major <u>disadvantage</u>, that being **vulnerability to foreign invasion**.*

The three terrorists thus tend to endorse the harm/care foundation to present themselves as 'good' action-takers and dislikers of harm targeting the ingroup, portraying themselves as allegedly compassionate violent agents. The evaluative couplings deployed serve to morally justify violence in reaction to alleged vulnerability, and to urge protecting the vulnerable 'We' group. The evaluative couplings can contribute to constructing a positive image of the terrorists, who responds in language to what they view as harmful to the ingroup.

Conclusion and further research

This chapter has contributed to the understanding of how terrorists enact moral disaffiliation as part of the social semiotic practice of incitement to hatred and violence, which is a critical social cybercrime facing the global community. The chapter has emphasised, Canning's (2014, p. 47) argument for, the usefulness of the metafunctional approach to forensic stylistics and providing valuable insights into criminal contexts, the morality of terrorism, and the ethical motives for crimes and online deviance. An extremist's appraisal signature has been found to be revelatory of opposing clusters of key bonds, enacted in discourse as collocative values. The findings reveal: (i) key social bonds at stake, realised in the extremists' appraisal signature as collocating values – i.e. axiological meanings and positively charged 'we' versus negatively charged 'they'; and (ii) inciter-incitee-victims' relationships and interpersonal treatment that are regulated and underpinned by a discursively constructed moral order of six meta-values that the extremists endorse ('ingroup/(dis)loyalty', 'authority/(dis)respect', 'purity/degradation', 'liberty/oppression', 'fairness/cheating', and 'harm/care').

Discourse meaning as constructed in cyber incitement texts has been found useful in embodying not only opinions (van Dijk, 1995) but also on-/off-line communities and their moral system. A terrorist text tends to construct—in White's (1997) terms—a model of social and moral order; that is, a model of what is normal and aberrant, beneficial and harmful, praiseworthy and blameworthy, and thus of what is (dis)approved of social actors in response towards a moral order disruption or a breach of a group's moral order. In addition, in Martin and White's (2005, p. 211) terms, the nuances of discourse semantics have offered insights into the incitement texts as being: axiologically speaking, unfolding rhetorically as an invitation to a social and actional affiliation against disaffiliative Others; and ideologically speaking, tending to unfold as moralised rationality (i.e. in a quest for 'truth') that is subjected to an extremist's "truth criteria" (van Dijk, 1998, p. 30), since they encourage the incitees to favour the ingroup and to delegitimise the outgroups.

The concept of disaffiliation and the coupling approach to disaffiliation have offered a tool whereby we view language in incitement texts as "a network of bonds and obligations" (Firth, 1964, p. 113). Evaluative couplings are found to be regulated reactions to allegedly immoral Others, a regulation that serves to view hostility as being justified and violence as legitimate. In other words, evaluative acts are found to be not only situationally constructed but also morally informed. In addition, the coupling approach has been revelatory of the linguistic resources that extremists use to manage to reverse the disdain a society may feel for a terrorist into a common enterprise against a shared enemy. This kind of cultural appropriation (e.g. van Langenhove, 2017) enables the extremists to turn violence into a communal goal (e.g. seeking justice) via the incitees' involvement in changing the world (e.g. toppling 'bad' rulers). This interpersonal influence accords with Reicher et al.'s (2008) argument that positive representation of the ingroup and negative representation of outgroups serve to make eradicating outgroups justified. In Hodge and Kress's (1988, pp. 3–4) terms,

437

by producing and constructing the complex moral-inciting behaviour, members of a social group can become constrained by means of linguistic structuring of "versions of reality" upon which the incited action is based and the incitees' interpretation for the inciting text relies. The meta-values taxonomy identified can help criminal investigators: (i) to interpret what links social structure to people's action; that is, how structures influence agents and are created through agency (see also van Langenhove, 2017); and (ii) to explore what binds inciters and incitees into certain roles, duties and obligations (see also Graham et al., 2011).

Unlike Smith et al. (2014, p. 1560) who found that binding (i.e. relational) meta-values (e.g. loyalty and respect for authority) do not "necessarily lead to in-group favoritism and outgroup derogation", these moral foundations have been found here doing so. This means that the role of meta-values varies across discourses, contexts and users. Terrorists coming from "individualistic cultures" yet condemning their dominant cultures (e.g. Tarrant), and those coming from "sociocentric cultures" (e.g. OBL and al-Baghdadi) (Haidt, 2012, p. 30) are found using the same meta-values, which ultimately serve to enhance the terrorists' moral regard. The similarities between the terrorists' moral foundations could be ascribed to the similarity in the function of incitement texts and their purposes, as well as to the fact that these foundations are—in Spencer-Oatey and Kádár's (2016) terms—universally applicable yet socio-culturally and contextually sensitive.

Finally, understanding the morality of violence and digital deviance, as well as the inherent moral appeal of extremists to potential followers, is crucial for maintaining global stability. The analytical strategy showcased in this study offers a valuable complementary method to the investigative approaches of law enforcement, intelligence and security organisations. This method can provide investigators with linguistic evidence and insights into the moral motives behind incitement and digital deviance, as well as into the social semiotic processes involved in enacting extreme forms of social (dis)affiliations, including identity fusion, discord, cancelling, and selective moral (dis)engagement.

References

Anderson, B. (2016). *Imagined communities*. Verso.

Atran, S. (2015). Recommendations to the UN Security Council Committee on counter terrorism. *Journal of Political Risk*, 3(12). Retrieved August 21, 2022, from www.jpolrisk.com/response-to-a-request-for-recommendations-to-the-un-security-council-committee-on-counter-terrorism/

Bandura, A. (2016). *Moral disengagement: How people do harm and live with themselves*. Worth Publishers.

Borum, R. (2004). *Psychology of terrorism*. University of South Florida. Retrieved August 21, 2022, from www.ojp.gov/pdffiles1/nij/grants/208552.pdf.

Braddock, K. (2019). Communicatively countering violent extremism online. In *The handbook of communication and security* (pp. 247–261). Routledge.

Buhrmester, M. D., Newson, M., Vázquez, A., Hattori, W. T., & Whitehouse, H. (2018). Winning at any cost: Identity fusion, group essence, and maximizing ingroup advantage. *Self and Identity*, 17(5), 500–516. https://doi.org/10.1080/15298868.2018.1452788

Canning, P. (2014). Functionalist stylistics. In M. Burke (Ed.), *The Routledge handbook of stylistics* (pp. 45–67). Routledge.

Cap, P. (2017). *The language of fear: Communicating fear in public discourse*. Palgrave Macmillan.

Chen, H., Thoms, C., & Fun, T. (2008). Cyber extremism in Web 2.0: An exploratory study of international Jihadist groups. In *2008 IEEE international conference on intelligence and security informatics* (pp. 98–103). Institute of Electrical and Electronics Engineers.

Conway, M. (2012). From al-Zarqawi to al-Awlaki: The emergence and development of an online radical milieu. *CTX: Combating Terrorism Exchange*, 2(4), 12–14. Retrieved August 21, 2022, from https://doras.dcu.ie/17596/2/PUBLISHED_VERSION%20(3).pdf

Dauber, C. E. (2009). *YouTube war: Fighting in a world of cameras in every cell phone and photoshop on every computer*. Strategic Studies Institute.

Du Bois, J. (2007). The stance triangle. In R. Englebretson (Ed.), *Stancetaking in discourse: Subjectivity, evaluation, interaction* (pp. 139–182). John Benjamins.

Elley, B. (2021). "The rebirth of the West begins with you!"—Self-improvement as radicalisation on 4chan. *Humanities and Social Sciences Communications, 8*(1), 1–10

Etaywe, A. (2021). *The role of (de)bonding in the legitimation of violence in extremists' public threatening communication*. [Conference paper]. Systemic Functional Linguistics Interest Groups Conference. Retrieved from https://doi.org/10.21203/rs.3.rs-1662949/v1

Etaywe, A. (2022a). Exploring the grammar of othering and antagonism as enacted in terrorist discourse: Verbal aggression in service of radicalisation. *Humanities and Social Sciences Communications, 9*, 177. https://doi.org/10.1057/s41599-022-01178-5

Etaywe, A. (2022b). Language as evidence: A discourse semantic and corpus linguistic approach to examining written terrorist threatening communication (Doctoral dissertation, UNSW Sydney). https://doi.org/10.26190/unsworks/24434

Etaywe, A., & Zappavigna, M. (2021). Identity, ideology and threatening communication: An investigation of patterns of attitude in terrorist discourse. *Journal of Language Aggression and Conflict, 10*(2), 315–350. https://doi.org/10.1075/jlac.00058.eta

Etaywe, A. (2023a). The role of (de)bonding in the legitimation of violence in extremists' public threatening communication. In To, V., Amundrud, T., & Humphrey, S. (Eds.), *Systemic functional linguistics theory and application in global contexts*, (12–24). University of Tasmania.

Etaywe, A. (2023b). Heteroglossia and identifying victims of violence and its purpose as constructed in terrorist threatening discourse online. *International Journal for the Semiotics of Law, 36*(2):907–937. https://link.springer.com/article/10.1007/s11196-023-09974-1

Etaywe, A. & Zappavigna, M. (2023). The role of social affiliation in incitement: A social semiotic approach to far-right terrorists' incitement to violence. *Language in Society (Cambridge)*, 1–26. https://doi.org/10.1017/S0047404523000404

FBIS Report. (2006). *Compilation of Usama bin Laden statements 1994-January 2004*. Retrieved June 29, 2022 from https://file.wikileaks.org/file/cia-fbis-bin-laden-statments-1994-2004.pdf.

Firth, J. (1964). *The tongues of men, and speech*. Oxford University Press.

Global Terrorism Index. (2020). *Global terrorism index: Measuring the impact of terrorism*. Institute for Economics and Peace. Retrieved August 21, 2022, from https://visionofhumanity.org/wp-content/uploads/2020/11/GTI-2020-web-1.pdf

Graham, J., Nosek, B., Haidt, J., Iyer, R., Koleva, S., & Ditto, P. (2011). Mapping the moral domain. *Journal of Personality and Social Psychology, 101*(2), 366–385. https://doi.org/10.1037/a0021847

Graham, R., & Smith, S. (2020). *Cybercrime and digital deviance*. Routledge.

Haidt, J. (2012). *The righteous mind: Why good people are divided by politics and religion*. Vintage.

Haidt, J., Graham, J., & Joseph, C. (2009). Above and below left—Right: Ideological narratives and moral foundations. *Psychological Inquiry, 20*(2–3), 110–119. https://doi.org/10.1080/10478400903028573.

Haidt, J., & Kesebir, S. (2010). Morality. In S. Fiske, D. Gilbert, & G. Lindzey (Eds.), *Handbook of social psychology* (pp. 797–852). John Wiley.

Halliday, M. A. K. (1973). *Explorations in the functions of language*. Edward Arnold.

Halliday, M. A. K. (1978). *Language as social semiotic: The social interpretation of language and meaning*. Edward Arnold.

Halliday, M. A. K., & Hasan, R. (1985). *Language, context, and text*. Deakin University Press.

Halliday, M. A. K., & Matthiessen, C. (2014). *Halliday's introduction to functional grammar*. Routledge.

Haugh, M. (2015). *Im/politeness implicatures*. Walter de Gruyter.

Hodge, R., & Kress, G. (1988). *Social semiotics*. Cornell University Press.

Jaconelli, J. (2017). Incitement: A study in language crime. *Crime, Law and Philos, 2018*(12), 245–265. https://doi.org/10.1007/s11572-017-9427-8.

Kádár, D. (2017). *Politeness, impoliteness and ritual*. Cambridge University Press.

Kádár, D., Parvaresh, V., & Ning, P. (2019). Morality, moral order, and language conflict and aggression. *Journal of Language Aggression and Conflict*, 7(1), 6–31. https://doi.org/10.1075/jlac.00017.kad.

Knight, N. (2010b). Wrinkling complexity: Concepts of identity and affiliation in humour. In M. Bednarek & J. Martin (Eds.), *New discourse on language: Functional perspectives on multimodality, identity, and affiliation* (pp. 35–58). Continuum.

Lai, C., Haidt, J., & Nosek, B. (2014). Moral elevation reduces prejudice against gay men. *Cognition and Emotion*, 28(5), 781–794.

Malešević, S. (2019). Cultural and anthropological approaches to the study of Terrorism. In E. Chenoweth, R. English, A. Gofas, & S. Kalyvas (Eds.), *The Oxford handbook of terrorism* (pp. 177–193). Oxford University Press.

Mandaville, P. (2007). *Global political islam*. Routledge.

Martin, J. (2010). Semantic variation—Modelling realisation, instantiation and individuation in social semiosis. In M. Bednarek & J. Martin (Eds.), *New discourse on language: Functional perspective on multimodality, identity, and affiliation* (pp. 1–34). Continuum International Publishing Group.

Martin, J., & White, P. (2005). *The language of evaluation: Appraisal in English*. Palgrave Macmillan.

Martin, J., Zappavigna, M., Dwyer, P., & Cléirigh, C. (2013). Users in uses of language: Embodied identity in Youth Justice Conferencing. *Text & Talk*, 33(45), 467–496.

Maton, K. (2014). *Knowledge and knowers: Towards a realist sociology of education*. Routledge.

May, A., Sousa-Silva, R., & Coulthard, M. (2021). Introduction. In M. Coulthard, A. May, & R. Sousa-Silva (Eds.), *The Routledge handbook of forensic linguistics* (pp. 1–8). Wiley Blackwell.

Miller, F. (2015). *The audacious ascetic: What the bin Laden tapes reveal about al-Qa'ida*. Hurst & Company.

Munn, L. (2020). Angry by design: Toxic communication and technical architectures. *Humanities and Social Sciences Communications*, 7(1), 1–11.

Olsson, J. (2021). Forensic discourse analysis: A work in progress. In Hyland, K., Paltridge, B., & Wong, L. (Eds.), *The Bloomsbury handbook of discourse analysis* (pp. 335–346). Bloomsbury Publishing.

Önnerfors, A. (2019). 'The great replacement'—Decoding the Christchurch terrorist manifesto. Centre for Analysis of the Radical Right. Retrieved August 21, 2022, from www.radicalrightanalysis.com/2019/03/18/the-great-replacement-decoding-the-christchurch-terrorist-manifesto/

Parvaresh, V. (2019). Moral impoliteness. *Journal of Language Aggression and Conflict*, 7(1), 79–104.

Parvaresh, V., & Tayebi, T. (2018). Impoliteness, aggression and the moral order. *Journal of Pragmatics*, 132, 91–107.

Rai, T., & Fiske, A. (2011). Moral psychology is relationship regulation: Moral motives for unity, hierarchy, equality, and proportionality. *Psychological Review*, 118(1), 57–75. https://doi.org/10.1037/a0021867

Rediker, E. (2015). The Incitement of Terrorism on the Internet: Legal Standards, Enforcement, and the Role of the European Union, 36 MICH. J. INT'L L. 321. Retrieved August 21, 2022, from https://repository.law.umich.edu/cgi/viewcontent.cgi?article=1077&context=mjil

Reicher, S., Haslam, A., & Rath, R. (2008). Making a virtue of evil: A five-step social identity model of the development of collective hate. *Social and Personality Psychology Compass*, 2/3, 1313–1344. https://doi.org/10.1111/j.1751-9004.2008.00113.x

Reid, E. F., & Chen, H. (2007). Mapping the contemporary terrorism research domain. *International Journal of Human Computer Studies*, 65(1), 42–56. https://doi.org/10.1016/j.ijhcs.2006.08.006

Sacks, H. (1992). *Lectures on conversation*. Blackwell.

Seto, T. (2002). The morality of terrorism. *Loyola of Los Angeles Law Review*, 35, 1272–1264.

Shuy, R. (2021). Terrorism and forensic linguistics: Linguistics in terrorism cases. In M. Coulthard, M. Alison, & R. Sousa-Silva (Eds.), *The Routledge handbook of forensic linguistics* (pp. 445–462). Wiley Blackwell.

Smith, I., Aquino K., Koleva, S., & Graham, J. (2014). The moral ties that bind . . . Even to out-groups: The interactive effect of moral identity and the binding moral foundations. *Psychological Science*, 25(8), 1554–1562. https://doi.org/10.1177/0956797614534450

Smith, S., & Shuy, R. (2002). Forensic psycholinguistics: Using language analysis for identifying and assessing offenders. *FBI Law Enforcement Bulletin*, 16–21.

Spencer-Oatey, H., & Kádár, D. (2016). The bases of (im)politeness evaluations: Culture, the moral order and the East—West debate. *East Asian Pragmatics*, *1*(1), 73–106. https://doi.org/10.1558/eap.v1i1.29084

Ståhl, T., Zaal, M., & Skitka, L. (2016). Moralized rationality: Relying on logic and evidence in the formation and evaluation of belief can be seen as a moral Issue. *Plos One*, *11*(11), e0166332. https://doi.org/10.1371/journal.pone.0166332.

Tarrant, B. (2019). *The great replacement manifesto*. Retrieved August 21, 2022, from https://web.archive.org/web/20190315144811/; https://observer.news/featured/the-manifesto-of-brenton-tarrant-a-right-wing-terrorist-on-a-crusade

Taylor, B. C., & Bean, H. (Eds.). (2019). *The handbook of communication and security*. Routledge.

Thompson, G., & Hunston, S. (2000). Evaluation: An introduction. In S. Hunston & G. Thompson (Eds.), *Evaluation in text: Authorial stance and the construction of discourse* (pp. 1–27). Oxford University Press.

Tsesis, A. (2017). Terrorist incitement on the Internet. *Fordham Law Review*, *68*(2), 367–377.

Turner, M., & Kühn, F. (2019). 'The West' and 'the rest' in international interventions: Eurocentrism and the competition for order. *Conflict, Security & Development*, *19*(3), 237–243. https://doi.org/10.1080/14678802.2019.1608014.

van der Dussen, J. (2016). The West and the rest. In J. van der Dussen (Ed.), *Studies on collingwood, history and civilization* (pp. 341–365). Springer. Retrieved from https://doi.org/10.1007/978-3-319-20672-1_15.

Van Dijk, T. (1998). Opinions and ideologies in the press. In P. Garrett & A. Bell (Eds.), *Approaches to media discourse* (pp. 21–63). Blackwell.

Van Dijk, T. A. (1995). Discourse semantics and ideology. *Discourse & Society*, *6*(2), 243–289. Retrieved August 21, 2022, from www.jstor.org/stable/42887977.

Van Langenhove, L. (2017). Varieties of moral orders and the dual structure of society: A perspective from Positioning Theory. *Frontiers in Sociology*, *2*(9). https://doi.org/10.3389/fsoc.2017.00009.

White, P. (1997). Death, disruption and the moral order: The narrative impulse in mass-media hard news reporting. In F. Christie & J. R. Martin (Eds.), *Genres and institutions: Social processes in the workplace and school* (pp. 101–133). Cassell.

Wignell, P., Tan, S., & O'Halloran, K. (2017). Violent extremism and iconisation: Commanding good and forbidding evil? *Critical Discourse Studies*, *14*(1), 1–22. https://doi.org/10.1080/17405904.2016.1250652.

Youngblood, M. (2020). Extremist ideology as a complex contagion: The spread of far-right radicalization in the United States between 2005 and 2017. *Humanities and Social Sciences Communications*, *7*(1), 1–10.

Zappavigna, M., Dwyer, P., & Martin, J. (2008). Syndromes of meaning: Exploring patterned coupling in a NSW Youth Justice Conference. In A. Mahboob & K. Knight (Eds.), *Questioning linguistics* (pp. 103–117). Cambridge Scholars Publishing.

24

FOLLOWER WEAPONIZATION

Reimagining violence in the technological landscape

Alice Fox

Academic discussions on technological weaponization

During the rise and reign of Donald Trump (2015–2020) and the reports generated by the Cambridge Analytica scandal (2018–2019), many scholars across political science, criminal justice, ethics, data science, and social science disciplines turned a much more critical eye to human-technology relationships. As a result, the field of technology-facilitated violence and abuse benefited from the increased curiosity, especially when compounded with the Covid-19 pandemic and wider engagement with social media platforms standing in for in-person socialization. From this point, several important articles, chapters, and books have been developed that call for a new approach to violence and abuse that centers the conversation on the dynamic socio-technical landscape and the way technologies open new and different possibilities for harm than our institutions and infrastructures currently consider.

While *follower weaponization* is the definition I propose and develop within this chapter, the phenomenon makes an appearance—albeit by different names, contexts, and pieces—throughout a variety of academic disciplines and public entities. The primary text leaned on in this chapter will be Sarah Sobieraj's detailed account of targeted harassment against vulnerable community members (particularly women of color) in *Credible Threat* (2020). Sobieraj presents a unique perspective in this emerging field of research as she investigates the uniquely intimate experience of experiencing targeted harassment online from strangers. Further, Sobieraj focuses on the *chilling effect* of targeted harassment on these vulnerable populations, arguing that one of the primary consequences of poor moderation and platform policies is the silencing of voices who are already at the margins. Sobieraj's work reveals a critical new facet of this type of technologically facilitated violence because of its deeply personal nature and focus on the qualitative, narrative accounts from experiencers of targeted harassment.

Along with this perspective, Vinay Prasad and John P. A. Ioannidis (2022) observe a similar pattern impacting researchers across a variety of disciplines, where these scholars are targeted with incessant bad-faith interpretations and negative comments on their

DOI: 10.4324/9781003277675-28

public-facing work on social media, to the point that it damages their reputation and becomes harmful to their work and their safety. In contrast to Sobieraj, these authors take a quantitative approach and call this phenomenon "obsessive criticism" while categorizing it as a type of academic bullying and harassment.

Other related scholarship on this topic focuses on the weaponization of social media *platforms*—as systems or structures—to manipulate socio-political dynamics of the public by political actors or entities or the weaponization of social media marketing and analytics data collected behind the scenes for this same purpose. From this perspective, Yochai Benkler, Robert Farris, and Hal Roberts' *Network Propaganda* (2018) offers a robust discussion grounded in case studies on how various actors and entities can manipulate social media algorithms and analytics for personal gain. Scholarship leaning into this approach often focuses on dis/misinformation and political campaigns and does not often view this phenomenon as one of violence or abuse, but instead a problem situated more within the framework of democracy, justice, fairness, and civic manipulation. As such, these articles are more within the realm of cybersecurity, platform politics/governance, and regulation, rather than identifying the common elements of follower weaponization itself (for examples of such approaches, see Woolley & Howard, 2018; Bay, 2018; Galeano et al., 2020).

More closely related to my approach in this chapter is the study of the *follower* element of these socio-technical problems. One of the most notable outcomes of mass consumption of social media has been the emergence of social media *influencers*. While sometimes these individuals act as an *argumentum ad verecundiam* by gaining fitness models or athletes to sell fitness gear or beauty gurus to collaborate with brands, these actors can also act as *cultural* or *political* influencers—capable of signaling to their followers who or what they should be supporting along with in-group norms and patterns. Andrew Tate, Elon Musk, and Ben Shapiro are all strong examples of cultural and (indirect) political influencers. Karen Savage's book chapter "Randy Rainbow's Musical and Social Media Activism: (Digital) Bodyguards and Politicizing/Weaponizing Audiences" (2021) provides a detailed account of this phenomenon that speaks more closely to the role of influencers and the way their audiences respond to them, while also offering a detailed analysis of Rainbow's *discourse* as a trail of breadcrumbs to understanding the subliminal power influencers have over their audiences.

This chapter embarks upon the project of synthesizing approaches to this specific kind of technologically-facilitated violence and abuse—something that has yet to be endeavored but is much needed to establish a shared understanding of the phenomenon and enhance discussions surrounding it. Thus, a cohesive account that seeks to clarify and define follower weaponization stands to better position scholars working across fields to have a clear schema to begin the important work of developing accounts with more nuance and accuracy to lived experiences. Accordingly, this account should not be seen as all-encompassing or an end to the discussion, but a starting point from which to build and position the variety of accounts currently in circulation.

Public perspectives on targeted harassment/online harassment

In one of the most detailed and recent sources for tracking and understanding abuse and harassment online, PEN America's *Online Harassment Field Manual* (2024) covers a wide variety of tactics utilized by both groups and individuals to abuse people through and with technology. They define 'online harassment' and 'online abuse' within an 'or' statement, indicating that these terms are interchangeable: "PEN America prefers the terms online harassment or online abuse, which we define as the 'pervasive or severe targeting of an individual or group online through harmful behavior.'" These tactics can include phishing, Zoombombing, and nonconsensual sharing of intimate images, but also (as most of this chapter will focus on) doxing, dog whistling, and astroturfing. These actions are presented without distinguishing between abuse and harassment.

Another prominent resource for defining and tracking types of target harassment comes from the Women's Media Center's (WMC) *Online Abuse 101* (n.d.). In this resource, they define targeted harassment as a *type* of online abuse, denoting that:

> Online abuse includes a diversity of tactics and malicious behaviors ranging from sharing embarrassing or cruel content about a person to impersonation, doxing, stalking and electronic surveillance to the nonconsensual use of photography and violent threats . . . The purpose of harassment differs with every incidence, but usually includes wanting to embarrass, humiliate, scare, threaten, silence, extort or, in some instances, encourage mob attacks or malevolent engagements.

The WMC focuses particularly on the gendered aspects of online abuse and targeted harassment, and as such identifies more specific tactics of online abuse such as deadnaming, supporter retaliation, and slut-shaming. Further, the WMC does not denote specific tactics as abusive, but instead maintains that any/all types of harassment can escalate to abuse when considering the context, duration, scope, and victim experience.

The third major resource that attempts to define and measure targeted harassment is the Pew Research Center (Vogels, 2021). In this case, Pew refers to targeted harassment as 'online harassment' and positions it as the primary category, with abusive actions falling under the wider umbrella of online harassment. Pew defines online harassment within the scope of their report as:

> six distinct behaviors: Offensive name-calling; Purposeful embarrassment; Stalking; Physical threats; Harassment over a sustained period of time; Sexual harassment; Respondents who indicate they have personally experienced any of these behaviors online are considered targets of online harassment in this report. Further, this report distinguishes between "more severe" and "less severe" forms of online harassment. Those who have only experienced name-calling or efforts to embarrass them are categorized in the "less severe" group, while those who have experienced any stalking, physical threats, sustained harassment or sexual harassment are categorized in the "more severe" group.

Pew is the only group that t distinguishes between the range of severity of online harassment in their data. However, the list of tactics is presented uniformly, and Pew does not explicitly note when these cases move from mere harassment to abuse. Further, the report uses online harassment and online abuse interchangeably. Lastly, Pew only analyzes the categories traditionally thought of as harassment within legal and social canons without incorporating the new tactics/types of harassment that are *emerging* from technology relations, such as Zoombombing, swatting, or phishing.

Challenges

So, what is targeted harassment, exactly? As the reader might assess from the divergent definitions here, the concept has not yet fully stabilized. Looking at these definitions from a more scientific lens using Thomas Kuhn's *The Structure of Scientific Revolutions* (1962), the study and definitions of targeted harassment/online harassment/digital harassment and online abuse/digital abuse are still in the *pre-paradigm* or *pre-science* phase. More simply put, the scientific, scholarly, and social communities have not yet reached a *consensus* for how to define and model these terms, how to differentiate between them, or how best to study/examine these phenomena. Importantly, that means that any/all contributions dedicated to understanding these phenomena are critical to developing the overall project of 'sorting things out', helping institutions recognize these problems, and providing help to those who are unfortunate enough to become targets of this type of harassment and abuse. Unfortunately, that means that while we are in the midst of the paradigm being established, several problems persist in the absence of firm legal, ethical, or institutional guidance.

Firstly, the blurring of definitions between harassment, abuse, and other asocial behaviors online creates several problems for scholars, policymakers, and targets alike. For one example, it results in actions such as trolling or flaming being seen as equivalent harms to revenge porn, stalking, doxing, hate speech, death threats, or swatting. Even when searching for 'targeted harassment' online, the top entries provided by Google are on cyberbullying—an important phenomenon, to be certain, but these phenomena are not the same. Cyberbullying has conceptually stabilized (Cyberbullying Research Center, n.d.) for at least the last decade as a particular interpersonal phenomenon between youths that oscillates between online and offline interactions. Importantly, bullying is defined as repeated, deliberate, and harmful, and the 'bully' is typically the same individual or group of individuals performing these actions on- and/or offline.

Most instances of cyberbullying, trolling, and flaming are more easily addressed because these actions usually are associated with specific and limited actors; it is much easier to identify an individual or entity as a troll, bully, or flamer. However, when we begin looking at the online harassment and/or abuse strategies that are more commonly associated with state or social entities, by individuals with large groups of followers, or by more technology-proficient individuals capable of harnessing bots, we start to look at a very different series of problems, risks, and potential consequences that begin to emerge that cannot be addressed by merely addressing assailants on an individual level or by instructing targets to avoid virtual spaces or technology use. Secondly, unclear and developing definitions often lead to an egalitarian or 'cover-all' approach to targeted harassment online. In an attempt to ensure that as few known cases/examples of online abuse/harassment are left out as possible, authors end up creating a list that includes multiple different types and kinds of abuse, harassment, and harm, without providing signposts for how one should interpret the list. For example, is online trolling truly as morally problematic as taking unsolicited intimate images of another person? Is flaming someone on their performance in a video game truly as reprehensible as threatening someone with rape or death on social media? Can (or should) instances of bot attacks be addressed under the same policy that focuses on cyberbullying?

As it stands, *all* of these cases are presently considered cases of targeted harassment/online harassment/online abuse, or some combination thereof. The lack of definitional fine-tuning encourages one-size-fits-all approaches to actions that vary widely in terms of severity, scope, scale, and potential for harm.

This results in the obfuscation or erasure of the power dynamics behind targeted harassment and abuse online. For example, cyberbullying is often conceptualized to be between *peers*—antisocial or damaging behaviors, words, or actions online that are harmful to individuals with equivalent levels of power. Even if the action remains the same, if the actor changes to a parent or teacher from another student/youth, the problem, harm, and potential solutions change dynamically alongside it. Public figures, state and social entities, and others with a high amount of social, political, or economic capital have a much larger potential to cause harm than an individual.

Moreover, when these power dynamics are rendered invisible by the presentation of the phenomenon and no consensus is established, it opens further potential for harm. As Sarah Schulman outlines in her book *Conflict is not Abuse* (2016), harm can be overstated in cases of conflict or disagreement (debate, discursive arguments, critiques, criticisms)—especially against state and social entities/groups, public figures, and policies by marginalized individuals or high-risk professions (journalists, human rights defenders)—and instances of abuse can be minimized, especially when these tables are turned (state and social entities or public figures targeting marginalized/politically vulnerable individuals). The point to be made here is that power dynamics play a key role in determining differences between conflict, harm, and abuse. When we lack definitional clarity and consensus, it becomes possible for groups with more power to control the narrative on what is harmful online and what is free speech.

Follower weaponization defined

Given the challenges of definitional blurring and obfuscation of power, I will provide a specific definition of targeted harassment that captures the specific phenomena of online targeted harassment and abuse that (hopefully) sidesteps the aforementioned concerns and more. The term I would like to propose and further illuminate is *follower weaponization*. In its most simple form, follower weaponization can be defined as the act of rallying one's online followers to silence or erase the lived experiences and perspectives of others through overwhelming amounts of negative engagement.

Negative engagement can cover a variety of creative strategies aimed to harness algorithmic dynamics and platform mechanics to disrupt or deplatform a target. Sometimes, this looks like burying content under a high influx of personal attacks or harmful content. But in other cases, it can work by recontextualizing events or bringing extreme virality to an unsuspecting target: a flood of copyright strikes can bog activists down with legal fees and challenges and prevent virality or continued exposure; a flood of negative reports or reviews can trip auto-mods to do the same or ensure actors no longer participate on a platform. When performed *par excellence*, weaponizers can harness algorithms to ensure that certain posts or people are made highly in/visible while recontextualizing the original content to negatively position the original poster. A strong example of this is Elon Musk banning the account tracking his private jet. After its removal, Elon threatened the owner of the account—a 24-year-old college student—with legal action for 'doxing' him (making sensitive personal information publicly available). Tying into the earlier remarks, Elon was able to use his much larger amount of social currency and financial position not only remove an account he did not like, but to also spin this action as doxing to recontextualize and amplify his support of the ban from followers and wealthy politicians, leading to further bans of similar accounts tracking other celebrities and elite citizens (Gollan, 2022).

I use *weaponization* here specifically to speak more toward the actor's armament of followers through a variety of tactics, rather than the entity's explicit participation, threats, or direct incitement of violence. This is one of the key defining features of this concept, as it makes it nearly impossible, under present legal definitions of harassment, hate speech, abuse, and credible threats, to tie the entity directly to the consequences of follower weaponization, thus, making it incredibly challenging to hold these social weaponizers accountable for the harms they cause both on and offline to their targets.

To define this term more thoroughly, we can begin to unpack the core features that make this phenomenon unique: weaponization tactics, platform dynamics, and communication strategy. Firstly, the weaponizer must have a subscriber base or followers. The severity and scope of follower weaponization scales with follower size. An individual with only 2–3 followers would struggle to carry out a mass, decentralized campaign against a target, whereas someone with 1,000 followers would have more success, and someone with hundreds of thousands would be very successful (widespread, constant, and overwhelming). Secondly, the weaponizer need not be an individual person. While some public figures and influencers, like Donald Trump or Kanye West, have massive individual followers, other entities include groups, like K-Pop artists BTS, or institutional entities like the University of Virginia, or social groups like PETA or Turning Point USA. In the case of collective entities, accountability and responsibility become much more challenging to because the membership of these entities is not always clear or public. Thirdly, the followers or subscriber base must be relatively engaged with the entity that they follow. Engagement can vary from platform to platform, but this usually involves user groups that like, share, or react to posts, purchase merchandise they recommend or create, or form parasocial relationships with the content creator (Kowert & Daniel, 2021). In qualitative research, this concept is often called 'insider-outsider positioning' (Woods, 2019). People who are insiders to the community can understand the implicit meanings of the group, the shared history and collective values, and 'read between the lines' of the group's social media creation on a discursive level. Fourthly, the entity must direct their followers to focus on a particular target: a personal photo, a name, an address, and/or other identifying information.

Primary goals of follower weaponization

First and foremost, one of the major goals of follower weaponization is to silence its targets. Silencing can happen in several ways including obfuscation, smothering, and erasure. All these methods constitute a kind of epistemic violence—identified by Kristie Dotson as:

> a refusal, intentional or unintentional, of an audience to communicatively reciprocate a linguistic exchange owing to pernicious ignorance. Pernicious ignorance should be understood to refer to any reliable ignorance that, in a given context, harms another person (or set of persons).
>
> *(Dotson, 2011, p. 238)*

This goal of follower weaponization focuses on the weaponizer's intent to silence the target by removing their audience through hiding their testimony, preventing their testimony, or forcing them to remove or delete their testimony.

Obfuscation refers to the manipulation and distortion of testimony—in all the cases mentioned, testimony is taken, purposefully misinterpreted or manipulated, and rendered more extreme through rage bait or dog whistling. It becomes almost impossible to tell what the target's initial audience, intention, or words even were by the time the time the weaponizers have cannibalized them. Thus, it becomes impossible for the target to communicate with their audience, or any audience, as the communication is being done for them, regurgitated by various followers on different platforms, and then used to justify attacks against them.

Smothering refers to Fricker's (2007) initial conceptualization within the framework of epistemic injustice when individuals *know* their testimony will be poorly received or put them at risk, and they choose not to say anything at all. This practice is best captured by the target of CM's follower weaponization attempt: "It's better to stay quiet, not make a sound, make it through my education" (Syed, 2019). The students were afraid to share their testimony online for fear of retaliation from CM and their followers. Further, they were afraid that CM's follower weaponization tactics would cause them to be kicked out of their universities and jeopardize their futures. One of the major goals of follower weaponization is to invoke enough fear that targets will self-censor and avoid speaking out again. This goal extends not only to the target themselves, but also to their support networks—people are afraid of even showing support to the target publicly because the followers might then target them. As such, being a target of follower weaponization is an extremely isolating experience.

Epistemic erasure focuses on attempting to get targets to delete their posts, stop their actions, and recant/retract their support for certain topics. In cases like Dr. Bernard's and the folks targeted by CM, it would be far easier for them to delete their posts and accounts and/or say that their initial narrative was untrue or misinterpreted, just to dodge the consequences of follower weaponization. This type of erasure is particularly insidious as it makes it seem as if the testimony never existed in the first place. As most websites do not keep digital archives of deleted posts, unless someone has the foresight to add a post to the Wayback Machine or take a screenshot, it's as if it never existed.

Second, another goal of follower weaponization is black marking. By associating the target with so many connected terms, like 'baby killer' in Dr. Bernard's case or 'antisemite' and 'nazi' in the case of the folks targeted by CM, the algorithms will populate search results with the pages and articles that have the highest amount of engagement. If potential employers or educational institutions search for the target on Google, the top results will be pages and posts that identify them as 'antisemitic' or 'baby killer'. For employers especially, it is unlikely that they would investigate far beyond the initial search results before opting to move forward with a candidate who does not have an online history. This presents a particular hardship to students, who will already be facing a challenging job market, with the uphill battle of figuring out how to also address the algorithmic black spot the weaponizer has placed on them.

Third, and finally, the goal of follower weaponization is to instill fear. By turning the target's entire digital ecosystem against them, weaponizers are not only able to effectively silence and black spot targets for an indefinite period of time; they are also able to scare off other possible dissidents by 'making an example' of the target: 'this is what happens if you want to speak out'. For those in precarious financial, residential, or educational situations, participating in actions that may even run the risk of being a target of follower weaponization is entirely out of the question. As such, weaponizers are further able to easily isolate targets from their social systems by making it seem as if they are the only person who has that position and experience. It is far easier for weaponizers to silence one or two individuals rather than hundreds or thousands. As such, weaponizers do not normally target entities that have more followers, that have more social currency (influence), or that have more money.

Follower weaponization tactics

With a working definition in mind, we can turn to the *how* of follower weaponization. The first technique, one also identified in the resources for targeted harassment here, is *dog whistling*. A dog whistle, without connotation, is a whistle that canines can hear, but produces sound at too high of a frequency for humans. Within politics, the term refers to discourse, media, or symbolism that group outsiders cannot 'hear', but community insiders can recognize and interpret. Differently put, groups or group members can use words, images, or actions that take on a double meaning or an implicit meaning to members within a community while not necessarily raising alarms to the general public. Some such examples provided by legal scholar and author of *Dog Whistle Politics* Ian Haney López include terms like "welfare queens" or "food stamp president" (2014). Other examples from recent contemporary discourse include: "abortion-inducing drugs" (when referring to birth control), "groomers" (when referring to parents of transgender persons), "woke" (when referring to someone non-conservative or beliefs that are non-conservative), "state's rights" (when signaling for support of segregation or other pre-civil rights policies), and "lazy" (when referring to workers unwilling to take jobs that do not compete with cost of living).

When dog whistling is used successfully, followers can be weaponized without tipping off outsider groups to what they are doing. Another key point of successful dog whistling is that it allows the weaponizer the coverage of *plausible deniability*. It is fairly easy for them to later reframe their statement when asked and say that 'wasn't what they meant'. This is particularly effective on social media websites that have strong restrictions in place for overt racism, sexism, homophobia, and threats of violence, but dog whistles can easily be chalked up to 'free speech'.

One of the major, and more successful, examples of follower weaponization in this way is Donald Trump and his supporters' use of dog whistling ahead of the January 6th insurrection attempt. During Trump's speech ahead of the insurrection attempt, he used several phrases that called out various supporters including white nationalist groups and QAnon supporters:

> "**American patriots** who are committed to the honesty of our elections and the integrity of our glorious republic"; "All of us here today do not want to see our election victory stolen by emboldened **radical-left Democrats**"; "He had **80 million computer votes**;" And don't worry, we will not take the name off the Washington Monument. **We will not cancel culture**"; "You hurt our monuments, **you hurt our heroes,** you go to jail for 10 years, and everything stopped"; "They've used the **pandemic as a way of defrauding the people** in a proper election"; "But this year, using the pretext of the **China virus** and the **scam of mail-in ballots,** Democrats attempted the most brazen and outrageous **election theft** and there's **never been anything like this**"; "So when you hear, when you hear, while there is no evidence to prove any wrongdoing, **this is the most fraudulent thing anybody has, this is a criminal enterprise. This is a criminal**

enterprise . . . I could go on for another hour reading this stuff to you and telling you about it. There's never been anything like it"; "And **we fight. We fight like hell.** And if you don't fight like hell, **you're not going to have a country anymore**"; "We're going to try and give them the kind of pride and boldness that they **need to take back our country**".

(Naylor, 2021)

While some of these statements from the speech may not seem particularly alarming at first glance, they hit on several of the major rallying points used by QAnon supporters and white nationalist groups online. QAnon supporters often refer to themselves as 'Patriots', as well as the subtle nod to white nationalist group the Patriot Front. Janet McIntosh's interview (Bencks, 2021) covered the social media discourse leading up to January 6th as noting followers being ready for the 'hammer to drop' or in their 'battle stations'—following the intensive QAnon belief in the deep state and the deep state's responsibility in 'the big lie' (that Trump lost the 2020 election) (Staff, 2021). These beliefs were further validated and weaponized throughout Trump's speech when he indicates that the pandemic was a plot to defraud people and dismantle the election, and that Joe Biden had 'computer votes'. Further, his frequent statements that 'there's never been anything like it/this' to indicate that there is more 'behind the scenes' amps up the secrecy and cryptic nature of 'how deep' the deep state goes.

In a further nod to white nationalism and hyper-conservative blocks, Trump speaks to 'cancel culture', the 'radical left', and the 'China virus'—all viewpoints that have percolated and been taken up throughout the pandemic and Twitter's crackdown on healthcare misinformation. Further, Trump provides a subtle nod to the Unite the Right Rally in Charlottesville, Virginia (which he had previously commented on at the time as having "very fine people on both sides") when removal of the Robert E. Lee monument sparked a violent protest. Some of the notable ultra-nationalist and white supremacy groups involved in the protest were the Loyal White Knights (KKK), League of the South, Vanguard America, and Hammer Brothers, amongst many others.

Creatively, Trump was able to weaponize followers through a hybrid format—making use of both Twitter and Facebook to pick up and harness talking points, gauge follower metrics and post-performance, and build expectations and anticipation for how and when followers could be impactful. In this case, social media technologies acted as an obfuscator—providing the cover of white noise to further obfuscate the discourse being used online from outsider groups and deny potential consequences. Additionally, social media acted as an *amplifier* for the various inside groups Trump was trying to connect with, reaching crowds that Trump may not have ever connected with otherwise.

Another tactic for follower weaponization that works through and with technology is the use of rage bait. Rage bait, or outrage bait, refers to the use of headlines or content that are written to purposefully drive anger and intrigue all at once. Timothy J. Ryan's article "What Makes Us Click? Demonstrating Incentives for Angry Discourse with Digital-Age Field Experiments" (2012) discusses how effective inducing feelings of anger and anxiety are for generating 'clicks' or engagement with content online. One popular example of this was the 2015 controversy over the Starbucks Christmas cups when they transitioned to a more minimalistic design. One of the prominent names in the debate, Josh Feuerstein, posted an 'expose' on YouTube saying "Do you realize that Starbucks wanted to take

Christ and Christmas off of their brand-new cups? . . . In fact, do you know that Starbucks isn't allowed to say Merry Christmas to their customers?". Feuerstein's post went viral within a few days and generated numerous articles and posts about Starbucks trying to "cancel Christmas" or starting a "war on Christmas" to generate clicks and engagement (Abad-Santos, 2016).

Generating clicks and engagement online is an extremely important tactic for follower weaponization. Engagement, or how many likes, reactions, comments, and views a post or article has, is a primary driver for how the recommendation algorithms curate content for their viewers. Once a user engages with a certain type of content, the algorithms working behind the scenes are more likely to recommend, or nudge, users toward similar types of content that are likely to cause them to engage as well. Further, advertisements and sponsored content (like political ads) will also shift to align with the type of content with which users are deemed more likely to engage. Within the fields of media studies, technology studies, and science and technology studies (STS), this phenomenon is called a 'filter bubble' or an 'echo chamber'.

Filter bubbles are also powerful tools when trying to weaponize followers because it helps the weaponizer submerge followers into a world of similarly minded individuals, advertisements, and social media content *without their direct awareness*. Recommender algorithms curate content on the back end of a platform—users are not able to turn these features off, and it is not made explicit when and how the algorithm is curating content. Thus, the user's experience is slowly and subtly changed to constantly reaffirm their values and interests online and whisk away anything that might disrupt their engagement. As found by Ping Liu and their co-authors in "The Interaction between Political Typology and Filter Bubbles in News Recommendation Algorithms" (2021), users with more extreme political leanings (on either side of the aisle) are more likely to be shown more content that reaffirms their views and content with less variety. As such, it is more likely that users will feel as if an increasing number of their friends, accounts they follow, and social media experience agree with their more extreme viewpoints. This echo chamber then also gives the user the impression that these viewpoints are not only socially acceptable but are *rewarded* through the social media platform with increasing followers, more likes, and even awards, in the cases of some social platforms like Reddit.

While weaponizers do not actively select these digital tactics for amassing followers and radicalizing them, the technologies and platforms readily lend themselves to be utilized for follower weaponization. Filter bubbles and rage bait work collaboratively alongside weaponizers to create a digital ecosystem to keep followers engaged and angry enough to recognize and act on dog whistles or other more direct requests. By algorithmically curating a community, followers are then exposed to an increasingly more extreme digital ecosystem that *normalizes* particular ways of interacting with perceived threats to the group or ideological opponents. Often, followers respond to these dog whistles or calls to action through two ways: One, sending the target of these posts, articles, or dog whistles an overwhelming amount of hate imagery and speech or threats of violence; two, posting the target's personally identifying information (email accounts, images, addresses, family members, cars/licenses) across other platforms to *amplify* the negative engagement across the follower base to avoid direct participation and maintain *plausible deniability* to their affiliations with the content and their level of involvement. Both acts of negative engagement will be discussed more in depth in the next section on the "Primary Goals" of follower weaponization. To exemplify follower weaponization in action, two recent cases can be examined: Dr. Caitlin Bernard's experience as a target of follower weaponization and the Canary Mission as an entity that weaponizes followers to silence activists.

Follower weaponization effects

Dr. Caitlin Bernard became the target of follower weaponization after providing a pregnant 10-year-old rape survivor a medication abortion. The child was an Ohio resident found in need of an abortion shortly after the heartbeat trigger-law went into effect banning all abortions after the detection of fetal poll activity with the fall of Roe v. Wade. Shortly after providing the abortion, which was still legal in Indiana, Attorney General of Indiana Todd Rokita went on Fox News claiming that Dr. Bernard was "An abortion activist acting as a doctor with a history of failing to report", before talking about opening a criminal investigation and showing an image of the doctor. After gaining traction on Fox News, conservative social media outlets began calling the story fake news (Choi, 2022). Soon after, the hospital began to receive consumer complaints from people of other states that had never interacted Dr. Bernard; additionally, Dr. Bernard began to receive harassment from conservative social media outlets and followers alongside continued attention from Fox News. As a result, Dr. Bernard and her family had to enlist 24/7 security.

In the second case, we can look at blacklist website the Canary Mission. The Canary Mission (CM) is a public blacklist that operates across various platforms including Twitter, Facebook, Instagram, and YouTube, but they also have an independent website. CM claims to "document people and groups that promote hatred of the USA, Israel and Jews" (Syed, 2019). The main website encourages individuals to report 'anti-Semitic activity' on their college campuses to the website. Once submitted, a full dossier of the student, faculty member, professional, or organization becomes publicly posted on their website, Twitter, and Facebook, including full names, personal websites, and contact information. Importantly, 'anti-Semitic activity' is expanded to target anyone critical of the State of Israel or trying to boycott, divest, or sanction (BDS) the State of Israel over their policy, politics, or statecraft. Allowing votes or discussions on BDS at the college level also qualifies as anti-Semitic activity under the 'Ethics Policy' of the CM, as does allowing those discussions or votes to be anonymous or secret. As such, the CM does not differentiate between Israeli state critics/anti-Zionists and Nazis/neo-Nazis, featuring both groups as equally engaging in antisemitism. The CM does not make its membership publicly visible, and it is unclear who determines whether individuals are worthy of posting across their platforms.

After being reported to CM, faculty and students alike have their images, emails, and other contact information posted across all of their social media pages. This results in hundreds and thousands of messages filling their university inboxes and bombarding them from across all major social media platforms—both publicly and privately. Social media posts often call the targets "antisemitic", accusing targets of "eliminating Israel" and "blood libel", and "nazism" while tagging other related groups with large follower bases. Jewish students who make their way onto CM's blacklist are particularly subjected to attack, being called "self-loathing Jews", "Jewish", "fake Jews", "Kapos", and sent Holocaust imagery.

In both cases, follower weaponization was *amplified* by tapping into the power of algorithms. In Dr. Bernard's case, Fox News was able to utilize its viewership and online audiences to spread doubt about the case using dog whistles like "fake news" and "acting" (invoking the 'crisis actors' discourse surrounding events like Sandy Hook) (Williamson,

2023). Further, by blasting Dr. Bernard's image on the news show immediately after these accusations, Fox News was able to activate its follower base and then point them in her direction. When their perspectives are further shared on social media and heavily engaged with, more and more people begin to see the content who would not have otherwise watched the news or engaged with it. Further, by linking the topic of abortion with terms such as "fake news" and "[crisis] acting", the ecosystem is expanded to begin normalizing and reinforcing these terms within groups that may not have engaged with Trump or Sandy Hook conspiracies but can now be added to the digital ecosystem. In addition, Fox News and AG Akita can maintain plausible deniability of wrongdoing because they did not explicitly direct their followers to harass Dr. Bernard; they merely provided the story and showed an image of whom they were referring to.

In the CM case, CM can harness their own followers and followers of similar groups online, via *amplification*. They 'at' (@) or tag various entities when they post their targets' information on their platforms to ensure as many eyes are on it as possible and to increase their engagement. Further, CM makes good use of rage bait, often phrasing their posts as "Student Organization Seeks to DESTROY Israel through Antisemitic Policy" or "[Redacted] wished painful deaths on innocent people" or "Free Palestine = the Jews must go!" Further, the CM will take quotes out of context and manipulate media to portray their targets more negatively (Syed, 2019). These posts generate immediate outrage from their follower base—and many others who are unaware of what CM is—and the algorithms detect this post engagement and spread it to various networks that would normally not see CM's content as 'posts others in your network are engaging with'. Additionally, CM and their followers will @ their targets along with other highly visible members of their target's community, especially those with perceived power over their targets. By connecting various points in an otherwise disconnected network, CM and their followers use the algorithms to amplify the potential for harm against targets by provoking their local networks as well. Again, CM and their followers maintain *plausible deniability* through only 'retweeting', 'liking', or 'sharing' their posts—not by directly engaging in harassment, threats, or harm.

Centering lived experiences

By bringing the lived experiences of targets to the fore of the discussion, the patterns and relational webs that underpin this type of violence and abuse become more salient. Integrating these patterns within the wider discussion of follower weaponization ensures that they are not overlooked, and that targets can be more readily identified and assisted by social and institutional support systems. Follower weaponization is experienced as an unceasing torrent of negative engagement online that bleeds into every aspect of the target's life. It is seemingly inescapable, isolating, and devastating to their work, finances, and relationships. Consider these opening remarks from Sobieraj's book *Credible Threat*:

> I find that most people can imagine what it would feel like to have a torrent of strangers flood your inbox, direct messages, comment sections, and @mentions with humiliating, frightening, and professional stigmatizing content. We understand why being photoshopped into violent or pornographic scenes, receiving rape and death threats, being called a 'cum dumpster' or 'yellow skank', and/or having our 'fuck-ability' debated in public—in full view of our colleagues, family, and community—might undermine our reputation, riddle us with anxiety, make us want to hole up, or

distract us from our work . . . People want to know the circumstances surrounding the tragedy. This desire is driven by concern and curiosity, but also by an implicit need to reassure ourselves that we are not in danger, because we do not smoke or drive under the influence.

(Sobieraj, 2020, p. 54)

People who hear the lived experiences of follower weaponization sometimes listen with sympathy and horror, but at the same time, they want to know *why* an individual is targeted and whether the target *deserved* to be targeted. One of the interviewees that Sobieraj featured noted people responded to her lived experience as a target of follower weaponization with "well, you chose this lifestyle. You chose to be doing this work. You chose to be vocal. This is [the] result". Another target noted that their partner reacted to their experience with "why do you put yourself in this position? Get out! Stop!" (p. 54–55)

While Sobieraj identifies this phenomenon as victim blaming, it also is another form of *just deserts* or *you reap what you sow*. There is this rather striking moment in conversations with victims, detailed in her book, where the people around them—even those within their deepest support networks—feel as if targets are getting what they deserve when it comes to follower weaponization. If the target did not speak up or speak out, they would not have become targets. It is the internet, after all. And if one does choose to speak up or out knowing these risks anyway, they must *deserve* whatever happens next. Problematically, when targets then reach out for help from support networks, institutions, or peers after becoming targeted, they are often met with this perverse sense of consequentialism via apathy or silence.

In Dr. Bernard's case, as an affiliate of Indiana University's healthcare system and an Assistant Professor of Clinical Obstetrics and Gynecology at IU, the institution was silent. When NPR interviewed other Indiana medical residents on their thoughts of Dr. Bernard's circumstances, one resident responded that "Watching what she went through was scary. I think that was part of the point for those who were putting her through that—was to scare other people out of doing the work that she does" (Summers, 2022). Dr. Bernard herself mentioned that she was afraid for herself and her family after being targeted by follower weaponization.

These experiences are echoed by students who were targeted by the CM and their affiliates. One of the students writes:

It is both scary and absurd to know that someone has convinced a human being in middle-of-nowhere Arkansas that you should be dead. Being targeted is a distinct mix of paranoia, frustration that there is no central organization to blame, and exhaustion as the constant harassment wears you down in a war of attrition.

(Anonymous Student, 2022)

Another target of the CM lists one of the comments they received from one of their followers as "I hope you are raped by 10,000 Arabs, but no, you would probably enjoy it" (Rothchild, 2019) and spoke more about the CM's impact on students:

The postings, selectively chosen and misinterpreted, are expansive and frequently updated. This constant surveillance and cyber-bullying leads students to feel anxious and paranoid as they find themselves the subjects of online death threats, and racial, homophobic and misogynist slurs. The website focuses disproportionately on students of color and Arabs.

(Rothchild, 2019)

Another target of CM's follower weaponization explains their perspective, noting:

Education is really important to us because, in my case, the reason my parents came is so that I could get a better education and I could thrive with the resources in America, following the American Dream . . . Canary Mission threatens that for us. I think that's a very real fear that first-generation Americans have . . . So a lot of people are immediately turned off. They're like, 'It's better to stay quiet, not make a sound, make it through my education,' because we don't have the privilege of being able to express our political opinions without having any consequences that affect not only us, but our families.

(Syed, 2019)

What these points highlight, especially between cases, is how the power differential between victims actually feels. When the targets of follower weaponization are vulnerable community members—particularly those who are poor or have a precarious residential status—their options for resistance are highly limited.

Looking at the difference between Dr. Bernard and the students, Dr. Bernard was able to afford a good lawyer and 24/7 security. Students are often expelled, put on leave, or minimized by their institutions; they do not have the funding to pursue defamation lawsuits or cease-and-desists; they do not have the money to hire security guards. Students are made to face these circumstances on their own—the institutions usually opt to try to protect their own reputations and social media image rather than use the institution to shield the students from harm. This touches on one of the other points Sobieraj (2020) makes in her text:

Those targeted are told not to give oxygen or attention to the trolls, to brush off and dismiss death threats and rape fantasies. If they leave Twitter or quit blogging, we reason that they have decided to stay above the fray, to save their thoughts for more fruitful venues—not that they have been effectively silenced. This kind of digital abuse must be understood as a struggle to control political discourse that reflects and reinforces existing social inequalities.

(pp. 2–3)

Tools for help

A few entities have published helpful guides for how to deal with having one's personal information posted online (doxxing), but far less has been posted for how to cope with follower weaponization. One of the most comprehensive resources, which was the product of the creator witnessing the experiences of follower weaponization targets, is the Faculty First Responders website (Kamola, n.d.). This website has a list of 'usual suspects', resources for faculty and students, resources for administrators, and a plethora of research explaining the impacts of targeted harassment and social media attacks.

Crash Override Network (n.d.) has a variety of online resources on how to cope with having personal information posted online and being subjected to online harassment. They also have various helpful guides discussing how to talk to one's employer, family, and the police (along with the pros and cons of each discussion level). They also note the difficulty of having these conversations with these groups, especially if they are not technologically affluent enough to understand the finer details and dangers of having sensitive information publicly available. Another good resource is the Online Harassment Field Manual created by PEN America (2024), mentioned earlier. While this resource is frequently updated, the contents of their website have a variety of resources and links for responding to online harassment from various stakeholder perspectives.

Conclusion

Follower weaponization constitutes a new and emerging type of socio-relational violence that transcends interpersonal, offline forms of violence and abuse that have long shaped legal definitions and practices. The current understanding of violence and abuse insufficiently recognizes the harm follower weaponization can cause and fails to recognize the lived experiences of targets and hold weaponizers accountable for the harm they cause. Without coordinated effort between social media platforms, advocacy groups, mutual aid, and changes to the classification and public understanding of violence and abuse in the technologically entangled live world, targets of follower weaponization will continue to be silenced and isolated. By creating more precise definitions and working with targets and former targets to better understand and catalogue their experiences, it becomes possible to not only understand the consequences of online abuse, but also to actively be able to identify it and prevent it within the platforms themselves.

References

Abad-Santos, A. (2016, September). *Starbucks's red cup controversy, explained*. Vox. Retrieved from www.vox.com/2015/11/10/9707034/starbucks-red-cup-controversy

America, P. (2022, September). *Online Harassment Field Editor*. Retrieved from https://onlineharassmentfieldmanual.pen.org/

Anonymous Student. (2022). Interview correspondence over signal messaging with the author.

Bay, M. (2018, November). Weaponizing the haters: The last jedi and the strategic politicization of pop culture through social media manipulation. *First Monday*, 23(11). https://dx.doi.org/10.5210/fm.v23i11.9388

Bencks, J. (2021, January 12). Trump and the language of insurrection. *BrandeisNOW*. Retrieved from www.brandeis.edu/now/2021/january/trump-language-capitol-riot-mcintosh.html

Benkler, Y., Farris, R., & Roberts, H. (2018). *Network propaganda*. Oxford University Press. Retrieved from https://library.oapen.org/handle/20.500.12657/28351

Choi, J. (2022). *Indiana AG says state will look at license of doctor who provided abortion to 10-year-old rape victim*. The Hill.

Cyberbullying Research Center. (n.d., September). *What is cyberbullying?* Retrieved from https://cyberbullying.org/what-is-cyberbullying

Gollan, D. (2022). @ElonMusk is not the only person @ElonJet is putting at risk. *Forbes*. Retrieved from www.forbes.com/sites/douggollan/2022/11/07/elonmusk-is-not-the-only-person-elonjet-is-putting-at-risk/?sh=2d1f1ad01711

Dotson, K. (2011). Tracking epistemic violence, tracking practices of silencing. *Hypatia*, 26(2), 236–257. Retrieved from www.jstor.org/stable/23016544

Fricker, M. (2007). Testimonial injustice. In *Epistemic injustice: Power and the ethics of knowing*. Oxford University Press. Retrieved from https://doi.org/10.1093/acprof:oso/9780198237907.003.0002

Galeano, K., Galeano, R., & Agarwal, N. (2020). An evolving (dis)information environment— How an engaging audience can spread narratives and shape perception: A trident juncture 2018 case study. In K. Shu, S. Wang, D. Lee, & H. Liu (Eds.), *Disinformation, misinformation, and fake news in social media*. Lecture Notes in Social Networks. Springer. https://doi.org/10.100 7/978-3-030-42699-6_13

Kamola, I. (n.d.). *Faculty First Responders*. Retrieved from https://facultyfirstresponders.com/

Kowert, R., & Daniel, E. (2021). The one-and-a-half sided parasocial relationship: The curious case of live streaming. *Computers in Human Behavior Reports, 4*. https://doi.org/10.1016/j.chbr.2021.100150.

Kuhn, T. S. (1962). *The structure of scientific revolutions* (3rd ed. reprint). University of Chicago Press.

Liu, P., Shivaram, K., Culotta, A., Shapiro, M. A., & Bilgic, M. (2021). The Interaction between Political Typology and Filter Bubbles in News Recommendation Algorithms. WWW 21, Ljubljana, Slovenia.

Lopez, I. H. (2014). *Dog whistle politics: How coded racial appeals have reinvented racism and wrecked the middle class*. Oxford University Press.

Naylor, B. (2021, 10/02/2021). Read Trump's Jan. 6 speech, a key part of Impeachment trial. *NPR*. Retrieved from www.npr.org/2021/02/10/966396848/read-trumps-jan-6-speech-a-key-part-of-impeachment-trial

Network, C. O. (n.d., September). *Resource center*. Retrieved from www.crashoverridenetwork.com/resources.html

PEN America. (2024). *Online harassment field manual*. Retrieved from https://onlineharassmentfield-manual.pen.org/

Prasad, V., & Ioannidis, J. P. A. (2022). Constructive and obsessive criticism in science. *European Journal of Clinical Investigation, 52*(11), e13839. https://doi.org/10.1111/eci.13839

Rothchild, A. (2019, December). Cyber bullies at canary mission muzzle free speech. *Washington Report on Middle East Affairs*. Retrieved from www.wrmea.org/2020-january-february/cyber-bullies-at-canary-mission-muzzle-free-speech.html

Ryan, T. J. (2012). What makes us click? Demonstrating incentives for angry discourse with digital-age field experiments. *The Journal of Politics, 74*(4). https://doi.org/10.1017/S0022381612000540

Savage, K. (2021). Randy Rainbow's musical and social media activism: (Digital) bodyguards and politicizing/weaponizing audiences. In L. Jarvis & K. Savage (Eds.), *Avatars, activism and postdigital performance*. Bloomsbury Publishing. ISBN: 9781350159327.

Schulman, S. (2016). *Conflict is not abuse: Overstating harm, community responsibility, and the duty of repair*. Arsenal Pulp Press.

Sobieraj, S. (2020). *Credible threat: Attacks against women online and the future of democracy*. Oxford University Press. Retrieved from https://doi.org/10.1093/oso/9780190089283.001.0001

Staff, R. (2021). Fact check: No evidence to support QAnon claims of mass arrests, military takeover, illegitimacy of Biden's presidency or Trump's return to power. *Reuters*. Retrieved from www.reuters.com/article/uk-factcheck-qanon-military-theories/fact-check-no-evidence-to-support-qanon-claims-of-mass-arrests-military-takeover-illegitimacy-of-bidens-presidency-or-trumps-return-to-power-idUSKBN29R1ZA

Summers, J. (2022). Their mentor was attacked. Now young OB-GYNs may leave Indiana In *All Things Considered*. Retrieved from www.npr.org/2022/08/15/1117605629/ob-gyn-residents-want-to-quit-in-indiana-after-states-abortion-law-harassment

Syed, Z. (2019). Canary mission blacklists students, faculty for pro-Palestine views. *The Michigan Daily*. Retrieved from www.michigandaily.com/news/community-affairs/canary-mission-blacklists-students-faculty-pro-palestine-views/

Vogels, E. A. (2021). *The state of online harassment*. Retrieved from www.pewresearch.org/internet/2021/01/13/the-state-of-online-harassment/

Williamson, E. (2023). *Sandy Hook: An American tragedy and the battle for truth*. Penguin Random House.

Women's Media Center. (n.d.). *Online abuse 101*. Retrieved from https://womensmediacenter.com/speech-project/online-abuse-101

Woods, H. (2019, September). *Examining the implications of insider-outsider positioning*. Retrieved from https://heatherawoods.ca/research/examining-the-implications-of-insider-outsider-positioning/

Woolley, S. C., & Howard, P. N. (Eds.). (2018). *Computational propaganda: Political parties, politicians, and political manipulation on social media*. Oxford University Press.

25
ATTACKS ON REFUGEE RECEPTION CENTRES IN FINLAND BETWEEN 2015 AND 2017—A CASE ANALYSIS OF HIVE TERRORISM

Tommi Kotonen and Heikki Kovalainen

Introduction

Between 2015 and 2017, at the wake of the so-called refugee crisis, dozens of attacks targeting refugee reception centres and other facilities accommodating refugees were conducted in Finland. Many of these cases are still unsolved. Nevertheless, in more than ten cases police managed to catch the attackers, providing data for a closer analysis. Based on this police and court data collected within a previous research project on attacks on refugee reception centres in Finland,[1] this chapter assesses the perpetrator profiles, focusing especially on their social media usage. The attacks are analysed as a form of "hive terrorism", a term conceptualized by Daniel Koehler.

Comparing the cases with previous research both in Sweden and Germany on similar types of attacks, we will argue that the attacks at least partly represented what Koehler has called hive terrorism, which he has defined as fluid networks centred around shared opposition to democratic government and immigration and mobilizing activists from mainstream society more or less spontaneously for terrorist and other violent acts.[2]

The perpetrators, 23 persons identified by the police, who were almost exclusively male, in most cases had no background in extremist organizations, but were however influenced by the far-right rhetoric via social media. The "hive" consisted especially of the anti-refugee Facebook groups, creating an interlinking ecosystem, in which several perpetrators participated, and in which arson attacks were supported and celebrated.

To contextualize the analysis, we will start with the analysis of the hive, focusing on the most popular anti-refugee Facebook group in Finland, called *Rajat Kiinni!* (Close the Borders!). At its height, the group had more than 10 000 members, and in the heated discussions attacking refugees was often incited, including arson attacks. The chapter analyses the role and significance of the hive for the attacks conducted and explores how the perpetrators shifted from online to offline activism.

According to an analysis by Koehler, during what has been called refugee crisis in Germany in 2015 and 2016, "more or less ordinary persons without previous ties to extremist

DOI: 10.4324/9781003277675-29

groups and movements got caught up in severe, but more or less spontaneous, plots or acts of violence".[3] The hive has no permanent structure, but the term "points to the continuously changing nature of the group involved, with dynamic and constantly shifting compositions" as well as "fluid networks centred around shared opposition to democratic government and immigration".[4]

In hive terrorism there may as well be "involvement of milieu outsiders in terror plots together with milieu insiders". Contact between outsiders and insiders happens often via social media, where the perpetrators "consumed extreme right-wing subcultural products like music and literature and voiced xenophobic or racist views".[5]

How online hate speech, which may also constitute a hate crime, correlates with offline extremist crimes has been the focus of several studies in recent years. Certain kinds of correlation have also been demonstrated. In their study on German Facebook groups, Müller and Schwarz have concluded that "short-run bursts in anti-refugee sentiment on social media can translate into real-life hate crimes", although they also acknowledge that in general causality is difficult to establish.[6]

In a recent study based on statistical analysis, Jackson concludes that the "growth in hate crimes overall reflects a wider base of popular support for them and for increasing levels of extremist violence incidents".[7] Studying social media data, Wahlström and Törnberg observe that the social media activity discussing refugees "correspond to a peak in the frequency of physical attacks on refugee facilities".[8] "Specific action forms (such as arson attacks in our case) can . . . become viral ideas, which are spread and perpetuated by mediated reporting and discussions about them".[9]

Also in a recent analysis, the arson attacks targeting refugees in Germany have been linked with far-right social media campaigns:

> The arson wave attracted the mass participation of people without any previous involvement in far-right structures. It showed dramatically how fast radicalization occurs, at first sight requiring little to no organizational structures. In hindsight, the arson attacks and riots of 2015–16 were hardly spontaneous and came in response to the social media campaign organized by the AfD and other representatives of the New Right.[10]

A Swedish study has made a similar connection between far-right social media and arson attacks.[11] The Finnish cases also suggest similar linkage.

In this study we explore this connection between social media activities, especially within certain "hate groups", and offline acts in more detail, looking at attacks in Finland that were motivated by anti-immigration attitudes, and as such constituted hate crimes or even terrorism. There is obviously lots of variation in these attacks; for example, in their relation to the "hive". As a previous study by Herath and Whittaker on online radicalization emphasizes, the role of the online aspect, although often relevant, may indeed appear in different types and levels of engagement and intensity.[12] This is also what our data indicates.

Research material

In this chapter, we will study the online aspects of the attacks on the refugee reception centres in Finland, primarily based on court records and police investigation files as well as media accounts. The court files and police investigation files are free to access by order from the authorities in Finland and do not require a research permit. However, as stipulated by the Act on the Openness of Government Activities (621/1999), the information is provided in masked format and sensitive data, including information on health or annual income, is removed. Handling of such data in research, as per the Data Protection Act (1050/2018), is allowed when it is "necessary for scientific or historical research purposes or statistical purposes and it is proportionate to the aim of public interest pursued". For a closer study, and to supplement the data provided by the authorities, limited online observations were also conducted of public webpages and social media pages of the perpetrators or groups they were associated with. This data was collected during our previous research project.[13] As is typical with the online data, especially with the social media accounts, some data has been removed online since our observation was conducted. When reporting the results and following the guidelines of the Data Protection Ombudsman in Finland, the direct links to the social media accounts have not been presented to secure the anonymity of the users.

There are certain obvious limitations in data gathered, which will be discussed later in more detail. The most obvious one is that in several cases the police did not manage to find the perpetrators. Considering the known number of attacks, 43, we find that 11 cases analysed here represent the phenomenon in general quite well. Another limitation is that online data may have disappeared before we conducted our observation, and some perpetrators may have had social media profiles we are not aware of. And lastly, the police investigations were sometimes very shallow. For example, in one case the perpetrators were caught right after the attack, but a detailed pre-trial investigation was not conducted as they were given only fines and no court process followed.[14]

Anti-refugee attacks as a phenomenon in Finland and elsewhere

Attacks against refugee reception centres, typically conducted as arson attacks, have in Finland as well as in some other European countries been connected with the rise of anti-immigration attitudes. Arson attacks have been also called a very common form of right-wing violence and are, according to Koehler, "essentially about sending a political statement or message to a wide audience and not primarily about killing a specified target".[15] There are no comprehensive previous studies on the phenomenon in Finland, especially regarding the earlier attack wave in the 1990s. The surge in attacks in the mid-2010s bears many similarities to the ones in Germany and in Sweden, in which the previous wave has also been analysed.

As has been noted in previous studies in Sweden[16] and in Germany,[17] anti-refugee attacks in 2015 were very similar to a wave of attacks in the early 1990s,[18] although certain differences can be detected.

In Germany, the first wave was clearly stronger than witnessed in 2015–2016; at the highest level in 2016, the authorities recorded 113 arson attacks whereas in 1992, at the peak of the previous wave, 708 attacks were conducted.[19] In Sweden the waves have also differed similarly in intensity. It has been assessed that this reflects to a certain extent the changes in far-right methods and organizations. Nowadays groups try to show a more acceptable façade, and the far-right more often uses parliamentary means for achieving their goals.[20]

Studying the previous analyses of the perpetrator profiles of the early 1990s attacks in Sweden and Germany, it is notable that around half of the attackers were intoxicated, and their ages were between 16–20 years. More than half had also a previous crime record, and all lived near the place of the attack.[21] According to a Swedish study by Lööw, perpetrators' motives can be classified into three categories: clearly personal motives, protest motives and hate motives. Especially in cases motivated by protest mentality, the perpetrators saw themselves as heroes, claiming that others just have no courage to conduct similar acts. According to Koehler,[22] in Germany only 21 per cent of the perpetrators were active members of any far-right organizations. As in Sweden, in Germany the attackers were also often intoxicated. The perpetrator profile in the mid-2010s wave was pretty similar, but only one in five of the perpetrators were intoxicated. Koehler has also detected certain radicalization in the attacks, as they more often targeted inhabited premises.[23]

Similar statistics are missing in Finland regarding the attacks in the early 1990s. More anecdotal evidence suggests, however, that there was a similar wave, and that the motives and perpetrator profiles were similar to the attacks in Sweden and Germany.[24] The new wave of attacks peaked in 2015, when 43 acts or attempts of arson or vandalism were recorded by the police.[25] More than half of the perpetrators were intoxicated. Like elsewhere, in Finland the solving rate of these crimes appears to be relatively low. Online activism, however, is mentioned only passingly in the aforementioned previous studies on attacks in Germany and Sweden. As will be shown here, the attacks in Finland nevertheless had an essential online element as well, and many of them were linked to a known online ecosystem focusing on anti-refugee mobilization.

The hive—breeding ground for the attacks?

In the wake of the arrival of a large number of refugees in Finland in 2015, an anti-immigration opposition demonstrated in several Finnish cities, at its height gathering thousands of participants. The movement started, at least ostensibly, as a rather spontaneous one, without any direct links to organized racist or far-right organizations. Key mobilization channels were different anti-immigration Facebook groups. These were created under the general umbrella of a movement which called itself Close the Borders! (Rajat Kiinni!).

Exposure to online hate speech in general, as shown in a study published in 2017, happened in Finland most often by using Facebook, and to a little lesser extent via YouTube or discussion boards.[26] Exposure to online hate speech among 15–30-year-old was much higher in Finland than in Germany,[27] with the most common form of hate content focusing on ethnicity.[28] The Rajat Kiinni! Facebook group was one of the key hate communities in Finland. In a recent study on hate crimes in Finland between 2016 and 2020, the Rajat Kiinni! community stands out as one of the key networks and as one of the platforms where hate crimes were committed, although the majority of crimes were committed by people without explicit links to any organizations or networks.[29]

Despite being to some extent a spontaneous movement in the sense that no formal organization was behind them and creating a counter-reaction to the arrival of the refugees, several Rajat Kiinni! activists had background in organized groups.[30] These included nationalist group Suomen Sisu and anti-immigration group Suomi Ensin (Finland First), which later transformed into a party.[31] The latter was built after the British model, even having a similar logo to the Britain First movement.

After the initial, more spontaneous phase, and reflecting the typical phases of the social movements,[32] the Rajat Kiinni! communities became closer to organized political groups, such as Suomen Sisu and different street patrol organizations.[33] This may be seen, as per typology by Bennet and Segerberg,[34] as a shift from personalized and network-based connective action towards organizationally enabled networks.

According to one of the key activists, the slogan "close the borders" was first used in August 2015[35] in an anti-refugee demonstration in Salo,[36] seen as a starting point of the movement. The Rajat Kiinni! Facebook group grew rapidly and had more than 11 000 members by 2016. In addition to the main group, there were also several local Facebook groups.[37] Furthermore, Rajat Kiinni! was one of the major hubs of a broader online far-right ecosystem[38] and had links to several similar but smaller groups. Some of these groups also organized off-line activities, including an Independence Day demonstration in December 2015.[39] The demonstration raised awareness about the refugee situation and threats caused by immigration and mobilized local resistance.

According to their now-defunct official webpages, Rajat Kiinni! was a non-revolutionary single-issue movement, which did not align itself politically.[40] However, following internal schisms,[41] some of the movement members established another webpage, on which political messages were quite openly far-right. They promoted anti-Semitic conspiracy theories and linked to neo-Nazi organizations.[42]

The centrality of the Rajat Kiinni! in hate speech networks also gave it much mainstream media attention. According to Saresma, "although the info channel of CB [Close the Borders!] is placed on the internet, the main aim is to organise demonstrations and mobilise people to take to the 'real' streets".[43] However, in a sense the Facebook group had a life of its own, and it lasted much longer than the actual demonstrations.

The Facebook page of Rajat Kiinni! was, unlike pages of some more organized far-right groups,[44] much less controlled, as any member could post in it and the feed was sometimes almost impossible to follow because of the flood of posts. In 2018, when discussion was less heated, there still appeared around 30 posts per day.[45] This, however, pales in comparison with 2015 and 2016. In a study analysing hate speech in Rajat Kiinni! and other groups during the first eight months of 2016, more than 50 000 posts and 350 000 comments were published.[46] On average, this means daily rates of more than 200 posts per day, with almost 1500 comments.

Aggressive or hateful comments comprised, depending on the analysis method, between 10 and 21 per cent of all comments.[47] Pohjonen suggests that the offensive language gradually became "the new 'normal'—a kind of ritualised opposition to mainstream norms and language".[48] Besides aggressive rhetoric, some posts and comments urged people to direct action.

Offline direct action developed in tandem with demonstrations and online group formations and was often mobilized online. First, the anti-refugee demonstrators tried to physically block the border between Sweden and Finland to prevent refugees from arriving. They also tried to prevent transfer of the refugees, violently demonstrating while they arrived at reception centres. Along with these forms of activism, some planned refugee reception centres were vandalized, and in some cases destroyed. After the refugees had arrived, arson attacks followed, which is the focus of this chapter. Later, in the autumn of 2015, vigilante street patrols were organized, the most successful of which became known as Soldiers of Odin.[49]

Arson attacks were celebrated and encouraged within the group. The attacks were often legitimized as defensive,[50] as scorched earth tactics to prevent the arrival of the refugees. A model for the attacks was provided by Swedish and German examples, which were also celebrated by the Rajat Kiinni! community. For example, some people commenting on the attacks in Sweden within the Rajat Kiinni! group saw violence as the only option: "Swedish people have not been given any other option and apparently they will not give in Finland either . . . just talk".[51]

More typical were sarcastic comments, alluding to also conducting attacks in Finland, without direct incitement. As the Rajat Kiinni! group was public, a more indirect approach was recommended. Often the comments would go along these lines (Facebook 20.12.2015):

Comment 1: "There has always been fires on New Year's Eve when ignited by rockets etc. smile"
Comment 2: "On New Years's Eve one can shoot rockets and other bombs. Every year something burns. What will it be this time"
Comment 3: "Some rockets may indeed go astray"

There were only a few cases that led to any legal consequences. One blogpost linked and published at the Rajat Kiinni! webpage urged people to lynch politicians and to conduct arson attacks. The author of the post was later convicted for public incitement to an offence after he instructed in a December 2015 blogpost how to destroy a refugee reception centre by using Molotov cocktails.[52]

The perpetrators and their shift from online to offline activities

In our analysis, we have identified in 11 different cases 23 perpetrators who were caught by the police and later convicted, typically for criminal mischief or criminal damage. Seven of these cases were arson attacks, and the rest included vandalism and menace. In some cases, electronic device searches were not conducted, and in most of the cases, although they were conducted, they were not considered to have provided enough relevant information to be attached to the investigation file. Sometimes, however, the suspects themselves talked about their online activities during the investigation. In some cases, their online profiles showed a connection.

A detailed analysis of the social media usage of the perpetrators shows that in most of the cases there is a link to Rajat Kiinni! community or to the online ecosystem surrounding it. Only in three cases were we unable to confirm a link between the perpetrators and the Facebook-based ecosystem. Here we will take a closer look at three cases where the link was most prominent, and which illuminate different aspects of online activities leading to offline attacks: arson attacks in Kouvola, Ylivieska and Oulu.

In September 2015, a 50-year-old local man with a Molotov cocktail attacked the refugee reception centre at Keltakangas, Kouvola. According to police investigation protocols, he was drunk during the act and took a taxi to the centre. He told the police he wanted to "protest current Finnish refugee policy, which causes an enormous burden for the society". The perpetrator used only one explosive but had another ready at his home. On the day of the attack, he had shared three anti-immigration writings calling to direct action on his Facebook profile.

During the investigation, the perpetrator told he had felt anger towards refugees for about three weeks, meaning he was radicalized very quickly, which also showed in his social media profile. Both three days and one day before the attack he shared news about arson attacks in Germany and Finland. The first link he shared was from a notorious anti-refugee news site MV-lehti, which called the refugees "jihadists" and "cultural enrichers" and celebrated the attack conducted by "Volksturm" "continuing its battle against the invaders".[53] In his own Facebook profile, the perpetrator also ranted that,

> Terrorist are coming through Western borders they can fuck off all the lot, now we have to establish in every community our own forces protecting the Finns for example prevent food delivery at Keltakangas they should fucking starve away from here we do not help terrorists, all join in[54]

The perpetrator was either a follower or a member of several anti-refugee Facebook groups which all linked to the Rajat Kiinni! community. Notably, he was also a member in a local group called "Save Kouvola from multiculturalism", which was protesting the opening of a refugee reception centre in Kouvola.

Besides anti-refugee webpages, it is worth mentioning that the traditional mass media also provided the attacks with visibility, resonance and legitimacy, which may have served as an inspiration as well. In this case too, another shared story originated from mainstream mass media.[55] This also happened in the Rajat Kiinni! Facebook-group, in which some mainstream media news stirred heated discussion, although MV-lehti was often their preferred and authoritative source for news.[56] According to Pohjonen, "where the extreme right information sources differed from other news sources was in the intensity of the conversations they provoked".[57]

The attack in October 2015 in Ylivieska was, according to police investigation, closely tied to online activism of the perpetrators. Four drunken perpetrators threw self-made Molotov cocktails, bottles filled with gasoline, against the wall of a refugee reception centre. The bottles did not ignite. The case did not lead to convictions on the arson attack itself; they had only to pay for the damages as the court considered their act as a "worthless attempt" that caused no real danger.[58] The court did not mention their online activities in its judgement.

It has however been possible to verify that at least one of the four perpetrators was a member of the Rajat Kiinni! Facebook group, and two of them were in a group they called "maahanmuutolle on tultava loppu" (immigration must stop). All perpetrators said during the investigation that they have nothing against "real refugees", but thought some of the male refugees were just seeking benefits and thus were showing moral indignation against them. According to them, they wanted to frighten the refugees by throwing Molotov cocktails, and one of them called it a political protest.

The person described by others as the agitator of the group was previously an active participant in the aforementioned group but was banned because of his too-radical opinions. He described his writings to the police, admitting that:

> in some of my writings I referred more or less directly to this kind of activity, like "one should do here like one does in Sweden" and I referred with this to some arson attacks

He added, however, that in his opinion, "joining this [Facebook] group is of no importance regarding our stupid act. My opinion is that we would have done it while drunken even if I had not joined the group".[59] Before the attack, the perpetrators had been drinking and discussing the current refugee policies.

Besides happening much later than the other attacks, the Oulu case in 2017 is an outlier in other respects as well. The person convicted for the attack was a member of the far-right street patrol organization Soldiers of Odin,[60] and thus the only case in our material in which a known member of a far-right group was directly involved. The attack, which was not successful as the bottles used did not ignite, targeted a tent of refugees at the city centre which was built for a demonstration.[61] In this case, too, the online element was relevant.

The attack happened on April 7, but the demonstration had already started in March and was discussed heatedly by local anti-refugee activists. Two weeks before the attack, members of Soldiers of Odin discussed the demonstration on Facebook, and one member suggested attacking it:

> I just guessing that if those tents will not be removed soon, it will be only a Molotov cocktail which will remove them!!!! And I do not classify myself as a racist, I'm just right now starting to freak out for those coddlers and coddled!!![62]

This comment was presented on the now-defunct Facebook page of the local leader of Soldiers of Odin (SOO). As has been noted in previous studies, the Rajat Kiinni! group has had several connections with the SOO,[63] and they have promoted each other as well as taken part in joint demonstrations.[64] SOO marched together with Rajat Kiinni! members in Tampere in 2017. During the march, a member of SOO Oulu, who was later fined for assisting the perpetrator of the Oulu arson attack, was arrested.[65] Overlapping online ecosystems seem to have thus evolved into joint offline activities.

Online roles of the perpetrators

The variations we can see in these three cases are interesting. Sometimes more or less direct online incitement is evident, as in the Oulu attack. In the Ylivieska case, the social media activities may have also directly affected the perpetrators' motivation for an attack. In that case, the link between online and offline activity is as close as it can get, as the perpetrators referred to venting hate online along with suggesting doing similar attacks. Whether banning the key perpetrator from Facebook led to offline activism is, however, impossible to prove, although it may have increased experienced frustration.

From the perspective of radicalization studies, the position of a perpetrator as a producer of hate speech is certainly interesting. As has been argued by Whittaker, the "online radicalization theories tend to focus heavily on the consumption of radical propaganda", although there are also those "who are at the same time producers and consumers of violent extremist materials".[66]

However, consumed material itself may also urge one to action. This was visible in the Kouvola case, in which the perpetrator was mostly a passive consumer, sharing only links that eventually inspired him. All three cases were somehow linked to far-right online ecosystems, but not as directly with organized groups as one would have perhaps expected. Online material consumed is only one part of an equation, and online experiences in general, such as bans or encounters with like-minded users, may also have an effect.

The share of passive consumers of online hate speech seems to be much higher in our arguably limited data, as out of 23 perpetrators only two could be identified as producers of hate speech, and even they do not appear to be high-frequency posters. It is also unknown whether any of them took part in any anti-refugee demonstrations.[67] Radicalization and subsequent action thus seem to have stemmed entirely from one's experiences within the online environment, without any help from formal organizations, or without the perpetrators later joining any such group.

What is also lacking, as far as is known in all the cases we identified, is the "feedback" to the online environment. None of the perpetrators shared or even tried to share media of their deeds with their online audiences. The only way some of the perpetrators were captured in the act was the surveillance cameras. Thus, there was no well-thought-out media strategy, suggesting the attacks were rather spontaneous by nature. Only in one case was it possible to confirm that the bottles used for the arson attacks were prepared several days before the attack, suggesting some level of premeditation.

A recent study comparing online posting between violent and non-violent extremists suggests that violent persons are not the most regular posters but may only be lurking and following discussions.[68] Our study shows a similar pattern: most of the perpetrators were merely consumers, not active producers of hate speech. As such, they could be characterized at best as sympathizers or followers of the far-right, but not as activists.[69] As far as is known so far, none of the perpetrators joined any organized far-right groups even after the attack.

Online activities, however, clearly had a role in target selection. Online groups showed the perpetrators a possible target, sharing the location of the refugee centres or informing them about the arrival of the refugees, and suggested weapons to be used for the attack.[70] Regarding explicitly stated motives, the perpetrators most often mentioned the refugee policy of the country; notably, religion was barely mentioned.

From hive to terror

Although hate speech was prevalent in Rajat Kiinni! and similar Facebook groups in 2015, authorities did not put much effort into investigating the matter, as is evident when studying the police investigations. The police only established its own team investigating the hate speech in 2017, which can then be seen producing more charges and convictions related to hate speech, such as incitement verdicts, in the following years.[71]

In the attacks against refugees studied in this chapter, a terrorist motive is also arguably present. If terrorism is defined as use of violence or of the threat of violence in the pursuit of political, religious, ideological or social objectives, trying to change the behaviour of a larger group of people than just the immediate target,[72] several of the attacks could be classified as terrorism. Many of them mentioned explicitly that their purpose was to change the politics of the country. On the other hand, the spontaneous nature of the attacks, as well as the lack of links to political organizations and lack of any media strategy resembles more of a hate crime.[73]

Applicable both to the online and offline environments, the concept of hive terrorism provides an interesting bridge between hate crimes and terrorism, and for analysing post-organizational far-right groups. The question remains, however, why these perpetrators decided to "go offline" and attack physical targets. One reason is obvious: to change the politics and scare the refugees, the online environment did not provide powerful enough tools for these activities. Frustrated, sometimes kicked off of social media, the often drunk perpetrators decide to do something more tangible to reach their political goals, however vaguely defined those goals may have been.

The hive studied here provided the critical mass: a large group of people who were incited within the online environment, and eventually some individuals shifted their activities offline. For the authorities, anticipating this kind of attack is more or less impossible. This is also partly due to the fact that the role of the online aspect, although often relevant, may appear in different types and levels of engagement and intensity and the perpetrators may assume very different online roles.

Of course, it is not social media itself which makes people to do harmful things, but it is also worth pondering whether the concept of "online" itself is too heavily demarcated from the offline. As is well known within, for example, online ethnography, the online environment is embedded into people's daily lives in such a manner that talking about them as different spheres or scenes is increasingly useless.[74]

The line between political agency and venting one's emotions is of interest here as well. As the argument sometimes goes, online hate speech is supposed to act as a safety valve, a relatively harmless environment for letting off steam. This does not seem to be the case. If anything, online venting increases one's frustration and anger. Terrorism studies have also suggested that "although the use of the Internet was increasing, it was not replacing offline interactions".[75]

In his study on what he calls a false dichotomy between online and offline radicalization, Whittaker argues for using a theory which "does not assume propaganda will influence its audience, nor does it preclude it, but instead attempts to understand why it may resonate with some, but not others, based on the individual and their environment". This also suggests that more focus should be put, instead of any general talk about "online", instead on the specific environments, such as certain platforms or even networks or groups within those platforms—the hives.

Notes

1 Tommi Kotonen & Heikki Kovalainen (2021): "Iskut vastaanottokeskuksiin Suomessa syksyllä 2015: terrorismia vai tihutöitä? [Attacks on refugee reception centres in Finland autumn 2015: terrorism or vandalism?]". *Kosmopolis*, *51*(1), 72–87.

2 Daniel Koehler (2016): "Right-wing extremism and terrorism in Europe. Developments and issues for the future". *PRISM*, *6*(2), 84–105, 97.

3 Daniel Koehler (2018): "Recent trends in German right-wing violence and terrorism: What are the contextual factors behind 'hive terrorism'?". *Perspectives on Terrorism*, *12*(6), 72–88, 73. www.jstor.org/stable/26544644

4 Ibid., 74.

5 Ibid., 77.

6 Karsten Müller & Carlo Schwarz (2021): "Fanning the flames of hate: Social media and hate crime". *Journal of the European Economic Association*, *19*(4), 2131–2167, 2163. https://doi.org/10.1093/jeea/jvaa045

7 Pamela Irving Jackson (2022): "Hate crimes nourish domestic terror in the United States and Europe". *Democracy and Security*, *18*(4), 349–380. https://doi.org/10.1080/17419166.2022.2039126, 15.

8 Mattias Wahlström & Anton Törnberg (2019): "Social media mechanisms for right-wing political violence in the 21st Century: Discursive opportunities, group dynamics, and co-ordination". *Terrorism and Political Violence*, *33*(4), 766–787. https://doi.org/10.1080/09546553.2019.1586676

9 ibid.

10 Julia Glathe and Mihai Varga (2021): "Cultural drivers of radicalization germany". Country Report of the project *De-Radicalisation in Europe and Beyond: Detect, Resolve, Re-integrate*. Online: https://dradproject.com/wp-content/uploads/2021/07/WP-5.1-Germany-report.pdf A typo corrected: in original the time frame was given as "2015–15".

11 Abby Peterson (2018): "The relationship between a movement party and its radical flank". https://doi.org/10.4324/9781315123851-9 In *Radical Right Movement Parties in Europe*. Edited by M. Caiani & O. Císař, 131–148, 140.

12 Chamin Herath & Joe Whittaker (2021): "Online radicalisation: Moving beyond a simple dichotomy". *Terrorism and Political Violence*, published online 22 November 2021. https://doi.org/10.1080/09546553.2021.1998008

13 Kotonen & Kovalainen, 2021.

14 National Prosecution Authority (n.d.): "Fine procedure". https://syyttajalaitos.fi/en/fine-procedure

15 Koehler Daniel (2017): *Right-wing terrorism in the 21st century. The national socialist underground and the history of terror from the far-right in Germany*. Routledge.

16 Heléne Lööw (2017): "I gränslandet—Symbiosen mellan det organiserade och det oorganiserade". In *Den ensamme terroristen? Om lone wolves, näthat och brinnande flyktingförläggningar*. Edited by H. Lööw, M. Gardell & M. Dahlberg-Grundberg. Ordfront.

17 Daniel Koehler (2019): "Anti-immigration militias and vigilante groups in Germany: an overview". In *Vigilantism against migrant and minorities*. Edited by T. Bjørgo & M. Mareš. Routledge, 86–102.

18 Cf. Esa Aallas (1991): *Somalishokki*. Suomen pakolaisapu.

19 Koehler, 2017.

20 Jacob Aasland Ravndal (2021): "From bombs to books, and back again? Mapping strategies of right-wing revolutionary resistance". *Studies in Conflict & Terrorism*. https//doi.org/10.1080/1057610X.2021.1907897

21 Lööw, 1995.

22 Koehler, 2017.

23 Koehler, 2019.

24 Aallas, 1991.

25 Polamk (2016): Poliisin tietoon tullut viharikollisuus Suomessa 2015. Poliisiammattikorkeakoulun katsauksia 10. *Tampere*. https://urn.fi/URN:ISBN:978-951-815-326-2

26 Teo Keipi, Matti Näsi, Atte Oksanen, & Pekka Räsänen (2017): *Online hate and harmful content: Cross-national perspectives*. Routledge, 64.

27 ibid. 62.

28 ibid. 68.

29 Tuija Saresma, Reeta Pöyhtäri, Aleksi Knuutila et al. (2022): *Verkkoviha Vihapuheen tuottajien ja levittäjien verkostot, toimintamuodot ja motiivit*. Valtioneuvoston selvitys- ja tutkimustoiminnan julkaisusarja 2022, 48. http://urn.fi/URN:ISBN:978-952-383-298-5

30 On similar developments in France and Italy, see Pietro Castelli Gattinara (2018): "Europeans, shut the borders! Anti-refugee mobilization in Italy and France". In *Contentious moves: Solidarity mobilizations in the 'long summer of migration'*. Edited by D. della Porta. Palgrave Macmillan, 271–297. https://doi.org/10.1007/978-3-319-71752-4_10

31 Daniel Sallamaa (2018): *Ulkoparlamentaarinen äärioikeistoliikehdintä ja maahanmuuttovastaisuus 2010-luvun Suomessa* (Publications of the Faculty of Social Sciences of the University of Helsinki 97). University of Helsinki. https://tuhat.helsinki.fi/ws/portalfiles/portal/117656530/Raportti_Sallamaa.pdf, 25.

32 Donatella Della Porta (1995): *Social movements, political violence, and the state: A comparative analysis of Italy and Germany*. Cambridge University Press. https://doi.org/10.1017/CBO9780511527555

33 See e.g. Facebook group Rajat Kiinni Etelä-Pohjanmaa. www.facebook.com/Rajatkiinniep/

34 W. Lance Bennett & Alexandra Segerberg (2012): "The logic of connective action". *Information, Communication & Society*, 15(5), 739–768. https://doi.org/10.1080/1369118X.2012.670661

35 Sallamaa, 2018, 21.

36 Kaisu Kinnunen (2017): *Pelon ja vihan voimalla: Rajat kiinni! -kansanliikkeen suomalaisuuden suojeluun verhottu rasistinen diskurssi vuosina 2015–2017*. Master Thesis in Political Science. University of Jyväskylän. https://jyx.jyu.fi/handle/123456789/56967, 19.2.2021.

37 Ibid., 43–44.

38 Maiju Tuomainen (2016): *The Online network of ethnonationalism: Exploring the discursive frames of the extreme right in Finland*. Master thesis. Lund University. https://lup.lub.lu.se/luur/download?func=downloadFile&recordOId=8878387&fileOId=8878391

39 Itsenäinen Suomi 2015. Archived webpage at https://web.archive.org/web/20151205193037/http://itsenainensuomi2015.fi/tervetuloa-tapahtumamme-kotisivulle/

40 Rajat Kiinni—infopalvelu. Archived webpage at https://web.archive.org/web/20160314201026/http://kansanliike.net/mielenosoituksen-jarjestaminen/

41 About the disintegration of the Rajat Kiinni! community, see Saresma, 2017; Sallamaa, 2018.

42 Rajat kiinni kansanliike. Archived webpage at https://web.archive.org/web/20160106200113/www.rajatkiinni.fi/

43 Saresma Tuija (2016): *'Close the borders!' Affective nationalism in the digital echo-chambers. 7th global conference of space and place.* University of Oxford. www.researchgate.net/publication/328449692_'Close_the_Borders'_Affective_Nationalism_in_Digital_Echo_Chambers

44 Katharina Neumann & Philip Baugut (2017): "In der Szene bist du wie in Trance. Da kommt nichts an dich heran. Entwicklung eines Modells zur Beschreibung von Medieneinflüssen in rechtsextremen Radikalisierungsprozessen". *Studies in Communication | Media*, 6, 39–70. https://doi.org/10.5771/2192-4007-2017-1-39

45 Anna-Marika Aalto (2018): *Suvakkiviha: Rasismia vai naisvihaa?* Master thesis. University of Lapland. https://lauda.ulapland.fi/bitstream/handle/10024/63371/Aalto.Anna-Marika.pdf?sequence=1

46 Matti Pohjonen (2018): *Horizons of hate: A comparative approach to social media hate speech.* © VOX-Pol Network of Excellence. www.voxpol.eu/download/vox-pol_publication/Horizons-of-Hate.pdf

47 ibid. 28.

48 Pohjonen 2018, 32.

49 Cf. Castelli Gattinara, 2018.

50 Cf. Robert J. VandenBerg (2019): "Legitimating extremism: A taxonomy of justifications for political violence". *Terrorism and Political Violence.* https://doi.org/10.1080/09546553.2019.1606800

51 Facebook group Rajat Kiinni!, 12.12.2015.

52 Rauma Police Station, pre-trial investigation 5650-R-13361–16.

53 "Saksassa poltettiin viime yönä pakolaisten hätämajoituskeskus". *MV-lehti*, 20 September 2015. https://mvlehti.net/2015/09/20/saksassa-poltettiin-viime-yona-pakolaisten-hatamajoituskeskus/

54 Kouvola District Court 20.11.2015, judgement 15/150275. Grammar mistakes following the style of the original text.

55 Cf. Wahlström & Törnberg, 2019 on discursive opportunity structures.

56 See Pohjonen, 2018, 33.

57 Ibid., 38.

58 Ylivieska-Raahe District Court, 4.4.2017, judgement in case 17/113988.

59 Oulu Police Station 13.1.2016: Pre-trial investigation file 5770/R/50954/15

60 On the organization, see Tommi Kotonen (2018): "The soldiers of odin in Finland: From local movement to international franchise". In *Vigilantism against migrant and minorities.* Edited by T. Bjørgo & M. Mareš. Routledge.

61 Description of the offense in judgement 21/116066 (20.4.2021), Oulu District Court.

62 Facebook 24.3.2017.

63 Tuomainen, 2016, 41; Saresma et al., 2022, 158.

64 Sallamaa, 2018, 24.

65 Varisverkosto (2017): "Tampereella ei ole tilaa natseille—Natsimarssin tapahtumista". https://varisverkosto.com/2017/10/tampereella-ei-ole-tilaa-natseille-natsimarssin-tapahtumista/

66 Joe Whittaker (2022): "Rethinking online radicalization". *Perspectives on Terrorism*, 16(4), 27–40.

67 cf. Koehler, 2017 and centrality of the Pegida in Germany.

68 Ryan Scrivens, Garth Davies, Tiana Gaudette, & Richard Frank (2022): "Comparing online posting typologies among violent and nonviolent right-wing extremists". *Studies in Conflict & Terrorism.* https://doi.org/10.1080/1057610X.2022.2099269

69 On the different roles of the far-right movement members, see e.g. Stefan Dierbach (2016): "Befunde und aktuelle Kontroversen im Problembereich der Kriminalität und Gewalt von rechts". In *Handbuch rechtsextremismus.* Edited by Fabian Virchow, F., Martin Langebach, & Alexander Häusle. Springer VS. https://doi.org/10.1007/978-3-531-19085-3_15

70 Cf. Müller & Schwarz, 2020, 32.

71 Milla Aaltonen (2019): *Viharikokset käräjäoikeuksissa vuonna 2018*. Oikeusministeriö. https://api.hankeikkuna.fi/asiakirjat/80ac0a59-5434-4983-b89e-e2ab0013ba21/f8cd2930-307a-4c79-9df3-d36defb38e91/MUISTIO_20190524105518.pdf

72 On definitions, see e.g. Hoffman Bruce (2006): *Inside terrorism*. Columbia University Press.

73 Colleen E. Mills, Joshua D. Freilich, & Steven M. Chermak M. (2015): "Extreme hatred: Revisiting the hate crime and terrorism relationship to determine whether they are 'close cousins' or 'distant relatives'". *Crime & Delinquency*, 63(10), 1191–1223.

74 Joe Whittaker (2022): "Rethinking online radicalization". *Perspectives on Terrorism*, 16(4), 71–84.

75 ibid.

26

YOU ARE UN-WELCOME

Caste-based hate speech online

Shivangi Narayan

Introduction

Caste-based discrimination, a major aspect of which is caste-based hate speech and which affects millions of South Asians across the world, is still not on the global list of recognised deviances. According to the report by the International Dalit Solidarity Network (IDSN) on caste hate speech, human rights organisations perpetually overlook this kind of hate speech as a distinctive category of humiliation for Dalits and other affected communities to this day (Shanmugavelan, 2021). This could be because the affected parties are not represented suitably to make a case against this at international or even local South Asian forums. Tech companies are also disproportionately majoritarian—whether it is race or caste—and while race and gender issues are acknowledged and discussed, caste remains invisible. In this chapter, I want to specifically look at caste-based hate speech as experienced by Dalits on the internet. The political assertion of Dalits has resulted in a backlash from the privileged *jati* groups, which has also extended to social media sites where Dalits have carved a space to talk about their discrimination and for assertion of their rights. This chapter looks at this backlash in the form of hate speech through detailed unstructured interviews with 12 participants belonging to Dalit, *Pasmanda Muslim* (Dalit Muslims) and Dalit Christian, *Ravidasi* Sikh (Dalit Sikh) communities.

A background on caste

Caste is a hierarchical division of people in South Asia according to their birth, originally occurring in the Hindu religion (Ambedkar, 2020). The popular version of this division propounds the fourfold classification of people known as the *varna* system, where the population is divided into four groups, *viz*. Brahmin (Clergy), Kshatriya (Warrior), Vaishya (Trader) and Sudra (Service), which practise the norms of purity and pollution amongst each other. However, in reality, the more accurate unit of division of people in South Asia is according to their '*jati*', which is a more localised division occurring at the level of the village community. There are more than 3000 *jatis* in India.

DOI: 10.4324/9781003277675-30

Though both 'Jati' and 'Varna' translate to caste in English, caste does not accurately translate to *jati*. 'Caste' is derived from the Portuguese word 'Casta', which came to India in the 15th century as a tool for the Europeans to understand the natives (Kumar, 2014). Caste denotes a one-person, one-occupation equation such that a person can be either a clergyman or a warrior or a trader or a service person, which is closer to a varna description than a jati description. It does not consider the many functions that one *jati* undertakes in the political economy of a village or the differences between *jatis* that share the same over-arching varna (ibid.). This difference between caste and *jati* needs to be clarified: any kind of 'caste' slurs or insults are directed not at the caste but at the localised *jati* of the person because more often than not, that is the identity people recognise and identify with. It is also because of this very localised existence of *jatis* that their corresponding slurs/insults are not recognised beyond the small radius of jati members or village residents. This becomes especially problematic in an online setting, where the moderators/platform creators might not be aware of such minutiae of social setting or of language and thus would not be aware to moderate it. Lack of representation of Dalits and other discriminated groups, such as Bahujans, Adivasis and minorities in the tech industry adds to this complexity. On the other hand, it is true that *jati* groups, especially those that share one overarching feature, such as a varna, political grouping or a linguistic identity, do come together to assert or identify as one 'caste', such as 'Tamil Brahmins' or Dalits, and are valorised or discriminated as such.

Dalit is a political term which refers to the ex-untouchable *jatis* who were not just considered untouchable but also unseeable (a *savarna*[1] can be ritually polluted by merely seeing such a person) and unapproachable (a *savarna* can be ritually polluted if such a person merely approaches them), who have come together politically to resist discrimination. Though other discriminated jatis, such as those belonging to the Bahujan (Sudra varna) or Adivasis (indigenous people of India) castes also suffer caste-based hate speech online, for this chapter, we will stick to studying the experience of Dalits online.

A number of ex-untouchable jatis converted to various religions such as Islam, Christianity and Sikhism to escape the stigma of their *jati*, but that was not meant to be. Even though division based on birth cannot be found in the scriptures or sacred texts of either Islam, Christianity or Sikhism, *jati*-based discrimination is practised in all three. Hence, in practice 'Dalits' are not only a phenomenon of the Hindu religion but can be found in all religions. In Islam, they are called the *Pasmanda* Muslims, Christian-Dalits in Christianity and *Ravidasi, Raidasi, Ramdasi* and *Mazhabi* Sikhs in Sikhism. The affirmative action or state support in jobs or education is only available to Dalits who were born in the Hindu religion and did not convert to any other religion, except in some cases Sikhism and Neo-Buddhism. Not only are Muslims and Christians devoid of the state's affirmative action to alleviate their condition, but they, along with Sikh Dalits, find it very difficult to even prove the existence of their discrimination because their scriptures do not mention caste-/jati-/varna-based division in their religion (for more discussion on prevalence of caste in religions such as Sikhism, Christianity and Islam and the quest for affirmative action see Samarendra, 2016; Fazal, 2017; Waughray, 2010; Judge, 2002).

Jati-based discrimination is common in India, especially against Dalits. In rural areas it is common for *savarna jati* groups such as Brahmins and Thakurs to unleash violence against Dalits for such acts as riding a horse in their own weddings or keeping a moustache, both markers of high status and thus high caste, and therefore disallowed for Dalits (Siddiqui, 2022). In urban areas, though such kinds of overt discrimination might not be present, lack of access to opportunities in jobs and education and segregation in housing are some of the biggest markers of such prejudice. Violence is also not uncommon in urban areas, where Dalits are routinely beaten or Dalit women raped for what are understood to be minor social infractions (The Indian Express, 2017). *Jati*-based discrimination is practised by South Asians, but it is in no way a phenomenon only concentrated in South Asia. Wherever there are South Asians, there are castes and their ensuing discrimination. Diaspora scholars have argued that Indians carry their caste identity to whichever foreign land they migrate to and that caste exclusion and discrimination is prevalent in the Indian diaspora (Ayyathurai, 2021; Mosse, 2020, Kumar, 2021). Recently, the state of Washington in the United States of America has passed a law banning caste discrimination (Matza, 2023). Clearly, caste is a global problem today, not something that exists only in India. Thus caste-based hate speech needs to be tackled adequately. The first step to doing that is to understand what caste-based hate speech online is.

Caste-based hate speech online

Jati-based hate speech, more commonly known as caste-based hate speech,[2] is defined as:

> any communication form such as speech, writing, behaviour, codes, signs, or memes that manifest hierarchies, invoke humiliation, serve to dehumanise, incite discrimination, degrade self-worth or perpetuate discrimination and are often the sources of physical, mental or material violence to a person or a group based on caste identity.
>
> *(Shanmugavelan, 2021)*

It has been used to vilify and exclude Dalits in real life as well as on the online medium, but it has not found the kind of attention that racial hate speech does. Hate speech against Dalits online is increasing exponentially and has become a cause for violent incidents, along with psychological damage to the members of the community. Though my research and anecdotal evidence shows that caste-based hate speech is increasing online, there was only one news report in 2017 that covered the issue (Agarwal, 2017). Hate speech acts as an amplifier of already existing prejudicial ideas in society, as found in the case of racist hate speech in the US (Bilewicz & Soral, 2020). This would also be true in the case of caste-based hate speech; in an environment of existing discrimination, hate speech only normalises and perpetuates discrimination against Dalits. Even with increasing incidents of caste-based hate speech, especially online, there is very little literature available on the subject, except for reports on caste-based hate speech by IDSN, theCentre for Internet and Society and a few academic articles (Shanmugavelan, 2021; Kain et al., 2022; Sajlan, 2021; Kumbhojkar, 2018). Though Twitter and Facebook recognise caste as a category for reporting online hate speech, it is also true that Facebook in India, according to its own report, did not remove 93 percent of posts that insulted Dalits (among other protected groups) (Rajagopalan, 2019).

In this chapter, I want to turn the spotlight on caste-based hate speech online that Dalits face, not just in India/south Asia but across the world. The report by IDSN (Shanmugavelan, 2021) on caste-based hate speech states that such hate speech works not only to reinforce the subconsciousness of the Dalits in accepting their inferior status as the natural order, but also helps to uphold the supremacy of the upper/*savarna*/dominant jatis. Upper castes, an umbrella term for all *jatis* that occupy a prominent place in the Indian hierarchical classification system, have dominated all forms of public life in India since forever. This has been possible by making education and any kind of social mobility impossible for them for decades. The online sphere is also dominated by the upper castes, with their technological know-how, access to media devices and knowledge of the English language keeping most Dalits away. The handful of Dalits who have been able to use the power of the internet to help other Dalits or politically mobilise based on identity have been attacked to keep their opinions in check, so much so that many of them have stopped interacting on social media completely. I argue that hate speech against Dalits is not just a call for violence or intimidation, but a huge part of it entails excluding them from online spaces where they have freedom to carve a niche for themselves, and can talk about their life experiences and mobilise support for their struggle against the oppressor castes (Singh, 2019).

Methods

This research is the result of data[3] obtained from 12 detailed unstructured interviews with respondents from oppressed communities in India, 10 of whom were Dalits, one of whom was Muslim, one Christian and another from Sikh religions. The remaining two belonged to a jati categorised as 'Other Backward Castes' in India and to Scheduled Tribes. This research incorporates only interviews from 10 Dalit respondents. While the respondents were broadly based in India, two of them were based in New York, USA and in Austria. The fact that they also experienced caste-based hate speech online strengthened our assumption that such hate speech is not just limited geographically to India. The analysis was done thematically. Rather than following an inductive or deductive approach, it follows a mixed approach (Schutt, 2004). I went with the assumption that Dalits face hate speech as a retaliation to their assertion, but I also let the interviews help me discover themes, such as those of overt and covert hate speech.

Jokes, innuendos, ridicule: hate speech before the internet—a case for Dalits in India

Even though hate speech definitions consider tacit psychological harms, it becomes legally punishable only when there is a proven case of tangible physical or mental harms. The Atrocity Act of 1989,[4] directed against hate crimes to those belonging to the scheduled caste[5] (SC) or tribes (ST) in India, recognises physical and psychological harm, it does so with a caveat. The psychological harm is restricted to when the hate crime is committed to an individual. The law does not recognise the psychological harms of hate speech to entire communities and the exclusion they could face due to it. It only punishes when there is evidence of violence due to the speech (Sajlan, 2021). Hate speech, however, just doesn't harm a community physically; the psychological damage on its dignity is well-known.

According to Arendt (1958), without speech, a person or even a community cannot divulge its true identity because they are not allowed to partake in the public sphere. They could then very well be robots performing tasks. Speech, therefore, is essential for human beings to distinguish themselves from humans (not in the sense of becoming the other, as Arendt clarifies, but to become specifically who they are). Hate speech silences people, and by not allowing them to partake in the public sphere, it takes away their ability to express and be who they are. Being invisibilized even when physically present is the highest degree of violence that can be inflicted on anyone.

Understanding hate speech only as a personal insult or only as a harbinger of violence does not explain the ways in which hate speech erodes the self of not just the person against whom the speech is directed but of the community as a whole. This performs the necessary task of keeping such communities away from participating in society and maintaining the hegemony of the oppressor caste. According to Delgado and Stefancic (2019), hate speech is one of the principal ways a race-based society maintains racial hierarchy and keeps the minorities in "their place". The authors argue that it teaches people at large that equality and equal dignity are of little value.

Similarly, Vivek Kumar (2005) notes that ridicule, another form of hate speech, was common to keep the Dalit communities from becoming equal citizens in the society (and continues to be). For example, before independence and even many years after independence, it was normal to not give proper names to Dalit kids. Their names were combinations of abstract words or garbled sounds such as *Dholu Ram* or *Khatpatiya Devi*, names occurring in the Hindi language that have no proper meaning in Hindi. A Dalit giving his child a proper name was unheard of and even frowned upon because only the *savarnas* were allowed to give their kids proper names. In North Indian villages, this is what Dalits (belonging to the *Chamar jati*) would hear if they named their kids with a proper name: "*Bitiya Chamaar ki, naam rajraniya.*" (ibid. 525–526)

This could be translated as: "The daughter of a Chamar (leather tanner) and named *Rajrani* (a name that could be loosely translated to Queen in Hindi)!"

Kumar gives more examples, including another couplet from the religious text of Hindus, 'Ramcharitramanas,' giving this advice: "*Shudra, ganvar, dhor, pashu, nari Yah sab taran ke adhikari.*" (ibid.) (Translated as "Shudras, villagers, ill-mannered, animals, women, All of them need a beating.") Kumar says that more often than not, in the Northern part of India, the *jati* '*Chamar*' and the Hindi word for thief, '*chor*,' were used interchangeably, demonstrating not just the stigma attached to these *jati* names but what they meant for a very local geographical region. This is significant because these local insults/ridicules take the form of hate speech online but are difficult to moderate because many platforms do not even recognise them.

These pejorative names related to *jatis* and the jokes/couplets that policed their everyday behaviour shows how social boundaries were strictly watched over, using ridicule as an effective gatekeeping mechanism to limit the social mobility of Dalits. Kumar gives similar examples for Dalit women wearing shoes or proper dresses showing the extent to which they were denied participating in the social life of the village. Respondents of this research also agreed that they have heard stories of hate speech from their elders and that online speech is still safe compared to what people in certain parts of India suffer in the name of casteism. Being called caste-based slurs as insults is common in urban language in India. A musician in Delhi even named his band using a caste slur, unaware that it was a caste slur until there was a row over an event by the band.[6] The period of 1932–1956, when Dr B R Ambedkar, seen as the leader of the depressed castes (now Dalits), was made a member of the Drafting Committee of India, which was responsible for drafting a constitution for independent India, saw a number of political cartoons in newspapers mocking him (Syama Sundar, 2019). The cartoons upheld the restrictive jati-based hierarchy in India and the functional rhythm of the caste system in India. They mocked Dr Ambedkar for breaking this rhythm, which was the hallmark of Indian life.

Insults and ridicule in real life are directly related to Dalit political assertions. Maharashtra, a state in West of India, is known for producing strong Dalit movements and leaders. One of our respondents from Maharashtra said that he always felt very safe in his class because most of his classmates belonged to his community. There was a power in numbers. However, it was completely different in the online space, where he was constantly harassed by his *savarna jati* classmates and schoolmates. According to this respondent, they posted memes related to Dr Ambedkar and his community online. They also made sure that he noticed these posts by tagging him in them. Dr Ambedkar is a revered figure; in our respondent's words, "almost like a father" to people in Maharashtra. Making jokes about him is akin to making jokes about our father, said our respondent. While our respondent felt that he could tackle such hate speech in the physical space, he did not know how to do that in the online one where there was very little support from the state and platforms themselves.

Dalits have also been called "dirty, drunkard and devoid of merit" in popular language as well as in novels and other literary compositions about them. One of the earliest references for this was in a speech by Annie Besant, quoted by Ambedkar in his original writings and speeches (Ambedkar, 1991). A famous novel about the life and struggles of Dalits, titled 'Beasts of Burden', indicates the normalised correlation between Dalits and this phrase (Imayam, 2019).

One of our respondents said that a number of Dalit kids do not avail reservation, a kind of affirmative action for marginalised castes who are represented according to their population in state-led institutions because of the stigma attached to it. Our respondent agreed that the idea that availing reservation somehow is anti-merit that has been perpetuated by the quote regarding Dalits being 'devoid of merit', and has led a number of Dalits to give up their constitutional right to prove themselves as meritorious. Availing reservation, even with its inefficiencies, has proven to be the most effective tool for social mobility for Dalits, kicking in the gatekeeping proclivities of the upper castes.[7] This got more intense when the Mandal Commission suggested increasing the ceiling of affirmative action to include hitherto unincluded communities that were also underrepresented in state institutions with respect to their populations.[8] States in India saw raging protests from the upper caste student community, a number of whom also attempted (and succeeded in) immolating themselves to register their angst against this constitutional provision (Balagopal, 1990).

As we will see in the next section, abuses regarding reservation have taken on a new life as hate speech on the internet and social media as well. This is one of the most prominent ways that we can see that ridicule and insult in real life has moved over to online life, though of course, online life has given birth to new ways of demeaning and disparaging Dalits.

Caste hate speech and the internet

Mainstream media in India is upper caste (Jeffrey, 2012) and urban, which means that issues related to marginalised populations and rural areas do not get represented there, except when there is a disaster. In this scenario, the internet opens up a democratic space where these sections of populations can express themselves and even organise and agitate against the discrimination meted out to them (Thakur, 2020). Though the internet comes with its own barriers of access to English language education, of infrastructure and of social and cultural capital to use its various sites and offerings, there are enough middle-class Dalits today who can tap into this resource for claiming their rightful place in society without the mediation of upper caste elites. The most significant incident that pushed Dalit activism online was the Rohith Vemula suicide case in 2016.[9] Most respondents called this the most defining moment of online Dalit activism in India and the coming of age of Dalit assertion in India.

However, before the explosion of social media which brought all online communication out into the public domain, the internet was full of closed user groups that attracted closed communications with members who were interested in similar things. One of our respondents said that the early internet interactions were more interesting, as people knew each other:

> That interaction is gone. Now interaction is only within similar caste groups, and inter-caste interaction is limited I would say. Unless you try to abuse someone or piss off someone—that is the only interaction that is left. But earlier I have been a member of many yahoo groups and google groups, around 10 years ago, and interactions there were much more enriching, and discussions were really good, and you could learn things. That has gone missing.

One of our female respondents said that she started writing blogs on the internet, again long before the advent of social media, in the late 90s and early 2000s. She and a male friend started a blog called the "fieryfeministblogpost", where they co-authored "basic feminist pieces . . . (which gave) a rudimentary sort of understanding of feminism". In response, she was called a "sex worker" and her male co-author was termed as her "pimp" in the comments section of the blog, apart from other names and ethnic slurs. "All this as a response to very basic, rudimentary understanding of feminism", she said. She said that at that point in time, they were reluctant to talk about caste so their blogs did not mention caste, but added that anyone could guess the direction those posts would have gone if she had mentioned caste.

The era of groups and forums heralded by such sites as USENET, text and picture-based forums such as 4Chan and AFU, though the innocent beginnings of online community living had their fair share of ugliness. 'Trolling', loosely understood as disruptive behaviour online that would render communication impossible, was a product of this era. This behaviour was more about pranks and tricks, and a performance that sought to entertain as much as enrage, than being about outright slurs and abuse (Kiberd, 2016). However, women-only USENET groups would vouch for abuse on their forums and a denigration of women to secondary users, even on groups about them (Zeavin, 2022, p. 657). Zeavin describes USENET as "frequently racist and hostile".

According to Elyse Graham (2019), trolling started as a strategy of boundary maintenance, i.e. to keep away those who were not privy to the internal codes and communication strategies of the group. It used hostile behaviour, jokes, puns and pranks to keep perceived outsiders away. Trolling fulfils this function and stands as proof of the existence of a boundary. The author agrees that "since its inception, an important function of trolling has been to police online communities and repel perceived outsiders—through either exposure or outright harassment" (Graham, 2019, p. 41).

The outsiders change, depending upon which minority group makes its presence felt on the internet and needs to be driven off, and with it the behaviours encapsulated under the umbrella term 'trolling'. For example, as Graham (2019) says, gaming sites are full of misogyny and rape threats to drive out the women gamers because they are understood as a particularly men-only sphere.[10] Similarly, I would argue that caste hate speech is a particular kind of trolling intended to drive out the Dalits who are now making their presence felt online. While the numbers of Dalits would be low enough to not garner much hate in Yahoo and Google groups, especially if one was not specifically talking about caste, these groups were not without expressing their hate towards Dalits and describing affirmative action (reservation) towards them as "evil" and a "crutch".[11]

The word 'crutch' is used in a pejorative sense, where the author of the post wants to describe those who avail reservation as people who are perpetually dependent on others for survival. Though the word 'reservation' is not a slur, it is used as such on social media platforms against Dalits, indicating the need to clarify the boundaries of those who are meritorious enough to be online and those who merely survive on state support. All 10 Dalit respondents across gender, religion and age agreed that every hate speech against them ended up reminding them about their 'merit', if they were even "worthy" of being online. A Christian Dalit respondent said that even though she had never availed reservation because it was not available for her religion, she was mocked online for being a product of India's affirmative action. Claiming that she never availed reservation only hurts her fellow Dalits, who themselves reel under stigma for the same reasons, she said.

When the Internet came to India (1990s), it was clearly the upper caste who had the means and the skills to explore social media long before Dalits were able to even make a mark there. The Internet also mirrored the social life of India in that it was a closed group where only the *savarnas* had access. Social media was also considered an exclusive space for them, denied to anyone who did not share their values and ethos. One respondent said, (in Hindi), "*Social media ko apni ghodi ya apni moonch samajh baithe hai . . . koi aur na karein istamal jaise yeh karte hai*", which translates to "these people consider social media their moustache or their horse . . . that no one can use it as they do it." The respondent alluded to caste-based practices in India where Dalits, especially in rural India, are not allowed to keep a moustache or ride a horse for their wedding processions, saying that the *savarnas* consider social media platforms as their own exclusive cultural artefacts, inaccessible to everyone else.

One of the respondents said that Dalit participants were at least 10 years late to the social media/online phenomenon in India. He said that when he looked into a sustained campaign on social media site Twitter insulting Ms Mayawati (a four-time woman chief minister of India's largest state by population, Uttar Pradesh, who belonged to the Dalit community), he found out that those tweets were at least 10 years old and that he had a chance to look at them only in the year 2021. He said that the users from socially marginalised castes are very new on the internet, "but this hate is not new, it is a product of a very long time".

This respondent was talking about a casual casteist banter that makes up not just online but offline spaces in India as well, which was normalised online due to lack of resistance. This respondent says that in a casual tweet on a cricket match between India and Pakistan, one of the actresses in the Hindi film industry said, "If India wins, Hina Rabbani is ours (India's) and if Pakistan wins, Mayawati is yours". Giving up on a Dalit woman leader in an event of a loss shows the casual ways in which misogyny and casteism plays out on social media. The respondent said that the replies celebrated the tweet, indicative of the caste and gender character of social media. The increase in numbers of Dalits who can oppose this has led to an increase in hate speech against them online.

If you do oppose such tweets, said a female Dalit respondent, you are attacked with hate speech:

People casually ask us to go and wash shit, and other things that would be punishable in real life[12] but go completely unreported online. (This is the case if you are a Dalit.) If you are a woman then it is twice the slurs, twice the problem.

"What people do offline, they bring online", a respondent said, hinting that prejudice from real life follows them online as well.

In real-life communication, a person is first heard and then seen. This gets turned around in social media where one is first 'seen', as in their presence registered, and then heard (Shepherd et al., 2015). Being 'someone' is therefore important on social media to be able to be heard and considered worthy of being heard. Hate is a low-lying fruit as far as online attention gathering is concerned. In a study on the curation of users' home Feeds in Facebook (Webfoundation, 2018), researchers found that content that garnered more 'emotional responses' was put out first compared to banal updates from their friends and family or other content that would not have an affective response. This was because affect-inducing responses drove more engagement, and more engagement meant more revenue for the users. Registering one's presence online using hate speech is easy because it attracts more eyeballs, both because of its content and the way platforms are designed. Caste is already a volatile topic for South Asians and is easily manipulated to provide instant fame for oppressor castes or *savarnas* online. These people amass hundreds of followers using inflammatory content to rile up their audiences, which gives them a formidable presence on social media platforms. With the current 'influencer' culture, this kind of following can be monetised for significant money/fame. Apart from gatekeeping the Dalits from the online world, *savarnas* also exploit the caste discriminatory system to make their careers online.

Overt vs covert: hate speech is not just slurs

According to Bhikhu Parekh, hate speech doesn't have to be only slurs and slang; "it can be subtle, moderate, non-emotive and even bland, and conveyed through ambiguous jokes, innuendoes and images" (Parekh, 2006, p. 2). However, he goes on to say that every utterance occurs in a particular historical context and becomes meaningful only in that context.

Caste-based hate speech becomes very complex because of the intrinsic involvement of caste with every aspect of South Asian life. And with 19500 languages spoken in India alone as mother tongues (The Indian Express, 2018), hate speech looks very different when one looks beyond the world of commonly known slurs and innuendos.

These commonly used slurs might also be known by the platform moderators and filtered out at the outset. However, there is a world of covert slang, the meanings of which are only known to a small community of people. The probability of these being known by the platform moderation system is negligible; therefore, they escape scrutiny but the harm done is sometimes more than that inflicted by slurs. For example, our Muslim Dalit respondent told us that women from their community are often called *Pasanda* online, which means a kind of a sweet. This is a take on the *Pasmanda* identity of Dalit Muslims. This is a misogynistic take on women (being compared to a sweet), enough to make them feel insulted and diminished. However, as the word is the harmless name of a sweet, the platforms would never know about it to filter it out. In Rajasthan, the local name for onion, *Kanda*, is used to denigrate a *jati* with the same name, as per our respondent. "People think that you are talking about an onion, but you and the person (who belongs to the jati) know what you are talking about", he said. Again, these insults are difficult for the moderating platform to catch and do not attract any attention because they are couched in harmless-sounding words.

One respondent said that *savarna jatis* have also infiltrated platforms such as 'Dank Meme' or 'Ted the Stoner', which are humourous meme pages that poke fun at everyday

479

happenings in the world. "There will be one or two posts insulting Dalits in the entire lot, which would be difficult to find, but we know that it is there. People think it is harmless because there are just one or two posts", she said. She said that the posts hide amongst the volume of thousands of posts on the site but perform their designated task of hate speech. Another respondent said that a lot of fake news and misinformation also circulates on social media, which makes life miserable for Dalits, but that there is no accountability.

Even the word "reservation" is not itself a slur and is not something that would be termed insulting by the moderation system of a platform. However, as mentioned earlier, this word is used most frequently to make Dalits feel as if they do not deserve their education/job/life. Different versions of this word, like 'quota', used in the sense of a certain quota of seats kept aside for Dalits, is used to mock those receiving these benefits from the government. Again, these words are unrecognisable as hate speech or even as an insult or derision on the internet.

Our respondent said that denial of caste-based discrimination, dismissive of the pain and suffering of Dalits and of atrocities committed against them, propagating stereotypes, are also forms of hate speech and should be considered as such. For another respondent, YouTube lessons on Hindu Dharma, in which the caste system is described as a functional system that keeps the village society in order (thus negating experiences of those out of such a society), is also a kind of hate speech, though again there is no foul language involved. More than insulting language or derogatory memes directed at their icons or caste location, respondents veered towards being made to feel "unwanted" on platforms. One respondent said that once she read a joke where the 'D' in Dalit was replaced with a 'B', so Dalit became 'Balit'. The joke continued with a question: "What is the difference between a stick and Balit Girl? One is roasted before something and another is roasted after". The joke alluded to the rape and murder of a Dalit girl in the Indian state of Uttar Pradesh, who was then secretly cremated by the state police to escape the media furore (Ara, 2020). The respondent said that they (the *savarna* crowd) change a letter here and there to escape scrutiny from moderation and covertly direct their attacks to their intended audience. I would add that such jokes do not even have to be understood by all but just the targeted population; they do not overtly insult but can make their targeted audience uncomfortable enough to leave social media entirely.

Caste is a club: a case for prohibition and moderation of caste-based hate speech

One of the primary objectives of this chapter was to educate academics and technologists about the existence of caste-based hate speech online. While hate speech and discrimination on the basis of race or gender or sexual orientation has been written about and discussed at great length in academia, the discussion on caste-based hate speech is still in its infancy. The legislation on caste-based discriminations in different states of the USA has woken up academia about the presence and persistence of this problem, which had been considered an issue belonging to the past in villages in India. It was not an urban phenomenon, certainly not amongst the 'educated' or people living in cities. This chapter counters all such assumptions to demonstrate the existence of caste-based discrimination and resultant hate speech as very much present on the internet.

This chapter also aimed to contribute to the nuances of caste-based hate speech and to inform about the difficulties in moderating such speech online and its impact on Dalits across the world. By showing the continuities of the physical world with the digital world and demonstrating how caste injustices follow the digital world from the physical, it makes the case of how injustices in the online world cannot be mitigated in a vacuum. To moderate caste-based hate speech online, one has to understand how it works in the physical world.

For starters, *Jati* identity is visible in one's name and hence is a very prominent part of one's identity. As one of our respondents said, "My last name is my clan name. People know who I am from my name". What he meant was that people not only know his clan name but also the fact that he is ripe for insults and jokes. That there is little or no support or protection at his disposal. That most of the time he would have no recourse but to bear it. It needs to be reiterated that the caste system as a whole is not just a discriminatory system, which means that it does not stop at everyday discrimination. Those at the top form a kind of a closed system with their own language, culture, dress code and food. The social, cultural and economic capital is earned per generation and cannot be amassed in a single or even in two or three generations.

For example, a Dalit respondent from a rural background, who came to study in the big city of Delhi (India's capital city), said that it was only in Delhi that he realised that it was the lower-caste women from poor families who wore flashy, colourful clothes. It was common knowledge amongst the upper-caste insiders to wear understated, sombre clothes. So was the case with language or food. He realised that even if he did not talk about his caste or kept it hidden from others, it was visible in his food and clothing and entertainment choices:

> I changed the colour of my clothes and started wearing only blues and whites. I read all the classic English texts. Listened to the music. But once when I was going back home and our bus stopped at a highway rest stop, a lady stopped me from using the community hand pump for drinking water. She knew my caste by my face. That was when I realised who I am kidding, this is who I am, this is who I will remain.

The discourse surrounding the caste system diminishes kids from a young age. If they are in a rural setting, they may face very obvious discriminatory actions such as being beaten up for drinking from the community well or not standing up when a village elder (from the *savarna* caste) turns up. At the time of writing this chapter, in August 2022, a child was beaten to death for drinking water from the vessel meant for *savarnas* in his school in Rajasthan, India (The Wire, 2022). In an urban setting, the exclusion might be slow and subtle, such as bypassing Dalits for promotions or not hiring them at all. In both cases, the oppressor castes, the *savarna jatis*, make sure that Dalits do not forget their station in life and remain oppressed forever. As I have mentioned before, the caste system works like an efficient gatekeeping mechanism for the *savarnas* and hence works to reproduce privilege, while resources and knowledge are kept hidden behind culture and customs to only be used by *savarna* kids. In such a scenario, a Dalit is questioned for their merit if they are able to make it in life. Caste-based hate speech replicates these gatekeeping mechanisms online, so that a space where Dalits could congregate without fear and express themselves freely has quickly started resembling their physical lives.

This chapter makes it clear that hate speech based on caste is not just a debate on free speech but a case against the dignity and human rights of Dalits. In India, the Prevention of Atrocity Law of 1989[13] is a formidable law against caste-based discrimination in India. However, it has no jurisdiction online. Respondents for this research said that they had all reported caste-based hate speech on various platforms but have never gotten a successful resolution. As mentioned earlier, most hate speech is so local (that only few people understand what it means) and so banal that it is difficult to prove it as hate speech. One of our respondents was working with Twitter/X (before it was bought by Musk) to help the organisation understand the nuances of caste-based hate speech in India, but the battle is a long way uphill, she said.

The business of technology across the world, including platforms, is dominated by White (racially) and *savarna* (caste) engineers, policy makers and moderators who do not understand (or want to understand) caste-based hate speech at a granular level. A granular-level understanding of caste hate speech would include diversifying these organisations to include representatives from the Dalit *jatis* across India, along with recording the different forms of caste-based hate speech in every corner of the country. Until then, communities will keep being insulted and ridiculed on the internet for merely existing.

Notes

1 In Hindi, adding the prefix '*sa*' to the word '*varna*' results in '*savarna*' Hindi, which is a word for those jatis who are attached to the first three varnas in the varna classification. These are upwardly mobile jatis who have amassed cultural, social and economic capital in India and have the maximum representation in state institutions. The prefix '*a*' to '*varna*' denotes the lack of a respectable varna or a *varna* essentially. '*Avarna*' is used to denote the bahujan and untouchable jatis.

2 Considering the differences between caste and jati are not explicitly understood in most literature on caste, caste-based hate speech is the most commonly understood phrase for jati-based hate speech. In this chapter, caste-based hate speech and jati-based hate speech would mean the same.

3 This data was also used to produce the Centre for Internet Society (CIS), India's report on caste-based hate speech, titled Online Caste-Based Hate Speech: Pervasive Discrimination and Humiliation on Social Media, authored by Damni Kain, Shivangi Narayan, Torsha Sarkar and Gurshabad Grover

4 Atrociety Act full text in English https://socialjustice.gov.in/writereaddata/UploadFile/The%20 Scheduled%20Castes%20and%20Scheduled%20Tribes.pdf accessed 11 April 2024.

5 'Scheduled Caste' (SC) is a legal category in India, along with Scheduled Tribes (ST) and Other Backward Caste (OBC). These categories were created by the British to include the most vulnerable sections of society to provide concessions and affirmative action. See Dushkin, 1967.

6 A Delhi Jazz club hosted a band with a name "Bhangi Jumping", where *Bhangi* is literally the name of one of the most oppressed *jatis* in India and used as a slur in the Hindi-speaking belt of North India. The band and the club feigned ignorance to the name or that it was used as a slur. www.thequint.com/news/india/piano-man-jazz-club-bhangijumping-controversy accessed 17 August 2022.

7 Reservation is not a foolproof method for affirmative action, as we have seen that a number of institutions, including the Delhi Police, do not offer reservations in hiring or selection of candidates in educational institutions. See Status of Policing of India Report 2019 for Delhi Police and affirmative action. Newspapers reported that a premier university in India did not honour the mandated reservation policy in higher education www.thehindu.com/news/cities/Delhi/jnu-v-c-following-anti-reservation-policy/article23409484.ece accessed 18 August 2022.

8 Mandal Commission was set up in 1979 to investigate and formulate a plan regarding the representation of *jatis* categorised as 'other backward castes' (OBCs) in India in government institutions and jobs. The report was released in 1980 and proposed increasing the ceiling of reservation to 50 percent, with a 27 percent reservation (correlated to population of the OBCs) to OBC *jatis*. See: Engineer, 1991; Maheshwari, 1991.

9 Rohith Vemula, a Dalit PhD student from the Indian state of Andhra Pradesh, died by suicide on January 16, 2017. Vemula was forced to take this extreme step because of extreme caste discrimination on the University of Hyderabad campus where he was a student. His monthly grad stipend

of Rs 25,000 was stopped and he was even evicted from his hostel on the complaint of an Indian right-wing student body called *Akhil Bhartiya Vidhyarthi Parishad* (ABVP). His suicide note became a strong indictment of the state of Dalits and Dalit students in India and spurned nationwide protests from Dalit bodies. See https://thewire.in/caste/rohith-vemula-letter-a-powerful-indictment-of-social-prejudices accessed 22 August 2022.

10 See also Gamergate, www.washingtonpost.com/news/the-intersect/wp/2014/10/14/the-only-guide-to-gamergate-you-will-ever-need-to-read/ accessed 29 July 2022.

11 This Reddit thread from 11 years ago (29 July 2022), talks about caste-based reservation (affirmative action) as crutches and doles handed out by the government; www.reddit.com/r/IAmA/comments/ot8ox/iama_higher_caste_indian_ama/ accessed 29 July 2022.

12 As per the Indian Atrocity Act of 1989 (see note 4) where discriminatory language, insult and derogatory language against Dalits (individuals) is punishable even if there is no evidence of physical violence.

13 See note 4.

References

Agarwal, D. (2017, July 15). Casteist remarks on social media now punishable: What fighting online hate speech in India entails. *Firstpost*. Retrieved from www.firstpost.com/india/casteist-remarks-on-social-media-now-punishable-what-fighting-online-hate-speech-in-india-entails-3815175.html

Ambedkar, B. R. (1991). *What congress and Gandhi have done for the untouchables*. Government of Maharashtra.

Ambedkar, B. R. (2020). *Caste in India their mechanism, genesis and development*. Neha Publishers & Distributors.

Ara, I. (2020, October 28). Hathras gang-rape and murder case: A timeline. *The Wire*. Retrieved from https://thewire.in/women/hathras-gang-rape-and-murder-case-a-timeline

Arendt, H. (1958). *The human condition* (Charles R. Walgreen Foundation Lectures). University of Chicago Press.

Ayyathurai, G. (2021). Emigration against caste, transformation of the self, and realization of the casteless society in Indian Diaspora. *Essays in Philosophy*, 22(1), 45–65. https://doi.org/10.5840/eip20212194

Balagopal, K. (1990). This anti-mandal mania. *Economic and Political Weekly*, 25(40), 2231–2234.

Bilewicz, M., & Wiktor, S. (2020). Hate speech epidemic. The dynamic effects of derogatory language on intergroup relations and political radicalization. *Political Psychology*, 41(S1), 3–33. https://doi.org/10.1111/pops.12670

Delgado, R., & Stefancic, J. (2019). *Understanding words that wound*. Routledge. https://doi.org/10.4324/9780429503351

Dushkin, L. (1967). Scheduled caste policy in India: History, problems, prospects. *Asian Survey*, 7(9), 626–636. https://doi.org/10.2307/2642619

Engineer, A. A. (1991). *Mandal commission controversy*. Ajanta Publications.

Fazal, T. (2017). Scheduled castes, reservations and religion: Revisiting a juridical debate. *Contributions to Indian Sociology*, 51(1), 1–24. https://doi.org/10.1177/0069966716680429

Graham, E. (2019). Boundary maintenance and the origins of trolling. *New Media & Society*, 21(9), 2029–2047. https://doi.org/10.1177/1461444819837561

Imayam. (2019). *Beasts of burden* (L. Holmstrom (trans.)). Niyogi Books Pvt. Ltd.

The Indian Express. (2017, December 4). Unequal spaces. *The Indian Express*. Retrieved from https://indianexpress.com/article/opinion/editorials/ncrb-dalit-caste-crime-sp-bsp-unequal-spaces-4966441/

The Indian Express. (2018, July 1). More than 19,500 mother tongues spoken in India: Census. *The Indian Express*. Retrieved from https://indianexpress.com/article/india/more-than-19500-mother-tongues-spoken-in-india-census-5241056/

Jeffrey, R. (2012, April 12). Missing from the Indian newsroom. *The Hindu*. Retrieved from www.thehindu.com/opinion/lead/missing-from-the-indian-newsroom/article62114053.ece

Judge, P. S. (2002). Religion, caste, and communalism in Punjab. *Sociological Bulletin*, 51(2), 175–194. https://doi.org/10.1177/0038022920020202

Kain, D., Shivangi, N., Torsha, S., & Gurshabad, G. (2021). Online caste based hate speech: Pervasive discrimination and humiliation on social media. *Centre for Internet and Society*. Retrieved from https://cis-india.org/internet-governance/blog/online_caste-hate_speech.pdf

Kiberd, R. (2016, July 8). Twenty years ago, trolling was repeatedly posting "Meow" in usenet groups. *Vice*. Retrieved from www.vice.com/en/article/78k4g4/twenty-years-ago-trolling-was-repeatedly-posting-meow-in-usenet-groups

Kumar, V. (2005). Situating dalits in Indian sociology. *Sociological Bulletin, 54*(3), 514–532.

Kumar, V. (2014). Caste and democracy in India: A perspective from below. Gyan Publishing House.

Kumar, V. (2021). Different shades of caste among the Indian diaspora in the US. *Transience, 12*(1).

Kumbhojkar, S. (2018). Dalits, internet and emancipatory politics. *Revista Científica Arbitrada de La Fundación MenteClara, 3*(April). https://doi.org/10.32351/rca.v3.1.42

Maheshwari, S. (1991). *The mandal commission and mandalisation: A critique*. Concept Publishing Company.

Matza, M. (2023, February 22). Seattle becomes first US city to ban caste discrimination. *BBC News*. Retrieved from www.bbc.com/news/world-us-canada-64727735

Mosse, D. (2020). Outside caste? The enclosure of caste and claims to castelessness in India and the United Kingdom. *Comparative Studies in Society and History, 62*(1), 4–34. https://doi.org/10.1017/S0010417519000392

Parekh, B. (2006). Hate speech. *Public Policy Research, 12*(4), 213–223. https://doi.org/10.1111/j.1070-3535.2005.00405.x

Rajagopalan, M. (2019, June 12). Facebook failed to delete 93% of posts containing speech violating its own rules in India. *BuzzFeed News*. Retrieved from www.buzzfeednews.com/article/meghara/facebook-india-hate-speech-equality-labs

Sajlan, D. (2021). Hate speech against dalits on social media: Would a penny sparrow be prosecuted in India for online hate speech? *CASTE/A Global Journal on Social Exclusion, 2*(1), 77–96. https://doi.org/10.26812/caste.v2i1.260

Samarendra, P. (2016). Religion and scheduled caste status. *Economic and Political Weekly, 51*(31), 13–16.

Schutt, R. K. (2004). *Investigating the social world: The process and practice of research* (4th ed.). Pine Forge Press. Retrieved from https://search.library.wisc.edu/catalog/999978763602121

Shanmugavelan, M. (2021). Caste hate speech: Addressing hate speech based on work and decent. *International Dalit Solidarity Network*. Retrieved from https://idsn.org/wp-content/uploads/2021/03/Caste-hate-speech-report-IDSN-2021.pdf

Shepherd, T., Alison, H., Tim, J., Sam, S., & Kate, M. (2015). Histories of hating. *Social Media + Society, 1*(2), 2056305115603997. https://doi.org/10.1177/2056305115603997

Siddiqui, I. (2022, January 25). In MP, dalit groom rides horse; Home attacked, Fir lodged. *The Indian Express* (blog). Retrieved from https://indianexpress.com/article/cities/bhopal/in-mp-dalit-groom-rides-horse-home-attacked-fir-lodged-7739982/

Singh, A. (2019, November 18). Social media has reshaped caste mobilisation. *Hindustan Times*. Retrieved from www.hindustantimes.com/columns/social-media-has-reshaped-caste-mobilisation/story-Hw1GIDJdCyZEWdliySowpJ.html

Sundar, U. S. (2019). *No laughing matter: The Ambedkar cartoons, 1932–1956*. Navayana.

Thakur, A. K. (2020). New media and the dalit counter-public sphere. *Television & New Media, 21*(4), 360–375. https://doi.org/10.1177/1527476419872133

Waughray, A. (2010). Caste discrimination and minority rights: The case of India's dalits. *International Journal on Minority and Group Rights, 17*(2), 327–353. https://doi.org/10.1163/157181110X495926

Webfoundation.org. (2018). *The invisible curation of content: Facebook's news feed and our information diets*. Web Foundation.

The Wire. (2022). Rajasthan: Nine-yr-old dalit boy passes away after alleged assault by schoolteacher. *The Wire*. Retrieved from https://thewire.in/caste/rajasthan-nine-yr-old-dalit-boy-passes-away-after-alleged-assault-by-schoolteacher (accessed 10 May 2023).

Zeavin, H. (2022). "This is womenspace": USENET and the fight for a digital backroom, 1983–86. *Technology and Culture, 63*(3), 634–664. https://doi.org/10.1353/tech.2022.0104

27

WHAT HAPPENS ON THE DIGITAL STREET, STAYS ON THE DIGITAL STREET? AN EXAMINATION OF PROVOCATIONS, THREATS, AND BEEFS IN THE ONLINE DRILL CULTURE IN ROTTERDAM

Robert A. Roks and Jeroen van den Broek

Introduction

In *The Digital Street*, Jeffrey Lane (2019, p. ix) documents how street life has "decoupled from its geographic location to split along the physical street and the digital street". Nowadays, experiences of youngsters get filtered through digital technology, resulting in the co-creation of the street code in physical and digital spaces. To date, studies have examined the integration of the internet and social media into street gang life (for a review, see Pyrooz & Moule, 2019; Moore & Stuart, 2022), concluding that for street-oriented persons, the digital street may now be "as meaningful and consequential as the physical street" (Lauger & Densley, 2018, p. 817). Lane (2019), for instance, describes how youngsters nowadays navigate both the physical and digital street which affects and sometimes alters the enactment of gender roles, code-switching, and the ways formal and informal control impact the (digital) lives of youngsters.

Urban violence is also one of the issues that is impacted by the rise of digital technologies, resulting in what Lane (2019) has called the digitization of the 'code of the street' (Anderson, 1999) or, in the words of Forrest Stuart (2020b) the "code of the Tweet". Although the relationship between urban violence and social media has gained increased scholarly attention (for an overview see Moore & Stuart, 2022), the research to date has been "surprisingly slow to disentangle the empirical relationship between violence and social media" (Lane & Stuart, 2022, p. 2). According to Lane and Stuart (2022, p. 2), the available studies seem to concur that "social media provide new and additional avenues for challenging rivals, displaying toughness, and building street cred". The debate, however, centers on the

DOI: 10.4324/9781003277675-31

question to what extent these acts of violence of the digital street spill onto physical streets and result in real life violence. Some scholars suggest "that social media play a causal role in exacerbating violence", whereas others are more skeptical about the role of social media in amplifying physical violence (Lane & Stuart, 2022, p. 2).

The issue of the relationship between social media usage and urban violence is at the heart of current public concerns about drill music, a subgenre of gangsta rap known for its hyperbolic communication of violence in music videos and other social media uploads (Stuart, 2020a, 2020b). Since its origin on the streets of Chicago (Stuart, 2020a, 2020b), drill music has spread to the UK (Fatsis, 2019; Ilan, 2020) and the European continent (Roks & Van den Broek, 2020). Since 2019, two violent incidents in the Netherlands—the death of 18-year-old Jay-Ronne Grootfaam, who was killed in the South-East of Amsterdam in September 2019, and 19-year-old Cennethson Janga from Rotterdam, who was stabbed to death in August 2020 on the pier of Scheveningen—have stirred up public concerns about the relationship between the growing popularity of drill music and youth violence, epitomized by headlines like "*Is drill music behind the recent wave of youth violence?*" (Bahara, 2019) and "*Whoever kills, scores in drill music*" (Bos & Van der Poel, 2020).

In this chapter, we aim to add to the academic debate on the relationship between urban violence and social media by drawing on a netnographic study into the online drill culture in Rotterdam. The term netnography was introduced to capture the application of the central principle of ethnographic research of *being there* to the study of digital data shared on the internet (Kozinets, 2002; Kozinets, 2015, p. 79; Costello et al., 2017). Using what Urbanik and Roks (2020, pp. 218–220) call the one-way-mirror approach (2020, pp. 218–220), we observed the digital content produced or shared by over 100 drillers from Rotterdam. We started our netnographic study by searching for drill music from Rotterdam on YouTube, Instagram, Telegram and Snapchat. In addition to watching video clips and other online content about drill in Rotterdam, we made an overview of Rotterdam drillers who were active on social media. In March 2020, we created the @*Crimin010gen* account on Instagram and Snapchat. In the bios of these accounts, we shared information about who we were, where we work and what our research was about. With these accounts we started following various drillers from Rotterdam, first by using our overview of drillers from Rotterdam and later by using search terms like 'drill' combined with 'Rotterdam'. Finally, we also added drillers we frequently encountered on the accounts we already followed.

In this way, we followed a total of 137 accounts on Instagram and 28 via Snapchat. Moreover, we participated in seven Telegram groups relevant to our research and manually checked several dozen YouTube channels. Twice a day—once at the beginning of the morning and once at the end of the evening—we made a digital tour of all the digital respondents and groups. We reviewed all the new online content and took screenshots of the posts that were relevant to our investigation; for instance, posts about music, drillers' involvement in phishing or narcotics sales via social media and conflicts between (rival) drillers. By immersing ourselves in the digital world of drill in Rotterdam twice a day, we gradually got to know and understand this online culture better. In total, we carried out netnographic fieldwork for seven months (between March and September 2020) and during that period we collected approximately 2,600 screenshots and videos that document the online behavior of Rotterdam drillers on social media (Roks & Van den Broek, 2020, pp. 154–160). Most of the empirical material presented in this chapter is based on the social media posts of a dozen drillers from Rotterdam and Amsterdam.

We begin this chapter with an overview of literature on the relationship between urban violence and social media. In the remainder of this chapter, we provide a thick description of the online drill rap culture in Rotterdam, an in-depth and detailed delineation of this context (Geertz, 1973). In our conclusion, we reflect on the meaning of our results in respect to the (changing) dynamics of violence by young people who navigate online and offline spaces.

Urban violence and social media

A growing body of literature examines the relationship between social media and violence (for an overview see Peterson & Densley, 2017; Irwin-Rogers et al., 2018; Moore & Stuart, 2022). The term cyber-violence—one of Wall's (2001) cybercrime typologies—is used to capture the ways individuals can cause harm in real or virtual environments, whereas street cultural acts of online violence have been colloquially coined "cyberbanging" (Haut, 2014) or "internet banging" (Patton et al., 2013). Because "cyber violence can lead to similar levels of fear and distress as real-world violence" (Peterson & Densley, 2017, p. 194), social media appears to be an effective tool for street-oriented people. To date, studies have documented how gang members use social media to challenge rival groups to violent confrontations, but also to harass and threaten others (Deuchar & Holligan, 2010; Pyrooz et al., 2015; Patton et al., 2016; Patton et al., 2017).

Some of the functionalities of social media facilitate traditional street cultural practices. Since posts on social media do not automatically include locations, individual users can decide whether and how they want to share information about their whereabouts. With the act of "spatial referencing" Patton et al. (2017, p. 1011) note how "gang-involved youth often referenced their location in home territory as a boast and/or challenge to rivals", but "they also stated opponents' geographic locations and disdain for those areas". Furthermore, symbolic acts like "incursion into rival territory" (Moule et al., 2017, p. 53) have an online equivalent in "spatial referencing". On blogs, Van Hellemont (2012) found "momentary captures of real life events" (Van Hellemont, 2012, p. 177), as youth uploaded pictures of themselves with the name sign of subway stations that were claimed by rival crews (Van Hellemont, 2012, pp. 175–176). Similarly, Patton et al. (2016, p. 594) note how "with social media platforms, youth can enter into rival gang territory and disrespect rivals' gang symbols without being witnessed—but still advertise this action as a threat" (Patton et al., 2016, p. 594). Nowadays, gang members can also post pictures on social media (pretending) to be hanging out on rival turf, including either real geotags or referencing fake locations (Stuart, 2020a, 2020b). Social media thus offers opportunities to threaten and challenge rivals without the immediate threat of violent retaliation such as during physical threats (Patton et al., 2017, p. 1012).

However, some aspects of internet banging move beyond merely challenging rivals on social media. For instance, Johnson and Schell-Busey (2016, p. 73) illustrate that for gang members, rap music and social media functions as "a new bottle for old messages": it is used to exchange threats with rival gangs, often resulting in increasingly violent back-and-forth retaliations. During threats of violence, or proactive acts of violence (Patton et al., 2017, p. 1007), gang members tend to reference the use of firearms to demonstrate a certain willingness to defend oneself or the group at all costs against outside attacks (Patton et al., 2017, p. 1008). Furthermore, gang members also utilize thoughtfully used emoji to imply a threat: "a gun pointed at an angry face, which could be interpreted as a murder; and a car and a bag of money, which may also suggest how and why this murder will occur" (Patton et al., 2017, p. 1008). However, threats also appear more subtle and may not be readily decipherable to outsiders, for example because gang members use deliberate emojis to communicate a threat (Patton et al., 2017, p. 1008).

Parallel to the street cultural acts of impression management online, some elements of internet banging remain analogous to violent acts on the physical streets (Haut, 2014; Lane, 2019), but there are some consequential differences. Social media platforms might provide ways to threaten or challenge rivals "without the immediate threat of violent retribution (e.g. shooting, stabbing, physical fighting) present in face-to-face neighborhood challenges" (Patton et al., 2017, p. 1012). Violent acts that do occur on the physical streets might also end up on the digital street. For instance, Irwin-Rogers et al. (2018, p. 404) state that videos and photographs of real-life incidents of serious violence are recorded and broadcasted online, "often involving additional acts of humiliation, for example, stripping the victim of their clothes or coercing them into denouncing their own gang". The potential virality of this digital or digitized violent content, where "people can be called out in front of thousands of far-flung audience members" (Urbanik & Haggerty, 2018, p. 1356), increases the rewards for posting, but also "can impose further social pressure on the gang member(s) being victimised or targeted to retaliate" (Irwin-Rogers et al., 2018, p. 406). Consecutive proactive and reactive acts of violence (Patton et al., 2017, p. 1007) lead to "vicious online-offline violence" (Irwin-Rogers et al., 2018, p. 404). However, these changing dynamics between violence on the physical and digital street might not just accelerate the process of conflicts; it can also result in an amplification of violence (Lane, 2019, p. xi).

Much of the available research identifies social media as a catalyst, vector or trigger for physical violence (Patton et al., 2013; Lauger & Densley, 2018; Moule et al., 2017; Irwin-Rogers et al., 2018; Urbanik & Haggerty, 2018). In these studies, the emphasis seems to be on the difference between so-called networked publics—a term referring to the ways (young) people's peer worlds are embedded in social media (boyd, 2014, pp. 11–14)—and traditional physical public spaces. Four affordances tend to shape the mediated environments created by social media: digital content is more persistent, visible to a larger audience, easily spreadable and searchable. Online violent displays, therefore, have the potential to reach a large audience of friends, rivals and outsiders, and thereby potentially impact real-world violent outcomes, but also dynamics of violence. In this line of thought, Stuart (2020b) signals a theoretical perspective of parallelism. By conceptualizing social media as a new or additional staging areas for (group) rivalries (Anderson, 1999, p. 77), the expectation is that online expressions of violence will amplify violence. However, studies note that social media might provide new opportunities for de-escalating or avoiding offline violence (Urbanik & Haggerty, 2018, Lane, 2019; Stuart, 2020a, 2020b; Lane & Stuart, 2022).

Stuart (2020a, 2020b) is the first scholar to date to shed light on the empirical reality of violence in the digital era. Based on ethnographic research, Stuart documents how young people use social media and how this impacts the origin and development of conflicts. His work highlights how young people who navigate both the physical and the digital street are increasingly aware of the performativity of online behavior. This specifically becomes apparent in young people's attempts to create "context collapse" (boyd, 2014): "to disrupt the key impression management practices associated with the 'code of the street'" (Stuart, 2020b, p. 192). Stuart (2020b, p. 192) discerns three strategies used by young people to "publicly invalidate the authenticity of their rivals' performances of toughness, strength, and street masculinity". "Cross referencing"—the first and easiest and most prevalent strategy—refers to "the process whereby challengers scrutinize and contradict their targets' online claims of violence by calling audience attention to past online content or private information that might otherwise go unnoticed" (Stuart, 2020b, p. 198). The second strategy—"calling bluffs"—sees young people openly challenging or daring their rivals "to act in accordance with their online claims of violence" (Stuart, 2020b, p. 198). "'Catching lacking' represents the last strategy employed by young people to exploit context collapse. This strategy entails confronting someone in non-gang-related social contexts (e.g., at work, at school, running errands with family), engaged in non-gang-related social roles and behaviors" (Stuart, 2020b, p. 199).

Each strategy differs in its likelihood to result in real life violence, with "catching lacking" running the highest risk of a violent conflict because of the possibility of a physical confrontation between rivals. However, as Stuart (2020b, p. 204) and Ilan (2020) stress, social media content makes it impossible to infer whether physical violence is imminent, because outsiders often lack the "street literacy" (Ilan, 2020) necessary to understand and interpret digital street content. Contrary to popular belief, the work of Stuart (2020a, 2020b) concludes that the majority of social media challenges remain confined to online spaces. In the majority of cases, online provocations are restored in non-violent ways. In a recent article, Lane and Stuart (2022) also stress the way social media offers new possibilities to de-escalate or avoid violent challenges.

Drill, violence and social media in Rotterdam

In the remainder of this chapter, we zoom in on the online drill culture in Rotterdam. First, we illustrate how the drillers in our study use social media and rap music videos on YouTube and Instagram to insult, challenge and threaten their rivals (or "opps"). Secondly, we zoom in on the ways the Rotterdam drillers actively contest each other's credibility as drillers, for instance by sharing compromising information about their rivals on social media. Thirdly, we provide an overview of the different types of beefs and provocations we came across in our research, with a specific focus on the online-offline dynamics in these group conflicts. It should be noted that the number of beefs that result in physical violence in our study is limited to a few cases, with the deadly stabbing incident on the pier of Scheveningen in August 2020 as the most striking example.

Digital provocations

Studies have illustrated how gang members use social media to provoke rival groups into violent confrontations (Deuchar & Holligan, 2010; Pyrooz et al., 2015; Patton et al., 2016, 2017; Lynes et al., 2020). Our empirical material also includes several examples where social media is used to challenge rivals. One example sees drillers photographing or filming themselves or their friends while they are on the territory of a rival group, a practice referred to as "opp block" in the drill culture, reflecting the postal code wars described in UK drill (Ilan, 2020, p. 12). For this practice, drillers use the same social media functionalities to signal that they are on their own "block" or in their own neighborhood, including the use of geotags to pinpoint their location or the use of specific filters.

Although these examples are meant as provocations, we found various examples that showcase that the presence of rivals on drillers turf is not always perceived as serious or threatening. For example, a driller from Amsterdam stated he was in Rotterdam by sending a direct message with photos from the local neighborhood to a rival driller from Rotterdam. On the shared screenshot, the driller from Rotterdam—who posted the screenshot on Instagram—added the comment: "*Yes, everyone is posted on the block at 6 o'clock in the morning*", indicating that he did not take the presence of a rival driller on his block in the early hours of the day that seriously.

In line with documenting being present *opp block* at times of day when rivals are unlikely to be nearby, we see other examples that highlight the symbolic nature of these digital provocations. For instance, we came across drillers who filmed or photographed themselves—sometimes while wearing a hoodie—in a moving car, while driving through rival territory, also limiting the chance of an actual violent confrontation. This is also apparent in a practice called "*Snap and go*", where young people give the impression that they have been on their rival's turf, but only for a very short period to take a photo. Afterwards, and often at a safe distance, they posted on social media that they were *opp block*.

In response to these symbolic provocations, our empirical data also contains a few examples where drillers call out their rivals to meet them in their neighborhood at a specific moment, like the following message on social media from a driller from Rotterdam: "*Come and get me at [street name], you know where I am*". We also came across posts on social media that are a lot more specific than the aforementioned examples. For instance, a driller from Amsterdam shared a private conversation on Snapchat with a rival from Rotterdam. The latter had sent him the following message: "*Don't chat much, come!*", mirroring the calling bluff strategy documented by Stuart (2020b, p. 198). However, the Amsterdam driller did not respond to this invitation by going to Rotterdam; instead, he shared his own whereabouts on social media, including his house number and zip code, and added the message: "*I am standing right here, don't chat much!! Call when you get here!!*"

During our digital fieldwork, we found one example of a driller responding to digital provocation. During a conflict with a rapper from the south of the country, the bluff of the driller from Rotterdam was called as he was challenged to meet up with his rival in his hometown. The driller from Rotterdam placed a series of videos online, documenting the search for his rival. In the first video, he sits in the passenger seat of a car and states, while filming his whereabouts:

Look, you are not even here bro, you are not here! Back the car up a bit, back it up, back it up, back it up. This fucking son of a bitch has to see that I'm here at this gas station mattie [Dutch street slang for friend]. Look man, I'm here bro, where are you? Huh? Where are you? Back the car up more, drive back so more. Fucking son of a bitch.

Soon after, the driller from Rotterdam shared a second video from a different location and states: "*Let's see if he is here*". Still seated in the passenger seat of the car, he summoned the driver to move in the direction of several cars in a parking lot. Because he also does not seem to be at the second location, the driller from Rotterdam decided to call his rival. In the last video, you can hear him shouting at his phone: "*Pussy boy! You wanted to meet me in the city, you're a pussy boy, you're a pussy!*" followed by a mention of his rival's name and the city he resides in. The driller from Rotterdam continues by saying:

You send me three different locations, and I came to all three, but you are not there, you're a pussy! Bro, if I catch you in the city mattie, fucking son of a bitch, your fucking mothers, your fucking children, your fucking son, fucking Zionist. Fucking punk, what's good bro?

At that moment, his rival hung up the phone and the camera of the driller from Rotterdam was directed at his stomach. Briefly, a gun behind his waistband could be made out. However, the digital provocations between these rivals did not result in a physical confrontation.

Online threats

In the material we collected on social media, we also saw digital content that went beyond publicly taunting or challenging rivals. For instance, a driller from Rotterdam posted an image of a young man on Snapchat with the following caption:

[Name boy] from [name school and location] (. . .)
    500 euros who beats his up and films it
    This is what happens when fans of KSB [drill group from Amsterdam] make fake accounts and talk about my child
    Then I'm doing research on you and I put a price on your head no matter how old you are

(June 2020, Snapchat)

In this message, the driller from Rotterdam offers a reward for whoever beats up the young man mentioned by name in the post. During our research, the same drillers made several of these threats. In addition to beating up specific individuals, he offered a reward for stabbing someone: "*Whoever stabs that [name] in front of me gets 1k [thousand euros). He doesn't have to die but just cheff [stab] that man haha*", followed by a smiling emoji.

We also came across examples of online threats that went a step further still. In various groups about drill in the Netherlands on Telegram Messenger, a death list was distributed, listing various drillers from Amsterdam, Rotterdam, and The Hague. During our research, it was not possible to determine who posted the list and to what extent this death list should be taken seriously. However, one of the drillers in our research did post various messages on Snapchat to find out who distributed the death list that bore his name. For example, he posted a photo of a specific location with the caption "*Who wants to find out if [name] lives here!!! You get paid to find out if he lives there!!!*" In a subsequent message, he even offered a reward for the person who finds and kills the alleged maker of the death list: "*7000,- [name] If you kill him you will get 5 thousand a month for 5 months.*" Similarly, we found a post about an amount of money that was offered to whoever stabs or lets two individuals run, followed by the caption: "*NO CAP YOU REALLY GET THE REWARD*". With the statement "no cap"—which is also written online as "no 🧢" or "❌🧢 "—the driller wants to indicate that he is not lying and that there actually is a monetary reward.

However, the (online) conflicts that we encountered during our research are not limited to those directly involved in beefs between drillers. In addition to several drillers promising amounts of money to make *opps* run, beat up or stab *opps*, we also encountered three different examples of threats against drillers' girlfriends. These posts contain a photo of the woman, an explanation that this was the girlfriend of a specific driller, and in one case the location where this girlfriend lived. In all cases, various amounts of money were made available to assault, stab, rape and in one case even kill these drillers' girlfriends.

Exposing drillers

In the examples of the symbolic practices of entering *opp block* and provoking rivals, we can recognize strategies directed at contesting the violent poses of the drillers and to inform the outside world about the performative nature of their online behavior. Our empirical material also contains examples that showcase how the drillers in our study attempt to create context collapse (boyd, 2014; Stuart, 2020a, 2020b) by exposing each other on social media, especially by sharing past social media posts, private information or information that not all the online followers of the drillers are privy to.

In September 2019, a driller from the city of Rotterdam posted the following message on his Instagram account: "*I am fed up with all that sneak dissing and gangster rap acting. You're only scary with a mask up, so don't let me expose these young niggas with their first names and faces*". In this post, sneak dissing refers to insulting other (drillers) without mentioning their name, even though it is clear from the context of the diss that this is aimed at a specific individual. In the last sentence of his post on Instagram, the driller from Rotterdam calls on his rivals from Amsterdam to be more specific with their insults or provocations, either by inviting him to a session of Instagram Live ("*Next time you diss me on Insta Life, invite me*") or by tagging him in the post ("*Or @ me*").

The second issue the driller from Rotterdam takes offense to is the "*gangster rap acting*", signaling that the persona his rivals proclaim is an act and not authentic. Exposing his rivals from Amsterdam—whose identity was unclear for a long time because they wore masks in their videos and posts on social media—would provide insight into the performativity of these drillers. Not long after his initial post, the driller from Rotterdam shared a series of photographs using the Story function on Instagram. Each individual photo is meant to expose the various members of the drill group from Amsterdam, among other things by sharing their first and last names and information about the school one of the drillers attends.

During our digital fieldwork, we found other examples of private information about the aforementioned members of this drill group from Amsterdam that was made public on social media, as the following information on Snapchat illustrates:

> Yoo
>
> You have beef with [name of Amsterdam driller], right?
>
> You shouldn't take this man seriously, he has no money. He's nothing. Supposedly robbing people, all he takes is a broken iPhone 5. He asks girls for money. Because he has no money. Not even €20 for groceries.
>
> *(August 2020, Snapchat)*

The sender explains that she was in a relationship with the Amsterdam driller for some time and therefore knows firsthand that the rapper should not be taken seriously because, in the words of the sender of the message, "*he is yusu [seriously] pathetic*". The response of the recipient of this message is: "*hhhhhhhhh you're awesome I swear*", followed by a smiling emoji and two red hearts.

Other information that is difficult to reconcile with drillers' violent poses is also shared online, as we can see in Figures 27.1 and 27.2—photos that seem to be taken from police files. In the first photo, we see a driller from Amsterdam running because he is being chased with a knife, something that according to the driller who posted the image is seen as particularly laughable and not in accordance with the way this driller presents himself in his

Figure 27.1 Snapchat

Figure 27.2 Snapchat

music and on social media. Figure 27.2 shows how a driller from Amsterdam is chased by three young men and is thrown onto the track of the metro with a machete in his hand. Here too we see that the pose of the driller is openly questioned, as witnessed by the caption: *"you had your machete in your hand you were thrown onto the railway and your knife was taken away what a driller ?? ?? ??"*

These examples show that the drillers in our study have information and photos from (ongoing) police investigations. For instance, a driller from Rotterdam shared a photo from a police file, highlighting a specific passage from an interrogation, with the caption: *"Okay, okay, I'll stop the beef I don't want beef anymore. Boys its resolved, can't beef no rats"*. In his post, the driller makes clear that he wholeheartedly disapproves with the statement made during the police interrogation, but also that he distances himself from the conflict with the young man. Despite the fact that this is not made explicit, he seems to allude to the likelihood that in the event of an escalation of the beef, this young man will once again violate the street code by snitching, with potentially adverse consequences for the Rotterdam driller.

Snitching—or talking to the police in general—is a practice that is condemned on the street (Rosenfeld et al., 2003). Because rumors about snitching can be disastrous for someone's reputation on both the physical and digital streets, young people—including drillers (Ilan, 2020, p. 9)—are very keen to quickly contradict such allegations. Social media provides a platform to communicate this high standard of silence and to indicate that someone has not snitched, for example by sharing excerpts from the interrogation (Roks, 2015, p. 423). We see this reflected in the following post by the aforementioned driller from Rotterdam, who himself shares the following fragment of part of his conversation with the local police officer via Snapchat:

> There are rumors that I made a statement about that time when I had to come to the police office but didn't want to make a statement and my mother went to talk. What's up with that? Because as far as I know, I said I didn't want anything to do with talking about the case. Exactly for these reasons.
>
> *(April 2020, Snapchat)*

In this case, the Rotterdam driller shares information to prove that he has not snitched. However, his approach does not have the desired effect. A driller from Amsterdam responded to his post:

> Wooow you have police officer saved in your phone you are an ORIGINAL SNITCH!!!
> But you're a driller?
> WTF is this
>
> *(April 2020, Snapchat)*

Moreover, he adds to his post that the driller from Rotterdam is *"worse than a rat"*, because he publicly blames his mother for the course of events. In turn, these Amsterdam drillers are called *"snitch gang"* by a different drillers from Rotterdam in a comment on a photo of a passage from an interrogation in which they were involved.

Beefs between drillers

Thus far, we have presented several examples that provide insight into violent conflicts between drillers on social media. In the remainder of this chapter, we zoom in on three beefs between the different drillers in our research. Two of these conflicts took place in the summer of 2020, during our digital fieldwork. One of these beefs dates from the period 2018–2019, but was referenced frequently by the drillers in our study. Based on the nature of our netnographic research, it is not always possible to determine the exact cause of these conflicts. Therefore, in our description, we mainly focus on explaining the development of these beefs between drillers, with specific attention to the online and offline dynamics of the conflicts.

"Fuck your dead homie"

The first example centers around a driller from Rotterdam and Amsterdam. A screenshot of a DM of the driller from Rotterdam indicates that the drillers have been in contact since 2018. In fact, the screenshot reveals that the driller from Amsterdam sent several positive reactions to an earlier post on the driller from Rotterdam's Instagram. Therefore, during the early moments of the beef the driller from Rotterdam stated: "*Men were fans in the past, you better chill*", followed by three smiling emojis. At some point, a beef between the drillers seemed to have started, something that based on his reaction "*But what is the deal? Beef or what?*" did not seem to be clear to the driller from Amsterdam at first.

Although the origin of the conflict remains unclear, the development of the beef is broadcast online in detail, with various recordings on YouTube of digital interactions between the drillers. In one of these videos, he interacts with the driller from Amsterdam on Instagram Live. This functionality of Instagram allows followers to watch a digital interaction between people in a split screen. At the start of the recording, more than 350 people see the driller from Rotterdam showing a gun. The driller from Amsterdam, visible on the split screen, does not seem to be impressed and responds with laughter and the statement: "*Such a sweet little pistol*". As the driller from Rotterdam walks through his living room with the gun, he asks: "*Ai no, where were you yesterday, G? Where were you yesterday?*" and he accused the other driller of hiding. Again, the driller from Amsterdam laughs. After mocking the first name of the driller from Rotterdam, he contests that the driller was in his neighborhood yesterday. Then, the drillers start talking over each other, specifically trading back-to-back accusations of not being "real" and being broke.

At that moment, more than 500 people are watching this session on Instagram Live. The interaction takes a turn when the driller from Amsterdam says: "*Fuck your dead mattie [Dutch slang for friend]*", a direct insult to the Rotterdam-based driller who recently lost a close friend. "*Good for you*", the Amsterdam driller repeats a number of times. With the number of viewers surpassing 650, the driller from Rotterdam seems to get more and more angry, saying: "*You are not a goon mattie, if I catch you mattie, if I catch you it's over.*" Quite abruptly, the live sessions ends. In another session on Instagram live between the two drillers, the deceased friend of the driller from Rotterdam is referenced again. Sitting in a car and repeatedly pointing his camera at his firearm, the Rotterdam driller says: "*Ey brother, DM, DM me that address, I'm coming G, I'm coming G, you're going to die brother for that disrespect to my homie*", and then, with more than 250 people watching live, the session ends again.

In addition to insulting the deceased friend of the Rotterdam driller in the earlier live sessions, the Amsterdam driller also posts a video on Snapchat in which he says: "*Fucking [name of Rotterdam driller], with your dead friend, do something about it buddy."* Based on various images and videos on social media, the driller from Rotterdam seems to travel to various locations in the Rotterdam area where the driller from Amsterdam would supposedly hang out. However, the latter does not show up and the Rotterdam driller shares various posts on social media as proof that he tried to call the driller from Amsterdam while he was at the agreed locations, but that he did not answer. Despite the heated discussions and a number of musical and digital provocations and threats back and forth, however, this did not result in a physical confrontation between these two drillers.

"Honestly, I can't give you a fist bump"

The second example concerns a short-lived beef that took place in the summer of 2020 and illustrates how violence that occurs on the physical street can end up on the digital street; for example, by posting photos and videos of violent incidents (cf. Irwin-Rogers et al., 2018, p. 404). In August 2020, images appear on various social media accounts of a fight between a driller from The Hague and various young people who claim to be part of a drill group from Rotterdam. Unlike the first example, it is possible to reconstruct how this conflict started, specifically because parts of the incident were filmed by several people and posted on social media. A Rotterdam driller directly involved in this beef shares various videos of the incident via Instagram Story. In a shot where he films himself, he heralds the sequence of posts:

> Those people come up to me, they just come up to me. I'm just with a few friends. Boy, I give those people a fist bump, I want to dab these people up. They don't want to give a fist bump, they just want to link with those people from [name of Amsterdam drill group] blablabla. I don't care, because I'm not doing, nothing, I'm just an artist, those people come to me.
>
> *(August 2020, Instagram)*

After this brief introduction, he posts the recording of the interaction he just described on Instagram. The video shows that the driller from Rotterdam wants to give a person, whose face is outside the frame of video but who is a driller from the city of The Hague, a fist bump. You can hear the driller from The Hague responding with: *"Honestly, I can't give you a fist bump. I'm really with boys, you know right? From the other side"*.

The next story of the driller from Rotterdam is a selfie with the caption *"3 minutes later . . . "* What follows is a video with shaky footage in which the driller from The Hague is held down and beaten by several people. A text has been added to the video: *"Do not link with [name of Amsterdam drill group] and [name of Amsterdam driller] I repeat, do not link with them"*. With this caption, the driller from Rotterdam explains that the driller from The Hague was beat up because he chose a side in a beef that has existed for some time between drillers from Amsterdam and Rotterdam. The recording clearly shows that the driller from The Hague is hit on the head by two different young men and the driller from Rotterdam who posted the videos can be heard shouting: *'We are [name Rotterdam drill group], we are [name Rotterdam drill group]. Don't bullshit, go to Damsco [street slang for Amsterdam]. Ey boys, beat that man to pieces"*. The video ends when the driller from The Hague stumbles away.

A few hours after the fight, the driller from The Hague posts an image of himself on Instagram with the following caption:

> Just got jumped in Scheveningen [city nearby The Hague] by 15 men was fucking drunk a nigga pulled both my chains, I grabbed back my chains and pulled his, they start to jump me I was with 5 men but I had to fight alone. Had to give up fighting because they jumped me get from all sides. I came home with my LV [Louis Vuitton] bag on me with my iphone 11 my necklaces and that guy's. Everything has stayed on me. God is great #OneManArmy
>
> *(August 2020, Snapchat)*

Later on, the driller from The Hague also posted photos online of the chains he had taken from his attackers. In another video he even professionally checks for how many carats of gold the chains are with the help of a specific liquid. In addition, he places a call on social media that he will take one of his followers to dinner with the proceeds from the sale of the chains.

The recording of the driller from The Hague being beaten by multiple people could be found on various social media accounts we followed during the course of our digital fieldwork. The result of posting this beef online for those directly involved—in this case the driller from The Hague—is that the (online) peer pressure may become so great, partly because the online audience on the digital street is many times larger and more anonymous than offline (Urbanik & Haggerty, 2018, p. 1356), that those involved feel compelled to respond with violence (Irwin-Rogers et al., 2018, p. 406). In this beef, however, that is not the case. In fact, the driller from The Hague posts the following message on his story on Instagram: *"Got a lot of love but The Hague stay calm I'm a man and make my own choices x ❤"*. Despite the fact that this beef was widely reported on social media, the driller from The Hague did not respond with violence.

"Tomorrow I'm at Skiffa my location stays on nobody wacks me"

The third and last beef we will discuss does have a violent outcome, with a young man dying after a stabbing incident. This violent encounter was preceded by a beef between rival drill groups from Amsterdam and Rotterdam. How the beef started could not be established based on the information on social media, and even one of the involved drillers from Rotterdam noted on social media that he was unclear on the origin of the conflict. The beef developed over the course of a few months on social media and saw a number of musical insults, but mostly digital provocations and online threats—some of which we discussed earlier in this chapter.

Most of the interactions between these rival drillers had a performative character and were aimed at establishing and reaffirming one's own authenticity as a driller and deconstructing the poses of the other drillers. However, in the days leading up to the lethal incident, a driller from Rotterdam posted the following message on social media:

> [Name Dutch drill groups], and everyone who links with them are fucking fag they are scared to do anything to me and my members. Only tough thing these guys do is threaten my girlfriend and expose our families. But we want to off them not their girls (two laughing emojis).

You are their fans, right. You tell them to meet somewhere in the middle of Amsterdam and Rotterdam, then we will fix that beef there at once.

I [name of Rotterdam driller] repeat I want to meet them all at once somewhere then we will fix it right there (wink emoji)

I know they don't want to do this and continue bullying my girlfriend [name of Rotterdam driller] bullying his girlfriend SAY THOSE MEN COME MEET ME

Today today we will fix it

(August 2020, Snapchat)

On the same day, an Amsterdam driller posts the following message on Snapchat: "*Tomorrow I'll be at Skiffa and my loca stays on nobody will wack me*", indicating that he will go to Scheveningen ("*Skiffa*") *the next day* and will keep his location function on his social media accounts on so that others can see where he is ("*my loca stays on*"), concluded by stating that no one will be able to harm him ("*nobody will wack me*").

Towards the end of the next day, messages appear on various social media accounts about an incident that took place in Scheveningen. Not much later, someone posts a video of part of the incident. On the video you can see and hear that panic breaks out on the pier in Scheveningen. Boys and girls push each other aside, scream and try to run away. A person with a firearm runs through the video and gunshots can be heard in the background. Photos of a young man lying on the ground fighting for his life are posted as wall. On August 10, 2020, 19-year-old Cennethson Janga—who was also known as "Chuchu"—lost his life on the pier of Scheveningen.

On social media, the death of this young men was celebrated by people who sided with the drillers from Amsterdam. Moreover, in the days and weeks following this incident, drillers from Amsterdam seemed to try to stir up the beef some more. Various messages appear on social media in which they ridicule the victim. At the end of October 2020, the drillers from Amsterdam even publish a song about that fatal day on the pier of Scheveningen in August 2020. In the song, which is called "The Pier", one of the drillers from Rotterdam is ridiculed for abandoning his friend. They also proclaim that it was a pity that another driller from Rotterdam was not the fatal victim. Overall, as one of the drillers from Amsterdam raps, "*Looking back, yes I am proud*".

Conclusion

Drill music, notoriously infamous for its references to violent criminality, is a musical genre that has gained popularity across the globe. In the Netherlands, drill has been explicitly linked to the recent rise of violent crimes among young people (Bahara, 2019, 2020). In this chapter, our focus was on the social media usage of drillers from an exploratory study into the drill culture in Rotterdam (Roks & Van den Broek, 2020). Based on the online content uploaded by the drillers from our research, we described the insults, challenges, threats and conflicts that could be observed in the social media posts of the drillers in our study. Our results, in line with previous studies on drill in the United States (Stuart, 2020a, 2020b) and the United Kingdom (Ilan, 2020), show that violence in drill is not limited to the music, but is embedded in a broader digital street culture on platforms such as YouTube, Instagram, and Snapchat. This digitization—or hybridization (Roks et al., 2021)—of street culture is increasingly studied, with an emphasis on the expressive practices on social media by street-oriented individuals and groups (see, among others, Lane, 2019; Moule et al., 2014;

Patton et al., 2017; Storrod & Densley, 2017; Stuart, 2020a, 2020b; Urbanik & Haggerty, 2018; Van Hellemont, 2012).

Where some such studies from the United States and the United Kingdom suggest that social media can act as a trigger or catalyst for physical, offline violence (Patton et al., 2013, 2017; Pyrooz et al., 2015; Moule et al., 2017; Irwin-Rogers et al., 2018; Irwin-Rogers & Pinkney, 2018; Lauger & Densley, 2018; Urbanik & Haggerty, 2018), some recent studies argue that social media also offers new opportunities and possibilities for de-escalating conflict and avoiding offline violence (Lane, 2019; Stuart, 2020a, 2020b; Lane & Stuart, 2022). What stands out in the examples in this chapter is the symbolic communication of violence. Even though the drillers in our study frequently post violent and provocative content online and allude to the ways in which they will act on these digital words and claims, the number of physical violence incidents as a result of these online expressions is limited. Much of the violence expressed by drillers on the social media platforms in this study can be seen as performative: geared toward communicating a dangerous and violent image more so than an actual willingness to commit physical violence (cf. Stuart, 2020a, 2020b). This is a first tentative indication that by no means does all the violence communicated online actually result in violent incidents, but also that young people use social media to settle online conflicts in a non-violent way (cf. Lane, 2019; Stuart, 2020b; Lane & Stuart, 2022).

Even though more violence is communicated in the online drill culture than actually takes place on the street, the course of the beefs that we have discussed in this chapter also makes clear that there is a certain risk associated with the online performance of violence. Communicating violence, certainly when it comes to specific provocations or threats, can result in physical violence. In fact, Stuart (2020a, p. 12) states that in Chicago "participation in drill and its related digital content greatly increases a young's risk of exposure to violence". This risk is increased when the authenticity of drillers is publicly questioned, but especially when rivals meet in real life (Stuart, 2020a, p. 7)—something that can be observed in the violent incident on the Pier of Scheveningen in August 2020.

Moreover, our research indicates that violence on the digital street, also symbolic acts of violence, have the potential to reach a large audience of friends, rivals, and other involved parties and, in this way, to influence the origin and developments of conflicts. Whereas in this chapter the focus has been on the digital interaction between drillers, expressions of violence and (group) conflicts on social media are not limited to those directly involved. After all, this digital content is visible online, is shared and thus reaches a much larger audience of fans and other consumers (of drill) who watch online (cf. boyd, 2014). How drillers, and young people in general, deal with this (online) pressure, however, needs to be examined in more detail in future research.

References

Anderson, E. (1999). *Code of the Street. Decency, violence, and the moral life of the inner city.* Norton.

Bahara, H. (2019, Oktober 23). Is drillmuziek de katalysator voor de recente geweldsgolf onder jongeren? *De Volkskrant.* Retrieved from www.volkskrant.nl/nieuws-achtergrond/is-drillmuziek-de-katalysator-voor-de-recente-geweldsgolf-onder-jongeren~b778afd9/ (accessed 22 August 2022).

Bahara, H. (2020, Augustus 23). Wie zijn de drillrapgroepen die zoveel zorgen baren? *De Volkskrant.* Retrieved from www.volkskrant.nl/nieuws-achtergrond/wie-zijn-de-drillrapgroepen-die-zoveel-zorgen-baren~bcedd124/ (accessed 22 August 2022).

Bahara, H., & Stoker, E. (2020, Augustus 23). Bedreigingen in de drillrapscene: 'Het is idioot, er staat een beloning van onlinepunten op het hoofd van jongeren'. *De Volkskrant*. Retrieved from www.volkskrant.nl/nieuws-achtergrond/bedreigingen-in-de-drillrapscene-het-is-idioot-er-staat-een-beloning-van-onlinepunten-op-het-hoofd-van-jongeren~b3028673/ (accessed 22 August 2022).

Bos, K., & van der, P. R. (2020, Augustus 25). Wie moordt, die scoort in drillrap. *NRC Handelsblad*. Retrived from www.nrc.nl/nieuws/2020/08/25/wie-moordt-die-scoort-in-drillrap-a4009827 (accessed 22 August 2022).

boyd, d. (2014). *It's complicated: The social lives of networked teens*. Yale University Press.

Costello, L., McDermott, M.-L., & Wallace, R. (2017). Netnography: Range of practices, misperceptions and missed opportunities. *International Journal of Qualitative Methods*, 16, 1–16. https://doi.org/10.1177/1609406917700647.

Deuchar, R., & Holligan, C. (2010). Gangs, sectarianism and social capital: A qualitative study of young people in Scotland. *Sociology*, 44(1), 13–30.

Fatsis, L. (2019). Policing the beats: The criminalisation of UK drill and grime music by the London Metropolitan Police. *The sociological review*, 67(6), 1300–1316.

Geertz, C. (1973). Thick description: Toward an interpretive theory of culture. In C. Geertz (Ed.), *The interpretation of cultures: Selected essays* (pp. 3–30). Basic Books.

Haut, F. (2014). Cyberbanging: When criminal reality and virtual reality meet. *International Journal on Criminology*, 2(2), 22–27.

Ilan, J. (2020). Digital street culture decoded: Why criminalizing drill music is street illiterate and counterproductive. *British Journal of Criminology*. Online first. https://doi.org/10.1093/bjc/azz086.

Irwin-Rogers, K., Densley, J., & Pinkney, C. (2018). Gang violence and social media. In J. L. Ireland, P. Birch, & C. A. Ireland (Eds.), *The Routledge international handbook of human aggression* (pp. 400–410). Routledge.

Irwin-Rogers, K., & Pinkney, C. (2017). *Social media as a catalyst and trigger for youth violence*. Catch22.

Johnson, J., & Schell-Busey, N. (2016). Old message in a New Bottle: Taking gang rivalries online through rap battle music videos on YouTube. *Journal of Qualitative Criminal Justice and Criminology*, 4(1), 42–81.

Kozinets, R. (2002). The field behind the screen: Using netnography for marketing research in online communities. *Journal of Marketing Research*, 39, 61–72. https://doi.org/10.1509/jmkr.39.1.61.18935.

Kozinets, R. (2015). *Netnography: Redefined*. Sage.

Lane, J. (2019). *The digital street*. Oxford University Press.

Lane, J., & Stuart, F. (2022). How social media use mitigates urban violence: Communication visibility and third-party intervention processes in digital urban contexts. *Qualitative Sociology*, 1–19.

Lauger, T. R., & Densley, J. A. (2018). Broadcasting badness: Violence, identity, and performance in the online gang rap scene. *Justice Quarterly*, 35(5), 816–841.

Lynes, A., Kelly, C., & Kelly, E. (2020). Thug life: Drill music as a periscope into urban violence in the consumer age. *The British Journal of Criminology*. Online first. https://doi-org.eur.idm.oclc.org/10.1093/bjc/azaa011.

Moore, C. L., & Stuart, F. (2022). Gang research in the twenty-first century. *Annual Review of Criminology*, 5, 299–320.

Moule, R. K., Decker, S. H., & Pyrooz, D. C. (2017). Technology and conflict: Group processes and collective violence in the Internet era. *Crime, Law and Social Change*, 68(1–2), 47–73.

Moule, R. K., Pyrooz, D. C., en Decker, S. H. (2014). Internet adoption and online behaviour among American street gangs: Integrating gangs and organizational theory. *British Journal of Criminology*, 54(6), 1186–1206.

Patton, D. U., Eschmann, R. D., & Butler, D. A. (2013). Internet banging: New trends in social media, gang violence, masculinity and hip hop. *Computers in Human Behavior*, 29(5), A54–A59.

Patton, D. U., Eschmann, R. D., Elsaesser, C., & Bocanegra, E. (2016). Sticks, stones and Facebook accounts: What violence outreach workers know about social media and urban-based gang violence in Chicago. *Computers in Human Behavior*, 65(1), 591–600.

Patton, D. U., Lane, J., Leonard, P., Macbeth, J., & Smith Lee, J. R. (2017). Gang violence on the digital street: Case study of a South Side Chicago gang member's Twitter communication. *New media and Society*, *19*(7), 1000–1018.

Peterson, J., & Densley, J. A. (2017). Cyber violence: What do we know and where do we go from here? *Aggression and Violent Behavior*, *34*(1), 193–200.

Pyrooz, D. C., Decker, S. H., & Moule, R. K. (2015). Criminal and Routine Activities in Online Settings. *Justice Quarterly*, *32*(3), 471–499.

Pyrooz, D. C., & Moule, R. K. (2019). Gangs and social media. In N. Rafter & M. Brown (Eds.), *Oxford research encyclopedia of criminology and criminal justice* (pp. 1–21). Oxford University Press.

Roks, R. A. (2015). Never snitch broertje, want de straat hoort het, *Ars Aequi*, *64*(5), 422–425.

Roks, R. A., Leukfeldt, E. R., & Densley, J. A. (2021). The hybridization of street offending in the Netherlands. *The British Journal of Criminology*, *61*(4), 926–945.

Roks, R. A., & Van den Broek, J. B. A. (2020). *Cappen voor Clout? Een verkennend onderzoek naar Rotterdamse jongeren, drill en geweld in het digitale tijdperk*. Erasmus Universiteit Rotterdam.

Rosenfeld, R., Jacobs, B. A., & Wright, R. (2003). Snitching and the code of the street. *British Journal of Criminology*, *43*(2), 291–309.

Storrod, M. L., en Densley, J. A. (2017). 'Going viral' and 'going country': The expressive and instrumental activities of street gangs on social media. *Journal of Youth Studies*, *20*(6), 677–696.

Stuart, F. (2020a). *Ballad of the bullet. gangs, drill music, and the power of online infamy*. Princeton University Press.

Stuart, F. (2020b). Code of the tweet: Urban gang violence in the social media age. *Social Problems* (Article first published online). https://doi.org/10.1093/socpro/spz010

Urbanik, M. M., & Haggerty, K. D. (2018). '#It's dangerous': The online world of drug dealers, rappers and the street code. *The British Journal of Criminology*, *58*(6), 1343–1360.

Urbanik, M. M., & Roks, R. A. (2020). GangstaLife: Fusing urban ethnography with netnography in gang studies. *Qualitative Sociology*, *43*, 213–233.

Van Hellemont, E. (2012). Gangland online. Performing the real imaginary world of gangstas and ghettos in Brussels. *European Journal of Crime, Criminal Law and Criminal Justice*, *20*(2), 165–180.

Wall, D. S. (2001). *Crime and the internet*. Routledge.

28

WHAT DRIVES AGGRESSIVE ONLINE BEHAVIOR AMONG ADULTS?

A literature review and explanatory model integrating individual, situational, and social status determinants

Lea Stahel

Introduction

Aggressive behavior on the internet is a major social challenge in the age of digitalization. It is easy to create, can be widely distributed, is highly visible, and is rarely removed or negatively sanctioned. It can have a negative impact on its targets at emotional, social, and economic levels and can interfere with freedom of expression and democracy (Ferguson, 2021; Tandoc et al., 2021). Consequently, developing countermeasures requires understanding what directly and indirectly stimulates online aggression (Siapera & Viejo-Otero, 2021). To examine these determinants, scholars have explored diverse forms of aggressive online behavior with different labels in various social domains, such as online hate speech and online incivility in politics, corporate harassment in business, and cyberbullying in the general population.

Theoretical overview

Online aggression

Online aggression is defined for the purposes of this review as digitally mediated content that includes but is not limited to insults, disparaging remarks, vulgarity, inappropriate generalizations, and threats. This content is sent via technology-enabled channels, mainly online via social media, discussion forums, chats, videotelephony, and email or, less frequently, via a mobile network such as SMS and telephone. In this chapter, the term "online aggression" serves as a catch-all term for the predominant phenomena of aggressive behavior identified in social science literature, including sociology, criminology, psychology, political science, and media and communications. It can be directed against both identifiable and unidentifiable targets, including individuals, social groups, corporations, and

DOI: 10.4324/9781003277675-32

institutions such as norms, traditions, and value systems. It is a condition that aggressive perpetrators consciously or unconsciously, directly or indirectly, have harmful intentions, even if this is usually difficult to demonstrate empirically (Anderson & Bushman, 2002). The same difficulty arises for the assumption that the perpetrator must envisage that the behavior will harm the target and that the target will attempt to avoid the behavior. A consequence of these assumptions is that accidental and consensual harm are not considered aggression. Finally, online aggression can be considered a form of online deviance, and in some cases cybercrime, because it violates accepted formal or informal rules and norms related to information and communication technology (Graham & Smith, 2019).

Manifestations of online aggression

Many diverse concepts circulate in the literature on aggressive online phenomena. To illustrate the range of their emphases, scientific definitions for these terms from literature reviews are presented in Table 28.1. The comprehensive listing (although without any claim

Table 28.1 Manifestations of aggressive online behavior

Concept	Definition
Trolling	"Deliberate, deceptive and mischievous attempts that are engineered to elicit a reaction from the target(s), are performed for the benefit of the troll(s) and their followers and may have negative consequences for people and firms involved." (Golf-Papez & Veer, 2017, p. 1339)
Online hate, cyberhate	"Posting online an explicitly negative assessment of a person or an object primarily for the purpose of expressing one's negative attitude toward that person or object." (Malecki et al., 2021, p. 3)
Online misogyny, online sexism	"Hatred of or contempt for women" occurring in virtual worlds (Moloney & Love, 2018, p. 3)
Virtual manhood acts (VMA)	Cues which "signal a masculine self, enforce hegemonic gender norms, oppress women, and keep men 'in the box'." (Moloney & Love, 2018, p. 1)
Cyber-racism	"Any form of communication via electronic or digital media by groups or individuals which seeks to denigrate or discriminate against individuals (by denying equal rights, freedom and opportunities) or groups because of their race or ethnicity." (Bliuc et al., 2018, p. 76)
Political online incivility	"A broad class of discursive behaviors . . . a *potentially* insidious social phenomenon that runs counter to the norms governing political interaction generally and political deliberation specifically." (Hopp, 2019, p. 204) This usually includes normative violations of speech and of the inclusion of others.
Cyberbullying	"The use of technology to deliberately and repeatedly threaten, insult, harass or tease another." (Jenaro et al., 2018, p. 113) This represents relational or interpersonal aggression, is intentional, repeated, occurs in asymmetrical situations, and is carried out via information and communications technology.

to completeness) focuses on manifestations that are either more established, such as trolling, or of particular sociological relevance, such as virtual manhood acts. There is usually little agreement between studies on a given concept's definition or operationalization (e.g., Hopp, 2019; Jane, 2015). However, there is substantial definitional overlap between the concepts. Similar terms are sometimes used interchangeably and sometimes for different phenomena. For example, "online hate" usually refers to generally negatively expressed attitudes, and "online hate speech" refers to ideologically based hostility that degrades the value of a particular social group. Some definitions have become established, although particular definitional aspects remain controversial, such as the repetition aspect of cyberbullying (Corcoran et al., 2015). For other typically used terms, such as online hostility, flaming, online abuse, and online harassment, no clear common denominators or research streams can be explicitly identified. Therefore, they have not been explicitly included in Table 28.1. One result of these definitional difficulties is that some authors have advocated using online aggression as a collective term for all kinds of hostile online phenomena (e.g., Corcoran et al., 2015).

Research gaps and objectives

To date, although some general reviews have been published of individual manifestations (Bliuc et al., 2018; Malecki et al., 2021; Moloney & Love, 2018), including on adults (Jenaro et al., 2018), these are very general and do not focus on the determinants of this behavior. To the author's best knowledge, no systematic review has covered the main determinants of the various manifestations of online aggression by adults from a sociological-criminological perspective. However, such a review would provide better meta-understanding of online aggression. This research gap is addressed by two key research questions:

1. What determinants of adult online aggression are addressed in the social sciences?
2. How can the identified determinants be integrated into a comprehensive model?

These issues are addressed by proposing an explanatory sociological model of online aggression and summarizing the empirical literature on the main determinants of various aggressive online phenomena in the context of adult perpetrators. The strong overlap in definitions identified feeds the assumption that similar determinants underlie various concepts, even though their explanatory power may vary for individual concepts. Therefore, transferring all identified determinants into a common, albeit rather general, sociological model seems justifiable.

EXPLANATORY MODEL OF AGGRESSIVE ONLINE BEHAVIOR

Existing empirical models usually treat a few determinants as parallel and independent factors at the same explanatory level (for an exception, see Lowry et al., 2016); by contrast, the theoretical model proposed here builds on work by Stahel and Weingartner (2023) to suggest a causal interplay between various types of determinants. This model follows an analytical approach in sociology (Elster, 2015; Hedström & Ylikoski, 2010) which views individual social behavior as embedded in social structures and explained by individual-based mechanisms such as beliefs. Individual-based determinants are thus not randomly distributed in a society but are systematically linked to the structure of social

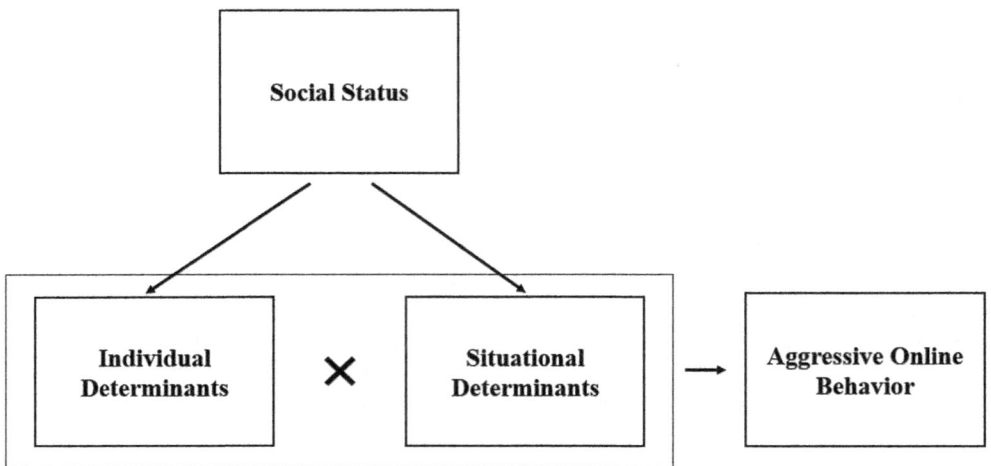

Figure 28.1   Explanatory model of aggressive online behavior

inequality and other social status differentiations. Another approach is situational action theory (Wikström & Treiber, 2009; McCuish et al., 2015). This theory conceptualizes violent behavior as a violation of moral rules of conduct. It explains it essentially through the interaction between the propensity to use violence as an alternative course of action (as influenced, for example, by personal moral rules, emotions, and self-control) and the social environment, which influences the individual's level of disinhibition (for instance through environmental moral rules, provocation, peer influence, and social control). Violent actions, or indeed nonactions, thus result from the convergence in time and space of people and situations that initiate a process of moral perception and moral decision.

These two approaches can be meaningfully combined. The model proposed here assumes that individual determinants interact with situational determinants to directly explain whether or not someone is aggressive online. In addition, it is believed that people's social status influences their individual characteristics and the situations in which they find themselves. This means that indicators of social status such as sociodemographic and socioeconomic factors indirectly influence online aggression through individual and situational factors (see Figure 28.1). This specific interaction in the proposed model is supported by general research on the social structuring of individual determinants as in the example of beliefs (Carvacho et al., 2013; Goubin & Hooghe, 2020), psychological symptoms (Lorant et al., 2003), and well-being (Wilkinson & Pickett, 2017).

Literature review: search strategy, selection, and inclusion criteria

The review was conducted according to the Preferred Reporting Items for Systematic Reviews and Meta-Analyses (PRISMA) guidelines. It represents an evidence-based minimum set of criteria for identifying and summarizing research in the social sciences (Moher et al., 2009). A loose adoption of PRISMA was chosen instead of a strict approach. This is because the goal is to identify the most important determinants and locate them within the theoretical model rather than claim complete inclusion of every single study on every single determinant.

Table 28.2 Selection terms and selection criteria

Search terms	Additional (narrowing) terms	Criteria for considering studies
Online OR digital in combination with: aggression hate hate speech abuse harassment hostility sexism misogyny racism cyber-racism cyberhate online incivility virtual manhood acts trolling trolls cyberbullying AND adults	causes motiv* driver*	a. they examine one of the defined manifestations of online aggression; b. they discuss one or more determinants that fit the proposed theoretical model; c. if they are surveys, they focus primarily on adults, even if they include the late adolescent years; d. they were published as original qualitative or quantitative empirical work; and e. they were written in English.

The literature available, including all published journal articles but excluding unpublished studies, dissertations, conference proceedings, monographs, and anthologies, was retrieved in August 2022 through the Web of Science, because of its inclusion of prestigious and high-ranking academic journals, and through Google Scholar, because of its emphasis on article citations as a dissemination measure. The selection of search terms was guided by widely familiar manifestations of online aggression, the restriction to adults, and the focus on determinants. Table 28.2 shows the search terms and selection criteria. All terms that are also examined in the offline context, such as "aggression" were only searched for in combination with "online" or "digital." For online-specific terms such as "trolling," such an addition was not necessary. Because most cyberbullying literature focuses on minors, "cyberbullying" was sought in combination with "adults." If a term or term combination returned an unmanageably large number of results, the search was narrowed by adding terms that indicated determinants such as "causes." Studies that met the five criteria listed in Table 28.2 were considered.

For each search, the titles of potentially relevant studies were examined individually to exclude studies that were obviously unrelated to the focus of the study. The abstracts were then reviewed to determine whether a study examined the determinants of online aggression. All selected studies were downloaded. The remaining studies were subjected to more detailed screening, and other irrelevant studies were excluded. This included those that examine intent to behave aggressively rather than actual aggression, focus on the nature of online aggression rather than clear determinants, focus on victims rather than perpetrators, and examine related but broader phenomena that may not be aggressive in nature, such as online firestorms and online moral outrage.

To avoid overlooking important determinants that were not identified by this search strategy, an additional snowballing procedure was used: The studies thus identified and additional literature reviews were examined, and relevant sources were added. The overall search resulted in 228 articles.

Individual determinants in each study were then identified and categorized on an Excel spreadsheet according to the specific online manifestation, domain (social status, individual, situational), subdomain, factors examined, specific determinants, and direction of each effect. A complete list of references is available on request. The studies included surveys, experiments, content analyses, network analyses, and conjunctive analyses of case configurations.

One limitation is that the geolinguistic breadth of the study is constrained by the exclusion of non-English items. Furthermore, the exclusion of some publication formats, such as monographs, may ignore thorough and critical studies. However, these constraints are compensated for by the fact that meta-analyses and literature reviews are referenced throughout the chapter. Finally, limiting the search to the defined key terms may have overlooked relevant research that uses synonymous niche terms such as "racist microaggressions on the internet," "technology-facilitated sexual violence," and "Zoombombing." However, the rather infrequent use of such niche terms justifies their exclusion.

Results

The results show that the determinants studied so far cover all three domains (see Table 28.3 for an overview). However, some determinants are primarily examined in the context of specific manifestations, such as some psychological symptoms associated with trolling behavior.

Individual determinants

The individual-level determinants identified are categorized into four subdomains: descriptive beliefs, evaluative beliefs, emotions and needs, and personality.

Descriptive beliefs refer to an individual's perception of facts and relationships in the external world (Elster, 2015). The results show that aggressive online users are more likely to hold particular beliefs about anonymity, social influence, and their social position and skills than nonaggressive users. Aggressive online users rationally consider anonymity on the internet, which offers them apparent protection from consequences: They perceive themselves as more anonymous online (Lee, 2017; Zhong et al., 2020), are more confident about not getting caught, and believe that online content is not permanent (Wright, 2013). These beliefs are based on the familiar online toxic disinhibition effect, which describes how people feel less restrained online than in person (Suler, 2004). Further, perceived social influence may contribute: People who are "toxically disinhibited" online are more likely to believe that their close social environment approves of such behaviors (Wu et al., 2017). Moreover, aggression can also compensate for perceived low status, such as in sexual hierarchy: Individuals who become abusive in digital dating perceive their value as partners to be lower than that of their partners (Bhogal et al., 2021). The opposite holds for communication technology skills: Individuals who rate their skills as high are more likely to engage in cyberbullying (Musharraf et al., 2019).

Evaluative beliefs, conversely, refer to individual judgments and evaluations of facts and relationships in the external world (Elster, 2015). Online aggression expresses preferences for particular sociopolitical orientations, social boundaries, and norms of interaction.

Table 28.3 Overview of determinants of online aggression

Domain	Subdomain	Factors examined
Individual determinants	Descriptive beliefs	Perceptions about anonymity, about social influence, and about position and skills
	Evaluative beliefs	Preferred socio-political orientations, social boundaries, and interaction norms
	Emotions and needs	Situation anger
		Depression, low self-esteem, self-contempt
		Emotionally motivated goals
	Personality	Dark triad
		Big Five
		Types of humor
		Psychological symptoms
		Tendency for social comparison
Situational determinants	Technical affordances	Technological infrastructure
		Design and governance structures of platforms
		Technological features
		Technology and internet use
	Social norms	Online groups
		Descriptive norms
		Injunctive norms
	Emotional-conflictive experiences	Informational triggers
		Social triggers
Social status	Achieved status	Socioeconomic factors (e.g., income, education, social capital)
	Ascribed status	Sociodemographic factors (e.g., gender, age, race)

Many studies suggest that both individual and institutional actors engage in aggressive online behavior to pursue specific sociopolitical preferences and goals. Individual users may react aggressively to a perceived threat, whether to their social identity (Glaser et al., 2002; Nauroth et al., 2015) or to their health, as in the COVID-19 pandemic (Alsawalqa, 2021), to a perceived social injustice (Erjavec & Kovačič, 2012), and to dissatisfaction with, for example, the quality of mass media (Eberwein, 2020). In their devotion to a political or other cause (Eberwein, 2020), they may aim to enforce a social order (Marwick, 2021; Rost et al., 2016) or an ideology, such as alt-right communities that seek "to facilitate the creation of a pan-national cultural identity centered on the fetishization of 'free speech' and 'troll culture'" (Hodge & Hallgrímsdóttir, 2020, p. 575). Misogynistic ideologies are particularly well studied: aggressive users in online gaming, online dating, and the manosphere and incel communities more strongly endorse unequal social hierarchies, espouse patriarchal norms, and see their masculinity threatened (Baele et al., 2021; Fox & Tang, 2014; Seo et al., 2022; Tang & Fox, 2016). They attempt to "(re)position women and femininity as sexually subordinate to masculinity and men" (Thompson, 2018, p. 69) and enforce a "cis-hetero-patriarchal gender order" (Richardson-Self, 2019, p. 573). Aggressive users often have distinct political opinions (Bernatzky et al., 2021; Rains et al., 2017) on both sides of the ideological left-right spectrum, albeit with a right-leaning and populist overhang (Frischlich et al., 2021; Golovchenko et al., 2020). Political orientations are closely related to the idea of trust: Although social trust as measured by regional voting turnout was not found to affect cyberhate (Denti & Faggian, 2021), aggressive online users showed a weaker sense of trust and belonging in their offline networks and a stronger one in their online networks (Kaakinen et al., 2018). Moreover, political institutions use sociopolitical aggression: State-organized trolls in Iran, Russia, and Turkey, among other countries, manipulate public opinion and suppress dissenting views (Bulut & Yörük, 2017; Kargar & Rauchfleisch, 2019). Another preference often connected with sociopolitical orientations is for establishing and maintaining social boundaries (inspired by Graham, 2019). For example, in online games and in YouTube streams of professional women's street-skating competitions, female competitors are harassed as perceived unlawful intruders to maintain an imagined exclusive territory for male players and skaters (McCarthy, 2022; Seo et al., 2022). Manosphere communities seek to enforce "the boundaries of a heterosexual, hegemonic masculinity" (Jones et al., 2020, p. 1903). Finally, racist YouTube commenters seek to maintain white online spaces and racial boundaries (Kettrey & Laster, 2014), and the American alt(ernative)-right seeks to create cultural boundaries for far-right online communities (Hodge & Hallgrímsdóttir, 2020). Moreover, aggressive users adjust their preferences for interaction norms so that these mentally prepare, and excuse, them for violations of commonly accepted interaction norms. They exhibit higher levels of moral disengagement by cognitively redefining their harmful actions, which causes them to feel less guilt and shame toward victims (Fang et al., 2020; Faulkner & Bliuc, 2016; Ye et al., 2021); this is supported by a meta-analysis (Zhao & Yu, 2021). Similarly, they generally view aggressive online behavior as more acceptable (Chan et al., 2019; Hilvert-Bruce & Neill, 2020).

Emotions and needs refer to the emotional basis of online aggression and the possibly unmet basic needs to be satisfied through aggression. Situational anger can lead to aggression, whether because of feeling unsafe and unfairly treated or due to inappropriate behavior by others (Johnson et al., 2009; Stephens et al., 2016). More chronically, depression, low self-esteem, and self-contempt are more common among cyberbullying and hateful users (Kaakinen et al., 2020; Kircaburun et al., 2020; Scotto di Carlo, 2022), although the effects of low self-esteem are inconsistent (March & Steele, 2020). Finally, trolls and hateful users are driven by diverse emotional motivation such as personal pleasure, thrill, attention, boredom, revenge, gaining rank, and against a backdrop of loneliness and a greater need for participation in social media (Ballard & Welch, 2017; Cook et al., 2018; Erjavec & Kovačič, 2012; Ozden Yildirim, 2019; Shachaf & Hara, 2010).

Personality refers to the personality traits and psychological symptoms that, according to the psychological literature, are more pronounced in aggressive online users than in nonaggressive ones. Probably the most commonly studied personality type is the dark triad; trolling users in particular show higher scores in sadism, psychopathy, and Machiavellianism, which means they are more cynical, emotionally detached, and willing to manipulate others (Buckels et al., 2014, 2018; Karlsson & Kajonius, 2020; Lee et al., 2021; March, 2019). A systematic literature review confirms the relevance of these traits, particularly of psychopathy, for diverse aggressive online behaviors (Moor & Anderson, 2019). The Big Five, a taxonomy for personality traits, have also been studied in this respect, with evidence of negative correlations with agreeableness, conscientiousness, and openness, and positive correlations with extraversion (Gylfason et al., 2021; Kim et al., 2020; Koban et al., 2018). In addition, particular types of humor are more pronounced among aggressive users. These include aggressive humor and the pleasure of laughing at others for their misfortune, termed schadenfreude, self-defeating humor and self-irony, and the pleasure of being laughed at (Brubaker et al., 2021; Craker & March, 2016; March, 2019; Navarro-Carrillo et al., 2021). Aggressive users also feel rewarded for causing discord in others, termed negative social potency. Moreover, cyberbullying and trolling users score higher on various psychological symptoms: impulsive, callous, and unemotional traits (Koban et al., 2018; Kokkinos et al., 2014; March et al., 2017); psychoticism (Arıcak, 2009); sensation seeking (Kokkinos et al., 2014); stress (Schenk et al., 2013); aggressive traits characterized by hostile cognition, anger, and readiness (Song et al., 2019); and autistic traits (Seigfried-Spellar et al., 2015). They are also more prone to suicidal behavior (Schenk et al., 2013). In addition, they tend to have lower empathy and lower mindfulness: conscious and nonjudgmental attention to one's current mind and body (Kokkinos et al., 2014; March, 2019; Wu et al., 2017). Finally, aggressive users are more inclined to make social comparisons: Trolling users feel more inferior (Hong & Cheng, 2018) and are more likely to make downward social comparisons on social media (Howard et al., 2019; Stephens et al., 2016). In this context, online misogyny increases among men who are more competitive with other men for mates and in regions with higher mating competition (Bhogal et al., 2021; Brooks et al., 2022).

Situational determinants

The situational-level determinants describe the remote and immediate characteristics of the digital media environment and the surrounding social context. They are categorized into three subdomains: technical affordances, social norms, and emotional-conflictive experiences.

Technical affordances describe the "possibilities for action . . . between an object/technology and the user that enables or constrains potential behavioral outcomes in a particular context" (Evans et al., 2017, p. 36). Affordances relevant to online aggression include the technological infrastructure, design, and governance structures of online platforms, specific technological features, and technology and internet use. At a global level, the fundamental technological infrastructure of the internet enables online aggression to thrive. Social media create "a new digital 'public agora' for the mass production, consumption and spread" of hateful content (Williams & Burnap, 2015, p. 234). The nature of social networks and the interconnectedness of the internet allow hate networks to form global "hate highways" across online platforms that, when banned, quickly adapt, rewire, and flourish (Johnson et al., 2019, p. 261). On a smaller scale, hashtag networks allow hate groups to unite, such as White supremacists' using Trump's "MAGA" campaign (Eddington, 2018). In addition, the design and governance structures of online platforms are influential. Matamoros-Fernández (2017) illustrates how platforms reinforce the spread of racist content through likes that influence algorithms, systems that recommend racist content, humor protection, and distributed content curation whose editorial practices are unclear and arbitrary enforcement of rules. Massanari (2017, p. 1) shows how the aggregation of material on Reddit, the ease of creating subreddits and user accounts, and the reward systems for gaining visibility provide fertile ground for misogynistic content and "toxic technocultures." From an economic perspective, the focus on videos, the logic of paying video creators, and the recommendation system determine the supply of and demand for hateful content on YouTube (Munger & Phillips, 2022). From a more abstract value perspective, Siapera and Viejo-Otero (2021, p. 112) believe that Facebook reproduces social inequality because it approaches hate speech as a race-blind, operational problem of "enforcement, data, and efficiency" rather than addressing issues of history, power, and injustice. In a similar vein, Salter (2018, p. 247) notes how a logic of "technological rationality" guides "the sociotechnical arrangements that make such abuse possible and impactful." Among specific technological features, studies have often highlighted anonymity. People are more aggressive if they are, for example, not visible to others, use unidentifiable names and fake accounts, and have no eye contact than those in identifiable circumstances (Lapidot-Lefler & Barak, 2012; Moore et al., 2012; Nitschinsk et al., 2022; Rowe, 2015). However, some studies have failed to find any effects of anonymity and have even identified circumstances under which aggressive users benefit from non-anonymity (Rost et al., 2016). Mobility is also relevant: Communication on mobile devices is more aggressive than on fixed web devices (Groshek & Cutino, 2016). In addition to these factors, aggressive users differ from nonaggressive users in their overall technology and internet use. Aggressive users spend more time using technology (Balakrishnan, 2015; Lowry et al., 2016) and appear to be occasional rather than frequent commenters (Coe et al., 2014; Costello & Hawdon, 2018). They exhibit more problematic or compulsive use of social media: They are cognitively more preoccupied with them, use them excessively, and show withdrawal symptoms (Kırcaburun et al., 2019; Zych et al., 2021). They also contribute content more frequently on particular social media platforms than on others (Costello & Hawdon, 2018; Hong & Cheng, 2018; Oz et al., 2018; Tang & Fox, 2016), underlining the significance of platform architecture.

Social norms describe the social rules that signal what behavior is acceptable. Online groups represent a source of normative and injunctive norms that influence whether online users choose to be aggressive or not. In some online communities and social networks, views that promote aggression are shared and normalized. Examples include like-minded online cliques and identity bubbles (Zych et al., 2021) that rally around, for example, misogyny, racism, and homophobia (Hardaker & McGlashan, 2016). Such community hate is more prevalent in smaller, more isolated, and hierarchical network clusters (Uyheng & Carley, 2021). However, such homogeneity processes are not always straightforward, as suggested by evidence of a decline in incivility the more online users are surrounded by members of their own group (Rains et al., 2017). One concrete mechanism is the behavior of other users, termed descriptive norms. Users tend to be aggressive when exposed to aggressive content and social interactions (Álvarez-Benjumea & Winter, 2018; Antoci et al., 2016; Kim et al., 2021; Seo et al., 2022; Shmargad et al., 2022). Some authors have taken a more dynamic perspective to show how imitation, social interactions, and reciprocity predict aggression on YouTube (Chen & Wang, 2022; Kwon & Gruzd, 2017). Such networked processes can lead, among other things, to an "affective economy of racialized affects" that motivates aggressive commenting (Murthy & Sharma, 2019, p. 209). Another mechanism is the rewards and disapprovals that users receive from others, termed injunctive norms. For example, up-votes for aggressive comments are motivating (Shmargad et al., 2022), and disapproving messages, comment moderation, and reputation management systems are deterring (Álvarez-Benjumea & Winter, 2018; Bilewicz et al., 2021; Chan et al., 2019; Lampe et al., 2014).

Emotional-conflictive experiences refer to stressful informational and social situational triggers that motivate online aggression. They can be informational in nature: Online aggression is reinforced by misinformation (Fichman & Vaughn, 2021), by sensitive, polarizing, and political topics, including racism, gender equality, sports, economy, political conflicts, and religion (Coe et al., 2014; Oz et al., 2018; Salminen et al., 2020), and by controversial policy debates and emotional political events such as terror attacks (Scharwächter & Müller, 2020; Theocharis et al., 2020). They can also be predominantly social in nature: Online users are more likely to be aggressive online if they experienced childhood emotional trauma (Kircaburun et al., 2020), live in regions where residents disagree in their attitudes toward racism (Rosenbusch et al., 2020), have their beliefs directly challenged (Hutchens et al., 2015), and experience threatening acts of rejection or criticism (Chen, 2015). Thus men, but not women, displace negative emotions resulting from work stress through online aggression (Vranjes et al., 2021). Moreover, if men perform poorly in shooter games, they attack female players who disrupt the male hierarchy by participating in the game (Kasumovic & Kuznekoff, 2015). Moreover, aggressive users experience more online victimization than nonaggressive users (Balakrishnan, 2015; Ballard & Welch, 2017; Costello & Hawdon, 2018; Wilson & Seigfried-Spellar, 2022), although the causality can run in both directions: Perpetrators attract aggression through their aggressive behavior, and victims respond with aggressive acts of revenge.

Social status

Social status refers to an individual's position in the social hierarchy and is usually signaled by the possession of a particular kind of capital, such as economic or social capital. This link to online aggression has been uncovered by a more recent line of research using individual-level survey data and social media data in combination with regional aggregate or collective data. The determinants are categorized into two subdomains: achieved status and ascribed status, although hardly any of the study authors refer to these concepts explicitly.

Achieved status describes positions that, in principle, can be taken by anyone and that can change over the life course (Bowles & Gintis, 2002). Achieved status is usually signaled by socioeconomic indicators. Associations with income, education, and social capital have been examined, with mixed results. More online aggression is identified in regions with greater economic inequality and economic insecurity (Denti & Faggian, 2021) and among individuals with lower incomes (Frischlich et al., 2021; Wilson & Seigfried-Spellar, 2022), as well as unemployment and rural residence (Stahel & Weingartner, 2023). Other studies have found no significant effects (Costello & Hawdon, 2018; Lowry et al., 2016). Moreover, online aggression is identified in regions with lower education (Vargo & Hopp, 2017), whereas individuals with higher education are less aggressive online (Frischlich et al., 2021; Stahel & Weingartner, 2023). Again, nonsignificant effects were also found (Costello & Hawdon, 2018; Lowry et al., 2016). Finally, online aggression has been associated with weaker social capital, at least offline. It is identified in regions with low potential for interconnected civic networks (Vargo & Hopp, 2017) and among individuals who enjoy less social support and feel lonelier (Masui, 2019; Wilson & Seigfried-Spellar, 2022).

Ascribed status describes positions that are socially classified as higher or lower but are difficult for individuals to control or change (Bowles & Gintis, 2002). Ascribed status is usually signaled by sociodemographic indicators. The only almost universally positive effect is that of male gender (Costello & Hawdon, 2018, 2018; Eriksson et al., 2023; March, 2019). While young age has been considered relevant (Buckels et al., 2014; Craker & March, 2016), Stahel and Weingartner (2023) identified aggression among individuals with ascribed social status associated with power claims, such as male gender, older age, and national citizenship. Finally, heterosexuals have been found to be more aggressive online than LGBTs (Ballard & Welch, 2017).

Conclusion

This chapter examined the literature on the determinants of online aggression appearing in journal articles published in the Web of Science and Google Scholar databases up to August 2022, followed by a snowballing process. This review contributes significantly to the fragmented literature on aggressive online behavior. It provides the first comprehensive overview of the determinants of adult online aggression. Moreover, the explanatory model proposed here, inspired by an analytical approach from sociology (Elster, 2015; Hedström & Ylikoski, 2010) and by situational action theory (Wikström & Treiber, 2009), helps to integrate the determinants identified thus far into a broad and theoretically meaningful framework. The proposed complex interplay contrasts with most previous empirical studies, which severely limit the number of determinants and domains considered and assume their parallel coexistence. It thus aligns with calls for more integrative and theory-based approaches to online aggression (Miller, 2021) and is consistent with DiMaggio et al.'s (2001, p. 329) general call for "explanatory models . . . of Internet use . . . that tie behavior directly to social and institutional context."

The results show that the determinants identified thus far can be grouped into three theoretically derived domains and associated newly proposed subdomains. Although some subdomains, such as evaluative beliefs, personality, and technical skills, are well established, others remain sparsely studied, including feelings and needs, social norms, and achieved and ascribed status. Overall, the findings suggest that the aggressive climate online is the result of diverse circumstances that make online aggression an appealing choice of action. One basic motivation seems consistent: to gain social status and rank, whether impulsive or instrumental and whether at the individual or group level (Bor & Petersen, 2022). This is indicated by personality traits that favor hierarchy, socioeconomic disadvantage and feelings of inferiority that call for aggressive compensation, and beliefs and stress that prepare for violence. This insight can also contribute to prevention and intervention measures. Addressing the underlying structural causes is one possible path. For example, attempts to change beliefs may be ineffective if the underlying structures of social inequality that produce them are not addressed or if the neutrality discourse of social media platforms remains unchallenged.

Three possible avenues are suggested for future research in this area. First, beyond the current predominance of correlations, more complex explanations of online aggression could be developed with causal models such as that proposed here, data collection, and designs such as panel designs. For example, individual and situational determinants may mediate the effects of social status on online aggression, and situational circumstances may moderate the effects of individual determinants on online aggression. Groundwork for such an approach has been laid by studies that assume interaction and mutual influence between the various determinants (Lim, 2017; Lowry et al., 2019; Stevens et al., 2021).

Second, more valid and additional determinants could be explored. Current self-reported online aggression may entail problems of social desirability, online content provides little information about its producers, and aggregate-level data risk ecological misconceptions. However, more valid results may be produced by data triangulation, for example of actual online behaviors and survey data (Hopp et al., 2020; Reiter-Haas et al., 2022). A sociological perspective may well be particularly instructive in examining potential "civility divides" in society more systematically: This term describes the idea that those endowed with resources and privileges offline also benefit disproportionately online while those disadvantaged offline find themselves in hostile and damaging spaces on the internet (Vargo & Hopp, 2017, p. 24). For example, resources such as the skills and time to produce aggression may be unequally distributed. An equally desirable research development is to increase variance in the characteristics of social groups examined, including age across the lifespan and similar demographic data.

Third, various possible patterns of aggressive online behavior could be differentiated. For example, users may differ in how often they are aggressive, how experienced they are, and what kind of aggressive manifestation they primarily use. This can affect the explanatory power of determinants, as already suggested by Lowry et al. (2019).

References

Alsawalqa, R. O. (2021). Cyberbullying, social stigma, and self-esteem: The impact of COVID-19 on students from East and Southeast Asia at the University of Jordan. *Heliyon, 7*(4), e06711.

Álvarez-Benjumea, A., & Winter, F. (2018). Normative change and culture of hate: An experiment in online environments. *European Sociological Review, 34*(3), 223–237.

Anderson, C. A., & Bushman, B. J. (2002). Human aggression. *Annual Review of Psychology, 53*, 27–51.

Antoci, A., Delfino, A., Paglieri, F., Panebianco, F., & Sabatini, F. (2016). Civility vs. Incivility in online social interactions: An evolutionary approach. *PLoS One, 11*(11), e0164286.

Arıcak, O. T. (2009). Psychiatric symptomatology as a predictor of cyberbullying among university students. *Eurasian Journal of Educational Research (EJER), 34*, 167–184.

Baele, S. J., Brace, L., & Coan, T. G. (2021). From "Incel" to "Saint": Analyzing the violent worldview behind the 2018 Toronto attack. *Terrorism and Political Violence, 33*(8), 1667–1691.

Balakrishnan, V. (2015). Cyberbullying among young adults in Malaysia: The roles of gender, age and Internet frequency. *Computers in Human Behavior, 46*, 149–157.

Ballard, M. E., & Welch, K. M. (2017). Virtual warfare: Cyberbullying and cyber-victimization in MMOG play. *Games and Culture, 12*(5), 466–491.

Bernatzky, C., Costello, M., & Hawdon, J. (2021). Who produces online hate?: An examination of the effects of self-control, social structure, & social learning. *American Journal of Criminal Justice*, 1–20. https://doi.org/10.1007/s12103-020-09597-3

Bhogal, M. S., Tudor, C., & Hira, S. (2021). The role of mating-relevant factors in the perpetration of digital dating abuse. *Journal of Interpersonal Violence, 37*(15–16), NP13707–NP13728.

Bilewicz, M., Tempska, P., Leliwa, G., Dowgiallo, M., Tańska, M., Urbaniak, R., & Wroczyński, M. (2021). Artificial intelligence against hate: Intervention reducing verbal aggression in the social network environment. *Aggressive Behavior, 47*(3), 260–266.

Bliuc, A.-M., Faulkner, N., Jakubowicz, A., & McGarty, C. (2018). Online networks of racial hate: A systematic review of 10 years of research on cyber-racism. *Computers in Human Behavior, 87*, 75–86.

Bor, A., & Petersen, M. B. (2022). The psychology of online political hostility: A comprehensive, cross-national test of the mismatch hypothesis. *American Political Science Review, 116*(1), 1–18.

Bowles, S., & Gintis, H. (2002). The inheritance of inequality. *Journal of Economic Perspectives, 16*(3), 3–30.

Brooks, R. C., Russo-Batterham, D., & Blake, K. R. (2022). Incel activity on social media linked to local mating ecology. *Psychological Science, 33*(2), 249–258.

Brubaker, P. J., Montez, D., & Church, S. H. (2021). The power of schadenfreude: Predicting behaviors and perceptions of trolling among reddit users. *Social Media+ Society, 7*(2), 1–13.

Buckels, E. E., Trapnell, P. D., Andjelovic, T., & Paulhus, D. L. (2018). Internet trolling and everyday sadism: Parallel effects on pain perception and moral judgment. *Journal of Personality, 87*, 328–340.

Buckels, E. E., Trapnell, P. D., & Paulhus, D. L. (2014). Trolls just want to have fun. *Personality and Individual Differences, 67*, 97–102.

Bulut, E., & Yörük, E. (2017). Digital populism: Trolls and political polarization of Twitter in Turkey. *International Journal of Communication, 11*, 4093–4117.

Carvacho, H., Zick, A., Haye, A., González, R., Manzi, J., Kocik, C., & Bertl, M. (2013). On the relation between social class and prejudice: The roles of education, income, and ideological attitudes. *European Journal of Social Psychology, 43*(4), 272–285.

Chan, T. K., Cheung, C. M., & Wong, R. Y. (2019). Cyberbullying on social networking sites: The crime opportunity and affordance perspectives. *Journal of Management Information Systems, 36*(2), 574–609.

Chen, G. M. (2015). Losing face on social media: Threats to positive face lead to an indirect effect on retaliatory aggression through negative affect. *Communication Research, 42*(6), 819–838.

Chen, Y., & Wang, L. (2022). Misleading political advertising fuels incivility online: A social network analysis of 2020 US presidential election campaign video comments on YouTube. *Computers in Human Behavior, 131*, 107202.

Coe, K., Kenski, K., & Rains, S. A. (2014). Online and uncivil? Patterns and determinants of incivility in newspaper website comments. *Journal of Communication, 64*(4), 658–679.

Cook, C., Schaafsma, J., & Antheunis, M. (2018). Under the bridge: An in-depth examination of online trolling in the gaming context. *New Media & Society, 20*(9), 3323–3340.

Corcoran, L., Mc Guckin, C., & Prentice, G. (2015). Cyberbullying or cyber aggression?: A review of existing definitions of cyber-based peer-to-peer aggression. *Societies, 5*(2), 245–255.

Costello, M., & Hawdon, J. (2018). Who are the online extremists among us? Sociodemographic characteristics, social networking, and online experiences of those who produce online hate materials. *Violence and Gender, 5*(1), 55–60. https://doi.org/10.1089/vio.2017.0048

Craker, N., & March, E. (2016). The dark side of Facebook®: The Dark Tetrad, negative social potency, and trolling behaviours. *Personality and Individual Differences, 102*, 79–84.

Denti, D., & Faggian, A. (2021). Where do angry birds tweet? Income inequality and online hate in Italy. *Cambridge Journal of Regions, Economy and Society, 14*(3), 483–506. https://doi.org/10.1093/cjres/rsab016

DiMaggio, P., Hargittai, E., Neuman, W. R., & Robinson, J. P. (2001). Social implications of the internet. *Annual Review of Sociology, 27*(1), 307–336.

Eberwein, T. (2020). "Trolls" or "warriors of faith"? Differentiating dysfunctional forms of media criticism in online comments. *Journal of Information, Communication and Ethics in Society, 18*(4), 575–587.

Eddington, S. M. (2018). The communicative constitution of hate organizations online: A semantic network analysis of "Make America Great Again". *Social Media + Society, 4*, 1–12. https://doi.org/10.1177/2056305118790763

Elster, J. (2015). *Explaining social behavior: More nuts and bolts for the social sciences* (2nd ed.). Cambridge University Press.

Eriksson, L., McGee, T. R., Rosse, V., Bond, C., & Horstman, N. (2023). When cyberaggression is personal: Gender differences in threats and betrayals of partners and friends. *Journal of Aggression, Conflict and Peace Research, 15*(2), 95–108.

Erjavec, K., & Kovačič, M. P. (2012). "You don't understand, this is a new war!" Analysis of hate speech in news web sites' comments. *Mass Communication and Society, 15*(6), 899–920.

Evans, S. K., Pearce, K. E., Vitak, J., & Treem, J. W. (2017). Explicating affordances: A conceptual framework for understanding affordances in communication research. *Journal of Computer-Mediated Communication, 22*(1), 35–52.

Fang, J., Wang, X., Yuan, K.-H., Wen, Z., Yu, X., & Zhang, G. (2020). Callous-Unemotional traits and cyberbullying perpetration: The mediating role of moral disengagement and the moderating role of empathy. *Personality and Individual Differences, 157*, 109829.

Faulkner, N., & Bliuc, A.-M. (2016). 'It's okay to be racist': Moral disengagement in online discussions of racist incidents in Australia. *Ethnic and Racial Studies, 39*(14), 2545–2563.

Ferguson, C. J. (2021). Does the internet make the world worse? Depression, aggression and polarization in the social media age. *Bulletin of Science, Technology & Society, 41*(4), 116–135.

Fichman, P., & Vaughn, M. (2021). The relationships between misinformation and outrage trolling tactics on two Yahoo! Answers categories. *Journal of the Association for Information Science and Technology, 72*(12), 1498–1510.

Fox, J., & Tang, W. Y. (2014). Sexism in online video games: The role of conformity to masculine norms and social dominance orientation. *Computers in Human Behavior, 33*, 314–320. https://doi.org/10.1016/j.chb.2013.07.014

Frischlich, L., Schatto-Eckrodt, T., Boberg, S., & Wintterlin, F. (2021). Roots of incivility: How personality, media use, and online experiences shape uncivil participation. *Media and Communication*, 9(1), 195–208.

Glaser, J., Dixit, J., & Green, D. P. (2002). Studying hate crime with the internet: What makes racists advocate racial violence? *Journal of Social Issues*, 58(1), 177–193.

Golf-Papez, M., & Veer, E. (2017). Don't feed the trolling: Rethinking how online trolling is being defined and combated. *Journal of Marketing Management*, 33(15–16), 1336–1354.

Golovchenko, Y., Buntain, C., Eady, G., Brown, M. A., & Tucker, J. A. (2020). Cross-platform state propaganda: Russian trolls on Twitter and YouTube during the 2016 US presidential election. *The International Journal of Press/Politics*, 25(3), 357–389.

Goubin, S., & Hooghe, M. (2020). The effect of inequality on the relation between socioeconomic stratification and political trust in Europe. *Social Justice Research*, 33, 219–247.

Graham, E. (2019). Boundary maintenance and the origins of trolling. *New Media & Society*, 21(9), 2029–2047.

Graham, R. S., & Smith, S. K. (2019). *Cybercrime and digital deviance*. Routledge.

Groshek, J., & Cutino, C. (2016). Meaner on mobile: Incivility and impoliteness in communicating contentious politics on sociotechnical networks. *Social Media+ Society*, 2(4), 1–10.

Gylfason, H. F., Sveinsdottir, A. H., Vésteinsdóttir, V., & Sigurvinsdottir, R. (2021). Haters gonna hate, trolls gonna troll: The personality profile of a Facebook troll. *International Journal of Environmental Research and Public Health*, 18(11), 5722.

Hardaker, C., & McGlashan, M. (2016). "Real men don't hate women": Twitter rape threats and group identity. *Journal of Pragmatics*, 91, 80–93.

Hedström, P., & Ylikoski, P. (2010). Causal mechanisms in the social sciences. *Annual review of Sociology*, 36, 49–67.

Hilvert-Bruce, Z., & Neill, J. T. (2020). I'm just trolling: The role of normative beliefs in aggressive behaviour in online gaming. *Computers in Human Behavior*, 102, 303–311.

Hodge, E., & Hallgrímsdóttir, H. K. (2020). Networks of hate: The alt-right, "troll culture", and the cultural geography of social movement spaces online. *Journal of Borderlands Studies*, 35(4), 563–580.

Hong, F.-Y., & Cheng, K.-T. (2018). Correlation between university students' online trolling behavior and online trolling victimization forms, current conditions, and personality traits. *Telematics and Informatics*, 35(2), 397–405.

Hopp, T. (2019). A network analysis of political incivility dimensions. *Communication and the Public*, 4(3), 204–223.

Hopp, T., Vargo, C. J., Dixon, L., & Thain, N. (2020). Correlating self-report and trace data measures of incivility: A proof of concept. *Social Science Computer Review*, 38(5), 584–599.

Howard, K., Zolnierek, K. H., Critz, K., Dailey, S., & Ceballos, N. (2019). An examination of psychosocial factors associated with malicious online trolling behaviors. *Personality and Individual Differences*, 149, 309–314.

Hutchens, M. J., Cicchirillo, V. J., & Hmielowski, J. D. (2015). How could you think that?!?!: Understanding intentions to engage in political flaming. *New Media & Society*, 17(8), 1201–1219.

Jane, E. A. (2015). Flaming? What flaming? The pitfalls and potentials of researching online hostility. *Ethics and Information Technology*, 17(1), 65–87.

Jenaro, C., Flores, N., & Frías, C. P. (2018). Systematic review of empirical studies on cyberbullying in adults: What we know and what we should investigate. *Aggression and Violent Behavior*, 38, 113–122.

Johnson, N. A., Cooper, R. B., & Chin, W. W. (2009). Anger and flaming in computer-mediated negotiation among strangers. *Decision Support Systems*, 46(3), 660–672.

Johnson, N. F., Leahy, R., Restrepo, N. J., Velasquez, N., Zheng, M., Manrique, P., Devkota, P., & Wuchty, S. (2019). Hidden resilience and adaptive dynamics of the global online hate ecology. *Nature*, 573(7773), 261–265. https://doi.org/10.1038/s41586-019-1494-7

Jones, C., Trott, V., & Wright, S. (2020). Sluts and soyboys: MGTOW and the production of misogynistic online harassment. *New Media & Society*, 22(10), 1903–1921.

Kaakinen, M., Räsänen, P., Näsi, M., Minkkinen, J., Keipi, T., & Oksanen, A. (2018). Social capital and online hate production: A four country survey. *Crime, Law and Social Change*, 69, 25–39. https://doi.org/10.1007/s10611-017-9764-5

Kaakinen, M., Sirola, A., Savolainen, I., & Oksanen, A. (2020). Impulsivity, internalizing symptoms, and online group behavior as determinants of online hate. *PLoS One, 15*(4), e0231052.

Kargar, S., & Rauchfleisch, A. (2019). State-aligned trolling in Iran and the double-edged affordances of Instagram. *New Media & Society, 21*(7), 1506–1527.

Karlsson, A. M. C., & Kajonius, P. J. (2020). Not only Trolls are Trolling the Internet: A study on dark personality traits, online environment, and commentary styles. *International Journal of Personality Psychology, 6*, 12–23.

Kasumovic, M. M., & Kuznekoff, J. H. (2015). Insights into sexism: Male status and performance moderates female-directed hostile and amicable behaviour. *PLoS One, 10*(7), e0131613.

Kettrey, H. H., & Laster, W. N. (2014). Staking territory in the "World White Web" an exploration of the roles of overt and color-blind racism in maintaining racial boundaries on a popular web site. *Social Currents, 1*(3), 257–274.

Kim, J. W., Guess, A., Nyhan, B., & Reifler, J. (2021). The distorting prism of social media: How self-selection and exposure to incivility fuel online comment toxicity. *Journal of Communication, 71*(6), 922–946.

Kim, M., Clark, S. L., Donnellan, M. B., & Burt, S. A. (2020). A multi-method investigation of the personality correlates of digital aggression. *Journal of Research in Personality, 85*, 103923.

Kircaburun, K., Demetrovics, Z., Király, O., & Griffiths, M. D. (2020). Childhood emotional trauma and cyberbullying perpetration among emerging adults: A multiple mediation model of the role of problematic social media use and psychopathology. *International Journal of Mental Health and Addiction, 18*(3), 548–566.

Kircaburun, K., Kokkinos, C. M., Demetrovics, Z., Király, O., Griffiths, M. D., & Çolak, T. S. (2019). Problematic online behaviors among adolescents and emerging adults: Associations between cyberbullying perpetration, problematic social media use, and psychosocial factors. *International Journal of Mental Health and Addiction, 17*(4), 891–908.

Koban, K., Stein, J.-P., Eckhardt, V., & Ohler, P. (2018). Quid pro quo in Web 2.0. Connecting personality traits and Facebook usage intensity to uncivil commenting intentions in public online discussions. *Computers in Human Behavior, 79*, 9–18.

Kokkinos, C. M., Antoniadou, N., & Markos, A. (2014). Cyber-bullying: An investigation of the psychological profile of university student participants. *Journal of Applied Developmental Psychology, 35*(3), 204–214.

Kwon, K. H., & Gruzd, A. (2017). Is offensive commenting contagious online? Examining public vs interpersonal swearing in response to Donald Trump's YouTube campaign videos. *Internet Research, 27*(4), 991–1010.

Lampe, C., Zube, P., Lee, J., Park, C. H., & Johnston, E. (2014). Crowdsourcing civility: A natural experiment examining the effects of distributed moderation in online forums. *Government Information Quarterly, 31*(2), 317–326.

Lapidot-Lefler, N., & Barak, A. (2012). Effects of anonymity, invisibility, and lack of eye-contact on toxic online disinhibition. *Computers in Human Behavior, 28*(2), 434–443.

Lee, E. B. (2017). Cyberbullying: Prevalence and predictors among African American young adults. *Journal of Black Studies, 48*(1), 57–73.

Lee, S. Y., Yao, M. Z., & Su, L. Y.-F. (2021). Expressing unpopular opinion or trolling: Can dark personalities differentiate them? *Telematics and Informatics, 63*, 101645.

Lim, M. (2017). Freedom to hate: Social media, algorithmic enclaves, and the rise of tribal nationalism in Indonesia. *Critical Asian Studies, 49*(3), 411–427. https://doi.org/10.1080/14672715.2017.1341188

Lorant, V., Deliège, D., Eaton, W., Robert, A., Philippot, P., & Ansseau, M. (2003). Socioeconomic inequalities in depression: A meta-analysis. *American Journal of Epidemiology, 157*(2), 98–112.

Lowry, P. B., Zhang, J., Moody, G. D., Chatterjee, S., Wang, C., & Wu, T. (2019). An integrative theory addressing cyberharassment in the light of technology-based opportunism. *Journal of Management Information Systems, 36*(4), 1142–1178.

Lowry, P. B., Zhang, J., Wang, C., & Siponen, M. (2016). Why do adults engage in cyberbullying on social media? An integration of online disinhibition and deindividuation effects with the social structure and social learning model. *Information Systems Research, 27*(4), 962–986. https://doi.org/10.1287/isre.2016.0671

Malecki, W. P., Kowal, M., Dobrowolska, M., & Sorokowski, P. (2021). Defining online hating and online haters. *Frontiers in Psychology*, *12*, 744614.

March, E. (2019). Psychopathy, sadism, empathy, and the motivation to cause harm: New evidence confirms malevolent nature of the Internet Troll. *Personality and Individual Differences*, *141*, 133–137.

March, E., Grieve, R., Marrington, J., & Jonason, P. K. (2017). Trolling on Tinder®(and other dating apps): Examining the role of the Dark Tetrad and impulsivity. *Personality and Individual Differences*, *110*, 139–143.

March, E., & Steele, G. (2020). High esteem and hurting others online: Trait sadism moderates the relationship between self-esteem and internet trolling. *Cyberpsychology, Behavior, and Social Networking*, *23*(7), 441–446.

Marwick, A. E. (2021). Morally motivated networked harassment as normative reinforcement. *Social Media+ Society*, *7*(2), 1–15.

Massanari, A. (2017). # Gamergate and The Fappening: How Reddit's algorithm, governance, and culture support toxic technocultures. *New Media & Society*, *19*(3), 329–346.

Masui, K. (2019). Loneliness moderates the relationship between Dark Tetrad personality traits and internet trolling. *Personality and Individual Differences*, *150*, 109475.

Matamoros-Fernández, A. (2017). Platformed racism: The mediation and circulation of an Australian race-based controversy on Twitter, Facebook and YouTube. *Information, Communication & Society*, *20*(6), 930–946. https://doi.org/10.1080/1369118X.2017.1293130

McCarthy, B. (2022). 'Who unlocked the kitchen?': Online misogyny, YouTube comments and women's professional street skateboarding. *International Review for the Sociology of Sport*, *57*(3), 362–380.

McCuish, E. C., Corrado, R. R., Hart, S. D., & DeLisi, M. (2015). The role of symptoms of psychopathy in persistent violence over the criminal career into full adulthood. *Journal of Criminal Justice*, *43*(4), 345–356.

Miller, K. C. (2021). Hostility toward the press: A synthesis of terms, research, and future directions in examining harassment of journalists. *Digital Journalism*, 1–20. https://doi.org/10.1080/21670 811.2021.1991824

Moher, D., Liberati, A., Tetzlaff, J., Altman, D. G., & Group*, P. (2009). Preferred reporting items for systematic reviews and meta-analyses: The PRISMA statement. *Annals of Internal Medicine*, *151*(4), 264–269.

Moloney, M. E., & Love, T. P. (2018). Assessing online misogyny: Perspectives from sociology and feminist media studies. *Sociology Compass*, *12*(5), 1–12.

Moor, L., & Anderson, J. R. (2019). A systematic literature review of the relationship between dark personality traits and antisocial online behaviours. *Personality and Individual Differences*, *144*, 40–55.

Moore, M. J., Nakano, T., Enomoto, A., & Suda, T. (2012). Anonymity and roles associated with aggressive posts in an online forum. *Computers in Human Behavior*, *28*(3), 861–867.

Munger, K., & Phillips, J. (2022). Right-wing YouTube: A supply and demand perspective. *The International Journal of Press/Politics*, *27*(1), 186–219.

Murthy, D., & Sharma, S. (2019). Visualizing YouTube's comment space: Online hostility as a networked phenomena. *New Media & Society*, *21*(1), 191–213. https://doi.org/10.1177/1461444818792393

Musharraf, S., Bauman, S., Anis-ul-Haque, M., & Malik, J. A. (2019). General and ICT self-efficacy in different participants roles in cyberbullying/victimization among Pakistani university students. *Frontiers in Psychology*, *10*, 1098.

Nauroth, P., Gollwitzer, M., Bender, J., & Rothmund, T. (2015). Social identity threat motivates science-discrediting online comments. *PLoS One*, *10*(2), e0117476.

Navarro-Carrillo, G., Torres-Marín, J., & Carretero-Dios, H. (2021). Do trolls just want to have fun? Assessing the role of humor-related traits in online trolling behavior. *Computers in Human Behavior*, *114*, 106551.

Nitschinsk, L., Tobin, S. J., & Vanman, E. J. (2022). The disinhibiting effects of anonymity increase online trolling. *Cyberpsychology, Behavior, and Social Networking*, *25*(6), 377–383.

Oz, M., Zheng, P., & Chen, G. M. (2018). Twitter versus Facebook: Comparing incivility, impoliteness, and deliberative attributes. *New Media & Society*, *20*(9), 3400–3419.

Ozden Yildirim, M. S. (2019). The relationship between loneliness, malicious envy, and cyberbullying in emerging adults. *Education in the Knowledge Society (EKS)*, 20, 1–10.

Rains, S. A., Kenski, K., Coe, K., & Harwood, J. (2017). Incivility and political identity on the internet: Intergroup factors as predictors of incivility in discussions of news online. *Journal of Computer-Mediated Communication*, 22(4), 163–178.

Reiter-Haas, M., Klösch, B., Hadler, M., & Lex, E. (2022). Polarization of opinions on COVID-19 measures: Integrating Twitter and survey data. *Social Science Computer Review*, 0. https://doi.org/10.1177/08944393221087662

Richardson-Self, L. (2019). Cis-hetero-misogyny online. *Ethical Theory and Moral Practice*, 22(3), 573–587.

Rosenbusch, H., Evans, A. M., & Zeelenberg, M. (2020). Interregional and intraregional variability of intergroup attitudes predict online hostility. *European Journal of Personality*, 34(5), 859–872.

Rost, K., Stahel, L., & Frey, B. S. (2016). Digital social norm enforcement: Online firestorms in social media. *PLoS One*, 11(6), e0155923.

Rowe, I. (2015). Civility 2.0: A comparative analysis of incivility in online political discussion. *Information, Communication & Society*, 18(2), 121–138.

Salminen, J., Sengün, S., Corporan, J., Jung, S., & Jansen, B. J. (2020). Topic-driven toxicity: Exploring the relationship between online toxicity and news topics. *PLoS One*, 15(2), e0228723. https://doi.org/10.1371/journal.pone.0228723

Salter, M. (2018). From geek masculinity to Gamergate: The technological rationality of online abuse. *Crime, Media, Culture*, 14(2), 247–264.

Scharwächter, E., & Müller, E. (2020). Does terrorism trigger online hate speech? On the association of events and time series. *The Annals of Applied Statistics*, 14(3), 1285–1303.

Schenk, A. M., Fremouw, W. J., & Keelan, C. M. (2013). Characteristics of college cyberbullies. *Computers in Human Behavior*, 29(6), 2320–2327.

Scotto di Carlo, G. (2022). An analysis of self-other representations in the incelosphere: Between online misogyny and self-contempt. *Discourse & Society*, 34(1), 3–21.

Seigfried-Spellar, K. C., O'Quinn, C. L., & Treadway, K. N. (2015). Assessing the relationship between autistic traits and cyberdeviancy in a sample of college students. *Behaviour & Information Technology*, 34(5), 533–542.

Seo, Y., Oh, P., & Kil, W. Y. (2022). Into the wolves' den: An investigation of predictors of sexism in online games. *Behaviour & Information Technology*, 41(8), 1740–1754.

Shachaf, P., & Hara, N. (2010). Beyond vandalism: Wikipedia trolls. *Journal of Information Science*, 36(3), 357–370.

Shmargad, Y., Coe, K., Kenski, K., & Rains, S. A. (2022). Social norms and the dynamics of online incivility. *Social Science Computer Review*, 40(3), 717–735.

Siapera, E., & Viejo-Otero, P. (2021). Governing hate: Facebook and digital racism. *Television & New Media*, 22(2), 112–130.

Song, M., Zhu, Z., Liu, S., Fan, H., Zhu, T., & Zhang, L. (2019). Effects of aggressive traits on cyberbullying: Mediated moderation or moderated mediation? *Computers in Human Behavior*, 97, 167–178.

Stahel, L., & Weingartner, S. (2023). Can political orientation explain the social structure of online aggression? Integrating social media and survey data. *Sociological Inquiry*, 94(1), 149–169.

Stephens, A. N., Trawley, S. L., & Ohtsuka, K. (2016). Venting anger in cyberspace: Self-entitlement versus self-preservation in# roadrage tweets. *Transportation Research Part F: Traffic Psychology and Behaviour*, 42, 400–410.

Stevens, H., Acic, I., & Taylor, L. D. (2021). Uncivil reactions to sexual assault online: Linguistic features of news reports predict discourse incivility. *Cyberpsychology, Behavior, and Social Networking*, 24(12), 815–821.

Suler, J. (2004). The online disinhibition effect. *Cyberpsychology & Behavior*, 7(3), 321–326. https://doi.org/10.1089/1094931041291295

Tandoc, E. C., Sagun, K. K., & Alvarez, K. P. (2021). The digitization of harassment: Women journalists' experiences with online harassment in the Philippines. *Journalism Practice*, 1–16. https://doi.org/10.1080/17512786.2021.1981774

Tang, W. Y., & Fox, J. (2016). Men's harassment behavior in online video games: Personality traits and game factors. *Aggressive Behavior*, 42(6), 513–521.

Theocharis, Y., Barberá, P., Fazekas, Z., & Popa, S. A. (2020). The dynamics of political incivility on Twitter. *Sage Open*, *10*(2), 1–15.

Thompson, L. (2018). "I can be your Tinder nightmare": Harassment and misogyny in the online sexual marketplace. *Feminism & Psychology*, *28*(1), 69–89.

Uyheng, J., & Carley, K. M. (2021). Characterizing network dynamics of online hate communities around the COVID-19 pandemic. *Applied Network Science*, *6*(1), 1–21.

Vargo, C. J., & Hopp, T. (2017). Socioeconomic status, social capital, and partisan polarity as predictors of political incivility on Twitter: A congressional district-level analysis. *Social Science Computer Review*, *35*(1), 10–32. https://doi.org/10.1177/0894439315602858

Vranjes, I., Baillien, E., Erreygers, S., Vandebosch, H., & De Witte, H. (2021). You wouldn't like me when I'm angry: A daily diary study of displaced online aggression in dual-earner couples. *Applied Psychology*, *70*(4), 1463–1491.

Wikström, P.-O. H., & Treiber, K. H. (2009). Violence as situational action. *International Journal of Conflict and Violence (IJCV)*, *3*(1), 75–96.

Wilkinson, R. G., & Pickett, K. E. (2017). The enemy between us: The psychological and social costs of inequality. *European Journal of Social Psychology*, *47*(1), 11–24.

Williams, M. L., & Burnap, P. (2015). Cyberhate on social media in the aftermath of Woolwich: A case study in computational criminology and big data. *British Journal of Criminology*, *56*(2), 211–238.

Wilson, N. C., & Seigfried-Spellar, K. C. (2022). Cybervictimization, social, and financial strains influence internet trolling behaviors: A general strain theory perspective. *Social Science Computer Review*, *41*(3), 967–982.

Wright, M. F. (2013). The relationship between young adults' beliefs about anonymity and subsequent cyber aggression. *Cyberpsychology, Behavior, And Social Networking*, *16*(12), 858–862.

Wu, S., Lin, T.-C., & Shih, J.-F. (2017). Examining the antecedents of online disinhibition. *Information Technology & People*, *30*(1), 189–209.

Ye, B., Zeng, Y., Im, H., Liu, M., Wang, X., & Yang, Q. (2021). The relationship between fear of COVID-19 and online aggressive behavior: A moderated mediation model. *Frontiers in Psychology*, *12*, 589615.

Zhao, L., & Yu, J. (2021). A meta-analytic review of moral disengagement and cyberbullying. *Frontiers in Psychology*, *12*, 681299.

Zhong, L. R., Kebbell, M. R., & Webster, J. L. (2020). An exploratory study of Technology-Facilitated Sexual Violence in online romantic interactions: Can the Internet's toxic disinhibition exacerbate sexual aggression? *Computers in Human Behavior*, *108*, 106314.

Zych, I., Kaakinen, M., Savolainen, I., Sirola, A., Paek, H.-J., & Oksanen, A. (2021). The role of impulsivity, social relations online and offline, and compulsive Internet use in cyberaggression: A four-country study. *New Media & Society*, *25*(1), 181–198.

29

SUB THEME: METHODS AND DATA

Online deviance through the lens of Sociotechnical Interaction Network (STIN): case study of cyber trolls

Dr Kanika Sharma

Introduction

In May 2021, a 17-year-old boy committed suicide due to cyber-trolling.[1] The parents were most shocked as they had had a pleasant dinner together and the adolescent was happy before going to bed. According to his parents, he was a victim of cyber-trolling and abuse, which was later confirmed by the police cyber investigation. It was discovered that he was targeted online allegedly by several accounts belonging to minor girls. The term 'cyber murder', as used by his parents, is significant.

In October 2018, a 23-year-old boy died by suicide due to online humiliation as he used to perform as a woman by wearing sarees.[2] In April 2017, a Mumbai boy died by suicide while on Facebook Live, after which the trolls started leaving hurtful comments on his Facebook account.[3] These two examples are the severe consequences of online trolling. However, instances of trolling happen on a regular basis. For example, a woman was being trolled as she tattooed an actor's face on her chest,[4] a Chief Justice of India was trolled because of a sub judice matter,[5] the leader of the opposition party was trolled heavily on his remarks,[6] and so on.

Cyber-trolling has been examined from multiple angles, including a focus on trolling conduct, the behavior of trolls, the gender-related elements of trolling, and its criminological aspects. Trolling in the online realm revolves around factors like accessibility,[7] affordability,[8] anonymity, engagement, and political implications. Nevertheless, the deviant aspect of this virtual form of trolling warrants further investigation. There have been many cases, such as the Amber Heard vs Johnny Depp domestic violence trial,[9] Samantha Ruth Prabhu and her divorce,[10] the MeToo movement,[11] electoral votes and speeches,[12] and so on. Before we explore the scholarly discussions on the topic, let's begin by examining the historical context of the term 'troll'.

When we discuss trolls, typically, cheerful characters from an endearing and delightful animated movie with the same name pops into the imagination, wherein trolls enjoy their own lives and do no harm until and unless it's for their defence (and they sing, too!!!).

DOI: 10.4324/9781003277675-33

However, trolls are part of Scandinavian mythology and were appalling and antagonistic.[13] According to one of the narratives, trolls emerged in the night from their underground habitat, as sunlight can turn them into stone. In the other narratives, they are described as savage with facial features like Neanderthals, and were said to be cunning thieves and tricksters[14] who loved to provoke reactions from people. The other potential origin is the technique of fishing; that is, putting the baited lines into the water.[15] The metaphorical use of internet troll comes from this mythological creature, as the behavior of the internet troll is similar to the mythological trolls: creating chaos, discord, and disruption within the communities in the digital realm. Additionally, it is like baiting people to diversify from the said discussion by heightening their sensibilities, causing mayhem and confusion.[16] There are numerous discussions over the definition of 'trolling' and 'trolls'.[17] Hardaker (2010) examined the phenomenon of trolling and its definition for academic usage from user discussions. She has highlighted four characteristics of trolling in her analysis: deception,[18] aggression,[19] disruption,[20] and success.[21] Trolling is a more intricate mechanism wherein it's not only about provoked attacks; but these attacks are open for scrutiny by the users for its efficiency, success, and potency (ibid). As per the global definition, cyber-trolling is "The act of starting arguments in online social spaces by emotion-based messaging, such as calling out others, name-calling, sharing inaccurate information, posting off-topic messaging, and otherwise sharing disagreeable messages (including potentially threats)".[22] Most of the studies have been conducted to analyse the psychology of the cyber/internet troll, which includes the portrayal of psychopathy, narcissism, sadism, and Machiavellianism traits.[23] Further, many suffer from low to negligible self-esteem, need of validation and to have a sense of superiority, mystery, and control, also offering anonymity.[24] Another perspective is where Papez (2018) utilises actor-network theory to understand lighthearted online trolling behaviour in consumerism.[25] However, this study too focuses on the dimension of behavior of trolls by highlighting the network/users not the facet of virtual space per se.

On the contrary, Centola (2010)[26] conducted studies by using social network or computer-mediated communication (Hardaker, 2010). Moreover, studies have been conducted on online deviance by the application of criminological theories such as routine activity theories, social cohesion theory, and so on.[27] In the next section, the focus is on types of cyber-trolls and trolling.

Classification of cyber-trolling

The classification could be based on the personality of the trolls or on the basis of nature of trolling. According to Bishop (2014), there are two types of trolling: *flame trolling*, where the intention is to abuse and antagonize; *kudos trolling* is to intentionally incite someone for shared amusement; thirdly, *electronic message faults*, which is the act of sharing inappropriate or harmful content with the intent of harming someone's reputation, well-being, or privacy. Fichman and Sanfilippo (2016) categorized trolls into six groups based on their motivations and the topics with which they engage. These categories include Grief and RIP, ideological, LOL, nonideological, religion, and political. Political trolls belong to a category of ideological trolls. In political trolling, various tactics are employed, ranging from enticing partisan arguments with ideological adversaries on news forums and comment sections, to organized endeavors aimed at inundating online platforms through civic demonstrations (Sanfillipo et al., 2017). Satirical trolling primarily revolves around the use of irony and aims to provoke individuals into expressing viewpoints that can be easily challenged, subsequently subjecting them to mockery and ridicule (Fichman & McClelland, 2021). Mantilla (2013) proposed the concept of gendertrolling, which refers to a specific category of trolling targeting women. Gendertrolling involves coordinated attacks by multiple trolls, utilizing gender-based insults, employing vicious language, issuing credible threats, and launching unusually intense and persistent attacks as a response to women expressing their opinions or speaking out on various issues (ibid).[28] Another type is global trolling (Fichman, 2020), which uses cross-cultural references. Patriotic trolling (Sombatpoonsiri, 2018) is an effective strategy of repression that involves capitalizing on nationalist sentiments to rally public hostility against dissidents. Other than classification, there were some studies conducted for the detection and prevention of trolling, such as domain-adapted sentiment analysis,[29] sentic analysis for detection of trolls,[30] and a machine learning with bilingual analytics solution implemented as a web application that can detect and identify trolling and sarcasm within comments posted on a user's online content.[31]

Like the definition of trolling still varies depending on the authors and their contexts, the classification is also both overlapping and distinct. Consolidating them into a single structure is not appropriate, nor does it align with the objective of this chapter. With diverse implementations and viewpoints, the method presented in this chapter at the intersection of cyber-deviance and STS becomes more engaging. While a few authors have touched on certain aspects such as computer-mediated communication,[32] their primary focus has been on defining trolling and its classifications.

When there is a discussion about the concept of online deviance, most of the literature focuses on the identified role of the user as deviant or as victim or for the usage as social actors. However, the medium, or the first component of this concept, is forgotten or ignored. With the understanding that social and technology are co-produced, the current chapter brings forth the embeddedness of both online and deviance as a practice,[33] with the example of cyber-trolling projected in the socio-technical interaction network (STIN) models. Prior to delving into the concept of STIN, it is important to introduce the field of science and technology studies.

Co-construction of science, technology, and society

Scientific knowledge was regarded as an embodiment of universal truth, yet it was human individuals and groups who made the actual inventions and innovations (Gonzalez, 2005). Furthermore, there was a belief that this knowledge, whether theoretical or practical, existed independently of society (Gonzalez, 2005). However, in recognizing the involvement of people and the practical implications of scientific knowledge, a new perspective emerged that sought to understand science and technology in their social context (Gonzalez, 2005). The shift in focus can be observed through various notable changes. These changes include: a) Moving away from solely examining the inherent nature of science and technology (primarily their epistemic contents) to understanding how they are socially constructed; b) Shifting attention from the language and structure of fundamental science to exploring the characteristics of applied science and the practical applications of scientific knowledge; c) Transitioning from perceiving technology merely as a means for humans to control their natural environment (advancing beyond the concept of 'technics' with the influence of science) to recognizing technology as a social practice and a tool of power; d) Moving from emphasizing the importance of internal values for the development of 'mature science' and 'innovative technology' to recognizing the significance of contextual or external values (such as cultural, political, and economic factors) in shaping science and technology (Gonzalez, 2005).

With the aforementioned background in mind, we can now explore the different theoretical stances within Science and Technology Studies (STS) that provide insight into the dynamic relationship between science and society. Sismondo (2008) has described the various perspectives which are prevalent in the stream of science and technology studies (STS). One of the most important characteristics of STS as described by Sismondo is "how the things . . . are constructed" (ibid: 13). The three postulations on social constructivism about science and technology are that they are *social*, *active*, and *not natural* (ibid, emphasis in the original). The history of STS can be traced back to the usage of this term in Merton's doctoral dissertation *Science, technology and Society in Seventeenth Century England* in 1938, in which he illustrated how the social interactions had an effect on the experimental science of the seventeenth century (Merton, 1938). He describes the embedded nature of science in the social and cultural factors (ibid); and *The Structure of Scientific Revolutions* by Thomas Kuhn (1972) forms the crucial study in which he argues that science is not only about breakthrough of facts but shifts from 'normal science' and revolution and opens the platform to the dissection of 'science' as a social process.

The work of Kuhn and other philosophers opened up new domains to study scientific knowledge, one of which is the use of technological paradigm in the form of technological 'trajectory' by Thomas Hughes in 1969 (MacKenzie & Wajcman, 1999). According to him, the innovation is embedded in the 'technological system' (ibid). The other is the sociology of scientific knowledge (SSK). The strong programme is the field of studying science as a knowledge system of both true and false beliefs, contrary to the 'weak' programme as described by Bloor, which only studied the false beliefs. In contradistinction to this weak programme, David Bloor's (1976) and Barry Barnes's (1974) study outlined the 'strong programme', the main idea of which is to study the causes of knowledge (Sismondo, 2008). This programme proposed four principles the scientific theory of knowledge should stick to: Principle of symmetry, which is the same kind of justifications for not only error but also for truth beliefs in science; Causality principle, that all the description of scientific knowledge systems should be causal; Impartiality principle, the unbiased account of the truth and falsity; Reflexivity principle, that the application of these principles in the discipline of sociology itself (Dusek, 2006). Harry Collin's empirical program of relativism (EPOR) is similar to the strong programme in which the principle of symmetry is achieved by concentrating on controversies during which knowledge is uncertain (Sismondo, 2008).

The approaches to analyse science, technology, and society studies can be described as technological determinism, social shaping of technology, and critical theory of technology. In technological determinism, technology has the agency and an autonomous nature which does not require human intervention for its progress (Salazar-Acosta & Holbrook, 2008). There are different views on this approach that have been classified by Bimber (1994) as cited in Salazar-Acosta and Holbrook (2008):

(i) *Normative*: based on Habermas; advances that if the standards of technology by which it is forwarded can be removed from political and ethical discourse, then technology can be regarded as autonomous and deterministic; Jacques Ellul can be considered as an exponent of this proposition;

(ii) *Unintended consequences*: suggests the observations from inadvertent and intractable results of technological progress; Langdon Winner advocates this approach (ibid). According to him, "technology is inherently political" (Winner, 1980, p. 133);

(iii) *Nomological*: states that technology progresses as naturally driven without any effects from social and cultural factors, and this advancement shapes the social changes (Salazar-Acosta & Holbrook, 2008). In order to understand *controversies*, many researchers such as Bruno Latour, Knorr Cetina, and others thought of studying the cultures and events that shaped these controversies (Sismondo, 2008). These researchers shifted their area of research in the laboratories to observe and analyse its claims displaying the "construction of data", which is not natural; rather, it is intertwined with human efforts (ibid, p. 15).

This shift from autonomy of the technology to construction of scientific knowledge signifying the human negotiation in it resulted in the development of social shaping of technology (SST)—the second approach to studying the intersections of science, technology, and society. Within SST there are two strands: one analyzes at the 'macro' level; i.e., technological change cannot only be explained on the basis of individual inventions; rather, the larger socio-economic factors such as funding needs to be considered; this approach is propounded by neo-Marxists (Mackay & Gillespie, 1992). The other strand analyses at the 'micro' level and again can be divided into various approaches (ibid)—Social Construction of Technology (SCOT) by Trevor Pinch and Wiebe Bijker, who argue that technological development is open to social negotiation and renegotiation, not only for their use but also their "design and technical content" (Bijker et al., 1993, p. 11). The other is a symbolic interactionist approach, which considers science and technology as work being done in various scientific and technical endeavours from labs to sponsorship and so on; that is, this approach focuses on work and its organization (A. Van House, 2003) by highlighting the participation of people who were not perceived as researchers or innovators (Sismondo, 2008). Actor-network theory (ANT) also expands that picture by illustrating the "work of technoscience" as the formation of networks (ibid: 16). The main characteristic of ANT is the heterogeneous nature of the networks, which is inclusive of nonhuman actors, such as materials, equipment, components, and human actors that can vary from individuals to organizations (ibid). The advocates of ANT argue that our society is made by actor-worlds, which associates heterogeneous entities. The principle of generalized symmetry suggests that both human and non-human actors are the same terms without making any distinction. However, ANT has been criticized as it generally reflects that at the centre of the network are often those humans who exercise power. The third approach to STS is the critical theory of technology by Andrew Feenberg, which emphasizes the democratic approach to technology (Liu & Feenberg, 1992). He argues that technology is not neutral; rather, it is ambivalent in nature at the level of design itself, which are the 'contingency' at choice of design and the 'constraints' put over by the privileged actors (Veak, 2006). The two principles which describe this ambivalence are: conservation of hierarchy, which states the persistent preservation of power in the social hierarchy despite changes in technology; the second is democratic rationalization, which states the utilization of the technology for the need which has been overlooked (ibid). For Feenberg, this democratization can disentangle the design of technology from authoritarian restraints (Veak, 2006). Feenberg's concept of democratization of technology entails that the technology should be user oriented and take into account the cultural connotations.

The foundation for cyber-trolling lies in the online platform facilitated by communication devices. Without this foundation, a discussion on cyber-trolling is incomplete. When we initiate a conversation about the concept of online deviance, our emphasis is primarily on behaviours and related aspects (as previously discussed in this chapter). Unfortunately, we tend to give insufficient attention to the role of online platforms and social media. Therefore, it is necessary to comprehend the intricacies of trolling on online platforms (such as social media) through communication devices and the concept of online deviance. To grasp this concept, it is essential to consider the principles of free expression and the ongoing democratization of technology

Democratization of technology and freedom of expression

Democratization of technology is the participation of the community/users/actors in designing and utilizing the technology for social upliftment. However, bringing the freedom of speech concept in the internet portrays the two sides of the same coin. On one hand, there are online support groups, connectivity, and a lot more for social upliftment, but there are also cybercrimes and their ramifications. To understand the complexity of online platforms, Feenberg's technical politics (based on democratization of technology) will be useful. In contemporary times, technology has become imperative for "social participation", which is not being enforced; rather it is seen "as a portal to opportunities for play, social connection and enjoyment" (Kirkpatrick, 2020, p. 9). The technology and its application have twin probabilities of being empowering and yet designed in "strategies of exploitation and manipulation" (ibid, p. 10).

Whereas per the international and national statutes, freedom of expression is a fundamental human right which includes freedom to have views without interference and to gather and disseminate information through any platform, the pattern of a network-based society depends on the digital technologies for access to information, citizen advocacy, and discerning alternatives (Danescu, 2021) to 'social participation'. Simultaneously, there is an increase in the impact of the virtual platforms for manipulations, exploitations, disruptions, and so on (ibid).

When we combine these two concepts, it forms the essential framework for comprehending how the actions, engagement, and viewpoints of individuals play a significant role in shaping various, albeit distinct, patterns related to deviant behavior on online platforms. When examining trolling behavior, these interconnected ideas become even more relevant. The freedom of expression, with its increasing importance in the online world, underscores how individuals exercise their rights and use technology to voice their opinions and engage in various online activities. Simultaneously, the democratization of technology emphasizes the widening access to online platforms and tools, enabling more people to become active participants.

Tying these two concepts together is crucial when exploring the dynamics of trolling on online platforms. Understanding how individuals participate, utilize technology, and bring their beliefs into the online space is fundamental in unraveling the complexities of trolling and its impact on the online environment. This chapter proposes the following method to study cyber deviance by the example of cyber-trolling.

Socio-Technical Information Network

A socio-technical information network must be considered when examining specific technologies associated with deviant behavior, such as cyber-trolling. This network underscores the mutual influence of technology and society, the integration of technology within its social context, and the flow of information that influences how technology is used within this network. Furthermore, it's essential to establish a socio-technical interaction network (STIN) that encompasses technological, social, and cultural dimensions. This STIN can serve as a foundation for further research into information and communication technologies (ICTs) and user behaviour, facilitating a deeper understanding of the intricate dynamics of participation within a network.

STIN's main goal is to achieve the intricate socio-technical arrangements included in a technology-intensive project, accentuating the correlative peculiarity of the inter-relationship among people, people and apparatus, and between technologies and political structure (Rosenbaum & Joung, 2004). This model comprises characteristics from social construction of technology and actor-network theory (Meyer, 2006). The four main assumptions are put forth to construct STIN: "the social and technical are not meaningfully separable; theories of social behavior not only can, but influence technical design choices; system participants are embedded in multiple, overlapping, and non-technologically mediated relationships; and sustainability and routine operations are critical" (Kling et al., 2003, p. 56). To grasp the STIN models and their application in unraveling the complexities of online deviance, cyber-trolling will be employed as a case study for examination. Cyber-trolling can be defined as a deliberate, disruptive online behaviour, where the 'troll' provokes and disrupts others (Fichman & Sanfilippo, 2016) for their own amusement.

Kling et al. (2003) have identified the steps for the method of STIN model formation:

• Identify system interactors

Determine all the interactors and their roles and participation. For instance, in the present case of cyber-trolling, interactors would be user-victim, technology-user-victim, technology-medium-user, anonymity-technology-users, culture-technology-freedom of expression, and so on.

• Identify the core interactor groups

Understanding the roles played by different interactor groups and who are the main players. In this case, the deviant, the victim, internet, app (Instagram, Facebook, or any other)

• Identify incentive structures

Analyzing the reasons behind the participation of relevant interactor groups: the deviant—anonymity, family patterns, socio-demographic aspects, socialization, victimization, school, and individual factors (Cioban et al., 2021); the victim—coverage, popularity, family patterns, socio-demographic aspects, socialization, victimization, school, and individual factors (ibid); interactions on applications used on the internet and so on.

- Identify excluded actors and undesired interactions

Analyzing interactions not only occurring in the system which is permissible by the interactors but also which they don't want to be part of. The case study on cyber-trolling is actually the undesired outcome. The major drawback is when there is a reply from the victim and they receive support from others. The troll feels like they are losing the edge over the numbers. Legislation is being established to deal with these trolling tactics, and simultaneously there is monitoring over the network.

- Identify existing communications systems

Understanding the communications systems used by the interactors: Does an algorithm have a part to play? How do the suggestions to interact or participate pop on the news feed of the applications? For instance, while trolling Indian actresses for their bodies, trolls use social media such as Instagram, Facebook, and the online news where the interaction is posted.

- Identify resource flows

To explore the flows of resources that can affect the interactions inside the system of interactors: the financial flow in the system and any financial aspect in trolling online. For instance, the trolling is mostly on the pages of celebrities or influencers; are any hidden competitive resources part of it?

- Identify architectural choice points

The choice point is a technological characteristic or social arrangement to select an alternative. There has been a change in trajectory from orkut to Facebook and nowadays Instagram, for more interaction, participation, and open domain for the aforementioned purpose. Facebook and Instagram are owned by one company.[34]

- Map socio-technical features to architectural choice points

After identification of socio-technical features and architectural choice points, attainable combinations and configurations are figured which could be sustainable. The identified architectural points provide the trajectory with the embeddedness in the socio-technical ensemble.

Case of cyber-trolling in STIN configuration

The socio-technical ensemble with online deviance provides the how and why of the trolling. Further, if required for the policy formation, this model will help in providing a holistic approach. To further elaborate on the utilization of the STIN model in the context of cyber-trolling, the following case-specific information is provided:

In this particular instance, the focus is on discussing the case of an individual's death, specifically through suicide or other means, which evokes strong emotions and sympathy. The trolling behavior in this case commenced after the suicide of a 17-year-old who

Figure 29.1 STIN model for cyber-trolling

livestreamed the act on Facebook while also providing instructions on how to commit suicide. According to the first component of the STIN model, the core interactor groups involved in this case are the family, the trolls, Facebook as a community network, and Facebook as an online platform. The incentive for the trolls in this scenario was to target the deceased victim to prevent similar incidents in the future, highlighting social status and the availability of drugs and alcohol for a 17-year-old. Additionally, the trolls discussed the victim's mental health conditions, such as depression, but deemed it insufficient as a reason for suicide. The trolls considered themselves emotionally more mature than the victim, despite being the same age. Notably, the excluded actors in this case were the police and Facebook as an organization,[35] which should have taken action to report such issues.

Furthermore, India is in the process of enacting the Digital India Act of 2023,[36] with a focus on freedom of expression, online safety, and social media policies. The communication system involved in this case was Facebook Live, prompting questions about the necessity of this live feature and how it is monitored. In terms of resource flows, Facebook management cannot be directly held accountable for the actions of a 17-year-old who livestreamed their suicide. However, questions arise regarding the presence of a tutorial on how to commit suicide. Is the popularity of such content driven by financial resources, increased profile visits, or the number of hits on the tutorial? The resource flow in this case involves emotional elements, including sympathy, anger, or the desire to exploit the situation for amusement.

Although Facebook Live was the initial platform of choice for the trolling, it has since migrated to Instagram, where users are now targeted through their reels.

The socio-technical ensemble model uncovers the motives and mechanisms behind trolling. It can provide a comprehensive approach for policy development. The case study reveals the dynamics surrounding a suicide livestream on Facebook, with trolls targeting the victim to prevent similar incidents. The model highlights interactor groups, such as the family, trolls, and Facebook, while excluded actors like the police and the platform itself should have taken action. The ongoing Digital India Act of 2023 addresses online safety and freedom of expression. Resource flows raise questions about the tutorial's popularity and its emotional impact. Trolling behavior has shifted from Facebook Live to Instagram reels. Considering the STIN model helps in understanding and addressing cyber-trolling, fostering a safer online environment.

Conclusion

STIN models[37] can help in the in-depth understanding of application, development, and sustainability (Kling et al., 2003). By employing these models, we can delve deeper into the interactions at play and uncover obstacles that may hinder progress. It is crucial to recognize the importance of contextualizing technologies within the dynamic socio-cultural milieu.

The case study on cyber-trolling exemplifies an undesirable outcome, but studying it through a socio-technical lens acknowledges the equal participation of technology and users. Rather than focusing solely on one aspect of the partnership, this framework examines the full spectrum of the dynamics between deviance and technology. By adopting this approach, we can gain insights into the complex interplay between human behavior, technological affordances, and societal influences.

By employing the STIN model, policymakers and stakeholders can develop a more nuanced understanding of cyber-trolling and its underlying causes. This holistic perspective allows for the identification of systemic issues and the formulation of comprehensive solutions. It sheds light on the motivations and incentives driving trolling behavior, the role of various actors, such as families, trolls, and platform providers, and the resource flows that sustain and perpetuate such actions and discussions about the right to freedom of expression.

Moreover, as technology continues to evolve, it is imperative to consider the socio-technical dynamics that shape its implementation and impact. The STIN model provides a framework to analyse the interdependencies between technology and society, facilitating a more informed approach to policy development. By incorporating socio-cultural factors and understanding the complex relationships between technology and deviant behavior, policymakers can develop strategies that address the root causes of cyber-trolling and foster a safer and more inclusive online environment.

In conclusion, the STIN model offers a comprehensive approach to understanding and addressing cyber-trolling. By studying the dynamics of deviance and technology within the socio-technical ensemble, policymakers can gain valuable insights and develop holistic strategies to tackle this issue effectively.

Acknowledgements

I would like to express my sincere appreciation to the editors and reviewers for their invaluable contributions. Your expertise, thoroughness, and dedication have greatly enhanced the quality and credibility of the work. Your feedback and guidance have been instrumental in shaping the final outcome. Heartfelt thanks for the support and cooperation.

Notes

1 https://theprobe.in/stories/gurugram-parents-allege-cyber-murder-of-son-await-justice/ accessed 1 May 2023.
2 www.dtnext.in/city/2018/10/17/friends-blame-online-trolls-for-youths-suicide accessed 1 May 2023.
3 www.indiatimes.com/news/india/mumbai-boy-who-died-of-chronic-depression-incur-the-wrath-of-those-who-fail-to-see-his-problems-274923.html accessed 1 May 2023.
4 www.indiatimes.com/entertainment/celebs/salman-khan-fan-getting-his-face-tattooed-on-her-chest-588780.html accessed 1 May 2023.
5 https://thefederal.com/news/online-trolling-of-cji-chandrachud-opposition-mps-write-to-president-murmu-seeking-action/ accessed 1 May 2023.
6 https://timesofindia.indiatimes.com/humour/53176096.cms accessed 1 May 2023. It is to be noted that this particular report, which is published by one of the prime news channels in India, used the concept of 'social humour' rather than the accurate terminology of trolling. See Fichman's (2020) discussion about the relationship between humour and the trolling.
7 In India, mobile in every household is approx. at 92.8% (Mohan et al., 2020) showing the level of access for this device; further, 52% of the population of India are active internet users (IAMAI Report, 2022), resulting in the probability of choice for the individual to troll. https://www.iamai.in/sites/default/files/research/Internet%20in%20India%202022_Print%20version.pdf accessed 1 May 2023.
8 As the devices and the internet usage increase (see note 17), so does the 'chance' and 'choice' of the individual for the usage of these.
9 For the summary of the trial, www.nbcnews.com/pop-culture/pop-culture-news/johnny-depp-amber-heard-defamation-trial-summary-timeline-rcna26136 accessed 1 October 2023. For trolling during the trial, see www.dazeddigital.com/life-culture/article/56586/1/how-amber-heards-trolls-weaponised-twitter-during-the-depp-trial-cyberstalking accessed 1 October 2023.
10 For further details and trolling please see www.womensweb.in/2023/01/trolls-samantha-ruth-prabhus-illness-is-karma-for-filing-divorce-jan23wk4sr/ accessed 1 October 2023.
11 See https://frontline.thehindu.com/dispatches/article25249976.ece accessed 1 October 2023.
12 See https://timesofindia.indiatimes.com/india/congress-vs-bjp-the-curious-case-of-trolls-and-politics/articleshow/23970818.cms accessed 1 October 2023.
13 www.theguardian.com/mythical-creatures/ng-interactive/2019/aug/26/most-legendary-mythical-creatures-history accessed 23 April 23.
14 ibid.
15 www.forbes5.pitt.edu/article/internet-trolls accessed 1 May 2023.
16 ibid.
17 See Jussinoja (2018).
18 A troll will try to present herself as a genuine member and, after establishing a fabricated identity, will actively disrupt the group while attempting to maintain her undercover status (Hardaker, 2010).
19 To characterize aggressive and malicious conduct aimed at deliberately irritating or provoking others into reacting negatively (ibid).
20 Engaging in behaviours that cause annoyance without specifically targeting a particular individual. This disruptive behaviour typically involves making meaningless, irrelevant, or repetitive posts with the intention of seeking attention or eliciting responses (ibid).
21 Users evaluate trolls based on their level of achievement, considering both the effectiveness of the trolling act itself and how others react to the troll (ibid).
22 www.igi-global.com/dictionary/being-and-a-trolling-state-of-electronic-hive-mind/74029 accessed 30 October 2022.

23 www.psychologytoday.com/intl/blog/your-online-secrets/201409/internet-trolls-are-narcissists-psychopaths-and-sadists accessed 13 September 2022 See further Cheng et al. (2017), Jenks (2019), Volkmer (2023), Maltby et al. (2016).

24 https://thewire.in/communalism/internet-trolls-psychology accessed 13 September 2022. Another perspective is of gender in trolling; this perspective needs to be taken in detail and will be dealt with somewhere else. For further reading, see, Lumsden and Morgon (2017), Paananen and Reichl (2019) for gender abuse and gendertrolling respectively.

25 I must acknowledge the extensive work done by Papez is commendable, as definition of trolling and its behaviour is debatable, but using the actor network theory opens the paradox of this behaviour.

26 Centola (2010) has focused on the spread of trolling behaviour using networks.

27 See Taylor, 2017.

28 See further Lumsden and Morgon (2017), Paananen and Reichl (2019)

29 Seah et al., 2015.

30 See further Cambria et al. https://assets.publishing.service.gov.uk/government/uploads/system/uploads/attachment_data/file/973971/DCMS_REA_Online_trolling__V2.pdf

31 Mane et al., 2021.

32 See Hardaker (2010) where she has discussed about the deduction of cyber-trolling definition by taking examples of various online platforms' trolls' statements.

33 Mol (2002).

34 See www.investopedia.com/articles/personal-finance/051815/top-11-companies-owned-facebook.asp accessed 5 October 2023.

35 www.insideedition.com/25564-the-dark-disturbing-trend-of-teens-live-streaming-suicide-and-how-it-can-be-stopped accessed 1 May 2023.

36 https://indiacsr.in/digital-india-act-2023/ accessed 1 May 2023.

37 Further read on the use of STIN models: Scacchi (2005), Barab et al. (2004), Meyer and Kling (2002), Rosenbaum and Joung (2004), Kling (2000).

References

Bijker, W. E, Hughes, T., & Pinch T. (1993). *The social construction of technological systems- new directions in the sociology and history of technology*. MIT Press.

Bishop, J. (2014). Digital teens and the 'antisocial network': Prevalence of troublesome online youth groups and internet trolling in Great Britain. *International Journal of E-Politics* (IJEP), 5(3), 1–15.

Centola, D. (2010). The spread of behavior in an online social network experiment. *Science, 329*, 1194–1197.

Cheng, J., Bernstein, M., Danescu-Niculescu-Mizil, C., & Leskovec, J. (2017). Anyone can become a troll: Causes of trolling behavior in online discussions. *CSCW: Proceedings of the Conference on Computer-Supported Cooperative Work. Conference on Computer-Supported Cooperative Work, 2017*, 1217–1230. https://doi.org/10.1145/2998181.2998213

Cioban, S., Lazăr, A. R., BaCter, C., & Hatos, A. (2021). Adolescent deviance and cyber-deviance. A systematic literature review. *Frontiers in Psychology, 12*.

Danescu, E. (2021). *Democracy, freedom and truth at a time of digital disruption: An equation with three unknowns?* IntechOpen. https://doi.org/10.5772/intechopen.97662

Dusek, V. (2006). *Philosophy of Technology: An Introduction*. Blackwell Publishing.

Fichman, P. (2020). Global trolling: The case of "America first". In *Proceedings of the 53rd Hawaii international conference on system sciences* (pp. 5903–5910).

Fichman, P., & McClelland, M. W. (2021). The impact of gender and political affiliation on trolling. *First Monday, 26*(1–4). Retrieved from https://firstmonday.org/ojs/index.php/fm/article/download/11061/10034; https://dx.doi.org/10.5210/fm.v26i1.11061

Fichman, P., & Sanfilippo, M. P. (2016). *Online trolling and its perpetrators: Under the cyberbridge*. Rowman and Little Field.

Gonzalez, W. J. (2005). The relevance of science, technology and society: The "social" turn. In *Science, technology and society: A philosophical perspective*. Netbiblo.

Hardaker, C. (2010). Trolling in asynchronous computer-mediated communication: From user discussions to theoretical concepts. *Journal of Politeness Research, 6*(2), 215–242.

Kling, R., McKim, G., & King, A. (2003). A bit more to IT: Scholarly communication forums as socio-technical interaction networks. *Journal of the American Society for Information Science and Technology, 54*(1), 46–67.

Kirkpatrick, G. (2020). *Technical politics.* Manchester University Press.

Kuhn, T. S. (1972). *The structure of scientific revolutions.* University of Chicago Press.

Liu, A., & Feenberg, A. (1992). Critical theory of technology. *MLN, 107*(5), 1032–1035.

Lumsden, K., & Morgon, H. M. (2017). Chapter 9: Cyber-trolling as symbolic violence: Deconstructing gendered abuse online. In N. Lombard (Ed.), *The Routledge handbook of gender and violence.* Routledge.

Mackay, H., & Gillespie. G. (1992). Extending the social shaping of technology approach: Ideology and appropriation. *Social Studies of Science, 22*(4), 685–716.

MacKenzie, D., & Wajcman, J. (1999). Introductory essay: The social shaping of technology. In *The social shaping of technology* (1st ed.). Open University Press.

Maltby, J., Day, L., Hatcher, R., Tazzyman, S., Flowe, H. D., Palmer, E. J., Frosch, C. A., O'Reilly, M., Jones, C., Buckley, C., Knieps, M., & Cutts, K. (2016). Implicit theories of online trolling: Evidence that attention-seeking conceptions are associated with increased psychological resilience. *British Journal of Psychology, 107*(3), 448–466.

Mane, P. H., et al. (2021). Prevention of cyber troll and sarcasm system on social networking using machine learning with bilingual analytics. *International Journal of Creative Research Thoughts, 9*(4), 3471–3475.

Mantilla, K. (2013). Gendertrolling: Misogyny adapts to new media. *Feminist Studies, 39*(2), 563–570.

Merton, R. K. (1938). Social structure and anomie. *American Sociological Review, 3*, 672–682.

Meyer, E. T. (2006). Socio-technical interaction networks: A discussion of the strengths, weaknesses and future of Kling's STIN model. In J. Berleur, M. I. Nurminen, & J. Impagliazzo (Eds.), *Social informatics: An information society for all? In remembrance of Rob Kling* (HCC 2006. IFIP International Federation for Information Processing, Vol. 223). Springer.

Mohan, D., Bashingwa, J. J. H., Tiffin, N., Dhar, D., Mulder, N., George, A., et al. (2020). Does having a mobile phone matter? Linking phone access among women to health in India: An exploratory analysis of the National Family Health Survey. *PLoS ONE, 15*(7), e0236078.

Paananen, A., & Reichl, A. J. (2019). Gendertrolls just want to have fun too. *Personality and Individual Differences, 141*, 152–156.

Papez, M. G. (2018). *Disassembling online trolling: Towards the better understanding and managing of online mischief-making consumer misbehaviours* [PhD Dissertation, University of Canterbury].

Rosenbaum, H., & KyoungHee, J. (2004). Socio-technical interaction networks as a tool for understanding digital libraries. In *Proceedings of the 67th ASIS&T annual meeting* (Vol. 41, pp. 206–212). Retrieved from https://asistdl.onlinelibrary.wiley.com/toc/15508390/2004/41/1#

Salazar-Acosta, M., & Adam, H. (2008). *Some notes on theories of technology, society and innovation systems for S&T policy studies.* Simon Fraser University. Retrieved from www.sfu.ca/sfublogs-archive/departments/cprost/uploads/2012/06/0802.pdf (accessed 13 October 2022).

Seah, C. W., et al. (2015). *Troll detection by domain-adapted sentiment analysis* [18th International Conference on Information Fusion, Washington].

Sismondo, S. (2008). Science and technology studies and an engaged program. In E. J. Hackett (Ed.), *The Handbook of science and technology studies* (1st ed.). MIT Press.

Sombatpoonsiri, J. (2018). Manipulating civic space: Cyber trolling in Thailand and the Philippines. *GIGA Focus Asien, 3* (Hamburg: GIGA German Institute of Global and Area Studies). Retrieved from https://nbn-resolving.org/urn:nbn:de:0168-ssoar-57960-4

Taylor, C. (2017). *Strategies and behaviors of cyberdeviance and cyber trolling* [All Master's Theses], p. 782.

Van House, N. (2003). Science and technology studies and information studies. *Annual Review of Information Science and Technology, 38*(1), 1–86.

Veak, T. J. (2006). *Democratising technology.* State University of New York Press.

Volkmer, S. A., Gaube, S., Raue, M., & Lermer, E. (2023). Troll story: The dark tetrad and online trolling revisited with a glance at humor. *PLoS One, 18*(3). https://doi.org/10.1371/journal.pone.0280271. PMID: 36897846; PMCID: PMC10004561.

Winner, L. (1980). Do artifacts have politics? *Daedalus, 109*(1), 121–136.

PART IV

Platforms, communities, and culture

30

INTERACTING WITH ONLINE DEVIANT SUBCULTURES

Gendered experiences of interviewing incels

Jan Christoffer Andersen and Lisa Sugiura

Introduction

This chapter presents reflections from two researchers, a man (Jan Christoffer Andersen) and a woman (Lisa Sugiura), who have conducted direct online interviews with incels (involuntary celibates) (see Andersen, 2023; Sugiura, 2021b). The incel subculture consists of men who believe they cannot escape their current situation of involuntary celibacy and lack of romantic success because of society's deterministic, hierarchical division of sex and attractiveness. Thus, incels are often known as deviant others who fully embrace a subcultural incel identity as a master status (Cottee, 2020). However, as we found in our research, some members are less invested in the subculture. Instead, they use *involuntary celibate* as a descriptive term for their life situation rather than an all-encompassing identity, highlighting the ongoing identity negotiation within the incel community.

This research contributes novel insights into incels, as most studies in the field involve secondary analysis of forums. We use a self-reflexive lens, and the chapter will demonstrate that our gender as researchers significantly influenced the content of interviews, the direction they took, and our data analysis. Our self-reflexive position of interviewing incels includes questions of anonymity (participants disclosing or hiding their identity), type of communication (text or video conversations), trust (participants withholding or revealing personal information), suspicion (participants questioning or accepting research legitimacy), investigation (incels testing or evaluating our specific knowledge), identity formation (how and why they identify as incel), and ideological commitment (participants' dedication to incel ideology and online participation).

There were commonalities in our research as well. For both of us, some interviewees were keen to impress their worldview onto us and change our perspectives, or what they thought our perspectives were. They participated primarily to share their personal experiences and research and statistics, and to challenge common misconceptions of the incel community and its members. However, even though some incels subverted, or at least attempted to subvert, the one-dimensional representation of incels as hateful, statements made by interviewees also indicated that they were deliberately curating themselves. This curation included furthering the incel victimhood narrative and retaining misogynistic and

DOI: 10.4324/9781003277675-35

anti-feminist beliefs, including claims of the existence of female supremacism. For example, one interviewee's reason for participating in the research was to clarify what an incel was by 'correcting the monolithic definition put forward by feminists and female supremacists and used by academics and mainstream media to describe incels as violent extremists'. The dilemma was that individuals keen to present themselves as non-hateful retained the hateful identifier of incel. Thus, incels inextricably associated misogyny and hate with their own identity and experiences, undermining the reality of structural misogyny.

The chapter will also highlight the importance of the researchers' safety and consider challenges such as self-care and maintaining personal boundaries. Researching fringe online groups requires constant ethical and methodical assessments that limit covert or deceptive research methods—personal exposure revealing our identities as researchers was thus unavoidable when recruiting participants. We therefore risked drawing unwanted attention to ourselves, as users of incel forums have publicly published private information about people they want to shame, harass, and harm, which differs somewhat according to the gender of the researcher.

However, being some of the few scholars who have directly engaged with persons from incel communities (for others, see Daly & Reed, 2022; Regehr, 2022), both of us discovered that our understanding of incels challenged media portrayals of them as inherently dangerous. As a relatively diverse community, participants varied in age, ethnicity, and background. None of the participants openly supported physical acts of violence or incel-related murders. A small subgroup of participants had little knowledge of the terms and theories used within the incel subculture, even though they frequented incel forums. This is not to say that the behaviour of some incels was unproblematic, particularly those espousing sexist and misogynistic attitudes. In some instances, participants acknowledged the harm done by other incels, but overwhelmingly their priority was to change our minds about what being an incel meant and what incels were really like. At times, interviewees elicited sympathy from us as their points (amongst the cacophony of animosity directed at feminism and women) about the societal importance of sexual and romantic relationships and conventional attractiveness were valid, even as they were distorted by incel ideology. It was thus important to draw on de Coning's (2021) methodological framework of critical empathy to navigate the challenging emotional dimensions of engaging in direct research and building rapport with individuals perpetuating discriminatory attitudes. Labelling of incels is problematic, but foregrounding the toxicity within incel communities is necessary; otherwise, we risk uncritical analyses of our interviewee responses. For example, for certain participants, the primary concern was not hating women or feminism but their own experiences and grievances of loneliness, poverty, family dysfunction, childhood trauma, or mental illness, leading us to question why such persons would want to be known as incels when the term is overwhelmingly associated with hate.

Incel

Incel is a portmanteau of involuntary and celibate. A self-ascribed term, it is adopted by those who consider themselves unsuccessful in having sexual and romantic relationships with those they desire (Sugiura, 2021b). The incel community was formed initially by a queer female student named Alana in 1997 who created a gender-inclusive, online space for anyone who was lonely, had never had sex, or who had not been in a relationship in a long time.[1] Early on, however, non-misogynist incels found themselves having to moderate violent and misogynist comments in incel forums, resulting in many misogynist incels moving to other forums such as *LoveShy* and *Pick Up Artist* (*PUA*), where they could openly espouse hate. After Alana left the site, there was a split between non-misogynist and misogynist incels, with the non-misogynist incel spaces decreasing, particularly after the 2014 Isla Vista attack (Baele et al., 2021). This development resulted in the co-option of the term *incel* by misogynist incels intersecting with and influenced by *PUA* (Bratich & Banet-Weiser, 2019). However, there are still some who align themselves with the original meaning of the term: in particular, female incels (femcels), those who identify as non-binary, men who actively reject misogyny on sites such as *Youarenotalone*, and some private Facebook communities (among some of the groups that Jan engaged during his interviews) trying to retain and revive incel's original non-misogynistic values.

Incel communities, the subject of this chapter, are often seen as monolithic by researchers, with the umbrella term being synonymous with male supremacist extremism, rather than researchers focusing on the problem of misogynist incels (Kelly et al., 2022). Nevertheless, men have appropriated the term *incel* and transformed the incel community into a notoriously misogynistic subculture, part of the broader online 'manosphere'. The incel community has also gained increased media, policy, law enforcement, and public attention following its association with mass murders, most notoriously in the UK (Plymouth), the US (Isla Vista, California, Oregon, New Mexico, Parkland and Tallahassee, Florida), and Canada (Toronto, Ontario, and Edmonton, Alberta) (Hoffman et al., 2020; Sugiura, 2021b). In reporting, there is an increasing tendency to name any misogynist-inspired attack as an incel attack rather than recognizing the broader issue of male supremacy (Bloom, 2022). In addition, it is essential to note that some incel-related attacks are just that—related—and the connection has been made by others rather than perpetrators self-identifying as incels. The situation is clearer when the perpetrators provide a manifesto or post a forewarning on social media (such as in the Isla Vista, 2014 (see Vito et al., 2018), and Toronto, 2018, attacks (see Cottee, 2020)), stipulating inceldom as the reason for the attacks. However, in many cases the true motives for abhorrent violence may never be known.

Scholarly work on incels is burgeoning. Studies have examined the underlying misogynistic framework of incel (blackpill) ideology (Baele et al., 2021; O'Malley et al., 2022; Sugiura, 2021b; Witt, 2020), compared incel terrorism with Islamist and right-wing terrorism (Cottee, 2020; Hoffman et al., 2020), and incorporated policy suggestions to prevent future attacks by the radicalized (Tomkinson et al., 2020). There have also been notable analyses of the content of specific online forums frequented by incels: its worldview (Baele et al., 2021), the presence of femmephobia and hatred of hyper-femininity (Chang, 2020; Menzie, 2022), and misogyny, victimhood, and fatalism (Cottee, 2020; Witt, 2020; see also Ging, 2019). This chapter, however, addresses a void in current scholarship by focusing on broader incel communities and how they negotiate their online deviant statuses. Importantly, we discuss our direct interactions with incels and reflect on our gendered experiences in conducting our research projects.

Media representation of incels

According to Howard Becker (1963), deviance results from labels or external control, altering the individual's self-concept and how others respond to the label. People or groups deviating from social norms risk homogeneously being labelled *outsiders* by the majority, thus constituting their behaviour as deviant. In the media, incels have been portrayed as figures of ridicule—losers, pathetic virgins, deviants, weirdos, misogynists, extremists, and terrorists. Some labels, such as underdog and sexually inexperienced, have been internalized and confirm the incel narrative of being victimized by women and other marginalized groups. However, other labels, especially that of terrorist, are actively rejected by most incels (Cottee, 2020) who want to distance themselves from violent associations while simultaneously engaging in discourse condoning acts of brutality against women. Still, incels are often demonized and seen as monolithic. For persons who already think they are hated, being the current 'folk devil' (Cohen, 1972) of choice means that what might have initially been self-perception is now validated by others. *Incel* is often the default word used for misogynists, but this overlooks how hatred and contempt of women is pervasive throughout societies, operationalized in the mainstream, and not confined to online spaces. Moreover, positioning incels as misogynistic folk devils situates misogyny solely in their domain and nowhere else.

Often in the immediate aftermath of lone terror attacks, the perpetrators are named incels even when there is no evidence to support such a claim (Jasser et al., 2020). This media coverage engages in what Jock Young (1971) famously referred to as 'deviance amplification', heightening the social reaction and amplifying the deviance itself. Additionally, much media coverage addresses the misogynistic angle of incels without addressing their link to male supremacist ideology. Such omissions mean that misogynists, and not just incels, can elicit sympathy for being victimized by having their reasons for hating women magnified and justified, for example, that 'women won't have sex with them'. Media coverage thus enables what Kate Manne (2017) conceptualizes as 'himpathy', the disproportionate or inappropriate sympathy extended to men over women even when they are engaged in or have engaged in violent or misogynistic behaviour. Tomkinson et al. (2020) describe how media reporting on incels, which publicly affirms feelings of victimhood and persecution among men, undermines political action on gender-based violence and encourages those who feel persecuted to engage in violence. The Institute for Research on Male Supremacism (IRMS) has called out the BBC, CNN, and the *New York Times* for portraying incels as ominous and distinct from wider society and broad patriarchal structures, and has created recommendations for media reporting on incels in response to misleading coverage.[2]

Online deviant subcultures

Subcultures develop to mitigate and create solidarity against stigmatization. This attracts individuals who feel society has rejected them, but ironically, by participating in a subculture, they are further ostracized, entrenching their sense of rejection (Braithwaite, 1989). As a subcultural group, incels present themselves as countercultural to mainstream society (Chang, 2020; O'Malley et al., 2022) and portray themselves as explicitly different from regular people, or 'normies' (Nagle, 2017). The alternative set of values and behaviours of the incel counterculture appeals to certain marginalized individuals because, as members of a deviant subculture, they can 'strike back' at, or provoke, mainstream audiences (Hebdige, 1979; Holt et al., 2017; Treadwell & Garland, 2011). As Cohen (1955, p. 27) states, they revel in 'an enjoyment in the discomfiture of others, a delight in the defiance of taboos'. In other words, online incels are a deviant subculture who reject larger social norms, which include countless narratives and tropes (e.g. the pill philosophy, victim narratives, portrayals of the sexual market), rituals and customs (e.g. gatekeeping, trolling, shitposting), artistic products (e.g. Internet memes, GIFs, music), and subcultural expressions (e.g. Chad, Stacy, Becky, truecel).

Much of what occurs in incel spaces is deliberately provocative and shocking, a form of shitposting and ironic humour, but this does not mean it does not impose harm or even that it is monolithic. Rheingold's (1993, p. 3) insight into the workings of virtual communities helps us appreciate the subtleties involved in navigating incel space and what, on the surface, appears to be a uniformity of misogynistic attitudes and behaviours: 'there is no such thing as a single, monolithic, online subculture; it's more like an ecosystem of subcultures, some frivolous, others serious'. Hence as researchers, we appreciate the complexity of the different groups of incels we studied and directly engaged with in our interviews. However, for our safety and well-being, we limited our involvement with the most hateful and overtly misogynistic incels.

Study design

This chapter compares our gendered experiences of interviewing incels online, reminiscent of an experiment. However, we recruited and interviewed members of the incel community as part of our respective research projects independently of each other. Our interviews were conducted at different times, using different recruitment platforms, and without us knowing about each other's work. The idea of working on this chapter came about when we shared our interview experiences after Lisa, the more experienced researcher, agreed to co-supervise the PhD project of Jan. Here we outline our specific recruitment and interview processes.

Jan undertook qualitative explorations of incel narratives involving non-participant observation, focusing on publicly available incel documents, discussions, and forums. Jan also conducted 13 interviews with self-identified former (n = 4) and current (n = 8) incels. One participant identified as voluntarily (n = 1) incel, meaning that although he was able to shed his inceldom status, he chose a lifestyle without dating, romance, or sex. The interviews, in which incels described their everyday experiences and stigma, explored the influence and philosophy of incels from a narrative and cultural criminological perspective (see Ferrell et al., 2008; Presser & Sandberg, 2015). Interview participants were identified using snowball and convenience sampling (Goodman, 1961; Sedgwick, 2013) and were all men between the ages of 20 and 50. Recruitment material did not specify that participants needed to be male, but only men responded. This was most likely due to recruitment taking place in male-dominated spaces. Although female incels were allowed in these spaces, their presence was less welcomed. Participants recognized the problematic and misogynistic aspects of the community, even as this acknowledgement undermined some participants' claims that incel spaces were non-misogynistic. As Cottee (2020, p. 2) points out, the incel subculture is often portrayed as 'exclusively male and the incel ideology is by definition anti-women'. It ultimately differentiates male and female sexuality within a dichotomous and hierarchical incel ideology, excluding women from the in-group. The male gender of Jan might also have made female incels reluctant to be involved.

Jan, a male researcher based in Norway, contacted his participants via private Facebook groups (n = 4). Two groups were found through the search engine on Facebook using phrases like *incels* and *incel groups*, but the two other groups did not show in the search engine. He discovered these groups by browsing the forum *Yourenotalone.co*, which has been shut down because of minimal activity but allowed Jan to follow its members' emigration to Facebook. The Facebook groups were selected based on convenience and with the safety of Jan in mind. Although the groups were private, they allowed outsiders, unlike large, puritanical incel forums, while prohibiting 'demotivational' and 'cult-like' posts that encouraged violence. Jan also used his personal Facebook account to establish trust and rapport. The relatively small sample size of the groups, varying from 300 to 1,200 members, reduced his overall exposure to the incel community. Participants in Jan's study were more comfortable disclosing their identity than participants in Lisa's study. Jan's interviews were conducted face-to-face via Zoom or Discord, depending on the platform participants were most comfortable using. Most participants had the camera on (n = 10) and openly shared personal information like their name, age, and country of origin. Similarly, Jan had his camera on throughout the interviews to maintain trust and build rapport. However, a small minority of participants remained anonymous by having their cameras off (n = 2), with one participant (n = 1) also using a voice modifier to hide his identity further. Full ethical approval was obtained from the Norwegian Agency for Shared Services in Education and Research (SIKT), with particular regard paid to topics of sensitivity and processing and storing personal data, including informed consent, confidentiality, and anonymity.

Lisa, a female researcher based in the UK, undertook a constructivist ethnographic study (Williamson, 2006) involving non-participant observation and reflexive thematic analysis (Braun & Clarke, 2019) of publicly available incel discussions, videos, memes, and comments on social media platforms. Lisa conducted 10 interviews with self-identified former (n = 7) and current (n = 3) incels to understand the influence and philosophy of incels from a gendered criminological perspective. Interview participants were all men, identified by snowball and convenience sampling (Goodman, 1961; Sedgwick, 2013). The recruiting advertisement did not specifically request men, but only men volunteered to be interviewed. As with Jan's experience, this might have been due to the male-dominated spaces in which recruitment was done and the reluctance of female incels to participate in interviews.

Participants were contacted via Reddit r/exredpill, r/incelswithouthate, and by searching Reddit for phrases like *I am/I used to be an incel*. Respondents were then messaged via Reddit's messaging service, inviting them for an interview. Lisa chose these forums with her safety in mind, deeming them less hostile than other incel spaces, as ascertained during her previous ethnographic explorations. Other interviews were conducted with incels who had contacted the researcher directly because they were aware of her work on this topic. The interviews were conducted via email or private messages on Reddit. Lisa offered interviewees the option of telephone or Skype interviews. However, none took her up on this offer, preferring instead to remain within the familiarity of the online spaces they usually frequented, which afforded them anonymity. Those who used email appeared less concerned about anonymity than those who wanted to remain on Reddit. They were happy to divulge what seemed to be their actual first names, as opposed to those on Reddit who remained masked by their Reddit usernames. Full ethical approval was obtained from Lisa's institutional faculty ethics committee, with particular regard paid to the sensitivity of the topic and the researcher's safety and well-being, alongside the usual considerations of informed consent, confidentiality, and anonymity.

Undertaking direct interviews with incels enabled us to consider how this shaped our perceptions of them and to contrast our work with media and other academic interpretations. Comparing our respective study experiences highlights the gendered distinctions we experienced and how we understood the narratives presented to us.

Gendered differences

The researcher is one of the most important instruments in qualitative research (Hanna, 2019). However, the gender of the researcher can have a substantial impact on observations and understandings and affect their reaction to participants in the field (Berger, 2015).

This issue can be pivotal in a hard-to-reach community such as incels, where members express suspicion and hostility towards outsiders, especially women. Both of us had experiences, determined by our gender, that significantly influenced the content and direction of our interviews and data analysis. Here we reflect on how these differences influenced participants' anonymity, their communication preferences, trust level, identity formation, and ideological commitment.

Few participants asked Jan probing or interrogating questions about his position, nor did they try to test his competence or tolerance. Participants who agreed to talk displayed little suspicion about Jan's bias or negative outlook about incels. To create rapport and trust, the recruitment advertisement and informational letter clearly stated that the interview would explore 'the diversity of the community' for the purpose of gaining a 'nuanced and humanized understanding of incels by looking more closely at the everyday-life, stigma, grievances, and life-stories of incels'. These measures might have eased the tension between the interviewer and participants as none tried to change his mind. Instead, being a male researcher seemingly generated a dimension of trust as Jan was able to take on the role of a friend. Many talked about why they identified as incel or involuntary celibate, how it affected their life, and their struggles. The question of anonymity between researcher and interviewer was, with few exceptions, not an issue as most incels openly shared personal stories of school, family, social life, work, and dating life. Still, attempts to relate to participants through shared gendered (as a male) or ethnic (as an Asian in Norway) dating experiences did not generate significant discussions, reminding Jan of their distinctive roles as interviewer and interviewee.

Anonymity, specific forum rules, and subcultural norms can affect incels' identity performance online, limiting what they say or do to shitposting and misogynistic diatribes (Preston et al., 2021). As Jan conducted the interviews face-to-face or through a blank screen, conversations rarely reflected the direct misogynistic or hateful speech found on incel forums. With a male interlocuter, participants nuanced their perspectives by recounting relatable personal issues, life stories, and grievances, such as the difficulty of living up to male ideals. At the same time, some participants might have wanted to portray themselves and the incel community more positively, thus not expressing misogynistic attitudes. However, there were instances where some participants mirrored misogynistic online rhetoric. For example, one participant was explicit in his hate for women: 'I hate women a lot. I hate women to such an extent . . . you can say I'm a very big misogynist, you can say that'.

Mistrust within the incel community means that members generally keep their identities hidden, but for Jan, snowball sampling was relatively successful in accessing this hard-to-reach population (Baltar & Brunet, 2012). Few participants were close to other incels or knew them personally, which reflects the overall attitude of mistrust among them. However, some were part of small chat groups on Facebook or Discord servers where they communicated more openly. One participant was most comfortable communicating via Discord, and Jan created a server to conduct the interview, which in turn allowed the participant to recruit two other incels with whom he had close contact to the server after completing his interview.

In contrast, participants interrogated Lisa about her worldview, and she experienced some suspicion and distrust. Her recruitment message highlighted her interest in why people self-identify as an incel. She did not refer to the community negatively, although stigma and apprehension would have been felt regardless of how she referred to the community. Throughout the interviews, she was often asked challenging or provocative questions to test her knowledge and competence, and efforts were made to catch her out. Yet, incels interviewed simultaneously referred to her as 'an intelligent female', an oxymoron according to misogynist incels. The use of this description by incels was an attempt to persuade Lisa of the validity of their thinking by claiming she was clever enough to appreciate their philosophies. Thus, unsurprisingly, being a female researcher appeared to generate a level of wariness, particularly as it was impossible to share gendered experiences. At the same time, participants often identified women as the reason for their problems. This gendered dynamic may have been the reason Lisa's participants were more concerned about anonymity than those interviewed by Jan. However, these interviewees also shared personal stories of school, family, social, work, and dating experiences, albeit with limited information to protect their identities. In this study, although the boundaries between the interviewer and the interviewee were clearly demarcated, with Lisa as the researcher other, participants also tried to assume a faux interviewer role in their questioning of Lisa. There were also instances in which Lisa found herself in the role of therapist for participants seeking sympathetic responses and support. The gendered stereotype that women are more nurturing and empathetic than men may have been at play here (Bem, 1974; Graham & Ickes, 1997; Sprague & Massoni, 2005), with Lisa placed in what Kate Manne (2017, p. XIII) describes as an 'asymmetrical moral support role'. Even though some participants openly made denigrating remarks about women, they still felt entitled to rely on a female researcher for comfort and care.

Impressing worldviews and assumptions about researchers' perceptions

Researchers working in the same area but with different field personas might end up with significantly different data, but this is not necessarily the case (Damsa & Ugelvik, 2017). Despite the differences, we found commonalities in our interactions and interviews with incels. Here we discuss mutual findings in our interviews, such as motives for participating, ideological framing, and identity formation.

Few participants asked Jan probing or interrogating questions about his motives or his identity as a researcher. However, during recruitment, potential participants expressed suspicion and scepticism. According to Goffman (1959), social interaction is comparable to 'onstage' and 'offstage' theatre performances. Similarly, potential participants' responses varied based on the community dynamic and the expectations of incel members' onstage performativity in the different incel groups. One group, posting mainly ironic and sarcastic memes mocking women and themselves, were sceptical about the validity of Jan's request. Group members questioned his role and whether he was out to 'villainize or actually learn about our struggle'. Others suspected that Jan was a federal agent, while others jokingly dismissed the request with memes saying, 'it's a trap'. However, despite their open dismissal, some members reached out for an interview later, and one member even recommended others Jan could contact.

Although participants did not push their ideology onto the researcher, some were curious about Jan's stance on specific incel theories and whether he considered them valid or sound. Some participants promoted a pseudo-scientific framework to substantiate their arguments and their position as an incel; for example, statistics and research explaining the unbalanced dating market, partner selection, and sexual attractiveness. This was to give 'a more scientific and accurate description of the incel phenomenon and its members' than what was portrayed in the media, as one interviewee said, even though media stories on incels often feature their focus on these issues. From one comprehensive pre-textual conversation leading up to the interview, Jan got the impression that the participant was determined to counter 'the perception of academics or mainstream media' with elaborate explanations, but the interview participant turned out to be more reserved and hesitant in the interview. He saw himself as 'not completely blackpilled' and used non-incel terms to explain the inconsistent dating market while focusing less on commonly held incel beliefs. It is also possible that the participant was more confident in written communication than oral, which made him more hesitant and less adamant in his argumentation than in previous conversations with Jan. Notably, he wanted to keep his identity hidden, thus excluding most of his lived experiences.

Lisa did not express particular viewpoints prior to the interviews. However, as conversations developed, participants indicated they had obtained information about Lisa elsewhere and made assumptions about her life experience and worldview. The gendered differences in experiences between Jan and Lisa here are palpable. In one interview, the participant repeatedly presented pseudo-scientific studies validating the incel blackpill philosophy, asking if these had 'changed her mind'. These studies comprised commonly held incel beliefs such as hypergamy (the belief that women will only mate with high-status males), the sexual racism theory (women will primarily choose white men to be their sexual or romantic partners), and the 80/20 rule of dating (80% of women desire and compete for the top 20% of men, and conversely, the bottom 80% of men compete for the bottom 20% of women), among others. Such behaviour led Lisa to question why these individuals had agreed to participate in an interview and whether they were attempting to impress their ideology on her for a reason. For example, were they seeking to 'turn' a feminist, as in the notorious case of Cassie Jaye, who became a poster girl for men's rights? Or was it an attempt to validate their ideology, which inevitably involves promoting it? These gendered differences raise the question of whether interviewees assumed that Jan as a man had some of this knowledge inherently or, by virtue of being a man, was more knowledgeable in general.

Ethical and methodological assessments

Researching fringe online groups requires constant ethical and methodological assessment. Contrary to journalists or law enforcement who use covert and deceptive research methods to investigate individuals online (Bates, 2021; Lavin, 2020), researchers have a more limited repertoire. The recruitment process therefore made it impossible for us to hide our roles as researchers and our identities. Thus, recruiting incels involved a certain level of personal risk to us since certain members of the incel community are notorious for doxing people they want to shame, harass, or harm (usually women). Here we discuss safety and the personal challenges we faced, negotiating boundaries with participants, and how they changed depending on the researcher's gender.

The virtual distance between participants and Jan was sometimes blurred. In addition to e-mail and Discord, Jan mainly used his personal Facebook account to recruit and communicate with participants before face-to-face interactions online. Jan's use of his personal social media account put him in a vulnerable position that made it easy for participants to investigate his personal life. At the same time, this form of recruitment was meant to build rapport and trust: communicating via a medium they were comfortable with while reassuring potential participants that the researcher was not a threat or out to demonize incels. Jan implemented specific security measures to ensure his safety online, such as changing and securing passwords, reviewing his online presence, and limiting social media exposure or personal contact information online to close friends. These measures included adjusting his work profile on the university webpage by toning down his previous emphasis on researching radicalization and terrorism (Andersen & Sandberg, 2020), so as not to equate incel activity with terrorism. However, the lines between the personal privacy of Jan as a professional researcher and informal recruiter became blurred as some participants sent him friend requests. These requests were politely rejected by explaining the need to keep a professional distance to 'both protect the identity of my participants, but also protect my own privacy'. Although Jan worried participants would react negatively to the rejection of their request, it never created conflict.

At the same time, upholding the security and privacy of interview participants was crucial. The majority of Jan's participants revealed their identities to the researcher, and a few people were even comfortable with him mentioning their names in publications. However, most asked that their identity remain anonymous and expressed concern and fear about social stigma, governmental control, and 'internal justice' meted out by bad actors within the incel community. Illustratively, one participant used a black ski mask when he turned on his camera for the interview. It looked uncomfortable, and Jan gave him the option of turning off his camera rather than wearing it—he took it off. He then explained that he was no longer a part of the incel community, but he feared the spitefulness of many users on incel forums, implying their cult-like propensity to harass. As he put it, 'they literally have nothing better to do than to spend ten-twenty-thirty hours trying to find out who you are, and what your job is, you know. And just find a way that they can mess with you.'

Lisa maintained a virtual distance between herself and her participants. The interviews only entailed textual conversations with no in-person or face-to-face interaction. However, tensions regarding online identity frequently blurred personal and professional boundaries, with participants able to access aspects of Lisa's online presence. In previous publications (Lavorgna & Sugiura, 2022; Sugiura, 2021a), Lisa has emphasized how certain forms of qualitative online research, such as digital ethnography, can cause tensions affecting researchers' private and public lives and result in power dynamics and conflicting agendas. For many academics, having a public presence and being active online is necessary to enhance their professional reputation and increase impact. This can include institutional requirements such as having university web pages and participating in media interviews. Researchers also use social media sites to connect with family, friends, and colleagues in their private lives. Lisa took some precautions before commencing her interviews; for instance, she reviewed what information was available about her online and checked the privacy settings of her social media profiles. However, during the research, it became clear that what was personal and what was professional were not distinct, certainly from the participants' perspectives. For instance, she received requests to connect on her personal (private) social media accounts, which she had obscured from public view. This means that participants had made an extra effort to discover her on these platforms, perhaps connecting with one of her friends in order to be able to send friend/follow requests. Even though there was no indication that these requests were sinister in nature, they made Lisa uneasy as they crossed her personal boundary. Her discomfort was exacerbated because of the incel community's association with misogyny, violence, and abuse.

Reflexivity is crucial throughout the research process, but it is essential during interviews related to sensitive or intimate topics (Hanna, 2019). Reflexivity enables researchers to interrogate the theories, assumptions, perceptions, emotions, and values they bring to their research and challenge the research to potentially be power-driven or politically influenced (Alvesson & Sköldberg, 2009; Bourdieu & Wacquant, 1992). It also acknowledges the potential impact of their work on research participants (Collins & McNulty, 2020; Gabriel, 2015). As a younger male academic venturing into a male-dominated community espousing anti-feminist and misogynistic views, reflexivity was important for Jan. This included assessing whether he presented himself as an ally or enemy to the participants. As a man researching men who hate women and blame them for their problems, would he unintentionally be giving the impression that he was an ally who would portray the incel community more favourably than a female researcher, even though this would be a betrayal of the trust of participants who shared private information about themselves? Participants revealed personal information about themselves such as their loneliness, poverty, family dysfunction, bullying, mental illness, and even ideation of and attempts to commit suicide. As the interview participants showed vulnerability, Jan had to critically evaluate his position as a researcher and the impact he had before, during, and after the interview (Berger, 2015). Discussions about depression and suicide are not uncommon on incel forums (Daly & Laskovtsov, 2021), so it was unsurprising that some participants brought it up. However, as a researcher, navigating the emotional work of an interviewee discussing the subject was not easy. For Jan, it was important not to be a source of distress for the interviewee by negatively impacting the interviewee's wellbeing. Expressing empathy and verifying that they consulted professional healthcare workers or were receiving treatment was done to alleviate some of the stress the interview might have put on the participants. Jan also regularly met with a therapist to help process his research experiences.

For Lisa, a female academic conducting research with people espousing misogynist perspectives, reflexivity was crucial to reconcile the challenging situations she encountered during her interviews. Lisa's experiences undeniably impacted her study, combined with an informed understanding of the harm to her arising from misogynist incels. She was also removed from participants in not being part of their community and holding diametrically opposing philosophies. Therefore, Lisa inhabited an exclusive space where she was both internal and external to the research, as a potential recipient of misogynist abuse and by being removed from incel ideology commonalities. Such positioning challenges impartiality in research; in this case, a woman researching male-dominated groups associated with misogynistic behaviours could lead to criticisms of bias. Critics raise similar concerns about studying a population linked to serious social harms or a population the researcher belongs to and advocates for. Yet research is not conducted in a vacuum. Therefore, researchers are unable to claim they occupy a neutral position no matter their research interests (Hammond & Kingston, 2014). Feminist epistemologies acknowledge and assert the researcher's position as part of, and influential in, the research process (Ahearne, 2021) and embrace critical participation in research in fraught settings (Jain, 2017). However, acknowledging a vested personal position could evoke criticism about professionalism and lack of impartiality. Tension can be intense when research participants are easily associated with social or political engagement. Depending on the circumstances, the researcher could be perceived as an ally or enemy. Nevertheless, ignoring one's identity would render the research and analyses artificial, betraying the researcher's lived experience (Sugiura, 2021a, 2021b). In Lisa's case, artificially divorcing her female identity from her researcher identity would have limited her understanding of the issues and the internal and external structural forces influencing her study.

Challenging the mediatized incel narrative

Direct interaction with members of the incel subculture allowed us to gain a more nuanced perspective than those represented in the media. Participants could explain why they self-identify or formerly identified as incel or involuntary celibate. The interview setting allowed them to delve into their ideological commitments, relationship experiences, and everyday feelings of loneliness and stigma. Thus, despite their problematic views, at times we acknowledged the validity of their views, eliciting our sympathy. However, post-interviews, when analysing the data and reflecting on our research experience, we also took issue with specific claims of the participants.

On several occasions, participants presented themselves in a way that challenged Jan's preconceived notions of who they were, how they would act, and what they would discuss. His previous explorations based on incel documents, discussions, and forums created initial expectations of ideological commitment, subcultural knowledge, and life experiences among self-identifying incels or people who frequent incel forums (Andersen, 2023). The media, which often describes incels as monolithic and inherently dangerous, also influenced his impressions. Incels are described demographically as white, cis-gendered males with a sense of entitlement about love and sex, ideologically blaming external factors for their failure in love while promoting violence (Daly & Laskovtsov, 2021). However, both Jan's and Lisa's research supports O'Malley and Helm's (2022) study that incel communities often comprise multiple ethnicities. Several participants were non-white, and some had little subcultural capital or specific knowledge about blackpill ideology. Interestingly, a few participants used blackpill language in texting but in interviews were hesitant to use it or did not use it at all, which suggests an intentionality in how they presented themselves. None of the participants supported physical acts of violence, and some did not embrace the term *incel* as a subcultural identity. In their ongoing status negotiation, they differentiated themselves as *involuntary celibates*. Illustratively, the framework of the initial interview guide created by Jan was ill-fitting for the life experience of one of his early participants, who had lived in foster care from a young age and struggled with alcohol and substance abuse. Even though he was not active or invested in incel ideology, he was preoccupied by his lack of sexual experience. He connected with the struggles shared within the incel group despite the hateful behaviour verbalized online. He highlighted the internal struggle of incels while reflecting on his agency when describing himself as involuntarily celibate. Instead of blaming external factors, like women, he turned the blame inwards—'I blame myself'.

Sensationalized media coverage propagates misconceptions about incels (DeCook & Kelly, 2022). They often present a one-dimensional portrayal of dangerous, isolated, misogynist men, overlooking vulnerabilities and pain suffered by some individuals within the community. Alternatively, the emphasis on incel-related perpetrators over victims—their names, backgrounds, manifestos (where applicable), social media presence, and, concerningly, their male supremacist ideologies—is given centre stage, which elicits sympathy and validation for their claims of misandry and anti-feminist rhetoric (Manne, 2017). Many people experience real vulnerabilities and pain but abstain from joining spaces propagating hate, regardless of how difficult their lives are. We point this out not to minimize their pain and vulnerabilities. However, we question why these men remain in these groups, retaining the name of incel when the term inextricably links them to misogyny.

Importantly, including misogynist narratives, whether about misogynist incels or not, in mainstream media reporting amplifies and legitimizes harmful channels uniting disillusioned

548

young men. As researchers, we realize the risk of giving voice to individual incels with misogynistic attitudes, as it could further their extremist and warped perspectives. Thus, we exercise caution in taking incel accounts at face value to avoid normalizing and validating the rhetoric of victimhood and misogyny that is ubiquitous in incel communities. Despite incels' claims to the contrary, they are not marginalized or silenced individuals. However, in addition to undertaking external observations of the incel communities, we felt it was important to directly engage with people to obtain a richer understanding of the incel dynamics without being unduly sympathetic. Without this interaction, we would not have been able to appreciate the heterogeneity within the incel community, especially the segment that does not hold to a worldview entrenched in misogyny. However, sometimes individuals portray themselves differently online than in person (Bullingham & Vasconcelos, 2013), which became evident in Jan's interviews. This has implications for how we interpreted our interviews. It does not necessarily mean that our participants were calculating and trying to manipulate us. The interview setting might have allowed them to express themselves more freely than they would on the forums, which often have strict norms and rules. Thus, the interviews allowed us to comprehend the humanity, vulnerability, and pain coexisting alongside the hatred and shocking and provoking behaviour in incel communities. This is not to excuse or minimize egregious behaviours and certainly not to platform or prioritize the purveyors of abuse. However, we recognize that the harms emanating from misogynistic incel ideology are both internal to incels and external, projected onto women and society.

Conclusion

The incel movement is a counter-cultural phenomenon that is gaining notoriety and attention from the media, law enforcement, and the public for its overt promotion of misogyny, anti-feminism, and violence. Direct contact with the online deviant incel subculture is necessary to obtain first-hand insight into the identity negotiation and motives of its members that challenge superficial media narratives. Our interviews led us to agree to some extent with Cottee (2020, p. 5), who stated that most incels are 'law-abiding and seek out other incels online not to coordinate acts of violence but to share their experiences and stave off feelings of loneliness'. However, this solidarity-seeking often involves the espousal of hate, emphasizing the need to move beyond spectacular mass violence as the only definition of violence or harm associated with incels. Furthermore, although incels do not coordinate acts of mass violence, it has been encouraged by them (Kelly et al., 2022; Scaptura & Boyle, 2020). For example, incels have organized participation in online harassment campaigns against women along with other groups in the manosphere, such as the THOTaudit meme (Kelly et al., 2022).[3]

Participation in the incel subculture provides its members with multiple ways to construct and perform an identity online, which is readily accessible to us as researchers. Nevertheless, underlying intentions and ambiguity are sometimes lost when we limit our research to observing online discussions of incels. Like other controversial subcultures, some of the loudest and most problematic opinions are amplified in the media and cemented as representative for every participant connected to the milieu. It is therefore critical to include the multiplicity of voices to understand the incel subculture fully by interacting with members who better illuminate their lived experiences and worldviews. Direct interviews provide nuance into what it means to be an incel by allowing incels to negotiate their online deviant status, explaining their understanding of the terms *incel* and *involuntary celibate*.

However, it is critical to assess the methodological and ethical challenges encountered when doing research and interviews with fringe online groups of hard-to-reach communities (Kaufmann & Tzanetakis, 2020) or 'unsavoury' populations (de Coning, 2021). As researchers of online communities, we must constantly evaluate the groups we engage with while maintaining boundaries of professionalism, personal privacy, and safety. At the same time, it is essential to clearly understand how our identities as researchers impact our study interactions before, during, and after an interview, highlighting the necessity of adopting a reflexive approach.

In this chapter, we have presented our reflections and experiences of interviewing incels directly. The differences in our interviews might have been affected by the type of platforms we used for recruitment. However, the gendered dimension is salient, and it too influenced the content of our interviews and the directions they took. The differences gender made were also manifested in the access we had to incel members and the trust we were able to establish between researcher and interviewee. This included participants' willingness to share personal and painful aspects of their lives, their style and platform of communication, and to what degree they wanted to stay anonymous throughout the interview. Therefore, we suggest that gender-impact assessments be part of the research design and ethics process when undertaking direct research with deviant online subcultures. Illustratively, Jan had to rethink some of his interpretations of incels because of his research collaboration with Lisa. He initially understood incels as somewhat contained within subcultural online spaces but came to recognize that it is impossible to separate their actions from social and cultural notions of misogyny. As a male researcher, most of his interactions with participants were benign and unproblematic, which could result in him failing to take into account unpleasant or harmful attitudes towards female researchers within the incel community. Thus, the risk of the pendulum swinging too much toward sympathy, or himpathy (Manne, 2017), for the incel community would have been present in his research without Lisa's input.

Lastly, forming a collective identity rooted in a shared sense of alienation and victimization is central to the incel subculture. However, this is not to justify loneliness as a basis for violent rhetoric grounded in misogyny and male supremacy. It is therefore imperative to recognize the diversity of incel members, or we risk emaciating the term *incel* by conflating it with all that is misogynistic, even though not all harm directed toward women is incel-related. In this respect, distinguishing *misogynist incel* from *incel* is necessary to make the connection with male supremacist ideologies, which may or may not underpin personal identification as an incel or involuntary celibate. However, if individuals are aware of the problems associated with misogynistic incels and want to distance themselves from them, why are they not addressing misogyny as a problem in society, and why do some even deny the existence of misogyny?

Further critical appraisal of why incels who consider themselves non-misogynistic use a term that is associated with misogyny and participate in misogynistic spaces is required. This appraisal must also include how misogyny and sexism, albeit in less overt forms, continue to thrive in supposedly non-misogynistic spaces and must be appreciated in the broader context of how misogyny is structurally embedded and experienced in women's daily lives (Kelly, 1987). Misogynist incels are not uniquely misogynistic but part of a societal pattern of gender-based abuse and violence. Without such considerations, misconceptions about the incel community will prevail, and the prevalence of misogyny and violence against women will continue to be normalized.

Notes

1 www.youtube.com/watch?v=X6yi8P03igQ
2 www.malesupremacism.org/tips-for-media/
3 https://knowyourmeme.com/memes/events/thot-audit

References

Ahearne, G. (2021). Criminologist or criminal? Liminal spaces as the site for auto/biography. *Methodological Innovations, 14*(1). https://doi.org/10.1177/20597991211012054

Alvesson, M., & Sköldberg, K. (2009). *Reflexive methodology: New vistas for qualitative research*. Sage.

Andersen, J. C. (2023). The symbolic boundary work of incels: Subcultural negotiation of meaning and identity online. *Deviant Behavior, 44*(7), 1081–1101. https://doi.org/10.1080/01639625.2022.2142864

Andersen, J. C., & Sandberg, S. (2020). Islamic State propaganda: Between social movement framing and subcultural provocation. *Terrorism and Political Violence, 32*(7), 1506–1526.

Baele, S. J., Brace, L., & Coan, T. G. (2021). From 'incel' to 'saint': Analyzing the violent worldview behind the 2018 Toronto attack. *Terrorism and Political Violence, 33*(8), 1667–1691. https://doi.org/10.1080/09546553.2019.1638256

Baltar, F., & Brunet, I. (2012). Social research 2.2: Virtual snowball sampling method using Facebook. *Internet Research, 22*(1), 57–74.

Bates, L. (2021). *Men who hate women: From incels to pickup artists: The truth about extreme misogyny and how it affects us all*. Sourcebooks.

Becker, H. S. (1963). *Outsiders: Studies in the sociology of deviance*. The Free Press.

Bem, S. L. (1974). The measurement of psychological androgyny. *Journal of Consulting and Clinical Psychology, 42*, 155–162.

Berger, R. (2015). Now I see it, now I don't: Researcher's position and reflexivity in qualitative research. *Qualitative Research, 15*(2), 219–234.

Bloom, M. M. (2022). The first incel? The legacy of Marc Lépine. *Journal of Intelligence, Conflict, and Warfare, 5*(1), 39–74.

Bourdieu, P., & Wacquant, L. J. C. (1992). *An invitation to reflexive sociology*. University of Chicago Press.

Braithwaite, J. (1989). *Crime, shame and reintegration*. Cambridge University Press.

Bratich, J., & Banet-Weiser, S. (2019). From pick-up artist to incels: Con(fidence) games, networked misogyny, and the failure of neoliberalism. *International Journal of Communication, 13*(25), 5003–5027.

Braun, V., & Clarke, V. (2019). Reflecting on reflexive thematic analysis. *Qualitative Research in Sport, Exercise and Health, 11*(4), 589–597.

Bullingham, L., & Vasconcelos, A. C. (2013). 'The presentation of self in the online world': Goffman and the study of online identities. *Journal of Information Science, 39*(1), 101–112.

Chang, W. (2020). The monstrous-feminine in the incel imagination: Investigating the representation of women as 'femoids' on/r/Braincels. *Feminist Media Studies*, 1–17. https://doi.org/10.1080/14680777.2020.1804976

Cohen, A. (1955). *Delinquent boys: The culture of the gang*. The Free Press.

Cohen, S. (1972). *Folk devils and moral panics: The creation of the mods and rockers*. Martin Robertson.

Collins H., & McNulty, Y. (2020). Insider status: (Re)framing researcher positionality in international human resource management studies. *German Journal of Human Resource Management, 34*(2), 202–227.

Cottee, S. (2020). Incel (e)motives: Resentment, shame and revenge. *Studies in Conflict & Terrorism, 44*(2), 93–114. https://doi.org/10.1080/1057610X.2020.1822589

Daly, S. E., & Laskovtsov, A. (2021). 'Goodbye, my friendcels': An analysis of incel suicide posts. *Journal of Qualitative Criminal Justice and Criminology*, *11*(1). https://doi.org/10.21428/88de04a1.b7b8b295

Daly, S. E., & Reed, S. M. (2022). 'I think most of society hates us': A qualitative thematic analysis of interviews with incels. *Sex Roles*, *86*, 14–33.

Damsa, D., & Ugelvik, T. (2017). A difference that makes a difference? Reflexivity and researcher effects in an all-foreign prison. *International Journal of Qualitative Methods*, *16*, 1–10.

de Coning, A. (2021). Seven theses on critical empathy: A methodological framework for 'unsavory' populations. *Qualitative Research*, 1–17. https://doi.org/10.1177/14687941211019563

DeCook, J. R., & Kelly, M. (2022). Interrogating the 'incel menace': Assessing the threat of male supremacy in terrorism studies. *Critical Studies on Terrorism*, *15*(3), 706–726.

Ferrell, J., Hayward, K., & Young, J. (2008). *Cultural criminology: An invitation*. Sage.

Gabriel, Y. (2015). Reflexivity and beyond: A plea for imagination in qualitative research methodology. *Qualitative Research in Organizations and Management: An International Journal*, *10*(4), 332–336.

Ging, D. (2019). Alphas, betas, and incels: Theorizing the masculinities of the manosphere. *Men and Masculinities*, *22*(4), 638–657. https://doi.org/10.1177/1097184X17706401

Goffman, E. (1959). *The presentation of self in everyday life*. Doubleday.

Goodman, L. A. (1961). Snowball sampling. *Annals of Mathematical Statistics*, *32*(1), 148–170.

Graham, T., & Ickes, W. (1997). When women's intuition isn't greater than men's. In W. Ickes (Ed.), *Empathic accuracy* (pp. 117–143). Guilford.

Hammond, N., & Kingston, S. (2014). Experiencing stigma as sex work researchers in professional and personal lives. *Sexualities*, *17*(3), 329–334.

Hanna, E. (2019). The emotional labour of researching sensitive topics online: Considerations and implications. *Qualitative Research*, *19*(5), 524–539.

Hebdige, D. (1979). *Subculture: The meaning of style*. Routledge.

Hoffman, B., Ware, J., & Shapiro, E. (2020). Assessing the threat of incel violence. *Studies in Conflict & Terrorism*, *43*(7), 565–587. https://doi.org/10.1080/1057610X.2020.1751459

Holt, T. J., Joshua D. F., & Chermak, S. M. (2017). Internet-based radicalization as enculturation to violent deviant subcultures. *Deviant Behavior*, *38*(8), 855–869.

Jain, T. (2017). Researcher vs. advocate: Ethnographic-ethical dilemmas in feminist scholarship. *Equality, Diversity and Inclusion*, *36*(6), 566–585.

Jasser, G., Kelly, M., & Rothermel, A. K. (2020). Male supremacism and the Hanau terrorist attack: Between online misogyny and far-right violence. *International Centre for Counter-Terrorism—The Hague*. Retrieved from www.icct.nl/publication/male-supremacism-and-hanau-terrorist-attack-between-online-misogyny-and-far-right

Kaufmann, M., & Tzanetakis, M. (2020). Doing Internet research with hard-to-reach communities: Methodological reflections on gaining meaningful access. *Qualitative Research*, *20*(6), 927–944.

Kelly, L. (1987). The continuum of sexual violence. In J. Hanmer & M. Maynard (Eds.). *Women, violence and social control* (pp. 46–60). Macmillan Press.

Kelly, M., DiBranco, A., & DeCook, J. R. (2022). Misogynist incels and male supremacist violence. In In E. K. Carian, A. DiBranco, & C. Ebin (Eds.), *Male supremacism in the United States: From patriarchal traditionalism to misogynist incels and the alt-right* (pp. 164–180). Routledge.

Lavin, T. (2020). *Culture warlords: My journey into the dark web of white supremacy*. Monoray.

Lavorgna, A., & Sugiura, L. (2022). Direct contacts with potential interviewees when carrying out online ethnography on controversial and polarized topics: A loophole in ethics guidelines. *International Journal of Social Research Methodology*, *25*(2), 261–267.

Manne, K. (2017). *Down girl: The logic of misogyny*. Oxford University Press.

Menzie, L. (2022). Stacys, Beckys, and Chads: The construction of femininity and hegemonic masculinity within incel rhetoric. *Psychology & Sexuality*, *13*(1), 69–85. https://doi.org/10.1080/19419899.2020.1806915

Nagle, A. (2017). *Kill all normies: Online culture wars from 4chan and Tumblr to Trump and the alt-right*. John Hunt Publishing.

O'Malley, R. L., & Helm, B. (2022). The role of perceived injustice and need for esteem on incel membership online. *Deviant Behavior*, 1–18. https://doi.org/10.1080/01639625.2022.2133650

O'Malley, R. L., Holt, K., & Holt, T. J. (2022). An exploration of the involuntary celibate (incel) subculture online. *Journal of Interpersonal Violence*, 37(7–8), NP4981–NP5008. https://doi.org/10.1177/0886260520959625

Presser, L., & Sandberg, S. (2015). *Narrative criminology: Understanding stories of crime*. New York University Press.

Preston, K., Halpin, M., & Maguire, F. (2021). The black pill: New technology and the male supremacy of involuntary celibate men. *Men and Masculinities*, 24(5), 823–841.

Regehr, K. (2022). In(cel)doctrination: How technologically facilitated misogyny moves violence off screens and on to streets. *New Media & Society*, 24(1), 138–155.

Rheingold, H. (1993). A slice of life in my virtual community. In L. M. Harasim (Ed.), *Global networks: Computers and international communication* (pp. 57–80). MIT Press.

Scaptura, M. N., & Boyle, K. M. (2020). Masculinity threat, 'incel' traits, and violent fantasies among heterosexual men in the United States. *Feminist Criminology*, 15(3), 278–298.

Sedgwick, P. (2013). Convenience sampling. *BMJ*, 347. https://doi.org/10.1136/bmj.f6304

Sprague, J., & Massoni, K. (2005). Student evaluations and gendered expectations: What we can't count can hurt us. *Sex Roles*, 53, 779–793.

Sugiura, L. (2021a). Engaging with incels: Reflexivity, identity and the female cybercrime ethnographic researcher. In A. Lavorgna & T. Holt (Eds.), *Researching cybercrimes: Methodologies, ethics, and critical approaches* (pp. 473–492). Palgrave Macmillan.

Sugiura, L. (2021b). *The incel rebellion: The rise of the manosphere and the virtual war against women*. Emerald Publishing.

Tomkinson, S., Harper, T., & Attwell, K. (2020). Confronting incel: Exploring possible policy responses to misogynistic violent extremism. *Australian Journal of Political Science*, 55(2), 152–169. https://doi.org/10.1080/10361146.2020.1747393

Treadwell, J., & Garland, J. (2011). Masculinity, marginalization and violence. A case study of the English Defence League. *British Journal of Criminology*, 51(4), 621–634.

Vito, C., Admire, A., & Hughes, E. (2018). Masculinity, aggrieved entitlement, and violence: Considering the Isla Vista mass shooting. *NORMA*, 13(2), 86–102.

Williamson, K. (2006). Research in constructivist frameworks using ethnographic techniques. *Library Trends*, 55(1), 83–101.

Witt, T. (2020). 'If I cannot have it, I will do everything I can to destroy it'. The canonization of Elliot Rodger: 'Incel' masculinities, secular sainthood, and justifications of ideological violence. *Social Identities*, 26(5), 675–689. https://doi.org/10.1080/13504630.2020.1787132

Young, J. (1971). *The drugtakers: The social meaning of drug use*. Paladin.

31

LEGITIMISATION OF GREY ACTIVITIES IN ONLINE SPACE

An example of metal detectorists

Diāna Bērziņa

Introduction

As far back as 1995, McRobbie and Thornton (1995) noted that 'folk devils' use their own niche- and micro-media to react to and contest their negative portrayal by mass media. McRobbie and Thornton's (1995) analysis mostly focused on analog media and niche-print cultures; however, the early 2000s saw an increase in connected media, which provided even more opportunities for different groups to contest negative portrayals. With connected media, information flow changed from one-way communication, where the general public was restricted in ways they could respond, to two-way communication with low entry barriers, allowing for a massive growth in user-generated content (Desjardins, 2022). This has provided digital media users with easily accessible opportunities to contest claims expressed on mass media outlets. As Hier (2019, p. 387) writes, 'digital communication networks are creating opportunities to subvert the traditional gatekeeping role of journalists and elites by providing spatially and temporally distant users with an unprecedented set of opportunities'.

The role of the digital has been explored in a number of contexts, such as the role of social media in elections (Allcott & Gentzkow, 2016; Fujiwara et al., 2021) or in hate crimes (Müller & Schwarz, 2019), and how social networking sites influence unionisation of workers (Maffie, 2020). This chapter will contribute to studies examining online communities by focusing on how the Internet is used by actors in grey markets to contest the illegality of their actions. This chapter will combine the ideas of 'contested illegality' (Hübschle, 2016) and exclusion of knowledge (Sibley, 1995) to create a theoretical framework which will analyze how online communities are able to successfully provide a counternarrative to portrayal of their actions as harmful or criminal. By providing a strong counternarrative, online communities in the grey markets are able to attract new participants by portraying norms, values, and advice on how to avoid legal trouble; fragment the opposition; influence laws and regulations; and neutralise potential wrongdoing in their eyes and in the eyes of others by contesting the illegality of their actions.

The concept of 'contested illegality' was first introduced by Hübschle (2016) through her doctoral research on the illegal rhino horn economy. Hübschle (2016, p. 53) used this

DOI: 10.4324/9781003277675-36

concept to refer to 'a legitimation strategy' used by key players to justify their involvement in illicit or grey aspects of rhino horn trade. In essence, contested illegality refers to the power of the actors to question or defy the label of illegality and the criminalisation process (Hübschle, 2017). The concept of contested illegality is embedded in power relations; not everyone can use it meaningfully to their advantage to achieve their goals. For instance, in the case of rhino horns, Hübschle argued that the illegal trade is facilitated by a multitude of actors, including legal actors such as wildlife professionals, who are 'bolstered by sentiments of contested illegality' (Hübschle, 2017, p. 194). Through this, actors distance themselves from the harms that illegal trade brings or neutralise their actions in a way that aligns with social, moral, or cultural norms but might diverge from the legal norms, therefore delegitimising the validity of the law (Hübschle, 2017).

This concept will be combined with the ideas of exclusion of knowledge (Sibley, 1995). In his book *Geographies of Exclusion*, Sibley argues that Western knowledge is built on the exclusion and ranking of knowledge. He argues that 'power in academia is reflected in the existence of hierarchies' and 'new ideas or subversive ideas can be as threatening as images of alien others' (Sibley, 1995, pp. 122, 183). In a similar way, Chan (2000, p. 130) describes the movement of knowledge as 'predominantly uni-directional, from the centre (mainly the US and to a lesser extent the UK) to the periphery'. This means that knowledge from the periphery 'has to appropriate the metropolitan vocabulary in order to be read and to be perceived 'as cutting edge' (Aas, 2012, p. 8). While this chapter does not cover the creation of academic knowledge, this idea of exclusion of knowledge adds another dimension in our understanding of how online communities are able to create a strong counter-narrative to the negative portrayal of their activities.

The combination of these two ideas provides a useful framework for looking at online communities that operate in grey markets. These are markets where 'flows of licit and illicit objects are intermixed' and there is not a clear separation between legal and illegal parts of the market (Mackenzie & Green, 2009, p. 154). Furthermore, even illicit objects, through changing hands, borders, and jurisdictions can move from illicit to licit 'but most likely ending up grey: not ethically clean, but legal' (Mackenzie & Yates, 2016, p. 82). On top of these more practical aspects, another facet of grey markets is the 'moral ambiguity' that is inherent when participating in these markets as through various neutralization techniques, actors can mould their activities from being illegal to being grey (Mackenzie & Yates, 2016, p. 83).

Ideas of contested illegality and exclusion of knowledge will be used to explore how online communities that participate in grey activities are able to create a narrative about their actions and contest claims made against them. To do so, this chapter will focus on one such community with a strong online presence, namely metal detectorists, who to varying degrees participate in the grey antiquities market.

Case study: metal detecting and the grey antiquities market

People use metal detectors to search for various metal objects such as lost jewellery, scrap metal, coins, archaeological objects, and even some types of meteorites (Zubacheva, 2017). This chapter will primarily focus on hobbyist treasure hunters who search for archaeological objects using metal detectors (from here on abbreviated as metal detectorists). Some have described this type of metal detecting as being a subculture (Ferguson, 2013; Immonen & Kinnunen, 2020; Moore, 2021a). Immonen and Kinnunen (2020, p. 330) describe metal detectorists in Finland as 'an amateur group with its own characteristics, traditions and attitudes—it is a subculture with a distinct heritage identity i.e. many define their hobby in terms of heritage and heritage institutions'. This is an apt description that applies to metal detectorists in other countries as well. As will be shown later, the hobby is often defended online by contrasting it with state-sponsored heritage preservation institutions and with profesional archaeologists.

The legality of metal detecting for archaeological objects varies—in some countries, such as France, metal detecting is prohibited unless official authorisation is given, and the Heritage code protects all objects on both private and public lands (Lecroere, 2016). In England and Wales, the situation is rather unique and favourable as metal detecting is mostly legal, but it is important to obtain the landowner's permission beforehand and to be aware of protected sites such as Scheduled Monuments (Lewis, 2016; Portable Antiquities Advisory Group, 2017). In other countries, metal detecting occupies a legal grey area. For instance, in Russia metal detecting is not completely forbidden; however, the legality of metal detecting activities depends on what type of objects are found and where the metal detectorist looks for them. It is forbidden to look for objects over 100 years old without a permit, and the use of metal detector counts as an aggravating circumstance (Zubacheva, 2017). It is possible to break the law even when looking for objects that are less than 100 years old; for instance, if a metal detectorist finds, transports, or keeps World War II weapons, their main parts, or ammunition, as these are covered by Article 222 of the Criminal Code of the Russian Federation.

Although the financial motivations of metal detectorists are continuously downplayed by metal detectorists themselves, who argue that metal detecting is not 'just about the treasure' (Crisp, 2014), the promise of potential financial rewards appears often on websites aimed at beginner metal detectorists. For example, one of the online metal detecting guides aimed at beginners states that 'financial gain is another benefit of the hobby' and then goes on to provide an example by saying, 'I did pay for my first metal detector with finds I made within the first 6 months' (The Detectorist, 2022). Therefore, metal detectorists often find themselves interacting with the grey antiquities market, both by selling their finds and also through the moral ambiguity mentioned earlier, that is prevalent in this antiquities-oriented space (see Mackenzie & Yates, 2016 for a detailed explanation of what makes the antiquities market grey).

Metal detectorists are active and vocal online—there are numerous guides, blogs, social media accounts, podcasts, and forums providing insights into this hobby. The data collection for this chapter involved collecting views expressed freely by metal detectorists on these various platforms. These primarily were in English with a selection of Russian language sources. These views were used to distil narratives that are created, used, and sustained by members of these online platforms. There are some limitations to the data gathered here; for example, statements on these platforms were made by individuals who are willing to express their views online and on open, publicly accessible discussion threads. It is reasonable to argue that there are some members of the metal detecting community who will not post anything online at all. Their views might represent a different viewpoint and/or demographic that might not fit the views collected during this study. Additionally, locked, members-only discussions or groups were not accessed, therefore some narratives might be missed. However, despite these limitations it is believed that open, publicly accessible sources provided well-rounded representation of narratives employed by metal detectorists in the digital space.

Some of these online spaces are also used for evaluations and/or selling of the finds (Bērziņa, 2021). However, this is not the topic of this chapter; instead, what this chapter explores is the power that "the digital" gives to those who operate in the grey spaces and markets. They might participate in activities that occupy a legal grey area depending on the location, but the greyness of the market facilitates their activities. In this chapter, the relationship between "the digital" and "the greyness" is viewed as symbiotic. The greyness allows for open digital interactions and creation of user-generated content, while this open digital space allows for blurring the lines between legal and illegal, therefore contributing to the existence of greyness. This chapter will focus on four ways that this particular online community uses the online spaces to control the narrative about the legality of their activities.

Sharing norms and values, avoiding legal problems

Using ideas by Ferrell et al. (2001, p. 179) and considering metal detectorists' strong online presence, metal detecting can be viewed as a community 'of mediated meaning and collective representation'. Moreover, among 'certain committed hobbyists' metal detecting has grown into a subculture (Moore, 2021a). However, it is arguably not a subculture with rigid boundaries, instead it can be conceptualised as 'culturally bounded (but not closed) networks of people who come to share the meaning of specific ideas, material objects, and practices through interaction' (Williams & Copes, 2005, p. 70).

While certainly people organise treasure hunting trips or participate in rallies, metal detecting is an individualistic hobby, described by some as a ' "hermit" hobby' (Ace, 2021). However, the online space brings the open-community aspect to this hobby, allowing people to share ideas, advice, and objects. In a study focusing on metal detecting in Norway, an interviewee said that 'it is more fun to show it [the object] off, posting it on Facebook and receive comments and such things' (Rasmussen, 2014, p. 95). Furthermore, by sharing stories and knowledge, metal detectorists earn anonymous peer respect. An analysis of Russian treasure hunting forums revealed that in certain object categories such as numismatics there are prominent users who help with identification and evaluation of objects, and their opinion is highly valued and sought after (Bērziņa, 2021). This is consistent with other studies focusing on deviance and online space such as digital piracy, where a hierarchy exists based on an individual's activity, interests, and on how the individual helps the larger community (Holt & Copes, 2010). Knowledge and experience in this space is important—more important than compliance with the law. A host of one of the episodes of the podcast Hardcore Metal Detecting Radio (2018)[1] praised a fellow metal detectorist, calling him a 'hardcore hunter' who 'does not obey the law that much', but he knows 'just about everything about this stuff'. Therefore, the amount of knowledge and experience this individual has gained provide 'a legitimation strategy' (Hübschle, 2016, p. 53) which disregards his noncompliance with the law.

There are certain recurring themes that come up when researching metal detecting in online spaces. Many guides and blogs warn that not everyone will make large sums of money from metal detecting, but there is a chance that it will happen. More importantly, however, the thrill of the hunt, adventure, the ability to hold in one's hands something that has been buried for hundreds if not thousands of years, and a way to spend more time outdoors are often highlighted as great incentives to pick up metal detecting (Ace, 2021; Sergei UpstateNY, 2020). Practicing metal detectorists describe the adventurous feel of metal detecting. For instance, one blog describes metal detecting in Russia as '[a]dventures of Indiana Jones are really nothing compared to searching for gold in Siberia' (Sergei UpstateNY, 2020). While legal aspects of this hobby have been discussed on more professional sales-oriented websites (e.g., article written by Kennedy, 2020 for Treasures in America website), this is a hobby of grey legality and as such guidelines which are often generalised might create an assumption that metal detecting is allowed in the reader's jurisdiction (Moore, 2021b). In cases where metal detecting might be legal but there exists some ambiguity, one of the forum's posts provides advice, saying, 'Basically the answer is NEVER ask gov authorities for permission. It [sic] the land does not say "no metal detecting" or "no trespassing" then you are free to hunt that gov property' (maxxkatt, 2022), which implies that explicitly asking for a permission will most likely result in no as an answer.

In cases where certain types of or all metal detecting is prohibited, blog or forum posts exist that describe how to behave to avoid unwanted attention while still engaging in metal detecting or how to avoid trouble if caught. A metal detectorist in Russia argues that rather than trying to change Russian laws pertaining to treasure hunting it is better to just dig, not flaunt great finds without a reason, and to not be overly impudent. In his eyes, the most important thing is 'to be in harmony with conscience' rather than follow the law (Vapour, 2020). Other strategies used by metal detectorists can be glimpsed from interviews given to local journalists. An anonymous digger operating in the Kirov region of Russia described to a journalist one of the strategies used by treasure hunters who post photos of their finds on online forums—metal detectorists cover their faces in the photographs to avoid potential trouble (Ляпунова, 2016). However, if the police approach a metal detectorist who is out on a treasure hunting trip in Russia, it is suggested to remain calm and simply say that they are looking for scrap metal or meteorites, and emphasise to the police that owning and carrying a metal detector is not prohibited (МД Арена, 2016).

The online space provides an opportunity to share advice from more mundane aspects of metal detecting related to the basics, such as which metal detector to choose to what to do if a metal detectorist is caught breaking the law, and what to do to avoid any trouble. The easy access to these online discussions and suggestions makes it more acceptable to skirt the line between legal and illegal. It creates an environment where certain behaviour is socially accepted, albeit not always legal or has some ambiguity attached to it. The defiance of the labels of crime and illegality, or in this case, ignoring these aspects, in itself serves as a 'legitimizing and enabling mechanism' (Hübschle, 2016, p. 50). Hübschle (2016, p. 51) argues that 'actors may find it less daunting to enter, transact in or establish markets, which are illegal but socially accepted'. Therefore, it appears that due to metal detectorists' self-legitimatisation on these online platforms, they are more willing to enter the grey or illegal space of this activity and feel more comfortable discussing it with fellow metal detectorists in open view of outsiders (including law enforcement), who might access these platforms.

Fragment the opposition

From the perspective of the academic archaeological community, metal detecting is a controversial and often discussed activity. The academics have generally divided into two opposite camps: one which endorses metal detecting and argues for permissive rather than restrictive conditions (Karl, 2016), while the other is against metal detecting as being destructive to the preservation of the past (Lecroere, 2016). However, some archaeologists purposefully participate in online metal detecting forums to encourage metal detectorists to report finds to them and are willing to identify objects found by metal detectorists (Lecroere, 2016). This indicates that online is an important space to engage with metal detectorists. The willingness of some archaeologists to participate in these online spaces and help with the identification of the objects provides further legitimisation to this activity for the metal detectorists who found the objects (Lecroere, 2016). What is interesting about the divide between opposite camps is that often the assumed financial motivations are used to make a distinction between different types of metal detectorists, such as 'the almost archaeologist', the ill-informed, and clear law-breakers who only care about the money (Lecroere, 2016, p. 186). Even within the metal detecting community itself pure financial motivation is frowned upon, while having a love for history is seen as a more noble motivation (Moorhouse, 2021). However, even those who are motivated by the love for history occasionally sell their finds (Moorhouse, 2021). This division is evident among other digitally connected groups as well, for example, in the previously mentioned case of digital piracy. As Holt and Copes (2010, p. 642) observed, 'the adherence to a non-profit mindset allowed pirates to portray themselves as non-criminals and, thus, morally acceptable'. Following this logic, people who metal detect arguably see themselves as motivated by some higher loyalties that overshadow fleeting monetary gain that they can receive from the occasional sale of an object.

While some deviant acts are strongly condemned by the majority of society, crimes with no apparent victim sow division in society. This is also the case for metal detecting. Take for example an article in the *Guardian*, which highlighted how illegal metal detecting in the United Kingdom continued even during the COVID-19 lockdowns (see Kale, 2020). Readers commenting under the digital version of the article were divided, with many seeing nothing wrong with this activity, saying that the law is wrong and if metal detectorists did not find these objects no one would and these objects would remain lost to humanity. Others argued for not putting all metal detectorists in the same category, as some do report their finds and follow procedures, while others keep finds for personal gains. In the comments under the *Guardian* article, one can also see the strong comparison between treasure hunters and archaeologists, with some arguing that treasure hunters are the ones bringing the majority of important archaeological finds to the public's attention. A similar notion has been expressed elsewhere, where it has been argued that 'its [sic] detectorists who have been finding the main important finds and not archaeologists' (vulcan800Geoff Bourne, 2012), and 'I have rescued literally thousands of objects from intensively cultivated land which otherwise would have been destroyed by modern farming methods' (Andrew, 2012). Statements like these portray this activity as a rescue and a greater good. As Rasmussen (2014, p. 91) points out, 'by labelling metal detecting as cultural heritage rescue, it cannot then at the same time be cultural heritage crime it appears'.

By advancing this idea of heritage rescue within the public digital sphere such as comment sections on prominent media outlets, metal detectorists create a lens through which they themselves and others view their activities. It makes metal detecting more socially acceptable, as it is portrayed in a way that it appears to contribute to the protection of cultural heritage. Through online platforms, this image can be shared with more people, regardless of geographic boundaries, differences, and local law. The blurring of the line between legal and illegal might seem less daunting if there are other people who are engaging in the same activity and even being acknowledged for their help. Rasmussen (2014, p. 102), using as a case study her work in Norway, observed that '[d]ubious acts are rationalized on the basis that they contribute to rescuing material that is perceived to be under severe threat. Archaeologists' praise seems to be an important confirmation of this impression'. This can be seen as a legitimation strategy that supersedes the potential illegality of treasure hunting activities.

Neutralisation and counternarrative

On online platforms, the love for history is presented as an impetus for this activity. Potential monetary gains are often downplayed. If anything, the resources, both in terms of time and money, are brought up to discuss how expensive metal detecting can be and that finding a perfect location to metal detect is a time-consuming task. As one of the metal detectorists summarised on a thread discussing research, '[t]he most important aspect to this hobby is location, most machines will find whatever is there regardless of price. If it ain't there you're not gonna find it' (kingman mikey, 2022). In terms of money spent on this activity, in the blog's Heritage Journal discussion section, metal detectorist Andrew (2012) claimed that he has been metal detecting for over 40 years and has spent over £100,000 on the hobby. He continued, saying that he has 'placed many items that would otherwise have been destroyed by modern farming methods into museum collections world-wide' (Andrew, 2012). This way, metal detecting is portrayed as a rescue, an activity that over the years costs a lot of money, but people are still doing it for a greater good, in this case saving the cultural heritage. Through this narrative metal detecting is portrayed as a harmless, even beneficial activity; they 'aren't hurting anyone' (Hardcore Metal Detecting Radio, 2018), and instead are rescuing archaeological objects. In one case, a speaker on a podcast recalls an encounter where someone told him that he 'quit a very good job in federal government and he actually become an outlaw relic hunter' in order to 'keep the government from getting their hands on as many civil war artefacts as possible because of the corruption he saw within a system' (All Metal Mode, 2020).

Some metal detectorists add objects to their personal collections. This is an interesting idea as by adding objects to their own collections, metal detectorists take up the role of a collector. This then allows them to expand their interactions with the antiquities trade and heritage sector, for example, by showing off their collections to the public and lending them to academics for research. This way, they can further legitimise their activities and contribute to the creation of new knowledge (see Herva et al., 2016; Labelle, 2003). Similarly, they can metal detect in a specific area with a goal of creating a display that can be donated to a local historical society museum (AceGVSU11, 2011). These collections then make metal detectorists as a community a strong challenger of official heritage discourse, which usually equates archaeologists as stewards of the heritage and advocates ' "conserve as found" conservation ethic' (Smith, 2012, para. 5). Through their activities and collections, metal detectorists can add the knowledge they have gained this way to the existing pool of knowledge or change it. A speaker on one of the episodes of the All Metal Mode podcast noted that 'metal detectorists can change history' and sometimes can 'do a better job of telling the story' than archaeologists can, especially when it involves large battlefields that cannot be fully excavated by archaeologists but can be surveyed by metal detectorists (All Metal Mode, 2020).

Metal detectorists are portrayed as knowledgeable and experienced, which often earns them peer respect. For instance, one of the hosts on the Hardcore Metal Detecting Radio podcast praised fellow metal detectorist Bob McWilliams by saying that 'it's unbelievable how much he knows about early man by digging artefacts up and just thinking about it [how they lived]' (Hardcore Metal Detecting Radio, 2018). Similarly, others through online podcasts have argued that metal detectorists

are becoming really great historians and a lot of them know a lot more about civil war history than the rangers and archaeologists do, because they have a passion for what they are doing and to these other people it is just a job.

(All Metal Mode, 2020)

These are just some of the narratives that run through this activity. Some of them resemble techniques of neutralisation as described by Sykes and Matza (1957), such as the condemnation of the condemners (e.g., metal detectorists versus archaeologists narrative), the denial of the victim (e.g., 'we aren't hurting anyone') and appeal to higher loyalties (e.g., 'outlaw relic hunter' protecting relics from the government). However, similarly to what Mackenzie and Yates (2015) note regarding the appeal to higher loyalties among high-end collectors of orchids and antiquities, these counternarratives and techniques of neutralisation appear to be used not to neutralise the guilt but instead to disagree with the illegality or potential harms of the activity. The contestation of the labels 'illegal' or 'illicit' is mostly done through two main narratives—metal detecting as a rescue and metal detecting versus archaeology. These two narratives appear prominently when looking at the portrayal of this activity in online space, especially when it comes to defending this activity from unfavourable legislations.

Influence laws and regulations

Metal detectorists are well equipped to contest the criminalisation of their actions and any legislation that might interfere with the status quo. This was expressed during the STOP (Stop Taking Our Past) campaign in the United Kingdom in the 1970s (see Bland, 2005), and metal detectorists' response to it, and recently in the United States with the opposing of the House Bill 6041 in Florida (The Florida Senate, 2018). In the 1970s, as a response to the STOP campaign, metal detectorists created DIG (Detector Information Group). The group was created by 'concerned individuals' whose main goal was to 'inform the Media and both Local and Central Government of the true facts about the hobby' (Hammond, 1998). DIG's chairman A. Hammond (1998) describes DIG's beginnings:

Dig burst upon the scene with a rally in Parliament square, and members of the executive presented a petition to 10 Downing Street. DIG's efforts were greatly welcomed . . . [and] many myths fabricated by the Council for British Archaeology were finally dispelled.

While in the 1970s DIG had to rely on national media and press to achieve their goals (DIG, 2003), nowadays with the advancement of digital media, the opportunities to oppose unfavourable legislations or to find out about proposed amendments to current legislations are far more diverse. As a metal detectorist expressed in 2009

we here and through out the web as metal detectorist [sic] need to really start standing up and getting our words in. It's a one sided conversation at this point driven by archaeologist [sic], their lobby and the crooked politicians that pass these laws.

(jocap, 2009)

It seems that metal detectorists did start to stand up. For instance, in April 2014 a thread titled 'Metal detecting illegal on Massachusetts state beaches July 1, 2014!!!!!!!' was created on Treasurenet.com. It was 'a call to arms' to sign a petition created by Roger Barbrick (see petition by Barbrick, 2014) to stop the banning of metal detecting on Massachusetts beaches through amendments to current regulations (Msbeepbeep, 2014). The topic was also discussed on NH Metal Detecting Forum. On a thread created on this forum, a text from email sent by Roger Barbrick was shared where he thanked all who signed the petition and said that the state official who he had a meeting with had said 'that they [Department of Conservation and Recreation (DRC)] have receive [sic] lots of phone calls and emails on this, it got their attention and they are very concerned' (NHBob, 2014). Later the whole email thread was shared, revealing that Roger Barbrick's efforts were successful, and it was confirmed by the DRC that metal detectorists would be allowed to continue metal detecting on all DCR coastal and inland beaches in Massachusetts without having to seek permission first. Roger Barbrick in the email thanked metal detectorists for their help saying 'it wouldn't have happened without your phone calls, emails and signing the petition!' (newfields, 2014)

Similarly, metal detectorists were quick to mobilise in 2018 to oppose Florida's House Bill 6041: Division of Historical Resources (The Florida Senate, 2018). Interestingly, the bill only dealt with artefact hunting, such as collecting arrowheads, rather than metal detecting itself. However, the host of the podcast Hardcore Metal Detecting Radio (2018), argued that it is only 'a half a step to us [metal detectorists] . . . we are all hobbyists' and urged listeners to look at a Facebook post where he provided a list of contact details of legislators, and to get in touch with them either by phone, email, or both to express their opposition to this bill. The host argued that 'them [archaeologists] are trying to take rights away' (Hardcore Metal Detecting Radio, 2018), essentially emphasising that metal detecting is a fundamental right which should not be opposed. The bill never passed; it is impossible to tell whether it was due to metal detectorists' efforts, but it is possible to assume that as with the Massachusetts situation described earlier, their efforts must have drawn at least some attention from the state officials.

These efforts by metal detectorists link to the concept of contested illegality, where actors can 'display a sense of entitlement' (Hübschle, 2016, p. 367) and believe that the use of the resource is their "right". In addition, to use the idea of exclusion of knowledge, it is easier to push for a change from within, which is further facilitated by the power of the digital world. In other words, metal detectorists come from similar backgrounds as many archaeologists and government officials, and by having access to an ever-increasing online audience, they are better equipped to enter into dialogue with policy makers and push for a change, as exemplified by the opposition of the House Bill 6041 and by the opposition to amendments to existing regulations in Massachusetts. Unlike physical rallies organised by DIG in the 1970s, regulations can now be challenged from the comforts of one's home, as long as there is a working Internet connection. Information about new developments can travel faster and mobilisation can happen almost immediately on these online platforms.

Discussion

This chapter provided an overarching view of metal detecting, but it was a necessary approach as online space transcends the boundaries of time and physical space. While metal detectorists and the contexts in which they operate may vary from one country to another, the narratives that they employ extend the boundaries of their specific geographical locations and are shared across different social media platforms.

This chapter explored how narratives pertaining to metal detecting activities are created, controlled, and used. Metal detectorists operate within a larger antiquities-oriented space wrought with moral ambiguity. This moral ambiguity is also sustained on metal detecting and treasure hunting platforms through several legitimation strategies. As discussed earlier, these might involve weighting or stacking different norms against each other such as following the law versus accruing as much knowledge as possible or breaking the law while still being in harmony with one's own conscience. Furthermore, some legal ambiguity is even encouraged on these online platforms to avoid the denial of access to metal detect. For example, this could be done by not specifically asking for permission to metal detect on government's property because if there are no signs explicitly forbidding it, then it is either allowed or it is a legal grey area (maxxkatt, 2022). All these discussions on online platforms create an image of an activity that skirts the line between legal and illegal; it is a grey activity that moves between these two poles.

Metal detectorists' "label" is not set; it is constantly being re-negotiated depending on the context and on the power that metal detectorists have to legitimise their actions. This idea has been expressed in similar studies dealing with activities, which like metal detecting can be both licit and illicit. For instance, Ferrell et al. (2001, p. 179) based on their research on BASE jumping concluded that 'the pervasiveness of mediated practices and image production in . . . illicit worlds suggests an emerging reconceptualization of deviant and criminal subcultures'. Through the use of "the digital", metal detectorists create a counternarrative to the negative portrayals. Their label is not set as might be the case for some other non-digital groups committing crimes against heritage. This is not to say that all metal detectorists are committing heritage crimes but instead to note how labels attached to those that are committing crimes are different than those from other non-digital communities. For example, those who illegally excavate archaeological objects due to poverty or lack of economic alternatives (see Hardy, 2012 on subsistence digging) are labelled either looters or diggers. Looter is a label which 'is meant to instil shame and shows strong moral opposition' to this activity (Hollowell, 2006, p. 71). However, illegal metal detectorists in the United Kingdom are more often than not called nighthawks, rather than looters. This was also noted by one of the commenters, who criticised the term 'nighthawk' used in the online article by the *Guardian*. Instead, they called illegal metal detectorists thieves and looters and asked to 'stop calling them "Nighthawks"; they're criminals, not Robin Hood' (scouseexile, 2017).

If someone is looking at metal detecting online and is interested in this activity, they will inevitably come across the specific narratives and counternarratives employed by metal detectorists. These narratives are used to fragment the opposition to this activity by portraying metal detectorists' activities as beneficial, as a harmless pastime, and as being more productive in terms of objects "discovered" than archaeologists. This is something that non-digital communities engaging in parallel behaviour are unable to do. They are unable to contest the illegality of their activities to a point where it enters grey area or to challenge unfavourable legislation with online means.

However, the contestation of illegality using "the digital" is only part of the equation. While metal detectorists might represent "the other" if looked at from the perspective of some archaeologists, many metal detectorists come from similar cultural backgrounds as professional archaeologists. Metal detectorists as a community do not quite fit the label of the deviant other. Perhaps this is one of the reasons why those who do break the law are not labelled looters. Instead, categories such as 'nighthawk' are used as a 'scapegoat' (Rasmussen, 2014 p. 102). This perhaps allows the shifting of the blame and allows unproblematic engagement with the rest of the community. Class disagreements in archaeology have already been noted by McGuire and Walker (1999, p. 160), where they argue that 'the dominance of middle-class interests and ideologies . . . encourages archaeologists to see the middle-class perspective as universal and to disdain other class interests and perceptions of the past'. While academic archaeological community is divided when it comes to metal detecting, there are people who are collaborating with metal detectorists, even with those who might have broken the law to acquire archaeological objects (Lecroere, 2016; Rasmussen, 2014). Sibley (1995, p. 129) argues that

> [i]n order to secure a place in the knowledge business, it may be necessary for dissenting groups to lunch their own journals and form their own study groups . . . If they do not become a part of mainstream discourses, they may remain invisible or, at least, be considered irrelevant and unimportant.

While Sibley was referring mostly to academic knowledge, these ideas also apply to metal detecting. Metal detectorists are able to 'secure a place in the knowledge business' through their own journals and online platforms. The gatekeeping by archaeologists is not as high of a threat as it might have been in the past since nowadays, with the help of digital means, metal detectorists are not invisible. Instead, their ideas, finds, and knowledge are shared online with other members of the community as well as with heritage sector specialists. Metal detectorists and their experiences are not as excluded as those of others; for example, those who might be participating in subsistence digging.

By looking at metal detectorists as an online community through the ideas of contested illegality and exclusion of knowledge, it was possible to see how metal detectorists create, shape, disseminate, and use the narrative related to their activities. By looking at the online spaces where this community interacts, it was possible to see a subculture as conceptualised by Williams and Copes (2005). They participate in activity that often can be individualistic, but through this online space they are part of a larger community that shares 'the meaning of specific ideas, material objects, and practices through interaction' (Williams & Copes, 2005, p. 70). As a subculture, they share some core values that they feel strongly about and use to defend this activity from those who might want to limit or outlaw it, as was exemplified by opposition to proposed regulations in Florida and Massachusetts. While the laws regulating metal detecting vary from one setting to another, the digital space is employed to blur the line between legal and illegal. Digital space provides a safe place for sharing tips and strategies to either bend the law, avoid getting caught, or explain what to do if caught. It provides ready-made neutralisation or enabling techniques which reverberate through different platforms, reaching different segments of the community that can be used to alleviate guilt or as a justification of why the law is not just and therefore should not be used as a guiding framework. Through the online platforms these views can be shared not only on metal detecting and treasure hunting oriented platforms but also in comments sections of prominent mainstream newspapers. These ideas trickle through to a wider online space, where they can then be picked up by non-metal detectorists, who can use these ideas to defend this activity or perhaps dismiss them and argue against it. Regardless, this contributes to the fragmentation of the views pertaining to this activity, making it harder to create a uniformed policy on how to approach or perhaps police this activity.

Conclusion

Online communities participating in grey activities create a challenge for legislators. Through the use of various social media platforms, they can further blur the line between legal and illegal, and between acceptable and unacceptable activities. Online communities are able to write their own narrative and sustain beliefs that reaffirm their convictions. Social, moral, or cultural norms appear to be held in higher regard than legal norms. Adherence to a specific mindset, in this case study characterised by narratives such as metal detecting being a heritage rescue, a harmless behaviour, and financial motivations not being the primary aim of this activity, allows metal detectorists to portray themselves as hobbyists, motivated by love for history. Even in the cases where the law is bent to suit their needs or broken, there is still room for those individuals to be morally accepted and not viewed as criminals, as some of the quotes from podcasts and forums highlighted. Engagement with the people who allegedly have broken the law also continues from outside the metal detecting community, for instance, by professional archaeologists. All of this complicates the development, interpretation, and application of the law.

Acknowledgements

The funding for this research was provided by the European Research Council (ERC) under the European Union's Horizon 2020 research and innovation programme (grant agreement n° 804851).

Note

1 It is a podcast dedicated to 'people who eat, sleep and breath metal detecting'. Episodes are available online at: www.radioline.co/podcast-spreaker-hardcore-metal-detecting-radio

References

Aas, K. F. (2012). The Earth is one but the world is not: Criminological theory and its geopolitical divisions. *Debating Theoretical Criminology*, 16(1), 5–20.

Ace. (2021, December 1). Is metal detecting worth it? *Metal Detecting Life*. Retrieved from www.metaldetectinglife.com/blog-posts/is-metal-detecting-worth-it

AceGVSU11. (2011, October 25). *WWII POW camp (Round 2)* [Forum post]. Retrieved from http://metaldetectingforum.com/showthread.php?t=90739&highlight=POW+Camp

All Metal Mode. (2020, March 11). *In archeology Vs metal detecting*. T. Vortex. Retrieved from www.iheart.com/podcast/966-all-metal-modes-sho-28893850/episode/archeology-vs-metal-detecting-59037234/

Allcott, H., & Gentzkow, M. (2016). Social media and fake news in the 2016 election. *Journal of Economic Perspectives*, 31(2), 211–236.

Andrew. (2012, December 2). *Re: Metal detecting: A landowners' guide to "finds agreements"—Part 2* [Comment]. The Heritage Journal. Retrieved from https://heritageaction.wordpress.com/2012/10/14/metal-detecting-a-landowners-guide-to-finds-agreements-part-2/

Barbrick, R. (2014). *Commissioner Jack Murray: Stop the banning of metal detecting on Massachusetts beaches*. Move On. Retrieved August, 22, 2022, from https://sign.moveon.org/petitions/commissioner-jack-murray?r_by=10393894&source=s.icn.fb

Bērziņa, D. (2021). More than just money: Human-object relationships in low-end collecting. In N. Oosterman & D. Yates (Eds.), *Crime and art* (pp. 225–239). Springer.

Bland, R. (2005). Rescuing our neglected heritage: The evolution of the government's policy on portable antiquities in England and Wales. *Cultural Trends, 14*(4), 257–296.

Chan, J. (2000). Globalisation, reflexivity and the practice of criminology. *Australian & New Zealand Journal of Criminology, 33*(2), 118–135.

Crisp, D. (2014, August 29). The joy of metal detecting—It's not just about the treasure. *The Guardian*. Retrieved August, 4, 2022, from www.theguardian.com/commentisfree/2014/aug/29/joy-metal-detecting-treasure-antiquities-folkestone-beach

Desjardins, J. (2022). The evolution of media: Visualizing a data-driven future. *Visual Capitalist*. Retrieved from www.visualcapitalist.com/evolution-of-media-data-future/

DIG. (2003). *The detector information group*. Retrieved from http://wood.newbury.net/dig.html

Ferguson, N. (2013). Biting the bullet: The role of hobbyist metal detecting within battlefield archaeology. *Internet Archaeology, 33*. https://doi.org/10.11141/ia.33.3

Ferrell, J., Milovanovic, D., & Lyng, S. (2001). Edgework, media practices, and the elongation of meaning: A theoretical ethnography of the Bridge Day event. *Theoretical Criminology, 5*(2), 177–202.

The Florida Senate. (2018). *HB 6041: Division of historical resources*. Retrieved from www.flsenate.gov/Session/Bill/2018/6041/ByVersion

Fujiwara, T., Müller, K., & Schwarz, C. (2021). *The effect of social media on elections: Evidence from the United State*. Retrieved from www.nber.org/system/files/working_papers/w28849/w28849.pdf

Hammond, A. (1998). *The detector information group*. Retrieved July 13, 2022, from http://wood.newbury.net/dig2.html

Hardcore Metal Detecting Radio. (2018, February 4). *Protecting our hobby*. Retrieved from www.radioline.co/podcasts/spreaker_hardcore_metal_detecting_radio

Hardy, S. A. (2012, April 3). Looting, the subsistence digging economy in Mali; and stemming the flow of looted antiquities from Mali to the USA. *Conflict Antiquities*. Retrieved from https://conflictantiquities.wordpress.com/2012/04/03/mali-looting-export-usa-import/

Herva, V. P., Koskinen-Koivisto, E., Seitsonen, O., & Thomas, S. (2016). 'I have better stuff at home': Treasure hunting and private collecting of World War II artefacts in Finnish Lapland. *World Archaeology, 48*(2), 267–281.

Hier, S. (2019). Moral panics and digital-media logic: Notes on a changing research agenda. *Crime Media Culture, 15*(2), 379–388.

Hollowell, J. (2006). Moral arguments on subsistence digging. In C. Scarre & G. Scarre (Eds.), *The ethics of archaeology: Philosophical perspectives on the practice of archaeology* (pp. 69–94). Cambridge University Press.

Holt, T. J., & Copes, H. (2010). Transferring subcultural knowledge on-line: Practices and beliefs of persistent digital pirates. *Deviant Behavior, 31*(7), 625–654.

Hübschle, A. (2016). *A game of horns: Transnational flows of rhino horn* [International Max Planck Research School on the Social and Political Constitution of the Economy]. Cologne.

Hübschle, A. (2017). Contested illegality: Processing the trade prohibition of rhino horn. In J. Beckert & M. Dewey (Eds.), *The architecture of illegal markets*. Oxford University Press.

Immonen, V., & Kinnunen, J. (2020). Metal detecting as a social formation: A longitudinal survey study from Finland. *Journal of Social Archaeology, 20*(3), 313–334.

jocap. (2009, February 21). Harmless hobby or blatant vandalism? [Forum post]. *Treasurenet.com*. Retrieved from www.treasurenet.com/threads/harmless-hobby-or-blatant-vandalism.117233/

Kale, S. (2020). Stealing Britain's history: When metal detectorists go rogue. *The Guardian*. Retrieved August, 11, 2022, from www.theguardian.com/culture/2020/jun/02/theres-a-romanticism-about-nighthawking-but-its-theft-when-metal-detectorists-go-rogue#comments

Karl, R. (2016). More tales from heritage hell: Law, policy and practice of archaeological heritage protection in Austria. *The Historic Environment: Policy & Practice, 7*(4), 283–300.

Kennedy, R. (2020). *Beginners guide to metal detecting*. Retrieved August, 23, 2022, from https://treasuresinamerica.com/metal-detectors/beginners-guide-to-metal-detecting/

Kingman, M. (2022, July 1). Re: Research! Research! Research! [Reply to forum post]. *Friendly Metal Detecting Forum*. Retrieved from https://metaldetectingforum.com/showthread.php?t=297670

Labelle, J. M. (2003). Coffee cans and folsom points: Why we cannot continue to ignore the artifact collectors. In L. J. Zimmerman, K. D. Vitelli, & J. Hollowell—Zimmer (Eds.), *Ethical issues in archaeology* (pp. 115–127). AltaMira.

Lecroere, T. (2016). "There is none so blind as those who won't see": Metal detecting and archaeology in France. *Open Archaeology*, 2(1), 182–193.

Lewis, M. (2016). A detectorist's Utopia? Archaeology and metal-detecting in England and Wales. *Open Archaeology*, 2, 127–139.

Mackenzie, S., & Green, P. (2009). Criminalising the market in Illicit antiquities: An evaluation of the dealing in cultural objects (Offences) Act 2003 in England and Wales. In S. Mackenzie & P. Green (Eds.), *Criminology and archaeology: Studies in looted antiquities* (pp. 145–170). Hart.

Mackenzie, S., & Yates, D. (2015). Collectors on illicit collecting: Higher loyalties and other techniques of neutralization in the unlawful collecting of rare and precious orchids and antiquities. *Theoretical Criminology*, 20(3), 340–357.

Mackenzie, S., & Yates, D. (2016). What is grey about the "grey market" in antiquities. In J. Beckert & M. Dewey (Eds.), *The architecture of illegal markets: Towards an economic sociology of illegality in the economy* (pp. 70–86). Oxford University Press.

Maffie, M. D. (2020). The role of digital communities in organizing gig workers. *Industrial Relations*, 59(1), 123–149.

МД Арена. (2016). Если на ваш коп приехала полиция. Что делать? *МД Арена*. Retrieved from https://md-arena.com/esli-na-vash-kop-priexala-policiya-chto-delat/

maxxkatt. (2022, June 16). Tips for beginners [Forum post]. *Friendly Metal Detecting Forum*. Retrieved from https://metaldetectingforum.com/showthread.php?p=3401607&nojs=1

McGuire, R. H., & Walker, M. (1999). Class confrontations in archaeology. *Historical Archaeology*, 33(1), 159–183.

McRobbie, A., & Thornton, S. L. (1995). Rethinking 'moral panic' for multi-mediated social worlds. *The British Journal of Sociology*, 46(4), 559–574.

Moore, M. (2021a). Metal detecting for beginners: 101 Things I wish I'd known when I started. *DetectHistory*. Retrieved from https://detecthistory.com/metal-detecting/metal-detecting-for-beginners-101-things-i-wish-i-d-known-when-i-started/

Moore, M. (2021b). Metal detecting laws in different countries. *Detect History*. Retrieved from https://detecthistory.com/metal-detecting-laws-in-different-countries/

Moorhouse, J. (2021). *Searching for something: Dualisms in metal detecting*. University of Amsterdam. Retrieved from https://scripties.uba.uva.nl/search?id=c4339573

Msbeepbeep. (2014, April 22). Metal detecting illegal on Massachusetts state beaches July 1, 2014!!!!!!! [Forum post]. *Treasurenet.com*. Retrieved from www.treasurenet.com/threads/metal-detecting-illegal-on-massachusetts-state-beaches-july-1-2014.411849/

Müller, K., & Schwarz, C. (2019). Fanning the flames of hate: Social media and hate crime. *Journal of the European Economic Association*, 19(4), 2131–2167.

newfields. (2014, June 18). Re: Massachusetts planning on banning metal detecting on state beaches, July 1st? [Reply to forum post]. *NH Metal Detecting Forum*. Retrieved from http://nhmetaldetectingforum.com/index.php?topic=12978.45

NHBob. (2014, May 7). Re: Massachusetts planning on banning metal detecting on state beaches, July 1st? *NH Metal Detecting Forum*. Retrieved from http://nhmetaldetectingforum.com/index.php?topic=12978.45

Portable Antiquities Advisory Group. (2017). *Code of practice for responsible metal detecting in England & Wales*. Retrieved from https://finds.org.uk/documents/file/Code-2017.pdf

Rasmussen, J. M. (2014). Securing cultural heritage objects and fencing stolen goods? A case study on museums and metal detecting in Norway. *Norwegian Archaeological Review*, 47(1), 83–107.

scouseexile. (2017, December 18). Re: The tense truce between detectorists and archaeologists [Commentary under an article]. *The Guardian*. Retrieved August, 24, 2022, from www.theguardian.com/science/2017/dec/18/the-tense-truce-between-detectorists-and-archaeologists

Sergei UpstateNY. (2020). Metal detecting in Russia. *Metal Detecting World*. Retrieved from www.metaldetectingworld.com/detecting_in_russia.shtml

Sibley, D. (1995). *Geographies of exclusion*. Routledge.

Smith, L. (2012). Discourses of heritage: Implications for archaeological community practice. *Nuevo mundo mundos nuevos* [Online]. Retrieved August, 4, 2022, from https://journals.openedition.org/nuevomundo/64148

Sykes, G. M., & Matza, D. (1957). Techniques of neutralization: A theory of delinquency. *American Sociological Review*, 22(6), 664–670.

The Detectorist. (2022). *Metal detecting UK—The complete guide*. Retrieved August, 4, 2022, from www.thedetectorist.co.uk/metal-detecting/

Vapour. (2020). Где заканчивается наука и начинается кладоискательство? *Записки раздолбая*. Retrieved from https://zen.yandex.ru/media/razdolbye/gde-zakanchivaetsia-nauka-i-nachinaetsia-kladoiskatelstvo-5e25507d04af1f00b15e4fa2

vulcan800Geoff Bourne. (2012, August 31). Re: Nighthawk caught. Great job, but . . . [Comment]. *The Heritage Journal*. Retrieved August, 10, 2022, from https://heritageaction.wordpress.com/2012/08/29/nighthawk-caught-great-job-but/

Williams, J. P., & Copes, H. (2005). "How edge are you?" Constructing authentic identities and subcultural boundaries in a straightedge internet forum. *Symbolic Interaction*, 28(1), 67–89.

Zubacheva, K. (2017). How to find hidden treasures in Russia and not get thrown into prison. *Russia Beyond*. Retrieved April, 5, 2022, from https://web.archive.org/web/20220405090046/www.rbth.com/arts/2017/05/17/how-to-find-hidden-treasures-in-russia-and-not-get-thrown-into-prison_764761

Ляпунова, О. (2016). В поисках вятских сокровищ: как найти клад и не попасть за решётку? *Kirov Portal*. Retrieved from https://kirov-portal.ru/blog/v-poiskakh-vyatskikh-sokrovishch-kak-nayti-klad-i-ne-popast-za-reshyetku-3237/?auth_service_id=Twitter&check_key=85023617d9bf326e3c2b1ea39e31b309&ELEMENT_ID=3237

32

COLLECTIVE CRIMINAL EFFICACY IN ONLINE ILLICIT COMMUNITIES

Taylor Fisher

Collective criminal efficacy in online illicit communities

Across the fields of sociology, public health, social work, and criminology, collective efficacy has guided the assessment of group dynamics in neighborhoods, schools, teacher groups, and social organizations (Stajkovic et al., 2009). Specific to its relationship to crime, collective efficacy is traditionally used to explain how groups or organizations (e.g., neighborhoods) can avoid higher crime rates. Collective efficacy has been shown to influence the community members' perception of the future within these neighborhoods and how they plan to seek out resources through collective action (Bandura, 2000). Collective efficacy, an expansion of Bandura's self-efficacy, consists of social cohesion which can then be used to employ informal social control, thus reducing crime in the area (Sampson et al., 1997). Sampson and colleagues studied collective efficacy as it relates to traditional communities, both in England and Chicago; however, more recently, online communities have developed that mirror some of the characteristics of traditional neighborhoods discussed in the context of collective efficacy. Since these online communities operate like traditional neighborhoods and organizations, the concepts of social cohesion, collective action, and ultimately collective efficacy can be, and likely are, present within the community. Furthermore, online illicit communities, which share a need for risk avoidance and general security practices, present collective efficacy as it relates to the successful avoidance of law enforcement and other adversaries.

Within traditional communities, social cohesion is developed through various avenues, including the environment, the institutions present in the community, relationships or bonds, conflict management, and individual perceptions of norms and values (Fonseca et al., 2018). Online communities operate similarly, with social relationships forming a network and cohesion just as traditional networks do, with cohesion being a strong indicator of a group's "community-ness" (Friggeri et al., 2011). These online communities can be organized around any similarity, including physical closeness (i.e., online neighborhood watch forums), interests in popular culture (i.e., fandom groups), or even criminality (i.e., online markets for drugs, guns, or child pornography). Within the latter interest group, risk avoidant behaviors become vital to the creation and continued operation of the

DOI: 10.4324/9781003277675-37

communities. Furthermore, personal experiences with risk avoidant behaviors (e.g., using aliases and cryptocurrency) become normalized to protect the interest of the group. This behavioral pattern of group-level risk avoidance is related to collective efficacy and the expectations of privacy and security that individuals within illicit online communities have come to expect. This application of collective efficacy has not yet been addressed empirically or theoretically.

Collective efficacy traditionally describes a group's ability to avoid crime, yet the underlying concepts of social cohesion and expectations of action on behalf of the community exist in groups of individuals whose collective aim is to commit crime. While criminal efficacy has been developed and explored at the individual level (Brezina & Topalli, 2012; Bandura, 2000), collective criminal efficacy research is incredibly rare. With the addition of online communities, the application of collective efficacy must be adapted to fit the new norms of online communication and group formation. It then becomes a theoretical question whether the concept of collective efficacy can apply to online illicit communities. By focusing on online forums and marketplaces where criminal behavior and interests are most likely to be shared, discussed, and acted upon, the concept of collective efficacy will be discussed as it relates to group-level risk avoidance behaviors within these communities. This chapter will first include a discussion of collective efficacy, its major components, and the lack of a consensus on measurement of the concept and how this has allowed for its broad application. Second, a comparison of online and offline social groups and a discussion about how online communities have similar features to traditional neighborhoods and other social organizations. Third, the differences between Clearnet and darknet communities will be explored as the inherent privacy concerns (or lack thereof) may influence collective efficacy as it relates to the online communities. Fourth, by using risk avoidance and self-efficacy as the basis for individual behavior, an argument will be made as to the applicability of collective efficacy to online illicit communities. Specifically, it is argued that while research on online collective efficacy has improved in recent years, the need for an exploration of the concept within online illicit communities is not only possible but necessary. Lastly, a list of empirical questions necessary to support this argument is presented and future policy implications are discussed.

Collective efficacy

Building on the foundations of self-efficacy developed by Bandura in 1977, Robert Sampson sought to better understand why residential mobility had such an impact on neighborhood violent crime rates. Sampson recognized that social disorganization was the inability of the community to recognize their common goals and that a lack of social capital could be the reason these bonds were not forming. Social capital refers to the network of relationships among people with common goals that allows for collective action to achieve those goals (Siisiainen, 2003). Once a group of individuals recognizes their common goals and develop relationships, they rely on each other and trust that they will act on behalf of the group if need be. Sampson evaluated two main concepts related to collective efficacy: the effect of unsupervised groups of children in the community and the willingness of neighbors to intervene and to assess street crime, finding that both unsupervised peer groups and the lack of willingness to intervene influenced crime (Sampson et al., 1997; Sampson, 1999). Ultimately, Sampson and colleagues (1997) concluded that cohesion amongst members of the community will lead to a mutual trust that is linked to their shared expectations for intervention on behalf of the neighborhood, ultimately resulting in greater social control. This became Sampson's definition of collective efficacy.

Collective efficacy relies on social cohesion among members of the community to enact social control. Many different types of communities can experience social cohesion, most notably physical neighborhoods (where the bond is the shared space, living near each other) and organizations (groups that form bonds over shared interests or needs) (Pratt & Cullen, 2005). As with self-efficacy, the creation of collective efficacy is reliant on the motivation behind an individual's own behavior; however, instead of their own capacity for action, the perception of interest is of community members' ability and willingness to act on behalf of the group (Carroll et al., 2005).

Community type and collective efficacy

Collective efficacy was originally developed to describe physical neighborhoods' ability to address crime and delinquency through social organization and a shared commitment to the neighborhood group. The factors typically associated with low collective efficacy include having low socioeconomic status throughout the community, racial-ethnic diversity, residential instability, and high levels of single parenthood (Leventhal & Brooks-Gunn, 2000). These factors of structural disadvantage lead to a lack of social organization, which in turn results in an inability to manage social problems that arise, like crime and delinquency. Applying these factors to assess collective efficacy in groups has included assessments of neighborhoods (Sampson et al., 1997), schools (Hoy et al., 2002), sports teams (Allen et al., 2009), and social organizations (Goddard & Salloum, 2011). Findings generally show that collective efficacy forms through cohesion among the group and the similarity of goals and aspirations. Many applications of collective efficacy have been explored; however, there is less consensus on how to measure the concept.

Measuring collective efficacy

Two competing models of collective efficacy have been embodied over the years, including Sampson's sociological model, which considers it a "fairly stable" attribute of the neighborhood itself, and Bandura's psychological model, which views collective efficacy as an emergent feature of goal-directed groups (Glassman et al., 2021). This division (described in more detail in Pajares, 1997), as well as the non-consensus on how to measure collective efficacy (i.e., via aggregated individual perceptions, group level discussions, etc.) has led to a variety of measures for collective efficacy to be developed and tested across multiple fields. In the community health field, a review of collective efficacy and its effect on health disparities included measures of collective efficacy that were generally within five domains: social cohesion, social trust, social control, willingness to intervene, and empowerment (Butel & Braun, 2019), indicating that there is more to the concept within the field of public health than the traditional cohesion and action components commonly used in criminology and other fields. In the education field, collective efficacy is applied to both teachers and students regularly to assess the effectiveness of classroom strategies using measurements that reflect classroom goal achievement. Reviewing education-related collective efficacy Goddard and colleagues (2004) found that in relation to group goal attainment (i.e., student achievement) collective efficacy had a greater impact on outcomes than student race or socioeconomic status. Additionally, they found that for teachers, beliefs about the collective capability of their faculty were strongly linked to student achievement as well (Goddard et al., 2004), indicating that regardless of the position within the group (i.e., student or teacher), if the goal is the same (i.e., student achievement), collective efficacy is likely to have an impact on the outcome. In social work, collective efficacy is applied to neighborhoods to improve community health, safety, and child development, and it is believed that through relationship building, bystander education, and restorative justice practices, neighborhood violence can be reduced (Beck et al., 2012). Within social work, measurements of neighborhood resources and capacity to engage with those resources is an important consideration within the operationalization of collective efficacy. Lastly, within psychology, the issue of type of measurement, rather than operationalization of the concept, has been greatly discussed with meta-analytic results indicating that using group discussions to assess agreement is more accurate than aggregating perceptions at the individual level (Stajkovic et al., 2009). Overall, the measurement and operationalization of collective efficacy in other fields is varied and among criminologists, there has not yet been a consensus reached as to a central scale/operationalization of collective efficacy.

In criminology, the first test of collective efficacy was by Sampson and colleagues (1997), using data from Chicago neighborhoods, and they determined collective efficacy was ultimately a combination of informal social control and social cohesion/trust. They used five Likert-type items to form a scale of informal social control. This scale included questions about how likely it was that neighbors could be counted on to intervene in various ways if "children were skipping school and hanging out on a street corner" or if "children were showing disrespect to an adult." The second scale included in their measure of collective efficacy was a five-item measure of social cohesion and trust. Respondents were asked if they agreed with statements like "people around here are willing to help their neighbors" and "people in this neighborhood do not share the same values (reverse coded)." Studies to follow this have not agreed on a universal application of the concept but rather have adapted the concept to fit the groups being assessed.

Within the field of criminology, the issues related to measuring collective efficacy are well described by Hipp & Wo (2015). Arguing that precise definitions and measurement of the concept is missing in criminology, they discuss whether general cohesion and trust within the neighborhood is conceptually included in or simply related to collective efficacy. While the general assessment of collective efficacy and crime indicates a negative relationship, questions as to its effect in high- versus low-disorder communities still exist and the impact of longitudinal tests of collective efficacy remain under-studied. While the relative instability of measurement causes a methodological concern for the field, the wide range of applications and its versatility as a concept allows for adaptation to groups in which traditional neighborhood concepts may not apply (i.e., physical closeness). The shared values of the group and the development of the social cohesion necessary for collective efficacy to exist have been documented in studies addressing crime and deviance in various neighborhoods and organizations.

Group dynamics and social cohesion in traditional neighborhoods and organizations

Social relationships are necessary in human life, as they allow for growth and development at various parts of the life course (Hartup, 1989). Communities typically consist of interactions, commonalities, and coresidency (Brower, 2011). These interactions and commonalities are determined by relationships that exist within the community and the social network that is built within it over time. Social cohesion then builds as home ownership levels rise and core, long-term residents begin to network with each other due to close proximity (Higgins & Hunt, 2016). Additionally, once these individuals develop relationships and engage with community resources (schools, parks, recreation centers, and/ or libraries), collective efficacy begins to form. The needs of the individual, particularly in terms of crime prevention, become the needs of the community. For instance, in a socially cohesive neighborhood, having your home broken into influences you as well as your neighbors, as crime can hurt home values and the housing market in the area. Further, having high levels of violent crime can inhibit the sale of homes and results in a higher level of vacancies in the area (Boggess et al., 2013). The collective goals of the community and the cohesion that develops over time allow collective efficacy to develop in neighborhoods and social groups. Online communities form in similar ways where shared goals are identified and self-efficacy morphs into collective efficacy.

Online communities

Communities that form online reflect many similarities with traditional social group formation, simply without the commonality of physical closeness (which may sometimes be present). In a cross-cultural study of social networking sites, Kim and colleagues (2011) found that social networks developed online maintained the cultural norms of the countries in which the users belonged to. Their findings indicated that American college students had a larger network with weaker bonds and Korean students had smaller, denser networks, each reflecting the norms of their particular cultures and the development of social networks offline in their respective countries (Kim et al., 2011). This commonality among social networking both offline and online extends to the formation of organizations based on shared interests. Commonalities, like topics of interest among group members and the existing relationships someone has with the network, affect both movement into and overall growth of the group (Backstrom et al., 2006). Additionally, just like traditional social groups, membership in an online social organization enables experimentation and development of one's identity and provides an outlet for individuals to be themselves with likeminded others (Code & Zaparyniuk, 2010).

While there are many commonalities between online and offline network formation, one key difference is the lack of physical proximity. Online networks of individuals who reside in physical proximity do exist (e.g., online neighborhood watch groups); however, most online communities lack the physical closeness of these groups. This difference could impact group cohesion, as general communication of the group is unlikely to occur face-to-face, limiting any physical risk present. Online forums and markets provide an opportunity for individuals seeking criminal activity (or related conversation) to interact with each other in a way that provides individuals far more privacy and security than face-to-face interactions. For this reason, it may be easier for individuals to trust each other, considering that the risk they are taking on can be mitigated to some extent by addressing risk as a group in a virtual setting.

To explore the application of collective efficacy in online communities that focus on illicit interests (i.e., forums that discuss pedophilia or markets that sell drugs), it must first be argued that online communities rely on social cohesion and develop collective efficacy in the first place. It has been shown that online relationships can and do form social capital through networking for both personal and professional needs (Rice, 2013; Spottswood & Wohn, 2020), albeit individuals may not form as high-quality bonds with others online as they might in traditional communities (Lee & Lee, 2010). By developing extensive online networks of both personal and private relationships, the individual is providing a sort of social safety net that they can rely on should they need to. The online nature of the network allows individuals to carefully curate their connections to maximize the potential reward and minimize potential risk. This practice would logically extend to online networks that deal in illicit practices, as they too would have an individualized need for security and protection from possible adversaries within the illicit community.

Online illicit communities—forums and marketplaces

Two of the most common places to find evidence of internet-related crimes are forums (Costello, et al., 2017) and marketplaces (Ball & Broadhurst, 2021). While neither community type is inherently illicit, the content and items for sale are what create their illicit nature. Furthermore, when the community is illicit, the need for risk avoidance/management is much higher. Both community types share a need for risk management, which includes staying out of the public view (Holt et al., 2015). For this reason, many forums and marketplaces are housed on the darknet to avoid identification.

Darknet forums and markets

To minimize risk, organizers of forums and marketplaces may choose to house their website on the darknet, or the unindexed portion of the internet, to avoid detection. Darknet markets operate like traditional online marketplaces (e.g., Amazon or eBay) providing an online space for vendors to connect with buyers; however, they are notorious for the sale of illicit products like drugs (Christin & Thomas, 2019; Rhumorbarbe et al., 2016), firearms (Lee et al., 2022; Holt & Lee, 2022), stolen data (Howell et al., 2023; Ouellet et al., 2022), and malware or illicit software (Meland et al., 2020). Darknet forums are equally notorious in that they are known for both the trade of illicit products and confidential information (Nazah et al., 2021). The TOR (The Onion Router) browser is one way to gain access to darknet sites. Onion routing (the basis of the TOR project) was originally designed by the US Navy as a way to protect communications within the military; however, it was made independent as a browser that bounces traffic across multiple relays in order to provide multiple levels of encryption (Jadoon et al., 2019), thus providing the user with multi-level protection. This level of privacy, mixed with the use of cryptocurrency, creates a near-perfect (virtual) location for vendors and buyers to make transactions. Once these transactions begin, a social network begins to form.

Social networking in online illicit communities

Using social network analysis, two notable studies have explored network formation and structure in online illicit communities on the darknet. Ouellet and colleagues (2022) used social network analysis to map out networks of vendors to assess movement across marketplaces within the larger illicit marketplace ecosystem. Findings of this study indicate that the vendor network covers many markets and that vendors sell on multiple markets. They also found that vendors make deliberate choices about which markets to join, depending on the financial opportunities available on the market (Ouellet et al., 2022). It is possible that, if financial opportunities influence vendor decisions to join markets, security practices of the market and its administrators could also influence decisions to join new markets.

In a second study utilizing social network analysis, Pete and colleagues (2020) compared six dark web forums and assessed the forum structure finding that there were differences in network behavior dependent on the position within the network. They found that while there are nodes of some members who are highly connected, the majority of members had a lower number of connections and posted in sub-forums with more specific topics (Pete et al., 2020). This study reflects similar findings in traditional communities where strong bonds are not required to build social cohesion and collective efficacy (Wilson, 1987). Wilson argues that the strength of the ties does not have as large of an impact as how those ties interact with resource availability within the group (1987). In online illicit communities, the strength of the ties may not be as strong, but the shared experiences of risk avoidance are enough to build social cohesion and therefore collective efficacy.

Community characteristics of online illicit communities

The characteristics of online illicit markets are similar to traditional communities. Within the world of child sexual exploitation, communities develop structures that serve both associational and entrepreneurial purposes to meet social and criminal needs of the members (van der Bruggen & Blokland, 2021), just as traditionally social networking has been used to build both personal and professional networks (Rice, 2013; Spottswood & Wohn, 2020). Other studies have found that operational security (i.e., logistics of the transaction) is an important component of market structure. Forums that are associated with markets will have posts specific to logistics to ensure successful transactions for all parties (Kamphausen & Werse, 2019). Trust is an important component of online illicit markets as not only does a strong reputation led to cooperation and loyalty from customers, but also better earnings (Kamphausen & Werse, 2019). Overall, the characteristics of online illicit communities mirror many of the characteristics of traditional communities.

Collective criminal efficacy in online illicit communities

Building on concepts of self-efficacy, criminal efficacy has come to describe any self-efficacy that is related to nonconventional (i.e., criminal or deviant) pursuits (Brezina & Topalli, 2012). For this criminal self-efficacy to translate to collective criminal efficacy, there would need to exist social cohesion within the online, illicit community. Assuming the ties are adequate to form social cohesion, the collective goals and aspirations must be agreed upon and the expectation of action to achieve these goals must be present. In illicit communities, the individual goal of risk avoidance (e.g., detection by law enforcement, victimization from other members of the community) aggregates to form a collective goal of risk avoidance and thus, collective criminal efficacy.

Criminal self-efficacy

Using Bandura's concept of self-efficacy (1977) and borrowing from the body of research on offender decision making, past performance becomes a key determinant of criminal self-efficacy. Brezina and Topalli (2012) took this approach, describing indicators of criminal self-efficacy as the ability to make quick money through crime, the ability to "beat the system" and avoid detection/apprehension, and the display of skill. The belief that an offender can successfully avoid detection is not only key to individual criminal efficacy, but also an important component of online risk avoidance for members of online illicit communities.

Research on criminal self-efficacy is rare; however, a few notable studies do exist. Tremblay and Morselli (2000) studied prison inmates and found that beliefs in personal "success" in crime was positively associated with higher earnings, indicating that these individuals' perceptions of criminal self-efficacy may be rooted in objective truth to some degree. The Brezina & Topalli study mentioned earlier consisted of a multi-method approach with prison inmates as well. Their findings indicated similar patterns, acknowledging the need to assess efficacy perceptions in non-institutionalized offender samples, as the individuals in jails and prison inherently have a different perspective of "success" when it comes to avoiding law enforcement detection. Online illicit environments provide this population of non-institutionalized offenders who portray self-efficacious behaviors.

Risk avoidance and self-efficacy in online illicit environments

Any individual who engages in crime, online or offline, takes on some level of risk. In online illicit environments, the risk comes from both formal (i.e., law enforcement) and informal (i.e., adversaries or other illicit actors) sources. What makes the darknet so intriguing as a form of illicit community formation is the large amount of risk that is not present online. In interviews with darknet vendors (i.e., individuals who sell drugs on darknet markets), Martin and colleagues found that the risk was perceived as much lower and the possible rewards much higher by selling online. One vendor described selling offline as "borderline stupid" due to the necessity for physical proximity. By selling online, these vendors were able to avoid the limitations and associated risks that come with selling offline (Martin et al., 2020). Another respondent in the Martin study reported that "shady" customers in "shady" parts of town was enough risk to convince them to move their business online. Citing law enforcement and potentially risky customers (e.g., those willing to "snitch" on the seller), this respondent believed that dealing online is significantly safer for themself (Martin et al., 2020). This need for safety and security being met by online environments is also seen in darknet forums. Identifying risk perception as a major theme, Bada and Chua (2021) found that individuals posted not only about odds of getting caught but also about tactics to avoid getting caught at all.

Other forms of risk come from other illicit actors within the group who may have ulterior motives for being a member. There is no way to ensure members are not informants, undercover law enforcement, or just impulsive individuals whose interactions put the user at risk (Tremblay & Morselli, 2000; Weerman, 2003). By engaging with these individuals, the user is at a higher risk of being caught by law enforcement and of possible victimization by other members of the community. Self-efficacy in online illicit environments helps protect the users, but to protect the entire network (e.g., forum or marketplace) there is a need for collective action on behalf of the group. The networking and need for risk avoidance indicates that there is a possibility for collective efficacy to be present in illicit online communities. The mechanism through which self-efficacy and risk avoidant behavior becomes collective efficacy is yet to be established. One possible explanation could be that individuals who wish to engage in criminal behavior but are low risk-takers might seek out online communities for their lower level of risk, as reported by users in the studies discussed earlier. This selection bias could mean that online communities are inherently more risk aversive, therefore creating a "safer" environment for criminals online than offline. If users choose to engage in online illicit communities, this could reveal that risk avoidance is the key to building online collective efficacy.

Collective efficacy in online illicit markets

Forums

In online forums where illicit content is discussed, there is typically evidence of group-level efforts to avoid detection and individual-level efforts to avoid being ripped off or scammed by other users. These efforts usually meet security needs for both the individuals and the group. When the entire group engages with these practices, it creates a safer environment (i.e., where law enforcement and scammers cannot access the users). Through moderators, established forum rules, and the engagement in informal social control (i.e., individual action with the goal of group-level protection), forum users employ adapted versions of collective efficacy to avoid risk.

Moderators are typically users or administrators of a site whose responsibility it is to maintain order in the forum and enforce any rules that they may have (Radianti, 2010). It is common for mediators of forums to manage any complaints by users of a related market about vendors who are scammers, provide poor quality product, or "ghost" potential buyers by not responding to interested customers (Bancroft et al., 2020). Moderators and administrators also work to establish and enforce rules that benefit the entire forum population. Rules may include limits on what can be discussed or procedures on how transactions are to be conducted (Barratt, 2011). For example, Reddit (a clearnet forum) posts content rules on their page to establish basic guidelines for what can be posted in their forums (Reddit Content Policy, 2022). The Ares marketplace (a darknet market with an associated forum) has a general rules page which outlines what can be sold (i.e., anything but child pornography) and has requirements for vendors looking to sell on their site, including experience and positive reviews (Ares Market, 2023).[1]

Additionally, there seem to exist various avenues to establish informal social control on illicit forums. Many posts, particularly in the world of hacking and cyber threats, include information on how to avoid detection or victimization. For example, forums will include tutorials on how to complete transactions or just generally how to find what they are looking for on the darknet (Dwyer et al., 2022). Educating other users on secure practices and procedures to maintain privacy is important in building rapport and trust among users, ultimately leading to greater social cohesion. Other forms of education allow users to learn from previous mistakes. Bada and Chua (2021) identify a post on a darknet forum that informs users that they could "boot" a program (presumably an illicit form of malware) up to three times on a single network without detection. The initial user did not have to share this information; however, by helping others avoid detection, that program (and the vulnerability it was exploiting) will remain operational and successful. If one user of the malware gets taken down by law enforcement, all other users of the same malware are now under greater scrutiny and are likely to be less successful once the vulnerability is addressed.

Other ways informal social control is present on illicit forums is by the open discussion about illicit behaviors and the shared risk of engaging in potentially incriminating discussions and exchanges. Forums are a hub for file sharing (i.e., child pornography or pirated content distribution), and the collective goal is to be able to engage in these practices and not get caught. This collective goal develops because in these online illicit environments, if one individual goes down, it puts the rest of the group at higher risk. Therefore, if the group not only educates new members on individual risk avoidance but also works together to achieve the overall goal of group-level risk avoidance, collective efficacy is likely present and will protect the group from adversaries.

Illicit marketplaces

Like forums, marketplaces also have sets of rules that determine what is allowed on the site and what is not. For example, Joy Market has a rule that clearly states any mention of police or law enforcement is punishable by a permanent ban, no matter what stage their order is at (this could mean losing out on money already paid for a product) (Joy Market, 2023). Other rules relate to account creation and say that nobody can create a username with the words "support" or "moderator" to avoid any deceptive behavior by a vendor or other users posing as an administrator. Additionally, Joy Market also has a support page, something regularly seen on traditional e-commerce sites, where registered users can work with market administrators to learn how to engage with the market or to resolve any issues they may experience. These rules and support systems exist on these pages to help make the market operate more efficiently and to help avoid any behaviors that put the group at risk. Lastly, by providing support for customers, these markets and their vendors are more likely to have loyal customers than those with poor or no support available. Loyal customers and loyalty to vendors could be an indicator of collective efficacy unique to online illicit marketplaces.

In addition to rules and customer support, markets also include both security measures and escrow systems to ensure a fair transaction between customer and vendor. For example, the White House market is a popular market which utilizes a security system, which labels transactions as varying levels of secure, depending on the user behavior of those involved (White House Market, 2023). It can identify a vendor who has poor ratings or a customer who does not use two-factor authentication to protect their accounts. This allows vendors to build strong reputations, which would include a loyal customer base. New customers have an easy way to determine whether the transaction is good for them based on the behavioral patterns of previous transactions. In a way, this is similar to the process of developing self-efficacy based on past performance; however, in this case, it is the vendor and market network that is developing efficacy based on past performance. Furthermore, escrow systems are common practice for darknet markets as they can protect both parties in the transaction. Escrow systems operate by allowing money to be held until the transaction is completed, to ensure neither party is able to scam the other (Horton-Eddison & Di Cristofaro, 2017; Janze, 2017).

Market administrators take security seriously and many will go after both vendors and buyers who engage in scams on their market. This helps to ensure that the entire market is free from scams and ensures a secure environment. For example, in the ASAP market there exists a "scam hunter" process which is operated by the administrators and aims to identify and remove scams from the market. Once they receive enough evidence that a scam is occurring (i.e., a vendor is taking payment and not delivering product) the market removes the vendor's access, takes down their advertisements, and gives any money currently in escrow back to the buyers (ASAP Market, 2023). By ensuring that all parties who misuse the market are held accountable, the administrators build a network of vendors and buyers who trust each other and are loyal to both their vendors and the markets that house them.

The use of Bitcoin and other cryptocurrencies provides an extra layer of protection for both vendors and potential buyers. Cryptocurrencies are virtually anonymous, albeit traceable, digital currency that are verified using cryptography, rather than through a centralized authority (e.g., the US Treasury) (Liu & Tsyvinski, 2021). While most Bitcoin users are not using it for illicit purposes, the privacy and lack of regulation allows transactions to occur with a lower level of risk than face-to-face exchanges of traditional currency (Kethineni et al., 2018). By using cryptocurrency, both the buyer and vendor are protected. This mutually beneficial system helps to create an environment that is safe and secure for all users. As with the transition from self-efficacy to collective efficacy in traditional settings, having a system where individual risks are aggregated to become representative of the group (i.e., one user being at risk leaves the entire group at risk) shows how social cohesion can form through needs for risk avoidance.

Lastly, markets recognize that any sale of drugs that leads to a death (e.g., overdose) will bring higher scrutiny onto the source of the drugs (in this case, the market or specific vendor). For this reason, vendors sometimes warn against the risks of fentanyl-laced products. In Figure 32.4, a Cypher Market vendor specifically includes the warning signs of a fentanyl overdose and outlines what to do in the case of a suspected overdose (Cypher Market, 2023). Additionally, some markets will mark vendors as having sold products that were laced with fentanyl to inform consumers that this vendor either purposely or inadvertently allowed fentanyl into their product, thus marking them as an untrustworthy source. Not only does this behavior alleviate the risk of exposing the market to law enforcement scrutiny, but it also helps to protect the population of consumers from dying of a fentanyl overdose. The rules, policies, and procedures for market engagement are outlined explicitly so that all parties are aware of the risk they pose to themselves and the market population. By limiting this risk across engagement, the market is able to protect itself from scrutiny by adversaries.

Future empirical questions

As with any theoretical concept, the argument presented in this chapter is nothing without empirical support. The following list of empirical questions is by no means exhaustive; however, included are pertinent empirical questions that require data analysis to better understand the concept of online collective criminal efficacy.

Are the bonds between members, and by extension their social cohesion, different in purely online communities versus communities who have some face-to-face contact but use technology as a form of communication? This question is an important distinction that could help to answer whether the concept of collective efficacy is applicable to all online communities as compared to just those who have some face-to-face contact. Further, considering the concept of risk avoidance in illicit online communities, determining if (and how) face-to-face contact affects the development of these concepts is also necessary. Establishing that all communities share the mechanisms of developing social control would strengthen the argument that traditional collective efficacy is applicable to all online communities, including illicit ones.

Which perspective on self-efficacy (Bandura's psychological or Sampson's sociological perspective) is more successful in explaining collective efficacy in online communities? Online illicit communities? Considering the lack of consensus on measurement and the lack of a universally agreed-upon scale of collective efficacy, the question of its application to online communities is highly under-studied and its application to online illicit communities is nonexistent. With that said, consensus on the measurement and operationalization of the underlying concept of self-efficacy is the first step in developing a strong measure of collective efficacy.

Do previous measures of collective efficacy apply to online communities? Online illicit communities? A strong conceptual model of collective efficacy in traditional communities (those most studied within this theoretical framework) is needed before it can be adapted to online communities, whether licit or illicit. The collective efficacy scale developed by Glassman et al. (2021) to assess online learning communities utilizes concepts from both perspectives and measures both participant and community-level collective efficacy. This scale may be a good starting point to build a similar scale for online illicit communities by adapting their constructs to fit online illicit community goals. For instance, their measure of participant-level social presence includes the perceived ability of the individual to write posts and contribute to the community. However, in an illicit marketplace this may not apply, but the perceived ability to engage in transactions (either as a vendor or a buyer) could indicate the participant-level social presence. Other constructs may not need adapting but could apply as they stand. This should be tested in online communities that have different goals, both licit and illicit.

Does social cohesion develop through the same mechanisms in both illicit and licit communities? Presumably no, as the collective goals are likely to be different. In both communities, risk avoidant behaviors will exist; however, the source of that risk is what differs. In illicit communities, the source of risk comes from law enforcement and other criminals online while in traditional communities, the source of the risk is the criminals themselves. In illicit communities, the self-selection bias of communicating and engaging with other criminals would mean the source of social cohesion is different. Determining mechanisms that operate in each community type and the extent of overlap in the measurement of social cohesion would help to better understand the concept as it applies to all community types.

Do the perceptions of ability and willingness to act on behalf of the group weigh differently in traditional v. online communities, and illicit v. licit communities? While traditionally the ability to act on behalf of the group would stem from social cohesion, evidence that online relationships may not be as cohesive (Lee & Lee, 2010) indicates that the willingness of a community to act may be stronger. This could be due to the shared risk that the community experiences. While traditionally the shared goal is to eliminate crime, the shared goal in illicit communities is to avoid detection and victimization by other illicit actors, so the importance of the collective goal to the group may outweigh differences in perceptions of ability. Additionally, there may exist differences in the perception of the ability to protect each other online, particularly on the darknet where privacy is much stronger, but the technological knowledge needed to participate is higher. The need to understand how to use both the darknet and cryptocurrency requires a standard level of skill that may be assumed by other members of the community (whether accurate or not).

In online illicit communities, is risk avoidance a strong enough collective goal to result in collective action on behalf of the group? In other words, if the traditional concept of social cohesion is not strong enough to result in collective action, is the need for risk avoidance as a group strong enough to counteract weaker bonds? Research has shown in traditional communities that strength of ties is not as influential as its interaction with community resource access and utilization and that online relationships may have weaker ties than those with face-to-face contact (Lee & Lee, 2010). If this is the case with the online illicit communities, is the potential risk so severe in these environments (coming from both law enforcement and adversaries within the community) that collective efficacy forms with looser bonds than is required in traditional or conventional communities?

Does social cohesion exist in darknet environments where anonymity is the standard practice? Or does the lack of "identity" lead to less involvement and commitment to the ⁻group? If individuals in illicit online environments purposely hide their true identity, does their relation to the group differ? It could be that when individuals are not sharing their identity, they take on personas or engage in behavior that they would not normally. How this relates to their ability to build and maintain relationships with other online illicit actors should be assessed to determine whether social cohesion develops differently, if at all, in online illicit communities.

Does the inherent difference in privacy between the Clearnet and darknet affect the development of social cohesion and by extension collective efficacy? If so, how does vendor loyalty relate to and possibly influence social cohesion in darknet communities? In the darknet environment, standard anonymity provides a level of protection that is not present on the Clearnet. For this reason, the perceptions of reliability and trustworthiness may develop differently in darknet environments. Different mechanisms in the development of social cohesion could mean differences in the establishment and actionability of collective efficacy. Furthermore, vendor loyalty has been assessed in the literature (Décary-Hétu & Quessy-Doré, 2017) and could provide insight on the development of social cohesion in online illicit environments.

Does social cohesion, collective action, and collective criminal efficacy exist in other forms of illicit online environments, like Telegram and other encrypted chat applications? Research has found that many criminal transactions are now taking place in encrypted channels like Telegram (Shah et al., 2020). These environments are not always openly available and can require an invitation to access. Does this threshold for inclusion into the group change the group dynamics? If so, what changes? If group dynamics are different, social cohesion would presumably develop differently, if at all. These encrypted channels are going to continue to host criminal transactions in the future and any discussion of disrupting online illicit communities should include encrypted messaging applications.

Is there a threshold for the actionability of collective criminal efficacy in online illicit environments? In other words, at what point does the risk become too severe to the whole that the lack of prevention (or intervention) is risky to the group as an entity beyond the individuals who make it up? If collective efficacy is present in online illicit environments, at what point does it become actionable, meaning individuals will act on behalf of the group? Level of engagement (i.e., level of commitment or involvement to the group) may affect the individual's perception of their own risk, and by extension their risk as it associates with the group. This question aims to address what level of engagement is required for an individual to act and engage in collectively efficacious behaviors to avoid risk. If there is a threshold and collective efficacy only exists when a certain percentage of members are engaged and willing to act, how can knowledge of that threshold be used for disruption techniques? If it is possible to alter the threshold, what does that look like and how would that affect the illicit online environment as a whole?

Conclusions and policy implications

Collective efficacy has been studied in traditional neighborhoods since the development of the concept in 1986 by Bandura and has just recently been assessed in the context of online communities (Bandura, 1986). While little agreement has been achieved on how to measure collective efficacy, the basic concepts of social cohesion and willingness to act on behalf of the group are consistent. These concepts can be used to assess collective efficacy in online communities. With a shift in focus regarding risk avoidance, these concepts can also be applied to illicit environments when the collective goal is risk aversion. The risk to these communities is not the existence of crime (as it is in traditional communities), but rather the possibility of detection by law enforcement or victimization by adversaries. Online communities form in similar ways to traditional communities, so the social cohesion concept can logically be adapted to describe mechanisms of collective efficacy in online illicit communities. While existing measures of collective efficacy are varied not only within criminology but across disciplines, the first step should be either further validating existing scales or creating measures to adequately assess collective efficacy in licit communities.

To contextualize this concept of collective criminal efficacy in online communities, policy implications should be considered. The collective ability of a group to achieve a goal is important to consider when the group is illicit in nature and their goal is to avoid law enforcement. For these reasons, if law enforcement wishes to disrupt these environments and cut down on crime facilitated by these groups, they must understand what factors lead to collective efficacy and aim to disrupt the cohesive nature of the group. With criminal self-efficacy there are associated risks that confident illicit actors show higher commitment (Brezina & Topalli, 2012) and are known to take higher risks (Tremblay & Morselli, 2000). If a criminal group develops collective criminal efficacy, the entire community becomes stronger as a result, leading (presumably) to greater social cohesion. Disruption efforts should focus on relationships and disrupting trust among administrators, vendors, and buyers. Specific to the darknet environment, intervening and establishing distrust in new markets is more successful than attempting to disrupt larger more established markets who have had time to build strong reputations. The importance here is of the identification of new communities through automated efforts. Methodologies that involve the use of web crawlers (programs that search the environment for key pieces of information) and scrapers (programs that collect data from identified sources) allow for robust assessments of the online illicit environment. By assessing the environment as a whole, the effects of disruption techniques, based on collective criminal efficacy, can be determined.

Note

1 At the time of this publication, the Ares market was no longer active. It is common for markets to switch between active and inactive states and switch onion links (Tor browser-specific URLs) regularly. While this helps to conceal their identity and location from adversaries, it makes it incredibly difficult to cite and reference content. All the onion links used to access the market content in this piece are no longer active. In this paper, markets accessed on Tor will be cited as ("Name" Market, 2023). The markets accessed in this chapter include: Ares, Joy, White House, ASAP, and Cypher. As of early 2024, Ares, ASAP, and Cypher are active and onion links for each can be found at https://darknetlive.com/markets. The White House Market was taken down by its administrators as a form of retirement. The status of Joy Market is unknown.

References

Allen, M. S., Jones, M. V., & Sheffield, D. (2009). Attribution, emotion, and collective efficacy in sports teams. *Group Dynamics: Theory, Research, and Practice*, 13(3), 205.

Backstrom, L., Huttenlocher, D., Kleinberg, J., & Lan, X. (2006, August). Group formation in large social networks: Membership, growth, and evolution. In *Proceedings of the 12th ACM SIGKDD international conference on knowledge discovery and datamining* (pp. 44–54). Association for Computing Machinery.

Bada, M., & Chua, Y. T. (2021, December). Understanding risk and risk perceptions of cybercrime in underground forums. In *2021 APWG symposium on electronic crime research (eCrime)* (pp. 1–11). IEEE.

Ball, M., & Broadhurst, R. (2021). Data capture and analysis of darknet markets [Working Paper]. Available at SSRN 3344936.

Bancroft, A., Squirrell, T., Zaunseder, A., & Rafanell, I. (2020). Producing trust among illicit actors: A techno-social approach to an online illicit market. *Sociological Research Online*, 25(3), 456–472.

Bandura, A. (1977). Self-efficacy: Toward a unifying theory of behavioral change. *Psychological Review*, 84(2), 191.

Bandura, A. (1986). *Social foundations of thought and action*. Prentice Hall.

Bandura, A. (2000). Exercise of human agency through collective efficacy. *Current Directions in Psychological Science*, 9(3), 75–78.

Barratt, M. J. (2011, June). Discussing illicit drugs in public internet forums: Visibility, stigma, and pseudonymity. In *Proceedings of the 5th international conference on communities and technologies* (pp. 159–168). Association for Computing Machinery.

Beck, E., Ohmer, M., & Warner, B. (2012). Strategies for preventing neighborhood violence: Toward bringing collective efficacy into social work practice. *Journal of Community Practice*, 20(3), 225–240.

Boggess, L., Greenbaum, R. T., & Tita, G. E. (2013). Does crime drive housing sales? Evidence from Los Angeles. *Journal of Crime and Justice*, 36(3), 299–318.

Brezina, T., & Topalli, V. (2012). Criminal self-efficacy: Exploring the correlates and consequences of a "successful criminal" identity. *Criminal Justice and Behavior*, 39(8), 1042–1062.

Brower, S. (2011). *Neighbors & neighborhoods: Elements of successful community design*. Routledge.

Butel, J., & Braun, K. L. (2019). The role of collective efficacy in reducing health disparities: A systematic review. *Family & Community Health*, 42(1), 8.

Carroll, J. M., Rosson, M. B., & Zhou, J. (2005, April). Collective efficacy as a measure of community. In *Proceedings of the SIGCHI conference on human factors in computing systems* (pp. 1–10). Association for Computing Machinery.

Christin, N., & Thomas, J. (2019). Analysis of the supply of drugs and new psychoactive substances by Europe-based vendors via darknet markets in 2017–18. *EMCDDA*. Retrieved from https://www.emcdda.europa.eu/drugs-library/analysis-supply-drugs-and-new-psychoactive-substances-europe-based-vendors-darknet-markets-2017-18_en

Code, J. R., & Zaparyniuk, N. E. (2010). Social identities, group formation, and the analysis of online communities. In *Social computing: Concepts, methodologies, tools, and applications* (pp. 1346–1361). IGI Global.

Costello, K. L., Martin III, J. D., & Edwards Brinegar, A. (2017). Online disclosure of illicit information: Information behaviors in two drug forums. *Journal of the Association for Information Science and Technology*, 68(10), 2439–2448.

Décary-Hétu, D., & Quessy-Doré, O. (2017). Are repeat buyers in cryptomarkets loyal customers? Repeat business between dyads of cryptomarket vendors and users. *American Behavioral Scientist*, 61(11), 1341–1357.

Dwyer, A. C., Hallett, J., Peersman, C., Edwards, M., Davidson, B. I., & Rashid, A. (2022). *How darknet market users learned to worry more and love PGP: Analysis of security advice on darknet marketplaces*. Retrieved from https://arxiv.org/abs/2203.08557

Fonseca, X., Lukosch, S., & Brazier, F. (2018). Social cohesion revisited: A new definition and how to characterize it. *Innovation: The European Journal of Social Science Research*, 32(2), 231–253.

Friggeri, A., Chelius, G., & Fleury, E. (2011, October). Triangles to capture social cohesion. In *2011 IEEE third international conference on privacy, security, risk and trust and 2011 IEEE third international conference on social computing* (pp. 258–265). IEEE.

Glassman, M., Kuznetcova, I., Peri, J., & Kim, Y. (2021). Cohesion, collaboration and the struggle of creating online learning communities: Development and validation of an online collective efficacy scale. *Computers and Education Open, 2*.

Goddard, R. D., Hoy, W. K., & Hoy, A. W. (2004). Collective efficacy beliefs: Theoretical developments, empirical evidence, and future directions. *Educational Researcher, 33*(3), 3–13.

Goddard, R. D., & Salloum, S. (2011). Collective efficacy beliefs, organizational excellence, and leadership. *Positive Organizational Scholarship Handbook, 642–650*.

Hartup, W. W. (1989). Social relationships and their developmental significance. *American Psychologist, 44*(2), 120–126.

Higgins, B. R., & Hunt, J. (2016). Collective efficacy: Taking action to improve neighborhoods. *NIJ Journal, 277*, 18–21.

Hipp, J. R., & Wo, J. C. (2015). Collective efficacy and crime. *International Encyclopedia of Social and Behavioral Sciences, 4*, 169–173.

Holt, T. J., & Lee, J. R. (2022). A crime script model of Dark web Firearms Purchasing. *American Journal of Criminal Justice, 1–21*.

Holt, T. J., Smirnova, O., Chua, Y. T., & Copes, H. (2015). Examining the risk reduction strategies of actors in online criminal markets. *Global Crime, 16*(2), 81–103.

Horton-Eddison, M., & Di Cristofaro, M. (2017). Hard interventions and innovation in crypto-drug markets: The escrow example. *Policy Brief, 11*, 16–27.

Howell, C. J., Fisher, T., Muniz, C. N., Maimon, D., & Rotzinger, Y. (2023). A depiction and classification of the stolen data market ecosystem and comprising darknet markets: A multidisciplinary approach. *Journal of Contemporary Criminal Justice, 39*(2), 298–317.

Hoy, W. K., Sweetland, S. R., & Smith, P. A. (2002). Toward an organizational model of achievement in high schools: The significance of collective efficacy. *Educational Administration Quarterly, 38*(1), 77–93.

Jadoon, A. K., Iqbal, W., Amjad, M. F., Afzal, H., & Bangash, Y. A. (2019). Forensic analysis of Tor browser: A case study for privacy and anonymity on the web. *Forensic Science International, 299*, 59–73.

Janze, C. (2017). Are cryptocurrencies criminals best friends? Examining the co-evolution of bitcoin and darknet markets. In *AMCIS 2017 proceedings*. Retrieved from https://aisel.aisnet.org/amcis2017/InformationSystems/Presentations/2

Kamphausen, G., & Werse, B. (2019). Digital figurations in the online trade of illicit drugs: A qualitative content analysis of darknet forums. *International Journal of Drug Policy, 73*, 281–287.

Kethineni, S., Cao, Y., & Dodge, C. (2018). Use of bitcoin in darknet markets: Examining facilitative factors on bitcoin-related crimes. *American Journal of Criminal Justice, 43*(2), 141–157.

Kim, Y., Sohn, D., & Choi, S. M. (2011). Cultural difference in motivations for using social network sites: A comparative study of American and Korean college students. *Computers in Human Behavior, 27*(1), 365–372.

Lee, J. R., Holt, T. J., & Smirnova, O. (2022). An assessment of the state of firearm sales on the Dark Web. *Journal of Crime and Justice, 1–15*.

Lee, J. R., & Lee, H. (2010). The computer-mediated communication network: Exploring the linkage between the online community and social capital. *New Media & Society, 12*(5), 711–727.

Leventhal, T., & Brooks-Gunn, J. (2000). The neighborhoods they live in: The effects of neighborhood residence on child and adolescent outcomes. *Psychological Bulletin, 126*(2), 309.

Liu, Y., & Tsyvinski, A. (2021). Risks and returns of cryptocurrency. *The Review of Financial Studies, 34*(6), 2689–2727.

Martin, J., Munksgaard, R., Coomber, R., Demant, J., & Barratt, M. J. (2020). Selling drugs on darkweb cryptomarkets: Differentiated pathways, risks and rewards. *The British Journal of Criminology, 60*(3), 559–578.

Meland, P. H., Bayoumy, Y. F. F., & Sindre, G. (2020). The Ransomware-as-a-Service economy within the darknet. *Computers & Security, 92*, 101762.

Nazah, S., Huda, S., Abawajy, J. H., & Hassan, M. M. (2021). An unsupervised model for identifying and characterizing dark web forums. *IEEE Access, 9*, 112871–112892.

Ouellet, M., Maimon, D., Howell, C. J., & Wu, Y. (2022). The network of online stolen data markets: How vendor flows connect digital marketplaces. *The British Journal of Criminology*, 62(6), 1518–1536.

Pajares, F. (1997). Current directions in self-efficacy research. In M. Maehr & P. R. Pintrich (Eds.), *Advances in motivation and achievement* (Vol. 10, pp. 1–49). JAI.

Pete, I., Hughes, J., Chua, Y. T., & Bada, M. (2020, September). A social network analysis and comparison of six dark web forums. In *2020 IEEE European symposium on security and privacy workshops* (pp. 484–493). IEEE.

Pratt, T. C., & Cullen, F. T. (2005). Assessing macro-level predictors and theories of crime: A meta-analysis. *Crime and Justice*, 32, 373–450.

Radianti, J. (2010, July). A study of a social behavior inside the online black markets. In *2010 Fourth international conference on emerging security information, systems and technologies* (pp. 189–194). IEEE.

Reddit Content Policy. (2022). Retrieved from www.redditinc.com/policies/content-policy

Rhumorbarbe, D., Staehli, L., Broséus, J., Rossy, Q., & Esseiva, P. (2016). Buying drugs on a Darknet market: A better deal? Studying the online illicit drug market through the analysis of digital, physical and chemical data. *Forensic Science International*, 267, 173–182.

Rice, A. (2013). We are all friends nowadays: But what is the outcome of online friendship for young people in terms of individual social capital? In C. Fowley, C. English, & S. Thouësny (Eds.), *Internet research, theory, and practice: Perspectives from Ireland* (pp. 177–197). Dublin.

Sampson, R. J., Morenoff, J. D., & Earls, F. (1999). Beyond social capital: Spatial dynamics of collective efficacy for children. *American Sociological Review*, 633–660.

Sampson, R. J., Raudenbush, S. W., & Earls, F. (1997). Neighborhoods and violent crime: A multilevel study of collective efficacy. *Science*, 277(5328), 918–924.

Shah, D., Harrison, T. G., Freas, C. B., Maimon, D., & Harrison, R. W. (2020, December). Illicit activity detection in large-scale dark and opaque web social networks. In *2020 IEEE international conference on big data (Big Data)* (pp. 4341–4350). IEEE.

Siisiainen, M. (2003). Two concepts of social capital: Bourdieu vs. Putnam. *International Journal of Contemporary Sociology*, 40(2), 183–204.

Spottswood, E. L., & Wohn, D. Y. (2020). Online social capital: Recent trends in research. *Current Opinion in Psychology*, 36, 147–152.

Stajkovic, A. D., Lee, D., & Nyberg, A. J. (2009). Collective efficacy, group potency, and group performance: Meta-analyses of their relationships, and test of a mediation model. *Journal of Applied Psychology*, 94(3), 814.

Tremblay, P., & Morselli, C. (2000). Patterns in criminal achievement: Wilson and Abrahamse revisited. *Criminology*, 38, 633–659.

van der Bruggen, M., & Blokland, A. (2021). Child sexual exploitation communities on the darkweb: How organized are they? In *Cybercrime in context* (pp. 259–280). Springer.

Weerman, F. M. (2003). Co-offending as social exchange. explaining characteristics of co-offending. *British Journal of Criminology*, 43(2), 398–416.

Wilson, W. J. (1987). *The truly disadvantaged*. University of Chicago Press.

33

CHARACTERISTICS OF THE DARK WEB'S ONLINE DRUG CULTURE

Ari Haasio, Piotr Siuda and J. Tuomas Harviainen

Introduction

This chapter focuses on analysing the special features of the Dark Web's drug culture. According to Gehl (2018), the Dark Web can only be reached by using specially configured routing software, such as the Tor browser. It is also anonymous and therefore more private to use, which is the main reason why the Dark Web is used for illicit drug marketing and as a platform to communicate drug-related questions. Due to these reasons, the importance of the Dark Web in the drug trade has increased significantly (Martin et al., 2020).

There are also drug-related sites on the clear web and drug dealing may take place on social media (Demant et al., 2019; Anderdal Bakken & Kirstine Harder, 2022; van der Sanden, 2022). In this chapter, we have focused on the specifics of the Dark Web drug culture, as it has become the main online marketplace for illicit drugs (Haasio et al., 2022). Because of this, users also discuss different aspects of the drug culture there, which makes the environment of high interest to scholars looking at not just drug trading.

Although Dark Web sites play a key role in the drug trade, several websites also have discussions about drug use, give peer information to other users and discuss topics related to drug culture, from music to information security. Some image boards likewise have discussion forums related to reducing and quitting drug use. Those sections are primarily based on peer support and the possibility to anonymously ask for advice without fear of being stigmatized (Haasio et al., 2022). Maddox et al. (2016) have pointed out that cryptomarkets are not just for selling and buying drugs. Their research about Silk Road's activism proves that discussions about drug policies and personal freedom within a libertarian framework in drugs is a frequently discussed topic.

Drug use is a cultural phenomenon that gives rise to its own subcultures. Allaste (2006) has pointed out that using drugs is partly a consequence of youth cultures. There are also subcultures on the internet based on lifestyles and people's interests and hobbies. Since drug users have their own subculture, it is natural that it can also be seen as a cultural community forming on the internet. Parts of it exist on image boards, but the discussions in many countries are now moving on to private groups on instant messaging services (Zambiasi, 2022).

DOI: 10.4324/9781003277675-38

The present study contributes to a conceptual framework to the drug user culture on the Dark Web. Our investigation opens a new perspective on the study of Dark Web drug culture by pointing out the main feelings and thoughts, which are typical to the discussion, that dominate the discussion culture on marketplaces and image boards specializing in the drug scene. For instance, personal stories about usage history are examples of this kind of cultural feature.

Previous research

The Dark Web's drug scene as a cultural phenomenon has not been widely studied. Research on the drug trade has mostly dealt with the types of products for sale, market shares of different drugs (e.g., Dolliver, 2015; Dolliver & Kuhns, 2016; Scourfield et al., 2019; Windle, 2021), sellers' reputations (Nurmi et al., 2017) or selling practices (Childs et al., 2020). Information needs and information sharing (Harviainen et al., 2020; Haasio et al., 2022), cultural and socioeconomic factors related to the lives of drug on the Dark Web (Harviainen et al., 2021) and information protection on the Dark Web market sites (Harviainen et al., 2021) have been also studied, but to a lesser degree. Bilgrei (2019) has studied risk management and trust in online drug communities. He points out that a new subculture of drug users has emerged on the internet. It makes interaction between people with same interests possible. Trust is one of the key factors in the Dark Web's drug markets. Its significance has been studied in several articles and dissertations (e.g. Holt et al., 2016; Duxbury, 2018; Bakken & Demant, 2019; Norbutas, 2020; Munksgaard, 2021). A comprehensive study on the drug culture of the Dark Web and its special features is still waiting to be done.

Drug users' subculture and way of life has been studied in various research articles (e.g. Marin et al., 2017; Kajanová & Mrhálek, 2019; Giraudo, 2020), but these studies are focused on the cultural features of the real world and do not consider the role of the virtual world in the culture and lifestyle of drug users. By the term "real world", we mean the physical environment, and by the term "virtual world", we mean services in the information network.

Conceptual framework and research questions

The theoretical framework of this chapter is based on Maslow's hierarchy of needs, the information needs derived from it (Wilson, 1981, 1984) and the analysis of the triggers of those information needs (Wilson, 1981, 1984; Haasio et al., 2020). Also, the idea of otherness presented by Zygmunt Bauman (1990) has influenced our work. Otherness can be understood as the quality or state of being other or different from others, and it is often used to describe someone's being part of a minority group, e.g. being a member of a group like outlaw bikers.

Culture can be defined in many ways. We use Hofstede's (1991–1994, p. 5) definition: "culture is the collective programming of the mind which distinguishes the members of one group or category of people from another". In this case, the drug users can be understood as a cultural group that represents a subculture of disnormative behaviour and disnormative information behaviour (Haasio, 2015; Haasio, 2019; Haasio et al., 2020). This disnormative behaviour and disnormative information behaviour can be understood as actions which are either against the law or against the generally accepted norms of the surrounding society. For example, when using drugs is illegal in most countries, the information seeking process concerning drug usage and sales, as well as the act of usage, can be understood to be disnormative.

The background of the drug culture on the internet is also the experience of otherness (see Bauman, 1990). Drug use is something that creates its mark on a person from the perspective of the rest of society. Stigmatization is something that many users fear (e.g. Ezell et al., 2021). The fact that someone uses drugs unites the users of drug forums on the Dark Web and acts as a factor promoting a similar otherness (Haasio, 2015). It is also a way of life, and in some cases it dominates everyday life, depending on the usage frequency, life situation and the substance used (Haasio et al., 2020).

Way of life also affects the things people do in their everyday life. For example, way of life can be understood as a major motive that affects information seeking behavior (e.g. Savolainen, 2008; Haasio et al., 2020). Actually, selling and buying drugs on the Dark Web is a good example of information seeking and information sharing.

Our main research questions are:

1) What are the typical features of the Dark Web's drug culture?
2) What characteristics are typical of the drug culture on the Dark Web in particular, and what kind of explanatory factors can be found for them?

We approach these questions broadly and seek the common shared features of Dark Web drug culture. On the margins of these two questions, we also signal that 3) there could be differences in this culture in different countries. The Internet is an international, border-crossing platform, but in many cases the illicit drug trafficking and communication happen mostly in domestic sites, in which just the local language is used. This may cause differences in the Dark Web's drug culture in different countries, due to both local culture and legislation as well as the differences in the availability of certain narcotics, and customers' purchasing power, which affects the market especially for higher-priced drugs, particularly heroin. For example, Finland stands out as a place where a heroin substitute, Subutex, is particularly popular (Haasio et al., 2022). When it comes to regional differences, we do not give any definite answers, and we are only looking for clues based on the first two questions.

Based on the analysis the authors have done for several articles (Haasio et al., 2020; Harviainen et al., 2021; Haasio et al., 2022) and using the qualitative and quantitative analysis of the data discussed later, we claim that there are three dimensions that can be considered special features of the Dark Web's drug culture. These dimensions are thoughts/feelings, values and actions. This chapter summarizes the observations we have made about the cultural features typical for the Dark Web's discussions and actions about drugs.

This chapter analyses the discussion culture of the Dark Web's image boards specializing in the drug scene—selling, buying and discussing drugs and drug culture as part of the user's life and lifestyle. It is based on a qualitative content analysis. In the background, there is an idea of a netnographic way to approach the research object. In other words, "it surveys the nature of online social experience and interaction: the phenomenon we wish to study" (Kozinets, 2015, p. 2). Netnography is a qualitative approach to social media and it analyses where cultural focus on the data is at the centre of the research (Kozinets, 2019).

Data and methods

This study uses data from both Finland and Poland. The Finnish data set contains almost 10000 closely read and analysed messages collected from the Finnish Dark Web site Sipulitori, and 3,104,971 messages submitted between 2017–2020 to another Dark Web site called Torilauta, analysed with directed searches followed by close readings. Polish Dark Web boards and markets, e.g. Cebulka (which currently lists around 18000 registered users), and forums dedicated to the discussion of illicit drugs (e.g., hyperreal; narkotyki.pl) have also been used as background material for this chapter. The data here was gathered less systematically as a confirmation of what was seen on Finnish sites. Samples of these data have been used in this chapter to illustrate and verify what is argued.

Our point of view is conceptual and based on the research we have done before. We also lean on the previous studies about drug culture on the web. Our goal has been to summarize and create an interpretation framework that illustrates the special features of the discussion culture of drug sites on the Dark Web.

Results

Multifaced drug culture

Drug culture is not a uniform culture. Rather, it can be understood as a subculture or a counterculture, which is divided into different smaller cultures. Which drugs and how often a person uses them has great importance in the cultural context. The users do make the differentiation themselves based on the type of use. For example, recreational users and the "junkies" who represent the lowest caste within the communities are very different cultural groups. It is the same way with users of cocaine or ecstasy, who have their own demographics distinct from users of other narcotics, possibly excluding amphetamine, which seems to hold a general interest. These differences are also clearly stated in the online discussions belonging to our data. Likewise, cannabis users who use nothing else form their own group, which may also have way of life associated with the use (see e.g. Giraudo, 2020; Haasio et al., 2022). Many, however, seem to use it alongside other drugs, so we postulate that two very different demographics relating to cannabis exist.

In a cultural sense, a person's lifestyle and life management are important. Is all the activity focused on getting the next dose, or is the user a working recreational user? The writings on online forums clearly show that some users have drifted or are drifting outside of mainstream society, and in the worst cases they have lost control of their lives. People who work and have family lives, whose life management is quite good according to them, represent the other extreme (see e.g. Haasio et al., 2020; Haasio et al., 2022). Allaste (2006), who studied the lives of Estonian drug users, has found that there are different types of drug users. This has been observed in several other studies, too (see e.g. Pitkänen et al., 2016). Tiberg and Nordgren (2022), for instance, have studied Swedish court descriptions of convicted users. They distinguish four different user groups in their research: criminals, addicts, ordinary people and recreational users. These groups have very different lifestyles, and the cultural environment differs between them.

Cannabis users can restrict their drug use and are established within their respective societies, in contrast to heroin users who quickly lose control of their lives. It is therefore important to point out the cultural and social context within which a narcotic substance is used. Drug use forms one's identity; for example, the label "cannabis user" is important in a person's identity formation (Lavie-Ajayi et al., 2022). Di Placido (2019) studied Italian working-class subculture and observed that using drugs is an important aspect of identity. In our view, this supports the idea that a person adopts the cultural features that are typical of cannabis users. He/she becomes attached to this subculture and adopts its core values, which include a normalization of drug use. Another important subcultural group is recreational users, whose drug usage is linked to relaxing on the weekends and also to parties and festivals (Wilson et al., 2010).

Three dimensions of drug culture

In Finland, the legislation is very strict. The law prohibits possession, use and selling of all kinds of illegal drugs. In Poland, the legislation is equally restrictive (Malinowska-Sempruch, 2016). Legislation has a significant impact on what kind of drug culture is coming online. Because of the harsh punishments in Finland and Poland, communication cannot be open, and the fear of being punished is always present. It also explains the willingness to use the Dark Web because of the anonymity (Haasio et al., 2022).

In the following, we analyze the characteristics of the Dark Web's drug culture with the help of three variables typical of the network. They are thoughts/feelings, actions and values which arose from the data (Table 33.1).

The three dimensions of Dark Web culture

Three elements of thoughts and feelings were observed from the data. These were fear, safety and caring. In some posts only one of these elements was noticeable; in some other posts, two or three elements were existing.

Confidence

Confidence plays an important role in Dark Web forums. Especially in drug deals, the trust between seller and buyer seems to be important and is discussed widely on the forums. When the information needs of Finnish Dark Web drug forum Torilauta were analysed, 5.2 percent of the information needs concerned a drug user's identity. There were also many racist comments about certain vendors and buyers, with Roma and immigrants being seen

Table 33.1 Characteristics of the Dark Web's drug culture analyzed with the help of three variables typical of the network

Thoughts/Feelings	Objects	Actions	Values
Fear, safety	Robbery	Sharing warnings	Safety
Fear, safety	Violence	Sharing warnings	Safety
Caring	Overdose	Sharing own experiences of use	Safety
Caring	Detoxification	Sharing own experiences of detoxification	Safety, peer support, peer information
Fear	Police, customs	Using Dark Net & Wickr	Anonymity

as particularly unreliable as trading partners (Haasio et al., 2020). According to Laferrière and Décary-Hètu (2022), there are four kinds of trust: the ones related to identity, marketing, security and signals that directly express trust.

In the Dark Web's drug culture, vendors have to build trust. One of the ways to convince customers about reliability is reputation, which is formed over time. On the other hand, vendors have to trust the customers, too. In our data there are many examples of mistrust and fear of robberies. If the customer is a new one, there is always a risk of being robbed. Vice versa, the vendors fear scams. On the discussion forums analysed there are warnings about the vendors one should not trust. In some cases, one may lose money or alternatively get a low-quality drug or even something other than what one was buying. In the messages sent by the vendors, "honest deals" and "excellent quality" are often mentioned. Many vendors also state their ethnicity as a sign of better reliability. Vendors fear customers and customers fear vendors (for an exploration of the conflict experiences of drug dealers in online and offline illicit drug markets, see Bergeron et al., 2022). In addition, both groups fear the police, because there is always the possibility of being caught for selling or buying drugs—both of which are illegal in Finland and Poland.

In this chapter, we surveyed 49 online illicit drug market vendors to explore the conflict experiences of drug dealers who participate in online and offline illicit drug markets. The results indicate that conflict and victimization experiences are rare for online drug dealers, but there are still many situations that are not mitigated by using anonymizing technologies like those used on online illicit markets. We demonstrate how these conflicts differ between online and physical drug markets.

In addition to the trading situation, thoughts are also focused on the quality of drugs and the consequences of their use. The quality of the drugs is widely discussed and on different forums, users give feedback on quality (see e.g., Aldridge & Decary-Hétu, 2015; Laferrière & Décary-Hètu, 2022). Health issues and rehabilitation are also themes that are commonly mentioned. When considering rehabilitation, many of the users do not want to quit all of their drug use. Instead, they may consider stopping use of opioids, but do not want to give up cannabis (Haasio et al., 2022). Safety plays an important role here, too, as posters are afraid of overdoses and the results of mixed use of different substances or drugs and alcohol.

In addition, technical issues are discussed in forums surprisingly often. Some participants have a significantly high level of knowledge about information technology. Information security and operational security are especially popular subjects. The instant messaging system Wickr and other anonymous services are used for communication, but the anonymity and safety of the Dark Web and Tor network is constantly a topic of discussion.

The discussion is motivated by the fact that the police in these countries have succeeded in shutting down several drug websites on the Dark Web, both in Finland and in Poland, pointing towards strong cooperation between law enforcement agencies. The anonymity of the Tor network and Wickr have been questioned many times in the forums. In terms of fears and feelings, it is typical for drug users to easily assume that their activities are being monitored, and they are more alert than average web users due to frauds and robberies related to the drug trade. Currently, setting up sales based on initial posts on image boards has moved from Wickr to Telegram, which has raised significant forum discussions on potential backdoors in the software, due to its origin.

Thoughts and feelings

When analysing the cultural features of the Dark Web's drug forums, thoughts and feelings are the motives that guide the activity. Anonymity is a prerequisite for an open discussion since the topics deal with illegal activities. Even detoxification and reducing usage are topics that not all the drug users are willing to speak about other than anonymously. Haasio et al. (2022) have observed from a Finnish forum that many participants in the discussions about detoxification are afraid of being identified. The fear of being stigmatized, especially by those users who have children or who are working, is general. This is due to Finland's strict drug policy. Because of this, the users find peer support very important.

On the Dark Web, the noteworthy thing is anonymity. The anonymity on Dark Web makes it possible to express feelings and ask questions one would not dare to say with one's own name (Gehl, 2018). In the chapter, we go through the actions and activities typical of the drug culture of the Dark Web that we have observed in our data. The aforementioned thoughts and feelings can be found in the background of all such actions.

Information seeking plays a big role in these forums. Information needs are shared in most of the posts, and the role of peer information is important (Haasio et al., 2020). For many users, Dark Web forums offer multiple opportunities for both trading and support. Such users do not want to be in contact with the authorities or social workers, because the use of drugs already fulfills the characteristics of a crime and carries a strong stigma of lacking control over one's life.

Caring also plays an important role in discussions. It is all about sharing peer information and peer support with other users. Even though people communicate anonymously, their background as drug users is the unifying thing. For example, when talking about one's own drug usage, problems related to life management or willingness to reduce drug use, peer support is important. Here Bauman's (1990) idea of otherness is clearly visible, as is Becker's (1963) concept of outsider ethos and identity. The fact that everyone participating in the discussions has experienced similar things makes it possible to acquire peer information and peer support that is considered reliable. Due to the illicit and sensitive subject, many questions cannot be answered by social workers or medical doctors (see also Haasio et al., 2020; Haasio et al., 2022). For example, questions related to optimal dosing and cross effects of different drugs are subjects where one may find answers only from the more experienced drug users.

Sharing information and experiences

According to our data, sharing experiences is common, and people do it to help other users. In our opinion, this shows that drug use is a unifying thing, which is also reflected in the desire to share experiences and thus acts as a community-creating factor. In the background of all of it, there is Bauman's idea of otherness that is experienced by the users. The experienced otherness is not just a unifying thing, but also an important basis to the Dark Web's drug culture, which relies on outsiderness and perceived authenticity (Gehl, 2018).

Sharing one's own experiences can also be understood as caring. A good example is dosing: how much can one take, if one has not used a certain drug before? How can a person avoid an overdose? More experienced users guide in dosage and warn about the effects of mixing substances, and recommend what drugs one should take in which order to get a certain effect. According to the participants of the discussions, these points of advice are perceived as very important. Although we may consider these instructions and advice questionable, in some cases they can prevent overdoses and represent strong community support in a marginalized group.

The information that is shared is mostly disnormative (Haasio, 2015; Haasio, 2019). A large part of it relates to illegal things, such as discussions about the sale of drugs. Other discussions which do not deal with selling or buying drugs can be classified disnormative, too. This is because the subjects are, if not illegal, at least questionable and even likely considered reprehensible by most people. Very typical information needs concern, for example, growing cannabis. That is prohibited by the law, but information about the techniques is often shared in these forums.

Although the Dark Web forums we examined are primarily places to initiate trading, there are plenty of discussions on other topics as well. However, the discussions are directly or indirectly related to drug use, the financing of drug use or drug trafficking. Drug-themed music and literature have also occasionally been discussed in these forums. Interesting manifestations of the drug culture of the Dark Web are the previously mentioned discussions about stopping or reducing drug use. Also, health is a topic that users discuss very often.

One cultural feature in Finnish Dark Web sites is prostitution. There is plenty of supply of this kind of service on the clear web, which is targeted for the common people. Drug users, however, publish their advertisements on the Dark Web and regularly ask for drugs as payment and/or want to use drugs with their customers, as well as have sex. These dating ads are clearly targeted at other drug users. Average citizens would not even find them on the Dark Web. On the contrary, the mere mention of drugs would drive them away. There are also ads on the Finnish Dark Web dating sites where the person is not looking for a sex partner, but just wants to find a person with whom they can use drugs. This too potentially denotes issues of safety, as well as a need to share one's experiences with others.

Cultural differences in regional Dark Web markets

On the margins of presenting the features of drug culture on the Dark Web, this study asks whether there could be any differences in this culture in different countries. One must note that the chapter cannot give a definitive answer here, as the data is limited to two countries and does not include the national/regional component. The thoughts/feelings, values and actions are treated universally here. However, we believe that the studied sites signal that Dark Web markets may have some localized features.

Having said this, the research on these features is almost non-existent. Some rare studies show how there are clear geographical differences when it comes to the use of the Dark Web for the drug trade. Van Buskirk et al. (2016) show that there are country-specific differences for the number of sellers, and Cunliffe et al. (2017) demonstrate that in Australia different risks in Dark Web trading depend on the given location. Similarly, Norbutas (2018) claims that "online drug trade networks might still be heavily shaped by offline (geographic) constraints" (2018, p. 92), and "might be more localized and less international than thought before" (2018, p. 92).

As mentioned, though, research on Dark Web locality is still rare. Existing studies focus on English-language sites and not so much on the culture of the drug trade but the numbers and kinds of drugs being sold—similarly to the aforementioned fact that Finland stands out as a place for trading Subutex, a heroin substitute (something that became visible while we studied the Finnish sites). Nevertheless, we believe that the regional cultural context could also be fundamental for the presented elements, i.e., thoughts/feelings, values and actions of drug users on the Dark Web.

For example, the drug policy of different countries affects the national culture of Dark Web drug forums. Since in Finland possession, use and the purchase and sale of drugs is prohibited by the law, practically all the contents of these sites are by their nature leading to punishable acts. This partially explains why fear is a typical feature of Finnish drug websites, which can be seen in the messages sent there.

The strictness of the legislation may explain the expressions of fear and prejudice observed in online discussions in both Finland and Poland (Malinowska-Sempruch, 2016). In Poland, the so-called "Act on legal highs" (introduced on August 21, 2018), an amendment to the Act counteracting drug addiction, had a major impact on the change in selling drugs and new psychoactive substances (NPS) on the Polish internet. Entering new substances on the list of prohibited compounds became much faster than before. It could be that the main consequence here is the moving of the drug market to the Dark Web and the building of drug culture of fear in online spaces, like other Polish reforms before 2018. A 2010 response resulted in the closure of some 1,400 brick-and-mortar shops where NPS used to be sold, and these impacted migrations of vendors online (European Monitoring Centre for Drugs and Drug Addiction & Europol, 2017; Martinez et al., 2016).

That the drug users represent a special kind of a subculture, and that the drug use is a common feature that unites this group and positions members to the surrounding world and each other, is highly visible and specific in Poland. Wanke et al. (2022) show how in Poland cannabis users are engaged in a boundary-making processes to "detach themselves" from Polish social conservativism (2022, p. 1). In Poland, drug subcultures are linked to the general intoxication cultures. The most obvious and significant dimension of these is alcohol consumption remaining the leading cause of morbidity and premature mortality among young and middle-aged adults (Nowak et al., 2018; Zatoński et al., 2019). The rate of both alcohol and illicit substance use in Poland is generally high and increasing, but the former is not stigmatized like the latter in the highly conservative society. It is very probable that this kind of social surrounding strongly impacts thoughts/feelings, values and actions of drug users in Dark Web environments, especially the fears they are experiencing.

Discussion

One can say that drug users' subculture on the Dark Web is a culture of otherness and outsiderness. The values it represents are largely against the values of the majority of society. Whereas a society sees drug use as a problem and related activities as punishable, on these discussion boards drugs are perceived as a positive thing, or at least as a natural part of everyday life. They are considered to enable expansion of consciousness and escapism. In addition, cannabis users defend their use with the substance's health effects, and users of certain other substances likewise use self-medication for mental health issues.

Fear is a key characteristic of Dark Web culture. It is strongly visible, especially when negotiating drug deals, both for buyers and sellers. Violence, robberies, frauds and police are the main factors that create the fear. Trust can be seen as an important factor and its necessity is often underlined when selling or buying drugs. Fear is also related to many other topics that are central to the drug culture of the web. Dangers of overdose, harmful cross effects of different substances and safety of information technology are some examples.

Anonymity is a prerequisite to all actions because of the subculture's illicit nature. Although the Tor browser is considered quite safe, security-related questions are constantly on users' minds. Information sharing is common, and people are keen to help each other in terms of drug use, plant growing etc.

Peer information and peer support are highly respected and play an important role in drug user's subculture. The communicative aspect and information sharing are important especially on the Dark Web, because often it is the only way to get informed about usage and issues related to it. The information needs and the information shared on the Dark Web's drug forums can be described as disnormative (see Haasio, 2019).

The results raise a question of decriminalization of drug use. The fears that users have are partly the result of strict legislation and the fear of being caught. When you do not dare to ask healthcare professionals or social workers for advice on the safe use of drugs or health problems, you rely on peer information. This is typical of Dark Web online drug culture.

Funding

The present research was supported by the Polish National Science Centre (Narodowe Centrum Nauki) grant 2021/43/B/HS6/00710.

References

Aldridge, J., & Decary-Hétu, D. (2015). Cryptomarkets and the future of illicit drug markets. In *The internet and drug markets* (pp. 23–32). Publications Office of the European Union.

Allaste, A.-A. (2006). *Drug cultures in Estonia: Contexts, meanings and patterns of illicit drug use* [Dissertation, University of Helsinki, Faculty of Social Sciences, Department of Sociology]. Retrieved from http://urn.fi/URN:ISBN:9985-58-458-9

Anderdal Bakken, S., & Kirstine Harder, S. (2022). From dealing to influencing: Online marketing of cannabis on Instagram. *Crime, Media, Culture*, 17416590221081166.

Bakken, S. A., & Demant, J. J. (2019). Sellers' risk perceptions in public and private social media drug markets. *International Journal of Drug Policy, 73*, 255–262.

Bauman, Z. (1990). *Thinking sociologically: An introduction for everyone*. Blackwell.

Becker, H. S. (1963). *Outsiders: Studies in the sociology of deviance*. MacMillan.

Bergeron, A., Décary-Hétu, D., & Ouellet, M. (2022). Conflict and victimization in online drug markets. *Victims & Offenders, 17*(3), 350–371. https://doi.org/10.1080/15564886.2021.1943090

Bilgrei, O. R. (2019). *Drugs and community on the internet-a study of drug trends, risk management and trust in online drug communities* [Dissertation, Department of Sociology and Human GEOGRAPH; University of Oslo]. Retrieved from www.duo.uio.no/handle/10852/69513

Childs, A., Coomber, R., Bull, M., & Barratt, M. J. (2020). Evolving and diversifying selling practices on drug cryptomarkets: An exploration of off-platform "direct dealing". *Journal of Drug Issues, 50*(2), 173–190.

Cunliffe, J., Martin, J., Décary-Hétu, D., & Aldridge, J. (2017). An island apart? Risks and prices in the Australian cryptomarket drug trade. *International Journal of Drug Policy, 50*, 64–73. https://doi.org/10.1016/j.drugpo.2017.09.005

Demant, J., Bakken, S. A., Oksanen, A., & Gunnlaugsson, H. (2019). Drug dealing on Facebook, Snapchat and Instagram: A qualitative analysis of novel drug markets in the Nordic countries. *Drug and Alcohol Review, 38*(4), 377–385.

Di Placido, M. (2019). Between pleasure and resistance: The role of substance consumption in an Italian working-class subculture. *Societies, 9*(3), 58.

Dolliver, D. (2015). Evaluating drug trafficking on the Tor network: Silk Road 2, the sequel. *The International Journal of Drug Policy, 26*, 1113–1123.

Dolliver, D. S., & Kuhns, J. B. (2016). The Presence of New Psychoactive Substances in a Tor Network Marketplace Environment. *Journal of Psychoactive Drugs, 48*, 321–329. https://doi.org/10.1080/02791072.2016.1229877

Duxbury, S. W. (2018). Information creation on online drug forums: How drug use becomes moral on the margins of science. *Current Sociology, 66*(3), 431–448.

European Monitoring Centre for Drugs and Drug Addiction & Europol. (2017). *Drugs and the darknet: Perspectives for enforcement, research and policy.* EMCDDA—Europol Joint publications, Publications Office of the European Union. Retrieved from www.emcdda.europa.eu/publications/joint-publications/drugs-and-the-darknet

Ezell, J. M., Walters, S., Friedman, S. R., Bolinski, R., Jenkins, W. D., Schneider, J., Link, B., & Pho, M. T. (2021). Stigmatize the use, not the user? Attitudes on opioid use, drug injection, treatment, and overdose prevention in rural communities. *Social Science & Medicine, 268*, 113470.

Gehl, R. W. (2018). *Weaving the dark web: Legitimacy on freenet, tor, and I2P.* MIT Press.

Giraudo, R. F. (2020). Cannabis culture on display: Deviant heritage comes out of the shadows. *Museum Worlds, 8*(1), 7–24.

Haasio, A. (2015). *Toiseus, tiedontarpeet ja tiedon jakaminen tietoverkon "pienessä maailmassa": Tutkimus sosiaalisesti vetäytyneiden henkilöiden informaatiokäyttäytymisestä* [Dissertation, Tampere University; Otherness, information needs and information sharing in the "small world" of the Internet: A study of socially withdrawn people's information behaviour]. Retrieved from https://urn.fi/URN:ISBN:978-951-44-9878-7

Haasio, A. (2019). What is disnormative information?. *Information and Communication Sciences Research, 23*, 9–16. Retrieved from http://icsr.unibuc.ro/pdf/23-haasio.pdf

Haasio, A., Harviainen, J. T., & Hämäläinen, L. (2022). "Biodynamically cultivated hash, confidentially": Information sharing on the dark web. *Information Research, 27*(Special issue) [ISIC 2041]. https://doi.org/10.47989/irisic2241

Haasio, A., Harviainen, J. T., & Savolainen, R. (2020). Information needs of drug users on a local dark Web marketplace. *Information Processing & Management, 57*(2), 102080.

Haasio, A., Harviainen, J. T., Ylinen, A., & Oksanen, A. (2022). TOR-verkossa tapahtuvien keskustelujen merkitys huumevieroituksessa. *Janus, 1*(30), 65–80. https://doi.org/10.30668/janus.101602

Harviainen, J. T., Haasio, A., & Hämäläinen, L. (2020, January). Drug traders on a local dark web marketplace. In *Proceedings of the 23rd international conference on academic mindtrek* (pp. 20–26). Academic Mindtrek 2020.

Harviainen, J. T., Haasio, A., Ruokolainen, T., Hassan, L., Siuda, P., & Hamari, J. (2021). Information protection in dark web drug markets research. In *Proceedings of the 54th Hawaii international conference on system sciences.* HICSS.

Hofstede, G. (1991–1994). *Cultures and organizations: Software of the mind.* Harper Collins Business.

Holt, T. J., Smirnova, O., & Hutchings, A. (2016). Examining signals of trust in criminal markets online. *Journal of Cybersecurity, 2*(2), 137–145.

Kajanová, A., & Mrhálek, T. (2019). Drugs as part of the psychedelic trance dance party. *Human Affairs, 29*(2), 145–156.

Kozinets, R. V. (2015). *Netnography: Redefined.* Sage.

Kozinets, R. V. (2019). *Netnography: The essential guide to qualitative social media research.* Sage.

Laferrière, D., & Décary-Hétu, D. (2022). Examining the uncharted dark web: Trust signalling on single vendor shops. *Deviant Behavior*, 1–20. https://doi.org/10.1080/01639625.2021.2011479

Lavie-Ajayi, M., Ziv, A., Pinson, H., Ram, H., Avieli, N., Zur, E., Tzur, E., & Nimrod, G. (2022). Recreational cannabis use and identity formation: A collective memory work study. *World Leisure Journal*, 1–17.

Maddox, A., Barratt, M. J., Allen, M., & Lenton, S. (2016). Constructive activism in the dark web: Cryptomarkets and illicit drugs in the digital 'demimonde'. *Information, Communication & Society, 19*(1), 111–126.

Malinowska-Sempruch, K. (2016). Shaping drug policy in Poland. *International Journal on Drug Policy, 31*, 32–38. https://doi.org/10.1016/j.drugpo.2016.02.018

Marin, A. C., Kelly, B. C., & Parsons, J. T. (2017). The other side of the story: Knowledge transfer and advice-giving in a drug subculture. *Deviant Behavior, 38*(5), 514–532

Martin, J., Munksgaard, R., Coomber, R., Demant, J., & Barratt, M. J. (2020). Selling drugs on dark-web cryptomarkets: Differentiated pathways, risks and rewards. *The British Journal of Criminology*, *60*(3), 559–578. Retrieved from www.gwern.net/docs/sr/2019-martin.pdf

Martinez, M., Kmetanyova, D., & Belackova, V. (2016). A method of exploring the number of online shops selling new psychoactive substances: Initial I-trend project results. In *The internet and drug markets (European Monitoring Center for Drugs and Drug Addiction: Insight 21)*. Publication Office of European Union.

Munksgaard, R. (2021). *Trust and exchange: The production of trust in illicit online drug markets* [Dissertation, University of Montreal].

Norbutas, L. (2018). Offline constraints in online drug marketplaces: An exploratory analysis of a cryptomarket trade network. *International Journal of Drug Policy*, *56*, 92–100. https://doi.org/10.1016/j.drugpo.2018.03.016

Norbutas, L. (2020). *Trust on the dark web: An analysis of illegal online drug markets* [Dissertation, Utrecht University]. Retrieved from https://dspace.library.uu.nl/handle/1874/401445

Nowak, M., Papiernik, M., Mikulska, A., & Czarkowska-Paczek, B. (2018). Smoking, alcohol consumption, and illicit substances use among adolescents in Poland. *Substance Abuse Treatment, Prevention, and Policy*, *13*(1), 42. https://doi.org/10.1186/s13011-018-0179-9

Nurmi, J., Kaskela, T., Perälä, J., & Oksanen, A. (2017). Seller's reputation and capacity on the illicit drug markets: 11-month study on the Finnish version of the Silk Road. *Drug and Alcohol Dependence*, *178*, 201–207.

Pitkänen, T., Perälä, J., & Tammi, T. (2016). *Huumeiden käyttäjiä on monenlaisia: kahdensadan helsinkiläisen huumeiden aktiivikäyttäjän elämäntilanne ja päihteiden käyttö [Different kinds of drug users: life situation and substance use of two hundred active drug users in Helsinki]*. Tietopuu: Tutkimussarja; 1–10. [In Finnish].

Savolainen, R. (2008). *Everyday information practices. A social phenomenological perspective*. Scarecrow.

Scourfield, A., Flick, C., Ross, J., Wood, D. M., Thurtle, N., Stellmach, D., & Dargan, P. I. (2019). Synthetic cannabinoid availability on darknet drug markets—Changes during 2016–2017. *Toxicology Communications*, *3*(1), 7–15.

Tiberg, F., & Nordgren, J. (2022). Ordinary people, criminals, addicts and recreational users: Swedish court of law descriptions of persons sentenced for online drug purchases. *Nordic Studies on Alcohol and Drugs*. https://doi.org/10.1177/14550725221079524

Van Buskirk, J., Naicker, S., Roxburgh, A., Bruno, R., & Burns, L. (2016). Who sells what? Country specific differences in substance availability on the Agora cryptomarket. *International Journal of Drug Policy*, *35*, 16–23. https://doi.org/10.1016/j.drugpo.2016.07.004

van der Sanden, R., Wilkins, C., Rychert, M., & Barratt, M. J. (2022). 'Choice' of social media platform or encrypted messaging app to buy and sell illegal drugs. *International Journal of Drug Policy*, *108*, 103819.

Wanke, M., Piejko-Płonka, M., & Deutschmann, M. (2022). Social worlds and symbolic boundaries of cannabis users in Poland. *Drugs: Education, Prevention and Policy*, 1–11. https://doi.org/10.1080/09687637.2022.2046706

Wilson, H., Bryant, J., Holt, M., & Treloar, C. (2010). Normalisation of recreational drug use among young people: Evidence about accessibility, use and contact with other drug users. *Health Sociology Review*, *19*(2), 164–175. https://doi.org/10.5172/hesr.2010.19.2.164

Wilson, T. D. (1981). On user studies and information needs. *Journal of Documentation*, *37*(1), 3–15.

Wilson, T. D. (1984). The cognitive approach to information seeking behavior and information use. *Social Science Information Studies*, *4*(2–3), 197–204.

Windle, J. (2021). How a Taliban ban on opium could affect the Irish drugs market. *RTÉ Brainstorm*, 1–2.

Zambiasi, D. (2022). Drugs on the web, crime in the streets. The impact of shutdowns of dark net marketplaces on street crime. *Journal of Economic Behavior & Organization*, *202*, 274–306. https://doi.org/10.1016/j.jebo.2022.08.008

Zatoński, W., Młoźniak, I., Zatoński, M., & Gruszczynski, L. (2019). *Small bottles—Huge problem? A new phase of Poland's ongoing alcohol epidemic* [SSRN Scholarly Paper No. 3460145]. Social Science Research Network. Retrieved from https://papers.ssrn.com/abstract=3460145

34

OPINION FORMATION THROUGH SOCIAL NETWORKS IN THE *BABY BOOMER* GENERATION

Susanne Ardisson and Laura Kobsch

Introduction

While a few years ago classical journalism, "professionally run and editorially organised" (Neuberger & Quandt, 2010, p. 59), was primarily the opinion-making medium in the form of daily newspapers or news broadcasts, this type of reporting is losing its monopoly position as the sole gatekeeper due to the digital transformation. Traditional journalism is increasingly being expanded, and partly replaced, by "internet journalism" (ibid.), which is also increasingly taking place via social media platforms. One component that has always played a central role for journalism, and is at least as relevant for news disseminated via social media, is trust in the producers of the published content (Prochazka, 2022, pp. 62–63). The evaluation competence regarding trust in a media source is particularly relevant in algorithmically personalised news channels on social media platforms, such as Facebook, Instagram or Twitter/X. These partly detach news from their original context, reassembling them for users in algorithmically and user-personalised news feeds or suggestion pages (Schweiger et al., 2019, p. 9).

One of the phenomena that has gained importance through news reports in social media offerings is fake news. Since the 2016 US presidential election, the terms "fake news", "post-truth" and "disinformation" have been declared words of the year in the *Collins Dictionary*, the *Oxford Dictionary* and *Dictionary.com*, respectively. Although the term "fake news" existed before 2016, its characteristics were defined differently from today's understanding (Brashier & Schacter, 2020, p. 316). The increasing presence of fake news in the media requires all users of (social) media to be trained in dealing with the flood of information and the associated risks of false news—not only the young ones. Active consumers of news provided on the internet or via social media platforms can also be found in the older generations. These *digital immigrants* are older adults who were not born into the digital world and have had to learn the language of it. According to Prensky (2001), *digital immigrants* include members of the post-war generation and those of the *Baby Boomer*s, who are the focus of this chapter (Prensky, 2001, pp. 3–4).

Guess et al. (2019) suggest that research should focus on the so-called *digital immigrants* (p. 4) and their internet usage behaviour. In the media usage environment in particular, a

DOI: 10.4324/9781003277675-39

digital divide is emerging that is evident between the younger generations, but especially between *digital natives* and *digital immigrants* (Guess et al., 2019, p. 4; Venter, 2017, p. 499). In the case of *digital immigrants*, it is often assumed that there is a disadvantage in understanding the information provided by the media, and in dealing with digital media and content due to digital illiteracy (Brashier & Schacter, 2020, p. 320; Venter, 2017, p. 499). It should be noted, however, that there are studies that show that even younger people, who are considered *digital natives*, have difficulties evaluating information and facts on the internet in terms of their trustworthiness (e.g. McGrew et al., 2018).

The spread of fake news plays a significant role across all age groups. There are already numerous studies on media usage behaviour and the understanding along with the handling of fake news in the younger generations. For the *Baby Boomer* generation, the number of studies is lower. However, studies by Brashier and Schacter (2020), for instance, show that the older generations are the ones who share the most Fake News (Brashier & Schacter, 2020, p. 317). Older adults, defined in the aforementioned study as people aged 30 and over, are more likely to forget where they found certain information. The information found may be passed on even though it comes from an unreliable source. Although the distinction between true and false news works for a large part of the age group, there is a high level of uncertainty when news content is repeatedly displayed in news feeds, as well as when questioning the content presented (Brashier & Schacter, 2020, p. 317ff.).

The central question of this study is, how do *Baby Boomer*s use social media for news consumption? The handling of political reports on social media platforms and fake news will be focused on for this generation in particular.

In order to answer these questions, a definition of social media (Section 2) on which the study is based, as well as usage behaviour in Germany (Section 2.1) and social media in the context of political opinion-forming (Section 2.2), will be explained. Since the focus of the study is on the *Baby Boomer* generation, it will be examined in more detail in the third section. In Section 4, the topic of fake news will be addressed in detail, and then in Section 5, the three components of social media, fake news and *Baby Boomer*s will be brought together, and the theoretical framework of the study will be concluded. The methodological procedure is explained in more detail (Section 6). A discussion of the results can be found in Section 7.

Social media

There are numerous approaches to defining the term "social media", most of which overlap and complement each other. Social media are digital platforms that are primarily used for the exchange of all kinds of content. Due to the progressive mediatisation of society, the content provided here is connected to almost all areas of citizens' lives and influences people's actions (Margetts, 2019, pp. 107–108). Social media platforms are virtual spaces of exchange on diverse life situations and topics. An example is the provision of news from politics, which can have an influence on the attitudes and opinions of platform users due to the direct and partly unfiltered provision (see Section 2.2). Internet-based channels usually feature a large number of users with different opinions and values, who interact with each other in heterogeneous or homogeneous circumstances. A central point in social media platforms is the possibility to create and disseminate one's own content (Carr & Hayes, 2015, pp. 47–48).

Social media usage behaviour in Germany

According to *Statista*, the number of active social media users in Germany is around 87% (Statista, 2022a, p. 25). On average, the age group of 14- to 29-year-olds is the most strongly represented. The 50- to 69-year-olds, who are the focus of this chapter, primarily use Facebook and Instagram (Statista, 2022a, p. 28).

Rohleder (2018) was able to find out in the context of a *BITKOM* study with 1,000 respondents, that social media are used across the age groups surveyed (internet users aged 14 and over) primarily to maintain private contacts (68%), directly followed by the function as a source of information on current events, which also includes the consumption of news (57%). As shown in Figure 34.1, this is followed by searches for products and services (38%), as well as research on companies and brands (31%) along with the retrieval of information on public figures (30%). In addition, it was stated that social media are used for job searches (18%), partner searches (11%) and for complaining about brands or companies (10%) (Rohleder, 2018, p. 7).

The Reuters Digital News Report provides further insight into media usage behaviour in Germany. The results of a 2021 survey of 2,000 people over the age of 18 show that 92% of respondents read, listen to or watch the news several times a week. 69% say they consume the news via the internet (Hölig et al., 2021, p. 5). Social media are the most important resource for news consumption for 10% of respondents, and a quarter of 18–24-year-olds. Social media platforms are relied on as the sole resource for news by 4% (in 2018, this figure was still 2%) (Hölig & Hasebrink, 2018, p. 8; Hölig et al., 2021, p. 5).

With regard to the detection of false reports, 37% expressed concerns. In a study from 2018, concerns were already being expressed about individual reports in which facts were twisted or distorted with factual errors, oversimplifications or misleading headlines (Hölig &

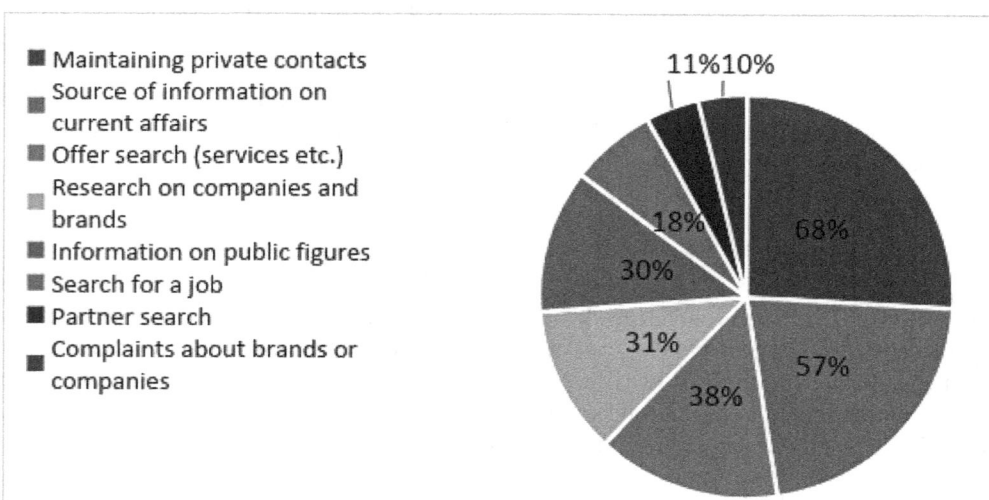

Figure 34.1   Use of social media platforms in Germany

(*Source*: Own representation based on *Rohleder, 2018*, p. 7)

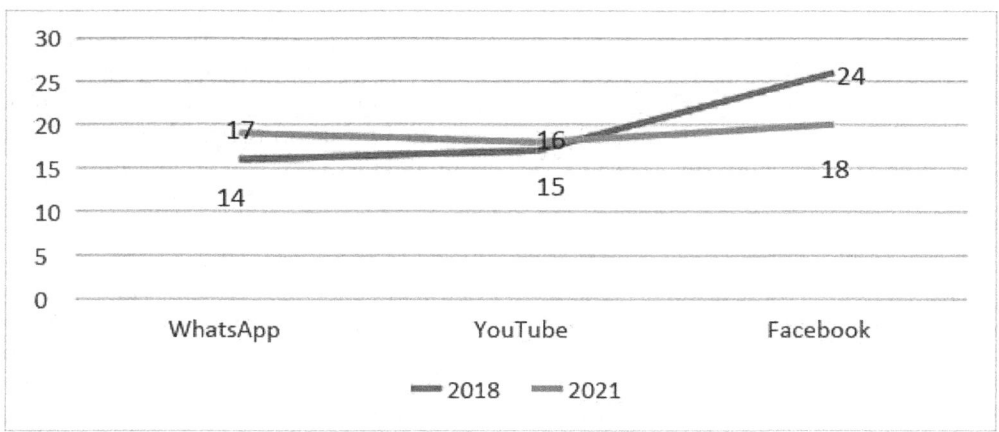

Figure 34.2   Most-used social media platforms for news consumption

(*Source*: Own representation based on Hölig & Hasebrink, 2018; Hölig et al., 2021)

Hasebrink, 2018, p. 8). In 2021, this explicitly referred to false reporting regarding the COVID 19 pandemic. The greatest concerns about the spread of false news are about Facebook, as well as messenger apps such as Telegram (Hölig et al., 2021, p. 6).

The most commonly used social media platforms for consuming news content in 2018 were WhatsApp, YouTube and Facebook. These have not changed in 2021. However, it should be noted that Facebook is used less and less as a news source, and the use of both WhatsApp and YouTube has slightly increased (see Figure 34.2).

Furthermore, it can be noted that in 2021, as in 2018, most social media users did not actively participate in news reporting on the internet. 12% regularly liked posts on social media platforms, 8% commented on them and only 7% shared their own posts. Users who place themselves more on the left or right of the political spectrum are more active than those who place themselves in the political centre (Hölig et al., 2021, p. 7).

Due to the negative characteristics of "junk science,[1] computerised propaganda, aggressive microtargeting, and political advertising" (Margetts, 2019, p. 107), which are directly associated with social media, platforms often have the reputation of being responsible for negative developments in democracies (ibid). Social media are said to create (political) filter bubbles[2] in which opinion-forming content is provided in the newsfeed and can thus influence citizens' views (Margetts, 2019, p. 107). By choosing the information offered by providers on social media platforms, they can determine the opinion of the target group more precisely, and disseminate their self-interests more efficiently than providers of journalistically prepared information (Prochazka, 2022, pp. 63–64).

Social media and political opinion-forming

Due to the media shift, which is primarily driven by digital interactive media and new communication technologies, social media are playing an increasingly central role in direct contact between voters and politics (Geise & Podschuweit, 2019, pp. 161–162).

The use of social media, particularly the formation of opinions through them, has been extensively researched with regard to *Generation Y* (birth years 1981–1995). Studies have also focused more frequently on *Generation X* (birth years 1966–1980) than on the *Baby Boomer* generation (birth years 1956–1965) and subsequent generations, although these are equally active users of the internet and social media platforms (Sheldon et al., 2021, p. 5). In particular, politically motivated behaviour and the formation of political opinions through various online offerings have hardly been considered for research in these age groups (Guess et al., 2019, p. 4).

Due to the firm anchoring of social media platforms in everyday life, they have become indispensable for the political opinion-forming of citizens (Rohleder, 2018, p. 14). Critical reflection, as well as competent handling of the information provided, are considered relevant skills in this day and age. In a society in which sometimes contradictory and non-fact-based news are circulating, the ability to critically question plays a central role—not only for the younger generations, who are *digital natives*, but also for *digital immigrants* (Andersen et al., 2021, p. 61ff).

On the occasion of the aforementioned anchoring in political decision-making and opinion-forming, the use of social media, and in particular communication via the same channels, plays an increasingly important role in political participation. By using them as a tool in election campaigns, they can have a direct connection to the everyday life of citizens, as well as direct communication with them (Engelmann, 2019, p. 9ff). Before social media usage for election campaigns, direct and analogue communication between candidates and voters was an important aspect in this field. Social media platforms provide another opportunity to get in touch with voters and candidates.

Especially in the USA, and increasingly in Germany, social media are used for two-way communication (Geise & Podschuweit, 2019, p. 161). They enable candidates to enter into direct exchange with their (potential) voters, to disseminate information or to respond directly to voter enquiries (Hernandez, 2019, p. 8). Information and dialogue are conducive to citizens' political participation. With the help of social media, democratic political concerns can be directly promoted and disseminated to specific target groups (Geise & Podschuweit, 2019, pp. 161–162). By means of social media, there is a possibility of a more pronounced participation in the political environment, on both the candidate and voter side. Political participation means "all behaviours and actions that citizens undertake voluntarily with the aim of directly influencing or directly participating in political opinion-forming and decision-making processes at the various political levels" (Geise & Podschuweit, 2019, p. 159). Thanks to social media, voters can engage directly in media-mediated exchange, organise among themselves and place expectations along with wishes more directly, and without barriers (Geise & Podschuweit, 2019, p. 160). Social media do not only provide direct communication with politicians, but also social interaction with other interested parties and the possibility of shaping political content themselves, as well as the theoretical option of being able to demand direct feedback. Some examples of political participation via social media, or the internet in general, include "e-petitions, blog posts, online votes or Twitter messages [in order] to participate in or at least influence decision-making processes on political personnel and factual issues" (Geise & Podschuweit, 2019, p. 162). The introduction and usage of social networks in active political communication opens up new participation opportunities for citizens. "Following, liking, tweeting, retweeting, sharing texts or images on a political issue or signing a digital campaign are . . . acts of political participation that had no equivalent in the pre-social media era" (Margetts, 2019, p. 108).

Participatory action within social media gives an increase to other aspects that need to be considered. Filter bubbles and algorithmically generated news feeds are components of opinion formation through social media, and they should not be underestimated (Zweig et al., 2017, pp. 324–325).

It is important that users internalise and understand the principal functionality of filter bubbles and news feeds. In this way, they can be designers of the "personal public sphere" and determine the content that is being displayed to them. In addition to theoretical knowledge, it is vital to have a capacity for reflection as well as an awareness that there are aspects, opinions and attitudes that need to be considered outside of this personal social media public sphere. With regard to this ability, discrepancies can be found between individuals in each age group, but especially among older adults who have not grown up with digital media (Geise & Podschuweit, 2019, pp. 162–163). As a result of the recipients' contact with many individual messages in their own newsfeed on a similar topic, there is a danger that perspectives become blurred, and that differences between fact and fiction, as well as the origin of the information, can no longer be clearly determined (Prochazka, 2022, p. 65). As already mentioned, there is a divergence in requirements in the older age group category regarding this matter. The *Baby Boomers*, who use digital media to a large extent but not as naturally as the younger generations, should be looked at from a closer angle.

Baby Boomer

The characteristics of the *Baby Boomer* generation (see Section 3.1) will be explain. In addition, we will focus on the media usage behaviour of this generation, especially in regards to social media (see Section 4.2).

Who is the Baby Boomer?

With 12.53 million members (as of December 2021), the *Baby Boomer* generation makes up a significant proportion of the German population. Considering that the selectivity of the birth years is not always clear, depending on the definition, members from the neighbouring generations (*Gen X/post-war generation*) can also be included (Statista, 2022b). The generation that is the focus of this research belongs to the *digital immigrants* already mentioned (Venter, 2017, p. 499).

First of all, it should be noted that there is no clear definition of generations in terms of characteristics, naming and birth year. As with other generational concepts, there are variations regarding individual aspects. Venter (2017) has summarised the generation concept of numerous authors on the following generations: the *Silent Generation*, the *Baby Boomers*, *Generation X, Generation Y* and *Generation Z* (Venter, 2017, p. 499). It should be noted here that Generation Alpha has not yet been considered. The Statistisches Bundesamt (2021) published an overview of the membership of the individual generations in Germany, which also took the youngest generation into account:

- *Generation Alpha* (from birth year 2010)
- *Generation Z* (birth year 1996–2009)
- *Generation Y* (birth year 1981–1995)
- *Generation X* (birth year 1966–1980)
- *Baby Boomers* (birth year 1956–1965)

- *Post-war generation* (birth year 1946–1955)
- *Generation up to '45* (before birth year 1945) (Statistisches Bundesamt, 2021, o.S.).

In some cases, the generations are combined or shifted by a few years. For example, Venter (2017) includes the *Baby Boomer*s in the birth years 1946 to 1964 (Venter, 2017, p. 500).

The *Baby Boomer* generation, which is the focus of this study, grew up without digital media, gradually learning to use these technologies through children and grandchildren, but also through everyday and professional embedding. The experiences and skills of using digital media vary within the generation (Venter, 2017, p. 498). *Baby Boomer*s, as already mentioned, belong to the *Digital immigrants*. "Digital" is the second language they had to learn, unlike the generations that grew up with digital media from an early age and are *Digital natives* (Venter, 2017, p. 499). *Baby Boomer*s are considered loyal, committed and reliable in daily life situations, especially in the work context. They are characterised by their strong work ethic as well as a trained awareness of hierarchy. Multimedia and multitasking in relation to the use of media offered in private as well as professional contexts is sometimes difficult for *Baby Boomer*s. In formal situations, they tend to rely on direct, personal communication, and use blogs, wikis and social media less than the next generation (Venter, 2017, p. 500).

(Social) media use behaviour of the Baby Boomers

Nowadays, *Baby Boomer*s use classic digital media (internet, smart TVs, etc.) in everyday life and work just as much as the younger generations. This can be proven by studies and research approaches (e.g. Deloitte, 2015, Ziegler, 2015)

The use of social media to exchange with certain contact circles, such as friends or family, is increasingly seen as beneficial by *Baby Boomer*s and adjacent generations, as the perception of social support is improved, and a sense of belonging to a group is created (Sheldon et al., 2021, p. 1).

According to a survey conducted by *PwC* with 1,000 participants in Germany, trust in social media decreases significantly with age. While 59% of 30- to 39-year-olds trust the content on social media platforms, only 29% of respondents over the age of 60 do (PwC, 2018, p. 14). Nevertheless, social media are still being used (Faktenkontor, 2022). One point for the low level of trust could be the spread, as well as the discussions, on the topic of fake news in the media.

Fake news/disinformation

There is currently no generally accepted definition of the term "fake news" (Guess et al., 2019, p. 6; Zimmermann & Kohring, 2018, p. 527). Furthermore, it should be noted that the term Fake News, according to today's understanding with its rather negative connotations, only became common during the 2016 US election. Before the 2016 election, fake news was exclusively understood as political news satire or platforms for news parodies (e.g. *Daily Show, heute-Show, Postillon*, etc.). Due to the US election, the focus is now on the (deliberate) manipulation of reports through which so-called fake news is created (Zimmermann & Kohring, 2018, p. 527).

In order to create a uniform understanding for this chapter, some characteristics of Fake News derived from the literature should be noted. According to Zimmermann and Kohring (2018), fake news reports are online publications that can occur in any form and in all digital media genres. At first glance, fake news is designed like real news reports, although it can certainly have stylistic flaws (Zimmermann & Kohring, 2018, p. 528). For the most part, there is conformity in the literature on the points mentioned. One feature, which is discussed ambivalently, is the deliberate intention to deceive when creating and sharing the reports (Zimmermann & Kohring, 2018, p. 529).

Social media increases the distribution of fake news. Social media platforms offer the sharing user the opportunity to make fake news available to a potentially unlimited and unfiltered public (Zimmermann & Kohring, 2018, p. 526). In addition to the term Fake News, other terms are used at the same time, each with slightly different meanings. Margetts (2019) defines fake news as false or distorted versions of information or events that serve the purpose of causing disruption among consumers. A related circumstance is so-called "echo chambers". Here, social media users go through a process of opinion formation by exchanging with like-minded people, and the consumption of opinions that reinforce and support their own belief systems. If Fake News is frequently shared in groups, newsfeeds and chronicles on social media platforms, they adapt accordingly and the user is influenced in regard to their own views. (Margetts, 2019, pp. 111–112; Cinelli et al., 2021, pp. 1–2). This process can have an influence on the formation of political opinion. In conclusion, the consumption of fake news, not only via social media platforms, can be problematic for any age group, especially for users who have little experience with digital messages. The interplay between the use of social media and the increasing dissemination of fake news, some of which is prepared in an increasingly professional manner, poses a particular challenge when considering older generations (e.g. *Baby Boomer*s).

Social media, fake news and Baby Boomer

The few studies that exist on the topic of social media used by *Baby Boomer*s often focus on the 2016 US election campaign and the social media behaviour of this age group. So far, there are hardly any results for the use of social media in Germany, especially if the focus is on the political opinion-forming of *Baby Boomer*s through social media (Merten et al., 2022, p. 1130). In regard to the current state of research in Germany, only assumptions can be derived based on research, like that in the US.

A differentiation can be shown in the educational level of news consumers. Woo-Yoo and Gil de Zúñiga (2014) found that highly educated US citizens who frequently used Facebook to read political content knew more about current issues and political structures than similarly educated users with lower Facebook use (Woo-Yoo & Gil-de-Zúñiga, 2014, pp. 43–44). Users with lower levels of education who used Facebook for news were often less well informed than similarly educated users who did not use Facebook as often for news. For users with low political interest, incidental contact with news on Facebook may even lead to an illusion of knowledge, rather than factual knowledge (Feezell & Ortiz, 2021).

Users over the age of 50 were overrepresented among the "supersharers", i.e. people who share an above-average number of (false) reports. During the 2016 US election campaign, they were responsible for approximately 80% of fake news shares (Grinberg et al., 2019, pp. 375–376). A similar pattern emerged on Facebook. Compared to younger users, those over 65 shared seven times more links to fake news topics (see Fig. 34.3) (Guess et al., 2019, p. 3).

Unlike younger users, older adults use Facebook and Instagram to compensate for the lack of social interactions in everyday life. This particular motivation has become more important during the COVID 19 pandemic. The isolation that prevailed in many countries,

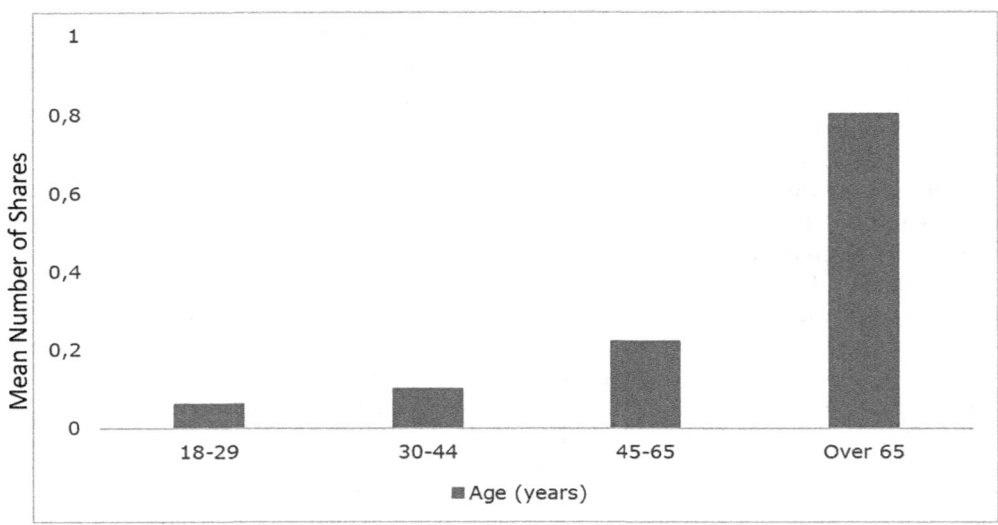

Figure 34.3   Number of shares of reports by age group

especially at the beginning of the pandemic, increased the need to create group belonging through digital communication options (Sheldon et al., 2021, p. 6).

Method

The study commissioned by the authors provides insights into the social media use of *Baby Boomers* in Germany. The topics of political opinion-forming and fake news are examined in more detail. A full survey was not carried out due to the diversity of experiences with digital media in the *Baby Boomer* generation. Therefore, the study can only provide certain insights.

Sampling

The sample is made up of 1,500 respondents who are representative of the *Baby Boomers*. These people are from Germany, regardless of their place of residence, gender, political orientation, level of education or current professional situation. Due to the ambiguous delimitation of birth years for the generations, the period of birth years from 1950 to 1969 was chosen for this study. The delimitation is based on the data of the Federal Statistical Office from the year 2021 (Statistisches Bundesamt, 2021, o.S.). In order to be able to derive differentiation between the core group of *Baby Boomers* and the adjacent generations, three age groups were determined to be considered in more detail:

- Birth years 1950 to 1954
- Birth years 1955 to 1964 (core group of *Baby Boomers*)
- Birth years 1965 to 1969

1,498 respondents were included in the evaluation. 736 men and 761 women participated. One person did not indicate their gender. From the birth years 1950 to 1954, 294 persons took part. From the group born between 1955 and 1964, 754 persons answered the questionnaire. From the age range between 1965 and 1969, 450 people took part.

Questionnaire and implementation

The survey was based on a set of eight content-related questions. Additionally, various demographic data were requested and evaluated. This includes

- the perceived gender affiliation (male/female),
- the classification into one of the following birth year groups (1950 to 1954, 1955 to 1964, 1965 to 1969),
- the place of residence (broken down by federal state),
- net household income (five groups between "less than 1,000 euros" and "4,000 euros or more" as well as one group for "don't know/no information"),
- employment status (eight groups, e.g. "employed full-time (35 hours or more per week)"; "looking for work" or "retired"),
- self-positioning of political views ("left of centre"; "centre"; "right of centre"; "don't know/no answer") and
- educational attainment (e.g. "no school leaving certificate or vocational qualification"; "secondary school leaving certificate or equivalent" or "(technical) university degree and higher").

In order for the respondents to comprehend how news is perceived in the context of the study, the term was defined at the beginning as "information about international, national, regional/local or other current events that is accessible via radio, television, print media or online" (Hölig et al., 2021, p. 12).

Since some of the questions asked provide predefined answer options, the questions along with the answer options will be briefly presented here.

In order to find out which social media channels are used for news consumption by the respondents, the question F1: **Which social media channels have you used in the last week to search for, read, watch, share and/or discuss news?** was asked. Response options were Facebook, YouTube, Instagram, Twitter/X, other, none, don't know and didn't specify.

Since the trustworthiness of the source of information is relevant for news consumption, the second question F2: **All in all: How trustworthy or untrustworthy do you consider the following social media channels in terms of the news published there (regardless of the topic)?** was intended to find out how trustworthy Facebook, Instagram, Twitter/X and YouTube are generally considered to be as news distributors. For each social media platform, respondents could choose between the options very trustworthy, rather trustworthy, rather not trustworthy, not trustworthy at all, don't know and no information. F3: **How trustworthy or untrustworthy do you consider the following social media channels regarding the political news published?** also aims at the trustworthiness of social media platforms, but explicitly with regard to the political news disseminated. The answer options, including the scales for assessing trustworthiness, are identical to F2.

Question F4: **How do you feel about the following statements? (I think you can trust most of the political news/When it comes to online news shared on social media, I have concerns about what is factual and what is fake news?)** is supported by a study conducted by the market and social research institute Ipsos (2018). In the study conducted on worldwide political sentiment regarding the topic of fake news, it was found that it is hardly perceived as such in Germany. Only 42% of Germans say they rarely or never actively identify fake news (Ipsos, 2018, p. 15). Germans reflect that they do not see themselves as being able to specifically distinguish between facts and fake news when consuming media (47%) (Ipsos, 2018, p. 8). No breakdown by age group was carried out in this study. In the context of the current survey, the answer to the fourth question intends to find out what the self-assessment of the *Baby Boomer* group surveyed is in regard to the ability to evaluate fake news.

In order to be able to critically question news, it is often recommended to verify information by comparing it to other sources (e.g. lmz, 2022a; Die Bundesregierung, 2022; bpb, 2022; klicksafe, 2022). The fifth question F5: **When you consume political news via social media, do you usually inform yourself via one or more sources?** intends to find out whether the *Baby Boomer*s who took the survey use this procedure. Here, always via several sources, mainly via several sources, mainly via one source, always via one source, I do not consume political news via social media, don't know and no information were given as possible answers.

The use of social media is mostly passive. *Baby Boomer*s are also more likely to use digital media in this manner (Beisch & Schäfer, 2020, p. 474). Whether there is passive consumption or not in the use of social media platforms is to be learned through question F6: **What activities do you carry out in an average week in relation to online political reporting?** Respondents could choose between the following response options: Rate or "Like" posts, share posts via short message services (e.g. WhatsApp), participate in polls from news sites or on social media, comment on posts on news websites (e.g. *n-tv, Bild*), comment on posts on social media, share posts on social media, talk about posts online (e.g. in chats), share posts via email, (co-)write blog about political issues, other, none, don't know or didn't specify. To gain insights into the *Baby Boomer* respondents' understanding of how personal news feeds are generated, question F7: **How do you think most decisions are made about what news stories are shown to specific people on Facebook?** Respondents chose between the items by computer analytics that monitor and analyse user behaviour, by editors/journalists who work for Facebook, by editors/journalists who work for news companies, random selection, don't know or no answer. For the eighth question F8: **How trustworthy or untrustworthy do you consider the online presences of the following media with regard to the published political news?** a selection of popular internet news platforms in Germany was given. Care was taken to provide a compilation of divergent providers with varying reputations. The selection was based on a survey by the Reuters Institute for the Study of Journalism. The survey was conducted by *Statista* on behalf of the institute in 2022. It generated a ranking of the most trusted German news sources (Statista, 2022b). A selection from the providers as well as a focus on the online platform was included for the present survey. The following platforms were provided as response options: *Bild. de, Spiegel.de, Stern.de, Zeitonline, FAZ.net, Focus.de, tagesschau.de, zdfheute.de, n-tv.de*, online presence of the regional/local newspaper, *rtl.de, sat1.de* and *t-online.de*.

The online survey was conducted by the opinion research institute *INSAConsulere* in Germany in May 2022.

Results

The most used social media platform among the respondents for consuming news is Facebook (42.7%), followed by YouTube (35.1%). Instagram is used by 16.3% to consume news and Twitter is used for this purpose by 11.1%. 33.8% say they do not use any of the four social media channels.

Regarding the trustworthiness of the news on social media platforms, it can be stated that a large number of respondents generally do not consider them as trustworthy in regard to general news reports. Only YouTube is considered trustworthy by 49% but is considered not trustworthy by 32%. 19% abstain (don't know/no answer). Facebook, Instagram and Twitter/X tend to be perceived as untrustworthy. This tendency remains the same when the individual age groups are differentiated (see Table 34.1).

A similar breakdown can be seen regarding trustworthiness for published political news. However, the percentage distance in this category is smaller for YouTube than for general news reports. 603 (40%) of the respondents consider YouTube to be trustworthy. Not trustworthy was selected by 591 (39%). Figure 34.4 shows that the percentages for the Facebook, Instagram and Twitter platforms are slightly different, but tend to remain similar.

It should be noted that a dependency between the assessment of the trustworthiness of the sources, and school education is recognisable. People without an educational qualification generally consider social media platforms to be more trustworthy as a source of political news than people with a school-leaving qualification (regardless of level). In general, it is

Table 34.1 Trustworthiness of social media platforms with regard to general news reports

Platform	Answer item	Total years of birth	1965–1969	1955–1964	1950–1954
Facebook	Trustworthy	32,2%	34,9%	32,7%	26,7%
	Not trustworthy	55,0%	52,5%	54,6%	59,5%
	Don't know/no answer	12,9%	12,5%	12,7%	13,8%
Instagram	Trustworthy	24,4%	27,7%	23,7%	21,1%
	Not trustworthy	46,4%	47,0%	45,8%	47,2%
	Don't know/no answer	29,2%	25,4%	30,5%	31,6%
Twitter/X	Trustworthy	21,9%	23,0%	22,9%	17,8%
	Not trustworthy	46,7%	44,8%	45,9%	51,4%
	Don't know/no answer	31,4%	32,2%	31,1%	30,8%
YouTube	Trustworthy	49,4%	55,0%	48,9%	41,9%
	Not trustworthy	31,8%	29,6%	32,2%	34,2%
	Don't know/no answer	18,8%	15,4%	18,9%	23,9%

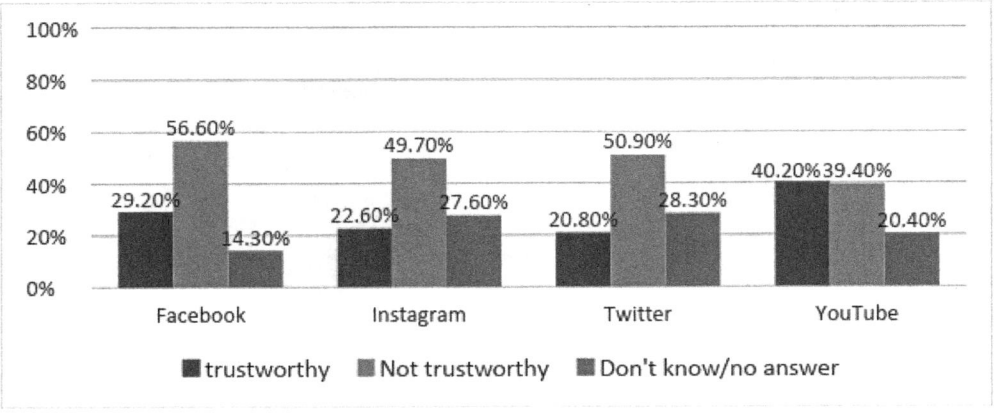

Figure 34.4 Trustworthiness of social media platforms with regard to political news reports

not those with a high school diploma who are the most critical, but those with a secondary school diploma. For the statement "very trustworthy", high school graduates are the ones with the highest percentage.

When it comes to online news shared on social media, 68% of respondents born between 1955 to 1964, as well as those born between 1965 and 1969, agree with the statement that they have concerns about what is factual and what is false news. The percentage is slightly higher among the oldest age group surveyed. In that case, 73% share these concerns, while 15% neither agree nor disagree with this statement. 7% do not agree at all and 4% abstained from answering. Among those born between 1955 and 1964, 20% neither agree nor disagree, and among those born between 1965 and 1969, 23% disagree.

In response to the fifth question, whether multiple sources are used when consuming political news via social media, the majority of respondents answered that they use multiple sources (55%). 8% say they use only one source for consuming political news. Differentiated by self-designated political orientation (right, centre, left), 6.8% of left-leaning and 6.6% of right-leaning respondents say they use only one source. 10.9 % of those located in the political centre say that they only use one source. 36.8% of the left-leaning respondents state that they do not consume any political news at all via social media. For those in the political centre, the percentage is 31.5%, and for those with a more right-wing political orientation, it is 28.9%.

The majority of respondents across all birth years say that they do not actively engage in any activity regarding the dissemination of political news in social media content (47%). 23% answered that they actively "like" posts, and 16% regularly "share" posts in their news feeds.

When asked how decisions are made about what news stories are shown to certain people on Facebook, the distribution of responses across the age groups surveyed is relatively stringent. The correct answer, namely through computer analytics that monitor and analyse usage behaviour, was chosen by 34% (1965–69), 32% (1955–1964) and 30% (1950–1954), respectively. The answer "don't know" was chosen by 31% (1965–69), 32% (1955–1964) and 37% (1950–1954), respectively. As seen in Figure 34.5, the remaining answer options are distributed evenly in their percentage share.

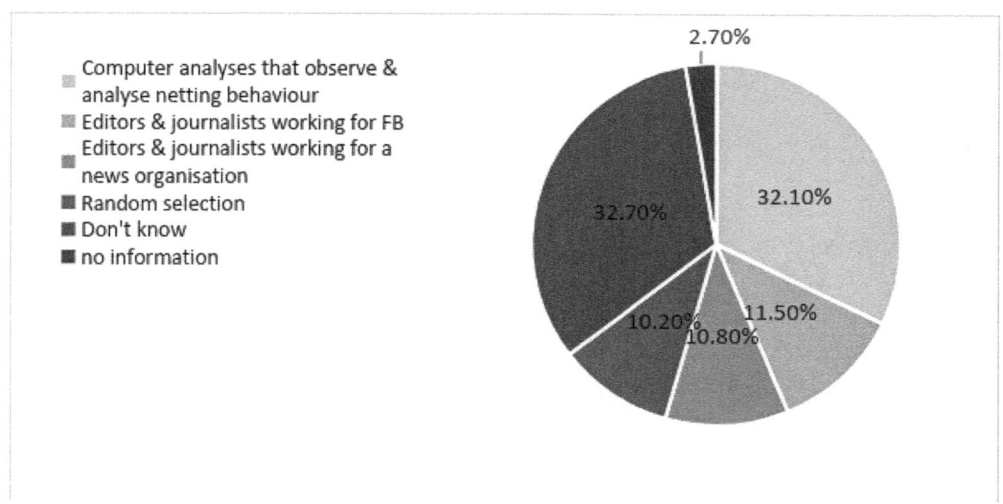

Figure 34.5 How does the news get into the newsfeed? (Answers across all age groups surveyed)

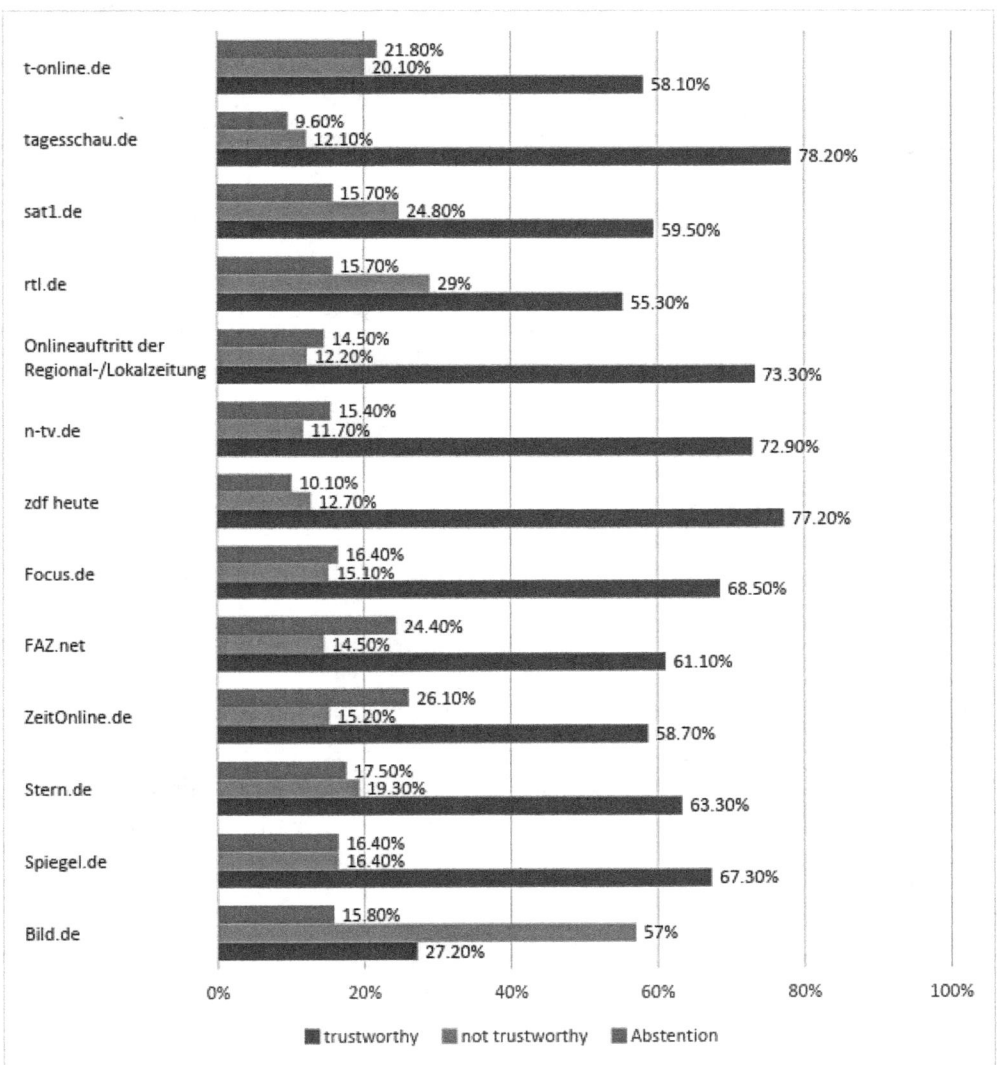

Figure 34.6 Trustworthiness of German online media with regard to political reporting (All espondents)

The eight questions were about how trustworthy or untrustworthy the online presences of the following media: *Bild.de, Spiegel.de, Stern.de, Zeitonline, FAZ.net, Focus.de, tagesschau.de, zdfheute.de, n-tv.de*, and the online presences of regional/local newspapers, *rtl.de, sat1.de* and *t-online.de*, are considered in terms of the political news published. The answers obtained vary. Figure 34.6 shows the distribution of responses in the entire age group surveyed. Here it can be seen that for all media, except *Bild.de*, the trustworthiness regarding the provision of political news is comparatively high.

If a distinction is made according to the level of education, the results are different to the average of the entire age group surveyed. Table 34.2 shows that *Bild.de* is more trusted

Table 34.2 Trustworthiness of online media in Germany with regard to political reporting (by level of education)

* Number of respondents allocated in this group	No school-leaving qualification (9)*	Secondary school leaving certificate/ Comparable (282)*	Realschulabschluss/ Comparable (632)*	Abitur/ Comparable (262)*	University degree/ Comparable (311)*	No indication of the degree (4)*
Bild.de						
Trustworthy	74,3%	30,7%	26,5%	27,2%	24,1%	23,1%
Not trustworthy	7,2%	45,9%	57,9%	60,6%	63,8%	53,3%
Spiegel.de						
Trustworthy	43,8%	58,9%	67,5%	73,3%	70,1%	53,3%
Not trustworthy	42,8%	16,3%	16,1%	13,6%	18,7%	0,0%
Stern.de						
Trustworthy	30,5%	58,1%	65,8%	65,7%	62,3%	23,1%
Not trustworthy	48,9%	14,5%	17,9%	21,0%	24,0%	30,2%
ZeitOnline.de						
Trustworthy	41,6%	47,7%	57,4%	65,3%	66,6%	23,1%
Not trustworthy	20,5%	14,4%	14,6%	18,8%	14,0%	0,0%
FAZ.net						
Trustworthy	16,2%	51,0%	59,0%	69,8%	68,6%	46,2%
Not trustworthy	31,5%	13,9%	14,3%	14,9%	14,7%	0,0%
Focus.de						
Trustworthy	10,8%	62,1%	69,5%	73,8%	69,7%	53,3%
Not trustworthy	31,5%	14,0%	14,3%	14,4%	17,8%	23,1%
zdf.heute						
Trustworthy	42,7%	74,6%	78,1%	78,4%	78,1%	46,2%
Not trustworthy	20,5%	10,3%	11,9%	16,3%	13,4%	0,0%
n-tv.de						
Trustworthy	40,3%	67,4%	74,8%	75,2%	73,3%	53,3%
Not trustworthy	18,2%	10,5%	10,2%	14,0%	13,7%	23,1%

(Continued)

Table 34.2 (Continued)

*Number of respondents allocated in this group	No school-leaving qualification (9)*	Secondary school leaving certificate/ Comparable (282)*	Realschul-abschluss/ Comparable (632)*	Abitur/ Comparable (262)*	University degree/ Comparable (311)*	No indication of the degree (4)*
Onlineauftritt der Regional-/Lokalzeitung						
Trustworthy	19,4%	65,2%	76,8%	72,0%	76,6%	46,2%
Not trustworthy	43,7%	10,1%	10,4%	18,2%	11,8%	0,0%
Rtl.de						
Trustworthy	55,0%	61,1%	57,8%	52,1%	48,1%	23,1%
Not trustworthy	31,5%	17,1%	27,7%	36,0%	36,3%	53,3%
Sat1.de						
Trustworthy	68,3%	63,3%	63,3%	55,3%	52,1%	23,1%
Not trustworthy	18,2%	14,6%	22,8%	30,3%	33,3%	53,3%
Tagesschau.de						
Trustworthy	61,1%	74,3%	79,3%	79,3%	79,6%	53,3%
Not trustworthy	18,2%	8,7%	12,0%	14,8%	13,1%	0,0%
t-online.de						
Trustworthy	27,0%	56,7%	57,6%	61,2%	59,2%	23,1%
Not trustworthy	43,7%	15,9%	20,6%	21,5%	21,1%	30,2%

by people without an education, for instance, than *Stern.de* or the online presence of the *Frankfurter Allgemeine Zeitung (FAZ.net)*.

Discussion and limitation

For the majority of users, social media are merely a supplementary source to their news repertoire from TV, radio, newspapers and the online channels of various providers (Hölig & Wunderlich, 2022, p. 39). Due to the digitalisation taking place in the media landscape, and the changes regarding the formats provided, like the increased streaming in the TV sector, news reporting is in a phase of change (Bitkom, 2022). Even if the *Baby Boomer*s surveyed are not entirely on the social media platforms, these channels are still present in this age group. Therefore, not taking them into account as a tool for forming political opinions would be a mistake. While new platforms, such as TikTok, are constantly being added to the younger generations, and these are already used and studied here as a distribution platform, social networks such as Facebook should not be disregarded as such in research, as it is the most used platform by *Baby Boomers* (Statista, 2021). In the present survey alone, 42.7% of the 1,500 respondents would be reached via Facebook and 35.1% via YouTube.

Since every user can upload content on the platforms and make their own views and opinions public, there are only a few rules regarding the content and preparation of the information. Concepts and possibilities should be developed, especially for the *digital immigrant* generations, on how to recognise and critically examine false information. While the existing offers and demands for opportunities to promote information and media competence are increasing among the *digital natives*, the offers are only sporadically focused on the older generation. The relevance of increasing such offers is once again made clear by the current study. The results of the survey show that 69.1% of respondents have concerns about their own competence in identifying fact and fiction or fake news in reporting. This result is supported by an Ipsos study conducted worldwide in 2018. Here, 47% of Germans said they do not feel sufficiently empowered to identify fake news. It should be noted that the Ipsos study only included adults between the ages of 16 and 64, which means that a small proportion of *Baby Boomer*s are not included in the results (Ipsos, 2018, p. 8).

In addition to the lack of knowledge regarding handling the information provided, the perceived trustworthiness of the *Baby Boomer*s towards social media platforms, is problematic. On the other hand, reporting on fake news in social media through "classic" distribution channels provides education on the topic. It is precisely this that presumably causes the trust of *Baby Boomer*s to decline further in reporting on social media platforms. While general news provided via Facebook is considered trustworthy by about 32% of respondents, the value for political news drops to 29%. For YouTube, the value shows a larger gap. Nevertheless, about 49% consider YouTube to be a trustworthy platform for general information. When it comes to political reporting, the figure is still around 40%. It should be mentioned that YouTube is underestimated, and thus underrepresented in the little amount of research available, as a possible relevant platform for the *Baby Boomer* generation. Obviously, the video platform is a significant consumption channel, which is trusted more than Facebook. At the same time, it must be specified that the present results are only a small intersection.

The understanding of how messages get into news feeds and suggestion pages of social media platforms is lacking among many of the *Baby Boomer*s surveyed. For instance, only just under a third were able to answer the seventh question correctly ("through computer analyses that observe and analyse user behaviour"). Here it cannot be ruled out that some of the respondents guessed when answering and have no knowledge regarding the matter. The knowledge of the technical possibilities decreases in the oldest group surveyed (birth year 1950–1954). Within this group the use of social media in general, and in relation to the consumption of (political) news, is the lowest. It can be assumed that the interest in educational offers provided will also be lower.

*Baby Boomer*s are rather passive users of social media platforms, which can be confirmed by the study. As many as 47% say they do not engage in active activities such as "sharing" or "liking" posts. 23% "like" and 16% "share" posts. It is unclear whether the passive users are aware that they are also adapting their own newsfeed thematically by simply reading or viewing posts. It can be assumed that many are not aware of this, as the majority of respondents are generally unaware of how exactly the feed is generated. Newsfeeds adapted to search and usage behaviour can trigger opinion-forming processes among users (Zweig et al., 2017, pp. 325–326). Looking at opinion formation in the political groups, the results of the study should take into account that several sources are used for the consumption of (political news), regardless of political orientation (right, centre, left).

No conclusions can be drawn about the quality of the sources. Thus, it may be that by using several sources, all of which generate news that is in line with the user's values, an opinion formation is further strengthened.

It should be made clear to *Baby Boomer*s that algorithmically generated feeds and filter bubbles exist. Raising awareness on this topic could help to improve the status of active users as "super-spreaders" of fake news. It should be made clear that they can influence and shape their own news feeds, suggestion pages, reading behaviour, along with a critical and polarised approach to the information provided. There are offers that deal with the media literacy of older adults. However, these are mostly designed for the administrative handling of media. These offers are mostly formats that are explicitly offered for seniors, which includes at least a part of the interviewed *Baby Boomer*s (lmz, 2022b, Deutscher Bildungsserver, 2022, Die Medienanstalt für Baden-Württemberg [lfk], 2022).

It should be emphasised once again that the group surveyed is only a section of the *Baby Boomer*s, which nevertheless reflects the heterogeneity of this generation.

The trustworthiness of news sources in Germany differs from the general picture within the country, depending on the group evaluated (which can be found in Figure 34.7). Further studies would have to be conducted to get a more precise picture. The figure also shows the trustworthiness in news sources of all kinds (print, digital, online) and not exclusively in the online formats that were queried in this study. For example, approximately 74% of those surveyed without a school-leaving certificate, and approximately 31% of those with a secondary school leaving certificate consider the news on *Bild.de* to be trustworthy. In the case of the online presence of regional and local newspapers, there is also an increased deviation in these groups. Only 19% of those without a school-leaving certificate consider the news to be trustworthy, whereas the respondents with a secondary school leaving certificate come closest to the results of the *Statista* study with 66% (see Figure 34.7).

The results show that there are significant differences between the survey groups when considering the level of education. In order to generate more precise and well-founded conclusions, further research should be pursued that focuses mainly on the connection between school education and the topic of fake news in social media.

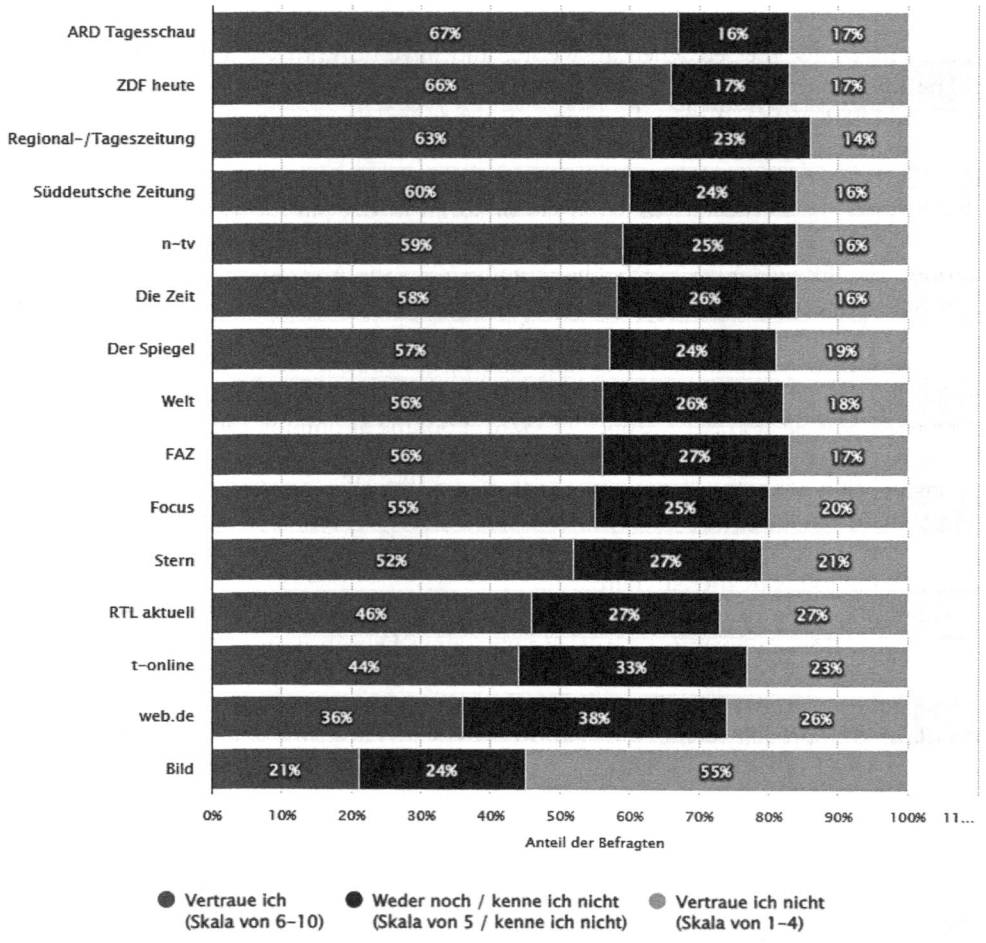

Figure 34.7 Trustworthiness ranking of news sources in Germany
(*Source*: Statista, 2021)

Conclusion

The central questions of the study were about how *Baby Boomer*s use social media for news consumption, and how this generation deals with political news on social media platforms, along with fake news. It should be noted that *Baby Boomer*s are social media users, even though they did not grow up with it. Their usage behaviour is different compared to younger people. *Baby Boomer*s do consume news via social media, but for the majority they do so rather passively. They do not always seem to realise that this passive reading and viewing of the news also leads to a certain selection of news items being displayed to them, which match their search and usage behaviour. Since this self-designed "personal public sphere" (see Section 2.2) can shape and drive opinion-forming processes, it is recommended to do more educational work with the older generations. Further research is needed to ensure that offers are perceived and used by this generation.

It should also be noted that *Baby Boomers* often do not know how to recognise fake news and thus become "super sharers". There are already studies regarding this particular topic, especially in the US. However, the results of the study suggest that a high number of this generation in Germany also share false news unknowingly.

Finally, it can be said that *Baby Boomers*, and other generations that belong to the group of *digital immigrants*, are categorised in the group of "older adults". Research that deals with this significant mass of the population in more detail would be desirable.

Notes

1 **Junk Science:** According to the *APA Dictionary of Psychology*, Junk Science is "invalid or fraudulent research findings, especially when admitted into court. Junk science is a cause of concern because judges, attorneys, and juries often lack the scientific training to identify unsound research" (APA 2022, o.S.).
2 **Filter Bubble:** According to the *Cambridge Dictionary*: "a situation in which someone only hears or sees news and information that support what they already believe and like, especially a situation created on the internet as a result of algorithms" (Cambridge University Press 2022, o. S.).

References

American Psychology Association [APA]. (2022). *Junk science*. Retrieved from https://dictionary.apa.org/junk-science (accessed 8 August 2022).

Andersen, K., Ohme, J., Bjarnøe, C., Bordaconni, M. J., Albæk, E., & de Vreese, C. (2021). *Generational gaps in political media use and civic engagement: From baby boomers to Generation Z*. Routledge.

Beisch, N., & Schäfer, C. (2020). Ergebnisse der ARD/ZDF-Onlinestudie 2020 Internetnutzung mit großer Dynamik: Medien, Kommunikation, Social Media. Retrieved from www.ard-zdf-onlinestudie.de/files/2020/0920_Beisch_Schaefer.pdf (accessed 8 August 2022).

Bitkom. (2022). *Fact sheet: Videostreaming 2021/22*. Retrieved from www.bitkom.org/sites/main/files/2021-10/211001_ct_fact-sheet_videostreaming.pdf (accessed 24 August 2022).

Brashier, N. M., & Schacter, D. L. (2020). Aging in an era of fake news. *Current Directions in Psychological Science*, 29(3), 316–323. https://doi.org/10.1177/0963721420915872

Bundeszentrale für politische Bildung [bpb]. (2022). *#StopFakeNews: Fake News erkennen*. Retrieved from www.bpb.de/themen/medien-journalismus/stopfakenews/ (accessed 13 August 2022).

Cambridge University Press. (2022). *Filter bubble*. Retrieved from https://dictionary.cambridge.org/dictionary/english/filter-bubble (accessed 13 August 2022).

Carr, C. T., & Hayes, R. A. (2015). Social media: Defining, developing, and divining. *Atlantic Journal of Communication*, 23(1), 46–65. https://doi.org/10.1080/15456870.2015.972282

Cinelli, M., De Francisci Morales, G., Galeazzi, A., Quattrociocchid, W., & Starnini, M. (2021). The echo chamber effect on social media. *Computer Sciences*, 118(9). https://doi.org/10.1073/pnas.2023301118

Deloitte. (2015). *Datenland Deutschland. Die Generationenlücke*. Retrieved from https://www2.deloitte.com/content/dam/Deloitte/de/Documents/deloitte-analytics/DAI-Datenland-Deutschland-Generationenluecke-s.pdf (accessed 8 August 2022).

Deutscher Bildungsserver. (2022). *Erwerb von Medienkompetenz—Seniorennetze*. Retrieved from www.bildungsserver.de/erwerb-von-medienkompetenz-seniorennetze-1446-de.html (accessed 23 August 2022).

Die Bundesregierung. (2022). *Woran Sie Falschmeldungen erkennen können*. Retrieved from www.bundesregierung.de/breg-de/themen/umgang-mit-desinformation/falschmeldungen-erkennen-1750146 (accessed 13 August 2022).

Die Medienanstalt für Baden-Württemberg [lfk]. (2022). *Seniorinnen und Senioren*. Retrieved from www.lfk.de/medienkompetenz/seniorinnen-und-senioren (accessed 23 August 2022).

Engelmann, I. (2019). Politische partizipation im medienwandel. In I. Engelmann, M. Legrand, & H. Marzinkowski (Hrsg.), *Politische Partizipation im Medienwandel* (S. 9–25). https://doi.org/10.17174/dcr.v6.1

Faktenkontor. (2022). *Social-media-atlas 2022*. Retrieved from www.faktenkontor.de/studien/social-media-atlas-2022/ (accessed 15 August 2022).

Feezell, J. T., & Ortiz, B. (2021). 'I saw it on Facebook': An experimental analysis of political learning through social media. *Information, Communication & Society*, 24(9), 1283–1302. https://doi.org/10.1080/1369118X.2019.1697340

Geise, S., & Podschuweit, N. (2019). Partizipation durch Dialog? Mobilisierungsstrategien politischer Akteure im Bundestagswahlkampf 2017. In I. Engelmann, M. Legrand, & H. Marzinkowski (Hrsg.), *Politische Partizipation im Medienwandel* (S. 157–191). Berlin. Retrieved from https://doi.org/10.17174/dcr.v6.7

Guess, A., Nagler, J., & Tucker, J. (2019). Less then you think: Prevalence and predictors of fake news dissemination on Facebook. *Science Advances*, 2019(5), 1–8. https://doi.org/10.1126/sciadv.aau4586

Grinberg, N., Joseph, K., Friedland, L., Swire-Thompson, S., & Lazer, D. (2019). Fake news on *Twitter* during the 2016 U.S. presidential election. *Science*, 363, 374–378. Retrieved from www.science.org/doi/10.1126/science.aau2706

Hernandez, Y. (2019). The technology gap across generations: How social media affects the youth vote. *Political Analysis*, 20(1). Retrieved from https://scholarship.shu.edu/pa/vol20/iss1/1 (accessed 9 June 2022).

Hölig, S., & Hasebrink, U. (2018). *Reuters institute digital news report 2018: Ergebnisse für Deutschland*. Retrieved from https://hans-bredow-institut.de/uploads/media/Publikationen/cms/media/t611qnd_44RDNR18_Deutschland.pdf (accessed 9 June 2022).

Hölig, S., Hasebrink, U., & Behre, J. (2021). *Reuters institute digital news report 2021: Ergebnisse für Deutschland*. Retrieved from https://leibniz-hbi.de/uploads/media/Publikationen/cms/media/v9drj2w_AP58_RDNR21_Deutschland.pdf (accessed 9 June 2022).

Hölig, S., & Wunderlich, L. (2022). *Instagram* statt tagesschau? Die Rolle Sozialer Medien in der Nachrichtennutzung. Über Chancen und Risiken. In J. Schützeneder & M. Graßl (Hrsg.), *Journalismus und Instagram: Analysen, Strategien, Perspektiven aus Wissenschaft und Praxis* (S. 59–75). Wiesbaden. Retrieved from https://doi.org/10.1007/978-3-658-34603-4_3

Ipsos Public Affairs. (2018). *Fake news, filter bubbles, post-truth and trust*. Retrieved from www.ipsos.com/sites/default/files/ct/news/documents/2018-09/fake_news_july_2018_v_final_30th_august.pdf (accessed 15 August 2022).

Klicksafe. (2022). *Desinformation und Meinung: von Deepfakes bis Fake News*. Retrieved from www.klicksafe.de/desinformation-und-meinung/fake-news (accessed 15 August 2022).

Landesmedienzentrum Baden-Württemberg [lmz]. (2022a). *Wie kann man Fake News erkennen?*. Retrieved from www.lmz-bw.de/medien-und-bildung/jugendmedienschutz/fake-news/wie-kann-man-fake-news-erkennen/ (accessed 13 August 2022).

Landesmedienzentrum Baden-Württemberg [lmz]. (2022b). *Senioren-Medienmentoren-Programm*. Retrieved from www.lmz-bw.de/medien-und-bildung/jugendmedienschutz/fake-news/wie-kann-man-fake-news-erkennen/ (accessed 23 August 2022).

Margetts, H. (2019). Rethinking democracy with social media. *The Political Quarterly*, 90, 107–123. https://doi.org/10.1111/1467-923X.12574

McGrew, S., Breakstone, J., Ortega, T., Smith, M., & Wineburg, S. (2018). Can students evaluate online sources? Learning from assessments of civic online reasoning. *Theory & Research in Social Education*, 46(2). Retrieved from https://doi.org/10.1080/00933104.2017.1416320

Merten, L., Metoui, N., Makhortykh, M., Trilling, D., & Moeller, J. (2022). News won't find me? Exploring inequalities in social media news use with tracking data. *International Journal Of Communication*, 16(21). Retrieved from https://ijoc.org/index.php/ijoc/article/view/17068/3694 (09.06.2022)

Neuberger, C., & Quandt, T. (2010). Internet-Journalismus: Vom traditionellen Gatekeeping zum partizipativen Journalismus?. In W. Schweiger & K. Beck (Eds.), *Handbuch Online-Kommunikation*. *VS Verlag für Sozialwissenschaften*. Retrieved from https://doi.org/10.1007/978-3-531-92437-3_3

Prensky, M. (2001). Digital natives, digital immigrants part 2: Do they really think differently?. *ON the Horizon*, *9*(6), 1–6. https://doi.org/10.1108/10748120110424843

Prochazka, F. (2022). Vertrauen in Journalismus unter social-media-bedingungen. In J. Schützeneder & M. Graßl (Hrsg.), *Journalismus und Instagram: Analysen, strategien, perspektiven aus Wissenschaft und Praxis* (S. 59–75). Wiesbaden. Retrieved from https://doi.org/10.1007/978-3-658-34603-4_3

PwC. (2018). *Vertrauen in Medien.* Retrieved from www.pwc.de/de/technologie-medien-und-telekommunikation/pwc-studie-vertrauen-in-medien-2018.pdf (accessed 15 August 2022).

Rohleder, B. (2018). *Social-media-trends 2018.* Retrieved from www.bitkom.org/sites/default/files/file/import/180227-Bitkom-PK-Charts-Social-Media-Trends-2.pdf (accessed 9 June 2022)

Schweiger, W., Weber, P., Prochazka, F., & Brückner, L. (2019). *Algorithmisch personalisierte Nachrichtenkanäle: Begriffe, Nutzung, Wirkung.* Wiesbaden.

Statista. (2021). *Anteil der Nutzer von Social-Media-Plattformen nach Altersgruppen in Deutschland im Jahr 2021.* Retrieved from https://de.statista.com/statistik/daten/studie/543605/umfrage/verteilung-der-nutzer-von-social-media-plattformen-nach-altersgruppen-in-deutschland/ (accessed 24 August 2022).

Statista. (2022a). *Soziale Netzwerke.* Retrieved from https://de.Statista.com/statistik/studie/id/11852/dokument/soziale-netzwerke-Statista-dossier/ (accessed 3 August 2022).

Statista. (2022b). *Anzahl der Einwohner in Deutschland nach Generationen.* Retrieved from https://de.statista.com/statistik/daten/studie/1130193/umfrage/bevoelkerung-in-deutschland-nach-generationen/ (accessed 13 August 2022).

Sheldon, P., Anony, M. G., & Ware, L. J. (2021). *Baby Boomers* use of Facebook and *Instagram*: Uses and gratifications theory and contextual age indicators. *Heliyon*, *7*(4), 1–7. https://doi.org/10.1016/j.heliyon.2021.e06670

Statistisches Bundesamt. (2021, December 2020). *Anzahl der Einwohner in Deutschland nach Generationen am 31.* Retrieved from https://de.Statista.com/statistik/daten/studie/1130193/umfrage/bevoelkerung-in-deutschland-nach-generationen/

Venter, E. (2017). Bridging the communication gap between Generation Y and the *Baby Boomer* generation. *International Journal of Adolescence and Youth*, *22*(4), 497–507. https://doi.org/10.1080/02673843.2016.1267022

Woo-Yoo, S., & Gil-de-Zúñiga, H. (2014). Connecting blog, *Twitter*, and Facebook use with gaps in knowledge and participation. *Communication & Society*, *27*(4), 33–48. https://doi.org/10.15581/003.27.4.33-48

Ziegler, K. (2015). *Mediennutzung in der Generation 50+: Untersuchung des Umgangs von 50- bis 79-Jährigen mit den Gütern des Medienkonsums* [Diss]. Retrieved from https://ediss.sub.uni-hamburg.de/handle/ediss/6554 (accessed 5 August 2022).

Zimmermann, F., & Kohring, M. (2018). "Fake news" als Aktuelle desinformation. *M&K Medien & Kommunikationswissenschaften*, *66*(4), 526–541. https://doi.org/10.5771/1615-634X-2018-4

Zweig, K., Deussen, O., & Krafft, T. (2017). Algorithmen und Meinungsbildung. *Informatik Spektrum*, *40*, 318–326 (2017). https://doi.org/10.1007/s00287-017-1050-5

35

NARRATIVES OF BLAME AND ABSOLUTION

Framing and managing digital risks in harmful sharenting practices

Anita Lavorgna, Morena Tartari and Pamela Ugwudike

Introduction

'Sharenting'—that is, the potentially harmful sharing of identifying and sensitive information of minors who are exposed online by parents or other legal guardians—is a phenomenon that has been under-investigated from a criminological perspective. Yet, recent research (Lavorgna et al., 2022, 2023) has shown how this topic matters for criminology and similar disciplines because it has direct implications for cyber safety. Additionally, the harms that can be caused by sharenting create a behavioural puzzle: in many cases, sharenting is done with the best of intention, or at worst with (lawful) negligence (Plunkett, 2019). Yet, even when sharenting is well-intended, the sharers have a Janus-faced role. Sharenters are responsible for the information they give and share, as well as enabling those digital risks to occur.

It is important to note that the digital platforms where sharenting takes place are best understood as sociotechnical assemblages formed by both human actors and algorithm-driven nonhuman entities embedded in their users' general communicative practices (see Prochazka, 2019). As such, as discussed in detail in Lavorgna and colleagues (2022), even if users maintain their agentic capacities (Lupton & Sutherton, 2021), their ability to act is both enabled and constrained by technological and regulatory social media affordances (Gibson, 1977; Hutchby, 2001; Bloomfield et al., 2010). Affordances in this context refer to the opportunities provided by social media platforms to anyone with a compatible device (e.g., a smartphone) to broadcast their opinions, criticisms, resistance and other discursive expressions to a global audience in real time. The affordances leave space for human (individual or collective) action. We argue that understanding sharers' actions, as well as accompanying choices, stories and motivations, is vital for comprehending sharenting in its complexity, hopefully envisaging ways to prevent and mitigate its potential harms. From this perspective, it is equally important to explore the counternarratives employed by those populating the same digital fields[1] and resisting or condemning sharenting practices: being subject to the same social media affordances, why do people have different takes on sharenting and the digital risks it may pose?

This study, developed in the context of the UK ESRC-funded project *ProTechThem: Building Awareness for Safer and Technology-Savvy Sharenting*,[2] investigates this puzzle

DOI: 10.4324/9781003277675-40

with the aim of advancing current understanding of how social media users frame and manage digital risks in the context of harmful sharenting. By relying on a digital ethnography carried out on a range of social media (British and Italian) groups and focusing on users' narratives about sharenting practices, it uses Sykes and Matza's theoretical model known as 'techniques of neutralisation' (1957) to unravel how sharers justify their actions. It also explores counternarratives against sharenting. In doing so, this chapter provides new insights on the contested nature of what is or can be considered as 'deviant' or socially harmful in digital fields.

Share with care: why sharenting matters for online safety

Sharenting is becoming increasingly relevant from a social perspective; it can accompany children's lives from the very start, with ultrasound images being shared online (Leaver, 2017; Nottingham, 2019). And if asking for the minor's consent does not makes much sense with unborn or very small children, with older ones, lack of consent can be problematic, causing distress in their relationship with the sharer (Lipu & Siibak, 2019; Siibak & Traks, 2019).

In popular imagination, the sharer is generally a social media influencer parent (or 'sharent'; see Plunkett, 2019), usually the mother, with attention focusing around accounts of mumbloggers, Instamums and occasionally Instadads (Archer, 2019; Bonanomi, 2020; Campana et al., 2020). While, indeed, the sharent is often the parent and especially the mother, it is important to note that sharenting is not only limited to parents. Extended family, friends and even teachers can share personal information on social media about minors in their care (Fox & Grubbs, 2019; Lavorgna et al., 2023). Additionally, not all sharenting is linked to social media influencers using children as characters in sponsorships or other money-making opportunities. Rather, sharenting has been linked to very diverse motivations, ranging from the willingness to increase social capital and influence to manifesting parental pride, from overcoming social isolation to looking for specific forms of expertise online (Brosch, 2018; Archer, 2019; Ranzini et al., 2020; Lavorgna et al., 2023). And these motivations are troubled by ethical puzzles, with sharers often facing dilemmas and hesitations in exposing minors' information online (Chalklen & Anderson, 2017; Steinber, 2017; Buchanan et al., 2019; Cino & Formenti, 2021; Greyson et al., 2021, Cino, 2022).

Sharenting is a key aspect of digital parenting, even if—until now—most attention to digital parenting has been linked to parental mediation strategies for the use of the internet by their children and adolescents, to increase safety-protective behaviours online (Clark, 2011; Sonck et al., 2013; Uhls, 2015; Livingstone et al., 2017; Greyson et al., 2021). Meanwhile, sharers themselves feel underprepared for the role of being digital custodians, even if they seem to have some awareness of the importance of digital footprints in the context of cyber safety (Buchanan et al., 2019).

Cyber safety is generally conceptualised as the protection of people who use devices and networks; it includes a range of overlapping risks relating to privacy, personal reputation management, bullying and predation (Greyson et al., 2021). Sharenting, even in its more innocent manifestations, can have major implications for online safety.

First, shared information, by interfering with minors' interpersonal connections and personal lives and leaving a digital data trail, might lead to negative consequences that could impact both personal and professional lives in the medium and long term (Keith & Steinberg, 2017). This could affect both minors' (current and future) reputation and their sense of self, as data once shared become transformed in terms of audience, purpose and longevity (Plunkett, 2019, p. 45). And it could potentially foster dangerous forms of 'data determinism that can look suspiciously like a caste system' (Plunkett, 2019, p. 142). Studies looking at the children's perspective have already shown that, even when the sharenting is well-intended, minors are not always happy to have their information shared (Smahel et al., 2020; Garmendia et al., 2021). Although individual privacy is increasingly recognised as a fundamental human right to be protected (Gligorijevic, 2019), minors' opinion and agency on this matter, unfortunately, are not always respected in sharenting choices (Lipu & Siibak, 2019).

Similarly, beside privacy and reputation management issues, there are risks linked to the misuse of the potentially sensitive identity information shared that can hinder the possibility to have a clean and curated digital identity in the future, as the wealth of information shared about the children of today (i.e., the adults of tomorrow) could be exploited for profiling practices or contribute to an increase in digital monitoring (Barassi, 2019; Mascheroni & Holloway, 2019; Lavorgna et al., 2022, 2023). Identity is indeed at the core of citizens' interactions in our information society. Nonetheless, despite the increasing awareness that identity is sensitive and can be used for criminal and harmful activities, much focus so far has been on security and data breaches (e.g., protecting identity data from unauthorised access, which is also linked to securitisation moves; see Levi & Wall, 2004). In contrast, the willing disclosure of information has received insufficient attention.

Additionally, there can be a range of direct harm and crime risks associated with certain forms of sharenting, as minors' data can become the target of deviant or criminal activities, such as identity theft, pornography (a seemingly innocent image may be used if taken out of context), antagonistic online behaviours (which include hate speech, harassment, stalking, bullying and trolling; see Lavorgna et al., 2023) and grooming (see, for instance, Minkus et al., 2015; Ebadifar & Steinberg, 2017; Plunkett, 2019, p. 21ff; Smahel et al., 2020; Bezáková et al., 2021; Wachs et al., 2021; Williams-Ceci et al., 2021). As detailed in Lavorgna and colleagues (2023), while reliable data on actual harm or crime manifestations is currently scarce because of the paucity of reported cases, there are systemic vulnerabilities (e.g., inadequate platform regulations) in current sharenting practices suggesting that risks are a genuine concern.

Narratives in a contested field

In the study presented here, we were particularly interested in the narratives adopted by our target population (i.e. the sharers) to justify their actions, and the counternarratives used by those opposing sharenting practices. We hypothesise that this can help us untangle a puzzling dichotomy pertaining to two contrasting narratives about sharenting practices. As the literature discussed earlier suggests, on the one hand, potentially harmful sharenting practices seem to be normalised by some, mainly the sharenters, although in many digital contexts such practices may involve risk behaviours. On the other hand, however, there seems to be an increasing awareness of the existence of certain digital risks, and where these and other concerns about sharenting are amplified through both traditional and digital media, moral panics can occur (e.g., Saner, 2018, as discussed further in Ugwudike et al., 2023). From a criminological perspective, this dichotomy translates into a conundrum of interest in the context of this handbook: what is to be considered as 'non-deviant' behaviour on one hand or 'socially deviant' on the other when the same social field is occupied by contrasting narratives, or when the narrative associated with risk behaviours is the 'nor-malised' (mainstream) one which depicts such behaviours as non-deviant, regardless of the social harms it may produce?

Of course, as mentioned in the Introduction, technological and regulatory social media affordances cannot be ignored when we explore communicative and behavioural practices online. Consider, for instance, how the architecture of social media platforms is gener-ally built to facilitate information exchange among users, or how these platforms often rely on a business model that involves monetising personal information and data (Grey-son et al., 2021). These structural characteristics are a direct reflection of the power that digital platforms exert over social, economic and political life and interactions, and create systemic changes and harms (Barassi, 2019; Cohen, 2019). But social media platforms also offer a range of affordances generating affective forces, relational connections among users, and even a sense of self or of personal branding (Bucher, 2012; Kuntsman, 2012; Sauter, 2014; Davis & Chouinard, 2016; Draper & Turow, 2019; Lupton & Sutherton, 2021). As such, they create various types of 'thing-power'—i.e. the dynamic interaction across the components of assemblages, encompassing a more-then-human approach (Bennet, 2004, 2009)—a concept that helps us to conceptualise the forces at the basis of users' willingness and need to use certain social media to expose certain information online (see also Lupton, 2019). Sharing on social media, for instance, creates visibility and invites responses from other users; and often in social media, visibility is something sought after, not something considered problematic (Marwick, 2012; Lupton, 2014).

In this digital context, discourses traditionally linked to a private sphere (such as on health) have increasingly become a public experience (Conrad et al., 2016), as people embrace the opportunity to open up to others with similar experiences, for instance in dedicated forums, social media pages or groups (Joinson, 2001; Lupton, 2014; Heckscher, 2015; Tsay-Vogel et al., 2018). Additionally, we should not forget that we live in a con-text where an increasing number of people are geographically dispersed from friends and family, and digital connections are irreplaceable lines of connection for both personal and professional lives (Lupton & Sutherton, 2021). Hence, (over)sharing is often a process of negotiation between possibilities and risks: sharing fosters opportunities for intimate con-nections (Kennedy, 2018) and other benefits stemming from active online participation (Facer, 2012; boyd, 2014; Buchanan et al., 2019), but the need for disclosure is in tension with the need to withhold information. Researchers have discussed how self-monitoring or self-censoring certain content in digital fields is an integral part of the ways in which human embodiment and concepts of selfhood are represented and configured, generally in an effort to present a certain kind of desired identity while adapting to or reproducing (digital) social norms and expectations (Marwick, 2012; Goodings & Tucker, 2014; Lupton, 2014).

To better untangle these (at least apparent) contradictions, we decided to investigate social media users' accounts of their own actions, and how they construct both the world and themselves (Presser, 2009). By looking at both the breath (i.e., the amount of disclosed information) and the depth (the level of intimacy) of self-disclosed information (Wheeles & Grotz, 1976) we can obtain narrative scripts framed by users through which selfhoods emerge: by telling stories, we narrate our vision of the word and of ourselves, but also how we want others to see us. In line with the narrative criminology tradition, which in itself can be traced back to narrative psychology, to the sociological work of Goffman with regard to the view of narratives as self-presentations, to structuralism for narratives' links to the broader sociocultural context and also to the postmodernism (as discussed in Verde, 2017), we are interested in focusing on the subjectivity of the storytelling itself more than on the events (Maruna & Liem, 2021). Our aim is to investigate 'stories as instigating, sustaining or effecting desistance from harmful action' (Presser & Sandberg, 2015, p. 1). It is, however, worth repeating that we are not looking at narratives by/about offenders or victims as in most narrative criminology work, but at individuals who, in some cases, carry out potentially harmful behaviours, or refrain from committing it. We move away from tendency of the narrative criminology tradition to focus on offenders' or victims' narratives. In doing so, we add a new dimension to the field.

In this context techniques of neutralisation (that is, rationalisations people use to convince themselves that it is justifiable to transcend dominant norms of conduct, thereby vindicating themselves; see Sykes & Matza, 1957) become very important, as they play out through internal and external dialogue which evolves into the narratives observed, and influence the decision to either engage in or desist from potentially harmful action. The five techniques recognised by Sykes and Matza are: denial of responsibility, denial of injury, denial of the victim, condemnation of condemners and the appeal to higher loyalties. As we will see, in the sharenting practices we will soon discuss in this study, all these techniques are used by sharers to rationalise their actions, supporting them in the construction of coherent digital selves.

Methodology

The study presented in this chapter is based on a passive (i.e. limited to observation only) digital ethnography. Digital ethnography (Androutsopoulos, 2008; Kozinets, 2019; Gibbs & Hall, 2021), similar to traditional types of ethnography, is an immersive type of research that allows an iterative-inductive approach, which evolves and adapts in design as the study progresses, and acknowledges the researcher's own role in this process (O'Reilly, 2005; Pink et al., 2016). In our application of the method, we: observed research participants in their online conversations; annotated the material available (in our case, textual and audiovisual material) through a detailed observation grid;[3] and analysed the data thematically. Researchers using this data gathering and analysis strategy do not generally discover life-stories, but rather, stories about particular events, and at times tropes hinting at stories with narratives to be actively reconstructed (Sandberg, 2016), keeping in mind that narratives extend beyond linguistics (e.g., Copes et al., 2019; Laws, 2020).

In the context of digital ethnography, it is important to remember that ethical standards to be applied are under refinement, yet still vary across disciplines and jurisdictions (Zimmer & Kinder-Kurlanda, 2017; Lavorgna & Holt, 2021). At times, the frameworks and standards traditionally used by researchers and ethical boards are inadequate to respond to some of the challenges and possibilities of online research (e.g., Lavorgna & Sugiura, 2022a, 2022b). In our study, data were manually collected online only in public digital fields (e.g., on open Facebook groups and pages, but not from private groups). The data were anonymised at the moment of data collection and only research notes were taken if socially sensitive information was discussed. When quotes are reported in this chapter, they have been slightly modified to make them not directly retrievable by a simple browser search (as approved by the Ethics Committee of the University of Southampton, Faculty of Social Sciences).

Of course, it would be impossible to explore all of cyberspace for sharenting practices. We purposively sampled a range of openly accessible social media pages and groups through some preliminary exploratory searches, and through discussions with project partners and members of our advisory board,[4] aiming for maximum variation strategy in terms of sharenting cases, while looking for comparable groups and pages with discussions both in English and in Italian (as the *ProTechThem* project has built in a comparative element). In this stage of the project, the digital ethnography was carried out on Facebook, starting from more recent posts and comments and going forward and then, after data saturation was reached, going back until data saturation was reached again (generally the observation lasted for three months for each group depending on the group or page, as most posts displayed the same characteristics; additionally, older posts and discussion specific about sharenting practices were retrieved through the search option available on each group or page, going back up to 2013). Despite the frequent criticisms of some of its practices (see, for instance, Bright et al., 2019), Facebook remains the most used social media platform globally because of a combination of affective forces, relational connections and agential capacities (Lupton & Sutherton, 2021). The platform also offers ethically accessible fields for digital ethnography and is mostly populated by users 'old enough' to be parents or legal guardians (Statista, 2022). Table 35.1 summarises our selection.

Contested practices in uncontested fields

While parents were present and active in all the Facebook groups and pages observed, sharing different types of their children's information depending on the scope of the group or page, it is first important to note that discussions about sharenting, or sharing sensitive information, were never a primary aim of/in the fields analysed. For this analysis we did not consider social media influencers' online activities, where sharing children's pictures or information might be at the core of their digital presence, as we were instead interested in the framing and managing of more disengaged sharenting practices, done by common users

Table 35.1 The digital fields for the ethnography

Group topic	Sub-topics/Notes	Users (number)	Country of reference
Parenting (general)	Parenting in general	3.8K	Italy
	Motherhood and beyond. Page associated to digital forum community	230K	UK/other EN-speaking countries
Children's health and wellbeing	Sleep and health issues	2.5K	Italy
		284K	UK/US
	ADHD	5K	Italy
		15K	UK
	Special needs	37.9K	Italy
		46.7K	UK
Legal issues	Requests for legal advice mostly on management of children custody/ children custody litigations	2.2K	Italy
	Requests for legal advice/ representation mostly on management of children custody/ children custody litigations	1.7K	UK

with no specific digital managing skills. We wanted to observe how forms of potentially harmful sharenting were used in their digital narratives (for instance, when presenting stories about themselves, their children, their families) and, whenever possible, what narratives and counternarratives they relied on when explicitly discussing online their own sharenting practices, as these narratives influence patterns and trajectories of digital behaviours, and offer insights on digital risk management. As such, in the ethnography information relevant for our analysis was relatively scarce and dispersed, often clustering around specific posts and rebuttals, with narratives to be carefully reconstructed. In this exercise, specific attention was given to the presence of techniques of neutralisation as they emerged in our analysis.

For a detailed analysis of how online and offline parenting cultures affect sharenting practices (including how parents negotiate their own and their children's needs in online communities even in terms of digital security) and how the consequences of sharenting are addressed in online communities, we refer the reader to Lavorgna & colleagues, 2023; Tartari & colleagues, 2023. In the remaining part of this chapter, we focus on the narratives adopted by the sharers and the counternarratives used by those opposing sharenting practices—when counternarratives were present—in the same digital fields, presenting them per group topic.

Parenting (general)

The generalist groups and pages on parenting, explicitly targeting mothers, offered frequent types of potentially harmful sharenting practices (mostly photos, some information on mental or physical health and a broad range of intimate information regarding minors presented as part of personal stories shared by mothers or occasionally grandmothers). More importantly for the scope of this work, these groups offered some animated discussions among users focusing specifically on sharenting and its harmful potential, prompted (especially in the English-speaking group) by articles posted by the group administrators.

Indeed, many forms of sharenting were normalised, or at least well tolerated, in the groups observed, as an inherent part of their practices. However, when the topic was explicitly discussed, a fracture of divergent imaginaries of digital risks emerged. Also, sharenting practices (or the lack of) were explicitly debated (please note: in the discussions the focus was only on the sharing of pictures), showing users' lines of reasoning behind the negotiation between possibilities and risks.

We could identify different attitudes emerging from the narratives and counternarratives, which allowed us to conceptualise users as (1) uninhibited sharers, (2) moderate sharers and (3) non-sharers.

Uninhibited sharers

The uninhibited sharers unapologetically share pictures of their own children and occasionally also of other children, as they consider the practice safe (*'If the photo is taken in a public space, it is ok to share, even if other people children are in it'*; *'I am going to do what I want, whether legal or not, because it is safe'*), in line with the 'denial of injury' appeal. Their sharenting practices are at times described as linked to the need to maintain relational and affective connections with those geographically distant (*'I have family and friends living far away, it's a way of keeping in contact'*; *'I want to keep my family in the loop, they live several thousand miles away*'), but in most cases the sharers recognise how their sharenting is merely linked to their desire to build a sense of self online, confirming how visibility (for themselves and their families) is something sought after by them ('*What is the meaning of life if you cannot boast about your children online? [smile]*'; '*I want everyone to see how beautiful my daughter is [laughing face]*'; '*My baby is simply too cute [blinking face]*'; '*As a parent I am just too proud of my son, I cannot contain myself and posted thousands of pictures of him on various social media sites*'; '*I am a stay at home and single mum, my children are a huge part of my life and if I do not post about them I would have hardly anything to post!*'). Both 'absolving' rationalisations are aligned with the 'appeal to higher loyalties' and 'denying the (potential) victim' techniques.

Smiles and humour are often used to reinforce uninhibited sharers' claims, and their lighthearted approach to (over)sharing their children's information ('*My daughter will sue me when she becomes a teen [smile]*'; '*My children will have no privacy until they start paying me rent [winkie smile]*'). Digital risks are ridiculed ('*It is a risk you need to live with as you see fit, personally I am happy to live with it [smile]*') or minimised as irrational fears ('*We should not have to live fearing that the wrong people will access pictures*').

The uninhibited sharers active in the conversation are often dismissive of the concerns raised by others ('*Boring, yawn*'), and lament the 'negativity' these cause, 'condemning the condemners' ('*You should try to be positive, if you do not want to share there is no need to write a long comment about that*'; '*You must have too much time to waste to find time to be so negative online*'; '*I think I will unfollow this page, too much negativity and making you question something you happily do as a parent. This is not supporting and does not make you feel good about your mothering skills! [Thumbs down]*'). As parents, they stress their agency in the matter ('*Hopefully parents know what type of pictures to take and post*'; '*It is the parents' choice*'), and do not like to feel judged about their choice ('*People should just mind their own business*').

Their sharenting practices are normalised in line with the 'denial of responsibility' technique ('*It is normal to share some pictures of your child online*'; '*It is unreasonable to ask people not to take and share pictures at large gatherings*'), while those opposing their views are ignored or attacked ('*This is being paranoid*'; '*These comments are ridiculous and funny [laughing face], you are a bunch of snowflakes, if I take a picture I own the copyright and do what I want with it. You are pathetic [laughing face]*', '*I cannot stand those parents who stop pictures being taken during plays. It is pathetic, get over yourself!*').

Moderate sharers

The moderate sharers best reflect the sharers' descriptions we could find in the recent literature describing the dilemmas and hesitations sharers face in exposing minors' information online (as mentioned previously in the literature review; see Chalklen & Anderson, 2017; Buchanan et al., 2019; Greyson et al., 2021; Cino, 2022 among others). Moderate sharers tend to use some precautions to mitigate digital risks ('*as an adult, I have to try and protect the children*'): for instance they do post '*occasional pictures*' but friend online only people they personally know, and try to keep their profile private; or they use '*another app, accessible by invitation only, to share pictures within the family*'. They avoid posting '*embarrassing stuff [their] children would not be happy to see online when they grow older*', '*close-ups, or half-naked pictures*', or pictures of their children when they '*look poorly or are ill*'. Some '*use nicknames rather than their [children's] unusual and therefore easy to find names*' when posting about them, or '*obscure the logo of the school uniform so no one can look up where [the child] is*'. Those with pre-teens and teens might ask their children permission to post their pictures.

Overall, they tend to agree that it is necessary to ask other parents' permission before posting pictures of their children online. One moderate sharer discussed how a child of one of her friends was groomed online (and thankfully stopped), and in later posts she became very assertive in responding to one of the uninhibited sharers ('*It is not like keeping children inside all the time to protect them, you do not go around naked. The danger is when people post hundreds of pictures of their children naked, making them vulnerable to paedophiles, it is sickening*').

Using techniques of neutralisation as absolving rationalisations is not common practice among this group, which is more concerned with mitigating risk. Instead, they emphasise that their sharing practices are non-harmful and blame the uninhibited sharers for their risky practices. However, some moderate sharers who seem to be influenced by how they perceive social desirability in the digital space rather than by considerations of digital risks when deciding to limit their posting did use techniques of neutralisation, e.g., denial of potential harm by minimising of ignoring risks (e.g., '*I am not scared but I limit the number of pictures I post as I think other people are not that interested in my children*'), or when complaining about other people posting pictures without asking permission first (one user, for instance, complained that she '*would never forget*' a relative for announcing the birth of her son before she did it online—hence the focus is on the parent's management of her (family) social media identity, not on the potential risks posed to the digital identity of her son himself).

Non-sharers

Finally, the non-sharers offered a range of counternarratives opposing the normalisation of potentially harmful sharenting practices observed in the groups. Importantly, these counternarratives were not found commenting directly other users' sharenting practices, but non-sharers were vocal in presenting their opinions in posts prompting specifically discussions on sharenting, and their comments had a role in raising awareness towards other users ('*I will be more mindful in the future about what and how to share*'). Their counternarratives pivot around issues of horizontal privacy ('*Children should be entitled to privacy online*'; '*I would not be happy to have pictures of when I was a baby online, so I am not posting those of my child*'), vertical privacy towards social media companies ('*I do not trust social media companies, might use the picture in the future*'; '*I do not want my pictures to become property of Facebook*'), and other forms of digital risk, at times including comments blaming the sharers ('*I hate sharing as you do not know who is out there*'; '*I feel the risks outweigh the benefits*'; '*You make your child a target, and that is unnecessary*'; '*There might be children at risk, someone might not want to be found*').

Some are possibilistic regarding sharing some images of their children ('*I might post some pictures when my children are old enough to decide*'), but overall they feel '*nervous about posting pictures of [their] children*' because of unspecified digital risks ('*My son is an IT expert, he asked me to never post pictures of my grandson, our address or where his day-care is, and I trust his instructions*') or, more generally, because of children's right to privacy ('*Children have a right to privacy, especially the younger ones who cannot make informed decisions*'). Not surprisingly, they do not accept having pictures of their children posted by '*careless*' others ('*If someone posts a picture of my child, I will ask them to take it down*'; '*How can you think it is ok to put online pictures of other people children?*'; '*This is so selfish, it is a matter of common decency*'). Interestingly, in one case a non-sharer tried to enforce her counternarrative by claiming that she easily downloaded some children's pictures that were posted in the group (to prove the point that everyone could do that, as there were no reliable security settings in place), and she was immediately attacked as a '*freak*' and '*weirdo*' and asked to immediately remove the pictures from her devices (in another instance of 'condemning the condemner').

Children's health and wellbeing

In the groups analysed under this label, we could observe three main dimensions of potentially harmful sharenting. A first one, image-based, was to be found in the standard practice of sharing pictures of children, especially small babies, in posts (to retrieve them/for pride) or in comments (for pride); here, the main issue was linked to the nudity present in some images. A second dimension, potentially posing a broader set of risks, was observed when pictures, videos or posts were shared to show or describe a potential illness, a behaviour or a routine (e.g., how they have a bath): here, alongside issues of nudity, there were at times descriptions of long-term health issues and treatments, mental conditions and several intimate aspects. Finally, a third dimension was linked to users with an online presence specifically dedicated to discussing their children's health (as they have a physical or mental disability), where alongside detailed information on diagnoses and treatments, the impact of the disability on the whole family and relations and conflicts with institutions are specifically discussed. In this latter case, the sharing of information was mostly linked to raising awareness on a specific issue and/or creating a community of support to others (similarly to the cause-based communities analysed in the context of commercial sharenting by Plunkett, 2019).

Also in these groups and pages, even if children's identifying information where not explicitly mentioned (in the first two manifestations as discussed earlier, and in the third manifestation identifying details are generally explicitly present), it would have been often easy to retrieve them as many sharers' profiles were open and/or publicly displaying information that could become sensitive especially once triangulated (place of living, work contact details, etc.).

When a formal netiquette was publicised in the group, it was about promoting in-group kindness (probably necessary as there were at times heated debates on issues such as sleep training or safety guidelines) or to remind that medical advice should not be sought, while explicit rules or suggestions on the sharing of potentially sensitive information were never explicitly discussed by the administrators/moderators of the group (with the exception of one Italian group, run by a psychologist and presenting a note on the fact that '*mutual trust*' was needed to be in the group, and that '*shared information should be treated with confidence and respect*'). Nonetheless, it was possible to retrieve some discussions directly relevant to the scope of this work, prompted in two cases (in English-speaking groups) by post of users lamenting the fact that a post with picture was shared outside the group (something enabled by the public setting of the group, while the private settings of the re-sharer made their identification impossible), or by the fact that comments to a post asking other users to share pictures were at a certain point closed.

Overall, also in these groups and pages sharenting was normalised, with users minimising the re-sharing of pictures, even if the practice was considered '*creepy*' ('*maybe I'm just being paranoid?'*), praising the fact that the moderation of the group was not restrictive on the material posted (*'I like that our posts do not have to be approved or denied'*) or even mocking the few stressing potential risks (*'someone might find sharing a picture of a child dangerous . . . but in any case here is a picture of my little one!'*). Again, a range of neutralisation techniques (e.g., 'denial of injury/of the victim') could be identified.

The very few comments presenting counternarratives, for instance advising the other users to be *'safe and smart'* and avoid posting nude photos, or stressing that the group was open and in any case had thousands of members, were marginalised (with generally fewer than 10 likes each, and only a couple of replies in total seconding them in total). A couple of users asked about the possibility to make at least the group private *'to safeguard the children'*, other two stressed that making a group private was not sufficient as screenshots could be taken (*'if you do not want pictures of your children shared online, do not share them in the first place'*, hence blaming the sharers), another three emphasised that they never posted children's faces or always blanked them out when posting pictures in the group as they do not trust *'weirdos or companies'*. Only one user admitted she never thought that sharenting could be harmful before the counternarrative comments, and one reacted by saying that she was taking her daughter's pictures down from the group. In one case, the administrator and founder of a group intervened, stressing (before turning off the comments) that it is a user's decision what to post, that she could not do anything about re-sharing and advising users to use stock image pictures if pictures are used to make a post more easily findable.

In an additional case (an Italian-speaking group), a post shared from another group and reflecting on the opportunity/importance of sharing information of minors with health conditions was published, without receiving attention from group members. To us, this was an important post as it was the only one reflecting on the third manifestation of sharenting as discussed earlier. The sharenting choice was presented as a *'dilemma'*, with the author of the post concluding that children, especially those with a mental disability, could not provide an informed consensus in any case, and that the sharing of certain stories is necessary to enable social changes, giving large-scale visibility to certain *'struggles'*. However, he also admitted that he reflected whether he disclosed too much about his daughter (with disabilities) and his family, and that *ex post* he modified and deleted some posts to remove some details.

Legal issues

In the groups analysed, minors' information (including personal judicial information) was mostly shared to get legal advice (e.g., in children custody litigations), or to lament institutional malfunctioning (especially in cases where users lamented forms of emotional abuse or referred to the contested and disproven concept of 'parental alienation'[5]). To us, this group was particularly interesting as the posts and comments encountered in the course of the ethnography provided examples of a 'less obvious' yet high-risk type of sharenting, with the publication of sensitive information by both people posting and by those commenting, often providing details of personal life histories, or even pictures of relevant legal documents; in some cases, links to local news articles narrating their stories were posted. Even if the name or location of the minors involved were generally obscured, it was often very easy to trace back this information as many sharers had accessible social media profiles, where they often also displayed pictures of the minors involved.

Sharenting was discussed explicitly only once, in an old post published in the Italian group back in 2013, with one user sharing the link of a media article focusing on harmful sharenting and stressing that it might contain important information for those '*a bit care-less in posting pictures and other information*'—the only post suggesting the presence of a counternarrative in the groups observed dealing with legal issues. The post received limited attention, with only a couple of users commenting and rejecting the alert raised on the basis that there would not be a physical risk for children, as '*it would not be easy for paedophile to get close to them*' and certain articles are '*written to scare people*'. Interestingly, shar-enting harms were only recognised with reference to the potential sexual exploitation of children, and non-physical harms were minimised.

Regardless of the sensitive information shared, there was an apparent consensus in the groups observed on the perceived appropriateness of their sharenting behaviours, seen as something necessary in their attempt '*to seek justice*'. As such, in this case a range of neu-tralisation techniques (namely, 'denial of injury'; 'appeal to higher loyalties') could also be identified as key dimensions framing the narratives of absolution observed. Certain posts lamented that, offline, the children were put through the fire, for instance with a user com-plaining that her partner shared with their children details of their divorce, impacting them psychologically and violating court requirements. Online, however, personal and highly conflictual stories about the users themselves or their beloved ones (e.g., the conflictual separation of a nephew) are constantly shared, with no consideration of the fact that other relatives or acquaintances, or the minors themselves, might read them sooner or later. When another user asked for advice on whether sharing online her story and the behaviours of her partner by copy-pasting parts of her divorce petition, would cause legal problems, only one user advised her not to do so on the basis that this could be used against her in a legal proceeding. As such, the risks recognised are those affecting the sharers themselves, while digital harms suffered by the minors go unrecognised ('denial of injury/of the victim').

Further discussion and conclusion

In this chapter we have investigated narratives and counternarratives on forms of poten-tially harmful sharenting practices that were presented by users populating the same digital fields. As such, we explored how forms of 'less obvious' digital risks are framed and man-aged by social media users. This entailed adopting a narrative criminology approach that transcends issues of crime and criminal justice to focus on social harms (Presser, 2018), in line with narrative research taking place in other fields (Maruna & Liem, 2021, p. 143).

We have presented our ethnographic observations by organising the analysis around the topic at the core of the digital fields shared by our population of interest. In doing so, we were able to identify different types of users depending on their sharenting attitudes (uninhibited sharers, moderate sharers and non-sharers), and to observe different dimen-sions of potentially harmful sharenting, posing different sets of digital risks (sharing of images and occasional private information; sharing of information on health issues and treatments, mental conditions, financial issues and other intimate details related to the chil-dren or their family. Additional digital risks observed were sharing detailed information on diagnoses, treatments, legal disputes, relations and conflicts with institutions and their impact on the children and their family). According to Brosch (2018)'s model of sharent-ing, we focused in detail only on one of its four elements—that is the content of posted information, highlighting the narratives of absolution (denoting the techniques of neutralisation used especially by uninhibited sharers to rationalise their actions) and the rarer narratives of blame (directed at the uninhibited sharers) that were neglected by the existing studies on the topic, who mostly stressed the risk mitigation strategies and the dilemmas faced by moderate sharers. While we have not analysed in detail the elements of amount and frequency as identified by Brosch, we can note that (over)sharenting was customary in all the groups observed; moreover, it is worth noting that amount and frequency might have an effect on the normalisation of certain sharenting practices in the fields observed, but harmful sharenting can manifest itself also with one single post (consider, for instance, a single detailed post in an open group detailing very sensitive health or legal information). The fourth element identified by Brosch (2018) is the audience. In this regard, it is worth emphasising once more that we focused only on open groups for ethical reasons, but it is likely that potentially harmful sharenting is further exacerbated in closed groups (even if with thousands of users).

If we look at the various sharenting practices observed, we can notice how they originate from a series of individual needs, which in turn are related to the kind of selves that are digitally presented and the techniques of neutralisation adopted by the sharers. Beyond the use of the traditional techniques of neutralisation, a sixth technique enabled by digital affordances could be observed: the creation and management of a digital desired self, this being the image of a lighthearted, a devoted-but-separated, or a careful parent. This technique was manifesting itself for instance in the use of humour and ridicule, or in the search for social desirability online, through impression management (Goffman, 1959).[6] Overall, all these techniques were used by sharers to rationalise their actions and absolve themselves from blame, concurring with the construction of a coherent self even when this meant clinging to narratives that could motivate and sustain harm (Fleetwood, 2016).

Of course, by relying on a theoretical construct (that of neutralisation techniques) developed for the study of crime and deviance, there is no implication that even harmful forms of sharenting should be acritically considered socially deviant. Yet, theories of deviance can help us to provide important insights on the contested nature of what is or can be considered as 'deviant' in digital fields: as potentially harmful behaviour are prevalent in certain social groups, it is difficult to classify them as 'against the norm' (as discussed also in Lavorgna, 2021). This prevalence, however, could be difficult to assess and be less clear-cut than generally assumed. We have seen how, coexisting in the same digital fields, there are certain practices that are at first sight accepted, normalised or even encouraged; the digital risks relating to (over)sharenting were in this respect neglected, ignored or even ridiculed. However, we have also noted the presence of a (generally) silent userbase that, especially when the chance is explicitly given, presents counternarratives detailing the how and the why of their different sharenting choices. Here digital risks are recognised and potentially amplified, creating a very different sociotechnical imaginary where our digital fields of interest are also populated by dangers. Hence, even in apparently uncontested fields where there is an apparent consensus towards practices that can be harmful (for online safety, in our case) the presence of counternarratives—if they are given a chance to emerge—challenge the idea that we can assume in-group cohesiveness, as these counternarratives become forms of narrative resistance that could be used to oppose (potential) harm (Presser & Sandberg, 2019; Sandberg & Andersen, 2019).

While narratives at the meso-level are generally used to understand the shaping of group identities (Loseke, 2007; Copes et al., 2019), we highlight the importance not to neglect the micro-level also within group dynamics, nor to lose precious in-group dynamics. We believe this point has significant implications in the study of online communities and, for what concerns more traditional criminological endeavours in the study of deviant subcultures online, reminding us that those are not monolithic groups. Additionally, this point suggests the key role of social media administrators and moderators in allowing counternarratives to emerge, defusing techniques of neutralisation and minimising risks, and creating opportunities to raise awareness about digital safety—something that should be explored by future research.

Notes

1 In line with Bordieu (1993), fields can be seen as structured spaces in which agents and their social positions are located.
2 www.protechthem.org/
3 The observation grid focuses on practices and discourses on sharenting by parents, guardians, pages and groups' administrators and moderators, and other users of the same community/group (including reactions). The grid collects data on the sharer's characteristics (e.g., gender, ethnicity, age, social status), explicit sharer's motivations, any relevant information on the child/children who are the 'object' of sharenting, characteristics of the photos, videos, texts which are shared, type of activities or issues addressed by the post, type of sharenting, any additional violation, type of audience, any additional sharenting practice by someone else in the same thread in response, comments on sharenting practices by users and moderators, relevant interactions between users on the platform, sharenting jargon, information about the social context which frames a specific post, sharenters' activities, any relevant group dynamics on the sharenting topic and explicit rules of the community/group about sharenting.
4 See www.protechthem.org/people/
5 Parental alienation can occur in conflictual separations of parents and refers to psychological manipulation of a child by saying and doing things that lead the child to look unfavourably on one of the parents and reject the bond with him or her. It was defined as a syndrome by the psychiatrist Richard Gardner in 1987. It has been considered a controversial diagnostic category since its creation. In Italy, recently the Civil Cassation Court sec. I—24/03/2022, n. 9691 with order on appeal 21633/2021—definitively declared the application of the parental alienation syndrome (PAS) illegitimate in proceedings concerning the exercise of parental responsibility.
6 As stressed by Laws (2020), traditionally in Criminology notions of the self have been rarely explored or defined: at the core of narrative analyses we generally find 'the reflexive self' (the person *we think* we are); followed by 'the unconscious self' (suggesting that our selfhood is also shaped by less-than-rational forces); and 'the experiencing self' (the in-the-moment or transcendental feeling of being alive, whose immediacy typically preceded narrative expression). Here, a 'digital self' is rather observable, carefully or inattentively crafting itself while presenting a selection of stories, tropes and visual elements.

References

Androutsopoulos, J. (2008). Potential and limitations of discourse-centred online ethnography. *Language@Internet*, 5.

Archer, C. (2019). How influencer 'mumpreneur' bloggers and 'everyday' mums frame presenting their children online. *Media International Australia*, 170(1), 47–56.

Barassi, V. (2019). Datafied citizens in the age of coerced digital participation. *Sociological Research Online*, 24(3), 414–429.

Bennett, J. (2004). The force of things: Steps toward an ecology of matter. *Political Theory*, 32(3), 347–372.

Bennett, J. (2009). *Vibrant matter: A political ecology of things*. Duke University Press.

Bezáková, Z., Madleňák, A., & Švec, M. (2021). Security risks of sharing content based on minors by their family members on social media in times of technology interference. *Media Literacy and Academic Research*, 4, 53–69.

Bloomfield, B. P., Latham, V., & Vurdubakis, T. (2010). Bodies, technologies and action possibilities: When is an affordance? *Sociology, 44*(3), 415–433.

Bonanomi, G. (2020). *Sharenting. Genitori e rischi della sovrapposizione dei figli online.* Mondadori.

boyd, D. (2014). *It's complicated: The social lives of networked teens.* Yale University Press.

Bright, L. F., Wilcox, G. B., & Rodriguez, H. (2019). #DeleteFacebook and the consumer backlash of 2018: How social media fatigue, consumer (Mis)Trust and privacy concerns shape the new social media reality for consumers. *Journal of Digital & Social Media Marketing, 7*(2), 177–188.

Brosch, A. (2018). Sharenting: Why do parents violate their children's privacy? *The New Educational Review, 54*(4), 75–85.

Buchanan, R., Southgate, E., & Smith, S. P. (2019). 'The whole world's watching really': Parental and educator perspectives on managing children's digital lives. *Global Studies of Childhood, 9*(2), 167–180.

Bucher, T. (2012). Want to be on the top? Algorithmic power and the threat of invisibility on Facebook. *New Media & Society, 14*(7), 1164–1180.

Campana, M., Van den Bossche A., & Miller, B. (2020). #dadtribe: Performing sharenting labour to commercialise involved fatherhood. *Journal of Macromarketing, 40*(4), 475–491.

Chalklen, C., & Anderson, H. (2017). Mothering on Facebook: Exploring the privacy/openness paradox. *Social Media + Society.* https://doi.org/10.1177/2056305117707187.

Cino, D. (2022). Beyond the surface: Sharenting as a source of family quandaries: Mapping parents' social media dilemmas. *Western Journal of Communication, 86*(1), 128–153.

Cino, D., & Formenti, L. (2021). To share or not to share? That is the (social media) dilemma. Expectant mothers questioning and making sense of performing pregnancy on social media. *Convergence, 27*(2), 491–507.

Clark, L. (2011). Parental mediation theory for the digital age. *Communication Theory, 21,* 323–343.

Cohen, J. E. (2019). *Between truth and power. The legal constructions of information capitalism.* Oxford University Press.

Conrad, P., Bandini, J., & Vasquez, A. (2016). Illness and the internet: From private to public experience. *Health, 20*(1), 22–32.

Copes, H., Hochstetler, A., & Ragland, J. (2019). The stories in the images; The value of the visual for narrative criminology. In J. Fleetwood, L. Presser, S. Sandberg, & T. Uggelvik (Eds.), *The Emerald handbook of narrative criminology.* Emerald.

Davis, J. L., & Chouinard J. B. (2016). Theorizing affordances: From request to refuse. *Bulletin of Science, Technology & Society, 36*(4), 241–248.

Draper, N. A., & Turow, J. (2019). The corporate cultivation of digital resignation. *New Media & Society, 21*(8), 1824–1839.

Ebadifar, K. B., & Steinberg, S. (2017). Parental sharing on the Internet child privacy in the age of social media and the pediatrician's role. *JAMA Pediatrics, 171*(5), 413–414.

Facer, K. (2012). After the moral panic? Reframing the debate about child safety online. *Discourse, 33*(3), 397–413.

Fleetwood, J. (2016). Narrative habitus: Thinking through structure/agency in the narratives of offenders. *Crime, Media, Culture, 12*(2), 173–192.

Fox, A., & Grubbs, M. (2019). Smart devices, smart decisions? Implications of parents' sharenting for children's online privacy: An investigation of mothers. *Journal of Public Policy & Marketing, 38*(4), 414–432.

Garmendia, M., Martínez, G., & Garitaonandia, C. (2021). Sharenting, parental mediation and privacy among Spanish children. *European Journal of Communication.* https://doi.org/10.1177/02673231211012146.

Gibbs, N., & Hall, A. (2021). Digital ethnography in cybercrime research: Some notes from the virtual field. In A. Lavorgna & T. J. Holt (Eds.), *Researching cybercrimes: Methodologies, ethics and critical approaches* (pp. 283–299). Palgrave MacMillan.

Gibson, J. (1977). The theory of affordances. In R. Shaw & J. Bransford (Eds.), *Perceiving, acting, and knowing: Toward an ecological psychology* (pp. 67–82). Erlbaum.

Gligorijevic, J. (2019). Children's privacy: The role of parental control and consent. *Human Rights Law Review, 19,* 201–229.

Goffman, E. (1959). *The presentation of the self in everyday life.* Anchor.

Goodings, L., & Tucker, I. (2014). Social media and the co-production of bodies online: Bergson, Serres and Facebook's timeline. *Media, Culture & Society*, 36(1), 37–51.

Greyson, D., Chabot, C., Mniszak, C., & Shoveller, J. A. (2021). Social media and online safety practices of young parents. *Journal of Information Science*. https://doi.org/10.1177/01655515211053808.

Heckscher, C. (2015). *Trust in a complex world. Enriching community*. Oxford University Press.

Hutchby, I. (2001). Technologies, texts and affordances. *Sociology*, 35(2), 441–456.

Joinson, A. N. (2001). Self-disclosure in computer-mediated communication: The role of self-awareness and visual anonymity. *European Journal of Social Psychology*, 31, 177–192.

Keith, B. E., & Steinberg, S. (2017). Parental sharing on the Internet. *JAMA Pediatrics*, 171(5), 413.

Kennedy, J. (2018). Oversharing is the norm. In A. S. Dobson, B. Robards, & N. Carah (Eds.), *Digital intimate publics and social media* (p. 265–280). Springer.

Kozinets, R. V. (2019). *Netnography: The essential guide to qualitative social media research*. Sage.

Kuntsman, A. (2012). Introduction: Affective fabrics of digital cultures. In A. Karatzogianni & A. Kuntsman (Eds.), *Digital cultures and the politics of emotion: Feelings, affect and technological change* (pp. 1–17). Palgrave.

Lavorgna, A. (2021). *Information pollution as social harm: Investigating the digital drift of medical misinformation in a time of crisis*. Emerald Group Publishing.

Lavorgna, A., & Holt, T. J. (Eds.). (2021). *Researching cybercrimes: Methodologies, ethics and critical approaches*. Palgrave.

Lavorgna, A., & Sugiura, L. (2022a). Direct contacts with potential interviewees when carrying out online ethnography on controversial and polarized topics: A loophole in ethics guidelines. *International Journal of Social Research Methodology*, 25(2), 261–267.

Lavorgna, A., & Sugiura, L. (2022b). Blurring boundaries: Negotiating researchers' positionality and identities in digital qualitative research. *Italian Sociological Review*, 12(7S), 709–727.

Lavorgna, A., Tartari, M., & Ugwudike, P. (2022). Criminogenic features of social media platforms: The case of harmful sharenting practices. *European Journal of Criminology*, https://doi.org/10.1177/14773708221131659.

Lavorgna, A., Ugwudike, P., & Tartari, M. (2023). Online sharenting: Identifying existing vulnerabilities and demystifying media reported crime risks. *Crime, Media, Culture*, 19(4), 472–490.

Laws, B. (2020). Reimaging 'the Self' in Criminology: Transcendence, unconscious states and the limits of narrative criminology. *Theoretical Criminology*, https://doi.org/10.1177/1362480620919102

Leaver, T. (2017). Intimate surveillance: Normalizing parental monitoring and mediation of infants online. *Social Media+Society*, 3(2), 707192.

Levi, M., & Wall, D. (2004). Technologies, security & privacy in the post-9/11 European information society. *Journal of Law & Society*, 31(2), 194–220.

Lipu, M., & Siibak, A. (2019). 'Take it down!': Estonian parents' and pre-teens' opinions and experiences with sharenting. *Media International Australia*, 170(1), 57–67.

Livingstone, S., Ólafsson, K., Helsper, E. J., et al. (2017). Maximizing opportunities and minimizing risks for children online: The role of digital skills in emerging strategies of parental mediation. *Journal of Communication*, 67(1), 82–105.

Loseke, D. R. (2007). The study of identity as cultural, institutional, organizational and personal narratives: Theoretical and empirical integrations. *The Sociological Quarterly*, 48(4), 661–668.

Lupton, D. (2019). The thing-power of the human-app health assemblage: Thinking with vital materialism. *Social Theory & Health*, 17(2), 125–139.

Lupton, D., & Sutherton, C. (2021). The thing-power of the Facebook assemblage: Why do users stay on the platform? *Journal of Sociology*, 57(4), 969–985.

Lupton, S. (2014). *Digital sociology*. Routledge.

Maruna, S., & Liem, M. (2021). Where is this story going? A critical analysis of the emerging field of narrative criminology. *Annual Review of Criminology*, 4(1), 125–146.

Marwick, A. (2012). The public domain: Social surveillance in everyday life. *Surveillance & Society*, 9(4), 378–393.

Mascheroni, G., & Holloway, D. (2019). The quantified child: Discourses and practices of dataveillance in different life stages. In O. Erstad, R. Flewitt, B. Kümmerling-Meibauer, et al. (Eds.), *The Routledge handbook of digital literacies in early childhood* (pp. 354–365). Routledge.

Minkus, T., Kelvin, L., & Ross, K. W. (2015). Children seen but not heard: When parents compromise children's online privacy. In *Proceedings of the 24th international conference on World Wide Web*. ACM.

Nottingham, E. (2019). 'Dad! Cut that part out!' Children's rights to privacy in the age of 'generation tagged': Sharenting, digital kidnapping and the child micro-celebrity. In J. Murray, B. Swadener, & K. Smith (Eds.), *International handbook of young children's rights*. Routledge.

O'Reilly, K. (2005). *Ethnographic methods*. Routledge.

Pink, S., Horst, H., Postill, J., Hjorth, L., Lewis, T., & Tacchi, J. (2016). *Digital ethnography: Principles and practice*. Sage.

Plunkett, L. A. (2019). *Sharenthood. Why we should think before we talk about our kids online*. MIT Press.

Presser, L. (2009). The narratives of offenders. *Theoretical Criminology, 13*(2), 177–200.

Presser, L. (2018). *Inside Story: How Narratives Drive Mass Harm*. Berkeley: Univ. Calif. Press.

Presser, L., & Sandberg, S. (2015). Introduction: What is the story? In L. Presser & S. S. Sandberg (Eds.), *Narrative criminology: Understanding the stories of crime*. New York University Press.

Presser, L., & Sandberg, S. (2019). Narrative criminology as critical criminology. *Critical Crimininology, 27*, 131–143.

Prochazka, O. (2019). Making sense of Facebook's content moderation: A posthumanist perspective on communicative competence and internet memes. *Signs and Society, 7*(3), 362–397.

Ranzini, G., Newlands, G., & Lutz, C. (2020). Sharenting, peer influence, and privacy concerns: A study on the instagram-sharing behaviors of parents in the United Kingdom. *Social Media + Society*. https://doi.org/10.1177/2056305120978376.

Sandberg, S. (2016). The importance of stories untold: Life-story, event-story and trope. *Crime, Media, Culture, 12*(2), 153–171.

Sandberg, S., & Andersen, J. C. (2019). Opposing violent extremism through counternarratives: Four forms of narrative resistance. In J. Fleetwood, L. Presser, S. Sandberg, & T. Uggelvik (Eds.), *The Emerald handbook of narrative criminology*. Emerald.

Saner, E. (2018). The 'sharent' trap—Should you ever put your children on social media?, *The Guardian*. Retrieved from www.theguardian.com/lifeandstyle/2018/may/24/sharent-trap-should-parents-put-their-children-on-social-media-instagram

Sauter, T. (2014). 'What's on your mind?' Writing on Facebook as a tool for self-formation. *New Media & Society, 16*(5), 823–839.

Siibak, A., & Traks, K. (2019). The dark sides of sharenting. *Catalan Journal of Communication & Cultural Studies, 11*(1), 115–121.

Smahel, D., Machackova, H., Mascheroni, G., et al., with with Members of the EU Kids Online Network. (2020). EU kids online 2020: Survey results from 19 countries. *EU Kids Online*. Retrieved from www.eukidsonline.net/.

Sonck, N., Nikken, P., & de Haan, J. (2013). Determinants of internet mediation: A comparison of the reports by Dutch parents and children. *Journal of Children and Media, 7*(1), 96–113.

Statista. (2022). Retrieved from www.statista.com/statistics/376128/facebook-global-user-age-distribution/.

Steinberg, S. (2017). Sharenting: Children's privacy in the age of social media. *Emory Law Journal, 66*, 839–883.

Sykes, G., & Matza, D. (1957). Techniques of neutralization: A theory of delinquency. *American Sociological Review, 22*(6), 664–670.

Tartari, M., Lavorgna, A., & Ugwudike, P. (2023). Share with care: Negotiating children's health and safety in sharenting practices. *Media, Culture & Society, 45*(7), 1453–1470.

Tsay-Vogel, M., Shanahan, J., & Signorielli, N. (2018). Social media cultivating perceptions of privacy: A 5-year analysis of privacy attitudes and self-disclosure behaviors among Facebook users. *New Media & Society, 20*(1), 141–161.

Ugwudike, P., Lavorgna, A., & Tartari, M. (2023). Sharenting in digital society: Exploring the prospects of an emerging moral panic. *Deviant Behavior*, 1–18.

Uhls, Y. (2015). *Media mums and digital dads: A fact-not-fear approach to parenting in the digital age*. Routledge.

Verde, A. (2017). Narrative criminology: Crime as produced by and re-lived through narratives. In *Oxford research encyclopedia of criminology and criminal justice*. Retrieved from https://doi.org/10.1093/acrefore/9780190264079.013.156

Wachs, S., Mazzone, A., Milosevic, T., Wright, M. F., Blaya, C., Gámez-Guadix, M., & O'Higgins Norman, J. (2021). Online correlates of cyberhate involvement among young people from ten European countries: An application of the routine activity and problem behaviour theory. *Computers in Human Behavior, 123*, 106872.

Wheeless, L. R., & Grotz, J. (1976). Conceptualization and measurement of reported self-disclosure. *Human Communication Research, 2*(4), 338–346.

Williams-Ceci, S., Grose, G. E., Pinch, A. C., Kizilcec, R. F., & Lewis, N. A. (2021). Combating sharenting: Interventions to alter parents' attitudes toward posting about their children online. *Computers in Human Behavior, 125*, 106939.

Zimmer, M., & Kinder-Kurlanda, K. (Eds.). (2017). *Research ethics for the social age. New challenges, cases, and contexts*. Peter Lang.

36

THE RISKS OF DIGITAL GOVERNANCE

Automatisation of crime politics

Veronika Nagy

Introduction

Shall we trust data-driven justice in the Era of Information societies? Digital technologies introduced new opportunities in crime control practices, extending the role of public services in sanctioning civilians outside the realm of penal institutions. In the landscape of contemporary governance, the advent of algorithmic systems has ushered in a techsolutionist paradigm shift, marked by an extension of control and sanctions within the administrative realm of public authorities. This transformation, also associated with preventive policing, has engendered a complex web of implications for societal dynamics and individual rights. This chapter provides critical reflections on algorithmic governance, spotlighting the burgeoning risks stemming from automated decision-making processes, in particular fraud detection in social services. Through a poignant case study, namely the child benefit scandal in the Netherlands, this chapter illustrates the perils inherent in relying on algorithmic solutions, showcasing how digital profiling can inadvertently exacerbate social exclusion and perpetuate criminalisation and debtfarism. Moreover, this chapter serves as a cautionary tale against the allure of tech-solutionist security policies, highlighting the insidious nature of automated decision-making strategies employed by local authorities. By shedding light on the disproportionate impact on marginalised communities, we underscore the transformative power of algorithmic surveillance strategies wielded by data service providers, lest it further victimise the poor and marginalise vulnerable segments of society.

Rapid technological developments and populist neoliberal principles increasingly fuel digital innovations in national and global policing practices to ensure safe, fast, easy and cost-efficient methods of crime prevention (Carr, 2016; Williams & Levi, 2017; Weiss, 2018). As a response to the public demands on crime prevention, increasing research has engaged with different concerns regarding the risks of digitalisation and predictive policing (Holt, 2017; Tilley & Sidebottom, 2017). Beside technological studies working on pre-policing and crime-mapping algorithms (Ratcliffe, 2010; Bowers et al., 2004), security and surveillance studies (Lyon, 2014; Candamo et al., 2010), social sciences (Hajian et al., 2011; Malleson & Andresen, 2015) media and economic sciences have extended their field to digital security governance (Chen et al., 2012; Silver & Miller, 2002; Loader, 1997;

DOI: 10.4324/9781003277675-41

Dunleavy, 2017). These disciplines often emphasise the advantages of current technologies in terms of data collection and analysis (Witten et al., 2016; Khan et al., 2015), such as how they facilitate better research opportunities. Others are concerned about the replacement of human decision-making (Kleinberg et al., 2015), the legitimacy of machine learning (Ridgeway, 2013a; Shalev-Shwartz & Ben-David, 2014) and lack of accountability or transparency (Brennan et al., 2013; Diakopoulos, 2016). Current studies stress the risks of fast digitalisation (Ridgeway, 2013b), the ethical concerns of AI (Lin et al., 2011) and how these changes might lead to unintended (or even uncontrolled) governmental structures (Hannah-Moffat, 2018) in which autonomous algorithms take the lead in decision-making processes (Just & Latzer, 2017). Recently, criminological studies shifted towards broader administrative domains, such as governmental data collection (Ephraim, 2017), private surveillance practices (Wonders, 2016), national intelligence like anti-terrorism measures and the vulnerability of critical infrastructures (Brassett & Vaughan-Williams, 2015). Scholars from different fields raised alarm about limitations on transparency in data processing (Wolak et al., 2007), alongside the privacy concerns of internet users and legislative limitations on corporate data security (Pearson & Benameur, 2010). After 20 years of scholarship, tech-solutionist notions got gradually extended by tech-pessimism regarding the digitisation and automation of public services, transforming the daily practices of administrative justice.

Critical social scientists, like STS and internet governance scholars, turned their attention to the normalisation of security narratives in the political discourse, exploring the digitisation of government bureaucracies and the ways the legitimacy of automatisation in decision-making processes (Cooke, 2017). In addition, there is a growing concern in academia about the role of corporate digital service providers, offering cheap, objective and efficient services, promising magical tools to governmental service providers, in particular for crime prevention and policing (Stenning & Shearing, 2015). Since local and national authorities are unable to provide the necessary digital literacy among their employees, external experts are contracted to ensure online data protection of the bureaucratic infrastructure (Van Erp, 2017). As it will be illustrated in the next case study, the need to ensure efficiency and public security—the key neoliberal managerialist principles—forces authorities to cooperate with corporate actors who collect, store and analyse all kinds of data and predict future risks and behaviours in their geopolitical territory. This dependency relationship in corporate governance is not only problematic regarding its influence on the local decision-makers, but it also ensures the position and the political influence of the new elite: the algorithm-literate state-contracted service provider.

While many studies adopt critical perspectives, the majority of disciplines related to policing remains entrenched in normative epistemic frameworks, endorsing automated technological investments for crime prevention, even when they contribute to widespread discrimination and social harms. Using the Dutch Child Tax scandal as a case study, this chapter examines how the accountability gap in the state-contracted security market leads to unforeseen harms inflicted by tech vendors, thereby shifting the responsibility of street level bureaucrats in legal decision-making processes. Initially, I will introduce the case study, outlining how the profiling system of Dutch tax authorities resulted in the discrimination and criminalisation of hundreds of thousands of child tax benefit applicants. Subsequently, I will delineate the key objectives of digital criminology as a positivist critique and discuss the detrimental effects of Zuboff's surveillance capitalism within the public sector. Lastly, I will underscore the involvement of tech corporations in law enforcement decisions and highlight the transparency issues arising from a new computational power structure. This discussion will elucidate how shifts towards public surveillance in the administrative sector replace the legitimacy of traditional law enforcement experts with programmers, who facilitate data collection and analysis and influence future policing priorities. Consequently, I will explore the negative ramifications of the related accountability issues and emphasise the risks associated with nondisclosure agreements signed by tech elites.

1 The child care benefit scandal

Algorithmic decision-making systems are increasingly prevalent in global government functions, particularly in tasks related to identifying potential lawbreakers and combating fraud (Konaté & Pali, 2023). This case description delves into the Dutch childcare allowance scandal, where an algorithmic decision-making system known as the "risk classification model" was employed by the tax authorities. This system, designed to detect fraudulent applications, has raised ethical concerns and led to a national scandal with far-reaching consequences (Fenger & Simonse, 2024). As I previously discussed the risks of these systems in the case of HMRC using fraud analysis software of Capgemini (Nagy, 2018), the harms of these tech model-based profiling systems are far more than discrimination practices. The normalisation of such technologies might also legitimise social injustices, commodify security and undermine well-regulated law enforcement practices.

The so-called Dutch child tax credit scandal is a symbolic case in critical governance studies, raising awareness about the need of accountability protocols of automated decision-making process (Peeters & Widlak, 2023).

Tax authorities are one of the key administrative organs of national authorities using excessive financial sanctions without penal court protocols. Though these authorities are generally associated with controlling income, they are also responsible for the digital administration and regulation of several social service provisions, like childcare allowance (Simonse et al, 2023).

Every parent or caregiver who legally resides and works or studies in the Netherlands is eligible for childcare allowance if the child goes to a registered daycare center. The division of costs between the government and the parent or caregiver depends on various factors, including total family income (Hummel et al., 2023). For example, parents or caregivers in a low-income household can have up to 96% of their childcare costs reimbursed through the childcare allowance system. Families with a high income receive 33.3% of the costs reimbursed for childcare. The allowances are paid in advance; the final amount to which the parent or caregiver is entitled is calculated afterwards, which means that any surplus must be refunded.[1]

In addition to automatically evaluating applications and modifications related to the allocation, disbursement and recovery of childcare allowances, the tax authorities conduct ongoing monitoring of all applications. This monitoring aims to identify discrepancies and potential instances of fraud. A key component of this oversight is the utilisation of a risk classification model, incorporating a self-learning algorithm designed to assess the risk associated with inaccurate requests and modifications (Alon-Barkat & Busuioc, 2023). Self-learning algorithms enable these systems to autonomously assimilate experiences over time, adapting their functioning without explicit programming by humans. Applications for childcare allowance that receive a low-risk score from the risk classification model are automatically approved by the tax authorities (Busuioc, 2022). According to the latest analysis of Amnesty International (2021), parents and caregivers were selected by the risk classification model because they had a high-risk score and were subsequently investigated by officials. The immediate consequence of the selection by the risk classification model included suspension of advance payments without clear justification so the decision was difficult to challenge by legal aid.[2] Officials responsible for manually processing the applications identified as high-risk by the risk classification model had the authority to label parents or caregivers as fraudulent, irrespective of the gravity of any errors (Zajko, 2023). This designation had significant repercussions, compelling parents and caregivers to repay the childcare allowance in full or in part, often amounting to tens of thousands of euros. Furthermore, the absence of a signature on the childcare contract or a delayed or incomplete payment of the mandatory personal contribution provided grounds for the tax authorities to reclaim all previously disbursed benefits and cease future benefits (Fenger & Simonse, 2024).

Parents and caregivers with lower incomes frequently found themselves obligated to reimburse larger sums solely because they had received higher allowances reflecting their financial circumstances. Additionally, those labelled as fraudsters and who had received benefits exceeding 10,000 euros per year were compelled to repay sums exceeding 3,000 euros. Furthermore, the blanket application of the "intent & gross negligence (OGS)" label, without due scrutiny, meant that parents and caregivers were deemed ineligible for a structured repayment plan for the reclaimed allowances (Damen, 2023). This standardised approach, using the OGS label, was applied uniformly, disregarding individual circumstances, and the 3,000 euros threshold served as a tool to swiftly clear backlogs and adjudicate thousands of applications from parents and caregivers seeking payment plans (Hayes de Kalaf & Fernandes, 2023).

In December 2020, a parliamentary interrogation committee concluded that the injustices inflicted on the victims of this policy were unprecedented. A series of parliamentary debates ensued, culminating in the downfall of the Dutch government in January 2021 and the resignation of the entire Council of Ministers of the Netherlands. Following the report from the parliamentary interrogation committee, the government acknowledged that parents and caregivers with non-Dutch nationality and/or dual nationality were more likely to be subjected to scrutiny by the Tax Authorities (Frerks & Terpstra, 2021).

One critical aspect of the scandal is the invisible incentive structure created by the tax authorities. Also, the financial motivation to accuse individuals of fraud to cover the costs of implementing data-driven fraud detection methods has compromised the accuracy of fraud allegations. This financial motive raises questions about the ethical foundation of the algorithmic decision-making system and highlights the importance of transparent and unbiased implementation and clear lines for accountability in the decision-making process. The consequences of false accusations stemming from the algorithmic decision-making system were profound, adversely affecting individuals and families (Giest & Klievink, 2024). Accordingly, the significant societal impact, including financial distress, unemployment and broken families, underscores the need for responsible implementation and robust oversight of such systems to prevent unintended harm.

As the report of Amnesty International explored in 2021, the tax authorities introduced an algorithmic decision-making system in 2013 for the detection of inaccuracies and fraud in applications for and changes to childcare benefits. This system, known as the risk classification model (SyRI), contains self-learning elements (Newman & Mintrom, 2023) that make it possible to draw up risk profiles of applicants for childcare benefits who may have more opportunity to submit incorrect and false information and potentially commit fraud.[3] The risk classification model operated as a black box system, concealing the input and operation details from users and external parties. The lack of transparency hindered accountability, as users were unaware of the factors contributing to high-risk scores. This opacity is incompatible with principles of legality and the rule of law, emphasising the necessity for explainable algorithms in sensitive government functions (Hirvonen, 2024). The Dutch benefit scandal exposes myriad legal and procedural failures, including inadequate investigation procedures, incorrect information and government unresponsiveness (Sattlegger et al., 2022). This systemic breakdown in digital governance not only highlights the importance of comprehensive legal frameworks and effective procedural mechanisms to rectify issues related to algorithmic decision-making systems but also its social implications, including the role of data experts.

Such a concerning aspect of the risk classification model is the dataset that has been developed by normative value stuctures, translating the analog lives into a digital index, like its utilisation of nationality as a parameter, leading to discriminatory outcomes. The algorithm incorporated "Dutchness: yes/no" as a risk factor, resulting in a higher risk score for individuals with non-Dutch nationality. Aside from incorporating the nationality of applicants into the risk classification model for the purpose of combating fraud, the tax authorities have employed nationality in various other capacities to identify potential organised fraud among individuals whose applications were initially approved. For instance, when suspicions arose regarding fraudulent activities by individuals with connections to or roots in a specific country, officials conducted searches in their databases to identify others with the same nationality (Bodó & Janssen, 2022). Subsequently, additional information about all applicants sharing that nationality was requested. As an illustration, a fraud report implicating 120 to 150 individuals with Ghanaian nationality triggered an investigation encompassing all 6047 applicants with Ghanaian nationality. This form of ethnic profiling perpetuates stereotypes and demonstrates a fundamental flaw in assuming a link between nationality and fraudulent behavior. The discriminatory impact of the risk classification model was also exacerbated by its intersectional nature (Fernandes Da Silva Ranchordas & Scarcella, 2021). Individuals with lower economic status, often belonging to ethnic minorities, were disproportionately affected. Accordingly, this intersectionality further amplifies the societal disparities created by the algorithmic decision-making system, emphasising the need for a controlled, traceable and inclusive approach to algorithm design and implementation.

2 Surveillance capitalism in the public sector

Several theoretical objectives try to explain the complexity of algorithmic harms and how digitised risk assessment processes create a new control scheme, transforming current power asymmetries by prediction-based administrative governance. Some studies focus on the surveillance power of such technologies, others are studying the results in terms of financial or social impact and some current scholars introduced new theoretical schools that highlight the changes in late modern state-corporate relations. According to this critical school, tech service providers and data companies in the globalised information society rapidly changed the biopolitics of policing and crime prevention by a new rationalisation principle, legitimising algorithmic predictions and selection of risk attributes. According to Stratton et al. (2017), we need to study the current technosocial cultures and therefore we need an epistemic framework that covers not only crime and criminal justice practices but also social harms, social justice, inequality and meaning-making. Arguably, "where conventional cybercriminologies have fallen short is that much of the field succumbs to degrees of techno-criminal determinism and of individualism." In this digital epistemology, 'technosociality' opens new avenues for exploration to emerge. Technology in discriminative practices, for example, is not understood to cause racism or race-based hate speech, but as I will illustrate, race certainly orders contemporary digital life in particular ways. Furthermore, such new social technologies contribute not only to individual criminal acts, but also to social practices of communication and action that can and do result in collective harms. Following the digital epistemology of Barry, current critical theory in criminology should extend this paradigm with computational economy to understand how anticipatory computing shifts the rationales behind contemporary data collection by softwarisation of society. Here, technology is understood neither as a cause of harm nor as a tool of harm, but rather as enmeshed in both pre-existing and newly emerging social practices.

Accordingly, those digital governance principles that legitimise digital governance tools, like preventive policing strategies, fuel harmful security measures based on outcomes of primitive machine learning products (Barocas et al., 2023). These assessment tools in crime-prevention methods raise new concerns around policing practices and professional expertise. On the one hand, manual interpretation of crime data is condemned due to its limitations, such as the size of data or the complexity among different socio-economic attributes. On the other hand, by integration of multiple methods such as classification, clustering, evaluation and data visualisation, digital data mining has established a dominant role in identifying patterns rapidly to detect risk behaviour. As the current examples of law enforcement software illustrates, these algorithm-based policing measures are considered as objective calculations and rationalise expensive investments in crime prevention strategies (De Mul, 2023). Such digitalisation process received several criticisms in particular in the field of crime prevention and the privatisation of policing.

A rapidly accelerating phase of capitalism funded by asymmetrical personal data accumulation poses significant concerns for democratic societies, yet the concepts used to understand and challenge practices of dataveillance are insufficient or poorly elaborated. Against a backdrop of growing corporate power enabled by legal lethargy and the secrecy of the personal data industry (Boggs, 2001), this chapter aims to highlight the practices inherent in what Shoshana Zuboff calls 'surveillance capitalism,' understanding these as threats to social justice. Based on Nancy Fraser's theory of 'abnormal justice' to characterise the separation of people from their personal data and its accumulation by corporations as an economic injustice of maldistribution, this injustice is explained as the key mechanism by which further opaque but significant forms of injustice are enabled in surveillance capitalism (Lehtiniemi, 2017). This sociocultural misrecognition occurs when personal data are subject to categorisation and political misrepresentation which renders people democratically voiceless, unable to challenge misuses of their data.

3 Surveillance Capitalism and 'Big Other'

Technology theorist Shoshana Zuboff poignantly foreshadowed the implications of increasingly corporate "digital sovereigns" (in MacKinnon's terms). In her influential 1988 book, *In the Age of the Smart Machine*, she articulated 'Zuboff's three laws' of information computing. First, everything that can be automated will be automated (Zuboff, 1988). Second, everything that can be informed will be informed. Third, and of most relevance here, "every digital application that can be used for surveillance and control will be used for surveillance and control, irrespective of its originating intention" (Zuboff, 2013, n.p.). Though I cannot agree fully with the power dynamics of her theory, Zuboff's three laws underpin an emerging logic of capital accumulation that she describes as surveillance capitalism: a "new form of information capitalism [that] aims to predict and modify human behaviour as a means to produce revenue and market control" (Zuboff, 2015, p. 75). Rather than the panopticon-style of surveillance typified by 'Big Brother', Zuboff identifies a new kind of sovereign power emerging in the information age: 'Big Other' (2015). Big Other emerges in the context of pervasive computer mediation, in which people's interactions, experiences and behaviours are commodified: reborn as data that are collectable, knowable and manipulable, and resulting in behaviour modification through rewards and punishments distributed by 'a new kind of invisible hand' from which there is no escape (Zuboff, 2015):

> False consciousness is no longer produced by the hidden facts of class and their relation to production, but rather by the hidden facts of commoditized behavior modification. If power was once identified with the ownership of the means of production, it is now identified with the ownership of the means of behavioral modification.
>
> *(p. 82)*

A key implication of surveillance capitalism, then, is that while the accumulation of information (from the deeply sensitive to the seemingly banal) is automatically analysed and fed back into the network to improve the 'consumer experience' (and thereby increase corporate profit margins), there is a simultaneous merging of corporate and state surveillance apparatuses (Giroux, 2015). The dual promises of greater security from the state and greater convenience from technology corporations have arguably acculturated the vast bulk of citizen-consumers "into accepting the intrusion of surveillance technologies and privatised commodified values into all aspects of their lives" (Giroux, 2015, p. 156). At the same time, the extent, nature, accessibility and uses of this personal information are not transparent; information that consumers share willingly with private companies in return for convenience, may in turn be shared with state authorities, as citizens are "now considered as both potential terrorists and a vast consumer market" (Giroux, 2015, p. 156). As Zuboff (2015, p. 86) further describes: "Since Edward Snowden, we have learned of the blurring of public and private boundaries in surveillance activities including collaborations and constructive interdependencies between state security authorities and high-tech firms".

The influence of corporate regulation of networked flows can be seen most directly in the behaviour of businesses and the ownership and control of intellectual property and user data (Darmody & Zwick, 2020). At a broad and diffuse level, however, it equally shapes and controls the behaviour and norms of all members of digital society who use these platforms. The ability to determine community standards policies and the form and function for communicating via digitally networked communications means that "companies are even more powerful because not only do they create and sell products, but they also provide and shape the digital space upon which citizens increasingly depend" (MacKinnon, 2012). The risk classification model implemented by the tax authorities exemplifies surveillance capitalism in action. By automating the assessment of childcare allowance applications and changes, the system surveils individuals, collecting vast amounts of personal data to feed its self-learning algorithm. This algorithm, operating as a black box system, maximises data extraction while maintaining opacity, a characteristic hallmark of surveillance capitalism. Accordingly, the utilisation of nationality as a parameter in the risk classification model exemplifies how surveillance capitalism exacerbates discriminatory practices. By using data related to applicants' nationality, the tax authorities perpetuate stereotypes and reinforce biases, linking ethnicity to the perceived risk of fraudulent behavior. This aligns with surveillance capitalism's profit-driven motive, as the algorithmic system exploits personal information to make discriminatory decisions, further entrenching social inequalities.

According to the late-modern neoliberal agenda, this process inherently thrives on the collection of data for profit. In the Dutch benefit scandal, the tax authorities' financial interest in accusing individuals of fraud aligns with the profit motive of surveillance capitalism. The perverse incentives created a situation where the algorithmic system was not merely a tool for fraud detection but a mechanism for extracting financial returns, amplifying the impact on vulnerable individuals, especially those with lower incomes. Also, the black box nature of the risk classification model contributes to the opacity of governance, a common feature of surveillance capitalism. The lack of transparency hinders accountability, allowing the tax authorities to operate with minimal scrutiny. This opacity is not only a breach of good governance principles but also a reflection of surveillance capitalism's penchant for operating in the shadows to maximise data extraction.

Discriminating algorithms

The intersectional discrimination observed in the Dutch benefit scandal further illustrates how surveillance capitalism exploits vulnerable populations. Individuals with lower economic status, often belonging to ethnic minorities, faced disproportionate consequences. This intersectionality is a byproduct of surveillance capitalism's relentless pursuit of data and its consequences on already marginalised groups, which amplify social disparities. As such, this child tax benefit case proves how surveillance capitalism manifests in governmental functions, exploiting personal data for financial gain and perpetuating discrimination and highlights the urgent need for ethical considerations and regulatory frameworks to curb the excesses of algorithmic decision-making in public institutions, especially in contexts where vulnerable populations are at risk of exploitation. Chilling effects of other algorithmic surveillance mechanisms also intensify any pre-existing inequalities of already disadvantaged individuals. As has been previously studied, there are new disadvantages created by machine learning due to the stigma of criminal justice contact and inequality (Becker, 1963; Brayne, 2014; Goffman, 2014; Goffman, 1963; Lyon, 2006).

With algorithmic assemblages, personal data in policing files may effectively extend the mark of a criminal record into other institutions. This creep of data across institutional contexts can lead to "cascading disadvantages" (Allen-Robertson, 2015). Online internet users leave more digital traces, so a new economy of moral judgement" (Fourcade & Healy, 2017, p. 24) becomes possible. A big data environment creates digitised collateral as consequences of groups' involvement in the criminal justice system. The burden of new surveillance practices is not borne equally, nor are the errors they produce (Guzik, 2009). Barocas and Selbst (2016) argue that discrimination may be an artefact of the data collection and analysis process itself. Algorithmic decision procedures can "reproduce existing patterns of discrimination, inherit the prejudice of prior decision makers, or simply reflect the widespread biases that persist in society" (Brayne, 2017, p. 999).

Algorithms are being designed without consideration of how user feedback inserts biases into the system and how users interact with them. People and organisations with vested social, political and economic interests can leverage the feedback loops that exist within these systems to actively and intentionally insert bias into recommendation systems and other algorithmic-based services Ethics and Information Technology. Friedman and Nissenbaum (1996) show that bias can manifest itself in a computer system in different ways: pre-existing bias in society can affect the system design; technical bias can occur due to technical limitations; and emergent bias can arise sometime after software implementation is completed and released (Friedman & Nissenbaum, 1996). Although there is a strong body of work demonstrating that marking someone in the criminal justice system is consequential for life outcomes and patterns of inequality (Becker, 1963; Brayne, 2014; Kohler-Hausmann, 2013; Pager, 2007; Rios, 2011), we know relatively little about whether and how the marking process has changed in the age of big data (Brayne, 2017). Consequently, there is a dearth of theoretically informed empirical research on the relationship between surveillance, big data and the social consequences of the intersection of the two forces.

FPF has outlined key areas of algorithmic discrimination, encompassing loss of opportunity, economic setbacks, social harm and curtailment of liberty (See Chart 1). This delineation illustrates the diverse aspects of life where automated decision-making can lead to negative consequences. Concurrently, due to the absence of legal accountability, algorithms are progressively assuming the role of social categorisation, altering traditional surveillance mechanisms through the involvement of privatised business entities.

According to the Future of Privacy Forum Report published in 2017, these digitalisation methods manifest in several ways: (1) subjective risk assessments are complemented and quantified through the use of risk scores; (2) data is increasingly employed for predictive purposes rather than reactive or explanatory functions; (3) the widespread use of automated alerts facilitates systematic surveillance of an unprecedentedly large population; (4) datasets now incorporate information about individuals with no prior direct police interactions; and (5) previously distinct data systems are amalgamated into relational systems, encompassing data originally gathered from non-criminal-justice institutions. These transformations carry significant implications for inequality, legal frameworks, and organisational practices across various institutional domains, particularly in the realm of crime prevention. Since then even more issues has been identified. "The problem is technology legitimises somehow (p. 242) the problematic policing that was the origination of the data to begin with" (Lane, 2014). Gary T. Marx says technology such as predictive policing creates "categorical suspicion" of people in predicted crime areas, which can lead to unnecessary questioning. "The power of algorithms here is in their ability to make choices, to classify, to sort, to order and to rank" (Beer, 2009, p. 6); that is, to decide what matters and to decide what should be most visible. Also, the performative role of algorithms and the algorithmic sealing effect, called 'filter bubbles', are often out of sight. As Prariser (2011) explains, as part of the algorithmic sorting, these might narrow down or close off external influences since algorithms repeat patterns and thus close down interactions to those who fit existing patterns (Kennedy et al., 2015). In short, algorithms create and maintain norms of abnormality (Crandall, 2010, p. 83) without real accountability for these harmful effects. In this context, achieving transparency and legitimacy necessitates a more profound comprehension of the technology involved, accompanied by intricate discussions regarding reasonable expectations of its use in the penal context. It is imperative to divulge not only the data being analysed, which extends beyond just user-contributed data to encompass metadata collected by the system, potentially unbeknownst to the user, but also to clarify whether this information is genuinely public. Similar to discussions on OSINT use of financial authorities, this depth of understanding is crucial for establishing trust and ensuring that individuals are fully aware of the scope and nature of data analysis conducted on their behalf. Furthermore, "even if individual data is provided voluntarily by users, there should still be a reasonable expectation of privacy when it comes to automated analytics carried out upon a vast collection of data linked across different platforms" (Scassa, 2017, p. 88).

But how could it have gone wrong for so long? How could tax authorities cover up this case even after many concerning reports? The answer lies in the new accountability principle of digitised bureaucracies, often referred to as structural negligence. First of all, as the political elite has a lack of understanding of big data calculations and programmed crime prevention models, they might accept the outcomes without valorisation. These digital predictions might strengthen technocratic bureaucracies and justify the limits of discretionary power among political stakeholders. In short, in modern E-governance it is not a moral entrepreneur who seeks to influence a group to adopt or maintain a norm, but risk assessments generated from data-mining designs. Therefore, not humans but software propagates the core moral viewpoints based on untraceable calculations. Data patterns presented by subcontracted tech services, described as neutral and objective indicators, determine the surveillance objectives of authorities by triggering an accountability gap (Cardona et al., 2013) wherein blame can potentially be assigned to several moral agents simultaneously. In these conditions, the machine is taking over the role of the moral entrepreneur by predicting future deviance and social concerns (Mittelstadt et al., 2016).

The algorithm 'learns' by defining rules to determine how new inputs will be classified. The model can be taught to the algorithm via hand labelled inputs (supervised learning); in other cases, the algorithm itself defines best-fit models to make sense of a set of inputs (unsupervised learning).

(Schermer, 2011; Van Otterlo, 2013)

"In both cases, the algorithm defines decision-making rules to handle new inputs. Critically, the human operator does not need to understand the rationale of decision-making rules produced by the algorithm" (Matthias, 2004, p. 179). As this explanation suggests, learning capacities grant algorithms some degree of autonomy. However, the impact of this autonomy is growing with the consumption logic of state authorities who adapt to the increasing prevalence of self-learning algorithmic systems to avoid accountability of the political elite, due to their efficiency in law enforcement practices.

Considering the discretionary power of professionals, there is a growing tendency towards reduced authority and freedom in case-based decision making. By justifying the normative value of data-mining possibilities, a digitalised risk-based governance approach undermines the discretionary power of civil servants (Amoore, 2013) and the professional value of human recourses. In contrast to the use of data mining in areas such as healthcare, credit scoring and general business analytics, where such techniques have a long tradition, the impact of algorithms on the public sphere, like security, poses novel challenges.

As media infrastructures and social environments become increasingly datafied, digital analysis and self-learning algorithms surpass the legitimacy of empirical studies to predict future security concerns without any methodological transparency (Berry, 2014). While these software predictions were mainly applied for situational crime prevention to define future crime spots or to serve crowd management, recent pre-crime policies have been initiated based on new technologies like nonlinear backpropagation algorithms, including attribute-based data-mining programs, to predict future behaviour that ought to be defined as a security risk. As the child tax scandal illustrated, statistical of learning approach has changed the role of statistics from empirical risk minimisation towards fluid self-programming systems that can combine all types of data from social reality. In neoliberal democracies, these sophisticated technical tools extend existing surveillance practices with electronic databases, enabling a new digital "bureaucracy" in favour of "national security" and "commercial competition" (Bauman & Lyon, 2013; Lyon, 2003).

Second, several concerns have been raised about the unintended effects of these predictive methods, as they may result in discriminatory data-mining effects such as the social, physical or financial exclusion of targeted groups (Barocas & Selbst, 2016). There are several critical factors that facilitate this social sorting. First of all, machine learning wipes out the traditional model of responsibility because "nobody has enough control over the machine's actions to be able to assume the responsibility for them" (Matthias, 2004, p. 177). This process raises concerns about 'machine ethics': "the modular design of systems can mean that no single person or group can fully grasp the manner in which the system will interact or respond to a complex flow of new inputs" (Allen et al., 2006, p. 14). Second, from traditional linear programming through to autonomous algorithms, behavioural control is gradually transferred from the programmer to the algorithm and its operating environment (Matthias, 2004, p. 182). When data collection, data storage and even the data analysis tools of public services are taken over by corporate companies, scholars warn about accountability issues in regard to governing these outsourced technologies. Mackenzie (2006) asserts that how algorithms make choices or how they provide information that informs and shapes predictions should be made public. Agents who design the algorithms, whose designs then shape how these processes play out or how desired outcomes are modelled into those systems, should be included in datafied decision-making processes (Beer, 2009).

The promotion of reliability of algorithmic data and the emphasis on online risks are a part of the conscious security narrative engineered by the program-literate elite that deliberately undertakes a campaign to generate and sustain fear and concern on the part of the public, undermining police trust regarding cyber security and promoting the legitimacy of their engagement. Typically, this profit-oriented marketing strategy of security experts intends to divert attention from individual responsibility of online ID protection and amplify the risks of users. These narratives undermine the role of professionals who might educate themselves or develop special expert units instead of serving the indicators of external experts (Reinarman & Levine, 1989). This tech-elite engineered model of moral panics (Hall, 1978) is based on the view that elites, such as algorithm-literate experts, have "immense power over the other members of the society, they dominate the media, determine the content of legislation and the direction of law enforcement, and control much of the resources on which action groups and social movements depend" (Goode, 1994, p. 165).

The argument presented by Hall et al. (1978) posits that societal panics, like the perceived threat of cybercrime, serve as mechanisms for constructing definitions of social and political reality that benefit those in power. Drawing parallels with the 1970s panic about street crime, which legitimised law-and-order initiatives and diverted attention from economic issues, today's security algorithm market emphasises cyber risks to extend state corporate influence in the data-mining sector. This lobbying compels governments to abandon a facade of neutrality and assume 'total social authority' over subordinate classes, shaping the direction of social life. This dominance by a new elite is portrayed as legitimate for the sake of security, concealing its exploitative nature.

This intrusion of formal governance, justified by exceptional threats such as the migration crisis or terrorist attacks, involves private companies exerting undue influence on public police practices. The consequences of this influence extend beyond concerns of privacy and security, impacting the entire legal system. Notably: A. The undue influence of surveillance technology companies can distort or hinder the development of privacy protection law. B. Nondisclosure agreements surrounding new surveillance technologies impede challenges by criminal defendants, preventing judicial review and undermining defendants' claims. C. Private companies' insistence on secrecy removes legal issues from judicial oversight, contributing to police accountability and social discrimination concerns.

In short, law enforcement expertise has not been achieved by the employment and training of civil servants and policing experts, but subcontracted vendors have been hired for the technological tasks to facilitate and sustain the information household of government data. This power of vendors has released the state authorities from the accountability of mistakes but has left their formal legitimacy and autonomy in the public domain. This shift in the field of biopolitics leads to new risks as the norms of vendors replace the constitutional values and unobtrusively invent the individual bias of tech experts in systemic data-mining strategies of national authorities. While the role of these experts concerns international law enforcement practices, the role of machine-equipped risks and the principles coded into policing algorithms of 'pure' information for rational consumption (Carey, 1989) has raised even more apprehension from academics and professionals alike.

In order to understand how personal bias of the programmer elite gets into governmental pre-crime algorithms, we should consider these values that might remain out of sight of the users. To understand how these human perceptions play a role in technological designs of data experts, the way the bias of software designers is transmitted in self-learning algorithms should be discussed. Ananny invented the concept of a "networked information algorithm" (2016, p. 97) as an assemblage (DeLanda, 2006; Latour, 2007) to understand the ethics of sociotechnical relationships that shape and rely on the formation processed by computational algorithms. Technology ethics emerges from a mix of institutionalised codes, professional cultures, technological capabilities, social practices and individual decision-making (Seele, 2022).

Big Bang Bias: algorithm-based governance creates an accountability gap

The emergence of the 'data paradigm' or the 'datafication' of society has introduced new power dynamics in risk governance, particularly in the realm of law enforcement practices. While the application of algorithms in crime prevention is touted for its promises of value-neutral information and enhanced crime prediction capabilities, there are profound concerns regarding social and economic exclusion, autonomy and ethical considerations. Algorithms in law enforcement not only act as filters and mirrors, reflecting information within their computational logic, but also play a significant role in shaping the legitimacy of information in society. The ethical evaluation of algorithms involves not only deciphering the black boxes of code but also critiquing the broader assemblages that govern daily life, challenging issues of accountability and transparency.

Critics argue that the lack of accountability in the use of algorithmic power, both by program designers and public authorities, is a significant concern. The opaque nature of algorithmic decision-making processes and a lack of transparency contribute to ethical ambiguities, hindering the understanding and verification of their outcomes. The concept of a 'black box society' is introduced, suggesting that values and rights encoded in algorithmic rules are hidden, creating a society governed by enigmatic technologies instead of transparent governance determinants. This lack of clarity raises questions about accountability and the potential crisis of governmental oversight in the face of algorithms' increasing influence in crime prevention.

Such a point opens up a series of questions about the role of algorithmic analysis in the deployment or expression of power and how it shapes risk-prevention measures. Algorithms can also anticipate future actions. Police departments in Los Angeles and New York use 'predictive policing' algorithms to combine historical crime data with real-time, geolocated tweets, deploying officers "where and when crime is most likely to occur" (Morrison, 2014). Pennsylvania is considering allowing judges to use statistical estimates of future offences to determine an inmate's current sentence—punishing them not only for crimes they have committed but crimes that algorithms think they might commit (Barry-Jester et al., 2015).

So, the impact of such digital governance in law enforcement practices seems not only far from the assumption that it eliminates human discretion and bias, but by self-learning, these algorithms anticipate and rewrite socio-economic opportunities. On the one hand, big data analytics may be a rationalising force with the potential to reduce bias, increase efficiency and improve prediction accuracy. On the other hand, the use of predictive analytics has the potential to technologically reify bias and deepen existing patterns of inequality. Today, in place of political stakeholders or corporate lobbies, software-based data analyses predict the crimes of tomorrow. Moral entrepreneurs of modern society are self-programming algorithms constructing policy needs from metadata, which is justified by the new faith in digital positivism. The power in these technologies is thus far more than observation. By individualising pathology through bureaucratic codification, risk is defined by digitalised characteristics and classified into risk categories of decision-makers (Lyon, 2003, p. 250). As Pasquale (2015) puts it: "critical decisions are made not on the basis of the data per se, but on the basis of data analysed algorithmically." Here, we see the role of algorithms as decision-making parts of code (see Beer, 2009). Napoli (2014) goes so far as to define algorithms as institutions because of their power to structure, behaviour, influence preferences, guide consumption, produce content, signal quality and sway commodification.

Today, predictive analytics are used for many law enforcement-related activities, including algorithms predicting the occurrence of crime (Perry et al., 2013), network models (Papachristos et al., 2013) and risk models. The proliferation of big data-driven decision-making in governmental organisations is mainly to improve both efficiency and accountability and to deploy resources more efficiently. Data-driven policing also holds potential as an accountability mechanism and response to criticisms organisations are facing over discriminatory practices. Although part of the appeal of big data lies in its promise of less discretionary and more objective decision-making, current algorithms embody the purposes of their creators (Boyd & Crawford, 2012; Gitelman, 2013; Kitchin, 2014) and undermine the ability of individual officers or law enforcement agencies to give an account of their decisions in important ways. Brayne argues that organisations operate in technically ambiguous fields in which they adopt big data analytics "not because of empirical evidence that it actually improves efficiency, but in response to wider beliefs of what organizations should be doing with big data (Willis, Mastrofski, and Weisburd, 2007). In other words, using big data may confer legitimacy" (Brayne, 2017, p. 980). Considering these limitations, the core concern is how this legitimacy of algorithmic accountability contributes to existing inequalities or serves to entrench power dynamics within policing organisations (Brayne, 2017, p. 982).

Conclusion

This examination reveals critical implications, particularly when considering the child tax benefit case, concerning the risks associated with algorithmic discrimination. Corporate governance structures in this context establish a concerning dependency between formal authorities and digital experts, who provide data analysis tools for administrative crime detection practices. In the child tax benefit case, where self-learning algorithms shape governance software, the endorsement of big data analysis for law enforcement practices exacerbates the accountability gap in the public-private relationship, thereby absolving authorities of their responsibilities.

Despite growing awareness of discrimination resulting from biased data-mining processes, the legitimacy of data-driven governance, particularly evident in the child tax benefit case, remains largely unchallenged. Digitization of administrative services constructs a new social divide, criminalising the poor and punish the non-conform by technocolonial economic objectives. Data scientists are contracted to support state authorities to transform the values and decision-making practices of street level bureaucrats and invisibly undermine the fundamental principles of fair treatment, even outside the traditional framework of penal law. The child tax benefit case underscores the urgency of addressing these concerns, emphasising the need to challenge the exceptionalist narrative upheld by the program-literate elite in the security market. This case illustrates that the discriminatory outcomes of algorithmic decision-making are not mere theoretical concerns but have real, tangible consequences, particularly in the context of child tax benefits. By externalising governance legitimacy to algorithms, the child tax benefit case becomes emblematic of broader shifts that risk turning constitutional states into dystopian landscapes governed by tech elites, posing significant ethical and social challenges that demand immediate attention.

Notes

1 Algemene wet inkomensafhankelijke regelingen, 23 juni 2005, artikel 9 tweede lid jo. Vreemdelingenwet, artikel 11. Wet kinderopvang, artikel 1.1.

Wet kinderopvang, artikel 1.7.
Besluit kinderopvangtoeslag, artikelen 3 t/m 8.
Besluit kinderopvangtoeslag, artikel 6

2 See further here https://www.amnesty.org/en/latest/news/2021/10/xenophobic-machines-dutch-child-benefit-scandal/
3 Amnesty International (2021) Xenofobe machines- discriminatie door ongereguleerd gebruik van algoritmen in het nederlandse toeslagenschandaal

Bibliography

Allen, C., Wallach, W., & Smit, I. (2006). Why machine ethics? *IEEE Intelligent Systems*, 21(4), 12–17.
Allen-Robertson, J. (2015, October 22). *Fundamental inequities in algorithmic space: What do games teach us about power in a software mediated society?* Retrieved from https://ssrn.com/abstract=2678770. https://dx.doi.org/10.2139/ssrn.2678770
Alon-Barkat, S., & Busuioc, M. (2023). Human–AI interactions in public sector decision making: "Automation bias" and "selective adherence" to algorithmic advice. *Journal of Public Administration Research and Theory*, 33(1), 153–169.
Amoore, L. (2013). *The politics of possibility: Risk and security beyond probability*. Duke University Press.

Ananny, Mike. "Toward an Ethics of Algorithms: Convening, Observation, Probability, and Timeliness." *Science, Technology, & Human Values*, 41(1), 2016, pp. 93–117, https://doi.org/10.1177/0162243915606523

Ananny, M. (2016). Toward an ethics of algorithms: Convening, observation, probability, and timeliness. *Science, Technology, & Human Values*, 41(1), 93–117.

Anderson, C. (2008). The end of theory: The data deluge makes the scientific method obsolete. *Wired Magazine*, 16(7), 16–07.

Barocas, S., Hardt, M., & Narayanan, A. (2023). *Fairness and machine learning: Limitations and opportunities*. MIT Press.

Barocas, S., & Selbst, A. D. (2016). Big data's disparate impact. *The California Law Review*, 104, 671.

Barry, M., Levin, C., MacCuaig, M., Mulley, A., Sepucha, K., & Boston ISDM Planning Committee. (2011). Shared decision making: Vision to reality. *Health Expectations*, 14, 1–5.

Barry-Jester, A. M., Casselman, B., & Goldstein, D. (2015). Should prison sentences be based on crimes that haven't been committed yet?. *FiveThirtyEight, August, 4*.

Bauman, Z., Bigo, D., Esteves, P., Guild, E., Jabri, V., Lyon, D., & Walker, R. B. (2014). After Snowden: Rethinking the impact of surveillance. *International Political Sociology*, 8(2), 121–144.

Bauman, Z., & Lyon, D. (2013). *Liquid surveillance: A conversation*. John Wiley & Sons.

Becker, H. S. (1963). *Outsiders: Studies in the sociology of deviance*. Free Press.

Beer, D. (2009). Power through the algorithm? Participatory web cultures and the technological unconscious. *New Media & Society*, 11(6), 985–1002. https://doi.org/10.1177/1461444809336551

Berry, D. (2014). *Critical theory and the digital*. Bloomsbury.

Bodó, B., & Janssen, H. (2022). Maintaining trust in a technologized public sector. *Policy and Society*, 41(3), 414–429.

Boggs, C. (2001). *The end of politics: Corporate power and the decline of the public sphere*. Guilford Press.

Boyd, D., & Crawford, K. (2012). Critical questions for big data: Provocations for a cultural, technological, and scholarly phenomenon. *Information, Communication & Society*, 15(5), 662–679.

Bowers, K. J., Johnson, S. D., & Pease, K. (2004). Prospective hot-spotting: The future of crime mapping?. *British Journal of Criminology*, 44(5), 641–658.

Brassett, J., & Vaughan-Williams, N. (2015). Security and the performative politics of resilience: Critical infrastructure protection and humanitarian emergency preparedness. *Security Dialogue*, 46(1), 32–50.

Brayne, S. (2014). Surveillance and system avoidance: Criminal justice contact and institutional attachment. *American Sociological Review*, 79(3), 367–391.

Brayne, S. (2017). Big data surveillance: The case of policing. *American Sociological Review*, 82(5), 977–1008.

Brennan, T., & Oliver, W. L. (2013). The emergence of machine learning techniques in criminology. *Criminology & Public Policy*, 12(3), 551–562.

Brunton, F., & Nissenbaum, H. (2011). Vernacular resistance to data collection and analysis: A political theory of obfuscation. *First Monday*, 16(5).

Busuioc, M. (2022). Chapter 31: AI algorithmic oversight: New frontiers in regulation. In Maggetti M, Di Mascio F, Natalini A, editors, *Handbook of Regulatory Authorities*. Edward Elgar Publishers. 2022. p. 470–486 Epub 2022 Aug 12. doi: 10.4337/9781839108990.00043

Candamo, J., Shreve, M., Goldgof, D. B., Sapper, D. B., & Kasturi, R. (2010). Understanding transit scenes: A survey on human behavior-recognition algorithms. *IEEE Transactions on Intelligent Transportation Systems*, 11(1), 206–224.

Cardona, M., Kretschmer, T., & Strobel, T. (2013). ICT and productivity: Conclusions from the empirical literature. *Information Economics and Policy*, 25(3), 109–125.

Carey, J. W. (1989). *Communication as culture*. Unwin Hyman.

Carr, M. (2016). Public—Private partnerships in national cyber-security strategies. *International Affairs*, 92(1), 43–62.

Chen, H., Chiang, R. H., & Storey, V. C. (2012). Business intelligence and analytics: From big data to big impact. *MIS Quarterly*, 1165–1188.

Cooke, P. (2017). 'Digital tech' and the public sector: What new role after public funding?. *European Planning Studies*, 25(5), 739–754.

Crandall, (2010). The geospatialization of calculative operations: Tracking, sensing and mega-cities. *Theory Culture Society*, 27(6), 68–90.

Crang, M., & Graham, S. (2007). Sentient cities Ambient intelligence and the politics of urban space. *Information, Communication & Society*, 10(6), 789–817.

Crawford, K. (2016). Can an algorithm be agonistic? Ten scenes from life in calculated publics. *Science, Technology & Human Values*, 41, 77–92.

Damen, W. (2023, July). Sounds good, doesn't work: The GDPR principle of transparency and data-driven welfare fraud detection. In *ISLSSL European Regional Congress-the lighthouse function of social law* (pp. 527–544). Springer International Publishing.

Darmody, A., & Zwick, D. (2020). Manipulate to empower: Hyper-relevance and the contradictions of marketing in the age of surveillance capitalism. *Big Data & Society*, 7(1). https://doi.org/10.1177/2053951720904112

De Giorgi, A. (2017). *Re-thinking the political economy of punishment: Perspectives on post-Fordism and penal politics*. Routledge.

De Mul, J. (2023). Metaphors we nudge by: Reflections on the impact of predictive algorithms on our self-understanding. In *Nudging choices through media: Ethical and philosophical implications for humanity* (pp. 33–57). Springer International Publishing.

DeLanda, M. (2006). Deleuzian social ontology and assemblage theory. In Fuglsang, Martin, and Bent Meier Sørensen (Eds). *Deleuze and the Social*. Edinburgh University Press, 2006. JSTOR, http://www.jstor.org/stable/10.3366/j.ctt1r23wb. Accessed 29 July 2024.

Diakopoulos, N. (2016). Accountability in algorithmic decision making. *Communications of the ACM*, 59(2), 56–62.

Duffield, M. (2014). *Global governance and the new wars: The merging of development and security*. Zed Books Ltd.

Dunleavy, P. (2007). Governance and state organization in the digital era', in Chrisanthi Avgerou, and others (Eds.), *The Oxford Handbook of Information and Communication Technologies* (2009; online edn, Oxford Academic, 2 Sept. 2009), https://doi.org/10.1093/oxfordhb/9780199548798.003.0017

Dunleavy, P. (2017). Public sector productivity: Measurement challenges, performance information and prospects for improvement. *OECD Journal on Budgeting*, 17(1). https://doi.org/10.1787/budget-17-5jfj7vb36p5c

Ephraim, P. E. (2017). Whistleblowing and social responsibility in a surveillance system: Appraising the morality of the Snowden disclosures. *Mapping Media Responsibility. Contemporary Aspects of Morals, Ethics and Social Discourse*, 50.

Fenger, M., & Simonse, R. (2024). The implosion of the Dutch surveillance welfare state. *Social Policy & Administration*, 58(2), 264–276.

Fernandes Da Silva Ranchordas, S. H., & Scarcella, L. (2021). Automated government for vulnerable citizens: Intermediating rights. *William and Mary Bill of Rights Journal*, 30(2), 373–418. https://www.wired.com/story/welfare-fraud-industry/

Flanagan, M., Howe, D., & Nissenbaum, H. (2008). Embodying values in technology: Theory and practice. *Information Technology and Moral Philosophy*, 322–353.

Fourcade, M., & Healy, K. (2013). Classification situations: Life-chances in the neoliberal era. *Accounting, Organizations and Society*, 38, 559–572.

Fourcade, M., & Healy, K. (2017). Seeing like a market. *Socio-Economic Review*, 15(1), 9–29.

Frerks, G., & Terpstra, N. (2021). *Contested institutional legitimacy*. A Think Paper Series #3 - Institutions for Open Societies, Utrecht University.

Friedman, B., Kahn, P. H., & Alan, B. (2006). Value sensitive design and information systems. *Human-Computer Interaction in Management Information Systems: Foundations*, 4, 348–372.

Friedman, B., Kahn, P. H., & Borning, A. (2006–2014). Value sensitive design and information systems. In *Human-computer interaction in management information systems: Foundations* (pp. 348–372). ME Sharpe, Inc.

Friedman, B., & Nissenbaum, H. (1996). Bias in computer systems. *ACM Transactions on Information Systems (TOIS)*, 14(3), 330–347. DOI:10.1007/s10676-013-9321-6

Giardullo, P. (2016). Does 'bigger' mean 'better'? Pitfalls and shortcuts associated with big data for social research. *Quality & Quantity*, 50(2), 529–547.

Giest, S. N., & Klievink, B. (2024). More than a digital system: How AI is changing the role of bureaucrats in different organizational contexts. *Public Management Review, 26*(2), 379–398.

Gillespie, T. (2014). The relevance of algorithms. *Media Technologies: Essays on Communication, Materiality, and Society, 167*.

Giroux, H. A. (2015). Selfie culture in the age of corporate and state surveillance. *Third Text, 29*(3), 155–164.

Gitelman, L. (2013). *Raw data is an oxymoron.* MIT Press.

Goffman, A. (2014). *On the run: Fugitive life in an American City.* University of Chicago Press.

Goffman, E. (1963). *Stigma: Notes on the management of spoiled identity.* Prentice-Hall.

Goode, E., & Ben-Yehuda, N. (1994). Moral panics: Culture, politics, and social construction. *Annual review of sociology, 20*(1), 149–171

Gordon, G. R., Rebovich, D. J., & Gordon, J. B. (2007). *Identity fraud trends and patterns: Building a data-based foundation for proactive enforcement.* Center for Identity Management and Information Protection, Utica College.

Guzik, K. (2009). Discrimination by Design: Predictive data mining as security practice in the United States' 'war on terrorism'. *Surveillance & Society, 7*(1), 3–20.

Hajian, S., Domingo-Ferrer, J., & Martinez-Balleste, A. (2011, April). Discrimination prevention in data mining for intrusion and crime detection. In *Computational Intelligence in Cyber Security (CICS), 2011 IEEE Symposium on* (pp. 47–54). IEEE.

Hall, S., Critcher, C., Jefferson, T., Clarke, J., & Roberts, B. (1978). The social history of a 'moral panic'. In *Policing the crisis: Mugging, the state, and the law and order* (pp. 53–77). The Mac Millan Press Ltd.

Hannah-Moffat, K. (2018). Algorithmic risk governance: Big data analytics, race and information activism in criminal justice debates. *Theoretical Criminology*, 1362480618763582.

Hayes de Kalaf, E., & Fernandes, K. (2023). *Digital identity: Emerging trends, debates and controversies.* [Guide or manual]

Hirvonen, H. (2024). Just accountability structures–a way to promote the safe use of automated decision-making in the public sector. *AI & Society, 39*(1), 155–167.

Holt, T. J. (2017). Identifying gaps in the research literature on illicit markets on-line. *Global Crime, 18*(1), 1–10.

Hummel, B., Yerkes, M. A., & Bal, M. (2023). 'Unprecedented injustice': Digitalisation and the perceived accessibility of childcare benefits. *Journal of Social Policy*, 1–20.

Jasanoff, S. (2010). A new climate for society. *Theory, Culture & Society, 27*(2–3), 233–253.

Joh, E. E. (2016). The new surveillance discretion: Automated suspicion, big data, and policing. *The Harvard Law & Policy Review, 10*(15), 38.

Just, N., & Latzer, M. (2017). Governance by algorithms: Reality construction by algorithmic selection on the Internet. *Media, Culture & Society, 39*(2), 238–258.

Kennedy, H., Poell, T., & van Dijk, J. (2015). Data and agency. *Big Data & Society, 3*, 1–2.

Khan, Z., Anjum, A., Soomro, K., & Tahir, M. A. (2015). Towards cloud based big data analytics for smart future cities. *Journal of Cloud Computing, 4*(1), 2.

Kitchin, R. (2014). Big Data, new epistemologies and paradigm shifts. *Big Data & Society, 1*(1), 2053951714528481.

Kleinberg, J., Ludwig, J., Mullainathan, S., & Obermeyer, Z. (2015). Prediction policy problems. *American Economic Review, 105*(5), 491–95.

Kohler-Hausmann, I. (2013). Misdemeanor justice: Control without conviction. *American Journal of Sociology, 119*(2), 351–393.

Konaté, S., & Pali, B. (2023). "You have to talk with us, not about us": Exploring the harms of wrongful accusation on those affected in the case of the Dutch 'childcare-benefit scandal'. *Revista de Victimología/Journal of Victimology*, (16), 139–164.

Lane, J., et al. (Eds.). (2014). *Privacy, big data, and the public good: Frameworks for engagement* (Daniel Solove, Understanding Privacy). Cambridge University Press.

Latour, B. (2007). *Reassembling the social: An introduction to actor-network-theory.* Oup Oxford.

Lehtiniemi, T. (2017). Personal data spaces: An intervention in surveillance capitalism? *Surveillance & Society, 15*(5), 626–639.

Lewis, S. C., & Westlund, O. (2015). Big data and journalism: Epistemology, expertise, economics, and ethics. *Digital Journalism, 3*(3), 447–466.

Lin, P., Abney, K., & Bekey, G. (2011). Robot ethics: Mapping the issues for a mechanized world. *Artificial Intelligence, 175*(5–6), 942–949.

Livingstone, S., & Helsper, E. J. (2007). Taking risks when communicating on the Internet: The role of offline social-psychological factors in young people's vulnerability to online risks. *Information, Communication & Society, 10*(5), 619–644.

Livingstone, S., & Smith, P. K. (2014). Annual research review: Harms experienced by child users of online and mobile technologies: The nature, prevalence and management of sexual and aggressive risks in the digital age. *Journal of child psychology and psychiatry, 55*(6), 635–654.

Loader, B. (Ed.). (1997). *The governance of cyberspace: Politics, technology and global restructuring.* Psychology Press.

Low, S. (2017). Security at home: How private securitization practices increase state and capitalist control. *Anthropological Theory, 17*(3), 365–381.

Lyon, D. (Ed.). (2003). *Surveillance as social sorting: Privacy, risk, and digital discrimination.* Psychology Press.

Lyon, D. (Ed.). (2006). *Theorizing surveillance: The panopticon and beyond.* Polity.

Lyon, D. (2014). Surveillance, Snowden, and big data: Capacities, consequences, critique. *Big Data & Society, 1*(2), 2053951714541861.

Mackenzie, A. (2006). *Cutting code: Software and sociality.* Peter Lang.

MacKinnon, D. (2012). Beyond strategic coupling: reassessing the firm-region nexus in global production networks. *Journal of Economic Geography, 12*(1), 227–245.

Malleson, N., & Andresen, M. A. (2015). The impact of using social media data in crime rate calculations: Shifting hot spots and changing spatial patterns. *Cartography and Geographic Information Science, 42*(2), 112–121.

Matthias, A. (2004). The responsibility gap: Ascribing responsibility for the actions of learning automata. *Ethics and Information Technology, 6*(3), 175–183.

Mittelstadt, B. D., Allo, P., Taddeo, M., Wachter, S., & Floridi, L. (2016). The ethics of algorithms: Mapping the debate. *Big Data & Society, 3*(2), 2053951716679679.

Morrison, J. (2014). The social license. In *The social license: How to keep your organization legitimate* (pp. 12–28). Palgrave Macmillan.

Nagy, V. (2018). *Crime prevention, migration control and surveillance practices: Welfare bureaucracy as mobility deterrent.* Routledge.

Napoli, P. M. (2014). Automated media: An institutional theory perspective on algorithmic media production and consumption. *Communication Theory, 24*(3), 340–360.

Newman, J., & Mintrom, M. (2023). Mapping the discourse on evidence-based policy, artificial intelligence, and the ethical practice of policy analysis. *Journal of European Public Policy, 30*(9), 1839–1859.

Pager, D. (2007). *Marked: Race, crime, and finding work in an era of mass incarceration.* University of Chicago Press.

Papachristos, A. V., Hureau, D. M., & Braga, A. A. (2013). The corner and the crew: The influence of geography and social networks on gang violence. *American Sociological Review, 78*(3), 417–447.

Pasquale, F. (2015). *The black Box society: The secret algorithms that control money and information.* Harvard University Press

Pearson, S., & Benameur, A. (2010, November). Privacy, security and trust issues arising from cloud computing. In *Cloud computing technology and science (CloudCom), 2010 IEEE second international conference on* (pp. 693–702). IEEE.

Peeters, R., & Widlak, A. C. (2023). Administrative exclusion in the infrastructure-level bureaucracy: The case of the Dutch daycare benefit scandal. *Public Administration Review, 83*(4), 863–877.

Perry, W. L., McInnis, B., Price, C. C., Smith, S. C., & Hollywood, J. S. (2013). Predictive policing: The role of crime forecasting in law enforcement operations. *RAND Safety and Justice Program.*

Prariser, E. (2011). *The filter bubble: What the internet is hiding from you.* Viking.

Ratcliffe, J. (2010). Crime mapping: Spatial and temporal challenges. In *Handbook of quantitative criminology* (pp. 5–24). Springer.

Reinarman, C., & Levine, H. G. (1989). Crack in context: Politics and media in the making of a drug scare. *Contemporary Drug Problems, 16*, 535.

Ridgeway, G. (2013a). Linking prediction and prevention. *Criminology & Public Policy, 12*(3), 545–550. https://doi.org/10.1111/1745-9133.12057

Ridgeway, G. (2013b). The pitfalls of prediction. *NIJ Journal, 271*, 34–40.

Rios, V. M. (2011). *Punished: Policing the lives of black and Latino boys.* New York University Press

Rose, J. A., & Lacher, D. C. (2016). *Managing public safety technology: Deploying systems in police, courts, corrections, and fire organizations.* Taylor & Francis.

Sandvig, C., Hamilton, K., Karahalios, K., & Langbort, C. (2014). Auditing algorithms: Research methods for detecting discrimination on internet platforms. *Data and Discrimination: Converting Critical Concerns into Productive Inquiry, 1*–23.

Sattlegger, A., Van Den Hoven, J., & Bharosa, N. (2022, June). Designing for Responsibility. In DG.O 2022: *The 23rd Annual International Conference on Digital Government Research* (dg.o 2022), June 15–17, 2022, Virtual Event, Republic of Korea. ACM, New York, NY, USA, 12 pages. https://doi.org/10.1145/3543434.3543581

Scassa, T. (2017). Law Enforcement in the Age of Big Data and Surveillance Intermediaries: Transparency Challenges. *SCRIPT-Ed, 14*(2), 239–284. https://doi.org/10.2966/scrip.140217.239

Schermer, B. W. (2011). The limits of privacy in automated profiling and data mining. *Computer Law & Security Review, 27*(1), 45–52.

Shalev-Shwartz, S., & Ben-David, S. (2014). *Understanding machine learning: From theory to algorithms.* Cambridge University Press.

Shilton, K. (2012). Participatory personal data: An emerging research challenge for the information sciences. *Journal of the American Society for Information Science and Technology, 63*(10), 1905–1915. http://dx.doi.org/10.1002/asi.22655

Silver, E., & Miller, L. L. (2002). A cautionary note on the use of actuarial risk assessment tools for social control. *Crime & Delinquency, 48*(1), 138–161.

Simonse, O., Vanderveen, G., van Dillen, L. F., Van Dijk, W. W., & van Dijk, E. (2023). Social security or insecurity? The experience of welfare participation by financially vulnerable households in the Netherlands. *Social Policy & Administration, 57*(3), 255–271.

Seele, P. (2022). Technology Ethics: Origins, Paradigms and Implications for Business and Society. In: Poff, D.C., Michalos, A.C. (Eds.), *Encyclopedia of Business and Professional Ethics.* Springer, Cham. https://doi.org/10.1007/978-3-319-23514-1_1268-1

Stenning, P., & Shearing, C. (October 14, 2015). Stenning, P. & Shearing, C. 2015. Privatisation, Pluralisation and the Globalisation of Policing. *Research Focus, 3*(1), 1–8. Available at SSRN: https://ssrn.com/abstract=2674028 or http://dx.doi.org/10.2139/ssrn.2674028

Stratton, G., Powell, A., & Cameron, R. (2017). Crime and justice in digital society: Towards a 'digital criminology'? *International Journal for Crime, Justice and Social Democracy, 6*(2), 17–33. https://doi.org/10.5204/ijcjsd.v6i2.355

Sweeney, L. (2013). Discrimination in online ad delivery. *Queue, 11*(3), 10.

Tilley, N., & Sidebottom, A. (Eds.). (2017). *Handbook of crime prevention and community safety.* Taylor & Francis.

van Erp, J. (2017). New governance of corporate cybersecurity: A case study of the petrochemical industry in the Port of Rotterdam. *Crime, Law and Social Change, 68*(1–2), 75–93.

Van Otterlo, M. (2013). A machine learning view on profiling. In M. Hildebrandt & K. de Vries (Eds.), *Privacy, due process and the computational turn-philosophers of law meet philosophers of technology* (pp. 41–64). Routledge.

Weiss, R. P. (2018). Vanishing boundaries of control: Implications for security and sovereignty of the changing nature and global expansion of neoliberal criminal justice provision. In *The Private Sector and Criminal Justice* (pp. 23–63). Palgrave Macmillan.

Williams, A. L., & Merten, M. J. (2009). Adolescents' online social networking following the death of a peer. *Journal of Adolescent Research, 24*(1), 67–90.

Williams, M. L., & Levi, M. (2017). Cybercrime prevention. *Handbook of Crime Prevention and Community Safety,* 454.

Willis, James J., Mastrofski, Stephen D., & Weisburd, D. (2007). Making sense of COMPSTAT: A theory-based analysis of organizational change in three police departments. *Law and Society Review, 41*(1), 147–188.

Winner, L. (1993). Upon opening the black box and finding it empty: Social constructivism and the philosophy of technology. *Science, Technology, & Human Values, 18*(3), 362–378.

Witten, I. H., Frank, E., Hall, M. A., & Pal, C. J. (2016). *Data mining: Practical machine learning tools and techniques.* Morgan Kaufmann.

Wolak, J., Mitchell, K., & Finkelhor, D. (2007). Unwanted and wanted exposure to online pornography in a national sample of youth Internet users. *Pediatrics, 119*(2), 247–257.

Wonders, N. A. (2016). Just-in-time justice: Globalization and the changing character of law, order, and power. *Critical Criminology, 24*(2), 201–216.

Zajko, M. (2023). Automated government benefits and welfare surveillance. *Surveillance & Society, 21*(3), 246–258.

Ziewitz, M. (2016b). Governing algorithms: Myth, mess, and methods. *Science, Technology & Human Values, 41*, 3–16.

Zuboff, S. (1988). *In the age of the smart machine: The future of work and power.* Basic Books, Inc.

Zuboff, S. (2013, June 25). Be the friction: Our response to the new lords of the ring. *Frankfurter Allgemeine Zeitung.* Retrieved from http://www.faz.net/aktuell/feuilleton/the-surveillance-paradigm-be-the-friction-our-response-tothe-new-lords-of-the-ring-12241996.html

Zuboff, S. (2015). Big other: Surveillance capitalism and the prospects of an information civilization. *Journal of Information Technology, 30*, 75–89.

Potential Harms from Automated Decision-Making

Individual Harms		Collective / Societal Harms
Illegal	**Unfair**	
Loss of Opportunity		
Employment Discrimination		**Differential Access to Job Opportunities**
E.g. Filtering job candidates by race or genetic/health information	E.g. Filtering candidates by work proximity leads to excluding minorities	
Insurance & Social Benefit Discrimination		**Differential Access to Insurance & Benefits**
E.g. Higher termination rate for benefit eligibility by religious group	E.g. Increasing auto insurance prices for night-shift workers	
Housing Discrimination		**Differential Access to Housing**
E.g. Landlord relies on search results suggesting criminal history by race	E.g. Matching algorithm less likely to provide suitable housing for minorities	
Education Discrimination		**Differential Access to Education**
E.g. Denial of opportunity for a student in a certain ability category	E.g. Presenting only ads on for-profit colleges to low-income individuals	
Economic Loss		
Credit Discrimination		**Differential Access to Credit**
E.g. Denying credit to all residents in specified neighborhoods ("redlining")	E.g. Not presenting certain credit offers to members of certain groups	
Differential Pricing of Goods and Services		**Differential Access to Goods and Services**
E.g. Raising online prices based on membership in a protected class	E.g. Presenting product discounts based on "ethnic affinity"	
	Narrowing of Choice	**Narrowing of Choice for Groups**
	E.g. Presenting ads based solely on past "clicks"	
Social Detriment		
	Network Bubbles	**Filter Bubbles**
	E.g. Varied exposure to opportunity or evaluation based on "who you know"	E.g. Algorithms that promote only familiar news and information
	Dignitary Harms	**Stereotype Reinforcement**
	E.g. Emotional distress due to bias or a decision based on incorrect data	E.g. Assumption that computed decisions are inherently unbiased
	Constraints of Bias	**Confirmation Bias**
	E.g. Constrained conceptions of career prospects based on search results	E.g. All-male image search results for "CEO," all-female results for "teacher"
Loss of Liberty		
	Constraints of Suspicion	**Increased Surveillance**
	E.g. Emotional, dignitary, and social impacts of increased surveillance	E.g. Use of "predictive policing" to police minority neighborhoods more
Individual Incarceration		**Disproportionate Incarceration**
E.g. Use of "recidivism scores" to determine prison sentence length (legal status uncertain)		E.g. Incarceration of groups at higher rates based on historic policing data

Chart 1   https://fpf.org/wp-content/uploads/2017/12/FPF-Automated-Decision-Making-Harms-and-Mitigation-Charts.pdf

PART V

Contextualizing online deviance

37

BRANDING THE "BANDITO INFLUENCER"

Studying cross-platform fame and deviance in the cases of Er Brasiliano and 1727wrldstar

Nicola Bozzi and Stefano Brilli

Introduction

While we have grown accustomed to seeing violent acts go viral, media scholarship has paid minor attention to the intertwining of social media influence and "criminal" lifestyles in everyday digital cultures. From a criminology perspective, recent studies on "internet banging" (Patton et al., 2013) have highlighted the role of social media in the escalation of gang violence (Lauger & Densley, 2018; Stuart, 2020), but their attention to the dynamics of celebrification of gang members is limited. From a celebrity studies perspective, while scholars have shown a particular interest in the relationship between celebrity and criminality (Penfold-Mounce, 2009), most of these analyses focus on mass media, where the media framing of the "criminal" is a product of centralised and professionalised dynamics.

To bridge these gaps, this chapter builds on previous research on the collective definition of the "gangsta" identity on social media (Bozzi, 2021) to investigate the "criminal" persona as a visibility strategy in influencer culture. By observing the fame management of two self-styled "criminal" influencers, the chapter examines how the cultures and affordances of digital platforms shape the framing of deviance and the performance of a "criminal" persona. To this end, the first part combines literature from criminology, celebrity studies and internet studies to explore scholarly debates on celebrity and criminal deviance, as well as "gangsta" identity in digital culture. We also emphasise how the discursive practice of the "dissing", popularised by hip-hop culture and specifically gangsta rap, has increasing relevance to the collective dimension of platformed digital environments. In this respect, we highlight the fraught implications that the acceleration and scalability afforded by social media fame can have in relation to criminalisation along social and racial lines.

This is especially important given the recent turn towards ephemerality and live streaming. The rising centrality of liveness in digital environments (Auslander, 2012; Gemini, 2016; Lupinacci, 2021) complicates, in fact, content moderation processes and lowers entry barriers to online performativity. These circumstances provide new conditions for self-exposure and celebrification of individuals with a criminal past or who revolve their persona around a criminal lifestyle (alleged or not). To address this issue and to explore localised variations of the gangsta influencer, the second part of the chapter looks at the

DOI: 10.4324/9781003277675-43

cases of two self-styled "criminal" influencers whose fame exploded during the 2020 lock-down in Italy: Algero Corretini aka "1727wrldstar" and Massimiliano Minnocci aka "Er Brasiliano". These personalities are examples of what we identify as "*bandito* influencers", where the Italian word "*bandito*" is intended both as "street thug" and "banned" from a specific site or group. The two characters share many common traits: they both boast street credibility and fashion their persona around the "borgataro" vernacular (a register that resonates with suburban areas of Rome but that also has national pop-cultural appeal); they have criminal records of violence; they owe their fame to viral videos in which they perform law-breaking actions; they have developed successful careers as influencers; they have been invited to mainstream television and radio programmes. The two, however, also differ significantly in the way they responded to media exposure. While, to a large extent, Minnocci's mainstream visibility has been framed through a narrative of rehabilitation and deviation from criminal life, Corretini's criminal parable was amplified alongside his growing popularity, arguably accelerating the staging of his own self-destruction (steroid addiction) and, much more seriously, acts of violence towards his partner.

The chapter thus aims to discuss the platformisation and celebrification of criminal deviance, emphasising how the self-representation afforded by social media platforms does not necessarily result in de-stigmatisation. On the one hand, criminal discourse and aesthetics sometimes become necessary to engage with one's audience; on the other, the labelling of the criminal on social media is a necessarily distributed and multi-sided dynamic that is hard to fully control with self-branding. With our account, we also wish to contribute a more localised perspective on the Italian context, which appears to be understudied. While the "criminal" or "gangsta" persona is a globally mediated, circulating collective subject, it still needs to be studied in its different contextual instances. The "*bandito*", in this respect, helps us outline this critical dialectic between the global and local dimensions of the criminal influencer.

Criminality, deviance and media celebrity

The role of media in the labelling of the criminal is a central issue when studying the social construction of deviance, and it has been a relevant topic in cultural criminology, sociology of deviance and media studies. The relationship between media representation, deviance and crime is indeed multifaceted and calls for critical examination. On the one hand, it has been shown how mass media can contribute to strengthening the labelling processes. For example, LaChance and Kaplan (2019) analysed the genre of *crimesploitation* reality TV, showing how it reinforces the ideology of "law and order punitivism". In their view, "real justice entertainment" shows—from the series *Cops* (which premiered in 1988) to the more recent *To Catch a Predator* (2004–2007)—share a kind of ideological discourse that:

> celebrates police or executive authority while casting suspicion on judicial decision making; bemoans commitments to due process and the rights of criminal defendants; constructs criminals in simplistic terms as evil and monstrous others; presents victims as innocents whose purity and goodness the community affirms in the act of punishment; and, finally, authorizes the harsh, extra-legal, and humiliating elements of punishment as a crucial and necessary counterpart to its modern, rule-bound, institutional logics.
>
> *(LaChance & Kaplan, 2019, pp. 129–130)*

On the other hand, mainstream media may occasionally participate in de-stigmatising the criminal individual. This process happens, however, without necessarily reforming the hegemonic labelling of the criminal. Media, in this sense, maintain their power over the conditions of visibility of individuals or groups framed as deviants. For instance, they do so by spectacularising the deviant through enfreakment strategies in talk shows (Gamson, 1998; Grindstaff, 2002) or through media rituals (Couldry, 2003) of shaming and rehabilitation (Boudana, 2014). In other words, both the social inclusion and social exclusion of criminals through media exposure are often inseparable from othering strategies (Greer & Jewkes, 2005).

Underlying these representational dynamics is the ambiguous fascination that criminal stories and subjectivities exert on the audience, which makes the securitarian frame and the fetishisation of criminal life coexist. A seminal contribution to trying to understand this attachment is offered by Paul Kooistra (1989), who distinguishes various motivations for the fascination with criminal deviance. Kooistra identifies three groups of motivations: psychological, cultural and social.

Among the psychological motivations are those whereby crime stories fulfil the audience's need for catharsis or tickle a fascination for radical otherness in a manner not dissimilar to the consumption of horror or thriller fiction.

The cultural motivations involve an appreciation for the role of the criminal as a rule-breaker who challenges social norms. In this sense, the same type of criminal activity may stimulate opposite reactions in different audiences depending on their compliance with the norm. In this regard, Heckert and Heckert (2002), studying "deviance admiration" in the American context, emphasise how it is based on conduct that breaks the over-conformity with normative expectations of middle-class behaviour. The subversion of the social norm of "moderation", for example, can be both condemned as negative deviance when it takes the form of hedonism, but also as deviance admiration in the character of roguishness, typical of the figures of the "charming rogue" or the "lovable drunk" (Heckert & Heckert, 2004).

Finally, we find social motivations when the admiration of the criminal is based on the sense of retaliation of certain social groups against the hegemonic order. Disenchantment or resentment towards this order leads to positively framing the criminal's actions (with whom the individual often shares a background to some extent) in the sense of a transgression of the oppressive order.

Stardom is one of the fields of analysis in which the ambiguity of the attraction of law-breaking has been most extensively investigated. Celebrity studies have shown a particular interest in the relationship between celebrity and criminality, exploring both the reactions to the illegal conduct of stars and the media visibility of criminal individuals. Since the beginning of the Hollywood industry, attention to celebrity wrongdoing has been an integral part of the construction of the stardom, as masterfully recounted in *Hollywood Babylon* (1959) by cult filmmaker Kenneth Anger. Some scholars have argued that the "criminalisation of the star" and "celebrification of the criminal" are increasingly intertwined (Rojek, 2001) and that we are witnessing a "collapse of the difference between fame and notoriety" (Schmid, 2006, p. 297).

The fame of the media celebrity and that of the criminal do indeed share a common function as objects on which the public experiments with their moral expectations. However, those expectations also contain a profound ambiguity. We can in fact distinguish two opposing spectator-positions prevalent in celebrity culture. On one side, celebrities and criminals are regarded as subjects on whom the public's condemnation is disinhibited (Connor, 2016), so much so that they are characteristic scapegoats for the tabloid industries. On another side, however, both live in a condition of a partial "moral moratorium" for the general public: Rojek (2012) calls "frontierism" this expectation addressed to celebrities to challenge social conventions and living borderline or "larger-than-life" lifestyles.

However, as Penfold-Mounce (2009) points out in what is still the most comprehensive analysis of the relationship between crime and celebrity, it is not quite correct to speak of "blurred boundaries" between these two figures. Instead, it is necessary to analyse the specific conditions (type of crime, historical context, type of constructed image) that can lead to either *glamorisation* (crime fuelling celebrity glamour) or *deglamorisation* (crime causing celebrity status to be lost). While it is true that crime is a powerful tool for the construction of media visibility, it is not necessarily the case that this visibility will result in celebrity capital (Driessens, 2013): the lack of an acceptable reputation in most cases prevents the accumulated fame from being converted into economic, social, cultural and symbolic capital.

Particularly useful in this regard is the distinction that Penfold-Mounce (2009) makes between *criminal celebrities* —criminals who acquire celebrity status—and *rogue celebrities*—i.e. stars who engage in criminal conduct.

Among criminal celebrities, the author identifies four sub-types: the *social bandit*, figures who appear to be criminals according to the law but are admired by the general public as defenders of the oppressed (the classic example in this respect is Robin Hood); the *criminal hero*, i.e. the criminal who, although recognised as a criminal even by the general public, maintains an admired style or code of moral conduct; the *underworld exhibitionst*, a criminal who actively pursues methods to attract fame by publicising his actions and using crime to build his celebrity persona; *iniquitous criminal*, criminals whose condemnation is unanimous and who do not attract appreciation but only morbid fascination (as in the case of serial killers).

Rogue celebrities, instead, can be distinguished into: *celebrity suspect*, celebrities who are suspected of crimes but still awaiting trial and who can therefore trigger a split in the audience between defenders and condemners; *celebrity deviant*, celebrities who are attributed deviant traits, not necessarily of a criminal nature, but who engage in transgressive conduct that oscillates between disapproval and desirability; *celebrity criminal*, when the celebrity is actually convicted of a crime and must therefore go through a rehabilitation process to regain their star status.

Then there are cases in which it is not easy to distinguish whether crime temporally precedes or follows celebrity clearly. Sometimes these two dynamics of visibility feed circularly when the very acquisition of fame takes place through shady or entirely illegal dynamics. Although they represent the exception rather than the rule, these are cases where the boundaries between celebrity and criminal activity are indeed blurred. In the Italian context, one notable example is Fabrizio Corona, the "tamarro celebrity" (Ricci, 2014)—the Italian equivalent of the "celebrity chav" (Tyler & Bennett, 2010)—who acquired fame through his borderline illegal activity as a *paparazzo*.

The limitation of the presented body of studies, however, is that it is mostly based on legacy media, which have centralised power and procedures to determine frames and representations of the deviant. In digital cultures, there are at least three factors that complicate the picture and require us to observe new declinations of the relationship between deviance and celebrity:

- The increase in self-representation: on social media platforms, people with alleged or proven criminal conduct can construct their presence more independently than television framing.
- The growing role of vilification in online fame (Brilli, 2018): there is a growing influence that affects of aversion, derision and disgust have in the construction of fame in digital environments. This can be observed in the way social media afford to coordinate and make visible the work of anti-fandoms (Harman & Jones, 2013), but also in the emergence of anti-celebrities whose fame stems primarily from mockery (Gamson, 2011; Brilli, 2017).
- The multiplicity of governance arrangements in digital platforms (Poell et al., 2021): the variety of affordances, regulations and cultures in digital environments produces a heterogeneity of contexts in which deviance can be defined in conflicting manners. This state of affairs has important consequences in the transformation of the ways in which deviance is constructed, in line with Lauderdale's (2015) hypothesis that "where power is more diffuse, deviance may still persist but is more likely to be construed positively . . . If power approaches complete diffusion, deviance often comes to be seen as 'diversity' and not as abnormal, immoral, or unlawful" (Lauderdale, 2015, p. 551).

The chapter thus seeks to address this gap by examining how criminal labelling is employed in influencer culture as a means of visibility and profit. A key node in this regard, and one that has recently been the subject of several analyses, is that of the "gangsta" persona on social media, given how "gangsta" identity and culture represent a widespread interface between deviant labelling, online self-exposure and cultural production.

Making the gangsta influencer: from gangsta rap to the dissing economy

In recent years, many studies have discussed the relationship between social media and gang culture, often highlighting how certain sub-genres of rap music (in particular "trap" and "drill") are used both to uphold gang values or criminalise young artists (Pinkney & Robinson-Edwards, 2018; Lauger & Densley, 2018). Some studies are preoccupied with the impact of social media on the acceleration of gang violence (Patton et al., 2013; Irwin-Rogers & Pinkney, 2017), while others focus on the literal and symbolic minefield from which rap artists from disadvantaged neighbourhoods can emerge to establish a musical career (Harkness, 2013; Evans & Baym, 2022). A common thread, however, is the emphasis on the fraught nature of maintaining a "gangsta" persona through identity and authenticity work, especially in the context of rap fame. While scholars have studied the performative nature of gang identity before (Garot, 2007) and its function as an "empty signifier" in mainstream media (Richardson & Kennedy, 2012), studying criminal identity in the age of social media, and social media-driven celebrity, is particularly needed.

We frame the "gangsta" as a dynamic fame template. In other words, although music and gang subcultures are the primary symbolical sources for a "gangsta" persona, the social media-famous gangsta rapper represents an aspirational figure who casts their influence beyond the field of music fandoms and producers, providing a set of styles and practices for digital influencers outside the music industry. This is interesting from several perspectives. Firstly, such influencers draw their following not from musical talent, but rather from mediated authenticity work as well as vernacular creativity (Burgess, 2006). Secondly, the dynamism of the "gangsta" template needs to be studied also in relation to the many territorial, national and diasporic contexts it encounters. In this respect, it should be noted that, while rap music has been culturally racialised for generations in the US, the fact that mainstream media in Europe often reinforce a narrative of moral panic around young trap and drill artists has fraught implications for second-generation immigrants. In Italy, for example, these youths often struggle to find representation in Italian culture and might search for it through music (Cuconato, 2021), while the social media-driven cultural appropriation of these genres by white Italian rappers can result in "racial evasion" (Oware, 2016).

Therefore, this section discusses how the "gangsta" influencer is doubly affected by the expectation of authenticity and how the rap "dissing" can be seen as a proto-viral cultural format that combines vernacular/oral creativity, deviance admiration and the testing of street credibility.

Gangsta identity at the crossroad of fame and authenticity

When studying the connections between the criminal persona and online fame, "gangsta" and "drill" rappers offer a contextually meaningful example of visibility that is both historically significant and social media-specific. Discussions of rap as a genre all too commonly focus on the most controversial and stereotypical aspects of rap music (Racine, 2018), arguably because the genre's emphasis on authenticity invites even more scrutiny of artists' lifestyles (Chang, 2005). In analysing social media influencers labelled as "deviant", we need to look at how the expectation of authenticity towards rap artists converges with and differs from the authenticity labour of social media influencers (Banet-Weiser, 2012; Arriagada & Bishop, 2021).

The controversial quality of their subcultural appeal is one way that the "criminal" rapper embodies a more fraught form of authenticity than other types of influencers. Since the early days of gangsta rap, the genre was both hailed as a powerful (and commercially successful) representation of life in low-income, primarily African-American neighbourhoods, as well as criticised for encouraging stereotypical depiction of Black people and misogynistic content for the benefit of white audiences (LaGrone, 2000). Cultural critiques have highlighted the ambivalent relationship between the genre and authenticity: while the rapper is expected to be close enough to gang life to write and perform about it, most rappers get inspiration from scenarios lived by people they know but do not necessarily experience first-hand (Chang, 2005; Quinn, 2005). If "gangsta rap" now reads more like a nostalgic nod to 1990s culture, the hip-hop sub-genres of "trap" in early-2000s Atlanta and "drill" in 2010s Chicago (the latter especially native to social media) have drawn comparable commercial and critical attention for similar reasons. Studies by Patton and colleagues (2013) in Chicago and Irwin-Rogers and Pinkney (2017) in London (the two global capitals of drill) highlight how social media can accelerate violent conflicts between gangs as well as lead to the involuntary involvement of innocent social media users in police investigations and arrests. Stuart (2020), on the other hand, emphasises the dangerous tendency of overestimating the harmful effects of online behaviour. Drill videos are not the root cause of violence but rather a catalyst at most, especially when they contain incriminating or specific information about particular crimes (Irwin-Rogers & Pinkney, 2017). The emphasis on authenticity has led to further stigmatisation of the genre and to rap lyrics increasingly being consulted and used as evidence in court cases (Kubrin & Nielson, 2014; Dunbar, 2018). Drill has thus become another example of how "street culture" is being commodified (Ilan, 2012) at the same time as criminalised along racial lines (Meena, 2022).

While gang identity is itself a volatile subjectification and can be evoked strategically in specific situations (Garot, 2007), rappers affiliated with certain environments are even more encouraged to engage in strategic identification with and distancing from their status (Harkness, 2013). Rap and drill music videos also play a role in gang-related mythmaking: they offer people on the outside a "periscope" into the gang-related habitus (Lynes et al., 2020) but they do so by regularly exaggerating the gang's capacity for lethal violence (Lauger & Densley, 2018). As noted by Racine (2018, p. 260), "Rap's self-representation is an internal struggle fought within the conscience of all MCs, a conflict between the sensational, the enlightening, and ultimately, the commercially viable".

This aspect resonates with the challenges that digital creators encounter. As Arriagada and Bishop argue, "(d)eveloping and maintaining an authentic artistic identity is central to commercial success in creative industries, but at the same time commercial success can jeopardise a perception of artists as real" (2021, p. 570). There is a conflictual element to this contrast, as "any and all claims of authenticity are tested continuously in a call-and-response rhetorical field with the community called into being by such claims" (Craig & Cunningham, 2019, p. 154).

From a gender perspective, however, if authenticity labour is gendered as feminine in many digital contexts, especially those involving emotional labour (Arriagada & Bishop, 2021), the gangsta rapper usually requires a heavy investment into a hyper-masculine impression.

From a racial standpoint, "authenticity policing" is a routine that more heavily impacts members of marginalised communities (Duffy et al., 2022). However, the visibility and relational labour of the urban poor involved in hip-hop have been underexplored. In their examination of the drill scene, Evans and Baym find the cultural influence achieved through amassing social media engagement and "clout" as a potential propelling force to empower disadvantaged youth since "artists and those working with them often sought to use their entrepreneurialism to lift their communities out of poverty together" (Evans & Baym, 2022, p. 2672). Unlike other creative producers and artists, the drill rapper is thus a converging point of different orders of value: creative talent, profitability and street credibility—the latter being a particular attribute that other types of influencers do not need to live by.

Digital affordances for networked credibility

To understand how the subcultural style of authenticity inherent to gang culture transitions into a cultural commodity that circulates on social media, this section looks at some of the cultural practices that enforce the testing of such authenticity and how they intersect with social media affordances.

Evans and Baym (2022) discuss three strategies that musical artists within the Chicago music scene utilise on social media to gain "clout": *capping*—projecting a self-aggrandising public persona; *cosigning* —establishing relationships with more established figures within the scene; *corralling*—creating a collective of supporters or posse to support the artist in the work. Evans and Baym also clarify that pursuing clout often requires exaggerating street credibility to the point of having harmful consequences for the producers.

Besides strategies to maximise self-popularity, other online techniques are aimed at reducing the visibility of competitors. When performing a street-savvy persona, rappers may be exposed to assessments that are embedded in the street code and rematerialise on the Internet. Stuart (2020) outlines several strategies that gang-associated youth rely on to exploit social media to invalidate their rivals' authenticity and masculine toughness publicly: *cross-referencing*, re-posting content from a rival's past; *calling bluffs*, urging a rival to escalate confrontation, and *catching lacking*, surprising a rival in a situation where their gang identity cannot be enacted. These confrontational methods can result in dangerous escalations of violence as well.

Bozzi (2021) discusses the practice of *tagging*, drawing a connection between the social labelling as a way of "making the criminal" (Tannenbaum, 1938) and its use in self-branding practices on social media. According to Bozzi, the practice of dissing is also especially relevant as a cultural format that is both embedded within hip-hop subcultures and appropriated as a click-bait strategy that dangerously amplifies the stereotypical ambiguity of the authenticity paradox outlined before. Social media affordances intensify the inherently scalable cultural relevance of the dissing. In terms of its specific contextual resonance, Johnson and Schell-Busey (2016) highlighted how the verbal contests exemplified by rap battles stem from the tradition of "the dozens" documented in African-American vaudeville (Wald, 2012) and among crowds of lower-class African-American boys (Abrahams, 1962) for a long time. Transported to the social and subcultural context of hip-hop, the confrontational tone of such exchanges in rap battles may occasionally lead to violence, but rappers have their ways of framing the clash as only verbal and de-escalate the tension (Johnson & Schell-Busey, 2016).

The reason for a dissing can often be to elevate a lesser-known rapper's fame at the expense of a more-established one. Dissing someone can result in a "beef", that is, an ongoing feud with a rival (mostly another rapper) publicly displayed through either recorded "diss tracks" or, in the age of social media, tweets, snaps or Instagram Stories. Regardless of who "wins" the beef, however, exposure can usually be beneficial to all involved.

Dissing, in conjunction with social media affordances, has thus become a visibility practice employed by numerous public figures, from micro-celebrities to business celebrities,[1] even outside the rap scene. Instagram Stories are especially interesting in this respect (Bozzi, 2021). Stories allow rappers or influencers to artfully curate "front" stage performances for the viewing public, also materialising the public "making" of the criminal by @-ing rivals or friends as either a form of provocation, endorsement, or an attempt to plug into their viewership. Given its conflictual, sensationalistic nature, the dissing is notable as a proto-viral cultural format that combines community-based authenticity and popularity boosting. It is therefore not surprising that dissing has emerged from its subcultural context to become a widespread visibility practice across the current attention economy. Beyond music as a creative endeavour, the avatar of the "platformed gangsta" is then an asset for creators, cultural producers and influencers that capitalise on online mischiefs and transgressive lifestyles.

If the gangsta persona's front- and backstage performance is individually crafted, the audience also participates in the overall persona construction. Followers provide their labour by saving, filtering, curating and editing content (for example, Stories but also live streams), isolating the more controversial bits. Content deleted from a platform for ToS infringement, or because of digital ephemerality, can be saved and reuploaded by users elsewhere, for example, as YouTube compilations of Instagram Stories. Furthermore, by saving that content and recirculating them in private contexts where moderation is looser (e.g., from Instagram to porn sites or Telegram channels), users co-construct those gestures as "transgressive". In this sense, whether they are fans or freebooters driven by personal profit, they don't just take part in the "participatory branding" (Meisner & Ledbetter, 2022) of the gangsta influencer, but also in its "participatory labelling". Not only do they perpetuate the content's existence but also substantiate the framing of the gangsta character between deviance and desire. The gangsta influencer thus becomes associated with a growing repository of banned videos that continue to exist in the undergrowth of the Internet.

As maintained by Bozzi (2021, p. 22):

> The exploded figure of the YouTube or Instagram Gangsta is, therefore, a dramatised stereotype and an aspirational figure at once—one that can help re-problematise the supposedly neutral infrastructure that allows users to leverage hyper-ritualised narrations of violence as if they were routine branding' best practices.

The many facets of the dissing economy

Moving beyond the idea that celebrity and notoriety merely mix in the economy of online visibility, the link between a "gangsta" or "criminal" persona and visibility strategies ought to be examined through different dimensions and frames. In other words, there are multiple ways in which transgressions (actual or performed) and criminal narratives can lead to influencing labour and the accumulation of celebrity capital. It is also crucial to emphasise how the digital environment implies the convergence of many intersecting normative systems, which can be consistent, coexistent or contrasting with each other: local street code, platform regulations, community customs and legacy media framing. Digital influencers can deliberately deploy such tensions. The online deviant who strategically brings street slang to social media (making it clash with native linguistic standards) or live-broadcasts contents that might be subject to censorship (semi-pornographic acts, drug consumption, verbal or non-verbal violence) are examples of a "weaponisation of contexts" (Abidin, 2021), useful to create sensationalism and enhance deviance admiration (Heckert & Heckert, 2002) from digital audiences.

While in mainstream media the framing of deviant fame is the product of centralised and professionalised dynamics, in the platform economy, it results from clashes between different regulation, labelling and monetisation systems. Therefore, this section proposes a taxonomy of how gangsta identity intersects with the construction of an online persona and the different ways in which dissing is practised. We can thus distinguish six dimensions that need to be taken into account when studying this phenomenon.

Consensus on the recognition of deviance

A first dimension to observing the use of the "gangsta" persona online is the degree of unanimity in recognising the subject and their actions as deviant. The moral heterogeneity of online exposure, especially in a cross-platform landscape, allows individuals framed as criminals for one audience to be seen as heroes for another. Thus, one can apply Penfold-Mounce's (2009) classification of criminal celebrities. In the most successful cases, the online gangsta person is regarded as a *social bandit* when they commit legal offences that are viewed favourably by followers (drug use is the most emblematic case). Sometimes they can also be *criminal heroes* when the public recognises specific actions of the character as criminal but respects their path to redemption. Cases of *underworld exhibitionists* and *iniquitous criminals* are rare in this sphere, especially given the slight chance they would not get banned from the major platforms and their remunerations. However, they are not impossible and occur mainly with short-term exposure; for instance, when the criminal posts first-hand videos of violent actions that quickly disappear from public platforms and circulate in private spaces.

Connection with music production

The media exposure of the gangsta persona is primarily linked to the rap, trap and drill scenes, but not all gangsta influencers have connections to music production. On the one hand, we thus find the use of the gangsta persona in conjunction with promoting one's musical career; on the other, influencers or creators who use their transgressive lifestyle to accumulate visibility. An example is the Italian streamer Don Alì, now excluded from all platforms, who has gangsta influencer traits without ever participating in music production. Don Alì became famous in 2021 thanks to IRL (in real life) lives on Twitch, where he filmed himself performing shenanigans bordering on illegality (provoking passers-by, disturbing underground passengers, clashing with the police, leaving McDonald's without paying). Between these two poles, there are numerous figures who, although not primarily pursuing a musical career, do feature and occasionally put out their rap tracks, either because they are connected with the local rap scene or as an additional branding tool.[2] Some individuals are artists whose criminal background is instrumental in their ascent and fall from grace narrative.[3]

Collective or individual dimension

Online criminal identity can be built around established gang membership (as highlighted in the previously cited literature). Alternatively, it may provide the basis for online networking among characters that form groups somewhere between "online gangs" and strategic Instagram pods (O'Meara, 2019) to increase visibility. Conversely, they may play their persona on the identity of the "lone wolf" with no gang or community membership, as in the case we will explore of 1727wrldstar.

Narration vs. exhibition of transgression

There are different degrees to which a "criminal" influencer might be engaged in illegal activities or boasting about them. On the one hand, deviant behaviour may be the subject of the narration of the influencer's story. On the other hand, the influencer may use the online space to directly display their borderline-illegal stunts directly. Then, a distinction has to be made between ex-post narration (i.e. when it is directed at recounting a criminal past from which one detaches oneself) and the simultaneous narration of a criminal lifestyle still in progress.

Role of intermediaries

The "gangsta" influencer is usually a phenomenon of self-exposure, but there are also intermediaries who narrate and elaborate on the transgressive or criminal lifestyle of the gangsta personality. In this respect, the constellation of "street-cred intermediaries" that also feed the dissing economy is heterogeneous. In a music industry context, well-structured channels such as VlatTV offer extensive and in-depth interviews with the protagonists, complete with context and, often, the necessary disclaimers.[4] A second format comprises channels bordering between documentary and true crime entertainment, which favour a de-stigmatising perspective and are careful not to celebrate or romanticise the criminal lifestyle.[5] There are also a range of derivative accounts that showcase curated compilations of news stories, Instagram Stories, music videos and news headlines. They generally feature extensive commentary and sometimes moral judgements or justifications, with varying degrees of nuance.[6] Others are more in the style of YouTube "drama" or "tea" (Christin & Lewis, 2021), keeping social commentary to a minimum and exploiting dissing as gossip material.[7]

Impact of locality

Finally, a "gangsta" persona takes on different forms in relation to locality and urban contexts. At one level, it draws from a repertoire of signs circulating internationally, with rap often acting as a meta-language. At the same time, "gangsta" takes on specific meanings and nuances according to local contexts, ranging concentrically from neighbourhood to city to region to nation. The "gangsta" influencer embodies a tripolar tension between local vernacular, digital vernacular and global subjectivity. Authenticity and street credibility, in this sense, should not be seen simply as adherence to locality, but as a relationship between "gangsta" as a general "*langue*", and a "gangsta *parole*", by which we mean the legitimacy in using idiolects belonging to specific communities. For this reason, we now briefly present the "*bandito* influencer" case study to clarify the mobility of the "gangsta" between nations, platforms, media and between physical and digital contexts.

Cross-platform transgression: framing the bandito influencer

Having established the platformed and globalised character of the "criminal" influencer, and its relevance to the study of online deviance, this section finally zooms in on the "*bandito* influencer". The double meaning of the word "*bandito*" as "street thug" and "banned" serves to emphasise the complex link between online and offline transgression and, at the same time, the importance that locality has in shaping the gangsta phenomenon. The two influencers discussed here, Er Brasiliano and 1727wrldstar, have many things in common: they share a geographic area of cultural reference, the wider metropolitan area of Rome; both gained national notoriety through verbally and sometimes physically violent behaviour; both mix the vernacular creativity of oral suburban cultures, gangsta imagery and influencing strategies based on global social media metrics and affordances; not leash, both figures represent controversial role models in terms of nationalist identity and misogynistic behaviour. Despite these commonalities, their framing by mainstream media and online audiences gradually diverged over time. Er Brasiliano has become a figure between the *social bandit* and the *celebrity deviant* (Penfold-Mounce, 2009), controversial for some audiences but still a "voice of the suburbs" for others. 1727wrldstar, on the other hand, has followed a downward parable that led him to become an "internet villain" and documented offender. This last part of the chapter briefly examines their case by looking at their rise to fame in relation to various media frames, the role of locality in authenticity construction and the relationship with the live/ephemeral affordances of social media.

Er Brasiliano and 1727wrldstar: rise to fame and cross-platform framing

The first example of *bandito* influencer is Massimiliano Minnocci, from the Pietralata suburb area of Rome. Known as "Er Brasiliano" (The Brazilian), Minnocci came to national fame around 2018, when he was interviewed on national TV as a member of a hooligan group who got banned from the stadium for 8 years. In November 2018, a video where he confronted the police bare-chested went viral. Given his large Facebook following, he was interviewed again by national TV and radios, especially concerning the fascist symbols he had tattooed. Since then, Er Brasiliano has become a regular figure in Italian media, notably on the popular radio show *La Zanzara*, where two hosts regularly interview controversial characters. In these appearances, Er Brasiliano is routinely confronted about his past behaviour, criminal affiliation and serving jail time—all aspects of his life that he publicly acknowledges with an apologetic attitude. Significantly, he also regularly uses his own platform on Instagram Stories and Live to give his own version to his followers and often project a narrative of repentance.

The second example is Algero Corretini, aka "1727wrldstar". Corretini's ascent to fame is tightly related to the first Covid lockdown in mid-2020, during the exploding popularity of digital livestream on Instagram and Twitch. Before the pandemic, 1727 had a Spotify profile where he posted rap songs, clearly influenced by different generations of the local rap and trap scene. While not musically successful, Corretini started to have some traction when he started doing frequent live sessions, during which he confronted "callers" and random followers creatively insulting them live for the amusement of his audience. Corretini scaled up from his social media fame and gained national notoriety through a viral video in which he crashed his car while live streaming on Instagram. His line uttered just after the crash—"*ho preso il muro fratelli*" (I caught the wall bro)—followed by—"*se ve siete salvati la diretta siete miliardari, fratelli*" (If you saved the stream you're billionaires, fam)—quickly became a popular meme nationwide, especially in the Rome area. This marked a turning point for his influencer career, which led to sponsorships (especially from urban fashion brands, jewellery, fitness products and local businesses such as barber shops, restaurants and gyms) and an explicit re-branding of his Instagram feed, as well as attention from some of the more famous Instagram gossip accounts.

This also attracted attention from mainstream media. Similarly to Er Brasiliano, 1727 was also invited on radio and TV and presented as a problematic figure emerging from social media. While Er Brasiliano managed to leverage the self-representation afforded by digital platforms, putting it in a productive dialogue with his more mainstream appearances, 1727's "transformation" was chronicled in more judgemental terms, emphasising his steroid use, sprawling face tattoos, nihilistic attitude and controversial rise to fame. Eventually, when he was incarcerated at the beginning of 2021 on allegations of domestic violence (some episodes of which had partially been captured live during his sessions), he disappeared from the scene for ten months.

The two personalities, and their reciprocal relationship, are helpful to understand the changing framing of the criminal personality in the cross-platform media ecology. Both were initially exoticised through the script of the "violent lowlife who finds online fame through sensationalism", and both are offered the same transformation proposal in the televised arena: to move away from their violent lifestyle and make their visibility productive to help the peripheries they come from. Although they have several similarities, there is a relevant generational difference between them: Er Brasiliano is in his forties, while

1727 is in his twenties. This generational gap also defines a different attitude towards their media visibility. While the former maintains a "criminal" persona based on honour, amoral familism and loyalty to the neighbourhood, the latter is portrayed as the embodiment of a new generation interested solely in visibility and significantly poorer in social and subcultural capital.

This reflects in the way the two have responded differently to the aforementioned media framing. Er Brasiliano seems to have accepted the mainstream media visibility and proposal to change his image (the two go hand in hand). Er Brasiliano seems to have accepted the mainstream media visibility and proposal to change his image (the two go hand in hand). This transformation happened through highly symbolic gestures in televised rites of passage: he erased his tattoos with fascist icons, almost physically clashed on live television with left-wing cartoonist Vauro and then becomes his friend, promises to give up cocaine consumption, was filmed promoting activities to help the suburbs. 1727wrldstar, on the contrary, treated journalists who invited him to convert his online presence into constructive and altruistic activities with condescension, trolled television by faking his own disappearance and continued cultivating his online persona based on provoking everyone and everything. However, he was not only excluded from mainstream media visibility, but also began to be banned from Twitch as well for his threats and aggressive behaviour towards other streamers.

More generally, Er Brasiliano adjusts to cross-platform and cross-media mobility, strategically modelling his figure to the different visibilities and regulations of each space. 1727wrldstar, on the other hand, creates his own "locality" entirely centred on his Instagram channel, where he ensures he maintains control of his own presentation. Therefore, what emerges is a conflict not only between two ways of dealing with the "criminal" persona but also a conflict between two conditions of visibility. On the one hand, TV and radio, where visibility is connected to the framing of the deviant personality through cautionary tales and exoticisation; on the other hand, the influencer economy, where visibility does not necessarily hinge on a univocal subjectivation or a unitary moral code but on a pact not to break community guidelines or foreclose commercial sponsorship. Mainstream media framing, in this case, offers de-stigmatisation on the condition of accepting conversion through media rituals and thus subordination to legacy media power. Conversely, online self-framing produces a memetic character that amplifies controversial and sensationalist traits, where deviant behaviour is the source for retaining the attention of followers.

Plugged-in locality: Roman vernacular between authenticity and theatricality

The second point of interest to focus on is the dynamic of interaction between the two characters and the way they employed dissing as a preferred form for establishing an initial contact and then sustaining their ongoing relationship. The first relevant documented moment in Er Brasiliano and 1727's evolving relationship is the live session in which they finally met on Instagram in April 2020. This is a significant moment because, in previous weeks, 1727 had been systematically calling for Er Brasiliano to have him on his profile. The meeting came after 1727wrldstar had already proven his vernacular creativity and confrontational attitude by targeting other rappers and influencers in Er Brasiliano's entourage.

While occasionally they included more introspective moments (e.g., 1727 crying while reflecting on his past or having a rather nuanced conversation with a psychologist), the most saved and re-uploaded interactions in 1727wrldstar's livestreams typically involved reciprocal insults in Roman dialect. These interactions have the characteristic form of the urban dozens (Abrahams, 1962), remediated through the social media dissing format and the affordances of Instagram Live. The strategically conflictual dynamics of 1727's insults, combined with Roman vernacular to grant both authenticity and cinematic charisma, was also accentuated by the pandemic backdrop. With the impossibility of physical meetings, the transgressive stakes were *raised* and *deflated* simultaneously: raised because the distance allowed for an escalation of verbal confrontation that would otherwise be impossible, but also deflated because the online context emphasised the performative "safe" nature of the confrontation.

Although the practice of verbal confrontation was employed as a performance of genuineness, strongly dependent on local cultural identity, at the same time it was a highly dramatised one. Both characters have stated on several occasions that almost all their dissings are totally artificial and used as a visibility device.[8] Er Brasiliano is quick to explain "this is all theatrics" and Instagram is his job, while 1727 calls it a "format" on several occasions. 1727 also confesses that he chose Er Brasiliano as his target because he was the most visible target, the king he had to claim his throne from. This way, the two figures quickly struck a playful rivalry and complicity. Since their first meeting, it was apparent how Minnocci recognises the rival's character in terms of cultural affinity, but also as a strategic asset. Eventually, rather than the dramatic climax of a long-announced confrontation, the first meeting (which had a live audience ranging from 8000 to 20000 viewers) proved to be the beginning of a troubled and much dramatised partnership, with Er Brasiliano eventually taking 1727 under his wing to capitalise on his strong ability to attract sponsorships and online attention.

Once again, we find a substantial ambiguity in the "gangsta" construct concerning the performance of authenticity. Here, the work of authenticity does not emerge from the values of consistency or honesty, as tends to be the case with the branding practices of popular influencers. This construction of authenticity is indeed based on establishing a link with past biography, but this link is merely a precondition to enable the use of a thoroughly affected performative language. Street credibility and criminal past work as guarantees that allow a theatrical staging of confrontations without it being perceived as cultural appropriation. In other words: if the specific conflict is fake, it is nonetheless substantiated by the general conflictuality that characterises their lifestyle. Deviance functions here as a legitimiser of violence that is false in actuality but true in virtuality.

Live/ephemeral digital affordances in the bandito influencer construction

The third theme to be emphasised is the centrality of liveness, temporariness and ephemerality in the digital environment (Boccia Artieri et al., 2021) to the construction of the *bandito* persona. This specific discursive construction of the criminal appears inseparable from the use of stories and live streams. Nevertheless, it also appears inseparable from how the pandemic has accelerated the shift from an urban arena to the online space.

With the immediacy of digital live streams, the entry skills required to reach visibility change from textual and audio-visual literacies to oral literacy. This is a type of literacy in line with a lower level of schooling, but it is also a kind of verbal duelling one learns to master in street interaction. In this sense, these affordances valorise social expertise scarcely valued by other media.

Secondly, the performance of the *bandito* influencer intensifies the unpredictability of liveness. The fame of Er Brasiliano and 1727 is built on rule-breaking, despite rule-breaking also being a factor that leads to being banned from platforms. In this sense, liveness fuels the promise that "anything could happen", which is a much more valuable promise in their case compared to the "clean" creators and influencers who are expected to have a long-term presence. Our two characters play with the limits of censorship, so the expectation of a violent escalation is always around the corner. Therefore, their contents are linked to *double ephemerality:* they are temporary by default, due to platform's affordances, and because they are likely to be deleted. The audience is then engaged in a game of constant attention, where they are the bottom-up curators of this otherwise volatile video heritage. The two influencers are very aware of this spectatorial pact. After all, the phrase that made 1727 famous is *"se ve siete salvati la diretta siete miliardari, fratelli"* (if you saved the stream you are billionaires, fam).

Thirdly, the two *bandito* influencers exploit the live stream's interactive affordances to transform dissing into a format of engagement with followers. In this case, dissing goes from being a practice of face-keeping to becoming the main course of their media offers. This format is not only based on their vernacular competence but also on how they branded their perceived dangerousness. This case thus shows an example of the construction of online deviance that oscillates between labelling processes that aim to contain it, and its instrumental use in conjunction with influencer culture and the affordances of digital platforms.

Conclusions

In this chapter, we examined the "criminal" persona in relation to the processes of platformisation and celebrification. To this end, we focused on the "gangsta" identity in online environments and analysed the increasingly widespread practice of dissing, from rap to influencer cultures. Then, the chapter proceeded to present the case study of the *"bandito influencer"*.

The *bandito* influencer is a compelling figure in terms of identity, self-branding and representation on social media. This figure confirms existing stereotypes of anti-social behaviour, including hypermasculinity and misogyny, while at the same time defending the fictional quality of such depiction, a non-essentialist notion of "criminal", and promoting a narrative of redemption and self-made entrepreneurship. A "criminal" background is instrumental to gaining the right to use an intimidating relational style that is highly dramatised, but also credible and unique. Er Brasiliano and 1727wrldstar trademarked memetic brands that cannot be easily copied since the connection to documented illegality fortifies them. This outcome partially contradicts those perspectives that see an automatic transition from mass media labelling to self-presentation on social media as a process of voice acquisition by marginalised subjects. While it is true that this shift allows empowerment to gain visibility and economic gain, this does not necessarily correspond to the construction of a more inclusive social narrative, but rather of an established pathway to fame that cannot discount a significant "overhead" in terms of conflict, stigma, misogyny and potentially violence. Like in the case of drill music, one cannot but wonder if the costs and affordances of online fame in countries like Italy (which at the moment are politically, if not demographically, white) might also vary significantly by identity markers such as ethnicity and nationality.

Significantly, in our case study, it was televised intervention that widened the frame on the influencers' story to include the account of the suburban reality from which they came (albeit by accepting media power, its moralistic stance and exoticising display). This type of storytelling requires a certain kind of literacy and organisation that goes beyond the stylistic immediacy and the rawness of Instagram livestreams and stories, which are centred on a single subject and sponsorship work alone. Therefore, if live affordances lower the entry barriers to influencer culture, such lowering could produce new social distinctions between digital creators. On the one hand, a class of creators with a high level of media literacy who master scripting, editing and performative proficiencies. On the other hand, a class of creators that rely on the exposure of their individuality (sometimes relying on widespread notions of deviance), prevalence of oral literacy and impermanence instead of persistent content. Future studies should further investigate how social difference and intersectional forms of oppression factor into this complex interplay of celebrification, platform affordances and increasingly individualised business models.

Notes

1 The beef between "Pharma Bro" Martin Shkreli and the Wu Tang Clan rapper Ghostface Killah is a case in point of the broad cultural influence of this practice.
2 Boonk Gang, a rapper who became a very active Instagrammer, is an example of this phenomenon within the US social media ecosystem. Although technically a rapper, Boonk Gang became famous online through his pranks and mischiefs (stealing snacks or jumping on the counter at Dunkin Donuts, having live sex on Instagram), which he uploaded and streamed online. While banned from Instagram, most of his clips found a new life on YouTube.
3 The most globally recognised figure to have emerged from this sort of "dissing economy" is rapper Tekashi 69, who famously used an aggressive communicative style and engaged in online dissings and occasionally real-life confrontations with other rappers. Importantly, Tekashi's affiliations with the Nine Trey gang people and imagery were also key factors in his rise to fame, as well as to the controversies following his arrest and later his early release with the widespread accusations of him for being a "snitch". His persona embodies the ambiguity inherent to the gangsta rap and the conundrum about the genre's authenticity, especially in the way he was able to leverage the dissing economy to his own favour (Roks, 2021).
4 This type of content integrates celebrity YouTube channels like TMZ, WorldStarHipHop or VladTV, which has built a large following interviewing rappers and focusing especially on the more street-adjacent aspects of their lives. Speculating or amplifying an idea of authenticity and street proximity seems to be one of the most central foci. VladTV in particular is worthy of mention, especially in relation to drill and authenticity: DJ Vlad's interview with Slim Jesus, a white drill rapper who admitted using the style because it was "cool" rather than for affinities with the criminal lifestyle, was at one point the most viewed on his channel.
5 A case in Italy is the former boxer, trainer and YouTuber Cicalone displays life in Rome's struggling suburbs with ex-criminals, rappers and influencers (including Er Brasiliano).
6 Examples are DJ Akademics in the US or Trap Lore Ross in the UK. Both accounts chronicle rappers' criminal vicissitudes in an entertaining fashion.
7 It is the case of Social Boom, an Italian account that has paid special attention to trap dissings and even trended as #1 on YouTube Italia by reposting a video of a group of rappers and boxers beating up and harassing other trappers (the video was later removed).
8 For example, in this "confessional" video www.youtube.com/watch?v=Y_ZbSpu3Fus

References

Abidin, C. (2021). From "networked publics" to "refracted publics": A companion framework for researching "below the radar" studies. *Social Media+ Society*, 7(1), 2056305120984458.
Abrahams, R. D. (1962). Playing the dozens. *The Journal of American Folklore*, 75(297), 209–220.
Anger, K. (1959). *Hollywood Babylon*. Pauvert.
Arriagada, A., & Bishop, S. (2021). Between commerciality and authenticity: The imaginary of social media influencers in the platform economy. *Communication, Culture and Critique*, 14(4), 568–586.

Auslander, P. (2012). Digital liveness: A historico-philosophical perspective. *PAJ: A journal of Performance and Art, 34*(3), 3–11.

Banet-Weiser, S. (2012). Authentic™. In *Authentic™*. New York University Press.

Boccia Artieri, G., Brilli, S., & Zurovac, E. (2021). Below the radar: Private groups, locked platforms, and ephemeral content—Introduction to the special issue. *Social media+ Society, 7*(1), 2056305121988930.

Boudana, S. (2014). Shaming rituals in the age of global media: How DSK's perp walk generated estrangement. *European Journal of Communication, 29*(1), 50–67.

Bozzi, N. (2021). Dramatization of the@ GANGSTA: Instagram Cred in the Age of Glocalized Gang Culture. In J. B. Wiest (Ed.), *Theorizing criminality and policing in the digital media age* (pp. 69–88). Emerald Publishing Limited.

Brilli, S. (2017). Zwischen Trash und Transzendenz. Zur kollektiven Produktion von lächerlichen Stars auf YouTube. *Zeitschrift für Medienwissenschaft, 9*(1), 21–36.

Brilli, S. (2018). Where is the sacred in online celebrity? Praise, loath and physical interaction with Italian webstars. *Mediascapes Journal, 11*, 64–79.

Burgess, J. (2006). Hearing ordinary voices: Cultural studies, vernacular creativity and digital storytelling. *Continuum, 20*(2), 201–214.

Chang, J. (2005). *Can't stop won't stop: A history of the hip-hop generation*. St. Martin's Press.

Christin, A., & Lewis, R. (2021). The drama of metrics: Status, spectacle, and resistance among YouTube drama creators. *Social Media+ Society, 7*(1), 2056305121999660.

Connor, S. (2016). Defiling celebrity. In A. Jaffe & J. Goldman (Eds.), *Modernist star maps* (pp. 235–250). Routledge.

Couldry, N. (2003). *Media rituals: A critical approach*. Routledge.

Craig, D., & Cunningham, S. (2019). *Social media entertainment: The new intersection of Hollywood and Silicon Valley*. New York University Press.

Cuconato, M. (2021). 'I rap therefore I am'. Second generation rappers and Italian citizenship. In S. Gonçalves & S. Majhanovich (Eds.), *Art in diverse social settings* (pp. 131–142). Emerald Publishing Limited.

Driessens, O. (2013). Celebrity capital: Redefining celebrity using field theory. *Theory and Society, 42*(5), 543–560.

Duffy, B. E., Miltner, K. M., & Wahlstedt, A. (2022). Policing "fake" femininity: Authenticity, accountability, and influencer antifandom. *New Media & Society, 24*(7), 1657–1676.

Dunbar, A. (2018). Art or confession?: Evaluating rap lyrics as evidence in criminal cases. *Race and Justice, 10*(3), 320–340.

Evans, J. M., & Baym, N. K. (2022). The audacity of clout (chasing): Digital strategies of black youth in Chicago DIY Hip-Hop. *International Journal of Communication, 16*, 19.

Gamson, J. (1998). *Freaks talk back: Tabloid talk shows and sexual nonconformity*. University of Chicago Press.

Gamson, J. (2011). The unwatched life is not worth living: The elevation of the ordinary in celebrity culture. *Pmla, 126*(4), 1061–1069.

Garot, R. (2007). "Where you from!" Gang identity as performance. *Journal of contemporary Ethnography, 36*(1), 50–84.

Gemini, L. (2016). Liveness: le logiche mediali nella comunicazione dal vivo. *Sociologia Della Comunicazione, 51*, 43–63.

Greer, C., & Jewkes, Y. (2005). Extremes of otherness: Media images of social exclusion. *Social Justice, 32*(1), 20–31.

Grindstaff, L. (2002). *The money shot: Trash, class, and the making of TV talk shows*. University of Chicago Press.

Harkness, G. (2013). Gangs and gangsta rap in Chicago: A microscenes perspective. *Poetics, 41*(2), 151–176.

Harman, S., & Jones, B. (2013). Fifty shades of ghey: Snark fandom and the figure of the anti-fan. *Sexualities, 16*(8), 951–968.

Heckert, A., & Heckert, D. M. (2002). A new typology of deviance: Integrating normative and reactivist definitions of deviance. *Deviant Behavior, 23*(5), 449–479.

Heckert, A., & Heckert, D. M. (2004). Using an integrated typology of deviance to analyze ten common norms of the US middle class. *Sociological Quarterly, 45*(2), 209–228.

Ilan, J. (2012). 'The industry's the new road': Crime, commodification and street cultural tropes in UK urban music. *Crime, Media, Culture, 8*(1), 39–55.

Irwin-Rogers, K., & Pinkney, C. (2017). Social media as a catalyst and trigger for youth violence. *Catch22*. Retrieved from www.catch-22.org.uk/social-media-as-acatalyst-and-trigger-for-youth-violence

Johnson, J., & Schell-Busey, N. (2016). Old message in a new bottle: Taking gang rivalries online through rap battle music videos on YouTube. *Journal of Qualitative Criminal Justice & Criminology, 4*(1), 42–81.

Kooistra, P. (1989). *Criminals as heroes: Structure, power & identity.* Popular Pressof Bowling Green State.

Kubrin, C. E., & Nielson, E. (2014). Rap on trial. *Race and Justice, 4*(3), 185–211.

LaChance, D., & Kaplan, P. (2019). The seductions of crimesploitation: The apprehension of sex offenders on primetime television. *Law, Culture and the Humanities, 15*(1), 127–150.

LaGrone, K. L. (2000). From minstrelsy to gangsta rap: The" nigger" as commodity for popular American entertainment. *Journal of African American Men*, 117–131.

Lauderdale, P. (2015). Political deviance as positive action: Against hegemony. In E. Goode (Ed.), *Research on deviance* (pp. 119–130). Wiley Blackwell.

Lauger, T. R., & Densley, J. A. (2018). Broadcasting badness: Violence, identity, and performance in the online gang rap scene. *Justice Quarterly, 35*(5), 816–841.

Lupinacci, L. (2021). 'Absentmindedly scrolling through nothing': Liveness and compulsory continuous connectedness in social media. *Media, Culture & Society, 43*(2), 273–290.

Lynes, A., Kelly, C., & Kelly, E. (2020). THUG LIFE: Drill music as a periscope into urban violence in the consumer age. *The British Journal of Criminology, 60*(5), 1201–1219.

Meena, B. (2022). *How the criminalisation of drill music perpetuates the historical marginalisation of black people.* Retrieved from https://ssrn.com/abstract=4038029

Meisner, C., & Ledbetter, A. M. (2022). Participatory branding on social media: The affordances of live streaming for creative labor. *New Media & Society, 24*(5), 1179–1195.

O'Meara, V. (2019). Weapons of the chic: Instagram influencer engagement pods as practices of resistance to Instagram platform labor. *Social Media+ Society, 5*(4), 2056305119879671.

Oware, M. (2016). "We stick out like a sore thumb . . ." Underground white rappers' hegemonic masculinity and racial evasion. *Sociology of Race and Ethnicity, 2*(3), 372–386.

Patton, D. U., Eschmann, R. D., & Butler, D. A. (2013). Internet banging: New trends in social media, gang violence, masculinity and hip hop. *Computers in Human Behavior, 29*(5), 54–59.

Penfold-Mounce, R. (2009). *Celebrity culture and crime: The joy of transgression.* Springer.

Pinkney, C., & Robinson-Edwards, S. (2018). Gangs, music and the mediatisation of crime: Expressions, violations, and validations. *Safer Communities, 17*(2), 103–118.

Poell, T., Nieborg, D. B., & Duffy, B. E. (2021). *Platforms and cultural production.* John Wiley & Sons.

Quinn, E. (2005). *Nuthin' but a 'G' thang: The culture and commerce of gangsta rap.* Columbia University Press.

Racine, J. P. (2018). The death of dissent and the decline of dissin': A diachronic study of race, gender, and genre in Mainstream American rap. In A. S., Ross &, D. J. Rivers (Eds.), *The sociolinguistics of hip-hop as critical conscience* (pp. 237–268). Palgrave Macmillan.

Ricci, O. (2014). Celebrità da disprezzare? Star di cattivo gusto, classe, genere e distinzione. *Studi Culturali, 11*(3), 449–468.

Richardson, C., & Kennedy, L. (2012). "Gang" as empty signifier in contemporary Canadian newspapers. *Canadian Journal of Criminology and Criminal Justice, 54*(4), 443–479.

Rojek, C. (2001). *Celebrity.* Reaktion Books.

Rojek, C. (2012). *Fame attack: The inflation of celebrity and its consequences.* A&C Black.

Roks, R. A. (2021). "Keeping it (hyper) real": A musical history of rap's quest beyond authenticity. In D. Siegel & F. Bovenkerk (Eds.), *Crime and music* (pp. 271–285). Springer.

Schmid, D. (2006). Idols of destruction: Celebrity and the serial killer. In S. Redmond & S. Holmes (Eds.), *Framing celebrity: New directions in celebrity culture* (pp. 295–310). Routledge.

Stuart, F. (2020). *Ballad of the bullet: Gangs drill music and the power of online infamy.* Princeton University Press.

Tannenbaum, F. (1938). *Crime and the community.* Ginn.

Tyler, I., & Bennett, B. (2010). 'Celebrity chav': Fame, femininity and social class. *European Journal of Cultural Studies, 13*(3), 375–393.

Wald, E. (2012). *The dozens: A history of rap's mama.* Oxford University Press.

38

ANTI-MIGRANT GROUPS IN CALAIS AND DOVER

Protecting online resources while engaging in digital vigilantism and hate speech

Matthijs Gardenier

Introduction

This chapter focuses on the online social movement activity of anti-migrant groups in Calais and Dover from 2015 to 2021. It stems from research conducted during a British Academy Newton International Fellowship at the University of Manchester between 2019 and 2021. These groups, most of which have a far-right background, are engaged in a *repertoire* of action that may be understood simultaneously as social movement activity and as vigilantism. While part of their activity takes place on the streets with demonstrations and direct actions, most of their activity takes place online, through social media platforms, and most of their street presence may be understood as performances aimed at social media audiences. Therefore, the activity of these groups falls within the scope of online deviance for two reasons. Firstly, they attempt to frame refugees as criminal populations to be policed, so these groups intend to define what constitutes deviance through a series of online campaigns. Secondly, their actions can be considered as a form of deviance: vigilantism, but also hate speech. This has pushed these groups to implement mitigating strategies in order to avoid falling under the law or being deplatformed.

This chapter aims to propose a new approach to understanding anti-migrant mobilisations. These have already been considered in terms of their political characterisation, following the example of the work of Cas Mudde (2019). Other researchers have studied them from the angle of radicality and cumulative or interactional radicalisation (Busher Macklin, 2015). Their inclusion in the field of social movements has also been documented by approaches such as that of Hilary Pilkington (2016) or Fabien Virchow (2007). Similarly, anti-migrant movements in Europe have been thought of from the perspective of vigilantism (Bjørgo & Mares, 2019). The present chapter intends to think of the action of anti-migrant groups through their online activity. Let us be reminded that online social life has become an essential element of the activity of social movements (Susca, 2016). The activity of these groups can be understood more particularly in relation to digital vigilantism (Tanner Campana, 2020) as well as hate speech, allowing us to consider the activity of these moral entrepreneurs as simultaneously an attempt to securitise migrations and thus to decree who is deviant or not, but also an online activity pertaining to deviance in itself.

DOI: 10.4324/9781003277675-44

These groups engage in a form of social control which, as Ray Abrahams pointed out (1998), is a form of crime control that is itself criminal. Intending to construct migrant populations as inherently criminal, anti-migrant groups engage in vigilantism both performatively and through street actions. Social media are extremely important to these groups: they use them to stage their vigilante actions, mobilise and call their supporters to participate. This inscribes their action within the field of digital vigilantism. This term has been coined to refer to 'direct forms of online intervention, targeting individuals, their behaviour or organisations in order to deter or punish them outside institutional frameworks and accepted norms of "civility"' (Loveluck, 2020). Loveluck characterises these online actions as: "flagging", "investigation", "stalking" (including doxing) and "organised exposure".

These groups therefore try to define through their online action who is criminal and who is not. Their vigilantism is not only aimed at repressing criminal acts but above all at framing the presence of refugees as criminal in itself. This vigilantism also takes the form of calls for self-justice against migrants (sometimes followed by acts of violence) and campaigns to support the perpetrators of violence, who are presented as martyrs (such as a Hungarian driver who ran over migrants on the motorway in Calais). Finally, vigilante street actions are staged for online audiences. These actions seem essential to the construction of the communitarian audiences of these groups. For example, British groups broadcasted online the patrols they carried out on the beaches of Dover. They also staged 'hotel exposures' by filming and posting online intrusions into hotels housing asylum seekers, who were filmed against their will. On the other hand, these performances can be double-edged and make the vigilantes enter the field of deviance: surveillance and even more intervention are subject of laws that leave the monopoly of such policing to the forces of order. The vigilantes thus become deviant. This is the case of the group Calaisiens en Colère, which published a live video of a demonstration in which a member flashed a rubber bullet gun before shooting it in the direction of refugees (Gardenier, 2018). If the spectacular posting of this video allowed for a massive audience, it also drew the negative attention of mainstream media, leading the group to scale down its activity.

The chapter will continue by examining the online discourse of anti-migrant groups. The core of their discourse portrays migrants as a security problem, an existential threat to local populations, who are supposed to be at 'war' with migrants. These anti-migration discourses are linked to related campaign themes of the far right such as Islam, terrorism or, for the most radical anti-migrant groups, theories of 'white genocide' or 'great replacement'. Very often, these speeches fall under hate speech laws of the countries where they are published, but also under the rules of use of platforms.

Let us be reminded that hate speech has been defined Raphael Cohen-Almagor (2011) as

> bias-motivated, hostile, malicious speech aimed at a person or a group of people because of some of their actual or perceived innate characteristics. It expresses discriminatory, intimidating, disapproving, antagonistic, and/or prejudicial attitudes toward those characteristics, which include gender, race, religion, ethnicity, color, national origin, disability, or sexual orientation.

This type of online discourse risks leading to judicial sanctions and deplatforming.

Without going into a lengthy debate, it should be noted that the definition of hate speech is complex and generates a series of ambivalences. Definitions vary according to different national legislation, but also according to the conditions of use of different platforms

(Courbet et al., 2015), as well as different practices of interpretation of moderation by these platforms. Moreover, the definition of what constitutes hate speech may also come into contradiction with the fundamental freedom of expression. While some publications can easily be classified as hate speech, such as those calling for violence against specific social groups, what about negative comments about groups that are not necessarily protected by specific legislative texts? Arbitrating and interpreting such boundaries may be difficult, creating additional ambivalence (Badouard, 2022). Moreover, the issue of hate speech arises above all on so-called social media platforms where users publish their own content.

In these private and transnational spaces where everything is played out very quickly, it is not the courts that regulate what constitutes hate speech or not, but the platforms themselves. They regulate content in a relatively obscure and arbitrary manner: let us be reminded that hate speech, at the forefront of which is anti-migrant hate speech, arouses strong interest among numerous users of these media, and therefore generates value and potential income for the platforms (Badouard, 2022). In some cases, platforms can be led to a certain tolerance for these types of content in order to attract audiences, unless the political context forces them to crack down on such contents; for example, in reaction to the January 6 Capitol riots, which subsequently led to an unprecedented movement of deplatforming of far-right content.[1]

It is thus within these ambivalences and ambiguities that the anti-migrant groups in Dover and Calais position themselves: strongly opposed to immigration and very often to any presence of immigrants on European territory, their communication is perpetually on the edge. Indeed, the identitarian construction of the far right is determined by the permanent designation of an enemy. Keeping this enemy at a distance would be the sine qua non condition of the possibility of a political community. The discourse of the far right is characterised by the invariance of the function of the enemy in its identitarian construction. For Caterina Froio, this specific construction in relation to the enemy is specific to the extreme right (Froio, 2017, p. 46):

> For any individual, the construction of identity(ies) is based on a distinction between ingroup and outgroup, between 'us' and 'them'. However, on the far right, the construction of identity takes an exclusionary form and presents at least two specificities. First, a Manichean view of the world in which human beings and their interactions are represented as 'good' or 'bad'. Secondly, researchers believe that right-wing extremes tend to define in-group characteristics primarily through the description of out-group characteristics. Often, then, the characteristics of 'us' are vaguer than those of 'them', and representations of 'us' are usually a mirror image of those of 'them'.

In order to avoid falling within the scope of hate speech laws, these groups have used various strategies. For example, there is the French far-right tradition of "speech on the edge", which consists of implying ideas that could fall under the law but using sufficiently vague and suggestive terms in order to avoid legal proceedings. While this tactic is effective in the courts, it is less effective in regard to the rules of social media platforms that do not require the same level of characterisation to deplatform a page. Other tactics have been used such as the use of code words that tend to recreate an online right-wing subculture often based on humour (such as the use of terms like 'Swedish' to refer to people of North African background). Humour is sometimes used to euphemise calls for violence. For instance, the group *Sauvons Calais* posted jokes about "hunting migrants", making a pun (in French) with the hunting season of migratory birds which allowed the post to an extremely massive audience. Finally, another discursive strategy will be that of the 'citizen journalism' posture, which tries to position the action of anti-migrants in a posture of journalism, when in reality it is more a matter of video activism. That is to say, of an image production that belongs to another regime of truth, following the example of the 'alternative facts' of Donald Trump's team (Rasmussen, 2019). Finally, it will be important to note the importance of online and offline counter-mobilisations in order to achieve a 'deplatforming' of these groups, defining through mobilisation the limits of what is acceptable and unacceptable discourse on these platforms.

Methodology

The results presented in this chapter are the result of a mixed methodology combining two tools: *Semi-structured interviews* with activists of the groups included in the study have been conducted in order to understand the trajectories of their activists and the actions they have undertaken. Access to such primary data is very interesting because it allows us to understand the motives that lead individuals to participate in such groups, as well as to grasp the ideological divergences within these groups that cannot be understood by a study limited to such groups' official communications.

Social media content analysis: semi-structured interviews were supplemented with content analysis of the social media output of 15 groups in Dover and Calais. This output has been analysed thematically, identifying categories that allows us to understand the contours of the group's communication framework. 700 social media postings have been drawn at random. This timespan includes a time of significant social movement activity, especially around the summer of 2020 for Dover, while the data in Calais is older and was collected during a timespan stretching from April 2015 and March 2016. This output has been analysed lexicometrically using the Reinhert method using the free software Voyant Tools, which proceeds in the same manner as the Alceste method. The lexicometric analysis was carried out on the corpus of postings which were treated as a single text; each posting treated as a paragraph. The advantage of this methodology is that by taking into account the structure of the text (sentences, paragraphs), it defines coherent sets of word usages and allows the researcher to free himself from his methodological *a priori*. In addition, six corpora of five videos produced by video activists have also been analysed thematically, as well as hermeneutically.

The chapter is divided in three separate sections. The first focuses on far-right framings of migration and how the phenomena of migration is connected to other issues central to the discourse of the far right. The second focuses on video activism and practices of online performative vigilantism in Dover, while the final section emphasises the steps taken by Calaisian groups to preserve their social media from being deplatformed.

I. The framing of migrations in Dover, from security dangers and competition with domestic national vulnerable publics to connecting issues: Islam and the decline of the West

Describing thoroughly the field research conducted in the nexus of the border between France and Britain could be a chapter in itself. However, as this specific chapter is centred on online deviance, the focus will be on the online part of the mobilisation of anti-migrant groups. Nevertheless, before discussing strategies of publication and mitigation tactics, it

Table 38.1 Detail of corpuses and interviews

	Single issue social movement structures	Far-right Political Organisations	Video activists	Total
Actors active in the field of social movements contentious of immigration in the UK and in France	Migration Watch UK, Protest against Penally Camp (Wales), Little Boats, Stop UK Marriage Fraud. South East Coast Defence, Sauvons Calais, Calaisiens en Colère	Britain First, The For Britain Party, Patriotic Alternative	Active Patriot, Steve Laws, John Lawrence, Chris Johnson, Darren Edmundson (Voice of Wales)	15 groups or video-activists
Semi structured interviews	South East Coast Defence, Protest against Penally Camp, Little Boats, Stop UK Marriage Fraud, Migration Watch UK Sauvons Calais, Calaisiens en Colère	The For Britain Party, Patriotic Alternative	John Lawrence, Darren Edmundson (Voice of Wales)	15 interviews
Social media publication corpuses (text + image) (50 social media postings by corpus randomly selected)	South East Coast Defence, Protest against Penally Camp, Little Boats, Stop UK Marriage Fraud, Sauvons Calais, Calaisiens en Colère	Britain First, The For Britain Party, Patriotic Alternative	Chris Johnson, Active Patriot, Steve Laws,	12 publication corpuses
Video corpuses (analysis of 5 videos)	Protest against Penally Camp	The For Britain Party, Britain First	John Lawrence, Active Patriot, Steve Laws	6 video corpuses

seems necessary to outline the contents of the online activities of the groups. Most of the publications offer a description of the migration process as the theatre of a conflict similar to warfare, opposing the refugees to the nationals (French and British) that would be subject to an immediate and deadly thread supposedly posed by the migratory process. We will start by discussing the immediate narrow framing of migration by these groups and continue by elaborating on how their communication is connected to broader themes characteristic to the political framing of the far right.

The narrow framing of immigration relies on two elements. The first is the illegality of the migratory process. This tends to frame migrants arriving in Dover as individuals whose status is ontologically illegal. The second element is the lack of knowledge about incoming migrants, and given the impossibility of prior checks, it raises the possibility that some migrants may be potential criminals or terrorists. According to activists, not every immigrant is a terrorist, but they oppose the risk that the uncontrolled nature of the migration process supposedly poses to the British public. It is possible to draw a parallel between these discourses and those in the 17th and 18th centuries regarding vagrants outside of local communities, who were not eligible for assistance, and because of their outsider status, would pose a potential threat to the local community (Castel, 1999). Thus E. tells us:

> I have been called a xenophobe a million times. [This is] absolute rubbish and I keep saying to people it is not about skin colour, it is not about race, religion, creed or skin colour[;] it is about National security and that's what they don't get. [Migrants have] no fingerprints, no Interpol checks, no Police checks, no background checks at all, no passports or identification for people, and these people are flooding into our country, [and] a lot of them are just disappearing.

J., head of a single-issue organisation, presents a similar viewpoint:

> We are not targeting the people in those boats, because they are human beings . . . The thing is, our problem is we have people arriving on our shores that we don't know anything about, and it is totally different if they were to come here via the normal channels. . . We are not complaining about that, but we are complaining about those people who we don't know anything about. . . . I'm more angry at the government than the migrants themselves. If they are genuinely coming from a war zone that's totally different. We had it in Vietnam in years gone by, the '70s, people came here and started new lives because they were being killed. . . . But this is economic migrancy on a massive scale, and as we just said earlier, they need to be deported. But this has to be a no-go area.

The issue of government assistance is juxtaposed with the position of the Britons who need assistance. This can also found in Hilary Pilkington's research that revealed the feeling of competition between white British and immigrants in securing access to social housing and benefits was a key driver behind support for far-right social movements (Pilkingon, 2016). It is also worth referencing the work of Olivier Schwartz, who describes the social perception of the French working classes as characterised by a 'triangular social consciousness' (Collovald and Schwartz, 2006). According to Schwartz, theirs is an identity defined in relation to the 'they' of the dominant classes, but also to the 'them' of immigrants who are insecure and in need of assistance. They are likewise perceived as potentially criminogenic and competition for access to the benefits system. It is in this perspective that the discourse on migrants must be understood. Furthermore, migrants are set side by side with army veterans, with the latter deemed to be worthy of assistance and yet denied it, whereas the former are deemed unworthy and yet benefit. In this perspective, and in a context of scarcity of resources where it would not be possible to provide for everyone, priority should be given to people who are legitimate by virtue of their nationality, and even more so to veterans who have fought for the national community. Thus J. told us that:

> I think one of the big problems we have . . . is the homeless in Britain. I am sure it is the same in France. We have a lot of members who are British, who worked . . . or for whatever reason whether they were in the military or had drug or alcohol problems, they are on the streets and to us that is wrong. . . . The other thing is we noticed a great deal of the migrants coming here, a lot of them have the latest mobile phones that we

can't afford, a lot of them. We see it. We saw it, you know, the other . . . last week, and you will see them and you wonder 'who are these people and why are we putting them in hotels', and some of them have thousands and thousands of euros on them.

Anne-Marie Waters., leader of The For Britain Movement shared this view:

The vast majority don't work, so we are told they are paying tax. Give me a break! Give me a break! The Benefit bill just gets bigger, and bigger, and bigger. . . . the vast majority do not work, will not work, so the idea that it's an economic opportunity is ridiculous. We are paying through the nose for this. We have 13,000 British veterans sleeping on the streets in this country. People who put their life on the line to fight for their country and to do, at the behest of a corrupt government, to put their lives on the line for a corrupt government. 13,000 of them sleep on the streets in this country every night. Migrants arrive, strangers, and are housed in 4-star hotels by our government. Well look, if you, look, if we are talking about immigration of people coming in to work in the financial district or to work in technology or medicine and sciences, that would be fine. That would be an economic addition to the UK. This is not what is happening in the vast majority of cases. The vast majority are coming here as refugees, asylum seekers. They meet the definition of neither and will spend the bulk of their life on benefits, so I don't understand. So, what we are doing is taking millions of people from these cultures, third world cultures, and putting them into Europe. Now a lot of them are illiterate in their own language, much less in ours and this has been, the Benefit Bill is astronomical. The vast majority of people who come to the UK from these countries don't work, will never work.[2]

Activists do not simply develop a discourse on immigration at Dover and small boat crossings. This issue is linked with related political issues. The first is the security threat supposedly posed by Islam. Anne Marie Waters, leader of a political organisation, shared this point of view and articulated it with a negative feeling towards Islam itself, and added that she was specifically against immigration originating from Muslim countries:

I am very, very clear that I don't like Islam. I think it's a dangerous, violent religion and I've studied it in depth for years. . . . as someone who knows the religion, has studied the Quran, has studied the Hadith, the Sunnah, the Muhai, . . . I know that it's a violent religion and it's a massive threat to our safety and our freedom, and that is proven every day. For that reason, I don't believe there should be immigration from Muslim Societies into ours. We are not compatible. There are individuals, of course, but as a collective. I'm not suggesting every individual Muslim is the same, that would be absurd, but as a collective, we are not compatible. Free democracies, for example, France is not compatible with Pakistani culture. . . . So, what we've done is move millions of people from the Muslim world into Europe, without any regard for the cultural differences, the religious differences, the difference in values. We were told that everyone was the same, which is an absolute lie, a blatant lie, and an absurdity and now we are reaping the reward of that. People are being beheaded in France for cartoons is the reward of that. You cannot, you simply cannot put oil and water together and expect it to mix.

No[w] this may sound trivial to you, but it is just an example of how different we are. We've had take-aways, fast food, run by Pakistanis, for example, where we've found faecal matter, human faeces around the place . . . even our toilet habits are so spectacularly different, that we ended up with take-away venues being found to have human faecal matter strewn around the place . . . What I am trying to say is we are completely different.

The civilisational danger supposedly posed by Islam is also linked to sexuality. The sexuality of Muslims, driven by different cultural values, is deemed a threat to British women. Thus M., organiser of a single-issue social movement organisation, told us that:

I've obviously been around a lot of Muslims myself, and they are, some of them can be quite fanatical about their religion and I do think that the extremists talk within religion itself. Muslims basically believe that Western woman are whores and this is across, and the two reasons are, as I say, because I have also worked in the Middle East as I have said, the two reasons are because we don't cover up and we generally have relationships before marriage.

Finally, for some activists (it is not the case for all of interviewees), migration endangers Western civilization. Some activists consider that immigrants are fighters against Britain. One interviewee considered that the youth of migrants implied that they would be fighters and immigration is thereby considered part of a governmental design:

Why is it only men and why are they taking over our army barracks? . . . why is it fighting age men from the age of 20 to 35 only allowed in? I don't know. I said, the people that are migrating into this country and taking over our army barracks they're at fighting age, 20 to 35[,] and ISIS said years ago that they will take over Europe and it looks like they're starting to. Now, are these men actually ISIS soldiers? We don't know. . . . Yeah, exactly, yeah, but is the government forced? Why is the government allowing all these in? . . . I don't really know.

Another activist linked the migratory processes to a possible disappearance of the 'white race' planned in a New World Order plot in which the British government is supposedly participating, the Coudenhove-Kalergi conspiracy:[3]

Coudenhove-Kalergi was an Austrian, I think, and he came out with this, it is literally called the Coudenhove-Kalergi plan. . . every single thing of this seems to be aimed at getting rid of the white man, and the thing is I didn't actually know until the other day, if you Google it up. Whites only take up I think it is between 8 and 9 percent of the global population? . . . Whites are the minority on earth. . . . I was really shocked. I had no idea, you know, the way all of this anti-white stuff is going on . . . We've got Muslim-only housing in London under Sadiq Khan. . . . This is blatant racism against whites in a predominantly white country, and our Government are doing nothing about it. They want to depopulate the world[;] I mean you must have seen 'The Great Reset' . . . you must know about Bill Gates wanting to depopulate via a vaccine? . . . The invasion continues, they are trying to wipe out the white man. . . . Coudenhove's plan was to flood Europe with people from the Middle East and from Africa, so that they breed with the white race so that there is one race on earth, and the whites need to be gone and it[']s all in this plan . . . There is an anti-white agenda and the British Government are very much playing their part.

Most discourses on immigration around Dover present the same lines of argument. These start with the illegality of immigration, highlight its uncontrolled and potential criminogenic character, and connect it to economic pressure on the benefit system, Islam, sexual peril and for some of them, to an existential civilisational threat.

Video-activism, exposure and vigilantism in Dover

This framing of migration is also present in the online posts of all the groups that have been studied. User-generated content, especially images and videos, are used to provide a visual anchor to this framing. The specific way this is achieved by these groups is what we call performative vigilantism, or video vigilantism: the activists stage themselves as engaging in vigilantism against migrants. This action intends to frame asylum seekers and refugees as a security threat rather than vulnerable persons entitled to assistance. In a nutshell, video vigilantism is a performative action aiming at changing the status of refugees in the views of the social media audiences of anti-migrant groups.

This type of activism has been rendered possible by what we call video activism. Let us be reminded that as a result of technological but also cultural changes, the possibility of producing images and films and immediately broadcasting them has become much more accessible. This phenomenon started with the spread of digital cameras and camcorders, followed by their incorporation into smartphones. From a dissemination point of view, the advent of social media has considerably increased the possibility of broadcasting user-produced content (Susca, 2016). Thus, certain platforms such as YouTube and TikTok or Twitch are dedicated almost exclusively to user-generated video content, while the algorithms of platforms such as Facebook and Instagram increasingly push video content.

The sharp drop in the cost of producing images, the possibility of distributing them directly on various platforms and the growing importance of images in the political sphere are background factors that may help the understanding of the emergence of video activism; that is, the more or less artisanal production of images in the context of social movement activity and campaigning. These images are then broadcast either immediately (live) or after summary editing. This activist-produced content can reach a mass audience, sometimes worldwide. In the case of the British far right, videos published by Tommy Robinson during the London Bridge attacks on the now-defunct live-streaming Periscope platform have reached a million views, numbers that compete with mainstream media audiences.[4]

As a result, the production of images by social movements actors has become a central issue. In the 1980s, Patrick Champagne described some French mobilisations as 'paper demonstrations' in the sense that some social movements seemed to orient their repertoire of action solely to the perspective of producing a certain image in newspapers and media (Champagne, 2015). It can be hypothesised that the situation has somewhat changed since the 1980s. Nowadays, demonstrations are simultaneously events that take place both physically and online through different news coverage, Twitter/X threads and live videos on different platforms. For instance, while observing a demonstration against grooming gangs in Manchester just before the Covid-19 lockdown, this dimension was prevalent: there were only a few dozen participants, and more than half of them were filming and some speaking to their phones addressing their community of followers. The attention of participants was focused on the speeches of the organisers. The first rows of the (sparse) audience participants were holding their phones in front of them in order to film the speeches. Several video-activists, some of them widely-followed, such as "The Little Veteran", displayed professional or semi-professional cameras printed with the name of their 'media'.

Without necessarily being the dominant type of social movement activism in Britain, practices of vigilantism have become an anchored part of their repertoire. The staging of vigilantism—linked to the citizen action against 'criminal' activity—tends to offer an alternative framing on migration to that of the mainstream media, or at least parts of it. Refugees would not be vulnerable populations in need of protection but criminogenic populations whose very presence constitutes a criminal offence.

The 'traditional' definition of vigilantism provided by Les Johnston (1996) divides functions of vigilantism into three categories: surveillance, intervention and administration of justice. These seem to allow for only a partial understanding of the phenomenon in Dover, contrary to Calais, where the categories of intervention and surveillance perfectly characterise the action of *Sauvons Calais* and *Calaisiens en Colère*. In Dover, it is the visibilisation of migration that seems to be the key consideration behind these actions rather than direct security intervention. Usually the implementation of 'classic' vigilantism is geared towards asserting a form of power on a territory. This is not the objective here. On the contrary, it is the production of images of vigilantism that seems to be what is important. To take up Rasmussen's (2019) point of view, the images produced are located at the heart of far-right politics as these images provide a 'framing of reality' to the audiences that consume the social media of these groups.

Accordingly, these practices of vigilantism can be more easily understood through the concept of digital vigilantism, which mainly takes the form of unsolicited attention (Trottier, 2017). This dimension is to be found in the practice of 'exposure', which corresponds to the online revelation of illegal or supposedly illegal activities. The first activity, the practice of patrolling, has been very important to anti-migrant groups in Calais, which will be developed further later in the text. But this practice seems less central in Dover, as the flow of small boat arrivals is more tightly controlled by British authorities: boats are most often intercepted before reaching British shores and asylum seekers are then taken to hotels and camps where their applications are directly processed. This implies that the chances of encounters with migrants during patrols are relatively low. Nevertheless, a number of actors carry out patrols, although their dimension seems to be primarily performative rather than directed towards the implementation of direct action on the ground. For instance, Britain First uses social media to stage patrols on the beaches of Dover in the hope of alerting the public.

However, this activity appears to be primarily symbolic, directed for the consumption of those following the group on social media. During the summer of 2020, the group broadcast videos featuring naval patrols trying to intercept small boats. It did not achieve any success in terms of interception, although it did invite attention from the local press.[5] Britain First is not the only organisation claiming to organise naval patrols. In the spring of 2021, the leader of Little Boats launched a fundraising campaign in order to buy a small boat that would allow his group to patrol the waters around Dover and thus challenge the actions of the Border Force and the French Navy, which were accused of encouraging illegal immigration.

Britain First

Ashlea in the cliff top bunker on a migrant patrol at Dover.....

👁 375   15:12

Figure 38.1   Britain First activist selfie taken while patrolling the coastline in Dover

Figure 38.2   Images of Britain First activists on patrol in Dover

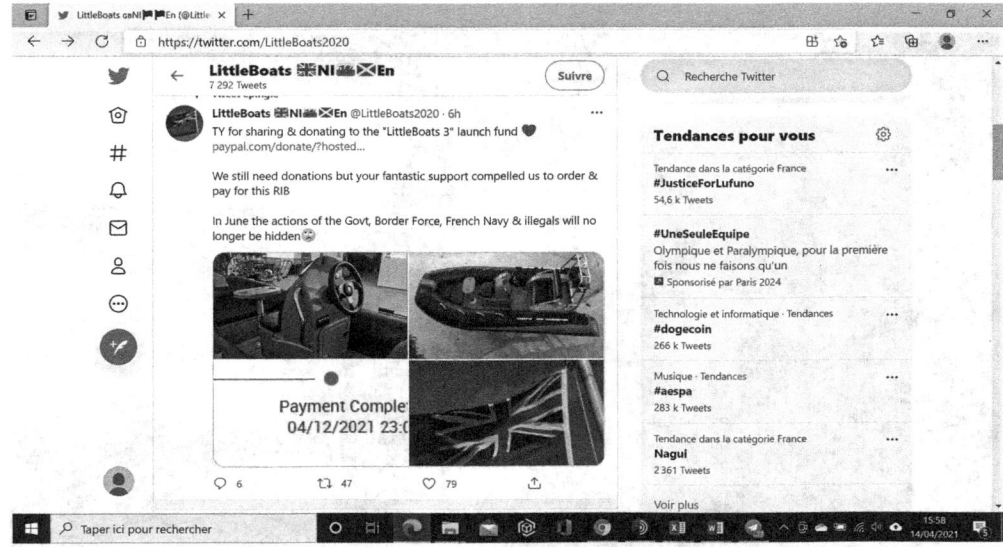

Figure 38.3   Little Boats Twitter publication announcing patrols for the summer of 2022

A further practice of digital vigilantism, mainly implemented by Britain First, is 'exposure', i.e. the giving of unwanted attention to 'deviant' and 'criminal' practices. In addition to its patrol campaign entitled Operation White Cliffs, Britain First has organised video-patrols to "expose" hotels. On a dedicated website, a form allows Internet users to report a hotel that might be hosting migrants, asking for a certain amount of information on the number of migrants, but also to report "any anti-social behaviour from illegal immigrants in the local area".[6] On the basis of the information collected through this form, but also information gleaned from local activists, an activist team then goes onsite to film a video.

The activists travel in the 'Battle Bus', which is a minibus equipped with megaphones. It displays a banner with the organisation's name and riot grates, which results in singular images that give a specific aesthetic to the videos. As visual sociology tells us, the produced image represents the situated gaze of the actor who produces them (La Rocca, 2007). As such, the images produced by the activists who go to meet the migrants present the construction of this gaze. This image presents an activist chanting nationalist slogans into the Battle Bus' megaphone while driving through an immigrant-populated area of Birmingham. The riot protection of the bus is particularly symbolic because as a security device it builds similarity with the British police minibuses it mimicks and immediately hints at the idea that the area where immigrants live is a zone of potential danger.

The tension is then highlighted as passers-by react to the activists' slogans by shouting "racist white motherfuckers". The camera then turns to the area where the shouting seems to originate, and the slur is subtitled to make it more obvious: the activists label these insults "bitter abuse by an Islamist".[7]

The same type of activism is conducted in hotels that house asylum seekers. On the group's website there are dozens of videos of 'migrant hotel exposures' that follow a similar *modus operandi*. The activists (filmed throughout the action) arrive at the hotel and try

Figure 38.4   Photogram of Britain First activist campaigning in an immigrant-populated neighbourhood in Birmingham

Figure 38.5   Photogram of the video is subtitled with an insult

Source: 'racist white m***********s'

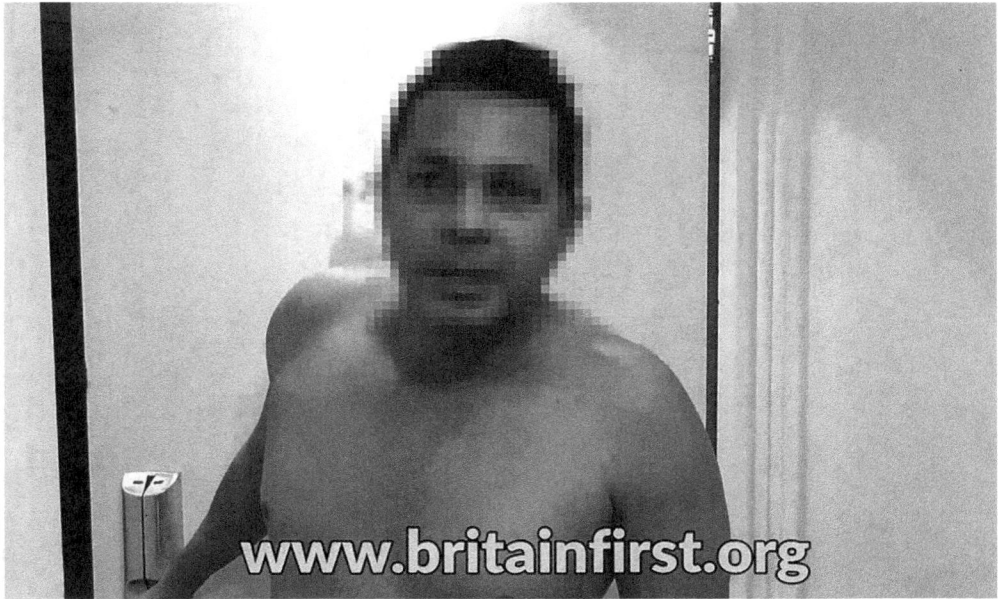

Figure 38.6 Photogram of an asylum seeker filmed while coming out of his hotel room during a Britain First 'migrant hotel exposure'

to get inside with or without permission from the hotel staff. When they manage to enter the premises, they question the people present, explaining that these hotels are financed by taxpayers' money and that many British people sleep on the street. They then insert these conversations into the edited video in order to 'expose' the scandal that they consider the reception of asylum seekers to be. Some activists ask the men in the hotel why, if they are refugees, they are not accompanied by their families. For example, see the image on the following photogram:[8]

This exposure of hotel migrants was regularly linked to a third campaign, called Operation Downes.[9] It was presented as a "major campaign to suffocate the scourge of Islamist grooming gangs". As part of the campaign, activists distributed leaflets about grooming gangs in Preston, showing the faces of men who have been convicted for being part of grooming gangs. They asked the public to email their findings to Britain First (rather than the police) if they witnessed any activity related to grooming gangs, such as seeing "older men with younger girls". The typical video begins when activists inform the police of the campaign that they will be running in the city: "to raise awareness, because we feel that the police have not done enough". The activists then distribute leaflets asking to report to Britain First any suspicious activity in mainly immigrant-owned businesses. In a video shot in Preston, when a taxi rank owner angrily asks them to leave his business, the activists seemed surprised by this refusal and wonder about the links between this business and grooming gangs: "I would like to know what goes on inside this taxi rank". The front of the business with its name and phone number is then displayed in the video:[10]

In our view, theses various practices of Britain First belong to the repertoire of 'spectacular' social media vigilantism. The patrols, and the exposure intend to construct a figure

Figure 38.7   Photogram of a Britain First patrol in Preston exposing a taxi-rank whose owner refused to display their leaflet

of the immigrant, of the Muslim as potentially complicit to grooming gangs, in a word as a potentially criminal figure. It should be noted that the very militant emphasis of the discourse, the use of megaphones, military vocabulary and aggressive postures have a performative dimension: they seem aimed at provoking an aggressive reaction from immigrants and thus creating a situation of inter-community conflict corresponding to the group's reading of social reality, creating images (and therefore truths for the viewer) that 'validate' Britain First's world view.

To conclude, these practices of vigilantism are above all symbolic. The 'supposed criminals' are never caught; to date, Britain First's Channel patrols didn't send any small boats back to French waters or dismantle any grooming gangs. In reality, the activists do not seem too concerned about achieving the goals put forward in their vigilante action. Their priority is to highlight the need for vigilance and above all to produce images that are consistent with their vision of the world, thus rendering its 'reality' through imagery.

Online discursive practices and minimisation of hate speech in Calais

As mentioned earlier, the agonistic relationship to the enemy is essential to the identity of anti-migrant groups. It is the extremely strong opposition to the migrant social group that forms the driver for collective action (Schmitt, 2009). Anti-migrant groups in Calais, like anti-migrant groups in Dover, present the Calaisian identity as 'ruined' and in 'decay': in a nutshell, a debilitated identity. They propose to recover it through participation in a fighting community bringing together activists in a political struggle. This opposition to migrants who represent an external enemy is supplemented by an internal enemy: NGOs and above all No Border have been portrayed as a treacherous fifth column.

The figure of the enemy

These two extremely strong oppositions were in evidence at a press conference on 7 June 2015. Migrants were referred to by terms such as "invasion" and "colonisation". The situation in Calais was described as an "abscess". Yvan Benedetti (leader of the *Parti Nationaliste Français*) spoke about a "migratory flood", which would presage not only an apocalyptic future for the city, but also for the whole of France.[11]

Speakers insisted that the French government would not allow the police to do their job. A lack of political will on the part of the state justified the use of vigilantism. *Sauvons Calais* called for the dissolution of "migrationist" groups supposedly bringing migrants to the slaughterhouse "like slave traders" for the benefit of "international finance and the oligarchy". They also demanded the "dissolution of all NGOs" that help migrants in one way or another, especially No Border, perceived as "the worst enemy of the French people".

This was coupled with a call for the closure of borders and a total halt to extra-European immigration. According to Yvan Benedetti, "when the plate is empty, there should no question of bringing in extra mouths, foreign mouths to share what little we have left". Moreover, this closure was a humanitarian response—to avoid "human trafficking". Over the longer term, non-European populations should be repatriated in order to "protect the French". Labelling immigration as "shared suffering", for Benedetti, mass deportation would end suffering for both the "uprooted" and the "native populations". Finally, Benedetti adds, there is no need to welcome refugees or asylum seekers: according to him, refugees are "cowards". If a situation is unbearable in a country at war, refugees should stay and fight against oppression, rather than flee to Europe. Challenging the notion itself of political refugee, he even called into question their masculinity: "These men have no courage, what do they have between their legs?"

Publication activities focused on vigilantism

This framing of migrations can also be found on the Facebook pages of Calais groups. This section will compare and analyse the publications of both Calais anti-migrant groups in regard to vigilantism with a specific focus on the measures taken by these groups to avoid being accused of hate speech and violence.

The publications of the two pages of *Sauvons Calais* and *Calaisiens en Colère* have been compared over the period from 15 November 2015 to 17 March 2016 using a thematic classification. The following table categorises the different contents published on Facebook by anti-migrant groups. It can be seen that they are mainly centred on various variations of the representation of the 'enemy', personified by *No Borders* activists and migrants. Calls for demonstrations and publications directly related to vigilantism can also be found. The main thematic contents of the *Sauvons Calais* page are the designation of the enemy with 38% of the contents, followed by the affirmation of a Calaisian identity, calls for demonstrations (16%) and then contents that directly concern vigilantism.

Catégories	Nombre de publications		Pourcentage	
	Sauvons Calais	Calaisiens en colère	Sauvons Calais	Calaisiens en colère
I.Désignation de l'ennemi	39	11	38,24%	10,58%
II. Affirmation du nous	22	3	21,57%	2,88%
III. Appels à manifestation	17	5	16,67%	4,81%
IV. Mentions d'autre groupes d'extrême droite	4	2	3,92%	1,92%
V. Posts appelant à ne pas poster de commentaires racistes	2	1	1,96%	0,96%
VI. Vigilantisme	18	82	17,65%	78,85%
VI. 1 Appels au vigilantisme	*10*	*0*	*9,80%*	*0,00%*
VI. 2 Surveillance de terrain	*8*	*58*	*7,84%*	*55,77%*
VI. 3 Publicisation des actions de vigilantisme de terrain	*0*	*24*	*0,00%*	*23,08%*
Total	102	104	100,00%	100,00%

Figure 38.8   Typological classification of the publications of Sauvons Calais and Calaisiens en Colère

It is also possible to notice differences between the two pages. On the *Calaisiens en Colère* page, the designation of the enemy accounts for only 10% of the publications, the affirmation of identity only for 2% of the publications and calls to demonstrations for 2.88%. The share of by vigilantism is overwhelming: more than 78% of the content of the *Calaisiens en Colère* page is directly related to vigilantism, four times more than *Sauvons Calais*.

The content related to vigilantism can be divided into three sub-categories. The first is the call to the public to engage in vigilantism and self-justice against migrants, which accounts for most of the publications on the subject by *Sauvons Calais* (10 out of 18) but has no occurrences on the page of *Calaisiens en Colère*. These publications legitimise violent attacks on migrants. For example, several publications support David and Gaël Rougemont, who pulled out a gun during an altercation on the margins of a pro-refugee demonstration.[12] It should be noted that Gaël Rougemont, who flashed the gun, is a member of *Sauvons Calais*. There are also postings in support of a Hungarian lorry driver who tried to run over migrants while filming himself live. The group supports him and challenges his dismissal by his employer following this attack.[13]

These many calls to action have sometimes been translated into violent action. A., a solicitor, has drawn to our attention to attacks that have been directly linked to the content published on these pages. After having interacted in one way or another on *Sauvons Calais*' Facebook page, these persons then attacked refugees. This was the case of a supermarket security guard. After posting his "exasperation" on the Facebook page of *Sauvons Calais*, he fired at migrants several times with a pellet gun, which led to his imprisonment for one year.[14]

There has also been the case of three young people from Calais. After publishing comments calling for self-justice against the supposed criminal actions of the refugees and participating in a demonstration organised by *Sauvons Calais* on 7 September 2014, they attacked a squat inhabited by Egyptian asylum seekers with Molotov cocktails.[15]

The second and third sub-categories concern surveillance and the designation of the 'enemy'. These are real-time posts informing the public about the 'danger' supposedly posed by migrants: rather blurred videos filmed with a mobile phone, as well as photos

taken in the field. These publications account for 55.77% of all publications. They constitute the core of the vigilantism of the *Calaisiens en Colère*, who picture themselves as the
'reporters' of this 'war zone' that is the Calaisis, making it possible to provide viewers with
live information, much like video-activists across the channel. This category falls into what
Benjamin Loveluck calls a vigilantism of denunciation (Loveluck, 2020).

The *Calaisiens en Colère* implemented a strategy of publicising their field actions, including violent ones, with a view to spectacularisation. Furthermore, social media followers
are regularly invited to join the groups actions as situations of tension are broadcasted live
online. For example, a publication on 17 December 2015 simply stated, "Illegals are attacking us!!!" (189 shares, 395 'likes') Very quickly, and even more explicitly, a second posting
followed, sharing a video of the supposed attack, stating bluntly, "It's war, come and help
us"[16] (39K views).

Sauvons Calais and *Calaisiens en Colère* have an ambiguous relationship with violence.
On the one hand, they aspire to be a broad, respectable and credible social protest movement (Grinshpun, 2014). On the other hand, they advocate direct action and vigilantism.
Unlike other forms of vigilantism (Clark, 1988), *Sauvons Calais* and *Calaisiens en Colère*
have denied their participation in such violence, blaming it on outsiders attracted by their
activity. The ambiguous relationship with violence of these collectives is reflected in their
online publications. These clearly identify migrants as the enemy and promote vigilantism,
whether through calls for self-justice or the staging of patrols or even fights with migrants.
However, in order to avoid legal proceedings or the risk of the page being closed down, the
groups also publish calls to avoid certain wordings that are too 'divisive' or use humour
to partially defuse the violence of certain comments. The communication of these groups
laid the groundwork for a dynamic of persuasion. This is, however, a posture fraught with
contradictions, reflected in the speeches of its leaders. As will be shown later, while some
of them make an effort to present their group in a positive light, others do not make the
effort to euphemise their words. These two differentiated forms of position-taking are often
intertwined.

Avoiding being deplatformed

When asked about their possible participation in violent actions, activists presented a categorical answer: they claim to condemn violence. This is the case of *Sauvons Calais*, whose
activists denied having participated in the violence against a squatted house in Coulogne
(Gardenier, 2018). However, the violence arising in the wake of their activity can impact
the respectability of these groups, who insisted on presenting themselves as "apolitical
locals".[17] For example, a video of clashes posted by *Calaisiens en colère* caused a mediatic
row. In the winter of 2016, the group was conducting 'security patrols' around the Jules
Ferry Jungle, in a context of regular skirmishes between the French police and refugees.
The activists pretended to conduct these patrols to secure the homes of the neighbouring
residents. On a livestreamed video, one of the patrollers could be heard declaring, "I'm
getting my gun out". He was then seen drawing what looks like a rubber bullet gun (the
Flashball model, which also equipped French police forces). Afterwards, it is possible to
hear detonations, but the video is blurred enough so that the viewer may not know precisely
if the detonations originate from the rubber bullet gun being fired or not. This video went
viral before being quickly taken offline. In the meanwhile, it attracted the attention of mainstream media, who highlighted the illegality of the patrols of the *Calaisiens en Colère*,[18] To

mitigate these accusations the activists declared that these patrols, where violence erupted, regularly attracted outsiders, members of far-right groups whose "action was uncontrollable".[19] Thus, 'Laurent', a member of the group, accused by pro-refugee activists of patrolling armed with a club, tried to deny his participation in violent actions in the columns of the local newspaper *Nord Littoral*: "Wednesday I was there, yes, but I was not armed with a club". He confided, however, that members of the patrol were armed with clubs and pepper spray, "but it wasn't us! That is also why we are standing down". And he adds: "Some people want to come with pepper spray and clubs, etc. We don't want to be assimilated to these people. We don't want to be seen as violent". After being identified in a photograph by pro-refugee activists, he sidestepped: "Three people had the same jacket as me that night". A simple coincidence, according to him.

Censoring comments and moderating social media content

However, beyond distancing themselves from violence, these groups are aware of what is at stake and the risks that their activities entail: those of legal proceedings, of course, but also—and above all—the deplatforming of their social media, which are essential to their political strategy.

In this context, the community managers of these pages have made several postings calling for restraint in order to avoid deplatforming. The examples of other deplatformed anti-immigration pages (e.g. *Calais Libre*) have been given. A publication that encourages the community to self-moderate can be seen in the following. Interestingly, there is no ethical condemnation of the comments being posted. On the contrary, the call not to publish such comments only argues about the risks of falling under the category of hate speech and losing the communicative resource constituted by the page.

> *Sauvons Calais*
> September 19, 2015
> I have just deleted several dozen comments from the page. Please moderate your comments, don't give food to our opponents who are just waiting for that. As a reminder, only the administrators of this page (and me in particular) are responsible for YOUR comments. Thank you and have a good weekend!:-)
>
> *(202 "likes")*

M., an activist with the *Sauvons Calais* group, shared these concerns. He claimed to be "law-abiding" and that he tried to remove comments that were openly racist or called for violence against migrants. According to him, if it was sometimes possible to find such comments on their Facebook page, it was because of the "mass of comments" which made "the work of moderation difficult". He did not make a link between the content published by the group and the presence of such hateful comments. He added that it was the "antifas" who posted the majority of the "worst racist comments" in order to have the page deplatformed.

An interview with A., a solicitor charged by the League of Human Rights (LDH) with filing a complaint for hate speech, held a completely different point of view. She told us that moderation only began after several months of existence, after an important demonstration which put the collective under the spotlight of the national media, after more than a year of 'liberated' and unmoderated hate speech on the page. She told us that a "big clean-up" had been done to avoid the deplatforming of the Facebook page. She showed us screenshots taken before this "clean-up" that had remained on the Facebook page for several months. For example, a user under the pseudonym "Mengele"[20] declared: "Stop these crabs, these migrants, save the laboratory animals and save Calais".

A. also focused on the comments following the shooting of migrants with a pellet gun by a security guard (mentioned earlier). She found many comments that supported this action and justified anti-migrant vigilantism. Here are some of these comments:

"If they weren't out there pissing people off, they wouldn't get shot".
"Only injured, people have to buy glasses to the security guard".
"When you shoot a rifle, it's like a zombie, you have to aim at the head".
"He deserves a medal for patriotic acts, one day Calais will end up like Oslo [reference to the terrorist attack carried out by Lars Anders Breivik in 2011]".
"France should give us a hunting licence".
"This is the only solution, arm yourselves people".

It should be noted that the stakes surrounding the moderating of publications are high. What the members of the collective seem to fear most is not so much a trial, which would take a long time and be an occasion to campaign around freedom of expression, but an immediate endangerment of the resource that is the page by deplatforming. On the one hand, the collectives cannot afford to actually respect the spirit of Facebook's terms of use, because their raison d'être and what explains their success is precisely their virulent denunciation of migrants. The challenge for community managers is to provide a communication 'on the edge': provocative enough to serve as an outlet and to drain mass audiences, but not so provocative as to lead to prosecution or to deplatforming.

Using humour to mitigate hate speech

The use of humour as an "argumentative construction" (Plantin, 2011) is another component of this communication strategy. A good example is the iconic and massively shared Decathlon advert, whose display within an anti-migrant group can easily be interpreted as a call to aggression against migrants.

Initially, it was an advert displayed in one of the Decathlon group's shops showing shotgun shells topped by a bird with its wings spread. The caption explains the message of the advert: "Special migration".[21] Published on 12 October 2016 on the Facebook page of *Sauvons Calais*, this posting generated 1,300 comments and more than 37,000 shares, which is a very large audience. This viral posting was even covered by the French live news channel BFM. Beyond the initial intentions of the designers of this advertisement for the sporting goods company, the addition of the words "Humour Décathlon", followed by an associated emoticon, metaphorically reframes the reading of the advert, playing on the polysemy of the term 'migration'. As an emblematic sign of the vagaries of moderation in social and digital networks, the strategy used in this particular example seems to work, as the publication was not deleted by Facebook moderators.

In another publication, the community manager of *Sauvons Calais* invited the public, with a photograph taken by the activists, *not* to compare a refugee having a bowel movement in the woods to a dog. Here again, he provoked dehumanising comments by posting

Humour Décathlon. 😊

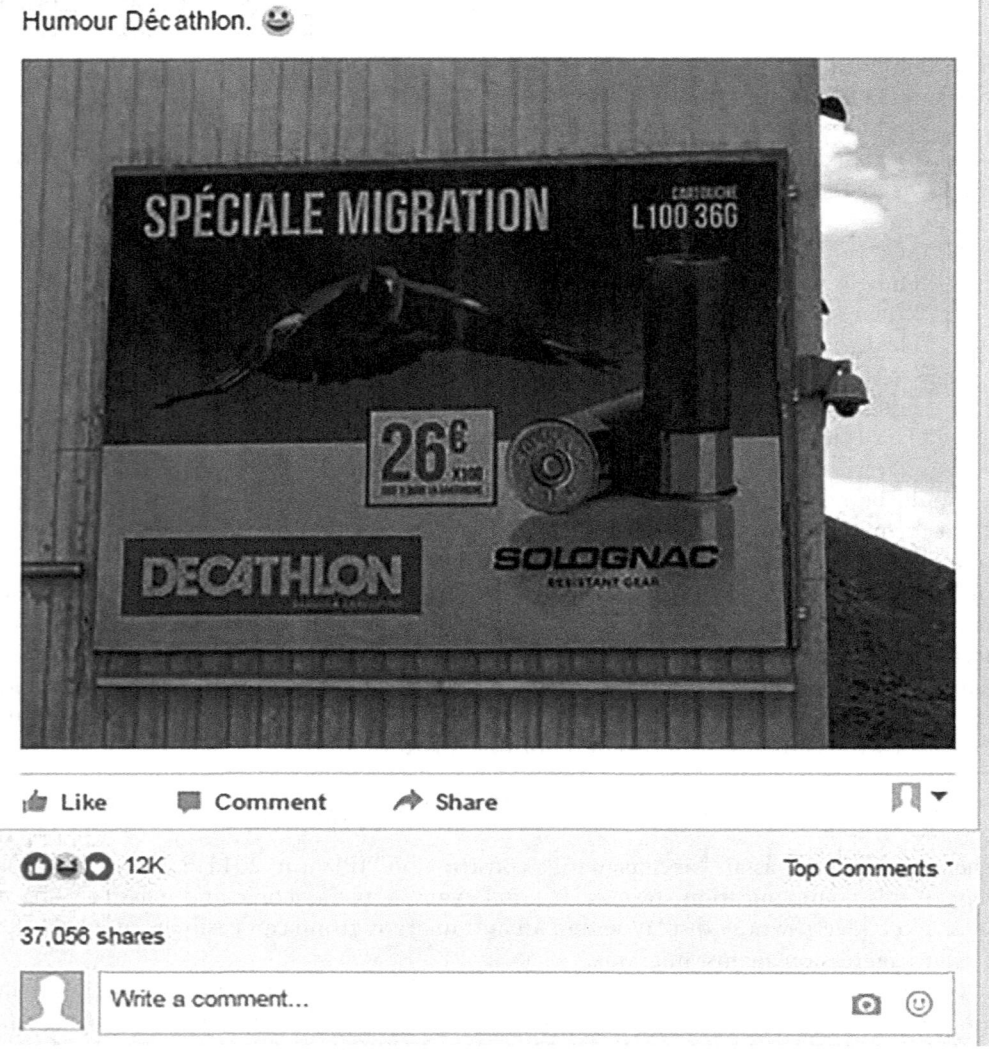

Figure 38.9 Posting "Decathlon humor" associating hunting migratory bird and potentially firing at migrants in Calais

the photograph online, while using an ironic tone to dissociate himself from the potential violence of the comments caused by the posting.

Sauvons Calais
    23 October 2015
    "Comparing this migrant woman relieving herself in the grass near the City to a dog is against the law. In advance, thank you."

266 "likes", 133 shares, 93 comments, including:

> "Did she pick up as dog owners should?"
>> "They don't like pigs, but they themselves are real pigs!"
>> "And we have to pick up dog poop".

Another example of a publication using humour targets the group's political enemies, the *No Border*: "The life of a cockroach is worth more than the opinion of a No Border. #Let's save Calais" (In French: La vie d'un cafard vaut plus que l'avis d'un No Border). In French the pun (*la vie* means life and *avis* means opinion) serves to undermine the violence of the statement. Instead of comparing the "life" of a *No Border* activist to that of a cockroach, a harmful insect, it is his "opinion", and therefore his speech and his enunciative capacity, that is judged inferior to the life of the insect.

A final case of a publication that illustrates the use of humour to mitigate the potentially offensive nature of the subject matter. It features a blonde woman and an African man in 'tribal' clothing who appears to be almost completely naked, with his sex covered by an image of the European Union flag. The image is accompanied by a parody of the logo of the online dating site Meetic, parodied as "Meegrants". The slogan "Think bigger and cheaper when dating" seems to be a reference to the sex of the partially naked African man. This 'meme'[22] is accompanied by an incitement addressed to "No borders, humanists and other left-wing extremists of all kinds: we are opening our own dating site . . . go to our site for more information!" In the form of a joke, activists in the migrant support movement are invited to enter into romantic relationships with migrants. This humorous image echoes one of the first campaigns of the German Nazi Party in 1923: when French troops occupied the left bank of the Rhine, the NSDAP (National Socialist Party) launched a campaign denouncing the so-called rape of German women by soldiers from sub-Saharan African countries of the French army's colonial troops. These campaigns emphasised the threat to German 'racial identity' posed by interbreeding with 'black blood', which was presented as inferior. In addition to the humiliation of the French invasion, the Nazis added a second attack, that of the 'defilement' of 'Germanic blood' called *Rassenschande, i.e.* 'racial shame' (Chapoutot, 2014). The *Sauvons Calais* meme is clearly part of this imagery, showing a blonde woman who appears to be engaged in a flirtatious situation, reactivating the imaginary of the defilement linked to the relationship between African men and European women. Here again, the distancing induced by the humorous discourse makes it possible to euphemise the symbolic charge of extremely violent remarks.

Conclusion

This chapter aims analyse the action of anti-migrant groups in Calais and Dover through the lens of online deviance. As is often the case with vigilantism (Abrahams, 1998), anti-migrants are 'order *amateurs*' who intend to police but whose activity paradoxically constitutes a form of deviance in itself. The acts of violence that emerge in the wake of the Calais groups, sometimes posted directly online, and the video patrols of Britain First constitute deviance in terms of the use of violence but also from the point of view of hate speech, defined by various legislative texts and user guidelines of social media platforms. A complex game of ambivalence is played out around these postings that stage vigilantism, which is either real (in France) or above all performative (in Britain).

Sauvons Calais
September 15, 2015

Nous ouvrons notre propre site de rencontre.

No Borders, "humanistes" et extrémistes de gauches en tout genre,
rendezvous sur notre site pour plus de renseignements !

Figure 38.10 Publication mocking a dating site

Indeed, the discourse and framing of anti-migrant groups aims to frame refugees crossing the Channel as a securitarian and not a humanitarian issue. They go so far as to present the figure of the migrant, the stranger to the community who is vulnerable and in need of assistance, as the enemy, echoing and building on the pre-modernist substrate of the late Middle Ages and Renaissance, which saw assistance as conditional on longstanding membership of the community and which saw the vagrant outside the group as an absolute peril (Castel, 1999).

These groups' communication around vigilantism necessarily comes up against legal regulations against hate speech, prohibiting calls to hatred and violence. Nevertheless, the rules allowing the removal of user-generated content are vague and ambiguous: not all platforms have the same standards or the same moderation capacities, especially as this type of content generates an economic ambiguity: although hate speech is prohibited by law, it generates massive traffic and therefore economic value for these platforms. This difficulty in controlling content and sometimes a lack of will to do so opens up spaces for these groups to develop this 'on the edge' communication.

This discourse remains close enough to hate speech and incitement to violence to generate strong reactions of support from the community audience of these groups, but it uses delaying tactics to preserve the communicative resource. We identify three main mitigation tactics for this hate speech: denial, the call for self-moderation and minimisation through humour. These are an example of how these groups manage to build significant communitarian audiences and exercise social movement activity that is not without influence. It should also be noted that these techniques renew social movement practices notably around video-activism, as the production of images becomes central to their anti-migration framing of the situation in the Channel.

Notes

1 "The Storm and the Web: Communication Technology and the Ecumenical Far Right". www. sv.uio.no/c-rex/english/news-and-events/right-now/2020/the-storm-and-the-web.html accessed 29 August 2022.
2 Interview with Anne Marie Waters on 27 November 2020
3 'Exposed: For Britain and the "white genocide" conspiracy theory'. www.hopenothate.org. uk/2019/04/18/exposed-for-britain-and-white-genocide-conspiracy-theory/ Seen 25 May 2021.
4 'Facebook supprime les comptes de Tommy Robinson, figure de l'extrême droite britannique'. www.lemonde.fr/pixels/article/2019/02/26/facebook-supprime-les-comptes-de-tommy-robinson-figure-de-l-extreme-droite-britannique_5428589_4408996.html Seen 25 May 2021.
5 'Royal Navy veteran captains Britain First 'HMS' patrol boat deterring migrants in English Channel'. www.plymouthherald.co.uk/news/uk-world-news/royal-navy-veteran-captains-britain-4412048 Seen 21 August 2021.
6 'Report migrant hotels to britain first'. www.patriot-campaigns.uk/report-migrant-hotels Seen 25 May 2021.
7 'Video: Britain first battle bus receives racial abuse and missiles in birmingham and coventry!'. www.patriot-campaigns.uk/video_britain_first_battle_bus_receives_racial_abuse_and_missiles_ in_birmingham_and_coventry Seen 25 May 2021.
8 'Video: Huge hotel in sheffield housing illegal immigrants!'. www.patriot-campaigns.uk/video_ huge_hotel_in_sheffield_housing_illegal_immigrants Seen 25 May 2021.
9 Why Downes?
10 'Video: Britain first takes action against grooming gangs in preston!'. www.patriot-campaigns.uk/ video_britain_first_takes_action_against_grooming_gangs_in_preston Seen 25 May 2021.
11 For more information regarding Yvan Benedetti, important leader of the French far right, refer to Pujol, P. (2017). *Mon cousin le fasciste*. Le Seuil.
12 Accessed: www.huffingtonpost.fr/2016/03/10/fusil-calais-gael-rougemont-droite-justice_n_9426886. html accessed 28 July 2017.
13 http://france3-regions.francetvinfo.fr/nord-pas-de-calais/le-chauffeur-qui-effraye-des-migrants-calais-avec-son-camion-ete-licencie-871035.html accessed 28 Septembre 2016.
14 http://tempsreel.nouvelobs.com/justice/20140709.OBS3225/calais-un-an-de-prison-pour-avoir-tire-sur-des-migrants.html accessed 28 Septembre 2016.
15 The attack did not result in any deaths or injuries and the perpetrators were quickly arrested and imprisoned. Read more: www.associationsalam.org/Des-cocktails-Molotov-lances Consulté 28 Septembre 2016.
16 In all the comments extracted from the social-numerical networks, we respect the spelling and syntax used by the authors of the posts, taking into account the language mistakes of the original documents.
17 "Calais: Angry Calaisians, an 'apolitical' collective, gathered 300 people". www.lavoixdunord. fr/archive/recup/region/calais-les-calaisiens-en-colere-collectif-apolitique-ia33b48581n3083793 Last accessed 5 July 2019.
18 "Controversial videos". *Nord Littoral*, Friday 8 January 2016, p. 13.
19 "Migrants: angry Calaisians temporarily halt nightly rounds". www.lavoixdunord.fr/archive/recu p%3A%252Fregion%252Fmigrants-les-calaisiens-en-colere-arretent-ia33b48581n3264028 Last accessed 5 July 2019.
20 Nazi doctor who conducted numerous experiments on Jewish prisoners in Auschwitz during the Second World War.
21 BFMTV, "Immigration: une affiche de Decathlon crée la polémique". www.bfmtv.com/societe/ immigration-une-affiche-de-decathlon-cree-la-polemique-1047889.html Last accessed 5 July 2019.
22 The "Internet meme" refers to an element, often visual, that is taken up and distributed en masse within the social-digital networks.

References

Abrahams, R. (1998). *Vigilant citizens: Vigilantism and the state*. Polity Press.
Badouard, R. (2022). Hate speech, fake news and content regulation on social networks in Europe. In A. Monnier, A. Boursier, & A. Seoane (Eds.), *Cyberhate in the context of migrations* (pp. 215–231). Palgrave Macmillan.

Bjørgo, T., & Mares, M. (Eds.). (2019). *Vigilantism against migrants and minorities*. Routledge.

Busher J., & Macklin G. (2015). Interpreting "cumulative extremism": Six proposals for enhancing conceptual clarity. *Terrorism and Political Violence, 27*(5), 884–905.

Castel, R. (1999). *Les métamorphoses de la question sociale*. Folio.

Champagne, P. (2015). *Faire l'opinion : Le nouveau jeu politique*. Les Editions de Minuit.

Chapoutot J. (2014). *La loi du sang: Penser et agir en nazi*. Gallimard.

Clark, M. (1988). Italian squadrismo and contemporary vigilantism. *European History Quarterly, 18*, 33–49.

Cohen-Almagor, R. (2011). Fighting hate and bigotry on the internet. *Policy and Internet, 3*(3), 1–2.

Collovald, A., & Schwartz O. (2006). Haut, bas, fragile: Sociologies du populaire. *Vacarme, 37*, 19–26.

Courbet, D., Fourquet-Courbet, M. P., & Marchioli, A. (2015). Les médias sociaux, régulateurs d'émotions collectives. *Hermès-La Revue, 71*, 287–292.

Froio, C. (2017). Nous et les autres. L'altérité sur les sites web des extrêmes droites en France. *Réseaux, 202–203*(2–3), 39–78.

Gardenier, M. (2018). Sauvons Calais, un groupe anti-migrants. Une perspective: Rétablir l'ordre. *Revue Européenne des migrations internationales, 34–1*, 235–257.

Grinshpun, Y. (2014). Ethos discursif. *Langage et Société, 149*, 85–101

Johnston, L. (1996). What is vigilantism?. *The British Journal of Criminology, 36*(2), 220–236.

La Rocca, F. (2007). Introduction à la sociologie visuelle. *Sociétés, 95*, 33–40.

Loveluck, B. (2020). The many shades of digital vigilantism. A typology of online self-justice. *Global Crime, 21*(3–4), 213–241.

Mudde, C. (2019). *The far right today*. Polity Press.

Pilkington, H. (2016). *Loud and proud: Passion and politics in the English defence league*. Manchester University Press.

Plantin, C. (2011). *Les bonnes raisons des émotions*. Peter Lang.

Pujol, P. (2017). *Mon cousin le fasciste*. Le Seuil.

Rasmussen, M. (2019). *La contre-révolution de Trump*. Divergences.

Schmitt, C. (2009). *La notion de politique: Théorie du partisan*. Éditions Flammarion.

Susca, V. (2016). *Les Affinités connectives*. Editions du Cerf.

Tanner, S., & Campana, A. (2020). Watchful citizens and digital vigilantism: A case study of the far right in Quebec. *Global Crime, 21*(3–4), 262–282.

Trottier, D. (2017). Digital vigilantism as weaponisation of visibility. *Philosophy and Technology, 30*(1), 52–64.

Virchow F. (2007). 'Capturing the streets': Marches as a political instrument of the extreme right in contemporary Germany. In M. Reiss (Ed.), *The street as stage, protest marches and public rallies since the nineteenth century*. Oxford University Press.

39

DOXXING AS A DEVIANT BEHAVIOUR

A critical analysis of Hong Kong's criminal law reform against doxxing activities

Aaron H. L. Wong, Paul Vinod Khiatani and Wing Hong Chui

Introduction

"Doxxing" is defined as "the intentional public release onto the internet of personal information about an individual by a third party, often with the intent to humiliate, threaten, intimidate or punish the identified individual" (Douglas, 2016, p. 199).[1] It was first used in the 1990s to describe internet hackers' activities of illegitimately acquiring and disclosing the identities or personal details of people who were supposed to be anonymous (Honan, 2014; Douglas, 2016). In contemporary times, doxxing is no longer seen as an activity exclusive to internet hackers; rather, it is widely recognised that anybody could potentially engage in doxxing activities, insofar as they possess personal data belonging to another and choose to disclose it publicly without the consent of the data subject.

Doxxing is not a new phenomenon in Hong Kong and has often been used as a means of cyber-bullying. However, Hong Kong's legal control of doxxing has not undergone major change until the outbreak of the 2019 Hong Kong Anti-Extradition Bill protests ("the 2019 protests"). In response to the widespread doxxing activities during the 2019 protests, the new two-tier criminal offences targeting doxxing were enacted in October 2021. This chapter explores the context for the recent development, explicating why and how the changes came about and their implications for doxxing activities. The chapter is divided into four parts. The first part traces Hong Kong's changing regulatory approach towards doxxing before and after the 2019 protests. The second part reflects on why and under what circumstances should doxxing be regarded as deviant behaviour. Following the identification of certain non-deviant/ legitimate doxxing activities, the third part reviews the scope of Hong Kong's new doxxing offences and evaluates whether the legislation is excessively broad in its coverage. The final part of the chapter explores whether legal control of doxxing through criminalisation is effective.

Hong Kong's changing approach towards doxxing: the pre-2019 context

As far back as two decades ago, doxxing activities could be observed in online discussion forums. At the time, however, the public and media outlets had not paid much attention to the nature and harms of doxxing (Lee, 2022). Doxxing behaviours were then known as

DOI: 10.4324/9781003277675-45

"Human Flesh Searching" ("HFS"), which is defined as "a collective online [behaviour] where netizens contribute knowledge and information through social media or networking platforms to expose alleged facts related to certain events and/or to publish information on a target individual or group" (Chang & Zhu, 2020, p.2). Before 2014, most HFS cases in Hong Kong were related to minor crimes, immoral incidents, personal affairs and sex-related topics (Chang & Leung, 2015). Since 2014, however, with the emergence of the "Occupy Central Movement" (another large-scale protest in Hong Kong), the targets of HFS changed to police officers and people involved in the protest (Office of the Privacy Commissioner for Personal Data ("PCPD"), 2014a). This change marked the beginning of a trend of politically motivated doxxing in Hong Kong. Despite this trend, and in light of the relatively small number of enquiries and complaints (i.e., 81 cases) received by the PCPD during the "Occupy Central Movement" (PCPD, 2014a), doxxing did not emerge as a matter of high importance for the Hong Kong government. Consequently, during the 2019 protests, the government lacked effective mechanisms to adequately respond to politically motivated doxxing activities. Four reasons are provided to substantiate and provide greater context to this argument.

Firstly, before the outbreak of the mass protests in June 2019, the PCPD, an independent public body established to enforce and promote compliance with the Personal Data (Privacy) Ordinance ("PDPO"), regarded doxxing merely as a form of cyber-bullying (PCPD, 2011, 2014b, 2018b). The PCPD has only formally classified a complaint as a "doxxing" case for the first time on 14 June 2019 (The Government of the Hong Kong Special Administrative Region [HKSAR Government], 2020). Before this, all "doxxing-related" complaints were classified as "cyber-bullying" cases in PCPD's annual reports. It was not until the publication of the PCPD's 2020–21 annual report that doxxing had been singled out as an independent category of complaint (PCPD, 2021a). While scholars have always treated HFS as a form of doxxing (Douglas, 2016), the PCPD has only started using the term "doxxing" after 2019.

Secondly, before and during the 2019 protests, there was no specific legislation that prohibited doxxing. Before 2021, there was no statute law in Hong Kong to specifically deal with cyber-bullying or doxxing activities (HKSAR Government, 2012). The PCPD (2014b, p.3) stated that as "cyber-bullying activities are wide-ranging and cover defamation, criminal intimidation and infringement of intellectual property", actions from different law enforcement bodies are required to address the violations of different breaches of the law.

Thirdly, the "enforcement notice" mechanism under the PDPO was unable to effectively combat doxxing activities. Pursuant to Section 4 of the PDPO, any person or organisation that collects, holds, processes or uses personal data (i.e., "data user" as defined in Section 2 of the PDPO) must comply with the six Data Protection Principles ("DPPs") laid down in Schedule 1 of the PDPO. In particular, DPP1 requires a data user to only collect personal data for a purpose directly related to the data user's function or activity; collect data as necessary and not excessively; and collect data by means which are lawful and fair. Also, DPP3 stipulates that unless the data subject (i.e., the individual who is the subject of the data) has given explicit and voluntary consent, personal data should only be used for the purpose(s) for which it was originally collected or for a directly related purpose. As doxxing occurs without the consent of the data subject, it may violate DPP1 and DPP3. Any person who suspects that their personal data privacy has been infringed, and can provide *prima facie* evidence, may make a complaint to the PCPD (*Wu Yin Nei Wenny v The*

Privacy Commissioner for Personal Data, 2012). If the Privacy Commissioner for Personal Data(hereafter, referred to as "the Commissioner") finds that the relevant data user has contravened the PDPO, the Commissioner may direct the relevant data user to remedy the contravention and prevent any recurrences of the contravention by issuing an enforcement notice under Section 50(1) of the PDPO. However, this "enforcement notice" mechanism has largely failed to control doxxing activities, because the contravention of the DPPs is not itself an offence. Instead, criminal liability only arises when the data user receives the enforcement notice and refuses to comply with it (Section 50A of the PDPO). Furthermore, the penalty for non-compliance is usually lenient and lacks deterrence. Before 2020, the courts had only issued fines between HK$1,000 and HK$5,000 under the relevant law (Constitutional and Mainland Affairs Bureau of the Government of Hong Kong Special Administrative Region [CMAB], 2020).

Fourthly, Section 64(2) of the pre-amended PDPO (i.e., effective from 2012 to 2021) provided that a person commits an offence if (i) the person discloses any personal data of a data subject which was obtained from a data user without the data user's consent; and (ii) the disclosure causes psychological harm to the data subject. While convictions for doxxing behaviour have been secured under this Section (CMAB, 2021a), the law gave rise to serious difficulties in enforcement. The law required proof that the disclosed data was obtained from a data user without consent. However, it is nearly impossible to ascertain the source of data (i.e., the data user involved) in doxxing cases, as the disclosed data are often reposted on online platforms by many users (CMAB, 2021a). At most, the PCPD or the Police may be able to ascertain the identities of some users who reposted the content. However, they may not have sufficient information to further trace and identify the original data user of the doxxed content and confirm whether the data user had given consent for the disclosure (CMAB, 2021a). As a result, the PCPD or the police cannot prove that the personal data concerned was obtained from the data user without his/her consent. In fact, the legislative purpose of this Section was to prohibit the non-consensual dissemination of personal data arising from incidences of personal data leakage or unauthorised sales of personal data (CMAB, 2009). Hence, before the 2021 amendment to the PDPO, the PCPD or the police were often unable to initiate prosecutions against doxxing activities (CMAB, 2021b).

The post-2019 context

A series of protests occurred during the second half of 2019 in Hong Kong. Although its demands later diversified and the protests escalated into city-wide riots, the protests originally started as a resistance against the government's intended introduction of an extradition bill. Over time, briefly put, various developments had driven a wedge between two major political camps in the city: pro-government and anti-government. During the 2019 protests, doxxing activities became prevalent among sympathisers and protesters of both camps in Hong Kong (Lam, 2021). The victims of doxxing came from various backgrounds, including, but not limited to, protesters, government officials, police officers, judges and their family members (PCPD, 2019). Even journalists and ordinary citizens, whether they were for or against the government, were not exempted from being doxxed (Lau & Ng, 2019; PCPD, 2019).

The personal data, such as the name, address, telephone number, photo, academic qualification, date of birth and identity card number, of the victims were released on online social platforms. Doxxing activities were particularly visible on Telegram, LIHKG,[2] and Facebook. Some platforms were even specifically created to disseminate these personal data. Notable examples include:

- The "Dadfindboy" Telegram channel had disseminated the personal information of over 1,100 police officers, as of August 2020 (*HKSAR v Chan King Hei,* 2021).
- The website "Hong Kong Chronicles" released a large amount of personal information and pictures of police officers and pro-government supporters (Fox News, 2021).
- The pro-government doxxing site "HKleaks" hosted 3,434 files of personal data belonging to, among others, protestors, journalists, teachers, medical workers and artists (Lam, 2021).

Up to May 2021, the police reported that over 3,800 of its officers and their family members were doxxed (*HKSAR v Hung Wing Sum,* 2021). Affected officers and their family members were greatly concerned about their personal safety (Hong Kong Police Force, 2019). The victims of doxxing often reported emotional distress and psychological harm caused by the repeated harassment and intimidation, following the online disclosure of their personal data (Legislative Council Secretariat of the Hong Kong Special Administrative Region [LegCo Secretariat of HK], 2020). In addition, one journalist reported being physically assaulted in September 2019 after being doxxed (Committee to Protect Journalists, 2019).

Doxxing activities became increasingly prevalent as the series of protests progressed over time (Hale, 2019). To prohibit doxxing activities, court injunctions were granted to protect certain groups of victims, including police officers, judges and their family members (*Secretary for Justice and Another v Persons Unlawfully and Wilfully Conducting Themselves in Any of the Acts Prohibited Under Paragraph 1(a), (b) or (c) of the Indorsement of Claim, 2019; Secretary for Justice v Persons Unlawfully and Wilfully Conducting Themselves in Any of the Acts Prohibited Under Paragraph 1(a), (b) or (c) of the Indorsement of Claim,* 2020). The newspaper "Apple Daily" and its staff also received protection (Lau & Ng, 2019). The court injunctions further prohibited the incitement of violence on any online platform or medium (*Secretary for Justice v Persons Unlawfully and Wilfully Conducting Themselves in Any of the Acts Prohibited Under Paragraph 1(a) and (b) of the Indorsement of Claim,* 2019). Multiple persons have been convicted of civil contempt of court for breaching these injunctions (PCPD, n.d.).

Between June 2019 and April 2021 (i.e., since the beginning of the 2019 protests and before the 2021 amendment to the PDPO), the PCPD had requested online service or website operators to remove over 5,900 hyperlinks. However, as such requests were not mandatory in nature (and had even less persuasive effects on overseas operators), only about 70% of the web links were removed (CMAB, 2021a; PCPD, 2021b).

As discussed above, the criminal law before the 2021 amendment was inadequate to curb doxxing activities. Notably, the PCPD and the Police were often unable to prosecute doxxers. Also, they lacked the statutory power to demand the cessation of doxxing content on overseas platforms. Against this backdrop, the Personal Data (Privacy) (Amendment) Bill 2021 ("PD(P)(A) Bill") was introduced to amend the PDPO. It came into force in October 2021.

The PD(P)(A) Bill creates a system of two-tier offences. The first-tier offence is a summary offence, criminalising the disclosure of personal data without the data subject's consent, with the intention to cause a specified harm or being reckless as to whether a specified harm would or would likely be caused to the data subject or their family member(s) (Section 64(3A) of the PDPO). The second-tier offence is an indictable offence. A person could be found culpable of this offence if, on top of satisfying the elements of the first-tier offence, a specified harm is actually caused to the data subject or their family member(s) (Section 64(3C) of the PDPO). The specified harm is defined as harassment, molestation, pestering, threat or intimidation; bodily harm or psychological harm; causing the person reasonably to be concerned for the person's safety or well-being; or damage to the property of the person (Section 64(6) of the PDPO). The maximum sentences for the first-tier and second-tier offences are two years' and five years' imprisonment respectively.

Previously, because the PCPD lacked criminal investigation and prosecutorial powers in handling doxxing cases, they had to refer all such cases to the Police or the Department of Justice. Under the PD(P)(A) Bill, the Commissioner is vested with new investigation powers. These powers include requiring persons to provide materials and assistance, entering and searching premises and seizing materials with a warrant, accessing and searching an electronic device with a warrant, and stopping, searching, and arresting persons. The Commissioner may now also institute prosecution for summary offences in the Magistrates' Courts. Furthermore, when there is a disclosure of personal data without the data subject's consent, the Commissioner may serve a cessation notice to anyone (including internet service providers), ordering the removal of the doxxing content. It can thus be seen that the scope of criminalisation, the investigative powers of the PCPD and the deterrence effect against doxxing have been greatly widened and strengthened under the new Bill.

Doxxing as a deviant behaviour

Deviance is broadly defined as behaviour that differs from what is normatively expected and that is negatively evaluated by the majority in society. This chapter adopts the same definition. The right to privacy is well-recognised in Hong Kong and internationally (Hong Kong Bill of Rights Ordinance, 1991, Article 14; International Covenant on Civil and Political Rights, 1966, Article 17). As doxxing behaviours infringe upon such rights, they are naturally worrisome. As Mr Justice Coleman observed, doxxing could cause real nuisance, harassment and anxiety to victims, and these impacts on victims may be long-lasting (*Secretary for Justice v Chan Oi Yau Riyo*, 2020). Recent studies have found that the disclosure of almost all types of personal information brings negative emotions, including stress, anxiety and depression, to the victims (Bravo et al, 2019; Chen et al., 2018; Chen et al, 2019). It is noteworthy that once the doxxing content is posted online, it would be difficult to get such content removed. Even if one manages to remove the online content, it is impossible to know if the removed content will re-emerge in the future, as some users may back up the content on their personal devices (before the deletion) with the intention of spreading it on other platforms (Douglas, 2016). Doxxing activities thus have the potential to cause prolonged perceived and/or actual harm to the victims.

Another worrying aspect of doxxing activities is that they generate the risk of conse-quential harm. The published personal data might be further misused by others to commit identity theft. Worse still, the victims might be physically harassed or even assaulted. In the context of the 2019 protests, the personal data of many police officers, government officials and judicial officers, as well as their family members, were doxxed, giving rise to the fear that protesters may tail behind and attack them. As mentioned earlier, the reported attack on a journalist who was doxxed also illustrates the real risks of such events happening. Apart from that, the victims often received persistent and frequent nuisance calls (*Secretary for Justice v Persons Unlawfully and Wilfully Conducting*, 2020). These nuisance calls typically contained "hate messages, incitements or statements and threats that there will be revenge, injury or even killing" (*Secretary for Justice and Another*, 2019, para. 16). Some unscrupulous users have even used publicised personal data to impersonate the victims. For example, some victims discovered that they were enrolled for organ donation, received unsolicited deliveries and/or became applicants for loan programs – all ploys to cause harm, loss and/or nuisance to data subjects (PCPD, 2020). Similarly, pro-government supporters have employed the same doxxing techniques to target anti-government protesters (PCPD, 2019). Following data leaks of their personal information, various protestors have received threatening calls, demanding them not to further engage in protests (Agence France-Presse, 2020).

As doxxing activities became increasingly prevalent among both political camps, there was a foreseeable danger that such practices could further deepen existing social cleavages and political polarizations in society. Apart from the intended targets of doxxing (e.g., indi-viduals or groups actively engaging in the protests or police officers), their family members, sympathizers in the community and other citizens might also be "intimidated into silence or suppressed in expressing their opinions openly and honestly or conducting their affairs or pursuing their life in the way they would wish for fear of being victimised by doxxing" (*Secretary for Justice v Chan Oi Yau Riyo*, 2020, para. 77).

Given that doxxing causes harm to individuals and society at large, it is not difficult to see why many acts of doxxing should be regarded as deviant behaviour. However, are there doxxing activities that are neither deviant nor illegitimate?

Could doxxing ever be legitimate?

Previous literature has considered whether doxxing could be seen as legitimate if it strikes the "right" balance between exercising the freedom of expression and protecting the right to privacy (Chang & Poon, 2017). On one hand, freedom of expression, which includes the right to publish information, might be legitimately restricted for respecting the rights of others (e.g., right to privacy) (Hong Kong Bill of Rights Ordinance, 1991, Article 16). On the other hand, an individual's right to privacy is not absolute. For example, it may be permissible to infringe a person's right to privacy if doing so would protect the public interest, e.g., for the detection and prevention of crime (The Law Reform Commission of Hong Kong, 2004). Thus, the permissibility of doxxing may be contingent on the line that is drawn between the two competing rights.

How should this "line" be drawn? An understanding of the varieties of doxxing activi-ties provides a suitable starting point to address this inquiry. Douglas (2016) differentiates doxxing activities into three types, namely deanonymising doxxing; target doxxing; and delegitimising doxxing. Their definitions are set out below:

Table 39.1 Types of doxxing

Type	Definition
Deanonymising doxxing	The target loses their anonymity, either in a professional or personal capacity.
Targeting doxxing	The target loses their obscurity. For example, the target's home address is revealed online.
Delegitimising doxxing	The target loses credibility and legitimacy. For example, a doxxer releases evidence that the target engaged in willful deception or immoral activity.

Source: Anderson & Wood, 2021

Douglas (2016, p.207) argued that deanonymising and delegitimising doxxing are only acceptable if their motive concerns public interest and public welfare, such that "the benefits to the public of exposing wrongdoing or deception outweigh the foreseeable harms to the subject". These types of doxxing may be acceptable when there are allegations that the target performed legal wrongdoing or serious misconduct. In contrast, targeting doxxing is generally not acceptable because these activities are intended to intimidate and harass the target (Douglas, 2016). In contrast to the two other forms of doxxing, targeting doxxing does not have a strong public interest justification. Thus, it is suggested that the legitimacy of doxxing activities depends upon the doxxer's motive (Douglas, 2016).

Douglas (2016, p.208) also remarked that deanonymising doxxing is a form of "private enforcement of public laws and morals standards", which has the potential to develop into vigilantism. "Digital vigilantism" is defined as "a process where people are collectively offended by other citizen activity and respond through coordinated retaliation on digital media" (Trottier, 2017, p.56). Vigilantes act as "the informal community guards to offset the inadequacy of the formal justice system" (Burrows, 1976, cited in Chang & Poon, 2017, p.1915). They use informal means to punish deviants who were not adequately disciplined, sanctioned or penalized by the formal justice system (Chang & Poon, 2017). In this sense, vigilantism, or "netilantism" (i.e., vigilantism on the internet) (Chang & Poon, 2017), may be regarded as a new type of citizen policing.

During the 2019 protests, some anti-government protestors engaged in deanonymising and delegitimising doxxing by disclosing the names and identification numbers of individual police officers who were accused of using excessive force or performing other forms of misconduct (Chang, 2020; Cheung, 2021). These doxxing activities represented not only the former's exasperation and dissatisfaction against the latter, but also their distrust of the justice system's fairness and its capability to resolve allegations of wrongdoing by police officers (Chang & Zhu, 2020; Cheung, 2021). In other words, some anti-government protestors chose to take justice into their own hands by attempting to hold the authorities accountable through digital vigilantism (Cheung, 2021).

In the cases of disclosing alleged misconduct committed by the authorities, it has been suggested that such doxxing activities, if limited to disclosing the relevant wrongdoers' names and identification numbers, should not be perceived as deviant since they were aimed at advancing public interest (and therefore should be protected under the right to freedom of expression) (Cheung, 2021). More generally, deanonymising and delegitimising persons who have committed immoral conduct (e.g., fraudsters) to advance the public interest (e.g., by warning potential victims) should also be deemed acceptable and non-deviant on this basis. Another illustration of doxxing in the public interest is the act of exposing "predatory Tinder dates". Some victims of predatory dates shared the details of the persons who were abusive and manipulative during the dates, in order to warn other Tinder users to avoid meeting the abusive persons (Tariq, 2022). It would be difficult to classify such activities as deviant behaviour.

While digital vigilantism may facilitate social justice, it could also jeopardise it. Zetter (2007) warned that digital vigilantism may weaken systems of social control and provide momentum for society to fall towards a state of anarchy, because cyber-activities are too hard to regulate and stop once the practice has been developed (Chang & Poon, 2017). By taking justice into doxxers' own hands, digital vigilantism could also be arbitrary in the target selection process and lead to injustice when the victims have no opportunity to rebut false allegations made against them (Chang & Poon, 2017; Chang & Zhu, 2020). It could also bring about a "chilling effect" and intimidate those holding unpopular opinions into silence. During the 2019 protests, many protestors went beyond doxxing those officers who were accused of legal wrongdoings; for example, they widely engaged in targeting doxxing and doxxed other police officers, judges and even their family members, causing considerable nuisance to those who were not morally reprehensible in any way. It could be argued that digital vigilantism develops into deviant behaviour once it becomes uncontrollable and unreasonably (or disproportionately) intrudes upon the right to privacy of the victim.

In determining whether a particular doxxing activity is legitimate or illegitimate, (i) the purpose of the disclosure; (ii) the target who is being exposed; and (iii) the type and scope of the personal data disclosed, should all be considered (Cheung, 2021). Doxxing is only justifiable as a form of freedom of expression if there is a legitimate public interest reason for the disclosure of personal data. If such public interest reason(s) can be established, the scope of the disclosure still must not be more than necessary in advancing the public interest (Chan, 2019). Doxxing activities that satisfy such a proportionality test should be seen as legitimate and should not be regarded as deviant. For example, in cases of exposing alleged misconduct in public office or financial scams, it may be acceptable to disclose the culprit's name and/or staff number. However, it would not be acceptable to disclose their residential address and/or their family members' personal information. The disclosure of the former class of information (i.e., name and/or staff number) assists in delegitimising wrongful behaviour by holding wrongdoers accountable, while the disclosure of the latter class of information (i.e., residential address and/or family members' personal information) facilitates future harassment or intimidation of the relevant persons. Of course, the extent to which personal information might be properly disclosed is a fact-sensitive issue. If there is no proper purpose for disclosing another's personal information, even mere disclosure of names should be deemed deviant. When doxxing is done to intimidate protesters from participating in lawful protests or police officers from lawfully executing their duties, such acts infringe on others' lawful rights and have no moral legitimacy (Cheung, 2021).

Re-thinking the scope of Hong Kong's 2021 amendment

With the abovementioned standard for evaluating the legitimacy of doxxing activities, as suggested by Cheung (2021), and the classification of doxxing activities as proposed by Douglas (2016), we turn our attention to examining Hong Kong's two-tier doxxing offences.

Have the new offences struck an appropriate balance between protecting the right to privacy and the right to freedom of expression? There is of course a strong policy reason to protect the right to privacy. Yet, if the law is over-ambitious in curbing all forms of personal information disclosure, it would unavoidably undermine the competing right to freedom of expression (Hong Kong Bill of Rights Ordinance, 1991, Article 16). Thus, it is necessary to explore whether legitimate doxxing activities are punishable or not under Hong Kong's new law.

As mentioned earlier, the recently enacted two-tier offences criminalise a doxxer who intended to cause a specified harm or was reckless "as to whether [a] specified harm would be, or would likely be, caused" (Section 64(3A) of the PDPO). For doxxing activities done with the intent to cause harm to others, there is no doubt that the criminal law should prohibit such behaviours, based on the harm principle (Baker, 2008).

However, the issue becomes more complicated when the *mens rea* of recklessness is considered. Case law has established the legal definition of recklessness(*R v G and Another*, 2003; *Sin Kam Wah and Another v HKSAR*, 2005). In the context of doxxing, the defendant is reckless if: (i) the defendant is aware of the risk that a specified harm would (or would likely) occur, and (ii) in the circumstances known to the defendant, it is unreasonable to take the risk. It should be noted that under the recklessness test, in deciding whether it is unreasonable for the defendant to take the risk, the court is concerned about whether the risk of causing a specified harm is negligible (so that it is reasonable to take the risk), rather than whether the reason behind the performance of a doxxing activity is reasonable.

There are many reasons that could prompt a person to disclose another person's personal information. Some may do so with a good motive and their conduct would by no means be morally reprehensible. For example, a victim of romance fraud or a financial scam may disclose the personal data (e.g., the name and home/work address) of the culprit to prevent others from being further victimised. However, if the victim realises that there is an actual risk that the culprit may suffer from a specified harm (e.g., being harassed) following the disclosure of personal information, it would inevitably be unreasonable, in the eyes of the law, for the victim to take that risk and, as a result, he/she would be found reckless.

There is also a risk of "derivative abuse" (i.e., subsequent doxxing or harassment) arising from the initially legitimate disclosure of data (*Secretary for Justice and Another v Persons Unlawfully and Wilfully Conducting Themselves in Any of the Acts Prohibited Under Paragraph 1(a), (b) or (c) of the Indorsement of Claim*, 2019). For example, ill-intentioned persons may act on personal data reported by media outlets. In an actual case, after the name of a police officer was read out in court and reported by the media, the officer was doxxed online and death threats were made against him (*Secretary for Justice and Another v Persons Unlawfully and Wilfully Conducting Themselves in Any of the Acts Prohibited Under Paragraph 1(a), (b) or (c) of the Indorsement of Claim*, 2019). Applying the recklessness test, if a reporter realised that disclosing a defendant/officer's name or other personal information in the news report may likely lead to derivative abuse performed by readers, it is at least arguable that the reporter could be charged under the new doxxing offences (subject to any available defence).

Thus, the problem with recklessness being a mens rea of doxxing offences is that prima facie it is excessively broad in its coverage. It applies to both illegitimate and legitimate doxxing and has the potential of criminalising persons who are acting in good faith and not morally reprehensible. A similar observation can be made regarding the *actus reus* of a person who "discloses any personal data of a data subject" (Section 64 (3A) and (3C) of the PDPO). In the PDPO, personal data is defined as data that relates to a living individual and "from which it is practicable for the identity of the individual to be directly or indirectly ascertained" (Section 2 of the PDPO). Among other information, a person's name, sex, age, occupation, nationality and telephone number are considered to be personal data (PCPD, 2018a). There are countless lawful and non-deviant situations in which one or more of the personal data mentioned above might be disclosed. For example, news reports would often mention a person's name, age, sex, nationality and occupation. Similarly, advocacy groups or victim support groups would often list the contact information of the relevant government officials or police officers on their websites, including the person's name, office address and phone number (and these kinds of information are sometimes already made publicly available). It is unfortunate that the legitimate disclosure of certain non-sensitive personal information would still be included in the scope of criminalisation. This wide net of criminalisation is, moreover, inadequately limited by the equally wide *mens rea* of recklessness as discussed above. If such a wide net is not limited by appropriate defences, the ensuing result is potential over-criminalisation.

Defences for the new doxxing offences

Section 64(4) of the new PDPO has provided four defences for the doxxing offences. They are: (i) having a reasonable belief that the disclosure is necessary to prevent or detect crime (the "crime prevention defence"); (ii) making disclosure as required by the law; (iii) having a reasonable belief that the disclosure was with the data subject's consent; and (iv) disclosure made "solely for the purpose of a lawful news activity . . . or a directly related activity" and that the defendant "had reasonable grounds to believe that the publishing or broadcasting of the personal data was in the public interest" (the "news activity defence").

The crime prevention and the news activity defences require further discussion, as they are more controversial in application and there may be confusion as to what amounts to lawful doxxing behaviour. The crime prevention defence only applies when the disclosure is necessary to prevent or detect crime. In the example of posting the personal information of the culprit of financial fraud on a public forum to warn others, it is possible that the defence does not apply because a better way to prevent future crime is to report the information to the police. Thus, the disclosure of personal information through the internet might not be seen as "necessary" for crime prevention or detection in the eyes of the law. Therefore, this defence arguably only applies in very limited circumstances, such as when a victim discloses the personal data of a perpetrator to law enforcement agencies. The "crime" requirement also presents a separate hurdle to overcome. In cases of exposing persons who perform immoral acts, such as "predatory Tinder dates", defendants are not covered by this defence because no crime is involved.

Regarding the news activity defence, it is only applicable when the defendant had reasonable grounds to believe that the information he/she disclosed (when conducting a lawful news activity) was in the public interest. Three obstacles could be observed in relying on the defence. Firstly, public interest is difficult to define. Given that the PDPO does not further define the concept of "public interest", further judicial interpretation is needed to clarify this concept. For example, when a journalist reports the defendant/police officer's name in a newspaper, it advances the public's right to know. However, considering the risk that the victim may suffer a specified harm, it is unclear whether the benefits of advancing the public's right to know outweigh the potential harm(s) caused to the victim. Secondly, having a subjective belief that such disclosure was in the public interest itself is not a valid defence. Rather, there must also be reasonable grounds from an objective standpoint to support such a belief. This further limits the applicability of the defence. Thirdly, the defence only applies to disclosure(s) made "solely for the purpose of" news activity (Section 64(4) of the PDPO). Thus, regardless of the benefits of the disclosure to public interest and welfare, ordinary citizens who engage in legitimate doxxing activities (e.g., to expose fraudsters) cannot rely on the defence.

The defences provided under the 2021 PD(P)(A) Bill are arguably too limited in scope. Ordinary citizens who performed legitimate doxxing activities are hardly able to rely on any of the defences. As a result, the new doxxing offences risk over-criminalising legitimate doxxing activities together with the illegitimate ones. While in practice it is highly unlikely that prosecutions will be initiated against most legitimate doxxing activities, it is far from legally certain that those engaging in legitimate doxxing activities would not be convicted, as prosecutorial discretion to not prosecute is a discretionary power held in the executive's hands, not a legal right that the defendants could rely on in court.

It is proposed that the public interest defence should not be limited to news activities. The general public should be able to perform legitimate doxxing activities without being criminalised (Cheung, 2021). For example, similar legislation in the United Kingdom, which can be used to criminalise doxxing behaviour, contains a defence available for anyone if, in the particular circumstances, the disclosure of personal data was justified as being in the public interest (Data Protection Act, 2018, Section 170(2)). It is suggested that such a defence can be adopted in Hong Kong. The Law Reform Commission of Hong Kong (2004) previously suggested a non-exhaustive list of public interest considerations in the context of discussing the civil liability for invasion of privacy. These non-exhaustive factors, such as the prevention of serious improper conduct and establishing whether a person was fit for public office, might be included in future amendments of the PDPO to make the law more accessible. If the legislation provides for a general public interest defence, it would be wide enough to cover situations of exposing fraud or other immoral activities.

The effectiveness of controlling doxxing through criminalisation

To a considerable extent, the law amendment has been successful in curbing doxxing. From 8 October 2021 (the commencement of the new PDPO) to 31 December 2022, the PCPD handled 2,128 cases relating to the new doxxing offences, and 114 criminal investigations were initiated (PCPD, 2023). As of August 2023, at least ten offenders have been convicted under the new doxxing offences. (PCPD, n.d.). The PCPD also issued 1,500 cessation notices to request the removal of 17,703 doxxing messages (PCPD, 2023). Around 90% of these messages have been removed (PCPD, 2023). Furthermore, the penalties imposed for violating doxxing injunctions and offences (ranging from community service order to eight months' imprisonment) have also delivered a clear message of deterrence (PCPD, n.d.). As explained earlier, after the amendment, the PCPD has been vested with wider investigative and prosecutorial powers. As a result, their capacity to combat doxxing activities has been significantly strengthened. The new doxxing law is hence effective in reducing the number of doxxing activities performed in Hong Kong.

That being said, limitations remain for the new law to fully halt doxxing activities in Hong Kong. There are at least two reasons for this.

Firstly, technological advancements have restricted the effectiveness of the cessation notice mechanism. While extra-territorial effect is introduced in the amended law so that a cessation notice can be served regardless of whether the doxxing activity is performed in Hong Kong or not (Section 66K of the PDPO), its actual enforcement remains difficult because the PCPD (2022) has neither the capacity nor authority to arrest overseas persons who are identified as being non-compliant. As a result, doxxing content remains publicly accessible on some overseas platforms. For example, even if it is blocked in Hong Kong, the "Hong Kong Chronicles" website remains accessible through the use of a Virtual Private Network (Kwan, 2021). Also, the "HKleaks" website, which was anonymously registered on a Russian server and disclosed the personal data of over 3,000 persons (mainly persons being identified as anti-government protestors and journalists), remained in operation until 2023 (Chan & Blundy, 2019; Ho, 2022; Lam, 2021).After the 2021 amendment, the PCPD observed that government officials, legislators and police officers were still the main targets of doxxing (LegCo Secretariat of HK, 2022). The number of politically motivated doxxing cases only began to noticeably decrease in 2022, which is likely due to the general social stability that has gradually been restored since the end of the 2019 protests (PCPD, 2022).

Secondly, apart from the technical difficulties encountered in removing online doxxing content, another complication arises from the controversial nature of doxxing and the blurry moral lines between legitimate and illegitimate doxxing. Unlike child pornography, which is clearly immoral and is outlawed in almost every jurisdiction, many jurisdictions would not treat doxxing content in the same way. Equally, overseas platforms would hardly feel compelled to abide by the laws of Hong Kong to remove those content. These challenges explain why, regardless of how wide the net of criminalisation is, it will be hard for Hong Kong's local legislation to effectively force the removal of doxxing content from all online platforms.

Conclusion

Although doxxing was not regarded as a serious public issue in Hong Kong before 2019, it has since attracted more attention following a series of social events. It has also led the Government to amend the PDPO. While the adverse consequences of doxxing activities should not be ignored, it is suggested that not all forms of doxxing activities are illegitimate and deviant in nature. It is proposed that doxxing activities that proportionately advance the public interest (e.g., exposing fraudsters or serious misconduct) should be regarded as legitimate and be protected by the law. The new two-tier doxxing offences in Hong Kong are arguably too broad in their coverage, potentially criminalising even legitimate doxxing activities. It may be worth considering to introduce a general public interest defence in the future.

While most online service providers have complied with the PCPD's cessation notices and removed the doxxing content, there remains to been enforcement challenges to remove the doxxing content hosted on overseas platforms. It is imperative that future research explore ways to better combat illegitimate doxxing activities, while also safeguarding the right to perform legitimate doxxing activities. Single and multiple-case study designs of policy and practice solutions in other jurisdictions would be particularly advantageous in this regard.

Notes

1 Although they are interchangeable, "Doxxing" is used instead of "Doxing" in this chapter for consistency with Hong Kong's regulatory regime.
2 Telegram Messenger is an instant messaging application commonly used for communicating messages, file storage and transfer, and social networking. LIHKG is an online discussion forum based in Hong Kong.

References

Agence France-Presse. (2020, September 18). *Anonymous site ramps up 'doxxing' campaign against HK activists*. MENAFN. Retrieved February 1, 2023, from https://menafn.com/1100816816/Anonymous-site-ramps-up-doxxing-campaign-against-HK-activists

Anderson, B., & Wood, M. A. (2021). Doxxing: A scoping review and typology. In A. Flynn, J. Bailey, & N. Henry (Eds.), *The Emerald international handbook of technology-facilitated violence and abuse* (pp. 205–226). Emerald Publishing Limited.

Baker, D. J. (2008). Constitutionalizing the harm principle. *Criminal Justice Ethics, 27*(2), 3–28. https://doi.org/10.1080/0731129X.2008.9992238

Bravo, D. Y., Jefferies, J., Epps, A., & Hill, N. E. (2019). When things go viral: Youth's discrimination exposure in the world of social media. In H. E. Fitzgerald, D. J. Johnson, D. B. Qin, F. A. Villarruel, & J. Norder (Eds.), *Handbook of children and prejudice* (pp. 269–287). Springer.

Chan, J. (2019). Proportionality after Hysan: fair balance, manifestly without reasonable foundation and Wednesbury unreasonableness. *Hong Kong Law Journal, 49*, 265.

Chan, E., & Blundy, R. (2019, November 1). *'Bulletproof' China-backed doxxing site attacks Hong Kong's democracy activists*. Hong Kong Free Press. Retrieved February 1, 2023, from https://hongkongfp.com/2019/11/01/bulletproof-china-backed-doxxing-site-attacks-hong-kongs-democracy-activists/

Chang, L. Y. C. (2020). Taking justice into their own hands: 'Netilantism' in Hong Kong. In L. Jaivin, B. Hillman, J. Golley, & S. Strange (Eds.), *China dreams* (pp. 217–219). ANU Press.

Chang, L. Y. C., & Leung, A. K. H. (2015). An introduction to cyber crowdsourcing (Human Flesh Search) in the Greater China region. In R. G. Smith, R. C.-C. Cheung, & L. Y.-C. Lau (Eds.), *Cybercrime risks and responses: Eastern and western perspectives* (pp. 240–252). Palgrave Macmillan.

Chang, L. Y. C., & Poon, R. (2017). Internet vigilantism: Attitudes and experiences of university students toward cyber crowdsourcing in Hong Kong. *International Journal of Offender Therapy and Comparative Criminology, 61*(16), 1912–1932. https://doi.org/10.1177/0306624X16639037

Chang, L. Y. C., & Zhu, J. (2020). Taking justice into their own hands: Predictors of Netilantism among cyber citizens in Hong Kong. *Frontiers in Psychology, 11*, Article 556903. https://doi.org/10.3389/fpsyg.2020.556903

Chen, M. T., Cheung, A. S. Y., & Chan, K. L. (2019). Doxing: What adolescents look for and their intentions. *International Journal of Environmental Research and Public Health, 16*(2), Article 218. https://doi.org/10.3390/ijerph16020218

Chen, Q., Chan, K. L., & Cheung, A. S. Y. (2018). Doxing victimization and emotional problems among secondary school students in Hong Kong. *International Journal of Environmental Research and Public Health, 15*(12), Article 2665. https://doi.org/10.3390%2Fijerph15122665

Cheung, A. (2021). Doxing and the challenge to legal regulation: When personal data become a weapon. In J. Bailey, A. Flynn, & N. Henry (Eds.), *The Emerald international handbook of technology-facilitated violence and abuse* (pp. 577–594). Emerald Publishing.

Committee to Protect Journalists. (2019, September 25). *Unidentified men assault journalist from pro-democracy Apple Daily newspaper in Hong Kong*. Retrieved February 1, 2023, from https://cpj.org/2019/09/unidentified-men-assault-journalist-at-pro-democra/

Constitutional and Mainland Affairs Bureau of the Government of Hong Kong Special Administrative Region [CMAB]. (2009, August). *Consultation document on review of the personal data (privacy) ordinance*. Retrieved February 1, 2023, from www.cmab.gov.hk/doc/issues/PDPO_Consultation_Document_en.pdf

Constitutional and Mainland Affairs Bureau of the Government of Hong Kong Special Administrative Region [CMAB]. (2020, January 20). *Legislative council panel on constitutional affairs: Review of the personal data (privacy) ordinance* [Paper for Discussion]. Retrieved February 1, 2023, from www.legco.gov.hk/yr19-20/english/panels/ca/papers/ca20200120cb2-512-3-e.pdf

Constitutional and Mainland Affairs Bureau of the Government of Hong Kong Special Administrative Region [CMAB]. (2021a, May 17). *Legislative council panel on constitutional affairs: Proposed amendments to the personal data (privacy) ordinance (Cap. 486)* [Paper for Discussion]. Retrieved February 1, 2023, from www.pcpd.org.hk/english/whatsnew/files/ca20210517cb4_974_3_e.pdf

Constitutional and Mainland Affairs Bureau of the Government of Hong Kong Special Administrative Region [CMAB]. (2021b, July 14). *Personal data (privacy) (Amendment) Bill 2021* [Legislative Council Brief]. Retrieved February 1, 2023, from www.legco.gov.hk/yr20-21/english/brief/cmabcr72245_20210714-e.pdf

Data Protection Act 2018, c. 12, section 170. (2018). Retrieved from www.legislation.gov.uk/ukpga/2018/12/

Douglas, D. M. (2016). Doxing: A conceptual analysis. *Ethics and Information Technology, 18*(3), 199–210. https://doi.org/10.1007/s10676-016-9406-0

Fox News. (2021, January 14). Hong Kong ISP blocks access to pro-democracy website under national security law. *Fox News.* Retrieved February 1, 2023, from www.foxnews.com/world/hong-kong-internet-firm-blocks-access-to-pro-democracy-site-over-national-security-law

Hale, E. (2019, September 20). Hong Kong protests: Tech war opens up with doxxing of protesters and police. *The Guardian.* Retrieved February 1, 2023, from www.theguardian.com/world/2019/sep/20/hong-kong-protests-tech-war-opens-up-with-doxxing-of-protesters-and-police

HKSAR v Chan King Hei, (2021). HKCA 1144, CACC 191/2020 (Hong Kong Court of Appeal). (2021, August 4).

HKSAR v Hung Wing Sum, (2021). HKDC 1347, DCCC 344/2021 (Hong Kong District Court). (2021, September 27).

Ho, K. (2022, May 17). Hong Kong officials, police, and lawmakers remain targets of doxxing, despite new law, says privacy watchdog. *Hong Kong Free Press.* Retrieved February 1, 2023, from https://hongkongfp.com/2022/05/17/hong-kong-officials-police-and-lawmakers-remain-targets-of-doxxing-despite-new-law-says-privacy-watchdog/

Honan, M. (2014, March 6). What is doxing? *WIRED.* Retrieved February 1, 2023, from www.wired.com/2014/03/doxing/

Hong Kong Bill of Rights Ordinance (Cap.383, Laws of Hong Kong). (1991).

Hong Kong Police Force. (2019, December 11). Interim injunction order of the High Court (HCA 1957/2019)—Doxxing and harassment against police officers, special constables and their families. *Police Messages.* Retrieved February 1, 2023, from www.police.gov.hk/ppp_en/03_police_message/iio_1957.html

International Covenant on Civil and Political Rights (United Nations). (1966).

Kwan, R. (2021, January 11). In a first under security law, Hong Kong police order telecom firms to block anti-gov't doxing website—Report. *Hong Kong Free Press.* Retrieved February 1, 2023, from https://hongkongfp.com/2021/01/11/in-a-first-under-security-law-hong-kong-police-order-telecoms-firms-to-block-anti-govt-doxing-website/

Lam, O. (2021, May 20). Hong Kong to toughen up privacy law against doxxing. *Global Voices Advox.* Retrieved February 1, 2023, from https://advox.globalvoices.org/2021/05/20/hong-kong-to-toughen-up-privacy-law-against-doxxing/

Lau, C., & Ng, K. (2019, September 20). Hong Kong newspaper gets injunction against reporters' doxxing. *South China Morning Post.* Retrieved February 1, 2023, from www.scmp.com/news/hong-kong-law-and-crime/article/3029573/hong-kong-newspaper-apply-daily-gets-injunction

Lee, C. (2022). Doxxing as discursive action in a social movement. *Critical Discourse Studies, 19*(3), 326–344. https://doi.org/10.1080/17405904.2020.1852093

Legislative Council Secretariat of the Hong Kong Special Administrative Region [LegCo Secretariat of HK]. (2020). *Replies to initial written questions raised by finance committee members in examining the estimates of expenditure 2021–22: Secretary for constitutional and mainland affairs: Session No.: 3.* Retrieved February 1, 2023, from www.legco.gov.hk/yr20-21/english/fc/fc/w_q/cmab-e.pdf

Legislative Council Secretariat of the Hong Kong Special Administrative Region [LegCo Secretariat of HK]. (2022, July 11). *Panel on constitutional affairs: Minutes of meeting held on Monday, 16 May 2022, at 2:30 pm in conference room 1 of the legislative council complex* [Minutes of

Meeting]. Retrieved February 1, 2023, from www.legco.gov.hk/yr2022/english/panels/ca/minutes/ca20220516.pdf

Office of the Privacy Commissioner for Personal Data, Hong Kong. (2011). *Newsletter (August 2011 Issue No.25)*. Office of the Privacy Commissioner for Personal Data, Hong Kong. Retrieved February 1, 2023, from www.pcpd.org.hk/english/resources_centre/publications/newsletter/newsletter_issue25.html

Office of the Privacy Commissioner for Personal Data, Hong Kong. (2014a, October 30). Privacy commissioner published leaflet reminding internet users to abide by the law as cyber-bullying arouses public concern. *Media Statement*. Retrieved February 1, 2023, from www.pcpd.org.hk/english/news_events/media_statements/press_20141030.html

Office of the Privacy Commissioner for Personal Data, Hong Kong. (2014b, October). Cyber-bullying—What you need to know [Leaflet]. *PCPD*. Retrieved February 1, 2023, from www.pcpd.org.hk/english/news_events/media_statements/files/cyberbullying_e.pdf

Office of the Privacy Commissioner for Personal Data, Hong Kong. (2018a). Introduction to the personal data (privacy) ordinance [PowerPoint slides]. *PDPO Public Seminar*. Retrieved February 1, 2023, from www.pcpd.org.hk/english/education_training/individuals/public_seminars/files/PDPO_PublicSeminar_2018_Eng.pdf

Office of the Privacy Commissioner for Personal Data, Hong Kong. (2018b, September 4). *Cyberbullying from a personal data privacy perspective* [PowerPoint slides]. Retrieved February 1, 2023, from www.pcpd.org.hk/english/news_events/speech/files/HKU_Cyberbullying_Conference_4Sept2018.pdf

Office of the Privacy Commissioner for Personal Data, Hong Kong. (2019, December 23). Privacy Commissioner provides updates on doxxing and cyberbullying: Reiterating criminal and social liability of doxxers and assisting platforms. *Media Statement*. Retrieved February 1, 2023, from www.pcpd.org.hk/english/news_events/media_statements/press_20191223.html

Office of the Privacy Commissioner for Personal Data, Hong Kong. (2020, December). "Doxxing can bring serious legal consequences" -- Privacy Commissioner's article contribution at Hong Kong Lawyer (December 2020). *Speeches, Presentations & Articles*. Retrieved February 1, 2023, from www.pcpd.org.hk/english/news_events/speech/speeches_202012.html

Office of the Privacy Commissioner for Personal Data, Hong Kong. (2021a). *2020–21 Annual report*. Retrieved February 1, 2023, from www.pcpd.org.hk/english/resources_centre/publications/annual_report/files/anreport21_full.pdf

Office of the Privacy Commissioner for Personal Data, Hong Kong. (2021b, November). "The personal data (privacy) (amendment) ordinance 2021 a new regulatory regime" -- Privacy Commissioner's article contribution at Hong Kong Lawyer (November 2021). *PCPD in Media*. Retrieved February 1, 2023, from www.pcpd.org.hk/english/news_events/newspaper/newspaper_202111.html

Office of the Privacy Commissioner for Personal Data, Hong Kong. (2022, October 10). *Feature interview with privacy commissioner by sing tao daily*. (In Chinese). Retrieved February 1, 2023, from www.pcpd.org.hk/tc_chi/news_events/newspaper/interview_20221010a.html

Office of the Privacy Commissioner for Personal Data, Hong Kong. (n.d.). Court Judgment. *PCPD*. Retrieved October 28, 2023, from www.pcpd.org.hk/english/enforcement/judgments/court_judgement.html

Personal Data (Privacy) Ordinance (Cap. 486, Laws of Hong Kong). (2022).

R v G and Another, (2003) UKHL 50, (2004) 1 AC 1034 (United Kingdom House of Lords). (2003, October 16).

Secretary for Justice and Another v Persons Unlawfully and Wilfully Conducting Themselves in Any of the Acts Prohibited Under Paragraph 1(a), (b) or (c) of the Indorsement of Claim, (2019). HKCFI 2773, HCA 1957/2019 (Hong Kong Court of First Instance of the High Court). (2019, November 8).

Secretary for Justice v Chan Oi Yau Riyo, (2020). HKCFI 1194, HCMP 249/2020 (Hong Kong Court of First Instance of the High Court). (2020, June 17).

Secretary for Justice v Persons Unlawfully and Wilfully Conducting Themselves in Any of the Acts Prohibited Under Paragraph 1(a) and (b) of the Indorsement of Claim, (2019). HKCFI 2809, HCA 2007/2019 (Hong Kong Court of First Instance of the High Court). (2019, November 15).

Secretary for Justice v Persons Unlawfully and Wilfully Conducting Themselves in Any of the Acts Prohibited Under Paragraph 1(a), (b) or (c) of the Indorsement of Claim, (2020). HKCFI 2785, HCA 1847/2020 (Hong Kong Court of First Instance of the High Court). (2020, November 13).

Sin Kam Wah and Another v HKSAR, (2005) 8 HKCFAR 192, FACC 14/2004 (Hong Kong Court of Final Appeal). (2005, May 26).

Tariq, F. (2022, September 12). Tinder app uncovers 'dangerous' date as 25 single women agree—Leicestershire Live. *Leicester Mercury*. Retrieved February 1, 2023, from www.leicestermercury. co.uk/news/uk-world-news/tinder-app-uncovers-dangerous-date-7576087

The Government of the Hong Kong Special Administrative Region [HKSAR Government]. (2012, December 19). LCQ12: Cyber-bullying. *Press Releases*. Retrieved February 1, 2023, from www. info.gov.hk/gia/general/201212/19/P201212190360.htm

The Government of the Hong Kong Special Administrative Region [HKSAR Government]. (2020, November 4). LCQ7: Measures against doxxing and cyber-bullying. *Press Release, The Government of the Hong Kong Special Administrative Region*. Retrieved February 1, 2023, from www. info.gov.hk/gia/general/202011/04/P2020110400462.htm

The Law Reform Commission of Hong Kong. (2004, December). *Report: Civil liability for invasion of privacy*. Retrieved February 1, 2023, from www.hkreform.gov.hk/en/docs/rprivacy-e.pdf

To, G. (2022, May 17). War on doxxing stepped up. *The Standard*. Retrieved February 1, 2023, from www.thestandard.com.hk/section-news/section/11/241742/War-on-doxxing-stepped-up

Trottier, D. (2017). Digital vigilantism as weaponisation of visibility. *Philosophy & Technology, 30*, 55–72. https://doi.org/10.1007/s13347-016-0216-4

Wu Yin Nei Wenny v The Privacy Commissioner for Personal Data, AAB 50/2011 (Hong Kong Administrative Appeals Board). (2012, May 23). Retrieved 22 October 2023, from https://www. pcpd.org.hk/tc_chi/enforcement/decisions/files/AAB_50_2011.pdf

Zetter, K. (2007, November 21). Cyberbullying suicide stokes the Internet fury machine. *WIRED*. Retrieved February 1, 2023, from www.wired.com/2007/11/cyberbullying-suicide-stokes-the-internet-fury-machine/

40

ADDRESSING CYBER DEVIANCE IN HYBRID POLITICAL SYSTEMS

Insights from Bangladesh

Syed Mahfujul Haque Marjan

Introduction

Bangladesh has a long history with the internet. As of now, the country has 123.82 million internet users (Bangladesh Telecommunication Regulatory Commission, 2022) and 44.7 million Facebook users (Statista, 2022). With the emergence of the internet, Bangladesh has also faced a rise in cyber deviance over the past few years. Since 2013, around 4,500 cybercrime cases have been filed in Bangladesh, with only 21 of those cases convicting the accused (Biswas, 2021). To address rising cybercrime and acquittal rates of filed cases, the Bangladesh government adopted a new Digital Security Act (DSA) in 2018. However, this law has become one of the most used tools for intimidating freedom of expression in Bangladesh (Mostofa & Subedi, 2021; Rahman & Or Rashid, 2020). During the COVID-19 pandemic, more cases were filed under the Digital Security Act. The goals were to suppress the protestors who challenged the health mismanagement and lack of government efficiency during that time. Statistics showed that 89 cases were filed against 179 people during the pandemic (Rabbi, 2020). The Awami League, the ruling party of Bangladesh, displays a trend of transforming democracy into a hybrid model. In this model, the country's democratic system has both democratic and authoritarian traits that resemble a hybrid political system (Riaz & Parvez, 2021). When a government has authoritarian traits, it reduces the freedom of expression in the country. The goal of the present chapter is to focus on the background of the enacted Digital Security Act and how the Bangladesh government is using the law to oppress freedom of speech from free thinkers, journalists, and government critics in the country. The chapter also addresses the relationship between freedom of expression and a hybrid regime.

Bangladesh's journey to a hybrid regime

Bangladesh is one of the youngest nations in the Indian subcontinent, liberated in 1971 after the Liberation War with Pakistan, in which 3 million people died. After the war, Bangabandhu Sheikh Mujibur Rahman, the present prime minister Sheikh Hasina's

DOI: 10.4324/9781003277675-46

father, became the country's first prime minister. He was in power from 1972 to 1975, and many criticized him for rampant corruption, shrinking democracy, economic misconduct, and worsening law-and-order situation (Riaz, 2015). In 1974, Sheikh Mujibur Rahman amended the constitution and made Bangladesh a one-party state (Rahaman, 2014). After the assassination of Sheikh Mujibur Rahman, Bangladesh went through the military regimes of Ziaur Rahman and Hussain Muhammad Ershad. Bangladesh entered the parliamentary democracy in 1991. From 1991 to 2018, Bangladesh had five general elections. The ruling Awami League secured victory in 2014 and 2018. However, Bangladesh started the journey toward a hybrid regime in the last two decades (Riaz, 2019a).

The hybrid regime's paradigm is divided into three schools (Adeney, 2017). The first school, led by O'Donnell and Zakaria, defined the hybrid regime as a weak and faulty democracy (Merkel, 2004). In the second school, intellectuals like Schedler and Cassani said it is better to portray the hybrid regime as an authoritarian form of government rather than define it as a faulty democracy (Cassani, 2014). However, the third school defined a hybrid regime as a distinct regime that intersects with authoritarian and democratic trends. Scholars like Bogaards, Gilbert, Mohseni, and Wigell followed this school (Bogaards, 2009).

Among the three schools, Bangladesh fits well with the third school, which blends democracy and autocracy. This blending trait is a legacy of the long, adverse, and competitive politics of Bangladesh. Historically, Bangladesh has been divided into two major political parties: the Bangladesh Awami League and the Bangladesh Nationalist Party. They have almost equal popularity among the voters. So, whenever a party comes to power, there is a lack of balance of power for fragile democratic institutions (Riaz & Parvez, 2021). From 1991 to 2001, the nonparty caretaker government held all the general elections in Bangladesh. And the Awami League amended the constitution to demolish the nonparty caretaker government before the 2014 general election. This provision allows elections under the incumbent government. The Bangladesh Nationalist Party boycotted the 2014 election, which ultimately led Bangladesh to become a one-party state that has subsequent traits of a hybrid regime (Riaz, 2019b). Most hybrid regimes attempt to curb freedom of speech, reduce the independence of the judiciary, and manipulate the electoral system (Seefeldt, 2013; Morgenbesser, 2014; Voltmer et al., 2021). Bangladesh engages in all three. The present Awami League government cracked down on the mass media with different laws and regulations, filled courts with supporters, and created an environment where opposition parties would not participate in elections (Fair, 2019). The Awami League completed two significant steps to hold power for a long time. The party came to power in 2009 after eight years. In 2011, the Awami League overturned the nonpartisan caretaker government, claiming that non-elected people should not be allowed to oversee the general election (BBC News Bangla, 2011). And just two months before the general election, the Awami League passed the Digital Security Act in the name of curbing cybercrime in the country (Tribune Desk, 2018). However, the final goal was to silence dissent permanently and to frighten people from dissenting directly before a manipulated general election (Blair, 2020; Mostofa & Subedi, 2021; Riaz & Parvez, 2021). The present chapter highlights how the present government uses the Digital Security Act to silence dissent and the outcomes of curbing cyber security after its enactment.

Conceptualizing a hybrid regime

Studying pseudo-democratic regimes that oppress freedom of speech through different laws and regulations is becoming a popular way to examine hybrid regimes. The European Center for Populism Studies (n.d.) defined a *hybrid regime* as:

> Hybrid regimes are nations with regular electoral frauds, preventing them from being fair and free democracies. These nations commonly have governments that apply pressure on political opposition, non-independent judiciaries, widespread corruption, harassment, and pressure placed on the media, anemic rule of law, and more pronounced faults than flawed democracies in the realms of underdeveloped political culture, low levels of participation in politics and issues in the functioning of governance.

The term hybrid regime emerged after the Cold War era. The wake of democracy and liberalism forced different authoritarian rulers to adopt a new way to rule the country.

Many academicians tried to conceptualize the hybrid regime as competitive authoritarianism, which relies on the election for legitimacy. The ending of the Cold War pushed a threat to tyrant leaders across the globe. So, the incumbents relied on the influence of the electoral process, biased mass media, oppression of dissent, and abuse of democratic institutions to be in power. Competitive authoritarianism's lack of three traits differentiates it from democracy: (a) free and fair elections, (b) distinct safety of civic rights, and (c) a level playing field for all political parties (Levitsky & Way, 2010). An interesting trait is that competitive authoritarianism does not have any level playing field for all political parties; however, it arranges elections frequently. The ruler makes election difficult for opposition parties, which leads the ruler to be in power (Kleinsteuber, 2019); for example, the most prominent opposition leader of Russia, Aleksei A. Navalny, returned to Russia in 2021. His return scared Mr. Putin, who had Navalny arrested at the Moscow airport and imprisoned for fraud and contempt. Navalny was sentenced to 9 years in prison for the convictions in 2022 (Reuters, 2022; Yablokov, 2021). He died in a remote prison in February, 2024 (Hopkins & Kramer, 2024). Levitsky and Way (2010) conceptualized this as a "legal repression" where the ruler takes away civil liberties using "legal instruments such as tax, libel, or defamation laws to punish the opponents."

In addition, hybrid regimes conduct the most violent attacks on journalists, bloggers, opinion leaders, online activists, and dissenting media outlets. According to Human Rights Watch (2021a), Malaysia has at least four different laws that have "overbroad and vaguely worded provisions": (a) The Penal Code, (b) The Sedition Act, (c) The Peaceful Assembly Act, and (d) The Communications and Multimedia Act, which allow the police to probe or detain dissidents anytime. Like Malaysia and Russia, Cameroon enacted different laws to regulate the mass media (Levitsky & Way, 2010). Bangladesh has demonstrated the same traits in the last two decades. Various characteristics, including suppressing mass and social media, have made Bangladesh a hybrid regime for the second year in a row (Diplomatic Correspondent, 2022). Among the many hybrid regime characteristics, censorship on mass and social media has become very common in the country. The present Awami League government uses the Digital Security Act of 2018 efficiently to silence the opposition and government critics. The law also caused self-censorship among journalists in Bangladesh

(Riaz & Parvez, 2021). The present chapter focuses on the hybrid regime where suppressing and censoring in the name of fighting cybercrime is a tool the government uses to remain in power.

Cyber world, cybercrime, and internet users in Bangladesh

Bangladesh has one of the highest-growing internet subscriber populations in the world. The latest Population and Housing Census 2022 report of the Bangladesh Statistics Bureau (BBS) reported that 37.01% of the adult population uses the Internet (The Business Standard Report, 2022). According to recent data, Bangladesh has an internet penetration rate of 31.5% of the population in January 2022 (Kemp, 2022). Among them, 47% have smartphones, and the percentage is projected to increase to 63% by 2025 (Islam, 2022). Many internet users are social networking users as well. Through May 2021, according to Facebook, Bangladesh has 47.2 million Facebook users, which is 28% of the country's total population (Staff Correspondent, 2021b).

This large number of internet users has caused a rise of cybercrime in the country. From April 30, 2022, to November 16, 2022, to April 30, 2022, 4,094 cybercrime cases were filed in the country. From November 2020 to November 2021, approximately 12,641 cybercrimes were reported to the police (Ali, 2022). According to research by the nonprofit organization CyberLine, almost 79% of social media users in the country face cybercrime. The study also found that 83.98% of the female victims of cybercrimes did not file any complaints, so their victimizations were unaddressed (Khan, 2022). *The Daily Prothom Alo*, a leading Bengali newspaper, surveyed the international non-governmental organization (NGO) Plan International on the victimization of women in the cyber sphere. The study found that 53% of female internet users were victimized online at least once. They were victims of fake profiles, shared personal information and pictures, and photo editing (Akhter, 2020).

Furthermore, Bangladesh was a victim of one of the most expensive cyber heists in the history of the world. North Korean hackers attempted to steal $951 million from the central bank of Bangladesh in 2016. The magnitude of this heist was so intense that the chief of the central bank, Bangladesh Bank, resigned after the incident. The hackers conducted a phishing attack to heist the money from the Foreign Exchange Reserves (Forex reserves) of Bangladesh (Gladstone, 2016; Hammer, 2018). At the micro level, a study found that 60% of social networking users in Bangladesh experienced cybercrime at least once (Mahmud et al., 2020). Identity theft has become a common cybercrime in Bangladesh. The banking sector is the most targeted victim of this type of theft; hackers install skimming devices in ATMs. With these devices, hackers clone debit and credit cards across the country. Police arrested hackers of different nationalities, including Turkish and Ukrainian citizens, for credit and debit card fraud. Bangladesh has become a corridor for transnational cybercrimes (Staff Correspondent, 2019; TBS Report, 2022). The cybercrime response team of the Bangladesh government expressed concern that the information of 46.03% of traditional cards and 89.54% of Visa card users in Bangladesh was leaked on the dark web and the credentials of a large portion of debit and credit card users in the country were jeopardized (Rahman, 2022). Online scamming is very common in the country. According to the Cyber Crime Awareness Foundation (CCA Foundation) of Bangladesh, 11.48% of online-shopping customers had been victims of online scamming. But most of the time, these incidents go unnoticed (Hossain, 2021). Hacking emails, social media accounts, and websites have been a very common issue in Bangladesh since the internet's inception. In 2008, a hacker accessed the Rapid Action Battalion (RAB) website, the elite paramilitary force of Bangladesh police (Staff Correspondent, 2008).

Bangladesh security agencies were accused of state-sponsored hacking of activists, bloggers, and dissidents from other countries. The hacker groups also attempted to compromise user accounts and conduct cyber espionage in other countries. Even Facebook authorities had to act against these violent hacker groups. The most interesting point is that there are two groups, Don's Team (also known as Defense of Nation) and the Crime Research and Analysis Foundation (CRAF), that target activists, journalists, religious minorities, and dissenters living abroad (Gleicher & Dvilyanski, 2020). Various cybercrime specialists labeled these as state-sponsored attacks to mute dissent and opposition to the ruling party (Netra News, 2020). Surprisingly, different state-sponsored security agencies in Bangladesh were also accused of hacking government critics and dissidents (Chowdhury, 2020; Netra News, 2020). As the fourth-largest Muslim country in the world, Bangladesh does not have any diplomatic relationship with Israel historically. Israel was one of the earliest countries that acknowledged the independence of Bangladesh. However, Bangladesh did not acknowledge the acknowledgment. A- Jazeera's Investigative Unit (I-Unit) and the Israeli newspaper *Haaretz* uncovered that the Bangladesh government paid around $330,000 for phone-hacking gear made by an Israeli company, though the countries do not have any official relationship. With this gear, the Bangladesh government now has access to and can extract data from cell phones (Ritzen & Al Jazeera Investigative Unit, 2021). I-Unit also revealed that in 2018 the Bangladesh military collected cellphone interceptors from an Israeli security company to access citizens' cell phones (Al Jazeera Investigative Unit, 2021).

The country has been used as a fertile ground for organized cybercrime with people from other countries scamming Bangladesh citizens. Undoubtedly, Bangladesh needs a strict cyber security law to prevent cybercrimes. When the government proposed the Digital Security Act, they said the goal of this law was to prevent cybercrimes; however, the government shaped the law in such a way that now it has become a tool for silencing dissent and opposition.

History of the Digital Security Act

Historically, Bangladesh's ruling parties have had an oppressive character. The DSA is the legacy of the Information and Communication Technology (ICT) Act enacted in 2006. Some of the Act's provisions restricted freedom of expression in the country. There were criticisms against Sections 46, 57, and 71. First, Section 71 allows judges to grant bail under certain strict circumstances. Next, Section 57 allows the government to treat as a crime someone tainting the image of the state or any person. Finally, Section 46 allows the authorities and the government to stop broadcasts of any content that are a threat to the sovereignty of Bangladesh, thereby hampering Bangladesh's relationships with other countries (Babu, 2021). Human rights activists, bloggers, and journalists also criticized Section 57, which the Bangladesh government used to arrest journalists and free thinkers in the country. From October 2013 to September 2018, approximately 1,300 cases were filed and around 1,200 people were arrested under Section 57 (Bari & Dey, 2019).

To impose restrictions on freedom of expression in the country, the Awami League changed the existing ICT Act and modified it to the harsher DSA directly before the general election in December 2018. Many critics say the government enacted the DSA to ensure the victory of the Awami League by curtailing freedom of expression. Under the ICT Act, law enforcement agencies could arrest anybody for committing cybercrime (Mamun, 2018). The new law is much more harmful because it gives security forces unrestricted power. Since its passage, academics, human rights advocates, reporters, and bloggers have been among the first to suffer the consequences of the new law, which limits freedom of expression (Hasan, 2018; Mostofa & Subedi, 2021, Rahman & Rashid, 2020, Nishat et al., 2022).

Overview of the Digital Security Act

When the government enacted the law, the general perception was that this time the government had taken care of the loopholes of the ICT Act. However, the Digital Security Act has a more repressive approach to limiting freedom of expression. The Act allows the government to transform various incidents and activities into criminal matters. The Act criminalizes cybercrime, unlawful entry to computer systems, unauthorized access to computer systems, unlawful changes to computer source codes, electronic fraud, cyberterrorism, and hacking (Bari & Dey, 2019). It seems plausible that the Digital Security Act would curb cybercrime. However, the Act contains a few subsections that contradict the freedom of expression that the Bangladesh constitution ensures. These subsections limit the dissemination of free speech and citizens' online activities. The Digital Security Act formed a Digital Security Council led by the prime minister of Bangladesh to oversee digital and cybercrime in the country.

Section 8

A watchdog agency, the Digital Security Agency, was formed under the DSA. The agency conducts surveillance of all the country's data and information. An additional secretary leads the agency. Section 8 allows the director general of the Digital Security Agency to block any information or data in Bangladesh in the name of national security, law enforcement, or maintaining public discipline. Under this section, the director general has enormous power to control information. For example, if any journalist publishes news regarding bureaucratic corruption, the director general can censor the news in the name of public discipline (Bari & Dey, 2019). So, this section grants immense power to bureaucrats.

Section 21

Bangladesh has always been a politically polarized nation. The country has two major political parties—the Awami League and the Bangladesh Nationalist Party (Rahman, 2019). Sheikh Mujibur Rahman was the father of the present prime minister of Bangladesh. Sheikh Mujibur Rahman led the Liberation War with Pakistan and is the Father of the Nation of Bangladesh. He was in power from 1972 to 1975 until his assassination, along with other family members. Sheikh Mujibur Rahman passed the Fourth Amendment to the Bangladesh Constitution in the first few months of 1975, converting the nation from a parliamentary to a presidential government, consolidating a considerable amount of authority in his own hands, and severely restricting human rights. His authority over the government was further strengthened after he founded the Bangladesh Krishak Sramik Awami League (BAKSAL), which brought all political parties together under a single umbrella (Hashmi, 2022). In the same year, he banned all newspapers except four government-owned newspapers (Index on Censorship, 2010). In that current scenario, a researcher or journalist may not criticize Sheikh Mujibur Rahman because he is the Father of the Nation and the father of the prime minister. Section 21 allows a judge to punish a person who did so for up to 10 years. Furthermore, Section 21 is one of the most criticized sections of the Act. The Section says:

> Punishment for making any kind of propaganda or campaign against liberation war, the spirit of the liberation war, the father of the nation, the national anthem, or the national flag.
>
> *(Riaz, 2021a)*

No single ruler is above all criticism. The Digital Security Act does not allow any critical comments against the founder of the ruling party or the government. The dangerous part is that this Section does not define criticism; there is a gray line. Gray lines in law enable misuse, as described later in this chapter.

Section 25

Digital platforms, social media, and the internet have become an integral part of political communication. In recent years, online activists used memes to protest (Makhortykh & González Aguilar, 2020). However, Section 25 of the Digital Security Act does not allow memes because they are an "insult" and "humiliation," and the punishment is three years of imprisonment. Under this Section, anyone who "intentionally or knowingly transmits, publishes or propagates any data-information" commits a punishable offense as well. Like Section 21, Section 25 contains gray-area language, such as "annoy, insult, humiliate, or malign." These words are not well-defined, which is very dangerous. Hypothetically, someone can make a fake profile on a social networking site and publish anti-government memes, and under this Section, police may arrest the person for damaging a political leader's image.

Section 28

Historically, Bangladesh is a secular country with a diversified ethnolinguistic Bengali identity (Siddiqi, 2010). The constitution of the ruling party, the Awami League, is also secular. There are several examples of the ruling party arresting editors or banning books that criticized Islam in particular. There is debate about whether the ruling party is Islamizing the socio-political atmosphere of the country (Lorch, 2019). Here, Section 28 prevents the publication or dissemination of any content that offends any religion. However, most of the cases filed under this Section are based on criticisms of Islam. Very few cases were filed for demeaning other religions.

Section 29

Section 29 prohibits the publication and transmission of derogatory information on a digital platform under the defamation clause of the Bangladesh Penal Code of 1860. The problem is that, rather than relying on the archaic Bangladesh Penal Code of 1860, the Digital Security Act does not define "defamation of a person." Hypothetically, in Bangladesh, someone may work at a newspaper as a cartoonist. If they draw a cartoon portraying political leaders engaging in corruption and mismanagement of COVID-19, the political leader, or someone on behalf of him/her, can sue the cartoonist and throw them into jail.

Section 31

Section 31 prohibits publishing or transmitting any news or content that deteriorates the law enforcement situation in Bangladesh. This Section has some long-term repercussions. In the future, the government can censor news about social movements or information that activates any movement against the government. Any type of anti-government protest will be a breach of the law-and-order situation in the country. Mass media and social networking sites alleviate the silencing of protests. In that case, the government can suppress the content and hold the person for seven years of imprisonment.

Section 32

Section 32, followed by the historical repressive act (Azad, 2021), poses threats to Bangladesh journalists. British colonial rulers formulated the Act to prevent government officers from leaking confidential information to journalists. However, after the British Empire, Bangladesh followed colonial law (Yasmin, 2021). Though the Constitution of Bangladesh ensures freedom of speech, Section 32 strengthens the Official Secrets Act by adding secrecy to digital versions of the information. The Section prohibits whistleblowing or gathering information on government bodies.

Section 43

The Bangladesh police have always been accused of brutality and biased investigations. The ruling party always tries to influence the police to work under its agenda. In terms of structures, functions, and regulatory mechanisms, the modern Bangladeshi police owe a great deal to the British colonial legacy (Shafiqul Islam et al., 2021). The Digital Security Act permits police officers to search, seize, and arrest without a warrant under reasonable belief or probable cause, even though the Bangladesh police have a long history of brutality and extrajudicial killings (Adil, 2020; Shafiqul Islam et al., 2021; Uddin, 2018). The Digital Security Act itself is repressive law, bestowing more power to law enforcement agencies already accused of various types of misconduct.

Discussion

Since the Digital Security Act's inception on October 8, 2018, Bangladesh experienced a rise in cases filed under the Act. Approximately three cases per day were filed under the Act in 2020. There were 4,657 cases filed from 2018 to April 2022. Cases are even being filed against adolescents for Facebook posts, insulting, blaspheming, and online gambling. An investigative report from the *Daily Prothom Alo*, one of the leading dailies in Bangladesh, found that in 12 districts of Bangladesh, there were 18 cases filed against 20 teenagers with sentences from 13 years to 17 years. Police, government supporters, and media activists filed those cases (Alam, 2022). In 2020, along with adolescents and teenagers, 38 journalists were arrested under the Act (Alam, 2020). Riaz (2018) identified the accusers of the 508 cases in his database of 890 cases. Among them, law enforcement agencies filed 111 cases, government officials filed 43 cases, and accusers of the 154 cases have blessings from the ruling party or officials. In terms of political affiliation, 81% of accusers are supporters of the ruling Awami League.

Case Study 1

Place: Pirgaccha, Rangpur District. In 2021, police arrested child "X" at his home. He was using his cell phone for online classes during the pandemic. One day the police came to his house and looked for him. Police informed the parents that he insulted Prime Minister Sheikh Hasina and her father Shiekh Mujibur Rahman online. Police filed the case, arrested the boy, and sent him to prison. He was bailed after 17 days when the news was published; he frequently had to appear in court (Alam, 2022).

Case Study 2

Place: Mymensingh District. Under the Digital Security Act, a case was filed against a schoolboy. He posted on Facebook against Prime Minister Sheikh Hasina. He removed the post shortly afterward, though. He had to seek forgiveness from local ruling party leaders for the negative post against their supreme leader. But he did not. On the same night, police came to his home. His parents left him at the nearby police station. The boy was bailed after 15 days. He was scared after the incident, and he went through post-traumatic stress disorder (Alam, 2022).

Case Study 3

Place: Rangpur District. A teenage boy shared a sarcastic picture of Sheikh Mujibur Rahman, the father of the present Prime Minister, wearing a mask. His picture went viral. A police officer at his nearby police station filed a case against him and he was arrested (Alam, 2022).

Bangladesh inherited an archaic judiciary from British colonial rulers. Most Bangladesh laws originated 200 years ago during the colonial period, though some can be traced further back to the pre-colonial period (Panday & Mollah, 2011). Around 3.4 million cases are still pending in the country, which is one of the major reasons for the lack of justice (United News Bangladesh, 2022). Bangladesh has a high dismissal rate of cybercrime cases of around 97%. As of 2019, Bangladesh had 3.7 million pending cases in the judiciary. Additionally, the archaic judiciary and lack of proper investigation caused the high dismissal rates of cybercrime cases. Many of the accused had to remain in prison until the end of their case. Many had to compromise with the plaintiff to live their lives. Undoubtedly, they had to go through physical, financial, and psychological stressors to overcome the situation (Asaduzzaman, 2021).

It can be assumed that when a case under the Digital Security Act moves to the trial process, there is a high chance the accused will be released. For example, from 2019 to 2020, the Cyber Tribunal rejected 329 cases for lack of substance (Asaduzzaman, 2020). Nevertheless, the accused still underwent a similarly stressful procedure. For example, journalist Prabir Sikder posted a Facebook status on August 10, 2015, about the current minister of the government Khandaker Mosharraf Hossain, whose son married the daughter of present Prime Minister Sheikh Hasina. Mr. Sikder was arrested under the Information and

Technology Act, the base Act of the Digital Security Act. He was acquitted 5 years after the case was originally filed (Court Correspondent, 2021).

Mr. Sikder was lucky to get bail in the middle of the trial; some were not as fortunate. Writer Mushtaq Ahmed died after being in jail for almost a year. He was a critic of Prime Minister Sheikh Hasina and how she dealt with mismanagement and corruption during the pandemic (Manik & Mashal, 2021). The Center for Governance Studies reported that most of the cases under the Digital Security Act were filed for criticizing the prime minister, ministers, and parliament members. Leaders and activists of the ruling party filed most of these cases (Editorial, 2022). Additionally, most cases were filed against journalists, teachers, human rights activists, politicians, students, government officials, business people, religious leaders, and other professionals (Riaz, 2022b).

During the pandemic, there has been a rising trend of filing cases under this Act. It was challenging for the government to tackle the scenario, and they demonstrated poor management and offered inadequate services (Islam et al., 2020). When journalists wrote about the mismanagement, cases were filed against them. During the pandemic, 22 cases were filed against 42 journalists (Rabbi, 2020).

The Digital Security Act was introduced in the name of protecting people from different types of cybercrime. However, shortly after its enactment, the DSA turned out to be an oppressive Act, creating an environment of self-censorship. The law is being used to save the ruling parties, politicians, and society's affluent class rather than dealing with cybercrime (Rashid, 2021). Furthermore, the Act has another frightening trait. Riaz (2022a) researched cases filed under the Digital Security Act from January 2020 to October 2021. During this time, they managed to collect data on 754 cases. The government has set up eight cybercrime tribunals in eight divisions of the country. However, these tribunals have failed to dispose of the cases promptly. Rather, the Act is being used to subdue opponents, critics, and dissenters. The study reported that 80% of people who lodged a complaint or filed a case were supporters of the ruling party. The sad part is that the state mechanism handles detainee information—such as the charges against them or the duration of their detention—in a way that makes it difficult for journalists or researchers to uncover the real situation.

Enactments of laws in Bangladesh have a separate procedure. Before sending a law to the parliament for a decision, the ministry of law and the parliamentary committee seek suggestions from stakeholders and the general public. The Awami League-led government was so adamant to enact the law that it did not pay any attention to any recommendations made by the stakeholders. The *Daily Prothom Alo*, one of the leading dailies in the country, analyzed the 197 cases filed under the Digital Security Act in 2020. The daily found that most of the cases were on charges such as "slander," "defamatory speech," "sharing distorted images," "spreading rumors," and "conspiracy against the government." In 80% of cases, the plaintiffs were the police and the ruling party's leaders and workers (Staff Correspondent, 2021a). Moreover, some people are misusing the Act for their gain and personal enmity. The next case study details this scenario.

Case Study 4

Abu Zaman was an illiterate rural farmer. He did not have a Facebook account or a smartphone. However, he was on the run for an alleged Facebook post that someone else posted. The allegation was that Zaman defamed the plaintiff's father, Mizanur Rahman, on a Facebook post and shared it through Messenger. Both Mizanur Rahman's and Abu Zaman's families had been fighting each other for a long time over a piece of land. By filing the case under the Act, Mizanur Rahman tried to subdue Abu Zaman and take his land (Star Report, 2021).

Case Study 5

Journalist Shafiqul Islam Kajol was missing for 53 days after a lawmaker of the ruling party Awami League back in 2019 sued him under the Digital Security Act. The lawmaker sued Kajol after he reported the connection of the lawmaker with an alleged escort service (Tribune Report, 2020). In an interview with *The Daily Star*, Mr. Kajol claimed that he was victimized by personal enmity and that a small group from the government was responsible for his disappearance. There is an allegation that the ruling Awami League uses enforced disappearances to instill a culture of fear and to hold power (Bari, 2021). Human Rights Watch reported that around 600 people have forcibly disappeared since the present prime minister Sheikh Hasina took power in 2010 (Human Rights Watch, 2021b).

The Digital Security Act in the hybrid regime

The Constitution of Bangladesh ensures freedom of speech. However, seven restrictions affect that freedom: state security, friendly relations with foreign states, public order, decency or morality, contempt of court, defamation, and incitement to an offense (Shupto, 2020). Most of these restrictions are portrayed in different sections of the Digital Security Act. That was the beginning. Fifty years after the constitution's adaptation, the ruling party, the Awami League, is following the same path. Consequently, the party has transformed the country into a hybrid regime established by the rigging of the general election of 2018. Riaz and Parvez (2021) argued that the ruling Awami League government used two subtle tactics to manipulate the election. They created a culture of fear among opposition leaders, and they controlled the election. Additionally, the ruling party cultivated fear among netizens, opposers, and human rights activists through the new draconian Digital Security Act, which was enacted 3 months before the national election. From October 8, 2018, to January 15, 2019, 63 people were arrested under the Act. It can be assumed that this Act was a fear factor during pre- and post-election scenarios in Bangladesh (Rashid, 2019). So, it can likewise be assumed that the hybrid regime's mutation was initiated with the election of 2018 (Riaz, 2021b). The DSA played an important role to mute opposition and dissent in the country. Bangladesh is not the only country where this type of Act was enacted; Vietnam, Thailand, and Singapore legislated repressive acts during the pandemic (Honstein, 2022).

Conclusion

In conclusion, Bangladesh's rapid advancement in internet usage and economic growth has brought significant transformations, but it has also introduced challenges concerning freedom of speech and democracy. The introduction of the Digital Security Act (DSA) in 2018, under the pretense of fighting cybercrime, has sparked concern about the erosion of freedom of speech in the country. The ruling Awami League party has employed the Act to suppress and censor dissenting voices, thus showcasing traits of a hybrid regime that straddles both democratic and authoritarian tendencies. To fully grasp the situation, it's necessary to delve into the rich political history of the country, a complex tale interwoven with shifting patterns of democracy. The Digital Security Act (DSA) of Bangladesh didn't emerge in isolation. It has morphed into a formidable weapon that seems to target thinkers who dare to question—the intellectual, the journalists, and the critics among the general public. A palpable sense of fear shrouds the country, creating an environment of self-censorship where journalists and citizens alike feel the sting of their right to free speech being challenged. The government may have introduced the DSA with the noble intention of addressing cybercrime, but the Act's language leaves ample room for interpretation and misuse, becoming a backdoor to further restrict freedom of speech. This precarious situation, a delicate mix of democracy and authoritarianism, hints at the possible misuse of laws like the DSA. It underscores the critical importance of adhering to democratic values and the necessity of staunchly protecting freedom of expression. For a robust and thriving democracy to flourish, the right to freedom of speech must not be smothered under the pretense of safeguarding national security.

References

Adeney, K. (2017). How to understand Pakistan's hybrid regime: The importance of a multidimensional continuum. *Democratization*, 24(1), 119–137. https://doi.org/10.1080/13510347.2015.1110574

Adil, M. S. R. (2020). Policing ethics: Context Bangladesh. *Bangladesh Journal of Bioethics*, 11(1), 9–23. https://doi.org/10.3329/bioethics.v11i1.49192

Akhter, N. (2020, November 25). Online a 53% Nari Sohingsotar Shikar (53% of Female Online Users are Victims of Violence and Harassment). *Prothomalo*. Retrieved from www.prothomalo.com/bangladeshঅনলাইনে-৫৩-নারী-সহিংসতাহয়রানরি-শকিার

Al Jazeera Investigative Unit. (2021). All the Prime Minister's Men. *Al Jazeera Investigative Unit*. Retrieved from www.ajiunit.com/investigation/all-the-prime-ministers-men/

Alam, S. S. (2020, June 26). Digital Nirapotta Aine Gore Protidin Tin Mamla (An average of three cases per day under the digital security act). *Prothomalo*. Retrieved from www.prothomalo.com/bangladesh/%E0%A6%A1%E0%A6%BF%E0%A6%9C%E0%A6%BF%E0%A6%9F%E0%A6%BE%E0%A6%B2-%E0%A6%A8%E0%A6%BF%E0%A6%B0%E0%A6%BE%E0%A6%AA%E0%A6%A4%E0%A7%8D%E0%A6%A4%E0%A6%BE-%E0%A6%86%E0%A6%87%E0%A6%A8%E0%A7%87-%E0%A6%97%E0%A7%9C%E0%A7%87-%E0%A6%AA%E0%A7%8D%E0%A6%B0%E0%A6%A4%E0%A6%BF%E0%A6%A6%E0%A6%BF%E0%A6%A8-%E0%A6%A4%E0%A6%BF%E0%A6%A8-%E0%A6%AE%E0%A6%BE%E0%A6%AE%E0%A6%B2%E0%A6%BE

Alam, S. S. (2022, April 2). Digitial NIrapotta Ain: Shishu KIshorerao Mamla Theke Rehai Pacce na [Digital Security Act: Children and teenagers are also not exempted from the case]. *Prothomalo*. Retrieved from www.prothomalo.com

Ali, I. (2022, June 19). Barche cyber oporadh (Cybercrimes are rising). *Bangladesher Khabor*. Retrieved from www.bangladesherkhabor.net/Information%20Technology%20%E0%A6%AB%E0%A7%87%E0%A6%B8%E0%A6%AC%E0%A7%81%E0%A6%95%20/85709

Asaduzzaman. (2020, September 19). Digital Security Act: Over 1000 cases filed in two years. *Prothomalo*. Retrieved from https://en.prothomalo.com/bangladesh/crime-and-law/digital-security-act-over-1000-cases-filed-in-two-years

Asaduzzaman. (2021, September 20). Cybercrime: 97 per cent cases dismissed. *Prothomalo*. Retrieved from https://en.prothomalo.com/bangladesh/crime-and-law/cyber-crime-97-per-cent-cases-dismissed#:~:text=Legal%20experts%20contend%20that%20the,57%20of%20the%20ICT%20Act

Azad, A. (2021). *Digital Security Act in Bangladesh: The death of dissent and of freedom of expression* [Master's thesis, Central European University]. Retrieved from https://www.etd.ceu.edu/2021/azad_ananya.pdf

Babu, K.-E.-K. (2021). Cyber security and its reality in Bangladesh: An analysis of existing legal frameworks. *Journal of Information System Security*, 17(3), 145–162.

Bangladesh Telecommunication Regulatory Commission. (2022, February 22). Internet subscribers [Government Website]. *Bangladesh Telecommunication Regulatory Commission*. Retrieved from www.btrc.gov.bd/site/page/347df7fe-409f-451e-a415-65b109a207f5/http%3A%2F%2Fwww. btrc.gov.bd%2Fsite%2Fpage%2F347df7fe-409f-451e-a415-65b109a207f5%2F-

Bari, M. E. (2021). The use of enforced disappearance in Bangladesh as a tool of political oppression: Human Rights in retreat. *Michigan State International Law Review*, 29, 413.

Bari, M. E., & Dey, P. (2019). *The enactment of digital security laws in Bangladesh: No place for dissent* [SSRN Scholarly Paper No. 3590287]. Retrieved from https://papers.ssrn.com/abstract=3590287

BBC News Bangla. (2011, June 30). Bangladesh ends caretaker government arrangement. *BBC News*. Retrieved from www.bbc.com/news/world-south-asia-13973576

Biswas, P. (2021, September 6). Cybercrime cases rise in Bangladesh, but suspects are mostly acquitted [News Site]. *Bdnews24.Com*. Retrieved from https://bdnews24.com/bangladesh/2021/09/06/cybercrime-cases-rise-in-bangladesh-but-suspects-are-mostly-acquitted

Blair, H. (2020). The Bangladesh paradox. *Journal of Democracy*, 31(4), 138–150. https://doi.org/10.1353/jod.2020.0061

Bogaards, M. (2009). How to classify hybrid regimes? Defective democracy and electoral authoritarianism. *Democratization*, 16(2), 399–423. https://doi.org/10.1080/13510340902777800

Cassani, A. (2014). Hybrid what? Partial consensus and persistent divergences in the analysis of hybrid regimes. *International Political Science Review*, 35(5), 542–558. https://doi.org/10.1177/0192512113495756

Chowdhury, K. R. (2020, December 11). Bangladesh: Facebook blocks 2 groups over hacking allegations. *Benar News*. Retrieved from www.benarnews.org/english/news/bengali/facebook-action-12112020160712.html

Court Correspondent. (2021, September 9). Journalist Prabir Sikder acquitted of ICT charge. *New Age | The Most Popular Outspoken English Daily in Bangladesh*. Retrieved from www.newagebd.net/article/148616/journalist-prabir-sikder-acquitted-of-ict-charge

Diplomatic Correspondent. (2022, February 10). Bangladesh again marked as hybrid regime [News Site]. *New Age | The Most Popular Outspoken English Daily in Bangladesh*. Retrieved from www.newagebd.net/article/162419/bangladesh-again-marked-as-hybrid-regime

Editorial. (2022, April 24). Ar Koto Mamla, Ar Koto Hoirani [How many cases and how much harassment]. *Prothomalo*. Retrieved from www.prothomalo.com

European Center for Populism Studies. (n.d.). *Hybrid Regime—ECPS*. Retrieved February 26, 2022, from www.populismstudies.org/Vocabulary/hybrid-regime/

Fair, C. C. (2019). Bangladesh in 2018: Careening toward one-woman rule. *Asian Survey*, 59(1), 124.

Gladstone, R. (2016, March 15). Bangladesh bank chief resigns after cyber theft of $81 million. *The New York Times*. Retrieved from www.nytimes.com/2016/03/16/world/asia/bangladesh-bank-chief-resigns-after-cyber-theft-of-81-million.html

Gleicher, N., & Dvilyanski, M. (2020, December 11). Taking action against hackers in Bangladesh and Vietnam [Facebook Blog]. *Meta*. Retrieved from https://about.fb.com/news/2020/12/taking-action-against-hackers-in-bangladesh-and-vietnam/

Hammer, J. (2018, May 3). The billion-dollar bank job. *The New York Times*. Retrieved from www.nytimes.com/interactive/2018/05/03/magazine/money-issue-bangladesh-billion-dollar-bank-heist.html, www.nytimes.com/interactive/2018/05/03/magazine/money-issue-bangladesh-billion-dollar-bank-heist.html

Hasan, R. (2018, September 20). Digital Security Bill passed. *The Daily Star*. Retrieved from www.thedailystar.net/politics/bangladesh-jatiya-sangsad-passes-digital-security-bill-2018-amid-concerns-journalists-1636114

Hashmi, T. (2022). The decline and fall of Sheikh Mujibur Rahman, 1972–1975. In T. Hashmi (Ed.), *Fifty years of Bangladesh, 1971–2021: Crises of culture, development, governance, and identity* (pp. 111–161). Springer International Publishing. Retrieved from https://doi.org/10.1007/978-3-030-97158-8_4

Honstein, E. (2022, April 13). A pandemic of silence. *ICNL*. Retrieved from www.icnl.org/post/analysis/a-pandemic-of-silence

Hopkins, V., & Kramer, A. E. (2024, February 16). Aleksei Navalny, Russian opposition leader, dies in prison at 47. *The New York Times*. Retrieved from https://www.nytimes.com/2024/02/16/world/europe/aleksei-navalny-dead.html

Hossain, S. (2021, June 20). 11.48% customers victim of online shopping scams in 2020. *Dhaka Tribune*. Retrieved from https://archive.dhakatribune.com/business/commerce/2021/06/20/11-48-cust omers-victim-of-online-shopping-scams-in-2020

Human Rights Watch. (2021a, May 19). Malaysia: Free speech under increasing threat. *Human Rights Watch*. Retrieved from www.hrw.org/news/2021/05/19/malaysia-free-speech-under-increasing-threat

Human Rights Watch. (2021b). "Where no sun can enter": A decade of enforced disappearances in Bangladesh. *Human Rights Watch*. Retrieved from www.hrw.org/report/2021/08/16/where-no-sun-can-enter/decade-enforced-disappearances-bangladesh

Index on Censorship. (2010, June 2). Bangladesh shuts down pro-opposition newspaper. *Index on Censorship*. Retrieved from www.indexoncensorship.org/2010/06/bangladesh-shuts-down-pro-opposition-newspaper/

Islam, H. B. (2022, July 8). Smartphone users will grow to 63% by 2025: Report. *The Business Standard*. Retrieved from www.tbsnews.net/tech/smartphone-users-will-grow-63-2025-report-455654

Islam, Md. T., Talukder, A. K., Siddiqui, Md. N., & Islam, T. (2020). Tackling the COVID-19 pandemic: The Bangladesh perspective. *Journal of Public Health Research*, 9(4), 1794. https://doi.org/10.4081/jphr.2020.1794

Kemp, S. (2022, February 15). Digital 2022: Bangladesh. *DataReportal—Global Digital Insights*. Retrieved from https://datareportal.com/reports/digital-2022-bangladesh

Khan, M. J. (2022, June 16). Evolution Of Cybercrime: Women, the worst sufferers as usual. *The Daily Star*. Retrieved from www.thedailystar.net/news/bangladesh/crime-justice/news/evolution-cybercrime-part-3-women-the-worst-sufferers-usual-3048576

Kleinsteuber, B. (2019). *Hybridity and political disorder: A mixed method approach to understanding the hybrid regime*. University of Louisville. Retrieved from https://ir.library.louisville.edu/etd/3190

Levitsky, S., & Way, L. A. (2010). *Competitive authoritarianism: Hybrid regimes after the cold war*. Cambridge University Press. Retrieved from https://doi.org/10.1017/CBO9780511781353

Lorch, J. (2019). Islamization by secular ruling parties: The case of Bangladesh. *Politics and Religion*, 12(2), 257–282. https://doi.org/10.1017/S1755048318000573

Mahmud, S., Chakraborty, D., Tasnim, L., Tahira, N., & Ferdous, M. (2020). *The Economic Impact of Social Media Fraud in Bangladesh and it's Remedies*. 4(1), 30–39. https://doi.org/10.30991/IJMLNCE.2020v04i01.004

Makhortykh, M., & González Aguilar, J. M. (2020). Memory, politics and emotions: Internet memes and protests in Venezuela and Ukraine. *Continuum*, 34(3), 342–362. https://doi.org/10.1080/10304312.2020.1764782

Mamun. (2018, August 10). How section 57 morphed into digital security Act provisions [News Site]. *Dhaka Tribune*. Retrieved from https://archive.dhakatribune.com/bangladesh/law-rights/2018/08/10/how-section-57-morphed-into-digital-security-act-provisions

Manik, J. A., & Mashal, M. (2021, February 26). Bangladeshi writer, detained over social media posts, dies in Jail. *The New York Times*. Retrieved from www.nytimes.com/2021/02/26/world/asia/bangladesh-mushtaq-ahmed-dead.html

Merkel, W. (2004). Embedded and defective democracies. *Democratization*, 11(5), 33–58. https://doi.org/10.1080/13510340412331304598

Morgenbesser, L. (2014). Elections in hybrid regimes: Conceptual stretching revived. *Political Studies*, 62. https://doi.org/10.1111/1467-9248.12020

Mostofa, S. M., & Subedi, D. B. (2021). Rise of competitive authoritarianism in Bangladesh. *Politics and Religion*, 14(3), 431–459. https://doi.org/10.1017/S1755048320000401

Netra News. (2020, May 30). We hack Facebook: State-sponsored cybercrime in Bangladesh. *Netra News — নেত্র নিউজ*. Retrieved from https://netra.news/2020/we-hack-facebook-state-sponsored-cybercrime-in-bangladesh/

Nishat, S. K., Islam, M. N., & Sharmin, S. (2022). Comparison between freedom of expression and the Digital Security Act, 2018: Bangladesh perspective. *British Journal of Arts and Humanities*, 4(5), 148–153.

Panday, P., & Mollah, Md. A. H. (2011). The judicial system of Bangladesh: An overview from historical viewpoint. *International Journal of Law and Management*, 53, 6–31. https://doi.org/10.1108/17542431111111863

Rabbi, A. R. (2020, June 28). Upsurge in Digital Security Act cases during the COVID-19 pandemic. *Dhaka Tribune*. Retrieved from https://archive.dhakatribune.com/bangladesh/2020/06/28/upsurge-in-digital-security-act-cases-during-the-covid-19-pandemic

Rahaman, M. (2014). *Basic structures of the constitution of Bangladesh* [SSRN Scholarly Paper No. 2439906]. https://doi.org/10.2139/ssrn.2439906

Rahman, A., & Or Rashid, H. (2020). Digital Security Act and investigative journalism in Bangladesh: A critical analysis. *CenRaPS Journal of Social Sciences*, 2, 216–236. https://doi.org/10.46291/cenraps.v2i2.32

Rahman, S. (2022, September 10). Bank cardholders losing credentials to cybercriminals. *The Financial Express*. Retrieved from https://today.thefinancialexpress.com.bd/first-page/bank-cardholders-losing-credentials-to-cybercriminals-1662745716

Rahman, T. (2019). Party system institutionalization and pernicious polarization in Bangladesh. *The Annals of the American Academy of Political and Social Science*, *681*(1), 173–192. https://doi.org/10.1177/0002716218817280

Rashid, M. (2019, January 15). 63 people held since October. *New Age | The Most Popular Outspoken English Daily in Bangladesh*. Retrieved from www.newagebd.net/article/61819/63-people-held-since-october

Rashid, M. (2021, October 1). Law widely used against journalists, govt critics. *New Age | The Most Popular Outspoken English Daily in Bangladesh*. Retrieved from www.newagebd.net/print/article/150590

Reuters. (2022, March 22). Alexei Navalny sentenced to 9 more years in prison after fraud conviction. *The Guardian*. Retrieved from www.theguardian.com/world/2022/mar/22/alexei-navalny-13-years-more-jail-fraud

Riaz, A. (2015). Bangladesh. In *An introduction to South Asian politics*. Routledge.

Riaz, A. (2019a). Bangladesh: From an electoral democracy to a hybrid regime (1991–2018). In A. Riaz (Ed.), *Voting in a hybrid regime: Explaining the 2018 Bangladeshi election* (pp. 21–31). Springer. Retrieved from https://doi.org/10.1007/978-981-13-7956-7_3

Riaz, A. (2019b, November 29). How new autocrats curb press freedom. *The Daily Star*. Retrieved from www.thedailystar.net/star-weekend/news/how-new-autocrats-curb-press-freedom-1833091

Riaz, A. (2021a). Bangladesh: In pursuit of a one-party state? In *Routledge handbook of autocratization in South Asia*. Routledge.

Riaz, A. (2021b, December 9). *How Bangladesh's Digital Security Act is creating a culture of fear*. Carnegie Endowment for International Peace.

Riaz, A. (2022a, January 15). Digital Nirapotta Ainer Totto Pete Keno Ai Badha (Why is this a barrier to getting information about the Digital Security Act?). *Prothomalo*. Retrieved from www.prothomalo.com/opinion/column/%E0%A6%A1%E0%A6%BF%E0%A6%9C%E0%A6%BF%E0%A6%9F%E0%A6%BE%E0%A6%B2-%E0%A6%A8%E0%A6%BF%E0%A6%B0%E0%A6%BE%E0%A6%AA%E0%A6%A4%E0%A7%8D%E0%A6%A4%E0%A6%BE-%E0%A6%86%E0%A6%87%E0%A6%A8%E0%A7%87%E0%A6%B0-%E0%A6%A4%E0%A6%A5%E0%A7%8D%E0%A6%AF-%E0%A6%AA%E0%A7%87%E0%A6%A4%E0%A7%87-%E0%A6%95%E0%A7%87%E0%A6%A8-%E0%A6%8F%E0%A6%87-%E0%A6%AC%E0%A6%BE%E0%A6%A7%E0%A6%BE

Riaz, A. (2022b). *The unending nightmare: Impacts of Bangladesh's Digital Security Act 2018* (p. 33) [Research Report]. Centre for Governance Studies.

Riaz, A., & Parvez, S. (2021). Anatomy of a rigged election in a hybrid regime: The lessons from Bangladesh. *Democratization*, *28*(4), 801–820. https://doi.org/10.1080/13510347.2020.1867110

Ritzen, Y., & Al Jazeera Investigative Unit. (2021, March 8). Bangladesh bought phone-hacking tools from Israel, documents show. *Al Jazeera*. Retrieved from www.aljazeera.com/news/2021/3/8/bangladesh-bought-hacking-tools-from-israel-documents-show

Seefeldt, J. L. (2013, January). *Hybrid regime repression of free expression rights: A case study using Venezuela and Bolivia* [Paper Presented at the Northeastern Political Science Association's Annual Conference].

Shafiqul Islam, A. K. M., Islam, N., & Ehsan, S. M. A. (2021). *Public perception regarding the efficiency of Bangladesh police: Quest for a new paradigm* [SSRN Scholarly Paper No. 3768083]. Retrieved from https://papers.ssrn.com/abstract=3768083

Shupto, N. A. (2020, May 14). Freedom of thought, conscience and of speech in Bangladesh. *New Age | The Most Popular Outspoken English Daily in Bangladesh*. Retrieved from www.newagebd. net/article/106406/freedom-of-thought-conscience-and-of-speech-in-bangladesh

Siddiqi, D. M. (2010). Political culture in contemporary Bangladesh: Histories, ruptures and contradictions. In *Political Islam and governance in Bangladesh*. Routledge.

Staff Correspondent. (2008, September 6). RAB website hacked. *The Daily Star*. Retrieved from www.thedailystar.net/news-detail-53558

Staff Correspondent. (2019, June 3). 6 Ukrainians held over ATM fraud. *The Daily Star*. Retrieved from www.thedailystar.net/city/news/6-ukrainians-arrested-over-atm-fraud-1752547

Staff Correspondent. (2021a, February 27). Karo Apotti Amole Nea Hoini [No one's objection was taken into account]. *Prothomalo*. Retrieved from www.prothomalo.com

Staff Correspondent. (2021b, June 10). Facebook users increase by 10 million in Bangladesh. *Prothomalo*. Retrieved from https://en.prothomalo.com/science-technology/social-media/facebook-users-increase-by-10-million-in-bangladesh

Statista. (2022, January). Facebook users by country 2021. *Statista*. Retrieved from www.statista.com/statistics/268136/top-15-countries-based-on-number-of-facebook-users/

TBS Report. (2022, January 19). 2 including Turkish citizen arrested for ATM fraud [News Site]. *The Business Standard*. Retrieved from www.tbsnews.net/bangladesh/crime/2-including-turkish-citizen-arrested-atm-fraud-359512

The Business Standard Report. (2022, July 27). 37% adults in country are internet users. *The Business Standard*. Retrieved from www.tbsnews.net/37-adults-country-are-internet-users-466238

Tribune Desk. (2018, September 19). Digital Security Bill passes amid free speech concerns. *Dhaka Tribune*. Retrieved from https://archive.dhakatribune.com/bangladesh/parliament/2018/09/19/digital-security-bill-2018-passed-with-provision-of-tougher-punishment

Tribune Report. (2020, May 7). Digital Security Act: More journalists facing arrest, cases amid hard days of Covid-19 crisis. *Dhaka Tribune*. Retrieved from https://archive.dhakatribune.com/bangladesh/2020/05/07/digital-security-act-more-journalists-facing-arrest-cases-amidst-hard-days-of-corona-crisis

Uddin, Md. K. (2018). A Southern perspective on extrajudicial police killings in Bangladesh. In K. Carrington, R. Hogg, J. Scott, & M. Sozzo (Eds.), *The Palgrave handbook of criminology and the Global South* (pp. 451–472). Springer International Publishing. Retrieved from https://doi.org/10.1007/978-3-319-65021-0_23

United News Bangladesh. (2022, January 9). Law minister: Govt to do everything to ease case backlog. *Dhaka Tribune*. Retrieved from www.dhakatribune.com/bangladesh/2022/01/09/law-minister-govt-to-do-everything-to-ease-case-backlog

Voltmer, K., Selvik, K., & Høigilt, J. (2021). Hybrid media and hybrid politics: Contesting informational uncertainty in Lebanon and Tunisia. *The International Journal of Press/Politics*, 26(4), 842–860. https://doi.org/10.1177/1940161221999266

Yablokov, I. (2021, September 19). Opinion | There's a reason Putin keeps winning. *The New York Times*. Retrieved from www.nytimes.com/2021/09/19/opinion/putin-russia-election.html

Yasmin, T. (2021, June 17). Whistleblowing and secrecy law: Where is the balance? [News Site]. *The Daily Star*. Retrieved from www.thedailystar.net/opinion/news/whistleblowing-and-secrecy-law-where-the-balance-2112365

Funding

This chapter was written without any specific funding from agencies in the public, commercial, or not-for-profit sectors.

41

STUDYING NATIONALISM IN AN ONLINE SETTING

A Russian far-right community on *Vkontakte* social media platform

Petr Oskolkov

Introduction and methods

It could be disputable whether any ideology might be regarded as "deviant behavior" since there is a certain controversy with the inherent right to self-expression and freedom of speech (sometimes referred to as Popper's paradox of tolerance). However, any kind of radicalism, like political actions that transcend the conventional framework of public discourse, and certainly extremism, that is placed *a priori* beyond the field of legal politics, might be conceptualized as deviant from the (though also highly disputable) "mainstream". In this regard, far-right (as well as far-left) movements might serve as an example of political deviation; the "far" predicate is already enough to situate them in the respective narrative.

There is a certain terminological uncertainty when we speak about the far-right: it might be also called "right-wing", "radical right", or even "extreme right". However, these concepts are not identical. Right-wing discourse is presumably part of the mainstream and is often found in the rhetoric of "moderate" parties and movements when different "hot issues", such as foreign immigration and social welfare, are brought to the table. The "radical right" narrative is less acceptable in public debates; however, it is still an inherent part of "politics as usual" in most Western democracies. "Extreme right" is already a bridge too far: most illegal anti-immigrant or anti-Semitic actions are associated with this phenomenon. "Far-right" is a kind of an umbrella denominator for both radical and extreme right: they are, for sure, also right-wing, but not every right-wing actor deserves to be called "far-right". This latter term includes "all those ultranationalist collective actors sharing a common exclusionary and authoritarian worldview—predominantly determined on socio-cultural criteria" (Pirro, 2022, p. 3).

The common basis under all these concepts is right-wing ideology, in its modern form. While associated initially with economic and freedom axes, since approximately the 1960s we speak about right-wingers as nationalists. Indeed, the main issue that unites all kinds of contemporary far-right actors is their attitude toward such issues as nation, race, and ethnicity. Cas Mudde (2007, p. 30) wrote: "the populist radical right is a specific form of nationalism"; Michael Minkenberg (2002, p. 337) specified the core element of right-wing radicalism as a "myth of a homogeneous nation, a romantic and populist ultranationalism

DOI: 10.4324/9781003277675-47

directed against the concept of liberal and pluralistic democracy and its underlying principles of individualism and universalism." For the adherents of right-wing ideology, the main signifier is not only the understanding of the nation as a value in itself and a homogenous object of veneration, but also all the possible ways to "purify" this nation. These ways include not only such extreme forms as ethnic cleansing or racial segregation but also restrictive immigration quotas, biopolitics, and certain religious, traditionalist, or ideological requirements for the "members of the club". It is hard to disagree with Aurelien Mondon (2013, p. 18) who reduces the core of far-right ideology to the notion of inequality: he argues that it is "the principle of fundamental human inequality" that "lies at the heart of right-wing extremism".

Studying far-right sentiments in the online setting has been in the academic spotlight for two decades already; nowadays, it often seems even more "fashionable" than traditional offline fieldwork. There are certain reasons for this trend. In the 21st century, most people in the "global North" have access to the Internet and use social networking sites for communicating and sharing their beliefs publicly. If initially the "online" aspect was seen as parallel with "real life", now it is commonly agreed that these two realms are inseparable parts of individual and group social behavior. Acting online transforms offline behavior, and vice versa (Hine, 2015); cyberspace might be regarded as a "distorting mirror of reality" (Branthonne & Waldispuehl, 2019, p. 8). The affordances of online networking make it possible for individuals not only to conceal their real objectives and identities, but to convey their messages to an even larger public since the core feature of Web 2.0 is user-generated content (Phillips, 2015). For political movements, Web 2.0 has really launched a new era, since now everyone may act as a political being not only by going to the polls but just by opening the browser. As Kristof Jacobs and Niels Spierings (2016, p. 20) note, "social media are 1) unmediated, 2) personal, 3) interactive, 4) cheap and easy to use, and 5) able to go viral". All these qualities make social networking sites an ideal arena for producing and disseminating deviant behavior while significantly lowering the risk of being spotted; Sabina Mihelj and César Jiménez-Martínez (2021, p. 339) agree that the proliferation of social media leads to a situation when "more extreme opinions get greater visibility and support than they would have in an offline media setting".

Far-right movements were among the first to discover the affordances of the online world and user-generated content, with the website of the American Stormfront frequently cited as a pioneer. It all started with the imageboards, such as *4chan* and *8chan* and other kinds of web forums. These resources are still in use, though now a substantial part of the far-right online activities is situated on social media that "broaden exposure to and amplify extreme content and far-right ideas", as well as "help those on the far right communicate with one another, broadening networks" (Miller-Idriss, 2020, p. 145). In Western Europe and the Americas, it is primarily Facebook and Twitter, as well as the newly discovered realm of "channels" in Telegram. However, Russia is different in this aspect as well: here, most online users prefer "*Vkontakte*" (or *VK*), a social networking site developed in the 2000s by Pavel Durov and later acquired by the more influential and partly state-sponsored "Mail.Ru Group".

A "community" and its potential boundaries should also be defined here. Robert Kozinets (2010, p. 10), one of the pioneers of *Netnography*, referred to a community as to a "group of people who share social interaction, social ties, and a common interactional format". However, in the subsequent research on the topic, he stressed the interactional element of this definition—with social ties (at least in their offline format) becoming less and less important. Therefore, Kozinets later modified his own definition, proposing to understand (virtual) community as a *consociality*, that is, "the physical and/or virtual co-presence of social actors in a network, providing an opportunity for social interaction between them" (Perren & Kozinets, 2018, p. 23; Kozinets, 2019, p. 113). For the present chapter, I suggest following this understanding of online community; that is, as a virtual co-presence of social actors sharing a common interest and characterized by a common interaction format.

It is however problematic to the scholars studying right-wing presence online to distinguish between the "real" adherents of the respective ideology and occasional visitors of the right-wing pages who come there in search of an alternative viewpoint, for some additional information about different aspects of social life, or even just for fun or "trolling" (Bartlett et al., 2011). Therefore, it would be probably reasonable to look not at the "community members" but at the public image of a far-right group itself, formed by its most active representatives who do not spare their efforts to express their views publicly for a broad audience. Certainly, it is also possible and valuable to establish direct contact with active users in private messages or comments, but that strategy would require additional time and other resources, and the results would deserve a special research presentation.

Methodologically, I have opted here for frame analysis as interpreted by Scott A. Hunt et al. (1994). Frame analysis was introduced into social sciences by Erving Goffman (1974) and is commonly associated with his name. However, I find Goffman's micro-sociological approach most suitable for the study of events and performances, while the analytical framework developed by Hunt, Snow, and Benford is more applicable to the research in discursive practices of socio-political movements. This methodological tool has proved its efficacy in studying various ideologically-driven communities, both offline and online (see, for instance: Lindekilde, 2014; Nissen, 2020). A frame is defined by Snow and his colleagues as "an interpretive schemata that simplifies and condenses the 'world out there' by selectively punctuating and encoding objects, situations, events, experiences, and sequences of actions within one's present or past environments" (Snow & Benford, 1992, p. 137). The aforementioned authors suppose that there are three "core framing tasks" that social movement organizations "must accomplish in order to affect consensus and action mobilization: diagnostic framing, and prognostic framing, and motivational framing" (Hunt et al., 1994, p. 191). To make a long story short, diagnostic framing identifies the problem, prognostic framing prescribes a solution to this problem, and motivational framing explains why the audience has to address this problem in the prescribed way. Thus, out of the many possible frames created by the far-right movement actors, the attitudes towards migration and government were chosen. I've searched for different framing strategies in the corpus of texts produced by the selected webpage; some of the most exemplifying excerpts are quoted here.

In the broad field of far-right studies, the Russian case is interesting. Russian nationalism is a model example of East European nationalist sentiments, combined with a mix of imperial ambitions, post-Soviet nostalgia, and resentment, as well as attempts to find its unique image at the crossroads of East and West. In this context, it deserves to be studied both in offline and online settings.

In this chapter, I aim to discover the forms and meanings of Russian far-right ideology in the online realm. For this purpose, I focused on the *Vkontakte (VK)* social networking site, which had 72 million registered users in 2021. In the first part of the chapter, the Russian far-right scene and the peculiarities of Russian nationalism are overviewed. Then, I proceed with the frame analysis of one of the biggest Russian online far-right communities, while identifying the framing strategies employed by this page to create a certain image of migration and government actions. The chapter ends with an attempt to draw some more general conclusions for both Russian nationalism and online deviance studies.

Russian far-right scene: an overview

There have been several attempts made to classify Russian nationalism. Vera Tolz (1998) pointed at five possible definitions of the Russian nation adopted by Russian nationalists: "union identity", "eastern Slavs", "Russian speakers", "racial Russians", and "civic Russian nation". Aleksandr Verkhovskii and Emil Pain (2012) distinguished between "Red Patriots", "Black Hundreds", "Orthodox Fundamentalists", "Neo-Eurasianists", and "Neo-Nazis", according to the nationalists' perception of the Russian civilization. Marlene Laruelle (2017) underlined the importance of the relationship between nationalist groups and the Russian state, thus grouping all nationalists into "nonstate", "parastate", and "state" actors. No less important seems to be the classical distinction between empire-essentialist nationalists on the one hand and ethnic national-democratic, anti-Soviet nationalists on the other (Pain, 2016).

I propose to underline the importance of the main object to which nationalists express loyalty: in the Russian case, it can be 1) empires of the past (including not only the Russian Empire itself but also the Soviet Union), 2) current Russian state, 3) Russian ethnic group, 4) the "white race" that the Russians constitute a part of.

For the first group, the idealized image of the Russian Empire or the Soviet Union (or even both) is the main discursive narrative. The return to the Golden Age should go hand in hand with the prevalence of Russian "national interests". Most commonly, this group is also characterized by anti-Semitism, violent actions, and a skeptical attitude toward the current Russian state (as an institution betraying the great empire's ancestors). The most striking examples here are the National-Patriotic Front "Memory" (*Pamyat*) of Dmitry Vasilyev and the "National-Bolshevik Party" of Eduard Limonov (Likhachev, 2002).

The second group is not as obvious to describe in the works on Russian nationalism, since in the Putin era it started to dominate the official discourse and propaganda and is now hardly discernible from the official Russian etatism. For instance, in the rhetoric of Evgeniy Fyodorov's "National Liberation Movement", it is exactly the current Russian state (and the president) that are idealized and venerated as the single possible loyalty object. Quite naturally, more "moderate" actors, such as the ruling "United Russia" party or the right-wing Liberal Democratic Party of Russia (Shenfield, 2001), might also be included in this group, especially after the annexation of Crimea, the war in Ukraine, and the 2020 Constitution amendments (with the Russian people designated now as "state-forming", according to Article 68). Neo-Eurasianism is also quite popular among the representatives of group 2, with Aleksandr Dugin as the ideological mastermind and Konstantin Malofeyev's "*Tsargrad*" TV channel as the main mouthpiece. Also, the role of the Russian Orthodox Church is usually emphasized mostly within this group of actors. Though some members of groups 1 and 3 also underline their affinity with Orthodox Christianity, for most of them, it does not play an important role in the Russian identity (unlike "blood ties"). For some actors of groups 3 and 4, Orthodoxy even presents a natural threat to the Russian people, since they proclaim the importance of Russian neo-Paganism. The Western world (mostly Europe and the US) is seen by this group usually as an enemy, with the former important exception of Aleksandr Dugin, who was among the first to introduce the ideas of the French and Italian

New Right to the Russian-speaking readers (see Clover, 2016); however, in the past two decades, Dugin has also joined the ranks of outspoken anti-Westerners.

The third group emphasizes the Russian ethnic group and its "natural interests". It is sometimes blurred with group 1; however, the discursive difference is usually quite evident. The entire "national democratic" movement fits into this category, with Konstantin Krylov's "National Democratic Party" and Alexei Shiropaev's "National Democratic Alliance" as the most evident actors. These "national democrats" promote a kind of ethnonationalism "of European populist movements that are able to work within a democratic environment" (Laruelle, 2017, p. 92). A certain methodological problem arises when we address paramilitary groupings such as Aleksandr Barkashov's "Russian National Unity" (later split into several descendants), since they also demonstrate some features of neo-Nazi ideology, and were active in the early 1990s in the "red-brown" alliance with Vasilyev, Limonov, and other actors from group 1 (Likhachev, 2002). However, upon closer scrutiny, we still see that neither racial nor palingenetic ideals dominate the RNU discourse, but rather exclusively "Russian Order", "Russian Power", etc. As a rule, organizations of this kind are also quite hostile toward the current Russian state; this time not because it betrays the "Golden Age" but because it neglects the "Russian ethnic[1] interests".

The idea of Russians as an inalienable element of the "white race" is most obviously formulated by the Russian right-wing skinheads ("boneheads") who form the fourth group, the loosest of all. As an influential force, they emerged in Russia in the early 1990s, with the mid-2000s as the peak of their activities and media attention. One of the main ideas shared by the Russian Nazi-skins is the preservation of the "genetic purity" of the "Slavic European race" that is a part of the "constellation of the great white nations" (Belikov, 2011, p. 99); they cherish "the sentiment of belonging to an endangered white world" (Laruelle, 2010, p. 29; see also: Parland, 2004). As one of the most renowned scholars of Russian violent nationalism notes, "'white race', 'Slavic brotherhood' and 'Russian race' frequently merge for them into an intractable alloy, and racism seems to be equaled to nationalism" (Shnirelman, 2011, p. 397). Various skinhead groups such as Dmitry Bobrov's "Schulz-88", Dmitry Borovikov and Ruslan Melnik's "Mad Crowd", and Ilya Goryachev's "Military Organization of Russian Nationalists" (BORN) may be cited here. Since these organizations are based on the ideas of national socialism, they are all characterized by overt anti-Semitism and the need to "clean" Russian streets of anyone who looks different. Aleksandr Belov's "Movement Against Illegal Immigration" (DPNI) is also frequently included in this category since it initially tried to rely on loosely organized skinheads before its leader embarked upon the path of turning DPNI into a "respectable nationalist movement with European tendencies" (Laruelle, 2019, p. 166). The Russian Federation in its current form (in any form, actually) is a natural enemy to skinheads and their allies, because their main activities occur outside the legal framework and are punishable under the Russian Criminal Code.

Vkontakte Russian nationalism: a case study

The classification outlined here is mostly applicable to offline Russian far-right groups. However, since the online realm echoes offline developments to a large extent (and vice versa), it is also highly relevant to the online community that is going to be examined.

In the online world of social media, the creation of a community is much less costly and takes just a few mouse clicks. However, most such communities do not transcend the limit of several hundred subscribers and are unable to produce original content. That is why a researcher has to focus their attention on just a few communities with the largest outreach, since only they might be regarded as having some influence and acting not merely as a "gentlemen club" but as a deviant political force creating and spreading informational items.

As a case study, the "Pravye" online community was chosen (its name means "The Right-Wing" in English). The choice might be justified for several reasons. With 151k followers, it's one of the biggest daily active online communities on *Vkontakte* (this "Olympus" could be challenged only by the "Yar" community, with 152–153k followers); its ideological profile is explicitly stated in its very name; the community content is highly textual, the preference is given to original texts over meme pictures and reposts. Remarkably, "Pravye" was already dominating the far-right online scene in Russia in the early 2010s (Prostakov, 2016), though this community was several times replaced (with the address change) and revived.

Taking into account the organizational mode of the "Pravye", it could be argued that it is not a community but rather a public page or text resource. However, I'd still prefer to call it an online community, since there are a huge number of members/followers whose names are displayed openly on the webpage; there is a set of permanent contributors and frequent commentators; the latter may actively take part in the discussions and successfully transcend the boundary between the two clusters. Overall, the "Pravye" meets the criteria for an online community outlined earlier—it is indeed a "virtual co-presence of social actors sharing a common interest and characterized by a common interaction format."

Dino Villegas (2021, p. 108) proposed a set of questions that we should ask ourselves to identify an online community's ideological profile:

> how do the members define themselves . . . what specific actions define the group, do group members posit a specific reason for the group to exist, can we interpret group norms and values . . . do they have a particular position in society?

While answering these questions, it could be useful to look at the group/community description. The group presents itself as a "community of kind Russian, ethnically-thinking people".[2]

> We write about history, literature, and politics. Our goal is for the Russians to acquire an ethnic well-reflected consciousness and sovereignty, and for the Russian people to gain a nation-state. We are the journal that shapes the ideology of political struggle of the right-wing Russian people.

So, the community initiators (and the members/followers who agree to be a part of the gang and accept the initiators' self-representation) present themselves as right-wing, ethnically (and "consciously") Russian. The community is depicted as a "journal"; however, a journal usually means a monological style of narrative, but comment threads in the "Pravye" are mostly quite populated. It might be suggested that by calling their community a "journal", the authors try to create an image of some hierarchically organized unit. The "specific actions" that define the group are thus the production of "mobilizing" texts that must frame the reality in a particular way, and the subsequent discussion. The "specific reason for the group to exist" is the inconsistency between the reality and the idealized image of a "Russian nation-state" with the exclusive rights reserved for the ethnic majority;

the need to foster "ethnic consciousness" and the lack of "sovereignty". The "group norms and values" speak for themselves and will be discussed in more detail. Finally, a "particular position in society" that is occupied by the group's ideological adherents (though certainly not by *all* the followers) is primarily on the right edge of the ideological spectrum.

Trying to match the ideological profile of the "Pravye" with the fourfold Russian nationalism classification presented in the previous section turns out to be a challenging task. The texts that are posted in the community are mostly original products or those derived from the contributors' *Telegram* channels; sometimes we also come across interviews with eminent Russian nationalists, statistical data (mostly about the so-called "ethnic crimes"), as well as news items accompanied by short commentaries demonstrating the administration's position. Quite a large number of texts published in the community are written by Dmitry Bobrov a.k.a. Schulz, the founder and leader of "Schulz-88", a skinhead grouping that committed violent offenses between 2001 and 2003. In 2009–2015, he was also a leader of the "National Socialist Initiative". Schulz was in jail from 2003–2009; now he is also an active *Telegram* blogger and the main author (and founder) of the project "Institute for the Studies of Ethnic Crimes". So, Bobrov is obviously the representative of the fourth group, i.e., of the Nazi skinheads (although he himself claims to have become more "moderate" in his views). However, many influential (according to the number of "likes" and "reposts") texts are produced by Andrey Pesotskiy, a former member of Limonov's National Bolshevik Party and its successor, *Drugaya Rossiya* (The Other Russia). He is a clear representative of the chauvinistic-imperial-style project, and some of his texts in the "Pravye" are clearly directed against skinhead ideas: "Russian is not just white, it's a great culture and not just a skinhead subculture. It's an imperial mission, the Russian World uniting different peoples".[3] Also, texts by and interviews with Konstantin Krylov (1967–2020), a prominent representative of the national-democratic camp (i.e., the third group), are frequently quoted. So, we might conclude that the overall ideological profile of the "Pravye" is "just" right-wing nationalist; the broadest possible audience of those who support Russian nationalist sentiments can be attracted to the community.

Pravye online community: framing strategies

The overall framing strategies that are employed by the community under scrutiny are quite predictable and are situated in the general framework of Russian nationalism. I think it would be reasonable to outline briefly the most common frames here and to investigate two framing strategies: namely, regarding migration and the Russian state authorities in more detail.

For most right-wing nationalist communities, both offline and online, national (ethnic) identity is the main focus, along with some wishful thinking about the idealized national state where the dominant (in the case presented here) ethnicity would feel the most comfortable. The idea of Russian ethnicity in the case of "Pravye" is perceived as something understood intuitively; it is not just the "white race" or the community of the Russian-speaking people. The "Pravye" aims to create the umbrella notion of some Russian identity that is simultaneously ethno-racial, cultural, and imperial-messianic (it will be further demonstrated in a number of framing examples).

Emil Pain (2014, p. 18) defines the "ideological minimum", or the lowest common denominator, of a Russian Internet nationalist as a view of Russia as an ethnic Russian state, migrantophobia, and "straight edge" propaganda. Migrantophobia (and other forms of xenophobia) is an important element of the negative identity shared by most Russian far-right activists: they rarely propose some positive agenda (except for the most radical prophets of "national revolution"), but rather consolidate around the negative demands against migration, Islam, Jews, or the anti-hatred articles of the Russian Criminal Code (notably Article 282). However, all kinds of Russian nationalism mentioned in the previous sections cannot be confined to xenophobia: "the targets . . . are not only ethnic minorities but also representatives of the ethnic majority who are labeled as 'tolerant' and 'liberal' intellectuals, human rights organizations, 'antifa' . . . and xenophobia-monitoring organizations" (Zuev, 2011, p. 132). So to the "ideological minimum" coined by Emil Pain, I might also add the "anti-liberal" political dimension: because of the peculiarities of the Russian political history, "liberalism" is often used as a label for all kinds of tolerance, human rights advocacy, and in the recent years also anti-Putin activism (however, some, if not a majority of, groups of radical nationalists are also opposed to the incumbent political regime).

Another frequently occurring frame is biopolitics, the image of the "white/Russian body" that is a reliquary for the "Russian blood". As for the German Nazis, biopolitics is of utmost importance for the Russian boneheads: in most of the groupings, the use of drugs is strictly prohibited, and physical training is an inherent part of the daily routine. This is to be traced to the "straight edge" tradition popular among British and American skins. Though among some skinhead groups, especially those allied with soccer fans, drinking beer is more than acceptable (Belikov, 2011), the idea of an absolutely "healthy lifestyle" is quite popular, which is expressed in such mottos as "Russian Means Sober". "Straight edge" propaganda as a kind of nationalist biopolitics is often a way to attract supporters by non-political means, together with other forms of formally non-political mobilization, such as fundraising and support for the imprisoned nationalists. The human "white" body is seen as the property of the nation or race. For instance, it is a common practice in the right-wing (mostly NS/WP) online communities to publish pictures shaming Russian girls dating immigrants, Jews, and people from South/North Caucasus: these girls are pejoratively named "*chernilnitsy*" ("inkpots").

An illustrative example from the community I analyze here is the idea of "alcoholic genocide of the [Russian] population",[4] performed by the "ethnic criminals" with indirect support from the (allegedly anti-Russian) authorities (*diagnostic frame*). To stop this "genocide", "the psycho-physiological quality of human life should be improved", and "the activities of criminal groupings that produce and sell hazardous alcoholic surrogate should be firmly stopped"[5] (*prognostic frame*).

Notably, some of the possibly divisive topics tend to be avoided in the public discourse. For instance, topic starters prefer not to initiate discussions on the role of the Russian Orthodox Church in society, because a significant part of the community members do not identify with this congregation. The same is also true for other potentially "dangerous" discussions, such as about the Third Reich heritage (Prostakov, 2016, p. 115).

It is very important to mention here that, after 24 February 2022, the war in Ukraine became the main subject of discussion in most Russian far-right online communities. Most of them reacted to the start of the war positively, seeing it as a long-awaited move, though not justifying the rest of the governmental actions. An exception is the hard-core skinhead camp, with *Telegram* channels such as "Oderint, dum metuant" (giving voice to the active participants of the "NS/WP crew") being the mouthpiece of anti-war sentiments on the far-right edge of the spectrum. For the rest of the Russian right-wing online communities, the war supplanted to a large extent (though not completely) the other important frames. Notably, this supplanting did not lead to a great (or any significant) reduction in the number of followers/members.

Migration

Migrants are the main "constituting Other" for most European and American far-right communities, and those based in Russia make no exception here. The motto of fighting "the blacks" (*chornye*) is one of the most consolidating initiatives for the Russian nationalists of all subgroups (though especially for the Nazi skinheads and "national democrats"). The notion of an "immigrant" is mostly used not in its initial legal and economic meaning, but as a relatively "politically correct" substitute for a "person looking differently", or "person of non-Slavic origin" (Alexseev, 2010). So, not only foreign citizens (coming mostly from Asian and African countries) fall under this category, but also the people coming from the North Caucasus (Chechen Republic, Northern Ossetia, Dagestan) and "Asian" regions of Russia (Buryatia, Tuva, Yakutia), who mostly are Russian citizens. Even the late Alexey Navalny, the iconic figure of the anti-Putin opposition, successfully launched the campaign "Stop Feeding the Caucasus" (*Khvatit kormit' Kavkaz*) in 2011 (Laruelle, 2019, p. 185). Some authors (e.g., Prostakov, 2016, p. 109) state that after the so-called "Russian spring" (the annexation of Crimea in 2014 and the subsequent events in Donbas) had come to replace the "Russian winter" (the "cold war" between nationalists and the authorities), the shift occurred in the nationalist discourse, and anti-immigrant rhetoric was sidelined by the events in Ukraine. However, a more long-term observation demonstrates that this trend was short-lived; rather, the war in Ukraine (before and after February 24, 2022) just added another issue to the discussion, and anti-immigrant mottos stayed in their place.

One of the key terms used by the Russian nationalists to refer to the issue of migration is "ethnic crimes". This term was initially used to designate the crimes committed by organized crime groups that were formed by the representatives of ethnic minority diasporas (see, for instance: Herzog, 2003; Poynting, 2001). However, in the nationalist discourse, it evolved quickly into an all-encompassing category that denotes all criminal acts committed by anyone of a "non-Slavic" origin. Again, the Russian nationalists are not exceptional here since the strategy of securitization of migration and creating a "moral panic" is widespread among the Western far-right as well. Notably, some Russia-based criminologists tend to consider the very term "ethnic crime", which is used not only in the overtly nationalist discourse but also in the media and academia, as inciting hatred and potentially punishable in itself (see Dikaev, 2012).

Also, it should be taken into account by researchers studying anti-migration sentiments in Russian society that, to avoid persecution, many keywords that might be identified as pejorative and have extremist connotations (such as "*churka*" for the Central Asian immigrants) are replaced with sarcastically tainted synonyms (e.g., "*mnogonatsional*", literally "multinational"; "A Typical Multinational" is also a name of one of the right-wing anti-immigrant Internet communities).

Diagnostically, the "Pravye" frame migration as some unchecked process that is inherently dangerous to social security, the state, and the "Russian interests". "Ethnic criminals undermine social security, damage Russian citizens and the Russian state, and worsen the quality of life of our people". In the war context, migrants are suspected of "subversive activities in the back".[6] They inevitably are "not prone to law-abiding behavior and form gangs to commit crimes".[7] The state is seen as both unable to control the migration flows and turning a blind eye to the potential conflicts because of indifference and corruption. Here, the strategy of *frame bridging* is clearly employed; that is, the "linkage of two or more ideologically congruent but structurally unconnected frames regarding a particular issue or problem" (Snow et al., 1986, p. 467). In the presented case, the frames of criminality and migration are linked in a way to create an image of an umbilical cord between the two.

Prognostically, the community proposes mainly administrative measures in the field of regulating immigration flows: for instance, to introduce a visa regime with the Central Asian and South Caucasian countries, and even abandon completely "mass labor migration from Central Asia to the Russian regions, because it is a region with a high ethnocultural distance". Priority should be given to "internal labor migration from ethnically and culturally close regions, as well as from Slavic countries". "Migrants from Central Asian and South Caucasian Muslim countries should be reoriented to Muslim and ethnically close regions of Russia if these regions officially ask for foreign specialists". The latter is true not only for external, but also for internal migration: "migrants should be sent from Russian regions to Russian regions, from Caucasian ones to Caucasian ones".[8] Here we see the strategy of *frame amplification*, i.e., "the clarification and invigoration of an interpretative frame that bears on a particular issue, problem, or set of events" (Snow et al., 1986, p. 469): the reform of migration policy is seen as only posing additional restrictions on the migration process and the migrants' rights.

Another set of proposed measures concerns law-and-order policies and financial measures. For labor migrants, the punishment for various crimes should be more severe than for Russian citizens, and no amnesty should be possible. Deportation should be paid for by the culprits themselves, and not from taxpayers' money. Migrants should be deprived of free educational and medical services (also to reduce the burden on the Russian taxpayers). Finally, a special committee is to be set up to scrutinize and reconsider the status of those of non-Slavic and non-indigenous origin who have acquired citizenship after 1992.

Motivationally, these measures are supposed to "preserve ethnocultural balance and avoid inter-ethnic tensions and conflicts".[9] The "Pravye" also argue that the strict policies proposed can "protect the Russian population from discrimination and unlawful infringements".[10] Thus, the Russian majority is framed as vulnerable and discriminated against. It is a nice example of *frame extension* strategy: encompassing "interests or points of view that are incidental to its [social movement organization's] primary objectives but of considerable salience to potential adherents" (Snow et al., 1986, p. 472). Restricting migration and "preserving ethnocultural balance" is presented as a remedy against "discrimination" (that is highly abstract and rarely concretized) or further "infringements". Overall, this framing strategy is supposed to build a bridge between "zero tolerance towards migration" on the one side and some imaginary "feeling comfortable and safe" on the other side (since the latter goal is much broader than the former one, I still call it here frame extension, and not frame bridging).

Government

Generally, Russian nationalists, except for those representing the pro-state fourth group of the far-right, assess the country's authorities (after 1917 or at least after 1991) quite critically. Even if some steps undertaken by the president or the government might be perceived as "moving in the correct direction", the overall attitude is rather negative. As Sergey

Prostakov notes, the so-called "Russian spring", though met with cautious admiration, was seen in the far-right camp "not as a phenomenon linked directly to the Russian authorities' actions in Ukraine, but as the awakening of the Russian self-consciousness", or even as a "unique coincidence of the interests of the 'anti-Russian' Kremlin powers with the true interests of the Russian nation" (Prostakov, 2016, p. 115). The Russian state in its current form is usually perceived as some unnatural and unsatisfying form of governance that oppresses, or at least does not give a true meaning to, the Russian "national interests". Even the very official name of the Russian state, "Russian Federation", might be used in a negative context, since federalism presupposes equal rights of the peoples coming from different semi-autonomous regions of the country. In this vein, some pejorative euphemisms are used to refer to it, such as "*erefiya*" (from the abbreviature "RF" that stands for the Russian Federation) or "*mnogonatsionaliya*" ("Multinational-land") (Zuev, 2011, p. 127). Moscow, the Russian capital, is also sometimes sarcastically referred to as "*Moskvabad*" (in a mockingly "oriental" style). The nationalist ideal is the unitary and ethnically homogenous Russia, or "Rus"; obviously, the current Russian federative statehood does not reflect this pattern.

The *diagnostic* framing strategy of the "Pravye" is quite obviously formulated in a number of postings; it clearly makes the followers see the incumbent Russian state as a unit inherently hostile to the Russian "national (i.e., ethnic) interests", even despite some supposedly correct minor or major steps.

Russian Federation is still an evil stepmother for the Russians, though the fight against the Banderites [a pejorative nickname of Ukrainian nationalists] is in accordance with the Russian national interests. But even here we see a strange war that resembles a series of betrayals. On 24 February, the clock showed the correct time but it is still irreparably broken.[11]

"The authorities consist of the Soviet people whose consciousness is filled with Russophobia, and they continue to systematically oppress the Russians".[12]

The *prognostic* framing provides a possible solution to the "problems" described here. The "Pravye" see the solution in a complete transformation of the Russian Federation into an ethnic nation-state, while acquiring more awareness and "national consciousness". To do this, nationalists must organize themselves into some institutional structures that eventually win the struggle for political power. They should "develop horizontal and vertical networks, acquire the skills of self-organizing, master political and informational technologies".[13]

A few more examples of the respective framing strategy:

The existing state cannot be hoped for, because to become finally a Russian national state, it has to be completely transformed . . . to become aware of ourselves, of our interests, to discover our enemies, both internal and external, to overflow with hatred towards them—this all is very useful for the people that has been taken hostage by hostile politics and ideas for more than a century.[14]

Schematically, the recipe is as follows:

We the Russians should become a subject, a collective actor that is aware of itself and acts as a united whole. . . . Many groups should emerge that advocate the Russian agenda, charity, culture, recreation, etc. When the moment is ripe, the political ideology will provide for the creation of a political party, of an organization that fights for political power. The victory in the political fight will lead to the creation of a Russian nation-state—the supreme way to protect our interests.[15]

The *motivational* framing strategy consists of presenting the respective solution as the only way to secure "Russian interests", to "make Russia free and prosperous, to bring order and development".[16] The "ethnic interests" are defined not just in terms of some abstract ideals, but also as a quite materialistic objective:

> if the authorities in Russia act in accordance with the ethnic interests of the Russian people, the quality of life in Russia will grow twice at least. . . . I think we deserve it . . . . We just want to live in comfort in a free country.[17]

Here we see, at the same time, strategies of *frame extension* and *frame bridging*. The frame of desirable "nation-state solution" is extended to freedom, prosperity, order, and development. To achieve all these nice things, Russia should be transformed into a nation-state with the most rights reserved for the ethnic majority. Just one "small" detail (though entailing a lot of incremental reforms) is supposed to significantly improve the lives of ordinary Russians. Simultaneously, the "ethnic interests" (that can allegedly be ensured in a nation-state only) are speculatively coupled with the quality of life, freedom, and comfort, although obviously these are far broader categories, irreducible to ethnicity.

Conclusion

This chapter analyzed framing strategies employed by the Russian online nationalist community "Pravye". The far-right group's activities are viewed as an example of deviant behavior in the online domain: literally, every construct with a "far" predicate might be considered as deviance from the ideological and practical mainstream. The case proved to be exemplifying not only in the Russian context but also in the broader continuum of the far-right online presence. The "Pravye" could be considered as a community defined by online consociality with shared interactive patterns. The analysis revealed that the "Pravye" is hard to locate the proposed scheme of the Russian nationalist scene since its goal is to attract the broadest possible audience of those who support far-right ideas: so, the elements of ethnic, civilizational, and racial nationalism can be found in the community's discourse.

Apart from the common and omnipresent far-right frames of ethnic identity, anti-liberalism, and biopolitics, the chapter focused on the strategies employed to frame the attitude toward migration and the modern Russian state. Diagnostically, migration is framed in terms of securitization and the so-called "ethnic crimes", as a presumably unchecked and dangerous process that is to be restricted administratively to protect the Russian people from the alleged "discrimination" and "infringements". The incumbent political regime is viewed highly negatively, as some unnatural and even "anti-Russian" state of affairs, though certain measures are perceived as correct. Prognostically, in the "Pravye"'s view, Russia should be transformed into an ethnic nation-state by means of nationalist self-organization and political struggle. This should be done to ensure freedom and prosperity for the Russian people. The strategies of frame bridging, frame amplification, and frame extension are widely employed in both framing clusters. The further qualitative comparative analysis of the Russian far-right sector (mostly in the Vkontakte social media site, as the most populated in Russia) might reveal other shades of online deviant behavior typical of East European nationalist movements.

Notes

1 In most cases, I translate "*natsional'nyi*" (literally, *national*) as *ethnic*, because in the Russian discourse (stemming from the "Soviet theory of ethnos"), *natsional'nost'* stands mostly not for *nationality* but for *ethnicity*.
2 All translations are my own.
3 https://vk.com/rus.prav?w=wall-23486475_1970723
4 https://vk.com/rus.prav?w=wall-23486475_1962218
5 https://vk.com/rus.prav?w=wall-23486475_1962218
6 https://vk.com/rus.prav?w=wall-23486475_1971958
7 https://vk.com/rus.prav?w=wall-23486475_1971767
8 https://vk.com/rus.prav?w=wall-23486475_1965987
9 https://vk.com/rus.prav?w=wall-23486475_1965987
10 https://vk.com/rus.prav?w=wall-23486475_1971175
11 https://vk.com/rus.prav?w=wall-23486475_1972026
12 https://vk.com/rus.prav?w=wall-23486475_1971907
13 https://vk.com/rus.prav?w=wall-23486475_1971237
14 https://vk.com/rus.prav?w=wall-23486475_1972026
15 https://vk.com/rus.prav?w=wall-23486475_1971208
16 https://vk.com/rus.prav?w=wall-23486475_1971907
17 https://vk.com/rus.prav?w=wall-23486475_1962200

References

Alexseev, M. A. (2010). Majority and minority xenophobia in Russia: The importance of being titulars. *Post-Soviet Affairs*, 26(2), 89–120. https://doi.org/10.2747/1060-586X.26.2.89

Bartlett, J., Birdwell, J., & Littler, M. (2011). *The new face of digital populism*. Demos.

Belikov, S. V. (2011). *Britogolovye: Vse o skinchedach* [Skinheads: All about the Skins]. Knizhny Mir.

Branthonne, A., & Waldispuehl, E. (2019). La netnographie pour étudier une communauté masculiniste en ligne: Contributions méthodologiques d'un e-terrain. *Recherches Qualitatives*, 24, 6–19.

Clover, C. (2016). *Black wind, white snow: The rise of Russia's new nationalism*. Yale University Press.

Dikaev, S. (2012). O tak nazyvayemoy etnicheskoy prestupnosti i ekstremizme [On So-Called Ethnic Crime and Extremism]. *Criminology*, 24(1), 38–44.

Goffman, E. (1974). *Frame analysis: An essay on the organization of experience*. Harvard University Press.

Herzog, S. (2003). Does the ethnicity of offenders in crime scenarios affect public perceptions of crime seriousness? A randomized survey experiment in Israel. *Social Forces*, 82(2), 757–781. https://doi.org/10.1353/sof.2004.0011

Hine, C. M. (2015). *Ethnography for the internet: Embedded, embodied and everyday*. Routledge.

Hunt, S. A., Benford, R. D., & Snow, D. A. (1994). Identity fields: Framing processes and the social construction of movement identities. In E. Laraña, H. Johnston, & J. R. Gusfield (Eds.), *New social movements: From ideology to identity* (pp. 187–208). Temple University Press.

Jacobs, K., & Spierings, N. (2016). *Social media, parties, and political inequalities*. Palgrave Macmillan.

Kozinets, R. (2019). *Netnography: The essential guide to qualitative social media research* (3rd ed.). Sage Publications.

Kozinets, R. V. (2010). *Netnography: Ethnographic research in the age of the internet* (1st ed.). Sage Publications.

Laruelle, M. (2010). The ideological shift on the Russian radical right: From demonizing the west to fear of migrants. *Problems of Post-Communism, 57*(6), 19–31. https://doi.org/10.2753/PPC1075-8216570602

Laruelle, M. (2017). Is nationalism a force for change in Russia? *Daedalus, 146*(2), 89–100. https://doi.org/10.1162/DAED_a_00437

Laruelle, M. (2019). *Russian nationalism: Imaginaries, doctrines, and political battlefields.* Routledge.

Likhachev, V. (2002). *Natsizm v Rossii* [Nazism in Russia]. Panorama.

Lindekilde, L. (2014). Discourse and frame analysis. In D. della Porta (Ed.), *Methodological practices in social movement research* (pp. 195–227). Oxford University Press. Retrieved from https://doi.org/10.1093/acprof:oso/9780198719571.003.0009

Mihelj, S., & Jiménez-Martínez, C. (2021). Digital nationalism: Understanding the role of digital media in the rise of 'new' nationalism. *Nations and Nationalism, 27*(2), 331–346. https://doi.org/10.1111/nana.12685

Miller-Idriss, C. (2020). *Hate in the homeland: The new global far right.* Princeton University Press. Retrieved from https://doi.org/10.1515/9780691234298

Minkenberg, M. (2002). The radical right in postsocialist central and eastern Europe: Comparative observations and interpretations. *East European Politics and Societies: And Cultures, 16*(2), 335–362. https://doi.org/10.1177/088832540201600201

Mondon, A. (2013). *The mainstreaming of the extreme right in France and Australia: A populist hegemony?* Ashgate.

Mudde, C. (2007). *Populist radical right parties in Europe.* Cambridge University Press. Retrieved from https://doi.org/10.1017/CBO9780511492037

Nissen, A. (2020). The trans-European mobilization of "generation identity." In O. C. Norocel, A. Hellström, & M. B. Jørgensen (Eds.), *Nostalgia and hope: Intersections between politics of culture, welfare, and migration in Europe* (pp. 85–100). Springer International Publishing. Retrieved from https://doi.org/10.1007/978-3-030-41694-2_6

Pain, E. (2016). Evolutsiya natsionalizma v Rossii [Evolution of Nationalism in Russia]. *Politicheskaya Kontseptologiya, 3*, 231–251.

Pain, E. (2014). Modern Russian nationalism in the mirror of the runet. In A. Verkhovskii (Ed.), *Rossiya—ne Ukraina: Sovremennye aspekty natsionalizma* [Russia is not Ukraine: Modern Aspects of Nationalism] (pp. 8–31). Sova Center.

Parland, T. (2004). *The extreme nationalist threat in Russia.* Routledge. Retrieved from https://doi.org/10.4324/9780203480229

Perren, R., & Kozinets, R. V. (2018). Lateral exchange markets: How social platforms operate in a networked economy. *Journal of Marketing, 82*(1), 20–36. https://doi.org/10.1509/jm.14.0250

Phillips, W. (2015). *This is why we can't have nice things: Mapping the relationship between online trolling and mainstream culture.* The MIT Press.

Pirro, A. L. P. (2022). Far right: The significance of an umbrella concept. *Nations and Nationalism.* https://doi.org/10.1111/nana.12860

Poynting, S. (2001). Appearances and "ethnic crime". *Current Issues in Criminal Justice, 13*(1), 110–113. https://doi.org/10.1080/10345329.2001.12036219

Prostakov, S. (2016). Nationalists 2.0: Companions of the empire. In G. Nikiporets-Takigawa & E. Pain (Eds.), *Internet i ideologicheskiye dvizheniya v Rossii* [The Internet and Ideological Movements in Russia] (pp. 74–134). Liberal Mission Foundation.

Shenfield, S. (2001). *Russian fascism: Traditions, tendencies, movements.* M.E. Sharpe.

Shnirelman, V. A. (2011). *"Porog tolerantnosti": Ideologiia i praktika novogo rasizma* [Threshold of Tolerance: Ideology and Practice of New Racism]. Novoe literaturnoe obozrenie.

Snow, D. A., & Benford, R. D. (1992). Master frames and cycles of protest. In B. Klandermans, H. Kriesi, & S. Tarrow (Eds.), *From structure to action* (pp. 133–155). JAI Press.

Snow, D. A., Rochford, E. B., Worden, S. K., & Benford, R. D. (1986). Frame alignment processes, micromobilization, and movement participation. *American Sociological Review, 51*(4), 464–481. https://doi.org/10.2307/2095581

Tolz, V. (1998). Forging the nation: National identity and nation building in post-communist Russia. *Europe-Asia Studies, 50*(6), 993–1022. https://doi.org/10.1080/09668139808412578

Verkhovskii, A., & Pain, E. (2012). Civilizational nationalism: The Russian version of the "special path." *Russian Politics & Law, 50*(5), 52–86. https://doi.org/10.2753/RUP1061-1940500503

Villegas, D. (2021). Political Netnography: A Method for Studying Power and Ideology in Social Media. In R. Kozinets & R. Gambetti (Eds.), *Netnography Unlimited: Understanding Technoculture using Qualitative Social Media Research*, (pp. 100–115). Routledge.

Zuev, D. (2011). The Russian ultranationalist movement on the internet: Actors, communities, and organization of joint actions. *Post-Soviet Affairs, 27*(2), 121–157. https://doi.org/10.2747/1060-586X.27.2.121

INDEX

Please note that page numbers in *italics* in this index indicate a figure and page numbers in **bold** indicate a table on the corresponding page.

9781032234472